ABORTION, MEDICINE, AND THE LAW

Fourth Edition, Completely Revised

Edited By

J. DOUGLAS BUTLER

and DAVID F. WALBERT

Facts On File

New York • Oxford

Acknowledgments

We would like to express our gratitude to Colleen Butler and Jeremy Blank for their time and their interest in this book.

Abortion, Medicine, and the Law, Fourth Edition, Completely Revised

Copyright © 1992 by J. Douglas Butler and David F. Walbert

Facts On File, Inc.	Facts On File Limited
460 Park Avenue South	% Roundhouse Publishing Ltd.
New York NY 10016	P.O. Box 140
USA	Oxford OX2 7SF
	United Kingdom

Library of Congress Cataloging-in-Publication Data
Abortion, medicine, and the law / edited by J. Douglas Butler and
David F. Walbert.—4th ed., completely rev.
p.   cm.
Includes bibliographical references and index.
ISBN 0-8160-2535-5 (alk. paper)
1. Abortion—United States.   2. Abortion—Law and legislation—
United States.   3. Abortion—Moral and ethical aspects.
I. Butler, J. Douglas (John Douglas), 1941–   .   II. Walbert, David
F.
[DNLM: 1. Abortion, Induced.   2. Ethics, Medical.   3. Forensic
Medicine.   HQ 767.5.U5 A1536]
HQ767.5.U5A265   1992
363.4'6—dc20
DNLM/DLC
for Library of Congress   91-43021

A British CIP catalogue record for this book is available from the British Library.

Facts On File books are available at special discounts when purchased in bulk quantities for businesses, associations, institutions or sales promotions. Please call our Special Sales Department in New York at 212/683-2244 (dial 800/322-8755 except in NY, AK or HI) or in Oxford at 865/728399.

Composition by the Maple-Vail Composition Services
Manufacturing by Hamilton Printing
Printed in the United States of America

10 9 8 7 6 5 4 3 2 1

This book is printed on acid-free paper.

The authors gratefully acknowledge the following publications for permission to reprint several articles:
Stanley Henshaw, *Induced Abortion: A World Review 1990* 22(2) Family Planning Perspectives (March/April 1990). © The Alan Guttmacher Institute.
Stanley Henshaw and Jennifer Van Vort, *Abortion Services in the United States, 1987 and 1988,* 22(3) Family Planning Perspectives (May/June 1990). © The Alan Guttmacher Institute.
Richard Stith, *New Constitutional and Penal Theory in Spanish Abortion Law* 35(3) The American Journal of Comparative Law. © 1987 by the American Association for the Comparative Study of Law, Inc.
Charles A. Gardner, *Is An Embryo A Person?* from the November 13, 1991, issue of The Nation. The Nation Magazine/The Nation Co., Inc. © 1990.

Dedication

The editors of the fourth edition of *Abortion, Medicine and the Law* would like to dedicate this book to Professor B. J. George Jr. Professor George received his B.A. from the University of Michigan in 1949 and received his J.D. degree with distinction from the University of Michigan in 1951. He was a member of the Order of the Coif and associate editor of the Michigan Law Review and is currently an M.Div. degree candidate at the New York Theological Seminary. He has been a professor of law at the University of Michigan Law School from 1958 to 1968, professor of law at Wayne State University from 1971 to 1977 and professor of law at the New York Law School from 1980 through the present. He has been deputy dean of the New York Law School and acting dean of the Wayne State University Law School. Additionally, he was a visiting professor at the Baylor Law School, Yale Law School, Tokyo University Law School, Churo University Law School, Kyoto University Law School, the University of Chicago Law School and the University of the Ryukyus.

An article by Professor George, entitled "Current Abortion Laws: Proposals and Movements for Reform," appeared in the first edition of this book, titled *Abortion and the Law,* published in 1967. His articles quickly became the keystones for all future editions of the book. A quarter of a century after his original work, Professor George has once again contributed to this anthology. His scholarly writing on the issue of abortion has made him one of the leading legal authorities in the area. We are indeed privileged to have a man of his stature included in this book.

Contents

Introduction

In preparing this fourth edition of *Abortion, Medicine, and the Law,* we looked back a quarter of a century to the genesis of this collection. In 1966, the editors of the *Case Western Reserve Law Review* (then the *Western Reserve Law Review*) commissioned a series of essays that addressed the central issues of the subject of abortion. Those essays appeared in a special issue of the *Law Review,* and because of the extraordinary interest in them, they were also published by Case Western Reserve University in 1967 under the title *Abortion and the Law*. That volume was the first book on the subject of abortion that addressed the legal issues in depth.

In 1972, because of the reception given the earlier volume and because of the rapidly changing legal, ethical, medical and political environment of abortion, another volume was undertaken at Case Western Reserve University by the current editors, then recent graduates of the law school. David F. Walbert had been the editor-in-chief of the *Law Review* and J. Douglas Butler had graduated with the class of 1972. Their first efforts culminated in the publication of several articles in the *Case Western Reserve University Law Review* in 1972 and in the publication of *Abortion, Society and the Law* in 1973.

The 1973 volume became the authoritative treatise for lawyers, legislators, doctors, students and others. It was our hope that the book would be a comprehensive resource that touched on as many of the legal, ethical, religious, psychological and medical aspects of the subject as possible. Among other things, that edition contained a detailed compilation of the status of the abortion laws in every state in the nation as well as an overview of the evolving law of abortion by Professor B. J. George Jr. It included an article by Alan F. Guttmacher, who has frequently been described as the nestor of the abortion movement, and commentary on ethical and religious issues by Daniel Callahan,

Rabbi Immanuel Jakobovitz and then-congressman Robert F. Drinan, S.J. It also included commentary on abortion practices as they had existed in the United States, psychiatric aspects of abortion and considerations of genetic and prenatal diagnosis that are inherent in liberalized abortion choices. Other articles in the legal arena addressed the rights of minors and abortion counseling.

Back in 1973, no one who was close to the subject of abortion could have foreseen the controversy the subject would provoke in the next two decades. Although it was easy to see in Justice Blackmun's opinions in *Roe v. Wade* and *Doe v. Bolton* the analytical weaknesses that might leave the opinions open to second-guessing—including his decision to predicate the trimester analysis on the shifting sands of present medical technology—such weaknesses in justices' opinions do not usually lead to protracted debate over constitutional legitimacy.

What has transpired in the abortion arena since 1973 is nothing short of remarkable. It has probably been the single most prominent political issue, and it promises to be so in the future. A fundamental tenet of the Republican party in recent years has been to appoint federal judges dedicated to overruling *Roe* and *Doe*. A remarkable amount of political activity both in favor of and in opposition to widely available abortion has coursed through state houses around the country and through Capitol Hill as well. In the wake of *Roe* and *Doe,* there has also been a host of legal and constitutional developments in other countries. Politics has influenced the issue in those places as well, although generally not to the same extent as in the United States.

It was because of the extended controversy concerning the abortion issue that we published a third edition of collected essays, now titled *Abortion, Medicine, and the Law,* in 1986. Much had happened since the 1973 edition, and it was important to commission articles for a new volume that illuminated the issues of the ongoing debate. In the 1986 volume, again, Professor George provided an extraordinary review of the law on abortion in the United States. Other legal articles looked closely at what Congress had done since the *Roe* decision, at the rights of minors and at emerging theories of liability in tort cases claiming wrongful birth and wrongful life. The book also contained significant scholarly commentary on the *Roe* and *Doe* decisions themselves. Six chapters were devoted to different medical and psychiatric aspects of abortion, and one article provided an in-depth look at the public health sector's response to legal abortion since the *Roe* and *Doe* decisions.

As in the 1973 volume, we included a chapter on prenatal diagnosis and selective abortion of fetuses that show evidence of a genetic disease or other abnormality. Ethical issues in the 1986 edition were addressed by Daniel Callahan and John T. Noonan Jr., as well as by Ronald Reagan, who is probably as responsible as anyone for strengthening the anti–*Roe v. Wade* movement. The 1986 edition also included, as one of its appendixes, excerpts of testimony before the United States Senate from a range of legal scholars who addressed proposed abortion-limiting legislation.

In the six years since our last volume appeared, the abortion controversy, if anything, rages even more heatedly. The need for a new comprehensive treatment of the subject is clear. Although much has been written in recent years on abortion, there is no single source that provides a broad range of scholarly commentary on the subject. We have tried to provide that here, and we hope that we have been successful. We know we have succeeded in bringing to this volume authors and contributors who are surpassed in their areas of expertise by none. No one individual or several individuals could have written a book of this sort, and we give our utmost appreciation and gratitude to all of the contributors. Their work provides an extremely valuable source of information concerning all aspects of abortion—from constitutional history to the leading edge of medical technology—that readers of all levels of interest and knowledge will find both useful and interesting. We want to especially thank Professor George. He has contributed to every edition, and here, as always, has provided the single most comprehensive review of current abortion law.

The legal topics. In addition to B. J. George's compendium and review, Professors Van Alstyne and Dellinger, two giants of constitutional law, look at the *Roe v. Wade* decision and provide new insights both into that case and into related questions. They examine the Utah law that was recently enacted and what effects the restrictions of that law might have upon the medical and legal community. Paige Cunningham and Clarke Forsythe provide some very different and thought-provoking comments on abortion law in the United States. They look at the level of knowledge that Americans have concerning the rights of women to obtain abortions, and they look at the impact of abortions on women's health. They conclude that the abortion privacy doctrine has spawned a range of ills without remedying the real historical injustices against women. James Bopp Jr. argues that there is no constitutional right to abortion and he assesses the extent to which the fourteenth amendment's equal protection clause might restrict state abortion laws. He predicts that, with the demise of *Roe v. Wade,* the states will again regulate abortion as they did prior to 1973. Michael J. Malinowski provides an excellent review of the rights of minors to obtain an abortion confidentially and without the involvement of their parents or others. Susan Davies gives thorough consideration to what role men might have with respect to abortion decisions, however limited, and she reviews the state of the law in this area in a variety of contexts where the issue has arisen. Michele Beasley has written the chapter on wrongful birth and wrongful life, an area of law that has changed and developed significantly since our last volume. Ms. Beasley also looks at what might happen to these legal issues if *Roe v. Wade* is overturned. Christopher and Corinne Yates analyze the question of fetal rights, giving us historical perspective and explaining the recent changes in the law expanding those rights even since *Roe v. Wade.* They also present their views on the question of fetal rights vis-à-vis the rights and health interests of women.

One of the most significant additions to the present volume is several excellent chapters on comparative law. Donald Kommers gives a comparative legal analysis of abortion law in six different countries. Anne McLellan presents an in-depth treatment of how the Canadian courts have responded to abortion issues. She writes about the fascinating history of Dr. Morgentaler, whose campaign of civil disobedience against restrictive abortion laws precipitated much of the definitive litigation in Canada. Stanley K. Henshaw gives a review of abortion laws and policies of countries around the world as well as the related social and medical questions of the frequency of abortion, mortality, demographic characteristics and the like. Richard Stith looks specifically at the legal issues in Spain. The experiences, laws and constitutional decisions in different countries should provide readers with unusual new insights into the particular laws and policies of their own country. An interesting example is the juxtaposition of the *Roe v. Wade* theory of constitutional law with the German constitutional decision that found that liberal abortion laws were *unconstitutional* because they allowed the destruction of fetuses that were entitled to constitutional protection, just as ''persons'' are protected under the fourteenth amendment to the United States Constitution.

Medical topics. Michael Flower writes about prenatal human development, which he describes as a continuous process with four major and distinct transitions. Charles Gardner questions the claim that a person is created at the moment of conception and argues that, at the early stages of development, the humanness of the individual has not yet been determined. Up-to-date statistics about the incidence of abortion in the United States are discussed in chapters by Stanley K. Henshaw and Lisa Koonin. Etienne-Emile Baulieu is known throughout the world for his developmental work with RU486, the drug used instead of abortive surgery by thousands of women in France with a high success rate. Here, Dr. Baulieu discusses both the mechanisms and the applications of RU486. Because of the drug's potential importance throughout the world, Dr. Baulieu's contribution is of special value.

M. Neil Macintyre, Llew Keltner and Dorothy Kovacevich write about the issue of prenatal diagnosis and selective abortion where there is an abnormal fetus. Given our rapidly expanding knowledge of genetics and the increasing ability to determine the presence of problems, this chapter, too, should be of great interest to many. Alan Guttmacher's now-historic personal insight into the genesis of liberalized abortion is included as a chapter, with an update by Irwin Kaiser. Kenneth Niswander and Manuel Porto detail the history of abortion practices in the United States as well as the contemporary indications for therapeutic abortions. Kenneth Ryan discusses the medical and research applications of fetal tissues. And Nancy Russo discusses the psychological aspects of unwanted pregnancies and their resolution.

Government action, ethics and religion. Senator Packwood's chapter describes the right-to-life movement in Congress from 1973 to 1983. Sharon Block then gives a detailed review of congressional action on all varieties of abortion-related issues from 1984 to 1991. Professor Linda Przybyszewski gives some new insights into the historic right to privacy. She argues that the right in fact is much broader than is commonly believed, and its origins in our body of law go back before the famous article by Warren and Brandeis. Daniel Callahan again addresses ethical issues of abortion. Thomas Murray examines the many arguments both for and against fetal tissue research and whether it really is beneficial; what, if any, is the relationship between the abortion issue and the use of fetal tissue; and whether the ethical dilemma raised by the use of fetal tissue may be avoided. Paul Simmons broadly reviews religious approaches to abortion questions.

J. Douglas Butler
David F. Walbert

Contributors

Etienne-Emile Baulieu, Ph.D.
    Professeur, Director Laboratoire D Pr E-E Baulieu
    Hospital De Bicetre
Michele E. Beasley, J.D.
    Georgetown University Law Center
Sharon Block, J.D.
    Georgetown University Law Center
James Bopp Jr., J.D.
    Partner, Brames, McCormick, Bopp & Abel; General Counsel, National Right to
    Life Committee Inc.
Daniel Callahan, Ph.D.
    Director, Hastings Center, New York, New York
Paige Comstock Cunningham, J.D.
    Board of Directors, Americans United for Life
Susan M. Davies, J.D.
    Office of the Solicitor General, U.S. Department of Justice
Walter Dellinger, LL.B.
    Professor, Duke University School of Law
Michael J. Flower, Ph.D.
    Associate Professor, University Honors Program and Department of Biology, Port-
    land State University
Clarke D. Forsythe, J.D.
    General Counsel for Americans United for Life

Charles A. Gardner, Ph.D.
    University of Michigan
B. J. George Jr., J.D.
    Professor, New York School of Law
Alan F. Guttmacher, M.D.
    Past President of Planned Parenthood—World Population (deceased), New York, New York
Stanley Henshaw, Ph.D.
    The Alan Guttmacher Institute
Dawn Johnsen, J.D.
    The National Abortion Rights Action League
Irwin H. Kaiser, M.D.
    Professor of Obstetrics and Gynecology, Albert Einstein College of Medicine, New York, New York
Donald P. Kommers, Ph.D.
    Professor of Law, University of Notre Dame School of Law
Lisa M. Koonin, M.N., M.P.H.
    Statistics and Computer Resources Branch, Division of Reproductive Health, National Center for Chronic Disease Prevention and Health Promotion, U.S. Dept. of Health and Human Services, Public Health Service Centers for Disease Control
M. Neil Macintyre, Ph.D.
    Professor Emeritus of Developmental Genetics, Medicine and Pediatrics, Case Western Reserve University School of Medicine, Cleveland, Ohio
Michael Malinowski, J.D.
    Yale University School of Law
A. Anne McLellan, LL.B., LL.M.
    Professor, University of Alberta, Edmonton School of Law
Thomas H. Murray, Ph.D.
    Professor and Director, Center for Biomedical Ethics, Case Western Reserve University School of Medicine
Kenneth R. Niswander, M.D.
    Professor of Obstetrics and Gynecology and Chairman of the Department at the School of Medicine, University of California, Davis, Sacramento, California
Bob Packwood
    U.S. Senator from Oregon
Manuel Porto, M.D.
    Assistant Professor of Obstetrics and Gynecology, School of Medicine at the University of California, Davis, Sacramento, California
Linda C. A. Przybyszewski, Ph.D.
    Assistant Professor of History, University of Cincinnati
Nancy Felipe Russo, Ph.D.
    Professor, Women's Studies Program, Arizona State University
Kenneth J. Ryan, M.D.
    Chairman, Department of Obstetrics and Gynecology, Brigham & Women's Hospital; Chairman, Department of Obstetrics and Gynecology, Harvard Medical School; Kate Macy Ladd Professor, Harvard Medical School
Paul D. Simmons, Th.M., Ph.D.
    Professor of Christian Ethics, Southern Baptist Theological Seminary

Richard Stith, J.D., Ph.D.
Professor of Law, Valparaiso University School of Law
William Van Alstyne, J.D.
William R. and Thomas R. Perkins Professor of Law, Duke University School of Law
Christopher P. Yates, J.D., M.B.A.
Assistant United States Attorney for the Eastern District of Michigan
Corinne Beckwith Yates, J.D.
Editor-in-Chief, Volume 90, Michigan Law Review, University of Michigan, School of Law

Planned Parenthood of Southeastern Pennyslvania v. Casey: An Analysis ——————

B. J. George Jr., J.D.

I. Introduction

The holding of the Third Circuit in *Planned Parenthood of Southeastern Pennsylvania v. Casey*[1] invalidating certain provisions of Pennsylvania's Abortion Control Act of 1982, as amended in 1988,[2] was important in its own right, in particular, because of its premise that none of the contested statutory provisions could be sustained as constitutional without overruling *Roe v. Wade*.[3] The Supreme Court's grant of certiorari appeared to create a possibility, if not the probability, that a substantially reconstituted Supreme Court might indeed overrule *Roe v. Wade*. Because it seemed inappropriate to suspend the manufacture of this book so that the implications of the Supreme Court's ruling in *Planned Parenthood of Southeastern Pennsylvania v. Casey*[4] might be discussed in a number of the chapters that follow, the pragmatic decision was made to present the Court's holding through this analytical note in the book's front matter, leaving it to the readers to integrate it in their understanding of abortion law and practice as addressed in this book as an entirety.

II. The *Casey* Holding

A. Scope of the Judgment
The Supreme Court handed down its *Casey* judgment on the last day of its 1991–1992 term, June 29, 1992.[5] In evaluating *Casey*, it is important to recognize that a five-Justice

---

[1]947 F.2d 682 (3d Cir. 1991), *rev'd in part & aff'd in part*, 112 S. Ct. (1992).
[2]18 Pa. Cons. Stat §§ 3203–3220 (1990).
[3]410 U.S. 113 (1973). The Third Circuit's specific holdings are noted *passim* in the author's chapter *infra*.
[4]For convenience, the case will be referred to hereinafter as "*Casey*."

majority[6] coalesced on only certain issues. As a consquence, some of the terms that have attracted substantial media and commentators' attention, for example, "undue burden" as a standard for determining the validity of legislation governing abortion,[7] have no present legal doctrinal significance simply because a majority of the Court has not adopted them.[8]

B. *Roe* Doctrine Reaffirmed

The *Casey* majority declined to make of the litigation an opportunity to overturn *Roe;* the four dissenting Justices were almost vituperative[9] in condemning the five majority Justices for not overturning *Roe.*[10] As far as the majority Justices were concerned, however, "the essential holding of *Roe* v. *Wade* should be retained and once again reaffirmed."[11] As the Court summarized that "essential holding":

> *[I]t has three parts. First is a recognition of the right of the woman to choose to have an abortion before viability and to obtain it without undue interference from the State. Before viability, the State's interests are not strong enough to support a prohibition of abortion or the imposition of a substantial obstacle to the woman's effective right to elect the procedure. Second is a confirmation of the State's power to restrict abortions after fetal viability, if the law contains exceptions for pregnancies which endanger a woman's life or health. And third is the principle that the State has legitimate interests from the outset of the pregnancy in protecting the health of the woman and the life of the fetus that may become a child. These principles do not contradict one another, and we adhere to each.*[12]

In taking that position, the majority refused to hold that the term "liberty," as protected by the Constitution, is restricted either to whatever is specific in the Constitution or whatever was viewed as protected under precedents in force when the Fourteenth Amendment was ratified in 1868. Were either controlling, the Court could not correctly have ruled (as it did) that marriage is included in "a realm of personal liberty

---

[5]112 S. Ct. (1992). Because *Supreme Court Reporter* pagination would not have been available until late August 1992, all page references that follow are to the Court's preliminary (slip) opinions.

[6]Justices O'Connor, Kennedy and Souter issued a joint opinion on parts of which they were joined by Justices Blackmun and Stevens to form the five-Justice majority. Slip op. at x.

[7]*Id.* at 34–37.

[8]*See* the concluding portion of this analysis.

[9]Justice Scalia, joined by the Chief Justice and Justices White and Thomas, characterized the majority's arguments as "outrageous," Scalia, J. (concurring in part and dissenting in part), slip op. at 3, and "Orwellian," *id.* at 18, and attributed to the majority "almost czarist arrogance," *id.* at 21. Chief Justice Rehnquist characterized the joint opinion "as a sort of judicial Potemkin Village, which may be pointed out to passers by as a monument to the importance of adhering to precedent." Rehnquist, C. J. (concurring in part and dissenting in part), slip op. at 23. Justice Blackmun was somewhat more restrained in his analysis of Chief Justice Rehnquist's position, calling it a "stunted conception [and] cramped notion of individual liberty." Blackmun, J. (concurring in part, concurring in the judgment in part, and dissenting in part), slip op. at 19, 20.

[10]Chief Justice Rehnquist commenced his opinion concurring in the judgment in part and dissenting in part thus: "We believe that *Roe* was wrongly decided, and that it can and should be overruled consistently with our traditional approach to *stare decisis* in constitutional cases." Rehnquist, C. J. (concurring in part and dissenting in part), slip op. at 1.

[11]Slip op. at 3.

[12]*Id.* at 3–4.

which the government may not enter."[13] Instead, the appropriate approach is through "reasoned judgment," the "boundaries [of which] are not susceptible of expression as a simple rule."[14] In the abortion context, "[t]he underlying constitutional issue is whether the State can resolve [the questions revolving about the profound moral and spiritual implications of terminating a pregnancy, even in its earliest stage] in such a definitive way that a woman lacks all choice in the matter, except perhaps in those rare circumstances in which the pregnancy is itself a danger to her own life or health, or is the result of rape or incest."[15]

Though a government can adopt one from among competing positions when reasonable people disagree, that does not operate if a final choice thus made can intrude upon a protected liberty, particularly in such areas as "personal decisions relating to marriage, procreation, contraception, family relationships, child rearing, and education."[16] An abortion decision can commence within the zone of conscience and belief, but it is more than a "philosophic exercise" because abortion is a unique act, "an act fraught with consequences for others: for the woman who must live with the implications of her decision; for the persons who perform and assist in the procedure; for the spouse, family, and society which must confront the knowledge that these procedures exist, procedures some deem nothing short of an act of violence against innocent human life; and, depending on one's beliefs, for the life or potential life that is aborted."[17] In that context, a woman's liberty "is at stake in a sense unique to the human condition and so unique to the law[; h]er suffering is too intimate and personal for the State to insist, without more, upon its own vision of the woman's role[, and t]he destiny of the woman must be shaped to a large extent on her own conception of her spiritual imperatives and her place in society."[18] *Roe* sought to protect that dimension of personal liberty; "the reservations any of us may have in reaffirming the central holding of *Roe* are outweighed by the explication of individual liberty we have given combined with the force of *stare decisis.*"[19]

C. The Force of *Stare Decisis*

The *Casey* majority next advanced certain policy reasons supporting its continuation of the Court's *Roe*-engendered jurisprudence.[20] One reason for rejecting an application of *stare decisis* principles is that an existing rule has proven unworkable, but that cannot be said of *Roe:* "[a]lthough [it] has engendered opposition, it has in no sense proven

---

[13]*Id.* at 5 (citing Loving v. Virginia, 388 U.S. 1 [1967] [invalidating on due process grounds state legislation prohibiting and penalizing mixed-racial marriages]). The Court noted that marriage is nowhere mentioned in the Constitution itself, and interracial marriages were illegal in most states during the 19th century. *Id.*

[14]*Id.* at 7.

[15]*Id.* at 8.

[16]*Id.* at 9 (summarizing the Court's holdings in, *e.g.,* Carey v. Population Services International, 431 U.S. 678, 685 [1977]).

[17]*Id.* at 9–10.

[18]*Id.* at 10. The *Carey* majority thought that in some critical respects the abortion decision is of the same character as the decision whether or not to use contraception: despite conflicting views as to whether procreation should be furthered or prevented, a woman is at liberty to decide whether to become pregnant or not. "The same concerns are present when the woman confronts the reality that, perhaps despite her attempts to avoid it, she has become pregnant." *Id.* at 11.

[19]*Id.* at 11.

[20]Chief Justice Rehnquist, joined by the other three doctrinal dissenters, was scathing in his attack on this portion of the majority's *stare decisis* analysis. Rehnquist, C. J. (concurring in part and dissenting in part), slip op. at 11–24.

'unworkable,' . . . . representing as it does a simple limitation beyond which a state law is unenforceable.''[21] A second important factor is that of reliance. There is, of course, no dimension of reliance in the setting of *Roe* as there might be in property and contract matters. Nevertheless:

> *for two decades of economic and social developments, people have organized intimate relationships and made choices that define their views of themselves and their places in society, in reliance on the availability of abortion in the event that contraception should fail. The ability of women to participate equally in the economic and social life of the Nation has been facilitated by their ability to control their reproductive lives . . . The Constitution serves human values, and while the effect of reliance on* Roe *cannot be exactly measured, neither can the certain cost of overruling* Roe *for people who have ordered their thinking and living around that case be dismissed.*[22]

Nor should *Roe* by dismissed ''as a mere survivor of obsolete constitutional thinking.''[23] It stands at an intersection of two lines of constitutional precedents, neither of which has been weakened in the interim. One is the ''scope of recognized protection accorded to the liberty relating to intimate relationships, the family, and decisions about whether or not to beget or bear a child.''[24] The other is the Court's recognition of limits ''on governmental power to mandate medical treatment or to bar its rejection,'' which bears on *Roe*'s treatment of abortion as a rule ''of personal autonomy and personal integrity'';[25] that precedential source likewise is fully operational.

Even if *Roe* is *sui generis,* however, the joint-opinion authors thought there had been no erosion of its focal determination. Even though the size of the majority had shrunk, the basic premise to which it had adhered had remained intact. Nor would other courts building on *Roe* be likely to go astray, should the *Roe* doctrine be continued in force; if it should be assumed that ''the central holding of *Roe* was in error, that error would go only to the strength of the state interest in fetal protection, not to the recognition afforded by the Constitution to the woman's liberty.''[26] That liberty has been sufficiently defined in scope by the Court that erroneous determinations are not likely. ''In any event, because *Roe*'s scope is confined by the fact of its concern with postconception potential life, a concern otherwise likely to be implicated only by some forms of contraception protected independently under *Griswold* and later cases,[[27]] any error

---

[21] Slip op. at 13.

[22] *Id.* at 14.

[23] *Id.*

[24] *Id.* at 15 (citing the Court's contraception holdings commencing with Griswold v. Connecticut, 381 U.S. 479 [1965]).

[25] *Id.* (citing Cruzan v. Director, Missouri Dept. of Health, 497 U.S. 261, 178 [1990]).

[26] *Id.* at 16.

[27] To the author, this would seem to suggest that RU-486 and like pharmaceuticals that can prevent implantation of a zygote on the walls of the uterus would be viewed by the joint-opinion authors as forms of contraception and thus not subject to a governmental ban. At this writing, a class action had just commenced in federal district court in New York attacking on constitutional grounds a United States Customs Service administrative ban on importation of RU-486 undergirding the seizure at Kennedy International Airport from a returning pregnant American citizen of a supply of RU-486 acquired in France. *See* Elyse Tanouye, *Abortion-Rights Activists File Lawsuit to Overturn U.S. Ban on French Drug,* Wall Street Journal, July 8, 1992, at B4.

in *Roe* is unlikely to have serious ramifications in future cases."[28] In addition, changes in views on viability go only to whether, for example, the usual time of viability is now 23 to 24 weeks, rather than the 28 weeks assumed in *Roe;* any changes "in *Roe*'s factual underpinning [have not] left its central holding obsolete, and none supports an argument for overruling it."[29]

Beyond that, for the Court to overrule *Roe* "would seriously weaken the Court's capacity to exercise the judicial power and to function as the Supreme Court of a Nation dedicated to the rule of law."[30] Something more than apposite legal principle is required; the "Court must take care to speak and act in ways that allow people to accept its decisions on the terms the Court claims for them, as grounded truly in principle, not as compromises with social and political pressures having, as such, no bearing on the principled choices that the Court is obliged to make."[31] The public may well be willing to give the Court the benefit of the doubt when it overrules precedents, replacing one judicially derived rule with another.

That process, however, does not pertain in two circumstances. One is when frequent overturning would overtax the country's belief in the Court's good faith; "[t]here is a limit to the amount of error that can plausibly be imputed to prior courts,"[32] because "[t]he legitimacy of the Court would fade with the frquency of its vacillation."[33] The second is when a decision overruling an earlier doctrinal precedent may be taken as "a surrender to political pressure, and an unjustified repudiation of the principle on which the Court staked its authority in the first instance[;] to overrule under fire in the absence of the most compelling reason to reexamine a watershed decision would subvert the Court's legitimacy beyond any serious question."[34] To the majority, the Court's duty was clear as it confronted once more the issue of governmental power to limit personal choice to undergo abortion:

> *A decision to overrule* Roe's *essential holding under the existing circumstances would address error, if error there was, at the cost of both profound and unnecessary damage to the Court's legitimacy, and to the Nation's commitment to the rule of law. It is therefore imperative to adhere to the essence of* Roe's *original decision, and we do so today.*[35]

D. The Pennsylvania Legislation

The Court summoned a doctrinal majority to address only two dimensions of the Pennsylvania statute.[36] The first had to do with the statutory definition of a medical emer-

---

[28] Slip op. at 17. The fact that advances in medical knowledge and techniques since 1973 allow for safe abortions later in pregnancy and neonatal care that promotes advanced viability does not counteract the stronger argument for "affirming *Roe*'s central holding, with whatever degree of personal reluctance any of us may have, not for overruling it." *Id.* at 19.

[29] *Id.* at 18. The joint-opinion discussion of the significance of viability, *id.* at 27–37, did not attract an endorsement from two additional Justices, *id.* at x. *See infra,* text accompanying note 47.

[30] Sip op. at 22.

[31] *Id.* at 23.

[32] *Id.* at 24.

[33] *Id.*

[34] *Id.* at 25. "If the Court's legitimacy should be undermined, then, so would the country be in its very ability to see itself through its constitutional ideals[; t]he Court's concern with legitimacy is not for the sake of the Court but for the sake of the Nation to which it is responsible." *Id.* at 26.

[35] *Id.* at 27.

gency.[37] Planned Parenthood attacked the language because it foreclosed the possibility of an immediate abortion despite some significant health risks. The Court acknowledged that if such a contention were correct, the Court would invalidate it, "for the essential holding of *Roe* forbids a State from interfering with a woman's choice to undergo an abortion procedure if continuing her pregnancy would constitute a threat to her health."[38] However, the federal district court had concluded that the statutory term "serious risk" would include three serious conditions that the petitioners had contended would not constitute such a risk.[39] Lower federal courts are better equipped to interpret state law than the Supreme Court; as construed by the district court and Third Circuit, the medical emergency definition imposed no undue burden on a woman's abortion right.[40]

The second dimension of the Pennsylvnaia statute concerning which the Court mustered a majority was section 3209, which barred the performance of an abortion on a married woman unless the attending physician had received either (a) a signed statement from the woman that she had notified her spouse she was about to undergo an abortion, or (b) her certification that her husband was not the man who impregnated her, that her husband could not be located, that the pregnancy resulted from a spousal sexual assault which she had reported, or that the woman believed that notifying the husband would cause him or someone else to inflict bodily injury on her. Should a physician perform an abortion without an appropriate signed statement, her or his medical license was to be revoked and she or he was to be liable to the husband for damages.[41]

The Court accepted the district court's findings concerning the potential for spousal abuse and marital rape bearing on the possible consequences of women's compliance with the spousal notification process, as well as the thrust of related research literature. It concluded that the statutory requirement would impose an "undue burden" on

---

[36] Initial press comments on *Casey* generally failed to note that a doctrinal majority assembled itself only on parts I–III, V-A, V-C and VI of the joint opinion. *Id.* at x. Justice Stevens joined part V-E (relating to the state statutory record-keeping requirements), but Justice Blackmun did not. *Id.* The four dissenting members of the Court joined the *Court's judgment* affirming in turn the Third Circuit judgment affirming the constitutionality of certain parts of the Pennsylvania legislation (other than the spousal notice portion which five Justices found unconstitutional). However, as noted *passim* in this Analysis, their grounds for doing so were diametrically opposed to the rationale of the majority: The majority found *Roe* still to be controlling constitutional doctrine but found no violation of *Roe* principles in certain portions of the statute; the dissenters thought *Roe* should have been repudiated and, in accord with that principle, thought there was nothing unconstitutional in the exercise of legislative judgment to restrict the availability of abortions.

[37] "Under the statute, a medical emergency is

'[t]hat condition which, on the basis of the physician's good faith clinical judgment, so complicates the medical condition of a pregnant woman as to necessitate the immediate abortion of her pregnancy to avert her death or for which a delay will create serious risk of substantial and irreversible impairment of a major bodily function.' 18 Pa. Cons. Stat. (1990). § 3203.

Slip op. at 37.

[38] Slip op. at 37.

[39] Preclampsia, inevitable abortion and premature ruptured membrane, each of which under some circumstances "could lead to an illness with substantial and irreversible consequences." *Id.* at 38.

[40] *Id.*

[41] *Id.* at 45.

abortions permitted under *Roe*, and hence was invalid.[42] Because the statutory spousal notification requirement likely would prevent a significant number of women from obtaining abortions by imposing a substantial obstacle in their path, it was constitutionally vulnerable. Section 3209 in effect

> *embodies a view of marriage consonant with the common-law status of married women but repugnant to our present understanding of marriage and of the nature of the rights secured by the Constitution. Women do not lose their constitutionally protected liberty when they marry. The Constitution protects all individuals, male or female, married or unmarried, from the abuse of governmental power, even where that power is employed for the supposed benefit of a member of the individual's family. These considerations confirm our conclusion that § 3209 is invalid.*[43]

It should be noted that there was no majority opinion concerning the constitutionality of the statutory informed consent requirements,[44] the parental consent provisions[45] and the statutory recordkeeping requirements.[46] On these issues, there was simply a majority of the Court affirming the Third Circuit's action in sustaining the constitutionality of these aspects of the Pennsylvania legislation; no doctrinal majority exists on these points, and no valid doctrinal conclusions can be drawn on the basis of the Court's majority action affirming the Third Circuit's judgmental action. Nor did the discussion by the joint-opinion authors of viability[47] attract the endorsement of another two of their colleagues. However, the Court's earlier jurisprudence on these matters[48] remains unaffected by *Casey,* and thus continues to provide needed guidance for state and lower federal courts.

III. Future Prosepcts of *Roe*

The author believes it is a nonproductive exercise to speculate at this time about what federal constitutional jurisprudence might look like were *Roe* to be overruled; it approximates a debate on the question, ''If I had a brother, would he like cheese?'' Nor does there seem to be profit in asking what the ''undue burden'' standard means, either in the abstract or as applied to state legislative efforts to limit abortion.[49] The five-Justice

---

[42] The Court distinguished parental notification as ''based on the quite reasonable assumption that minors will benefit from consultation with their parents and that children will often not realize that their parents have their best interests at heart[; w]e cannot adopt a parallel assumption about adult women.'' *Id.* at 53.

[43] *Id.* at 56–57.

[44] *See* Joint Opinion, slip op. at 38–45, in which Justice Blackmun joined, slip op. at x.

[45] *Id.* at 57–58.

[46] *Id.* at 58–59.

[47] *Id.* at 27–37.

[48] *See* the relevant portions of the author's chapter *infra.*

[49] The joint-opinion authors characterized a ''finding of an undue burden [as] a shorthand for the conclusion that a state regulation has the purpose or effect of placing a substantial obstacle in the path of a woman seeking an abortion of a nonviable fetus.'' Slip op. at 34. Justice Stevens' concept was that ''[a] burden may be 'undue' either because the burden is too severe or because it lacks a legitimate, rational justification.'' Stevens, J. (concurring in part and dissenting in part), slip op. at 10. Neither formulation attracted the endorsement of five members of the Court required to convert it into controlling constitutional doctrine.

majority's restatement and reaffirmation of *Roe* principles obviously renders unconstitutional legislative efforts like those in Guam, Louisiana and Utah to outlaw abortions unnecessary to preserve the life of pregnant women. As noted, the three aspects of the Pennsylvania legislation concerning which no doctrinal majority assembled itself are rather well targeted by the Court's existing precedents which remain in functional effect as long as *Roe* continues as a foundational precedent. State and lower federal courts probably have as much guidance as they need to resolve the constitutionality of legislative experimentation with the details of abortion regulation.

At the same time, *Casey*'s majority Justices seem not essentially concerned about the economic and logistical impediment that the restrictions imposed by legislative requirements approved by the Court place in the way of financially-unable or lower-income women, and on those without access to sophisticated advice who may prove incapable in the real world of meeting legislative requirements instituted for that very purpose. Undesirable as this may be in the author's view, however, that process has been manifest for more than a decade without effective hindrance from a majority of the Supreme Court; *Casey* has not innovated in that respect.

In short, *Roe*'s basic constitutional doctrine remains in force after, and perhaps because of, *Casey*. Its longevity,[50] however, probably will be determined at the presidential polls in November 1992, as the next president will almost certainly have the opportunity to appoint a Justice. There is poignancy in Justice Blackmun's concluding lines:

> *I am 83 years old. I cannot remain on this Court forever, and when I do step down, the confirmation process for my successor well may focus on the issue before us today. That, I regret, may be exactly where the choice between the two worlds will be made.*[51]

---

[50] Whatever the outcome of future federal constitutional litigation, Congress arguably would have the power, as would state legislatures, to legislate the equivalent to the broad abortion-rights legislation approved on June 26, 1992, by the German *Bundestag:* pregnant women may elect abortions in the first 12 weeks of pregnancy after submitting to nonbinding medical counseling. *See* Marc Fisher, *Germany Gives Women the Right to Abortion: End of Bitter Dispute Is a Defeat for Kohl,* Washington Post, June 26, 1992, at A25. No original documentation was available at this writing.

[51] Blackmun, J. (concurring in part and dissenting in part), slip op. at 22–23.

1 · LAW

Professor George begins with what he see as the conflicting interests affected by abortion legislation. He separates these into four foci: the fetus, the pregnant woman, the family and the surrounding community. The next section concerns the legal regulations of abortion before 1967 and trends toward legalized therapeutic abortion between 1968 and 1973. Finally, he looks at basic constitutional doctrines and the scope and constitutionality of current abortion legislation. This detailed review by Professor George takes on enhanced significance because the *Webster* case has allowed the individual states to have additional freedom in determing their own abortion laws. It is obvious that if *Roe* is ever overturned, state laws will once again be as significant as they were prior to 1973.

1 · State Legislatures Versus the Supreme Court: Abortion Legislation into the 1990s ____

B. J. George Jr., J.D.

Abortion regulation was a matter exclusively for state legislatures until 1973, when the United States Supreme Court brought medically indicated abortions within the protection of the fourteenth amendment in *Roe v. Wade*[1] and *Doe v. Bolton*.[2] As will be surveyed in parts I and II of this chapter, some liberalization in the scope of lawful abortions was evident in several legislatures before 1973,[3] but few statutes approached the breadth of the privacy right decreed by the Court in *Roe* and *Doe*.

Since 1973, and with increasing celerity since 1988, when the possibility emerged that *Roe* might be overturned by a reconstituted Supreme Court, a majority of state legislatures have tried to impose functional limitations on the availability of abortions both before and after viability.[4] Many (but not all) of these efforts have been invalidated in subsequent decisions by the Court, but in many instances the legislatures have left their statutes unrevised, despite their patent unconstitutionality. Thus, the onus is on the courts to squelch efforts to invoke unconstitutional laws against pregnant women and their physicians. Unconstitutional laws still exist because, in many states, a majority of

---

[1] 410 U.S. 113 (1973).

[2] 410 U.S. 179 (1973).

[3] In parts II and III of this chapter, only the names of the states and not specific statutory citations appear. For more information, see *infra* note 31.

[4] For a detailed coverage of state legislation, see Linton, *Enforcement of State Abortion Statutes After Roe: A State-by-State Analysis,* 67 U. Det. L. Rev. 157 (1990) [hereinafter Linton]. NARAL, Who Decides?: A State-by-State Review of Abortion Rights (1991), contains a limited summary of laws and legislative proposals on selected categories of problems and major political party platforms, arranged jurisdiction by jurisdiction.

legislators are hostile to freely available abortions,[5] whereas in others they appear to be cowed by threats of reprisals at the polls from the so-called "right-to-life" movement.

A pragmatic understanding of the causes of unsatisfactory legislative coverage of abortion law does not change the fact that state statutes in too many jurisdictions provide no guidance to, or protection for, pregnant women and their medical advisors. Consequently, a legislative limbo occurs in which one of two phenomena is likely to appear.

The first possibility is that medical abortion becomes an out-of-view dimension of hospital administration governed by local or state public health regulations. This alternative may prove a practical accommodation acceptable to both legislators and physicians. Legislators are not called on to take action visible to their constituents that the latter will view as approving abortions, and the medical profession can treat abortion like any other dimension of medical practice. The second possibility is official disapproval of therapeutic abortions that will force pregnant women, their physicians and the administrators of clinics to turn to the judiciary for redress.

At this writing, the best conclusion one can assay is that there is a widespread anticipation or fear (depending on one's point of view) that *Roe* will be abrogated or significantly restricted by a reconstituted Supreme Court; it is at least a strong possibility that the Court will retreat from its earlier interpretation of the Constitution. Several legislatures in 1990 and 1991 have begun to legislate in anticipation of such a change—most by enacting highly restrictive legislation but in some instances[6] by endeavoring to guarantee a perpetuation of *Roe* analysis as a matter of state law.

The following pages offer a brief review of the conflicting interests recognized in or affected by abortion legislation; then a summary of the basic constitutional principles set forth by the Court in 1973 and thereafter; and finally, an evaluation of the compatibility of state legislation as of 1991 with the federal Constitution.

I. Conflicting Interests Affected by Abortion Legislation

Discussions of the desirability or illicitness of abortion revolve about four foci: the fetus, the pregnant woman, the family into which a child will be born if a pregnancy goes to term and the surrounding community.

As to the first focus, there clearly is a semantic issue. A choice from among an array of terms—conceptus, zygote, embryo, fertilized ovum, fetus or prenatal infant—advertises the thinking of the speaker and not a scientifically impeccable choice of terms.[7] Whichever term is selected, concern about fetuses typically reflects two contradictory schools of thought.

According to one of these schools, inviolate life comes into being from the time an ovum is fertilized.[8] The strongest adherence to this view has been found within the

---

[5] *See infra* notes 147–54 and accompanying text.

[6] Connecticut and Maryland.

[7] On other semantic aspects of the abortion debate, see Bell, *Toward a New Analysis of the Abortion Debate,* 33 Ariz. L. Rev. 907, 913–14 (1991) [hereafter Bell]; Fromer, *Abortion Ethics,* 30 Nursing Outlook 234, 234–35 (April 1982) [hereinafter cited as Fromer]; Hardin, *Semantic Aspects of Abortion,* 24 ETC.: A Review of General Semantics 263 (1967); Murray, *Nature and Rights of the Foetus,* 1990 Am. J. Juris. 149, 157 [hereinafter Murray]. *See also* Chemerinsky, *Rationalizing the Abortion Debate: Legal Rhetoric and the Abortion Controversy,* 31 Buffalo L. Rev. 107 (1982) [hereinafter cited as Chemerinsky].

[8] *See generally* Rubenfeld, *On the Legal Status of the Proposition that "Life Begins at Conception,"* 43 Stan. L. Rev. 599 (1991).

Roman Catholic faith, which has condemned abortion under all circumstances.[9] There is, however, also Protestant support for the idea.[10] The second view is that the possible fate of a full-term fetus should be taken into account. If a child would be born deformed, mentally defective or otherwise incapable of living a normal life or would be born into a highly detrimental environment for which it could not be adequately compensated,[11] it may be preferable to terminate its incipient life. This premise is likely to be an argument incidental to advocacy of liberalized abortion based on social necessity.[12] Adoption of the first view of fetal life impels rejection of all abortion.[13] Yet to adopt the second is usually to favor abortion in a relatively wider array of instances.

The second focus is on pregnant women.[14] Most women concerned with their legal positions favor a free choice on their part. Indeed, this is a strong dimension of the

---

[9] Canon 1398 (1983): "A person who actually procures an abortion incurs a *latae sententiae* [automatic] excommunication." On the corresponding predecessor provision, canon 2350, § 1, see 8 C. Bachofen, Commentary on Canon Law 397–402 (1931).

In support of the Roman Catholic position, see, *e.g.,* Brown, *Recent Statutes and the Crime of Abortion,* 16 Loy. L. Rev. 275 (1970); Decker & Decker, *The Credibility Gap That Kills,* 131 America 47 (Aug. 10, 1974); Giannella, *The Difficult Quest for a Truly Humane Abortion Law,* 13 Vill. L. Rev. 257, 292 (1968) [hereinafter cited as Giannella]; Granfield, *Law and Morals,* 4 Criminologica 11 (Feb. 1967); Heaney, *On the Legal Status of the Unborn,* 33 Cath. Law. 305 (1990); McConnell, *The Unalienable Right to Life,* 1990 J. Christ. Juris. 53; Noonan, *Abortion: From "An Almost Absolute Value in History,"* in Moral Problems in Medicine 290 (S. Gorovitz *et al.* ed. 1976); Murray, *supra* note 7, *passim.*

[10] *See, e.g.,* H. Thielicke, Ethics of Sex 226–47 (J. Doberstein trans. 1964) [hereinafter cited as H. Thielicke]; Baum, *Abortion: An Ecumenical Dilemma,* 99 Commonweal 231 (Nov. 30, 1973); Brown, *An Evangelical Looks at the Abortion Phenomenon,* 135 America 161 (Sept. 25, 1976); Eller, *Let's Get Honest About Abortion,* 92 Christian Century 16 (Jan. 1–8, 1975); Ramsey, *Ethics of a Cottage Industry in an Age of Community and Research Medicine,* 284 New England J. of Med. 700, 701–03 (1971); Note, *Abortion, Laws, Religious Beliefs and the First Amendment,* 14 Val. U.L. Rev. 487, 497–503 (1980).

Mainline Protestant denominations generally take a contrary position. For example, the United Methodist Church at its 1988 quadrennial general conference supported the "legal option of abortion under proper medical procedures"; because "[g]overnmental laws and regulations do not provide all the guidance required by the informed Christian conscience," "a decision concerning abortion should be made only after thoughtful and prayerful consideration by the parties involved, with medical, pastoral, and other appropriate counsel." United Methodist Church, *Book of Resolutions* 96, para. 71G (1988).

For a general survey of contemporary religious positions, see Nelson, *The Churches and Abortion Law Reform,* 1983 J. Christ. Juris. 29.

Traditional Jewish law views abortion as a tort, not a criminal activity. However, some contemporary rabbinic sources speak of it in terms of homicide. *See* Sinclair, *Legal Basis for the Prohibition on Abortion in Jewish Law,* 15 Israel L. Rev. 109 (1980).

[11] *See* Dahlberg, *Abortion,* in Sexual Behavior and the Law 379, 389 (R. Slovenko ed. 1965); Krimmel & Foley, *Abortion: An Inspection Into the Nature of Human Life and Potential Consequences of Legalizing Its Destruction,* 46 U. Cin. L. Rev. 725, 780–89 (1977) [hereinafter cited as Krimmel & Foley].

[12] *See* Hardin, *Abortion—Or Compulsory Pregnancy?,* 30 J. Marriage & the Family 246, 247 (1968); Samuels, *Termination of Pregnancy: A Lawyer Considers the Arguments,* 7 Med., Sci. & L. 10, 12–13 (1967).

[13] *See* H. Thielicke, *supra* note 10; *but see* Giannella, *supra* note 9, at 301–02.

[14] *See* Jones, *Abortion and the Consideration of Fundamental Irreconcilable Interests,* 33 Syracuse L. Rev. 565, 612–13 (1982) [hereinafter cited as Jones]; Thomson, *A Defense of Abortion,* 1 Philosophy & Pub. Affairs 47 (1971); *cf.* Note, *Isolating the Male Bias Against Reform of Abortion Legislation,* 10 Santa Clara L. Rev. 301 (1970).

Maternal life and health are increasingly recognized as grounds for lawful therapeutic abortions in other countries through legislation. For a survey of national laws, see Bulfinch, *Introduction: Symposium on Abortion Law and Public Policy,* 7 Comp. L. Y.B. 3 (1984) [hereinafter cited as Bulfinch]; Dourlen-Rollier, *Legal Problems Related to Abortion and Menstrual Regulation,* 7 Colum. Human Rts. L. Rev. 120, 126–32 (1975). For a summary of abortion laws and policies in 32 countries, see International Handbook on Abortion (P. Sachdev ed. 1988).

Supreme Court's constitutional analysis.[15] One exception is the contention that inter-course producing pregnancy is licit only if done within marriage and for procreation.[16] Hence, an unwanted pregnancy is unfortunate, but the fulfillment of divine mandate. Therefore, a woman must carry a fetus to term, whatever the consequences. This school of thought aside, most statements of policy are sympathetic toward pregnant women. This is based on the importance of health concerns rather than the complete favoring of free choice.[17]

A third focus is on the family unit to which the pregnant woman belongs and into which the baby will be born. Some schools of thought stress concern for the freedom of sexual partners to decide whether they will have children.[18] Others emphasize the economic and emotional well-being of the whole family. The family unit may be ad-versely affected if limited resources must be stretched to care for another member or if siblings experience emotional deprivation because parental care is diluted by yet another child.[19] The use of abortion for purposes of gender selection likewise can be germane to the shaping of family units, for example, in a culture in which male heirs are impor-

---

Austrian legislation in 1977 allowed medical interruptions of pregnancy during the first three months of pregnancy, and thereafter if founded on medical or eugenic indications or if the pregnant female was under age 14 at the time of conception. The Austrian Constitutional Court ultimately sustained its lawful-ness in the face of contentions that it violated the European Convention on Human Rights. *See* Mock, *Symposium on Abortion Law and Public Policy: Austria,* 7 Comp. L. Y.B. 19 (1984).

The English Abortion Act, 1967, adopted a relatively liberal view concerning the availability of ther-apeutic abortion. *See generally* Grubb, *Abortion Law—An English Perspective,* 20 N.M.L. Rev. 649 (1990). The English legislation has influenced other Commonwealth nations. *See* Dickens & Cook, *Development of Commonwealth Abortion Laws,* 28 Int'l & Comp. L.Q. 424, 442–56 (1979) [hereinafter cited as Dickens & Cook]; Menon, *The Law of Abortion With Special Reference to the Commonwealth Caribbean,* 5 Anglo-Am. L. Rev. 311, 327–37 (1976) [hereinafter cited as Menon]. Barbados legislation substantially resembles the English legislation. *See* Menon, *The Medical Termination of Pregnancy Act 1983 (Barbados),* 32 Int. & Comp. L.Q. 630 (1985). In 1990 the Human Fertilisation and Embryology Act, § 37, made certain changes in the available grounds for lawful abortion, imposed time limits within which lawful abortions may be performed, included within the scope of regulated abortion the practice of selective reduction and authorized the use of medicinal abortifacient substances. *See* Grubb, *The New Law of Abortion: Clarifica-tion or Ambiguity?,* [1991] Crim. L. Rev. 659.

The Canadian Criminal Code § 251(4) allows licensed medical practitioners to terminate pregnancies in licensed hospitals if necessary to preserve a woman's life or health. *See generally The Abortion Debate in the United States and Canada: A Source Book* 173–81, 212–22 (M. Muldoon ed. 1991); Beschle, *Judicial Review and Abortion in Canada: Lessons for the United States in the Wake of Webster v. Repro-ductive Health Services,* 61 U. Colo. L. Rev. 537 (1990); Dickens, *Reproduction Law and Medical Con-sent,* 35 U. Toronto L.J. 255, 271–78 (1985); Dickens, *Eugenic Recognition in Canadian Law,* 13 Osgoode Hall L.J. 547, 562–65 (1975) [hereinafter cited as Dickens]; Marshall, *Liberty, Abortion and Constitutional Review in Canada,* 1988 Public Law 199; Micallef, *Meaning and Interpretation of "Unlawful" in Cana-da's Abortion Law,* 23 C. de D. 1029 (1982); Shumlatcher, *"I Set Before You Life and Death" (Abortion—Borowski and the Constitution),* 24 U. West. Ont. L. Rev. 1 (1987); Note, *A Comparison of United States and Canadian Approaches to the Rights of Privacy and Abortion,* 15 Brooklyn Int. L.J. 759, 785–98 (1989).

On the availability of abortions in francophonic nations, primarily those in Europe, see Knoppers, Brault & Sloss, *Abortion Law in Francophone Countries,* 38 Am. J. Comp. L. 889 (1990).

Therapeutic abortion is asserted to be contrary to the Irish Constitution. Mathew, *Quantitative Inter-ference with the Right to Life: Abortion and Irish Law,* 22 Cath. Law. 344, 356–58 (1976). On a right-to-life amendment to that constitution, see *Recent Developments: This Amendment Could Kill Women,* 7 Harv. Women's L.J. 287 (1984).

In India, the Medical Termination of Pregnancy Act, 1971 (MTPA), replaced § 312 of the Indian Penal Code, which had allowed abortions only to save maternal life. MTPA § 3(2) allows termination of pregnancy by an individual medical practitioner during the first trimester and from the 13th through the

tant to achieving the care of parents in their old age.[20] Concentration on factors like these almost always leads to support of liberal abortion.

A final focus is on the needs of the community. Any of the concerns already listed, of course, can be restated in terms of social interests (e.g., protection of the life of the fetus, protection of maternal health or protection of the health of a viable family unit). But within the community dimension there are at least two additional concerns. One is the factor of population control. Abortion clearly can be a means of birth control, albeit a much less satisfactory form than mechanical or chemical contraceptive methods.[21] In the past, the population control use of abortion has been evident in some cultures.[22] With improved contraceptive methods, reliance on abortion for that purpose has become less necessary. Some writers have suggested that legalized abortion as a means of population control manifests an impermissible exercise of state power[23] or have expressed fear that it will result in too stark a decline in population levels to permit the state to survive.[24] In reality, however, abortion produces only incidental population control

---

20th week on the good faith medical opinion of two practitioners that continuation of pregnancy would risk the life of a pregnant woman or threaten grave injury to her physical or mental health or that there is a substantial risk that the child, if born, will suffer from physical or mental abnormalities that will seriously handicap it. Grave injury to mental health is presumed in instances of rape and contraceptive failure, and a woman's "actual or reasonably foreseeable environment" may be taken into account in determining the risk to maternal health. Abortions can be performed only by registered practitioners in a government-approved facility and must be consented to by the patient or her guardian if she is younger than 18. After the 20th week of pregnancy, abortions are allowed only if necessary to preserve a woman's life; life-threatening emergencies also justify performance of abortions without the concurrence of a second practitioner in other than licensed facilities. *See generally* Bose, *Abortion in India: A Legal Study,* 16 Indian L. Inst. J. 535 (1974) [hereinafter cited as Bose]; Menon, *Population Policy, Law Enforcement and the Liberalization of Abortion: A Socio-Legal Inquiry Into the Implementation of the Abortion Law in India,* 16 Indian L. Inst. J. 626 (1974).

In Israel, the Criminal Law Amendment (Abortion) Law, 1977, allows consensual abortion for women under 17 or over 40, women pregnant because of illegal, consanguineous or nonmarital relations, women whose fetuses are likely to be born with physical or mental handicaps or women whose pregnancies might cause grievous harm to them or their other children because of difficult family or social conditions experienced by them or their families. *See* Falk, *The New Abortion Law of Israel,* 13 Israel L. Rev. 103 (1978) (containing English translation of text at 109–10); Shnit, *Induced Abortion in Israeli Law,* 15 Israel Y.B. on Human Rights 155 (1985); Slater, Weiner & Davies, *Illegal Abortion in Israel,* 13 Israel L. Rev. 411 (1978).

In Italy, medical abortion was liberalized by statute in 1978; the new statute was sustained by the Constitutional Court, at least indirectly, and is assumed, therefore, to be constitutional. *See generally* Bognetti, *Symposium on Abortion Law and Public Policy: Italy,* 7 Comp. L. Y.B. 83 (1984).

In Christian League of South Africa v. Rall. [1981] 2 S.A. 820, the court denied the petitioning organization's claim to be appointed curator ad litem for the unborn child of an unmarried woman, pregnant as the result of rape, who had obtained a judicial certification for an abortion. *See* Bedil, *Can a Fetus Be Protected From Its Mother?,* 98 S. Afr. L.J. 462 (1981).

The West German therapeutic abortion statute, Law of June 18, 1974, [1974] Bundesgesetzblatt, Teil I, § 1297 (see legislative history in Horton, *Abortion Law Reform in the German Federal Republic,* 28 Int'l & Comp. L.Q. 288 (1979)), was declared unconstitutional by the Federal Constitutional Court, Jt. of Feb. 25, 1975, 39 Bundesverfassungsgericht, 1975 Juristenzeitung 206, on the basis that it conflicted with the Grundgesetz (Basic Law), art. 2(2), which guarantees everyone "the right to life and to inviolability of his person"; the term *"Jeder"* (everyone) was construed to embrace fetal life. *See* Gerstein & Lowry, *Abortion, Abstract Norms, and Social Control: The Decision of the West German Federal Constitutional Court,* 25 Emory L.J. 849, 859, 863 (1976); Lommers, *Abortion and Constitution: United States and West Germany,* 25 Am. J. Comp. L. 255 (1977); Mezey, *Civil Law and Common Law Traditions: Judicial Review and Legislative Supremacy in West Germany and Canada,* 32 Int. & Comp. L.Q. 689, 696–700 (1983);

consequences[25] and so poses no serious threat either to population levels or citizens' liberties.[26]

A second social factor addresses the freedom of the medical profession to approach termination of pregnancies on the same basis as other medical problems, free from arbitrary controls. This, too, has found strong support in the United States Supreme Court's constitutional jurisprudence.[27]

These concerns, although not necessarily comprehensive, demonstrate the principal policy interests implicated by abortion legislation and constitutional precedents governing it. In most jurisdictions in the United States to 1967, abortions were allowed only to save the lives of pregnant women.[28] Activists within the self-proclaimed "right-to-life" movement believe the United States Constitution should be amended to prohibit all abortions or, at a minimum, to allow only those necessary to save maternal life. In contrast, the supreme Court's current constitutional analysis recognizes a woman's freedom of choice. Any woman early in pregnancy may, in consultation with a willing physician, choose to have an abortion. As pregnancy advances, medical considerations

---

Morris, *Abortion and Liberalism: A Comparison Between the Abortion Decisions of the Supreme Court of the United States and the Constitutional Court of West Germany*, 11 Hastings Int'l & Comp. L. Rev. 159 (1988). Thereafter, the West German *Bundestag* enacted replacement legislation, an English translation of which may be found in Bulfinch, *supra*, at 15–17; see also Eser, *Reform of German Abortion Law: First Experiences*, 34 Am. J. Comp. L. 369 (1986); Quaas, *Symposium on Abortion Law and Public Policy: Federal Republic of Germany*, 7 Comp. L. Y.B. 41 (1984). (At this writing, it does not appear that the German law has yet been reconsidered following the reunification of Germany in 1990; the basic principle adopted at reunification is that the former West German penal and civil law will apply throughout the country.)

On subsequent unsuccessful efforts by pro-choice proponents to invoke art. 8(1) of the European Convention before the European Commission on Human Rights, see Note, *Abortion Law Reform in Europe: The European Commission on Human Rights Upholds German Restrictions on Abortion (Brueggemann and Scheuten v. Federal Republic of Germany)*, 15 Tex. Int'l. L.J. 162 (1980) (also surveying contemporary legislative developments in Austria, France and Italy).

On developments in abortion legislation in Poland, see Fuszara, *Legal Regulation of Abortion in Poland*, in Signs: Journal of Women in Culture & Soc. 117 (1991).

On the status of abortion in the People's Republic of China and the U.S.S.R., see Savage, *The Law of Abortion in the Union of Soviet Socialist Republics and the People's Republic of China: Women's Rights in Two Socialist Countries*, 40 Stanford L. Rev. 1027 (1988).

[15] *See* Roe v. Wade, 410 U.S. 113, 152–54 (1973) (concerning privacy implications).

[16] For an interpretation of Saint Augustine's view of sexual relations not too removed from this, see D. Bromley, Catholics and Birth Control 9–15 (1965).

[17] *See, e.g.*, Johnsen, *From Driving to Drugs: Governmental Regulation of Pregnant Women's Lives After Webster*, 138 U. Pa. L. Rev. 179 (1989); Comment, *The Right to Privacy: Does It Allow a Woman the Right to Determine Whether to Bear Children?*, 20 Am. U. L. Rev. 136 (1970). *See also* Roe v. Wade, 410 U.S. at 154 (Court rejected absolute constitutional protection for abortions of choice not based on medical considerations).

[18] *See* J. Fletcher, Morals and Medicine 92–99 (Beacon Press ed. 1960); Thompson, *A Defense of Abortion*, 1 Philosophy & Pub. Affairs 47 (1971).

[19] *See* Krimmel & Foley, *supra* note 11, at 792–96. Only Japan appears to embody this specifically in its statute. Eugenic Protection Law *(Yûseihogohô)* (Law No. 156, 1948, as amended), art. 3(5) permits abortion "if there are several children and the mother's health will be seriously impaired if she again delivers." Article 14 permits a doctor authorized by a district medical association to terminate a pregnancy at his or her discretion, with consent of both husband and wife, for several reasons, including the likelihood of substantial injury to the mother's health for either physical or economic reasons if the pregnancy continues to term (author's translation and paraphrase). Some Scandinavian legislation extends about as broadly. *See* Clemmesen, *State of Legal Abortion in Denmark*, 112 Am. J. Psych. 662 (1956); Klintskog, *Survey of Legislation on Legal Abortion in Europe and North America*, 21 Medico-Legal J. 79 (1953).

become more significant but can never be eclipsed by a desire solely to preserve fetal life. Of course, as noted *passim* below, future terms of the Supreme Court may see a change on the Court's part concerning its doctrines in place since 1973.[29] Until or unless there is change, however, the tension will continue as it was in the 1980s, namely, between abortion as a dimension of medical practice and prohibition of abortion as unwarranted termination of human fetal life. Abortion for purposes of population control, eugenics or preservation of family strength and harmony is not within the ambit of the Supreme Court's constitutional concerns and finds no home in today's legislative chambers. For now, concerns of this nature continue to be matters for moral, ethical and theological debate, not litigation or the legislative process.

II. Legal Regulation of Abortion Before 1967[30]

A. Criminal Statutes

1. STATUTES PENALIZING ABORTION   Criminal statutes outlawing abortion date from 1821.[31] Common law precedent was so scant that it played an insignificant role in evaluating the legality of abortions.[32] Statutes were roughly classifiable into those that

---

The English Abortion Act, 1967, c. 87, § 1(2), permits medical practitioners to take account of "the pregnant woman's actual or reasonably foreseeable environment" in deciding whether, under § 1(1)(a), there is risk of "injury to the physical or mental health of the pregnant woman or any existing children of her family, greater than if the pregnancy were terminated." *Id.* at § 1(1)(a). *See* G. Williams, *Textbook of Criminal Law* 256 (1978) [hereinafter cited as G. Williams, *Criminal Law*]; Simms, *Abortion Law Reform: How the Controversy Changed*, 1970 Crim. L. Rev. 567, 568–71. India's Medical Termination of Pregnancy Act, 1971, § 3(2) embodies similar considerations. *See supra* note 14.

[20] Pennsylvania legislation declares that no abortion sought solely because of the sex of the fetus is to be deemed a necessary abortion. Pa. Cons. Stat. Ann. § 3204(c) (Purdon Supp. 1992).

[21] The dividing line between abortion, on the one hand, and contraceptive devices or pharmaceuticals preventing the implantation on the uterine wall of a fertilized ovum, on the other, is not intrinsically clear. *See* Roe v. Wade, 410 U.S. at 160–61; Brahams, *Postcoital Pill and Intrauterine Device: Contraceptive or Abortifacient?*, 1983 Lancet, vol. 1, no. 8332, p. 1039 (May 7, 1983); Cole, *The End of the Abortion Debate*, 138 U. Pa. L. Rev. 217 (1989) [hereinafter cited as Cole] (on the implications of RU486, the "French abortion pill," for surgical abortion); Knoppers, *Modern Birth Technology and Human Rights*, 33 Am. J. Comp. L. 1 (1985); Tunkel, *Modern Anti-Pregnancy Techniques and the Criminal Law*, 1974 Crim. L. Rev. 461. On amniocentesis and other sex-determining and sex-selecting techniques, see Dickens, *Abortion, Amniocentesis and the Law*, 34 Am. J. Comp. L. 249 (1986); Nolan-Haley, *Amniocentesis and the Apotheosis of Human Quality Control*, 2 J. Legal Med. 347 (1981); Warren, *Law of Human Reproduction: An Overview*, 3 J. Legal Med. 1, 49–51 (1982) [hereinafter cited as Warren]; Note, *Genetic Screening, Eugenic Abortion, and Roe v. Wade: How Viable Is Roe's Viability Standard?*, 50 Brooklyn L. Rev. 113, 125–30 (1983); Note, *Sex Selection Abortion: A Constitutional Analysis of the Abortion Liberty and a Person's Right to Know*, 56 Ind. L.J. 281, 284–88 (1981); Comment, *Legal Status of the Morning-After Pill: Abortion or Birth Control?*, 25 U.S.F.L. Rev. 402 (1991).

On other socioeconomic concerns, see Menon, *supra* note 14, at 317–18.

[22] *See* Roemer, *Abortion Law Reform and Repeal: Legislative and Judicial Developments*, 61 Am. J. Pub. Health 500, 505–06 (1971) [hereinafter cited as Roemer], describing such a reliance on abortion in several Pacific Basin nations. India's Medical Termination of Pregnancy Act, 1971, seems strongly aimed at population control. *See* Kelkar, *Impact of the Medical Termination of Pregnancy Act, 1971: A Case Study*, 16 Indian L. Inst. J. 603, 693 (1974) [hereinafter cited as Kelkar].

Traditional Japanese attitudes encouraged large families and therefor viewed the use of contraceptives as improper, even by married couples, see R. Beardsley, J. Hall & R. Ward, *Village Japan* 335–36 (1959), but that view has weakened substantially, particularly in urban areas where nuclear families have replaced the extended family units typical of rural Japan. *See* R. Dore, *City Life in Japan* 205 n.196 (1958). Kelkar, *supra* at 619, records advice by Japan's former Premier Sato to Indian authorities not to rely heavily on abortion as a means of population control, based on Japanese experience.

prohibited all abortions and those that allowed some abortions under carefully limited circumstances. The laws of four states[33] provided no exceptions to a general prohibition against abortion, although judicial interpretations softened the harsh impact of the legislation.[34] In the remaining states and the District of Columbia, abortions were permissible to preserve maternal life.

Even during that era, a few states went beyond saving the lives of pregnant women. Some permitted abortions to preserve the life of an unborn child,[35] a qualification with little or no effect other than to exempt induced labor at or near term from the scope of abortion law.[36] Two states allowed abortions necessary to forestall serious and permanent bodily injury,[37] and two other jurisdictions recognized any maternal health considerations.[38]

A number of difficult legal problems arose in administering restrictive legislation. The first had to do with classes of persons authorized to perform abortions in instances of exigency. Twenty-six states appeared to allow anyone to perform an abortion,[39] and the rest required that abortions be done by physicians or surgeons.

---

[23] See H. Thielicke, *supra* note 10, at 215–25; Cole, *supra* note 21 *passim;* Krimmel & Foley, *supra* note 11, at 796–97. *Cf.* Planned Parenthood Ass'n of Kansas City v. Ashcroft, 655 F.2d 848, 868–69 (8th Cir. 1981), *aff'd on other grounds,* 462 U.S. 476 (1983) (requirement that woman be told approximate length of pregnancy found unconstitutional because it would eliminate use of menstrual extraction and similar techniques, which under the state law would be an abortion); Margaret S. v. Edwards, 488 F. Supp. 181, 190–91 (E.D. La. 1980) (definition of abortion was not impermissibly vague even though it might have included IUDs and morning-after pills [two forms of birth control], since no other statutory formulation would be more precise, and abortion does not include contraceptive measures). N.M. Stat. Ann. § 30-5-1(A) (1989) defines pregnancy as implantation of an embryo in the uterus, which excludes morning-after pills from the scope of abortion provisions. Okla. Stat. Ann. tit. 63, § 1-730(8) (West 1984) excludes from the definition of abortion birth control devices or medications. 18 Pa. Cons. Stat. Ann. § 3203 (1983) excludes from the statutory definition of abortion the use of IUDs or birth control pills ''to inhibit or prevent ovulation, fertilization or the implantation of a fertilized ovum within the uterus.'' W. Va. Code § 16-2B-2 (1991) states that abortion is not considered an approved method of family planning and is excluded from state-supported family planning programs, and Wis. Stat. Ann. § 146.80(1) (West 1989) prohibits family planning services from promoting, encouraging or performing voluntary terminations of pregnancy.

On contraception as a desirable alternative to abortion, see Sneideman, *Abortion: A Public Health and Social Policy Perspective,* 7 N.Y.U. Rev. L. & Soc. Change 187, 206–12 (1978) [hereinafter cited as Sneideman].

The matter of *in vitro* fertilization is also addressed in some legislation, *e.g.,* Minn. Stat. Ann. § 145.422(3) (West Supp. 1989) (gross misdemeanor to buy or sell living human conceptus); 18 Pa. Cons. Stat. Ann. § 3213(e)(5) (1983) (various data to be reported, including ''number of fertilized eggs destroyed or discarded''). *See* Dickens, *supra* note 14, at 573–74; Noonan, *Christian Tradition and the Control of Human Reproduction,* 1983 J. Christ. Juris. 1, 11–15; Warren, *supra* note 21, at 5.

[24] That may have underlain the rescission in 1956 of the U.S.S.R. law allowing easy abortion. *See* G. Williams, *The Sanctity of Life and the Criminal Law* 219–20 (1957) [hereinafter cited as G. Williams, *Sanctity*]. That rescission in turn, however, is reported to have been modified. P. Gebhard, W. Pomeroy, C. Martin & C. Christenson, *Pregnancy, Birth and Abortion* 208–11 (1958). So was a similar change in Bulgarian law. Roemer, *supra* note 22, at 504.

[25] Sulloway, *The Legal and Political Aspects of Population Control in the United States,* 25 L. & Contemp. Probs. 593, 597–98 (1960); Tietze, *The Current Status of Fertility Control,* 25 L. & Contemp. Probs. 426, 442–44 (1960). Abortion as a means of population control appears to be significant in the People's Republic of China. Luk, *Abortion in Chinese Law,* 25 Am. J. Comp. L. 372, 389 (1977).

[26] Indeed, Dr. Thielicke's concerns (*see supra* note 23 and accompanying text) find no home in American constitutional jurisprudence, which stresses the right of married and unmarried persons to have information about contraception and access to contraceptives. *See* Bolger v. Youngs Drug Prods. Corp., 463 U.S. 60 (1983) (holding federal statute prohibiting mailing of unsolicited advertisements for contraceptives unconstitutional); Carey v. Population Servs. Int'l, 431 U.S. 678 (1977); Eisenstadt v. Baird, 405 U.S. 438

The second turned on whether necessity was to be determined on an objective or strict liability basis or whether a good faith belief in the existence of justifying medical grounds would suffice. Many statutes seemingly defined necessity as an objective element,[40] although some courts embraced a good faith professional belief that necessity existed, despite the rather plain statutory language to the contrary.[41] The impact on physicians of this usual language was ameliorated to some extent where the burden of proving want of medical necessity was placed on the prosecution.[42] Legislation in three states[43] and the District of Columbia was specific in stating that belief or motivation, and not objective necessity, governed the statutory exception from coverage.

The common law requirement that a fetus be quick before there could be a criminal abortion[44] had disappeared from statutory law: Twenty-three states[45] referred only to pregnancy, and four other states used "whether quick or not."[46] In a handful of states, duration of pregnancy had begun to reemerge as a legal element of abortion, which had begun to expand the scope of noncriminal abortion.[47] Therapeutic abortions were limited in three states to the period of nonviability.[48]

(1972) (legislation allowing distribution of contraceptives to married couples but not to single persons violated the equal protection clause); Griswold v. Connecticut, 381 U.S. 479 (1965) (overturning state law banning use of contraceptives).

[27] See Roe v. Wade, 410 U.S. 113, 156 (1973); see also infra notes 116–37 and accompanying text.

[28] See infra, notes 33–38 and accompanying text.

[29] Linton, supra note 4, is written from a right-to-life perspective and indicates passim the impact on state statutes of a reversal of Roe. See id. at 255–56 (table showing status of pre-Roe state abortion laws "after Roe is overruled").

[30] In parts II and III of this chapter, only the names of the states and not specific statutory citations appear. This is because almost all the legislation in force through 1973 has been replaced. Persons wishing then-contemporary citations may find them in George, The Evolving Law of Abortion, 23 Case W. Res. L. Rev. 708 (1972) (passim).

[31] See G. Williams, Sanctity, supra note 24, at 152–56; Quay, Justifiable Abortion—Medical and Legal Foundations, 49 Geo. L.J. 173, 231–38 (1960); Special Project: Survey of Abortion Law, 1980 Ariz. St. L.J. 87, 93–100 [hereinafter cited as Special Project].

[32] Most common-law cases covered only conduct that caused miscarriages after fetuses had quickened. See R. Perkins & R. Boyce, Criminal Law 186–88 (3d ed. 1983) [hereinafter Perkins & Boyce].

On the historical antecedents and development of the law of abortion, see Dellapena, The History of Abortion: Technology, Morality, and Law, 40 U. Pitt. L. Rev. 359, 365–407 (1979) [hereinafter cited as Dellapena]; Destro, Abortion and the Constitutions: The Need for a Life-Protective Amendment, 63 Calif. L. Rev. 1250, 1267–82 (1975) [hereinafter cited as Destro]; Dickens & Cook, supra note 14, at 425–41; Menon, supra note 14, at 323–26; Special Project, supra note 31, at 73–100.

[33] Louisiana, Massachusetts, New Jersey, Pennsylvania. In New Hampshire, the attempted abortion statute allowed no exceptions, while a companion provision penalizing completed abortions justified acts necessary to save maternal life.

[34] Commonwealth v. Brunelle, 341 Mass. 675, 677, 171 N.E.2d 850, 852 (1961) (physicians who acted in an honest belief that abortions were necessary to avoid great peril to maternal life or health did not violate the statute, if their judgments corresponded with the average judgment of doctors in the communities where they practiced); State v. Brandenburg, 137 N.J.L. 124, 126–28, 58 A.2d 709, 710–11 (1948) (abortions necessary to save life, but not health).

[35] Connecticut, Minnesota, Missouri, South Carolina, Washington.

[36] This is dealt with today in statutory definitions of abortion. See infra, notes 155–65 and accompanying text.

[37] Colorado, New Mexico.

[38] Alabama, District of Columbia. Occasionally, broad judicial interpretations achieved the same result. See, e.g., Walsingham v. State, 250 So. 2d 857 (Fla. 1971) (physical and mental health); Commonwealth v. Brunell, 341 Mass. 675, 171 N.E.2d 850 (1961) (physical and mental health).

[39] Alabama, Arizona, Connecticut, Idaho, Indiana, Iowa, Kentucky, Maine, Michigan, Minnesota, Montana, Nebraska, Nevada, North Dakota, Ohio, Oklahoma, Rhode Island, South Dakota, Tennessee, Texas, Utah,

Another array of legal problems arose when, despite efforts to abort a fetus, no miscarriage occurred. This might have resulted from an interrupted or incompletely performed abortion or from the fact the woman was not pregnant. Some 32 states[49] and the District of Columbia eliminated the first problem by penalizing the administration of drugs, use of an instrument or any other means intended to produce an abortion. If a woman was not pregnant, however, it might have been argued under common law concepts that the crime was "impossible" to attempt.[50] Such a defense was unavailable under abortion statutes that prohibited abortion activity affecting "any woman,"[51] a woman "whether pregnant or not,"[52] or a woman believed by a defendant to be pregnant.[53] Several courts relied on such language to affirm convictions for abortion even though the affected women were not pregnant.[54]

2. STATUTES PROHIBITING KILLING AN UNBORN QUICK CHILD   Before 1963 six states had statutes making it a separate offense to kill willfully an unborn quick child under circumstances in which, had the mother and not the fetus been killed, the crime would have been murder or manslaughter.[55] The aim of these statutes was not entirely

---

Vermont, West Virginia, Wyoming. Missouri legislation appeared to favor unlicensed abortionists. Abortion was proscribed unless necessary to preserve the life of a woman or her unborn child, but if the person performing an abortion was not a licensed physician, it was a defense that the performance had been advised by a duly licensed physician to be necessary for the purpose. Thus, a licensed physician was held to a standard of objective necessity while an unlicensed person could rely on medical advice whether or not the abortion was objectively necessary. The statute probably was intended to protect registered nurses and other hospital and medical staff personnel but was not so limited.

[40] Alabama, Arizona, Connecticut, Idaho, Illinois, Indiana, Iowa, Kentucky, Maine (good faith belief no defense: State v. Rudman, 126 Me. 177, 136 A. 817 (1927)); Michigan, Minnesota, Missouri, Montana, Nevada, North Dakota (good faith belief no defense: State v. Shortridge, 54 N.D. 779, 211 N.W. 336 (1929)); Oklahoma, Rhode Island, South Dakota, Utah, Vermont, Wyoming.

[41] Honnard v. People, 77 Ill. 481 (1875); State v. Dunklebarger, 206 Iowa 971, 221 N.W. 592 (1928).

[42] *Compare* the Supreme Court interpretation of the District of Columbia Code to that effect, in United States v. Vuitch, 402 U.S. 62 (1971).

[43] Tennessee, Texas, West Virginia. Several statutes enacted after 1967 in Arkansas, Florida, Georgia, New York, North Carolina, Oregon and South Carolina set a standard of "reasonable belief." That was a compromise position between strict liability and criminality turning on exclusively subjective considerations, but it achieved criminality based on criminal negligence. That standard of culpability seems inappropriate in the context of abortion, although perhaps recognizable in manslaughter prosecutions if a woman dies from the effects of a bungled abortion.

[44] *See generally* G. Williams, Criminal Law, *supra* note 19, at 252–53; Note, *Abortion Reform: History, Status, and Prognosis,* 21 Case W. Res. L. Rev. 521, 526–27 (1970).

[45] Alabama, Arizona, Colorado, Delaware, Florida, Georgia, Idaho, Illinois, Indiana, Kansas, Kentucky, Louisiana, Michigan, Mississippi, Montana, Nebraska, Nevada, New Jersey, New Mexico, North Carolina, North Dakota, Oklahoma, South Carolina, South Dakota, Tennessee, Texas, Utah, Wyoming.

[46] Arkansas, Kentucky, Maine, Tennessee. Statutes punishing attempted abortion also reduced the practical significance of pregnancy as an element of the crime of abortion. *See infra* notes 45–50 and accompanying text.

[47] California, Colorado, Delaware, New York, Oregon, Washington.

[48] Alaska, Hawaii, Washington.

[49] Alabama, Arizona, Arkansas, California, Connecticut, Delaware, Georgia, Idaho, Illinois, Indiana, Iowa, Kentucky, Louisiana, Maine, Massachusetts, Michigan, Missouri, Montana, Nebraska, Nevada, New Hampshire, New Jersey, New York, North Carolina, North Dakota, Ohio, South Carolina, South Dakota, Tennessee, Utah, Virginia, Washington. Texas had a special attempt provision that achieved the same result.

[50] *See generally* W. Lafave & A. Scott, *Criminal Law* 438–46 (1972); Perkins & Boyce, *supra* note 32, at 627–35. The doctrine of impossibility is repudiated in Model Penal Code § 5.01(1)(a) (1980). *See also* N.Y. Penal Law § 110.10 (McKinney 1987).

evident from either language or interpreting precedent, but their targets probably were those who intended to cause pregnant women to miscarry without their consent and who used physical violence against them for that purpose.[56]

3. STATUTES PENALIZING DEATH OF PREGNANT WOMEN RESULTING FROM ABORTION   Under classical criminal-law theory, should a pregnant woman die as a result of a criminal abortion, the abortionist should be guilty of either second-degree murder based on felony murder in the commission of a felony not enumerated under traditional first-degree murder statutes, the intentional infliction of grave bodily injury or the reckless performance of activity with known dangerous consequences or be guilty of manslaughter based on criminal negligence.[57] Several states confronted such cases directly by providing augmented punishment for performing an abortion should a woman die as a result[58] or by characterizing the death as either murder[59] or manslaughter.[60]

4. STATUES PENALIZING WOMEN WHO SEEK ABORTIONS   In default of special legislation, women who sought or submitted to abortions were generally not viewed as accomplices to the crime.[61] Rhode Island and Vermont preserved the doctrine by statute.[62] In several states, however, legislatures decreed that women who solicited or sub-

---

[51] California, District of Columbia, Iowa, Louisiana, Massachusetts, Ohio, Pennsylvania, Virginia, Washington, West Virginia.

[52] Illinois.

[53] Indiana, Kentucky, Rhode Island, Vermont, Wyoming.

[54] People v. Kutz, 187 Cal. App. 2d 431, 435, 9 Cal. Rptr. 626, 629 (1960); Urga v. State, 155 So. 2d 719, 723 (Fla.. Dist. Ct. App. 1963), cert. denied, 379 U.S. 829 (1964); People v. Marra, 27 Mich. App. 1, 5, 183 N.W.2d 418, 419 (1971); Wyatt v. State, 77 Nev. 490, 503, 367 P.2d 104, 111 (1961). Cf. Williams v. State, 218 Tenn. 359, 363–66, 403 S.W.2d 319, 322–23 (1966) (no defense that substances and instruments could not cause miscarriage). The Kentucky and Maine statutes, however, varied punishment levels according to whether a miscarriage actually resulted.

[55] Arkansas, Florida, Michigan, Mississippi, North Dakota, Oklahoma.

[56] Such statutes clearly accorded independent personality to fetuses, because the crime was called manslaughter and usually placed with other homicide offenses (where abortion legislation did not usually appear).

[57] See G. Williams, Criminal Law, supra note 19, at 244–45; Wechsler & Michael, Rationale of the Law of Homicide, 37 Colum. L. Rev. 701, 702–23 (1937).

[58] Colorado, Massachusetts, New Jersey, New Mexico, Rhode Island, South Carolina, Vermont.

[59] District of Columbia, New Hampshire, Texas, West Virginia.

[60] Michigan, Missouri, New York, North Dakota.

[61] See, e.g., Heath v. State, 249 Ark. 217, 219, 459 S.W.2d 420, 422 (1970), cert. denied, 404 U.S. 910 (1971); Commonwealth v. Rollansbee, 155 Mass. 274, 277, 29 N.E. 471, 471 (1892); In re Vickers, 371 Mich. 114, 118–19, 123 N.W.2d 253, 254–55 (1963) (woman could not be held for commission of abortion on herself and thus was not an aider or abettor thereof); In re Vince, 2 N.J. 443, 450, 67 A.2d 141, 144 (1949) (interpreted statute failing to denounce participation in abortion by pregnant woman as evidencing legislative policy to leave woman involved unpunished); State v. Shaft, 166 N.C. 407, 409, 81 S.E. 932, 933 (1914); Smartt v. State, 112 Tenn. 539, 553, 80 S.W. 586, 589 (1904); Willingham v. State, 33 Tex. Crim. 98, 99, 25 S.W. 424, 424 (1894). Compare State v. Clifford, 133 Iowa 478, 480, 110 N.W. 921, 922 (1907) (victim could not be charged because she had died as a result of the abortion, but court characterized her as a conspirator so that her statements were admissible against the abortionist as a declaration promoting the common criminal enterprise), with Snyder Appeal (Commonwealth v. Fisher), 398 Pa. 237, 246, 157 A.2d 207, 212 (1960) (woman is a victim and cannot be a conspirator). Contra, Steed v. State, 27 Ala. App. 263, 170 So. 489, aff'd, 233 Ala. 159, 170 So. 490 (1936); State v. McCoy, 52 Ohio St. 157, 160, 39 N.E. 316, 316 (1894).

On the English law, see 11 Halsbury's Laws of England ¶¶ 1191–92 (4th ed. 1976); G. Williams, Criminal Law, supra note 19, at 253.

[62] Revisers' comments to the Louisiana statute indicated an intent to preserve earlier case law to the same effect.

mitted to abortions that were not necessary to preserve their lives were criminals.[63] These statutes had two significant legal consequences and one practical result as well.

One consequence was that accompanying statutes sometimes required corroboration of a woman's testimony,[64] or were interpreted in that way.[65] A second was that women who underwent abortions, as putative criminal defendants, could claim privilege against self-incrimination when summoned to testify for the prosecution against an abortionist.[66] Because, however, that testimony frequently is critical to establishing guilt, some legislatures either purported to abolish privilege in such cases[67] or conferred immunity against prosecution for complicity in abortion on women who testified.[68] That brought the matter around full circle to where it would have been had participating women not been denominated criminals in the first place.[69] However, legislation penalizing abortion patients may have conferred a practical advantage on prosecutors by allowing them to threaten prosecution if a woman did not cooperate and to promise her immunity from prosecution if she did.

5. STATUTES PENALIZING ACTIVITY FACILITATING PERFORMANCE OF ABORTIONS Physicians performing abortions use instruments that are part of the ordinary equipment of gynecologists and obstetricians.[70] It is unrealistic for law enforcement officials to attempt to control the use of such instruments; in any event, the very nature of physician and hospital supply channels makes it unlikely that laypersons could procure them. In the decades before *Roe v. Wade*, however, self-induced abortions were a major public health problem,[71] and the devices and chemical substances used were clearly identifiable and devoid of legitimate modern uses. Since they were controllable without adverse impact on legitimate medical practice, legislatures consistently tried to control their availability.

The advertising of abortifacients was penalized in 23 states. In 19 of them, a special statute covered abortifacients either alone or in the context of medicines preventing conception, curing venereal disease and the like[72] while in others the prohibition appeared in the context of obscenity regulation.[73] The unconstitutionality of this form of legislation was recognized only recently.[74] State legislatures also sought to regulate

---

[63] Arizona, California, Connecticut, Idaho, Indiana, Minnesota, New York, North Dakota, Oklahoma, South Carolina, Utah, Washington, Wisconsin, Wyoming. State courts did not always apply the literal language of these statutes outside their specific coverage and thus held that women were not accomplices under the primary abortion statutes. *See* State v. Burlingame, 47 S.D. 332, 198 N.W. 824 (1924); State v. Cragun, 85 Utah 149, 38 P.2d 1071 (1934).

[64] California, Idaho, Montana, North Dakota, South Carolina.

[65] People v. Peyser, 380 Ill. 404, 44 N.E.2d 58 (1942); State v. McCoy, 52 Ohio St. 157, 39 N.E. 316 (1894).

[66] *See* Snyder Appeal (Commonwealth v. Fisher), 398 Pa. 237, 157 A.2d 207 (1960).

[67] Minnesota, Washington. Such statutes were obviously unconstitutional under Murphy v. Waterfront Comm'n, 378 U.S. 52 (1964); Malloy v. Hogan, 378 U.S. 1 (1964).

[68] Nevada, New Jersey, Ohio, South Carolina.

[69] *See, e.g., In re* Vickers, 371 Mich. 114, 123 N.W.2d 253 (1963); *In re* Vince, 2 N.J. 443, 67 A.2d 141 (1949).

[70] *See* J. Bates & E. Zawadski, Criminal Abortion 38–39 (1964).

[71] *Id.* at 85–91.

[72] Arizona, California, Connecticut, Delaware, Florida, Idaho, Illinois, Indiana, Louisiana, Massachusetts, Michigan, Missouri, Pennsylvania, Rhode Island, South Dakota, Vermont, Virginia, Wisconsin, Wyoming. Like statutes were repealed in 1967 and 1968 in Maine and Maryland.

[73] *E.g.,* Colorado, Mississippi.

[74] *See infra,* note 488 and accompanying text.

commerce in abortifacients by prohibiting their manufacture,[75] distribution,[76] furnishing,[77] keeping or exposing for sale,[78] giving away[79] or lending.[80] Two states required all sales to be under registerable prescriptions.[81] Oregon penalized people who furnished premises knowing that nontherapeutic abortions would be performed there. Most of this legislation, too, is incompatible with modern first amendment notions.[82]

III. Accelerating Trends Toward Legalized Therapeutic Abortion: 1968–1973

A. Coverage of Revised Abortion Legislation

1.   GROUNDS FOR THERAPEUTIC ABORTIONS   The Model Penal Code,[83] promulgated by the American Law Institute in 1962, asserted a strong and perhaps paramount influence on a legislative expansion of the grounds for legal abortion during the period 1968–1973. The code posited the lawfulness of abortions necessary to safeguard the physical and mental health of pregnant women; 13 states had recognized this ground by 1973.[84] A second ground for abortion, accepted in 12 states, allowed pregnancies to be terminated on eugenic grounds, that is, because a fetus if born would be seriously mentally or physically handicapped.[85] A third, based on humanitarian considerations, permitted victims of rape[86] or incest[87] to have their pregnancies terminated. Three states, however, went far beyond the Model Penal Code pattern to eliminate all restrictions on medically indicated abortions.[88] Consequently, only those jurisdictions were relatively

---

[75] Massachusetts (subsequently declared unconstitutional in Eisenstadt v. Baird, 405 U.S. 438 (1972), in its application to contraceptives), Minnesota, Nevada, New York, Washington.

[76] Colorado, Illinois, Louisiana, Maryland.

[77] Texas (invalidated in Roe v. Wade, 314 F. Supp. 1217 (N.D. Tex. 1970), *aff'd on other grounds,* 410 U.S. 113 (1973)).

[78] Colorado, Delaware, Illinois, Iowa, Maryland, Massachusetts, Michigan, Minnesota, Mississippi, Missouri, Nevada, Rhode Island, Vermont, Washington.

[79] Colorado, Delaware, Iowa, Massachusetts, Minnesota, Mississippi, Missouri, Nevada, Vermont, Washington.

[80] Colorado, Massachusetts, Mississippi.

[81] Colorado, Michigan.

[82] *See infra,* note 484 and accompanying text. On the English law, see 11 Halsbury's Laws of England ¶ 1193 (4th ed. 1976); G. Williams, Criminal Law, *supra* note 19, at 264–65.

[83] Model Penal Code § 230.3 (1980).

[84] Arkansas, California, Colorado, Delaware, Florida, Georgia, Kansas, Maryland, New Mexico, North Carolina, Oregon, South Carolina, Virginia. English legislation adopted the same position. English Abortion Act, 1967, c. 87, § 1(1)(a). *See* G. Williams, Criminal Law, *supra* note 19, at 257–60.

[85] Arkansas, Colorado, Delaware, Florida, Georgia, Kansas, Maryland, New Mexico, North Carolina, Oregon, South Carolina, Virginia. The English Abortion Act contains similar coverage. English Abortion Act, 1967, c. 87, § 1(1)(b) ("substantial risk" of "such physical abnormalities as to be seriously handicapped"). *See* G. Williams, Criminal Law, *supra* note 19, at 256–57. Similar legislation is found in Singapore (Singapore Abortion Act, 1969) and South Australia. *See* Roemer, *supra* note 22.

[86] Arkansas, California, Colorado, Delaware, Florida, Georgia, Kansas, Maryland, Mississippi, New Mexico, North Carolina, Oregon, South Carolina, Virginia. Whether statutory as well as forcible rape was included had to be determined in each state in light of statutory cross-references.

Parliament declined to recognize rape as an independent basis for abortion. *See* G. Williams, Criminal Law, *supra* note 19, at 260–61.

[87] Arkansas, California, Colorado, Delaware, Florida, Kansas, New Mexico, North Carolina, Oregon, South Carolina, Virginia.

[88] Alaska, Hawaii, Washington. The English Abortion Act, 1967, c. 87, §§ 1(1)(a), (2), reaches about the same result by permitting medical practitioners to consider the actual or reasonably foreseeable environment

free of impact from the 1973 Supreme Court decisions in *Roe* and *Doe,* as far as grounds for justifiable abortion were concerned.

2.   LENGTH OF PREGNANCY   As mentioned earlier,[89] length of pregnancy often bore on the lawfulness of therapeutic abortions. Thus, even the three most liberal states before 1973 found this dimension of their statutes invalidated.

3.   RESIDENCY REQUIREMENTS   Some legislatures that expanded the permissible scope of therapeutic abortions manifested a fear that their states would become abortion havens for residents of other jurisdictions with restrictive laws. Therefore, a number required periods of residency before an abortion could be performed.[90] Such legislation usually placed the burden on pregnant women to assert residency, not on physicians to ascertain the truth of claims of residency; only the Georgia and Virginia statutes attached perjury consequences to declarations of residency. These statutes fell under *Doe v. Bolton.*[91]

4.   PRELIMINARY APPROVAL BY MEDICAL PEERS   Even before the abortion law revision movement, a number of states required[92] or permitted, as an alternative to an operating physician's personal professional judgment, the advice of other independent physicians.[93] Later legislation generally mandated preliminary consultation with or approval by medical colleagues before abortions could be performed. Approval could be gained through certification by medical practitioners other than a physician wishing to terminate a pregnancy,[94] by a hospital review committee[95] or by both.[96] Because peer concurrence took time, several states legislated an emergency exception for situations in which a woman's life would be put in jeopardy unless an abortion was performed immediately. A ratification of medical necessity then had to be obtained swiftly after an abortion.[97] The degree to which such requirements have survived the Court's 1973 abortion decisions is discussed below.[98]

5.   SPECIAL APPROVAL IN RAPE AND INCEST CASES   Statutes that allowed abortion

---

of pregnant women in deciding whether their physical or mental health may be injured by pregnancy, as well as the risk to siblings if an additional child is born. *See also supra,* note 19.

[89] *See supra,* notes 44–48 and accompanying text.

[90] Alaska, Arkansas, Delaware, Georgia, Hawaii, North Carolina, Oregon, South Carolina, Virginia, Washington.

[91] *See infra,* notes 338–40 and accompanying text.

[92] Louisiana, Mississippi.

[93] Florida (repealed 1972), Nebraska, New Hampshire, Ohio, Wisconsin. Missouri provided for advice by one duly licensed physician if an abortion was performed by one who was not a duly licensed physician. On this anomaly, see *supra,* note 39.

[94] Arkansas, Delaware, Georgia, Kansas, North Carolina, Oregon, South Carolina. Concurring physicians generally could not be relatives of or associated in medical practice with a doctor who wished to perform an abortion. The English Abortion Act, 1967, c. 7, § 1(1), requires the good faith opinion of two medical practitioners as does India's Medical Termination of Pregnancy Act, 1971, § 3(2).

[95] California, Colorado, Delaware, Georgia, Maryland, New Mexico, Virginia. Alaska left the matter to administrative regulation. On the counterpart requirement under the Canadian Criminal Code § 251(4), see Harris & Tupper, *Study of Therapeutic Abortion Committees in British Columbia,* 11 U. Brit. Colum. L. Rev. 81 (1977) (in comparison with the English Abortion Act, 1967).

[96] Delaware, Georgia.

[97] Arkansas, Kansas, North Carolina, Oregon, South Carolina, Washington. The English Abortion Act, 1967, c. 87, § 1(4), creates an emergency exception if abortion is necessary to save the life or prevent grave permanent injury to a pregnant woman's physical or mental health.

[98] *See infra,* notes 358–65 and accompanying text.

in rape and incest cases on humanitarian grounds[99] generally required some form of substantiation. A woman's claim of violation was not an automatic reason because medical grounds did not necessarily justify abortion in all instances of sexual assaults. Sometimes some form of complaint or affidavit by a victim sufficed,[100] but more commonly, approval or certification by prosecuting authorities was needed.[101]

6. PERSONS AUTHORIZED TO PERFORM ABORTIONS   Revised statutes before 1973 required terminations of pregnancy to be performed by physicians licensed in the jurisdiction.[102] The statutes did not touch on the legal status of nurses and medical paraprofessionals who performed or participated in lawful therapeutic abortions, but one may assume that prosecuting authorities were unenthusiastic about prosecuting persons acting in such a capacity. At any rate, no precedent on the matter emerged.

7. PLACE OF PERFORMANCE OF ABORTIONS   Statutes that restricted the grounds for lawful abortion to health, eugenic or humanitarian concerns almost always required abortions to be performed in accredited hospitals.[103] Two states, however, allowed abortions to be performed in approved clinics away from full-service hospitals.[104] The unconstitutionality of some situs restrictions is discussed below.[105]

8. REQUIRED RECORDS AND REPORTS   As legislatures began to recognize the licitness of medically indicated abortions, they also instituted record-keeping and reporting requirements. Sometimes, applications or certificates needed only to be retained in medical office or hospital patient files,[106] but periodic reports to state agencies increasingly came to be mandated.[107] Requirements were imposed that the identity of abortion patients be kept confidential. The constitutionality of much broader contemporary reporting legislation is commented on below.[108]

9. FREEDOM OF CONSCIENCE EXEMPTIONS   Many doctors, nurses and hospital employees have strong religious or moral scruples against abortion, and many private, particularly church-affiliated, hospitals will not tolerate the performance of abortions on their premises. As therapeutic abortion came increasingly to be recognized, the question arose whether individuals or hospitals could refrain legally from participation. Many states had legislated to allow a freedom of conscience exemption.[109] The number of such statutes has markedly increased since *Roe* and *Doe* were decided.[110]

---

[99] *See supra,* notes 86–87 and accompanying text.

[100] Arkansas, Georgia, New Mexico, North Carolina, South Carolina, Virginia.

[101] California, Colorado, Delaware, Georgia, Maryland, Oregon, South Carolina.

[102] Arkansas, California, Colorado, Delaware, Florida, Georgia, Hawaii, Kansas, Maryland, New Mexico, New York, North Carolina, South Carolina, Virginia, Washington. England's Abortion Act, 1967, c. 87, §§ 1(1), 2(1)(b), contains a like requirement.

[103] Arkansas, California, Colorado, Delaware, Florida, Georgia, Hawaii, Kansas, Maryland, New Mexico, North Carolina, South Carolina, Virginia, Washington, Wisconsin.

[104] Alaska, Washington. England's Abortion Act, 1967, c. 87, § 1(3), allows abortions to be performed in a hospital or place approved by the Minister of Health or Secretary of State, subject to an emergency exception. *Id.* at § 1(4).

[105] *See infra,* notes 341–53 and accompanying text.

[106] Arkansas, Colorado, New Mexico. Sometimes this form of record keeping was imposed in addition to reporting requirements, as in Georgia, Maryland and Oregon.

[107] Delaware, Florida, Maryland, South Carolina. Oregon left the matter to administrative regulation, which also is the stance of the English Abortion Act, 1967, c. 87, § 2.

[108] *See infra,* 408–20 and accompanying text.

[109] Alaska, Arkansas, Colorado, Delaware, Florida, Georgia, Hawaii, Maryland, New Mexico, Oregon, South Carolina, Virginia, Washington. A similar exemption for medical practitioners is provided in England's

B. Resort to Litigation: The New Frontier

The wave or, perhaps more accurately, ripple of legislative reform probably had peaked by 1973. In any event, advocacy increased rapidly for constitutional invalidation of legislative restrictions on therapeutic abortion.[111] The principal grounds advanced were the following: vagueness and indefiniteness in abortion legislation denying due process of law;[112] infringement of equal protection, through either an arbitrary legislative classification of eligibility and ineligibility for abortion[113] or financial discrimination against financially-unable persons;[114] or invasion of a constitutionally protected right of privacy.[115] What might have evolved from a long process of constitutional litigation is unknowable, because the Supreme Court in 1973 asserted its primacy in the constitutional regulation of abortion legislation.

IV. Basic Constitutional Doctrine

As matters eventuated, the Court built its doctrinal framework on the constitutional right to privacy, which it thought "broad enough to encompass a woman's decision whether or not to terminate her pregnancy."[116] This analysis has been followed in all subsequent cases,[117] although it may be repudiated if a reconstituted majority of the Court determines to overturn *Roe v. Wade*.[118] In selecting a "right to privacy" rationale, the Court specifically repudiated the claim that fetuses are persons within the meaning of the fourteenth amendment: "[T]he unborn have never been recognized in the law as persons

---

Abortion Act, 1967, c. 87, § 4(1), but the burden of proof is on a practitioner who refuses an abortion on that basis. For a criticism of India's Medical Termination of Pregnancy Act, 1971, based on a failure to include similar language, *see* Minnattur, *Medical Termination of Pregnancy and Conscientious Objection,* 16 Indian L. Inst. J. 704 (1974).

[110] *See infra,* notes 425–51 and accompanying text.

[111] *See generally* Baude, *Constitutional Reflections on Abortion Reform,* 4 J. L. Reform 1 (1970); Lucas, *Federal Constitutional Limitations on the Enforcement and Administration of State Abortion Statutes,* 46 N.C.L. Rev. 730 (1968); Comment, *Abortion Laws: A Constitutional Right to Abortion,* 49 N.C.L. Rev. 487 (1971).

For a retrospective view, see Moore, *Moral Sentiment in Judicial Opinions on Abortion,* 15 Santa Clara L. Rev. 591 (1975).

[112] *See generally* Kolender v. Lawson, 461 U.S. 352 (1983); Smith v. Goguen, 415 U.S. 566 (1974); Papachristou v. City of Jacksonville, 405 U.S. 156 (1972).

[113] *See, e.g.,* City of Dallas v. Stanglin, 490 U.S. 19 (1989) (sustaining constitutionality of ordinance limiting the admission to dance halls and other regulated establishments between the hours of 1:00 P.M. and midnight of persons between ages 14 and 18); Craig v. Boren, 429 U.S. 190 (1976) (invalidating legislation penalizing sale of alcoholic beverages to males at a greater age than females).

[114] *See, e.g.,* Harris v. McRae, 448 U.S. 297 (1980); Mayer v. Chicago, 404 U.S. 189 (1971).

[115] *See* the contraceptive cases cited *supra* note 26; Stanley v. Georgia, 394 U.S. 557 (1969) (private possession of pornography). *Stanley,* however, has been substantially limited to its factual circumstances. *See* Osborne v. Ohio, 495 U.S. 103 (1990).

[116] Roe v. Wade, 410 U.S. 113, 153 (1973). *See generally* Chemerinsky, *supra* note 7; Jones, *supra* note 14, at 605–12; King, *The Juridical Status of the Fetus: A Proposal for the Legal Protection of the Unborn,* 77 Mich. L. Rev. 1647, 1650–57 (1979); Krimmel & Foley, *supra* note 11; Moore, *Moral Sentiment in Judicial Opinions on Abortion,* 15 Santa Clara L. Rev. 591, 625–34 (1975); Morgan, *Roe v. Wade and the Lesson of the Pre-Roe Case Law,* 77 Mich. L. Rev. 1724 (1979); Parness & Pritchard, *To Be or Not To Be: Protecting the Unborn's Potentiality of Life,* 51 U. Cin. L. Rev. 257 (1982) [hereinafter cited as Parness & Pritchard]; Regan, *Rewriting Roe v. Wade,* 77 Mich. L. Rev. 1569 (1979).

[117] In particular, City of Akron v. Akron Center for Reproductive Health, 462 U.S. 416 (1983); Colautti v. Franklin, 439 U.S. 379, 386 (1979); Planned Parenthood v. Danforth, 428 U.S. 52, 60 (1976).

[118] *See infra,* note 536 and accompanying text.

in the whole sense."[119] Thus, a human being entitled to direct constitutional protection emerges at live birth, not conception.[120] This premise has since been reaffirmed by the Court.[121]

The Court's basic constitution premise was also attested to by the Court's ruling on standing to attack abortion legislation. A woman who is pregnant at the time legal action commences[122] has standing because her right of privacy is directly affected by legal prohibitions against abortion.[123] On the other hand, married women (with their husbands) who assert that they might become pregnant in the future and require termination of pregnancy for health reasons do not have standing.[124] Doctors who may be prosecuted or otherwise interfered with in their practice also are directly affected,[125] as are clinics and facilities providing abortion services.[126]

Having recognized that women's claims to abortion find support in a constitutional right to privacy, the Court nevertheless rejected the contention that such a right is absolute, allowing a woman "to terminate her pregnancy at whatever time, in whatever way, and for whatever reason she alone chooses."[127] A "pregnant woman cannot be

---

[119] Roe v. Wade, 410 U.S. at 162. In Webster v. Reproductive Health Services, Inc., 492 U.S. 490 (1989), a majority of the Court refused to consider the constitutionality of the preamble to the Missouri abortion statute setting forth a legislative finding that life begins at conception and unborn children have protectable interests in life, health and well-being because by its terms the language regulated neither abortion nor the practice of medicine. Id. at 504–07.

[120] Roe v. Wade, 410 U.S. at 161–62.

[121] City of Akron v. Akron Center for Reproductive Health, Inc., 462 U.S. 416, 444 (1983):

> [The ordinance] requires the physician to inform [a] patient that "the unborn child is a human life from the moment of conception," a requirement inconsistent with the Court's holding in Roe v. Wade that a State may not adopt one theory of when life begins to justify its regulation of abortions.

Id. (citation omitted).

That this is the crux of the Court's abortion rationale is reflected in efforts to persuade Congress to adopt for presentation to the states for ratification a right-to-life amendment or to enact a human life statute on the strength of § 5 of the fourteenth amendment. On the constitutionality of the latter approach, see Emerson, The Power of Congress to Change Constitutional Decisions of the Supreme Court: The Human Life Bill, 77 Nw. U.L. Rev. 129 (1982) (questioning constitutionality); Estreicher, Congressional Power and Constitutional Rights: Reflections on Proposed "Human Life" Legislation, 68 Va. L. Rev. 333 (1982) (questioning constitutionality); Gordon, The Nature and Uses of Congressional Power Under Section Five of the Fourteenth Amendment to Overcome Decisions of the Supreme Court, 72 Nw. U.L. Rev. 656, 689–94 (1976) (questioning constitutionality); Hyde, The Human Life Bill: Some Issues and Answers, 27 N.Y.L. Sch. L. Rev. 1077 (1982); Isaacs, The Law of Fertility Regulation in the United States: A 1980 Review, 19 J. Fam. L. 65, 70–71 (1980) [hereinafter cited as Isaacs]; Pilpel, Hyde and Go Seek: A Response to Representative Hyde, 27 N.Y.L. Sch. L. Rev. 1101 (1982); Note, Constitutionality of the Human Life Bill, 61 Wash. U.L.Q. 219 (1983) (suggesting constitutionality). The implications of such a bill for certain forms of contraception are discussed in Note, Personhood and the Contraceptive Right, 57 Ind. L.J. 579 (1982).

On the constitutional amendment, see Destro, supra note 32, at 1319–51. A survey of constitutional provisions in other nations may be found in Mukerjee, World Constitutions and Population: A Preliminary Survey of World Constitutions, 16 Indian L. Inst. J. 675, 679–87 (1974).

The right-to-life controversy manifests itself in other ways. See Federal Election Comm'n v. Mass. Citizens for Life, 479 U.S. 238 (1986) (FEC could not invoke 2 U.S.C. § 441b (1988) to prevent antiabortion group from expending funds for a special election issue of its prolife publication, distributed at the time of an election for federal office; the activity fell within the language of § 441b, but its invocation violated the appellee's first amendment rights because it was an organization formed to disseminate political ideas); Fausto v. Diamond, 589 F. Supp. 451 (D.R.I. 1984) (city sponsorship of fountain as memorial to "The Unborn Child," with plaque quoting Deut. 30:19, "Choose life, then, that you and your descendants

isolated in her privacy,'' for she ''carries an embryo and, later, a fetus . . .'' [128] Accordingly, abortion is never completely free from state regulation, although the scope of state powers grows slowly with a pregnancy and has ceiling limitations far lower than those recognized in state legislation before 1973.

During approximately the first trimester of pregnancy,[129] '' 'the abortion decision and its effectuation must be left to the medical judgment of the pregnant woman's attending physician,' without interference from the State.'' [130] ''The participation by the attending physician in the abortion decision, and his [or her] responsibility in that decision'' [131] underlie the standing accorded to physicians to litigate abortion decisions.[132] Throughout early pregnancy, minor regulations can be imposed if they further ''important health-related State concerns'' but only if they do not ''interfere with the physician-patient consultation or with the woman's choice between abortion and childbirth.'' [133]

After the first stage, states may choose to impose reasonable restrictions relating to the preservation and protection of maternal health,[134] but state regulation cannot ''depart

---

may live,'' did not amount to establishment of religion; plaintiffs pointed out Roman Catholic sponsorship of the memorial had a declared objective of including aborted fetuses).

On efforts to attack the tax exempt status of the Roman Catholic Church based on its efforts to influence antiabortion legislation, *see* Capetanakis, *Abortion Rights Mobilization and Religious Tax Exemptions*, 34 Cath. Law. 169 (1991).

[122] In Roe v. Wade, 410 U.S. at 124–25, the Court rejected the appellee's contention that the case had been mooted because Roe's pregnancy long since had been terminated by birth or abortion. Pregnancies will come to term before usual appellate processes can be completed, but ''[p]regnancy often comes more than once to the same woman, and in the general population, if man is to survive, it will always be with us.'' Therefore, pregnancy truly ''could be 'capable of repetition, yet evading review . . .' '' *Id.* (quoting Southern Pacific Terminal Co. v. ICC, 219 U.S. 498, 515 (1911)).

[123] *Id.* at 153.

[124] *Id.* at 127–29.

[125] Doe v. Bolton, 410 U.S. 179, 188–89 (1973). *See also* Colautti v. Franklin, 439 U.S. 379 (1979). In Roe v. Wade, 410 U.S. at 124–27, a medical doctor, a defendant in a pending criminal prosecution, was not allowed to appeal. This was not because of a want of standing but because the Court's doctrine of preclusion, set forth in Samuels v. Mackell, 401 U.S. 66 (1971), and Younger v. Harris, 401 U.S. 37 (1971), prohibits federal courts from intervening in matters pending in state courts; potential prosecutions are not within the doctrine. In Doe v. Bolton, 410 U.S. at 189, the Court thought it unnecessary to decide whether nurses, clergy, social workers and counseling services had standing because it resolved all the issues affecting them in connection with the physicians' attack on the state statute.

In Harris v. McRae, 448 U.S. 297, 318 n.21 (1980), discussed *infra* in notes 470–74 and accompanying text, the Court found that the constitutional entitlement of a physician advising financially unable Medicaid recipients was no greater than the entitlement of the patient; therefore, he or she had no greater due process protections.

In Diamond v. Charles, 476 U.S. 54 (1986), the Court first noted probable jurisdiction but then dismissed an appeal on the basis of a lack of a case or controversy required by Article III of the Constitution. After an action had commenced challenging provisions of the Illinois abortion statute, Dr. Diamond was allowed to intervene, over the objection of the plaintiffs, based on his assertion of a conscientious objection to abortion and his status as a pediatrician and father of an unemancipated minor daughter. The district court found for the plaintiffs, and the State of Illinois decided not to appeal. Nevertheless, Diamond filed a notice of appeal and jurisdictional statement with the Supreme Court, and Illinois submitted a ''letter of interest'' in the outcome of the appeal under Supreme Court R. 10.4. The Court found that Illinois was not an appellant because it had not filed the required timely notice of appeal; that destroyed the controversy.

The Court found that Dr. Diamond had no standing. The physicians who had commenced the action had standing because they faced prosecution if the statute was valid. But Diamond, in seeking review before the Supreme Court, was actually trying to pursue a review on behalf of the State of Illinois that the state itself had not pursued. Diamond showed no cognizable impact on his practice from an invalidated statute.

from accepted medical practice'' or increase the costs and limit the availability of abortions ''without promoting important health benefits.''[135] After viability,[136] a state ''may regulate an abortion to protect the life of the fetus and even may proscribe abortion except where it is necessary, in appropriate medical judgment, for the preservation of the life or health of the mother.''[137]

These, then, are the basics of the Court's regulation of abortion, the constitutional structure for most of its decisions on specific aspects of abortion law. This does not mean, however, that no other constitutional rationale will be invoked. For example, the Court has relied on the vagueness and indefiniteness concept under the due process clause[138] to strike down penal statutes invoked against physicians.[139] Equal protection, in contrast, has not had significant impact on abortion law.[140]

V. Scope and Constitutionality of Current Abortion Legislation

A. Legislative Responses to the 1973 Decisions

The initial impact of *Roe* and *Doe* was manifested by state high court decisions invalidating traditional abortion legislation.[141] On occasion, legislatures have apparently

---

His parental claim did not strengthen his position. His appeal did not extend to the parental notification dimension of the statute, and he failed to show that his daughter was a minor or incapable of asserting her own rights, and thus lacked standing to pursue the issue of whether his daughter might be supplied or administered an abortifacient without her informed consent. Finally, he could not assert constitutional claims on behalf of an unborn fetus because only the state may invoke regulatory measures to protect that interest.

[126] Abortion clinics were allowed to litigate constitutional issues in Planned Parenthood v. Danforth, 428 U.S. 52 (1976), and City of Akron v. Akron Center for Reproductive Health, Inc., 462 U.S. 416 (1983). *See also* Deerfield Medical Center v. City of Deerfield Beach, 661 F.2d 328 (5th Cir. 1981) (abortion clinic had standing to assert privacy rights of women who might be unable to obtain abortions if municipality denied occupational license to clinic on basis of zoning ordinance).

[127] Roe v. Wade, 410 U.S. at 153.

[128] *Id.* at 159.

[129] The Court's definition of ''trimester'' is discussed *infra* in notes 178–79 and accompanying text.

[130] Planned Parenthood v. Danforth, 428 U.S. at 61 (quoting Roe v. Wade, 410 U.S. at 164).

[131] *Id.*

[132] *See supra*, note 125 and accompanying text.

[133] City of Akron v. Akron Center for Reproductive Health, Inc., 462 U.S. at 430 (footnote omitted).

[134] Roe v. Wade, 410 U.S. at 163.

[135] City of Akron v. Akron Center for Reproductive Health, Inc., 462 U.S. at 431. On the minimal risk of medically-administered abortion, *see* Sneideman, *supra* note 23, at 194–97.

[136] ''''[A] point purposefully left flexible for professional determination, and dependent upon developing medical skill and technical ability . . .'' Planned Parenthood v. Danforth, 428 U.S. at 61 (footnote omitted). *See also infra*, notes 185–88 and accompanying text.

[137] Planned Parenthood v. Danforth, 428 U.S. at 61 (paraphrasing Roe v. Wade, 410 U.S. at 163–65).

[138] *See* precedents cited *supra*, note 112.

[139] City of Akron v. Akron Center for Reproductive Health, Inc., 462 U.S. at 451–52 (ordinance making it a misdemeanor not to dispose of remains of unborn children in ''a humane and sanitary manner,'' held vague and indefinite); Colautti v. Franklin, 439 U.S. at 390–401 (viability determination and standard of care provisions in felony statute voided for vagueness).

[140] *See infra*, notes 503–10, 514–16 and accompanying text. Efforts to claim a right to abortion based on free exercise of religion under the first amendment likewise have been rejected. Harris v. McRae, 448 U.S. 297, 318–21 (1980); Women's Servs. v. Thone, 636 F.2d 206, 209 (8th Cir. 1980).

[141] *E.g.*, People v. Norton, 181 Colo. 47, 507 P.2d 862 (1973); State v. Mirmelli, 54 Ill. 2d 28, 294 N.E.2d 257 (1973) (per curiam); State v. Hultgren, 295 Minn. 299, 204 N.W.2d 197 (1973) (per curiam) (nonphysician); State v. Hodgson, 295 Minn. 294, 204 N.W.2d 199 (1973) (per curiam) (physician); Spears v.

decided to do nothing. The New Jersey criminal code contains no abortion provisions.[142] Likewise, the text of the Texas provisions no longer appears; they have been replaced by a compiler's notation of "unconstitutional."[143] Most legislatures, however, revamped their statutes in response to or anticipation of judicial invalidation of pre-1973 legislation.

A handful of states retained[144] or adopted[145] a policy of leaving regulation of therapeutic abortion to administrative agencies. Most have accomplished substantial revisions with the Supreme Court's reversal of its constitutional principles as their guide.[146]

Several legislatures, however, voiced their restiveness or outright opposition to the Court's doctrine. Some stated a preference for normal childbirth over abortion,[147] and others affirmed the state's obligation to protect human life whether unborn or not.[148] Nebraska objected to Supreme Court "intrusion" and "deplored" the destruction of unborn human lives that would result,[149] and Montana announced its intent to restrict abortions to the extent it could do so constitutionally.[150] Illinois[151] and Kentucky[152] declared their intent to prohibit abortions should the Supreme Court reverse its consti-

---

State, 287 So. 2d 443 (Miss. 1973); Commonwealth v. Jackson, 454 Pa. 429, 312 A.2d 13 (1973) (per curiam) (nonphysician); State v. Lawrence, 261 S.C. 18, 198 S.E.2d 253 (1973); State v. Munson, 87 S.D. 245, 206 N.W.2d 434 (1973); Doe v. Burk, 513 P.2d 643 (Wyo. 1973). Although the court in State v. Sulman, 165 Conn. 556, 339 A.2d 62 (1973), held that the unconstitutionality of its abortion statute rendered it unenforceable against all offenders, in State v. Menillo, 171 Conn. 141, 368 A.2d 136 (1976) (on remand from Connecticut v. Menillo, 423 U.S. 9 (1975)), it held later that the statute's unconstitutionality as applied to physicians did not destroy its effectiveness as to nonphysicians.

[142] The matter was left to a legislative study commission. New Jersey Criminal Law Revision Comm'n Final Report, Commentary 259 (1971). A comprehensive abortion regulation statute was approved by the New Jersey Legislature, Assembly Bill No. 1285, but was vetoed by Governor Brendan Byrne on Jan. 3, 1980.

Illegal abortions can be prosecuted under simple assault provisions, N.J. Stat. Ann. § 2C:12-1(a)(1) (West Supp. 1992), since consent to acts causing more than trifling inconvenience is legally irrelevant to criminality. Id. § 2C:2-10(b); Model Penal code § 2.11(2) (1980).

[143] Tex. Rev. Civ. Stat. Ann. arts. 4512.1–4512.4, 4512.6 (Vernon 1976) (compiler's note). Criminal abortions could be prosecuted as assault under Tex. Penal Code Ann. §§ 22.01(a)(1), 22.02(a)(1) (Vernon Supp. 1992), however, and consent is valid only if a victim knows the injury to be a risk of "recognized medical treatment." Id. § 22.06(2)(B). See generally Johnson, Abortion, Personhood, and Privacy in Texas, 68 Tex. L. Rev. 1521 (1990).

[144] Alaska Stat. § 08.64.105 (1991). See Cleveland v. Municipality of Anchorage, 631 P.2d 1073 (Alaska 1981). The state had taken this approach to the problem before 1973. See supra, note 88 and accompanying text.

[145] E.g., Nev. Rev. Stat. § 442.260(1) (1991) (although § 442.250 tracks the Roe grounds for lawful abortion); Ohio Rev. Code Ann. § 3701.341(A) (Page 1992) (although the provision lists only some matters for regulation without an ejusdem generis clause). Failure to comply with procedures in an administrative procedure act (APA) governing promulgation of regulations can invalidate regulations. See, e.g., McKee v. Likins, 261 N.W.2d 566 (Minn. 1977) (regulation restricting use of public funds for therapeutic abortion invalidated for failure to comply with APA notice requirements).

[146] Cf. Mo. Ann. Stat. § 188.010 (Vernon Supp. 1992) ("It is the intention of the [legislature] to regulate abortion to the full extent permitted by the Constitution of the United States, the decisions of the United States Supreme Court, and federal statutes"); 18 Pa. Cons. Stat. Ann. § 3202(c) (Purdon 1983) ("In every relevant civil or criminal proceeding in which it is possible to do so without violating the Federal Constitution, the common and statutory law of Pennsylvania shall be construed so as to extend to the unborn the equal protection of the laws and to further the public policy of this Commonwealth encouraging childbirth over abortion.").

Articles on current abortion legislation from the standpoint of theology and ethics include Eidsmoe, A Biblical View of Abortion, 1983 J. Christ. Juris. 17; Fletcher, Abortion and the True Believer, 91 Christian Century 1126 (Nov. 27, 1974); Fromer, supra note 7, at 239–40; Nelson, The Churches and Abortion Law

tutional stance or should the Constitution be amended to permit them to do so. Idaho has gone the furthest in that regard. It has standby provisions[153] to come into force through gubernatorial proclamation should the constitutional picture change.[154] Obviously, legislative resonations of this nature, although therapeutic for antiabortion legislators and their constituents, have no legal force and must be ignored by state judges, at least as long as the basic federal constitutional concepts espoused by the Supreme Court in *Roe v. Wade* remain substantially intact.

States vary in the placement of therapeutic abortion provisions within the body of statutes. Some have continued the tradition of penal code regulation supported by ancillary provisions elsewhere, but a great many have chosen the context of laws governing the healing professions with residual or ancillary criminal provisions. The statutory analysis that follows looks first at civil or civil-oriented legislation, then at criminal law provisions and finally at restrictions affecting publicly funded abortion services.

B. Noncriminal Regulation of Therapeutic[155] Abortion

1. DEFINITIONS a. *"Abortion"* The new focus on abortion as a medical technique has brought about modernized legal definitions, usually of the term "abortion" but sometimes of "miscarriage"[156] or "feticide."[157] A few states content themselves

---

Reform, 1983 J. Christ. Juris. 29; Orloski, *Abortion: Legal Questions and Legislative Alternatives*, 131 America 50 (Aug. 10, 1974).

[147]*E.g.*, Ind. Code Ann. § 16-10-3-4 (Burns 1990); Minn. Stat. Ann. § 256B.011 (West 1982); N.D. Cent. Code § 14-02.3-01 (1991).

The Supreme Court indicated that states are not prevented from making such a value judgment and implementing it by allocation of public funds. Maher v. Roe, 432 U.S. 464, 474 (1977). *See also* Harris v. McRae, 448 U.S. 297, 314–15 (1980) (utilizing *Maher v. Roe* principles in the context of the Hyde amendment prohibiting the use of Medicaid funds for abortions; see *infra*, text accompanying notes 511–16).

[148]*E.g.*, Ill. Ann. Stat. ch. 38, § 81-21 (Smith-Hurd Supp. 1991 & 1992) ("the unborn child is a human being from the time of conception and is, therefore, a legal person for purposes of the unborn child's right to life and is entitled to the right to life from conception under the laws and Constitution of this State"); Ky. Rev. Stat. § 311.710(5) (1990) ("declared policy . . . to recognize and to protect the lives of all human beings regardless of their degree of biological development . . ."); Mont. Code Ann. § 50-20-102 (1991) ("tradition of the state of Montana to protect every human life, whether unborn or aged, healthy or sick . . . [and] intent to extend the protection of the laws of Montana in favor of all human life"); Neb. Rev. Stat. § 28-325(4) (1989) ("this state is prevented from providing adequate legal remedies to protect . . . unborn human life"); N.D. Cent. Code § 14-02.1-01 (1991) ("purpose . . . is to protect unborn human life . . . [and] reaffirms the tradition of the state of North Dakota to protect every human life whether unborn or aged, health or sick").

[149]Neb. Rev. Stat. § 28-325 (1989).

[150]Mont. Code Ann. § 50-20-102-103 (1991).

[151]Ill. Ann. Stat. ch. 38, § 81-21 (Smith-Hurd Supp. 1991 & 1992).

[152]Ky. Rev. Stat. § 311.710(5) (1990).

[153]Idaho Code §§ 18-614–18-615 (1987).

[154]*Id.* § 18-613.

[155]The word "therapeutic" refers to medically indicated abortions, to be contrasted with terminations of pregnancy motivated solely, for example, by a desire to limit family size, a concern with the economic consequences of the birth of a child, a desire to engage in gender selection, a fear of the eugenic consequences of childbirth (for example, birth of a severely mentally impaired or physically handicapped child) or cosmetic considerations (for example, avoiding the loss of physical slimness). One or more such motivations might be camouflaged by a claim of therapeutic need, but none can be directly acknowledged as a licit ground for an abortion. *See generally* text accompanying notes 18–26, *supra*.

[156]Me. Rev. Stat. Ann. tit. 22, § 1596(1)(B) (1980).

with defining abortion as termination of pregnancy[158] while others specify methods in a comprehensive way.[159]

Abortion implies intent or purpose, but statutes frequently spell it out anyway, either generally[160] or in terms of intent to produce fetal death.[161] More frequently, the intent element is stated inversely, that is, a purpose other than to induce live birth[162] or to remove a dead fetus.[163] Only rarely does a definition of abortion include references to viability[164] or period of gestation;[165] such matters usually are dealt with in substantive provisions.

b. *"Conception"* A definition of "conception" probably is functionally unnecessary to delineate the scope of therapeutic abortion. Nevertheless, some states have specifically provided one in neutral terms such as "fecundation of the ovum by the spermatozoa."[166] Sometimes the definition relates to some other term like "pregnancy," while at other times it is synonymous with "fetus" or "unborn child." These terms are of doubtful constitutionality if invoked to limit therapeutic abortions.[167]

---

[157] Iowa Code Ann. § 707.7 (West 1979). This may well reflect a legislative bias against abortion. *See supra,* notes 147–54 and accompanying text.

[158] *E.g.,* La. Rev. Stat. Ann. § 37:1285(8)–(9) (West 1988); Md. Pub. Health Code Ann. § 20-208(a) (1990); Va Code § 18.2-72 (1988); Wash. Rev. Code Ann. § Repealed.

[159] *E.g.,* Ill. Ann. Stat. ch. 38, § 81-22(6) (Smith-Hurd Supp. 1991 & 1992) (criminal code context); Me. Rev. Stat. Ann. tit. 22, §§ 1596(1)(A) (1992), 1598(2)(A) (1992); 18 Pa. Cons. Stat. Ann. § 3203 (Purdon 1983); Utah Code Ann. § 76-7-301(1) (Supp. 1991) (including all procedures undertaken to kill a live unborn child and to produce miscarriage). *See generally* Warren, *supra* note 21, at 27; Note, *Criminal Liability of Physicians: An Encroachment on the Abortion Right?,* 18 Am. Crim. L. Rev. 591, 592–93 (1981).

[160] *E.g.,* Idaho Code § 18-604(1) (1987) (intentional); Iowa Code Ann. § 707.7 (West 1979) (intentional); Kan. Stat. Ann. § 21-3407(1) (1988) (purposeful); Me. Rev. Stat. Ann. tit. 22, §§ 1596(1)(A) (1992), 1598(2)(A) (1992) (intentional); Mass. Gen. Laws Ann. ch. 112, § 12K (West 1983) (knowing destruction or intentional expulsion or removal); Mich. Stat. Ann. § 1415(2835)(1) (Callaghan 1988) (purposeful); Mo. Ann. Stat. § 188.015(1) (Vernon Supp. 1992) (intentional); Neb. Rev. Stat. § 28-326(1) 1989) (intent); N.Y. Penal Law § 125.05(2) (McKinney 1987) (intent); Okla. Stat. Ann. tit. 63, § 1-730(1) (West 1984) (purposeful); R.I. Gen. Laws § 23-4.7-1 (1989) (intent); Va. Code § 18.2-71 (1988) (intent); Wyo. Stat. § 35-6-101(a)(i) (Supp. 1991) (intent).

[161] *E.g.,* Ill. Ann. Stat. ch. 38, § 81-22(4) (Smith-Hurd Supp. 1991 & 1992); Ky. Rev. Stat. § 311.720(1) (1990); Tenn. Code Ann. § 39-15-201(a)(1) (1991).

[162] *E.g.,* Fla. Stat. Ann. § 390.011(1) (West 1986) ("intention other than to produce live birth"); Idaho Code § 18-604(1) (1987) (viable birth); Ind. Code Ann. § 35-1-58.5-1(b) (Burns Supp. 1992); Iowa Code Ann. § 702.20 (West 1979); Nev. Rev. Stat. § 442.240 (1991); N.D. Cent. Code § 14-02.1-02(1) (1991) (not including completion of incomplete spontaneous miscarriage); S.C. Code Ann. § 44-41-10(a) (Law. Co-op. Supp. 1991) (other than delivery of viable birth); S.D. Codified Laws Ann. § 34-23A-1(1) (1984); Utah Code Ann. § 76-7-301(1) (Supp. 1991) ("undertaken to kill a live unborn child [or] produce a miscarriage"); V.I. Code Ann. tit. 14, § 151(a) (Supp. 1991). *See also supra* note 160.

[163] *E.g.,* Fla. Stat. Ann. § 390.011(1) (West 1986); Ind. Code Ann. § 35-1-58.5-1(b) (Burns Supp. 1991); Iowa Code Ann. § 702.20 (West 1979); Me. Rev. Stat. Ann. tit. 22, §§ 1596(1)(A) (1992), 1598(2)(A) (1980); Mass. Gen. Laws Ann. ch. 112, § 12K (West 1983); Mo. Ann. Stat. § 188.015(1) (Vernon Supp. 1992); Nev. Rev. Stat. § 442.240 (1991); N.D. Cent. Code § 14-02.1-02(1) (1991) (embryo or fetus); Okla. Stat. Ann. tit. 63, § 1-730(1) (West 1984); S.C. Code Ann. § 44-41-10(a) (Law. Co-op. Supp. 1991); S.D. Codified Laws Ann. § 34-23A-1(1) (1986); Utah Code Ann. § 76-7-301(1) (Supp. 1991) ("removal of a dead unborn child"); V.I. Code Ann. tit. 14, § 151(a) (Supp. 1991).

[164] Alaska Stat. § 18.16.010 (1991) (nonviable fetus). On the unconstitutionality of prohibitions against all abortions after viability, see *supra,* notes 136–37; *infra,* notes 185–88 and accompanying text.

[165] *E.g.,* Iowa Code Ann. § 707.7 (West 1979) (after end of second trimester); Me. Rev. Stat. Ann. tit. 22, § 1596(1)(B) (1992) (miscarriage defined as interruption of pregnancy of less than 20 weeks duration).

c. *"Pregnancy"* The term "pregnancy" is defined variously as implantation of an embryo in the uterus[168] or as the condition of a woman carrying a fetus or embryo within her body as a result of conception.[169] The first definition is another legislative means of exempting contraceptive techniques that prevent implantation ("morning-after pills") from the coverage of abortion statutes,[170] and the second definition usually is tied to legislative descriptions of fetuses or unborn children.

d. *"Fetus and Related Definitions"* Those state legislatures that have defined "fetus" have not been motivated by a desire to assure medical personnel that medical terminology is recognized in the law. Instead, they seem to have used such definitions as another way of sniping at the Supreme Court.[171]

For example, Illinois states that "fetus" and "unborn child" each means a human being from fertilization until birth.[172] Kentucky defines "fetus" the same way.[173] Other states use the term "unborn child" to the same effect.[174] To the extent that these provisions serve to vent legislative steam and soothe right-to-life constituents, no harm is done. If, however, they are intended to limit the availability of medically indicated abortions, they are a nullity under the Supreme Court's constitutional doctrine, at least until the Court concludes to change that doctrine.

e. *"Trimester"* A few statutes contain definitions of trimesters, perhaps because that is significant under *Roe v. Wade.*[175] Idaho defines the first trimester as the initial 13 weeks of pregnancy,[176] the second trimester as the portion of gestation between the 14th week and viability[177] and the third as the segment after viability.[178] Pennsylvania uses a period of 12 weeks for the first trimester.[179] South Carolina computes the first

---

[166] *E.g.*, Okla. Stat. Ann. tit. 63, § 1-730(4) (West 1984) ("fertilization . . . by the sperm of a male individual"); S.C. Code Ann. § 44-41-10(g) (Law. Co-op. Supp. 1991); Wyo. Stat. § 35-6-101a(iii) (Supp. 1991).

[167] *See infra,* notes 229–32 and accompanying text.

[168] N.M. Stat. Ann. § 30-5-1(A) (1984).

[169] *E.g.*, Mass. Gen. Laws Ann. ch. 112, § 12K (West 1983); Pa. Stat. Ann. tit. 18, § 3203 (Purdon Supp. 1991); S.C. Code Ann. § 44-41-10(f) (Law. Co-op. Supp. 1991); Wyo. Stat. § 35-6-101(a)(vi) (Supp. 1991).

[170] *See supra,* note 23.

[171] *See supra,* notes 147–54 and accompanying text. In State v. Green, 245 Kan. 398, 781 P.2d 678 (1989), the court ruled that imposing criminal liability for the killing of a fetus was a legislative function, so that the Kansas Supreme Court was prohibited from construing the term "human being" in the state's first-degree murder statute to include a "viable fetus." The court noted that it had ruled the same way in construing the state's aggravated vehicular homicide statute, in State v. Trudell, 243 Kan. 29, 755 P.2d 511 (1988).

[172] Ill. Ann. Stat. ch. 38, § 81-22(6) (Smith-Hurd Supp. 1991 & 1992).

[173] Ky. Rev. Stat. § 311.720(5) (1990).

[174] *E.g.*, Mass. Gen. Laws Ann. ch. 112, § 12K (West 1983); Mo. Ann. Stat. § 188.015(6) (Vernon 1992) ("[h]uman offspring from conception until birth at every stage of biological development"); Okla. Stat. Ann. tit. 63, § 1-730(2) (West 1984) ("from the moment of conception, through pregnancy, and until live birth including the human conceptus, zygote, morula, blastocyst, embryo and fetus").

On Canadian doctrine, see Weiler & Catton, *The Unborn child in Canadian Law,* 14 Osgoode Hall L.J. 643, 645–47 (1976) [hereinafter cited as Weiler & Catton]; Note, *Abortion Law in Canada: A Need for Reform,* 42 Sask. L. Rev. 221, 232–38 (1977).

[175] *See supra,* notes 129–37 and accompanying text.

[176] Idaho Code § 18-604(4) (1987).

[177] *Id.* § 18-604(5). The provision sets out a conclusive, irrebuttable presumption in favor of licensed physicians that the second trimester does not end before the beginning of the 25th week of pregnancy. *Id.*

[178] *Id.* § 18-604(6).

[179] Pa. Stat. Ann. tit. 18, § 3203 (Purdon 1983).

trimester from conception.[180] Indiana divides each pregnancy into three equal parts of three months each.[181]

In 1983 the Supreme Court selected the beginning of the last menstrual period experienced by a woman before impregnation as the means by which to define trimester.[182] The Court adhered to this trimester analysis as "a reasonable legal framework for limiting a State's authority to regulate abortions."[183] To the extent that state legislatures use a variant definition to limit the availability of abortions that the federal constitution guarantees, they invite invalidation of the offending provisions.[184]

f. *"Viability"* The point of viability is important under the Supreme Court's delineation of constitutionally protected abortion.[185] The Court defined viability as the point in a pregnancy at which "the fetus is 'potentially able to live outside the mother's womb, albeit with artificial aid.' Presumably the fetus is capable of 'meaningful life outside the mother's womb,' . . . [which] 'is usually placed' at about seven months or 28 weeks, but may occur earlier."[186] Quite a number of states have utilized that language or a near variant of it.[187] This is obviously the only safe course, because the

---

[180] S.C. Code Ann. § 44-41-10(i) (Law. Co-op. Supp. 1991) (through 12th week); conception is defined *id.* § 44-41-10(g). The second trimester extends from the 13th through the 24th week, *id.* § 44-41-10(j), and the third trimester from the 25th week through termination of pregnancy, *id.* § 44-41-10(k).

[181] Ind. Code Ann. § 35-1-58.5-1(a) (Burns Supp. 1991).

[182] City of Akron v. Akron Center for Reproductive Health, Inc., 462 U.S. 416, 431 n.15 (1983).

[183] *Id.* at 429 n.11. *See also* Comment, *The Trimester Approach: How Long Can the Legal Fiction Last?,* 35 Mercer L. Rev. 891, 909–13 (1984).

[184] A declaration of unconstitutionality is even more likely if criminal penalties turn on ascertaining the stage of pregnancy. Ind. Code Ann. § 35-1-58.5-3 (Burns 1985) requires a physician to determine and certify which trimester of pregnancy the patient is in and whether the fetus is viable. *Id.* § 35-1-58.5-4 makes performance of an abortion "not expressly provided for" a class C felony. If such a standard functions as an impediment to free implementation of a pregnant woman's constitutional claim to a therapeutic abortion, it will be struck down. *See* City of Akron v. Akron Center for Reproductive Health, Inc., 462 U.S. at 429–30.

[185] *See supra,* notes 136–38 and accompanying text. *See also* Special Project, *supra* note 31, at 128–47; Note, *Criminal Liability of Physicians: An Encroachment on the Abortion Right?,* 18 Am. Crim. L. Rev. 591, 600–01 (1981); Note, *Viability and Fetal Life in State Criminal Abortion Laws,* 72 J. Crim. L. & Criminology 324 (1981); Note, *Current Technology Affecting Supreme Court Abortion Jurisprudence,* 27 N.Y.L. Sch. L. Rev. 1221, 1239–42 (1982); Comment, *Fetal Viability and Individual Autonomy: Resolving Medical and Legal Standards for Abortion,* 27 U.C.L.A. L. Rev. 1340, 1356–63 (1980); Comment, *Technological Advances and Roe v. Wade: The Need to Rethink Abortion Law,* 29 U.C.L.A. L. Rev. 1194, 1202–14 (1982).

[186] Planned Parenthood v. Danforth, 428 U.S. at 63 (quoting Roe v. Wade, 410 U.S. at 160, 163). *See also* Colautti v. Franklin, 439 U.S. at 386.

[187] *E.g.,* Idaho Code § 18-604(7) (1987); Ill. Ann. Stat. ch. 38, § 81-22(2) (Smith-Hurd Supp. 1991 & 1992) (reasonable likelihood of sustained survival of fetus outside womb, with or without artificial support); Ind. Code Ann. § 35-1-58.5-1(e) (Burns Supp. 1991); Iowa Code Ann. § 702.20 (West 1979) ("indefinitely outside womb"; "[t]he time . . . may vary with each pregnancy, and the determination of whether a particular fetus is viable is a matter of responsible medical judgment"); Ky. Rev. Stat. § 311.720(8) (1990); La. Rev. Stat. Ann. § 14:87.5 (West 1986) (when life may be continued indefinitely outside womb); Minn. Stat. Ann. § 145.411(2) (West 1989); Mo. Ann. Stat. § 188.015(6) (Vernon 1992); Neb. Rev. Stat. § 28-326(6) (1989); N.D. Cent. Code § 14-02.1-02(7) (1991); Okla. Stat. Ann. tit. 63, § 1-730(3) (West 1984); Pa. Stat. Ann. tit. 18, § 3203 (Purdon 1983) (stage of fetal development, when in the physician's judgment "in light of the most advanced medical technology and information available . . . there is a reasonable likelihood of sustained survival of the unborn child outside the body of . . . [the] mother, with or without artificial support"); S.C. Code Ann. § 44-41-10(*l*) (Law. Co-op. Supp. 1991); Tenn. Code Ann. § 39-15-202(b)(3) (1991) (in providing information for women, physician must describe in equivalent terms); Wyo. Stat. § 35-6-101(a)(vii) (Supp. 1991).

Court has made it clear that viability cannot be determined arbitrarily in terms of life but must rest on each woman's pregnancy.[188]

g. *Live Born*   Four statutes contain definitions of live birth and live born.[189] These do not impact directly on abortion but are relevant in connection with legal responsibility to safeguard the lives of viable fetuses born alive during or as a consequence of an abortion.[190]

2. PERSONS PERFORMING ABORTIONS   *Roe v. Wade* was explicit that abortion is a medical matter and that licit abortions must be performed by professionally qualified persons.[191] Accordingly, therapeutic abortion laws are uniform in restricting the performance of abortions to licensed physicians.[192] The converse of this is that persons other than physicians who perform abortions can be punished.[193] Perhaps a potential area of litigation lurks concerning whether nurses or medical paraprofessionals can be prosecuted under such statutes. Often these individuals, who are supervised by licensed physicians and who follow accepted medical techniques in performing therapeutic abortions, appear to be covered by criminal statute because they are not licensed physicians. One

---

[188] Planned Parenthood v. Danforth, 428 U.S. at 64–65. There is latent difficulty in, *e.g.*, Minn. Stat. Ann. § 145.411(2) (West 1989) (''[d]uring the second half of its gestation period a fetus shall be considered potentially 'viable' ''), if that is intended to extend the limitations on postviability abortions to women whose fetuses are not yet viable. South Carolina establishes a presumption of viability no sooner than the 24th week of pregnancy. S.C. Code Ann. § 44-41-10*(l)* (Law. Co-op. Supp. 1991). This is acceptable if a woman with a viable fetus can obtain an abortion based on medical considerations not related to her life and health (assuming that does not infringe the constitutional status of the fetus, an implication of its *Roe v. Wade* analysis the Court has not yet explored) but unacceptable if invoked to deny an otherwise proper abortion to a woman who has not experienced fetal life by the 24th week of pregnancy.

   Viability constitutionally may be defined in terms of a reasonable likelihood that a fetus is capable of sustained survival outside the uterus. Charles v. Carey, 579 F. Supp. 464, 468,69 (N.D. Ill. 1983).

   See also Fromer, *supra* note 7, at 237–39.

[189] Ill. Ann. Stat. ch. 38, § 81-26(3) (Smith-Hurd Supp. 1991 & 1992) (''[i]t shall not be construed to imply that any human being aborted is not an individual under the Criminal 'Code of 1961' ''); Me. Rev. Stat. Ann. tit. 22, § 1595 (1992); N.D. Cent. Code § 14-02.1-02(4) (1991); 18 Pa. Cons. Stat. Ann. § 3203 (Purdon 1983) (''human being was completely expelled or extracted from her or his mother and after such separation breathed or showed evidence of any of the following: beating of the heart, pulsation of the umbilical cord, definite movement of voluntary muscles or any brain-wave activity'').

[190] *See infra*, notes 387–92, 478–80 and accompanying text. In Constitutional Right to Life Comm. v. Cannon, 117 R.I. 52, 363 A.2d 215 (1976), the court held that states are bound by the chronological approach of the Supreme Court to accommodate the conflicting private and public interests.

[191] 410 U.S. at 165. Abortion may be inferred to be a medical matter from the wording (i.e., the first trimester decision is left to the ''medical judgment of the pregnant woman's physician''). *Id.*

[192] *E.g.*, Alaska Stat. § 18.16.010 (1991); Cal. Health & Safety Code § 25951 (West 1984); Colo. Rev. Stat. § 18-6-101(1) (1986); Conn. Gen. Stat. Ann. § 53-31a(c) (Repealed); Del. Code Ann. tit. 24, § 1790(a) (Supp. 1990); Fla. Stat. Ann. § 390.001(1)(a), (3) (West 1986); Ga. Code Ann. § 16-12-141(a) (1988); Idaho code §§ 18-604(2), 18-608, 18-609 (1987), *and see id.* § 18-606(2) (hospital, nurse or other health care personnel do not commit a crime if in good faith they provide abortion-related services in reliance on the directions of a physician or pursuant to a hospital admission authorized by a physician); Ill. Ann. Stat. ch. 38, §§ 81-22(2), 81-23.1 (Smith-Hurd Supp. 1992); Ind. Code Ann. §§ 35-1-58.5-1(d), 35-1-58.5-2(1)(A) (Burns 1985 & Supp. 1991); Iowa Code Ann. § 707.7 (West 1979); Kan. Stat. Ann. § 21-3407(2) (1988); Ky. Rev. Stat. §§ 311.720(7), 311.750 (1990); La. Rev. Stat. Ann. § 37:1285(8.1), (9) (West 1988) (unless physician lacks training and experience to perform the procedure); Me. Rev. Stat. Ann. tit. 22, § 1598(1), (3)(A) (1980); Md. Pub. Health Code Ann. §§ 20-207, 20-208(a) (1990); Mass. Gen. Laws Ann. ch. 112, §§ 12L, 12M (West 1983); Minn. Stat. Ann. § 145.412(1)(1) (West 1989) (or physician in training under supervision of licensed physician); Mo. Ann. Stat. § 188.020 (Vernon 1983); Mont. Code Ann. § 50-20-109(1)(a) (1991); Neb. Rev. Stat § 28-335 (1989) (abortion by other than a licensed physician a felony); Nev. Rev. Stat. § 442.250(1)(a) (1991) (including physician in employ of United States); N.M.

may assume that if a restriction of lawful abortion to licensed physicians is not consonant with accepted medical practice and a consequence is the impediment of pregnant
women in their quest for lawful abortions, the restriction is constitutionally unacceptable.[194]

  3. PHYSICIAN-PATIENT CONSULTATION   The Supreme Court has spoken of abortion as something based on physician-patient consultation[195] because consent by the
patient is a condition to lawful abortion.[196] Counseling is reflected in different ways in
legislation. It may be sanctioned in the context of pregnancy of or abortions for minors[197]
or posited as an appropriate subject of administrative regulation.[198] As a form of consumer protection law, institutions announcing the availability of counseling services
must have qualified staff members to provide them.[199] Pennsylvania specifically requires
it as a condition for a determination that an abortion is necessary.[200]

  Some legislation,[201] however, clearly states that it is ancillary to more elaborate
statutory requirements concerning information that must be communicated to pregnant
women before they can consent to abortion. If the informational process functions to

---

Stat. Ann. § 30-5-1(C) (1984); N.Y. Penal Law § 125.05(3) (McKinney 1987) (abortion by duly licensed
physician is justifiable under certain circumstances); N.C. Gen. Stat. § 14.45.1(a), (b) (1986); N.D. Cent.
Code § 14.02.1-04(1) (1991); Okla. Stat. Ann. tit. 63, § 1-731(A) (West 1984); 18 Pa. Cons. Stat. Ann.
§ 3204(a) (Purdon 1983); S.C. Code Ann. § 44-41-20 (Law. Co-op. 1984); S.D. Codified Laws Ann.
§§ 34-23A-1(2) (including physician in employ of United States), 34-23A-3 to -5 (1986); Tenn. Code Ann.
§ 39-15-201(c) (1991); Utah Code Ann. §§ 76-6-301(2), 76-7-302(1) (Supp. 1991) (including qualified
physician in federal employment); Va. Code §§ 18.2-72 to .2-74 (1988); Wash. Rev. Code Ann. § 9.02.070
(Repealed); Wyo. Stat §§ 35-6-101 (a)(v), 35-6-103, 35-6-111 (1988 & Supp. 1991) (statutory references
are to physicians performing abortions, and abortion by other than a physician is punishable as a felony).

  V.I. Code Ann. tit. 14, § 151(b)(1) (Supp. 1991), refers to licensed physicians during the first 12
weeks of pregnancy, but subsections (2) and (3) limit abortions thereafter to those performed by licensed
surgeons or gynecologists. If there is no supportable medical basis for that limitation and it serves to make
otherwise lawful abortions less readily available than would normally be the case, the latter limitation is
unconstitutional under City of Akron v. Akron Center for Reproductive Health, Inc., 462 U.S. 416, 426–
31 (1983).

  If a state legislature does not legitimate therapeutic abortions performed by licensed physicians, a court
must read in that exemption from penal law coverage. See, e.g., People v. Bricker, 389 Mich. 524, 208
N.W.2d 172 (1973).

[193]Connecticut v. Menillo, 423 U.S. 9 (1975) (per curiam). See infra, notes 461–63 and accompanying text.

[194]See City of Akron v. Akron Center for Reproductive Health, Inc., 462 U.S. at 426–31.

[195]See id. at 426–27.

[196]Planned Parenthood v. Danforth, 428 U.S. at 65–67. See infra, notes 233–43 and accompanying text.

[197]E.g., V.I. Code Ann. tit. 19, § 292(c) (1976).

[198]E.g., Ill. Ann. Stat. ch. 38, § 81–23.1(B)(1) (Smith-Hurd Supp. 1991 & 1992) (with legislatively mandated content); Ky. Rev. Stat. § 311.723(b)(2)(a) (1990) (but with legislative objectives specified); Ohio
Rev. Code Ann. § 3701.341(A)(5) (Page 1988).

[199]Okla. Stat. Ann. tit. 63, § 1-736 (West 1984).

[200]18 Pa. Cons. Stat. Ann. § 3204(b) (Purdon 1983). In Planned Parenthood of Southeastern Pennsylvania,
947 F.2d 682, 703–04 (3d Cir.), cert. granted, 112 S. Ct. 931 (1991), the court approved the statutory
requirement that a referring or performing physican advise a pregnant woman of the nature of the abortion
procedure and of the risks and alternatives to the procedure or treatment that a reasonable patient would
consider material to an abortion decision, the probable gestational age of the fetus and the medical risks
associated with carrying a fetus to term. It thought the legislature could decide that information of that sort
should come from a doctor rather than a counselor. The Casey court also sustained the constitutionality of
a provision requiring either a physician or a counselor to give specified information about financial aspects
of abortion and childbirth. Id. at 704–05 (rejecting also a claim based on the first amendment that these
requirements dictated the expression of views contrary to personally-held beliefs, id. at 705–06).

deter or impede decisions to have abortions, it is unconstitutional,[202] and associated counseling requirements will fall with it.

4.   INFORMATION TO PATIENTS   An informed consent is a prerequisite to a lawful therapeutic abortion.[203] A patient must be given information about ''just what would be done and . . . its consequences,''[204] and state legislation may ensure that the abortion decision is made ''in the light of all attendant circumstances—psychological and emotional as well as physical—that might be relevant to the well-being of the patient.''[205] In the case of immature minors, state concerns to protect pregnant girls and to promote family integrity justify special measures to ensure that ''the abortion decision is made with understanding and after careful deliberation.''[206] A sizable number of states have picked up on this dimension of the Court's jurisprudence, in some instances to implement its intent but at other times with an obvious purpose of scaring patients away from decisions to seek abortions. The latter form of legislation has produced a new level of constitutional intervention by the Court.[207] Statutes call for communicating information that, in a physician's best professional judgment, a woman is pregnant[208] and about the

---

[201] Okla. Stat. Ann. tit. 63, § 1-736 (West 1984); S.D. Codified Laws Ann. § 34-23A-10 (1986) (physicians must make available to patients at request information about professional social service and counseling service agencies in the state providing a full spectrum of alternative solutions for problem pregnancies).

[202] See infra, notes 226–28 and accompanying text. In Thornburgh v. American College of Obstetricians and Gynecologists, 476 U.S. 747 (1986), the Supreme Court invalidated a number of statutorily-prescribed warning requirements because they ''wholly subordinate[d] constitutional privacy interests and concerns with maternal health in an effort to deter a woman from making a decision that, with her physician, is hers to make.'' Id. at 759.

[203] Planned Parenthood v. Danforth, 428 U.S. at 67, 85. See also City of Akron v. Akron Center for Reproductive Health, Inc., 462 U.S. at 442–44.

[204] Planned Parenthood v. Danforth, 428 U.S. at 67 n.7.

[205] Colautti v. Franklin, 439 U.S. at 394.

[206] City of Akron v. Akron Center for Reproductive Health, Inc., 462 U.S. at 443 n.32.

[207] See infra, notes 225–33 and accompanying text.

[208] E.g., Me. Rev. Stat. Ann. tit. 22, § 1599 (1992); Mo. Ann. Stat. § 188.039(2)(1) (Vernon Supp. 1992); Nev. Rev. Stat. § 442.253(1)(a) (1991) (a copy of the pregnancy test results should be made available); N.D. Cent. Code § 14-02.1-02(5)(a) (1991); R.I. Gen. Laws § 23-4.7.3(b) (1989); Tenn. Code Ann. § 39-15-202(b)(1) (1991).

[209] E.g., Ky. Rev. Stat. § 311.726(2)(c) (1990) (probable gestational age of the fetus at the time an abortion is to be performed); Me. Rev. Stat. Ann. tit. 22, § 1599 (Supp. 1992) (number of weeks from probable time of conception); Mo. Ann. Stat. § 188.039(2)(2) (Vernon Supp. 1992) (same); Nev. Rev. Stat. § 442.253(1)(b) (1991) (same); N.D. Cent. Code § 14-02.1-02(5)(b) (1991) (based on information provided by patient or medical and laboratory evaluations); 18 Pa. Cons. Stat. Ann. § 3205(a)(1)(ii) (Purdon Supp. 1991 & 1992) (probable gestational age of unborn child at time abortion is to be performed); R.I. Gen. Laws § 23-4.7-3(b) (1989) (gestational age of fetus at time of disclosure); Tenn. Code Ann. § 39-15-202(b)(2) (1991) (based on information provided by patient or medical and laboratory evaluation).

[210] E.g., Del. Code Ann. tit. 24, § 1794(a)(1) (1987); Fla. Stat. Ann. § 390.025(2) (West 1986); Ind. Code Ann. § 35-1-58.5-1(f) (Burns Supp. 1991); Mass. Gen. Laws Ann. ch. 112, § 12S (West 1983); Minn. Stat. Ann. § 145.412(1)(4) (West 1989); Mont. Code Ann. § 50-20-104(3)(a) (1991); Neb. Rev. Stat. § 28-326(8)(b) (1989); Okla. Stat. Ann. tit. 63, § 1-736 (West 1984) (such information must be given before a hospital can advertise that it offers counseling services); R.I. Gen. Laws § 23-4.7-3 (1989); S.C. Dep't of Health & Envtl. Control R. 61-12, § 203(C)(3) (1992); Utah Code Ann. § 76-7-305(1) (1990); Va. Code § 18.2-76 (1988).

[211] E.g., Del. Code Ann. tit. 24, § 1794(a)(2) (1987) (probable effects of procedure on woman, including effects on child-bearing ability and possible future pregnancies); Fla. Stat. Ann. § 390.025(2) (West 1986); Minn. Stat. Ann. § 145.412(1)(4) (West 1989); Mo. Ann. Stat. § 188.039(2)(2) (Vernon Supp. 1992) (possible emotional or psychological consequences); Mont. Code Ann. § 50-20-104(3)(b) (1991) (physical and psychological effect); Nev. Rev. Stat. § 442.253(1)(c) (1991) (any known immediate and long-term

length of the pregnancy at the time of consultation.[209] They require information about the abortion procedure to be used,[210] and the effects[211] and risks[212] associated with abortion. Three states call for patients to be provided with the name of the physician who will perform the abortion.[213] Several authorize communication of any other information a counselor believes significant to an informed consent.[214] With the possible exception of certain language in the Missouri, Nevada and North Dakota statutes bearing on the consequences of abortion, which may or may not be supportable by current medical knowledge,[215] the information required to be given is compatible with the Supreme Court's expectations.[216] This cannot be said, however, of requirements that pregnant women be given information that abortion is a major surgical technique[217] or that they be told of the drawbacks and medical risks associated with abortion.[218]

A common legislative requirement is that a pregnant woman be told about alternatives to abortion,[219] including the availability of services and financial aid,[220] adoption[221] and counseling.[222] In several states, public agencies supply forms and other information concerning public and private agencies available to help women if the women request

---

physical or psychological dangers); 18 Pa. Cons. Stat. Ann. § 3205(a)(1)(i) (Purdon Supp. 1991 & 1992) ("[t]he fact that there may be detrimental physical and psychological effects which are not accurately foreseeable"); S.C. Dep't of Health & Envtl. Control R. 61-12, § 203(C) (1992).

[212] *E.g.*, Del. Code Ann. tit. 24, § 1794(a)(4) (1987); Ky. Rev. Stat. § 311.726(2) (1990) (same); Me. Rev. Stat. Ann. tit. 22, § 1599 (1992) (same); Mass. Gen. Laws Ann. ch. 112, § 12S (West 1983) (possible complications associated with use of procedure and performance of abortion itself); Mo. Ann. Stat. § 188.039(2)(2) (Vernon 1983) ("immediate and long-term physical dangers of abortion and psychological trauma resulting from abortion and any increased incidence of premature births, tubal pregnancies and stillbirths following abortion"); Nev. Rev. Stat. § 442.253(1)(c) (1991) (similar language to Missouri); N.D. Cent. Code § 14-02.1-02(5)(d) (1981) (same); 18 Pa. Cons. Stat. Ann. § 3205(a)(1)(iii) (Purdon Supp. 1991 & 1992) ("[t]he particular medical risks associated with the particular abortion procedure to be employed including, when medically accurate, the risks of infection, hemorrhage, danger to subsequent pregnancies and infertility"), § 3205(a)(1)(v) (medical risks associated with carrying child to term) (Purdon 1983); R.I. Gen. Laws § 23-4.7-3(d) (1989) (but information need not be communicated if there is a medical basis, certified in writing in patient's record, for nondisclosure); Tenn. Code Ann. §§ 39-15-202(b)(6) (numerous benefits and risks are attendant on either continued pregnancy and childbirth or abortion depending on patient's circumstances; physician to explain benefits and risks to best of ability and knowledge of circumstances), 39-15-202(c) (particular risks associated with pregnancy and childbirth and abortion or child delivery technique to be employed, including at least a general description of medical instructions to be followed after abortion or childbirth to insure safe recovery) (1991); Utah Code Ann. § 76-7-305.5(4) (1990); Va. Code § 18.2-76 (1988) (risks, if any, in her particular case to her health).

[213] *E.g.*, Ky. Rev. Stat. § 311.726(2) (1990).

[214] *E.g.*, Mo. Ann. Stat. § 188.039(3) (Vernon Supp. 1992); N.D. Cent. Code § 14-02.1-02(5) (1991) (any other explanation of information that in the exercise of the physician's best medical judgment is reasonably necessary to allow the woman to give an informed consent with full knowledge of the nature and consequences of abortion); R.I. Gen. Laws § 23-4.7-3(b) (1989) (same); Utah Code Ann. § 76-7-305(2) (1990) (other factors deemed necessary to a voluntary and informed consent).

At least four states, Kentucky, Ky. Rev. Stat. § 311.729(1) (1990); Nevada, Nev. Rev. Stat. § 442.253(3) (1991); Pennsylvania, 18 Pa. Cons. Stat. Ann. § 3208(a) (Purdon Supp. 1991 & 1992) (English, Spanish and Vietnamese); and Rhode Island, R.I. Gen. Laws § 23-4.7-5(c) (1989), require women to receive printed information in a language they can understand, with a notation whether an interpreter has been used during counseling. Statutes in Rhode Island, *id.* § 23-4.7-5(d), and South Dakota, S.D. Codified Laws Ann. § 34-23A-10.1 (1986), allow for a copy to the patient at her request.

[215] To the extent there is no significantly greater risk of premature births, tubal pregnancies and stillbirths following induced abortion in comparison to spontaneous miscarriages and normal childbirth, based on current medical experience, the statutory language probably provides the "parade of horribles" that leads to constitutional invalidation. *See* City of Akron v. Akron Center for Reproductive Health, Inc., 426 U.S. at 445. *See also infra,* notes 230–33 and accompanying text.

this information.[223] One state provides that a woman cannot be denied public assistance if she refuses to consent to an abortion.[224]

However, in *Thornburgh v. American College of Obstetricians and Gynecologists*,[225] the Supreme Court ruled unconstitutional statutory provisions requiring advice about medical assistance benefits and paternal financial responsibilities because they constituted "poorly disguised elements of discouragement for the abortion decision."[226] Much of the content was "nonmedical information beyond the physician's area of expertise and, for many patients, would be irrelevant and inappropriate."[227] Such information in a life-threatening situation might well prove cruel as well as detrimental to the relationship between physician and patient.[228] The required information was irrelevant to informed consent and thus advanced no legitimate state interest.

Therefore, one can assume that only warning requirements relating to medical matters that embody legitimate medical implications of abortion may be imposed constitutionally. Nevertheless, the Supreme Court has noted that "a State is not always foreclosed from asserting an interest in whether pregnancies end in abortion or childbirth."[229]

---

[216] This pattern of legislation is constitutional, from indications in City of Akron v. Akron Center for Reproductive Health, Inc., 462 U.S. at 446–47, sustaining ordinance language similar to most of the cited statutes.

[217] Tenn. Code Ann. § 39-15-202(b)(4) (1991) (abortion in a considerable number of cases constitutes a major surgical procedure). Such a warning was invalidated in City of Akron v. Akron Center for Reproductive Health, Inc., 462 U.S. at 444 ("a dubious statement"; trial court expert evidence supported a conclusion that it is a minor surgical procedure. *Id.* at 444 n.35).

[218] In Thornburgh v. American College of Obstetricians and Gynecologists, 476 U.S. 747 (1986), the Court held unconstitutional the Pennsylvania statutory requirement that physicians communicate information of these sorts to patients because it inappropriately impeded the professional activities of physicians. The Court noted that the state "does not, and surely would not, compel similar disclosure of every possible peril of necessary surgery or of simple vaccination, [thus revealing] the anti-abortion character of the statute and its real purpose." *Id.* at 764. Physicians were compelled under the statute to repeat the prescribed information whether or not they believed it pertinent to a patient's personal decision. Hence, the provision was facially unconstitutional.

[219] *E.g.*, Del. Code Ann. tit. 24, § 1794(a)(5) (1987); Fla. Stat. Ann. § 390.025(2) (West 1986); Ky. Rev. Stat. § 311.729(1) (1990); Me. Rev. Stat. Ann. tit. 22, § 1599 (1992); Mass. Gen. Laws Ann. ch. 112, § 12S (West 1983); Mo. Ann. Stat. § 188.039(2)(3) (Vernon Supp. 1992); Mont. Code Ann. § 50-20-104(3)(c) (1991); Neb. Rev. Stat. § 28-326(8) (1989); Nev. Rev. Stat. § 442.253 (1991); N.D. Cent. Code § 14-02.1-02(5)(f) (1991); 18 Pa. Cons. Stat. Ann. § 3205(a)(2)(i–iii) (Purdon Supp. 1991 & 1992); R.I. Gen. Laws § 23-4.7-5(b)(1) (1989); S.C. Dep't of Health & Envtl. Control R. 61–12, § 203(C)(1) (1992); Tenn. Code Ann. § 39-15-202(b)(5) (1991). The Massachusetts statute was held constitutional in Planned Parenthood League v. Bellotti, 641 F.2d 1006, 1020–26 (1st Cir. 1981).

[220] *E.g.*, Ky. Rev. Stat. § 311.729(1) (1990); Me. Rev. Stat. Ann. tit. 22, § 1599(2)(D) (1992); 18 Pa. Cons. Stat. Ann. §§ 3205(a)(2)(ii) (medical assistance benefits may be available for prenatal care, childbirth and neonatal care), 3205(a)(2)(iii) (father is liable to assist in support of child, even if father has offered to pay for abortion) (Purdon Supp. 1991).

[221] *E.g.*, R.I. Gen. Laws § 23-4.7-5(b)(1) (1989); Utah Code Ann. § 76-7-305(2)(a) (1990).

[222] S.D. Codified Laws Ann. § 34-23A-10 (1987).

[223] *E.g.*, Ky. Rev. Stat. § 311.729(1) (1990); Mass. Gen. Laws Ann. ch. 112, § 12S (West 1983); 18 Pa. Cons. Stat. Ann. § 3208(a)(1) (Purdon Supp. 1991 & 1992); R.I. Gen. Laws § 23-4.7-5(b)(1) (1989); Utah Code Ann. § 76-7-305.5(2)(a) (1990).

[224] Mass. Gen. Laws Ann. ch. 112, § 12S (West 1983). The statute was sustained as constitutional in Planned Parenthood League v. Bellotti, 641 F.2d 1006, 1020–21 (1st Cir. 1981). *See also infra,* notes 527–31 and accompanying text.

[225] 476 U.S. 747 (1986).

[226] *Id.* at 763.

[227] *Id.*

If statutorily mandated information reflects a good-faith legislative effort to see that patients are informed about alternatives to abortion, including public financial assistance and support services, and no legislative motivation is perceptible to discourage abortion, one may posit that state legislation on the point is as valid as legislation governing information about the legitimate medical dimensions of abortion and childbirth.

The same cannot be said, however, of statutory requirements that patients be told the specifics of fetal development and characteristics. Utah has gone the farthest in this regard,[230] but several other states require similar information.[231] The Supreme Court voided language typical of these statutes because it "would involve at best speculation by the physician."[232] Therefore, one may doubt that a physician or counselor constitutionally could be prosecuted for a failure to comply with legislative requirements that appear on their face to be intended to discourage free choice of abortion and not to provide neutral information relevant to a woman's decision.

In sum, although some of the specific information required under several state laws cannot constitutionally be required of physicians, most of the individual requirements are probably valid. Nevertheless, if one stands apart and surveys the totality of information mandated in some jurisdictions, particularly Kentucky, Nevada, North Dakota,

---

[228] The Court observed that theoretical financial assistance from a father is frequently not realized. *Id.* In addition, "a victim of rape should not have to hear gratuitous advice that an unidentified perpetrator is liable for support if she continues the pregnancy to term." *Id.*

[229] City of Akron v. Akron Center for Reproductive Health, Inc., 462 U.S. at 444 n.33.

[230] Utah Code Ann. § 76-7-305.5(1)(b) (1990) requires the state department of health to provide descriptions of "physical characteristics" of normal unborn children at two-week intervals, "beginning with the fourth week and ending with the twenty-fourth week . . . accompanied by scientifically verified photographs of an unborn child" at each stage of development, including "information about physiological and anatomical characteristics, brain and heart function and the presence of external members and internal organs during the applicable stages of development."

[231] *E.g.,* Del. Code Ann. tit. 24, § 1794(a)(3) (1987) ("[f]acts of fetal development as of the time proposed abortion is to be performed"); Idaho Code § 18-609(2)(b) (1987) (similar); Ky. Rev. Stat. § 311.729(3) (1990) (probable anatomical and physical characteristics of the fetus at the various gestational ages at which abortion might be performed, including any relevant information on the possibility of fetal survival); Mass. Gen. Laws Ann. ch. 112, § 12S (West 1983) (information about stage of development of unborn child); Mont. Code Ann. § 50-20-104(3)(a) (1991) (similar to Delaware language, *supra*); N.D. Cent. Code § 14-02.1-02(5)(c) (1991) (similar); 18 Pa. Cons. Stat. Ann. § 3202(b)(i) (Purdon 1983).

[232] City of Akron v. Akron Center for Reproductive Health, Inc., 462 U.S. at 444 (footnoted omitted). In Thornburgh v. American College of Obstetrics and Gynecologists, 476 U.S. 747 (1986), the Court invalidated several statutory requirements concerning information to be communicated by physicians to pregnant patients because they were "nothing less than an outright attempt to wedge the Commonwealth's message discouraging abortion into the privacy of the informed-consent dialogue between the woman and her physician." *Id.* at 762. A requirement that a physician describe the characteristics of a fetus every two weeks was overinclusive, since this information is not always relevant to a woman's decision, and "may serve only to confuse and punish her and . . . heighten her anxiety, contrary to accepted medical practice." *Id.*

On *Webster,* see generally Dellinger & Sperling, *Abortion and the Supreme Court: The Retreat from Roe v. Wade,* 138 U. Pa. L. Rev. 83 (1989); Heaney, *On the Legal Status of the Unborn,* 33 Cath. Law. 305 (1990).

See also Planned Parenthood Ass'n v. Ashcroft, 655 F.2d 848, 867–68 (8th Cir. 1981), *aff'd on other grounds,* 462 U.S. 475 (1983) (plurality opinion) (woman's decision was burdened insofar as anxiety and tension involved in such a decision are increased without medical justification); Planned Parenthood League v. Bellotti, 641 F.2d 1006, 1021–22 (1st Cir. 1981) (information not directly related to any medically relevant fact would cause many women "emotional distress, anxiety, guilt, and in some cases increased physical pain"). There is no impediment to state regulations requiring patient counseling without specifying the content. Birth Control Centers, Inc. v. Reizen, 743 F.2d 352, 362–63 (6th Cir. 1984).

Pennsylvania, Tennessee and Utah, the legislative purpose seems clear—to discourage consents to abortion, a governmental motive that the Supreme Court has declared unconstitutional.[233]

There is one other dimension of unconstitutionality in many information statutes. Some do not specify who must impart the information[234] or allow for alternative sources to physicians.[235] A number of states, however, require physicians, often on threat of criminal penalties, to communicate the information personally.[236] The Supreme Court invalidated that approach in *City of Akron v. Akron Center for Reproductive Health*,[237] although it confirmed that a physician cannot abdicate his or her ultimate responsibility for the medical aspects of abortion. Therefore, states can require physicians to verify that adequate counseling has been provided by qualified persons and that a patient's consent is informed.

5. NOTICE TO OTHERS   In the years when notice requirements appeared clearly to be unconstitutional, states repealed legislation requiring information to be given to spouses[238] or the consent of a minor female's parents or guardian.[239] However, in anticipation of a Supreme Court repudiation of *Roe v. Wade,* the Pennsylvania legislature enacted a statute[240] requiring notice to spouses, subject to certain exceptions, including a fear of spousal violence.[241] The legitimacy of mandates of these sorts turns on the constitutionality of requiring spousal or parental consent.[242]

6. CONSENT   a. *General Requirements*   As noted, medically indicated abortions must be consented to.[243] This means a free choice on a woman's part—freedom from

---

[233] City of Akron v. Akron Center for Reproductive Health, Inc., 462 U.S. at 445: "By insisting upon recitation of a lengthy and inflexible list of information, Akron unreasonably has placed 'obstacles in the path of the doctor upon whom [a woman is] entitled to rely for advice in connection with her decision.' " *Id.* (quoting Whalen v. Roe, 429 U.S. 589, 604 n.33 (1977)).

[234] *E.g.,* Del. Code Ann. tit. 24, § 1794(a) (1987); Minn. Stat. Ann. § 145.412(1)(4) (West 1989); Neb. Rev. Stat. § 28-326(8) (1989); 18 Pa. Cons. Stat. Ann. §§ 3205(a)(4)(woman to certify in writing that she has received the information required), 3205(a)(4) (physician must receive copy of woman's certification before performing abortion) (Purdon Supp. 1991 & 1992).

[235] *E.g.,* Fla. Stat. Ann. § 390.025(2) (West 1986) (covers only abortion counseling or referral agencies); Idaho Code § 18-609(3) (1987); Ky. Rev. Stat. § 311.726(3) (1990); R.I. Gen. Laws § 23-4.7-3(a) (1989) (either a physician or associated personnel or authorized agents to give information); S.C. Codified Laws Ann. § 34-23A-10 (1987) (triggered only by a patient's request for information about counseling service agencies).

[236] *E.g.,* Me. Rev. Stat. Ann. tit. 22, § 1599 (1992); Mo. Ann. Stat. § 188.039(2) (Vernon Supp. 1992); Mont. Code Ann. § 50-20-106(2) (1991); Nev. Rev. Stat. § 442.253 (1991); N.D. Cent. Code §§ 14-02.1-02(5), 14-02.1-03(1) (1991); Tenn. Code Ann. § 39-15-202(b) (1991) (patient must sign form indicating physician has orally informed her); Utah Code Ann. § 76-7-305(2) (1989); Va. Code § 18.2-76 (1988).

[237] 462 U.S. at 446–49. The Court reasoned that consent of a woman can still be informed even though the physician has allowed another "qualified individual" to counsel her. *Id.* at 448.

[238] The Illinois statute requiring that, Ill. Ann. Stat. ch. 38, § 18-23.4 (Smith-Hurd Supp. 1984–1985), was repealed in 1984.

[239] A Missouri provision so requiring was held invalid in Planned Parenthood Ass'n v. Ashcroft, 655 F.2d 848, 866 (8th Cir. 1981), *aff'd on other grounds,* 462 U.S. 476 (1983) (plurality opinion).

[240] 18 Pa. Cons. Stat. Ann. § 3209 (Supp. 1992).

[241] The statute was declared unconstitutional in Planned Parenthood of Southeastern Pennsylvania v. Casey, 947 F.2d 682, 709–15 (3rd Cir.), *cert. granted,* 112 S. Ct. 931 (1991).

[242] *See infra* notes 263–67 and accompanying text (spousal consent); *infra* notes 255–62 and accompanying text (parental consent).

[243] Planned Parenthood v. Danforth, 428 U.S. at 65–67. *Cf.* Guste v. Jackson, 429 U.S. 399 (1977) (court should not have invalidated state consent statute as far as women generally were concerned). *See also* Smith v. Bentley, 493 F. Supp. 916, 928 (E.D. Ark. 1980).

any coercion.[244] It is common to include the requirement of consent in legislation,[245] quite frequently with the additional mandate that a consent be in writing[246] or certified.[247] Consent may be dispensed with only in cases of immediate threat to a woman's life[248] or health.[249] Otherwise, criminal[250] or civil[251] sanctions may be pursued against those who perform abortions.

b. *Consent by Minor*   A pregnant minor must consent to an abortion like her elders. This is noted specifically in some statutes,[252] subject to an emergency exception.[253] The bulk of litigation, however, has been generated by requirements of consent by parents or legal guardians.[254]

c. *Consent by Parent or Guardian*   It has been common to require consent by both parents,[255] one parent[256] or a guardian[257] before an unmarried, unemancipated minor can have an abortion. A guardian may be given the exclusive power to decide whether someone judicially determined to be mentally incompetent may have an abortion.[258]

The constitutionality of these provisions has been the object of considerable deci-

---

[244] That norm appears occasionally in legislation. *See, e.g.,* Iowa Code Ann. § 707.8(3) (West Supp. 1991) (procuring consent through force or intimidation a felony); 18 Pa. Cons. Stat. Ann. § 3206(g) (Purdon Supp. 1991) (coercion of minor or mental incompetent); Tenn. Code Ann. § 39-15-201(b)(3) (1991) (obtain or procure abortion); Utah Code Ann. § 76-7-312 (1990) (coercion to obtain abortion).

The issue arises indirectly from time to time. *See, e.g.,* People v. Pointer, 151 Cal. App. 3d 1128, 199 Cal. Rptr. 357 (1984) (court could not require as a condition of probation following conviction of child endangerment that the defendant not conceive again; this might force an abortion when there were other methods of forestalling future child endangerment); Planned Parenthood Ass'n v. Department of Human Resources, 297 Or. 562, 687 P.2d 785 (1984) (court invoked state constitutional provisions to invalidate administrative regulation limiting number of elective abortions a woman could have under public funding). *Cf.* Sanchez v. Sirmons, 121 Misc. 2d 249, 467 N.Y.S.2d 757 (Sup. Ct. 1983) (arbitration clause in a medical consent form was not binding in malpractice suit based on bungled abortion unless defendant physician established that the woman knew she was waiving the right to a jury trial; the circumstances of an abortion decision made such an awareness unlikely).

A refusal to undergo an abortion cannot be asserted as a defense in a "wrongful birth" action (*see infra* note 424) based on a claim that a plaintiff had brought about the damages through her own choice. Morris v. Frudenfeld, 135 Cal. App. 3d 23, 185 Cal. Rptr. 76 (1982); Rivera v. State, 94 Misc. 2d 157, 163, 404 N.Y.S.2d 950, 954 (Ct. Cl. 1978) (any interpretation of traditional doctrine that would require an abortion would be "an invasion of privacy of the grossest and most pernicious kind"). Nor is a plaintiff required to mitigate damages by undergoing a second abortion after a bungled one by a physician defendant. Delaney v. Krafte, 98 A.D.2d 128, 470 N.Y.S.2d 936 (1984).

A constitutional issue is inherent in statutory provisions, *e.g.,* Mont. Code Ann. § 50-20-108(2) (1991); N.D. Cent. Code § 14-02.1-03 (1981); S.D. Codified Laws Ann. § 34-23A-18 (1986) (all facts and circumstances involving birth and abortion are relevant and material evidence in parental rights termination, dependency or neglect proceedings; state department of social services may commence proceedings); Tenn. Code Ann. § 39-15-207 (1991); Tex. Fam. Code Ann. § 15.022(a) (Vernon 1986) (action to terminate parental rights may be based on abortion).

The constitutionality of such provisions appears suspect. *Cf.* Freiman v. Ashcroft, 584 F.2d 247 (8th Cir. 1978), *aff'd,* 440 U.S. 941 (1979) (court invalidated statutory requirement that physician inform patient of that consequence). The Supreme Court in Planned Parenthood v. Danforth, 428 U.S. at 62 n.2, found that the physician-plaintiffs lacked standing to attack this portion of the Missouri statute. *See also* Parness & Pritchard, *supra* note 116, at 293–95.

In instances of termination of the rights of a mother, one should consider Lassiter v. Department of Social Servs., 452 U.S. 18, 27 (1981), in which the Court acknowledged that "a parent's desire for and right to 'the companionship, care, custody, and management of his or her children' is an important interest that 'undeniably warrants deference and, absent a powerful countervailing interest, protection' " (quoting Stanley v. Illinois, 405 U.S. 645, 651 (1972)). Hence, a state that terminates that interest "will have worked a unique kind of deprivation." *Id.* "A parent's interest in the accuracy and justice of the decision

sional law. During the first trimester of pregnancy, a state cannot impose a blanket requirement that every pregnant minor obtain the consent of a parent or guardian.[259] If a pregnant minor is capable of giving an informed consent,[260] her consent controls. However, if a minor is unmarried and emancipated and there is doubt whether the minor can make an informed consent to an abortion, the Court has indicated that either parental[261] or judicial[262] consent may be required.

If state statutes recognize complete discretion on the part of emancipated (or married) minors to select abortion as the mode of terminating their pregnancies and provide expeditious judicial proceedings to determine whether unemancipated minors are capable of choice, they are constitutional. Many states, however, have not revised their legislation to reflect the refinements expected by the Supreme Court.

d. *Spousal Consent*   The Supreme Court invalidated all requirements of spousal consent,[263] which has shifted legislative attention in most jurisdictions to spousal notification as a condition to abortion.[264] Nevertheless, one still may encounter occasionally a requirement of spousal consent.[265] This probably reflects a disinclination to recognize

---

to terminate his or her parental status is, therefore, a commanding one." *Id.* Consequently, a hearing meeting the administrative due process requirements established in Mathews v. Eldridge, 424 U.S. 319 (1976), is a prerequisite to termination of parental rights. An automatic termination by statute, or based on presumptions of neglect resting on consents to lawful postviability abortions, does not meet that constitutional standard. *Cf.* Smith v. Organization of Foster Families, 431 U.S. 816, 847–56 (1977) (foster parents had a limited liberty interest in termination of custodial status, but state procedures amply recognized *Mathews v. Eldridge* concerns). A husband presumably would have equivalent claims.

As to putative fathers (fathers of children born outside marriage), the Court has indicated that they must be given an opportunity to develop a relationship with their children. Lehr v. Robertson, 463 U.S. 248, 261–63, 265 (1983). Only if they do not avail themselves of such an opportunity can their claims to parental status be terminated summarily through abortion proceedings. *Id. See also* Quilloin v. Walcott, 434 U.S. 246 (1978). Otherwise, they have procedural protections, Stanley v. Illinois, 405 U.S. 645 (1972), which as a matter of equal protection must be equal to those an illegitimate child's mother enjoys. Caban v. Mohammed, 441 U.S. 380 (1979) (sex bias violates equal protection clause). These holdings, too, appear to preclude invocation of the above state statutes against fathers of illegitimate children. *See generally* Note, *Potential Fathers and Abortion: A Woman's Womb Is Not a Man's Castle,* 55 Brooklyn L. Rev. 1359 (1990) [hereinafter Fathers and Abortion Note].

[245] *E.g.,* Colo. Rev. Stat. § 18-6-101(1) (1986) (at woman's request); Idaho Code §§ 18-609–610 (1987) (consent required; refusal to consent is binding irrespective of nonage or incompetency); Iowa Code Ann. § 707.8(2) (West 1979); Ky. Rev. Stat. § 311.726 (1990); Minn. Stat. Ann. § 145.412(1)(4) (West 1989); N.M. Stat. Ann. § 30-5-1(C) (1984); N.Y. Penal Law § 125.05(3) (McKinney 1987) (abortion not justified without consent); N.D. Cent. Code § 14-02.1-03(1) (1991); Wash. Rev. Code Ann. § 9.02.070(a) (Repealed).

18 Pa. Cons. Stat. Ann. § 3215(f) (Purdon 1983) forbids any court, judge, executive officer or administrative agency to issue orders, other than in instances of a medical emergency, to require abortions without express, voluntary consent, and Wis. Stat. Ann. § 66.04(1)(m) (West 1990) prohibits payment of incentive funds for abortions.

[246] *E.g.,* Del. Code Ann. tit. 24, § 1794(a) (1987); Fla. Stat. Ann. § 390.001(4) (West Supp. 1992); Md. Pub. Health Code Ann. § 20-214(c)(1) (1990) (refusal to consent cannot be penalized); Mass. Gen. Laws. Ann. ch. 112, §§ 12S, 12Q (West 1983) (must be delivered to physician performing abortion [presumably, in referral case]); Mo. Ann. Stat. § 188.027 (Vernon 1983); Mont. Code Ann. §§ 50-20-104(3), 50-20-106(2) (1991); Neb. Rev. Stat. §§ 28-326(8), 28-327 (1989); Nev. Rev. Stat. § 442.252 (1991); Okla. Stat. Ann. tit. 63, § 1-738(A)(2) (West 1984) (physician's report must indicate who signed consent form); Or. Rev. Stat. § 435.435(1) (1991) (refusal to consent cannot be penalized); 18 Pa. Cons. Stat. Ann. § 3205(3) (Purdon 1983) (informed consent requires certification by woman that required information has been given her); R.I. Gen. Laws § 23-4.7-2 (1989); S.C. Code Ann. §§ 44-41-10(h), 44-41-20(a) (Law. Co-op. 1984); S.D. Codified Laws Ann. § 34-23A-7 (1987); Tenn. Code Ann. § 39-15-202(a) (1991); Utah

Supreme Court doctrine but serves only to impel judicial nullification. If statutes refer to spousal consent for minor married women and mental incompetents,[266] issues of constitutionality should be resolved on the basis of parental consent in such instances.[267]

  e. *Judicial Approval for Abortions*   The Supreme Court has ruled that if a minor is not emancipated, a state may require either parental consent or a judicial determination in lieu of it.[268] If there is no specific legislation, a parental consent requirement will be ruled unconstitutional.[269] A number of states have provided for such a judicial avenue.[270]

If the procedures are clear and expeditious, such legislation will be sustained as a legitimate alternative to parental consent for minors incapable of giving it. However, if a court concludes that a minor is competent to give an informed consent, it can only certify that fact, allowing the minor to exercise her *Roe v. Wade* rights. The state cannot forbid an abortion because it believes a woman should not have one. The latter determination is to be made only if the minor is not capable of consenting; denial of an abortion then must rest on a showing that abortion is inimical to her best interests.[271]

Code Ann. § 76-7-305(1) (1990); V.I. Code Ann. tit. 14, § 151(b) (Supp. 1991); Va. Code § 18.2-76 (1988).

[247] Women may be required to certify they have been given the information required by statute. *See, e.g.,* Me. Rev. Stat. Ann. tit. 22, § 1598(1) (1992); Md. Health Occ. Code Ann. § 20-211(d) (1990); 18 Pa. Cons. Stat. Ann. § 3205(3) (Purdon 1983). A physician may be required to certify the same thing as a condition to receiving a valid consent. *See, e.g.,* Mont. Code Ann. § 50-20-106(2) (1991).

[248] *E.g.,* Del. Code Ann. tit. 24, § 1794(b) (1987); Ind. Code Ann. § 35-1-58.5-2(1)(B) (Burns 1990); Minn. Stat. Ann. § 145.412(2) (West 1989) (unlawful to perform abortion on unconscious woman unless unconscious for purpose of abortion or necessary to save woman's life); Mont. Code Ann. § 50-20-106(3) (1991); Neb. Rev. Stat. § 28-327 (1989); S.C. Code Ann. § 44-41-30(b) (Law. Co-op. Supp. 1991) (or unless woman has been adjudicated mentally incompetent).

[249] *E.g.,* Iowa Code Ann. § 707.8(2) (West 1979) (life or health of pregnant woman or fetus).

[250] *E.g.,* 18 Pa. Cons. Stat. Ann. § 3205(c) (Purdon Supp. 1991 & 1992); S.D. Codified Laws Ann. § 34-23A-10.2 (1986) (conviction also to be reported to professional disciplinary authority): Utah Code Ann. § 76-7-314(2) (Supp. 1991).

[251] 18 Pa. Cons. Stat. Ann. § 3205(d) (Purdon Supp. 1991 & 1992) (physician who complies with consent provisions is not civilly liable).

[252] *E.g.,* Mo. Ann. Stat. § 188.027(3) (Vernon 1983) (emancipated minor must consent like adult); N.M. Stat. Ann. § 30-5-1(C) (1984) (at request of minor and parent or guardian); Okla. Stat. Ann. tit. 63, § 2602(A)(3) (West 1984) (general consent law); 18 Pa. Cons. Stat. Ann. § 3206(a) (Purdon Supp. 1991 & 1992) (pregnant minor and a parent). Occasionally, a general consent law allowing minors, capable of doing so, to consent to medical techniques contains a specific exception in cases of abortion. *See, e.g.,* Ga. Code Ann. § 88-2902 (1988). That might suggest an equal protection violation, unless there is a medical basis to support the conclusion—a medical basis difficult to document in light of, *e.g.,* Roe v. Wade, 410 U.S. 113 (1973), and City of Akron v. Akron Center for Reproductive Health, Inc., 462 U.S. 416 (1983).

[253] *E.g.,* Mo. Ann Stat. § 188.028(3) (Vernon Supp. 1992); Nev. Rev. Stat. § 129.030(2) (1991); Okla. Stat. Ann. tit. 63, § 2602(A)(3) (West 1984).

[254] *See infra* notes 259–62 and accompanying text. *Cf.* State v. Norflett, 67 N.J. 2678, 287–89, 337 A.2d 609, 619–20 (1975) (in prosecution against lay abortionist for contributing to delinquency of minor, a minor can manifest delinquency by consenting to abortion).

[255] *E.g.,* Alaska Stat. § 18.16.010 (1991); Ariz. Rev. Stat. Ann. § 36-2271 (1986) (surgical consent law); Ill. Ann. Stat. ch. 38, 81.51–54 (Smith-Hurd Supp. 1991 & 1992); Ky. Rev. Stat. § 311.732(1) (1990); Mass. Gen. Laws Ann. ch. 112, § 12S (West 1983); Minn. Stat. Ann. § 144.343(4)(b) (West 1989) (if parent or guardian authorizes abortion in writing, doctor need not comply with parental notice provision); N.D. Cent. Code § 14-02.1-03.1(1)(a) (1991); Okla. Stat. Ann. tit. 63, § 1-738(A)(2) (West 1984) (reporting form must indicate who signed consent, including parents).

The Supreme Court addressed several details of procedure affecting judicial approval of a minor's request to have an abortion performed in *Ohio v. Akron Center for Reproductive Health.*[272] It found no merit in the appellees' concern that a physician could perform an abortion without notifying a parent if either the juvenile court or state court of appeals should fail to act on a petition within specified time limits; the appellees contended that the absence of an affirmative order of approval of a minor's petition would deter physicians from acting. The Court declined to pursue such a speculation because it assumed that state courts will follow mandated procedures and the appellees had shown no demonstrated pattern of abuse or defiance of law on the courts' part. Although the Ohio attorney general represented that physicians in fact can obtain a judicial certification that constructive authorization has occurred, that is not required by the Court's applicable precedent;[273] the Ohio statute was not defective in that regard.[274]

The appellees objected next to the placement on minors of a burden of persuasion at the level of clear and convincing evidence to prove their maturity or the fact that parental notification was not in their best interests.[275] The Court thought the Constitution

---

[256] *E.g.,* Colo. Rev. Stat. § 18-6-101(1) (1986); Del. Code Ann. tit. 24, § 1790(b)(3) (1987) (if minor not residing in household with either of parents or guardian); Fla. Stat. Ann. § 390.001(4)(a) (West Supp.1992); Ill. Ann. Stat. ch. 38, § 81-54(3) (Smith-Hurd Supp. 1991 & 1992) (remaining parent if one parent has died, deserted his or her family or is unavailable); Mass. Gen. Laws Ann. ch. 112, § 12S (West 1983) (surviving parent or divorced parent with custody); Mo. Ann. Stat. § 188.028(1)(1) (Vernon Supp. 1992); N.M. Stat. Ann. § 30-5-1(C) (1984); N.D. Cent. Code §§ 14-02.1-03(2)(b), 14-02.1-03.1(1)(a) (1991) (for abortion after viability, a parent if living, a surviving parent or custodial parent in cases of separation or divorce); 18 Pa. Const. Stat. Ann. § 3206(a) (Purdon 1983) (one parent); R.I. Gen. Laws § 23-4.7-6 (1989) (one parent); S.C. Code Ann. § 44-41-30(b), (c) (Law. Co-op. Supp. 1991) (unmarried and less than 16 years of age or adjudicated a mentally incompetent); Va. Code § 18.2-76 (1988) (parent of woman adjudicated mentally incompetent).

[257] *E.g.,* Alaska Stat. § 18.16.010 (1986); Del. Code Ann. tit. 24, § 1790(b)(3) (1987); Ill. Ann. Stat. ch. 38, § 81-54(3) (Smith-Hurd Supp. 1991); Ky. Rev. Stat. § 311.732(2) (1990) (or person in loco parentis if no parent or guardian); Mass. Gen. Laws Ann. ch. 112, § 12S (West 1983); Minn. Stat. Ann. § 144.343(4)(b) (West 1989) (if guardian authorizes abortion in advance, physician need not comply with parental notice requirement); Mo. Ann. Stat. § 188.028)(1)(1) (Vernon Supp. 1990); N.M. Stat. Ann. § 30-5-1-(C) (1984); N.D. Cent. Code §§ 14-02.1-03.1(1)(b), 14-02.1-03.1(1)(a) (1981); Okla. Stat. Ann. tit. 63, § 1-738(2) (West 1984) (reporting form must indicate whether guardian signed consent); R.I. Gen. Laws § 23-4.7-6 (1989); S.C. Code Ann. § 44-41-30(b) (Law. Co-op. 1988); Wash. Rev. Code Ann. § 9.02.070(a) (Repealed).

[258] *E.g.,* Del. Code Ann. tit. 24, § 1790(b)(3) (1987); Fla. Stat. Ann. § 390.001(4) (West Supp. 1992); Ill. Ann. Stat. ch. 38, § 81-54(3) (Smith-Hurd Supp. 1992); Ky. Rev. Stat. § 311.732(1) (1990); 18 Pa. Cons. Stat. Ann. § 3206(a) (Purdon Supp. 1991 & 1992); S.C. Code Ann. § 44-41-30(B) (Law. Co-op. Supp. 1991); Va. Code § 18.2-76 (1988).

[259] Planned Parenthood v. Danforth, 428 U.S. at 72–75. *See also* Bellotti v. Baird, 443 U.S. 622 (1979) (Massachusetts statute requiring parental consultation and consent).

[260] *See* Planned Parenthood v. Danforth, 428 U.S. at 75. *See generally* Buchanan, *The Constitution and the Anomaly of the Pregnant Teenager,* 24 Ariz. L. Rev. 553 (1982).

In Arnold v. Bd. of Educ., 880 F.2d 305 (11th Cir. 1989), the court held that allegations by the parents of a pregnant minor student that a school counselor and vice-principal had coerced the student and putative father not to consult their parents before proceeding with an abortion stated a cause of action under the Federal Civil Rights Act, 42 U.S.C. § 1983 (1988) (the district court had dismissed the action on the pleadings).

Analogies for resolving the constitutionality and lawfulness of a guardian's or parent's decision concerning abortion probably must be drawn from the jurisprudence relating to sterilization of mental retardates. *See, e.g.,* Buck v. Bell, 274 U.S. 200 (1927) (Court sustained constitutionality of sterilization statute invokable against "feeble-minded" persons); *In re* C.D.M., 627 P.2d 607, 612–13 (Alaska 1981) (court approved use of the same conditions as those established in *In re* Grady, 85 N.J. 235, 264–65, 426 A.2d

did not require that the burden of persuasion be placed on the state; a heightened burden of persuasion on an applicant was in order, granted that the bypass procedure was to be ex parte and approval was to be based only on the minor's testimony. States are not required by the Constitution to fix a burden at a lower level than clear and convincing proof.[276]

The appellees then asserted that the pleading requirements of the statute, which necessitated that a minor choose from among three different forms of pleadings,[277] constituted a trap for an unwary minor. The Court thought not, since it appeared unlikely that Ohio courts would treat a minor's choice of complaint form without appropriate care for and understanding of her unrepresented status.[278] The statute therefore could survive a facial challenge.

Although the appellees failed to prevail on their narrowly focused objections to details of procedure, they nonetheless asserted that the entire procedure failed to accord a minor her state substantive right "to avoid unnecessary or hostile parental involvement" if she could demonstrate that her maturity or best interests favored abortion

---

467, 482–83 (1981)); *In re* Guardianship of Tulley, 83 Cal. App. 3d 698, 146 Cal. Rptr. 266 (1978), *cert. denied sub nom.* Tulley v. Tulley, 440 U.S. 967 (1979) (father of a mentally-retarded woman has no statutory authority to request a sterilization order); *In re* A.W., 637 P.2d 366 (Colo. 1981) (general parental consent statute did not allow parents to approve sterilization of a mentally-retarded child); P.S. by Harbin v. W.S., 452 N.E.2d 969 (Ind. 1983) (juvenile court had power to order sterilization of mentally retarded son with parental consent without specific enabling statute); Wentzel v. Montgomery General Hosp., 293 Md. 685, 447 A.2d 1244 (1982), *cert. denied,* 459 U.S. 1147 (1983) (court has inherent parens patriae authority to entertain parental application for sterilization of incompetent minor); *In re* M.K.R., 515 S.W.2d 467 (Mo. 1974) (juvenile court has no authority to order sterilization of minor female at parents' request); *In re* Grady, 85 N.J. 235, 426 A.2d 467 (1981) (court has inherent parens patriae jurisdiction to allow sterilization of noninstitutionalized female, at parental request, but must find, among other things, that minor cannot understand nature and significance of sterilization, incompetency is probably permanent, incompetent person is fertile and capable of procreation); *In re* Moore, 289 N.C. 95, 221 S.E.2d 307 (1976) (court approved sterilization order for mental retardate at parents' request); *In re* Guardianship of Hayes, 93 Wash. 2d 228, 608 P.2d 635 (1980) (court has inherent power to order sterilization of mentally-incompetent person at parental request but should not do so unless substantial medical evidence has been adduced establishing that sterilization is in the best interest of the retardate; court established a presumption against sterilization that proponents must overcome by clear, cogent and convincing evidence); *In re* Guardianship of Eberhardy, 102 Wis. 2d 539, 307 N.W.2d 881 (1981) (established public policy to allow sterilization of 22-year-old woman, incapable of consent, at insistence of parents should be matter for legislation).

[261] City of Akron v. Akron Center for Reproductive Health, Inc., 462 U.S. at 439–40 (explaining the Court's ruling in *Bellotti*). *See also* Planned Parenthood League v. Bellotti, 641 F.2d 1006, 1011–13 (1st Cir. 1981) (court rejected due process and equal protection attacks on Massachusetts statute that required either parental consent or judicial determination that minor was competent to consent).

[262] *See infra* notes 268–79 and accompanying text.

[263] Planned Parenthood v. Danforth, 428 U.S. at 67–72. *Cf.* Hagerstown Reproductive Health Servs. v. Fritz, 295 Md. 268, 454 A.2d 846, *cert. denied,* 463 U.S. 1208 (1983) (court vacated as moot an appeal of a lower court injunction, issued at a husband's request, against performance of an abortion until he consented because the abortion already had been performed); Coleman v. Coleman, 57 Md. App. 755, 471 A.2d 1115 (1984) (husband cannot enjoin medically indicated abortion for wife). English case law adopts a similar position, although not, of course, on constitutional grounds. *See* Paton v. Trustees of British Pregnancy Advisory Service, [1978] 2 All E.R. 987, [1978] 3 W.L.R. 687.

A corollary is that the father of a child cannot defeat his duty to provide financial support for his child on the basis that he had not been given an opportunity to decide whether a fetus should be aborted or that he had offered to pay for a first-trimester abortion. *See* People *ex rel.* S.P.B., 651 P.2d 1213 (Colo. 1982) (citing authorities).

[264] *See infra,* notes 281, 302 and accompanying text.

without notification of one of her parents. The Court did not agree. The confidentiality provisions, expedited procedures and pleading form requirements satisfied facially the minimum dictates of due process; the Court saw little risk of erroneous deprivation of a minor's rights in the course of the statutory procedures and hence no need to require additional procedural safeguards.[279]

7.   NOTICE TO PARENTS AND SPOUSES   When most legislation requiring parental or spousal consent to abortion fell before the Court's constitutional axe, a number of states substituted requirements that parents[280] or spouses[281] be given notice[282] before an abortion is performed.[283] Sometimes the same litany of information required to be given a patient[284] must be given along with the basic notice.[285]

In 1990 the Court addressed in detail the extent to which states may impose parental notification requirements when minor females wish abortions. In *Hodgson v. Minnesota,*[286] the Court addressed a Minnesota statute that required physicians contemplating a consensual abortion to be performed on an unemancipated minor give notice to both the minor's living parents personally or by certified mail at least 48 hours before

---

[265]*E.g.,* Colo. Rev. Stat. § 18-6-101(1) (1986) (abortion must be at request of woman and husband). One should note the precedent that denies to a putative father and parents of the putative father standing to contest the constitutionality of an abortion decision reached by a pregnant minor. Arnold v. Bd. of Educ., 880 F.2d 307, 312 (11th Cir. 1989). *See generally* Fathers and Abortion Note, *supra* note 244.

[266]*E.g.,* S.C. Code Ann. § 44-41-30(B) (Law. Co-op. Supp. 1991).

[267]*See supra,* notes 259–62 and accompanying text.

[268]*See supra,* note 261.

[269]City of Akron v. Akron Center for Reproductive Health, Inc., 462 U.S. at 439–42. *See also* Planned Parenthood v. Ashcroft, 462 U.S. 476, 490–93 (1983) (plurality opinion).

[270]*E.g.,* Ariz. Rev. Stat. Ann. § 36-2152(B)(2) (Supp. 1991); Fla. Stat. Ann. § 390.001(4)(a) (West Supp. 1992); Ill. Ann. Stat. ch. 38, § 81-54(3) (Smith-Hurd Supp. 1991 & 1992); Ind. Code Ann. § 35-1-58.5-2.5 (Burns Supp. 1991); Ky. Rev. Stat. § 311.732(3)–(6) (1990); Mass. Gen. Laws Ann. ch. 112, § 12S (West 1983); Minn. Stat. Ann. § 144.343(6) (West 1989); Mo. Ann. Stat. § 188.028(2) (Vernon 1983 & Supp. 1991); N.D. Cent. Code § 14-02.1-03.1(2) (1991); 18 Pa. Cons. Stat. Ann. § 3206(c)–(f), (h) (Purdon 1983 & Supp. 1991 & 1992); R.I. Gen. Laws § 23-4.7-6 (1989). In *In re* T.W., 543 So. 2d 837 (Fla. Dist. Ct. App. 1989) (per curiam), *stay granted* and *stay vacated sub nom.* Boylston v. T.W., 490 U.S. 1077, *approved,* 1989 Fla. LEXIS 972 (Fla. 1989), the court invalidated the Florida judicial-alternative statute, *supra,* because its language was vague and indefinite and hence insufficient to safeguard against possibly arbitrary denials of minors' petitions; the court also invalidated the statutory parental consent requirement.

[271]*See* City of Akron v. Akron Center for Reproductive Health, Inc., 462 U.S. at 439–42. When a recipient court failed to act on a minor's petition within the time period set out in the statute, the petition was deemed granted as of the expiration of the time limit. *In re* J.V., 548 So. 2d 749 (Fla. Dist. Ct. App. 1989) (per curiam).

Although abortion legislation does not address the matter, a similar approach is taken when a pregnant woman has become comatose and cannot decide for herself whether to terminate or continue her pregnancy. *See* Matter of Klein, 145 A.D.2d 145, 538 N.Y.S.2d 274, *app. denied,* 73 N.Y.2d 705, 536 N.E.2d 627, 539 N.Y.S.2d 298, *stay denied,* 489 U.S. 1003 (1989). In *Klein,* the court rejected the petitions of two right-to-life activists, one to be appointed guardian for Mrs. Klein and the other guardian for the fetus (the latter on the *Roe v. Wade* principle that fetuses are not persons. However, the court utilized the filed petition to appoint Mr. Klein a legal guardian with full authority to consent to medical procedures including abortion; it noted that the outside petitioner had shown no adverse interest between Klein and the comatose Mrs. Klein.

[272]110 S. Ct. 2972 (1990). In Hodgson v. Minnestoa, 110 S. Ct. 2926 (1990), the Court found that the judicial bypass provision made contingent in the statute on an invalidation of the primary parental notification provision, see note 287 *infra,* and in effect made permanent through the Court's invalidation of the two-parent notification scheme, was constitutional. *Id.* at 2947.

the abortion was to be performed.[287] The Court affirmed the action of lower federal courts finding the statutory requirement unconstitutional.[288] It believed that the statute furthered no legitimate state interest and indeed disserved the state interest in protecting and assisting minors in dysfunctional families.[289] In the Court's belief, Minnesota had no more a legitimate interest in compelling family members to talk with one another than it had to require them to live together; nor could its interest in protecting a parental interest in shaping a child's values and lifestyle overcome the child's liberty interest in acting with the consent of a single parent or a court.[290] The Minnesota two-parent notification requirement, which was at odds with all other state and federal consent statutes governing the health, welfare and education of minors,[291] was unreasonable and hence unconstitutional.[292]

In the companion case of *Ohio v. Akron Center for Reproductive Health*,[293] the Court affirmed the constitutionality of Ohio legislation[294] imposing restrictions on the medical performance of abortions on pregnant minors.[295] The appellees asserted that the statute in its entirely should be invalidated because it imposed the duty of parental

---

[273] Planned Parenthood Ass'n of Kansas City, Mo., Inc. v. Ashcroft, 462 U.S. 476, 479–80 n.4 (1983). Although the Court in *Akron Center*, 110 S. Ct. at 2981, stated "[w]e did not require . . . ," there was no majority opinion in the 1983 case.

[274] 110 S. Ct. at 2981.

[275] Ohio Rev. Code Ann. § 2151.85(A)(1)–(5) (Page 1990), *See* 110 S. Ct. at 2977.

[276] 110 S. Ct. at 2981–82.

[277] One alleged only maturity, a second only best interests and a third both maturity and best interests; a minor would have to select the third if she were to be allowed to attempt to prove both. Ohio Rev. Code Ann. § 2151.85(C) (Page Supp. 1991). *See* 110 S. Ct. at 2982.

[278] 110 S. Ct. at 2982. The Court noted also that a petitioning minor was to be supplied with counsel and accorded the ability to move for leave to amend the pleadings. *Id.*

In *Re* Anonymous, 549 So. 2d 1347 (Ala. Civ. App. 1989) (per curiam), the court characterized as an abuse of judicial discretion a trial court's finding that a minor petitioner was not mature enough to make an informed decision regarding abortion. The lower court had adduced no evidence to support its conclusion, and the appellate court thought that no other conclusion could be reached on the record but that the minor had met the statutory criteria for judicial waiver of parental consent.

[279] 110 S. Ct. at 2982. The Court noted the statutory provisions for assistance of counsel and a guardian ad litem, an ex parte proceeding, a judicial responsibility to take special care in deciding whether a minor's consent should suffice without parental notification, and the definite and reasonable time limits in the statute as promoting procedures compatible with due process of law. *Id.*

[280] *E.g.*, Ariz. Rev. Stat. Ann. § 36-2152(A) (1986); Md. Pub. Health Code Ann. § 20-103 (1990 & Supp. 1991 (subject to referendum)) (notice not required if minor does not live with parent or guardian and a reasonable effort to give notice is unsuccessful or if notice may led to physical or emotional abuse of minor; physician is not civilly or criminally liable for decision not to give notice on latter basis); Minn. Stat. Ann. § 144.343(4)(c) (West 1989) (not required if minor declares she is a victim of sexual abuse as defined in § 626.556); Mont. Code Ann. § 50-20-107(1)(b) (1991); Nev. Rev. Stat. § 442.255 (1991) (if possible to notify); Tenn. Code Ann. § 39-15-202(f) (1991) (if parents cannot be located, then to agency or other individual to whom the minor's custody has been transferred).

[281] *E.g.*, Ky. Rev. Stat. § 311.735 (1990) (within 30 days after abortion if reasonably possible); Mont. Code Ann. § 50-20-107(1)(a) (1991) (unless husband is voluntarily separated); 18 Pa. Cons. Stat. Ann. § 3209 (Purdon 1988 & Supp. 1991 & 1992) (woman must sign statement that she has notified her husband of her intended abortion, subject to specified emergency exceptions); R.I. Gen. Laws §§ 23-4.8-2 (1989) (if notice is reasonably possible), 23-4.8-3 (unnecessary if woman furnishes written statement that she has given notice to her husband, that the fetus was not fathered by the husband, that the woman is separated from her husband, or that she has filed for divorce or if husband gives physician written notice that he has been notified); Utah Code Ann. § 76-7-304(2) (1990).

See Note, *Spousal Notification: An Unconstitutional Limitation on a Woman's Right to Privacy in the Abortion Decision*, 12 Hofstra L. Rev. 531 (1984).

notification on the physician who was to perform the abortion.[296] The Court saw a significant distinction, however, between notification of minors' parents and informing patients about the routine risks of an abortion.[297] Therefore, it adhered to the position that states may require physicians to take reasonable steps to notify minors' parents because the latter often will provide important medical data; physician-parental conversations also may enable parents to provide better advice to their children. Practical impositions on physicians' schedules were minor enough[298] that the facial challenge to the constitutionality of the physician notification requirement failed.[299]

If notice is restricted to the fact of abortion but goes to one whose consent cannot be required constitutionally, one may ask what function it is to play. Language in some of the opinions in *H.L. v. Matheson*[300] suggests that if a pregnant minor is not emancipated but still a part of a family unit, a parental notice requirement promotes familial harmony and an ability on the part of parents to help a daughter make an informed choice. Alternatively, if a minor is emancipated or alienated from her parent, a requirement of parental notice would appear to impose a burden on the minor's free choice and thus be unconstitutional.[301]

---

[282] Some statutes provide for notice by certified or registered mail if notice is not communicated orally. *See, e.g.*, Me. Rev. Stat. tit. 22, § 1597(2) (1992) (if cannot notify orally or by mail, must notify state department of human services in writing of inability to give notice and of intention to perform abortion); Md. Pub. Health Code Ann. § 20-103(d) (1987) (proof of mailing is conclusive evidence of notice); N.D. Cent. Code § 14-02.1-03(1) (1991).

[283] Notice statutes frequently require a 24- or 48-hour waiting period after notice before an abortion can be performed. The constitutionality of waiting periods generally is discussed *infra*, notes 334–44 and accompanying text.

[284] *See infra*, notes 366–76 and accompanying text.

[285] *E.g.*, N.D. Cent. Code § 14-02.1-03(1) (1991).

[286] 110 S. Ct. 2926 (1990).

[287] Minn. Stat. Ann. §§ 144.343, 144.346 (West 1989). The Minnesota legislation is the ''most intrusive'' of the 38 state statutes addressing parental notification. *See Hodgson*, 110 S. Ct. at 2931–32 n.5. The legislative purpose was identified as the protection of the well-being of pregnant minors by encouraging them to discuss with their parents a decision whether or not to terminate their pregnancies, as well as to deter and dissuade them from choosing abortion. *Id.* at 2933–34.

[288] The Court noted the district court's findings that only about half of all Minnesota minors reside with both biological parents and that notification requirements have a particularly harmful effect in cases of divorce and separation in which the custodial and noncustodial parents are at odds; there were also significant difficulties in two-parent homes in which family violence was a problem. Under the Minnesota statute, the judicial bypass alternative was available only if the notification provision was temporarily or permanently enjoined by judicial order. *See* 110 S. Ct. at 2932–33. The federal district court entered a temporary restraining order and then a preliminary injunction against enforcement of the statute, which continued in effect throughout the litigation. *Id.* at 2934. A rather substantial number of judicial bypass petitions had been filed and approved over nearly a five-year period, during which 3,573 bypass petitions were filed in state courts; all but 15 were granted, *id.* at 2940, although not without incidental traumatic effects for a number of the minors. *Id.*

[289] *Id.* at 2945–46.

[290] *Id.* at 2946.

[291] The Court noted that only one other Minnesota statute, that pertaining to minor's change of name, required consent by both parents. *Id.* at 2947.

[292] *Id.*

[293] 110 S. Ct. 2972 (1990). *See generally* Graziano, *Parental Notification and a Minor's Right to an Abortion After Hodgson & Akron II*, 17 Ohio N.U.L. Rev. 581 (1991).

[294] Ohio Rev. Code Ann. §§ 2919.12 (1987), 2151.85 (1990), 2505.073 (Page 1991). *See* 110 S. Ct. at 2977–78.

Spousal consent requirements appear to be unconstitutional as long as the fundamental *Roe v. Wade* doctrine remains substantially intact. However, *Hodgson v. Minnesota*[302] did not dispose of the matter of the constitutionality of spousal notice requirements.[303] The Supreme Court has the question under review at the time of this writing.[304] Recent Pennsylvania legislation[305] requires a woman seeking an abortion to sign a statement that she has notified her husband of the intended abortion, subject to certain statutory exceptions.[306] The Third Circuit found the provision an unconstitutional burden on a pregnant woman's free decision to have an abortion—the state could not legitimate the requirement as a means of promoting the integrity of the marital relationship, protecting a spouse's interest in having children within marriage or protecting a spousal interest in the prenatal life of the woman's fetus.[307] Should the Court not overturn or limit substantially its earlier abortion precedents, it might adopt the Third Circuit's rationale. If it writes *finis* to *Roe v. Wade,* spousal notice and perhaps spousal consent as well will become available legislative options to restrict abortions, assuming any at all are licit under restrictive state legislation.

---

[295] To avoid criminal penalties, physicians wishing to perform consensual abortions on pregnant minors were required to comply with at least one of four statutory alternatives. One was to give a minimum of 24 hours' advance notice in person or by telephone to one of the female minor's parents (or guardian or custodian) of the intent to perform an abortion. A second was to obtain written consent from a parent, guardian or custodian. Ohio Rev. Code Ann. § 2919.12(B)(1)(a)(ii) (Page 1987). *See* 110 S. Ct. at 2977. A third and fourth related to alternative judicial bypass procedures. *See* the summary of these alternatives in 110 S. Ct. at 2977–78.

[296] Appellees placed reliance on Akron v. Akron Center for Reproductive Health, Inc., 462 U.S. 416, 446–49 (1983), which had invalidated a requirement that an attending physician provide the information and counseling bearing on an informed consent. *See* 110 S. Ct. at 2983.

[297] *Id.* The Court indicated as a basis for the distinction its action in H.L. v. Matheson, 450 U.S. 398 (1981). However, there was no majority opinion in *H.L.*

[298] The Court noted the statutory authorization for the use of the mails if a minor's parent cannot be reached after a reasonable effort and for dispensing with notice entirely in the event of specified emergencies. *See* 110 S. Ct. at 2983.

[299] *Id.*

[300] 450 U.S. 398 (1981).

[301] Planned Parenthood Ass'n v. Ashcroft, 655 F.2d 848, 858–59 (8th Cir. 1981), *aff'd on other grounds,* 462 U.S. 476 (1983) (plurality opinion). *Cf.* Planned Parenthood Ass'n v. Matheson, 582 F. Supp. 1001 (D. Utah 1983) (requirement that notice be given minor's parents concerning provision of contraceptives invalidated as contrary to federal statutory policy and invasive of minor's privacy); Note, *The "Squeal Rule" and a Minor's Right to Privacy,* 12 Hofstra L. Rev. 497 (1984) (discussion of federal Department of Health and Human Services proposed "squeal rule" requiring federally-funded family planning agencies to notify parents that their minor children have obtained prescription contraceptives).

[302] 110 S. Ct. 2926 (1990). *See supra,* text accompanying notes 286–92.

[303] The issue came up seldom and essentially collaterally, *See* Scheinberg v. Smith, 659 F.2d 476, 482–87 (5th Cir. 1981) (remanding for a district court determination whether a husband's concern for a more than de minimis decrease in his wife's procreative potential following an abortion, outweighed the influence of a spousal notice requirement on the wife's abortion decision). *Cf.* Hagerstown Reproductive Health Servs. v. Fritz, 295 Md. 268, 454 A.2d 846, cert. denied, 463 U.S. 1208 (1983) (court vacated as moot an appeal against a lower court's issuance of an injunction of an abortion, at a husband's request, because abortion had already been performed).

[304] Planned Parenthood of Southeastern Pennsylvania, 947 F.2d 682 (3d Cir.), *cert. granted,* 112 S. Ct. 931 (1991).

[305] 18 Pa. Cons. Stat. Ann. § 3209 (Purdon 1988 & Supp. 1992). The statement need not be notarized but must contain a notice that false statements in a declaration are punishable by law. *Id.* § 3209(b).

[306] The exceptions are (1) the husband is not the father of the child, (2) the husband could not be located after diligent effort, (3) the pregnancy was the consequence of spousal sexual assault which had been reported

8. GROUNDS FOR ABORTION   a. *Incest*   Several states have continued their pre-*Wade* coverage of incest as a humanitarian basis for abortion[308] in current statutes.[309] Laws of this nature should be unconstitutional if they are invoked to prevent abortions otherwise medically justified under *Roe v. Wade*,[310] but if they legitimate abortions not based strictly on medical consideration (assuming pregnancies from such causes do not cause sufficient emotional trauma to constitute a medical ground), they probably are constitutional.[311]

b. *Rape*   Rape as a humanitarian ground for abortion, recognized before 1973,[312] continues to be acknowledged in some legislation.[313] In some instances, the individual is subject to reporting or confirmation requirements.[314] The constitutionality of such provisions turns on the same considerations mentioned in the context of incest as a ground for abortion.[315]

c. *Physical or Mental Defect in Child If Born Alive*   Abortion based on eugenic considerations was acknowledged in some states before *Roe v. Wade*[316] and continues today.[317] The constitutionality of this form of legislation turns on whether, in an obverse

---

to a law enforcement agency having jurisdiction over the matter and (4) the woman has reason to believe that giving notice is likely to result in the infliction of bodily injury on her by her spouse or someone else. *Id.* § 3290(b). Any one will suffice. *Id.*

[307] Planned Parenthood of Southeastern Pennsylvania, 947 F.2d at 709–15.

[308] *See supra* note 87 and accompanying text.

[309] *E.g.,* Cal. Health & Safety Code § 25951(C)(2) (West 1984), Cal. Penal Code § 274 (West 1988) (exempts such abortions); Colo. Rev. Stat. § 18-6-101(b) (1986) (within first 16 weeks of pregnancy; limitation held unconstitutional in People v. Norton, 181 Colo. 47, 507 P.2d 862 (1973); Del. Code Ann. tit. 24, § 1790(a)(3)(a) (1987); Idaho Code § 18-608(1) (1987) (limited to first trimester); Kan. Stat. Ann. § 21-3407(2) (1988); N.M. Stat. Ann. § 30-5-1(C)(4) (1984).

[310] Because they are not reported or are not within time limitations, for example, Colo. Rev. Stat. § 18-6-101(b) (1986) (within first 16 weeks of pregnancy); Idaho Code § 18-608(1) (1987) (within first trimester).

[311] This would require a consideration of whether the Court's concern in Roe v. Wade, 410 U.S. at 164–65, over the "potentiality of human life" translates into a restriction on abortions based other than on medical necessity. In context, however, the Court's language is a limitation on a state's power to regulate abortions following viability. *Cf.* the Court's language in Harris v. McRae, 448 U.S. 297, 325 (1980), quoted *infra* note 474 and accompanying text.

[312] *See supra,* note 86 and accompanying text.

[313] *E.g.,* Cal. Health & Safety Code § 25951(C)(2) (West 1984), Cal. Penal Code § 274 (West 1988) (exempting such cases); Del. Code Ann. tit. 24, § 1790(a)(3)(b) (Supp. 1990); Idaho Code § 18-608(1) (1987) (first trimester only; in cases of rape or felonious intercourse; all illicit intercourse with female under 16 deemed felonious intercourse); Kan. Stat. Ann. § 21-3407(2) (1988); Md. Pub. Health Code Ann. § 20-208(a)(4) (1990); Miss. Code. Ann. § 97-3-3(1)(B) (1972); N.M. Stat. Ann. § 30-5-1(C)(3) (1984).

[314] *E.g.,* Md. Pub. Health Code Ann. § 20-208(a)(4) (1990) (if state's attorney for county informs hospital abortion review authority in signed writing that probable cause exists to believe alleged rape occurred); N.M. Stat. Ann. § 30-5-1(C)(3) (1984) (woman must submit to special hospital board an affidavit that she has been raped and that rape has been or will be reported to appropriate law enforcement officials).

[315] *See supra,* notes 310–13 and accompanying text.

[316] *See supra,* note 88 and accompanying text.

[317] *E.g.,* Del. Code Ann. tit. 24, § 1790(a)(2) (1987) (substantial risk of grave and permanent physical deformity or mental retardation); Idaho Code § 18-608(1) (1987) (physical or mental health, first trimester only); Iowa Code Ann. § 707.7 (West 1979) (life or health of fetus, final trimester coverage); Kan. Stat. Ann. § 21-3407(2) (1988) (child born with physical or mental defect); Md. Pub. Health Code Ann. § 20-208(A)(3) (1990) (substantial risk of grave and permanent physical deformity or mental retardation); N.M. Stat. Ann. § 30-5-1(C)(2) (1984) (child probably will have grave physical or mental defect). Public funds are available for abortion on this ground in Virginia, Va. Code § 32.1-92.2 (1988) (if qualified physician certifies in writing after appropriate tests a belief that fetus will be born with gross and totally incapacitating physical deformity or mental deficiency).

application of *Roe v. Wade* principles,[318] the potentiality of human life in a fetus precludes abortions on this basis if not otherwise medically indicated from the standpoint of maternal life or health.

d. *Maternal Life*   As discussed earlier, for many years, in almost every jurisdiction, abortions could be performed only to save the life of a pregnant woman.[319] Some states have continued this as the sole basis for lawful abortions,[320] in some instances only in later stages of gestation.[321] There may be no constitutional barrier to recognizing this as an exception to an aggravating factor under penal statutes when abortions are performed other than by licensed physicians in later stages of pregnancies[322] (even granted the rarity of cases in which a layperson could manage abortions properly) or in limiting availability of public funds for abortions unless preservation of maternal life is involved.[323] But limiting legislation of this sort is unconstitutional if invoked to prevent a woman and her physician from reaching an abortion decision within the parameters of *Roe v. Wade*. Perpetuation of such statutes can be attributed only to legislative inertia or reluctance to acknowledge Supreme Court doctrine.[324]

e. *Maternal Life or Health*   Several states have continued a requirement that all abortions be based on considerations of maternal life or health,[325] frequently restricted by a qualifying phrase such as "gravely impair[ed]."[326] This form of legislation, however, is unconstitutional under *Roe v. Wade*,[327] which makes "medical judgment" the criterion during the first trimester of pregnancy and regulation of abortion procedures "reasonably related to maternal health" the standard during the period before viability.

---

[318] *See supra* note 311. For a discussion of the matter of whether others may intervene to contest a parental-physician decision not to use life support systems to preserve an infant born with serious birth defects, *see* Weber v. Stony Brook Hosp., 60 N.Y.2d 208, 456 N.E.2d 1186, 469 N.Y.S.2d 63, *cert. denied*, 464 U.S. 1026 (1983) (lawyer with no disclosed relationship to infant or her family could not obtain judicial authorization for surgery, overriding parental and physicians' decision not to provide extraordinary medical treatment for infant born with spina bifida and other serious complications). *See also* Maguire, *Can Technology Solve the Abortion Dilemma?*, 93 Christian Century 918 (Oct. 27, 1976); Smith, *Life and Death Decisions in the Nursery: Standards and Procedures for Withholding Lifesaving Treatments From Infants*, 27 N.Y.L. Sch. L. Rev. 1125 (1982).

[319] *See supra*, note 34 and accompanying text.

[320] *E.g.*, Ariz. Rev. Stat. Ann. § 13-3603 (1989); Mich. Comp. Laws Ann. § 750.14 (West 1968); N.H. Rev. Stat. Ann. § 585:13 (1986) (certified by two physicians to be necessary); Vt. Stat. Ann. tit. 13, § 101 (1974); W. Va. Code § 61-2-8 (1989) (good faith belief in necessity); Wis. Stat. Ann. § 940.04(5)(b) (West 1982).

[321] *E.g.*, N.H. Rev. Stat. Ann. § 585:13 (1986) (quick child); R.I. Gen. Laws § 11-23.5 (1989) (quick child).

[322] *E.g.*, R.I. Gen. Laws § 11-23-5 (1989); Wash. Rev. Code Ann. § 9.02.010 (1988). A similar restriction may be imposed through judicial interpretation. *See, e.g.*, People v. Bricker, 389 Mich. 524, 208 N.W.2d 172 (1973).

[323] *E.g.*, Minn. Stat. Ann. § 256B.02(8)(13)(a) (West Supp. 1990) (public employee health insurance plans may include abortions in which woman's life would be endangered by carrying pregnancy to term). Constitutional aspects of withholding public funding are discussed *infra*, notes 503–26 and accompanying text.

[324] *See supra*, notes 147–54 and accompanying text.

[325] *E.g.*, Ala. Code § 13A-13-7 (Michie 1982) (criminal code); D.C. Code Ann. § 22-201 (1989) (see also United States v. Vuitch, 402 U.S. 62 (1971); Kan. Stat. Ann. § 21-3407(2) (1988); P.R. Laws Ann. tit. 33, § 4010 (1983); Tenn. Code Ann. § 39-15-201(c)(3) (1991).

[326] *E.g.*, Cal. Health & Safety Code § 25951(c)(1) (West 1984); Del. Code Ann. tit. 24, § 1790(a)(4) (1987) ("substantial risk of permanent injury"); Md. Pub. Health Code Ann. § 20-208(a)(1)–(2) (1990); N.M. Stat. Ann. § 30-5-1(C)(1) (1984); Va. Code § 18.2-74 (1988) (substantial or irremediable impairment). The pattern for the "gravely impair[ed]" qualifier is the Uniform Abortion Act § 1(b)(2) (1972). *See* Roe v. Wade, 410 U.S. at 146 n.40 (quoting the act).

[327] 410 U.S. at 164.

Only after viability does the criterion of "preservation of life or health of the mother" become valid.[328] Many states, therefore, have legislated the "life or health" standard only for abortions following viability[329] or after a stated number of weeks of gestation.[330]

The difficulty with the latter standard, however, is that, although there may have been a basis in *Roe v. Wade* for use of a time standard as an alternative to viability, the Supreme Court has rejected it in the setting of the place of performance of abortions. Viability is the sole acceptable criterion in that context.[331] Hence, application of the "life or health" standard before actual viability in each pregnancy risks a declaration of unconstitutionality if physicians are prosecuted, sued or disciplined for performing medically indicated (therapeutic) abortions in the period between the beginning of the statutorily prescribed period and viability.

f. *General Medical Grounds*   *Roe v. Wade* legitimates the constitutional right of pregnant women to abortions before viability if medically indicated.[332] Some states acknowledge the constitutional norm only indirectly by legislating specific standards following viability.[333] Several others, however, have enacted the Supreme Court standard or an equivalent.[334] Such legislation has no observable constitutional defect but is superfluous.

---

[328] *Id.* at 164–65. *See* Coleman v. Coleman, 57 Md. App. 755, 471 A.2d 1115 (1984) (invalidated state legislative restriction of abortions to those based on grave impairment of maternal health, rape or likelihood of a seriously deformed child).

[329] *E.g.*, Ill. Ann. Stat. ch. 38, § 81-25(2) (Smith-Hurd Supp. 1991 & 1992); Ind. Code Ann. § 35-1-58.5-2(3)(C) (Burns Supp. 1991); Ky. Rev. Stat. § 311.780 (1990); La. Rev. Stat. Ann. § 37:1285(8) (West 1988) (third trimester or after viability); Me. Rev. Stat. Ann. tit. 22, § 1598(4) (1992); Mo. Ann. Stat. § 188.030)(1) (Vernon 1983); Mont. Code Ann. § 50-20-109(1)(c) (1991); Neb. Rev. Stat. § 28-329 (1989); Okla. Stat. Ann. tit. 63, § 1-732(A) (West 1984); Utah Code Ann. § 76-7-302(3) (1990) (if child is sufficiently developed to have any reasonable possibility of survival outside womb).

[330] *E.g.*, Fla. Stat. Ann. § 390.001(2) (West 1986) (third trimester); Iowa Code Ann. § 707.7 (West 1979); Mass. Gen. Laws Ann. ch. 112, § 12M (West 1983) (24 weeks or later); Minn. Stat. Ann. § 145.412(3) (West 1989) (potentially viable); Nev. Rev. Stat. § 442.250(1)(c) (1991) (after 24th week); N.Y. Penal Law § 125.05(3) (McKinney 1991) (after 24 weeks); N.C. Gen. Stat. § 14-45.1(b) (1986) (after 20th week); N.D. Cent. Code § 14-02.1-04(3) (1991) (after point at which fetus may reasonably be expected to have reached viability); S.C. Codified Laws Ann. § 44-41-20(c) (Law. Co-op. 1988) (third trimester); S.D. Codified Laws Ann. § 34-23A-5 (1986) (after 24th week of pregnancy).

[331] City of Akron v. Akron Center for Reproductive Health, Inc., 462 U.S. at 433–34 (the Court endorsed a viability standard over a trimester test).

[332] *See* Roe v. Wade, 410 U.S. at 165–66. The medical determination may be reached in light of all attendant circumstances. *Id. See also* Colautti v. Franklin, 439 U.S. at 387–89; Doe v. Bolton, 410 U.S. at 190–91.

[333] *E.g.*, Fla. Stat. Ann. § 390.001(5) (West 1986) (must use professional skill to keep fetus alive if at all possible after viability); Me. Rev. Stat. Ann. tit. 22, § 1598(4)(A) (1992) (criminal liability for knowing disregard of fetus viability); N.Y. Pub. Health Law § 4164 (McKinney 1985) (viably born fetus given immediate legal protection).

[334] *E.g.*, Ga. Code Ann. § 16-12-141 (West 1988) (best clinical judgment that abortion is necessary); Idaho Code § 18-608(1) (1987) (appropriate in medical judgment based on factors including but not limited to physical, emotional, psychological or familial); Ill. Ann. Stat. ch. 38, § 81-23.1(A) (Smith-Hurd Supp. 1991 & 1992) (best medical judgment; first trimester only); La. Rev. Stat. Ann. § 37:1285(A)(8), (9) (West 1988) (unprofessional conduct to terminate pregnancy if contrary to or unnecessary in best medical judgment of physician); Mass. Gen. Laws Ann. ch. 112, § 12L (West 1983) (best medical judgment under all attendant circumstances); Nev. Rev. Stat. § 442.250(1)(b) (1991) (same); S.C. Code Ann. § 44-41-20 (Law. Co-op. 1988) (pursuant to professional medical judgment); S.D. Codified Laws Ann.8 §§ 34-23A-3, 34-23A-4 (1986) (medically indicated); Tenn. Code Ann. § 39-15-201(c)(1)–(2) (1991) (medical judg-

9. RESIDENCY REQUIREMENTS   A small number of states[335] retain a residency requirement[336] limiting the availability of abortions. These statutes are unconstitutional.[337] Hence, their continued presence in statute books reflects legislative inertia or unwillingness to acknowledge constitutional doctrine.

10. PLACE OF PERFORMANCE   A few states retain requirements that all abortions be performed in hospitals licensed by the state,[338] accredited by outside agencies[339] or both.[340] Invoked as a limitation on performance of first-trimester abortions, such restrictions violate the constitutional rights of pregnant women and their physicians.[341] Language in *Doe v. Bolton,* however, approved a prohibition against abortions performed after the first trimester other than in a hospital. Accordingly, a lengthy roster of states has legislated an in-hospital requirement.[342]

In hindsight, reliance on Supreme Court dicta proved unfortunate because in 1983 the Court invalidated all statutes requiring performance of abortions in general hospitals from the beginning of the second trimester of pregnancy through viability.[343] A state must allow abortions during that time to be performed in clinics and outpatient facilities

---

ment of attending physician); Utah Code Ann. §§ 76-7-303 (concurrence of attending physician based on best medical judgment), 76-7-304(1) (best medical judgment; must consider all facts relevant to woman's well-being including but not limited to physical, emotional and psychological health and safety, age and familial situation) (1990). *Cf.* Wyo. Stat. § 35-6-112 (1988) (a felony to use other than accepted medical procedures to abort).

[335] *E.g.,* Alaska Stat. § 18.16.010 (1991) (30 days); Del. Code Ann. tit. 24, § 1793 (1987) (120 days; inapplicable if woman or spouse is employed in state, if woman is a patient of a Delaware physician or if there is a life-threatening emergency); Tenn. Code Ann. § 39-15-201(d) (1991) (woman must prove bona fide residency; hospital records must retain supporting documentation); Wash. Rev. Code Ann. § 9.02.070(b) (1988) (Repealed).

[336] *See supra,* notes 90–91 and accompanying text.

[337] Doe v. Bolton, 410 U.S. at 200; Smith v. Bentley, 493 F. Supp. 916, 929 (E.D. Ark. 1980). Residency requirements affecting access to nonemergency hospitalization or medical care at public expense constitute an invidious classification violating equal protection and the constitutional right of interstate travel. Memorial Hosp. v. Maricopa County, 415 U.S. 250, 254 (1974).

[338] *See, e.g.,* Alaska Stat. § 18.16.010(a)(2) (1991) (or hospital operated by federal government or agency); Colo. Rev. Stat. § 18-6-101(1) (1986) (held unconstitutional in People v. Norton, 181 Colo. 47, 507 P.2d 862 (1973)); Wis. Stat. Ann. § 940.04(5)(c) (West 1989) (unless emergency prevents).

[339] *E.g.,* Cal. Health & Safety Code § 25951(a) (West 1984) (accredited by Joint Commission on Accreditation of Hospitals [JCAH]); Del. Code Ann. tit. 24, § 1790(a) (1987 & Supp. 1990) (accredited by nationally recognized medical or hospital accreditation authority); N.M. Stat. Ann. § 30-5-1(C) (1984) (accredited hospital).

[340] *E.g.,* Kan. Stat. Ann. § 21-3407(2)(a) (1988) (certificate of necessity for abortion to be filed in hospital licensed by state and accredited by JCAH); Md. Pub. Health Code Ann. § 20-208(a) (1990) (state licensed and JCAH accredited).

[341] Doe v. Bolton, 410 U.S. at 193–95. *See also* Roe v. Wade, 410 U.S. at 163.

[342] *E.g.,* Idaho Code § 18-608(2)–(3) (1987) (second and third trimester); Ky. Rev. Stat. § 311.760(2) (1990) (after first trimester, unless emergency to protect woman's life or health); La. Rev. Stat. Ann. § 37:1285(A)(8)(b) (West 1988) (after first trimester, unprofessional conduct); Mass. Gen. Laws Ann. ch. 112, § 12Q (West 1983) (13th week or after); Mo. Ann. Stat. § 188.025 (Vernon Supp. 1992) (16-week gestational age or later); Mont. Code Ann. § 50-20-109(1)(b) (1991) (after first three months of pregnancy); N.Y. Pub. Health Law § 4164(1) (McKinney 1985) (after 12th week, on hospital inpatient basis); N.C. Gen. Stat. § 14-45.1(b) (1986) (after 20th week); N.D. Cent. Code § 14-02.1-04(2), (3) (1991) (after first 12 weeks of pregnancy); Okla. Stat. Ann. tit. 63, § 1-731(B) (West 1984) (subsequent to first trimester); S.C. Code Ann. § 44-41-20(c) (Law. Co-op. 1988) (third trimester); Tenn. Code Ann. § 39-15-201(c)(2)– (3) (1991) (after three months).

On abortion services for women prisoners, see Cal. Welf. & Inst. Code § 220 (West 1984) (pregnant females in local juvenile facilities may obtain lawful abortions).

as well as hospitals. Statutes so providing are constitutional.[344] Several states have had such legislation in place for many years.[345]

A few states have provided specifically for the licensing and regulation of abortion clinics.[346] Although the limited authority is not unanimous, licensing is constitutional as long as its attendant requirements promote maternal health and do not impose unacceptable barriers against a woman's free exercise of the right to choose abortion.[347] Requirements that designated personnel be in attendance although not mandated by medical needs,[348] that equipment be provided not dictated by good medical practice[349] or that clinic physicians maintain a hospital affiliation[350] have been declared unconstitutional.

One may assume a similar vulnerability in statutes prohibiting fees or compensation for abortion referrals[351] or abortion referrals for profit.[352] Administrative search provisions may also infringe patients' rights to privacy.[353] However, if regulations are otherwise constitutional, there should be no infirmity in legislation allowing nuisance abatement proceedings against places where abortions are performed in violation of law.[354]

11. PEER APPROVAL   A few states have retained statutes requiring that all abor-

---

[343] Planned Parenthood Ass'n v. Ashcroft, 462 U.S. at 481–82; City of Akron v. Akron Center for Reproductive Health, Inc., 462 U.S. at 434–39. The requirement imposed a significant burden on women wishing abortions, in terms of costs and restricted availability of abortion services in full-service general hospitals. Medical data recognized by the Court also established that abortions can be performed safely in clinics or outpatient facilities during the second trimester to the time of viability. City of Akron v. Akron Center for Reproductive Health, Inc. 462 U.S. at 436–37.

[344] In Simopoulos v. Virginia, 462 U.S. 506, 516–19 (1983), the Court sustained the constitutionality of a state requirement that second-trimester abortions be performed in a hospital, defined to include clinics and outpatient facilities; the legislation comported with good medical practice. Simopoulos had used the saline injection system in his office and allowed the pregnant minor to go to a motel where she aborted; his criminal conviction was held valid. *Id. See also* Birth Control Centers, Inc. v. Reizen, 743 F.2d 352, 366 (6th Cir. 1984) (invalidating state requirement that second-trimester abortions be performed at a clinic's parent hospital). *Birth Control Centers* rejected, however, an equal protection attack on a regulatory statute applicable to clinics but not to private doctor's offices where abortions might be performed; no selective enforcement was established. *Id.* at 359.

[345] *E.g.,* Ga. Code Ann. § 16-12-141(b) (1988) (after first trimester); Idaho Code § 18-608(1) (1987) (during first trimester only); Ind. Code Ann. § 35-1-58.5-2(3) (Burns Supp. 1991); Minn. Stat. Ann. § 145.412 (West 1989) (after first trimester); Nev. Rev. Stat. § 442.250(2) (1991); N.C. Gen. Stat. § 14-45.1(a) (1986) (within first 20 weeks; in hospital thereafter); S.C. Code Ann. § 44-41-20(b)-(c) (Law. Co-op. 1988) (second trimester; in certified hospitals during third trimester); S.D. Codified Laws Ann. § 34-23A-4 (1986) (between 12th and 24th week, if hospital facilities unavailable); Utah Code Ann. § 76-7-302(a) (Supp. 1991) (must be performed in hospital if 90 days or more after commencement of pregnancy as defined by competent medical practice); Va. Code §§ 18.2-73, 18.2-74 (1988) (validated in Simopoulos v. Virginia, 462 U.S. 506 (1983)); Wash. Rev. Code. Ann. § 9.02.070(c) (Repealed) (may terminate elsewhere if medical emergency makes abortion immediately necessary).

[346] *E.g.,* Fla. Stat. Ann. § 390.014 (West 1986 Supp. 1992); Ill. Ann. Stat. ch. 111½, §§ 157-8.1–8.16 (Smith-Hurd 1988); 18 Pa. Cons. Stat. Ann. § 3207 (Purdon 1983 & Supp. 1991 & 1992); S.C. Code Ann. § 44-41-70 (Law. Co-op. 1988).

[347] Baird v. Department of Pub. Health of Mass., 599 F.2d 1098 (1st Cir. 1979); Florida Women's Medical Clinic v. Smith, 536 F. Supp. 1048, 1057–58 (S.D. Fla. 1982), *appeal dismissed,* 706 F.2d 1172 (11th Cir. 1983); Westchester Women's Health Org. v. Whalen, 475 F. Supp. 734 (S.D.N.Y. 1979); Fox Valley Reproductive Health Care Center v. Arft, 446 F. Supp. 1072 (E.D. Wis. 1978); Village of Oak Lawn v. Marcowitz, 86 Ill. 2d 406, 427 N.E.2d 36 (1981); Indiana Hosp. Licensing Council v. Women's Pavilion of South Bend, Inc., 420 N.E.2d 1301 (Ind. App. 1981). *Contra,* Word v. Poelker, 495 F.2d 1349 (8th Cir. 1974) (facilities for first-trimester abortions); Margaret S. v. Edwards, 488 F. Supp. 181, 223–24 (E.D. La. 1980) (facilities for first-trimester abortions); Mahoning Women's Center v. Hunter, 444 F. Supp. 12, 17 (N.D. Ohio 1977), *aff'd,* 610 F.2d 456 (6th Cir. 1979), *vacated on other grounds and remanded,* 447 U.S. 918 (1980) (ordinance covering only abortion clinics denied equal protection because

tions be concurred in by other physicians,[355] hospital review committees[356] or both.[357] The Supreme Court invalidated both requirements, at least as they pertain to first-trimester abortions.[358] Accordingly, legislation was approved in some jurisdictions requiring such approval in the third trimester[359] or after viability.[360] Mandates of this sort are probably constitutional if applied after viability because the Supreme Court by its judgment approved a requirement that a second physician be in attendance at the time of an abortion after viability.[361] Between the beginning of the second trimester and viability, however, limitations of this sort are likely to be viewed as barriers to women's free choice, unless similar requirements govern other medical and surgical techniques of approximately the same seriousness. There should be no impediment to requirements that, if a consulting physician refers the case to another physician for performance of an abortion, full medical details be transmitted.[362]

12. WAITING PERIODS   One technique for delaying abortions is to impose waiting periods between receipt of information required to be imparted to a woman[363] or parent[364]

---

other surgery with equivalent medical risks could be performed in unlicensed facilities); Wright v. State, 351 So. 2d 708, 711 (Fla. 1977) (term "approved facility" unconstitutional in relation to first-trimester abortions, although it might be valid thereafter); People v. Dobbs Ferry Medical Pavilion, 33 N.Y.2d 584, 301 N.E.2d 435, 347 N.Y.S.2d 452 (1973) (terms "facility" and "clinic" in medical care facility licensing statute were overinclusive and thus unconstitutional).

Efforts to use zoning regulations targeted at abortion clinics alone constitute an impediment to exercise of *Roe v. Wade* rights. Deerfield Medical Center v. City of Deerfield Beach, 661 F.2d 328, 336–38 (5th Cir. 1981); West Side Women's Services, Inc. v. City of Cleveland, 573 F. Supp. 504 (N.D. Ohio 1983); Framingham Clinic v. Board of Southborough Selectmen, 373 Mass. 279, 283, 367 N.E.2d 606, 610 (1977).

A statutory prohibition against performance of abortions at an educational facility other than to save life, Ariz. Rev. Stat. Ann. § 15-730 (Supp. 1990), was sustained as constitutional in Roe v. Arizona Bd. of Regents, 113 Ariz. 178, 179, 549 P.2d 150, 151–52 (1976), in part because of the availability of abortion facilities elsewhere.

[348] Birth Control Centers, Inc. v. Reizen, 743 F.2d 352, 364–65 (6th Cir. 1984); Florida Women's Medical Clinic v. Smith, 536 F. Supp. 1048, 1057 (S.D. Fla. 1982), *appeal dismissed,* 706 F.2d 1172 (11th Cir. 1983).

[349] Florida Women's Medical Clinic v. Smith, 536 F. Supp. at 1056. *See also* Birth Control Centers, Inc. v. Reizen, 743 F.2d 352, 366 (6th Cir. 1984) (invalidating a requirement that clinic corridors be six feet wide, as not reasonably related to the purposes of clinic regulation).

[350] Women's Medical Center of Providence v. Cannon, 463 F. Supp. 531, 537–38 (D.R.I. 1978) (invalidating requirement that physician performing first-trimester abortions had to have unsupervised privileges at an accessible hospital).

[351] *E.g.,* Ky. Rev. Stat. § 311.820 (1990) (although some of the terms like "kickbacks" are probably not objectionable as long as the practice is condemned in every context; if only abortion is singled out, there is an equal protection problem); 18 Pa. Cons. Stat. Ann. § 3213(b) (Purdon 1983) (at least unless all other physicians and clinics are under a similar disability).

[352] *E.g.,* Md. Pub. Health Code Ann. § 20-204 (1990) (but repealed subject to referendum, *id.* Supp. 1991).

[353] Margaret S. v. Edwards, 488 F. Supp. 181, 214–17 (E.D. La. 1980). Basic administrative search doctrine is delineated, *e.g.,* in Donovan v. Dewey, 452 U.S. 594, 598–606 (1981); Michigan v. Tyler, 436 U.S. 499 (1978) (*and see* Michigan v. Clifford, 464 U.S. 287 (1984)); Marshall v. Barlow's, Inc. 436 U.S. 307, 313 (1978); United States v. Biswell, 406 U.S. 311 (1972); See v. Seattle, 387 U.S. 541 (1967); Camara v. Municipal Court, 387 U.S. 523 (1967).

[354] Antiabortion groups frequently picket, physically obstruct entrance to and even physically invade abortion clinics and counseling centers. Although peaceful picketing basically is a form of protected speech under the first amendment, the Supreme Court ruled in Frisby v. Schultz, 487 U.S. 474 (1988), that a local ordinance could prohibit focused picketing solely in front of a single residence that destroyed the privacy of the inhabitants; the picketing was directed at the residence of a doctor who performed lawful abortions

and performance of an abortion,[365] perhaps subject to an emergency exception if an abortion must be performed to protect maternal life or, in some instances, health.[366] Such requirements at times have been augmented by an ensuing waiting period between a woman's submission of a signed consent form and performance of an abortion,[367] again subject to an emergency exception.[368]

The Supreme Court has invalidated the latter form of waiting period[369] as an arbitrary, inflexible limitation without a medical basis and a costly imposition that could require two separate trips to an abortion facility.[370] Although the Court did not have before it a mandated waiting period between receipt of information and submission of a consent, its rationale in *Akron Center* appears germane, particularly in light of the Court's invalidation of several items of information intended to discourage decisions to undergo an abortion.[371]

Nevertheless, the Third Circuit[372] has read into Justice O'Connor's concurring opinion in *Hodgson v. Minnesota*[373] an indication that the Supreme Court stands ready to legit-

---

at clinics in adjacent towns. Trespassers and persons blocking access to clinics have been convicted of criminal trespass; appellate courts have affirmed the convictions and rejected claims of the necessity defense allegedly founded on the need to preserve fetal life. *See, e.g.,* State v. Aguillard, 567 So. 2d 674 (La. App.), *cert. denied,* 571 So. 2d 631 (La. 1990); State v. O'Brien, 784 S.W.2d 187 (Mo. App. 1989); State v. Migliorino, 150 Wis. 2d 513, 442 N.W.2d 36, *cert. denied sub nom.* Haines v. Wisconsin, 110 S. Ct. 565 (1989).

[355] *E.g.,* Kan. Stat. Ann. § 21-3407(2)(a) (1988) (three physicians); Wis. Stat. Ann. § 97-3-3(2) (1972) (two reputable licensed physicians); Wis. Stat. Ann. § 940.04(5)(b) (West 1989) (two physicians).

[356] *E.g.,* Cal. Health & Safety Code § 25951(b) (West 1984) (unanimous approval if no more than three licensed physicians and surgeons on staff committee); Colo. Rev. Stat. § 18-6-101(1), (4) (1986) (ruled unconstitutional in People v. Norton, 181 Colo. 47, 507 P.2d 862 (1973)); Md. Pub. Health Code Ann. § 20-208(b)(2) (1990) (hospital abortion review authority); N.M. Stat. Ann. § 30-5-1(C), (D) (1984) (same).

[357] *E.g.,* Del. Code Ann. tit. 24, § 1790(a), (b) (1987) (abortion review committee plus two licensed physicians certifying necessity).

[358] Doe v. Bolton, 410 U.S. at 195–200. *See also* Smith v. Bentley, 493 F. Supp 916, 927–28 (E.D. Ark. 1980).

[359] *E.g.,* Fla. Stat. Ann. § 390.001(2)(a)–(b) (West 1986) (two physicians); Ga. Code Ann. § 16-12-141(c) (1988); Idaho Code § 18-608(3) (1987) (one physician: corroborated by consulting physician); S.C. Codified Laws Ann. § 44-41-20(c) (Law. Co-op. 1988) (one other physician); Va. Code § 18.2-74(b) (1988) (two consulting physicians).

[360] *E.g.,* Mont. Code Ann. § 50-20-109(2)(b) (1991) (two other physicians); N.D. Cent. Code § 14-02.1-04(3) (1981) (two other physicians).

[361] This was the result in Planned Parenthood Ass'n v. Ashcroft, 462 U.S. 476, 482–86, 505 (1983), although there was no majority opinion. The provision related to protection of live-born fetuses. *See infra,* notes 387–91, 478–80 and accompanying text.

[362] *E.g.,* Ky. Rev. Stat. § 311.723(1)(b) (1990); Mass. Gen. Laws Ann. ch. 112, § 12R (West 1983).

[363] *See supra,* notes 203–33 and accompanying text.

[364] *See supra,* note 239 and accompanying text.

[365] Statutes triggered by information to pregnant women include Ind. Code Ann. § 35-1-58.5-2(d) (Burns 1990) (24-hour period between receipt of consent form and submission of signed form to physician); Me. Rev. Stat. Ann. tit. 22, § 1599(1) (1992) (48 hours); Mo. Ann. Stat. § 188.039(1) (Vernon 1983) (48 hours); 18 Pa. Cons. Stat. Ann. § 3205(a)(2) (Purdon 1983) (24 hours); S.D. Codified Laws Ann. § 34-23A-10.1 (1986) (24 hours); Tenn. Code Ann. § 39-15-202(d) (Supp. 1990) (two-day minimum excluding day on which information was given); Utah Code Ann. § 76-7-305.5(2) (1990) (24 hours if possible).

Spousal information laws imposing a waiting period include Ky. Rev. Stat. § 311.735 (1990) (before or, if not possible, within 30 days after); Nev. Rev. Stat. § 442.254 (1991) (24 hours if possible).

Waiting periods based on notice to parents or guardians of minor pregnant females are found in Me. Rev. Stat. Ann. tit. 22, § 1597 (1992) (24 hours; 48 hours if mail notice); Minn. Stat. Ann. § 144.343(2)

imate mandated waiting periods, in particular the 24-hour period required under a recent Pennsylvania statute.[374]

However, the Supreme Court concluded that a 48-hour-delay between parental notification and performance of an abortion on a minor was constitutional.[375] Legislatures are best advised to eliminate all time-delay requirements affecting pregnant adults in light of these Supreme Court precedents and in light of the Court's flexible, medically oriented approach to counseling and consent,[376] waiting times may be imposed only governing abortions for pregnant minors, as approved in *Hodgson*.

13. ABORTION TECHNIQUES   a. *General Standard of Care*   The Supreme Court's constitutional focus is on maternal health as the sole concern after the first trimester of pregnancy,[377] based on contemporary medical standards.[378] Hence, no legislative statement is required to establish positive medical standards for abortions; general licensing requirements suffice. Nevertheless, there is no constitutional defect in reaffirming, in the setting of therapeutic abortion legislation, the applicability of usual standards of professional care.[379] Constitutional problems arise only when statutes purport to restrict accepted medical practice.

(West 1989) (48 hours); Neb. Rev. Stat. § 28-347(1) (1989) (24 hours; 48 hours if mail notice); Nev. Rev. Stat. § 442.255 (1991) (24 hours); N.D. Cent. Code § 14-02.1-03(1) (1981) (24 hours; 48 hours if mail notice); Tenn. Code Ann. § 39-15-202(f) (Supp. 1990) (two days minimum).

[366] *E.g.,* Ky. Rev. Stat. § 311.735 (1990); Me. Rev. Stat. Ann. tit. 22, §§ 1597 (1992), 1599(1) (1992); Neb. Rev. Stat. § 28-347(3) (1985); Tenn. Code Ann. § 39-15-202(f) (Supp. 1990).

[367] *E.g.,* Del. Code Ann. tit. 24, § 1794(b) (1987) (24 hours); Ky. Rev. Stat. § 311.726(2) (1990) (2 hours); Mass. Gen. Laws Ann. ch. 112, § 12S (West 1983) (24 hours); Nev. Rev. Stat. § 442.252 (1991) (24-hour minimum, 30-day maximum validity of consent); N.D. Cent. Code § 14-02.1-03(1) (1991).

[368] *E.g.,* Del. Code Ann. tit. 24, § 1794(b) (1987); S.D. Codified Laws Ann. § 34-23A-10.1 (1986).

[369] City of Akron v. Akron Center for Reproductive Health, Inc., 462 U.S. at 449–51.

[370] The Kentucky imposition of a two-hour period might or might not run afoul of such criteria. The Nevada and North Carolina fixing of a 30-day maximum period during which consents are effective should prove valid, at least in the absence of an indication that other medical consent forms are not subject to equivalent time limitations. If only abortion consent forms are so limited, there would appear to be an invidious classification violative of equal protection.

[371] *See supra,* notes 225–28 and accompanying text.

[372] Planned Parenthood of Southeastern Pennsylvania v. Casey, 947 F.2d 682, 706–07 (3d Cir.), *cert. granted,* 112 S. Ct. 931 (1991).

[373] 110 S. Ct. 2926, 2950 (1990). *See supra,* text accompanying notes 285–92.

[374] 18 Pa. Cons. Stat. Ann. § 3205(a) (Purdon 1988 & Supp. 1991).

[375] Hodgson v. Minnesota, 110 S. Ct. 2926, 2944, 2969 (1990).

[376] City of Akron v. Akron Center for Reproductive Health, Inc., 462 U.S. at 450–51: ''In accordance with the ethical standards of the profession, a physician will advise the patient to defer the abortion when he thinks this will be beneficial to her. But if a woman, after appropriate counseling, is prepared to give her written informed consent and proceed with the abortion, a State may not demand that she delay the effectuation of her decision.''

[377] Roe v. Wade, 410 U.S. at 163: ''It follows that, from and after [the end of the first trimester], a State may regulate the abortion procedure to the extent that the regulation reasonably relates to the preservation and protection of maternal health.''

[378] City of Akron v. Akron Center for Reproductive Health, Inc., 462 U.S. at 436–37. The Court concluded that the dilitation and evacuation technique for abortion could be safely performed away from a general service hospital, at least until viability, rendering a city ordinance requirement that all abortions after the first trimester be performed at a hospital an unreasonable burden on women's free choice not justified on medical grounds. *Id.*

[379] *See, e.g.,* Colo. Rev. Stat. § 18-6-101(1) (1986) (licensed physician using accepted medical procedures); Wyo. Stat. § 35-6-112 (1988); Dellapena, *supra* note 32, at 361–65, 411–14. To the extent, however, that more severe penalties are visited on those otherwise allowed to perform abortions who use substandard

b. *Precluded Techniques*   At least one state continues to forbid the use of saline amniocentesis as an abortion technique after the first trimester of pregnancy, in the absence of a special justification.[380] The objective is to compel use of other techniques that increase the possibility that a viable fetus might be born alive. The Supreme Court has invalidated such prohibitions as not reasonably related to maternal health because they proscribe techniques that pose less of a risk to maternal health than those that would have to be used as an alternative.[381] Continuation of these statutes can only be attributed to a legislative unwillingness to bow to Supreme Court mandate. Essentially, they are dead letters as to enforceability.

There appears to be no constitutional objection to a legislative restatement of the Court's doctrine requiring medical personnel to use all reasonable medical procedures to enhance the chance of a live birth of a viable fetus if they are consistent with maternal health.[382] Only if maternal health were relegated to a subordinate status would there be a constitutional problem.[383]

c. *Testing Requirements*   Two states require blood typing and Rh factor testing before an abortion may be performed.[384] To the extent such a requirement applies to second-trimester abortions before viability (and perhaps the stage of viability), when survival after live birth is medically impossible, it is probably unconstitutional under the Supreme Court's doctrine that all limitations on abortion be supported by current medical practice standards and paramount concerns for maternal health. If, in contrast, such legislation is interpreted to govern only those stages of pregnancy when live fetal birth is a medical possibility, there is probably no impermissible barrier to an unfettered abortion decision and its effectuation.

d. *Attending Physician*   Statutes occasionally require a second physician to be present when a viable fetus is aborted.[385] The Supreme Court has sustained such a legisla-

---

abortion techniques, there may be an equal protection problem or a manifestation of disproportionality of punishment to offense, violative of the eighth amendment. On the latter, *see* Solem v. Helm, 463 U.S. 277 (1983). Cases considering and applying standard medical malpractice concepts in the abortion context include Brown v. University of the State of New York, 147 A.D.2d 784, 537 N.Y.S.2d 655 (1989); Dillon v. Silver, 134 A.D.2d 159, 520 N.Y.S.2d 751 (1987); Lynch v. Bay Ridge Obstetrical & Gynecological Assoc., P.C., 134 A.D.2d 240, 520 N.Y.S.2d 431 (1987), *aff'd,* 72 N.Y.2d 632, 532 N.E.2d 1239, 536 N.Y.S.2d 11 (1988).

[380] Ky. Rev. Stat. § 311.770 (1990). *Cf.* Wyo. Stat. § 35-6-103 (Supp. 1991) (physician is not intentionally to terminate viability of infant prior to, during or following abortion).

[381] Planned Parenthood Ass'n v. Danforth, 428 U.S. at 78–79: "Moreover, as a practical matter, [the proscription] forces a woman and her physician to terminate her pregnancy by methods more dangerous to her health than the method outlawed." *See also* Note, *Criminal Liability of Physicians: An Encroachment on the Abortion Right,* 18 Am Crim. L. Rev. 591, 604–05 (1981).

[382] *E.g.,* Fla. Stat. Ann. § 390.001(5) (West 1986); Idaho Code § 18-608(3) (1987); Ill. Ann. Stat. ch. 38, § 81-26(3)–(5) (Smith-Hurd Supp. 1991 & 1992); Mass. Gen. Laws Ann. ch. 112, § 12 (West 1983) (unless technique would create greater risk of death or serious bodily harm to mother at time of abortion or subsequently during future pregnancy; *query,* are the qualifiers constitutional under *Danforth,* 428 U.S. at 81–84?); Mo. Rev. Stat. § 188.030(a) (Vernon 1983); Neb. Rev. Stat. § 28-330 (1989); Okla. Stat. Ann. tit. 63, § 1-734(C) (West 1984); 18 Pa. Cons. Stat. Ann. § 3211(c)(4) (Purdon Supp. 1991 & 1992); Utah Code Ann. § 76-7-307 (Supp. 1991).

[383] On the required protection of live-born fetuses in the context of abortion, see *infra,* notes 387–92, 478–80 and accompanying text.

[384] Mass. Gen. Laws. Ann. ch. 112, § 12R (West 1983); S.D. Codified Laws Ann. § 34-23A-6 (1986).

[385] *E.g.,* Mo. Rev. Stat. § 188.030(3) (Vernon 1983); N.Y. Pub. Health Law § 4164(1) (McKinney 1985) (after 20th week of pregnancy); N.D. Cent. Code § 14-02.1-05 (1991); Okla. Stat. Ann. tit. 63, § 1-732(E) (West 1984); 18 Pa. Cons. Stat. Ann. § 3211(c)(5) (Purdon Supp. 1991 & 1992).

tive condition to abortion.[386] Its rationale, as far as can be gleaned from the judgmental majority's serial opinions, was that such a requirement reasonably relates to preservation of the life or health of a live-born fetus, without detrimental consequences to maternal health.

14. STATUS OF INFANTS, FETUSES AND FETAL TISSUE   a. *Live-born Infants*   There is no need for special statutes confirming that viable fetuses born alive are persons entitled to the full protection of civil and criminal law. Those who terminate human life, whether neonate or of greater duration, whether intentionally, recklessly or with criminal negligence, may be prosecuted for murder or manslaughter[387] and incur wrongful death liability. Nevertheless, some statutes confirm long-established general legal principles in the setting of abortion legislation by providing a definition of human life[388] or confirming a duty, usually enforced by criminal penalties,[389] to care for fetuses born alive.[390] Other provisions, perhaps reflecting difficult proof problems in establishing beyond a reasonable doubt the independent human existence of a fetus/child, mandate a special obligation to safeguard fetal life during abortion processes.[391] These are seem-

---

[386] Planned Parenthood Ass'n v. Ashcroft, 462 U.S. 476, 482–86, 505 (1983) (five justices concurring in separate opinions).

[387] If a fetus is born alive and becomes a child (a "person" in legal parlance), manslaughter criminality attaches even though the physiological cause of death was inflicted before birth processes began. *See, e.g.,* People v. Hall, 158 A.D.2d 69, 557 N.Y.S.2d 879, *appeal denied,* 76 N.Y.2d 940, 1021, 564 N.E.2d 679, 771, 565 N.Y.S.2d 69, 771 (1990) (citing and discussing precedents elsewhere). If there is a stillbirth, *e.g.,* People v. Vercelletto, 135 Misc. 2d 40, 514 N.Y.S.2d 177 (County Ct. 1987), or evidence is lacking that a live birth occurred, *e.g.,* State v. Green, 245 Kan. 398, 781 P.2d 678 (1989), homicide criminality does not exist.

[388] *See supra,* notes 189–90 and accompanying text. Tex. Fam. Code Ann. § 12.05(b) (Vernon 1986) provides alternative medical standards by which live birth is to be determined.

[389] *See infra,* notes 478–80 and accompanying text.

[390] *E.g.,* Cal. Health & Safety Code § 25955.9 (West 1984); Del. Code Ann. tit. 24, § 1795(a) (1987); Ga. Code Ann. § 16-12-141(c) (1988) ("if capable of meaningful or sustained life"); Ind. Code Ann. § 35-1-58.5-7 (Burns 1985); Iowa Code Ann. § 707.10 (West 1979); La. Rev. Stat. Ann. §§ 14:87.5 (West 1986), 37:1285(28) (West 1988) (taking life of viable fetus aborted alive is a basis for license revocation); Me. Rev. Stat. Ann. tit. 22, § 1594 (1991); Mass. Gen. Laws Ann. ch. 112, § 12P (West 1983); Minn. Stat. Ann. § 145.415 (West 1989); Mont. Code Ann. § 50-20-108(1) (1991); Neb. Rev. Stat. § 28-330 (1989); N.Y. Exec. Law § 291(3) (McKinney 1982), N.Y. Pub. Health Law § 4164(2) (McKinney 1985); N.D. Cent. Code § 14.02.1-08 (1991); Okla. Stat. Ann. tit. 63, § 1-734(A), (C) (West 1984); 18 Pa. Cons. Stat. Ann. §§ 3202(b)(3), 3212(b) (Purdon 1983); R.I. Gen. Laws § 11-9-18 (Supp. 1991); S.D. Codified Laws Ann. § 34-23A-16.1 (1986); Tenn. Code Ann. § 39-15-206(a) (1991); Tex. Fam. Code Ann. § 12.05(a) (Vernon 1986); Wyo. Stat. § 35-6-104 (1988).

[391] *E.g.,* Idaho Code § 18-608(3) (1987); Ill. Rev. Stat. ch. 38, § 81-26(3) (Smith-Hurd Supp. 1991 & 1992); Iowa Code Ann. § 707.7 (West 1979); Ky. Rev. Stat. § 311.780 (1990); La. Rev. Stat. Ann. § 14:87.1 (West 1986); Mass. Gen. Laws Ann. ch. 112, § 12P (West 1983) (must have life-support equipment, as defined by state department of public health, in room where abortion is performed); Neb. Rev. Stat. § 28-325(3) (1989); Okla. Stat. Ann. tit. 63, 1-734(C) (West 1984) (all reasonable measures to preserve life of child alive when partially or totally removed from uterus as long as such measures do not create a significant danger to woman's life or health); Tenn. Code Ann. § 39-15-206(a) (1991) (however, extraneous life support measures need not be attempted if it can be determined through amniocentesis or medical observation that a fetus is severly malformed); Tex. Rev. Civ. Stat. Ann. art. 4512.5 (Vernon 1976) (during parturition, destroying vitality or life if child would have been born alive); Utah Code Ann. § 76-7-308 (Supp. 1990); Va. Code § 18.2-74(c) (1988); Wyo. Stat. § 35-6-103 (1988).

The Tennessee exception is obviously based on eugenic considerations. *See supra,* notes 19–20, 85 and accompanying text.

See also the discussion of requirements that attending physicians be present during abortions during viability, *supra* notes 378–80 and accompanying text.

ingly constitutional as long as, expressly or through judicial interpretation, the protection of maternal life or health takes priority over the preservation of fetal life.[392]

b. *Experimentation Involving Fetuses*   Quite a number of states have prohibited experimentation with, and research on, embryos and fetuses before[393] and after[394] abortions and on stillborn[395] and live-born[396] infants. Exceptions, however, are provided to cover acts done to advance fetal[397] or maternal[398] health and for pathological examinations.[399] Traffickers in fetal or neonate tissue for such purposes may be penalized.[400] Limited authority sustains the constitutionality of such provisions.[401]

c. *Tissue Analysis*   Several states require that pathological examinations be performed on dead fetuses and on removed fetal tissue[402] or at least contemplate that such examinations may properly be conducted.[403] The Supreme Court has sustained the constitutionality of such a requirement,[404] apparently because tissue examinations are an incident to surgical techniques and do not impose a special economic hardship on women desiring abortions.

---

[392] *See supra,* notes 378–80 and accompanying text.

[393] *E.g.,* Ariz. Rev. Stat. Ann. § 36-2302(A) (1986); Fla. Stat. Ann. § 390.001(6) (West 1986); Ill. Ann. Stat. ch. 38, § 81-26(3) (Smith-Hurd Supp. 1991 & 1992); Me. Rev. Stat. Ann. tit. 22, § 1593 (1992); Okla. Stat. Ann. tit. 63, § 1-735(B) (West 1984); 18 Pa. Cons. Stat. Ann. § 3216(a) (Purdon Supp. 1991 & 1992); Utah Code Ann. § 76-7-310 (1990); Wyo. Stat. § 35-6-115 (1988) (persons consenting to, aiding or abetting traffic in viable aborted children commit a felony).

[394] *E.g.,* Ariz. Rev. Stat. Ann. § 36-2302(A) (1986); Cal. Health & Safety Code § 25956 (West 1984) (exempting public or private educational institutions); Fla. Stat. Ann. § 390.001(6) (West 1986); Ill. Rev. Stat. ch. 38, § 81-32 (Smith-Hurd Supp. 1992); Ind. Code Ann. § 35-1-58.5-6 (Burns 1985); Me. Rev. Stat. Ann. tit. 22, § 1593 (1992); Mass. Gen. Laws Ann. ch. 112, § 12J(a) (West 1983); Mich. Comp. Laws. Ann. § 333.2688(1) (West 1980); Minn. Stat. Ann. § 145.422 (West 1989); Neb. Rev. Stat. § 28-346 (1989); N.D. Cent. Code § 14-02.2-01 (1991); Okla. Stat. Ann. tit. 63, § 1-735 (West 1984); 18 Pa. Cons. Stat. Ann. § 3216 (Purdon Supp. 1991 & 1992); S.D. Codified Laws Ann. § 34-23A-17 (1986); Tenn. Code Ann. § 39-15-208(a) (1991) (including photography); Wyo. Stat. § 35-6-115 (1988).

[395] *E.g.,* N.D. Cent. Code § 14-02.2-02 (1981); 18 Pa. Cons. Stat. Ann. § 3216(b) (Purdon 1983).

[396] *E.g.,* Ill. Ann. Stat. ch. 38, § 81-26 (Smith-Hurd Supp. 1991 & 1992) (written consent from one parent in instances of stillbirth or fetal death not resulting from abortion); La. Rev. Stat. Ann. § 14:87.2 (West 1986); Minn. Stat. Ann. § 145.422 (West 1989); Mo. Ann. Stat. § 188.037 (Vernon 1983); Mont. Code Ann. § 50-20-108(3) (1991); Neb. Rev. Stat. § 28-346 (1989); N.D. Cent. Code § 14-02.2-01 (1991).

[397] *E.g.,* Fla. Stat. Ann. § 390.001(6) (West 1986) (protection of life or health); Ill. Ann. Stat. ch. 38, § 81-26 (Smith-Hurd Supp. 1992) (protection of life or health); La. Rev. Stat. Ann. § 14:87.2 (West 1986) (life and health of live-born child; preserve life or improve health of embryo or fetus); Minn. Stat. Ann. § 145.422 (West 1989) (protect life or health); Mo. Ann. Stat. § 188.037 (Vernon 1983) (same); Mont. Code Ann. § 50-20-108(3) (1991) (same); Neb. Rev. Stat. § 28-346 (1989) (same); Okla. Stat. Ann. tit. 63, § 1-735(A) (West 1984) (unless therapeutic to child or unborn child); 18 Pa. Cons. Stat. Ann. § 3216(a) (Purdon Supp. 1991 & 1992) (life or health of child); Utah Code Ann. § 76-7-310 (1990) (allowed when, in a physician's best medical judgment, a technique should be used to test for genetic defects).

[398] *E.g.,* Ariz. Rev. Stat. Ann. § 36-2302(A) (1986) (strictly necessary to diagnose disease or condition in mother, if abortion was performed because of that disease or condition).

[399] *E.g.,* Mass. Gen. Laws Ann. ch. 112, § 12J(a)(II) (West 1983); Mich. Comp. Laws Ann. § 333.2688(1) (West 1980); N.D. Cent. Code § 14-02.2-02(1) (1991); Okla. Stat. Ann. tit. 63, § 1-735(B) (West 1984). *See infra,* note 482.

[400] *E.g.,* Ind. Code Ann. § 35-1-58.5-6 (Burns 1985) (transporting fetus out-of-state); Me. Rev. Stat. Ann. tit. 22, § 1593 (1992); Neb. Rev. Stat. § 28-342 (1989); N.D. Cent. Code § 14-02.2-02 (1991).

[401] Margaret S. v. Edwards, 488 F. Supp 181, 219–21 (E.D. La. 1980). *See also* Destro, *supra* note 32, at 1315–16; Note, *Ethical Standards for Fetal Experimentation,* 43 Fordham L. Rev. 547 (1975).

[402] *E.g.,* Ill. Ann. Stat. ch. 38, § 83-32 (Smith-Hurd Supp. 1991 & 1992); Mo. Ann. Stat. § 188.047 (Vernon 1983); 18 Pa. Cons. Stat. Ann. § 3214(c) (Purdon 1983); S.D. Codified Laws Ann. § 34-23A-19(3) (1986) (if facility is equipped to complete pathology reports); Utah Code Ann. §§ 76-7-309, 76-7-313(8) (1990).

d. *Disposition of Fetal Remains*   Some states have legislated with reference to the disposition of fetal remains, sometimes through specific criminal legislation[405] and sometimes by recognizing the need for administrative regulations on the matter.[406] The Supreme Court invalidated a criminal statute requiring physicians to ensure that fetal remains be "disposed of in a humane and sanitary manner" on the ground of vagueness and indefiniteness.[407] Arguably, a purely administrative-law approach is not vulnerable as long as residual criminal penalties are not provided.

15. RECORDS AND REPORTS   With the recognition of therapeutic abortions came a concern for documentation of the fact of and medical grounds for abortion.[408] Since 1973 such requirements have become the norm. Physician and hospital records may have to reflect consents[409] and information given to patients[410] as well as data of purely medical significance.[411] In addition, physicians and institutions are expected to submit statistical information[412] or detailed information about each abortion.[413] The contents of reports may be left for determination through administrative regulation or provision of state reporting forms.[414] Most legislation reflects the Supreme Court's concern[415] over

---

[403] Ind. Code Ann. § 35-1-58.5-5(8) (Burns 1985) (physician's report to include results of pathological examination, if performed); Ohio Rev. Code Ann. § 3701.34.1(3) (Page 1992) (public health council to adopt rules concerning pathological reports following abortions).

[404] Planned Parenthood Ass'n v. Ashcroft, 462 U.S. at 486–90, 505. There was no majority opinion.

[405] E.g., N.D. Cent. Code § 14-02.1-09 (1991) (physician performing abortion).

[406] E.g., Fla. Stat. Ann. §§ 390.001(7), 390.012(1)(e) (West 1986 & Supp. 1992); Ill. Ann. Stat. ch. 38, § 81-32 (Smith-Hurd Supp. 1991 & 1992) (no exploitation of aborted fetus or tissue); Minn. Stat. Ann. § 145.423(3) (West 1989) (child born alive and dying after birth to be disposed of according to general statutes governing human burials); N.Y. Pub. Health Law § 4164(4) (McKinney 1985) (similar); Ohio Rev. Code Ann. § 3701.341(4) (Page 1992) (public health council to adopt rules relating to humane disposition of products of human conception); Wyo. Stat. § 35-6-109 (Supp. 1991) (state board of health to prescribe rules and regulations for disposal of bodies, tissues, organs and parts of unborn child, human fetus or aborted human embryo).

[407] City of Akron v. Akron Center for Reproductive Health, Inc., 462 U.S. at 451–52. In Planned Parenthood of Minnesota v. Minnesota, 910 F.2d 479 (8th Cir. 1990), the court sustained the constitutionality of the state fetal disposition law and reversed a district court holding that the law was unconstitutionally vague and indefinite, burdened abortion choices and was deficient in scope. Cf. Feminist Women's Health Center, Inc. v. Philibosian, 157 Cal. App. 3d 1076, 203 Cal. Rptr. 918 (1984) (district attorney could not contract for private interment of fetuses with Roman Catholic religious services without violating the first amendment prohibition against establishment of religion).

[408] See supra, notes 106–08 and accompanying text.

[409] E.g., Idaho Code § 18-611 (1987) (discretionary); Ind. Code Ann. § 35-1-58.5-2(d) (Burns 1985); Nev. Rev. Stat. § 442.252 (1991) (as well as marital status and age); R.I. Gen. Laws §§ 23-4.7-5, 23-4.8-3(d) (1989); Utah Code Ann. § 76-7-313 (1990).

[410] E.g., Ind. Code Ann. §§ 35-1-58.5-1(f) (Burns Supp. 1991); R.I. Gen. Laws § 23-4.7-5 (1989).

[411] E.g., Ill. Ann. Stat. ch. 38, § 81-25(2) (Smith-Hurd Supp. 1991 & 1992); Ind. Code Ann. §§ 35-1-58.5-2(3)(c), 35-1-58.5-3 (Burns 1985); Mo. Rev. Stat. § 188.052 (Vernon 1983); Nev. Rev. Stat. § 442.250(3) (1987); N.Y. Pub. Health Law § 4164(3) (McKinney 1985) (life-sustaining efforts for viable fetus born alive); N.D. Cent. Code § 14-02.1-07 (1991); Okla. Stat. Ann. tit. 63, §§ 1-732(B)–(D), 1-738, 1-739 (West 1984); R.I. Gen. Laws § 23-4.7-4 (1989) (medical emergency requiring immediate abortion).

Some statutes require medical records to be retained for a specified time. See, e.g., Mo. Ann. Stat. § 188.060 (Vernon 1983) (seven years); Nev. Rev. Stat. § 442.256 (1987) (consents and information documentation retained at least five years); N.D. Cent. Code § 14-02.1-07(1)(a) (1991) (seven years); Okla. Stat. Ann. tit. 63, § 1-739 (West 1984) (seven years). Courts disagree as to whether these are unreasonable requirements burdening therapeutic abortion decisions. Compare Planned Parenthood League v. Bellotti, 641 F.2d 1006, 1018 (1st Cir. 1981) (constitutional), with Margaret S. v. Edwards, 488 F. Supp. 181, 213–14 (E.D. La. 1980) (burdensome requirement attached only to abortion case records).

patient privacy by requiring the names of patients[416] and at times physicians[417] to be kept confidential, subject perhaps to a possibility of disclosure through court order.[418] Hospitals also may be required to report to authorities cases of complications apparently flowing from abortions.[419]

Reporting and record-maintenance requirements are constitutional as long as they are not abused or overdone to the point where they accomplish an unacceptable burden on the exercise of the constitutional right to abortion.[420] For the most part, state laws appear to respect that qualification. However, Illinois, Nevada, Oklahoma, Pennsylvania and Utah, for example, decree such detailed requirements or tie report contents to matters of consent and information (some of which are unconstitutional in isolation) that one may doubt they are consonant with the Supreme Court's concerns.

16. SANCTIONS   Many of the details regarding therapeutic abortion practice are found outside criminal codes. Nevertheless, supplementary criminal penalties may well be provided[421] in addition to criminal penalties attached to nontherapeutic abortions.[422] In general, the former are directed at medical personnel who fail to conform to statutory

---

[412] *E.g.,* Del. Code Ann. tit. 24, § 1790(c) (1987); Ga. Code Ann. § 16-12-141(d) (1988); Kan. Stat. Ann. § 65-445 (1985); Md. Pub. Health Code Ann. § 20-208(c) (1990); N.M. Stat. Ann. § 24-14-18 (1991); N.Y. Pub. Health Law § 4164(3) (McKinney 1985); N.D. Cent. Code § 14-02.1-07 (1991); 18 Pa. Cons. Stat. Ann. § 3214(e)–(f) (Purdon Supp. 1991 & 1992); Utah Code Ann. § 26-2-23(3) (1990); Va. Code § 32.1-264 (1982).

[413] *E.g.,* Cal. Health & Safety Code §§ 429.50(3), 25955.5 (West 1984); Ill. Ann. Stat. ch. 38, § 81-30 (Smith-Hurd Supp. 1991 & 1992); Ind. Code Ann. § 35-1-58.5-3 (Burns 1985); Mass. Gen. Law. Ann. ch. 112, § 12R (West 1983); Mich. Comp. Laws Ann. § 333.2835 (West 1980); Mo. Ann. Stat. § 188.052 (Vernon 1983); Neb. Rev. Stat. § 28-343 (1989); 18 Pa. Cons. Stat. Ann. § 3214(a) (Purdon 1983 & Supp. 1991 & 1992); P.R. Laws. Ann. tit. 24, § 232 (1979); S.D. Codified Laws Ann. § 34-23A-19 (1986); Tenn. Code Ann. § 39-15-201(c)(3) (1991); Utah Code Ann. § 76-7-313 (1990).

In Planned parenthood of Southeastern Pennsylvania v. Casey, 947 F.2d 682, 715–17 (3d Cir.), *cert. granted,* 112 S. Ct. 931 (1991), the court sustained the constitutionality of the reporting requirements of the Pennsylvania statute.

[414] *E.g.,* Cal. Health & Safety Code § 25955.5 (West 1984); Ky. Rev. Stat. § 211.027 (1991); Me. Rev. Stat. Ann. tit. 22, § 1596(2) (1992); Minn. Stat. Ann. § 145.413 (West 1989); Mont. Code Ann. § 50-20-106(2) (1991); Nev. Rev. Stat. § 442.260(2) (1991); Ohio Rev. Code Ann. § 3701.341(2) (Page 1992) (public health council to adopt rules relating to abortion reporting forms); Okla. Stat. Ann. tit. 63, § 1-738 (West 1984); P.R. Laws Ann. tit. 24, § 234 (1979); S.C. Code Ann. § 44-41-60 (Law. Co-op. 1988); Wyo. Stat. § 35-6-107 (Supp. 1991).

[415] Planned Parenthood v. Danforth, 428 U.S. at 80: Reporting and record-keeping requirements are constitutional as long as they "properly respect a patient's confidentiality and privacy." Despite the latter reservation, some courts have held that the names of patients and physicians reported to government offices become public records accessible under freedom of information laws. *See, e.g.,* State *ex rel.* Stephan v. Harder, 230 Kan. 573, 641 P.2d 366 (1982); Minnesota Medical Ass'n v. State, 274 N.W.2d 84 (Minn. 1978). In Planned Parenthood of Southeastern Pennsylvania v. Casey, 947 F.2d 682, 717–19 (3d Cir.), *cert. granted,* 112 S. Ct. 931 (1991), the court sustained the constitutionality of the reporting requirements of the Pennsylvania statute, 18 Pa. Cons. Stat. Ann. § 3207(b) (Purdon Supp. 1991), in the face of an objection that the reports were public records that, because of their availability, might discourage women from seeking abortions. *Cf.* Schulman v. New York City Health & Hosps. Corp., 38 N.Y.2d 234, 342 N.E.2d 501, 379 N.Y.S.2d 702 (1975) (reporting requirement sustained in absence of indications that identification information was leaked or made available to other governmental agencies for illegitimate purposes). If harassing use is made of information obtained by members of the public, release would appear to infringe through public action the privacy rights of patients and their physicians in the exercise of federal constitutional rights.

[416] *E.g.,* Cal. Health & Safety Code § 25955.5 (West 1984); Del. Code Ann. tit. 24, § 1790(c) (1987); Ga. Code Ann. § 16-12-141(d) (1988); Kan. Stat. Ann. § 65-445 (1985); Me. Rev. Stat. Ann. tit. 22, § 1596(2) (1980); Md. Pub. Health Code Ann. § 20-208(c) (1990); Mich. Comp. Laws Ann. § 333.2835 (West

requirements while the latter have laypersons as their targets. In addition, participation in criminal abortions is usually a basis for professional discipline.[423] Wrongful death liability also may be confirmed specifically in abortion legislation.[424]

17. CONSCIENCE EXCEPTION   The legalization of medically indicated abortions, which had begun to emerge before 1973 in some states, necessitated protective legislation for institutions and medical professionals whose religious, ethical or moral beliefs foreclosed their participation in abortion practice.[425] These statutes are nearly universal today. A number of states allow all hospitals,[426] including publicly-operated facilities,[427] to refuse to allow abortions or admit patients for the purpose of abortion. There is no constitutional infirmity in granting a conscience exception to public facilities.[428] A few states, however, limit the conscience exemption to private or religious institutions.[429] Hospitals cannot be held civilly liable[430] or denied public subsidies[431] because of refusals to allow abortions, although they may be required to notify patients beforehand of their policies.[432]

1980); Minn. Stat. Ann. § 145.413 (West 1989); Mo. Ann. Stat. §§ 188.055(2), 188.070 (Vernon 1983); Neb. Rev. Stat. § 28-343(10) (1989); N.M. Stat. Ann. § 24-14-18(B) (1991); N.C. Gen. Stat. § 90-14(2) (1990); N.D. Cent. Code § 14-02.1-07(2)(a) (1991); 18 Pa. Cons. Stat. Ann. § 3214(a) (Purdon 1991 & 1992) (patient identification); S.C. Code Ann. § 44-41-60 (Law. Co-op. Supp. 1991); S.D. Codified Laws Ann. § 34-23A-19 (1986); Tenn. Code Ann. § 68-3-505 (1987) (but some means of identification must be used in case further information is needed); Utah Code Ann. § 76-7-313 (1990); Wyo. Stat. § 35-6-108 (Supp. 1991).

On the interpretation of a confidentiality requirement, see Bell v. Elco Corp., 137 Misc. 2d 502, 521 N.Y.S.2d 368 (Sup. Ct. 1987) (an explanation of benefits report transmitted to the patient's estranged husband, and stating only "maternity" services, did not identify that abortion had been performed).

[417] E.g., Neb. Rev. Stat. § 28-343 (1989); N.M. Stat. Ann. § 24-14-18(B) (1991). See, however, the decisions cited supra at note 415.

[418] E.g., Ga. Code Ann. § 16-12-141(d) (West 1988) (shall be available to district attorney of circuit in which hospital or health facility is located); Ill. Ann. Stat. ch. 38, § 81-30 (Smith-Hurd Supp. 1991 & 1992); Neb. Rev. Stat. § 28-343(10) (1985); P.R. Laws Ann. tit. 24, § 233 (1979) (except as furnished to judges, prosecutors or police or peace officers for proper action).

[419] E.g., Ill. Ann. Stat. ch. 38, § 81-30.1 (Smith-Hurd Supp. 1991 & 1992); Minn. Stat. Ann. § 145.413(2) (West 1989); Nev. Rev. Stat. § 422.265 (1991); 18 Pa. Cons. Stat. Ann. § 3214(g)–(h) (Purdon 1983 & Supp. 1991).

[420] Planned Parenthood v. Danforth, 438 U.S. at 79–81.

[421] E.g., Alaska Stat. § 18.16.010(b) (1991); Ill. Ann. Stat. ch. 38, § 81-31 (Smith-Hurd Supp. 1991 & 1992); Me. Rev. Stat. Ann. tit. 22, § 1598(4) (1992); Mass. Gen. Laws Ann. ch. 112, § 12N (West 1983); Minn. Stat. Ann. § 145.412(4) (West 1989); Nev. Rev. Stat. § 442.257 (1991); N.D. Cent. Code § 14-02.1-04(4) (1991); S.D. Codified Laws Ann. § 22-17-5 (1988); Tenn. Code Ann. § 39-15-201(b) (1991); Utah Code Ann. § 76-7-314 (1990); Wash. Rev. Code Ann. § 9.02.070 (Repealed); Wyo. Stat. § 35-6-110 (1988).

[422] See infra, notes 452–59 and accompanying text.

[423] E.g., Ill. Ann. Stat. ch. 38, § 81-31 (Smith-Hurd Supp. 1992); Kan. Stat. Ann. § 65-2912(2) (Supp. 1990); La. Rev. Stat. Ann. § 37:1285(8)–(9) (West 1988); Me. Rev. Stat. Ann. tit. 32, § 3285(5)(A) (1980); Md. Pub. Health Code Ann. § 14-504(24) (1990); Minn. Stat. Ann. §§ 147.021(h), 147.101 (West 1989); Miss. Code Ann. § 73-25-29(5) (rev. 1989); Mo. Ann. Stat. § 188.065 (Vernon 1983); Neb. Rev. Stat. § 71-148(6) (1991); Nev. Rev. Stat. §§ 630.306(4) (physician), 632.320(6)(b) (nurse); 633A.100(1)(i) (naturopath) (1991); N.M. Stat. Ann. §§ 61-10A-5(A) (osteopathic physician's assistant) (1989), 61-6-14(B)(1) (medicine and surgery) (1984); N.C. Gen. Stat. § 90-14(2) (1990); Okla. Stat. Ann. tit. 59, § 509(1) (West 1984); 18 Pa. Cons. Stat. Ann. § 3219 (Purdon Supp. 1991 & 1992); R.I. Gen. Laws § 23-4.7-7 (1989) (failure to obtain consents is unprofessional conduct); S.D. Codified Laws Ann. §36-4-30(1) (1986); Tenn. Code Ann. §§ 63-6-214(6) (medicine and surgery), 63-9-111(6) (Supp. 1991) (osteopathic physicians); Tex. Rev. Civ. Stat. Ann. art. 4495b, § 3.08(14) (Vernon Supp. 1992); Utah Code Ann.

The private right of conscience is usually delineated in terms of religious, moral, ethical or professional scruples[433] but may be left unrestricted.[434] Most frequently, conscientious objectors are required to file a written statement of objection.[435] In some jurisdictions that burden is not specifically imposed.[436]

Laws may be drafted simply to allow the conscience exception to any person[437] or may designate physicians,[438] nurses[439] or other hospital, clinical or medical office personnel.[440] Those who invoke their personal conscience rights cannot be held criminally[441] or civilly[442] liable or subjected to administrative penalties[443] or to disciplinary[444] or recriminatory[445] action. Statutes also proscribe discrimination against those relying on their statutory rights,[446] particularly in connection with employment[447] or educational[448] opportunities.

On occasion, sanctions are supplied for violations of the conscience exception in the form of criminal penalties[449] and civil injunctive[450] and damage[451] remedies.

---

§§ 58-12-36(1) (medicine), 58-12-7(1) (osteopathy) (1990); Wash. Rev. Code Ann. §§ 18.36.140(1) (drugless healer), 18.50.100 (midwifery), 18.57.170(1) (osteopathy), 18.72.030(2) (physician) (1988).

If abortion is not specified, convicted abortionists can be disciplined on the basis of their criminal record. *See, e.g.,* Mich. Comp. Laws. Ann. § 333.16221(b)(v) (West 1980); N.H. Rev. Stat. Ann. § 329:17(VI)(d), (j) (1984); Vt. Stat. Ann. tit. 26, § 1354(3) (1990). On constitutional requirements of administrative due process governing professional discipline, see Withrow v. Larkin, 421 U.S. 35 (1975).

[424] This usually is aimed at failure to preserve the lives of live-born fetuses. *See, e.g.,* Ill. Ann. Stat. ch. 70, § 2.2 (Smith-Hurd 1989); Ind. Code Ann. § 35-1-58.5-7(c) (Burns 1985); Me. Rev. Stat. Ann. tit. 22, § 1594 (1992); Nev. Rev. Stat. § 442.270(2) (1991); Tenn. Code Ann. § 39-15-206(c) (1991); Utah Code Ann. § 78-11-24 (1992).

On the traditional refusal to consider a fetus a human being with a consonant right to sue for prenatal injuries persevering after live birth, *see* Roe v. Wade, 410 U.S. at 161–62. *Cf.* Mont. Code Ann. § 41-1-103 (1991) (''a child conceived but not yet born is to be deemed an existing person, so far as may be necessary for its interests in the event of its subsequent birth''). Precedent conflicts as to whether a wrongful death action may be maintained for injuries after viability that result in a stillbirth, although a majority of jurisdictions appear to allow such litigation. *See, e.g.,* Shirley v. Bacon, 154 Ga. App. 203, 267 S.E.2d 809 (1980); Chrisafogeorgis v. Brandenberg, 55 Ill. 2d 368, 304 N.E.2d 88 (1973); O'Neill v. Morse, 385 Mich. 130, 188 N.W.2d 785 (1971); Ryan v. Beth Israel Hosp., 96 Misc. 2d 816, 409 N.Y.S.2d 681 (N.Y. Sup. Ct. 1978) (guardian ad litem not allowed to maintain action that was an effort to attack a lawful abortion); Libbee v. Permanente Clinic, 268 Or. 258, 518 P.2d 636 (1974) (summarizing authorities to date of opinion). If the fetus is not viable, such an action appears not to be allowed. *See, e.g.,* Group Health Ass'n v. Blumenthal, 295 Md. 104, 453 A.2d 1198 (1983); Weiler & Catton, *supra* note 174, at 651–55; Special Project, *supra* note 31, at 152–55.

A now-repealed statute allowing the parents of a fetus aborted in noncompliance with abortion statutes to maintain a wrongful death action against a physician who performed the abortion was held unconstitutional as an unacceptable burden on the woman's and physician's abortion decision. Doe v. Rampton, 366 F. Supp. 189, 193 (D. Utah 1973) (three-judge court).

Courts generally rule out homicide criminality based on acts causing stillbirths. *See, eg.,* People v. Greer, 79 Ill. 2d 103, 402 N.E.2d 203 (1980); Hollis v. Commonwealth, 652 S.W.2d 61 (Ky. 1983); State v. Brown, 378 So. 2d 916 (La. 1979); People v. Guthrie, 97 Mich App. 226, 293 N.W.2d 775 (1980), *appeal denied,* 417 Mich. 1006, 334 N.W.2d 616 (1983); State v. Amaro, 448 A.2d 1257 (R.I. 1982). The same result is decreed if a crime of assault is charged based on injury to a fetus in a woman's uterus. Love v. State, 450 S. 2d 1191 (Fla. Dist. Ct. App. 1984) (prosecution charged ''aggravated assault of fetus''; court ruled that ''person'' in statute does not include a fetus). If a fetus is born alive and then dies, however, a contrary conclusion is appropriate. *See, e.g.,* People v. Bolar, 109 Ill. App. 3d 384, 440 N.E.2d 639 (1982) (defendant properly convicted of reckless homicide as drunken driver of car that struck car in which pregnant woman was riding, necessitating a caesarean section).

Because of the legitimacy of contraception and abortion, some parents have sued because bungled techniques have resulted in the birth of defective children. *See, e.g.,* Robak v. United States, 658 F.2d 471 (7th Cir. 1981) (rejecting argument that, because case facts arose in 1972 before *Roe v. Wade,* an abortion

C. Criminal Statutory Provisions Affecting Abortions

1. GENERAL PRINCIPLES   In the immediate aftermath of *Roe v. Wade,* a few states voided their abortion legislation entirely, eliminating criminality for non-physician abortionists as well as for medical practitioners performing therapeutic abortions.[452] This was judicial overkill. In *Connecticut v. Menillo,*[453] the Court confirmed that its 1973 *Roe* and *Doe* decisions were not intended to provide a constitutional exemption from criminal law coverage for nonphysician abortionists.[454] State decisions are now uniform in recognizing the governmental power to prosecute nonphysician abortionists.[455] This power extends as well to physicians who violate constitutionally acceptable regulations of therapeutic abortions.[456]

When prosecutions of the latter sort are initiated, however, federal constitutional principles require that the underlying legislation be sufficiently precise to give warning of the prohibited and acceptable activities. If the statute is vague and indefinite, it will be invalidated.[457] Beyond that, consistent with the Court's general approach to strict

---

would have been unavailable to a mother suffering rubella and the government should not be liable under the federal Tort Claims Act); Morris v. Frudenfeld, 135 Cal. App. 3d 23, 185 Cal. Rptr. 76 (1982); Fulton-Dekalb Hosp. Author. v. Graves, 252 Ga. 441, 314 S.E.2d 653 (1984); Jones v. Malinowski, 299 Md. 257, 473 A.2d 429 (1984) (court not required to instruct jury that woman could have had an abortion); Schroeder v. Perkel, 87 N.J. 53, 432 A.2d 834 (1981) (pediatricians treated first child for four years without diagnosing cystic fibrosis until mother was eight months pregnant with second child); Delaney v. Krafte, 98 A.D.2d 128, 470 N.Y.S.2d 936 (1984) (plaintiff not required to mitigate damages by undergoing later abortion); Speck v. Finegold, 497 Pa. 77, 439 A.2d 110 (1981); Certification *re* Harbeson v. Harbeson, 98 Wash. 2d 460, 656 P.2d 483 (1983). However, recoveries do not extend to the costs of rearing a healthy child to maturity. *See, e.g.,* Flowers v. District of Columbia, 478 A.2d 1073 (D.C. 1984) (bungled sterilization); Morse v. Soffer, 101 A.D.2d 856, 476 N.Y.S.2d 170 (1984) (defective abortion); Delaney v. Krafte, 98 A.D.2d 128, 470 N.Y.S.2d 936 (1984) (defective abortion); McKernan v. Aasheim, 102 Wash. 2d 411, 687 P.2d 850 (1884) (defective abortion); McKernan v. Aasheim, 102 Wash. 2d 411, 687 P.2d 850 (1984) (defective sterilzation).

See generally Parness & Pritchard, *supra* note 116, at 257, 270–75; Stoutamire, *Effect of Legalized Abortion on Wrongful Life Actions,* 9 Fla. St. U.L. Rev. 137 (1981); Warren, *supra* note 21, at 51–55; Weiler & Catton, *supra* note 174, at 651–55; Note, *Genetic Screening, Eugenic Abortion, and Roe v. Wade: How Viable Is Roe's Viability Standard?,* 50 Brooklyn L. Rev. 113, 137–41 (1983); Note, *Wrongful Birth in the Abortion Context—A Critique of Existing Case Law and a Proposal for Future Actions,* 53 Den. L.J. 501 (1976); Comment, *Wrongful Life: Birth Control Spawns a Tort,* 13 J. Mar. L. Rev. 401 (1980).

Utah Code Ann. § 78-11-25 (1992) states that a failure or refusal to prevent a live birth is not a defense in any action and is not to be considered in awarding damages or child support or in imposing a penalty in any action. Speck v. Finegold, 497 Pa. 77, 439 A.2d 110 (1981), disallowed a so-called wrongful life action, but there is contrary authority. *See, e.g.,* Procanik v. Cillo, 97 N.J. 339, 478 A.2d 755 (1984) (doctor failed to detect rubella in mother and to advise her to undergo an abortion; damages affirmed for extraordinary medical expenses); Rivera v. State, 94 Misc. 2d 157, 404 N.Y.S.2d 950 (Ct. Cl. 1978); Certification *re* Harbeso v. Parke-Davis, Inc., 98 Wash. 2d 460, 656 P.2d 483 (1983) (citing authorities). *See generally* Parness & Pritchard, *supra* note 116, at 275–81; Warren, *supra* note 21, at 55–57 (wrongful life).

Precedent allowing wrongful death actions based on the deaths of women resulting from improperly performed abortions, observable before 1973, Wolcott v. Gaines, 225 Ga. 373, 169 S.E.2d 165 (1969); Martin v. Hardesty, 91 Ind. App. 239, 163 N.E. 610 (1928); True v. Older, 227 Minn 154, 34 N.W.2d 700 (1948); Milliken v. Heddesheimer, 110 Ohio St. 381, 144 N.E. 264 (1924); Andrews v. Coulter, 163 Wash. 429, 1 P.2d 320 (1931) (only for negligent aftercare, not an abortion itself), clearly remains valid today, although the availability of therapeutic abortions and the low risk rate for previability abortions has caused such litigation to drop from sight.

On malpractice liability in abortion cases before *Roe v. Wade,* see Richey v. Darling, 183 Kan. 642, 331 P.2d 281 (1958); Lembo v. Donnell, 117 Me. 143, 103 A. 11 (1918); Henrie v. Griffith, 395 P.2d

liability criminal legislation,[458] abortion statutes imposing felony or serious misdemeanor penalties must include a scienter (intent or knowledge) component, or they will be invalidated.[459] There is no constitutional barrier to a statutory requirement that proof of a medical justification be advanced by a physician defendant as an affirmative defense.[460]

2. PERSONS COVERED   As noted above, criminal statutes can only be invoked constitutionally against nonphysicians in general or against physicians who depart from acceptable medical practices.[461] This is express in some statutes;[462] if not, courts must apply this meaning to the general term "any person" if constitutional problems are to be avoided.[463]

3. ACTUS REUS   The objective acts embodied in traditional abortion legislation, still in force in some jurisdictions, are administering drugs or substances[464] or using instruments or other means[465] to terminate pregnancy. A majority of states, particularly those that have modernized their criminal legislation, require that the woman be preg-

---

809 (Okla. 1964). After 1973 there has been no basis to treat abortion-related medical malpractice actions differently from all other such actions, at least if the abortion was lawful. *See, e.g.,* Salinetro v. Nystrom, 341 So. 2d 1059 (Fla. Dist. Ct. App. 1977) (no negligence in x-raying pregnant accident victim who did not know she was pregnant; pathologist report after abortion showed fetus already dead); Byrne v. Pilgrim Medical Group, Inc., 187 N.J. Super. 386, 454 A.2d 920 (1982) (husband allowed wages lost in caring for wife, to amount that would have been necessary to pay professional attendant); S.R. v. City of Fairmont, 280 S.E.2d 712 (W. Va. 1981) (state long-arm statute gave plaintiff ability to sue Pennsylvania facility for failure to provide proper care following lawful abortion there). *Compare* Reno v. D'Javid, 55 A.D.2d 876, 390 N.Y.S.2d 421, *aff'd,* 42 N.Y.2d 1040, 369 N.E.2d 766, 399 N.Y.S.2d 210 (1977) (no malpractice action is allowed arising from unlawful abortion that woman solicited, on principle that she could not profit from an illegal act in which she had participated).

[425] *See supra,* notes 109–10 and accompanying text; Isaacs, *supra* note 121, at 77–78; Warren, *supra* note 21, at 34–38. On the recognition of the conscience exception under the English Abortion Act, 1967, § 4, see Royal College of Nursing v. Dep't of Health & Social Security, [1981] A.C. 800 (H.L.).

[426] *E.g.,* Alaska Stat. § 18.16.010(a) (1991); Ariz. Rev. Stat. Ann. § 36-2151 (1986); Ark. Code Ann. § 20-16-601 (1991); Colo. Rev. Stat. § 18-6-104 (1986); Del. Code Ann. tit. 24, § 1791(b) (1987); Fla. Stat. Ann. § 390.001(8) (West 1986); Ga. Code Ann. § 16-12-142 (1988); Idaho Code § 18-612 (1987); Ill. Ann. Stat. ch. 111½, § 87-9 (Smith-Hurd 1988); Ind. Code Ann. § 16-10-1.5-8 (Burns 1990); Kan. Stat. Ann. § 65-444 (1985); Me. Rev. Stat. Ann. tit. 22, § 1591 (1992); Md. Pub. Health Code Ann. § 20-214(b) (Supp. 1991) (subject to referendum on amendment); Mass. Gen. Laws Ann. ch. 112, § 12*l* (West 1983), ch. 272, § 21B (West 1990) (private hospitals and facilities); Minn. Stat. Ann. §§ 145.414, 62D.20 (West 1989 & Supp. 1992) (health maintenance organizations); Neb. Rev. Stat. § 28-337 (1989); N.J. Stat. Ann. § 2A:65A-2 (West 1987); N.M. Stat. Ann. § 30-5-2 (1984); N.C. Gen. Stat. § 14-45.1(f) (1986); N.D. Cen. Code § 23-16-14 (1991); Tenn. Code Ann. §§ 39-15-204, 39-15-205 (1991); Va. Code § 18.2-75 (1988); Wash. Rev. Code Ann. § 9.02.080 (Repealed); Wis. Stat. Ann. § 140.42(1) (West 1988).

[427] *E.g.,* Ky. Rev. Stat. § 311.800(1) (public), (3) (religious or private) (1990); Mo. Ann. Stat. § 197.032 (public or private) (Vernon 1983); Ohio Rev. Code Ann. § 4731.91 (public or private) (Page Supp. 1991).

[428] Poelker v. Doe, 434 U.S. 880 (1977) (public hospitals may refuse to allow therapeutic abortions even though they subsidize childbirths).

[429] *E.g.,* Cal. Health & Safety Code § 25955(c) (West Supp. 1992) (religious or nonprofit); Mont. Code Ann. § 50-20-111(1) (1991) (private hospital or health care facility); Okla. Stat. Ann. tit. 63, § 1-741(A) (West 1984); S.C. Code Ann. § 44-41-40 (Law. Co-op. 1988) (private or nongovernmental hospital or clinic); S.D. Codified Laws Ann. §§ 34-23A-14, 34-23A-15 (1986) (public hospitals cannot adopt policy excluding or denying admissions for abortions); Tex. Rev. Civ. Stat. Ann. art 4512.7, § 2 (Vernon Supp. 1992) (private hospitals); Utah Code Ann. § 76-7-306(2) (1990) (private or denominational hospital not required to admit patients for abortions); Wyo. Stat. § 35-6-105 (1988) (private institutions).

Doe v. Bridgeton Hosp. Ass'n, 71 N.J. 478, 366 A.2d 641 (1976), *cert. denied,* 433 U.S. 914 (1977), interpreted state law to prohibit private, nonprofit, nonsectarian hospitals from closing their facilities to

nant,[466] although a minority do not include that specific requirement.[467] If pregnancy is required but the particular woman in fact was not pregnant, general attempt provisions in contemporary codes will cover the activity because traditional doctrines of impossibility have been abrogated.[468] However, statutes based on activities with intent to produce a miscarriage function as a crystallized application of attempt law;[469] at times, attempted abortion is covered specifically.[470]

Some statutes continue to embody distinctions based on the stage of a pregnancy in terms of time[471] or viability.[472] These cannot be invoked against physicians practicing within the constitutional bounds established by the Supreme Court. They are, however, appropriately applied to laypersons as a means of grading punishments. The further into the pregnancies that illicit abortions are performed, the greater the danger to maternal life and health and the greater the justification for augmented penalties. If, however, the statutes restrict the coverage of criminal abortion legislation as applied to nonphysicians, they are unwise because there should be no lawful scope for such abortions.[473]

---

first-trimester abortions. *See also* the case on remand, 160 N.J. Super. 266, 389 A.2d 526 (1978) (state decision unaffected by United States Supreme Court decisions in *Maher, Beal* and *Poelker* [discussed *infra* notes 503–10 and accompanying text]).

The European Court of Justice has recognized that medical facilities in one member state can refuse abortions for visiting workers, authorized by another member state, if abortion is prohibited in the competent institution's own nation. Bestuur van het Algemeen Ziekenfonds Drenthe-Platteland v. G. Pierele (Case 182/78), [1979] E.C.R. 1977, 1990.

[430] *E.g.,* Alaska Stat. § 18.16.010(a) (1991); Ark. Code Ann. § 20-16-601 (1991); Cal. Health & Safety Code § 25955(a) (West Supp. 1992); Colo. Rev. Stat. § 18-6-104 (1986); Del. Code Ann. tit. 24, § 1791(b) (1987); Ga. Code Ann. § 16-12-142 (1988); Idaho Code § 18-612 (1987); Ill. Ann. Stat. ch. 38, § 81-33 (Smith-Hurd Supp. 1991 & 1992); Kan. Stat. Ann. § 65-443 (1985); Ky. Rev. Stat. § 311.800(5)(a) (1990); Me. Rev. Stat. Ann. tit. 22, § 1591 (1992); Md. Pub. Health Code Ann. § 20-214(b)(2)(i) (Supp. 1991) (subject to referendum on amendment); Mass. Gen. Laws Ann. ch. 112, § 12I (West 1983); Minn. Stat. Ann. § 145.414 (West 1989); Mo. Ann. Stat. § 197.032(1) (Vernon 1983); Mont. Code Ann. § 50-20-111(1) (1991); Neb. Rev. Stat. § 28-337 (1989); N.J. Stat. Ann. § 2A:65A-3 (West 1987); N.Y. Civ. Rights Law § 79i (McKinney 1976); Ohio Rev. Code Ann. § 4731.91(d) (Page Supp. 1990); Okla Stat. Ann. tit. 63, § 1-741(A) (West 1984); 18 Pa. Cons. Stat. Ann. § 3213(d) (Purdon 1983); R.I. Gen. Laws § 23-17-11 (1989); S.C. Code Ann. § 44-41-40 (Law. Co-op. 1988); S.D. Codified Laws Ann. § 34-23A-14 (1986); Utah Code Ann. § 76-7-306(1) (1990); Va. Code § 18.2-75 (1988); Wis. Stat. Ann. § 140.42(2) (West 1989); Wyo. Stat. § 35-6-105 (1988).

Several jurisdictions reject invocation of the hospital conscience exemption in cases of emergency. *See, e.g.,* Cal. Health & Safety Code § 25955(d) (West Supp. 1992) (or in instances of spontaneous abortion); Fla. Stat. Ann. § 390.001(9) (West 1986) (inapplicable to induced labor); S.C. Code Ann. § 44-41-40 (Law. Co-op 1988) (emergency admittance).

[431] *E.g.,* Mont. Code Ann. § 50-20-111(4) (1991); 18 Pa. Cons. Stat. Ann. § 3213(d) (Purdon 1983).

[432] *E.g.,* Ill. Ann. Stat. ch. 38, § 81-33 (Smith-Hurd Supp. 1991 & 1992); Neb. Rev. Stat. § 28-337 (1989); Or. Rev. Stat. § 435.485(1) (1991) (physician to advise patient); Wyo. Stat. § 35-6-105 (1988).

[433] *E.g.,* Ariz. Rev. Stat. Ann. § 36-2151 (1986); Cal. Health & Safety Code § 25955(a) (West Supp. 1992); Colo. Rev. Stat. § 18-6-104 (1986); Fla. Stat. Ann. § 390.001(8) (West 1986); Ga. Code Ann. § 16-12-142 (1988); Idaho Code § 18-612 (1987); Ind. Code Ann. § 16-10-3-2 (Burns 1990); Ky. Rev. Stat. § 311.800(4) (1990); Mo. Ann. Stat. § 197.032 (Vernon 1983); Mont. Code Ann. § 50-20-111(2) (1991); Nev. Rev. Stat. § 632.475(1) (1991); N.M. Stat. Ann. § 30-5-2 (1984); N.Y. Civ. Rights Law § 79i (McKinney 1976); N.C. Gen. Stat. § 14-45.1(e) (1986); 18 Pa. Cons. Stat. Ann § 3203 (Purdon 1983); R.I. Gen. Laws § 23-17-11 (1989); Utah Code Ann. § 76-7-306(1) (1990); Va. Code § 18.2-75 (1988); Wis. Stat. Ann. § 140.42(1) (West 1989).

[434] *E.g.,* Alaska Stat. § 18.16.00 (1991); Ill. Ann. Stat. ch. 38 § 81-33 (Smith-Hurd Supp. (1991 & 1992) ("conscience"); Kan. Stat. Ann. § 65-443 (1985); Me. Rev. Stat. Ann. tit. 11, § 1591 (1980); Md. Pub. Health Code Ann. § 20-214(a) (Supp. 1991) (subject to referendum on amendment); Minn. Stat. Ann.

4. SCIENTER Traditional statues are clear that abortions must be done with intent to produce an abortion or miscarriage. Thus, they create no constitutional infirmities as far as scienter requirements are concerned. That appears to be a problem exclusively generated by recent therapeutic abortion statutes supported by residual criminal penalty provisions.[474]

5. WEIGHT The overwhelming majority of abortion statutes carry felony-level punishment,[475] with few offenses punishable as misdemeanors.[476] It is possible that this field of penal law will prove susceptible to restriction under the eighth amendment prohibition against disproportionate punishments.[477]

6. CRIMINALITY BASED ON NEONATAL DEATH Statutory provisions governing care of neonates and fetuses during abortion and birth processes have been noted.[478] Specific criminal penalties usually are set forth governing what in most instances is a form of medical malpractice.[479] The chief deficiencies observable in some of these statutes are the lack of a clear scienter requirement, vagueness problems in statements of the standard of duty[480] and disproportionality of punishments.

---

§ 145.42 (West 1989); Neb. Rev. Stat. § 28-338 (1989); N.J. Stat. Ann. § 2A:65A-1 (West 1985); N.D. Cent. Code § 23-16-14 (1991); Ohio Rev. Code Ann. § 4731.91 (Page Supp. 1991); Okla. Stat. Ann. tit. 63, § 1-741(B) (West 1984); Or. Rev. Stat. § 435.485(1) (1991); S.C. Code Ann. § 44-51-50(a) (Law. Co-op. 1988); S.D. Codified Laws Ann. § 34-23A-13 (1986); Tenn. Code Ann. § 39-15-204 (1991); Tex. Rev. Civ. Stat. Ann. art. 4512.7 § 1 (Vernon Supp. 1992); Wash. Rev. Code Ann. § 9.02.080 (Repealed); Wyo. Stat. § 35-6-106 (1988).

The conscience exemption may not be invoked in emergency situations. *See, e.g.,* Fla. Stat. An. § 390.001(9) (West 1986) (induced labor); Iowa Code Ann. § 146.1 (West 1989); Nev. Rev. Stat. § 632.475(3) (1991); Okla. Stat. Ann. tit. 63, § 1-741(C) (West 1984).

[435] *E.g.,* Ariz. Rev. Stat. Ann. § 36-2151 (1986); Cal. Health & Safety Code § 25955(a) (West Supp. 1992); Colo. Rev. Stat. § 18-6-104 (1986); Ga. Code Ann. § 16-12-142 (1988); Idaho Code § 18-612 (1987); Ill. Ann. Stat. ch. 38, § 81-33 (Smith-Hurd Supp. 1992); Ky. Rev. Stat. § 311.800(5) (1990); Mass. Gen. Laws Ann. ch. 112, § 121 (West Supp. 1991); Nev. Rev. Stat. § 632.475 (1991); N.Y. Civ. Rights Law § 79i (McKinney 1976); 18 Pa. Cons. Stat. Ann. § 3213(d) (Purdon 1983); S.C. Code Ann. § 44-41-50(a) (Law. Co-op. 1988); Va. Code § 18.2-75 (1988); Wis. Stat. Ann. § 140.42(1) (West 1989).

[436] *E.g.,* Fla. Stat. Ann. § 390.001(8) (West 1986); Ind. Code Ann. § 16-10-3-2 (Burns 1990); Iowa Code Ann. § 146.1 (West 1989); Minn. Stat. Ann. § 145.42 (West 1989); N.M. Stat. Ann. § 30-5-2 (1984); N.D. Cent. Code § 23-16-14 (1991); Or. Rev. Stat. § 435.485 (1986); Utah Code Ann. § 76-7-306 (1990).

[437] *E.g.,* Ark. Code Ann. § 20-16-601 (1991); Colo. Rev. Stat. § 18-6-104 (1986); Del. Code Ann. tit. 24, § 1791(a) (1987); Fla. Stat. Ann. § 390.001(8) (West 1986); Ga. Code Ann. § 16-12-142 (1988); Iowa Code Ann. § 146.1 (West 1989); Kan. Stat. Ann. § 65-443 (1985); Md. Pub. Health Code Ann. § 20-214(a)(2) (Supp. 1991) (subject to referendum on amendment); Minn. Stat. Ann. § 145.42 (West 1989); Neb. Rev. Stat. § 28-338 (1989); N.J. Stat. Ann. § 2A:65A-1 (West 1987); N.Y. Civ. Rights Law § 79i(1) (McKinney 1976); Okla. Stat. Ann. tit. 63, § 1-741(B) (West 1984); Va. Code § 18.2-75 (1988); Wyo. Stat. § 35-6-106 (1988).

[438] *E.g.,* Cal. Health & Safety Code § 25955(a) (West Supp. 1992); Fla. Stat. Ann. § 390.001(8) (West 1986); Idaho Code § 16-612 (1987); Ill. Ann. Stat. ch. 38, § 81-33 (Smith-Hurd Supp. 1992); Ind. Code Ann. § 16-10-3-2 (Burns 1990); Ky. Rev. Stat. § 311.800(5)(b) (1990); Me. Rev. Stat. Ann. tit. 22, § 1591 (1992); Mass. Gen. Laws Ann. ch. 112, § 12*l* (West 1983); Minn. Stat. Ann. § 145.42 (West 1989); Mo. Ann. Stat. § 197.032(1) (Vernon 1983); N.C. Gen. Stat. § 14-45.1(e) (1986); N.D. Cent. Code § 23-16-14 (1991); Or. Rev. Stat. § 435.485(1) (1991); 18 Pa. Cons. Stat. Ann. § 3213(d) (Purdon 1983); R.I. Gen. Laws § 23-17-11 (1989); S.C. Code Ann. § 44-41-50 (Law. Co-op. 1988); S.D. Codified Laws Ann. § 34-23A-12 (1986); Tenn. Code Ann. § 39-15-204 (1991); Tex. Rev. Civ. Stat. Ann. art. 4512.7, § 1 (Vernon Supp. 1992); Utah Code Ann. § 76-7-306 (1990); Wash. Rev. Code Ann. § 9.02.080 (Repealed); Wis. Stat. Ann. § 140.42(1) (West 1989).

[439] *E.g.,* Cal. Health & Safety Code § 25955(a) (West Supp. 1992); Idaho Code § 16-612 (1987); Ky. Rev. Stat. § 311.800(5)(b) (1990); Me. Rev. Stat. Ann. tit. 22, § 1591 (1992); Minn. Stat. Ann. § 145.42 (West 1989); Mo. Ann. Stat. § 197.032(1) (Vernon 1983); Nev. Rev. Stat. § 632.475 (1991); N.C. Gen. Stat.

7. CRIMINALITY BASED ON MATERNAL DEATH   There is no need for special legislation governing the death of a woman in the course of an unlawful abortion or manifesting criminal negligence in the setting of therapeutic abortion.[481] Nevertheless, several states specially address that form of homicide.[482]

8. LIABILITY FOR SEEKING CRIMINAL ABORTION   Some jurisdictions penalized women before 1973 for seeking abortions.[483] Some continue such penal law coverage as far as nontherapeutic abortions are concerned.[484] Perpetuation of that form of criminality, however, is as unwise today as it was before 1973, because of the difficulties it creates in criminal justice administration.[485]

9. ADVERTISING ABORTIFACIENTS   Criminal statutes penalizing the advertising of abortions and abortifacients have been evident for generations.[486] A number of such provisions continue to exist in unmodified form.[487] They are unconstitutional because they do not exempt dissemination of information about lawful therapeutic abortions that constitutes a form of commercial speech protected by the first amendment.[488] Therefore,

---

§ 14-45.1(e) (1986); N.D. Cent. Code § 23-16-14 (1991); 18 Pa. Cons. Stat. Ann. § 3213(d) (Purdon 1983); S.C. Code Ann. § 44-41-50 (Law. Co-op. 1988); S.D. Codified Laws Ann. § 34-23A-12 (1986); Tex. Rev. Civ. Stat. Ann. art. 4512.7 § 1 (Vernon Supp. 1992); Wash. Rev. Code Ann. § 9.02.080 (Repealed). *See* Durham, Wood & Condie, *Accommodation of Conscientious Objection to Abortion: A Case Study of the Nursing Profession,* 1982 B.Y.U.L. Rev. 253.

[440]*E.g.,* Ariz. Rev. Stat. Ann. § 36-2151 (1986); Cal. Health & Safety Code § 25955(a) (West Supp. 1992); Fla. Stat. Ann. § 390.001(8) (West 1986); Idaho Code § 16-612 (1987); Ind. Code Ann. § 16-10-3-2 (Burns 1990); Ky. Rev. Stat. § 311.800(5)(b) (1990); Me. Rev. Stat. Ann. tit. 22, § 1591 (1992); Mass. Gen. Laws Ann. ch. 112, § 121 (West Supp. 1991); Minn. Stat. Ann. § 145.42 (West 1989); Nev. Rev. Stat. § 632.475 (1991); N.M. Stat. Ann. § 30-5-2 (1984); N.D. Cent. Code § 23-16-14 (1991); Or. Rev. Stat. § 435.485(2) (1991); 18 Pa. Cons. Stat. Ann. § 3213(d) (Purdon 1983); R.I. Gen. Laws § 23-17-11 (1989); S.C. Code Ann. § 44-41-50 (Law. Co-op. 1988); S.D. Codified Laws Ann. § 34-23A-12 (1986); Tex. Rev. Civ. Stat. Ann. art. 4512.7, § 1 (Vernon Supp. 1992); Utah Code Ann. § 76-7-306(1) (1990); Wash. Rev. Code Ann. § 9.02.080 (Repealed); Wis. Stat. Ann. § 140.42(1) (West 1989).

[441]*E.g.,* N.J. Stat. Ann. § 2A:65A-3 (West 1987); 18 Pa. Cons. Stat. Ann. § 3213(d) (Purdon 1983).

[442]*E.g.,* Alaska Stat. § 18.16.010(a) (1991); Ark. Code Ann. § 20-16-601(c) (1991); Cal. Health & Safety Code § 25955(a), (c) (West Supp. 1992); Colo. Rev. Stat. § 18-6-104 (1986); Del. Code Ann. tit. 24, § 1791(a), (b) (1987); Fla. Stat. Ann. § 390.001(8) (West 1986); Ga. Code Ann. § 16-12-142 (1988); Idaho Code § 18-612 (1987); Ill. Ann. Stat. ch. 38, § 81-33 (Smith-Hurd Supp. 1991 & 1992); Kan. Stat. Ann. § 65-443 (1985); Ky. Rev. Stat. § 311.800(5) (1990); Me. Rev. Stat. Ann. tit. 22, § 1591 (1992); Md. Pub. Health Code Ann. § 20-214(a)(i) (Supp. 1991) (subject to referendum on amendment); Mass. Gen. Laws Ann. ch. 112, § 12*l* (1983); Minn. Stat. Ann. § 145.42(1) (West 1989); Mo. Ann. Stat. § 197.032(1) (Vernon 1983); Mont. Code Ann. § 50-20-111(1) (1991); Neb. Rev. Stat. § 28-338 (1989); N.J. Stat. Ann. §§ 2A:65A-1 to 65A-3 (West 1987); N.Y. Civ. Rights Law § 79i(2) (McKinney 1976); N.C. Gen. Stat. § 14-45.1(e) (1986); Ohio Rev. Code Ann. § 4731.91 (Page Supp. 1991); Okla. Stat. Ann. tit. 63, § 1-741 (West 1984); 18 Pa. Cons. Stat. Ann. § 3213(d) (Purdon 1983); R.I. Gen. Laws § 23-17-11 (1989); S.C. Code Ann. § 44-41-50(b) (Law. Co-op. 1988); S.D. Codified Laws Ann. § 34-23A-12 (1986); Utah Code Ann. § 76-7-306 (1990); Va. Code & 18.2-75 (1988); Wis. Stat. Ann. § 140.42(2) (West 1989); Wyo. Stat. § 35-6-106 (1988).

[443]*E.g.,* Ill. Ann. Stat. ch. 38, § 81-33 (Smith-Hurd Supp. 1991 & 1992); 18 Pa. Cons. Stat. Ann. § 3213(d) (Purdon 1983).

[444]*E.g.,* Ark. Code. Ann. § 20-16-601 (1991); Colo. Rev. Stat. § 18-6-104 (1986); Del. Code Ann. tit. 24, § 1791(a) (1987); Fla. Stat. Ann. § 390.001(8) (West 1986); Ga. Code Ann. § 16-12-142 (1988); Ill. Ann. Stat. ch. 38, § 81-33 (Smith-Hurd Supp. 1992); Ind. Code Ann. § 16-10-3-2 (Burns 1990); Me. Rev. Stat. Ann. tit. 22, § 1592 (1992); Md. Pub. Health Code Ann. § 20-214(a)(2)(ii) (Supp. 1991) (subject to referendum on amendment); Minn. Stat. Ann. § 145-414 (West 1989); Mont. Code Ann. § 50-20-111(1) (1991); N.J. Stat. Ann. § 2A-65A-3 (West 1987); N.M. Stat. Ann. § 30-5-2 (1984); N.C. Gen. Stat. § 14-45.1(e) (1986); Ohio Rev. Code Ann. § 4731.91(C) (Page Supp. 1991); Okla. Stat. Ann. tit. 63, § 1-741

several statutes have been amended to conform with *Bigelow v. Virginia* concepts;[489] the residual coverage would appear to be constitutional.[490]

10. SOLICITING ABORTIONS   Some traditional statutes have penalized the act of soliciting women for abortions.[491] To the extent they fall within the advertising cases discussed immediately above, they are subject to equivalent constitutional attack. However, even if such statutes apply only to personal contacts, they seem clearly unconstitutional under *Roe v. Wade* because they impede access by women to lawful therapeutic abortions. Recent legislation reflects such concerns.[492]

11. TRAFFICKING IN ABORTIFACIENTS   Criminal regulation of abortifacients, like restrictions on advertising and solicitation, came into the statute books in the 19th century.[493] Many such laws have been continued in force without change.[494] However, to the extent they burden the availability of lawful therapeutic abortions, they are unconstitutional.[495] Consequently, most contemporary statutes either exempt therapeutic abortions[496] or limit their coverage to unlawful abortions.[497]

(West 1984); 18 Pa. Cons. Stat. Ann. § 3213(d) (Purdon 1983); R.I. Gen. Laws § 23-17-11 (1989); Utah Code Ann. § 78-11-25 (1992); Va. Code § 18.2-75 (1988); Wis. Stat. Ann. § 140.42(1) (West 1989).

[445] *E.g.,* Colo. Rev. Stat. § 18-6-104 (1986); Del. Code Ann. tit. 24, § 1791(a), (b) (1987); Fla. Stat. Ann. § 390.001(8) (West 1986); Ga. Code Ann. § 16-12-142 (1988); Idaho Code § 18-612 (1987); Me. Rev. Stat. Ann. tit. 22, § 1592 (1992); Md. Pub. Health Code Ann. § 20-214(a)(2)(ii) (Supp. 1991) (subject to referendum on amendment); Mass. Gen. Laws Ann. ch. 112, § 12*I* (West 1983); Mont. Code Ann. § 50-20-111(1) (1991); N.M. Stat. Ann. § 30-5-2 (1984); N.C. Gen. Stat. § 14-45.1(e) (1986); Okla. Stat. Ann. tit. 63, § 1-741 (West 1984); R.I. Gen. Laws § 23-17-11 (1989); Utah Code Ann. § 78-11-25 (1992); Va. Code § 18.2-75 (1988); Wis. Stat. Ann. § 140.42(1) (West 1989). Minn. Stat. Ann. § 145.414 (West 1989) proscribes coercion to allow abortions.

[446] *E.g.,* N.J. Stat. Ann. §§ 2A:65A-1, 2A:65A-3 (West 1987); N.Y. Civ. Rights Law § 79i (McKinney 1976); N.D. Cent. Code § 23-16-14 (1991); Ohio Rev. Code Ann. § 4731.91 (Page Supp. 1991).

[447] *E.g.,* Cal. Health & Safety Code § 25955(a) (West Supp. 1992) (but medical employer can inquire into conscience reservation before hiring); Ill. Ann. Stat. ch. 38,§ 81-33 (Smith-Hurd Supp. 1991 & 1992); Ind. Code Ann. § 16-10-3-2 (Burns 1990); Iowa Code Ann. § 146.1 (West 1989); Kan. Stat. Ann. § 65-443 (1985); Ky. Rev. Stat. § 311.800(5) (1990); Me. Rev. Stat. Ann. tit. 22, § 1592 (1992); Mass. Gen. Laws Ann. ch. 112, § 12*I* (West 1983); Minn. Stat. Ann. § 145.414 (West 1989); Mo. Ann. Stat. § 197.032(2) (Vernon 1983); Mont. Code Ann. § 50-20-111(1) (1991); Neb. Rev. Stat. § 28-341 (1989); Nev. Rev. Stat. § 632.475(2) (1991); 18 Pa. Cons. Stat. Ann. § 3213(d) (Purdon 1983); S.C. Code Ann. § 44-41-50(c) (Law. Co-op. 1988); S.D. Codified Laws Ann. § 34-23A-13 (1986); Tex. Rev. Civ. Stat. Ann. art. 4512.7, §§. 1, 3, 4 (Vernon Supp. 1992); Utah Code Ann. § 78-11-25 (1992) (including employment with other discrimination); Va. Code § 1802-75 (1988); Wash. Rev. Code Ann. § 9.02.080 (Repealed); Wis. Stat. Ann. § 140.42(3) (West 1989); Wyo. Stat. § 35-6-106 (1988).

[448] *E.g.,* Cal. Health & Safety Code § 25955(b) (West Supp. 1992) ("no medical school or other facility for the education or training of physicians, [or] nurses . . . shall refuse admission . . . or penalize . . . because of such person's unwillingness to participate in the performance of an abortion . . ."); Ky. Rev. Stat. § 311.800(5)(c) (1990); Mass. Gen. Laws Ann. ch. 112, § 12*I* (West 1983); 18 Pa. Cons. Stat. Ann. § 3213(d) (Purdon 1983); Tex. Rev. Civ. Stat. Ann. art. 4512.7, § 3 (Vernon Supp. 1992).

[449] *E.g.,* Neb. Rev. Stat. § 28-339 (1989) (class II misdemeanor); Nev. Rev. Stat. § 632.475(4) (1991) (misdemeanor); N.Y. Civ. Rights Law § 79i(1) (McKinney 1976) (misdemeanor); Wyo. Stat. § 35-6-113 (1988) ($10,000 fine).

[450] *E.g.,* Mont. Code Ann. § 50-20-111(3) (1991); Neb. Rev. Stat. § 28-341 (1989); Tex. Rev. Civ. Stat. Ann. art. 4512.7 § 4 (Vernon Supp. 1992); Wyo. Stat. § 35-6-114 (1988).

[451] *E.g.,* Ill. Ann. Stat. ch. 111½, § 5201(c) (Smith-Hurd 1988) (treble damages with minimum $2,000 recovery); Ind. Code Ann. § 16-10-3-2 (Burns 1990) (reinstatement of employment also available); Mo. Ann. Stat. § 197.032(3) (Vernon 1983) (may recover in action at law, suit in equity or other redress); Neb. Rev. Stat. §§ 28-340 (damages), 28-341 (injunctive relief) (1989); Ohio Rev. Code Ann. § 4731.91(e) (Page Supp. 1990) (civil damages available); 18 Pa. Cons. Stat. Ann. § 3213(d) (Purdon 1983) (civil liability in

12. SPECIAL EVIDENTIARY PROVISIONS   A few statutes require that a woman's testimony concerning a criminal abortion be corroborated.[498] Vermont's abortion statute allows a woman's statements in evidence as a dying declaration if she dies following an abortion.[499] Two jurisdictions immunize a woman's testimony against incriminating use so that she may be called as a prosecution witness.[500] Legislation of this sort is probably residual from earlier times and deserves repeal.

Rhode Island legislation states that it is unnecessary for the prosecution to prove that an abortion was not legally justified.[501] Current constitutional doctrine legitimates placement on the defendant of a burden of going forward with evidence; however, the legality of imposing the burden of persuasion on the defendant turns on the legal characterization to be placed upon the matter.[502]

D. Economic Aspects of Therapeutic Abortions

1. PUBLIC FUNDING OF ABORTIONS   A logical corollary of the Supreme Court's holding in *Roe v. Wade* seemingly would have been a requirement that states and the

---

addition to liability for punitive damages in the amount of $5,000); S.C. Code Ann. § 44-41-50(c) (Law. Co-op. 1988) (reinstatement of employment also available); Wyo. Stat. § 35-6-114 (1988).

[452] *See* State v. Hodgson, 295 Minn. 294, 204 N.W. 2d 199 (1973) (per curiam) (physician who performed abortion within first trimester secondary to the contraction of rubella by his pregnant patient not criminally convictable); Commonwealth v. Jackson, 454 Pa. 429, 312 A.2d 13 (1979) (per curiam) (nonphysician's conviction of committing an unlawful abortion reversed).

[453] 423 U.S. 9 (1975) (per curiam).

[454] The Court noted that it was concerned with maternal health and had only legitimated an "abortion . . . performed by medically competent personnel under conditions insuring maximum safety for the woman." *Id* at 11. Hence, prosecutions of nonphysicians for first-trimester abortions "infringe upon no realm of personal privacy secured by the Constitution against state interference." *Id.* "The ever-increasing state interest in maternal health provides additional justification for such prosecutions." *Id.*

[455] *See, e.g.,* State v. Orsini, 187 Conn. 264, 445 A.2d 887, *cert. denied,* 459 U.S. 861 (1982) (persistent felony offender claimed record of earlier conviction for aiding in criminal abortion was silent as to whether the principal was a physician; the court thought indications in the record that the abortion was performed in a motel room using a "shoehorn device" was a sufficient indication the abortion was criminal); State v. Menillo, 171 Conn. 141, 368 A.2d 136 (1976) (application of abortion statute held valid as to nonphysicians) (on remand from *Connecticut v. Menillo*); Rhim v. State, 264 Ind. 682, 348 N.E.2d 620 (1976) (statute regulating abortions performed by nonphysicians remained unchanged when legislature passed statute regulating abortions performed by physicians); Spears v. State, 278 S. 2d 443 (Miss. 1973) (nonphysician subject to criminal penalties for performing abortion); State v. Norflett, 67 N.J. 268, 337 A.2d 609 (1975) (one without medical degree can be convicted under criminal abortion law). *See also* Smith v. Bently, 493 F. Supp. 916, 924–27 (E.D. Ark. 1980) (states can prohibit nonphysicians from performing abortions during any stage of pregnancy).

[456] *See* Simopoulos v. Virginia, 462 U.S. 506 (1983) (requirement that second trimester abortions be performed in licensed clinics is not an unreasonable means of furthering state's compelling interest in protecting the woman's own health and safety).

[457] *See* City of Akron v. Akron Center for Reproductive Health, Inc., 462 U.S. at 451–52 (invalidating criminal statute requiring disposal of fetal remains "in a humane and sanitary manner" because it failed to give physicians fair notice that the contemplated conduct was forbidden); Colautti v. Franklin, 439 U.S. 379 (1979) (statutes turning on whether fetus is "viable" void for vagueness); Planned Parenthood v. Danforth, 428 U.S. at 81–84 (statute imposing criminal penalties for failure to exercise degree of professional skill, care and diligence necessary to preserve life and health of fetus held invalid).

[458] *See* United States v. United States Gypsum Co., 438 U.S. 422, 434–46 (1978) (refusal to construe the Sherman Act as embracing strict liability criminal offenses). *See also* Morrissette v. United States, 342 U.S. 246 (1952).

federal government provide the same financial support for therapeutic abortions as they offer for other medical services to financially-unable citizens. Otherwise, government would burden the free exercise of women's rights to have abortions and create invidious distinctions among classes of patients based on financial considerations. However, logic lost as the issue came before the Supreme Court.

In *Maher v. Roe*[503] welfare recipients attacked a state exclusion of Medicaid payments to patients receiving therapeutic abortions; a federal district court found the preclusion to deny equal protection. The Supreme Court disagreed. Although it did not depart its *Roe v. Wade* principle that the Constitution protects women from unduly burdensome interference with the freedom to terminate pregnancies, it held that there is no constitutional barrier to a state's making "a value judgment favoring childbirth over abortion and . . . implement[ing] that judgment by the allocation of public funds."[504] Financially-unable patients not wishing to take advantage of state-supported childbirth must depend on private sources:

---

[459] Colautti v. Franklin, 439 U.S. at 395 ("[b]ecause of the absence of a scienter requirement in the provision directing the physician to determine whether the fetus is or may be viable, the statute is little more than a 'trap for those who act in good faith.' ").

[460] *Simopoulos,* 462 U.S. at 510 (placing burden on a defendant of going forward with evidence on an affirmative defense generally is permissible).

[461] *See e.g.,* People v. Franklin, 683 P.2d 775 (Colo. 1984) (osteopath could be convicted for performing a nontherapeutic abortion even though criminal statute unconstitutionally outlawed certain theapeutic abortions by licensed medical practitioners). *See also supra,* notes 191–94 and accompanying text.

[462] *See, e.g.,* Alaska Stat. § 18.16.010 (1991); Colo. Rev. Stat. § 18-6-101 (1986); Del. Code Ann. tit. 24, § 1790(a) (1987); D.C. Code Ann. § 22-201 (1989); Fla. Stat. Ann. § 390.001(3) (West 1986); Ga. Code Ann. § 16-12-140(a) (1988); Idaho Code §§ 18-606(2), 18-608 (1987); Ind. Code Ann. §§ 35-1-58.5-2, 35-1-58.5-4 (Burns 1985); Iowa Code An. § 707.7, ¶ 3 (West 1979); Kan. Stat. Ann. § 21-3407(2) (1988); Ky. Rev. Stat. §§ 311.750, 311.760(2) (1990) (see also § 311.760(1) under which a woman herself is not a criminal for producing abortion during first trimester on advice of licensed physician); La. Rev. Stat. An. § 37:1285(8), (8.1), (9) (West 1988) (therapeutic abortions are dealt with under medical licensing statutes; this would seem to qualify § 14:874); Me. Rev. Stat. Ann. tit. 22, § 1598(3)(A) (1992); Md. Pub. Health Code Ann. § 20-210(a)(3) (Supp. 1991) (subject to referendum on amendment); Mass. Gen. Laws Ann. ch. 112, §§ 12L, 12M, 12N (West 1983); Minn. Stat. Ann. § 145.412(1) (West 1989); Mo. Ann. Stat. § 188.020 (Vernon 1983); Mont. Code Ann. § 50-20-109 (1991); Neb. Rev. Stat. § 28-335 (1989); Nev. Rev. Stat. § 442.250(1) (1987); N.M. Stat. Ann. § 30-5-1(C) (1984); N.Y. Penal Law § 125.05(3) (McKinney 1987); N.C. Gen. Stat. §§ 14-44, 14-45. 14-45.1(a), (b) (1986); N.D. Cent. Code § 14.02.1-04(5) (1991); Okla. Stat. Ann. tit. 63, § 1-731(A) (West 1984); P.R. Laws Ann. tit. 33, § 4010 (1983); S.C. Code Ann. § 44-41-20 (Law. Co-op. 1988) (defined in § 44-41-10[b]); S.D. Codified Laws Ann. § 34-23A-3 (1986); Tenn. Code Ann. § 39-15-201(c) (1991); Utah Code Ann. § 76-7-302(1) (Supp. 1991) (defined in § 76-7-301(2)); V.I. Code Ann. tit. 14 § 151(b) (Supp 1991); Va. Code §§ 18.2-72, 18.2, 74.1 (1988); Wash. Rev. Code Ann. § 9.02.070 (Repealed); Wis. Stat. Ann. § 940.04(5)(a) (West 1989); Wyo. Stat. 35-6-111 (1988).

[463] *See e.g.,* People v. Bricker, 389 Mich. 524, 208 N.W.2d 172 (1973) (conviction of nonphysician for conspiracy to commit an abortion); Beecham v. Leahy, 130 Vt. 164, 287 A.2d 836 (1972) (no justiciable controversy when physician sued for injunctive relief).

[464] *E.g.,* Ala. Code § 13A-13-7 (Michie 1982); Ariz. Rev. Stat. Ann. § 13-3603 (1989); Ark. Code Ann. § 5-61-102 (1987); Cal. Penal Code § 274 (West 1988); Del. Code Ann. tit. 11, § 654 (1987); D.C. Code Ann. § 22-201 (1989); Ga. Code Ann. § 16-12-140(a) (1988); Idaho Code § 18-605 (1987); Ill. Ann. Stat. ch. 38, § 81-22(7) (Smith-Hurd Supp. 1991 & 1992); La. Rev. Stat. Ann. § 14:87(1) (West 1986); Me. Rev. Stat. Ann. tit. 22 § 1596(1)(A) (1992); Mass. Gen. Laws Ann. ch. 272, § 19 (West 1990); Mich. Comp. Laws Ann. § 750.14 (1968); Miss. Code Ann. § 97-3-3(1) (1973); Nev. Rev. Stat. § 201.120(1) (1991); N.M. Stat. Ann. § 30-5-3 (1984); N.Y. Penal Law § 125.05(2) (McKinney 1987); N.C. Gen. Stat.

The State may have made childbirth a more attractive alternative, thereby influencing the woman's decision, but it has imposed no restriction on access to abortions that was not already there. The indigency that may make it difficult—and in some cases, perhaps, impossible—for some women to have abortions is neither created nor in any way affected by the [state] regulation.[505]

In short, the Court perceived a

basic difference between direct state interference with a protected activity and state encouragement of an alternative activity consonant with legislative policy. Constitutional concerns are greatest when the State attempts to impose its will by force of law; the State's power to encourage actions deemed to be in the public interest is necessarily far broader.[506]

---

§ 14-44 (1986); Okla. Stat. Ann. tit. 21 § 861 (West 1984); P.R. Laws Ann. tit. 33, § 4010 (1983); R.I. Gen. Laws § 11-23-5 (1989); S.C. Code Ann. § 44-41-80(a) (Law. Co-op. 1988); Tenn. Code Ann. § 39-15-201(1), (2) (1991); Vt. Stat. Ann. tit. 13, § 101 (1974); Va. Code § 18.2-71 (1988); Wash. Rev. Code Ann. § 9.02.010(1) (Repealed); W. Va. Code § 61-2-8 (1989).

[465] The statutes cited *supra* note 464 contain this alternative with the following exceptions and additions: Colo. Rev. Stat. § 18-6-102 (1) (1985); Del. Code Ann. tit. 11, §§ 651, 654 (Supp. 1991); Ky. Rev. Stat. § 311.720(1) (1990); Nev. Rev. Stat. § 201.120(2) (1991); Wash. Rev. Code Ann. § 9.02.020 (Repealed).

[466] E.g., Ala. Code § 13A-13-7 (Michie 1982); Ariz. Rev. Stat. Ann. § 13-3603 (1989); Ark. Code Ann. § 5-61-102 (1987); Colo. Rev. Stat. § 18-6-101(1) (1986) (terminating pregnancy); Del. Code Ann. tit. 11, § 651 (1987); Idaho Code § 18-605 (Supp. 1990); Ill. Ann. Stat. ch. 38, § 81-22(4) (Smith-Hurd Supp. 1991 & 1992) (woman known to be pregnant; but see § 81-31[4], making it a class 2 felony to perform abortions on women who are not pregnant); Ind. Code Ann. § 35-1-58.5-1(b) (Burns Supp. 1991) (termination of human pregnancy); Iowa Code Ann. §§ 707.7 ¶ 2, 707.8(2) (West 1979) (termination of pregnancy); Kan. Stat. Ann. § 21-3407(1) (1985); Ky. Rev. Stat. § 311.720(1) (1990) (woman known to be pregnant); Me. Rev. Stat. Ann. tit. 22, § 1596(1)(A) (1992) (interruption of pregnancy); Md. Pub. Health Code Ann. § 20-208 (1987) (terminating human pregnancy); Mass. Gen. Laws Ann. ch. 112, § 12K (West 1983); Minn. Stat. Ann. § 145.411(5) (West 1989) (must result in termination of pregnancy); Miss. Code Ann. § 97-3-3(1) (1973) (pregnant with child); Mo. Ann. Stat. § 188.015(1) (Vernon Supp. 1992) (termination of pregnancy); Mont. Code Ann. § 50-20-104(4) (1991) (terminate a pregnancy); Neb. Rev. Stat. § 28-326(1) (1989) (woman known to be pregnant); N.H. Rev. Stat. Ann. §§ 585:12, 585:13 (1986) (pregnant woman; pregnant with quick child); N.M. Stat. Ann. § 30-5-3 (1984) (pregnant woman); N.C. Gen. Stat. §§ 14-44, 14-45 (1986) (pregnant or quick with child; pregnant woman); N.D. Cent. Code § 14-02.1-02(1) (1991) (definition of abortion as termination of human pregnancy); P.R. Laws Ann. tit. 33, § 4010 (1983) (pregnant woman); R.I. Gen. Laws § 11-23-5 (1989) (unborn quick child); S.C. Code Ann. § 44-41-10(a) (Law. Co-op. Supp. 1991) (abortion defined as termination of human pregnancy); S.D. Codified Laws Ann. § 34-23A-1(1) (1986) (same); Tenn. Code Ann. § 39-15-201(a)(1) (1991) (pregnant, whether quick or not); Utah Code Ann. § 76-7-301(a) (Supp. 1991) (termination of pregnancy); V.I. Code Ann. tit. 14, § 151(a) (Supp. 1991) (termination of human pregnancy); Va. Code § 18.2-71 (1988) (intent to destroy unborn child, producing abortion or miscarriage and thus destroying child); W. Va. Code § 61-2-8 (1989) (producing abortion or miscarriage); Wis. Stat. Ann. § 940.04 (West 1989) (destruction of life of unborn child); Wyo. Stat. § 35-6-102 (1988) (after viability).

[467] E.g., Cal. Penal Code § 274 (West 1988); D.C. Code Ann. § 22-201 (1989); Ga. Code Ann. § 16-12-140(a) (1988); La. Rev. Stat. Ann. § 14:87(2) (West Supp. 1992); Nev. Rev. Stat. § 201.120(1) (1991) (whether pregnant or not); N.Y. Penal Code § 125.05(2) (McKinney 1987) (same); Okla. Stat. Ann. tit. 21 § 861 (West 1984); Vt. Stat. Ann. tit. 13 § 101 (1974) (pregnant or supposed to be pregnant); Wash. Rev. Code Ann. § 9.02.010(1) (Repealed).

[468] *See* authorities cited *supra* at note 50.

Two other decisions during the same term documented the Court's theme. In *Beal v. Doe*,[507] the Court applied an identical analysis to title XIX of the Social Security Act,[508] which it construed not to require state funding of nontherapeutic abortions but not to preclude such funding either.[509] In *Poelker v. Doe*,[510] it ruled that publicly-owned and -operated hospitals did not have to offer free hospital abortion services even though they provided free childbirth facilities. The rationale was that of *Mather v. Roe*.

While *Beal v. Doe* was awaiting final resolution, Congress had begun enacting an annual prohibition, the Hyde Amendment,[511] that in varying forms banned the use of federal Medicaid funding for nontherapeutic abortions or therapeutic abortions other than for certain restricted reasons.[512] Constitutional attacks on it were launched immediately, since *Beal v. Doe* had dealt only with construction of Medicaid provisions not bearing the Hyde Amendment limitation. In *Harris v. McRae*,[513] the Court reiterated its *Maher v. Roe* premise that legislative bodies, including Congress, can refuse to underwrite therapeutic abortions and, "by means of unequal subsidization of abortion and

---

[469] *E.g.,* Cal. Penal Code § 274 (West 1988); Colo. Rev. Stat. § 18-6-103 (1986) (pretending to end real or apparent pregnancy); Del. Code Ann. tit. 11, § 654 (1987); Ga. Code Ann. § 16-12-140(a) (1988); Idaho Code § 18-605 (1987); La. Rev. Stat. Ann. § 14:87 (Supp. 1992); Me. Rev. Stat. Ann. tit. 22 § 1596(1)(A) (1992); Mass. Gen. Laws Ann. ch. 272, § 19 (West 1990); Mont. Code Ann. § 50-20-104(4) (1991); Nev. Rev. Stat. § 201.120(1) (1991); N.H. Rev. Stat. Ann. § 585:12 (1986); Okla. Stat. Ann. tit. 21, § 861 (West 1984); Vt. Stat. Ann. tit. 13, § 101 (1974).

[470] *E.g.,* D.C. Code Ann. § 22-201 (1989); Md. Pub. Health Code Ann. § 20-208(a) (1990); N.M. Stat. Ann. § 30-5-3 (1984); Tenn. Code Ann. § 39-15-201(a)(2) (1991); Utah Code Ann. § 76-7-301(1) (Supp. 1991).

[471] *E.g.,* Del. Code Ann. tit. 24, § 1790(b)(1) (1987); Iowa Code Ann. § 707.7 (West 1979); Md. Pub. Health Code Ann. § 20-208(b)(1) (1990); Nev. Rev. Stat. § 442.250(b)–(c) (1991); N.Y. Penal Law § 125.45 (McKinney 1987); Wash. Rev. Code Ann. § 9.02.070 (Repealed).

[472] *E.g.,* Alaska Stat. § 18.16.010 (1991); Ark. Code Ann. § 5-61-102 (1987); Me. Rev. Stat. Ann. tit. 22, § 1598 (1992); Minn. Stat. Ann. § 145.411(2) (West 1989); Neb. Rev. Stat. § 28-329 (1989); N.H. Rev. Stat. Ann. § 585:13 (1986); N.C. Gen. Stat. § 14-44 (1986); R.I. Gen. Laws. § 11-23-5 (1989); Wis. Stat. Ann. § 940.04 (West 1989).

[473] *See* Connecticut v. Menillo, 423 U.S. at 11. *See also supra,* notes 453–54 and accompanying text. For illustrations of legislation apparently so limited, see Iowa Code Ann. § 707.7 West 1979); Wyo. Stat. § 35-6-101 (1988).

[474] *See supra,* notes 458–59 and accompanying text. *See also* Harris v. McRae, 448 U.S. 297, 311 n.17 (1980) (Hyde Amendment criminal sanctions were valid because they contained "a clear scienter requirement under which good-faith errors are not penalized").

[475] *See* the statutes cited *supra* in notes 474–82 all of which, except as listed *infra* in note 476, carry felony penalties.

[476] *E.g.,* Ala. Code § 13A-13-7 (Michie 1982) (fine not less than $100 nor more than $1,000 and imprisonment for not more than 12 months); Ill. Ann. Stat. ch. 38, § 81-31(1)-(3) (Smith-Hurd Supp. 1992) (remaining provisions are punishable as felonies); Me. Rev. Stat. Ann. tit. 22, § 1598(4) (1992) (abortion by a physician after viability is a class D crime, all other abortions are class C crimes); N.H. Rev. Stat. Ann. § 585:12 (1986) (imprisoned not more than one year, or fined not more than $1,000 or both); N.D. Cent. Code § 14-02.1-04(4) (1991) (class A misdemeanor if physician violates regulations); Wash. Rev. Code Ann. § 9.02.070 (1988) (gross misdemeanor, if physician performs the abortion without consent or if the woman has not resided in the state for 90 days or if the abortion is performed in other than an accredited hospital or medical facility).

[477] *See* Solem v. Helm, 463 U.S. 277 (1983) (eighth amendment barred life sentence of imprisonment without possibility of parole against fourth offender for writing a check of $100). *But see* Harmelin v. Michigan, 111 S. Ct. 2680 (1991) (eighth amendment does not forbid mandatory life term for a first offender convicted of possessing a substantial amount of cocaine; there was no majority opinion).

[478] *See supra,* notes 387–92 and accompanying text.

other medical services, encourage alternative activity deemed in the public interest.''[514] Moreover, it rejected a contention that the Hyde Amendment, by embodying Roman Catholic doctrine rejecting abortion, violated the establishment clause dimension of the first amendment.[515] The Court thought, as well, that the legislation embodied no invidious discrimination violating equal protection as guaranteed in the fifth and fourteenth amendments. Congress could authorize federal reimbursement for medically necessary services generally but need not do so for medically indicated abortions: ''Abortion is inherently different from other medical procedures, because no other procedure involves the purposeful termination of a potential life.''[516]

The Court reiterated its basic position on the economics of abortion-related funding in *Rust v. Sullivan*.[517] Federal legislation[518] provided that ''none of the funds appropriated under this subchapter shall be used in programs where abortion is a method of family planning.'' In 1988 the secretary of Health and Human Services issued regulations based on the statute prohibiting any recipient of federal funding for family planning services from referring pregnant women to abortion providers, even upon specific

---

[479]*E.g.*, Del. Code Ann. tit. 24, § 1795(b) (1987) (knowing and reckless conduct detrimental to life or health of live-born infant after abortion a class A misdemeanor); Fla. Stat. Ann. § 782.09 (West 1986) (killing unborn child by injury to mother deemed manslaughter); Ill. Rev. Stat. ch. 38, § 81-26(1) (Smith-Hurd Supp. 1991 & 1992) (class 3 felony); Ind. Code Ann. § 35-1-58.5-7(c) (Burns 1985) (subjected to homicide and manslaugher criminality); Iowa Code Ann. §§ 707.9 (intentional killing of live-born fetus a class B felony), 707.10 (failure to preserve life and health of viable fetus a serious misdemeanor) (West 1979); La. Rev. Stat. Ann. §§ 14:87.1 (killing child during delivery punishable by life imprisonment), 14:87.5 (intentional failure to sustain life and health of live-born viable infant punishable by up to 21 years imprisonment) (West 1986); Mass. Gen. Laws Ann. ch. 112, § 12T (West 1083) (failure to take reasonable steps to protect life and health of live-born child a misdemeanor, together with any other criminal liability); Mich. Comp. Laws Ann. § 750.322 (1968) (willful killing of unborn quick child by injury to mother is manslaughter), § 750.323 (1981) (successful efforts to kill unborn quick child is manslaughter); Mont. Code Ann. § 50-20-108(1) (1991) (purposely, knowingly or negligently to cause death of premature viable infant born alive is criminal homicide); Neb. Rev. Stat. § 28-332 (1989) (class IV felony to fail to take reasonable steps to preserve life of live-born infant); Nev. Rev. Stat. § 442.270(2) (1991) (failure to preserve life and health of live-born infant); Nev. Rev. Stat. § 442.270(2) (1991) (failure to preserve life and health of liveborn individual subjects person to general criminal statutes); N.D. Cent. Code §§ 14-02.1-05, 14-02.1-08 (1991) (class C felony to fail to preserve life and health of unborn child); Okla. Stat. Ann. tit. 63, § 1-734(D) (West 1984) (persons killing neonate or failing to take reasonable measures to preserve life of infant are guilty of homicide); 18 Pa. Cons. Stat. Ann. § 3210(b) (Purdon Supp. 1991 & 1992) (third-degree misdemeanor to fail to protect life of unborn viable child); R.I. Gen. Laws § 11-9-18 (1989) (knowingly and intentionally failing to provide reasonable medical care and treatment, causing death of live-born infant, is manslaughter); S.D. Codified Laws Ann. § 22-17-6 (1986) (intentional killing of human fetus by causing injury to mother, other than during therapeutic abortion, a class 4 felony); Tenn. Code Ann. § 39-15-206(b) (1991) (felony to fail to use good medical skill to preserve life and health of live-born infant); Tex. Rev. Civ. Stat. Ann. art. 4512.5 (Vernon 1976) (destroying life during parturition if child would have been born alive is a felony punishable by a minimum five years' imprisonment to life); Utah Code Ann. § 76-7-314(2) (1990) (thid-degree felony to fail to use medical skills to preserve life of unborn child); Wash. Rev. Code Ann. § 9A.32.060(b) (1988) (intentionally killing unborn quick child by injuring mother is first-degree manslaughter); Wyo. Stat. § 35-6-110 (1988) (felony intentionally to terminate viability of unborn infant or to fail to use accepted means of preserving live-born fetus).

See State v. Lewis, 429 N.E.2d 1110 (Ind. 1981), *cert. denied sub nom.* Lewis v. Indiana, 457 U.S. 1118 (1982) (doctor could be retried for unlawful postviability abortion performed at clinic rather than hospital; viability demonstrated by fact fetus had been born alive and had survived 2 hours).

[480]*See* materials cited *supra* at note 457. *See also* Commonwealth v. Edelin, 371 Mass. 497, 359, N.E.2d 4 (1976) (insufficient evidence that physician's conduct was negligent or reckless, so that verdict of acquittal should have been directed; court divided equally as to whether death of fetus could be manslaughter); Special Project, *supra* note 31, at 156–59; Note, *Criminal Liability of Physicians: An Encroachment on*

request. In reliance on its reasoning in *Maher v. Roe,* the Court rejected contentions that the limitation was unconstitutional because it invidiously discriminated on economic grounds, in violation of the equal protection concept, and that it impeded the constitutional right of women to determine whether to terminate their pregnancies.[519]

The Court's 1977, 1980 and 1988 rulings have served to legitimate legislation in about one-quarter of American jurisdictions limiting the use of state,[520] local[521] and, on occasion, federal pass-through[522] funding for purposes of abortion. Similar restrictions may govern public employee or other health insurance plans,[523] family-planning services[524] and miscellaneous benefits.[525] Exceptions may be indicated, however, to cover abortions necessary to preserve maternal life[526] or used to terminate pregnancies resulting from rape[527] or incest.[528] Moreover, a few state appellate courts have invalidated or limited the impact of restrictive legislation on state legal grounds.[529]

2. PROTECTING WOMEN ELECTING ABORTIONS   It would be a clear violation of *Roe v. Wade* standards for state officials in any way to coerce women to have or to decline abortions. A few states specifically prohibit the former.[530] Beyond that, legisla-

---

the Abortion Right?, 18 Am. Crim. L. Rev. 591, 609–15 (1981); Note, *Current Technology Affecting Supreme Court Abortion Jurisprudence,* 27 N.Y.L. Sch. L. Rev. 1221, 1249–55 (1982).

[481] *See supra,* notes 57–60 and accompanying text.

[482] *E.g.,* Colo. Rev. Stat. § 18-6-102(2) (1986) (class 2 felony); D.C. Code Ann. § 22-201 (1989) (second-degree murder); Mass. Gen. Laws Ann. ch. 272 § 19 (West 1990) (felony punishable by 5 to 20 years' imprisonment); Miss. Code Ann. § 97-3-3(1) (1973) (murder); N.H. Rev. Stat. Ann. § 585:14 (1986) (second-degree murder); N.M. Stat. Ann. § 30-5-3 (1984) (second-degree felony); N.Y. Penal Law § 125.15(2) (McKinney 1987) (second-degree manslaughter); Vt. Stat. Ann. tit. 13, § 101 (1974) (felony punishable by 5 to 20 years' imprisonment); Wis. Stat. Ann. § 940.04(2) (West 1989) (felony punishable by not more than 15 years' imprisonment).

Several statutes require coroners or medical examiners to inquire into deaths apparently resulting from criminal abortions. *See, e.g.,* Fla. Stat. Ann. § 406.11(1)(a)(9) (West 1986); La. Rev. Stat. Ann. § 33:1561 (West Supp. 1992); Mass. Gen. Laws Ann. ch. 38, § 6 (West Supp. 1991); Miss Code Ann. § 41-61-9 (1989).

On wrongful death civil liability, see *supra,* note 424 and accompanying text.

[483] *See supra,* notes 61–63 and accompanying text.

[484] *E.g.,* Ariz. Rev. Stat. Ann. § 13-3604 (1989); Cal. Penal Code § 274 (West 1988) (exempting therapeutic abortions); Del. Code Ann. tit. 11, § 651 (Supp. 1990); Idaho Code §§ 18-606(2) (soliciting, submitting to or self-inducing), 18-609(1) (except for lawful abortion) (1987); Ky. Rev. Stat. §§ 311.750 (prohibits self-abortion), 311.760(1) (except on advice of licensed physician) (1990); Mont. Code Ann. § 50-20-104(4) (1991) (abortion defined to include "submission to act or operation"); Nev. Rev. Stat. §§ 200.220 (submission to abortion after 24th week of gestation except as authorized under therapeutic abortion statute), 201.120(2) (self-abortion except as a therapeutic abortion on advice of licensed physician) (1991); N.Y. Penal Law §§ 125.05(3) (woman's act is justifiable if she believes it is done by physician performing lawful abortion), 125.50 (second-degree self-abortion through 24th week of pregnancy; class B misdemeanor), 125.55 (first-degree self-abortion if more than 24 weeks pregnant; class A misdemeanor) (McKinney 1987); Okla. Stat. Ann. tit. 21, § 862 (soliciting, taking substance or using means to procure miscarriage; misdemeanor), tit. 63, § 1-733 (no woman to perform or induce abortion on self except under supervision of licensed physician) (West 1984); P.R. Laws Ann. tit. 33, § 4011 (1983) (any solicitation for an abortion is a felony punishable by two to five years' imprisonment); S.C. Code Ann. § 44-41-80(b) (Law. Co-op. 1988) (misdemeanor to solicit abortion unless justified); V.I. Code Ann. tit. 14, §§ 152 (woman lawfully may submit when physician lawfully may perform abortion), 156 (violation a felony) (Supp. 1991); Wash. Rev. Code Ann. § 9.02.020 (Repealed).

Some states, *e.g.,* 18 Pa. Cons. Stat. Ann. § 3218 (Purdon 1983); Vt. Stat. Ann. tit. 13, § 101 (1974), specifically preclude a woman's criminality.

[485] *See supra,* notes 64–68 and accompanying text.

[486] *See supra,* notes 72–73 and accompanying text.

tion may bar discrimination or loss of privileges[531] or denial of public benefits[532] to women who refuse to have abortions[533] or, on occasion, consent.[534] The latter, of course, is a preferably neutral statement, but neutrality is not an evident objective of most such legislation.

VI. Conclusion and Recommendation: A Sunset Law Analogy for Abortion Legislation?

Unless a right-to-life amendment to the United States Constitution is ratified, which appears extraordinarily unlikely at this writing, the right of women to elect medically indicated abortions is protected. On the other hand, however, it continues to be most unlikely that the Court will depart from its position in *Harris v. McRae* that the Constitution does not require that therapeutic abortions be underwritten for financially-unable women because of the possible ripple effect a contrary interpretation would have on

---

[487] *E.g.*, Ariz. Rev. Stat. Ann. § 13-3605 (1989) (misdemeanor); Fla. Stat. Ann. § 797.02 (West 1986) (misdemeanor); Mass. Gen. Laws Ann. ch. 272, § 20 (West 1990) (felony); Mich. Comp. Laws Ann. §§ 750.15, 750.34 (1968) (immoral advertising); Miss. Code Ann. § 97-3-5 (1973); Mont. Code Ann. § 50-20-109(4) (1991); Nev. Rev. Stat. § 442.270(1) (1991); N.D. Cent. Code § 14-02.1-06 (1981); P.R. Laws Ann. tit. 10, § 315 (public display or advertising), tit. 33, § 4012 (Supp. 1983); Vt. Stat. Ann. tit. 13, § 104 (1985); Wash. Rev. Code Ann. § 9.68.030 (1988).

[488] *See* Bolger v. Youngs Drug Prods. Corp., 463 U.S. 60 (1983) (contraceptives and contraceptive information); Carey v. Population Servs. Int'l, 431 U.S. 678, 700–02 (1977) (same); Bigelow v. Virginia, 421 U.S. 809 (1975) (advertisement of lawful therapeutic abortion services).

See also Coalition for Abortion Rights and Against Sterilization Abuse v. Niagara Frontier Transp. Auth., 584 F. Supp. 985 (W.D.N.Y. 1984) (public transportation authority's refusal to allow advertising about the availability of therapeutic abortions at public service rates, when similar advertising bearing on reproductive choices had been accommodated at those rates, violated the Coalition's first and fourteenth amendment rights).

[489] 421 U.S. 809 (1975). *See, e.g.*, Idaho Code §§ 18-604 (physicians and licensed health care providers), 18-607 (except to physicians or druggists or distributors to others or in trade or professional channels unlikely to reach the general public) (1987); Md. Pub. Health Code Ann. § 20-210(a)(2) (Supp. 1992) (repealed subject to referendum) (other than by physicians in licensed and accredited hospitals [probably too limited an exception to meet *Bigelow* requirements]); Va. Code § 18.2-76.1 (1988) (amended after *Bigelow*); Wis. Stat. Ann. § 450.11(2) (West 1989).

[490] *Cf.* Baird v. La Follete, 72 Wis. 2d 1, 239 N.W.2d 536 (1976) (statute construed not to cover educational and informational exhibits in the context of free public lectures; could not ban even in a commercial setting good faith educational presentation of general information regarding contraception). *See generally* Warren, *supra* note 21, at 45–47. A telephone company acted properly in refusing to delete abortion clinic advertising in a classified directory as ordered by state public utilities commission based on the commission's ruling that the advertising was "deceptive." Neary v. Pennsylvania Public Utility Comm'n, 78 Pa. Commw. 636, 468 A.2d 520 (1983).

[491] *E.g.*, Idaho Code § 18-606(1) (1987); Mass. Gen. Laws Ann. ch. 272, § 20 (West 1990); Mont. Code Ann. § 50-20-109(4) (1991) (by physician, hospital or other person or agency); Nev. Rev. Stat. § 442.270(1) (1991) (person or organization not to advertise directly or indirectly abortion costs or conditions); N.D. Cent. Code § 14-02.1-06 (1991); V.I. Code Ann. tit. 14, § 153 (Supp. 1991) (no public or private organization or society is to be created for purpose of soliciting candidates for abortion).

[492] *E.g.*, Cal. Penal Code § 276 (West 1988); Del. Code Ann. tit. 24, § 1792(2) (1987).

[493] *See supra*, notes 75–81 and accompanying text.

[494] *E.g.*, La. Rev. Stat. Ann. § 14:88(1) (West 1986); Miss. Code Ann. § 97-3-5 (1973); Nev. Rev. Stat. § 201.130 (1991); Vt. Stat. Ann. tit. 13, § 104 (Supp. 1991).

[495] *See* Carey v. Population Servs. Int'l, 431 U.S. 678, 688 (1977):

allocation of public funds in other sensitive areas.[535] The want of public funding may in time impel women to resort to clandestine abortionists and thus recreate the public health problem manifest before 1973.[536]

State legislatures hostile to the Court's doctrine no doubt will stand pat with their present legislation[537] because they are unwilling to reopen the volatile issue of abortion reform; they may also be anticipating a Supreme Court overturning of *Roe*.[538] If legislatures, not so motivated, in good faith track the details of each Supreme Court decision, they may find themselves out of step with the next sequence of constitutional precedent, with defective or inadequate legislation productive of new litigation. Legislating the details of rights to privacy is as futile and unproductive as endeavoring to duplicate through statute the myriad of refined points to doctrine adjudicated under the fourth amendment.

Hence, until the Supreme Court drops the other shoe, the future of abortion legislation is as shrouded in mist as the mountains in a Chinese brush painting. If the Su-

---

[T]he same test must be applied to state regulations that burden an individual's right to . . . terminate pregnancy by substantially limiting access to the means of effectuating that decision as is applied to state statutes that prohibit the decision entirely. Both types of regulation "may be justified only by a 'compelling state interest' . . . and . . . must be narrowly drawn to express only the legitimate state interests at stake."

Id. (citing Roe v. Wade, 410 U.S. 113, 155 (1973)).

[496]*E.g.,* Cal. Penal Code § 274 (West 1988); Colo. Rev. Stat. § 18-6-105 (1985) (other than licensed physician); Del. Code Ann. tit. 24, § 1792(1) (1987) (exempting for purposes of lawful abortion under § 1790); Idaho Code § 18-607 (1987) (except to physician or druggist or distributor or on prescription or order of physician, or possession with intent to supply to lawful recipient); Ill. Ann. Stat. ch. 38, § 81-31(3) (Smith-Hurd Supp. 1991 & 1992) (without prescription); Iowa Code Ann. §§ 205.1 (exempting supply on prescription), 205.2 (exempts those supplying physicians, etc., for use in the practice of their profession) (West 1987); Mich. Comp. Laws Ann. § 750.15 (1968) (except on prescription [probably too narrow under *Carey*]); S.C. Code Ann. § 44-41-80(a) (Law. Co-op. 1988) (except in connection with therapeutic abortions; women on whom abortions performed are not within criminal provisions); Wis. Stat. Ann. § 450.11(2) (West 1989) (except to licensed physicians or medical services).

[497]*E.g.,* Mass. Gen. Laws Ann. ch. 272, § 21 (West 1990); N.Y. Penal Law § 125.60 (McKinney 1987); Wash. Rev. Code Ann. § 9.02.030 (Repealed).

[498]*E.g.,* Idaho Code § 19-2115 (1987); Nev. Rev. Stat. § 175.301 (1987) (unless the person against whom the offense was committed was at the time a police officer or deputy sheriff (legitimating use of police-women decoys)). *See also supra,* notes 64–65 and accompanying text.

[499]Vt. Stat. Ann. tit. 13, § 102 (1974).

[500]Nev. Rev. Stat. § 201.140 (1987) (abortion, attempted abortion or selling abortifacients); Wash. Rev. Code Ann. § 9.020.040 (Repealed) (no person can claim privilege against self-incrimination in prosecutions for abortion, attempted abortion or selling drugs but is immunized under Wash. Rev. Code Ann. § 10.52.090 (1990)). *See also supra,* notes 66–69 and accompanying text.

[501]R.I. Gen. Laws § 11-23-5 (1989) (unnecessary to save woman's life; this basic provision is unconstitutional under *Roe v. Wade* if applied to physicians and superfluous in actuality in instances of criminal abortion).

[502]*See* Simopoulos v. Virginia, 462 U.S. at 510. If the matter amounts to an affirmative defense, then the burden of persuasion on the issue may be imposed on the defendant. Martin v. Ohio, 480 U.S. 228 (1987); Patterson v. New York, 432 U.S. 197 (1977). If the element of the lack of justification constitutes an element of the offense, then, according to Mullaney v. Wilbur, 421 U.S. 684 (1975), the burden of establishing the existence of that justification cannot constitutionally be shifted to the defense.

[503]432 U.S. 464 (1971). *See generally* Appleton, *Beyond the Limits of Reproductive Choice: The Contribution of the Abortion-Funding Cases to Fundamental-Rights Analysis and to the Welfare-Rights Thesis,* 81 Colum. L. Rev. 721, 724–31 (1981) [hereinafter cited as Appleton]; Canby, *Government Funding, Abortions and*

preme Court overrules or fundamentally restricts the constitutional protections for women desiring therapeutic abortions, then one may expect a surge of legislative activity. Most of it will be directed at doing away with all abortions unnecessary to preserve the lives of pregnant women. Some states, however, may be expected to return to the positions they held immediately before 1973, when they confirmed a statutory claim to therapeutic abortions for their residents.[539]

If, however, the Supreme Court honors the doctrine of stare decisis and leaves *Roe* substantially untouched, then one may wonder whether abortion legislation of any sort is actually needed. Civil, administrative and disciplinary proceedings can be brought against medical providers who make professionally unsound decisions to abort, and hospitals and clinics can be required to provide appropriate personnel and equipment to safeguard maternal and fetal health and life. Laypersons who offer medically unsupervised abortion services can be prosecuted for unlawful practice of medicine just as if they had purported to offer any other form of surgical or pharmaceutical treatment.

---

the Public Forum, 1979 Ariz. St. L.J. 11; Horan & Marzen, *The Moral Interest of the State in Abortion Funding: A Comment on Beal, Maher and Poelker,* 22 St. Louis U.L.J. 566 (1978); Jones, *supra* note 14, at 594–600; Petersen, *The Public Funding of Abortion Services: Comparative Developments in the United States and Australia,* 33 Int'l & Comp. L.Q. 158 (1984).

[504] 432 U.S. at 474.

[505] *Id.*

[506] *Id.* at 475–76 (footnote omitted).

[507] 432 U.S. 438 (1977).

[508] 52 U.S.C §§ 1396a(a)(13)(B), (17), 1396d(a)(1)–(5) (1988).

[509] Beal v. Doe, 432 U.S. at 447.

[510] 432 U.S. 519 (1977). *Poelker* was distinguished by the Eighth Circuit Court of Appeals, however, when it enjoined a city hospital commission from refusing to allow staff at the only hospital in the community, publicly owned, to perform lawful abortions for paying patients. Nyberg v. City of Virginia, 667 F.2d 754, 757–58 (8th Cir. 1982), *appeal dismissed, cert. dismissed,* 462 U.S. 1125 (1983).

[511] Called the Hyde Amendment after its original congressional sponsor. *See* Harris v. McRae, 448 U.S. 297, 302–03 (1980); Vinovskis, *The Politics of Abortion in the House of Representatives in 1976,* 77 Mich. L. Rev. 1790 (1979).

[512] The 1977 version acknowledged only danger to maternal life; the 1979 language recognized "severe and long-lasting physical health damage"; the 1980 version included rape or incest if reported promptly to a law enforcement agency or public health service. *See* Harris v. McRae, 448 U.S. at 302–03. The fiscal year 1984 version covered only instances "where the life of the mother would be endangered if the fetus were carried to term." Departments of Labor, Health and Human Services, and Education Appropriations Act, Pub. L. No. 98-139, § 204, 97 Stat. 871, 887 (1983).

In 1979, the president instructed the director of the United States International Development and Cooperation Agency, through the Agency for International Development (AID), not to provide funds under the Foreign Assistance Act of 1961, 22 U.S.C. §§ 2151-2429a (1988), to foreign nongovernmental organizations that perform or promote abortions, even with separate funds. In Planned Parenthood Federation of America v. Agency for International Development, 915 F.2d 59 (2d Cir.), *application denied,* 111 S. Ct. 335 (1990), the court ruled that a standard clause containing the restriction, in grants to American organizations, did not violate Planned Parenthood Federation's constitutional rights of speech, association or privacy. This holding appears ratified after the fact by the Court's holding in Rust v. Sullivan, 111 S. Ct. 1759 (1991) that the executive branch could bar all advice whatever concerning the availability of an abortion office given by family planning organizations receiving federal funding. *See infra,* notes 517–19 and accompanying text.

[513] 448 U.S. 297 (1980). Later the same term, in Williams v. Zbaraz, 448 U.S. 358 (1980), the Court held that a state participating in the Medicaid program is not obligated to underwrite medically-indicated abortions for which federal reimbursement is unavailable under the Hyde Amendment; the Court confirmed that state funding restrictions patterned on the Hyde Amendment do not violate fourteenth amendment equal

Abortion regulation adds nothing not already achievable through existing general legislation and administrative regulations.

Nor is there a need for special criminal abortion statutes aimed at clandestine or nonmedically indicated abortions, even though they are constitutional.[540] If a pregnant woman dies as a result of a criminally negligent abortion or bungled aftercare or if a viable fetus born alive dies for similar reason, the coverage of manslaughter or criminally negligent homicide statutes is clear. If a neonate's life is intentionally snuffed out, murder or manslaughter provisions are fully available.

If an unqualified person performs an abortion or a medically qualified person departs the bounds of proper abortion techniques without causing maternal or neonatal death, criminality is clear under modern assault statutes. Administering a substance other than for lawful medical or therapeutic purpose can be made a form of assault,[541] and the use of instruments almost certainly causes physical injury[542] or serious physical injury.[543] If an abortion is unlawful, a woman's consent to it is legally irrelevant to the criminality of the abortionist because it does not tend to raise a reasonable doubt about

---

protection. *See generally* Appleton, *supra* note 503; Isaacs, *supra* note 121, at 71–75; Jones, *supra* note 14 at 600–05; Yarbrough, *The Abortion-Funding Issue: A Study in Mixed Constitutional Cues,* 59 N.C.L. Rev. 611 (1981).

[514] Harris v. McRae, 448 U.S. at 315.

[515] *Id.* at 318–20. The Court also found that the plaintiffs lacked standing to litigate whether the Hyde Amendment interfered with their "free exercise" rights under the amendment. *Id. See also* Note, *Abortion Laws, Religious Beliefs and the First Amendment,* 14 Val. U.L. Rev. 487 (1980); Comment, *The Establishment Clause and Religious Influences on Legislation,* 75 Nw. U.L. Rev. 944 (1980).

On the religious dimension of the Hyde Amendment and similar legislative efforts to limit the impact of *Roe v. Wade,* see *e.g.,* Symonds, *The Denial of Medi-Cal Funds for Abortion: An Establishment of Religion,* 9 Golden Gate 421 (1978–1979); Pilpel, *The Fetus as Person: Possible Legal Consequences of the Hogan-Helms Amendment,* 6 Fam. Planning Perspectives, No. 1, p. 6 (Winter 1974); Editorial, *Do Catholics Have Constitutional Rights?,* 105 Commonweal 771 (Dec. 8, 1978).

[516] Harris v. McRae, 448 U.S. at 325.

Following enactment of the Hyde Amendment, federal courts required interim funding for therapeutic abortions until welfare recipients could be notified about reductions in Medicaid benefits, Pennsylvania v. Dep't of Health & Human Services, 723 F.2d 1114 (3d Cir. 1983) (based on more general federal legislation creating the Medicaid system), and continued reimbursement to states for abortions performed pursuant to federal court order. Georgia Dep't of Medical Assistance v. Heckler, 583 F. Supp. 1377 (N.D. Ga. 1984) (based on federal legislation and implementing administrative regulations).

Organizations like Planned Parenthood that include abortion counseling among their services can be denied eligibility to participate in the Combined Federal Campaign (CFC) for charitable giving by federal employees. That is the doctrinal conclusion to be drawn from the Supreme Court's holding in Cornelius v. NAACP Legal Defense & Educational Fund, Inc., 473 U.S. 788 (1985). In *NAACP,* although the respondents were exercising a first amendment-protected right of commercial speech in the form of solicitation, CFC rather than government property was the relevant forum; the government's stated reasons for denying access to CFC satisfied the requirement of reasonableness governing a denial of access to a nonpublic forum. Arguably, advocacy of abortion rights is to be analogized to the public-issue advocacy in which various ethnic-rights and environmental groups wished to engage and for the funding of which they sought inclusion in the CFC fund-raising efforts directed at federal officials and employees.

See generally Benshoof, *The Chastity Act: Government Manipulation of Abortion Information and the First Amendment,* 101 Harv. L. Rev. 1916 (1988); Hirt, *Why the Government Is Not Required to Subsidize Abortion Counseling and Referral,* 101 Harv. L. Rev. 1895 (1988).

[517] 111 S. Ct. 1759 (1991).

[518] 42 U.S.C. § 300a-6 (1988).

[519] 111 S. Ct. at 1776–78. The Court refused to invalidate the regulation on grounds that it would prevent women whose lives were endangered by pregnancy from receiving abortion-related information. The attack

the existence of the actus reus element of physical injury or serious physical injury.[544] If there is an unclear area, it is the criminality of negligent or intentional activity that destroys fetal life during birth processes. If this is a problem, curative legislation should be addressed directly at the basic problem without regard to whether birth processes result from the abortion of a viable fetus, induced labor or spontaneous premature or near-term miscarriage.

Accordingly, just as some states have legislated the demise of a great many regulatory provisions affecting professions, occupations, businesses, industries and enterprises, which have no affirmative justification for perpetuation,[545] so legislatures should recognize that abortion legislation is currently unnecessary and unproductive and terminate all special legislation relating to abortions, whether lawful or unlawful. Granted, however, the symbolic importance that abortion legislation has in the contemporary United States, it is exceedingly unlikely that legislation action of this sort will ever be forthcoming.

---

was launched against the regulation on its face; specific applications of the regulation in instances of life-endangering pregnancies could be addressed should they arise. *Id.* at 1773–74.

The decision was based on a five-to-four alignment of the Court, with Justice Souter joining Justice Rehnquist's majority opinion (the remaining three in the majority bloc were Justices White, Scalia and Kennedy). Although contemporaneous press reports summarized the view of a number of influential commentators that *Rust* presaged an overruling of the Court's constitutional jurisprudence protecting medically indicated terminations of pregnancy, the majority opinion in fact evokes principles, discussed *supra* in the main text, to which the Court had adhered since 1977.

[520] *See, e.g.,* Ariz. Rev. Stat. Ann. § 35-196.02 (1990); Ill. Ann. Stat. ch. 23, §§ 5-5, 6-1 (Smith-Hurd Supp. 1991 & 1992); Ind. Code Ann. § 16-10-3.3 (Burns 1990); Ky. Rev. Stat. §§ 205.560(1) (1991), 311.715 (1990); Minn. Stat. Ann. §§ 145.925(2), 256B.40 (West 1989 & Supp. 1992); N.J. Stat. Ann. § 30:4D-6.1 (West 1981) (*but see* Right to Choose v. Byrne, 91 N.J. 287, 450 A.2d 925 (1982)); N.D. Cent. Code §§ 14-02.3-01, 14-02.3-05 (1991) (violation a class B misdemeanor); 18 Pa. Cons. Stat. Ann. § 3215(c) (Purdon 1983); Pa. Stat. Ann. tit. 62, § 453 (Purdon Supp. 1991 & 1992); Utah Code Ann. §§ 26-18-4(3)–(4) (violation a class B misdemeanor), § 26-18-10(7) (1990); W. Va. Code § 16-2B-2 (1991) (state funds not to be used for abortion as a means of family planning); Wis. Stat. Ann. § 20.927(1) (West 1989).

[521] *E.g.,* Ariz. Rev. Stat. Ann. § 35-195-02 (1990); Ind. Code Ann. § 16-10-3.3 (Burns 1990); Ky. Rev. Stat. § 311.715 (1990); Minn. Stat. Ann. §§ 261.28, 393.07(11) (West Supp. 1992); N.D. Cent. Code § 14-02.3-01 (1981); 18 Pa. Cons. Stat. Ann. § 3215(c) (Purdon Supp. 1991 & 1992); Pa. Stat. Ann. tit. 62, § 453 (Purdon Supp. 1991 & 1992); Utah Code Ann. § 26-18-10(6)–(7) (1990); W. Va. Code § 16-2B-2 (1991); Wis. Stat. Ann. § 20.927(1) (West 1989).

[522] *E.g.,* Minn. Stat. Ann. § 256B.40 (West Supp. 1992); N.D. Cent. Code § 14-02.3-01 (1991); 18 Pa. Cons. Stat. Ann. § 3215(c) (Purdon Supp. 1991 & 1992), Pa. Stat. Ann. tit. 62 § 453 (Purdon Supp. 1991); Wis. Stat. Ann. § 20.927(1) (West 1989).

[523] Ill. Ann. Stat. ch. 127, § 526 (Smith-Hurd Supp. 1991 & 1992) (noncontributory health insurance payments to state employees); N.D. Cent. Code § 14.02.3-03 (1991) (all health insurance policies, except by optional rider with extra premium); 18 Pa. Cons. Stat. Ann. § 3215(d) (Purdon 1983) (funded for employees out of public monies); R.I. Gen. Laws § 36-12-2.1 (1984) (state or local health insurance plans); S.C. Code Ann. § 1-13-30(1) (Law. Co-op. 1988) (sex discrimination statute does not require employer to pay health benefits for abortion, but employer may agree to do so through collective bargaining).

[524] Utah Code Ann. §§ 76-7-322, 76-7-323 (1990); W. Va. Code § 16-2B-2 (1991).

[525] Including prohibitions against providing hospital or nursing care services, *e.g.,* Ill. Ann. Stat. ch. 23, § 7-1 (Smith-Hurd 1988); N.D. Cent. Code § 14-02.3-04 (1991); 18 Pa. Cons. Stat. Ann. § 3215(a), (b) (Purdon 1983) (except for treatment of postabortion complications or when no other facility performing abortions is available within a radius of 20 miles), disability benefits, *e.g.,* Ill. Ann. Stat. ch. 23, § 6-1 (Smith-Hurd Supp. 1991 & 1992), or burial benefits. *Id.* § 7-1.

[526] *E.g.,* Ariz. Rev. Stat. Ann. § 35-196.02 (1990); Ill. Ann. Stat. ch. 23, § 6-1 ((Smith-Hurd Supp. 1991 & 1992); Ind. Code. Ann. § 16-10-3-3 (Burns 1990); Ky Rev. Stat. §§ 205.560(6) (1991), 311.715 (1990);

Minn. Stat. Ann. § 256B.02(8)(13)(a) (West 1982); N.J. Stat. Ann. § 30:4D-6-1 (West 1981); N.D. Cent. Code § 14-02.3-01 (1991); 18 Pa. Cons. Stat. Ann. § 3215(c)(2) (Purdon Supp. 1991 & 1992); Pa. Stat. Ann. tit. 62, § 453 (Purdon Supp. 1991 & 1992); Utah Code Ann. § 26-18-4(3) (1990); Wis. Stat. Ann. § 20.927(2)(a) (West 1989). In addition, Ill. Ann. Stat. ch. 23, § 6-1 (Smith-Hurd Supp. 1991 & 1992), exempts abortions necessary to the health of either mother or unborn viable child, while Wis. Stat. Ann. § 20.927(2)(b) (West 1989) exempts cases in which a preexisting condition will cause grave, long-lasting physical health damage to a woman if she is not given an abortion. The health of an unborn viable child may be recognized under Ill. Ann. Stat. ch. 23, §§ 6-1, 7-1 (Smith-Hurd Supp. 1991 & 1992), and Va. Code § 32.1-92.2 (1988) recognizes the eugenic ground of a physician's certification that a fetus will be born with a gross and totally incapacitating physical deformity or mental deficiency.

[527] *E.g.*, Minn. Stat. Ann. § 256B.02(13)(b) (West 1982); 18 Pa. Cons. Stat. Ann. § 3215(c)(3) (Purdon 1983); Va. Code § 32.1-92.1 (1988); Wis. Stat. Ann. § 20.927(2)(a) (West 1989).

[528] Minn. Stat. Ann. § 256B.02(13)(c) (West 1982); 18 Pa. Cons. Stat. Ann. § 3215(c)(2)(3) (Purdon 1983); Va. Code § 32.1-92.1 (1988); Wis. Stat. Ann. § 20.927(2)(a) (West 1989).

[529] *E.g.*, Committee to Defend Reproductive Rights v. Myers, 29 Cal. 3d 252, 625 P.2d 779, 172 Cal. Rptr. 866 (1981) (budget act excluding funds to underwrite therapeutic abortions was declared in violation of the state constitution); Committee to Defend Reproductive Rights, Inc. v. Rank, 151 Cal. App. 3d 83, 198 Cal. Rptr. 630 (1984) (budget act restricting use of public funds for abortions found in conflict with basic Medi-Cal statute authorizing funds for therapeutic abortions); Doe v. State, 216 Conn. 85, 579 A.2d 37 (1990) (class of financially-unable women had succeeded in enjoining state from enforcing restrictions on abortions for patients eligible for state medical assistance, but state constitutional provision guaranteeing access to the courts did not provide a basis for an award of attorney fees); Kindley v. Governor of Md., 289 Md. 620, 426 A.2d 908 (1981) (court construed state legislation to cover all abortions determined by physicians in the patients' best interest but noted the lack of a legal obligation to fund abortions); Bayne v. Secretary of State, 283 Md. 560, 392 A.2d 67 (1978) (budget appropriation for public funding of abortions was not subject to state constitutional provision for popular referendum, which specifically excluded budgetary legislation); Right to Choose v. Byrne, 91 N.J. 287, 450 A.2d 925 (1982) (state constitution required invalidation of state legislation tracking Hyde Amendment; public funding must extend to all abortions necessary to maternal health); Donovan v. Cuomo, 126 A.D.2d 305, 513 N.Y.S. 2d 878, *application denied*, 70 N.Y.2d 611, 581 N.E.2d 6, 523 N.Y.S.2d 495 (1987) (reliance by state department of social services on a physician's certificate of medical necessity as the sole basis for funding abortion services under Medicaid is not improper as amounting to a payment for an elective abortion not eligible for funding; mere allegation that many abortions not medically necessary were being performed was insufficient in the absence of proof to obtain a judicial invalidation of procedures by which the department accepted physicians' certificates of medical necessity as a sole basis of funding); Stam v. Hunt, 66 N.C. App. 116, 310 S.E.2d 623 (1984) (rejecting citizen attack on state funding for therapeutic abortions based on claim that $1 million appropriation for purpose had been exhausted; legislature had appropriated additional funds).

On state constitutional and legislative responses generally, *see* Corns, *The Impact of Public Abortion Funding Decisions on Indigent Women: A Proposal to Reform State Statutory and Constitutional Abortion Funding Provisions,* 24 U. Mich. J.L. Ref. 371 (1991).

In Reina v. Landeskreditbank Baden-Württemberg, 1982, C.J. Comm. E. Rec. 33, 40, the European Court of Justice held that special interest-free loans to residents upon childbirth were a "social advantage" that could not be denied workers from another member state under art. 7(1) of the EEC Treaty and art. 7(2) of Council Regulation (EEC) No. 1612/68 (the anti-discrimination regulation). The court rejected a justification advanced by Baden-Württemberg that childbirth loans were intended to encourage larger families among residents; demographic objectives of countering falling birth rates among a member state's nationals cannot be pursued in a way that discriminates against nationals of other member states.

[530] *E.g.,* Minn. Stat. Ann. § 145.925(8) (West 1989) (misdemeanor); Mont. Code Ann. § 50-20-106(4) (1991); N.D. Cent. Code § 14-02.1-03(3) (1991); 18 Pa. Cons. Stat. Ann. § 3215(f), (h) (Purdon 1983).

[531] *E.g.,* Ark. Code Ann. § 20-17-601(c) (1991); Cal Health & Safety Code § 25955.3 (West 1984); Del. Code Ann. tit. 24, § 1791(c) (1987); Ky. Rev. Stat. § 311.810 (1990); Minn. Stat. Ann. § 145.414 (West 1989); Mo. Ann. Stat. § 197.032(2) (Vernon 1983).

[532] *E.g.,* Ark. Code Ann. § 20-16-601(c) (1991); Cal. Health & Safety Code § 25955.3 (West 1984); Del. Code Ann. tit. 24, § 1791(c) (1987); Ky. Rev. Stat. § 311.810 (1990); Me. Rev. Stat. Ann. tit. 22, § 1591 (1992); Md. Pub. Health Code Ann. § 20-214(c)(2) (Supp. 1991) (subject to referendum on amendment); Mass. Gen. Laws Ann. ch. 112, § 12S (West 1983) (patients are to be informed that refusal to undergo abortion is not a ground for denial of public assistance); Mo. Ann. Stat. § 197.032(2) (Vernon 1983); Or. Rev. Stat. § 435.435 (1991); 18 Pa. Cons. Stat. Ann. § 3215(g) (Purdon 1983).

[533] *E.g.,* Ark. Code Ann. § 20-16-601(c) (1991); Cal. Health & Safety Code § 25955.3 (West 1984); Del. Code Ann. tit. 24, § 1791(c) (1987); Ky. Rev. Stat. § 311.810 (1990); Me. Rev. Stat. Ann. tit. 22, § 1591 (1992); Md. Pub. Health Code Ann. § 20-214(c) (Supp. 1991) (subject to referendum on amendment); Mass. Gen. Laws Ann. ch. 112, § 12S (West 1983); Minn. Stat. Ann. § 145.414 (West 1989); Mo. Ann. Stat. § 197.032(2) (Vernon 1983); Or. Rev. Stat. § 435.435 (1991); 18 Pa. Cons. Stat. Ann. § 3215(g) (Purdon 1983).

[534] *E.g.,* Cal. Health & Safety Code § 25955.3 (West 1984); Ky. Rev. Stat. § 311.810 (1990).

[535]   Although the liberty protected by the Due Process Clause affords protection against unwarranted government interference with freedom of choice in the context of certain personal decisions, it does not confer an entitlement to such funds as may be necessary to realize all the advantages of that freedom. To hold otherwise would mark a drastic change in our understanding of the Constitution. It cannot be that because government may not prohibit the use of contraceptives . . . or prevent parents from sending their child to a private school . . . government, therefore, has an affirmative constitutional obligation to ensure that all persons have the financial resources to obtain contraceptives or send their children to private schools. To translate the limitations on governmental power implicit in the Due Process Clause into an affirmative funding obligation would require Congress to subsidize

the medically necessary abortion of an indigent woman even if Congress had not enacted a Medicaid program to subsidize other medically necessary services. Nothing in the Due Process Clause supports such an extraordinary result.

Harris v. McRae, 448 U.S. at 317–18 (citations omitted).

[536] Clandestine abortion was viewed as a public health problem before 1973, see, *e.g.*, Claderone, *Illegal Abortion as a Public Health Problem*, 50 Am. J. Pub. Health 948 (1960), and has that potential today if the availability of lawful therapeutic abortion is restricted. *See* Sneideman, *supra* note 23, at 192–94.

[537] *See supra*, notes 147–54 and accompanying text.

[538] That is the premise on which Linton, *supra* note 4, premised his article. *See also* Note, *The Supreme Court's Abortion Jurisprudence: Will the Supreme Court Pass the "Albatross" Back to the States?*, 65 Notre Dame L. Rev. 731 (1990).

[539] *See supra*, notes 38, 88 and accompanying text.

[540] *See supra*, notes 453–56 and accompanying text.

[541] *See e.g.*, N.Y. Penal Law § 120.05(5) (McKinney 1987); 30 Halsbury's Laws of England ¶ 43 (4th ed. 1980); Model Penal Code § 211.1, comment 3–4 (Official Draft & Revised Comments 1980).

[542] *See* N.Y. Penal Law §§ 10.00(9) (physical injury defined as impairment of physical condition or substantial pain), 120.00(1), (2) (McKinney 1987).

[543] *See* N.Y. Penal Law §§ 10.00(10) (serious physical injury defined as that which creates a substantial risk of death or which causes death or serious and protracted disfigurement, protracted impairment of health or protracted loss or impairment of the function of any bodily organ), 120.05(1), (2), (4), 120.10(1), (3) (McKinney 1987). The crime of reckless endangerment also may be available in abortion cases not producing death or injury but substantially risking either. *See, e.g., id.* §§ 120.20, 120.25; Tex. Penal Code Ann. § 22.05(a) (Vernon 1974); Model Penal Code § 211.1 (1980).

[544] *See, e.g.*, State v. Brown, 143 N.J. Super. 571, 364A.2d 27 (Super. Ct. Law Div. 1976), *aff'd*, 154 N.J. Super. 511, 381 A.2d 1231 (Super Ct. App. Div. 1977); Model Penal Code § 211.1, (2)(a) (1980); Comment, *Mayhem: Consent of Maimed Party as a Defense*, 47 Iowa L. Rev. 1122, 1127 n.25 (1961–1962).

[545] *See, e.g.*, Ala. Code §§ 41-20-1 to 41-29-16 (Michie 1991); Fla. Stat. Ann. § 11.61 (West 1988); W. Va. Code §§ 4-10-1 to 4-10-14 (1990 & Supp. 1991) (sunset law).

For a model abortion law consistent with the Supreme Court's doctrines, see Comment, *A Decade of Cementing the Mosaic of Roe v. Wade: Is the Composite a Message to Leave Abortion Alone?*, 15 U. Tol. L. Rev. 681, 749–53 (1984). Other legislative proposals appear in Walker & Puzder, *State Protection of the Unborn After Roe v. Wade: A Legislative Proposal*, 13 Stetson L. Rev. 237 (1984).

This article takes a careful look at the holding of *Roe v. Wade* and looks at the constitutional debate surrounding that now famous case. Professor Van Alstyne compares *Roe* with the *Cruzan* decision and shows that both cases may revolve around the issue of ''meaningful life.''

2 · The Cycle of Constitutional Uncertainty in American Abortion Law

William W. Van Alstyne,* J.D.

Abortion is the induced termination of pregnancy before the fetus is capable of survival. In a word, it is termination of pregnancy by means involving fetal death.[1] Until 1973, the circumstances in which abortion was permitted in the United States varied considerably, depending principally on the law of each state in the United States. Contrary to the constitutional practice in many other countries, there has never been a single national law setting the conditions for lawful abortions in the United States. And as public attitude tended to differ considerably in different states, the scope of the pertinent laws differed as well. As of 1973, the differences were quite substantial, from New York in which abortions were generally lawful within the first 12 weeks of pregnancy, to Texas in which abortions were lawful only insofar as the pregnant woman's life was at risk.[2]

---

*Perkins Professor of Law, Duke University.

[1] "Abortion" is derived from Latin, *aboriri,* meaning "to die, disappear." Standardly, abortion contemplates the termination of a pregnancy by means that are understood to be fatal to the fetus. "*Abortion:* n. 1. Induced termination of pregnancy before the fetus is capable of survival. 2. Any fatally premature expulsion of an embryo or fetus from the womb. (Latin, *abortare,* frequentative of *aboriri* (past participle of *abortus*), to die, disappear . . .)." *Amer. Heritage Dictionary* 4 (1971 ed.).

[2] Whether the Congress might preempt state laws on abortion in favor of a uniform national rule is beyond the scope of this review, but within broad limits it is likely that Congress could do so if it felt so inclined. The sources of enumerated powers Congress could draw from include the commerce clause, the spending clause, the necessary and proper clause and the enabling clause of the fourteenth amendment. Each has been given an extraordinarily permissive interpretation in the twentieth century decisions of the Supreme Court. (Since 1937, only one act of Congress displacing state laws has been held to fail in an unoverruled decision by the Supreme Court. [Oregon v. Mitchell, 400 U.S. 112 (1970)].) Moreover, some members of the Supreme Court now regard "mere" federalism questions to be virtually nonjusticiable—*i.e.,* as not subject to meaningful constitutional review. (*See, e.g.,* Garcia v. San Antonio Metro. Transit Auth., 469

In 1973, however, by a vote of seven-to-two, the Supreme Court of the United States held unconstitutional the laws of 49 states that limited the circumstances in which physicians could assist women in terminating pregnancies by abortion.[3] Its decision has been unceasingly controversial ever since. It is this subject we mean to review in this chapter, the better to understand the ongoing constitutional debate, and why that decision is now once again regarded as doubtful and seriously at risk.

A. The Basis and Holding in *Roe v. Wade*

The Court's decision in *Roe v. Wade* was based on the due process clause of the fourteenth amendment. The fourteenth amendment itself was adopted in 1868, in the aftermath of the Civil War. The due process clause,[4] on which the Court relied in *Roe v. Wade,* reads specifically in the following way:

> *[N]or shall any State deprive any person of life, liberty, or property, without due process of law . . .*

Though the Court's decision in *Roe v. Wade* was dramatic,[5] the Court's use of the due process clause to invalidate a state law interfering with personal liberty was not new. Far from it. For nearly 90 years, the Court had construed this clause as a source of substantive protection for persons whose liberty or property was threatened by some state law or local regulation restricting them in some way they believed to be oppressive. In 1878, a mere decade following the adoption of the fourteenth amendment, for

---

U.S. 528 (1985).) Insofar as that policy may characterize the attitude of the Supreme Court, it is entirely plausible that direct congressional preemption of state laws regulating abortion would be sustained. Differences among state laws regulating abortion may obviously bear differently on different people, for instance, depending partly on their varying ability to travel and seek recourse to the more permissive laws of some other state or foreign country, irrespective of the law of the state in which they reside. Congress might presume to declare that the effects of such behavior on interstate commerce and/or the intolerability of such differences made possible by such behavior require the establishment of a uniform national rule. It is doubtful that the Supreme Court would declare such an act of Congress void.

[3] Roe v. Wade, 410 U.S. 113 (1973) (White, J., and Rehnquist, J., dissenting). The effect of the decision was to invalidate existing antiabortion laws in every state with the possible exception of New York, which had just recently relaxed its regulations of lawful abortions. Although there was considerable variation among state laws regulating abortion (some permitting abortions fairly freely at least through the first four months, others hardly at all), no state law, New York possibly excepted, permitted abortions as freely as the Supreme Court declared in *Roe* to be constitutionally required.

[4] The due process clause, though a part of the fourteenth amendment (1868), was adapted from an earlier clause in the fifth amendment that was adopted in 1791 as part of the Bill of Rights. The original clause as it appears in the fifth amendment reads in the following way: "[N]or shall any person . . . be deprived of life, liberty, or property, without due process of law." Despite its general wording, however, this fifth amendment provision was understood to apply only to actions by the national government and *not* to actions by the states. (*See* Barron v. Mayor and City Council of Baltimore, 32 U.S. (7 Pet.) 243 [1833].) In the aftermath of the Civil War, as part of Reconstruction, following the adoption of the thirteenth amendment, Congress moved to secure the same measure of protection the due process clause provided in respect to actions by the national government for all persons in each state against state action as well. Thus the proposal in Congress in 1866 to include a due process clause in § 1 of the fourteenth amendment expressly addressed to the states. (Note the very similar wording of the due process clause in the fifth and in the fourteenth amendments, the two being virtually identical except that the fourteenth amendment makes explicit that it applies to the states.)

[5] *See supra* note 3.

example, Justice Bradley had reflected this view of appealing under the due process clause for relief against such state laws. In a case reviewing a Louisiana state supreme court decision under the due process clause, Justice Bradley explained the Court's role in the following way:[6]

> *I think we are entitled under the fourteenth amendment, not only to see that there is some process of law, but* due process of law, *provided by the State law when a citizen is deprived of his property; and that, in judging what is "due process of law," respect must be had to the cause and object of the taking, whether occurring under the taxing power, the power of eminent domain, or the power of assessment for local improvements, or none of these: and if found to be suitable or admissible in the special case, it will be adjudged to be "due process of law;" but if found to be arbitrary, oppressive, and unjust, it may be declared to be not "due process of law."*

In *Roe v. Wade,* in 1973, in a large sense this is just what the Supreme Court did in protecting a pseudonymous Jane Roe in Texas from what it regarded as an oppressive state law affecting her interest in "personal liberty."[7] A century-old Texas statute made it a felony for any physician to assist another in terminating any pregnancy by abortion unless the pregnant woman's life was at stake.[8] Ms. Roe[9] sued to have enforcement of

---

[6]Davidson v. New Orleans, 96 U.S.97, 107 (1878) (Bradley, J., concurring) (emphasis added). An earlier statement of the same sort also appears with reference to the due process clause of the fifth amendment, from which, as we have noted, the due process clause of the fourteenth amendment was copied. In Dred Scott v. Sandford, 60 U.S. (19 How.) 393, 450 (1857), Chief Justice Roger Taney had declared:

[A]n Act of Congress which deprives a citizen of the United States of his liberty or property, merely because he came himself or brought his property into a particular Territory of the United States, and who had committed no offense against its laws, could hardly be dignified with the name of due process of law.

(This statement was used in *Dred Scott* by Chief Justice Taney to hold against an act of congress forbidding slaveholders from traveling with their slaves (their "property") into territories of the United States disallowing slavery—*i.e.,* the congressional restriction was deemed to be unconstitutional under the fifth amendment as a deprivation of property without due process. The decision in *Dred Scott* helped bring on the Civil War.)

[7]410 U.S. at 153.

[8]The statute applied as a restriction on providing lawful medical services—*i.e.,* the doctor (not the woman) was subject to criminal punishment for performing an unlawful abortion. The origin of the statute (1854) and the fact that it was enacted solely as a restriction on the lawful practice of medicine suggest that when it was enacted the impelling concern was a concern for the ethical standards of the medical profession (*i.e.,* that there was no medical abortion procedure regarded as sufficiently safe from serious health risks to warrant approval within the profession itself). If so, then in *Roe* the Court might merely have held that as of 1973, circumstances had so far changed in respect to medically safe abortion procedures as to have rendered the original concern of the Texas legislature obsolete, insofar as early term abortions, properly provided, would as of this time in the 20th century put a woman no more at risk (and often at less risk) than were she to carry even a normal pregnancy to full term. But the Court declined to address the Texas statute simply on this limited basis, preferring to treat it as if it were also a reflection of felt legislative concerns respecting the value of human life in gestation and a response to the community's sense of repugnance to the very idea of conceiving a child one might then seek to have aborted (destroyed) though it posed no threat to oneself of a medical kind.

[9]A pseudonym for an unmarried pregnant woman wishing to shield her anonymity and thus suing as "Jane Roe."

this statute enjoined. Her claim was that though her life was not at risk, the Texas law was nevertheless unconstitutional as an invasion of her personal liberty to terminate her unwanted pregnancy as she thought best—that is, it was her decision, not that of Texas, to determine the best balance of interests under the circumstances. In essence, the Court agreed and held that the Texas statute imposed an undue limitation on the plaintiff's personal liberty to decide for herself whether to secure a medically safe termination of an unwanted pregnancy though her life was not at risk. Accordingly, having reached that conclusion, it struck the state statute down.

Moreover, in the Court's view, expressed in a lengthy opinion by Justice Blackmun, a state could have no constitutionally acceptable reason to limit a pregnant woman's freedom of choice to secure an abortion during the first six months of her pregnancy, so long as she did so in a medically safe manner not threatening to her own health. Until the end of the sixth month, it was a matter to be decided privately between herself and her physician without hindrance interposed by the state except to assure her own safe treatment. Consistent with "due process," in the Court's view, a legislature could subordinate her "liberty" interest (to decide for herself either to continue or abort her pregnancy with a willing physician's professionally competent assistance) only in two circumstances:

(a)   to the extent necessary to avoid hazards to her own physical health;[10] or

(b)   to protect the life of a viable (but not a pre-viable) fetus.[11]

Any other restrictions limiting abortion by positive state law would not be regarded as due process of law.

B. Elaborations of the Holding in *Roe v. Wade*

In the aftermath of *Roe v. Wade,* but consistent with this description of the case, a large number of decisions flowed from the Supreme Court. We briefly examine here a representative number of these decisions to illustrate the extent to which laws on abortion have been affected pursuant to this case. Could the state require that two physicians (rather than merely one physician) concur before an abortion could be provided consistent with *Roe v. Wade?* No, the Court concluded, because standardly there is certainly no such requirement for medical services in general and there is no special condition peculiar to abortions in general that medically warrants the imposition of such a requirement in every abortion case. Legislating such a special requirement for abortions, therefore, unduly burdens the woman's abortion right established in *Roe* by subjecting it to an arbitrary condition. Accordingly, a law imposing such a condition is void.[12]

What, then, of a state law restricting abortions only to hospitals? Such a restriction, the Court held, must fall on the same ground. Since many medically safe abortions can be performed in much less elaborate, less costly, and more readily available facilities,

---

[10]*E.g.,* by restricting the kind of facility in which abortions could be provided, the medical procedures, and the qualifications of authorized personnel, but only to the extent necessary to insure medically responsible practices consistent with insuring the woman's own physical health.

[11]Subject, however, to the qualification that the law must permit an abortion at *any* time, whether or not in the last trimester, if "necessary to preserve the life or health of the mother."

[12]*See* Doe v. Bolton, 410 U.S. 179 (1973).

a general restriction of this sort is likewise an undue burden on women seeking termination of pregnancy by abortion. Accordingly, it too is arbitrary and void.[13]

But could the state forbid abortion to a married woman absent her husband's agreement? No, it could not do so, the Court was to hold. The decision is hers to make in the Court's view of her liberty interest under *Roe,* and the state could not subject the decision to third-party consent.[14]

At least in the case of an unemancipated and unmarried minor, absent a medical emergency, could a state require parental consent prior to abortion? The case may seem somewhat more problematic, but again the answer was no. Here, too, the majority thought such a requirement unduly burdens a (minor-age) woman's paramount interests and is also, therefore, unconstitutional as a denial of due process of law.[15]

Can the state forbid abortion unless those providing the service first read material the state itself deems suitable for the pregnant woman to consider and wants to be forcefully impressed on her? No, once again, not insofar as it exceeds what a competent physician might himself or herself find suitable to provide.[16] As these several decisions indicate, then, *Roe v. Wade* has had a very substantial career.

C. Countervailing Developments and Second Thoughts

On the other hand, the post-*Roe* decisions are not all of a piece. As we have seen, the Court has limited the states' interference with the protected liberty of women to control the critical decision in terminating or not terminating an unwanted pregnancy, but its decisions have not extended to any requirement of positive assistance of any kind, at least in respect to any abortion not medically advised. Concretely, the Court has held that no state is constitutionally obliged to subsidize nontherapeutic abortions even though the state will pay the medical expenses of low-income women who choose to carry the fetus to full term.[17] And it has held, likewise, that Congress can restrict any use of federal aid to defray medical costs related to nontherapeutic abortion while providing reimbursement assistance only to women electing childbirth.[18] Moreover, it has quite recently held that, except as necessary to save a pregnant woman's life, a state may forbid any abortion in any public hospital or public health care facility and may likewise forbid any health care professional in public service to perform, assist or counsel abortion.[19]

---

[13] *Id.* Could such a restriction be imposed at least for any abortion after the first trimester? (No. *See* City of Akron v. Akron Center for Reproductive Health, Inc., 472 U.S. 416 [1983]: same reasoning—too rigid a requirement as not all second trimester abortions require the facilities of a hospital).

[14] *See* Planned Parenthood v. Danforth, 428 U.S. 52 (1976). (The consequence is that the husband cannot gainsay his wife's choice of abortion for whatever reason is satisfactory solely to herself though the child is his, though he desires it and though abortion is not medically required for the woman's health.)

[15] *See* Planned Parenthood v. Danforth, 428 U.S. 52 (1976). On the other hand, a state may require parental *notice* prior to any nonemergency abortion procedure on an unmarried and unemancipated minor at least if an alternative judicial bypass procedure in lieu of such notice is also provided by the law. *See* Hodgson v. Minnesota, 497 U.S., 110 S.Ct. 2926 (1990); Ohio v. Akron Center for Reproductive Health, Inc., 497 U.S., 110 S.Ct. 2972 (1990).

[16] *See* Thornburgh v. American College of Obstetricians & Gynecologists, 476 U.S. 747 (1986).

[17] *See* Maher v. Roe, 432 U.S. 464 (1977). In the Court's words, the state is not obliged to remove cost barriers to abortion. *Roe v. Wade,* in brief, protects "liberty"—*i.e.,* freedom (from state restrictions); it does not create a "right" (of nontherapeutic abortion at public expense).

[18] *See* Harris v. McRae, 448 U.S. 297 (1980).

[19] *See* Webster v. Reproductive Health Services, 492 U.S. 490 (1989).

Accordingly, depending on the availability of private clinics and private physicians, the economic circumstances of the woman seeking a nontherapeutic abortion, travel distances, fees, personal knowledge, and so forth, practical access for nontherapeutic abortion may vary quite substantially for women in some American states.[20] None of this has raised any special question, however, about *Roe v. Wade* itself. Rather, the report we have thus far given is merely a dry report on developments—that is, merely as they have occurred.

The basic case (as well as several of the subsequent decisions), however, has in fact continued to engender deep controversy, including controversy within the Supreme Court itself. In fact, as of the day of this writing, it is fairly reckoned that a minimum of four justices on the Supreme Court now believe the basic decision in *Roe v. Wade* was improper, leaving aside cases as appeared to expand upon it in some way. The two justices originally in dissent (Justice White and Justice Rehnquist—now Chief Justice) remain active on the Court. Each has continued to express objections to *Roe,* and each has maintained a resolve to reconsider the decision under appropriate circumstances.[21] Before retiring from the Supreme Court, Chief Jutice Warren Burger, who originally joined in Justice Blackmun's opinion in *Roe,* expressed regret for having done so in view of the subsequent case law developments.[22] Two others, Justice Scalia and Justice Kennedy, more recently appointed by President Reagan, are on record as willing to reconsider *Roe* as well.[23] The newest justices, Justice Souter and Justice Thomas, have had no occasion thus far to express themselves one way or the other,[24] but the auspices

---

[20] As reported in the New York Times (April 26, 1991, p. A13, col.6), overall the number of induced abortions in the United States each year "has been relatively stable since 1980, at nearly 1.6 million each year," but the rate varies substantially, by age, location, and race (*e.g.,* teenage pregnancies are more common than in 1980 and abortions have risen by 18% since 1980 among girls under 15 years—nearly one in every 100 14-year-olds in the sample considered had undergone an abortion—even while overall, in proportion to population, the frequency of abortion has dropped since 1980 by 6%). About half the abortions, according to the study reported in the Times (from the Alan Guttmacher Institute), are performed in early pregnancy—*i.e.,* prior to the ninth week with somewhat less than 1% occurring later than the 20th week.

[21] Thornburgh v. American College of Obstetricians and Gynecologists, 476 U.S. 747, 786 (White, J., dissenting in an opinion for himself and Justice Rehnquist) ("I was in dissent in *Roe v. Wade* and am in dissent today . . . *Stare decisis* is not the only constraint upon judicial decisionmaking . . . [I]t is essential that this Court maintain the power to restore authority to its proper possessors by correcting constitutional decisions that, on reconsideration, are found to be mistaken.")

[22] *Id.* at 783–785 ("I regretfully conclude that some of the concerns of the dissenting Justices in Roe . . . have now materialized . . . If *Danforth* and today's holding really mean what they say, I agree we should reexamine *Roe.*")

[23] *See* Webster v. Reproductive Health Services, 490 U.S. 490, 532 (1989) (Scalia, J., calling for the explicit overruling of *Roe v. Wade* and agreeing with Justice Blackmun that a part of the decision [in which Justice Kennedy concurred] in *Webster* is inconsistent with, and a rejection of, *Roe*); Ohio v. Akron Center for Reproductive Health, 497 U.S., 110 S.Ct. 2972, 2984 (Scalia, J., concurring) (again expressing disapproval of *Roe,* adding also that "the Constitution contains no right to abortion"); see also opinion in this case by Kennedy, J., and in the companion case, Hodgson v. Minnesota, 497 U.S., 110 S.Ct. 2926 (1990) (Kennedy, J, voting to sustain two-parent notification requirement prior to abortion on unemancipated, unmarried minor), and *id.* at 2960 (concurring opinion by Scalia, J.).

[24] But *see* Rust v. Sullivan, 111 S.Ct. 1759 (1991) (sustaining as constitutional—against objections based on *Roe v. Wade* and on the first amendment—a restriction forbidding any referral to any abortion provider or any consideration of abortion as an alternative to child birth in any "family planning" project operating in whole or in part with federal funds, absent a medical emergency). Justice Souter wrote no separate opinion in *Rust.* Nevertheless, his vote was crucial to the outcome, to compose the five-member majority on the Court, sustaining the federal regulation pursuant to an opinion by Chief Justice Rehnquist (for himself,

of their nominations by President Bush (and their careful abstentions from any utterance with reference to *Roe* during their confirmation hearings held before a Democratically dominated Senate Committee) indicate at least something less than a foregone vote firmly committed to *Roe v. Wade*.

In fact, only Justice Blackmun (who is over 80 years old) and Justice Stevens are on record as committed to the full regime of *Roe v. Wade* as we have outlined it here. Justice O'Connor has several times said simply that no case coming to the Court thus far has required her to face the original case. Her statements on point, however, indicate a substantial repudiation of the simple trimester framework laid down in the advisory opinion by Justice Blackmun for the Court in the original case.[25]

These developments, plus the political fact that *Roe v. Wade* has simply not passed into history as being so settled as to be beyond reconsideration, are fully reflected in recent legislative developments in the United States as well. Here, it is useful to mention but two such developments, each quite pointedly illustrating the manner in which oppositely minded forces seem themselves to understand that *Roe v. Wade* is exceedingly insecure. In Congress, as of this writing, a bill has been introduced that proposes to have Congress forbid any state from adopting any law inconsistent with *Roe v. Wade*.[26] The obvious intention is to try by this means to take the issue from reconsideration by the Supreme Court under the fourteenth amendment by legislating a national abortion right. In Utah, in the meantime, a new statute has already passed and is in litigation. The Utah act limits abortion generally to pregnancies resulting from rape or from criminal incest, to cases where the woman's health is at serious risk and to cases in which the fetus is determined to be gravely defective.[27] The Utah statute is only modestly different from the current law incidentally, on permissible abortion in (West) Germany.[28] This statute, among several, may well put the original issue once more before the Supreme Court.[29]

Souter, Kennedy, White, and Scalia.) Instructively, the principal dissent written by Justice Blackmun for himself, Marshall and Stevens, based partly on *Roe* and separately on the first amendment, failed to carry Justice Souter. (There was a separate dissent by Justice O'Connor on the limited claim that the restrictive regulation was not clearly authorized by the act of Congress and, insofar as sustaining the regulation would require the Court to address a substantial first amendment question, canons of statutory construction applicable to acts of Congress in such circumstances mandated avoidance of a constitutional issue where an alternative construction was equally consistent with the language and legislative history of the act.)

[25] *See, e.g.* her comments in Akron v. Akron Center for Reproductive Health, Inc., 462 U.S. 416, 459–466 (1983); Thornburgh v. American College of Obstetricians and Gynecologists, 476 U.S. 747, 814, 828 (1986) (O'Connor, J., dissenting) ("This Court's abortion decisions have already worked a major distortion in the Court's constitutional jurisprudence . . . [T]he Court's unworkable scheme for constitutionalizing the regulation of abortion has had [a] debilitating effect . . . the Court is not suited to the expansive role it has claimed for itself in the series of cases that began with *Roe v. Wade*") Additionally, Justice O'Connor's dissent in *Rust v. Sullivan supra* note 24 places no reliance on *Roe v. Wade*.

[26] The original version is S. 1912, 101st Cong., 1st Sess., Nov. 17, 1989 (The "Freedom of Choice Act of 1989").

[27] Specifically that "in the professional judgment of the pregnant woman's attending physician, the child would be born with grave and irremediable physical or mental deformities incompatible with sustained survival."

[28] *See* 28 The American Series of Foreign Penal Codes (Federal Republic of Germany) §§ 211–219 (1987).

[29] On January 21, 1992, the Supreme Court granted review in *Planned Parenthood of Southeastern Pennsylvania v. Casey,* 947 F.2d 682 (3rd. Cir. 1991), *cert. granted,* 60 U.S.L. Wk. 3492. The case involves a challenge to a recent Pennsylvania act (the "Pennsylvania Abortion Control Act") imposing certain new restrictions on abortion procedures. Unlike the Utah statute, however, nothing challenged in the Pennsylvania act forbids any abortion otherwise allowed by *Roe v. Wade*. Consistent with the Pennsylvania act,

D. Once More on Protecting "Life" and "Liberty" in the United States

The litigation now outstanding in Utah, regardless of how it turns out, is symbolically useful to us in understanding the unconstitutional uncertainty that still hangs over *Roe v. Wade*. In electing a particular pseudonym for challenging the Utah law, the plaintiff has chosen to present herself as "Jane Liberty" rather than as "Jane Doe" or "Jane Roe," as has been most customary.[30] The pseudonym she has chosen may merely seem highly appropriate. After all, it is the liberty clause of the fourteenth amendment on which *Roe v. Wade* itself has made to rest. So her presentation of herself seems merely in keeping with that seminal case.

This is a phrase with a possible excess of cleverness in its use here, however, for it also puts the question raised in *Roe* very aggressively—just how far may one's liberty extend?[31] Does it extend to the extent of inflicting harm on others? Does it extend to inflicting death? Ordinarily, one's liberty has not been thought so to do. Ordinarily, moreover, it has been thought to be the function of legislative bodies to see that it does not. The avoidance of harm to others, that is, unjustified harm, is among the chief ends of a civilized community.[32] And when legislative bodies have drawn some conscionable

---

for example, a woman could still secure an abortion with any willing physician's help, though it were done late in the second trimester and done purely from disappointment after determining that the sex of the fetus made the pregnancy not worthwhile to continue—an abortion the Utah statute would forbid. In this respect the Pennsylvania statute still takes a very "hands off" position insofar as it continues to commit the life-or-death fate of the fetus entirely to the final decision of the pregnant woman and does so at *all* times during the same extended time frame as provided by *Roe*.

    Despite that fact, i.e., despite this clear difference distinguishing the Pennsylvania statute from the different kind of statute recently adopted in Utah, the Supreme Court's grant of certiorari generated instant national speculation that whatever decision the Court renders in this case may settle the extent to which a majority of the Court is prepared to overrule *Roe v. Wade*. Perhaps, but it is not obvious why it should unless the largely procedural regulations under review in this case are regarded by the Court as so substantial and burdensome in character as to be unsustainable, unless *Roe v. Wade* is unsustainable as well (just as some members of the Court have already declared). It is fairly arguable whether or not that is so, however, and presumably it is just to determine whether that is so that the Court agreed to hear this case. The Utah statute, though not yet adjudicated (and thus not yet eligible for review in the Supreme Court), is better designed as a direct challenge to *Roe*.

[30] The case is *Liberty v. Barngerter* (the second party being the governor of Utah whom the plaintiff seeks to enjoin from securing the enforcement of the Utah act). *See* N.Y. Times, May 10, 1991, p. B12, col. 1.

[31] *See,* for example, Holmes, J., dissenting in Lochner v. New York, 198 U.S. 45, 76 (1906): "[I] think the word 'liberty,' in the 14th amendment, is perverted when it is held to prevent the natural outcome of a dominant opinion, unless it can be said that a rational and fair man would necessarily admit that the statute proposed would infringe fundamental principles as they have been understood by the traditions of our people and our law." In respect to abortion, state statutes forbidding physicians to take fetal life other than under highly compelling circumstances (as *Roe* does not require) would *not* fail this test. (It is a point repeatedly stressed in many of the dissents.)

[32] *Cf.* John Stuart Mill's observation, in his essay titled as an essay "On Liberty," published in 1859 (Mill, *On Liberty* 10–11 [Norton edition, ed. D. Spitz, 1975]):

> The object of this Essay is to assert one very simple principle, as entitled to govern absolutely the dealings of society with the individual in the way of compulsion and control . . . [t]hat the only purpose for which power can be rightfully exercised over any member of a civilised community, against his will, is to prevent harm to others.

The question, then, is not whether society may intervene to prevent harm to others but rather who is to count (and who is to decide whether they should and for how much).

balance according to the harm principle[33] and when they have made that balance explicit in criminal laws, whether to protect small animals, large persons, other people's property or for that matter human life in gestation, the U.S. Supreme Court has generally found no basis in the due process clause of the fourteenth amendment to set it aside.[34] Least of all has the Court felt privileged to do so when the law it is asked to set aside is a law that forbids the infliction of death.

In *Cruzan v. Director*,[35] decided during the most recent term of the Supreme Court, for example, the Court had under review a due process "liberty" claim also involving a life weighed as worthwhile enough by a legislature to protect and a liberty as claimed by those seeking to exercise that liberty to terminate that life, this time in the setting of a person understood to exist in an irreversible vegetative state. Her closest family members desired to have her detached from nutritional tubes, allowing her to die (or, in a sense, merely to complete her death—for she lacked all consciousness and consciousness could never be regained). Absent clear and convincing evidence that the irreversibly stricken person would herself choose to have her "life" (such as it was) terminated, however, the Court held that the legislative act must control.

The decision in *Cruzan* is in some ways clearly distinguishable from *Roe v. Wade*, but it is also fundamentally at odds with *Roe v. Wade* in the manner in which it defers to conscionable legislative efforts in measuring life.[36] Eminently reasonable persons might conclude (indeed, they plainly had concluded) not merely that a person in Ms. Cruzan's condition was beyond all possibility of recovery[37] but that her present "existence" was so reduced as not at all to involve "meaningful life"—the only concern reflected in the state law.[38] In this respect, however, the statute involved (and sustained) in *Cruzan* is more than merely akin to an abortion statute that attaches value to a four-month healthy human fetus in gestation. Rather, it is just like it. It puts a value on a certain kind of human life. Yet, according to Justice Blackmun's opinion in *Roe v. Wade*, no legislature may constitutionally deem such a fetus sufficiently worthy of protection as to warrant protection against the termination of its life when done by abortion.[39] Indeed, what makes *Cruzan* so salient is to ask, consistent with the harm

---

[33] That abortion does "harm" to a fetus is not problematic (indeed, it is defined as a procedure to cause the fetus to die). *See supra* note 1.

[34] Never, in fact (prior to *Roe v. Wade*), unless the person were herself or himself at grave and immediate risk (in which case, it may be quite appropriate to speak of an imperative personal right to life—*i.e.*, a right of self-defense).

[35] 496 U.S., 110 S.Ct. 2841 (1990).

[36] Instructive of the possible value of this comparison of *Cruzan* and *Roe* is the fact that the justices in dissent in *Cruzan* are exactly *and only* the same justices still committed to *Roe v. Wade*—*i.e.*, Brennan and Marshall, both since retired, Blackmun and Stevens. The majority, sustaining the state law against a due process "liberty" claim, consisted of Justices O'Connor, Kennedy, White, Scalia, and Chief Justice Rehnquist, all still on the Court. We have already noted their expressed reservations about *Roe*.

[37] As was stipulated to be the case.

[38] She was described as existing in a state wholly bereft of consciousness, with irreversible brain loss of cognitive functions—a mere "vegetative" condition that could never improve. It was a point forcefully made in the case, in dissent. *Id.* at 2886 (Stevens, J., dissenting, describing the act as reflecting "[t]he State's unflagging determination to perpetuate the [vegetative person's] physical existence" as "comprehensible only as an effort to define life's meaning, not as an attempt to preserve its sanctity.")

[39] Recall that according to the Blackmun opinion, it is not until the end of the sixth month in gestation that a legislature may even "count" the fetus as having a life interest to weigh against the wishes of the person who desires it to be terminated. Only when it is "viable" may it for some reason be deemed a life worthy to be kept from harm.

principle and life and liberty, if the legislature may treat ''life'' in *Cruzan*-like circumstances as worthy of protection, how it can still be thought unconstitutional if the legislature treats ''life'' in gestation as worthy of protection as well? And if it may, as now seems likely—that is, if it may treat human life in gestation as worthy of protection—then that reopens the question just as it was prior to *Roe,* namely, to what extent?[40]

As a legislative matter, to be sure, there may be much to commend in leaving things pretty much as they now are. As a constitutional matter, however, *Roe v. Wade* is weak in its view of protectible ''life'' and is probably quite as perishable as was *Dred Scott.*[41] The fourteenth amendment may have little to say on such matters as those involved in this case, and what it says may by no means be all on one side.

Compare the West German Abortion Decision of 1975, holding *un*constitutional the *de*criminalization of abortion so long as it occurs prior to the thirteenth week of pregnancy (not the 24th week as Blackmun posited in *Roe*). The Constitutional Court held that the Basic Law itself forbids even the national legislature from ascribing *no* protectible worth to a fetus in gestation—''The state may not abdicate its responsibility . . . through the recognition of a 'legally free area,' by which the state abstains from the value judgment and abandons this judgment to the decision of the individual to be made on the basis of his own sense of responsibility.'' (Constitutional Court of the Federal Republic of Germany, Decision of February 25, 1975 [1975 BVerfG 1 (Jonas and Gorby translation, reprinted in 9 John Marshall Journal of Practice and Procedure 605-84 (1976)]). The decision rested on Article 2 of the Basic Law—the Constitution of West Germany—that, it declared, was drafted and enacted ''to avoid past faults and to learn not only from history—if ever possible—but from our own constitutional history'' (undoubtedly referring to the Holocaust and the disregard for categories of human life during the Nazi era). For the current law applicable in West Germany applicable to lawful abortion, *see supra* note 28.

[40] *E.g.,* to the extent of protecting that life except in circumstances compelling recognition that it cannot in all likelihood survive in gestation and/or that its continued gestation poses a grave threat?

[41] Dred Scott v. Sandford, 60 U.S. (19 How.) 393 (1857) (the case construing the due process clause of the fifth amendment as protecting private property in the form of slaves, noted and discussed at *supra* note 6).

This article presents the perils of compromise on abortion along with several legislative proposals to regulate abortion. Professor Dellinger interestingly states, ''even if only one 'reason' for having an abortion were prohibited by law, every woman would have to prove to some government board that the prohibited reason was not her reason.'' The article ends with a careful examination of the new Utah law and what effects it would have upon the medical and legal community.

3 · Abortion: The Case Against Compromise ⎯⎯⎯⎯⎯

Walter Dellinger,* LL.B.

As a result of the Supreme Court's decisions in *Webster v. Reproductive Health Services* (1989) and *Rust v. Sullivan* (1991), abortion has become a central issue of majoritarian politics: More than half a million Americans rallied in the nation's capital in the year following *Webster* to assert strongly pro-choice or pro-life views. Many prominent commentators are concluding, however, that the "extremists on both sides" must yield to the quieter voices of those who understand the necessity of moderate solutions and legislative compromise. That view, it seems to me, is profoundly mistaken.

The calls for compromise are appearing with increasing frequency. Historian Fred Seigel, for example, writes in the *Atlantic* that the abortion issue "pits advocates for women's rights against proponents of fetal rights on an issue that cries out for the compromise heartily desired by the vast majority of the American people." Once the "true believers" on each side have exhausted themselves, William Safire writes, the sensible "pro-compromise majority" will step forth to "reject politicians who slavishly follow pro-life or pro-choice fundamentalists." Opinion polls consistently show, says the *New York Times,* "a substantial middle ground in public opinion, an ambivalent majority that is opposed to an unlimited right to abortion but is also convinced that there are situations when abortion should be available."

⎯⎯⎯⎯⎯⎯⎯⎯⎯

*Walter Dellinger is a professor of law at Duke University. He was counsel of record for pro-choice members of the United States Congress in the United States Supreme Court's 1992 Pennsylvania abortion case, *Planned Parenthood v. Casey,* and he served as cocounsel on the amicus brief of the National Association of Women Lawyers in *Rust v. Sullivan.* He is the coauthor with Gene B. Sperling of *Abortion and the Supreme Court: The Retreat from Roe v. Wade,* 138 University of Pennsylvania Law Review 83 (1990). Some of the material in this chapter appeared in Dellinger, *Should We Compromise on Abortion?* in The American Prospect, Summer 1990.

Many argue that pro-choice supporters should not be unduly alarmed by the return of the abortion issue to state legislatures. In July of 1989, the editors of the *Washington Post* offered the reassuring opinion that

> *It is our suspicion . . . that even if the worst nightmare of the abortion rights groups came true and Roe were overturned entirely, not a single state would move to criminalize abortion. There will be skirmishing around the edges for years on questions such as funding and parental notification. Some legislatures will adopt some restrictions, but then the voters will have the final word. In a number of states, minor changes may be accepted. But basic rights will not be withdrawn.*

The argument that legislative compromise on abortion is inevitable and desirable has not been confined to popular publications. The argument that legislatures will (and should) gradually compromise on moderate legislative restrictions received serious scholarly support two years ago from the publication of the ambitious comparative law study *Abortion and Divorce in Western Law* by Harvard Law Professor Mary Ann Glendon. "Interest in her analysis," the *New York Times* reported, "has grown since last summer when the Supreme Court . . . at least partially returned legal authority over abortion to state legislatures."

In her complex critique of *Roe v. Wade,* Glendon argues that *Roe* endorsed an "extreme and isolating version of individual liberty" and contrasts that with the more "communitarian" approach she finds in Europe where most countries take a "middle position" of disapproving abortion in principle while permitting it in circumstances deemed by the legislature to constitute good cause. She draws a sharp contrast between the European situation and that of the United States where "to a greater extent than any other country, our courts have shut down the legislative process of bargaining, education, and persuasion on the abortion issue."

(Glendon misleadingly suggests that *Roe v. Wade* "insulated the pregnant women from the larger society" and that it precluded humane statutory initiatives and supportive communitarian approaches to the problem of abortion and unwanted pregnancy. Nothing in *Roe v. Wade,* however, precluded a woman from choosing to consult her parents, spouse, minister or supportive friends about her decision; nothing in *Roe* precluded governments from reducing the number of abortions by making more effective birth control widely available; nothing in *Roe v. Wade* precluded the community from providing the financial support that would make it easier for more women to choose to have more children. What *Roe* foreclosed was not communitarianism but compulsion.)

Arguing that a world without *Roe* "would not necessarily represent a setback for women" Glendon asserts that it is erroneous to conclude that "no compromise is possible" on abortion. The continental experience, she concluded, "shows that when the legislative process is allowed to operate, political compromise is not only possible but typical."

The Perils of Compromise

The widespread desire that some kind of compromise be found for the divisive abortion issue is understandable: Our public law should not appear wholly indifferent to the values that underlie the deeply held moral beliefs of large numbers of Americans. Even though I am naturally inclined to welcome suggestions for ameliorating contentious issues, I want to argue here that proposed "compromise" restrictions on abortion are unacceptable. What is proposed as compromise simply does not satisfy the concerns of people who find abortion morally troublesome. But the "moderate" restrictions in force and those now being introduced do impose real harm on many women and fall with such disproportionate force upon the less fortunate that they offend fundamental principles of equality.

The kinds of abortion legislation being advanced in the sheep's clothing of compromise fail to take into account the social and economic reality of abortion in America. Some "intermediate" restrictions now being proposed are coercive laws that would seriously curtail every woman's autonomy. Other proposals would retain access to safe and legal abortion for affluent urban women while compromising away the rights of young, poor, uneducated and rural women. Many compromise legislative proposals are disguised trades that would enable those who are affluent to retain access to abortion (for now at least) in exchange for "moderate" restrictions that place abortion out of the reach of less fortunate women. It is a devil's bargain and it must be rejected.

Legislative proposals to regulate abortion fall into these general categories: (1) *access restrictions,* such as mandatory waiting periods, abortion-specific health and safety regulations and parental or spousal notification and consent requirements; (2) *timing restrictions,* which require that abortions be performed only in the earlier weeks or months of gestation; and (3) *justification requirements,* limiting the reasons that count as acceptable grounds for terminating a pregnancy. Each type carries its own perils.

Restrictions on Access

Requirements that all second trimester abortions be performed either in hospitals or in clinics resembling small hospitals may raise the cost of abortion but do not seem wholly to preclude the exercise of choice. Similarly, a mandatory waiting period (recently enacted in Pennsylvania and now under consideration in several other states) may not seem an undue burden when viewed from the perspective of an urban professional woman. Viewed from the perspective of a young pregnant woman, 18 years old, unmarried and living in rural North Carolina, a different picture emerges. Seemingly innocuous requirements may have devastating consequences. A low-income, 11th-grade girl struggling to finish high school and prepare herself for a meaningful future may have limited access to transportation and may never, in fact, have traveled out of the rural county where she was born. An unnecessary hospitalization requirement can raise the cost of an abortion from $250 to more than $1000 and involve a trip of hundreds of miles; a 24- or 48-hour waiting period may necessitate *two* long trips and an overnight stay in a strange and distant city.

To some, such legislative requirements may seem no more than "skirmishing around the edges," minor impediments in a world of otherwise easy access to "abortion on demand." For much of America, however, the reality is far different. Steve Wermeil and Michel McQueen report in the *Wall Street Journal* that "abortion is already scarcer and more difficult to obtain in many parts of the country than the existence of a constitutional right implies . . . Women in western Missouri who want a second trimester abortion must either drive the 250 miles across the state or cross into Kansas." In North Dakota, Isabel Wilkerson writes in the *New York Times,* "what was always a difficult journey has become even more daunting since the only physician performing abortions in North Dakota retired." In part because of hostile pressure from pro-life activists, "none of the state's 1,200 physicians have stepped forward to fill the void." In Minnesota, 82 out of the 87 counties have no readily available abortion provider.

The critical fact is that even seemingly modest restrictions will increase the barriers to access in a system that already makes it extremely difficult for many women to secure abortions. Legislative restrictions can be, and often are, the final straw. The ban on Medicaid funding of abortions for the poor, coupled with a ban on performance of abortions in hospitals receiving public assistance (upheld in the *Webster* decision), severely curtailed access for many. Unnecessary clinic regulations and mandatory, though medically unnecessary, tests add even more to the cost. If hospitalization is required and public hospitals are barred from participation, only expensive private hospitals, often distant and inaccessible to the poor and the young, will remain.

One of the principal consequences of many abortion access restrictions is that they delay abortion. Delayed abortion creates a greater health risk, especially for teenagers. These delays may be lengthy for many young women, especially those who are poor and less informed: They may postpone state-mandated parental involvement and avoid as long as possible the alternative of going to court for judicial permission. Or they may find it necessary to delay the abortion while raising funds or seeking transportation to a distant location.

Delay is not the only adverse consequence of the mandatory parental involvement laws now on the books in more than 30 states. As one lower court noted, "Although family relationships benefit from voluntary and open communication, compelling parental notice has an opposite effect. It is almost always disastrous." New York Assemblywoman Gloria Davis notes that even parental involvement laws with judicial bypass provisions lead to "scared, pregnant teenagers being shuffled through an overburdened court system along with drug dealers and other violent criminals, or trying to scrape the money together to travel someplace with less restrictive laws." Evidence in the Minnesota parental involvement case decided by the Supreme Court in 1990 showed that some pregnant minors "were so afraid of the [judicial] proceeding that they turned mute in court, were 'wringing wet with perspiration,' and frequently required a sedative. Some vomited and one began to abort spontaneously during the court process." However well-intentioned in theory, mandatory parental involvement laws promoted by those who are hostile to all abortions often become a form of state-sponsored child abuse.

(Some state legislatures have recently crafted provisions on parental involvement that do far less harm than the mandatory notification laws adopted in other states. Wisconsin, Connecticut and Maine have recently adopted provisions that reflect the popular sentiment that some young women need family guidance but that do not impose unnecessary burdens on young women's access. These provisions generally encourage minors to consult a parent, other close family member, family friend or counselor but do not require notification where there is a valid reason for a minor not to notify her parents or guardian. These statutes do not require minors to go to court as the only means of avoiding notification, and they demonstrate that it is possible for legislatures to facilitate communication between a minor and a parent, guardian or other responsible adult by means that do not impede a minor woman's right to terminate a pregnancy.)

That so many abortion access regulations are dysfunctional in practice should not be surprising. Such laws are seldom actually motivated by their ostensible goals of enhancing family relationships or protecting women's health. They are instead intended to prevent as many women as possible from having abortions. At that unstated goal they often succeed. In the four years following the implementation of a two-parent notification law in Minnesota, the birth rate among Minneapolis women aged 15 to 17 rose 38.4%.

In May of 1991 the Supreme Court sustained federal family planning regulations that further restrict the access to abortion for low-income women. In *Rust v. Sullivan* the Court sustained the power of federal officials to "gag" medical professionals in family planning clinics that receive federal funds and prevent them from discussing abortion with low-income women who are diagnosed as pregnant. Congress had originally enacted Title X in 1970 to subsidize family planning by clinics and local public health departments. The act clearly prohibited using any of the funds for the actual performance of abortions. It did provide, however, for doctors to refer patients to other agencies for postconception services. For 18 years the administrative rules provided that when a woman was diagnosed as pregnant, the program with Title X funds could provide her with information concerning the full range of her options, including prenatal care, adoption and abortion. Then in the waning days of the Reagan administration, the rules were dramatically changed. Under the new regulations upheld in *Rust*, all nonpejorative discussion of abortion was prohibited. Doctors were to provide pregnant clients only with a list of prenatal care agencies "that promote the welfare of the mother and the unborn child." No clinics that principally performed abortions could be included on the referral list. Among the reasons cited for the change was a shift in public attitude against "the elimination of unborn children by abortion."

Consider what these regulations mean for a single mother of three children living in poverty whose doctor believes that continuing her new pregnancy will exacerbate an existing medical condition, such as lupus or diabetes. The doctor must still abstain from even mentioning abortion when discussing her referral options. The only exception is for an immediate medical emergency; then a doctor may refer to emergency treatment a woman "whose pregnancy places her life in imminent peril." No mention of abortion is permitted, even in the face of serious health complications, in the absence of "imminent peril" to a woman's life.

In sustaining the *Rust* regulations, the Court suggested that the constraints on an indigent woman's freedom of choice are a result not of the regulations but of the woman's indigence. "These Title X clients," the Court asserts, "are in no worse position than if Congress had never enacted Title X." This is not the case. The regulations do positive harm to low-income women by requiring doctors to provide these women with incomplete and misleading information. Instead of no information, or medical advice in her best interest, the Title X client is provided with the official federal line on childbirth, offered in the guise of independent medical judgment. A woman who believes that she has already been to "her" doctor has no way of knowing that she still needs honest medical advice about how abortion or pregnancy might particularly relate to a person in her medical condition or how she might locate a licensed responsible provider.

The federal regulations in *Rust* exacerbate the burdens on access to abortion that have been, or will in the future, be adopted by state legislatures in the "moderate" form of waiting periods, hospitilization and testing requirements and consent and notification hurdles. By pricing and regulating abortion beyond the reach of many women, "moderate" access restrictions draw a line across society on social and economic grounds. Above that line women would continue to have access to safe and legal abortions; below it women are relegated to illegal, dangerous alternatives or forced into continued pregnancy and childbirth. The more regulations the state imposes, the higher the line goes.

Restrictions on the Timing of Abortion

More than 90% of all abortions in America now occur within the first 12 weeks of pregnancy. Nonetheless, the pro-life movement has succeeded in making late-stage abortions a prominent public issue, often exemplified by graphic pictures of fetuses aborted at advanced stages of development. Proposed laws that limit the performance of abortions to the earlier months of gestation appear to respond to legitimate concerns. Later abortions are more dangerous than earlier abortions. And for many, abortion turns morally problematic as the months change a microscopic fertilized ovum into a fetus that at the end of pregnancy fully resembles a human infant.

There is no good reason why as many as 10% of American abortions should still take place at such an advanced stage of fetal development, especially considering the greater health risks to pregnant women caused by delaying abortion. As Mary Ann Glendon notes, "Unlike partisans on either side, the public seems to believe that there is an important difference between early and late stages of gestation."

Even so, attempts to deal with late abortions by prohibitory laws are profoundly misguided. There is bitter irony to the pro-life movement's public focus on late abortions. If anyone active on the abortion issue is responsible for the unnecessarily high percentage of late abortions still being performed in this country, it is those who march under the pro-life banner. As a result of *Roe v. Wade,* abortion became not only safer and cheaper but also far more likely to be performed very early in pregnancy.

Some late abortions will always be necessary as fetal abnormalities are discovered or as threats to a woman's health emerge during pregnancy. More importantly, *the way to prevent late abortions is to permit access to early abortions.* The women most likely to delay until the second trimester are those who are poor, young and without access to local, affordable providers. Already, the absence of funding for abortions and the presence of waiting periods, consent requirements and other needless regulations push many U.S. abortions into the second trimester. The adoption of a parental notification law in Minnesota, for example, caused the percentage of minors obtaining second-trimester abortions to rise by 26%. Adding to these burdens will increase the number of late abortions; eliminating restrictions would reduce the number.

Glendon praised European statutes for setting a gestational time limit for legal abortions. These statutes, however, operate in a wholly different context from ours. Glendon notes that Sweden's cutoff for abortion is 18 weeks, after which permission from a national board is required. But in Sweden the government does everything possible to insure that every woman who wants to terminate her pregnancy may readily do so in the first 18 weeks. A woman who wants to end a pregnancy may go to her well-publicized, accessible, free, neighborhood public health clinic and in complete confidence obtain an abortion. In most of the Western world outside the United States, Janet Maslow Cohen notes in the *Yale Law Journal,* a woman who is legally entitled to an abortion will find that "her government will support her abortion decision in the two most equality-promoting ways that government can—by providing her with the safest procedure available in her society and by helping to pay for it."

To enact in the United States laws that simply prohibit abortions after 12 or 18 weeks would constitute a strange and cruel response to the issue of late abortions. In this country, legislative deadlines beyond which abortion was prohibited would coexist with access regulations designed to *prevent* women from being able to meet the deadline. No state truly concerned about either the increased maternal health risks or the moral implications of late abortions should consider the coercive step of prohibiting second-trimester abortions[1] while simultaneously pursuing policies that cause abortions to be delayed. Bans on funding for abortions, shutting off access to public hospitals, parental consent/judicial bypass laws and testing requirements all fall into this category. Legislators who are troubled in principle by late abortions should reject funding bans, consent requirements and other "pro-life" proposals that cause delay and should support instead measures insuring that every woman who wants to terminate a pregnancy can do so as early and as safely as possible.

There are further ironies. Better access to abortion, as noted above, helps prevent late abortion. Better access to *contraception* helps prevent abortion altogether. Yet strong elements in the pro-life movement oppose contraception as well. The United States has fallen far behind other advanced countries in the research and development of birth control choices. According to a 1990 study by the National Academy of Sciences, as many as two million unwanted and unplanned pregnancies occur each year because of contraceptive failure; between one-third and one-half of all abortions in America could be prevented if more birth control options were available. The study states that "the stronger the desire to reduce abortion, the greater should be the investment to develop new methods of contraception."

Former Surgeon General C. Everett Koop noted, "We are at a very strange place in history, where the people most opposed to abortions are also opposed to the one thing that would stop them, which is contraceptive information."

Most pro-life groups strongly oppose making contraceptives more widely available, arguing that such a step might be seen as condoning adolescent sexuality. They seem to prefer subjecting all women to a coercive regime of abortion regulation or government-compelled childbirth to the slight risk of marginally encouraging premarital sex. That weighing of values is difficult to justify.

Mandatory Justification Requirements

The last category of legislative restrictions on abortion are enactments that would limit the reasons for which a woman may decide to terminate a pregnancy. Such laws affect every woman who seeks an abortion. If, despite their harshness, they seem to have significant public support, it is because of a deep confusion among commentators that erroneously translates widespread personal ambivalence about abortion into a positive prescription for coercive public policy.

Undoubtedly, many Americans personally favor abortion in some circumstances and personally oppose it others. A national poll by the *New York Times* showed that although most Americans approved of abortion when a woman's health was seriously endangered (87%) and when there was a danger of serious fetal defects (69%), majorities also thought that a woman "should not be able to get a legal abortion" when "a single woman did not want to marry the man who made her pregnant" (50% opposed,

---

[1] Third-trimester abortions—those near or after the point of fetal viability—are almost always a medical crisis and are usually tragic events. But they do not pose a public policy issue for a simple reason: *No one wants* to wait until the third trimester to have an abortion. Only 0.8% of all abortions occur after the 21st week, almost always for fetal abormalities, and 99% of those few abortions that do occur after the 21st week occur before the 24th week. Nancy Rhoden noted that "Essentially the only defect for which abortion will be performed after week twenty-four is anencephaly. Abortion should be permissible at any time for this defect, because the anencephalic fetus, or infant, is never viable." Mary Ann Glendon's harsh criticism of *Roe* for not requiring every state to forbid or regulate third-trimester abortions thus seems way off the mark. It is not clear how government regulators could provide any meaningful assistance in these very rare and tragic circumstances.

42% in favor) or when "a low-income family could not afford any more children" (49% opposed, 43% in favor).

It is a fundamental mistake, however, to suppose that these respondents would upon reflection want to enact into their state's code of laws their own personal assessment of when abortion is wrong. Although the literal wording of the above questions called for respondents to state when a "woman should be able to obtain a legal abortion," respondents were likely giving their own personal views of when one "should" or "should not" have an abortion. That interpretation is borne out by the answers given when respondents were directly asked the central public policy question: "If a woman wants to have an abortion and her doctor agrees to it, should she be allowed to have an abortion or not?" Sixty-three percent said that woman should be allowed to, and only 24% said no. The most plausible reading of the ambiguous polling data is that Americans personally condone or disapprove of abortion for a variety of reasons but, in the end, prefer to leave the choice to individual women.

Even if a majority of Americans did believe in the abstract that the law should determine what reasons justify an abortion, that majority would likely disappear if more people understood the mechanisms of government regulation required to enforce such a policy. Consider, for example, a law that prohibited abortion when "used as a means of birth control." As Gene B. Sperling and I wrote, "The fundamental flaw in these laws is what they would require of every woman who decides to terminate a pregnancy. Potentially, each woman could be subjected to an intrusive and humiliating process of proving to some official committee, or court, that she was using birth control when she became pregnant." Even if only one "reason" for having an abortion were prohibited by law, every woman would have to prove to some government board that the prohibited reason was not her reason. In the 1990s and beyond, people hostile to all abortions are likely to seek appointment to committees that would decide these questions. In such a case, choice could be replaced by cross-examination.

Chief Justice Rehnquist wrote in *Webster* that the suggestion that "legislative bodies . . . will treat our decision today as an invitation to enact abortion regulation reminiscent of the dark ages . . . misreads our views . . ." The Chief Justice's sanguine prediction that legislatures would act responsibly was shattered by legislation enacted not long after *Webster* was decided. Utah led the way by the enactment of a law (now being challenged in the courts) that bans virtually all abortions.

The narrow exceptions set out in the Utah law must be read in the context of the chilling effect on physicians created by the bill's severe criminal penalties. Any physician who performed *any abortion* after the enactment of this statute would do so at great personal peril. Unless the physician were able to establish that the abortion fell within one of the bill's narrow exceptions, he or she would face a felony conviction and five years imprisonment.

When the penalty is so great, the chilling effect of the statute on physicians will be substantial. As a result, the apparent exceptions in the Utah legislation are not in fact exceptions that a physician could ever be confident of establishing in court. If one considers, for example, the risk faced by a physician asked to terminate a pregnancy caused by rape or one that threatened a woman's health, it becomes evident that no physician could safely undertake to perform an abortion if this bill became law.

The Utah law purports to permit a woman who has been raped to terminate her pregnancy. In fact, it imposes severe criminal penalties on any physician who terminates a pregnancy for a rape victim unless the physician can establish that (1) the rape was reported to a law enforcement agency; (2) the woman was in fact raped; and (3) the woman's pregnancy *resulted from* the rape and not from some other act of intercourse she might have had with her husband or other partner. Reporting the event to a law enforcement agency would not establish the *separate* requirement that the pregnancy to be terminated was indeed "the result of" that rape.

If a suspect of the rape has not been apprehended and convicted, how can a physician establish that the pregnancy "is the result of rape" as defined by the terms of Utah Criminal Code? If there is no apprehension or conviction or if the suspect pleads guilty to a lesser offense, a physician cannot be confident that he will be able to establish that this requirement has been met.

Even if a physician could be confident of establishing that a woman had been raped, he or she could rarely, if ever, be confident of establishing that the pregnancy "is the result of rape" and not the result of some other act of "intercourse. Thus, a physician who performs any abortion on an "alleged" rape victim would do so at substantial risk of a felony conviction and substantial prison sentence.

Like the rape exception, the health exception to Utah's abortion ban is also so limited as to be virtually meaningless. In order to perform an abortion on a woman facing severe health risks from continuation of pregnancy, a physician must be confident of proving that the abortion was necessary to "prevent grave damage to the pregnant woman's medical health." Apparently, a serious medical *risk* from continued pregnancy would not be sufficient; it must be the case that the grave damage *would result* unless prevented by the abortion. A woman who was severely diabetic might face a significant *risk* from continued pregnancy without her physician being able to conclude that an abortion was necessary to prevent "grave damage to the pregnant woman's medical health." Any competent health care attorney, asked to advise a physician of the circumstances under which an abortion could be performed without the physician risking a felony conviction, would conclude that there are few, if any, circumstances under which a physician could be confident of avoiding the act's drastic criminal penalties. Many women who have been raped or face serious health risks will thus be unable to obtain safe and legal abortions under the new Utah law.

As a result of the legislation adopted since *Webster* in Utah and other states, we now know that some state legislatures will not be content with "moderate" restrictions that "merely" foreclose abortion for the most vulnerable women. And even if the line can be held in most states against enactment of the most draconian laws, the lesser, "marginal" restrictions now being adopted or proposed in many states severely harm those women who are hostage to geography, youth, poverty and inadequate education. For the affluent and the comfortable to sacrifice the right to abortion of the less fortunate would not really be a compromise. It would be a sell-out.

The authors present the 1990 Gallup Organization Abortion and Moral Beliefs Survey from which they conclude that Americans are woefully ignorant about the state of law on abortion. Basically, U.S. Americans know that a woman has a legal right to an abortion because of the landmark decision *Roe v. Wade*. However, there is great confusion as to when during a pregnancy a woman may exercise her legal right. Additionally, the authors look at such issues as abortion and free choice, the impact of abortion on women's health and the relationship of the equality of women to *Roe v. Wade*. In conclusion they find that ''the abortion privacy doctrine has spawned a great host of ills for women, without remedying any of the real historical injustices against them.''

4 · Is Abortion the "First Right" for Women?: Some Consequences of Legal Abortion ⸻⸻⸻

Paige Comstock Cunningham, J.D.,[1] *and*
Clarke D. Forsythe, J.D.[2]

I. Introduction

Freely available, legal abortion in the United States is of relatively recent vintage. Prior to 1960, abortion in virtually all circumstances was a crime in every state.[3] In the

[1] B.A., Taylor University, 1977; J.D., Northwestern University, 1982; formerly Associate General Counsel, Americans United for Life, Chicago.

[2] B.A., Allegheny College, 1980; J.D., Valparaiso University, 1983; Vice-President & General Counsel, Americans United for Life, Chicago. The authors are grateful to Edward Grant, Esq.; Amy T. Miller; Wendy Stone; Laurie Ramsey; Melodie Gage; Robert Destro, Esq.; Victor G. Rosenblum, Esq.; and Mary Beth Krane-Derr for comments on earlier drafts; to Mark Wells, Esq., and Tim Murphy for extensive research assistance; to Mary Ann Reardon for word processing and research assistance; and to Jeanette O'Connor for graphics support.

[3] Colorado (in 1968) and New Mexico (in 1919) permitted abortion only for "serious and permanent bodily injury." Maryland (in 1867) permitted abortion for the mother's "safety." Alabama (in 1951) and the District of Columbia (in 1901) allowed abortion when necessary for the mother's "life or health." By judicial interpretation, Massachusetts allowed abortion for the mother's life and physical or mental health. Kudish v. Board of Registration on Medicine, 356 Mass. 98, 99–100, 248 N.E. 2d. 264, 266 (1969) and cases cited therein. Linton, *Enforcement of State Abortion Statutes After Roe: A State-by-State Analysis,* 67 U. Detroit L. Rev. 157 (1990); Witherspoon, *Reexamining* Roe: *Nineteenth Century Abortion Statutes and the Fourteenth Amendment,* 17 St. Mary's Law Journal 29, 45–49 (1985).

The notion that legal abortion was available before the 19th century and at common law has been exploded by recent scholarship. J. Keown, *Abortion, Doctors & the Law* (1988); Dellapenna, *The Historical Case Against Abortion,* No. 13 Continuity 59 (1989); Dellapenna, *The History of Abortion: Technology, Morality & Law,* 40 U. Pitts. L. Rev. 359 (1979); Dellapenna, Brief of the American Academy of Medical Ethics as *Amicus Curiae,* in Hope v. Perales, No. 21073/90 (N.Y. Sup. Ct. App. Div. Jan. 1992).

1960s, a movement that sought to abolish abortion laws had some success: By the time of the Supreme Court's decision in *Roe v. Wade*[4] in 1973, 19 states had "liberalized" their abortion laws to various degrees.[5] Numerous rhetorical arguments were raised in justification of legalized abortion "as a humane solution to a critical social problem."[6] Legalized abortion was needed for population control,[7] to promote maternal health,[8] to reduce child abuse,[9] to alleviate poverty[10] and to eliminate unsafe "back-alley abortions."[11] Many of these arguments were implicitly relied upon in the Supreme Court's opinion in *Roe v. Wade*,[12] in which the Court legalized abortion on demand through all nine months of pregnancy.[13] In less than a decade, the status of abortion changed from being a crime in all 50 states to being widely perceived as a "constitutional right," a "fundamental freedom." As Lawrence Lader wrote, "[T]he Court went far beyond any of the 18 new state laws the movement had won since 1967, with only New York's law approaching its scope. It climaxed a social revolution whose magnitude and speed were probably unequaled in United States history."[14]

Yet the public rhetoric has shifted dramatically in the 20 years since *Roe:*

---

[4]410 U.S. 113 (1973).

[5]Linton, *supra* note 3; *See generally,* L. Lader, *Abortion II: Making the Revolution* (1973); F. Ginsburg, *Contested Lives: The Abortion Debate in an American Community* 35–37, 64–71 (1989). However, shortly before the Supreme Court's decision in *Roe v. Wade,* Michigan rejected a state referendum by a 61% majority that would have introduced elective abortion up to five months. J. Noonan, *A Private Choice: Abortion in America in the Seventies* 34 (1979); Destro, *Abortion and the Constitution,* 53 Cal. L. Rev. 1250, 1337–38 (1975). North Dakota rejected a similar referendum by a 77% majority. *Id.*

[6]L. Lader, *supra* note 5, at 43. *See generally,* Tietze & Lewit, *Abortion,* 220 Scientific Amer. 21 (Jan. 1969); A. Neier, *Only Judgment: The Limits of Litigation in Social Change* 116 (1982); Callahan, *An Ethical Challenge to Prochoice Advocates: Abortion & the Pluralistic Proposition,* Commonweal, Nov. 23, 1990, at 681, 682–83.

[7]L. Lader, *supra* note 5, at 14, 54; Hardin, *Abortion and Human Dignity,* in A. Guttmacher, ed., *The Case for Legalized Abortion Now* 83 (1967). For a more recent statement, *see* "Population size can't be overlooked as an environmental danger," New York Times, October 31, 1988, at A18.

[8]*Cf.* the statement of Mary Calderone, medical director of Planned Parenthood Federation of America, in 1960: ". . . medically speaking, that is, from the point of view of diseases of the various systems, cardiac, genitourinary, and so on, it is hardly ever necessary today to consider the life of the mother as threatened by a pregnancy." Calderone, *Illegal Abortion as a Public Health Problem,* 50 Am. J. Pub. Health 948 (July 1960). Ten years later, Christopher Tietze acknowledged: "Abortion is much more widely approved as an emergency measure than as an elective method of birth regulation." Tietze & Lewit, *Abortion,* 220 Scientific Amer. 21, 23 (Jan. 1969) (chart).

[9]L. Lader, *supra* note 5, at 23–24; Hardin, *supra* note 7, at 82. A more recent argument of this kind is made in H. P. David, et al., *Born Unwanted: Developmental Effects of Denied Abortion* (1988).

[10]Hardin, *supra* note 7, at 84–85. *Cf.* Beal v. Doe, 432 U.S. 438, 463 (1977) (Blackmun, J., dissenting) ("And so the cancer of poverty will continue to grow").

[11]Maginnis, *Elective Abortion as a Woman's Right,* in A. Guttmacher, *supra* note 7, at 132. For a recent version of this argument, *see* E. Messer & K. May, *Back Rooms: An Oral History of the Illegal Abortion Era* (Torchstone paperback ed. 1989).

[12]410 U.S. 113, 116, 153 (1973) ("In addition, population growth, pollution, poverty, and racial overtones tend to complicate and not to simplify the problem.").

[13]*See infra* note 21. The phrase "abortion on demand" appears first coined by abortion advocates, not opponents. B. Nathanson, *Aborting America* 176–77 (Life Cycle Books paperback 1979); Guttmacher, *Abortion—Yesterday, Today & Tomorrow,* in A. Guttmacher, *supra* note 7, at 13 ("Today, complete abortion license would do great violence to the beliefs and sentiments of most Americans. Therefore I doubt that the U.S. is as yet ready to legalize abortion on demand, and I am therefore reluctant to advocate it in the face of all the bitter dissension such a proposal would create.")

[14]L. Lader, *supra* note 5, at iii.

*The most striking ideological development has been the emergence into
leadership positions in the prochoice movement of some feminists who
have scanted many of the original arguments for abortion reform. They
have shifted the emphasis almost entirely to a woman's right to an abortion, whatever her reasons and whatever the consequences.*[15]

Today, the argument, almost exclusively, is that abortion—for any reason, at any time
of pregnancy—is the "first right" for women; that is, women's unlimited access to
abortion is essential for sexual equality and is the nonnegotiable prerequisite for all other
social, economic or legal rights.[16] As one abortion-rights activist has put it, "[w]e can
get all the rights in the world . . . and none of them means a doggone thing if we don't
own the flesh we stand in . . ."[17] Nevertheless, a sober assessment of this new justification for elective abortion suggests that it was not founded on a genuine consideration
of women and their needs or on an accurate understanding of elective abortion in practice.

The Supreme Court will have an opportunity to conform the legal reality more
closely to the philosophical and political reality of abortion's tragic impact on women
and society by upholding all provisions of the law challenged in *Planned Parenthood v.
Casey.*[18] The Pennsylvania law sets forth minimal protections for women's physical and
psychological well-being. For example, it requires fully informed consent, with a 24-

---

[15] Callahan, *supra* note 6, at 681, 683. *Cf.* A. Neier, *Only Judgment: The Limits of Litigation in Social
Change* 116 (1982).

[16] *See, e.g.,* R. Petchesky, *Abortion and Woman's Choice* 5 (Rev. ed. 1990) ("A woman's right to decide on
abortion when her health and her sexual self-determination are at stake is 'nearly allied to her right to
be' "); Wattleton, *Reproductive Rights Are Fundamental Rights,* The Humanist, Jan/Feb. 1991, at 21, 22
("Without reproductive autonomy, our other rights are meaningless"); Paul & Schaap, *Abortion and the
Law in 1980,* 25 N.Y.L. School L. Rev. 497, 498 (1980) ("without which other legal rights have little
significance"). *See generally,* B. Harrison, *Our Right to Choose* (1983).
    Lawrence Lader said much the same thing in 1973. L. Lader, *supra* note 5, at 18. But the message
was not so single-minded. Indeed, Lader claims that "Friedan, one of the most impressive militants of her
time, avoided the abortion issue at first" and that, early on, he urged on her (implicitly to no avail) the
proposition that "all feminist demands hinged on contraception and abortion and a woman's control over
her own body and procreation." *Id.* at 36.

[17] Quoted in K. Luker, *Abortion & the Politics of Motherhood* 97 (U. Cal. Press paperback 1985).
    Those who view abortion as the "first right" are generally the same advocates of abortion rights who
refuse to debate the morality of abortion because it is "off-limits" (DeParle, *Beyond the Legal Right: Why
Liberals and Feminists Don't Like to Talk about the Morality of Abortion,* Washington Monthly 28 (April
1989). Even some modern abortion-rights supporters recognize the incongruity here.

> If, for some people, to have choice is itself the beginning and end of morality, for most
> people it is just the beginning. It does not end until a supportable, justifiable choice has
> been made, one that can be judged right or wrong by the individual herself based on some
> reasonably serious, not patently self-interested way of thinking about ethics. That stan-
> dard—central to every major ethical system and tradition—applies to the moral life gener-
> ally, whether it be a matter of abortion or any other grave matter. An unwillingness to
> come to grips with that standard not only puts the prochoice movement in jeopardy as a
> political force. It has a still more deleterious effect: it is a basic threat to moral honesty and
> integrity. The cost of failing to take seriously the personal moral issues is to court self-
> deception, and to be drawn to employ arguments of expediency and evasion.

Callahan, *supra* note 6, at 682.

[18] 947 F.2d 682 (3rd Cir. 1991), *cert. granted,* 112 S. Ct. 931–932 (1992).

hour waiting period to digest the information, and abortion statistical reporting. As discussed below, in the profitable abortion marketplace, women are often deceived or coerced into undergoing abortions they do not want. With an opportunity to evaluate meaningful alternatives to abortions or to consult with a parent (in the case of a minor), many unnecessary, unwanted abortions may be avoided.

II. Do Women Consider Abortion the "First Right"?

A. Current Public Opinion

People who claim to speak for women and their fundamental reliance on completely accessible abortion dominate the airwaves, the press and academic journals. Yet opinion polls taken in recent years do not substantiate the alleged importance of abortion rights to the majority of American women. For example, a New York Times poll of July 1989 indicated that most women were concerned more about job discrimination, child care and balancing work and family than about abortion.[19] These opinion polls did not deeply probe underlying attitudes about abortion and other social issues.

In 1990, the Gallup Organization conducted the largest and most comprehensive survey of U.S. attitudes on abortion to date, the Abortion and Moral Beliefs Survey.[20] One of the most striking conclusions from the survey is that Americans are woefully ignorant about the state of U.S. law on abortion. *Roe v. Wade* legalized abortion throughout pregnancy for any or no reason.[21] Nine out of ten Americans simply do not know the extent to which abortion is legally available.

---

[19] Dionne, *Struggle for Work and Family Fueling Women's Movement*, New York Times, Aug. 22, 1989, at A18. *See infra* note 28 and accompanying text.

[20] Abortion and Moral Beliefs Survey (May 1990) [hereinafter Survey]. In this survey, the Gallup Organization conducted interviews with 2,174 adults and asked 200 questions concerning abortion and related areas of moral belief and public policy, requiring a 45-minute personal interview. Gallup conducted the survey interviews and tabulated the survey findings. Question design and development was conducted by a team of social scientists, including James Davison Hunter, Ph.D., of the University of Virginia, Carl Bowman, Ph.D., of Bridgewater College in Virginia, and Robert Wuthnow, Ph.D., of Princeton University. James Rogers, Ph.D., of Wheaton College, Wheaton, Illinois and a Senior Research Associate at Northwestern University School of Medicine, analyzed and interpreted the data. The margin of error does not exceed +/− 3% for questions asked of the entire sample. For questions asked of a subsample, the margin of error may be greater. This survey was commissioned by Americans United for Life and is on file with the authors.

[21] The Supreme Court in *Roe v. Wade* held that the states could not prohibit any abortions prior to viability. After viability, the Court said, the states may prohibit abortion, "except where it is necessary, in appropriate medical judgment, for the preservation of the life or health of the mother." *Roe*, 410 U.S. at 165. But the Court then expanded the exception for "health of the mother" in a way to make it impossible for states to prohibit abortions. The Court held that *Roe v. Wade* and *Doe v. Bolton* "are to be read together," *id.* at 165, and the Court defined "health" in *Doe* as "all factors—physical, emotional, psychological, familial and the woman's age—relevant to the well-being of the patient. All these factors may relate to health." Doe v. Bolton, 410 U.S. 179, 192 (1973). Both the Supreme Court and the lower federal courts have applied "health" in the third trimester in a very broad manner. Thornburgh v. American College of Obstetricians and Gynecologists, 476 U.S. 747 (1986); Colautti v. Franklin, 439 U.S. 379, 400 (1979) ("women's life and health" requires that "all factors relevant to the welfare of the woman may be taken into account by the physician in making his decision" after viability); American College of Obstetricians and Gynecologists v. Thornburgh, 737 F.2d 283, 299 (3d Cir. 1984), *aff'd*, 476 U.S. 747 (1986); Schulte v. Douglas, 567 F.Supp. 522 (D.Neb. 1981); Margaret S. v. Edwards, 488 F.Supp. 181, 196 (D.La. 1980).

Commentators, likewise, have also understood the third trimester "health" exception to be very broad. Wood & Hawkins, *State Regulation of Late Abortion and the Physician's Duty of Care to the Viable Fetus*, 45 Mo. L. Rev. 394 (1980); Ely, *The Wages of Crying Wolf: A Comment on* Roe v. Wade, 82 Yale L.J.

Survey respondents were asked whether they were "very familiar," "fairly familiar," "not too familiar" or "not at all familiar" with "the 1973 Supreme Court decision on abortion known as *Roe v. Wade*." Only one in four of those who said that they were "very familiar" with *Roe v. Wade* could accurately state its outcome. Forty-two percent of the sample who stated that they were "very familiar," "fairly familiar" or "not too familiar" thought *Roe* legalized elective abortion only in the first three months. Among women who claimed at least some familiarity with *Roe,* 24% thought *Roe* meant that "abortions are legal only during the first three months, and only when a mother's life or health is threatened"; 39% thought *Roe* meant that "abortions are legal during the first three months, regardless of a woman's reasons for wanting one." Only 18% of this subsample correctly indicated that *Roe* meant that "abortions are legal for the duration of pregnancy, regardless of a woman's reason for wanting one."

This ignorance applies as well to the Supreme Court's July 1989 decision in *Webster v. Reproductive Health Services.*[22] Although the Abortion and Moral Beliefs Survey was conducted 10 months after the decision, during which time there was extensive media coverage, 8 out of 10 respondents stated that they were "not at all familiar" with the decision. Respondents were asked whether they thought they were "very familiar," "fairly familiar" or "not at all familiar" with "the 1989 Supreme Court decision on abortion in the *Webster* case." Among women, 81% conceded that they were "not at all familiar" with *Webster.* Among women who stated that they were "very familiar" or "fairly familiar" with the decision, 23% thought that "the legal outcome of the *Webster* decision" was "best described" as "abortions are permitted only during the first three months and only when a mother's life or health is threatened"; 10% thought that "abortions are now legal during the first three months, regardless of a woman's reason for wanting one"; and another 51% thought that "abortions that are legal in one state may be illegal in another." Only 5% knew that *Webster* means "abortions are legal for the duration of the pregnancy regardless of a woman's reason for wanting one."[23]

920, 921 n.19 (1973); Editorial, *Abortion: The High Court Has Ruled,* 5 Fam. Plan. Perspect. i (Winter 1973) ("'Even New York's law appears to be overbroad in proscribing all abortions after 24 weeks except to preserve the woman's life, since the Court has held that an exception must also be made for preservation of the woman's health (interpreted very broadly)'").

[22] 492 U.S. 490 (1989).

[23] In *Webster,* the Supreme Court did not explicitly overrule *Roe v. Wade;* nor did the Court uphold any prohibition on abortion for any reason at any time of pregnancy. Rather, the Supreme Court upheld the constitutionality of several provisions of a Missouri abortion statute, including a preamble, tests for fetal viability at or after 20-weeks gestation and prohibitions on public funding for abortion.

The ACLU, in a brief filed before the Ninth Circuit Court of Appeals, has characterized *Webster* as follows:

> In *Webster,* the Court found constitutional provisions of a Missouri statute that, unlike those enjoined here, dealt with the use of public resources for abortions and required certain tests to determine viability. The Court determined only that "none of the challenged provisions of the Missouri Act properly before [it] conflict with the Constitution." 109 S. Ct. at 3058. The *Webster* plurality modified *Roe* only "to the extent" required to uphold the Missouri statute. 109 S. Ct. at 3058. Although Justice O'Connor, the critical fifth vote, mentions with approval her dissenting opinion in *Akron,* she uses the standards of *Roe,* and the majority opinions in *Akron* and *Thornburgh,* to measure the constitutionality of the viability testing requirement and sustains the Missouri law under that test. *Webster,* 109 S. Ct. at 3060–64 (O'Connor, J., concurring). Justice O'Connor agreed with the Chief Justice that

The survey demonstrates that, after 19 years of legalized abortion nationwide, the American public still does not understand *Roe* and its policy of abortion on demand throughout pregnancy. If they did, they might not select the "prochoice" label so readily.[24] In fact, the majority of Americans disapprove of the majority of abortions.[25] Approximately 25% of the sample disapproved of abortion in almost all circumstances except to save the life of the mother (the "consistently disapproves" group). Another 26% disapproved of abortion when it is used for "birth control" or "sex selection" (the "seldom disapprove" group). The largest group, which makes up nearly 50% of the sample, disapproved of abortion except for certain "hard cases"—including danger to the life or physical health of the mother, rape, incest or serious fetal deformity (the "often disapprove" group). Yet, these cases represent no more than 5 percent of the 1.6 million abortions performed each year.[26]

The survey also showed that Americans have strong opinions about the nature of the unborn. Seventy-seven percent of the respondents believed that abortion is either "an act of murder as bad as killing a born human being" (37%), "an act of murder but not as bad as killing a born human being" (12%) or "the taking of human life" (28%). Only 16% believed that abortion is merely a surgical procedure or the removal of tissue. Fully 50% of the respondents believed that, from the moment of the child's conception, the unborn child's right to be born supersedes the woman's "right to choose." Only 23% believed that "the child's right to be born" does not outweigh "the woman's right to choose" until viability (16%) or birth (7%).

Contrary to conventional wisdom, the survey demonstrated that there is no "gender gap" on abortion, or at least not the one commonly assumed.[27] More women than men

---

there was "no necessity to accept the State's invitation to reexamine the constitutional validity of *Roe v. Wade.*" *Id.* at 3060 (O'Connor, J., concurring). Thus, Justice Blackmun observed in his dissent, "the Court extricates itself from *[Webster]* without making a single, even incremental change in the law of abortion." 109 S. Ct. at 3067. And Justice Scalia severely chastises the Court for failing to take that step. *Id.* at 3064 (Scalia, J., concurring).

Brief of Appellees in Guam Society of Obstetricians and Gynecologists v. Ada, No. 90-16706 (9th Cir.), at 22–23.

The "legal outcome" of *Webster*, therefore, is that it leaves *Roe* undiluted. In the aftermath of *Webster*, abortions are still legal throughout pregnancy virtually for any reason in almost all states. The jurisprudential door has been opened, however, for potentially greater state regulation of abortion. The "practical outcome" is that abortion is perceived as less available and that abortion rights are in jeopardy.

[24] Thirty-three percent of the respondents identify themselves as "moderately prochoice" or "strongly prochoice."

[25] Answers to 29 questions in the survey were submitted to a statistical procedure known as "cluster analysis." The purpose of this analysis was to find groups of individuals who generally hold the same patterns of beliefs regarding abortion. The cluster analysis tests for the consistency of response through a range of questions and plots the attitudes of the survey respondents accordingly. As a result of this analysis, three clusters of public belief emerged:

- those who *"consistently disapprove"* of abortion (25%)
- those who *"often disapprove"* of abortion (49%)
- those who *"seldom disapprove"* of abortion (26%)

[26] *See infra* note 174–76 and accompanying text.

[27] The Abortion and Moral Beliefs Survey was designed by the Gallup Organization to represent the nation as a whole and not any subgroup of the total population. However, although a subgroup analysis may be suggestive of the views held by that particular segment of the population (women) and is valuable for purposes of guiding future research, it should not be portrayed as conclusive evidence of the views of the subgroup in the general population.

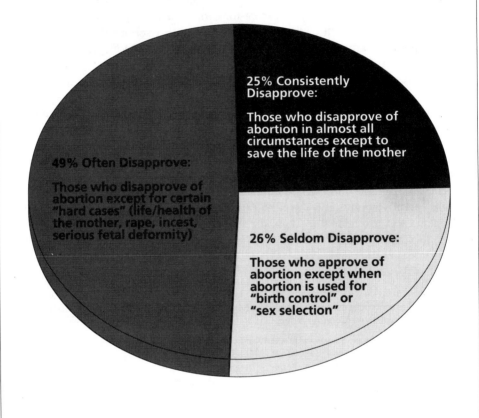

Cluster Analysis Identifying American Opinion on Abortion

25% Consistently Disapprove:

Those who disapprove of abortion in almost all circumstances except to save the life of the mother

49% Often Disapprove:

Those who disapprove of abortion except for certain "hard cases" (life/health of the mother, rape, incest, serious fetal deformity)

26% Seldom Disapprove:

Those who approve of abortion except when abortion is used for "birth control" or "sex selection"

Source: "Abortion and Moral Beliefs Survey," May 1990. The Gallup Organization conducted interviews with 2,174 adults and tabulated results. Study commissioned by Americans United for Life. Margin of error is not greater than ± 3 percent.

(53% to 46%) believed that "the unborn child's right to be born" outweighs the "woman's right to choose whether she wants to have the child *at the moment of conception*." Sixty-two percent of the women (49% of men) stated that "the fertilized egg inside a mother's womb first becomes a person at the moment of conception," compared to 15% of women (18% of men) who said "when the mother first feels movement," 13% of women (14% of men) who said "when the baby could survive on its own" and 5% of women (10% of men) who said at the "moment of birth." When women were asked, "[W]hich of these statements best describes your feelings about abortion," 42% (compared to 32% of men) responded that "abortion is just as bad as killing a person who has already been born; it is murder." In general, women in this sample were more protective of unborn human life than were men.[28]

Abortion is often portrayed as an issue that pits most women (assumed to be abortion supporters) against most men (assumed to be abortion opponents). This portrayal fails to explain why *more* men than women favor abortion rights in public opinion surveys. It may be that men perceive greater benefits from freely available, relatively cheap abortion. Why else is the Playboy Foundation such a strong supporter of abortion rights—securing the exercise of the Playboy ethic with no fault, no mess for men?[29] "It is difficult to be loving and caring. It is challenging, demanding, exhausting, and expensive to provide the care and support needed by women in distress. It is much easier, quicker, and cheaper to send a woman to an abortionist."[30] A recent article in *Esquire* about men and abortion reveals that in many cases the male partner suggested the abortion first.[31]

Not only are women less supportive of abortion than men are, public opinion surveys and studies consistently show that many other issues—whether personal or public—are more important to women than abortion.[32] Although women expressed concern about the abortion issue, they were more concerned about other issues nearly a year after the *Webster* decision. The Abortion and Moral Beliefs Survey revealed that, although 52% of the women were "very concerned" and 29% were "concerned" about abortion, a higher percentage were "very concerned" about other public issues: child abuse (85.8%), drug abuse (84.8%), AIDS (68.5%), environmental pollution (61.6%) and homelessness (58.2%).[33] In ranking abortion among personal issues, women are more concerned about equal pay (94%), day care (90%), rape (88%), maternity leave (84%) and job discrimination (82%) than they are about abortion (74%).[34] These levels of concern were expressed after the *Webster* decision when "abortion rights" were considered to be in jeopardy. The rankings are consistent with a poll taken just days before *Webster* when women were asked what should be the most important goal for

---

[28] Other surveys indicate that more women than men support criminal penalties for women who injure their unborn child *in utero* through drug use. Curriden, *Holding Mom Accountable*, 76 ABA Journal 50, 51 (March 1990) ("A survey of 15 southern states by the *Atlanta Constitution* found that 71 percent of the 1,500 people polled favored criminal penalties for pregnant women whose illegal drug use injures their babies. Another 45 percent favored prosecuting women whose use of alcohol and cigarettes during pregnancy harms their offspring. Surprisingly, the survey found that more women than men were in favor of criminalizing 'fetal abuse.' ").

[29] C. MacKinnon, *Feminism Unmodified: Discourses on Life and Law* 99 (1987); MacKinnon, Roe v. Wade: *A Study in Male Ideology*, in J. Garfield & P. Hennessey, eds., *Abortion: Moral and Legal Perspectives* 51 (1984).

[30] Smith, *Abortion as a Feminist Concern*, in J. Hensley, ed., *The Zero People* 79 (1983).

[31] Baker, *Men on Abortion*, Esquire 114 (March 1990). *See also*, Goodman, *Men and Abortion*, Glamour 178 (July 1989).

[32] *See, e.g.*, A. Hochschild, *The Second Shift: Working Parents and the Revolution at Home* (1989); Wallis, *Onward, Women!* Time 80 (Dec. 4, 1989).

[33] Survey, *supra* note 20.

[34] Wallis, *supra* note 32, at 82 (poll taken Oct. 23–25, 1989).

A Comparison of Male and Female Attitudes on Abortion

Question 124: Which of these statements best describes your feelings about abortion?

 Females

Males

1. Abortion is just as bad as killing a person who has already been born; it is murder.

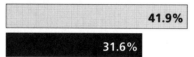
41.9%
31.6%

2. Abortion is murder, but it is not as bad as killing someone who has already been born.

11.3%
12.4%

3. Abortion is not murder, but it does involve the taking of human life.

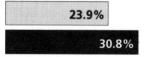
23.9%
30.8%

4. Abortion is not murder, it is a surgical procedure for removing human tissue.

16.4%
18.0%

5. Can't say.

6.6%
7.2%

Source: "Abortion and Moral Beliefs Survey," May 1990. The Gallup Organization conducted interviews with 2,174 adults and tabulated results. Study commissioned by Americans United for Life. Margin of error is not greater than ± 3.8 percent.

women's organizations. Abortion ranked last (2%) behind job equality (27%), equal rights (14%) and child care (5%).[35]

B. Women's Values and Self-Understanding

Despite the opinion of American women as revealed in polls, the organized women's movement has come to stand predominantly for abortion advocacy. There is an obvious discrepancy between the political agenda of the women's movement—and its philosophical underpinnings in academic feminism—and the needs of the majority of mainstream American women. There are several reasons why this may be the case. First, as the Abortion and Moral Beliefs Survey reveals, the women's movement is out of touch with the fact that for a majority of women access to abortion is a low priority. It is also out of touch with the feelings of the majority of women who consider abortion to be murder or killing. Finally, the claim that abortion is a *sine qua non* negates women's own understanding of themselves. One feminist legal scholar has characterized women as valuing intimacy, nurturance, community, responsibility and care.[36] Another observer— an approving male—lauded four virtues of feminist thought, virtues that he perceived abortion as violating: nonviolence, ecological harmony (the "deep connection between our bodies and the earth"), community (inclusivity) and egalitarian power-sharing (cooperation as a replacement for competition).[37] These "feminine" values contrast with allegedly "masculine" values.

> *Women respond to their natural state of inequality by developing a morality of nurturance that is responsible for the well-being of the dependent, and an ethic of care that responds to the greater needs of the weak. Men respond to the natural state of equality with an ethic of autonomy and rights.*[38]

Yet much of the rhetoric of and philosophical support for the abortion-rights movement is couched in "masculine" terms of autonomy ("it's my body") and rights ("not the church, not the state, women must decide their fate").

No matter what explanation is preferred, abortion advocacy fails both the political and philosophical analysis. Politically, the women's movement has abandoned the very people it claims to serve. Philosophically, the abortion ethic contradicts the essence of women by seeking to destroy, rather than protect and nurture, the one with whom the pregnant woman is so intimately connected. Abortion advocacy ignores, or at least buries, the intuitive knowledge of women throughout the centuries. Long before the emergence of rabbit tests or ultrasound, women (and therefore society) have intuitively known the obvious: The entity conceived through intercourse is a child, their child.[39]

---

[35] Dionne, *supra* note 19, at A1. Concern about abortion tied with balancing work and family (2%); the "all other problems" category was 18%.

[36] West, *Jurisprudence and Gender*, 56 U. Chi. L. Rev. 1, 28 (1988).

[37] Liias, *The Internal Threat to Feminism*, New Oxford Rev. 4 (Oct. 1990).

[38] West, *supra* note 36, at 28. Despite her recognition that nurturance is a feminine quality, West nonetheless defends the right to abort as necessary to defend against the "danger" of "invasion of the body by the fetus and the intrusion into the mother's existence following childbirth." *Id.* at 70.

[39] *See, e.g.,* Flodin, *Why I Don't March,* Newsweek, Feb. 12, 1990, at 8 ("I was pregnant, I carried two unborn children and I chose, for completely selfish reasons, to deny them life so that I could better my own"). In 1960, the medical director of Planned Parenthood Federation of America acknowledged that "abortion is the taking of a life . . . ." Calderone, *supra* note 8, at 951.

A recent, frank revelation on this score is that of California psychologist, Susan Nathanson, in her 1989 book, *Soul Crisis*.[40] Nathanson's account of her abortion, at four weeks' gestation, an abortion that occurred after she had previously given birth to three children, is unique for her candid, strongly stated certainty about the humanity of her fourth, unborn child from conception.[41] "My wish to have this unborn, though very alive, fourth child is so strong it is palpable."[42] In contrast, she writes, the baby "doesn't have much reality" for her husband.[43] Her experience is not unique. Women appear to identify and connect with the fetus as a child—their child—more than men do.[44] Nathanson cites an account of a friend who, upon revealing her own abortion of years ago, said she felt as though she had committed "murder."[45] Years later Nathanson continues to have these feelings: ". . . in ending the life of my child, I also annihilated a part of myself . . ."[46] Nathanson does not retreat from her conclusion. Rather, armed with this belief, she argues that abortion is a version of infanticide; women and society now must accept an ethic that allows (and perhaps encourages) women to both conceive and kill their children according to their individual and family needs.[47] Her goal is to help women reconcile and embrace their power as both life-givers and "murderers."[48] Pro-choice feminist periodicals ignored Nathanson's book, perhaps because she recognizes abortion as murder.[49]

Nathanson's conclusions pinpoint the basis of the profound conflict over abortion among women. Abortion advocacy illustrates the different views of self that women hold, as Faye Ginsburg recognized in *Contested Lives*, a study of women in the pro-choice and pro-life movements.[50] The essential difference in the two concepts of self

---

[40] S. Nathanson, *Soul Crisis: One Woman's Journey Through Abortion to Renewal* (Signet paperback ed. 1990).

[41] *Id.* at 2 ("Once a new life has been conceived, there is no turning back; an unalterable event—physical and psychological—has occurred"); *id.* at 26 ("but we are not talking about the choice of whether to conceive a child; this child is a reality, taking shape already deep within my body"); *id.* at 27 ("This fourth child exists, it's here, it's a reality. It's the fate of this child that we have to decide.").

[42] *Id.* at 29.

[43] *Id.* at 40.

[44] *Cf.* Goodman, *supra* note 31, at 210 ("For me, that fetus wasn't a child yet. For her, it was.").

[45] S. Nathanson, *supra* note 40, at 203–204 ("Liz").

[46] *Id.* at 194.

[47] *See id.* at 218 ("I wish now that my fourth child could have been sacrificed with my love and tears, even with my own hands, in the circle of a family or a community of women . . . and not as it was, in a cold and lonely hospital room with instruments of steel."); *id.* at 217 ("I meditate again upon what a different world it would be if we could each become aware of and take responsibility for our capacity to annihilate others!"); *id.* at 209 ("Women have to develop themselves psychologically so that they can accept the consciousness of having the power and capacity to choose to end a life that is also part of their very own being"); *id.* at 205 ("Someday I hope our culture will evolve a new attitude, one that will enable women to bear the responsibility for choosing life or death for our offspring in a different way than is possible now.").

[48] *Id.* at 204–206. "Women have to develop themselves psychologically so that they can accept the consciousness of having the power and capacity to choose to end a life that is also part of their very own being." *id.* at 209.

[49] The *Reader's Guide to Periodical Literature* reveals only one cursory review of *Soul Crisis*—85 Booklist 1493 (May 1, 1989). In addition, a manual review of many issues of Glamour, Ms. Ladies Home Journal, Mademoiselle, McCall's, Mother Jones, Working Woman, Savvy Woman, Vogue turns up no review of the book since publication.

[50] F. Ginsburg, *Contested Lives: The Abortion Debate in an American Community* (1989). *See also* S. Hewlett, *A Lessser Life: The Myth of Women's Liberation in America* 323–337 (1986); Callahan, *supra* note 6 at 684; Bayles, *Feminism and Abortion*, Atlantic Monthly 79 (April 1990); *cf.* Quarles, *Letter to the Editor,*

among women is between those who consider child-bearing to be essential to the definition of womanhood and those who see it as a mark of inequality with men that must be neutralized.[51] As moral philosopher Janet Smith has written:

> [B]ehind women's demands for unlimited access to abortion lies a profound displeasure with the way in which a woman's body works and hence a rejection of the value of being a woman. Whereas one might hope that the women's movement would be based on the assertion that it is great to be a woman and that women would endeavor to promote the powers and qualities which are theirs, the popularity of abortion indicates quite the opposite. Abortion is a denigration of women, a denial of one of the defining features of being a woman—her ability to bear children. Now some may deny that this is a defining characteristic of women. But is there any more certain criterion? A woman is a woman because she can bear children . . .
>
> Child-bearing is basic to them. We might expect that deliberate and violent denial of such a potential may be devastating. Some women argue that the fetus (be it a human being or not) is a part of their bodies and that they may do with it what they will. In one sense—a very different sense—the argument is true. Pregnancy and childbearing are perfectly normal conditions for women, and hence a part of her physical and psychological make-up. To have an abortion is to destroy part of one's self. It is normal for a woman to carry the children she conceives to term. To remove that child forcibly interrupts and harms the healthy functioning of her body. To put it bluntly, an abortion amounts to a mutilation of the woman's body and to a denial of her nature.[52]

Implicit in the position of those feminists who favor abortion rights is the view that men's inability to conceive is somehow superior to women's unique ability to bear children; women must be able "to have sex on a man's terms, not on a woman's."[53] It is this philosophical difference about the nature of unborn human life and pregnancy more than any other, that distinguishes women's positions on abortion in America and explains why, for many women, elective abortion can never be considered a basic right.

Pro-life women question whether the assertion of "choice" and "rights" in relation to aborting an unborn child can be reconciled with nurturance and other values cherished by feminists. Ginsburg writes that "[i]n opposition to the market relations of capitalism, nurturance stands for noncontingent and self-sacrificing support and love . . ."[54]

> One of the central notions in the modern American construct of The Family is that of nurturance . . . a relationship that entails affection and

---

Ms. Magazine, 19–20 (Jan./Feb. 1989) with Harmon, Letter to the Editor, Ms. Magazine 20 (Jan./Feb. 1989).

[51] Maggie Gallagher observed that some women consider a child to be "a crucial life goal, a primary form of self-identification." M. Gallagher, Enemies of Eros 68 (1989).

[52] Smith, supra note 30, at 81, 84.

[53] Id. at 86.

[54] F. Ginsburg, supra note 50, at 18.

love, that is based on cooperation as opposed to competition, that is enduring rather than temporary, that is noncontingent rather than contingent upon performance, and that is governed by feeling and morality instead of law and contract.[55]

Abortion, a self-centered act, contradicts the very notion of nurturance as "self-sacrificing support and love."[56] Abortion as a prerequisite for equality with men contradicts the value of cooperation. Abortion as a protection against the "invasion" of the unborn child contradicts connectedness with, and care for, that child. Ginsburg perceptively noted that, "[p]ro-life advocates critique a cultural and social system that assigns nurturance to women yet degrades it as a vocation."[57]

Commitment to the family and its associated values of nurturance, love, cooperation, and permanence is not limited to identifiable pro-life advocates. One woman attorney who had a "high-powered job as a commercial litigator" surprised herself when she gave up part-time day care for her infant son in order to be home with him full time. She observed:

> *It is easy to talk about combining kids and careers until you really do the mixing. The problem is not, as many of the young feminists I meet at the law school apparently believe, that some repressive male chauvinists are bent on keeping women in the home, and trying to recreate a stupid, sexist way of having a family. The problem is that women care too much about their children to abandon them to someone else . . .*
>
> *Women naturally love their children and want to spend time with them. To say otherwise, to try to fit ourselves into a new model, is itself a terrible oppression of women—an oppression often by the very people who call themselves feminists.*[58]

Only recently is the feminist movement waking up to this woman's concerns. Columnist Susanne Fields commented, "Almost every poll tells us that mothers of young children would like to spend more time at home with them. Liberal feminists, who have until now stressed individual rights of women over the collective needs of the family, are getting that message."[59] The continuing demand for elective abortion starkly contrasts with this reawakening to family needs. And this reawakening may further erode support for abortion rights.

No individual or group can tolerate forever a basic inconsistency with its human nature, whether this contradiction is imposed by government, religion or academia. Most women affirm their identity as life-giver, child-bearer, nurturer and cooperator and their connectedness with the vulnerable. A claim of the power and right to wield the knife of abortion, whether at her own hands or the physician's, violates the core of woman's values and being. Last but not least, it also stands starkly outside the mainstream of historical feminist thought.

---

[55] F. Ginsburg, *supra* note 50, at 254 n.19.

[56] *Id.* at 18.

[57] *Id.* at 18.

[58] Presser, *Mom, a sound concept,* Chicago Tribune, Nov. 20, 1989, sec. 1, p. 19, col. 2.

[59] Fields, *Even feminists now boost the family,* Chicago Sun-Times, May 7, 1991, at 23.

C. The Early Feminist Views on Abortion

Contemporary women's strong convictions against abortion were shared by the early American feminists in the 19th century, who "celebrated motherhood itself as a uniquely female power and strength that deserved genuine reverence."[60] Indeed, "the founding mothers of the women's movement staunchly opposed abortion, even to the point of supporting the late nineteenth century legislative campaign against it."[61]

Early feminist opposition to abortion has been dismissed as nothing more than an insufficient philosophical divorce from 19th century patriarchal society.[62] But this is a superficial reading. The 19th century leaders of the women's movement did not view legalized abortion as a solution to the oppression and disenfranchisement of women. They understood that abortion occurred *because* of that inequality. They understood that abortion is something done to women, by men, for men. Early feminists were uniformly opposed to abortion—including Susan B. Anthony, Elizabeth Cady Stanton, Matilda Gage, Victoria Woodhull, Sarah F. Norton and Mattie H. Brinkerhoff. They commonly called it "ante-natal child murder,"[63] "child murder"[64] and "infanticide."[65] They believed that "[l]ife must be present from the very moment of conception."[66]

The early feminists condemned not only the practice of abortion. They were equally concerned about its causes: ignorance about sexuality and reproduction, the view of pregnancy as a pathological condition, the double standard that promoted male irresponsibility, social pressures against illegitimacy and lack of economic support to single mothers.[67] Susan B. Anthony's and Elizabeth Cady Stanton's journal, *The Revolution*, often contained articles or editorials denouncing abortion's causes and tragic effects. Mattie Brinkerhoff wrote:

> [A]s law and custom give to the husband the absolute control of the wife's person, she is forced to not only violate physical law, but to outrage the holiest instincts of her being . . .
>
> When a man steals to satisfy hunger, we may safely conclude that there is something wrong with society—so when a woman destroys the life of her unborn child, it is an evidence that either by education or circumstances she has been greatly wronged.[68]

Dr. Charlotte Lozier, a New York physician, in 1869 reported to the authorities a man who brought a young woman to her for an abortion. She then extended other

---

[60] M. Derr, *"Man's Inhumanity to Woman, Makes Countless Infants Die"*: The Early Feminist Case Against Abortion i (1991) (privately published); on file with the authors.

[61] Derr, *supra* note 60, at i.

[62] R. Petchesky, *Abortion & Women's Choice* 44–45 (Rev. ed. 1990); J. Mohr, *Abortion in America: The Origins & Evolution of National Policy* 112–113 (1978).

[63] Woodhull & Claflin's Weekly, Nov. 19, 1876, (Sarah F. Norton).

[64] 1 The Revolution 215–16, April 9, 1868, (Matilda E. J. Gage).

[65] 1 The Revolution 65, Feb. 5, 1868, (Elizabeth Cady Stanton).

[66] A. Stockham, *Tokology* 246 (1887). Historian Carl Degler has noted that this valuation of fetal life at all stages "was in line with a number of movements to reduce cruelty and to expand the concept of the sanctity of life . . . the elimination of the death penalty, the peace movement, the abolition of torture and whipping in connection with crimes"—all movements that feminists supported. "The prohibiting of abortion was but the most recent effort in that larger concern." C. Degler, *At Odds: Women and Family in America From the Revolution to the Present* 247 (1980).

[67] *See generally Brief of Feminists for Life, et al.* in *Bray v. Alexandria Women's Health Clinic,* No. 90–985, at 10–25 (U.S. 1991).

[68] 3 The Revolution 138, Sept. 2, 1869.

assistance to the young woman. For this act, Lozier was praised in *The Revolution* and eulogized after her death by Pauline Wright Davis, an eminent suffragist:

> *[Lozier's] sense of justice would not allow her to let the wrong-doer escape the penalty of the law, while at the same time she pitied and tenderly cared for the victim. We have been amazed to hear her denounced for this brave, noble act on the ground of professional privacy. It is said she had no right to expose the outrage of having one thousand dollars offered her to commit murder. The murder of the innocents goes on. Shame and crime after crime darken the history of our whole land. Hence it was fitting that a true woman should protest with all the energy of her soul against this woeful crime.*[69]

The 19th century feminists forcefully wrote that the only remedy for this "fearful ravage" was "the education and enfranchisement of women."[70] They originated the then-radical philosophy of "voluntary motherhood," which declared a woman's right to avoid pregnancy as she chose, through birth control or abstinence but *not* through abortion. They sought "prevention, not merely punishment. We must reach the root of the evil."[71]

Their desire for legal reform to protect and improve the circumstances of women[72] was accompanied by support for legal sanctions against the proliferating abortion trade, known commonly as "Restellism." *The Revolution* editorialized in favor of legislation to restrict abortifacient drugs and remedies on grounds that "Restellism has long found in those broths of Bellzebub, its securest hiding place."[73]

In the early 20th century, opposition to abortion by feminists continued. Alice Paul, founder and chair of the National Woman's Party and author of the original Equal Rights Amendment in the 1920s, is recognized as "the foremost feminist of this century." She said that "[a]bortion is just another way of exploiting women."[74] Contemporary women's opposition to abortion thus has a clear philosophical link to the origins of American feminism.

D. Contemporary Feminist Understanding of Women

It was not until the late 1960s that the women's movement began demanding abortion rights. The movement was conceived and portrayed as a revolt against "the traditional female role," inspired in part by Betty Friedan's book, *The Feminine Mystique*.[75] The stated goal of the women's liberation movement was freedom and autonomy on an

---

[69] M. Derr, *supra* note 60, at 4 (citing 4 The Revolution 346, Dec. 2, 1869; 5 The Revolution 41–42, Jan. 20, 1870).

[70] 1 The Revolution 65, Feb. 5, 1868.

[71] 4 The Revolution 4, July 8, 1869.

[72] At the same time, these feminists sought reform in marital property laws, the right to vote and the right to trial by a jury of her peers—women—for women, including the "frenzied mother, who, to save herself from exposure and disgrace, ended the life that had but just begun . . ." S. Anthony, M. Gage, E. Stanton, eds., *History of Women Suffrage* 597–98 (1881).

[73] 1 The Revolution 2, Feb. 5, 1868.

[74] Personal correspondence from Evelyn K. S. Judge to Wendy E. Stone, Nov. 1, 1991 (copy on file with the authors). Judge was a longtime political coworker of Paul's and lobbied with her for 18 years on Capitol Hill and at the United Nations.

[75] B. Friedan, *The Feminine Mystique* (1963).

equal basis with men. This encompassed an effort to attain biological sameness as well. Some women hated the uniqueness of the female body and one called gender differences "metaphysical cannibalism."[76] Abortion was deemed necessary to avoid the burdens of pregnancy, which men would not share. This "female oppression" was seen as the "most deeply ingrained injustice in history."[77]

However, the reality of gender differences could not be ignored. Women came to the realization that being treated exactly like a man was not the panacea they had hoped. "Sameness" did not yield equality. Women learned that the rigors they encountered in the workplace were just as brutalizing to men. In addition, many women ended up going home from work to face the "second shift," where women perform 75% of the housework and child care.[78] Academic feminist thought eventually took into account the reality that this "first-stage" feminism or "equality feminism" lets men have it both ways—enjoying the second income of the wife while expecting her to fulfill a more traditional role at home.[79]

Even Betty Friedan now recognizes the "superwoman" fallacy. Speaking at Smith College's commencement, Ms. Friedan told the audience that "having it all" and being a "superwoman" have been

> a cruel illusion. Women have been spared petty prejudice only to be met with personal catastrophe. For the first time in American history, women work far harder than their mothers. And they miscarry more, are divorced more, abandoned more, abused more, and fall into poverty more.[80]

Contemporary feminism then tried to compensate for its disillusionment with "absolute equality" by developing "difference feminism" or "second-stage feminism,"[81]

> None of the very real problems facing women today, from finding ways to combine fruitful work with a nurturing family life, to rescuing women from the economic disaster of divorce, can be resolved without abandoning the failed doctrine of sexual androgyny. That is, without firmly and quite unashamedly acknowledging the distinctive needs, desires, and contributions of women.[82]

Difference feminism "questioned the move towards full assimilation of female identity with public male identity and argued that to see women's traditional roles and activities as *wholly* oppressive was itself oppressive to women, denying them historic subjective and moral agency."[83] Dr. Barbara Bardes, dean of the University College of Loyola University in Chicago, calls this the "post-feminist age:" "It represents a consciousness that women acknowledge their desire to be mothers—that they want to be different but

---

[76] Bayles, *supra* note 50, at 79, 84 (quoting Ti-Grace Atkinson).

[77] *Id.*

[78] *See generally* A. Hochschild, *supra* note 32.

[79] Wallis, *supra* note 32, at 86.

[80] As quoted in K. Monroe, *The Writing on the Wall,* The Harvard Salient 1 (Nov. 1990). *See also* Betty Friedan's recent book, *The Second Stage* (1986).

[81] Bayles, *supra* note 50, at 79.

[82] M. Gallagher, *supra* note 51, at 70. *See* Bayles, *supra* note 50, at 85.

[83] Bayles, *supra* note 50, at 85 (quoting Jean Bethke Elshtain, emphasis in original).

equal.''[84] This second-stage feminism (or difference feminism) acknowledges and accepts that women are biologically different than men. Second-stage feminism looks at each problem or human condition from the unique perspective of women. But not all feminists who acknowledge sexual differences seek equality. Some make ''. . . no pretense of [desiring] equal treatment but rather the pursuit of privilege to compensate for the great range of psycho-sexual differences between the genders.''[85]

Nonetheless, this trend in feminism acknowledges values that most women intuitively share: nurturing, responsibility, caring for others and a sense of community. Carol Gilligan concluded in *In a Different Voice* that men reason from ideas of individual rights and fair play, while women reason from ideas of individual responsibility and concern for others.[86] This, of course, is the age-old dichotomy between justice and mercy, that, together, establish the foundation of the human community. But these ''feminine'' values are not unique to women. Men, too, can be nurturing and care for others, just as women may pursue autonomy and individual rights. But to negate or compromise nurturance and inclusivity destroys the essence of women's self-concept, a deep, inseparable, part of who they are. Thus, the assumption that women need abortion as their ''first right'' represents a profound misunderstanding of the nature of women.

The commitment to abortion rights creates some glaring inconsistencies for feminism. ''Today, this inconsistency shows up in the heat of political debate, as pro-choice activists switch back and forth between the two kinds of feminism to defend the absolute right to abortion.''[87] The reason for this dilemma is not difficult to understand: ''It is not easy to reconcile the feminine metaphors of motherhood and community with the feminist defense of abortion on the grounds of individual right.''[88] This inability of abortion advocates to reconcile these conflicts, accompanied by determined adherence to abortion rights, leaves many American women—those who do not fit the trends in feminist theory—unpersuaded. Despite the self-proclaimed success of some women's organizations, particularly as abortion advocates, a 1989 survey found that only 25% of women agreed that women's organizations have done something that ''made your life better.''[89]

This confusion—about who women are, what women want and what women believe ''woman's role'' to be—is no more evident than in the view of unborn children. If feminine values are nurturing and inclusive, does abortion fit in? As individuals with abilities and aspirations, women make moral choices *as women,* in the context of relationships. Those relationships include those who are dependent and vulnerable. And the one who is most dependent on a woman—for her nurturance, compassion, strength, courage and wisdom—is the child in her womb. Mature feminism, therefore, would contemplate that society accommodate the reproductive capacities of women, that childbearing and rearing be valued just as much as, if not more, than establishing financial security and job satisfaction.

The deep needs and feelings of many American women may more accurately be reflected by what has been described as ''conservative feminism'' or ''classical femi-

---

[84] Dionne, *supra* note 19, at A1.

[85] Amiel, *Feminism Hits Middle Age,* National Review 23 (Nov. 24, 1989).

[86] C. Gilligan, *In a Different Voice: Psychological Theory and Women's Development* 19–22 (1982).

[87] Bayles, *supra* note 50, at 85.

[88] R. Bray, *No Feminist Is an Island,* The New York Times Book Review 12 (May 5, 1991) (quoting and reviewing E. Fox-Genovese, *Feminism Without Illusions* [1991]).

[89] Dionne, *supra* note 19, at A11.

nism." In her essay, "What Do Women Want?," Katherine Kersten concludes that classical feminism "teaches women that their horizons should be as limitless as men's."[90] She explains:

> *What sets me apart from most contemporary feminists is that—more than anger at the injustices done to women in the past—I feel gratitude toward the social and political system that has made much-needed reform possible . . .*
>
> *Consequently, I propose an alternative to the feminism of the women's studies departments and "public interest" lobbies. I envision a self-consciously conservative feminism, inspired by what is best in our tradition, that can speak to women's concerns in both the private and public spheres. Such a feminism is based on three premises: first, that uniform standards of equality and justice must apply to both sexes; second, that women have historically suffered from injustice, and continue to do so today; and third, that the problems that confront women can best be addressed by building on—rather than repudiating—the ideals and institutions of Western culture.*[91]

The conservative feminist seeks the full participation of women in all aspects of cultural and personal development "to develop their talents, to follow their interests to their natural conclusion, to seek adventure, to ask and answer the great questions, and to select from a multitude of social roles," Kersten says.[92]

This view embraces feminine values, seeing "the special bond of motherhood not as evidence of oppression, but as cause for thanksgiving."[93] Many women would agree. Abortion as the "first right" thus stands outside the early tradition of feminism and most contemporary women's self-perception. And although it may be politically correct to espouse abortion as the foundation for women's freedom and progress, it has not truly benefited women. Abortion promotes neither the core values of women, such as inclusiveness and nurturance, nor the premises of autonomy and choice upon which it is based.

III. Is Abortion Really a Free Choice?

A. Male Coercion, Pressure, Denial, Abandonment

Abortion as women's "first right" is premised on abortion as a free, self-determined choice. The abortion-rights movement raised up "freedom of choice" as its ubiquitous slogan in the 1980s. *Roe v. Wade* symbolizes "freedom" to choose abortion. Press releases and advertising suggest that, unless *Roe v. Wade* is overturned and restrictive abortion laws are reinstated, abortion will remain a "free choice." But is the abortion choice really free?

The creation and expansion of the unlimited abortion doctrine first enunciated in *Roe v. Wade* actually isolated women in their contemplation of abortion. First, in *Roe,*

---

[90] Kersten, *What Do Women Want?* Policy Review 4, 6 (Spring 1991).
[91] *Id.* at 4.
[92] *Id.* at 10.
[93] *Id.* at 9.

the Court held that a woman had the "right" to decide to have an abortion for any and every reason at any time of pregnancy. Three years later, in *Planned Parenthood v. Danforth*,[94] the Court imposed a revolutionary social law on American men, women, and children: Men have no rights whatever to protect their child before birth. Ironically, the Court recognized that although the woman presumably makes the abortion decision "with the approval of her physician but without the approval of her husband . . . it could be said that she is acting unilaterally."[95] Nonetheless, it approved the unilateral power of the woman to prevent her *husband* (much less a man to whom she is not married) from protecting his own offspring. These two decisions placed all "choice"— the choice to abort or not to abort—on the pregnant woman. By necessary implication, whether the child lives or dies is solely up to the pregnant woman. Since that exclusive power over the child's life is under the woman's control, the determination whether the father will become the father of born offspring and incur child-support obligations falls entirely on the mother. She becomes the only one who can eliminate this expense.

The logic of women's exclusive control over reproduction is not lost on men. By vesting all rights to abort in the mother alone and by stripping the man of all his parental rights, it psychologically divests the man of all responsibility as well. It undermines healthy relationships between men and women. It destroys responsible communication by creating an artificial barrier to discussing a matter that deeply affects not only the woman but her partner as well. Men naturally may respond with distrust. The motives of all women, both those who demand and those who refuse abortion, come under suspicion. True intimacy cannot develop when a relationship lacks trust and communication. Coercion, pressure, abandonment and denial of responsibility all result.

What exacerbates this legal wedge in the relationship between men and women is the fact that 80% of all abortions are performed on single women.[96] In such a relationship, the man bears no legal obligation unless the child survives. Frequently, he neither prepares for nor desires any child. By its very nature, such a relationship creates the greatest potential for male coercion, denial of responsibility and abandonment when pregnancy results.

One of the myths of the abortion liberty—and *Roe v. Wade*—is that it only created a right to choose abortion for women who wanted abortion; it did not force anyone to abort or to participate in abortion. But over the past 15 years, it has become increasingly clear that coercion and pressure on women play a significant role in many, if not most, decisions to have an abortion.[97]

One of the most compelling accounts is Susan Nathanson's story about her abortion and subsequent psychotherapy.[98] Nathanson is no pro-life advocate. Indeed, she wrote

---

[94] 428 U.S. 52 (1976).

[95] 428 U.S. at 71.

[96] Koonin, et al., *Abortion Surveillance, United States, 1988,* 40 *CDC [Centers for Disease Control] Surveillance Summaries, Morbidity and Mortality Weekly Report* 22 (July 1991) (Table 1) (79.7% in 1988).

[97] D. Reardon, *Aborted Women: Silent No More* x (1987). *See, e.g.,* Linda D. v. Fritz C., 38 Wash. App. 288, 687 P.2d 223, 225 (1984) ("When she informed the father [that she was pregnant], he asked her to have an abortion. She refused."); L. Francke, *The Ambivalence of Abortion* (1978). *See also* S. Nathanson, *supra* note 40, at 201; Baker, *supra* note 31; Goodman, *supra* note 31.

[98] S. Nathanson, *supra* note 40, at 3 ("I did not anticipate how profoundly I would suffer emotionally, or how long my suffering would endure").

[99] *Id.* at 2–5. *See also* Nathanson-Elkind, *Perspectives on the Abortion Debate,* San Francisco Examiner-Chronicle, July 8, 1990, at 1 (review of Laurence Tribe, *Abortion: The Clash of Absolutes*). Susan Nathanson is not related to Bernard Nathanson, M.D.

her book to make the argument for abortion rights and to support *Roe v. Wade*.[99] But she writes honestly. The night before her abortion she sat, watching out the window of her house: "But mostly I sit with the life of my fourth child growing inside me, trying to contemplate this ending, and I grieve and grieve and grieve and grieve."[100]

Coercion by her husband played a primary and determinative role in her abortion. "I am absolutely clear that I do not want a fourth child under any circumstances," he said.[101] "If you don't choose to abort this child, I will push you to do it."[102] Nathanson felt she had little alternative: "It is at this moment that I know that *I* will take responsibility for the decision that must be made and that I will have an abortion, even though Michael and I will repeat this discussion over the next few days with no variation in our positions."[103] Some time after the abortion, her husband realized that he "pushed [her] to make the decision to have an abortion."[104] Much of the last part of her book describes her post-abortion counseling. It does not seem to help when, five years later, her husband suggests that they could have had that fourth child after all: "I was so worried about my physical well-being then. I don't have that apprehension now. Now I feel as if we really could have managed to raise that child."[105] Unable to respond to his untimely admission, Nathanson has "no answer" for her husband. What is remarkable about this account is that it happened *within* an apparently healthy marriage—under ideal economic, social and emotional conditions to support mother and child. If the abortion liberty can prompt such coercion within an intact marriage, its impact on extramarital relationships can only breed more disastrous consequences.

Coercion or pressure to have an abortion is reflected in court cases of various kinds around the country.[106] In some cases, fathers raise the woman's "right to abortion" as an affirmative defense to child support. The defense is usually framed in the following terms: The woman got pregnant by a man to whom she was not married; he did not want to get married or to support the child; she could have had an abortion, and he offered to pay for that abortion; she has a constitutional right to get an abortion, and he is legally helpless to prevent it; by her failure to obtain an abortion, she took sole responsibility for the child; therefore, the man should not be liable for any child support. Fortunately for the women and children involved, all courts have apparently rejected this defense.[107] But they have done so only by evading the logic of *Roe v. Wade*. In other variations on this theme, men have sued to "enforce" a contract to undergo an

---

[100] S. Nathanson, *supra* note 40, at 41.

[101] *Id.* at 25.

[102] *Id.* at 28.

[103] *Id.* at 29 (emphasis in original); *id.* at 28 ("this man who is pressuring me to give up my fourth child"); *id.* at 29–30 ("the final responsibility for the choice clearly rests with me alone").

[104] *Id.* at 154.

[105] *Id.* at 287–88.

[106] *See, e.g.,* Noto v. St. Vincent's Hosp. & Med. Center, 142 Misc.2d 292, 537, N.Y.S.2d 446 (1988), *aff'd,* 559 N.Y.S.2d 510 (1990) (abortion after "affair" with hospital psychiatrist; pressure to have abortion alleged); J.L.S. v. W.C., No. PI 90-2333 (Hennepin County Dist. Ct., 4th Jud. Dist., Minn. filed Feb. 8, 1990) (coercion to have abortion alleged).

[107] People in Interest of S.P.B., 651 P.2d 1213 (Colo. 1982); D.W.L. v. M.J.B.C., 601 S.W.2d 475 (Tex. Civ. App. 1980); Harris v. State, 356 So.2d 623 (Ala. 1978); Dorsey v. English, 390 A.2d 1133 (Md. Ct. App. 1978); Dauksas v. Rataj, No. 87 CH 5206 (Cook Co. Ill. Cir. Ct. filed May 28, 1987). *See also In re* Ince, 28 Or. App. 71, 558 P.2d 1253 (1977), *appeal dismissed,* 434 U.S. 806 (1977); *In re* Goodwin, 30 Or.App. 425, 567 P.2d 144 (1977); Isabellita S. v. John S., 132 Misc.2d 475, 504 N.Y.S.2d 367 (1986). *See generally* Swan, *Abortion on Maternal Demand: Paternal Support Liability Implications,* 9 Val. U.L. Rev. 243 (1975).

abortion.[108] Women have been subjected to unconsented abortion performed by a physician-lover,[109] defenses to child support for "misrepresenting" the nonuse of contraception[110] or clauses in surrogate mother contracts requiring the surrogate mother to undergo an abortion for various reasons. Few disputes end up in court, and even fewer appear in published court decisions. There are countless scenarios in which the man threatened nonsupport but did not follow through with a lawsuit.[111]

Coercion to have an abortion is also reported in scholarly journals. A survey from the Medical College of Ohio examined a sample of 150 women who "identified themselves as having poorly assimilated the abortion experience."[112] Of the 81 women who responded, "more than one-third felt they had been coerced into their decision"; less than one-third of these women initially considered the abortion themselves.

There is a tendency to suggest that male coercion is simply a kink that needs to be worked out of our policy of legalized abortion.[113] But male coercion is an inevitable tragic consequence of legal abortion on demand inaugurated by *Roe*. This endemic coercion is revealed in Carol Gilligan's work, *In a Different Voice*.[114] Gilligan determined that the women she interviewed processed their abortion decision consistent with objective moral reasoning and based on principles of care, concern, responsibility and nonviolence. Gilligan suggested, "The sequence of women's moral judgment proceeds from an initial concern with survival to a focus on goodness and finally to a reflective understanding of care as the most adequate guide to the resolution of conflicts in human relationships."[115] Gilligan's sample, however, reveals that many decisions were not independent, moral choices. Male coercion played an important role in a number of cases.[116] Harvard Law Professor Mary Ann Glendon observed: "It is striking how many

---

[108] Breidenbach v. Hayden, No. 90-CI-00021 (Jefferson Co., Ky., Cir. Ct. Div. 2); Briedenbach v. Hayden, No. 91-CI-00591 (Jefferson Co., Ky., Cir. Ct. Div. 2) (custody action). A surgeon allegedly impregnated his secretary during an affair, paid her $20,500 to have an abortion, and then sued for breach of contract for her failure to comply. The physician alleged the woman's failure to return his money and also objected to fully supporting the child once it was born. After a paternity suit and proof that the physician was indeed the father of the child, he asked for visitation rights and custody or joint custody. Wolfson, *Lawsuit raises novel questions in abortion case,* Louisville Courier-Journal, Mar. 28, 1991, at 1.

[109] Collins v. Thakkar, 552 N.E.2d 507 (Ind. Ct. App. 1990), *appeal denied,* No. 30AO1-8911-CV-00460 (Ind. Oct. 11, 1990), *on remand,* Collins v. Thakkar, No. 73CO1-9005-CP-0074 (Shelby Co., Ind., Cir. Ct.) (physician allegedly aborted three-month-old fetus during pelvic examination against Collins' wishes). The same physician allegedly drugged another woman, aborted her eight-month-old unborn child, then killed the infant. Hertzinger v. Thakkar, No. 29CO1-8903-CT-00174 (Hamilton Co., Ind. Cir. Ct. 1991); Caleca, *Doctor sued over abortions can't move or hide assets,* Indianapolis Star, Feb. 21 1989, at 1. Dr. Thakkar was found guilty of seducing three women and aborting or attempting to abort their pregnancies without their consent. *Chicago Tribune,* June 13, 1991, at 24.

[110] Linda D. v. Fritz C. 38 Wash. App. 288, 687 P.2d 223 (1984); L. Pamela P. v. Frank S., 449 N.E.2d 713, 59 N.Y.2d 1 (1983); Hughes v. Hutt, 455 A.2d 623 (Pa. 1983); Stephen K. v. Roni L., 105 Cal. App. 3d 640, 164 Cal. Rptr. 618 (1980). *See also* Barbara A. v. John G., 145 Cal. App. 3d 369, 193 Cal. Rptr. 422 (1983).

[111] *See, e.g.,* D. Reardon, *Aborted Women: Silent No More* (1987).

[112] Franco, et al., *Psychological profile of dysphoric women postabortion,* 44 J. Amer. Med. Women's Assoc. 113 (July/August 1989). *See also* M. Zimmerman, *Passage Through Abortion: The Personal and Social Reality of Women's Experiences* (1977).

[113] Callahan, *supra* note 6, at 684.

[114] Gilligan, *supra* note 86. It should be noted that the interviewing group totaled 24 women and "no effort was made to select a representative sample of the clinic or counseling service population." *Id.* at 3.

[115] *Id.* at 105, 82–83, 99.

[116] *See, e.g., id.* at 80 (Cathy), 81 (Denise), 90–91 (Sarah).

of Carol Gilligan's subjects in her chapter on the abortion decision stated that one of the reasons they were seeking abortions was because the men in their lives were unwilling to give them moral and material support in continuing with pregnancy and childbirth. This fact surely must have been central to their moral dilemma, but Gilligan, surprisingly, never picks up on this aspect of her data."[117] Gilligan—who has a reputation as the foremost feminist analyst of women's abortion rights and independent decision-making—evidently could not distinguish independent judgment from coercion.

Gilligan's conclusions have been challenged by moral philosopher Janet Smith and others on precisely this point.[118] Gilligan does not approve of being "self-sacrificing." Nor does she believe that any act, including abortion, is intrinsically immoral, though she believes that abortion is often the "morally responsible" choice.[119] How can the demand for arbitrary life-and-death power over one's own children be morally "responsible," as Gilligan claims? This claim for exclusive dominion over the fetus is nothing short of viewing the child as property.[120] This directly conflicts with what women know about their own children: "This child is flesh of my flesh and bone of my bone." "This daughter has my blue eyes; this son has my dark hair." It was not so long ago that wives were treated as the property of their husbands (and, in some parts of the world, they still are).[121] If it is wrong for men to treat others as possessions, it is wrong for women, too.

Who has abortion freed? Legalized abortion has helped create a sexual climate throughout our country by which men are freed to engage in the most irresponsible sexual relations, and the consequences fall directly and solely upon the woman. Women are left to pay the price. Kathleen Kersten highlights the painful consequences of sex without commitment:

> *Feminists often explain traditional restraints on women's sexual freedom in one-dimensional terms, dismissing them as male attempts to wrest control of women's vital reproductive functions.*
>
> *. . . But women are wrong to assert that sex without commitment is no more dangerous for women than it is for men. We know now that sex of this sort has led to an epidemic of abortions, venereal disease, and female infertility; a host of unwanted children; and a sorry legacy of educations and careers—women's, not men's—cut short.*[122]

Contrary to what might be the popular impression, abortion does not solve or heal relationships. Indeed, it usually dissolves them. "When one partner wants a child and the other doesn't, an abortion often leads to a breakup."[123]

---

[117] M. Glendon, *Abortion and Divorce in Western Law* 52 (1987).

[118] Smith, *Abortion and Moral Development Theory: Listening with Different Ears,* 28 Inter. Phil. Q. (March 1988); reprinted in 13 Inter. Rev. 237 (Fall/Winter 1989).

[119] *Id.* at 246–248.

[120] *See* Ryan, *"The Argument for Unlimited Procreative Liberty: A Feminist Critique,"* Hastings Center Report 6 (July/Aug. 1990).

[121] Elizabeth Cady Stanton wrote in 1873, "When we consider that women are treated as property, it is degrading to women that we should treat our children as property to be disposed of as we wish." Monroe, *supra* note 80, at 12.

[122] Kersten, *supra* note 90, at 13.

[123] Goodman, *supra* note 31, at 179.

> *The most common male response to unwanted pregnancy when it occurs outside of marriage has been to "take off," leaving the woman to bear the physical, the emotional and, often, the financial brunt of either having an abortion or carrying the pregnancy to term. Studies of abortion and its aftermath reveal that, more often than not, relationships do not survive an abortion: the majority of unmarried couples break up either before or soon after an abortion.[124]*

Men are freed to engage in behavior without serious personal consequences, knowing that it is both the woman's "right" and "responsibility" to get an abortion if anything goes "wrong."[125] He has the "security" that the woman can obtain an "easy," "safe," "painless," "quick" abortion, for which he might pay $200 to $300.[126]

Freely available legal abortion thus encourages the very kind of male behavior that feminists have railed against for generations. "Modern ideology makes it easy for men to rationalize their defection from family life. . ."[127] Even an abortion rights advocate like Daniel Callahan can see this: "If legal abortion has given women more choice, it has also given men more choice as well. They now have a potent new weapon in the old business of manipulating and abandoning women."[128] Since 80% of abortions are performed on single women, who are outside the protective circle of family life, it is probable that the man is strongly inclined to not want their child.[129] His pressure on the woman to "choose" her legally endorsed alternative is virtually inevitable.[130] The notion among modern feminists that restrictive abortion laws *support* "male domination" is tragic foolishness. It is directly contradicted by real human experience with abortion on demand in the United States over the past 19 years.

B. Parental Coercion

Men are not the only source of coercion. Parental coercion of teens does occur, and it can be overwhelming.[131] The extent of this pressure is difficult to document, but one example illustrates the extremes to which parents may go to compel their daughter to have an abortion. ChristyAnne Collins is executive director of an organization that provides crisis pregnancy assistance: counseling, medical services and placement services. She was appointed by a Rockville, Maryland circuit judge as legal guardian for a 16-year-old woman ("Jane Doe") who wanted to continue her pregnancy.[132] The previous year, Jane Doe had been forced by her parents to abort an earlier pregnancy.[133]

---

[124] K. McDonnell, *Not an Easy Choice: A Feminist Re-examines Abortion* 59 (1984) (citing M. Zimmerman, *supra* note 112).

[125] D. Reardon, *supra* note 97, at xi (1989).

[126] Goodman, *supra* note 31, at 179, 209.

[127] M. Gallagher, *supra* note 51, at 116.

[128] Callahan, *supra* note 6, at 684.

[129] Goodman, *supra* note 31, at 209, 210.

[130] M. Gallagher, *supra* note 51, at 108–110.

[131] *See generally* Ciolli, *Abortion and Consent: Limiting minors' access in next court battleground*, New York Newsday, Sept. 25, 1989, pp. 3, 21; Feder, *Parents in the dark on abortion*, Boston Herald, Dec. 11, 1989; Herrmann, *Fifty percent of teens tell their parents*, Chicago Sun Times, June 26, 1991, p. 42.

[132] In the matter of Jane Doe, C.A. No. 70798 (Mont. Co. Md. Cir. Ct., Feb. 1, 1991).

[133] Telephone conversation with ChristyAnne Collins, May 10, 1991. Her parents appeared to acquiesce in their daughter's refusal. When Jane, accompanied by her parents, agreed to go to a clinic to test for sexually transmitted diseases, she again refused to sign abortion consent papers. The last thing she remembers is the nurse drawing blood for a test. She woke up from anesthesia two hours later with her unborn child aborted.

In order to exercise her choice to carry her second pregnancy to term, Jane Doe had to turn to the courts for protection from her parents. It is ironic that this occurred in Maryland, a state that excludes parental influence in *preventing* an abortion.

Another teenager, this time the victim of rape, was taken against her will to a Bremerton, Washington abortion clinic. Although she screamed that she did not want an abortion, the abortionist and nurse, in unsanitary clothing, forced this teen to undergo the procedure. Police detective Linda Johnson—who had been ordered against her will to gather the fetal remains as evidence against the rapist—attempted suicide more than a dozen times and was treated at a mental health clinic.[134]

A more widely published example of coercion—not choice—is that of Denise Lefebvre in Florida. Denise is apparently psychotic and routinely takes lithium, an antipsychotic drug known to cause birth defects. In 1990, she stopped taking the drug when she suspected she was pregnant, even though her condition renders her dangerous to herself and others when she is not medicated. She apparently stopped the medication to protect her unborn child, and spent virtually all her pregnancy confined to a hospital—strapped to the bed for her own protection. The assistant public defender who eventually represented her said, "This woman is very lucid regarding her baby. Everyone wanted to give the woman an abortion except her."[135] Indeed, the physicians involved, and even her father, sought to order an abortion against her will. They argued that there was a *chance* of fetal defect based on *possible* exposure to lithium. Florida law provides for "termination of pregnancy" for incompetent women if certain procedural safeguards are extended.[136] For example, a three-member examining committee must be appointed before a determination of incapacity is made, and written consent of the woman's court-appointed guardian must be obtained before the pregnancy can be terminated. Lefebvre was originally denied all the procedural protections due her, and the trial court ordered an abortion. The appeals court reversed the decision solely on procedural error. A healthy baby boy was born just after Christmas. At last report, the baby was scheduled to be adopted by other Lefebvre family members.[137]

C. Social Pressure

Perhaps as much as direct coercion, women cite a lack of alternatives—or their belief that they had no alternative—as the reason for abortion.[138] Some women view abortion as a "forced response to a problem, rather than an affirmative action in their lives."[139] This may be due, at least in part, to inadequate counseling.[140] This situation seems not to have changed in 30 years. In 1960, Mary Calderone, the medical director of Planned Parenthood Federation of America, wrote:

---

[134] Johnson v. City of Bremerton, No. 89-2-00218-5 (Kitsap Co., Wash. Sup. Ct. 1990); Marez, *Former police officer tells about "abortion duty,"* Bremerton (Wash.) Sun, Oct. 18, 1990, at B1, col. 1.

[135] *Psychotic's pregnancy stirs legal fight,* Chicago Tribune, Aug. 24, 1990, sec. 1, p. 20; *Baby born after abortion fight may be up for adoption,* Chicago Tribune, Jan. 2 , 1991, sec. 1, p. 3, col. 2.

[136] Fla. Stat. § 394.467 (1989); Fla. Stat. § 744.331 (1989); Fla. Stat. 390.001(4)(1989).

[137] Lefebvre v. North Broward Hosp. Dist., 566 So. 2d 568 (Fla App. 1990); Los Angeles Times, Jan. 1, sec. A-22, col. 1.

[138] D. Reardon, *supra* note 97; Quarles, Letter to the editor, Ms. Magazine, 19–20 (Jan./Feb. 1989); "Women who have the fewest choices of all exercise their right to abortion the most." Tisdale, *We Do Abortions Here: A Nurse's Story,* Harper's 66, 70 (Oct. 1987).

[139] Franco, *supra* note 109, at 115 (citing Freeman, *Influence of personality attributes on abortion experiences,* 47 Am. J. Orthopsychiatry 503 [1977]).

[140] Callahan, *supra* note 6, at 687.

> *Conference members agreed, and this was backed up by evidence from the Scandinavians, that when a woman seeking an abortion is given the chance of talking over her problem with a properly trained and oriented person, she will in the process very often resolve many of her qualms and will spontaneously decide to see the pregnancy through, particularly if she is assured that supportive help will continue to be available to her.*[141]

Besides feeling alone and without resources, a pregnant woman may also sense the pressure of the workplace. For example, a recent study of female medical residents reported open hostility to pregnant residents from program directors and colleagues.[142] The percent of abortion among female residents was *threefold* that of the control group.[143] And those residents and physicians who chose to carry their pregnancies to term were "more likely to underreport their symptoms in order to minimize the influence of their pregnancy on their work."[144]

Similarly, women lawyers are aware of the same subtle bias against having children. An article in the *National Law Journal* noted that law firms have been unable or unwilling to create an environment supportive of working mothers.[145] Women who want to make partner are told not to get pregnant until the partnership is secure. Those who do choose motherhood are often put on the "mommy track," with no likelihood of achieving partnership. In another recent incident, the New York City Department of Corrections settled a lawsuit filed by several female officers who had been told to have abortions; many who refused were given physically grueling jobs.[146]

D. Failure to Protect Wanted Children

Abortion-rights advocacy goes to such lengths as to vigorously fight against any legislative attempts to protect the child of the woman who chooses nurturance. For example, in 1991 the New Hampshire legislature considered and passed a fetal homicide bill that would penalize the killing of an unborn child by a third person (other than an abortionist). A criminally assaulted pregnant woman who did not previously choose abortion presumably desires to carry her child to term. The bill was opposed by the National Abortion Rights Action League of New Hampshire. Spokesperson Peg Dobbie argued that it would lead to limitations or restrictions on "a woman's reproductive right."[147] A similar bill was defeated by abortion-rights advocates in Delaware in 1991.[148] Thus the pro-choice position claims that a woman who *chooses* to give birth should be given no legal protection, even after viability, for the child she carries in her womb.

---

[141] Calderone, *supra* note 8, at 951.

[142] Shulkin & Bari, Letter to the editor, 324 New Eng. J. Med. 630 (Feb. 28, 1991).

[143] Klebanoff, Shiono & Rhoads, *Outcomes of Pregnancy in a National Sample of Resident Physicians,* 323 New Engl. J. Med. 1040, 1041 (Oct. 11, 1990).

[144] Letter, *supra* note 142, at 630.

[145] Stern, *Female Talent at Lawfirms,* National Law Journal 15–16 (Mar. 18, 1991).

[146] Martin, *Women Given Cruelest Choice Now Fight Back,* New York Times, Oct. 21, 1989, at A27. *See* New York Daily News, May 24, 1989 (More than a dozen women claimed they were told to have abortions or resign their jobs. One suffered a miscarriage, although she pleaded with supervisors to allow her to see a doctor. Another who became pregnant was told to "stay home and collect (welfare) checks or get rid of it.").

[147] Kenny, *What Is Life Worth in New Hampshire?* Manchester Union Leader, Feb. 14, 1991, at 45.

[148] Alan Guttmacher Institute, *State Reproductive Health Monitor,* vol. 2, no. 3 at 4 (Sep. 1991).

Nor does the pro-choice position permit state encouragement of healthy prenatal care. This has led to a strange alliance between the National Organization for Women (NOW) and tavern owners in New York, both of whom oppose mandatory posting of signs that warn pregnant women of the dangers of alcohol consumption. The warning-sign legislation is an attack on the woman's right to "choose," according to state NOW president Marilyn Fitterman.[149]

"Freedom of choice" appears to be a one-way street when the issue is abortion. For Denise Lefebvre and Jane Doe, their choice *not* to have an abortion was opposed by those with more power; this resonates of patriarchy and chauvinism. These women, and many like them, are vulnerable to a system that is geared to deal with problem pregnancies by eliminating the unborn child. Feminism supposedly stands against patriarchy and paternalism. Yet silence or outright opposition from the women's movement in the face of real harm to real women belies their claim to represent women. "Choice" has come to mean that abortion is a moral good, and any law that might influence a woman to consider an alternative to abortion or that establishes governmental protection for the child *in utero* is suspect. The "choice" agenda is not truly about protecting women; it is about promoting abortion.

IV. The Impact of Abortion on Women's Health

A. The Use and Misuse of Abortion Statistics

A current abortion-rights slogan is, "Keep abortions safe and legal!" The phrase fosters the assumption that, invariably, legal abortions are safe and illegal abortions are not. The evidence fails to support this claim.

Prior to *Roe v. Wade,* proponents of legalized abortion sought to eradicate "back-alley abortions," alleging they were dangerous because they were illegal. In their view, illegality meant that only criminal abortionists—unskilled and uncaring—performed abortions.[150] Liberalization of abortion laws should therefore eliminate, or at least substantially reduce, abortion morbidity. Part and parcel of this campaign was the claim about the large number of illegal abortions performed before 1973. Based on a 1955 conference sponsored by Planned Parenthood, a figure of 200,000 to 1,200,000 was widely cited for the next 20 years.[151] Although there is anecdotal evidence of illegal

---

[149] Sack, "Unlikely Union in Legislative Battle: Feminists and Liquor Sellers," New York Times, April 5, 1991, at A16.

[150] A typical example of this broad brush, undocumented "parade of horribles" is L. Lader, *supra* note 5, at 21–24.

[151] Both Calderone and Tietze relied on the 1955 conference estimate. The papers and discussion from the conference were later published in a book edited by Calderone. M. Calderone, ed., *Abortion in the United States* (1958). Calderone later said, "The best statistical experts we could find would only go so far as to estimate that, on the basis of present studies, the frequency of illegally induced abortion in the United States might be as low as 200,000 and as high as 1,200,000 per year." Calderone, *supra* note 8, at 950. *See also,* Schwartz *Abortion on Request: The Psychiatric Implications* in *Abortion, Medicine, and the Law* 331 (J. D. Butler & D. Walbert eds. 3d ed. 1986), ("1 million" each year, citing Tietze & Lewit, *Abortion,* 220 Scientific Amer. 21, 23 [1969]). Yet, Calderone wrote, "I would like to enlist public health in an effort to establish better figures on the incidence of illegal abortion. Actually, of course, we know that the nature of this problem is such that one will never get accurate ex post facto figures." Calderone, *supra* note 8, at 952.

A 1981 study arrived at a much lower estimate. "During the years 1940–1967, the largest possible number of criminal abortions in any one year was approximately 210,000 . . . in 1961 and the least number in this prelegalization era was 39,000 in 1950; the mean was 98,000." Syska, Hilgers & O'Hare,

abortions and illegal abortion counseling and referral, the actual number of abortions is very difficult to quantify. Most of the anecdotes appear to stem from the 1960s.[152] Just a few years later, both the incidence and dangers of abortion were in question. In 1960, Mary Calderone, Planned Parenthood's medical director, concluded that "90% of all illegal abortions are presently done by physicians."[153]

Calderone wrote:

> *Abortion is no longer a dangerous procedure. This applies not just to therapeutic abortions as performed in hospitals but also to so-called illegal abortions as done by physicians. In 1957 there were only 260 deaths in the whole country attributed to abortions of any kind . . . Two corollary factors must be mentioned here: first, chemotherapy and antibiotics have come in, benefiting all surgical procedures as well as abortion. Second, and even more important, the [1955 Planned Parenthood] conference estimated that 90 per cent of all illegal abortions are presently done by physicians. Call them what you will, abortionists or anything else, they are still physicians, trained as such; and many of them are in good standing in their communities.* They must do a pretty good job if the death rate is as low as it is. *Whatever trouble arises usually comes after self-induced abortions, which comprise approximately 8 per cent, or with the very small percentage that go to some kind of nonmedical abortionist. Another corollary fact: physicians of impeccable standing are referring their patients for these illegal abortions to the colleagues whom they know are willing to perform them, or they are sending their patients to certain sources outside of this country where abortion is performed under excellent medical conditions . . . So remember fact number three; abortion, whether therapeutic or illegal, is in the main no longer dangerous, because it is being done well by physicians.*[154]

Nonetheless, later reports exaggerated the numbers of maternal deaths from illegal abortion as ranging from 5,000 to 10,000 deaths annually.[155] One founder of the Na-

---

An *Objective Model for Estimating Criminal Abortions and Its Implications for Public Policy,* in Hilgers, Horan & Mall, *New Perspectives on Human Abortion* 171 (1981).

[152] F. Ginsburg, *supra* note 50, at 37, n. 20. Lader sets forth evidence tending to show that supply increased demand when clergy consultation services arose after the opening of the first service in New York City in May 1967. L. Lader, *supra* note 5, at 42–54, 72–79.

[153] Calderone, *supra* note 8, at 948, 949. Tietze repeated the 90% figure in 1969, relying on Kinsey's studies of sexual behavior. 220 *Scientific Amer.* at 23. Lader provides similar evidence at various points. Lader, *supra* note 5, at viii ("performed in the offices of licensed physicians").

[154] Calderone, *supra* note 8, at 949 (emphasis added).

[155] L. Lader, *Abortion* 3 (Beacon Press paperback 1967) ("5,000 to 10,000 abortion deaths annually"); Maginnis, *Elective Abortion as a Woman's Right,* in A. Guttmacher, ed., *supra* note 7, at 132 ("some 5,000 to 10,000 deaths yearly"); Editorial, *Start on Abortion Reform,* New York Times, April 29, 1967, at 34, col. 1 ("the needless death of 4000 mothers each year").

Lader acknowledged that "Dr. Tietze places the figure nearer 1,000" (*Abortion,* at 3). The late Dr. Christopher Tietze of the Alan Guttmacher Institute called the 10,000 figure "unmitigated nonsense." Graham, *Fetus Defects Pose Abortion Dilemma,* New York Times, Sept. 7, 1967, at 38, col. 2. He would have put the figure at under 1,000. Tietze & Lewit, *supra* note 8, at 21, 23. But Tietze also wrote: "Nor do we have reliable data for determining the number of deaths from illegal abortions in the United States."

tional Association for the Repeal of Abortion Laws (now the National Abortion Rights Action League—NARAL) later conceded, in retrospect, that such claims were completely false and were for rhetorical purposes only.[156] These allegations ignored evidence of the tremendous reduction in abortion-related deaths in the prior 30 years due to advances in medical care.[157] The Centers for Disease Control in Atlanta reported 39 *illegal* abortion-related deaths and 24 *legal* abortion-related deaths in 1972, the last full year before abortion was nationally legalized by *Roe v. Wade*.[158]

Abortion proponents, who argued that legalized abortion would prevent maternal deaths from childbirth, have cited national statistics to prove that abortion is physically safer than childbirth.[159] This argument is undermined, however, by technological advances in the 1960s by which "medical science has now made it possible for all but the most severely medically ill women to give birth safely."[160] Mary Calderone said in 1960, "Medically speaking, that is, from the point of view of diseases of the various systems . . . it is hardly ever necessary today to consider the life of a mother as threatened by a pregnancy."[161] Both general maternal mortality and abortion-related maternal mortality have been on a steady downward trend for decades. The legalization of abortion has had little effect on this trend.[162] Claims that "abortion is safer than childbirth"

Other sources cite other statistics. D. Callahan, *Abortion: Law, Choice, and Morality* 132–36 (1970); Louisell & Noonan, *Constitutional Balance,* in J. Noonan, ed., *The Morality of Abortion: Legal and Historical Perspectives* 231–32 n.53 ("[a]pproximately 250 women each year are known to have died as a result of abortions") (citing *Vital Statistics of the United States*—235 maternal deaths from abortion in 1965; 189 maternal deaths from abortion in 1966); Hilgers & O'Hare, *Abortion Related Maternal Mortality: An In-Depth Analysis,* in Hilgers, Horan & Mall, *New Perspectives on Human Abortion* 80 (1981) (abortion-related maternal deaths: 235 in 1965, 189 in 1966, 160 in 1967, 133 in 1968, 132 in 1969, 128 in 1970, 99 in 1971, 70 in 1972, 36 in 1973) (citing II *Vital Statistics of the United States: Mortality, Part A, 1960–1977*). Tietze also acknowledged the NCHS statistic of 235 from all abortions in 1965 but then said, without documentation or citation, "Total mortality from illegal abortions was undoubtedly higher than that figure . . . ." Tietze & Lewit, *supra* note 8, at 23.

[156] "How many deaths were we talking about when abortion was illegal? In N.A.R.A.L., we generally emphasized the drama of the individual case, not the mass statistics, but when we spoke of the latter it was always '5,000 to 10,000 deaths a year.' I confess that I knew the figures were totally false, and I suppose the others did too if they stopped to think of it. But in the 'morality' of the revolution, it was a useful figure, widely accepted, so why go out of our way to correct it with honest statistics. The overriding concern was to get the laws eliminated, and anything within reason which had to be done was permissible." B. Nathanson, *Aborting America* 193 (1979).

[157] Dr. Andre Hellegers, Professor of Obstetrics and Gynecology at Georgetown University Hospital, cited a reduction in abortion related deaths from 1,231 in 1942 to 120 in 1971. *Abortion—Part 2; Hearing Before the Subcommittee on Constitutional Amendments of the Committee on the Judiciary of the United States Senate on S.J. Res. 119 and S.J. Res. 130,* 93d Cong., 2d Sess. 107 (1976) (April 25, 1974, statement of Andre Hellegers).

[158] U.S. Public Health Service, Centers for Disease Control, *Abortion Surveillance* 61 (Nov. 1980).

[159] Cates, et al., *Mortality from Abortion and Childbirth: Are the Statistics Biased?,* 248 J.A.M.A. 192 (1982); Le Bolt, et al., *Mortality from Abortion and Childbirth: Are the Populations Comparable?,* 248 J.A.M.A. 188 (1982).

[160] Schwartz, *supra* note 151, at 325.

[161] Calderone, *supra* note 8, at 948.

[162] Hilgers & O'Hare, *supra* note 155, at 68, 73.

In Illinois, for example, maternal deaths (defined as deaths attributed to "complications of pregnancy, childbirth, and the puerperium") dropped from 1,141 in 1920, to 699 in 1930, to 114 in 1950, to 40 in 1972 (the last full year before *Roe*). Between 1972 and 1981, however, maternal deaths only dropped from 40 to 27, and the rate only dropped from 2.2 to 1.5. Illinois Dept. of Public health, *Vital Statistics Illinois 1981* I.11 (March, 1984) (Table A).

are compromised not only by the likelihood that deaths relating to abortion are underreported but also by the fact that the methods employed by some statisticians do not represent a valid comparison between abortion and childbirth: Most studies consider as deaths related to "childbirth" virtually all cases of maternal mortality not related to abortion, why and whenever they occur. When comparison is made between abortion and natural pregnancy during corresponding periods of gestation, natural pregnancy is shown to be safer than induced abortion at every stage.[163]

In contrast to unsubstantiated claims about the danger of illegal abortion and the risks of childbirth, legal abortion has been consistently publicized since *Roe* as "safe" and "easy." Abortion advocates vehemently assert that recriminalizing abortion will inevitably make it unsafe. Likewise, proponents allege that legal abortion has little negative psychological impact. At most, abortion advocates concede short-term negative psychological reaction but no long-term negative consequences. And in any case, psychological consequences from abortion are alleged to be less than, or no greater than, those following childbirth.[164] (The psychological impact of legal abortion is discussed in subsection E. below.)

In truth, the physical effects of legalized abortion are difficult to quantify accurately. The late Christopher Tietze, Planned Parenthood's statistician, wrote in a prior edition of this book:

> *Abortion-related deaths are of course only the proverbial tip of the iceberg. Nationwide information on the incidence of nonfatal complications of legal abortion, including major complications requiring inpatient care, is far less complete than information on abortion-related mortality. This is so because there is no agreement among investigators as to what constitutes a major complication, and no system of surveillance is in place.[165]*

Only two national agencies have the capacity to compile national data about abortion, the Centers for Disease Control (CDC) in Atlanta (a division of the federal Department

---

It is difficult to determine an objective relationship between legality and safety. "Legal abortion" is defined by CDC officials "as a procedure performed by a licensed physician or by someone acting under the supervision of a licensed physician," while an "illegal abortion" is defined "as a procedure performed by the woman herself or by someone who was not a licensed physician and was not acting under the supervision of a licensed physician." Atrash, et al., *Legal Abortion in the United States: Trends and Mortality,* 35 Contemp. Ob. Gyn. 58, 59 (Feb. 1990). But if any abortion is defined as "legal" merely if a physician is licensed and safety is attributed to this fact alone, then most abortions performed before 1973 were, in effect, "legal abortions" as well. Tietze & Lewit, *supra* note 8, at 23; Calderone, *supra* note 8, at 949.

[163] Hilgers & O'Hare, *supra* note 155, at 86–89 (comparison of maternal mortality rates from induced abortion and natural pregnancy during first 20 weeks and final 20 weeks of pregnancy); Lanska, et al., *Mortality from Abortion and Childbirth,* 250 J.A.M.A. 361–362 (1983) (correspondence, emphasizing that "maternal mortality caused by abortion should be compared with both vaginal delivery and cesarean delivery separately . . . the results suggest that the mortality rate among women who had an abortion is almost twice as high as maternal mortality rates for women who have vaginal deliveries.").

[164] Schwartz, *supra* note 151, at 331 (citing David, *Abortion in Psychological Perspective,* 42 Am. J. Orthopsychiat. 61 [1972]; Brewer, *Incidence of Post-Abortion Psychosis: A Prospective Study,* 1 Brit. Med. J. 476 [1977]).

[165] Tietze, *Demographic and Public Health Experience with Legal Abortion: 1973–1980,* in J. Douglas Butler & David F. Walbert, eds., *Abortion, Medicine, and the Law* 303 (3d Rev. ed. 1986).

of Health and Human Services) and the Alan Guttmacher Institute (AGI), a private organization that historically was the research arm of Planned Parenthood.[166] There is no federal abortion statistics reporting law.[167] The CDC relies on voluntary reporting and on reporting made to the individual state departments of health pursuant to state statute. This is a patchwork compilation since abortion reporting laws vary from state to state and some states have no reporting law in effect.[168] Many states have attempted to collect accurate medical data through confidential abortion reporting.[169] Yet these have been regularly struck down by the courts.[170] Some providers may not report or may underreport abortions, as well as deaths and complications, to state authorities.[171] The CDC admits that it annually underreports abortions and abortion deaths and complications.[172] As a result, the CDC reports are not entirely reliable. At the same time, the AGI's ideological support for the broadest abortion rights has enabled it to collect abortion statistics directly from providers for the past 15 years.[173] But the providers have an obvious interest in not releasing complete reports of deaths or complications. And these data are apparently unavailable to the CDC and even less available to the public. As a

---

[166] Gorney, *Abortion in the Heartland,* Washington Post Health Section, Oct. 2, 1990, at 12–13 ("the Alan Guttmacher Institute, a research organization formerly funded by Planned Parenthood . . .").

[167] *Teen Pregnancy: What Is Being Done? A State by State Look,* Report of the House Select Committee on Children, Youth and Families, 99th Cong., 2d Sess., 5 (Dec. 1986).

[168] Atrash, et al., *The Need for National Pregnancy Mortality Surveillance,* 21 Fam. Plan. Perspect. 25 (Jan./Feb. 1989). Francke noted this more than a decade ago: "The discrepancy in numbers [of abortions] results from the fact that the CDC receives its abortion data from state health departments, many of whom have not established complete or indeed any reporting systems since the legalization of abortion in 1973. The Alan Guttmacher Institute, on the other hand, seeks out abortion statistics from the actual providers of abortion, and the CDC generally accepts those statistics as more accurate." L. Francke, *The Ambivalence of Abortion* 16 (1978).

As a result of a suit by the ACLU, Illinois, for example, has been prevented by federal court injunction from collecting abortion statistics since 1984. *See* Keith v. Daley, No. 84-5602 (N.D. Ill. Sept. 28, 1984) (continuing temporary restraining order in effect, by agreement of the parties, for more than seven years).

[169] *See generally* Wardle, *infra* note 225, at 958 (citing, *e.g.,* Cal. Health & Safety Code § 25955.5 [West 1984]; Fla. Stat. § 390.002 [1989]; Rev. Stat. § 338-9 [1988]; Idaho Code § 18-609 [4] (1987); Ill. Rev. Stat. ch. 38, ¶ 81-30.1 [1989]; Ind. Code Ann. § 35-1-58.5-5 [Burns 1985]; Ky. Rev. Stat. Ann. § 213.055 [Baldwin 1982]; La. Rev. Stat. Ann. 40:1299.35.8 [West Supp. 1989]; Me. Rev. Stat. Ann. tit. 22, § 1596 [2] [1980]; Md. Health-Gen. Code Ann. § 20-208 [1987]; Mass. Ann. Law ch. 38, § 6, ch. 112, § 12R [1983]; Mich. Comp. Laws Ann. § 333.2835 [West 1980]; Minn. Stat. Ann. § 145.413 [West 1989]; Mo. Ann. Stat. § 188.052 [1983]; Mont. Code Ann. § 50-20-110 [1989]; Neb. Rev. Stat. § 28-343 [1985]; Nev. Rev. Stat. § 442.256, § 442.265 [1986]; N.J. Stat. Ann. § 30:4D-6.1 [1981]; N.M. Stat. Ann. § 24-14-18 [1978]; N.C. Gen. Stat. § 14-45.1 [1986]; N.D. Cent. Code § 14.02.1-07 [1981]; Okla. Stat. Ann. tit. 63, §§ 1-738, 1-739 [West 1984]; Or. Rev. Stat. § 435.496 [Supp. 1987]; 18 Pa. Cons. Stat. Ann. § 3207 [a]–[b], 3214 [Purdon Supp. 1989]; S.C. Code Ann. § 44-41-60 [1988]; S.D. Codified Laws Ann. § 34-23A-19 [1986]; Tenn. Code Ann. § 39-4-203 [1982]; Utah Code Ann. § 26-2-23 [3], 76-7-313 [1989]; Va. Code Ann. § 321.1-264 [1988]; Wash. Rev. Code Ann. § 43.20A.625 [West 1983]; W. Va. Code § 16-2F-6 [1985]; Wis. Stat. Ann. 69.186 [West Supp. 1989]; Wyo. Stat. §§ 35-6-107, 35-6-108 [Michie 1977]).

[170] Thornburgh v. American College of Obstetricians and Gynecologists, 476 U.S. 747 (1986). Compare the proposal of the medical director of Planned Parenthood in 1960:

> We will never find out how many illegal abortions have been performed, but how about trying to find out how many are being asked for? Suppose requests for abortion were made reportable? Why not? Suppose that every time a woman comes to a doctor asking for an abortion, he makes a note of it along with some easily obtained information and sends this note to his health officer. Suppose that after a few such efforts, physicians discovered that the sky did not fall in on them in the person of the law and that the privacy of their patients

result, there is substantial reason to doubt the accuracy of currently cited national abortion statistics. However, because they are the only available national statistics, the figures are common currency.

This underreporting of abortion deaths and complications is problematic. If women's health and well-being are truly served by "safe and legal abortions," then accurate statistics should confirm this. Abortion providers should have nothing to hide and nothing to fear from revelation of the truth. On the other hand, if women are maimed or killed by legal abortion, they need protective safeguards. Abortion advocates should be demanding comprehensive, nationwide reporting—open to public scrutiny—if only to substantiate their claim that legal abortions are safe.

Nor do statistics support the argument that legal abortion is necessory to protect women's health. A profile compiled from the available data indicates that few abortions are performed for reasons of "medical necessity."[174] That is, abortion is rarely sought because of a genuine health risk. The typical abortion patient today is white, single and young and is seeking abortion for reasons other than serious health concern, rape or incest.[175] "[T]wo percent of all abortions in this country are done for some clinically identifiable entity—physical health problem, amniocentesis, and identified genetic disease or something of that kind. The overwhelming majority of abortions . . . are performed on women who for various reasons do not wish to be pregnant at this time."[176]

Abortion advocates are thus relying on inaccurate, incomplete and unreliable statistics to support their campaign to keep "safe" legalized abortion on demand. As discussed below, legal abortion is not necessarily safe for women (and obviously is not "safe" for unborn children). Neither was illegal abortion the great killer of thousands of women. Abortion is not needed to avoid death by childbirth. And rarely is it sought for genuine reasons of medical necessity. Consequently, the proposition that legal abortion is needed to protect women's health rests on faulty assumptions.

B. Physical Effects and Legal, "Back Alley" Abortions

Despite the clamor to "keep abortions safe and legal," evidence from the CDC's own experts indicates that the incidence of abortion complications and even death is serious:

---

was being respected. At the end of two or three years we might really know something about this disease of society.

Calderone, *supra* note 8, at 952–53.

[171] Atrash, et al., *supra* note 162, at 58, 60. "[S]tate vital statistics have also been found to understate maternal deaths by 17–73 percent." Atrash, Ellerbrock, Hogue & Smith, *The Need for National Pregnancy Mortality Surveillance,* 21 Fam. Plan. Perspect. 25 (Jan/Feb. 1989).

[172] Francke cites former CDC official Willard Cates: " 'Go with the Guttmacher figures,' said Willard Cates, Jr., chief of the Abortion Surveillance Branch. 'Some states require the reporting of fetal deaths due to abortion. Others don't. We think we're pretty lucky to have 85 percent of them recorded.' " Francke, *supra* note 168, at 16. *See also,* Atrash, Ellerbrock, Hogue & Smith, *supra* note 171, at 25.

[173] Atrash, et al., *supra* note 162, at 60; Francke, *supra* note 168, at 16.

[174] Torres & Forrest, *Why Do Women Have Abortions?* 20 Fam. Plan. Perspect. 169 (1988).

[175] *Id.*; Atrash, et al., *supra* note 162, at 58.

[176] *Constitutional Amendments Relating to Abortion: Hearings on S.J. Res. 17, S.J. Res. 18, S.J. Res. 19 and S.J. Res. 110 Before the Subcommittee on the Constitution of the Senate Committee on the Judiciary,* 97th Cong. 1st Sess. 158 (Oct. 14, 1981) (statement of Irvin M. Cushner, M.D., M.P.H., U.C.L.A. School of Public Health). *See also* Torres & Forrest, *supra* note 174, at 169 (of 1,773 abortion patients surveyed, 3%

The scope of the problem of abortion complications is large, both numerically and economically. For example, in 1977, nearly 100,000 women in the United States sustained complications of abortion, and 16 died . . . . Excluding the indirect costs of lost productivity, the estimated direct cost of treating women who suffered complications in 1977 was over $22 million.[177]

Deaths from legal abortion do occur. One study, by the CDC's own statistician relying on CDC data, concluded that there were 213 "legal abortion-related" deaths between 1972 and 1985—an average of 15 per year.[178] Other studies report different totals for deaths of women from legal abortion.[179]

Follow-up on other abortion complications is compounded by women's refusal to admit to the procedure, even when questioned confidentially. Former Surgeon General C. Everett Koop, in a January 9, 1989, letter to President Reagan, noted that reliable assessment of the statistical impact of abortion on women is made difficult by the fact that an estimated "50 percent of women [who] have had an abortion apparently deny having had one when questioned."[180]

Observers, independently of the pro-life movement, agree that the legalization of abortion has not eliminated "back-alley" abortions; it has merely moved them to Park Avenue.[181] Investigative journalist Debbie Sontag, in her expose of the Dadeland Family Planning Center in Florida, wrote: "Even in the days of legal abortion, the back alley persists—on a commercial street, in a medical building, with a front door, and sometimes even with a state license."[182]

---

cited maternal health considerations as most important factor for choosing abortion; 1% cited rape or incest).

[177] Grimes & Cates, *Abortion: Methods and Complications,* in E. Hafez, ed. *Human Reproduction: Conception and Contraception* 796 (2d ed. 1980).

[178] Atrash, et al., *supra* note 162, at 58. But 540 deaths were examined as "possibly abortion-related." This article also concluded that among blacks, there is a higher rate of abortion and a higher rate of abortion mortality.

[179] Atrash, Cheek & Hogue, *Legal abortion mortality and general anesthesia,* 158 Am. J. Ob. Gyn. 420 (1988) (citing 193 deaths nationally between 1972 and 1985); Grimes, Kafrissen, O'Reilly & Binkin, *Fatal Hemorrhage from Legal Abortion in the United States,* 157 Surg. Gyn & Ob. 461 (1983) (citing 194 deaths nationally between 1972 and 1979); 248 J.A.M.A. 188 (1982) (citing 138 deaths nationally between 1972 and 1978); Cates, Smith, Rochat, Patterson & Dolman, *Assessment of Surveillance and Vital Statistics Data for Monitoring Abortion Mortality, United States, 1972–1975,* 108 Am. J. Epidemiol. 200 (1978) (citing 240 deaths, "legal," "illegal," and "spontaneous" between 1972 and 1975). In none of these articles is the critical criteria ("legal" abortion versus "illegal" abortion) ever clearly defined.

[180] Letter from C. Everett Koop, Surgeon General of the United States to President Ronald Reagan, January 9, 1989, 21 Fam. Plan. Perspect. 31, 32 (Jan/Feb 1989).

[181] The Louisville Courier Journal reported the temporary closing of an abortion clinic. Operating room equipment was dirty, dusty and in disrepair. Some intravenous medications were administered without any physician present. Patients were not given postoperative instructions. Gil, *Clinic can resume first trimester abortions,* Louisville Courier Journal, Nov 1, 1990, p. B1; Gil, *Doctor at abortion clinic not disciplined by board,* Louisville Courier Journal, May 17, 1991, p. B1.

[182] Sontag, *Do Not Enter,* Miami Herald, Sept. 17, 1989, at 8. "In 1983, four women died from botched abortions at Hipolito Barreiro's notorious Biscayne Boulevard clinic called the Women's Care Center. The media closely followed the closing of the clinic by court order, Barreiro's arrest on charges of manslaughter and his ultimate conviction of practicing medicine without a license." "And in response, the Dade County [Florida] grand jury called for greater state regulation of abortion clinics—regulations previously declared unconstitutional by the Florida Supreme Court." *Id.* at 22.

Legal, "unsafe" abortions are often ignored by abortion activists. Yet reported cases of maternal death and injury may indicate that more women die and are injured from legal abortion than many are willing to admit.[183] And countless more women are physically injured, often permanently. Enormous damages have been levied against physicians for botched abortions.[184] Countless more lawsuits are unreported because the case is settled prior to trial or appeal. Anecdotal information and lawsuits reveal that women suffer mild to severe physical injury and trauma from legal abortions, including punctured uterus,[185] incomplete abortions,[186] pelvic inflammatory disease[187] or stroke.[188]

Occasionally, abortion clinic abuses are publicized and investigated.[189] In Chicago, Illinois, the *Chicago Sun-Times* and the Better Government Association conducted an undercover investigation in the late 1970s into the practices of Chicago abortion clinics. This resulted in a 12-part series in the *Sun-Times*.[190] Their joint investigation discovered *a dozen previously unreported deaths from legal abortion*.[191] In addition, they found that abortions were performed by incompetent, unlicensed or unqualified physicians un-

---

[183] Atlanta Obstetrics v. Coleman, 260 Ga. 569, 398 S.E.2d 16 (1990), Collins v. Thakkar, 552 N.E.2d 507 (Ind. App. 1990); Kirby v. Jarrett, 190 Ill. App. 3d 8, 545 N.E. 2d 965 (1989); Joplin v. University of Mich. Bd. Regents, 173 Mich. App. 140, 433 N.W.2d 830 (1988); Sherman v. Ambassador Ins. Co., 670 F.2d 251 (D.C.Cir. 1981); Martinez v. Long Island Jewish Hillside Medical Center, 70 N.Y.2d 697, 518 N.Y.S.2d 955, 512 N.E.2d 538 (1987); Hunte v. Hinkley, 731 S.W.2d 570 (Tex. App. 1987); Jean-Charles v. Planned Parenthood, 99 A.D.2d 542, 471 N.Y.S.2d 622 (1984); Delaney v. Krafte, 98 A.D.2d 128, 470 N.Y.S.2d 936 (1984); Vuitch v. Furr, 482 A.2d 811 (D.C. Ct. App. 1984); Mears v. Alhadeff, 88 A.D.2d 827, 451 N.Y.S.2d 133 (1982); Pierce v. McCroskey, No. 69039 (Ham. Co., Tenn. Ch. Ct. Jan. 3, 1990) ($400,000 settlement for wrongful death from abortion on October 10, 1989); Keys v. Capitol Women's Center No. 90-00926 (D.C. Sup. Ct. 1991) ($565,000 settlement for alleged incomplete abortion and ruptured uterus). *See, generally,* Roberts, *Medical Malpractice in Abortion Cases,* 3 Am. J. Trial Ad. 259 (1979).

Thirteen-year-old Dawn Ravenell choked to death under anesthesia for a 21-week abortion at Eastern Women's Center, New York City's second-largest abortion center; her parents were awarded $1.2 million. Under cross-examination, defendant Dr. Allen Kline noted his lack of concern for her youth: "I've done 13-year-olds before. When they're 10, maybe I'll notice." Kerrison, *Horror tale of abortion,* New York Post, Jan. 7, 1991, at 2, 25; New York Post, Dec. 11, 1990, at 7. A second woman died after an abortion at Eastern Women's Center. She was 21. Kerrison, *Abort patients' naivete leads to another death,* New York Post, Aug. 5, 1991, at 2.

Sixteen-year-old Erica Kae Richardson of Cheltenham, Maryland was injured during an abortion without parental knowledge. She was left without attention on the operating table for four hours and died in a hospital emergency room. Perl, *Teen's death after abortion brings suit,* Prince George's Journal Weekly, May 30/31, 1990.

Teresa Causey, a 17-year-old, died a few hours after an abortion from which she never awakened. Fincher, *Macon teen dies after abortion,* Macon Telegraph and News, Dec. 5, 1988, at 1.

Angela Duarte, a 21-year-old mother of two, bled to death after an abortionist perforated her uterus. *Vegas abortion death investigated,* San Francisco Examiner, Nov. 4, 1991, at A-7.

Glenda Davis died on March 14, 1989, as a result of an abortion performed three days earlier at Aaron Family Planning Clinic of Houston. David Davis v. Aaron Family Planning Center of Houston, No. 89-028771 (Harris Co., Tex. July 12, 1989). Just a few months later, a woman died at another Houston clinic, Joe and Janet Montoya v. Women's Pavilion of Houston, No. 89-16747 (Harris Co., Tex. April 20, 1989).

Seventeen-year-old Latachie Veal died after an abortion performed by Dr. Robert Crist, who previously had been sued five times for botched abortions, one resulting in the woman's death. Most were second-trimester abortions. Bravley & McGuire, *Doctor investigated in post-abortion death,* Kansas City Star, Nov. 6, 1991, at A1.

Dr. Abu Hayat's medical license was suspended by the New York Department of Health after he severed the arm of an infant who survived a third-trimester abortion. He had been cited in eight previous

der unsterile conditions, on women who were not pregnant, without anesthesia or before anesthetics could take effect; results of pregnancy tests were intentionally withheld from patients; because of unsanitary conditions and haphazard clinic care, many women suffered debilitating cramps, massive infections and such severe internal damage that all of their reproductive organs were removed; because of assembly-line techniques and severe overcrowding, patients were forced to leave the recovery room while they were still in pain; medical records, including patients' vital signs, were fabricated or falsified; clinics failed to order critical postoperative pathology reports, and ignored the results or mixed up specimens; women received incompetent counseling by untrained staff who often were paid on a commission basis; unscrupulous sales techniques were used to pressure women into having abortions; and kickbacks were paid for abortion referrals. Some of the doctors investigated continued to practice.[192]

In subsequent years, dozens of abortion malpractice cases were filed against Chicago-area clinics and doctors, including the Michigan Avenue Medical Center,[193] Bio-

---

cases, including the death of a teenager. Belkin, *Manhattan doctor loses state license over abortion cases,* New York Times, Nov. 26, 1991, at A12.

Earle, Adm. v. Armstrong, No. 91-1343 (Lucas Co., Ohio Ct. Common Pleas, April 24, 1991).

[184] Thomas v. Family Planning Medical Center of Mobile, No. CV-87-000899 (Mobile Co., Ala. Cir Ct. June 5, 1991) ($10 million jury verdict); Ruckman v. Barrett and Central Center for Women, No. CV-188-675CC (Greene Co., Mo. Cir. Ct. Jan. 28, 1991), *appeal docketed,* No. 17453-2 (Mo. Ct. App. Mar. 26, 1991) ($330,000 actual damages and $25 million aggravating damages awarded by jury in wrongful death suit); Gallagher v. Barton, No. 80 L 1539 (Cook Co. Cir. Ct. April 14, 1989), *rev'd sub. nom.,* Northern Trust Co. v. *UpJohn Co.,* 213 Ill. App. 3d 390, 572 N.E.2d 1030 (1991) ($9.4 million jury award for severe brain damage reversed for failure to establish standard of care), Chicago Tribune, April 15, 1989, at sec. 1, p. 6, col. 2; Thompson v. Washington Hospital Center (D.C. Super. Ct.) ($4.6 million for irreversible brain damage), Abramowitz, *Brain damaged patient awarded $4.6 million,* Washington Post, March 24, 1989, at B4, col. 3.

Ellen Williams' family was awarded $1 million after her death at the hands of Dr. Chatoor Bisal Singh and Dr. Nabil Ghali in 1985, resulting from an infection due to a perforated uterus and bowel. Sontag, *supra* note 182, at 12.

[185] The New York Health Department suspended Brooklyn physician Dr. Colin Bailey on April 3, 1991, for cases in which one woman suffered a punctured uterus and another suffered a heart attack. *New York: Physician Suspended,* Abortion Report, April 5, 1991, at 2.

[186] Dr. Ming Kow Hah, a Queens, New York, doctor, was suspended from medical practice by the New York State Health Department in November 1990 after an alleged incomplete abortion in which the fetal head was retained by the woman. Holland, *State Mulls Fate of Queens Abortion Doctor,* New York Newsday, Feb. 4, 1991, at 29; Holland, *State Hears 1st Witnesses Against Doctor,* New York Newsday, Nov. 27, 1990, at 27; Holland, *Why They Suspended Doctor Hah,* New York Newsday, Nov. 25, 1990, at 1, 3, 65; Fischer, *"Danger" Cited in Suspension of Queens Doc,* New York Newsday, Nov. 17, 1990, at 3. This same physician was one of several physicians who were the focus of the Chicago Sun-Times 1978 series entitled, *The Abortion Profiteers, infra* note 190. *See also* Watson v. Ming Kow Hah, No. 79 L 24780 (Cook Co. Ill. Cir. Ct.).

[187] Flodin, *Why I Don't March,* Newsweek, Feb. 12, 1990, at 8.

[188] Atlanta Obstetrics v. Coleman, 260 Ga. 569, 398 S.E.2d 16 (1990).

[189] *See, e.g.,* People v. Florendo, 95 Ill.2d 155, 447 N.E.2d 282 (1983); People v. Bickham, 89 Ill.2d 1, 431 N.E.2d 365 (1982).

[190] Zekman & Warren, *The Abortion Profiteers,* Chicago Sun-Times, November 12, 1978, at 1; *Meet the Profiteers,* Nov. 13, 1978, at 1; Nov. 16, 1978, at 19; Nov. 19, 1978, at 25.

[191] *Id.* The series listed abortion deaths of the following women: Evelyn Dudley (March 16, 1973), Julia Rogers (March 28, 1973), Jane Roe No. 1 (no date), Dorothy Muzorewa (August 23, 1974), Linda Fondeen (Fondren) (Jan. 20, 1974), Dorothy Brown (Aug. 16, 1974), Sharon Floyd (Mar. 28, 1975), Sandra Chmiel

genetics Ltd.,[194] Albany Medical Corp.,[195] Concord Medical Center,[196] Women's Aid Clinic,[197] Park Medical Center,[198] American Women's Medical Group[199] and Dr. Ulrich Klopfer.[200] The clinic regulations adopted in Chicago in the 1970s—prior to the *Sun-Times* investigation—had been enjoined by a federal court.[201] The clinic regulations adopted by the Illinois General Assembly in the wake of the 1978 investigative series were also enjoined by a federal judge in 1985 and were eventually scrapped by the Illinois Attorney General in a settlement with the ACLU.[202]

Because of the lack of a nationwide reporting system, it is impossible to provide anything more than a sample of cases on a national scale. But identified abortion malpractice cases have been filed in Alabama,[203] California,[204] Illinois,[205] Michigan,[206] Minnesota,[207] Kentucky,[208] North Dakota,[209] Ohio,[210] Tennessee[211] and West Virginia,[212] among others. Los Angeles County is another metropolitan area with confirmed, but officially unreported abortion morbidity and mortality. Between 1970 and 1987, at least 20 deaths occurred from legal abortion.[213]

(June 3, 1975), Jane Roe No. 2 (Springfield, 1975), Jane Roe No. 3 (1975), Diane Smith (Sept. 11, 1976), Jane Roe No. 4 (1977), Sherry Emry (Jan. 2, 1978). Another woman, Barbalee Davis, died in Granite City, June 14, 1977. Subsequent cases were filed for wrongful death from abortion in Cook County, Illinois. Gilbert v. Women's Aid Clinic, No. 85 L 10455; Moore v. Bickham, No. 87 L 15971; Benton v. Biogenetics, No. 89 L 2906.

[192] *See supra* note 186 regarding Dr. Ming Kow Hah. *See infra* note 215 regarding Dr. Arnold Bickham.

[193] Dr. Florendo, was sued at least ten times between 1977 and 1990 for alleged abortion malpractice: Roberts v. Florendo, No. 77 L 20887; Mears v. Florendo, No. 79 L 19386; Magerkurth v. Florendo, No. 79 L 19366: Wallace v. Florendo, No. 82 L 19014; Tate v. Florendo, No. 83 L 18423; Forsythe v. Florendo, No. 84 L 4948; Henning v. Florendo, No. 85 L 9757; Boykins v. Florendo No. 85 L 18957; Taylor v. Florendo, No. 88 L 4085; Sottile v. Florendo, No. 88 L 22540. Other abortion malpractice suits were filed against other doctors at the clinic—Belisle v. Palmer, No. 78 L 16452; Davis v. Poma, No. 79 L 374; Watson v. MAMC, No. 79 L 24780; Chism v. Agustin, No. 82 L 8727; Liggett v. MAMC, 84 L 6197; Bates v. MAMC, No. 84 L 8588; Wolff v. MAMC, No. 85 L 7571; Jordan v. MAMC, No. 85 L 9488; Lyons v. MAMC, No. 85 L 12356; Williams v. MAMC, No. 85 L 14494; Lockwood v. MAMC, No. 85 L 18607; Parham v. Urban Health Services, MAMC, No. 85 L 18688; Washington v. Perez, No. 85 L 18882; Thomas v. Perez, No. 85 L 19262; Wilson v. Perez, No. 86 L 5824; Ross v. Urban, No. 88 L 5853; Cunningham v. Cruz, No. 89 L 8639; Scott v. Urban, No. 89 L 14859; Spagnola v. Agustin, No. 79 L 16622; Kernaghan v. Agustin, No. 87 L 2097; Colbert v. Agustin, No. 89 L 206. The authors are grateful for the original research identifying these suits by Timothy Murphy and the Pro-Life Action League of Chicago.

[194] Deane v. Bickham, No. 76 L 12753; Kim v. Bickham, No. 77 L 23879; Harrington v. Bickham, No. 78 L 9382; Kroetz v. Baldoceda, No. 78 L 23724; Young v. Baldoceda, No. 79 L 5313; Moreno v. Biogenetics, No. 79 L 8163; Rudowicz v. Zivkovic, No. 79 L 5639; Jones v. Zivkovic, No. 79 L 28651; Najera v. Biogenetics, No. 82 L 9851; Cole v. Baldoceda, No. 82 L 22100; Daylie v. Biogenetics, No. 83 L 12294; Mitchell v. Baldoceda, No. 83 L 13383; Payton v. Baldoceda, No. 83 L 20888; Weidner v. Baldoceda, No. 83 L 23448; Pitts v. Molina, No. 84 L 22841; Patterson v. Biogenetics, No. 85 L 16375; Stinger v. Biogenetics, No. 88 L 19456; Benton v. Biogenetics, No. 89 L 2906; Fernandez v. Okwuje, No. 89 L 13460. Other suits have been filed against physicians at this clinic: Hammond v. Obasi, No. 88 L 717; Pierce v. Obasi, No. 89 L 15575; Patterson v. Obasi, No. 89 L 17575; Harris v. Zapata, No. 84 L 2410; Kernaghan v. Zapata, No. 87 L 2097. *See also,* Robinson & Petacque, *Michigan Avenue abortionist slain,* Chicago Sun-Times, Nov. 4, 1979, at 1 (Biogenetics owner Kenneth Yellin shot to death). The authors are grateful for the original research identifying these suits by Timothy Murphy and the Pro-Life Action League of Chicago and for the research for footnotes 195–200, 213.

[195] Kozlowski v. Albany, No. 76 L 22826; Harris v. Albany, No. 77 L 4168; Mieles v. Myers, No. 79 L 1988; Budacki v. Taparia, No. 79 L 6074; Insalato v. Albany, No. 79 L 6562; Mourning v. Albany, No. 79 L 8864; Weston v. Albany, No. 79 L 18870; Archambeau v. Myers, No. 80 L 23068; Oshinski v. Myers, No. 81 L 448; Sadowski v. Albany, No. 81 L 10591; Hoffman v. Albany, No. 81 L 16554; Jaffe

It is apparent from abortion malpractice cases and from newspaper stories that the legalization of abortion has not eliminated abortion deaths and injuries or "back-alley abortions" and unskilled abortionists.[214] Many of these physicians are still in business and still operate their clinics in major metropolitan areas.[215] Because some abortion experts assert that the safety of abortion is directly related to the experience of the abortionist,[216] one might think that the physicians who have been sued for malpractice have performed relatively few abortions. Quite the opposite is true. Many of the physicians who are sued in such cases have performed thousands of abortions.[217] They continue to practice in the name of "choice," insulated from government regulation and largely immune from effective private redress.

Despite official support for abortion from major medical organizations like the American Medical Association and the American College of Obstetricians and Gynecologists, a strong and growing stigma against performing elective abortion exists among doctors. Perhaps for this reason, the number of physicians willing to perform abortions

---

v. Rebandel, No. 82 L 11472; McGowan v. Myers, No. 82 L 15203; McKenna v. Albany, No. 82 L 22499; Hawk v. Albany, No. 84 L 5490; Bartyzel v. Blumenthal, No. 84 L 18187; Schindel v. Albany, No. 84 L 23584; Schmidt v. Albany, No. 85 L 11809; Konczak v. Rebandel, No. 85 L 17203; Smiley v. Albany, No. 86 L 17935; Ahmed v. Albany, No. 87 L 15875; Mazalan v. Blumenthal, No. 88 L 2016; DiMartino v. Albany, 88 L 5723; Herskovitz v. Myers, No. 88 L 22225. All cases are filed in Cook County, Illinois, Circuit Court.

[196] Allen v. Concord, No. 75 L 17343; Bouwense v. Concord, 79 L 25110, Roe v. Zapata, No. 80 L 1301; Helm v. Zapata, No. 80 L 4880; Wiegand v. Hankin, No. 80 L 8508; Bynum v. Salimi, No. 80 L 25796; Penkala v. Kim, No. 81 L 7731; Burwell v. Kuo, No. 81 L 16352; Sowinski v. Bozorgi, No. 81 L 17059; Levy v. Pelta, No. 81 L 24691; Brandt v. Kim, No. 81 L 26210; Chomsky v. Ventura, No. 82 L 6446; Greve v. Ventura, No. 82 L 14030; Dunn v. Salimi, No. 82 L 17572; Deon v. Concord, No. 83 L 5203; Crum v. Salimi, No. 84 L 13660; Garcia v. Kuo, No. 87 L 7938; Kang v. Bozorgi, No. 88 L 18636; Robinson v. Hankin, No. 90 L 4882. All cases are filed in Cook County, Illinois, Circuit Court.

[197] Kerstein v. Turow, No. 75 L 15616; Jones v. Turow, No. 75 L 1; Vogel v. Turow, No. 76 L 10066; Jewell v. Olsen, No. 77 L 16890; Welninski v. Turow, No. 78 L 8125; Dobson v. Turow, No. 79 L 16059; Kahn v. Turow, No. 79 L 10033; Kelly v. Turow, No. 79 L 20392; Pinto v. Turow, No. 79 L 29343; Vanderhyden v. WAC, No. 80 L 18035; Alexandria v. Turow, No. 81 L 24043; Stanley v. Pirnazar, No. 82 L 19115; Mai v. Turow, No. 83 L 13861; Pope v. Turow, No. 84 L 13350; Cohen v. Olsen, No. 84 L 13571; Kuehne v. Turow, No. 84 L 20307; Goedecker v. Turow, No. 85 L 10455; Hamlin v. Turow, No. 85 L 14364; Skocz v. Pirnazar, No. 88 L 9809. All cases are filed in Cook County, Illinois, Circuit Court.

[198] Goryl v. Nemerovski, No. 80 L 23157; Robinson v. Nemerovski, No. 82 L 21661; Kenny v. Nemerovski, No. 82 L 21835; Peitti v. Arora, No. 85 L 12727; Powell v. Park Medical Center; No. 85 L 17633. See also Jackson v. Arora, No. 85 L 19584; Woolworth v. Moragne, No. 91 L 6791. All cases are filed in Cook County, Illinois, Circuit Court.

[199] Girton v. Barton, No. 75 L 1541; Caprio v. Barton, No. 76 L 5835; Duggins v. Barton, No. 78 L 21281; Besenhofer v. Barton, No. 79 L 4629; Guzik v. Barton, No. 81 L 3932; Szostak v. Barton, No. 85 L 19546; Walker v. Barton, 87 L 17994. All cases are filed in Cook County, Illinois, Circuit Court.

[200] Herrara v. Chicago Loop Mediclinic, No. 79 L 26661; Carson v. Chicago Loop Mediclinic, No. 80 L 3966; Tebbens v. Marcowitz Medical Service Corp., No. 82 L 6309. See also Zekman, Abortion Unit Under Fire Here Closed, Chicago Sun-Times, Jan. 3, 1980, at 18, col. 1. All cases are filed in Cook County, Illinois, Circuit Court.

[201] Friendship Medical Center v. Chicago Bd. of Health, 505 F.2d 1141 (7th Cir. 1974), cert. denied, 420 U.S. 997 (1975); Miner, Two more reports of hysterectomies after abortions at the Friendship center, Chicago Sun-Times, Mar. 24, 1973, at 12, col. 1 (noting three women undergoing hysterectomies in March 1973, after undergoing abortions at Friendship Medical Center).

[202] Ragsdale v. Turnock, 841 F.2d.3239 1358 (7th Cir. 1988), juris. postponed, 109 S. Ct. (1989) (stayed pending hearings below). Subsequently, the Illinois attorney general settled the case with the plaintiffs,

is declining.[218] At the same time, the stigma diminishes the number of hospitals that permit abortions, thereby increasing the extent to which abortions are performed in great numbers in specialty abortion centers. Today, most abortions are performed in approximately 800 specialty centers in the United States.[219]

In many clinics, abortion counseling is either nonexistent or inadequate. Physicians spend little time, if any, with their patients, even if the patients are young girls.[220] Bottom-line profitability controls most abortion practice, and the physician is typically paid per abortion, not for time spent in counseling.[221] The situation was effectively summarized by Justice Sandra Day O'Connor in her 1983 dissent in *City of Akron v. Akron Center for Reproductive Health:* "It is certainly difficult to understand how the Court believes that the physician-patient relationship is able to accommodate any interest that the State has in maternal physical and mental well-being in light of the fact that the record in this case shows that the relationship is nonexistent."[222] As a practical matter for women, this means that an increasing percentage of abortions are performed in assembly-line fashion by anonymous doctors who spend little time with their patients.

---

virtually eliminating the strength of many of the regulations, which was approved by the federal district court. The federal court of appeals affirmed, and the Supreme Court denied an appeal brought by intervenors, ending the litigation. Ragsdale v. Turnock, 734 F. Supp. 1457 (N.D. Ill. 1991), *aff'd in part, dismissed in part,* 941 F.2d 501 (7th Cir. 1991), *cert. denied sub. nom.,* Murphy v. Ragsdale, 112 S. Ct. 879 (U.S. Jan. 13, 1992).

[203] Staniford v. Planned Parenthood of Alabama No. 90-6411 (Jefferson Co., Ala., Cir. Ct. Aug. 21, 1990).

[204] Schlote v. Planned Parenthood, No. 349599 (San Mateo Co., Cal., filed Mar. 21, 1990).

[205] Shirk v. Kelsey, No. 84 L 13308 (Cook Co., Ill., Cir. Ct. Feb. 5, 1991), *appeal filed,* No. 91-0738 (Ill. App. Mar. 8, 1991) ($375,000 jury award of punitive and compensatory damages for abortion increased to $525,000; incomplete abortion at nine weeks gestation); Lamar v. Obasi, No. 89 L 13692 (Cook Co., Ill. Cir. Ct. filed Oct. 12, 1989) (alleged wrongful death); Patterson v. Obasi, No. 89 L 17575 (Cook Co., Ill. Cir. Ct. filed Dec. 6, 1989) (alleged incomplete abortion, perforated uterus). *See supra* notes 191–198.

[206] Stanton v. Detroit Macomb Hosp., No. 85-502-157 (Wayne Co., Mich., Cir. Ct.).

[207] Maki v. Mildred S. Hanson, M.D., No. 89-15330 (Minn. 4th Jud. Dist. Ct. filed Sept. 9, 1989) (alleging negligence, battery, infliction of emotional distress, lack of informed consent); Jodel Field v. Mildred S. Hanson, M.D., No. 91-5057 (Hennepin Co., Minn. 4th Jud. Dist. Ct. filed Mar. 1, 1991) (alleging negligence, battery, breach of implied contract); J.L.S. v. J.M., M.D. and G.H.I., No. 90-3303 (Minn. 4th Jud. Dist. Ct. filed Feb. 23, 1990) (alleging abortion on teenager, negligence, malpractice); M.G. v. Planned Parenthood of Minnesota and Dr. Valgamae, No. 90-9090 (Hennepin Co., Minn. 4th Jud. Dist. Ct. filed May 23, 1990) (alleging malpractice of abortion on teenager). The authors are grateful to Michael DeMoss, Esq., for identifying these cases.

[208] Muckle v. Banchongmanie, No. 89-CI-006286 (Jefferson Cir. Ct., Dist. 12) (twins aborted without mother being informed that she carried twins; mother expelled head of one twin at home after the abortion). This abortionist's Louisville clinic was shut down by the state of Kentucky in September 1990, but a state judge ordered the state to allow him to resume abortions up to 14 weeks gestation in November 1990. Gil, *Clinic can resume first-trimester abortions,* Louisville Courier Journal, Nov. 1, 1990, at B-1; State v. Women's Health Services, (Jefferson Co., Ky., Cir. Ct. Nov. 1, 1990).

[209] Tamera Green v. Robert Lucy, M.D., Jane Bovard, and Fargo Women's Health Organization, Inc., No. 901491 (Dist. Ct. E. Central Jud. Dist. Cass Co., N.D. filed Aug. 16, 1990) (alleging malpractice, excessive bleeding, hysterectomy); Nancy Sabot v. Fargo Women's Health Organization, Inc., and George Miks, M.D., No. 89-91 (Dist. Ct. E. Central Jud. Dist. Cass Co., N.D. served Nov. 2, 1988) (alleging malpractice, incomplete abortion, lack of anesthesia).

[210] Perrine v. Dayton Women's Clinic, No. 89-4426 (Montgomery Co., Ohio Ct. Common pleas, filed Dec. 18, 1989); Perrine v. Ray Robinson, M.D., No. 90-3266 (Montgomery Co., Ohio Ct. Common Pleas filed Aug. 9, 1990) (final appealable orders sent to all parties Feb. 26, 1992); Passmore v. Gaujean, No. 175142 (Cuyahoga Co., Com. Pleas Ct. filed Aug. 24, 1989); Tarr v. Mahoning Women's Center, No. 89 CV 1679 (Mahoning Co., Com. Pleas Ct. filed Aug. 11, 1989); Lofton v. Cleveland Center for Reproductive Health, No. 91977 (Cuyahoga Co., Com. Pleas Ct. filed May 23, 1985).

For the vast majority of women, the notion that abortion is "between a woman and *her* physician" is utterly a myth.

C. The Protection of Women's Health

How are women, as health care consumers, to be protected from abortion medical malpractice? In the aftermath of the Supreme Court's legalization of abortion on demand in every state in 1973, many states tried to enact consumer protection laws, including clinic regulations, informed consent requirements, waiting periods and confidential statistical data reporting requirements. All these were challenged immediately by abortion activists and have largely been invalidated by the federal courts. Abortion advocate Dr. Willard Cates has acknowledged that the judiciary "has influenced the practice of abortion most profoundly"—more than the mass media, legislators or regulatory agencies.[223] As a result, abortion in America is a largely unregulated industry.[224]

After *Roe,* many states enacted clinic regulations.[225] However, court decisions have effectively prevented the states from enforcing many of those regulations.[226] This out-

---

[211] Bradford v. Chattanooga Women's Clinic, No. 91CV0467 (Ham. Co., Tenn. Cir. Ct. filed Feb. 25, 1991) (patient alleged botched abortion, resulting in shock, massive bleeding and transfer to a hospital emergency room).

[212] CAB and BAB v. Women's Health Center of West Virginia, Inc. and Dr. John Hogan, M.D., No. 91C687 (Kanawha Co. Cir. Ct., W. Va. filed March 1, 1991) (alleging malpractice, perforated uterus, lacerated cervix).

[213] Sara Doe, No. 70-8468 (L.A. County Coroner's Report); Janet Doe, No. 71-9846 (L.A. County Coroner's Report); Blevins v. County of Los Angeles, No. C 24787 (Sup. Ct. Cal., L.A. Co.); Margaret Doe, No. 72-7647 (L.A County Coroner's Report); Kathryn Doe, No. 72-9587 (L.A. County Coroner's Report); Natalie Doe, No. 72-11445 (L.A. County Coroner's Report); Kathy Doe, No. 73-14675 (L.A County Coroner's Report); Cheryl Doe, No. 75-9493 (L.A County Coroner's Report); Mitsue Doe, No. 75-10935 (L.A County Coroner's Report); Lynette Doe, No. 75-11665 (L.A County Coroner's Report); Maria Doe, No. 76-5654 (L.A County Coroner's Report); Jacqueline Doe, No. 77-14563 (L.A County Coroner's Report); Jennifer Doe, No. 82-8251 (L.A County Coroner's Report); Cora Doe, No. 83-15079 (L.A County Coroner's Report); Chacon v. Avalon Memorial Hospital, No. 84-2948 (L.A County Coroner's Report); Tanner v.Inglewood Hospital, No. C 555 261 (Sup. Ct. Cal., L.A. Co.); Mary Doe, No. 84-16016 (L.A County Coroner's Report); Garcia v. Family Planning Associates Medical Group, No. SOC 82220 (Sup. Ct. Cal., L.A. Co.); Byrd v. Inglewood Women's Hospital, No. SWC 90298 (Sup. Ct. Cal., L.A. Co.).

Abortion-related deaths continue in California. In a 15-month period, one physician was allegedly responsible for the deaths of three women. Ellis, *State Panel Accuses MD of Negligence in 3 Deaths,* Los Angeles Times, May 5, 1990, at B1, Col. 5.

[214] *Tragic End of Ghanaian's Dream,* New York Newsday, June 9, 1989, at 6; *"Battlefield Conditions" Reported at Hospital in Inglewood,* Los Angeles Times, Dec. 3, 1987, at II-8, col. 4; *3 Die after Abortions at Clinic,* Los Angeles Herald Examiner, Feb. 22, 1988, at A-1; Rado, *Scrutiny of abortion clinic standards will continue,* St. Petersburg Times, Oct. 13, 1989, at 20A.

[215] Zekman, *supra* note 190, at 1. One of the physicians publicized in the series, Arnold Bickham, still practiced abortion until 1986, when an abortion he performed allegedly resulted in the death of an 18-year-old woman. *Board Urges Penalty for Doctor,* Chicago Tribune, Aug. 28, 1988, sec. 2, p. 2; *Charges Sought Against Doctor in Woman's Post-Abortion Death,* Chicago Tribune, Mar. 2, 1987, sec. 2, p. 3. *See also Under the Knife,* transcript of June 25, 1989, report of the Channel 2 Investigative Team, WBBM-TV, Chicago.

Dr. Ronachai Banchomangie, whose Louisville abortion clinic was shut down for operating illegally without a license (the clinic was dirty and in disrepair and performed abortions through the 22nd week of pregnancy), was allowed to reopen less than two months later. Gil, *supra* note 208, at B1.

[216] W. Hern, *Abortion Practice* (1984).

[217] The physician who performed the abortion on Dawn Ravenell (*supra* note 183), resulting in her death, had admittedly performed 5,000 abortions since 1971.

[218] "Under siege from protesters and largely isolated from medical colleagues, doctors who perform abortions say they are being heavily stigmatized, and fewer and fewer doctors are willing to enter the field." Kolata,

come is affirmed by abortion advocates. In an increasingly familiar pattern, people who call themselves pro-choice oppose clinic regulations, even for such blatantly abusive places as the Florida Dadeland Family Planning Center. Full-time activist Janis Compton-Carr explained, "In my gut, I am completely aghast at what goes on at that place. But I staunchly oppose anything that would correct this situation in law." [227] In a recent "60 Minutes" expose of the Hillview abortion clinic in Maryland, Meredith Vieira discovered that "Many pro-choice leaders knew about problems at Hillview, but didn't want them publicized." [228] When confronted with the opposition of Barbara Radford, executive director of the National Abortion Federation, Vieira concluded, "even though those laws could make clinics safer, they [pro-choice leaders] usually fight them." Pro-choice Maryland State Senator Mary Boergers found that her support of laws to make clinics safer made her "the enemy" of the pro-choice movement. She accurately perceived that "all arguments from the pro-choice community can become suspect." [229]

Just as relevant to women's health as clinic regulations, and apparently just as offensive to advocates of "choice," is fully informed consent. [230] Since *Roe v. Wade*,

---

Under Pressures and Stigma, More Doctors Shun Abortion, New York Times, Jan. 8, 1990, at 1. Gorney, *Abortion in the Heartland,* Washington Post Health Section, Oct. 2, 1990, at 13, col. 2 ("the increasing reluctance of physicians to participate directly in abortion"); Jouzaitis, *Group: Rural areas lose abortion access,* Chicago Tribune, May 1, 1991, sec. 1, at 10, col. 1. Apparently because of market forces, "abortion services are not available in 83 percent of the nation's counties." *Id.*; Wolinsky, *Doctor lag limits access to abortion, group says,"* Chicago Sun-Times May 1, 1991, at 3, col. 1; O'Hara, *Abortion: MDs who do them and those who won't,* Amer. Med. News, Dec. 8, 1989, at 17.

[219] Torres & Forrest, *supra* note 174, at 169 n.* (nonhospital facilities that performed 400 or more abortions in a year—constituting only 25% percent of all abortion providers—accounted for 81% of all abortions).

[220]
> The counseling . . . occurs entirely on the day the abortion is to be performed . . . It lasts for two hours and takes place in groups that include both minors and adults who are strangers to one another . . . The physician takes no part in this counseling process . . . Counseling is typically limited to a description of abortion procedures, possible complications, and birth control techniques . . . The abortion itself takes five to seven minutes . . . The physician has no prior contact with the minor, and on the days that abortions are being performed at the (clinic), the physician may be performing abortions on many other adults and minors . . . On busy days patients are scheduled in separate groups, consisting usually of five patients . . . After the abortion (the physician) spends a brief period with the minor and others in the group in the recovery room . . .
> Planned Parenthood v. Danforth, 428 U.S. 52, 91 n.2 (1976) (Stewart, J., concurring) (ellipses in original).

[221] *See* Sontag, *supra* note 182.

[222] 462 U.S. at 473 (citing 651 F.2d at 1217 [Kennedy, J., concurring in part and dissenting in part]). It is worthwhile noting that the only two women judges who considered the City of Akron's informed consent ordinance (Justice O'Connor and Circuit Judge Kennedy) would have upheld it.

[223] Cates, *The First Decade of Legal Abortion in the United States: Effects on Maternal Health,* in Butler & Walbert, *supra* note 151, at 307.

[224] CBS Television, *60 Minutes,* April 21, 1991, transcript at 17. Only in the most severe cases—usually involving abortion deaths—will state medical officials step in. *See, e.g.,* Department of Professional Regulation v. Obasi, No. 89-2096 (Ill. Dept. of Prof. Reg. Oct. 25, 1989) (temporarily suspending license of Inno Obasi, M.D., after three alleged botched abortions, including one abortion death and two perforated uteruses).

[225] *See generally* Wardle, *Time Enough: Webster v. Reproductive Health Services and the Prudent Pace of Justice,* 41 Fla. L. Rev. 881, 958 (1989) (citing, e.g., Alas. Stat. § 18.16.010 [a] [2]; Ark. Stat. Ann. § 20-9-302 [1987]; Fla. Stat. § 797.03 [1]–[2] [1989]; Ga. Code Ann. § 16-12-141 [b] [Supp. 1989]; Idaho Code § 18-608 [1987]; Ill. Rev. Stat. ch. 111 1/2, ¶ 157-8.1 to -8.16 [1989]; Kan. Stat. Ann. § 21-3407 [2] [a]; Ky. Rev. Stat. Ann. § 311.760 [1989]; Minn. Stat. Ann. § 145.412 [2] [West 1989]; 18 Pa. Cons. Stat. Ann. § 3207 [a]–[b] [Purdon Supp. 1989]; S.C. Code Regs. § 61–12 sec. 101-609 [1976]; S.B. No.

many states have enacted informed consent requirements.[231] The Supreme Court and lower federal courts have routinely struck down laws requiring the doctor to provide certain information to women contemplating abortion.[232]

The Supreme Court and the lower federal courts have also struck down even a brief, 24-hour waiting period before abortion.[233] (In France, by contrast, a week-long "reflection period" is required, as is a counseling session with a psychologist.[234]) These laws, modeled after other consumer protections, have been regularly struck down in the name of "women's choice." There seems to be an underlying fear that too much information might lead a woman to choose childbirth over abortion. Ironically, the result of judicial invalidation of virtually all abortion regulations is that women are forced to rely on private enforcement—on their individual effort to shed their anonymity and initiate a lengthy, emotionally draining lawsuit in court.

Whether or not the Court reverses *Roe* in *Planned Parenthood v. Casey,* it can at least rectify some aspects of abortion exploitation. If the Court upholds the Pennsylvania regulations, protections such as informed consent would be constitutional. As long as

---

804, General Assembly of Tennessee [June 2, 1989]; Tex. Rev. Civ. Stat. Ann. art. § 4512.8 [Vernon Supp. 1989]).

[226] Ragsdale v. Turnock, 841 F.2d 1358 (7th Cir. 1988), *juris. postponed,* 109 S. Ct. 3239 (1989) (stayed pending hearings below) *settlement approved,* 734 F.Supp. 1457 (N.D. Ill. 1990), *aff'd in part, dismissed in part,* 941 F.2d 501 (7th Cir. 1991), *cert. denied sub. nom.,* Murphy v. Ragsdale, 112 S. Ct. 879 (U.S. Jan 13, 1992). Birth Control Centers, Inc. v. Reizen, 743 F.2d 352 (6th Cir. 1984); Hallmark Clinic v. North Carolina Dept. of Hum. Res., 519 F.2d 1315 (4th Cir. 1975); Friendship Medical Center, Ltd. v. Chicago Board of Health, 505 F.2d 1141 (7th Cir. 1974), *cert denied,* 420 U.S. 997 (1975); Florida Women's Medical Center v. Smith, 746 F. Supp. 89 (S.D. Fla. 1990) (refusing to modify 1982 injunction against abortion clinic regulations); Pilgrim Medical Group v. New Jersey State Board of Medical Examiners, 613 F.Supp. 837 (D.N.J. 1985); Florida Women's Medical Clinic v. Smith, 536 F.Supp. 1048 (D.Fla. 1982), *appeal dismissed,* 706 F.2d 1172 (5th Cir. 1983); Florida Women's Medical Clinic v. Smith, 478 F.Supp. 233 (D.Fla. 1979), *appeal dismissed,* 620 F.2d 297 (5th Cir. 1980); Women's Medical Center of Providence v. Cannon, 463 F.Supp. 531 (D.R.I. 1978); Fox Valley Reproductive Health Care v. Arft, 446 F.Supp. 1072 (E.D. Wis. 1978); Mobile Women's Medical Clinic v. Board of Commissioners, 426 F.Supp. 331 (S.D. Ala. 1977); Village of Oak Lawn v. Marcowitz, 86 Ill.2d 406, 427 N.E.2d 36 (1981) (striking Illinois regulations).

[227] Sontag, *supra* note 182, at 14.

[228] *60 Minutes, supra* note 224, at 15.

[229] *Id.* at 16.

[230] *See generally* Renfer, Hegarty & Shaheen, *The Women's Right to Know: A Model Approach to the Informed Consent of Abortion,* 22 Loyola U. Law Rev. 409 (1991).

[231] *See generally* Wardle, *supra* note 225, at 962 (citing, *e.g.,* Del. Code Ann. tit. 24, § 1794 [1987]; Fla. Stat. § 390.001 [4] [1989]; Ga. Code Ann. § 15-11-112 [a] [2] [Supp. 1988]; Idaho Code § 18-609 [1987]; Ill. Rev. Stat. ch. 38, ¶ 81-26 [6] [1989]; Ind. Code Ann. § 35-1-58.5-2 [1] [B] [Burns 1985]; Iowa Code Ann. § 707.8 [West 1979]; Ky. Rev. Stat. Ann. § 311.726, 311.729 [Baldwin 1986 & Supp. 1988]; La. Rev. Stat. Ann. 40:1299.33 [D], 40:1299.35.6 [West 1977]; Me. Rev. Stat. Ann. tit. 22, § 1599 [Supp. 1988]; Md. Health-Gen. Code Ann. § 20-211 [d] [1987]; Mass. Ann. Law ch. 112, § 12S [1985]; Minn. Stat. Ann. § 145.412 [4] [West 1989]; Mo. Ann. Stat. § 188.027, 188.039 [Vernon 1983]; Mont. Code Ann. §§ 50-20-104 [3] [c], 50-20-106 [1987]; Neb. Rev. Stat. § 28-327 [1985]; Nev. Rev. Stat. Ann. § 442.252 [Michie 1987]; N.Y. Penal Law § 125.053 [Kinney 1987]; N.D. Cent. Code § 14-02.1-03 [1] [1981]; Ohio Rev. Code Ann. § 2929. 12 [A] [Anderson 1987]; Okla. Stat. Ann. tit. 63, § 1-738 [West 1984]; 18 Pa. Cons. Stat. Ann. §§ 3205, 3208 [Purdon Supp. 1989]; R.I. Gen Laws § 23-4.7-2 [1985]; S.C. Code Ann. § 44-41-20 [1985]; S.D. Codified Laws Ann. §§ 34-23A-7, 34-23A-10.1 [1986]; Tenn. Code Ann. §§ 39-4-201 [c], 39-4-202 [1982]; Utah Code Ann. § 76-7-305.5 [Supp. 1989]; Va. Code Ann. § 18.2-76 [1988]; Wash. Rev. Code Ann. § 9.02.070 [1988]; Wis. Stat. Ann. § 146.78 [West 1989]).

[232] Thornburgh v. American College of Obstetricians and Gynecologists, 476 U.S. 747 (1986); City of Akron v. Akron Center for Reproductive Health, 462 U.S. 416 (1983); Barnes v. Moore, No. J-91-0425 (S.D.

abortion remains legal, women should be protected from its most obvious abuses. Information about health risks, coupled with a meaningful opportunity to evaluate abortion outside the stress and pressures of a for-profit abortion center, should be provided to every woman contemplating an abortion.

D. RU486 as an Alternative to Surgical Abortion

As abortion advocates have become more aware of the physical trauma and complications of surgical abortion, as well as the very public nature of clinics, they have sought an alternative means for aborting a pregnancy. In the past two years, increasing publicity has been given to the abortifacient RU486 (Mifepristone), the so-called French abortion pill, and its potential effect on women and abortion in the United States.[235] The drug has also been touted as a treatment for brain tumors, but the benefits are minor and results are preliminary.[236] Congress has held hearings about the distribution of the drug in the United States.[237] It appears widely suggested, and believed, that RU486 is an easy, safe, preferable solution to surgical procedures, such that it will quickly replace surgical abortion and make abortion a safe, easy, at-home experience. Abortion clinics will become a thing of the past, and the accompanying demonstrations in front of clinics will be eliminated. Women will no longer need doctors to perform abortions. It will be a private matter, and no one will know the difference. The abortion issue will simply evaporate from the lack of an identifiable target.[238]

Miss. 1991), *appeal docketed,* No. 91-1953 (5th Cir. 1991); Fargo Women's Health Organization v. Sinner, No. 91-95 (D.ND. Aug. 23, 1991)

[233] City of Akron v. Akron Center for Reproductive Health, 462 U.S. 416, 449–51 (1983).

[234] Van Biema, *The Abortion Pill,* Life 75, 76 (July 1990). Nathanson records the irony that she could have proceeded with the abortion immediately but not with a tubal ligation. Her doctor said, "You'll need to sign a release in advance for permanent sterilization—that's to prevent impulsive decisions, since it's an irreversible procedure." Nathanson, *supra* note 40, at 36.

[235] *See, e.g.,* Wickenden, *Drug of choice: the side effects of RU 486,* 203 The New Republic 24 (Nov. 26, 1990); Van Biema, *supra* note 234, at 73; Sanders, *Whose Right to Choose?* 2 New Statesman & Society 29 (Sept. 29, 1989); Schumer, *The Pill that isn't,* 10 Savvy Woman 94 (Oct. 1989); Carey, *Can the 'abortion pill' save lives?* Business Week 56 (Dec. 17, 1990); *Pro-con (excerpts from congressional investigations concerning the drug RU-486),* 109 U.S. News & World Rep. 15 (Dec. 3, 1990); *A pill worth testing,* 54 The Progressive 9 (Dec. 1990); Wright, *Fertility Rites,* Scientific American 14 (Dec. 1988); *About-Face Over an Abortion Pill,* Time 103 (Nov. 7, 1988); Langone, *After-the-Fact Birth Control,* Time 103 (Oct. 10, 1988).

[236] Greenberg, Weiss, et al., *Treatment of Unresectable Meningiomes Antiprogesterone Agent Mifepristone,* 74 J. of Neurosurgery 861–866 (June 1991).

[237] Suplee, *Hill Holds Heated Hearing on RU 486,* Washington Post, Nov. 20, 1990, at A21, col. 2.

[238] *See, e.g.,* L. Lader, *RU486* (1991) (bookjacket: "RU486 is a pill that ends an unwanted pregnancy quickly, safely, and without an invasive procedure"); Editorial, *A Mayoral Boost for RU-486,* New York Times, April 8, 1991, at A14 ("would be as private a decision as it should be and considerably safer than it now is with surgical procedures"); Van Biema, *supra* note 234, at 78 ("If the pro-choice movement is founded on the proposition that abortion is a woman's private decision, here was a magic wand to make it a correspondingly private procedure. The woman would act alone, excluding the host of other participants and spectators . . ."); Goodman, *Abortion: By Pill,* Washington Post, July 29, 1989, at A-17, col. 1; *About-Face over An Abortion Pill,* Time 103 (Nov. 7, 1988) ("Administered within the first five weeks of pregnancy, it causes abortions by blocking the action of the hormone progesterone, thus provoking the uterine lining to slough off the embryo. If taken with a prostaglandin . . . RU 486 is about 95 percent effective. Some 8,000 women have used the pill, which has been available only in hospitals and medical clinics and has no harmful side effects"); Pogash, *Science v. Religion,* San Francisco Examiner (Image Sunday magazine), April 14, 1991 at 10 (Women anywhere in the world would be able to abort "in the privacy of their own homes").

However, a review of the medical and popular literature based on the drug's use in France suggests otherwise.[239] The process of using RU486 is more extensive and cumbersome than commonly known and requires, in France, four trips to a clinic.[240] First, the woman visits the clinic to have her pregnancy confirmed by a urine or blood test and clinical examination. If pregnant, she is a candidate for using RU486, which is most effective during the seventh week of pregnancy.[241] The woman returns a week later and is given a 600-mg. oral dose of RU486, which induces an abortion by inhibiting proper implantation or by inducing a sloughing from the uterine wall after implantation.[242] In short, the process induces a miscarriage with "heavy menstrual bleeding."[243] But because Mifepristone by itself is only 50% to 85% effective,[244] the woman must return a third time for administration of a prostaglandin to induce uterine contractions. This allegedly increases the effectiveness rate to 95%.[245] Nausea may set in before the prostaglandin is administered, and the prostaglandin may exacerbate the nausea. The woman spends a few hours in a hospital bed. "A few women . . . expel [the fetus] before coming in for the injection, most do so while at the hospital, and for some it will happen later, at home."[246] For some, the expulsion may be delayed at home as long as five days.[247] The woman must go to the clinic a fourth time, eight to twelve days later. If the abortion is not complete, a surgical abortion must be performed.[248] Even with the combination of RU486 and a prostaglandin, there is still an incomplete abortion rate of 3% to 4%, and a continued pregnancy rate of about 1%.[249]

For most women, the process is like a very heavy menstrual period, with bleeding lasting on average from six to 16 days. During this process, some women require analgesic shots for pain.[250] The French inventor of RU486, Etienne-Emile Baulieu, warns that, "In an out-patient setting, this method requires strict medical supervision in order to monitor cases of aggressive blood loss,"[251] which may continue for as much as three weeks after the prostaglandin is taken. Consequently, Baulieu recommends that any

---

[239] An exception to the rosier descriptions in the popular media is Wickenden, *supra* note 232, at 24; Allen, *The Mysteries of RU-486*, The American Spectator 17 (October 1989).

[240] Armstrong, *RU-486: The abortion pill*, Santa Clara Mercury News, Feb. 20, 1990, at 1C.

[241] Baulieu, *Contragestion and other clinical applications of RU486, an Antiprogesterone at the Receptor*, 245 Science 1351, 1354 (Sept. 22, 1989).

[242] Ulmann, Teutsch & Philibert, *RU 486*, 262 Scientific American 42 (June 1990). "RU" comes from the maker's name, Roussel-Uclaf. The authors of this article are employees of Roussel-Uclaf who oversaw the testing of the drug.

[243] Van Biema, *supra* note 234, at 75 (July 1990).

[244] Some reports say RU486 is only 60% effective alone. Riding, *Frenchwoman's Death Tied to the Use of Abortion Pill*, New York Times, April 10, 1991, at A4, col. 1. Baulieu reports 1% to 10% cases of complete failure, 10% to 30% cases of incomplete expulsion and 60% to 85% cases of complete expulsion Baulieu, *supra* note 241, at 1354.

[245] Prostaglandin is a naturally occurring compound that stimulates uterine contractions. It can also be synthesized chemically. There are several types. *Dorland's Illustrated Medical Dictionary* 1077–1078 (26th ed. 1985). Some World Health Organization studies are using a different prostaglandin—gemeprostin—as a vaginal suppository. A third type of prostaglandin is being tested. Riding, *supra* note 244, at A4 col. 1.

[246] Van Biema, *supra* note 234, at 80.

[247] *Id.*

[248] Armstrong, *supra* note 240, at 2C. "Also, follow-up is necessary in cases of failure that may be related to ectopic (extrauterine) pregnancies . . . ." Baulieu, *supra* note 241, at 1355.

[249] Baulieu, *supra* note 241, at 1355.

[250] *Id.*

[251] *Id.*

distribution of RU486 be done only by gynecologists in clinics.[252] *Life* magazine described the side effects this way: "The bleeding RU486 causes, the disagreeable cramps and nausea that sometimes results from the prostaglandin, and the extension of a process normally completed in a few traumatic hours over several emotionally taxing days. This last is the most surprising to those who expect the pill to be quick."[253] Dorothy Wickenden wrote in *The New Republic*, "There is no denying that RU486 is an eerie drug."[254]

Even aside from the complexity of the process, the literature indicates that RU486 is not the simple abortifacient that has been commonly thought. It is only effective for about a three-week period, between six and eight weeks of pregnancy.[255] The American Medical Association, which supports RU486 research, agrees with the FDA ban on importing the drug, noting that RU486 "poses a severe risk to patients unless the drug is administered as part of a complete treatment plan under the supervision of a physician."[256] The side effects of the drug make it anything but easy and effortless.[257] These side effects include incomplete abortion, heavy bleeding or hemorrhage, nausea and vomiting and abdominal pain. There is anecdotal evidence that RU486 is stressful and painful.[258] For women with undetected tubal (ectopic) pregnancies, taking RU486 would not end the pregnancy; undetected continuation of the pregnancy might result in a rupture of the fallopian tubes.[259] It is necessary to ensure that *every* woman returns after taking RU486 for the prostaglandin dosage; otherwise an incomplete abortion may result.[260] As a result, some researchers do not believe that RU486 will ever replace suction abortions.

The death of a French woman from RU486 was reported in April 1991.[261] French authorities had previously "recommended against nonsurgical abortion in cases when the women are smokers or have heart problems, diabetes and high cholesterol."[262] In

---

[252] Van Biema, *supra* note 234, at 83. A 1990 memo signed by the French director general of health, the director of hospitals and the director of pharmacy and medication noted that the use of the prostaglandin Nalador with RU486 caused "serious undesirable side effects of the cardio-vascular type." The memorandum recommended that the method of use be scrupulously noted and that "training of personnel and the proper use of material are indispensable." The procedures included: 1) the woman must be in a prone position during and after administration of the drug for several hours; 2) cardiorespiratory resuscitators must be available; 3) the patient should have blood pressure taken every half-hour for several hours; 4) electrocardiogram should be given if the patient notes chest pain. (Memorandum on file with authors.)

[253] Van Biema, *supra* note 234, at 76.

[254] Wickenden, *supra* note 235, at 27.

[255] Baulieu, *supra* note 241, at 1354; Allen, *supra* note 239, at 18.

[256] Suplee, *Hill Holds Heated Hearing on RU 486*, Washington Post, Nov. 20, 1990, at A21, col. 1.

[257] *See generally* Allen, *RU-486, the French Abortion Pill: What is Safe?* Wall Street Journal, A20 col. 3 (Oct. 31, 1989) (Midwest Edition); Allen, *supra* note 239, at 17.

[258] One patient stated during the process of taking the drug: "But what's really hard to take is the mental side of it. The emotional side. To feel the egg is in the process of dying. And you are almost . . . assisting in this death for forty-eight hours—forty-eight hours between the pills and the shot and what comes next." Van Biema, *supra* note 234, at 80.

[259] *Id.* at 83.

[260] *Id.* at 83.

[261] Riding, *Frenchwoman's death tied to the Use of Abortion Pill*, New York Times, April 10, 1991, at A4, col. 1. Her death was attributed to her reaction to the hormone prostaglandin injected with the Mifepristone. This article also reported that three other women had died and four had suffered heart attacks after taking the prostaglandin, Nalador, alone. At least another two had suffered heart attacks after taking RU486 with the prostaglandin in 1990.

[262] Riding, *supra* note 261, at A4.

April 1991, shortly after the woman's death, the French Ministry of Health banned the use of RU486 for women who are regular smokers or who are older than 35.[263]

RU486 has created a dilemma for abortion advocates who are also concerned about women's health. In addition to the risks from the procedure, the long-term effects are unknown. The drug may suppress ovulation for three to seven months after it is taken.[264] If RU486 is unsuccessful in aborting the pregnancy, although the effects on the fetus are uncertain,[265] it may cause birth defects.[266] It is not recommended either as a "morning after" pill or as a "once a month" menses inducer,[267] although NOW and the Fund for a Feminist Majority have promoted it as such.[268] Also, it can cause "dysynchrony," a phenomenon "in which a woman's ovulating and menstrual cycles become unlinked," reducing the drug's effectiveness in terminating any pregnancy.[269]

The National Women's Health Network "has serious qualms about introducing reproductive products onto the market without adequate testing."[270] In contrast to extensive testing with Norplant—a time-release contraceptive capsule placed in a woman's arm and allegedly effective for up to five years that underwent over 20 years of research—a coalition of NOW, Fund for a Feminist Majority, the Population Council and Planned Parenthood is pushing to have RU486 approved by the FDA within four years.[271] If protection of abortion availability were not the issue, one would expect aggressive feminist concern about the health ramifications of RU486. One of the few pro-choice feminist groups to question the safety of RU486 is the Institute on Women and Technology; it has been heatedly criticized by other pro-choice feminists.[272] Abortion advocates should still remember the devastation of the Dalkon shield and the first-generation birth control pills. But they ignore, apart from moral or philosophical concerns, the genuine health risks to American women. Their single-minded pursuit of abortion-on-demand by any means belies any legitimate claim to represent the interests of American women.

E. Psychological Effects

Even if aborted women escape physical trauma or death, they have another hurdle to overcome: damage to their psychological and emotional well-being. The psychological impact of abortion may be even more hotly denied by feminists than are physical complications. To admit that abortion causes guilt, remorse or regret violates the fundamental premise that abortion is a "first right." Margaret Liu McConnell, who had an all-too-easy abortion in college, discovered too late: "For all the pro-choice lobby's talk of abortion as a deep personal moral decision, casting abortion as a right takes the weight of morality out of the balance. For, by definition, *a right is something you need*

---

[263] *France Forbids Pill Treatment,* Wall Street Journal, May 14, 1991, at B1, col. 6; *How RU 486 Works,* USA Today, May 20, 1991, at 10A, col. 4.

[264] Allen, *supra* note 239, at 18.

[265] Baulieu, *supra* note 241, at 1355.

[266] Allen, *supra* note 239, at 18.

[267] *Id.*

[268] Allen, *supra* note 239, at 19.

[269] Allen, *supra* note 239, at 18.

[270] *Id.* at 20.

[271] *Id.* at 17.

[272] *Feminist Group Dissents on RU-486 Use for Abortion,* Science 199 (Oct. 11, 1991). *See* J. Raymond, et al., *RU 486: Misconceptions, Myths and Morals* (1991).

not feel guilty exercising.'' [273] Precisely. If abortion is a ''right,'' why does it feel so wrong?

Abortion has long been recognized to have devastating effects on at least some women. There is evidence that the psychological effects of abortion on women were publicized in the middle of the last century.[274] The contemporary debate over the psychological impact of abortion spans 30 years.[275] Studies prior to the liberalization of abortion concluded that abortion had negative psychological consequences.[276] Indeed, Dr. Mary Calderone stated in 1960, based on the 1955 conference of experts sponsored by Planned Parenthood: ''I am mindful of what was brought out by our psychologists . . . that in almost every case, abortion, whether legal or illegal, is a traumatic experience that may have severe consequences later on.''[277] But writings and research by abortion-rights advocates in the late 1960s concluded that abortion had neither negative nor positive psychological consequences.[278] Later articles by abortion-rights advocates admitted that negative consequences do in fact occur.[279] However, they minimized the impact by claiming that the psychological sequelae from abortion may be less than that following childbirth.[280] Mary Zimmerman, a sociologist who interviewed women who had aborted, suggests that the abortion experience is not uniform for women: Neither the ''abortion as crisis'' view (by the antiabortion movement) nor the ''abortion as harmless'' view (by those who favor abortion) fully explains the abortion experience. These two views result in abortion being seen as an ''either/or issue . . . either abortion

---

[273] McConnell, *Living With* Roe v. Wade, Commentary 34, 36 (Nov. 1990) (emphasis added).

[274] Elizabeth Evans, *The Abuse of Maternity* (Philadelphia: Lippincott 1875).

[275] *See, e.g.,* Schwartz, in Butler & Walbert, eds., *supra* note 151, at 323; Pfeiffer, *Psychiatric Indications or Psychiatric Justification of Therapeutic Abortion,* 23 Arch. of Gen. Psychiat. 402 (1970); Botler, *The Psychiatrist's Role in Therapeutic Abortion: The Unwitting Accomplice,* 119 Am. J. of Psychiat. 312 (1962).

[276] *See, e.g.,* Bolter, *supra* note 270, at 312; Galdston, *Other Aspects of the Abortion Problem: Psychiatric Aspects,* in M. Calderone, ed., *Abortion in the United States* (1958); Wilson, *The Abortion Problem in the General Hospital,* in *Therapeutic Abortion* (H. Rosen, ed. 1954); Taussig, *Effects of Abortion on the General Health and Reproductive Functions of the Individual,* in H. Taylor, ed., *The Abortion Problem* (1942).

[277] Calderone, *supra* note 8, at 951.

[278] *See, e.g.,* Notman, *Pregnancy and Abortion: Implications for Career Development of Professional Women,* 208 Annals of the N.Y. Acad. of Science 205 (1973); Payne, et al., *Methodological Issues in Therapeutic Abortion Research,* in H. Osofsky and J. Osofsky, eds., *The Abortion Experience: Psychological and Medical Impact,* (1973); Athanasiou, et al., *Psychiatric Sequelae to Term Birth and Induced Early and Late Abortion: A Longitudinal Study,* 5 Family Planning Persp. 227 (1973).

[279] Schwartz, in Butler & Walbert, *supra* note 151, at 331. Of the 32 articles that Schwartz examined, only 11 were written after 1973 (the year *Roe v. Wade* legalized abortion), and only 2 of the 32 were written as late as the 1980s. *See also* M. Zimmerman, *Passage Through Abortion: The Personal and Social Reality of Women's Experiences,* 3, 20–24 (1977).

One factor that may affect research outcome is that the attitudes of professional psychologists dramatically changed in the 1960s: ''Whereas in 1967 only 24 percent of members of the American Psychiatric Association responding to a poll favored abortion on request, 72 percent were in favor by 1969. By the end of the decade, two of the most influential organizations within the profession [the Group for the Advancement of Psychiatry and the American Psychiatric Association] had published official statements favoring legalization of abortion.'' Schwartz, *supra* note 151, at 324 (cit. omit.).

[280] Schwartz, in Butler & Walbert, *supra* note 151, at 331 (citing David, *Abortion in Psychological Perspective,* 42 Am. J. Orthopsychiat. 61 [1972]); Brewer, *Incidence of Post-Abortion Psychosis: A Prospective Study,* 1 Brit. Med. J. 476 (1977]).

is viewed as a crisis or not; either it constitutes a major disruption or it does not."[281] Women's responses vary.

In any case, because no longitudinal studies have been conducted, the scientific reliability of all previously completed studies has been questioned.[282] A recent article examined all studies published in English between January 1966 and April 1988 that "quantitatively examined psychological sequelae" from abortion through original empirical data.[283] The authors questioned the scientific reliability of many of those studies. Validity is compromised when, for example, "systematic attrition occurs, the reliability of an assessment instrument is unknown, or a sample size is too small to reliably generalize to the underlying population."[284]

Despite the lack of comprehensive national statistics, abortion does affect individual women deeply. Anecdotal evidence of negative reactions is plentiful.[285] In her autobiography, actress Patricia Neal wrote of her abortion of Gary Cooper's child and of the trauma she suffered for 30 years thereafter.[286] Sue Nathanson, in *Soul Crisis,* conveyed the devastation of her abortion in a startling and direct way. She wrote of "the psychological descent into despair I made after the abortion and tubal ligation."[287] She grieved on each anniversary of her abortion.[288] Even five years after her abortion, she felt compelled to "acknowledge the reality and permanence of the pain of my loss. My grief for my unborn fourth child, though perhaps different in quality than the grief I would have for any living child, is just as palpable."[289]

In *Passage Through Abortion,*[290] Mary Zimmerman conducted personal interviews with 40 women from one community who underwent abortion in 1975. She found that

---

[281] M. Zimmerman, *supra* note 279, at 3.

[282] Rogers, Stoms & Phifer, *Psychological Impact of Abortion: Methodological and Outcomes Summary of Empirical Research between 1966 and 1988,* 10 Health Care for Women Inter'l 347 (1989). *See also* Posovac & Miller, *Some Problems Caused By Not Having a Conceptual Foundation for Health Research: An Illustration From Studies of the Psychological Effects of Abortion,* 5 Psych. & Health 13 (1990).

[283] Rogers, Stoms & Phifer, *supra* note 282, at 369.

[284] *Id.* at 369.

[285] *See, e.g.,* Lyons, *After Abortion: Stress disorder strikes women (& men) years later,* New York Daily News, March 11, 1991, at 18.

Sandra Kaiser underwent an abortion, without her mother's knowledge, when she was 14. Prior to the abortion, she had been hospitalized three times for psychiatric problems, but the clinic failed to elicit this information. Sandra jumped to her death. Her mother sued the clinic but lost. Jackson, *Jury Considering Abortion-Suicide Suit,* St. Louis Post-Dispatch, March 1, 1991, at 3A, col. 1.

[286] P. O'Neal, *As I Am: An Autobiography* 134 (1988) ("But for over thirty years, alone, in the night, I cried. For years and years I cried over that baby. And whenever I had too much to drink, I would remember that I had not allowed him to exist. I admired Ingrid Bergman for having her son. She had guts, I did not. And I regret it with all my heart. If I had only one thing to do over in my life, I would have that baby."); N. Sorel, *Ever Since Eve: Personal Reflections on Childbirth* 243, 247 (1984) (Gloria Swanson: "The greatest regret of my life has always been that I didn't have my baby, Henri's child, in 1925. Nothing in the whole world is worth a baby, I realized as soon as it was too late, and I never stopped blaming myself.").

[287] *Id.* at 270.

[288] "At some deep place in my mind, I continue to track the development of my unborn child as if he or she were alive." *Id.* at 285.

[289] *Id.* at 268. *See id.* at 285 ("the permanent place occupied by the abortion and tubal ligation . . . ."); ". . . I understood yet another underpinning of the horror of abortion. The death of a child, whether unborn or living, triggers an archetypal panic . . ." *Id.* at 287.

[290] M. Zimmerman, *supra* note 112.

> *social change such as is involved in the legalization of abortion exacts severe personal costs from the women she studied. The legitimizing of abortion, followed by the provision of institutional settings where abortions are routinely obtainable—although not uniformly available—has not been accompanied by parallel changes in the moral definitions of abortion. Among many, abortion continues to be viewed as an immoral act. For the individuals involved in this study . . . the guilt feelings which result from the discrepancy between what is legally permissible and moral belief is the price which they must pay.*[291]

It is ironic that so many women are opposed to or ambivalent about an act they also claim as their legal, fundamental right. Zimmerman observed that "the most dramatic trend remains that by far the majority of women studied (70%) reported that they had disapproved of abortion to some degree prior to their own experience with it."[292] About half of the group Zimmerman interviewed were troubled in the first few weeks following their abortion.[293] It is worth noting that the women Zimmerman studied had abortions just two years after *Roe*. They grew up with abortion largely prohibited; few knew anything factual about abortion or had ever discussed it with anyone.[294] However, even for women who have no memory of the pre-*Roe* years, the moral uncertainty, ambivalence and secrecy remain.[295] Why?

One reason may be the inescapably human nature of the fetus, as illuminated by fetal photography and modern developments in medical science. Many women considering abortion have at least a general idea of what a developing fetus looks like.[296] Scientific confirmation of the humanity of the fetus cannot be attributed to the "moralists" in the pro-life movement or shrugged off as the survival of traditionalist or antifeminist morals. Medical care for the unborn child as a patient preceded the *in utero* photography and technology in the 1960s—and it will survive any demise of the pro-life movement.[297] Traditionally, concern for the fetus has been an essential aspect of prenatal care, intended to promote the health of mother *and* child.[298] That approach is

---

[291] *Id.* at vii (Foreword by Harold Finestone).

[292] Zimmerman, *supra* note 112, at 69–70.

[293] *Id.* at 182–185. This study covered only immediate aftereffects; most interviews were conducted between six and ten weeks after the abortion. *Id.* at 43.

[294] *Id.* at 62–63.

[295] McConnell, *supra* note 273, at 34, 35–36 ("I longed for those days I knew only from old movies and novels, those pre-60's days when boyfriends visiting from other colleges stayed in hotels (!) and dates ended with a lingering kiss at the door . . . I am not in the habit of exposing this innermost regret, this endless remorse to which I woke too late.")

[296] On a December 28, 1991, visit to the Museum of Service and Industry in Chicago, one of the coauthors was surprised that one of the longest lines was at the fetal development exhibit.

[297] *Cf.* Zimmerman, *supra* note 279, at 1–2; Callahan, *supra* note 6, at 683.

[298] *See generally* D. Danforth & J. Scott, *Obstetrics and Gynecology* 5 (5th ed. 1986); H. Speert, *Obstetrics and Gynecology in America: A History* 142–43 (A.C.O.G. 1980). Direct therapy for unborn infants appeared as far back as 1928, when transabdominal application of drugs for fetal asphyxia was introduced. Dudenhausen, *Historical and ethical aspects of direct treatment of the fetus*, 12 J. Perinatal Med. 17 (1984 Supp.). "Prior to the recent developments in fetal surgery, the fetus generally was considered a medical patient and certain defects were treated with medicines administered to the mother or directly into the amniotic fluid." Blank, *Emerging Notions of Women's Rights and Responsibilities During Gestation*, 7 J. Legal Med. 441, 461 (1986). "[T]he health of the fetus has always been a concern . . . In some obvious

reflected in current medical practice as well. The American College of Obstetricians and Gynecologists Ethics Committee, in their Opinion No. 55, states that the "current ethical position of the medical community is that a physician treating a pregnant woman in effect has two patients, the mother and the fetus, and should assess the risk and benefits attendant to each in advising the mother on the course of her treatment."[299]

A recent issue of *Discovery* magazine brought into popular view the latest developments in fetal surgery and medicine that have been growing throughout the 1970s and 1980s.[300] It is now possible to care for the unborn child *in utero* at virtually every stage of pregnancy.[301] *In utero* treatments have been performed successfully for hydrocephalus, hydrops fetalis associated with maternal Rh sensitization, congenital adrenal hyperplasia, urinary tract malformation, congenital hydronephrosis, perinatal asphyxia and congenital cystic adenomatoid malformation.[302] Intrauterine blood transfusions have been performed for a variety of fetal diseases.[303] Fetal surgery has also been performed to correct some fetal anomalies *in utero* by removing the fetus from the uterus, operating and then replacing the fetus into the uterus,[304] and to remove a dead fetal twin.[305] These medical developments reaffirm that the fetus is a human child, loved and cared for and highly valued by her parents and society.

Developing technology and surgical techniques, which reinforce traditional princi-

---

nontechnical sense, the fetus has always been regarded as a patient." Shinn, *The Fetus as Patient: A Philosophical and Ethical Perspective,* in Milunsky & Annas, eds., *Genetics and the Law III* 318 (1985).

[299] American College of Obstetricians and Gynecologists, *Patient Choice: Maternal-Fetal Conflict* (October 1987) (as cited in *In re A.C.,* 573 A.2d 1235, 1246 n.13 (D.C. Ct.App. 1990).

[300] Ohlendorf-Moffat, *Surgery Before Birth,* Discovery (Feb. 1991).

[301] Proper control of a diabetic mother's fuel metabolism at conception is advised and proper control at six to eight weeks of gestation can prevent fetal malformations. Nelson, *Diabetics and Pregnancy: Control Can Make a Difference,* 61 Mayo Clin. Proc. 825 (1986). Additional therapy available for previable, unborn children in the first trimester include treatments for congenital adrenal hyperplasia, some vitamin-responsive inborn errors of metabolism, neural tube defects and fetal cardiac arrhythmias. Schulman, *Treatment of the Embryo and the Fetus in the First Trimester,* 35 Am. J. Med. Genetics 197 (1990).

[302] Frigoletto, et al., *Antenatal Treatment of Hydrocephalus by Ventriculoamniotic Shunting,* 248 J.A.M.A. 2496 (1982); McCullough, *A History of the Treatment of Hydrocephalus,* 1 Fetal Ther. 38 (1986); Editorial, *Prenatal Treatment of Congenital Adrenal Hyperplasia,* 355 Lancet 510–511 (March 3, 1990); Golbus, et al., *In utero treatment of urinary tract obstruction,* 152 Am. J. Ob. Gyn. 383 (1982); Harrison, et al., *Management of the fetus with a urinary tract malformation,* 246 J.A.M.A. 635 (1981); Manning, et al., *Antepartum chronic fetal vesicoamniotic shunts for obstructive uropathy: a report of two cases,* 145 Am. J. Ob. Gyn. 819 (1983); Vallancien, et al., *Percutaneous Nephrostomy in Utero,* 20 Urology 647 (1982); Harrison, et al., *Fetal Surgery for Congenital hydronephrosis,* 306 N. Eng. J. Med 591 (1982); Kirkinen, et al., *Repeated transabdominal renocenteses in a case of fetal hydronephrotic kidney,* 142 Am. J. Ob. Gyn. 1049 (1982); Jacobs, et al., *Prevention, Recognition, and Treatment of Perinatal Asphyxia,* 16 Clin. Perin. 785 (1989); Nugent, et al., *Prenatal Treatment of Type I Congenital Cystic Adenomatoid Malformation by Intrauterine Fetal Thoracentesis,* 17 J. Clin. Ultra. 675 (1989).

[303] Gonsoulin, et al., *Serial Maternal Blood Donations for Intrauterine Transfusion,* 75 Ob. Gyn. 158 (1990); Keckstein, et al., *Intrauterine treatment of severe fetal erythroblastosis: intravascular transfusion with ultrasonic guidance,* 17 J. Perin. Med. 341 (1989); Pattison, et al., *The Management of Severe Erythroblastosis Fetalis by Fetal Transfusion: Survival of Transfused Adult Erythrocytes in the Fetus,* 74 Ob. Gyn. 901 (1989); Peters, et al., *Cordocentesis for the Diagnosis and Treatment of Human Fetal Parvovirus infection,* 75 Ob. & Gyn. 501 (1990); Pringle, *Fetal surgery: It has a Past, Has it a Future?* 1 Fetal Ther. 25 (1986).

[304] Harrison, *Successful Repair in Utero of a Fetal Diaphragmatic Hernia after Removal of Herniated Vicera from the Left Thorax,* 332 N. Eng. J. Med. 1582 (1990).

[305] Van, *Rare fetal surgery has happy ending,* Chicago Tribune, Apr. 20, 1991, at sec. 1, p. 1.

ples of medical ethics, will be promoted by physicians and sought out by parents, whether or not the pro-life movement disappears in this country.[306] Not only activists in the pro-life movement but physicians outside that movement ask the same ethical question: How and why do we provide surgery and treatment for one unborn child while another unborn child—at the same gestational age and in better health—is legally aborted?[307] Medical technology is thus another factor highlighting the tension over abortion as a legal "right" and a moral "wrong." Women contemplating abortion are vulnerable to this tension.

Not surprisingly, assessment of the psychological effects of abortion continues. Some accepted conclusions demand an appropriate response. One example is the frequent aborter—experts appear to agree that women who have multiple abortions suffer more.[308] The rate of repeat abortions has risen over the past 15 years and now stands at 42%.[309] Some women suffer "anniversary reactions" on the date of the abortion or the date of the predicted birth of the child.[310] An extreme example of mental and emotional suffering is the woman who commits suicide after her abortion.[311]

The aftermath of abortion is detrimental for many, if not most, women. For some of them, the effects may be both severe and long-lasting. As long as abortion is legal, women deserve to know about all possible risks before making any decision. These risks should give pause to those who espouse the position that abortion is an unqualified good, the "first right," "morally responsible," or "safe and easy."

---

[306] "The more that parents actually see the fetus and recognize a human form, the more valuable will that fetus become in their eyes . . . [S]ince ultrasound is being more routinely used in obstetrical practice and is indicated for many high-risk pregnancies, we have good reason to believe that a more complex and progressively more human relationship will begin to develop between parents and fetuses." M. Harrison, M. Golbus & R. Filly, *The Unborn Patient: Prenatal Diagnosis and Treatment* 165 (1984).

[307] "The fetus now begins to make serious claims for a right to nutrition, to protection, to therapy. How can tolerance of abortion be morally reconciled with those claims?" Ruddick & Wilcox, *Operating on the Fetus,* 12 Hast. Cent. Rep. 10, 11 (1982) (quoting Richard McCormick); "The paradox here for the abortion debate is evident: a moral status that is denied the fetus when abortion is sought is given the fetus when its future healthy development is desired, though the same generic organism is under consideration." Callahan, *How Technology Is Reframing the Abortion Debate,* 16 Hast. Cent. Rep. 33, 37 (1986). *See generally,* K. Maeda, ed., *The Fetus as a Patient '87 Proceedings of the Third Inter'l Symposium* (1987); A Kurjak, ed., *The Fetus as a Patient, Proceedings of the First International Symposium* (1985); M. Harrison, et al., *The Unborn Patient: Prenatal Diagnosis and Treatment* (1984); E. Volpe, *Patient in the Womb* (1984); Manning, *Reflections on Future Directions of Perinatal Medicine,* 13 Sem. Perin. 342 (1989); Mahoney, *Editorial: The Fetus as Patient,* 150 West. J. Med. 459 (1989); Newton, *The Fetus as a Patient,* 73 Med. Clin. N. Amer. 517 (1989); Rosner, et al., *Fetal Therapy and Surgery: Fetal rights versus maternal obligations,* 89 N.Y. State J. Med. 80 (1989); Brodner, et al., *Fetal Therapy: Ethical and Legal Implications of Prenatal Intervention and Clinical Application,* 2 Fetal Ther. 57, 58 (1987); Chernevak, et al., *Ethical Analysis of the intrapartum management of pregnancy complicated by fetal hydrocephalus and macrocephaly,* 68 Obst. & Gyn. 720 (Nov. 1986); Chervenak & McCullough, *Perinatal ethics: a practical method of analysis of obligations to mother and fetus,* 66 Obst. & Gyn. 442 (1985).

[308] Franco, et al., *Psychological profile of dysphoric women postabortion,* 44 J. Amer. Med. Women's Assoc. 113, 115 (1989).

[309] Henshaw, et al., *The Characteristics and Prior Contraception Use of U.S. Abortion Patients,* 20 Fam. Plan. Perspect. 158, 159 (1988) (Table 1).

[310] Franco, et al., *supra* note 308, at 113, 115 (42% of women studied who "poorly assimilated" their abortion reported "anniversary reactions").

[311] Eidson v. Reproductive Health Services, No. 87206358 (St. Louis City Cir. Ct. Div. 9 March 1, 1991). A verdict was rendered in favor of the defendants.

F. Effects on Minor Women

The impact of abortion on minor women can be particularly negative. Many of them are not sufficiently mature to receive and assimilate the information needed to make a life-impacting decision. These adolescents fluctuate back and forth between dependence on the familial/parental community and the need for self-expression and individuation. Ironically, many adults reflect this same ambiguity in their attitudes toward, and descriptions of, teenagers and pregnancy. There is a great deal of public concern about "children having children," implying that 14- and 15-year-olds are too young to become mothers (although if they are pregnant, they already *are* mothers). On the other hand, these same adults oppose parental involvement legislation that would promote communication and assist these "children" in making responsible decisions about their own children, claiming that the same 14- or 15-year-old—by virtue of her biological ability to get pregnant—is sufficiently mature to make an independent decision to abort.

The open bias toward abortion is clear. Abortion is invariably advocated as the best choice for minors, even when it conflicts with significant feminine values. Why do some feminists fight against another woman's ability and obligation to raise, rear and care for her minor daughter in the context of the minor's abortion? When a daughter is in the midst of a crisis pregnancy, the core values of feminism—connectedness, care, community—are implicated. The mother is connected to her daughter and also to her granddaughter. Her embrace is ample enough to encompass this tiny, vulnerable new member of the family. Both mother and father of a minor daughter are expected to care deeply for her and to prudently exercise their constitutional right to rear their child, along with their obligations and responsibilities toward her.

The need for parental connection with a minor daughter in a stressful time is substantiated by the social sciences and recent litigation concerning parental notice laws. The scope of the problems of teen pregnancy and abortion is vast. Adolescent psychology and targeted research into adolescent abortion provides evidence that elective abortion uniquely impacts minors. Nearly 200,000 abortions are performed every year on minors age 17 or younger, including more than 15,000 on girls 14 years old or younger.[312] More than 40% of all teenagers with confirmed pregnancies obtain abortion.[313] This is 60% higher than the abortion rate for teenagers in 1973, the first year of nationwide legalized abortion.[314]

Nearly 80% of all abortions performed on teenagers are done in abortion clinics.[315] In these unfamiliar surroundings, minors often are furtive, frightened visitors subjected to assembly-line techniques. One study of Minnesota found that, in 1982, four Minnesota abortion clinics performed 78% of the 5,082 abortions performed on minors under 19 years of age.[316]

---

[312] Henshaw, Benker, Blaine & Smith, *A Portrait of American Women who Obtain Abortions*, 17 Fam. Plan. Perspectives 90, 92 (1985).

[313] Henshaw, et al., *supra* note 312, at 93; Russo, *Adolescent Abortion: The Epidemiological Context*, in G. Melton, ed., *Adolescent Abortion: Psychological-Legal Issues* 40, 49 (1986).

[314] Russo, *supra* note 313, at 49.

[315] Henshaw & O'Reilly, *Characteristics of Abortion Patients in the United States 1979–1980*, 15 Fam. Plan. Perspect. 5, 11 (1983).

[316] Blum, et al., *The Impact of Parental Notification Law on Adolescent Abortion Decision-Making*, 77 Am. J. Pub. Health 619 (1987).

Despite this high incidence of teen pregnancy and abortion, few family planning clinics have parental consent policies. Less than half of the abortion clinics nationwide require parental notice even for teenagers 15 years of age or younger; even fewer require parental notification before performing abortions on minors age 16 or older.[317] This drives a deeper wedge in what may be fragile parent-child communication; teenagers in crisis often feel unable to confide in their parents. In one survey, nearly half (45%) of the 1,170 teenager abortion patients interviewed admitted to getting an abortion without parental knowledge; this figure obviously could not include teenagers who denied the clandestine nature of their abortion.[318]

Adolescence is a time of tremendous transition in the life of an individual. "Guidance is essential if the transition is to be made successfully and with minimum psychological damage."[319] There is enhanced risk of "replacement pregnancy" and multiple abortions for adolescents.[320] Ambivalence and confusion regarding the abortion decision are even greater for adolescents. "The here and now of an abortion decision for adolescents is more complicated than it is for most adult women."[321] One researcher found

> [t]he decision to have an abortion was not an easy one. One of the young women admitted getting off the table at the abortion clinic before the procedure began. Another was not told that she was having an abortion and was confused about what was occurring . . . Attitudes about the acceptability of abortion also demonstrate the ambivalence of many [adolescents] who had abortions. Looking back to the time before the abortion, less than one-half approved of abortion at that time . . . less than one-quarter approved of it after the abortion.[322]

One study found that "[a]lmost one third of the young women (31.8%) changed their minds once or twice about continuing the pregnancy or having the abortion, 18% changed their minds even more frequently, but 50% did not change their minds at all."[323] An-

---

[317] Torres, Forrest, & Eisman, *Telling Parents: Clinic Policies and Adolescents' Use of Family Planning and Abortion Services,* 12 Fam. Plan. Perspect. 284, 285 (1980) (Table 1) [hereinafter Torres].

[318] Torres, *supra* note 317, at 289 (Table 7), 287. *See also* Rosen, Benson & Stack, *Help or Hindrance: Parental Impact on Pregnant Teenagers' Resolution Decisions,* 31 Fam. Relations 271, 279 (1982); R. Mnookin, *In the Interests of Children* 158 (1985).

[319] E. Hurlock, *Adolescent Development* 15 (4th ed. 1973).

[320] Henshaw, et al., *supra* note 305, at 92; Teitze, *Repeat Abortions, Why More,* 10 Fam. Plan. Perspect. 205, 206 (1978); Steinhoff, et al., *Women Who Obtain Repeat Abortions: A Study Based on Record Linkage,* 11 Fam. Plan. Perspect. 30 (1979).

[321] Brown, *Adolescents and Abortion: A Theoretical Framework for Decision Making,* 12 J. Ob. Gyn. & Neonatal Nursing 241, 246 (1983).

[322] Horowitz, *Adolescent Mourning Reactions to Infant and Fetal Loss,* 59 Social Casework 551, 557 (Nov. 1978). *See also* L. Francke, *supra* note 165, at 178–206 (1978); Olson, *Social and Psychological Correlates of Pregnancy Resolution Among Adolescent Women,* 50 Am. J. Orthopsychiatry 432, 437–41 (1980); Babikan & Goldman, *A Study in Teenage Pregnancy,* 128 Am. J. Psychiat. 755 (1971).

[323] Klerman, Bracken, Jekel & Bracken, *The Delivery-Abortion Decision Among Adolescents,* in Stuart & Wells, ed., *Pregnancy in Adolescence: Needs, Problems, and Management* 219, 227 (1982); Wallerstein, Kurtz & Bar-Din, *Psychosocial Sequelae of Therapeutic Abortion in Young Unmarried Women,* 27 Arch. Gen. Psychiat. 828 (1972).

other study confirms this ambivalence: "About one-quarter of women having a later abortion [defined as 16 or more weeks' gestation] said their delay was attributable (at least in part) to the long time they had needed to make the abortion decision."[324]

Teenagers who choose abortion typically have more difficulty with the decision than pregnant teenagers who reach other decisions. They are also relatively uninformed. They typically talk with fewer people and receive substantially less counseling than pregnant teenagers who chose to keep the baby or place it for adoption.[325] However, adolescents who choose abortion typically make that decision much more hastily (nine days) than teens who choose to keep the baby (56 days) or place it for adoption (more than 100 days).[326]

There has been inadequate empirical study of the impact of parental notice of abortion statutes on minors and their abortions because the minimal ingredients for such a study—a simultaneous enforcement of a parental notice law and state abortion data reporting—have been in effect in only a handful of states over the past 20 years. Federal or state courts have repeatedly enjoined parental notice and parental consent statutes.[327] One notable exception is the Minnesota parental notice law, which was in effect from August 1, 1981 until it was enjoined by a federal district court on March 2, 1986. The notice requirement applied to teens below the age of 18.[328] The federal district court in Minnesota acknowledged that it was the first district court "ever to examine a parental notification or consent substitute statute in actual operation."[329] The experience of Minnesota during the four and one-half years that its parental notice of abortion law was in

---

[324] Torres & Forrest, *supra* note 171, at 169, 174, 175 (Table 5).

[325] Klerman, et al., *supra* note 323, at 231, 233; Paulsen, *Correlation of Outcomes of Premarital Pregnancy*, 18 Fam. Plan. Perspect. 25, 29 (Winter 1984).

[326] Paulsen, *supra* note 325, at 28.

[327] *See, e.g.*, Planned Parenthood v. Neeley, No. 89-489 (D. Ariz. 1989); Smith v. Bentley, 493 F. Supp. 916 (E.D. Ark. 1980); American Academy of Pediatrics v. Van de Kamp, No. 88457 (Cal. Super. Ct. Dec. 28, 1987), *aff'd*, 263 Cal. Rptr. 46, 214 Cal. App. 3d 831 (1989); In re T.W. 551 So.2d 1186 (Fla. 1989); Eubanks v. Brown, 604 F.Supp. 141 (W.D. Ky. 1984), *aff'd in part, rev'd in part, sub nom.* Eubanks v. Wilkinson, 937 F.2d 1118 (6th Cir. 1991); Glick v. McKay, 616 F.Supp. 322 (D.Nev. 1985), *aff'd*, 937 F2d 434 (9th Cir. 1991); Planned Parenthood v. Casey, 686 F.Supp. 2089 (E.D.Pa. 1988) (preliminary injunction), 744 F.Supp. 1323 (E.D. Pa. 1990), *aff'd in part, rev'd in part*, 947 F.2d 682 (3d Cir. 1991), *cert. granted*, 112 S. Ct. 931–932 (1992); Planned Parenthood Assoc. v. McWherter, 716 F.Supp. 1064 (M.D. Tenn. 1989), *vacated & remanded with instructions to dismiss the case*, No. 89-6026 (6th Cir. Sept. 30, 1991).

[328] Minn. Stat. Ann. 144.343 (2)–(7) (West 1989). In this analysis, it was assumed that any change in the incidence of pregnancy, abortion and childbirth because of the notice law would most heavily fall on teens 17 and below, who were directly affected by the notice law (Minn. Stat. Ann. 645.451 [West 1989]); less heavily on teens ages 18 to 19 who would have recently been subject to the law; somewhat less on women ages 20 to 24; and least on women ages 25 to 54. The notice law itself does not define "minor" by age, and thus it is possible that there was some confusion as to who, among 17- to 19-year-olds, was covered by the law. Moreover, some teens who gave birth at 18 might have been 17 at the time they became pregnant and thus were directly affected by the law. Those who were 18 or 19 in 1983–1986 were subject to the law in 1981, and the group as a whole could reasonably have been influenced by the law through socialization, including schooling and peer contacts. Similarly, some in the 20–24 age group in later years would have been subject to the law in earlier years of its enforcement. Women age 25–54 would never have been personally affected by the law.

[329] Hodgson v. Minnesota, 648 F.Supp. 756, 774 (D.Minn. 1986), *cert. denied*, 479 U.S. 1102 (1987), *rev'd*, 853 F.2d 1452 (8th Cir. 1988), *aff'd*, 110 S.Ct. 2926 (1990).

effect gives some indication of the positive effect of parental notice of abortion laws on minors.[330]

The data collected by the Minnesota Department of Health tell a broader public health story—not only about those Minnesota teens who aborted (.60% in 1982) but also about those who never got pregnant (98.7%) and those who carried their children to term (.66%). The department's data demonstrate that the notice law is reasonably related to protecting the health of minor women because it requires parental notice without causing any increased health problems for minors and, in fact, possibly decreases adolescent pregnancy and abortion rates *without* causing increased birth rates. There is apparently no evidence of even a single report of child abuse caused by the parental notification law or a single report of medical complications caused by the law, or a single case of parental prevention or coercion of an abortion.[331] This is an extraordinary benefit for teens in Minnesota.

The data show that pregnancies for Minnesota preteens and teens, ages 10 to 17, *declined* between 1981 and 1986 while the notice law was in effect. The number of pregnancies in this age group *increased* by 9.0 percent between 1975 and 1980 and *fell* by 27.4 percent from 1980 to 1986. In this age group, the highest number of adolescent pregnancies occurred in the year before the notice law went into effect. For the 18–19 age group, pregnancies *increased* 27.8 percent between 1975 and 1980 and *fell* by 33.8 percent between 1980 and 1986.

The department's data also show that abortions for preteens and teens, ages 10 to 17, declined between 1980 and 1986 while the notice law was in effect. Abortions in this age group *increased* 54.4% from 1975 through 1980 and *fell* by 33.6% from 1980 to 1986. For the eighteen-to-nineteen age group, abortions grew markedly between 1975 and 1980 before decreasing between 1980-1986. Abortions *rose* 92.3% between 1975 and 1980 before *falling* 29.8% between 1980 and 1986.

Finally, it might be speculated that if a parental notice law caused abortions to fall for teens, births would increase, but the Minnesota data show just the opposite. Births for girls ages 10 to 17 declined while the notice law was in effect. Births dropped 18.7% from 1975 to 1980, but they continued to drop 20.3% from 1980 to 1986. For the 18–19 age group, births *increased* by 4.0% from 1975 to 1980 but *decreased* by 36.6% from 1980 to 1986.

The rates of teen pregnancies, abortions and births also fell during the four and one-half years that the parental notice law was in effect.[332] The pregnancy rate for the 10–17 age group rose from 12.7 (12.7 per 1,000) in 1975 to a high of 15.6 in 1980, the year before the notice law took effect, and then declined to a low of 11.3 in 1983 and 12.4 in 1986. Thus, even though the population of 10- to 17-year-olds declined between 1975 and 1986, the pregnancy rate declined as well, by 20.5% between 1980

---

[330] Rogers, et al., *Impact of the Minnesota Parental Notification Law on Abortion and Birth*, 81 Am. J. Pub. Health 294 (March 1991). *See also, Brief of the Association of American Physicians and Surgeons (AAPS) as Amicus Curiae in Support of State of Minnesota*, in Hodgson v. Minnesota, 110 S. Ct. 2926 (1990). One of the authors was counsel of record in the U.S. Supreme Court on this brief.

[331] *Hodgson v. Minnesota*, 110 S. Ct. 2926 (1990), Cross Petitioners' Brief (Cross Pet.Br.) at 10–11, 18.

[332] Because raw figures do not take into account possible changes in Minnesota's population for a particular age group from year to year, rates for pregnancies, abortions and births were also calculated based on the department's data. Rates, in this study, equal the occurrence (incidence) of a phenomenon per 1,000 females. This data relies on the department's data for the entire population of Minnesota, not just on a sample.

and 1986. The pregnancy rate for the 18–19 age group rose substantially from 75.5 (75.5 per 1000) in 1975 to a high of 98.5 in 1980, the year before the notice law went into effect, but then fell after 1980 to 96.0 in 1981 and to 73.5 in 1986, *below the 1975 level*. Thus, again, even though the population in Minnesota for the 18–19 age group fell between 1976 and 1986, the pregnancy rate for 18- to 19-year-olds declined 25.4% between 1980 and 1986.

The abortion rate also declined. The abortion rate for the 10–17 age group rose from 4.9 in 1975 to a high of 8.4 in 1980 and then fell 27.4% percent between 1980 and 1986 for 10- to 17-year-olds. The abortion rate also fell for the 18–19 age group. The abortion rate rose from 20.4 in 1975 to a high of 40.1 in 1980 and then fell 4.8% to 38.20 in 1981 and a further 16.8% to a low of 31.80 in 1986. The abortion rate for 18- to 19-year-olds thus rose 96.6% between 1975 and 1980 and fell 20.7% between 1980 and 1986.

Finally, the birth rate fell for 10- to 17-year-olds and for 18-to 19-year-olds. The birth rate for the 10–17 age group fell from 7.8 in 1975 to 7.2 in 1980, but it continued to fall to 7.0 in 1981, to a low of 5.8 in 1983 and then to 6.3 in 1986. The birth rate for 10- to 17-year-olds thus fell 7.7% between 1975 and 1980 but fell 12.5% between 1980 and 1986. The birth rate for the 18–19 age group rose from 54.6 in 1975 to 58.0 in 1980 but fell to 57.4 in 1981 and to a low of 41.5 in 1986. Thus, the birth rate for 18-to-19 year-olds rose 6.2% from 1975 to 1980 but fell 28.4% between 1980 and 1986.

What does this public health story say for young women in Minnesota? The comparison of the pregnancy, abortion and birth rates in Minnesota between 1975–1980 and 1981–1986 supports the conclusion that the notice law effectively caused a decrease in the pregnancy rate in those years. This cannot be absolutely proven because this statistical study did not control for all other possible factors. However, since the abortion rate fell 27.4% for 10- to 17-year olds and 20.7% for 18- to 19-year-olds, while the birth rate throughout Minnesota simultaneously fell 12.5% for 10- to 17-year-olds and 28.4% for 18- to 19-year-olds, the pregnancy rate must have also declined, as the data confirm, supporting the conclusion that the notice law in fact changed adolescent behavior. In other words, since it seems undisputed that the notice law directly decreased abortion rates, while birth rates simultaneously decreased, the law must have decreased abortion rates by affecting pregnancy rates. Decreased unwed pregnancy for young women means decreased abortion and childbirth at a vulnerable age and time in their lives. A law that positively deters young women from pregnancy and abortion benefits young women.

V. Does Legal, Economic, and Social Equality for Women Hinge on *Roe v. Wade?*

As noted above, many feminist abortion advocates view abortion rights as the fundamental basis for all other freedoms. Abortion on demand is seen as necessary not only for freedom from male sexual oppression and domination,[333] but also as a legal basis

---

[333] Radical feminist Catherine MacKinnon believes abortion is an essential tool for women's liberation:

> A pregnant woman is the reification of male sexuality. Aggression, strength, and potency have triumphed over vulnerability, softness, and passivity. Pregnancy is the manifestation of male dominance and female submissiveness. A similar objectification of children from the male epistemology, in which children are defined in relation to male issues of potency, of continuity as a compensation for mortality, of the thrust to embody themselves or the

for other economic, educational and social rights. Thus, from this perspective, the legal guarantee of readily available abortion, whether based on a right of privacy or some other constitutional claim, is paramount. *Roe v. Wade* must be preserved in order to preserve and promote the development of female equality. In the face of often vociferous argument, it is worthwhile to examine the foundation for women's legal, social and economic rights.

Roe is rarely cited as a precedent for women's rights in any area other than abortion.[334] Virtually all progress in women's legal, social and employment rights over the past 30 years has come about through federal or state legislation and judicial interpretation wholly unrelated to and not derived from *Roe v. Wade*.[335] Many specific measures to advance women's rights over the past 30 years have been the result of congressional action. These developments began at least a decade before *Roe*. Congress passed the Equal Pay Act in 1963,[336] Title VII of the Civil Rights Act of 1964[337] and the Pregnancy Discrimination Act amendments in 1978.[338] Additional workplace protections have been added. For example, in 1978 the first appellate court held that sexual harassment

---

image of themselves, also underlies the issue of abortion. As MacKinnon notes: 'the idea that women can undo what men have done to them on this level seems to provoke insecurity sometimes bordering on hysteria.' Abortion, to MacKinnon, is a threat to the fundamental premise of male sexuality: the domination of female sexuality.

Cossman, *The Precarious Unity of Feminist Theory and Practice: The Praxis of Abortion*, 44 Toronto Fac. L. Rev. 85, 87 (1986) (citing to C. MacKinnon, *The Male Ideology of Privacy: A Feminist Perspective on the Right to Abortion* [1983] 17 Radical America 23 at 24 [footnote omitted]).

[334]   Although *Roe* has been cited in almost 100 cases by [the Supreme Court], and in more than 1,000 cases by other federal and state courts, these citations, outside the context of abortion regulation, have been largely superfluous to the issues decided in those cases. Hundreds of the cited cases involve some regulation of abortion; this body of law will understandably be altered by the reversal of *Roe*. Of the remaining cases, however, very few, if any, could not be resolved by principles other than those pronounced in *Roe*.

Westlaw indicates that *Roe* has been cited in 99 opinions or summary dispositions by this Court. Of these, 18 were cases involving state regulation of abortion, or limitations on abortion funding. Eleven more were summary dispositions, issued shortly after *Roe* reversing and remanding cases to lower courts in light of *Roe*. In 13 cases, *Roe* was cited for its holding on the issue of mootness. See e.g., *United States Parole Comm'n v. Geraughty*, 445 U.S. 388, 398 (1980); *Firefighters Local Union No. 1784 v. Stotts*, 467 U.S. 561, 593 (1984) (Blackmun, J., dissenting); *Edgar v. Mite Corp.*, 457 U.S. 624, 655 (1982) (Marshall, J., dissenting). In 16 cases *Roe* was cited in the body of an opinion, but as part of a string citation. See e.g., *Block v. Rutherford*, 468 U.S. 576, 597 (1984) (Blackmun, J., concurring); *Cleveland Board of Education v. LeFleur*, 414 U.S. 632, 639 (1974). In 23 cases, *Roe* was cited in memorandum opinions or dissents therefrom. See e.g., *Whisenhunt v. Spradlin*, 464 U.S. 965 (1983) (Brennan, J., dissenting).

The remaining cases, numbering 18, consist of more substantial reliance upon, or distinguishing of, *Roe*. See e.g. . . . *Carey v. Population Services Int'l*, 431 U.S. 678, 684 (1977); *Zablocki v. Redhail*, 434 U.S. 374, 386 (1978); *Kelley v. Johnson*, 425 U.S. 238, 244 (1976).

However, in no case has this Court relied on *Roe*, to the exclusion of other caselaw, in extending individual rights under the Due Process Clause of the Fourteenth Amendment.

Brief Amicus Curiae of Hon. Christopher Smith, et al., in Support of Appellants at 24–25 & n.53, in Webster v. Reproductive Health Services, 492 *U.S.* 490 (1989).

[335]See generally H. Kay, *Sex-Based Discrimination: Text, Cases and Materials* (2d ed. 1981); B. Babcock, A. Freedman, E. Norton & S. Ross, *Sex Discrimination and the Law: Causes and Remedies* (1975).

[336]77 Stat. 56, 29 U.S.C. § 206(d) (1988).

in the workplace was sex discrimination, prohibited by Title VII (equal employment opportunity).[339] Two years later, the Equal Employment Opportunity Commission (EEOC) adopted similar guidelines, prohibiting sexual harassment as a form of sex discrimination.[340] State agencies, as well as federal and state courts, have followed the EEOC's *Guidelines'* basic definition of sexual harassment.[341] Title IX of the Education Amendments of 1972 prohibits sexual discrimination against women in sports in federally funded schools.[342] Sex equity in education was established by the Women's Educational Equity Act of 1974[343] and expanded by the Women's Educational Equity Act of 1984.[344] The Federal Equal Credit Opportunity Act of 1974 prohibits sex discrimination in credit practices.[345] Other developments have come about through presidential order. For example, Executive Order No. 11,246 ensures equal opportunity in federal employment.[346] Progress has been facilitated simultaneously by state legislation. Some states have equal pay laws;[347] fair employment laws barring sex discrimination;[348] prohibitions on sex discrimination in state employment;[349] and prohibitions on sex discrimination in credit and financing practices,[350] sale, lease or rental of property,[351] insurance

---

[337] Pub. L. No. 88-352, 78 Stat. 241 (codified at 42 U.S.C. §§ 2000e to 2000e-17 [1988]). *See* Meritor Savings Bank, FSB v. Vinson, 477 U.S. 57 (1986) (holding that plaintiff may establish a violation of Title VII by proving that discrimination grounded in sexual harassment has created a hostile or abusive work environment); Arizona Governing Committee v. Norris, 463 U.S. 1073 (1983) (per curiam) (holding state annuity plan violates Title VII); Los Angeles Dept of Water & Power v. Manhart, 435 U.S. 702 (1978) (holding employer plan that required female employees to make larger contributions to pension fund violates Title VII).

[338] Pregnancy Discrimination Act of 1978, 92 Stat. 2076 (1978) (codified at 42 U.S.C. § 2000e [k] [1982] [overturning General Electric Co. v. Gilbert, 429 U.S. 125 (1976)]. *See* International Union, U.A.W. v. Johnson Controls, Inc., 111 S. Ct. 1196 (1991) (holding "fetal protection policy" that barred "all women, except those whose infertility was medically documented, from jobs involving actual or potential lead exposure" violates Pregnancy Discrimination Act); Newport News Shipbuilding and Dry Dock Co. v. EEOC, 462 U.S. 669 (1983) (holding pregnancy limitation in employer's health plan that provides for fewer benefits for spouses of male employees violates Pregnancy Discrimination Act); Nashville Gas Co. v. Satty, 434 U.S. 136 (1977) (denial of accumulated seniority to persons who take mandatory pregnancy leave violates Title VII).

[339] Barnes v. Costle, 561 F.2d 983 (D.C. Cir. 1978).

[340] *Equal Employment Opportunity Commission Guidelines on Sexual Harassment*, 29 C.F.R. § 1604.11 (1988).

[341] Littleton, *Feminist Jurisprudence: The Difference Method Makes*, 41 Stanford L. Rev. 751 at 769 (1989). *See also*, Meritor Savings Bank v. Vinson, 477 U.S. 57 1986).

[342] *See* M. Nelson, *Are We Winning Yet?: How Women are Changing Sports and Sports are Changing Women* (1991).

[343] Section 408 of P.L. 93-380.

[344] Title IV of the Education Amendments of 1984, P.L. 98-511, 98 Stat. 2389 (1984), *codified at* 20 U.S.C. § 3341 (1982).

[345] P.L. 93-495; 15 U.S.C. § 1601, 1691 (1982); 12 C.F.R. § 202 (1991).

[346] Exec. Order No. 11,246, 3 C.F.R. 339 (1964–1965), *reprinted in*, 42 U.S.C. § 2000e app. (1982).

[347] *See, e.g.*, Alas. Stat. § 18.80.220(5) (1986 & Supp. 1986); Ariz. Stat. § 23-341 (1983); Ark. Stat. § 11-4-601, -612 (1987); Cal. Lab. Code § 1197.5 (1989); Colo. § 8-5-102 (1986); Conn. § 31-75 (1987); Del. tit. 19, § 1107A (1985); D.C. Code Section 1-2502, -2512 (1987 & Supp. 1990); Fla. Stat. § 48.07 (02), 725.07 (1) (1988 & Supp. 1991); Ga. §§ 34-5-3, 34-5-1 (1991); Idaho § 67-5909 (1989); Ill. Rev. Stat. Ch. 48, ¶ 1004 (b) (Supp. 1990); Ind. § 22-2-2-4 (1986); Kan. § 44-1205 (1986); Ky. § 337.423 (Supp. 1990); La. § 23:1006 (1985); Me. Tit. 26, § 628 (1988); Mass. Ch. 149, 105A (1989); Minn. 181.67 (1) (Supp. 1990); Mo. § 290.410 (1965); Mont. § 39-3-104 (1) (1989); Neb. § 48-1219, -1221 (1984); Nev. § 608.017 (1987); N.H. § 275:37 (1987); N.M. § 28-1-7 (1987); N.Y. Labor 194 (1986); N.D. § 34-06.1-03 (1980); Ohio § 4111.17 (1991); Okla. Tit. 40, § 198.1 (1986); Ore. § 652.220 (1989); R.I. § 28-6-17, -18 (1986); S.C. § 1-13-80(a) (1) (1976 & Supp. 1990); S.D. § 60-12-15, (1978); Tenn. § 50-2-202 (1983); Tex. Civ. article 6825; article 5221(k), 2.01, 5.01 (1960 & Supp. 1991); Utah § 34-35-6 (1990); Vt. Tit.

practices[352] and public accommodations.[353] States have also enacted legislation targeted at domestic violence.[354] In the realm of education, "[t]he states too have been active partners in developing programs to achieve educational equity."[355] At least 14 states have laws modeled on the federal Title IX.[356]

Legislative progress was subsequently buttressed by judicial interpretation of the equal protection clause of the fourteenth amendment. Prior to 1971 the Supreme Court exercised great deference toward legislatively established gender classifications.[357] In 1971 the Court first held that sex discrimination violates the equal protection clause in *Reed v. Reed*.[358] Other similar decisions have followed, striking down some gender classifications.[359]

Few, if any, of these legal and legislative developments rest on *Roe v. Wade*. Some of these events preceded *Roe v. Wade*. And the judicial decisions rely on interpretations of congressional or state policy-making, rather than on *Roe*.

The single-minded pursuit of abortion rights has arguably sidetracked progress on the legal, economic and social issues that are most important to most women: equal

---

21, 465(1) (1987 & Supp. 1990); Va. § 40.1-28.6 (1990); Wash. § 49.12.175 (1990); W.Va. Section 21-5b-3 (1989); Wis. § 111.36(1) (a) (1988); Wyo. § 27-4-302 (1987).

[348] *See, e.g.,* Alas. Stat. § 18.80.200 (Supp. 1990); Ariz. Stat. 41-1461 (1985); Cal. Gov. Code §§ 12920, 12926 (1980 & Supp. 1990); Colo. § 24-34-402 (Supp. 1986); Conn. § 46a-51(17), -60(a) (1)2a(10) (Supp. 1991); Del. tit. 19, § 710, 711 (1985); D.C. Code § 1-2502-2512 (1987 & Supp. 1991); Fla. § 760.02, .10 (1986); Idaho § 67-5909 (1989); Ill. Rev. Stat. Ch. 68, ¶ 2-102 (1989); Ind. Stat. § 22-9-2-2, -1, -3 (1986); Iowa § 601A.6 (1988 & Supp. 1991); Kan. Stat. § 44-1009(1) (1986); Ky. Stat. § 344.030, .040, .050, .060, .070 (1983 & Supp. 1990); La. Rev. Stat. § 23:1006 (1985); Me. Tit. 5, 4553(4), 4572-a (1989 & Supp. 1990); Utah § 34-35-6 (1990); Mass. Ch. 151b, sec. 1 (1989 & Supp. 1990); Minn. § 363.02(1) (1991); Mont. § 49-2-310 (1989) ("reasonable maternity leave"); Neb. § 48-1101, -1102(2), -1104 (1984); Nev. § 613.330 (1987); N.H. § 354-8:8, -a:8(1) (Supp. 1990); N.J. § 10:5-5, -12 (Supp. 1990); N. M. § 28-1-7 (1987); Ohio § 4112.02(a); 4112.01(b) (1991) (pregnancy); Ore. § 659.010(6), .030(1)(a) (1989 & Supp. 1990); Pa. Cons. Stat. Tit. 43, § 955 (1991); R.I. § 28-5-5, -6(b), -7 (Supp. 1991); S.C. § 1-13-30, -80 (1986 & Supp. 1990); S.D. § 20-13-1, -10 to -12 (1987); Tenn. §§ 4-21-401, 4-21-404 (1985); Tex. Civ. art. 5221 (K), 2.01, 5.01 (Supp. 1991); Vt. Tit. 21, § 495 (1987 & Supp. 1990); Wash. § 49.60.180 (1990); W.Va. § 5-11-1 to 9 (1990); Wis. 111.31 to .36 (1988 & Supp. 1990); Wyo. § 27-9-102(b), -105 (1987 & Supp. 1990).

[349] *See, e.g.,* Alas. Governor's Code of Fair Practices by State Agencies, art. I (Aug. 11, 1967); Ariz. Exec. Order No. 83-5 (Aug. 31, 1983); Cal. Fair Employment & Housing Act, Cal. Gov. Code § 12926(c) (Supp. 1991); 4 Code of Colo. Regs. § 801-1 (1982); Conn. § 46a-70(a), -51(10) (1986 & Supp. 1991); Del. Exec. Order No. 9, Tit. 19, § 710(2) (1985); D.C. Code § 1-507, 1-607.7 (1987), Mayor's Order No. 79-89 (1979) (sexual harassment); Fla. § 110.105, 760.02 (1982), Exec. Order No. 80-69 (1981) (sexual harassment); Idaho § 67-5902(6)(b) (1989), Exec. Order No. 78-4 (1978); Ill. Rev. Stat. ch. 68, ¶ 2-101, -105(B) (1989 & Supp. 1990), Exec. Order No. 80-1 (1980) (sexual harassment); Ind. § 22-9-1-3(h) (1986).

[350] *See, e.g.,* Alas. Stat. § 18.80.200, .210, .250 (Supp. 1990); Ark. Stat. § 4-87-104 (1987).

[351] *See, e.g.,* Alas. Stat. § 18.80.200, .210, .240 (Supp 1990); Ariz. Stat. § 20-1548 (1990) (mortgage guaranty insurance only).

[352] *See, e.g.,* Alas. Stat. § 21.36.090 (Supp. 1990); Ariz. Stat. § 20-448 (1990).

[353] *See, e.g.,* Alas. Stat. 18.80.200, .230 (Supp. 1990).

[354] *See, e.g.,* Alas. Stat. § 25.35.060 (Supp. 1990); Ariz. Stat. § 13-3601 (1989); Cal. Welf. & Ins. Code § 18291 (1980 & Supp. 1991); Cal. Penal Code §§ 262, 264, 273.5 (1988 & Supp. 1991); Colo. §§ 14-2-101; 14-4-101 (1987); Conn. §§ 46b-15, 53a-71 (1986 & Supp. 1991); Del. tit. 10 §§ 901(9), 921(6) (1975 & Supp. 1990); D.C. Code §§ 16-1001, 22-2801 (marital rape) (1989); Fla. §§ 415.602, 415.603 (spousal abuse), § 741.30, § 794.011 (spousal rape) (1986 & Supp. 1991); Ga. § 19-13-1 (1990); Idaho § 39-5202 (1985); Illinois Domestic Violence Act of 1986, Ill. Rev. Stat. ch. 40, ¶ 2311-1 (1989); Ill. Stat. ch. 40, ¶ 2401 (1989) (domestic violence shelters).

[355] NOW Legal Defense Fund, *The State-By-State Guide to Women's Legal Rights* 48 (1987).

pay, day care, maternity leave, job discrimination. Minority women in particular are concerned about issues that directly affect the health and welfare of their families: access to education, adequate health care and safe neighborhoods for their children.[360] Despite the "success" of achieving freely available, legal abortion, women's economic rights in domestic-relations law have not progressed; in fact, the opposite has been true. "Divorce reform," which was achieved in the name of equality, has been devastating for women. The "feminization of poverty" is a reality caused, at least in part, by modern divorce laws.[361] With no-fault divorce laws in 43 states, women have suffered *more* than with previous divorce laws. No-fault laws eliminate alimony and force the sale of the family home. There is a 73% drop in the standard of living for the wife and children, and a 42% increase for the husband.[362] The presence of "abortion rights" is irrelevant at best, and at worst, has paralleled women's economic decline.

There may be countless other ways that *Roe* and the expansion of the abortion doctrine have been ineffective and irrelevant in advancing those issues and meeting the needs that are most important to women. The full impact on women and society may not be known for several generations.

VI. Conclusion

Abortion as the "first right" for women runs counter to all the principles of feminism and to the basic human value of protecting the weak and defenseless. By promoting the death of one's own offspring as a positive "good," abortion violently contradicts the core values that are the very essence of a woman's being: nurturance, care, compassion, cooperation, inclusivity, community and connectedness. It denies basic civil rights to an entire class of prenatal human beings. Women, who so recently have begun to achieve equality and opportunity, should be the first to recognize that the diminution of the rights of other human beings threatens the rights of women as well.

The abortion privacy doctrine has spawned a great host of ills for women without remedying any of the real historical injustices against them. Abortion on demand has isolated women, subjected them to coercion, maimed their bodies and wounded their psyches. The abortion-on-demand mentality that *Roe v. Wade,* more than anything else, fostered has not truly benefited women, whether examined from the perspective of women's self-perception, the psychological and physical consequences of abortion, the impact on minors or the relationships between women, their families and their communities. No

---

[356] *See, e.g.,* Alas. Stat. § 14.18.010 (1990); Cal. Educ. Code §§ 40, 230, 51500, 51501, 66016 (1978 & Supp. 1991); Cal. Gov. Code § 12943 (1980).

[357] *See, e.g.,* Hoyt v. Florida, 368 U.S. 57 (1961); Goesaert v. Cleary, 335 U.S. 464 (1948); Muller v. Oregon, 208 U.S. 412 (1908); Bradwell v. Illinois, 83 U.S. 130 (1873).

[358] 404 U.S. 71 (1971).

[359] Wengler v. Druggists Mut. Ins. Co., 446 U.S. 142 (1980); Califano v. Westcott, 443 U.S. 76 (1979); Califano v. Goldfarb, 430 U.S. 199 (1977); Stanton v. Stanton, 421 U.S. 7 (1975); Weinberger v. Wiesenfeld, 420 U.S. 636 (1975); Taylor v. Louisiana, 419 U.S. 522 (1975); Frontiero v. Richardson, 411 U.S. 677 (1973).

[360] Wallis, *Onward, Women!,* Time, Dec. 4, 1989 at 80.

[361] M. Fineman, *The Illusion of Equality: The Rhetoric and Reality of Divorce Reform* (1991); D. Medved, *The Case Against Abortion* (1989); L. Weitzman, *The Divorce Revolution* (1985); M. Gallagher, *Enemies of Eros* (1989).

[362] *See* Weitzman, *supra* note 354.

essential legal, economic and social rights for women will be undermined when *Roe v. Wade* is overruled. If anything, eradication of legalized abortion on demand will allow energy to be refocused on economic and social targets. Perhaps the most critical is the restoration of relationships of mutual responsibility between women and men and prompting society to affirm women and protect the fruit of their unique procreative ability: children.

This article presents the argument that if there is no constitutional right to abortion the Supreme Court will be able to use a "rational basis" test to uphold laws against abortion. Conversely, if there is a right to abortion in the Constitution, the Supreme Court will apply the "strict scrutiny" test. James Bopp Jr. avers that *there is no* constitutional right, specifically in the equal protection clause of the fourteenth amendment as well as in the rest of the Constitution. He predicts that with the demise of *Roe,* the states will once again regulate abortion, as they did prior to 1973.

5 · Is Equal Protection a Shelter for the Right to Abortion? ⸻

*James Bopp Jr., J.D.**

I. Introduction

In *Roe v. Wade,*[1] the Supreme Court found that the right of privacy, which it had previously discovered in *Griswold v. Connecticut,*[2] was "broad enough" to include the right to an abortion.[3] The *Roe* decision consisted of essentially three elements: a historical inquiry into abortion,[4] an inquiry into whether a fetus is a person within the meaning of the fourteenth amendment[5] and a balancing of the interests of the pregnant mother and the state.[6] The historical inquiry claimed that abortion regulations were a fairly recent statutory phenomenon.[7] The Court then concluded that the unborn were not persons within the meaning of the fourteenth amendment.[8] Finally, the Court formulated the "trimester framework" to balance the rights of the mother and the interests of the state. This framework curtailed state regulation of abortion until the second trimester of

*B.A., Indiana University, 1970; J.D., University of Florida School of Law, 1973; Partner, Brames, McCormick, Bopp & Abel, Terre Haute, Indiana; General Counsel, National Right to Life Committee, Inc.; former member, President's Committee on Mental Retardation; Editor, Issues in Law & Medicine.

    The author gratefully acknowledges the research and writing assistance of W. Tim Miller and funding by the Horatio R. Storer Foundation, Inc.

[1] 410 U.S. 113 (1973).
[2] 381 U.S. 479 (1965).
[3] 410 U.S. at 153.
[4] *Id.* at 129–152.
[5] *Id.* at 156–162.
[6] *Id.* at 162–166.
[7] *Id.* at 129.
[8] *Id.* at 158.

pregnancy and left the mother's decision to abort, made in consultation with her physician, unfettered until after viability.[9]

The *Roe* decision and its progeny have spawned a great deal of criticism by constitutional scholars.[10] John Hart Ely summed up the problem with *Roe* by stating that "it is bad because it is bad constitutional law, or rather because it is not constitutional law and gives almost no sense of an obligation to try to be."[11] Judge Robert Bork commented that "in the entire opinion there is not one line of explanation, not one sentence that qualifies as legal argument."[12] This weakness in *Roe* has become ever more apparent in recent decisions of the Court.

In an effort to protect the "right to abortion" from erosion, those supporting the "right" have recognized the need to give it some legitimate basis in the Constitution.[13] This article will explore the attempts by those favoring a right to abortion to ground that right in the equal protection clause of the fourteenth amendment.[14] Some argue that the real biological differences between the genders should be ignored and that men and women should be treated *as if* they are similarly situated. Others would point up these real biological differences between the genders and require that the government treat women with more deference than men in an effort to neutralize any negative effects that these differences cause women. Both of these approaches reach the conclusion that an unfettered right to an abortion is a prerequisite to gender equality.

This article will conclude, however, that these "equal protection" arguments for the right to an abortion are unavailing because pregnant women have never been recognized as a suspect or even as a quasi-suspect classification by the Supreme Court and because the genders are simply not similarly situated with respect to pregnancy. Furthermore, the right to abortion is not a fundamental right, as the Court has defined the term. Thus, under current equal protection analysis, regulations curtailing abortions should not be subjected to heightened scrutiny, rather such regulations should be reviewed under the rational basis test.

II. The Demise of *Roe*

The Supreme Court subsequently broadened its original holding in *Roe* in the context of cases that dealt with state-mandated abortion procedures and consent requirements. In *Planned Parenthood of Central Missouri v. Danforth*,[15] the Court invalidated provisions of a state abortion statute that required parental consent for an underage girl[16] and

---

[9] *Id.* at 162–166 (Although the state's interest in "potential life" was recognized by the Court, that interest did not become "compelling" until the fetus was viable. *Id.* at 163–164.).

[10] *See* Ely, *The Wages of Crying Wolf: A Comment on* Roe v. Wade, 82 Harv. L. Rev. 920, 935 (1973).

[11] *Id.* at 947.

[12] R. Bork, *The Tempting of America: The Political Seduction of the Law* 112 (1990).

[13] *See generally,* Bopp, *Will There Be a Constitutional Right to Abortion After the Reconsideration of* Roe v. Wade? 15 J. Contemp. L. 131, 136 (1989) (this article discusses several alternative rationales to *Roe v. Wade:* equal protection, self-defense, bodily integrity, establishment of religion, free exercise of religion, freedom of association, freedom of speech, involuntary servitude, the good samaritan doctrine, the physician's right to privacy and cruel and unusual punishment).

[14] The U.S. Supreme Court may face this issue in Bray v. Alexandria Women's Clinic, No. 90-985, which is scheduled to be decided by June 1992.

[15] 428 U.S. 52 (1976).

[16] *Id.* at 72–75.

spousal consent for a married woman to obtain an abortion.[17] The Court also struck down a section of the statute that prohibited the use of the saline amniocentesis method of abortion[18] and a section that required the physician performing the abortion to use a standard of care that would preserve the life of the fetus after viability.[19]

Similarly, in *Akron v. Akron Center for Reproductive Health*,[20] the Court found sections of an Akron city ordinance unconstitutional. These sections required hospitalization for second trimester abortions,[21] a twenty-four-hour waiting period before obtaining an abortion[22] and "humane and sanitary" disposal of the fetal remains.[23] Also held invalid were consent provisions. These provisions required parental consent for a minor and informed consent for any female desiring an abortion.[24] The *Akron* Court limited the state's ability to regulate abortion in the second trimester to those requirements that did not "depart from accepted medical practice."[25] The decision was based on the doctrine of stare decisis and a respect for the precedent embodied in *Roe v. Wade*.[26] Thus, with each case that came before the Court, the right discovered in *Roe* was accorded more and more protection.[27]

Webster v. Reproductive Health Services,[28] however, made substantial changes in the Court's analysis of abortion cases. In *Webster,* the Court upheld a state statute that restricted the use of public employees and facilities for nontherapeutic abortions.[29] The Court upheld a viability testing provision in spite of the fact that compliance with this provision would increase the cost of an abortion.[30] In so holding, the plurality of Chief Justice Rehnquist and Justices White and Kennedy overruled *Roe's* trimester framework,[31] and Justice Scalia would have expressly overruled *Roe* entirely.[32]

Most recently, in *Hodgson v. Minnesota*,[33] the Supreme Court upheld a state statute that required a minor to notify both her parents and then wait 48 hours before obtaining an abortion.[34] In *Hodgson's* companion case, *Ohio v. Akron Center for Re-*

---

[17] *Id.* at 67–71.

[18] *Id.* at 75–79.

[19] *Id.* at 81–83.

[20] 462 U.S. 416 (1983). *See also* Planned Parenthood Ass'n of Kansas City v. Ashcroft, 462 U.S. 476 (1983); Simopoulos v. Virginia, 462 U.S. 506 (1983).

[21] 462 U.S. at 434–439.

[22] *Id.* at 449–451.

[23] *Id.* at 451–452.

[24] *Id.* at 439–449.

[25] *Id.* at 431.

[26] *Id.* at 419–420.

[27] *See generally* Bopp & Coleson, *The Right to Abortion: Anomalous, Absolute, and Ripe for Reversal*, 3 B.Y.U. J. Pub. L. 181, 185–192 (1989).

[28] 109 S. Ct. 3040 (1989).

[29] *Id.* at 3050–3053.

[30] *Id.* at 3054–3057.

[31] *Id.* at 3056–3058; *see generally* Bopp & Coleson, *What Does* Webster *Mean?*, 138 U. Pa. L. Rev. 157, 162–164 (1989).

[32] 109 S. Ct. at 3067 (Scalia, J., concurring in part and concurring in the judgement); Justice O'Connor found no need to reexamine *Roe v. Wade. Id.* at 3060.

[33] 110 S. Ct. 2926 (1990).

[34] *Id.* at 2944 (Stevens, J., plurality) (48-hour waiting period is constitutional); at 2950–51 (O'Connor, J., concurring in part and concurring in the judgement in part) (two parent notification with judicial bypass is constitutional); at 2961–72 (Kennedy, J., concurring in the judgment in part and dissenting in part) (two parent notification without judicial bypass and 48-hour waiting period is constitutional).

productive Health,[35] the Court found constitutional a state statute requiring that one parent be notified twenty-four hours before a minor could obtain an abortion.[36] In each of these cases, the Court employed the rational basis test to uphold these abortion restrictions—a test inimical to *Roe.* These three cases, *Webster, Hodgson,* and *Ohio,* clearly indicate that the Court has abandoned the constitutionally weak rationale of *Roe,* adopted a less rigorous standard of review for abortion cases[37] and signaled a willingness to uphold substantial regulation of abortion.[38]

III. The Equal Protection Analysis

A. The Original Understanding

Both the history of section 1 of the fourteenth amendment and the scope of its originally intended enforcement are somewhat ambiguous. The Supreme Court first construed the fourteenth amendment in *The Slaughter-House Cases,*[39] only five years after the amendment had been ratified. As the Court noted, "[f]ortunately that history [of the fourteenth amendment] is fresh" that the "pervading purpose" of the amendment was "the freedom of the slave race, the security and the firm establishment of that freedom, and the protection of the newly made freemen and citizen from the oppressions of those who had formerly exercised unlimited dominion over him."[40]

More specifically, the Court stated that "[t]he existence of laws in the states where the newly emancipated negroes resided, which discriminated with gross injustice and hardship against them as a class, was the evil to be remedied by . . . [the equal protection] clause."[41] The Court concluded with a forecast: "We doubt very much whether any action of a state not directed by way of discrimination against the negroes as a class, or on account of their race, will ever be held to come within the purview of this provision."[42]

Seven years later in *Strauder v. West Virginia,*[43] the Court again had occasion to review the history of the fourteenth amendment. The *Strauder* Court found that the fourteenth amendment "was designed to assure to the colored race the enjoyment of all the civil rights that under the law are enjoyed by white persons, and to give to that race the protection of the General Government, in that enjoyment, whenever it should be denied by the States."[44] The Court, therefore, struck down a state statute that restricted jury duty to whites but indicated that the restriction limiting jury duty to male citizens over the age of 21 would he upheld. The Court held that the state could not discriminate

---

[35] 10 S. Ct. 2972 (1990).

[36] *Id.* at 2977 (the statute contained a judicial bypass provision).

[37] This change in the standard of review has been noted in recent federal court of appeals decisions on abortion, Planned Parenthood v. Minnesota, 910 F.2d 479 (8th Cir. 1990) ("Prior to *Webster,* we believe the statute would have been reviewed under the strict scrutiny standard . . . In *Webster,* however, the Supreme Court appears to have adopted a less rigorous standard of review than the strict scrutiny analysis . . ." *Id.* at 5.); Planned Parenthood v. Casey, 947 F.2d 682 (3rd Cir. 1991).

[38] *See generally* Bopp, Coleson & Bostrom, *Does the United States Supreme Court Have a Constitutional Duty to Expressly Reconsider and Overrule* Roe v. Wade?, 1 Seton Hall Const. L. J. 55, 73–82 (1990).

[39] 83 U.S. 57 (1873).

[40] *Id.* at 71.

[41] *Id.* at 81.

[42] *Id.*

[43] 100 U.S. 303 (1880).

[44] *Id.* at 306.

on the basis of race, but "[i]t may confine the selection to males, to freeholders, to citizens, to persons within certain ages, or to persons having educational qualifications. We do not believe the 14th Amendment was ever intended to prohibit this."[45]

In 1953 the Court looked again to the history of the fourteenth amendment to resolve the issue of school segregation.[46] Time appeared to have obscured the original meaning of the fourteenth amendment, and the *Brown* court dismissed the historical evidence as "inconclusive."[47] Shortly after *Brown* was handed down, Alexander Bickel made his own detailed inquiry into the circumstances surrounding the adoption of the fourteenth amendment.[48] By looking at both the impact of the amendment at the time of its ratification and considerations of its future effects, Professor Bickel concluded that "section I . . . deals not only with racial discrimination, but also with discrimination whether or not based on color."[49]

Professor Bickel based this finding on the fact that there was an earlier alternative to section I that would have applied specifically to race alone that was rejected in committee.[50] Bickel also believed that the drafters of the fourteenth amendment "emulated the technique of the original framers, who were . . . responsible to an electorate only partly receptive to the fullness of their principles, and who similarly avoided the explicit grant of some powers without foreclosing their future assumption."[51] In short, Bickel argued that the language of section I of the fourteenth amendment is purposefully broad enough to encompass "further strides toward the ideal of equality" that are consistent with "the trend in public opinion."[52]

Judge Robert Bork would not take such a broad view of the original intentions of the framers of the fourteenth amendment. Bork claims that "[i]t is clear that the ratifiers . . . did not think they were treating women as an oppressed class similar in legal disadvantages to the newly freed slaves,"[53] and, therefore, it was never contemplated that "racial and sexual groups needed [a] special protection to the same degree."[54] Regardless of whose analysis one accepts, both would probably agree that the 39th Congress would not have passed an amendment that would have given women immediate social and legal equality with men.[55] Regardless, Bork's analysis appears to reflect the approach that the Court has ultimately taken with respect to racial and gender classifications.

B. Present Equal Protection Analysis

The Court has traditionally subjected the classifications used in economic and social welfare legislation to a rational basis test.[56] For legislation to pass this test, "the classification must be reasonable, not arbitrary, and must rest upon some ground of differ-

---

[45] *Id.* at 310.
[46] Brown v. Board of Education, 347 U.S. 483 (1953).
[47] *Id.* at 489.
[48] Bickel, *The Original Understanding and the Segregation Decision,* 69 Harv. L. Rev. 1 (1955).
[49] *Id.* at 59–60.
[50] *See id.* at 59.
[51] *Id.* at 62.
[52] *Id.* at 63–64.
[53] Bork, *supra* note 12, at 329.
[54] *Id.* at 66 n.*.
[55] *See* Bickel, *supra* note 47, at 63–64; Bork, *supra* note 12, at 329.
[56] Lindsley v. Natural Carbonic Gas Co., 220 U.S. 61, 78 (1911).

ence having a fair and substantial relation to the object of the legislation, so that all persons similarly circumstanced shall be treated alike."[57] The Court's inquiry into the purpose of the classification generally does not go very far. "Where . . . there are plausible reasons for [the legislature's] action, our inquiry is at an end. It is, of course, 'constitutionally irrelevant whether this reasoning in fact underlay the legislative decision.' "[58] The rational basis test ensures against "arbitrary and unreasonable government,"[59] while allowing the legislature maximum latitude in drawing necessary statutory classifications.

Legislation that classifies on the basis of race or national origin, however, has historically been treated with less deference by the Court.[60] In *Korematsu v. United States,*[61] the Court stated that "all legal restrictions which curtail the civil rights of a single racial group are immediately suspect . . . [and] courts must subject them to the most rigid scrutiny."[62] As further developed by the Court, the strict scrutiny test requires that a classification be narrowly tailored to further a compelling government interest.[63] This test has come to be applied not only to statutes that classify on the basis of race and national origin but also those classifications that infringe upon the exercise of a fundamental right by a particular group.[64] This two-pronged use of the equal protection analysis owes its origin to Justice Stone's famous footnote in *United States v. Caroline Products Co.*[65]

Recently the Court has employed a test more rigorous than the rational basis test yet less searching than strict scrutiny. Intermediate scrutiny requires that the legislative classification be substantially related to an important government interest.[66] This standard has been applied in the context of discrimination based on gender,[67] alienage[68] and illegitimacy.[69]

---

[57] F. S. Royster Guano Co. v. Virginia, 253 U.S. 412, 415 (1919).

[58] United States Railroad Retirement Bd. v. Fritz, 449 U.S. 166, 179 (1980) (quoting Flemming v. Nestor, 363 U.S. 603, 612 [1960]).

[59] Railway Express Agency, Inc. v. New York, 336 U.S. 106, 112 (1948) (Jackson, J., concurring).

[60] *See, e.g., Strauder,* 100 U.S. 303 (1880); Yick Wo v. Hopkins, 118 U.S. 356 (1886).

[61] 323 U.S. 214 (1944).

[62] *Id.* at 216.

[63] Cleburne v. Cleburne Living Center, 473 U.S. 432, 440 (1985).

[64] *See, e.g.,* Harper v. Virginia State Bd. of Elections, 383 U.S. 663 (1966); Skinner v. Oklahoma, 316 U.S. 535 (1942); Shapiro v. Thompson, 394 U.S. 618 (1969).

[65] There may be a narrower scope for operation of the presumption of constitutionality when legislation appears on its face to be within a specific prohibition of the Constitution, such as those of the first 10 amendments, which are deemed equally specific when held to be embraced within the fourteenth amendment:

> It is unnecessary to consider now whether legislation which restricts those political processes which can ordinarily be expected to bring about repeal of undesirable legislation, is to be subjected to more exacting judicial scrutiny under the general prohibitions of the Fourteenth Amendment than are most other types of legislation.
>
> Nor need we inquire . . . whether prejudice against discrete and insular minorities may be a special condition, which tends seriously to curtail the operation of those political processes ordinarily to be relied upon to protect minorities, and which may call for a correspondingly more searching judicial inquiry.

304 U.S. 144, 152 n.4 (1938).

[66] Craig v. Boren, 429 U.S. 190, 197 (1976); Mills v. Habluetzel, 456 U.S. 91, 99 (1982).

[67] *See e.g., Craig,* 429 U.S. 190.

[68] *See, e.g.,* Plyler v. Doe, 457 U.S. 202 (1982); Graham v. Richardson, 403 U.S. 365 (1971).

As can be seen from this brief discussion, the Supreme Court's approach to the two-pronged equal protection analysis presently consists of three levels of scrutiny. Legislation that draws classifications on the basis of race or national origin or that impinges on a fundamental right is subject to strict scrutiny and is almost always found unconstitutional. Legislation classifying on the basis of gender, alienage or illegitimacy is scrutinized at an intermediate level, and all other statutory distinctions must be rationally related to a legitimate state purpose.

C. Gender Discrimination

The application of the intermediate standard of review in the context of gender discrimination is of fairly recent origin. In *Reed v. Reed*,[70] the Court used the rational basis test to strike down a state statute that favored men over women in determining who would administer the estate of one who dies intestate.[71] The *Reed* Court found that "[b]y providing dissimilar treatment for men and women who are . . . similarly situated, the challenged section violate[d] the Equal Protection Clause."[72] Conversely, in *Frontiero v. Richardson*,[73] Justice Brennan, writing for a plurality of four, stated that "classifications based upon sex, like classifications based upon race, alienage, and national origin, are inherently suspect and must therefore be subjected to close judicial scrutiny."[74] The *Frontiero* Court found unconstitutional a federal statute that provided larger military housing allowances and medical benefits to the spouses of male personnel than to the spouses of female personnel.[75]

After canvassing both of these approaches to equal protection analysis, the Court settled on an intermediate standard of review in *Craig v. Boren*.[76] *Craig* dealt with a state statute that prohibited the sale of 3.2% beer to males under 21 and females under 18 years of age.[77] Justice Brennan, again writing for the Court, stated that "[t]o withstand constitutional challenge . . . classifications by gender must serve important governmental objectives and must be substantially related to the achievement of those objectives."[78] Under this standard the statute was found violative of equal protection.[79] More recently, the Supreme Court applied this same standard of review to allow a male to attend all-female, state-supported nursing school.[80]

Some gender discrimination cases, however, have not invalidated the statutory distinctions drawn between men and women. In *Schlesinger v. Ballard*,[81] the Court was required to review a promotion policy of the United States Navy that allowed women a longer period of time for promotion prior to mandatory discharge than was allowed

---

[68] *See, e.g.*, Plyler v. Doe, 457 U.S. 202 (1982); Graham v. Richardson, 403 U.S. 365 (1971).

[69] *See, e.g.*, Matthews v. Lucas, 427 U.S. 495 (1976); Trimble v. Gordon, 430 U.S. 762 (1977).

[70] 404 U.S. 71 (1971).

[71] *Id.* at 76 (citing *Royster*, 253 U.S. at 412, 415).

[72] *Id.* at 77 (citation omitted).

[73] 411 U.S. 677 (1973).

[74] *Id.* at 682.

[75] *Id.* at 678–679.

[76] 429 U.S. 190 (1976).

[77] *Id.* at 192 n.1.

[78] *Id.* at 197.

[79] *Id.* at 210.

[80] *See* Mississippi University for Women v. Hogan, 458 U.S. 718 (1982).

[81] 419 U.S. 498 (1975).

men.[82] The Court found that, unlike the statutes at issue in *Reed* and *Frontiero*, "the different treatment of men and women naval officers . . . reflects, not archaic and overbroad generalizations, but, instead, the demonstrable fact that male and female line officers . . . are not similarly situated."[83] Similarly, in *Rostker v. Goldberg*,[84] a case dealing with the Military Selective Service Act that permitted only men to be drafted, the Court found that "[m]en and women . . . are simply not similarly situated for purposes of a draft or registration for a draft."[85] The *Rostker* Court went on to say that "The Constitution requires that Congress treat similarly situated persons similarly, not that it engage in gestures of superficial equality."[86] In both cases, the statutory classification was upheld based on the differences between the sexes.

Thus, in the area of gender discrimination, there is a distinction between those statutory classifications that bear no relationship to actual differences between men and women and those classifications that are predicated upon those differences. The former are held to a standard of intermediate scrutiny, and the latter are upheld as long as the distinction is rationally related to a legitimate government interest. Nowhere is this same distinction more apparent than in the context of pregnancy regulation.

Geduldig v. Aiello[87] presented the question of whether a state disability insurance program that excluded from coverage disabilities resulting from pregnancy denied women equal protection.[88] The Court found that there was no denial of equal protection because gender discrimination, as previously defined in *Reed* and *Frontiero*, did not exist with respect to the disability plan.[89] The *Geduldig* Court stated that

> *[t]he California insurance program does not exclude anyone from benefit eligibility because of gender but merely removes one physical condition— pregnancy—from the list of compensable disabilities. While it is true that only women can become pregnant it does not follow that every legislative classification concerning pregnancy is a sex based classification . . . The program divides potential recipients into two groups—pregnant women and nonpregnant persons. While the first group is exclusively female, the second includes members of both sexes.*[90]

This case has caused great consternation among those arguing for an equal protection right to abortion. Logically, if pregnant women are not similarly situated with respect to nonpregnant persons, a law prohibiting abortion would not be a denial of equal protection to all women as a class and, therefore, not gender discrimination.[91] The statute would only need pass the rational basis test for the purposes of equal protection analysis. Thus, several constitutional scholars have devised "equal protection

---

[82] *Id.* at 500.
[83] *Id.* at 508.
[84] 453 U.S. 57 (1981).
[85] *Id.* at 78.
[86] *Id.* at 79.
[87] 417 U.S. 484 (1974).
[88] *Id.* at 492.
[89] *Id.* at 496 n.20.
[90] *Id.*
[91] *See* Law, *Rethinking Sex and the Constitution,* 132 U. Pa. L. Rev. 955, 985 (1984).

models'' in an effort to get around *Geduldig* while at the same time trying to provide some sort of constitutional basis for the right to abortion.

IV. The Alternative Equal Protection Models

A. The Equal Treatment—Assimilationist—Approach

The assimilationist mode, as set forth by Professor Wendy Williams, is essentially based upon two propositions: first, generalizations that are based entirely on a person's sex, regardless of where those generalizations come from, are not permissible; and second, even if a law is not based on a sex generalization, those wishing to uphold the law should carry the ''burden of justification,'' if the law has ''a disproportionately negative effect upon one sex.''[92] Although Professor Williams agrees that both the assimilationist model and the special treatment model[93] can be the basis of ''positive rights'' for women,[94] she asserts that assimilation is the best approach because ''the equal protection clause is unlikely to ever be interpreted to require equal treatment because an excluded class is different from the included class.''[95]

The purpose of this model is to prevent legislators from classifying on the basis of sex and instead force them to ''classify on the basis of the trait or function or behavior for which sex was used as a proxy.''[96] The ultimate objective is ''to get the law out of the business of reinforcing traditional, sex-based family roles.''[97] To achieve this objective, Professor Williams would define equality by using an androgynous prototype that ''requires sex neutral schemes that take into account the normal range of human characteristics—including pregnancy.''[98] She would also subject all sex-based classifications to strict judicial scrutiny.[99] Thus, Williams' assimilationist approach redefines equality by using an androgenous standard rather than a male or female standard.

Feminist critics of the assimilationist model define it as a model that ''treat[s] men and women as if they were interchangeable,'' thereby ''minimiz[ing] the significance of . . . [their] reproductive differences.''[100] Others characterize it as a model that recognizes ''no real differences between the sexes . . . that cannot be dismissed as illusory sex-stereotypes.''[101] Oddly enough, these critics appear to agree that the worst problem with the model is that it accepts ''maleness'' as the standard by which assimilation is

---

[92] Williams, *Equality's Riddle: Pregnancy and the Equal Treatment/Special Treatment Debate,* 13 N.Y.U. Rev. L. & Social Change 325, 329–330 (1984–85) (the latter proposition Williams refers to as the ''disparate effects theory'' which would ''permit . . . a challenge to neutral rules based on a male prototype,'' *id.* at 364).

[93] *See infra* at note 122 and accompanying text.

[94] Williams, *supra* note 92, at 375.

[95] *Id.* at 361 n.143.

[96] *Id.* at 329 (as examples of these ''traits,'' Professor Williams states that ''[s]strength, not maleness, would be the criterion for certain jobs; economic dependency, not femaleness, the criterion for alimony,'' *id.*).

[97] *Id.* at 352.

[98] *Id.* at 369.

[99] *Id.* at 363 n.144.

[100] Kay, *Models of Equality,* 1985 U. Ill. L. Rev. 39, 40 (1985) (hereinafter cited as Kay I).

[101] Krieger & Cooney, *The Miller-Wohl Controversy: Equal Treatment, Positive Action and the Meaning of Women's Equality,* 13 Golden Gate U. L. Rev. 513, 538 (1983).

to occur.[102] In so doing, the model becomes "incapable of defining sexual equality in the context of sex-specific conditions,"[103] such as reproduction.

Krieger and Cooney argue that this flaw in the assimilationist model "permits a denial of equality of effect to women who are either unwilling or unable to assimilate to . . . [the male] norm."[104] To Krieger and Cooney, the model does not go far enough. Although the assimilationist view would assure equal treatment to those similarly situated (i.e., all those who fit within the male prototype), it would not avoid a result similar to that reached in *Geduldig* where women are not similarly situated to men with respect to pregnancy. Professor Herma Kay levels the same criticism when she states that the model is "inadequate . . . for those few situations where the law must confront immutable sexual reproductive differences."[105]

Obviously, if the assimilationist model uses a male prototype, there is no escaping the Court's result in *Geduldig*. The androgenous prototype, however, is just as problematic. First, what exactly is androgyny? It is defined as "[h]aving the characteristics or nature of both male and female."[106] But, for the purposes of equal protection analysis, which characteristics are included in the androgenous prototype? Certainly Professor Williams would include pregnancy, but beyond that, she offers little guidance. Second, Professor Williams, like others noted below, is simply redefining the relevant equal protection classification. The Court defines the relevant equal protection classifications as men and women for the purposes of gender discrimination, but Williams would define the classification as androgenous people. This definition means that any legislative distinction drawn between men and women, however unsimilarly situated, would be subjected to strict judicial scrutiny.

B. The Episodic Approach

Professor Kay's episodic model is premised on the belief that "reproductive behavior is episodic and temporary."[107] Kay advocates an "episodic" approach because pregnancy will "never satisfy the comparability standard inherent in the . . . [assimilationist approach] for, by definition, there are no similarly situated pregnant men."[108] The episodic model draws a distinction based on the duration and effects of reproductive behavior. For the purposes of the episodic approach, reproductive behavior of females lasts nine months, while that of males "is quite brief in duration."[109] Also, the effects of reproductive behavior are more debilitating to a woman's opportunities than to a man's.[110] Episodic analysis "enable[s] the law to treat women differently than men during a limited period when their needs may be greater . . . as a way of ensuring that women will be equal to men with respect to their overall . . . opportunities."[111]

---

[102] *Id.* at 539; *see also* Law, *supra* note 91, at 968; L. Tribe, *American Constitutional Law* § 16–29, 1583 (1988).

[103] Krieger & Cooney, *supra* note 101, at 538.

[104] *Id.* at 539.

[105] Kay I, *supra* note 100, at 41.

[106] *Webster's Ninth New Collegiate Dictionary* 84 (1985).

[107] Kay, *Equality and Difference: The Case of Pregnancy,* 1 Berkeley Women's L.J. 1, 24 (1985) [hereinafter cited as Kay II].

[108] Kay I, *supra* note 100, at 81.

[109] Kay II, *supra* note 107, at 24.

[110] *Id.* at 26, 27.

[111] *Id.* at 34.

The purpose of this model is to "compensate[e] for biological reproductive sex differences that would otherwise handicap women and impede their realization of equal . . . opportunity."[112] In the context of *Geduldig*, episodic analysis requires that the "relevant reference group . . . [be] limited to those persons who have engaged in reproductive behavior while continuing to work."[113] This reclassification results in the conclusion that pregnant women are similarly situated with respect to men and nonpregnant women and are therefore entitled to the same benefits that accrue to the latter class.[114] According to Professor Kay, this result furthers the concept of equality of opportunity by ensuring that, just like men, women are not disadvantaged by engaging in reproductive behavior.[115] The same reasoning would obviously apply to a woman's desire to terminate her pregnancy.[116] A law restricting abortion would treat some individuals who had engaged in reproductive behavior differently from others who had done the same.

The thought of the Court declaring "persons who engage in reproductive behavior" a suspect or even quasi-suspect class is ridiculous. People who engage in reproductive behavior can hardly be considered a "discrete and insular minority" in the sense that Justice Stone employed that term in his famous *Caroline Products* footnote.[117] Nor would this classification be considered suspect since "it is not saddled with such disabilities, or subjected to such a history of purposeful unequal treatment, or relegated to such a position of political powerlessness as to command extraordinary protection from the majoritarian political process."[118] Finally, if strict scrutiny is not applicable to classifications based on mental retardation,[119] wealth[120] and age,[121] it is hard to imagine that the Court will set aside for special consideration those who engage in reproductive behavior.

Secondly, the episodic model confuses reproductive behavior with the results of that behavior. A pregnant woman is obviously not engaging in reproductive behavior for nine months in the sense that she is perpetually engaging in sex during the term of her pregnancy. Rather, the pregnancy is a possible result of her having engaged in reproductive behavior (i.e., having had intercourse). This is an important distinction because it means that Professor Kay defines the duration of a male's reproductive behavior to include only the act but defines the duration of a female's reproductive behavior to include both the act and a possible result.

It is not a necessary result of engaging in reproductive behavior that a woman becomes pregnant. Therefore, all women who engage in reproductive behavior are not similarly situated, some become pregnant while others do not. For the purposes of the Court's equal protection analysis, Professor Kay's reproductive behavior classification, in reality, leads to the same result that the *Geduldig* Court found: Persons who engaged

---

[112] *Id.* at 18.

[113] *Id.* at 30.

[114] This obviously includes the benefit of being free of burdens from which others in the group are free, such as pregnancy.

[115] *Id.* at 26.

[116] *Id.* at 23 n.125.

[117] 304 U.S. at 144 n.4

[118] San Antonio Indep. School Dist. v. Rodriguez, 411 U.S. 1, 28 (1973).

[119] *See Cleburne*, 473 U.S. 432.

[120] *See Rodriguez*, 411 U.S. 1.

[121] *See* Massachusetts Bd. of Retirement v. Murgia, 427 U.S. 307 (1976).

in reproductive behavior and happened to become pregnant versus persons who engaged in reproductive behavior and did not become pregnant. Thus, there would be no gender-based discrimination because an abortion restriction would apply only to those who happened to become pregnant and not to an entire gender as a class.

C. The Special Treatment Approach

The special treatment model attempts to redefine equal protection analysis by focusing on the "biological reproductive differences between men and women."[122] This model, like the episodic approach, rejects the assimilationist premise that "sex-based biological differences are wholly insignificant . . . [because] changes in social, cultural, and legal arrangements [can] not make [biological] differences disappear . . . [and] assimilation seems often to mean assimilation to a male norm."[123] The purpose of the special treatment approach is to point up the biological differences between men and women that "have been used to justify sex-based legal and cultural limitations on human potential that do not reflect any real difference between men and women and that enforce the inferiority of women and the dominance of men."[124]

Professor Sylvia Law, a strong advocate of the special treatment approach, is not shy about stating her divergence from the traditional constitutional concept of equality. "[T]he appropriate function of the law is not to enforce a general vision of what men and women are really like."[125] According to Law's version of the special treatment approach,

> laws governing reproductive biology should be scrutinized by courts to ensure that (1) the law has no significant impact in perpetuating either the oppression of women or culturally imposed sex-role constraints on individual freedom or (2) if the law has this impact, it is justified as the best means of serving a compelling state interest . . . [T]he state should bear the burden of justifying its rule in relation to either proposition.[126]

The test requires a determination of whether the law applies to reproductive biology and a determination of whether the law perpetuates the oppression of women. If it does oppress women, the law is subjected to strict scrutiny.[127] As one can easily see, this is a far more searching inquiry than the Court has ever applied under the guise of equal protection analysis.

In applying this test to abortion, one finds immediately that any restriction of the "right" to abort could conceivably oppress women. "By restricting access to abortion, the state necessarily denies the capacity of women as independent moral decision makers."[128] A law impinging on a woman's inability to get an abortion "dramatically impairs the woman's capacity for individual self determination, [and] imposes a crushing restraint on the heterosexual woman's capacity for sexual expression."[129] Thus it is

---

[122] Law, *supra* note 91, at 955.

[123] *Id.* at 966, 968.

[124] *Id.* at 969.

[125] *Id.*

[126] *Id.* at 1008–1009.

[127] *Id.* at 1013–1014.

[128] *Id.* at 1019.

[129] *Id.* at 1017, 1019.

clear that, under Professor Law's analysis, any law restricting abortion would be subjected to strict scrutiny. Implicit in this realization is the conclusion that any such law should be struck down because "such laws enforce the invasion of women's bodies."[130]

It is in this camp—special treatment—that Professor Lawrence Tribe would pitch his tent. Although Tribe would agree with some of Professor Kay's analysis, his approach, in the main, is similar to the work of Professor Law. Like Kay, Tribe would agree that "the proper comparison in *Geduldig* was . . . between female employees who had engaged in reproductive behavior and male employees who had done likewise."[131] Tribe also agrees that equality of opportunity should be the focus of equal protection analysis for laws dealing with pregnancy.[132] Tribe would agree with Law, however, that a woman's role in reproduction is special and therefore requires special treatment by the courts and the legislatures.[133]

Tribe bases his equal protection analysis on "an antisubjugation principle, which aims to break down legally created or legally reinforced systems of subordination that treat some people as second-class citizens."[134] Under this analysis, strict scrutiny would be applied to legislation that "given . . . [its] history, context, source, and effect, seem[s] most likely not only to perpetuate subordination but also to reflect a tradition of hostility toward a subjugated group, or a pattern of indifference to the interests of that group."[135] Given that "[a]bortion . . . involve[es] the intensely public question of the subordination of women to men through the exploitation of pregnancy,"[136] there exists a "constitutionally problematic subjugation of women in the law's indifference to the biological reality that sometimes requires women but never men to resort to abortion . . . to . . . retain control of their own bodies."[137] Thus with Tribe, a law restricting abortion would violate his antisubjugation principle because carrying a child to term subordinates women as a class.[138]

D. A Critique

Proponents of the special treatment approach simply cannot escape the fact that not all women are pregnant women. Even though virtually all women have the capacity to become pregnant at least during a period of their lives, it does not follow that laws that draw distinctions on the basis of reproductive biology discriminate on the basis of gender. Contrary to Professor Tribe's assertions, such distinctions do not affect the female gender as a whole but instead affect only those members of the gender that happen to be pregnant. Absent gender discrimination or a determination that pregnancy is a suspect classification, the Court would apply a rational basis test to abortion legislation, even though Professor Tribe might wish to apply strict scrutiny.

---

[130] *Id.* at 1017.

[131] Tribe, *supra* note 102, § 16-29 at 1584 (citing Kay II, *supra* note 107, at 30, 31, 35).

[132] *Id.* (citing Kay II, *supra* note 107, at 26).

[133] *Id.* § 16-29 at 1583 (quoting Law, *supra* note 91, at 1007).

[134] *Id.* § 16-21 at 1515.

[135] *Id.* § 16-21 at 1520.

[136] *Id.* § 15-10 at 1353.

[137] *Id.* § 15-15 at 1385.

[138] *See id.* § 15-10 at 1354 ("Even a woman who is not pregnant is inevitably affected by her knowledge of the power relationships thereby created.").

The special treatment approach is antithetical to traditional equal protection jurisprudence. The Court has a long history of ensuring that similarly situated persons are treated similarly.[139] Special treatment analysis admits that men and women are not similarly situated with respect to reproductive biology but then requires the legislature to either ignore these differences or enact laws that will compensate women as a class for those differences. Men and women are then not treated equally, as the Constitution requires, but rather women as a class are given more protection of the laws than similarly situated men in an effort to equalize the effects of pregnancy. Women would certainly benefit from the special treatment approach, just as the poor would benefit from a redistribution of wealth, but this benefit would come at the expense of the constitutional concept of equality under the laws.

Ultimately, the special treatment model, like the episodic approach, is really not a model of equality—in the sense of equal treatment—but instead, it is a "liberal ratchet"[140] to be used to reach what some believe are socially desirable results. Professor Kay cites Professor Ronald Dworkin for the proposition that the equal protection clause embodies two different types of rights: the right to equal treatment and the right to treatment as an equal.[141] The latter of these two rights Dworkin defines as "the right . . . to be treated with the same respect and concern as anyone else."[142] Dworkin further states that "the right to treatment as an equal is fundamental, and the right to equal treatment, derivative."[143] From this, "[e]quality can be seen as an individual right to equal treatment or as a social policy promoting equality of effect."[144] Thus, the argument is that some classes of people are entitled to treatment as equals even though they are not similarly situated with those with whom they are asserting equality.[145]

In further discussing the "right to be treated as an equal," Dworkin warns that "we must be careful not to overstate what . . . [the right to be treated as an equal] means."[146] "An individual's right to be treated as an equal means that his potential loss must be treated as a matter of concern, but that loss may nevertheless be outweighed by the gain to the community as a whole."[147] Assuming for the sake of argument that such a right exists,[148] it in no way follows that a law restricting abortion denies pregnant women equal treatment as Dworkin defines that concept. Clearly, using Dworkin's analysis, the gain to society of its continued existence through successive generations outweighs the temporary inconvenience to those women who become preg-

---

[139] See Royster, 412 U.S. at 415.

[140] See Bork, supra note 12, at 92 (Judge Bork uses this term in characterizing Justice Brennan's view of section 5 of the fourteenth amendment. In discussing Brennan's opinion in Katzenbach v. Morgan, 384 U.S. 641 (1966), Bork states that "Justice Brennan was forced into the position that the power to enforce [under section 5] was a liberal ratchet, it could go only in one direction.").

[141] R. Dworkin, Taking Rights Seriously 276–277 (1977). See also Kay I, supra note 100, at 87; Krieger & Cooney, supra note 101, at 553–554.

[142] Dworkin, supra note 141, at 227.

[143] Id. (Dworkin gives the following example that is also quoted in Krieger & Cooney, supra note 101: "If I have two children, and one is dying from a disease that is making the other uncomfortable, I do not show equal concern if I flip a coin to decide which should have the remaining dose of a drug.").

[144] Krieger & Cooney, supra note 101, at 554.

[145] This, in short, is the underlying argument of both the episodic approach and the special treatment model.

[146] Dworkin, supra note 141, at 227.

[147] Id.

[148] The author neither admits nor condones the existence of such a right.

nant. Thus, even Dworkin's analysis would place limits upon the concept of equality of results.

The Court has never interpreted the equal protection clause to require that statutory distinctions between similarly situated people achieve equal results among those people. Similarly, the Court has never held that people who are *not* similarly situated must be treated equally by a legislature, if the statutory classification is rational. Therefore, it is beyond reason to assert that the Court should require legislatures to ensure equal results among groups that are clearly and admittedly *not* similarly situated.[149]

In analyzing Professor Tribe's version of the special treatment approach, its extremely broad application is immediately apparent. The antisubjugation principle would invalidate all types of legislative classifications, not just those based on the biological differences between men and women. Classifications based on age, sex, wealth, mental retardation, gender, illegitimacy and alienage would all be subjected to strict judicial scrutiny. In fact, any group, or for that matter any individual, who could lay claim to somehow being "subjugated" by the government, could seek redress in the courts. Actual, perceivable differences between groups of people could no longer be taken into account by legislatures. Instead, legislators would draw distinctions uneasily, knowing that if a class is somehow subjugated by the distinction, the law would have to be narrowly tailored to meet a compelling governmental objective.

This result clearly violates a statement of the Court that Professor Tribe is fond of quoting: "Sometimes the grossest discrimination can lie in treating things that are different as though they were exactly alike."[150] The Court has long recognized and given deferential treatment to the prerogative of a legislature to draw distinctions between groups that are not similarly situated.[151] In *Tigner v. Texas*,[152] the Supreme Court through Justice Frankfurter stated that

> [t]he equality at which the equal protection clause aims is not a disembodied equality. The Fourteenth Amendment enjoins 'the equal protection of the laws,' and the laws are not abstract propositions. They do not relate to abstract units A, B, and C, but are expressions of policy arising out of specific difficulties, addressed to the attainment of specific ends by the use of specific remedies. The Constitution does not require things which are different in fact or opinion to be treated in law as though they were the same.[153]

Tribe's antisubjugation principle posits a "disembodied equality" that would completely curtail the legislatures' ability to draw necessary statutory distinctions between people who are not similarly situated.

---

[149] *See* Coleman, Roe v. Wade: *A Retrospective Look at a Judicial Oxymoron*, 29 St. Louis U.L.J. 7, 38 (1984) ("Equal treatment [sometimes] produced unequal results, but the results are essential to preserve individual rights for everyone.").

[150] Jenness v. Fortson, 403 U.S. 431, 442 (1971) (Tribe uses this quote to attack the assimilationist model, Tribe, *supra* note 102, at 1583, but it is just as applicable to the special treatment approach).

[151] *See, e.g.*, Bain Peanut Co. v. Pinson, 282 U.S. 499 (1931); Nashville, Chattanooga & St. Louis Railway v. Browning, 310 U.S. 362 (1940); Patsone v. Pennsylvania, 232 U.S. 138 (1914); Miller v. Wilson, 236 U.S. 373 (1915); Quaker City Cab Co. v. Pennsylvania, 277 U.S. 389 (1928).

[152] 310 U.S. 141 (1940).

[153] *Id.* at 147.

Professor Law's version of the special treatment approach is a similar attempt at redefining the traditional concept of equality and would therefore violate the same accepted norms of constitutional adjudication. The oppression standard, as applied to legislative classifications, would result in the same evil that the antisubjugation principle would propagate. In the context of gender discrimination alone, it refuses equal treatment for both sexes because it is obsessed with compensating pregnant women for their pregnancy. In short, Professor Law does not want equal protection of the laws; she wants the law to effectuate her personal concept of equality.

All of the above equal protection models have thus failed to endow pregnancy with the necessary attributes that would compel the Court to apply heightened scrutiny to a legislative restriction on abortion. Both the assimilationist view and the episodic approach would redefine the constitutionally relevant group so that pregnant women would be viewed as similarly situated with nonpregnant persons. These approaches are unavailing because the Court is just as unlikely to recognize androgyny as a classification as it is to find that people who engage in reproductive behavior are a suspect class. In admitting that men and women are not similarly situated with respect to reproductive biology, episodic analysis and the special treatment approach both fail to invoke heightened scrutiny. Equality of the laws simply cannot and should no be perverted to require an equality of results ensured by the government among persons who are not similarly situated.

V. The Fundamental Rights Analysis

A legislative classification that does not implicate a suspect or quasi-suspect class can still be subjected to strict judicial scrutiny if that classification impinges upon a fundamental right.[154] In the equal protection realm, the Supreme Court has recognized three such fundamental rights: the right to procreation,[155] the right to vote[156] and the right to travel.[157] In substantive due process adjudication, the Court has deemed several rights to be fundamental.[158] In *Synder v. Massachusetts*[159] the Court defined a fundamental right as a "principle of justice so rooted in the traditions and conscience of our people as to be ranked as fundamental."[160] In *Palko v. Connecticut*[161] the Court defined fundamental rights as "immunities that are valid as against the federal government by force of the specific pledges of particular amendments [that] have been found to be implicit in the concept of ordered liberty."[162]

---

[154] *See supra* note 64 and accompanying text.

[155] Skinner v. Oklahoma, 316 U.S. 535 (1942).

[156] Harper v. Virginia State Bd. of Elections, 383 U.S. 663 (1966).

[157] Shapiro v. Thompson, 394 U.S. 618 (1969).

[158] *See* Meyer v. Nebraska, 262 U.S. 390 (1923) (right of students to acquire knowledge); Pierce v. Society of the Sisters, 268 U.S. 510 (1925) (rights of childrearing); Griswold v. Connecticut, 381 U.S. 479 (1965) (married persons' right of privacy in the use of contraceptives); Eisenstadt v. Baird, 405 U.S. 438 (1972) (general right of privacy in the use of contraceptives); Roe v. Wade, 410 U.S. 113 (1973) (privacy in the right to an abortion); Moore v. East Cleveland, 431 U.S. 494 (1977) (rights of family relations); Zablocki v. Redhail, 434 U.S. 374 (1978) (right to marry); Youngberg v. Romeo, 457 U.S. 307 (1982) (limited rights of people with retardation).

[159] 291 U.S. 97 (1934).

[160] *Id.* at 105.

[161] 302 U.S. 319 (1937).

[162] *Id.* at 324–325.

The Supreme Court has applied both of these standards in an effort to determine whether there existed a fundamental right to engage in homosexual sodomy.[163] The *Bowers* Court made an inquiry as to the history of the asserted sodomy right and found that sodomy had been proscribed at common law, by the laws of the original 13 states and by all states as late as 1961.[164] In concluding that there was no fundamental right to engage in homosexual sodomy, Justice White warned that

> *[t]he court is most vulnerable and comes nearest to illegitimacy when it deals with judge-made constitutional law having little or no cognizable roots in the language or design of the Constitution . . . There should be, therefore, great resistance to expand the substantive reach of . . . [the fourteenth amendment], particularly if it requires redefining the category of rights deemed to be fundamental. Otherwise, the Judiciary necessarily takes to itself further authority to govern the country without express constitutional authority.*[165]

More recently, the Supreme Court was confronted with the question of defining the scope of a right that was asserted as fundamental.[166] *Michael H.* involved a man asserting paternal rights to a child, in the face of a statutory presumption that the child born to a married woman cohabiting with her husband was a child of the marriage.[167] The plurality defined the proposed right as the right of an individual "to have himself declared the natural father and thereby to obtain parental prerogatives . . . over a child born into a woman's existing marriage with another man."[168] Justice Scalia reached this definition by "refer[ing] to the most specific level [of generality] at which a relevant tradition protecting, or denying protection to, the asserted right can be identified."[169] *Bowers* and *Michael H.* both require that a proposed fundamental right be formulated in a concrete, fact-sensitive manner.[170] Once the proposed right is defined in this manner, it is subjected to the historical inquiry to determine its fundamentality. The purpose of this two-step analysis is to mitigate the danger of constitutionally illegitimate, result-oriented decisions. A narrow, fact-sensitive definition of the proposed fundamental right necessarily excludes other tangentially related, proposed rights that are not before the Court. The historical inquiry then separates those proposed rights that are embodied in constitutional precedent from other activities that have never been sanctioned by the constitution.

The *Roe* Court devoted some 20 pages of its opinion to a historical inquiry into abortion[171] and concluded that "at common law, at the time of the adoption of our Constitution, and throughout the major portion of the 19th century, abortion was viewed

---

[163] *See* Bowers v. Hardwick, 478 U.S. 186, 191–192 (1986).

[164] *Id.* at 192–193.

[165] *Id.* at 194–195.

[166] Michael H. v. Gerald D., 109 S. Ct. 2333 (1989).

[167] *Id.* at 2338–2339.

[168] *Id.* at 2343.

[169] *Id.* at 2344 n.6 (Scalia, J., and Rehnquist, C. J.) (O'Connor, and Kennedy, JJ., the other members of the plurality, did not join in this footnote, *id.* at 2346–47 [O'Connor and Kennedy, JJ., concurring in part]).

[170] *See generally* Bopp & Coleson, Webster *and the Future of Substantive Due Process*, 28 Duq. L. Rev. 271, 281–291 (1990).

[171] 410 U.S. at 129–149.

with less disfavor than under most American statutes currently in effect.''[172] As has been subsequently pointed out, the Court relied heavily on the work of individuals associated with the National Association for the Reform of Abortion Laws (NARAL) for its source material regarding the history of abortion.[173] Articles by Cyril Means Jr., NARAL's legal counsel, were cited six times, and a book by L. Lader, the founder and chairman of NARAL, was cited seven times in the *Roe* opinion.[174] As has been shown by subsequent research, the *Roe* Court's analysis was somewhat flawed by a reliance on biased source material.[175]

Professor Dellapenna surveyed seven centuries of Anglo-American history to scrutinize the relationship between the changes in abortion law and the changes in abortion technology.[176] In the period from A.D. 1200 to 1600 A.D., Dellapenna found ''little reference to abortion in either treatises or reported common law cases . . . [but] abortion after quickening clearly was a crime under cannon law.''[177] Since ''knowledge of gestational processes was extremely rudimentary'' at this time, there were obvious causation problems associated with proving that the accused abortionist killed the unborn child.[178] Thus, ''[the] royal courts . . . [were] reluctant to convict a person for murder for performing an abortion . . . [and] instead relegated the crime to the less rigorous penalties of the church courts.''[179]

It was at this time that the ecclesiastical courts drew the quickening distinction between homicidal abortions and others.[180] Dellapenna asserts that ''the existing technology only permitted protection after the child had been felt to quicken.''[181] Due to the limited technology, abortions at the time were extremely dangerous to the mother,[182] and given this danger, Dellapenna claims that ''there were probably not many abortions in England before 1600.''[183] Abortion prosecutions were rare during this period due to the scarcity of the crime and the fact that the abortion usually involved a felonious assault against the mother for which the abortionist could more easily forfeit his life.[184] During the 17th century, jurisdiction over abortion cases was transferred from the ecclesiastical courts to the common law courts.[185] Abortion after quickening was denounced

---

[172]*Id.* at 140.

[173]Dellapenna, *The History of Abortion: Technology, Morality, and Law,* 40 U. Pitt L. Rev. 359, 363–364 (1979).

[174]*Id.* at 364 n.23.

[175]*See* Dellapenna, *supra* note 173; Destro, *Abortion and the Constitution: The Need for a Life-Protective Amendment,* 63 Calif. L. Rev. 1250 (1975) (''The Court's uncritical acceptance of an advocate's interpretation of the common law only served to confuse the issues and to rest an important constitutional holding on an erroneous historical foundation.'' *Id.* at 1273).

[176]Dellapenna, *supra* note 173, at 365.

[177]*Id.* at 366, 368.

[178]*Id.* at 370 (''Given the very limited technology (both information and tools) available to perform abortions, the judges could not determine that the child was alive before the abortional act, or that the act caused the misdelivery,'' *id.* at 377).

[179]*Id.* at 371.

[180]*Id.* at 377.

[181]*Id.* at 378.

[182]*Id.* at 371 (abortions at this time were performed by either ''a physical beating, or a noxious potion'').

[183]*Id.* at 377.

[184]*Id.* at 379 (given the technology, the assault against the mother was obviously far easier to prove than the abortion, and since all felonies at early common law were capital offenses, it really made no difference for which crime the abortionist hung).

[185]*Id.* at 379, 382–383.

as "a great misdemeanor."[186] Since technology had not made appreciable changes, the common law courts were confronted with the same evidentiary problems regarding abortions that also plagued the ecclesiastical courts.[187] Thus, the common law came to recognize "abortion after quickening . . . [as] a great misprision"[188] and "as felonious homicide if the child was born alive, and thereafter died—if the death were clearly caused by the abortion."[189] Dellapenna attributes this "broadening" of abortion laws to the English Reformation and the decline of the ecclesiastical courts in favor of the common law courts.[190]

Abortion technology changed considerably during the late 18th century with the use of insertion techniques to induce labor.[191] In response to this extremely dangerous technology and in an effort to clarify the already existing common law, Parliament enacted Lord Ellenborough's Act in 1803.[192] This act as originally written "prohibited all abortions by drugs or poisons," and by 1837, Parliament had outlawed all abortions by whatever means and at any stage of pregnancy.[193] At this same time, similar statutory prohibitions were enacted in the United States. In 1821, the Connecticut legislature passed the first antiabortion statute in the United States, and likewise several states that did not enact statutes recognized abortion as a common law crime.[194] Other states followed, and by the end of the Civil War, abortion was outlawed in 26 of 36 states and 6 of 10 territories.[195] Rhode Island was the last state to outlaw abortion in 1986, thus making abortion "a crime in every state and the District of Columbia."[196]

Professor Dellapenna argues that the overriding purpose of these abortion statutes was to protect the unborn child and that laws prohibiting abortion reflected the current technological awareness of fetal development.[197] At the time of the first statutory prohibitions on abortion, the quickening distinction was still prevalent due to the limited state of the technology.[198] "[E]ven scientifically sophisticated people conceded that they

---

[186]*Id.* at 379 (citing 1 W. Blackstone, *Commentaries* 129–30 [1765]; 4 Blackstone, *Commentaries* 198 [1769]; E. Coke, *Third Institute* 50–51 [1644]; M. Hale, *History of the Pleas of the Crown* 433 [1736]; W. Hawkins, *Treatise of the Pleas of the Crown* 80 [1716]) (other citations omitted);

> [T]he reticence of some early common law writers to classify abortion as a felony is traceable to two factors having little relevance to 20th century constitutional adjudication: (1) a lack of knowledge as to the nature of prenatal development; and (2) problems of proof, including an inability to ascertain with any degree of certainty whether or not the abortion was the cause of the child's death.

Destro, *supra* note 175, at 1270.

[187]Dellapenna, *supra* note 173, at 386–387.
[188]*Id.* at 381.
[189]*Id.* at 382.
[190]*Id.* at 382–383.
[191]*Id.* at 394 (Dellapenna refers to this technology as "premature" in the sense that "related technologies necessary to make it safe (control of infections and shock) did not yet exist." *Id.* at 395).
[192]*Id.* at 389.
[193]*Id.* at 389, 393.
[194]*Id.* at 389, 389 n.193.
[195]*Id.* at 389 ("Eight of the ten most populous states had prohibited abortions by 1860 . . . In 1850 about 75% of the United States population lived in states banning abortions, and the figure exceeded 85% by 1860." *Id.* at n.195).
[196]*Id.* at 389–390.
[197]*Id.* at 402–403.
[198]*Id.* at 402.

could not prove that a living thing had been killed before quickening.''[199] Thus early statutes such as Lord Ellenborough's Act imposed harsher penalties for abortions performed after quickening than for abortions performed prior to quickening, when it was not entirely certain that the fetus was in fact alive.[200]

Technology changed drastically in 1827 with the discovery of the mammalian ovum and with the subsequent fertilization of frogs' eggs in 1830.[201] ''These discoveries . . . provided support for the theory that a new being came into existence with the fertilization of the ovum, and that this being thereafter developed without any change of its essential substance.''[202] This change in technology coupled with an expressed desire to protect the unborn child, led to ''[a]bortion . . . [being] made uniformly criminal at any stage of pregnancy.''[203] There were, however, still problems proving that the abortion had actually caused the death of the unborn child. This was particularly true in the early stages of pregnancy due to the still-limited knowledge of gestational processes.[204] This explains why, in the United States, abortion was never penalized as harshly as were other homicides.[205]

Given the long history of judicial and statutory prohibitions on abortion, it becomes obvious that the *Roe* Court reached erroneous conclusions regarding the ''right to abortion.'' Abortion is not and can never be considered a fundamental right in the sense that the Court has defined that term. Abortion is clearly not so deeply rooted in our nation's conscience as to be considered fundamental, nor has it ever been considered implicit in the concept of ordered liberty. Although proponents of abortion would define the right more broadly to save it from its sordid past, these attempts are unavailing since a broadly defined right necessarily includes activities that have absolutely no history of being rooted in anyone's conscience.

Professor Tribe writes about the antisubjugation principle,[206] a right of ''individual autonomy''[207] and ''a right[] whose impairment serves to disempower women.''[208] Others mention the right to choose, a right to ''control reproductive capacity''[209] and a right to ''bodily integrity.''[210] But clearly all of these formulations of proposed rights include either activities by individuals or restraints on the government that, historically, have never been sanctioned by the American people. A right to individual autonomy or a right of individual choice could conceivably include a right to incest, adultery, polygamy or even a right to murder. Similarly, restricting the government from taking actions that might subjugate or disempower certain people could conceivably keep government from enacting any type of legislative classifications and could also do away with welfare programs, military conscription and even taxes. Thus, the Court's approach to defining

---

[199] *Id.* at 403.

[200] *Id.*

[201] *Id.* at 404.

[202] *Id.* at 404.

[203] *Id.* at 404 (''Ten states distinguished an abortion before quickening from one performed after quickening by imposing a different punishment for each stage,'' *id.* at 404–405.)

[204] *Id.* at 405 (''One could rarely prove beyond a reasonable doubt that the abortion was the cause of death, even if one could prove the abortion,'' *id.* at 406.)

[205] *Id.* at 405.

[206] See Tribe, *supra* note 102, § 16-21 at 1515.

[207] *See id.* § 15-10 at 1352.

[208] *See id.* § 16-33 at 1613.

[209] *See* Kay II, *supra* note 107, at 23 n.125.

[210] *See* Krieger & Cooney, *supra* note 101, at 561.

proposed fundamental rights[211] as employed in *Bowers* and *Michael H.* is best suited to the broad ranging effects of declaring an activity fundamental.

In summary, a statutory restriction on abortion would not be subjected to strict or heightened scrutiny under equal protection analysis because (1) pregnant women are not a suspect class, and the sexes are not similarly situated with respect to pregnancy and (2) abortion is not a fundamental right under an appropriate interpretation of the Constitution. A law restricting abortion would therefore only have to be rationally related to a legitimate state interest. Obviously, that interest is the protection of the life of the unborn child.[212]

VI. Conclusion

This article has explored various attempts to ground the "right to abortion" in the equal protection clause of the fourteenth amendment. All of these "alternative equal protection models" are unavailing because they fail to get past the basic fact that men and women are simply not similarly situated with respect to pregnancy. Furthermore, as subsequent scholarship has shown, there is no such thing as a fundamental right to abortion. Thus, given a legitimate state interest in the unborn child, the "right to abortion" would not survive either prong of the equal protection analysis.

---

[211] *See supra* note 166 and accompanying text.

[212] Even under *Roe's* progeny, the Court recognized a state's legitimate interest in protecting "the potential life of the fetus." Maher v. Roe, 4322 U.S. 464, 478 (1977); Harris v. McRae, 448 U.S. 297 (1980). A majority of the current Court has now declared that this interest is "compelling" and exists throughout pregnancy. *See* Bopp & Coleson, *supra* note 31, at 162–64.

The author compares both state laws and Supreme Court cases that concern themselves with the minor's right to an abortion. He carefully examines questions such as parental permission and parental notification. Ironically, the article begins with an episode from the TV show "Make Room for Daddy." The article concludes that abortion *access* is an issue on its way down into the states, and the poor and the young—the politically weak—are not likely to fare well when at the mercy of state legislatures.

6 · "Hello, Dad. This is your daughter. Can I get an abortion?": An Essay on the Minor's Right to a Confidential Abortion

Michael J. Malinowski, J.D.[*]

—1954—

The episode, entitled "Terry Grows Up," is from "Make Room for Daddy."[1] Rusty enters the apartment first, puts his books down and skips around the living room repeating, "Terry's in love, Terry's in love. . . ." In floats Terry with her eyes open wide, guiding her thoughts as if they were a kite trying to break away and escape into the heavens. Danny and Margaret walk into the room.

DANNY: What's going on here?
MARGARET (with concern): Terry—what? Rusty, Rusty be quiet. Rusty, shhhh. Honey, what is it? What's the matter?
TERRY: Oh, mommy. The most wonderful thing in the whole world just happened.
RUSTY: Terry's in *loove*.
DANNY: Terry's in *loove*? With *whoom*?
(laugh track/audience)

---

[*]B.A., Tufts University, *summa cum laude*, 1987; J.D. Yale Law School, 1991. I would like to thank Professor Mari Matsuda. It was through my experience editing for Professor Matsuda that I felt the full power of legal storytelling—a technique that has taught me so much, and now, I hope, enables me to communicate with and teach others. A special thanks to Diane Orentlicher who, on the eve of publication, improved the accuracy of my words. I would also like to thank Dr. Butler, Colleen Carey, Mark Malinowski, Theresa Rohr, Susan Schwartz, and Douglas Tookey—the family, friends, editors, and Fifth Circuit colleagues who shared their talent and purified my writing.
[1]The following was interpreted and transcribed from videotape by the author.

MARGARET: Terry, come on. Don't just stand there like a zombie. Tell us what happened.

TERRY: Of all the boys in the whole school, Johnny Lane asked *me* to go to the big annual dance. *Me*.

*   *   *

It is several minutes later, and Terry and Margaret are now sitting on the sofa. Danny is sitting across from them in an arm chair, listening as Terry gives Margaret all the details.

TERRY: All of a sudden we see Johnny Lane. And *I said,* "I bet he is going to take Priscilla Myers." And *Gertrude said,* "Ya, she always gets all the boys."

MARGARET: Wait a minute, wait a minute. What's the matter with you? Why should Priscilla Myers get all the best boys?

TERRY: Well, uh, (matter-of-factly) she goes after them.

DANNY: "She goes out after them"—What kind of talk is that?

TERRY (quickly): Well, you know. Uh, she makes *eyes* at them. And she's always looking. Well she laughs at everything they say. You know, she butters them up.

RUSTY: Is that how Mom got you?

(laugh track/audience)

DANNY (rising out of the chair): I don't understand this language. Are these *my* children talking? How are you bringing them up Kitten?

MARGARET (rising off the sofa to confront Danny): Something wrong with the way I'm bringing them up?

DANNY: Well, you listening? What is that—"girls looking at the boys . . . they butter them up"? What kind of generation is this? The battle of the sexes starts at 12?

MARGARET: *Starts?* Where have you been? At 12 it just comes out into the open.

(laugh track/audience)

Introduction

Times have changed. A lot more is now out in the open: Our children no longer live in a quiet, simple world—a world that blocks its children's ears and protects them from adult realities like sex and rape, keeping them children until they and their parents are ready. Although honesty is responsible for some of this change,[2] it does not account for all of it:

> *Eight years ago, according to the National Survey of Family Growth,*
> *only 19 percent of girls under the age of 15 were sexually experienced;*
> *today that number is nearly 50 percent higher, and some seven of 10*
> *teenagers have had sex by age 18. Five years ago the teenage birth rate*

---

[2] For example, although it is likely that many of our children were being victimized while our society was watching "Make Room for Daddy," we pretended incest did not exist. Ignorance was bliss—except for the victims. *See* Note, *Easing Access to the Courts for Incest Victims: Toward an Equitable Application of the Delayed Discovery Rule,* 100 Yale L.J. 2185, 2188 (1991) ("Yet despite its prevalence, until the late 1970s incest was rarely discussed, and the public was largely ignorant of the extent of the problem.").

was declining; now 9 percent of American girls become mothers before turning 18, and another 9 percent have abortions.[3]

The result? More than one million minors will become pregnant this year, just over 400,000 will obtain abortions, and nearly 470,000 will give birth.[4] It should come as no surprise that 84% of all these pregnancies and 92% of premarital teenage pregnancies are unintended.[5]

The numbers are frightening, especially to people who have lived in both worlds— children in the world of "Make Room for Daddy" who are today's parents. This essay is about our societal reaction to teenage pregnancy and the rights of minors to choose abortion; it is about who among us decides questions regarding abortion access, and it is about our decisions—what influences them and their impact on our lives, especially their impact on the lives of minors. It is also about what we as a society should consider before we make these decisions. Finally, it is an expression of my position on abortion: Although I am receptive to many of the moral and religious arguments against abortion and generally equate abortion with societal failure, I also believe that efforts (specifically, those fed with talk of respect for human life) to legislate away access to abortion are the products of misconception—that is, misconceptions about why our adolescents are getting pregnant, about the children born to them, and about the effects of parental involvement laws on adolescents and adolescent promiscuity.

This essay begins with a brief primer on abortion access. Its purpose is to introduce you to the decision tree growing out of this issue and to situate the abortion rights of minors in relation to the broader rights of adult women. As will be discussed below,

---

[3] Freeman, *Risky Business: One Day's Look at the Pleasures and Pressures of Sex at an Early Age,* Time, Nov. 5, 1990, at 50 (NEXIS, Magazines source file). *See* Henshaw, Koonin, & Smith, *Characteristics of U.S. Women Having Abortions, 1987,* 23 Fam. Plan. Persp. 75, 79 (1991) [hereinafter *Characteristics*] ("The abortion rate for teenagers aged 15–19 rose during the 1970s . . . but remained stable after 1980 at 43 to 44 abortions per 1,000 women (Table 4)."); Hofferth, Kahn, & Baldwin, *Premarital Sexual Activity Among U.S. Teenage Women Over the Past Three Decades,* 19 Fam. Plan. Persp. 46 (1987). For an explanation as to why today's teens are more sexually active, *see infra* note 138; *see generally* Comment, *Risking the Future: A Symposium On the National Academy of Sciences Report on Teenage Pregnancy,* 19 Fam. Plan. Persp. 119 (1987). Many attribute this increase in teen sexual activity to an increase in consumption of alcohol and drugs. For a discussion of the overt relationship over time of early substance use and early sexual activity, see Mott & Haurin, *Linkages Between Sexual Activity and Alcohol and Drug Use Among American Adolescents,* 20 Fam. Plan. Persp. 128 (1988).

[4] Comment, *supra* note 3, at 119; *see also Children's Defense Fund, A Children's Defense Budget FY '89* 165; Henshaw & Van Vort, *Teenage Abortion, Birth and Pregnancy Statistics,* 21 Fam. Plan. Persp. 85 (1989); Hewitt, Freeman, Nelson, & Shaw, *Mortal Choices at a Tender Age,* Time, July 23, 1990, at 30 (NEXIS, Magazines source file) [hereinafter Hewitt & Freeman] ("In 1987, the most recent year for which there are statistics, there were roughly 1,015,000 teenage pregnancies in the U.S., of which 407,000 ended in abortion."). And consider how the United States rates in the "developed world":

> In fact, the United States leads the developed world with the highest rates of teen pregnancies, abortions and births. Every 67 seconds a teenager has a baby in the United States. Every day, 28 girls under age 15 give birth to their first child. Fifteen 16-year-olds give birth to their second. Every day 500 school-age teens have abortions.

Foley, *Mothers Before Their Time: The Global Problem of Teen Pregnancy,* Calypso Log, April 1991, at 17.

[5] *Teenage Pregnancy in Industrialized Countries: A Study Sponsored By the Alan Guttmacher Institute* 40 (1986).

the abortion rights of minors were defined later than the abortion rights of adults and have never fully left state legislatures.

The second part of this essay is a closer look at the Supreme Court's abortion decisions. After a brief discussion of decisions ensuring the abortion rights of adult women—especially *Roe*,[6] which conceptualized the privacy right that undergirds the Court's abortion decisions—I analyze the minors' case law, emphasizing the implications that flow from the Court's very recent *Hodgson*[7] and *Ohio*[8] decisions. Part III is a fuller analysis of these implications. It suggests that the entire abortion issue is descending back down into the states and that this change will have an especially detrimental effect on the abortion rights of minors.

Part IV, a collection of stories about minors and abortions, introduces you to those affected by parental involvement laws; it is about the reality of these laws. Part V pulls this scrapbook of stories—letters, a magazine article, trial testimony, bits of narrative prose, and a book excerpt—together by reconsidering them in the light of their unifying theme. In response to these stories and the laws that generate them, Part VI is about what we *should* consider before accepting and drafting laws that limit our minors' access to abortion.

I. Who Decides and the Decisions that Have Been Made

Although the right of minors to choose abortion was not explicitly defined until *Bellotti v. Baird*,[9] *Roe*[10] has become synonymous with the right of all women to choose the option of abortion.[11] The reason is that *Roe* conceptualized reproduction as the product of personal choice—as decisionmaking snugly cloaked and protected within the right to privacy guaranteed under the fourteenth amendment.[12] It follows that adult women have

---

[6] Roe v. Wade, 410 U.S. 113, 93 S. Ct. 705 (1973). *Roe* is discussed *infra* at Part II.A.

[7] Hodgson v. Minnesota, 110 S. Ct. 2926 (1990). *Hodgson* is discussed *infra* at Part II.B.6.

[8] Ohio v. Akron Center for Reproductive Health, 110 S. Ct. 2972 (1990). *Ohio* is discussed *infra* at Part II.B.5.

[9] 443 U.S. 622, 99 S. Ct. 3035 (1979) [hereinafter *Bellotti II*]. *Bellotti II* is discussed *infra* at Part II.B.2.

[10] Roe v. Wade, 410 U.S. 113, 93 S. Ct. 705 (1973). The story of Norma McCorvey (alias Jane Roe) is told in *The Choices We Made* 137–43 (1991) [hereinafter *Choices*]. *Roe's* companion case, Doe v. Bolton, 410 U.S. 179 (1973), has slipped into *Roe's* shadow. In that case, the Court struck down a Georgia abortion law and reiterated many of the principles we have come to attribute to *Roe*.

[11] *Roe* actually *returned* the practice of legal abortion to our society. With the exception of some 50 years preceding *Roe*, our society has always had legal abortion:

> At that time—the 1920s—abortion had only relatively recently become illegal throughout the United States. In fact, abortions prior to the point of "quickening"—that is, when the pregnant woman first feels fetal movement, generally around eighteen to twenty weeks— were permitted by traditional common law until the middle of the 1880s. But by 1900, following stepped-up pressure by the medical profession to drive charlatans and competitors out of business and gain greater control over medical care, every state in the country had outlawed abortion.

Choices, supra note 10, at xxii.

[12] Many, including my former colleague Adrienne Davis, value *Roe* for what it accomplished but have little respect for the legal analysis undergirding the opinion. In Adrienne's words, "The politics surrounding the issue demanded that the right initially be prescribed by the Court. But, now that the right has been realized and women have come to expect it, the issue should be returned to our legislatures." Informal conversation

the right to choose abortion because the Supreme Court has so decided.[13] Women who are minors share this right, but the Court has allowed state legislatures to restrict their version of it.[14]

The United States Congress could decide our abortion questions.[15] In fact, *Roe* and *Bellotti II* are very much the product of Congress' silence: In the absence of a congressional response, state legislatures—namely Texas and Massachusetts—decided for themselves, and challenges to their decisions are what prodded the Court to deliver *Roe*.[16] Although there have been some grumblings within Congress on this issue, Congress as a body has remained silent.[17]

Nearly two decades have passed since the Court made its *Roe* decision. The faces and ideologies of those sitting on the bench—a bench that has supported *Roe* for some 18 years—have changed, as has our society. Ironically, although our society has grown more open and sexually permissive,[18] our Court has become more conservative—a trend that is likely to continue.[19] The Court has already begun to back away from providing the access to abortion established in *Roe*. I refer you to *Webster v. Reproductive Health*

---

in Yale Law Journal lounge (May 10, 1991). According to Professor Stephen Carter, *Roe* is not a logical outgrowth of the Court's privacy decisions—in particular, it is not an outgrowth of Griswold v. Connecticut, 381 U.S. 479, 85 S. Ct. 1678 (1965). Carter, Stephen L., Book Review, 100 Yale L.J. 2747 (1991) (review of L. Tribe, *infra* note 27 [1991]); *see also* Ely, *The Wages of Crying Wolf: A Comment on* Roe v. Wade, 82 Yale L.J. 920 (1973) (decision perceived as not being constitutional law "in any recognizable sense."); *The Most-Cited Articles from* The Yale Law Journal, 100 Yale L.J. 1449, 1474 (F. Shapiro ed. 1991) (commentary by John Hart Ely) ("[W]riting a convincing criticism of *Roe v. Wade* was hardly an assignment requiring a rocket scientist. Merely a kamikaze pilot."). For those who wish to defend *Roe,* Professor Carter points to the equality model as surer ground upon which to fight: "Surely the pro-choice advocate can better defend *Roe* on the model of equality, writing privacy out of the case altogether and challenging abortion restrictions as sex discrimination." Book Review, *supra,* at 2754 (citation omitted). Professor MacKinnon has already made this argument. *See* C. MacKinnon, *Privacy v. Equality: Beyond* Roe v. Wade, in *Feminism Unmodified: Discourses on Life and Law* 93–102 (1987). [hereinafter Feminism Unmodified].

[13] *See infra* Part II.A.

[14] *See infra* Part II.B.

[15] Webster v. Reproductive Health Servs., 492 U.S. 490, 109 S. Ct. 3040 (1989), discussed *infra* Part II.A, and its Rust v. Sullivan, (1991) 111 S. Ct. 1759 progeny, discussed *infra* note 31, have triggered congressional efforts such as the Freedom of Choice Act, which would prohibit all states from interfering with a woman's right to decide whether or not to have an abortion. *See* Birnbaum, *House Fails to Override Veto on Abortion,* Wall Street Journal, Nov. 20, 1991, at A18 (discussing failure of House to override President Bush's veto of bill that would have allowed federally-financed health clinics to counsel pregnant women about abortion); Hall, *Abortion Fight Shifts Gears,* USA Today, Apr. 30, 1991, at 3A (NEXIS, Major Papers source file) ("abortion rights supporters are pinning their hopes on the federal Freedom of Choice Act, a 13-line bill that says states 'may not restrict the right of a woman to choose to terminate a pregnancy before fetal viability . . . .' "); *House Panel OKs Bill on Right to Abortion,* Los Angeles Times, Oct. 5, 1990, at A24, col. 4 (NEXIS, Major Papers source file) ("A House subcommittee approved a bill Thursday that would put into federal law a woman's right to an abortion, as ruled on the Supreme Court's Roe vs. Wade decision."). Passage of such an act is not likely, for "the Congress is split on the issue of choice, with the House of Representative [sic] opposed to keeping abortion legal and the Senate supportive of abortion as a legal option." NARAL Foundation, *Who Decides?: A State-by-State Review of Abortion Rights* viii (1991) [hereinafter *Who Decides?*]; *see id.* at 171–77 for a discussion of abortion positions within the Bush Administration and a summary of proposed federal legislation; *see also* Matlack, *Abortion Wars,* Nat'l J., Mar. 16, 1991 (NEXIS, Magazines source file):

But while abortion-rights leaders talk bravely about federal legislation they are promoting to guarantee the right to abortion, most admit privately that chances of enactment are virtually nil with an anti-abortion President in the White House. . . . In this lobbyist's view,

Services, a decision the court handed down in 1989.[20] In *Webster,* the Court trimmed the edges of *Roe* by, among other things, adding two types of abortion restrictions to the restrictions states were already permitted to enforce: (1) prohibitions on the use of public facilities and the involvement of public employees in the performance of abortions and (2) mandatory testing for viability after a specified point in pregnancy were added to restrictions on (3) minors' access to abortion and (4) public funding.[21] And since *Webster,* two faces have changed (Justice Souter is now sitting in the seat once occupied by Justice Brennan and Justice Thomas has taken Justice Marshall's).[22]

If the Court does back further away from the abortion question (or turns its back to it altogether by shredding *Roe*[23]) and Congress maintains its silence—or if Congress generates legislation but the President vetoes that decision and Congress does not have the two-thirds vote of legislators elected in each house needed to override the President—the abortion rights of all women will be dangled within the reach of state legislatures. For some, this is simply returning the issue to where it belongs;[24] others flash back to a pre-*Roe* time and point out that these are the palms that were slapped by *Roe.*

---

it would be better to keep the bill alive in committee as a rallying point for the movement— and a magnet for donations—than to press for a doomed-to-fail showdown.

It should also be noted that, even when facing a conservative challenge in the February 1992 New Hampshire primary from Patrick J. Buchanan, President Bush recently anchored his position on abortion way over to the right:

According to the White House, Mr. Bush opposes abortions except "when the life of the mother is threatened or there is rape or incest." He supports a constitutional amendment that would reverse the Roe v. Wade ruling as well as an amendment to the Constitution that would outlaw abortion, with those same exceptions.

Rosenthal, *Bush and Republican Leaders Take Firm Anti-Abortion Stand,* N.Y. Times, Jan. 23, 1992, at A4.

[16] *See infra* Parts II.A and II.B.2.

[17] *See supra* note 15.

[18] *See supra* notes 2–5 and accompanying text.

[19] *See infra* notes 65–69 and accompanying text.

[20] 492 U.S. 490, 109 S. Ct. 3040 (1989). *Webster* is discussed *infra* Part II.A.

[21] *See infra* Part II.A. In Rust v. Sullivan, 111 S. Ct. 1759 (1991), the Court proceeded along the direction taken in *Webster. See infra* note 31.

[22] *See infra* note 65 and accompanying text regarding Justice Souter. Despite the nationally televised testimony of Professor Anita Hill and her graphic description of sexual harassment, not to mention the opposition of the NAACP, Clarence Thomas was confirmed by the United States Senate during the early evening of October 15, 1991. The vote was 52 to 48. *See* Benedicts, *Confirmation Conversion?: Thomas Backs Away from Former Stands; Democrats Question Process,* A.B.J. J. 18, 20, 21 (Nov. 1991) (tracing shifts and contradictions in Justice Thomas' positions); Berke, *Women Accusing Democrats of Betrayal,* N.Y. Times, Oct. 17, 1991, at A1, A12; Brill, *Where Have All Our Leaders Gone?,* Am. Law. 5, 74 (Nov. 1991); Robinson, *Surprises Stir Unease in Thomas Supporters,* Boston Sun. Globe, July 14, 1991, at A1; Rosenbaum, *Selection Process for Court Under Attack on All Sides,* N.Y. Times, Oct. 17, 1991, at A12; Suro, *Hill Sees Justice in Testifying in Senate Hearing on Thomas,* N.Y. Times, Oct. 17, 1991, at A12; Taylor, *What's Really Wrong with the Way We Choose Supreme Court Justices,* Am. Law. 5, 74, 76–78 (Nov. 1991) ("I, for one, learned that Thomas is not as sharp, nor as candid, and not as courageous as I had assumed him to be. And not good enough for the Supreme Court, even assuming that he *was* the victim of an outrageously false claim of sexual harassment.") (offering lists of nation's top legal minds based on interviews with some 50 law professors, practitioners, and judges); *see also infra* note 66.

[23] *See* D. Meyers, *The Human Body and the Law* 43–45 (2d ed. 1990) (addresses how *Webster* attacks *Roe* and implications that follow). The Court has agreed to decide the constitutionality of Pennsylvania's restric-

As will be discussed below, the right of minors to choose abortion has never been fully out of the reach of state legislatures; the implication is that further delegation of the abortion question will drop the abortion rights of minors squarely into their hands.[25] If these legislatures decide to take away abortion access—or, in the case of minors, further restrict abortion access—state courts may step in to protect that right under their state constitutions.[26] However, in comparison with our shared Constitution, state constitutions are more amenable.[27] State legislatures may constitutionalize decisions that limit abortion access.

II. A Closer Look at the Court's Abortion Decisions

A. The Adult Woman's Right to Choose

> *1. A state criminal abortion statute of the current Texas type, that excepts from criminality only a* life-saving *procedure on behalf of the mother,*

---

tive abortion law—the post-Justice Marshall Court's first opportunity to reconsider *Roe. See* Casey v. Planned Parenthood of Southeastern Pennsylvania, 947 F. 2d 682 (3d Cir. 1991), *cert. granted*, 112 S. Ct. 932 (1992); *See also* Greenhouse, *High Court Takes Pennsylvania Case on Abortion Right*, N.Y. Times, Jan. 22, 1992, at A1, A10; Hinds, *Appeals Court Upholds Limits for Abortions*, N.Y. Times, Oct. 22, 1991, at A1, A6. The Pennsylvania statute, one of the strictest in the nation, has provisions

- requiring minors to obtain the consent of either one parent or a judge before obtaining an abortion (the United States Court of Appeals for the Third Circuit upheld this provision);
- requiring married women who seek to exercise the abortion option to notify their spouse (the Third Circuit found this provision unconstitutional);
- requiring doctors to inform women about abortion alternatives, the risks associated with abortion, and the probable gestation of the fetus (the Third Circuit upheld this provision);
- requiring women to wait 24 hours after obtaining the above information before undergoing an abortion (the Third Circuit upheld this provision); and
- requiring abortion providers to file confidential reports on each abortion performed with the state health department and requiring health clinics receiving public funds to file similar reports detailing the number of abortions performed (the Third Circuit also upheld this provision).

A decision is expected this summer, and it is highly possible that, having spent last summer and fall as the subject of political press, the Court will delay the execution of *Roe* until after the 1992 presidential election. *See* Barrett, *Justices Agree to Rule on Abortion Law in Pennsylvania, but May Sidestep Roe*, Wall S. J. Jan. 22, 1992, at A4 ("[I]n an order issued yesterday, the Supreme Court indicated that it might not address the basic question of whether to overturn *Roe* . . . . The court instructed the parties in the Pennsylvania case to limit their arguments to the constitutionality of specific provisions of the state's law."). Nevertheless, more opportunities to overturn *Roe* are soon to follow: Louisiana, Utah, and Guam have enacted bans on abortion, and the United States Court of Appeals for the Fifth Circuit heard arguments on the constitutionality of Louisiana's abortion law in February 1992 and is expected to issue a decision shortly. *See* Sojourner v. Buddy Roemer, No. 91-3677 (5th Cir. briefs filed Oct. 1991).

[24] *See supra* note 12.

[25] *See infra* Part III.

[26] In fact, the Supreme Court of Florida ruled that a law prohibiting minors from obtaining an abortion without parental consent violated the right to privacy guaranteed by the Florida Constitution. *See In re T.W.*, 551 So.2d 1186, 1190 (Fla. 1989) (striking statute down under Florida law, noting "Florida is unusual in that it is one of at least four states having its own express constitutional provision guaranteeing an independent right to privacy . . . ."); *id.* at 1194 ("The challenged statute fails because it intrudes upon the privacy of the pregnant minor from conception to birth."). While *Roe* stands, we can also expect federal courts to

without regard to pregnancy stage and without recognition of the other interests involved, is violative of the Due Process Clause of the Fourteenth Amendment.

(a) For the stage prior to approximately the end of the first trimester, the abortion decision and its effectuation must be left to the medical judgment of the pregnant woman's attending physician.

(b) For the stage subsequent to approximately the end of the first trimester, the State, in promoting its interest in the health of the mother, may, if it chooses, regulate the abortion procedure in ways that are reasonably related to maternal health.

(c) For the stage subsequent to viability, the State in promoting its interest in the potentiality of human life may, if it chooses, regulate, and even proscribe, abortion except where it is necessary, in appropriate medical judgment, for the preservation of the life or health of the mother.
2. The State may define the term "physician," as it has been employed in the preceding paragraphs of this Part XI of this opinion, to mean only a physician currently licensed by the State, and may proscribe any abortion by a person who is not a physician as so defined.[28]

This is the capsule summary of *Roe*'s holding.[29] To make the Court's holding digestible, let me now attempt to dilute it with non-attorney verbiage: The Court held that the Texas criminal abortion law being challenged was unconstitutional—that it violated a woman's constitutional right to privacy guaranteed by the fourteenth amendment to the Constitution.[30] According to *Roe*, the right to choose abortion is a funda-

---

do their part. *See* Whitman, *Abortion Rights are Intact—so Far*, U.S. News & World Rep., Sept. 24, 1990, at 52 (NEXIS, Magazines source file):

> In fact, a U.S. News survey of the 41 abortion-related rulings by federal judges in the 14 months since *Webster* shows the decision plainly failed to stop women from having abortions. To date, U.S. district and appellate judges—many appointed by Ronald Reagan—have proved the main hurdle to states implementing stricter abortion laws.

[27] Amending the Constitution has lately proved virtually impossible, even for such broadly popular amendments as those that would guarantee equality for women or forbid desecration of the American flag. *See* Kaplan & Cerio, *Tinkering With the Constitution*, Newsweek, June 25, 1990, at 18 (NEXIS, Magazines source file): "Of the 10,000 proposals in its historical suggestion box, a mere 33 have been sent along to the states for ratification. (The most recent cases were the Equal Rights Amendment and an amendment giving the District of Columbia federal voting representation, both of which fell short of adoption in the 1980s)." Professor Tribe mentions the possibility of realizing an amendment without congressional approval through a constitutional convention: "Article V provides the method: A constitutional convention for the purpose of proposing amendments for ratification by the states *must* be called by the Congress upon the application of two-thirds of the state legislatures—the legislatures of thirty-four of our fifty states." L. Tribe, *Abortion: The Clash of Absolutes* 151 (1990).

[28] *Roe*, 410 U.S. at 165–65, 93 S. Ct. at 732–33.

[29] A more eloquent passage from the opinion reads that the "right of privacy, whether it be founded in the Fourteenth Amendment's concept of personal liberty and restrictions upon state action, as we feel it is, or, as the District Court determined, in the Ninth Amendment's reservation of rights to the people, is broad enough to encompass a woman's decision whether or not to terminate her pregnancy." *Id.* at 153.

[30] Professor MacKinnon rejects privacy law as a means to protect women: "Privacy law assumes women are equal to men in there. Through this perspective, the legal concept of privacy can and has shielded the place of battery, marital rape, and women's exploited domestic labor. It has preserved the central institutions

mental component of the constitutional right to privacy, and state regulations that interfere with that fundamental right are to be *strictly scrutinized* by courts—that is, they are to be upheld by courts only if they are drafted narrowly to further certain state interests. These interests are prescribed (and buried) within the jargon above: During the first trimester, there are no compelling state interests that justify interference; during the second, because of the increasing medical risks of abortion, states may clip into the right to choose abortion but only to the extent necessary to further their interests in women's health and medical standards; and during the third trimester, or after viability (when the fetus is capable of living apart from its mother), a state may regulate abortion to protect fetal life but must still provide exceptions that permit abortion for women whose health is at stake.

Although the right *Roe* protects was limited to those capable of affording to exercise it[31] and conditioned for minors,[32] *Roe* remained whole for nearly a decade, only to be reaffirmed by *Akron v. Akron Center for Reproductive Health*.[33] There the Court reiterated its rigorous "strict scrutiny" standard of judicial review, refusing to adopt an approach that would limit the use of strict scrutiny only to laws which "unduly burden"

---

whereby women are deprived of identity, autonomy, control, and self-definition. It has protected a primary activity through which male supremacy is expressed and enforced." C. MacKinnon, *Toward a Feminist Theory of the State* 193 (1989) [hereinafter *Feminist Theory*]; *see also* C. MacKinnon, *Feminism Unmodified*, *supra* note 12, at 93–102; *id.* at 102 ("This right to privacy is a right of men 'to be let alone' to oppress women one at a time."). *But see* Robenfield, *The Right of Privacy*, 102 Harv. L. Rev. 737, 737 (1989) ("This Article is about the constitutional right to privacy, a right that many believe has little to do with privacy and nothing to do with the Constitution. By all accounts, however, the right to privacy has everything to do with delineating the legitimate limits of governmental power").

[31] Maher v. Roe, 432 U.S. 464, 97 S. Ct. 2376 (1977) (holding that states are under no constitutional obligation to provide public funding for abortions of state welfare recipients—even though state provides funding for normal childbirth):

> The Connecticut regulation places no obstacles—absolute or otherwise—in the pregnant woman's path to an abortion. An indigent woman who desires an abortion suffers no disadvantage as a consequence of Connecticut's decision to fund childbirth; she continues as before to be dependent on private sources for the services she desires. The State may have made childbirth a more attractive alternative, thereby influencing the woman's decision, but it has imposed no restriction on access to abortions that was not already there.

Id. at 474. The Court pushed this point even further in Harris v. McRae, 448 U.S. 297, 100 S. Ct. 2671 (1980), when it upheld the Hyde Amendment, which prohibits the use of federal funds even for *medically necessary* abortions. In Webster v. Reproductive Health Servs., 492 U.S. 490, 507, 109 S. Ct. 3040, 3051 (1989) (quotation omitted), the Court reestablished its position: "[T]he Due Process Clauses generally confer no affirmative right to government aid, even where such aid may be necessary to secure life, liberty, or property interests of which the government itself may not deprive the individual." And now the Court has held that federally funded clinics can be banned from counseling about the abortion option. *See* Rust v. Sullivan, 111 S. Ct. 1759, 1775–76 n.s. (1991) (citations omitted):

> Potential grant recipients can choose between accepting Title X funds—subject to the Government's conditions that they provide matching funds and forgo abortion counseling and referral in the Title X project—or declining the subsidy and financing their own unsubsidized program. We have never held that the Government violates the First Amendment simply by offering that choice.

[32] *See infra* Part II.B.
[33] 103 S. Ct. 2481 (1983).

fundamental rights and reminded states that they have but two compelling interests—women's health after the first trimester and fetal life after viability—that justify interfering with an adult woman's right to choose abortion.[34]

Then came *Webster*.[35] Now states may reach into and restrict the right of women to choose abortion if states do it through prohibitions on the use of public facilities and the involvement of public employees in the performance of abortions, or through mandatory (and expensive) testing for viability after a specified point in pregnancy.[36]

Specifically, in a 5–4 vote, a majority of the Court upheld state laws banning the use of tax money for encouraging or counseling abortion, banning the performance of abortion by any public employee, and banning the use of a taxpayer-supported facility to perform an abortion, unless necessary to save the life of the mother. *Webster* also suggests that, in place of the strict scrutiny standard applied in *Roe,* Justice O'Connor's "undue burden" standard—a standard offering much less constitutional protection—may be the applicable standard of review.[37] Most importantly, *Webster* suggests a new Supreme Court tolerance for state restrictions on abortion; the Court is consciously lowering the abortion issue down into state legislatures.

B. Making Minors Ask

The abortion access rights of minors is an issue that has never really left state legislatures. The case law is plentiful, and how these cases relate to one another can be confusing. Notification/consent, judicial bypass/no judicial bypass, one parent/two parents—the issue of abortion access for minors shattered long ago, and the pieces are numerous. To help you through the following discussion, I have provided a matrix (page 192)—a map that situates the cases among these issue fragments.

1. DANFORTH (1976) *Danforth*[38] was brought by physicians on behalf of all physicians and surgeons wanting to perform abortions and the patients who desired them. The action was a challenge to a Missouri abortion statute that required, among other things, unmarried women under the age of 18 years to obtain the consent of at

---

[34] *Id.* at 452, 103 S. Ct. at 2504 (O'Connor, J., dissenting).

[35] Webster v. Reproductive Health Servs., 492 U.S. 490, 109 S. Ct. 3040 (1989). Let me share with you the *Webster* reaction of Judy Widdicombe, founder and president of Reproductive Health Services in St. Louis, the named plaintiff in *Webster:*

> But my real concern about the impact of *Webster* is a scenario as follows: The decision says, You cannot do abortions in publicly funded hospitals. What is a publicly funded hospital? A private hospital that got federal funds to be built? That gets Medicaid funds? There isn't a private institution that doesn't get some kind of federal money for something. Since *Webster,* some hospitals in Missouri are taking a very conservative interpretation and, even though they are not publicly funded institutions, choosing not to provide abortions. *Webster* just gives them one more excuse.

Choices, supra note 10, at 134.

[36] *See* 492 U.S. 491–521, 109 S. Ct. at 3042–58 (also see the progeny of *Webster,* Rust v. Sullivan, 111 S. Ct. 1759 (1991), *discussed supra* note 31). It should also be noted that the *Webster* Court upheld a legislative declaration that "[t]he life of each human being begins at conception." *Id.* at 3049–50.

[37] *See id.* at 3063; *see also Justices Agree, supra* note 23 (explaining that the Third Circuit applied Justice O'Connor's reasoning in upholding Pennsylvania's abortion statute) ("Justice O'Connor has urged that abortion regulations 'rationally' related to a 'legitimate' government purpose ought to be upheld unless they place an 'undue burden' on a woman's freedom to choose to terminate her pregnancy.").

[38] Planned Parenthood of Central Mo. v. Danforth, 428 U.S. 52, 96 S. Ct. 2831 (1976).

Matrix 1*

	With Judicial Bypass		Without Judicial Bypass	
	1 Parent	2 Parents	1 Parent	2 Parents
Parental Notification Statute	5. *Ohio* (Constitutional)	6. *Hodgson* (Constitutional) ↑	? Conditional Bypass	3. *Matheson* (Constitutional) 6. *Hodgson* (Unconstitutional) ↑
Parental Consent Statute	4. *Ashcroft* (Constitutional)	?	1. *Danforth* (Unconstitutional)	2. *Bellotti II* (Unconstitutional)

*This matrix was drafted from data compiled by the NARAL Foundation. *See* Who Decides?, *supra* note 15.

least one parent during their first 12 weeks of pregnancy.[39] An exception was made for abortions certified by a licensed physician as necessary to preserve the life of the mother.[40]

The Court used *Roe* and *Doe*[41] to strike down this consent statute, holding that:

> [T]he State does not have the constitutional authority to give a third party an absolute, and possibly arbitrary, veto over the decision of the physician and his patient to terminate the patient's pregnancy, regardless of the reason for withholding the consent.
>
>   *   *   *
>
>   Any independent interest the parent may have in the termination of the minor daughter's pregnancy is no more weighty than the right of privacy of the competent minor mature enough to have become pregnant.[42]

However, the Court also made clear "that the State has somewhat broader authority to regulate the activities of children than of adults"[43] and that, where minors are concerned, states may pass laws in furtherance of interests other than fetal viability or maternal health.[44]

    2. BELLOTTI II (1979) *Bellotti II*[45] is to minors what *Roe* is to adult women: it defines the minor's constitutional right to choose abortion, holding:

---

[39] *Quoted in Danforth,* 428 U.S. at 52, 98 S. Ct. at 2836: "§ 3(4), requiring, for [the first 12 weeks of pregnancy], the written consent of one parent or person in loco parentis of the woman if the woman is unmarried and under the age of eighteen years, unless . . . certified by a licensed physician as necessary in order to preserve the life of the mother."

[40] *Id.*

[41] "Other courts that have considered the parental-consent issue in the light of *Roe* and *Doe* have concluded that a statute like § 3(4) does not withstand constitutional scrutiny." *Id.* at 74.

[42] 428 U.S. at 74–75, 96 S. Ct. at 2843-44.

[43] *Id.* (citation omitted).

[44] *Cf. id* at 75, 96 S. Ct. at 2844.

[45] 443 U.S. 622, 99 S. Ct. 3035 (1979). The Court was introduced to the Massachusetts' parental involvement statute struck in *Bellotti II* in Bellotti v. Baird, 428 U.S. 132, 96 S. Ct. 2857 (1976) *(Bellotti I).* The

(1) that mature minors have a right to make their own decisions about abortion without parental involvement; (2) that mature and immature minors must, as a matter of constitutional law, have the opportunity, through an alternative judicial or administrative procedure, to obtain an abortion without parental consent or consultation; *and (3) that with respect to immature minors, the sole test must be their own best interests.*[46]

Despite the fact that it had a judicial bypass procedure (the means to test for maturity), the Massachusetts statute in question was found to violate the abortion rights of minors because it required them to go to their parents before going to court, to notify their parents about bypass proceedings—in short, the statute made minors inform their parents about their decision to pursue abortion even when they chose to obtain consent for the abortion from a judge, and because it allowed judges to withhold authorization even when the minor was mature.[47]

Eight of the Justices agreed that the Massachusetts statute was unconstitutional—a strong statement in and of itself.[48] As is evident in the Court's two separate opinions, the Justices disagreed as to how far a state may legislate away the right of minors to *confidential* abortion (the Powell opinion stresses that states may require parental involvement so long as it is tailored to protecting youths from their own immaturity).[49] Perhaps this disagreement is why the Court stopped short of scripting "the full procedural guarantees enabling 'mature' or 'best interests' minors to bypass their parents."[50]

3.   MATHESON (1981)   In *Matheson*,[51] the Court upheld a Utah statute requiring doctors to notify parents prior to performing abortions on all unemancipated minors under the age of 18. Although it contains no judicial bypass procedure, the statute is incredibly narrow,

requiring a physician to give notice to parents, "if possible," prior to performing an abortion on their minor daughter, (a) when the girl is living with and dependent upon her parents, (b) when she is not emancipated by marriage or otherwise, and (c) when she has made no claim or showing as to her maturity or as to her relations with her parents.[52]

4.   ASHCROFT (1983)   The *Ashcroft* Court upheld a Missouri statute requiring minors to secure parental or judicial consent to abortion, stressing that a "State's interest in protecting immature minors will sustain a requirement of a consent substitute, either

---

Bellotti I Court noted that the statute was susceptible to multiple constructions and certified questions to the Supreme Judicial Court of Massachusetts regarding the state's existing procedure.

[46] Benshoof & Pilpel, *Minors' Rights to Confidential Abortions: The Evolving Legal Scene,* in *Abortion, Medicine and the Law* 139–40, J. Butler & D. Walbert eds. (3d ed. 1986) (emphasis added).

[47] *Bellotti* II 443 U.S. at 644–50, 99 S. Ct. at 3048-52.

[48] The Court consisted of Justices Blackmun, Brennan, Marshall, Powell, Stewart, Rehnquist, Stevens, White, and Chief Justice Burger. Justice White was the isolationist.

[49] 443 U.S. at 634–42, 99 S. Ct. at 3043-47; *id.* at 634, 99 S. Ct. at 3043: "We have recognized three reasons justifying the conclusion that the constitutional rights of children cannot be equated with those of adults: the peculiar vulnerability of children; their inability to make critical decisions in an informed, mature manner; and the importance of the parental role in child rearing."

[50] Benshoof and Pilpel, *supra* note 46, at 141.

[51] H.L. v. Matheson, 450 U.S. 398, 101 S. Ct. 1164 (1981).

[52] *Id.* at 407, 101 S. Ct. at 1170.

parental or judicial.''[53] The statute was allowed to stand on the grounds that it contains a bypass procedure whereby a pregnant minor may demonstrate her maturity or that, despite her immaturity, abortion is in her best interest.[54]

5. OHIO (1990)   The *Ohio* one-parent notification statute at issue in this case—a statute that requires physicians to personally notify a patient's parent before performing an abortion—was upheld by a six-to-three vote.[55] "To obtain a judicial bypass of the notice requirement, the minor must present clear and convincing proof that she has sufficient maturity and information to make the abortion decision herself, that one of her parents has engaged in a pattern of physical, emotional, or sexual abuse against her, or that notice is not in her best interests.''[56] Although the statute does contain a bypass procedure accompanied by a "constructive authorization" procedure (this means, in essence, that the court pretends there is authorization) that is triggered whenever courts fail to act in a timely fashion,[57] it is a bypass procedure that pro-choice advocates argue is booby-trapped with the following procedural difficulties:

- *The Pleadings Trap.* A minor must choose among three forms, depending on whether she intends to argue that she is mature enough to make the decision on her own, or that abortion is in her best interest, or both;
- *Lack of Anonymity.* The forms require that minors identify their parents;
- *Expediency.* It was argued that the judicial procedure, including appellate review, could take up to 22 calendar days and, therefore, is not sufficiently expedited;
- *Excessive Burden of Proof.* Minors must prove by "clear and convincing evidence" that they are mature or that abortion is in their best interest. This means that, even if a judge is satisfied that the minor is mature or that abortion is in her best interest, she cannot authorize the abortion unless the evidence is clear and convincing; and
- *Chilling Effect on Physicians.* Since physicians will fear liability under the statute, they will not perform abortions unless they have actually notified parents. Therefore, it was argued that the statute's constructive authorization provision would not work.

6. HODGSON (1990)   *Hodgson*[58] was a test case—the first serious challenge to the bypass procedure prescribed in *Bellotti II*.[59] The statute in question was apparently written to test, for it is a notification statute devoid of any bypass that transforms itself into a notification statute *with* a judicial bypass if and when the bypassless version is ever "temporarily or permanently restrained or enjoined by judicial order," and then *transforms itself back* "if such temporary or permanent restraining order or injunction is ever stayed or dissolved, or otherwise ceases to have effect.''[60] Since the bypassless

---

[53] Planned Parenthood Ass'n of Kansas City, Mo., Inc. v. Ashcroft, 462 U.S. 476, 490–91 (1983).

[54] *Id.* at 492–94.

[55] Ohio v. Akron Center for Reproductive Health, 110 S. Ct. 2972 (1990).

[56] *Id.* at 2974, 103 S. Ct. at 2525-26.

[57] The statute provides constructive authorization of abortion when courts fail to act in a timely fashion. *Id.* at 2981.

[58] Hodgson v. Minnesota, 110 S. Ct. 2926 (1990).

[59] *Bellotti II* is discussed *infra* at Part II.B.2.

[60] Subdivision 6 of Minn. Stat. § 144.343 provides in full that:

> If subdivision 2 of this law is ever temporarily or permanently restrained or enjoined by judicial order, subdivision 2 shall be enforced as though the following paragraph were

form of the statute was struck down by the Court as unconstitutional, it follows that the Court actually considered the constitutionality of two different notification statutes—two two-parent notification statutes, one with and the other without a judicial bypass procedure. The second statute—the one that provided a judicial bypass procedure through which a minor may avoid notifying her parents by demonstrating her maturity or best interests to a judge—was upheld by the Court.[61]

Hodgson shattered the Court: there are five separate opinions, and not one of them is agreed upon in its entirety by a majority of the Court. To deduce the holdings of *Hodgson*, one must piecemeal the opinions together by writing up a score card on all of the pertinent issues and reading through all of the opinions. This work has been done,[62] and the results are as follows:

> *A majority of the Court, speaking through an opinion authored by Justice Kennedy, joined by Chief Justice Rehnquist and Justices Scalia and White and concurred in part by Justice O'Connor, upheld the provision of the Minnesota statute requiring a young woman who desires an abortion either to notify both biological parents of her decision to obtain an abortion or to go through a judicial bypass procedure to avoid notification to her parents. The same majority, with Justice Stevens, also upheld the provision requiring a 48-hour waiting period after written notice is sent to a minor's parents. However, a different majority of the Court, in an opinion authored by Justice Stevens and joined in part by Justices Marshall, Brennan, Blackmun and O'Connor, struck down the provision requiring a minor to notify both biological parents of her decision to obtain an abortion without allowing her the option of using a judicial bypass procedure.[63]*

So, for now, *Bellotti II* remains untouched: States must provide a bypass procedure through which the minor may demonstrate that she is mature enough to make her own decision or that her best interests would be served by abortion without her parents' involvement.[64] What has changed is that the votes have gotten closer: The notification

---

incorporated as paragraph (c) of that subdivision; provided, however, that if such temporary or permanent restraining order or injunction is ever stayed or dissolved, or otherwise ceases to have effect, subdivision 2 shall have full force and effect, without being modified by the addition to the following substitute paragraph which shall have no force or effect until or unless an injunction or restraining order is again in effect.

Quoted in 110 S. Ct. at 2933 n.9.

[61] Justice O'Connor cast the decisive vote on this provision. *See id.* at 2950–51.

[62] *See* ACLU Reproductive Freedom Project, *The Current Status of the Supreme Court and Abortion Law: Summary and Legal Analysis of* Hodgson v. Minnesota *and* Ohio v. Akron Center for Reproductive Health (undated).

[63] *Id.* at 6–7.

[64] Although such bypass procedures may sound appealing, consider how they have been implemented:

Although the Minnesota statute contains many facial procedural guarantees for the court bypass alternative, such as requiring that courts will be open 24 hours a day, seven days a week, in fact, the statute does not assure that mature or best interests minors have their right to a confidential abortion protected.

procedure without a bypass was struck down in a five-four vote, the majority of five consisting of Justices Blackmun, Brennan, Marshall, O'Connor, and Stevens. Now Justice Brennan's seat on the Court is occupied by Justice Souter,[65] and Justice Marshall's bears the weight of Justice Thomas.[66] Despite his close call with the Thomas confirmation, President Bush, an avid sportsman who savors a challenge, is not likely to temper his conservative taste when choosing another nominee.[67] Considering the ages of Justices Blackmun and Stevens, four more years means two more appointments.[68] But the president need not necessarily appoint more Justices nor wait much longer: Opportunities for the Court to further delegate the abortion issue are already visible along the horizon. In fact, a case involving Pennsylvania's abortion statute has already arrived, and similar opportunities from Louisiana, Utah, and Guam are expected to follow soon.[69]

III. Where We Are Now

The right to choose abortion is sinking down to the states, where public financing of abortions has already settled.[70] The constitutional question, which some argue was po-

---

> Courts are open in only three of the 87 counties, many judges will not hear these cases, and virtually all of the petitions are heard by three judges who now limit their hearings for minors to certain days a week and certain hours. . . . Older, white, more sophisticated and more affluent teenagers are the only ones who can "work" the judicial system.
>
> * * *
>
> In addition, the failure of states to appropriate any money for more judges, counselors, or additional court hours to implement the court bypass system, and facilitate minors' access to that system is one proof that the statutes are not, in fact, designed for their stated purposes, but rather for the purpose of deterring as many abortions as possible.

Benshoof & Pilpel, *supra* note 46, at 145 (citation omitted). For a discussion of inconsistencies in implementing bypass provisions (to determine "maturity"), see *Judges Divided on Minor Abortion Rulings,* United Press Int'l, Dec. 16, 1990 (NEXIS, Papers source file) ("Cuyahoga County Juvenile Judge Peter Sikora said, 'The real problem is that different judges could be applying different kinds of standards in the same court, in different counties, all across the state.' "). Massachusetts' experience confirms this:

> Some judges who are opposed to abortion rights decline to hear the petitions, one of the reasons a relatively small pool of judges hear the majority of the petitions. Balch said that most petitions—called Mary Moes because they are kept confidential—are granted because judges hear only one side and lawyers "judge shop" in order to direct their clients to judges who are known to be sympathetic. Abortion rights advocates say they seek out judges known to be supportive.

Mitchell, *Mass. Teen-agers Turn to the Courts for Access to Abortion,* Boston Globe, Aug. 2, 1991, at 1, 4.

To understand what it is like to go through one of these bypass procedures, consider Heather Pearson's story—the story behind *Hodgson,* in which Heather was the named party:

> Neither mother nor daughter considered notifying Heather's father, who had been absent since the couple's divorce 10 years before. "Are you kidding? I hardly knew him. And he has a terrible temper," says Heather of the man who calls her twice a year and whom she has never told of the pregnancy. And so on Aug. 16, Heather and her mother went to county court in downtown Minneapolis. "You could tell that everyone knew what you were there for," Heather recalls. "They'd stare, then walk off, whispering." After

litical all along, is now officially becoming a political one.[71] In the words of Professor Stephen Carter, "The reason, I suspect, that *Webster* came as such a stunning setback to both sides is that neither was well-prepared to cope with a world in which the political institutions would actually have to resolve a moral dilemma instead of letting the Supreme Court do it and taking potshots at the results."[72]

The states have responded to *Webster.*[73] The public is now demanding that adult women be allowed to keep their right to choose, and state legislatures are obliging:

> *Perhaps most noteworthy of all the findings is that thirty-four (or one-third of) state legislative bodies are viewed as being significantly more supportive of abortion as a legal option than they were eighteen months ago, just before the Supreme Court issued the* Webster *decision. Only three houses are considered to be significantly more opposed to keeping abortion legal.*[74]

---

enduring a battery of questions by a court-appointed guardian and a public defender—Why did she want an abortion? Had she been pressured? Why hadn't she told her father?—Heather arrived before the judge. Her request, like all but nine of the 3,573 petitions that came before the court from 1981 to 1986, was summarily approved.

Hewitt & Freeman, *supra* note 4.

[65] In response to questioning about his position on abortion during his confirmation hearings, Souter said only that he is open-minded about the issue. *See Whatever Happened to the Great Abortion Debate of 1990?*, Bus. Wk., Oct. 15, 1990 (NEXIS, Magazines source file). This response made both sides nervous. *See* Borger, *A Judge Rises Above His Trial by Litmus Test*, U.S. News & World Rep., Oct. 1, 1990 (NEXIS, Magazines source file). Now Justice Souter has cast his vote as a member of the *Rust* majority, voting to uphold a ban on abortion counseling at federally funded clinics. *See* Rust v. Sullivan, 111 S. Ct. 1759 (1991); *see supra* note 31 for a fuller discussion of *Rust*.

[66] Times have changed. A legal career spanning some six decades ended "with a terse letter to President Bush that stunned Washington when it was made public about two and a half hours after the Court recessed for the summer." *Marshall Leaves Bench: High Court Battle Begins*, New York Times News Service, June 28, 1991. Judge Thomas is young, conservative, inconsistent, and ambitious—ambitious to the point of changing positions to win friends, a quality much more acceptable in a politician than a Supreme Court Justice. *See* Benedicts, *Confirmation Conversion?*, *supra* note 22; Robinson, *Surprises*, *supra* note 22; Taylor, *The Way We Choose Justices*, *supra* note 22. Of course, now that he has been seated for life, perhaps Justice Thomas will just be himself—that is what scares so many, especially women. *See* Berke, *supra* note 22.

Early indications suggest that such concerns are justified. *See* Crovitz, *Justice Thomas's Opinions: No Wonder they Wanted to Stop Him*. Wall S. J., Jan. 29, 1992, at A13 ("Justice Thomas already has done more than solidify the intellectual conservative wing of the court. It also seems likely that his lifelong career on the Supreme Court will be a constant reminder to his critics of why they went to such lengths to try to block his nomination."). Beyond the fact that he was given merely a flat "qualified" ranking by the ABA, I find it hard to believe a mistake has not been made when the second African-American ever nominated to the United States Supreme Court is opposed by the NAACP in a vote of 49 to 1. *See* Cohn, *Liberals and the Lessons of Bork*, Newsweek, Aug. 12, 1991, at 26 (discussing Justice Thomas' lack of support).

[67] During President Bush's televised nomination speech from the "summer White House" in Kennebunkport, Maine on July 1, 1991, the president was asked about speculative nominees Emilio M. Garza and Edith Jones, both federal appellate judges sitting on the Fifth Circuit Court of Appeals.

Although inexperienced in appellate work (Judge Garza began his term on the Fifth Circuit in June 1991), Judge Garza is one of only a few Hispanic federal appellate judges. If elevated, he would be the first Hispanic ever appointed to the United States Supreme Court—a historic first for President Bush. As for Judge Jones, the Thomas nomination had to give the President something of a scare, and Judge Jones'

The same is true of these states' governors:

> *Significant movement toward support for the right to choose has occurred among state governors since the June 1989 NARAL Foundation/NARAL survey. Twenty-six governors—a bare majority—support keeping abortion legal, as compared to only sixteen governors in June 1989. This shift is due primarily to a greater willingness on the part of governors to take a pro-choice position, in response to an electorate that increasingly demands to know their position on choice. . . . Despite these pro-choice gains, the number of governors who oppose keeping abortion legal has not changed and remains ominously high at twenty-three, identical to the pre-*Webster *count.* [75]

However, there seems to be a tradeoff going on. Although people are openly supportive of the right to choose and unwilling to make abortion a crime, they apparently are

---

public record (meaning her statements in open court) may be as yellowed as Thomas' private one. Consider the following example:

> After New York lawyer Edward Chikofsky volunteered to aid a Texan on death row, he filed an appeal late because of illness and to take account of a recent Supreme Court ruling on the key issue. Jones refused to delay the execution, saying that the ''veil of civility that must protect us in society has been twice torn here''—by the murderer and by Chikofsky's conduct.

Gest & Miller, *Edith Jones: A Texas Hard-Liner Might be Next in Line for the Supreme Court,* U.S. News & World Rep., Dec. 31, 1990/Jan. 7, 1991 (NEXIS, Magazines source file). However, Judge Jones is intellectually gifted, young, and personable, and rumor on the Fifth Circuit is that the Bush administration has virtually promised her Justice O'Connor's seat should it become vacant while President Bush is still in power. Perhaps the most likely nominee is Solicitor General Kenneth Starr--''a conservative who would draw liberal flak over abortion but could likely win Senate approval.'' *Washington Wire,* Wall St. J., Oct. 18, 1991, at A1. For a full discussion of what President Bush has done to the federal judiciary, see Goldman, *The Bush Imprint on the Judiciary: Carrying on a Tradition,* 74 Judicature 294 (1991) (noting that, by 1993, about two-thirds of the federal judiciary will have been selected by Presidents Reagan and Bush); *id.* at 299 (table indicating that 89.6% of Bush appointees are male and 95.8% are white).

[68] A homogeneously conservative Court no longer appears inevitable. As this article goes into print, polls show that recession has sobered this nation—a nation once intoxicated with Operation Desert Storm spirit. *See* Toner, *Bad News for Bush as Poll Shows National Gloom,* N.Y. Times, Jan. 28, 1992, at A1, A10 (''Support for Mr. Bush continues to erode, with just 43 percent saying they approve of his performance as President, an astonishing drop of 45 points since his popularity rating reached 88 percent, a historic peak, after the Persian Gulf war.'').

[69] *See supra* note 23.

[70] *See supra* notes 31, 65–69, and accompanying text.

[71] *See* Webster, 492 U.S. at 490, 109 S. Ct. at 3040. For a personal account of the politics surrounding abortion from its illegal days, through *Roe* and the bombings of abortion clinics in the late 1970s, to *Webster,* see Judy Widdicombe's story, told in *Choices, supra* note 10, at 123–35; *see also supra* note 35 and accompanying text.

[72] *See* Book Review, *supra* note 12. *Webster* has now been followed by Rust v. Sullivan, 111 S. Ct. 1759, 114 L. Ed. 2d 233, 59 U.S.L.W. 4451 (1991), and both the public and Congress are responding. *See Marchers Protest Abortion 'Gag' Rule,* Worcester Sunday Telegram, July 7, 1991, at A4 (''About 5,000 protesters rallied yesterday against a U.S. Supreme Court ruling that bars employers of federally funded clinics from discussing abortion with patients.''); *Senate Approves Abortion Advising,* Worcester Telegram & Gazette, July 18, 1991, at A7 (''Congress moves closer to veto showdown''); *see also Rule to Bar Abortion Discussion Hit by AMA,* Worcester Telegram & Gazette, June 26, 1991, at A12 (''The American

Matrix 2*

	With Judicial Bypass		Without Judicial Bypass	
	1 Parent	2 Parents	1 Parent	2 Parents
Parental Notification Statute	Georgia Nebraska Nevada [Ohio] <u>West Virginia</u>	<u>Arizona</u> Illinois <u>Minnesota</u>	Maryland Montana	Idaho [Tennessee] <u>Utah</u>
Parental Consent Statute	<u>Alabama</u> Arizona California <u>Florida</u> <u>Indiana</u> [Louisiana] <u>Michigan</u> <u>Missouri</u> [Ohio] <u>Pennsylvania</u> <u>Rhode Island</u> <u>South Carolina</u> <u>Wyoming</u>	Kentucky <u>Massachusetts</u> <u>Mississippi</u> [North Dakota] [Tennessee]	Alaska Colorado [Delaware] New Mexico South Dakota Washington	[Delaware] [Louisiana]

*Underline indicates the statute is enforced; brackets indicate statute does not cleanly fit into categorization.
This matrix was drafted from data compiled by the NARAL Foundation. *See* Who Decides?, *supra* note 15.

Medical Association yesterday condemned a U.S. Supreme Court ruling barring federally funded clinics from discussing abortion with patients, saying it infringes upon the doctor-patient relationship.'').

[73] *See* Hinds, *supra* note 23, at A6 (''Since the *Webster* decision, state legislators across the country have considered nearly 600 bills restricting abortion. Only Louisiana, Utah and Guam have enacted bans on abortion. Pennsylvania, Mississippi, North Dakota, South Carolina, Michigan and Nebraska have enacted procedural restrictions.''); *see also Who Decides?, supra* note 15, at vi:

> [T]he changes documented reflect the effects of the post-*Webster* climate on the American public and their elected representatives, and in particular represent the cumulative effect of at least three factors: the number of individual legislators who have changed their positions because of the new post-*Webster* reality; changes that resulted from the election of more pro-choice candidates in 1989 and 1990; and the increased number of politicians willing— in the face of a demanding electorate—to state publicly their support for the right to choose.

[74] *Who Decides? supra* note 15, at vi–vii. The breakdown is as follows:

> Thirty-four houses received a more ''pro-choice'' characterization in this study than in the June 1989 study, including: 8 houses that were considered opposed to legal abortion but now are viewed as supporting legal abortion (FL, GA, ID and MT Senates; FL, GA, MA and MT Houses); 15 houses that were considered closely divided but now are viewed as supporting legal abortion (AZ, CA, KS, MD, NH, OR and VT Senates; AZ, DE, KS, MD, OR and VT Houses; CA Assembly; NJ General Assembly); and 11 houses that were considered opposed to legal abortion but are now viewed as closely divided (IL, IN, IA, NJ, OK, SC and TX Senates; IL, RI, SC and TX Houses).

Id. at vi; *see also Whatever Happened, supra* note 65 (''But after long agonizing, some politicians now find it safer to ease their opposition to abortion.'').

willing to add restrictions—especially if the restrictions are on minors. People want the choice, but they do not want their kids to exercise that choice without their knowledge.[76] This requirement has already been codified by many states.

Professor Matsuda has written that "[t]he places where the law does not go to redress harm have tended to be the places where women, children, people of color, and poor people live."[77] The poor and young—the politically weak—are unlikely to fare well under the new scheme. In comparison with financially able adult women, their right to abortion was never as protected by the Court,[78] and efforts to restrict abortion access have already been directed at them.[79] It seems that, especially when there is agreement to protect the abortion rights of adult women, restricting the abortion rights of minors is an easy sell.[80]

Although the abortion question is *perhaps* innately political and moral and therefore belongs in state legislatures,[81] there is a price that all sexually active women will have to pay. That price is uncertainty. As long as our society remains divided on the abortion issue,[82] women will have to keep fighting *for* their right and *against* subtle ways of

---

[75] *Id.* at iv. The breakdown is as follows:

> 26 governors and the [M]ayor of the District of Columbia support keeping abortion legal (AZ, AR, CA, CO, CT, DE, DC, FL, GA, IL, IN, ME, MD, MA, MN, MS, NJ, NM, NY, OK, OR, RI, TN, TX, VT, VA, WA); 23 governors favor outlawing abortion (AL, AK, ID, IA, KS, KY, LA, MI, MO, MT, NE, NV, NH, NC, ND, OH, PA, SC, SD, UT, WV, WI, WY); the position of one governor on this issue is unknown (HI).

Id. at iv–v. Perhaps fired up by the Court's recent *Rust* opinion (*see supra* note 72), Louisiana's legislature even went so far as to override a veto by former Governor Roemer who, although not pro-choice, believed the legislature had gone too far. *See Louisiana Abortion Ban Becomes Law,* Worcester Telegram & Gazette, June 19, 1991, at C8 (noting that Governor Roemer "became the first Louisiana governor this century to have a veto overridden, according to legislative historians."). Louisiana's statute banning abortion is now law, and the United States Court of Appeals for the Fifth Circuit is expected to soon render a decision regarding that statute's constitutionality—a question the United States Supreme Court is likely to consider soon after. *See supra* note 23.

[76] The position taken by Governor Schaefer of Maryland is typical:

> Democratic Gov. William Schaefer last week signed legislation that's being called the nation's most liberal abortion law. The measure guarantees access to abortion even if the U.S. Supreme Court's Roe v. Wade decision legalizing abortion is overturned. However, the new law requires that physicians inform the parents of minors seeking abortions in certain cases.

The Week in Healthcare: Regional News Digest, Northeast, Mod. Healthcare, Feb. 25, 1991, at 19 (NEXIS, Magazines source file).

[77] *Public Response to Racist Speech: Considering the Victim's Story,* 87 Mich. L. Rev. 2320, 2322 (1989) (citation omitted) [hereinafter *Public Response*].

[78] *See supra* note 31 and accompanying text; *supra* Part II.B.

[79] "Perhaps most alarming, despite the apparent increased opposition among lawmakers to total bans on abortion, the climate in the states is alarmingly conducive to the anti-choice incrementalist strategy of first enacting restrictions on choice aimed at the least politically powerful and most vulnerable women—poor women and young women." *Who Decides?, supra* note 15, at iii. Consider the following NARAL findings:

> • 35 states have laws on the books that prevent minors from obtaining abortions without parental consent or notice . . . ; of these, 15 are currently being enforced . . . In addition, 3 states require a minor to receive mandatory counseling that includes discussion of the possibility of consulting her parents . . . (*id.* at v [*see* matrix 2, *supra* text]);

restricting it.[83] But, then again, this uncertainty is not new, and the battle I speak of was waged long ago. The difference will be in its intensity, its consistency, where it is fought, and how much there is to lose.[84]

IV. Some Stories

The technique of legal storytelling is an effort to communicate insight gained through personal experience to those who have not shared in that experience. It is a highly personal, human approach—an effort to graft faces back onto the law; to restore the flesh seared away by pure utilitarian thought, such as the Chicago School of law and economics that was so popular during the 1980s. The legal community associates this technique of storytelling with a group of creative and often poetic scholars—such as Derrick Bell, Kimberlé Crenshaw, Richard Delgado, Mari Matsuda, and Patricia Williams—who are now enlightening us with the victim's story told through a body of legal scholarship known as "outsider jurisprudence."[85]

- 30 states and the District of Columbia will not provide Medicaid funding for abortions unless the woman's life is in danger . . . ; 8 states provide public funding in certain additional, though very limited, circumstances, such as when the pregnancy resulted from reported rape or incest . . . ; only the remaining 12 states fund most or all abortions . . . and 3 of these states do so only under a court order . . . (*id.*);
- Perhaps the most important current federal abortion restriction is that, under federal law, a woman may not obtain federal funds to pay for an abortion unless the procedure is necessary to prevent her death. This prohibition of federal funding of abortion affects approximately 44 million American women (*id.* at viii).

[80] Carlson, *Abortion's Hardest Cases*, Time, July 9, 1990, at 22 (NEXIS, Magazines source file):

> Even those who strongly favor a woman's right to choose find themselves troubled by the notion of a girl's right to choose, so parental consent or notification has been a comparatively easy sell: 33 states have passed such laws. By forcing the pro-choice movement to challenge this trend, the pro-life movement has been able to paint its opponents as antifamily, bent on weakening the bond between the generations, encouraging teenage promiscuity and fostering a libertine attitude toward sex that results in more than 400,000 teenage abortions a year.

[81] *See supra* notes 12, 71, and accompanying text. My position is that the United States Congress should construct a threshold—recognition of at least the most fundamental form of the right to choose—to abortion access that states cannot narrow.

[82] Carlson, *supra* note 80:

> The irreconcilable answers people give to pollsters are, in part, an expression of society's inability to come to grips publicly with so private an issue. In a Los Angeles Times poll last year, 61% of those interviewed said abortion is morally wrong; 57% of them believe it is murder, yet 51% think it should remain a woman's decision.

[83] Parental and spousal consent requirements; mandatory waiting periods; hospital board approval requirements; restrictions on public funding; burdensome licensing requirements for providers—a lack of creativity is the only limitation to how a state legislature may publicly support the right to choose abortion while actually restricting it. The following is a summary of what NARAL says state legislatures are brewing:

> The types of restrictions on abortion introduced range from bans on all abortions, including some bans that purport to prohibit abortions "as a means of birth control," to prohibitions of abortion for the purpose of selecting the sex of a child, restrictions on minors' access to

Although I do not possess personal experience involving the issue of abortion and minors, I now want to share some stories with you. They are the experiences of those who have lived with the issue that is the subject of this essay, and they are told from several different perspectives—from the perspective of an adult woman who had an abortion when she was a minor, the perspective of a minor about to get an abortion, the perspective of the parents of a minor who had an illegal abortion, the perspective of a judge who presides over bypass proceedings, the perspective of a counselor at a women's medical center in Mississippi, the perspective of an incest victim, and the perspective of the unborn. Moreover, the stories are a scrapbook compilation of letters, a magazine article, trial testimony, bits of narrative prose, and a book excerpt. This section of my essay is not balanced between pro-choice and pro-life factions; these are the stories *I* have found convincing. I urge you to read them and others.[86]

---

abortions, and requirements that a married woman must notify her husband before obtaining an abortion. During the same time-period, certain pro-choice bills were also introduced, such as clinic access protections, repeals of abortion restrictions and prohibitions, and attempts to codify the trimester framework established by the Supreme Court in *Roe*. In addition, the study summarizes the bills relating to bans on fetal tissue research, the disposition of fetal remains, bans on abortion counseling in sex education and contraception programs, and the prosecution for "prenatal child abuse" of women who use drugs and alcohol during pregnancy.

Who Decides?, supra note 15, at vii.

The major threat to abortion access is now coming through a diminishing number of abortion providers: "During the three-year period from 1985 to 1988, thirty-four states suffered a loss in the number of providers, which was attributable to a thirteen percent reduction in the number of hospitals offering abortion services." *Id.* at iv. The cause? NARAL suggests "existing and anticipated legal restrictions. Other causes include anti-choice harassment and violence aimed at providers and a sharp decline in the number of medical students who receive training in how to perform abortions." *Id.; see also supra* note 35 (Judy Widdicombe's explanation). As for harassment, consider the demonstrations in Wichita, Kansas during which more than 2,500 protestors were arrested. This demonstration was finally put to an end by Judge Patrick Kelly through implementation of a post–Civil War-era federal statute, known as the Klu Klux Klan Act, that prohibits conspiracies to deprive people of equal protection of the laws. *See* Denniston, *Abortion Blockade Case: Skepticism for Both Sides,* Am. Law. 106–08. (Jan./Feb. 1992); Lawson, *Operation Rescue: Was the Justice Dept. Right to Intervene in Wichita?,* A.B.A. J. 44 (Nov. 1991), *accompanied by* Davis & Paul, *No: A Case of Partisan Politics,* A.B.A. J. 45 (Nov. 1991). On October 16, 1991, the Supreme Court heard a case on this issue—Jayne Bray v. Alexandria Women's Health Clinic, No. 90-985—and is now considering the solicitor general's argument that, rather than singling out women for discriminatory treatment, demonstrators who block access to abortion clinics are seeking to prohibit the practice of abortion altogether. *See id.*

[84] It is clear that *Webster* triggered a lot of activity: "[U]nder its current president, Faye Wattleton, [Planned Parenthood] has sharply increased its activity on the abortion-rights front. Several months before the Supreme Court agreed to hear *Webster,* the group launched a nationwide advertising campaign under the slogan 'Keep abortion safe and legal.' " Matlack, *supra* note 15. By the end of 1990, NARAL spent $2 million just on its "Who Decides?" campaign, and another $1.5 million on political campaigns across the country. *Id.* Revenues are apparently growing for both sides. *Id.* ("Anti-abortion organizations are growing, too. Revenues at the National Right to Life Committee have risen 35 percent since 1988. The committee runs a massive direct-mail program, and its officials estimate they spent $1 million last year on anti-abortion advertising."). The biggest player is Planned Parenthood. "With an annual budget of about $300 million, the New York-based federation and its affiliates dwarf the other players in the arena (NARAL's 1990 revenues were about $12.8 million, and the National Right to Life Committee's were about $11.1 million)." *Id.* One interesting change is that even abortion clinics are now organizing as a lobbying force:

A. Anonymous: An Adult Woman's Story

May 3, 1985

Dear CARAL:

> *I am a 26 year old, single, Black woman. I have had 2 abortions: one when I was 12 years old, the other when I was 13. I got pregnant from my stepfather and my mother's boyfriend. My mother totally denied incest had been happening since I was 5.*
>
> *At the time, I felt having the abortions made my position safer by keeping it hidden. I was a child myself developing severe emotional problems from living in an intolerable situation from which I knew of no escape. I did later escape temporarily, by having a nervous breakdown, in which I attempted suicide and was placed in a mental hospital and*

> A group of about 80 clinic operators recently formed the National Coalition of Abortion Providers and hired Ron Fitzsimmons, a former NARAL employee and congressional aide, as their lobbyist. Abortion clinics already have a professional association, the National Abortion Federation. But some clinic operators, weary of continuing protests and bombings at their facilities, "wanted to come out of the trenches, get more aggressive," Fitzsimmons said.

Id.

Although ruckuses are now going on in state legislatures, *see* text accompanying *supra* notes 73-76, the real battle is going to be fought during the 1992 campaign. *See* Matlack, *supra* note 15 ("both sides are gearing up for even heavier investments in the 1992 elections. NARAL, for example, is working on a massive voter identification effort."). This campaign-focused battle has already been raging at the state level:

> But virtually all the groups—including Planned Parenthood, which is barred by federal law from partisan politicking [in exchange for the luxury of collecting tax deductible donations]—kept up a drumbeat of advertising and direct mail supporting their positions without targeting specific campaigns . . . NARAL won four of eight congressional and gubernatorial races that it had targeted; the best that Right to Life could say in a postelection analysis was that anti-abortion candidates "pretty much held their own."

Id.

Within the parties, Republicans are likely to feel the issue more sharply because they are more divided on abortion. *See Whatever Happened, supra* note 65 ("A deeply divided GOP faces a wrenching internal fight over abortion when it drafts its 1992 platform."); *see also* Loth, *A GOP Split on Abortion,* Boston Sun. Globe, July 14, 1991 ("The greatest anguish over the nomination of conservative jurist Clarence Thomas to the U.S. Supreme Court appears to be less among liberal Democrats than among moderate Republicans, who are lamenting that the nomination will move the incendiary issue of abortion front and center in the 1992 political debate."); Rosenthal, *supra* note 15; *Young Republicans Reject Antiabortion Plank,* Boston Sun. Globe, July 14, 1991. *And see Who Decides?, supra* note 15, at viii:

> The majority of state Democratic parties (twenty-seven states and the District of Columbia) support keeping abortion legal. No state Democratic Party opposes abortion as a legal option. Twenty-two state Democratic parties take no position on abortion. By contrast, only two state Republican parties (ME, NY) support keeping abortion legal. More than half (twenty-six) oppose abortion as a legal option. Twenty-two state Republican parties and the District of Columbia Republican party take no position on the legality of abortion.

later a children's home. I could hardly have raised 2 children, nor would it have been good for them to have taken my place in the home and begin their lives by being repeatedly and brutally raped.

Not having 2 children has enabled me to leave my home as soon as possible, (age 17), and go to school to try to improve my life and get off welfare.

I am writing this letter because I think it's important for abortion to remain legal so that other young women have options and ways out of devastating circumstances.

Sincerely,
[Signed] [87]

B. Anonymous: A Minor's Story

May 15, 1985

President Ronald Reagan
c/o CARAL
Box 14022
Cleveland, OH 22394

Dear President Reagan:

I am a 17 year old, and I will graduate this June. I'm a good student and have been on the honor roll most of my junior and senior year. I have a part-time job and I want to go to college, if I can get the tuition together.

---

[85] *See* Delgado, *Storytelling for Oppositionists and Others: A Plea for Narrative,* 87 Mich. L. Rev. 2411 (1989); Delgado, *When a Story is Just a Story: Does Voice Really Matter?,* 76 Va. L. Rev. 95 (1990); Matsuda, *Looking to the Bottom: Critical Legal Studies and Reparations,* 22 Harv. C.R.-C.L. L. Rev. 323 (1987); Matsuda, *Public Response, supra* note 77; Matsuda, *Voices of America: Accent, Antidiscrimination Law, and a Jurisprudence for the Last Reconstruction,* 100 Yale L.J. 1329 (1991); Williams, *The Obliging Shell: An Informal Essay on Formal Equal Opportunity,* 87 Mich. L. Rev. 2128 (1989) (Patricia Williams).

[86] *See generally Choices, supra* note 10; McMichael, Book Review, The Seattle Times, Feb. 17, 1991 (NEXIS, Papers source file):

> Editor Angela Bonavoglia includes the thoughts of a man who as a child of 4 lost his pregnant mother to an illegal abortion; from actress Whoopi Goldberg, who self-aborted with a coat hanger in a public restroom at 14; from a father who was able to obtain an abortion for his daughter after she had been gang-raped; and from Norma McCorvey, the "Jane Roe" in the historic Roe v. Wade Supreme Court decision that in 1973 made abortion legal for all women across the country.

Although many of the stories read as though they are in the same hand and voice (a noted exception is Whoopi Goldberg's, but, then again, I do not think it is possible to dilute Whoopi's personality beyond recognition—even in prose), I strongly recommend this collection of honesty, which opens with a beautiful foreword in the hand and voice of Gloria Steinem. For stories about teenage sexuality, I direct you to Freeman, *supra* note 3.

My boyfriend is 18 and he is graduating, too. He has been working since he was 14, and he gives his mom $10 a week.

My parents are ———.

My Mom gets ADC and I'm the oldest. She's really proud of me, and she'd be awfully disappointed if she knew I was pregnant. I just couldn't do that to her. She's always tried to make us kids try to better ourselves. She never had a chance, so she wanted us to have one. She used to take us to the library when we were little, even though she could hardly read herself. But she learned. But she just kept having babies, she never had a chance to do anything else.

I was really dumb to get pregnant. I just didn't have the money to get the prescription refilled, so we took a chance without using anything.

Well, I'm getting this abortion. My boyfriend is with me. We managed to borrow some of the money from his brother, and the clinic is letting us pay the rest of it in installments. If they hadn't done that, I don't know what I'd have done. I went to one of the places that is supposed to help you if you get pregnant. They offered me a baby bed, some bottles, and a few diapers, and said I didn't have to keep the baby, they'd help me get the baby adopted. I told them I don't plan to give up a baby if I can have it, I'll keep it. But I'm not raising any baby on welfare, and that's the kind of help they were offering me. They were going to help me get on welfare of my own. No. When I get married and have a family, it isn't going to be on welfare.

I didn't want to have an abortion, but it's better than being pregnant when you're just a kid.

[Signed][88]
Cleveland, Ohio

C. A Parent's Story

[O]ne Saturday night in September 1988, Becky came home early from a party, complaining of flulike symptoms. Her parents were not alarmed; Becky's father, Bill, a 47-year-old regional sales manager for an office-supplies firm, had lately been suffering from the flu himself. But after five days, when Becky's symptoms persisted and she ran a high fever, the Bells insisted on taking her to a doctor. At a local clinic a physician quickly diagnosed pneumonia and urged her to check into a hospital. The Bells drove to nearby St. Vincent hospital, where doctors administered oxygen to Becky to ease the congestion in her lungs. Relieved that their daughter was getting the proper medical care, the Bells went to Wendy's for a hamburger. "I love you, Mommy and Daddy," said Becky as they left.

When the Bells returned, some problem had arisen. For the next

---

[87] *Reproduced in* ACLU Reproductive Freedom Project, *Parental Notice Laws: Their Catastrophic Impact on Teenagers' Right to Abortion* 25–26 (1986).

[88] *Id.* at 26–27.

three hours they watched in growing panic as doctors and nurses scrambled in and out of Becky's room. Finally a doctor delivered the horrifying news: Their daughter had died, but not from pneumonia—she had been pregnant and the victom of a botched abortion that had caused blood poisoning. "Something dirty was stuck into her," Bill recalls the doctor saying. "Probably a coat hanger or a knitting needle."

* * *

"I don't want to hurt Mom and Dad. I love them so much," she wrote in a note the Bells later found.

* * *

Each evening after supper, Bill and Karen walk hand in hand to Bethel Cemetery, where their daughter lies. "We have to keep coming here because we're not finished being Mom and Dad yet," says Karen, sitting beside the white gravestone. "Why did she have to die?" For Bill, the answer is clear. "If I had heard of those laws before, I probably would have thought they were a good idea," he says. "But now I know what they do. These goddamned laws are killing kids." [89]

D. A Judge's Story

[Judge] Garrity, who presided over hundreds of judicial-bypass hearings, also believes that a youngster can be a good judge of whether parents can handle an unwanted pregnancy on top of their own difficulties or even whether the parents want to be involved. Of the teenagers who came before him, Garrity says, "To a person, they were scared to death, but they did know what they wanted." An alcoholic mother, a drug-addicted father, an absent or neglectful parent are some of the reasons teenagers cite for not going home for help. [90]

E. A Counselor's Story

[M]inors will go to tremendous lengths to keep their parents from finding out they are pregnant—even placing their need for secrecy before their own safety. On one occasion, for example, I received a call from a panicked young woman who was pregnant and bleeding profusely. The young woman had had an abortion. I told her that she had to get to a hospital immediately. She said this was impossible because she could not get to the hospital without her parents finding out. I offered to come and get her and take her myself. However, she refused to tell me where she was because strangers coming to the house would make her parents suspicious. I pleaded with her to let me take her to the hospital, but she was adamant about maintaining secrecy at all costs. The next day a friend of hers called to tell us that the young woman had bled to death in her room. [91]

---

[89] Hewitt & Freeman, *supra* note 4. Becky's story was also told on "60 Minutes," CBS, Feb. 24, 1991.

[90] Carlson, *supra* note 80.

[91] The narrator of this story is a counselor at a women's medical center in Mississippi. Declaration of Martha Fuqua, Barnes v. Mississippi, No. J86-0458(W), at 4-5 (S.D. Miss. filed June 30, 1986).

F. An Incest Victim's Story

Spring Adams was 13 years old when she became pregnant.[92] She was impregnated through sexual abuse inflicted upon her by her own father. Spring could not afford to travel six hours to Portland, Oregon to get an abortion—never mind paying for the procedure. Then, finally, two Portland organizations took care of the arrangements for her. But Spring never made it to Portland. She never woke up the morning she was supposed to leave for the clinic. That morning, Spring's father shot her to death with a .30-caliber rifle.

G. The Unborn's Story

> As early as the 56th day of gestation, the child has been observed to move in the womb. . . . If fetal bones and joints are beginning to develop this early, movement is necessary to the structural growth; and if Liley is correct, the occasion of movement is discomfort or pain. Hence, there would be some pain receptors present before the end of the second month. A physiologist places about the same point—day 59 or 60—the observation of "spinal reflexes" in the child. Tactile stimulation of the mouth produces a reflex action, and sensory receptors are present in the simple nerve endings of the mouth. Somewhere between day 60 and day 77 sensitivity to touch develops in the genital and anal areas. In the same period, the child begins to swallow. The rate of swallowing will vary with the sweetness of the injection. By day 77 both the palms of the hands and the soles of the feet will also respond to touch; by the same day, eyelids have been observed to squint to close out light.
>
> * * *
>
> The principle modern means of abortion are these. In early pregnancy sharp curettage is practiced: A knife is used to kill the unborn child. Alternatively, suction curettage is employed: a vacuum pump sucks up the unborn child by bits and pieces, and a knife detaches the remaining parts. In the second trimester of pregnancy and later, a hypertonic saline solution is injected into the amniotic fluid surrounding the fetus. The salt appears to act as a poison; the skin of the affected child appears, on delivery, to have been soaked in acid. Alternatively, prostaglandins are given to the mother; in sufficient dosage they will constrict the circulation and impair the cardiac functioning of the fetus. The child may be delivered dead or die after delivery.[93]

V. Pain: The Unifying Theme

I am not insensitive to the unborn's pain.[94] I too want abortion to stop. However, I am also sensitive to the child's pain—the pain that comes from an empty stomach; the

---

[92] This is my rendition of Spring Adam's story, which I compiled from the following: Miller, *Rocky Adams Stuns Court with New Plea,* Idaho Statesman, Mar. 6, 1990; Ensunsa, *Agencies Set Up Adams' Abortion,* Idaho Statesman, Aug. 30, 1989; Ensunsa, *Adams Charged with Murder,* Idaho Statesman, Aug. 23, 1989.

[93] Noonan, *The Experience of Pain by the Unborn,* in *Abortion, Medicine, and the Law* 360–69, 364–66, J. Butler & D. Walbert eds. (3d ed. 1986) (author is a United States Circuit Judge for the Ninth Circuit Court of Appeals in San Francisco).

thinking pain that swishes around and around, and never leaves; the pain of broken bones.

All of this pain bothers me. Unlike Judge Noonan, I do not think laws forbidding abortion will stop the unborn child's pain; they will simply delay it.[95] As horrible as the abortion scenario is,[96] remember that born children too are scalded in hot water, suffocated, beaten to death. . . . Forbidding this harm does not seem to work.[97]

We must let go of our misconceptions.[98] The choices are not abortion/adoption or abortion/poor-but-happy child. The children of teenage mothers are not healthy,[99] and adoptive parents can be cruelly—sometimes racistly—selective.[100] Our foster care system has authored volumes of its own horror stories.[101] And remember the minor's story:[102] Many of the teenagers who are forced to go through with their pregnancies are not going to part with their babies—even if they have no possible way to care for them.[103]

Remember Becky's parents' story.[104] Try not to forget the pain her parents are living through. Mandatory parental involvement is going to increase their pain, for teen-

---

[94] It should be noted that the accuracy of Judge Noonan's story has been rigorously challenged. *See* Flower, *Coming into Being: the Prenatal Development of Human Life,* in *Abortion, Medicine, and the Law,* J. Butler & D. Walbert eds. (4th ed.) (preliminary draft) (dismissing early fetal movement as "knee jerk" on grounds that neocortical cells do not *begin* connecting until some time between 19 and 22 weeks, meaning that higher brain is isolated from sensations until then); *cf.* Sarkin-Hughes, *Choice and Informed Request: The Answer to Abortion,* 1 Stellenbosch L. Rev. 372, 377–82 (1990) (South African law journal article advocating availability of abortion until 20th week of pregnancy based on, among other things, analysis of fetal development). I am using Judge Noonan's version of the unborn's story *because* it is so extreme. My overall objective is to show that, even if Judge Noonan's story proves true, there are other poignant stories about pain, stories that justify allowing minors access to confidential abortion.

[95] Pregnancies will not stop; children will be born: "The birth rate for 15–17 year-olds in Minneapolis rose 38.4% from 1980 to 1984, while the birth rate for 18–19 year-olds, who were unaffected by the law, rose only 0.3%." Plaintiff's Exhibit 116, Hodgson v. Minnesota, 648 F. Supp. 756 (D. Minn. 1986).

[96] It should be noted that many of those most sympathetic to the pain of the unborn are also opposed to drugs that promise to reduce their alleged pain. *See infra* note 131; *see also Choices, supra* note 10, at xxv:

> A critical alternative, especially for rape victims, the morning-after pill is available in clinics throughout the country, but thanks to anti-choice pressure, its use remains controversial and poorly publicized. That same pressure is depriving American women of access to the French abortifacient RU486, which studies show to be a safe, effective alternative to early surgical abortion.

[97] My authority on this point is Lisa Steinberg and the thousands of children like her. Lisa was beaten into a coma by Joel Steinberg, an attorney who illegally adopted Lisa after being entrusted with arranging her adoption. For the story of Michele Launders, Lisa's biological mother, see McMurran, *Michele Launders Learns to Live with a Mother's Nightmare,* People, Aug. 27, 1990 (NEXIS, Magazines source file). Keep in mind that there are 2.5 million cases of child abuse reported each year—Kantrowitz and Springen, *Parental Indiscretion,* Newsweek, Apr. 22, 1991 (NEXIS, Magazines source file)—and that reports of child abuse in the United States have been increasing steadily during the past decade. *Children's Crusade,* Newsweek, Oct. 8, 1990 (NEXIS, Magazines source file); *see generally Wounded Innocents: The Real Victims of the War Against Child Abuse* (1990) (Prometheus Books).

[98] We no longer live in a world

> where all children are born into families that will take care of them, whether their conception came about through love or violence. By contrast, the court decisions addressed a world that seems to have spun out of control, where pregnant children have to be forced to talk to their parents. Who would not wish for a *Father Knows Best* kind of life, where teenagers delayed becoming parents until they were no longer children, where youngsters

age girls are 24 times as likely to die of childbirth as of a first-trimester abortion,[105] and, based on Minneapolis' experience, parental involvement laws will make more teenage women give birth.[106] Also consider the danger of delay recognized in *Roe*[107] and that the Minnesota parental notification law upheld in *Hodgson* increased the percentage of minors who obtained *second* trimester abortions by 26.5%.[108] Moreover, remember Becky's desperation. Abortion is a desperate act and making abortion illegal will only increase that desperation.[109]

Remember Spring Adam's story.[110] To help you conceptualize her life with her father, I offer you his profile—the profile of a batterer: a person with low self-esteem and unpredictable mood swings; he is a person who confuses sexual and emotional intimacy and is pathologically jealous.[111] There was no boundary between Spring's father and herself, no distance—no perception of Spring as a separate individual with her own rights and feelings. It is "almost impossible [to communicate with Spring's father] in a human way because he decrees that he has the right to make all decisions and isn't

---

in trouble could turn to families full of wise advice, where rape and incest were unknown and abortion was an unusual remedy for a rare misfortune?

Carlson, *supra* note 80.

[99] *See infra* note 103. "Young mothers, in the absence of adequate nutrition and appropriate prenatal care, are at a heightened risk of pregnancy complications and poor birth outcomes . . ." Comment, *supra* note 3, at 119. Compared to children of mothers in their twenties, children of teenage mothers are twice as likely to die in infancy. Alan Guttmacher Institute, *Teenage Pregnancy: The Problem That Hasn't Gone Away* 29 (1981) [hereinafter *Teenage Pregnancy*]. These children are also more likely to be premature or of low birth weight than children of older child bearers. *Id.; Digest: Social Factors, Not Age, Are Found to Affect Risk of Low Birth Weight,* 16 Fam. Plan. Persp. 142–43 (1984) ("Adolescents continue to be more likely than adult women to have low birth-weight babies. . . ."). Low birth rate causes neurological defects, including mental retardation, and may even cause infant mortality. *See Substantially Higher Morbidity and Mortality Rates Found Among Infants Born to Adolescent Mothers,* 16 Fam. Persp. 91–92 (1984).

[100] Consider Whoopi Goldberg's response to the racism that scars our adoption practices:

The other thing, too, what would make it sort of a little bit easier, is if you could get some of these black and Puerto Rican and Chicano babies adopted. Nobody adopts these babies. They all want little white babies, cute white babies with blond hair and blue eyes. Why bring a child in that you know is going to spend its life in a fucking institution? What are those peoples' alternatives to *that*?

Choices, supra note 10, at 122 (1991); *see also infra* notes 125–27 and accompanying text.

[101] These stories are some of the ugliest. *See, e.g.,* K. H. Through Murphy v. Morgan, 914 F.2d 846 (7th Cir. 1990) (child discovered to have gonorrhea at age 17 months removed from parents and placed in foster care, only to be physically and sexually abused, repeatedly, and shuffled between nine homes—all before age six years) (case remanded for trial); Milburn v. Anne Arundel County DSS, 871 F.2d 474 (4th Cir. 1989), *cert. denied,* 110 S. Ct. 148 (1989) (child, put into questionable foster care at age 23 months and removed approximately two years later, medically treated on four separate occasions for injuries allegedly inflicted by foster parents: multiple bruises and fracture of right femur; deep laceration over left eye; severely burned hands—hands allegedly immersed in hot water as punishment—resulting in permanent disfigurement; and broken tibia); *id.* at 479 (affirming dismissal of complaint against former foster parents and others, noting that "plaintiff here has filed his parallel action in the state courts of Maryland, upon the merits of which we, of course, express no opinion."; Simpson v. State, 796 P.2d 840, 842 (Alaska App. 1990) (affirming conviction of foster parent who "entered [14-year-old foster son's] room, pulled off [foster son's] underwear, and sucked his penis until [foster son] ejaculated. Simpson also attempted to digitally penetrate [foster son's] anus."); *Brooklyn Woman and Boyfriend Charged in Sex Abuse of 4 Sisters,* N.Y. Times, Nov. 21, 1990, at B1, col. 4 (NEXIS, Major Papers source file) (woman and boyfriend charged

always interested in what other people think or feel or will do.''[112] The violence that ended Spring's life was an explosion of her father's ''inability to control his anger whenever there is frustration or stress.''[113]

There is no limit as to what batterers will demand or do, for their family members *belong to* them.[114] Batterers who rape and impregnate their children are often themselves the victims of childhood abuse.[115] Their abuse is a scar they carry, and their victims—their children—will be scarred in a way that is likely to affect their own parenting.[116] Untreated, the batterer's pain therefore regenerates by feeding upon child after child, after child . . .

VI. What We Should Consider

Even with some assurance by medical experts that it is exaggerated, if not pure fiction, why do I and so many others find the story narrated by Judge Noonan so difficult to dismiss?[117] I think, in part, it is because, like Judge Noonan, I am Catholic and I feel

---

with sexually abusing four sisters—ages six, nine, twelve, and sixteen years—placed in foster care) (''The man police identified as her boyfriend . . . was charged with rape, sodomy, endangering the welfare of a minor and more than 60 counts of sexual abuse involving all four girls.'').

[102] *See supra* Part IV.B.

[103] *See generally* Comment, *supra* note 3. To give you some idea of what the lives of such children and their mothers are like, I offer you the following empirical findings:

- ''Children born of teenagers are much more likely to grow up in poverty and be undereducated and poorly housed. Children born of teenage mothers are twice as likely to die in infancy as are those born of women in their 20s, and they are much more likely to be raised in resentment and rage.'' Carlson, *supra* note 80; *see* Foley, *supra* note 4, at 17.
- Eight in ten women who become mothers at 17 or younger drop out of high school and only one in fifty finishes college. Center for Population Options, Washington, D.C., *The Facts: Teenage Childbearing, Education, and Employment* (1987) (factsheet).
- Families headed by teenage mothers are seven times more likely to be poor. Alan Guttmacher Institute, *supra* note 99, at 33.
- ''[T]eenage mothers usually go on to have large families, adding to the growing number of individuals who are trapped in poverty and prevented from becoming productive citizens.'' Foley, *supra* note 4, at 17; *see* Newcomer, *Not Getting Pregnant Pays off for Teens,* Rocky Mtn. News, Dec. 25, 1988, at 7 (''Between 30% and 50% of teen-agers who have been pregnant once are likely to become pregnant again before they're 18.'').
- In 1985, 53% of the $15.69 billion in AFDC (Aid to Families with Dependent Children) payments went to families that began when the mother was a teenager. Center for Population Options, *Estimates of Public Costs for Teenage Childbearing* 28 (1986).
- Women who have children during their teens continue to earn less for the rest of their lives than women who postpone childbearing. *See Risking the Future: Adolescent Sexuality, Pregnancy, and Childbearing,* vol. 1, at 130 (C. Hayes ed. 1987) (National Academy Press) (hereinafter *Risking the Future*).
- Children of teenage parents tend to have lower I.Q. and achievement scores, and they are more likely to repeat at least one grade. *See* Baldwin & Cain, *The Children of Teenage Parents,* 12 Fam. Plan. Persp. 34, 37–38 (1980).
- Children born to teenagers will be disadvantaged educationally, socially, and psychologically. *See generally* Marecek, *Consequences of Adolescent Childbearing and Abortion,* in *Adolescent Abortion: Psychological and Legal Issues, Report of the Interdivisional Committee on Adolescent Abortion, American Psychological Association* 96 (G. Melton ed. 1986).

guilty about promoting a practice that causes the pain and destruction he describes.[118] I also mourn the lives that will never come into being—lives that would have been unique and cannot be replaced. Nevertheless, I stand behind the minor's right to a confidential abortion and alleviate my guilt by thinking about Spring and Becky.

Another reason for my reaction to Judge Noonan's argument, a reason suggested by Professor Catharine MacKinnon, is my gender. Professor MacKinnon proposes that men relate to the fetus and are, therefore, sympathetic to its pain: "Men may more readily identify with the fetus than with the pregnant woman if only because all have been fetuses and none will ever be a pregnant woman."[119] She also steps back from the fetus and, looking at the problem in its societal context, asks *why* we are having abortions. Her answer is sexism:

> *If sex equality existed, there would be no more forced sex; safe effective contraception would be available and the psychological pressures surrounding its use would be gone; whatever womanhood meant, women*

See also infra note 130 and accompanying text. It should be noted, however, that these consequences of teenage pregnancy may be softened as society becomes more tolerant and sympathetic toward teenage pregnancy—as more members of this society confront the reality that *their* daughters, granddaughters and nieces are sexually active. Moreover, recent studies by the Guttmacher Institute suggest that earlier predictions may be too pessimistic. *See* Furstenberg, Brooks-Gunn & Morgan, *Adolescent Mothers and Their Children in Later Life*, 19 Fam. Plan. Persp. 142, 150 (1987) ("The young mothers who participated in our study are far better off today than they were a decade ago; many more have advanced their schooling, found employment, become independent of welfare, established their own households and regulated their fertility."). However, I personally am a bit suspicious of the optimism surfacing in this latest Guttmacher study, for the study was completed during the 1980s while our society was binging on the fruits of an inflated economy—a time when we were *all* doing better.

[104] *See supra* Part IV.C.

[105] Carlson, *supra* note 80 (based on data compiled by the Alan Guttmacher Institute); *see Teenage Pregnancy, supra* note 99, at 29 (death rate among mothers under 15 years 2.5 times rate among mothers 20 to 24).

[106] *See supra* note 95.

[107] 410 U.S. at 148–50, 162–63.

[108] *Percent Abortions of Second Trimester: Minnesota Residents*, Plaintiff's Exhibit 122, Hodgson v. Minnesota, 648 F. Supp. 756 (D. Minn. 1986), *aff'd*, 110 S. Ct. 2926 (1990) (discussed *supra* at Part II.B.6).

[109] The desperation I speak of leads to death. *Choices, supra* note 10, at xxiii:

> In 1973, the risk was 3.4 deaths per 100,000; by 1985, it had dropped to .4 deaths per 100,000. The figures illustrate the enormous impact legalizing abortion has had on women's lives: Of the 1.6 million legal abortions done each year in the United States, only 6 result in the mother's death; of the 1.5 million done in Mexico, where abortion is illegal, 140,000 women die.

For a discussion of how illegalizing abortion has simply pushed it into South Africa's back alleys, see Sarkin-Hughes, *supra* note 94, at 386 (citations omitted): "With possibly a quarter of a million illegal backstreet abortions annually in South Africa, one has to conclude that abortion on request already exists."

[110] *See supra* Part IV.F.

[111] *See generally* D. Sonkin, D. Martin & L. Walker, *The Male Batterer: A Treatment Approach* (1985).

[112] Transcript of Record at 306, Hodgson v. Minnesota, Civ. No. 3-81538 (D.Minn. Jan. 23, 1985) (testimony Dr. Lenore Walker) (on file with ACLU Reproductive Freedom Project).

[113] *Id.* at 306, 310.

[114] *See* L. Walker, *The Battered Woman Syndrome* 38 (1984).

would need neither men nor intercourse nor babies to prove it; abortions for sex selection as now practiced would be unthinkable; the workplace would be organized with women as much in mind as men; the care of children would be a priority for adults without respect to gender; women would be able to support themselves and their families (in whatever form) in dignity through the work they do. Now imagine the woman who is pregnant without wanting to be.[120]

Professor MacKinnon sees *both* abortion and forced motherhood as the products of sex inequality.[121] Her approach is to take away the causes of abortion and thereby extinguish its need.[122] This may not be as difficult to realize as critics/skeptics would suggest, since "[n]o *free* woman, with 100 percent effective, nonharmful birth control readily available, would 'choose' abortion."[123] In the words of Professor MacKinnon, "Sex does not look a lot like freedom when it appears normatively less costly for women to risk an undesired, often painful, traumatic, dangerous, sometimes illegal, and potentially life-threatening procedure than to protect oneself in advance."[124]

---

[115] See Note, *supra* note 2, at 2190 ("[T]he internalization of the anger and anxiety that the incest victim has not been allowed to express frequently results in a profound self-hatred that causes self-destructive behavior later on: incestuous childhood victimization commonly leads to other abusive relationships, self-mutilation, prostitution, and drug and alcohol addiction") (citations omitted).

[116] *Id.*

[117] See *supra* note 94. Judge Noonan's article has had a profound impact: Fetal pain has been the subject of movies on abortion, and the issue has been debated in Congress. At least one of these movies, *The Silent Scream*, has received wide national exposure.

[118] The reaction of Catholics to abortion has been discussed in *Choices, supra* note 10, at xxvi:

> Those in the book who had grown up Catholic typically suffered great conflict about abortion. They spoke for the many Catholic women who, in spite of the Church's absolute prohibition, choose abortion in numbers that are close to the national average—in fact, at a rate that is 30 percent higher than the abortion rate for Protestant women. It is interesting to note that the Church's prohibition was not always so absolute. From A.D. 1150 to the nineteenth century, Catholic canon law held that abortion of an "unformed" embryo—up to forty days for a male and eighty for a female (it was thought that the male fetus quickened earlier)—was not murder, though it was considered a sexual sin. For centuries, Catholic theologians taught that ensoulment did not occur until the embryo began to show human form.

For a more personal account, consider Rita Moreno's story:

> When I grew up, there were very definitely good girls and bad girls. Bad girls did bad things, and sex was certainly a bad thing.
>
> I came to New York City from Puerto Rico and was raised a typical Catholic. I had to go to catechism, have my communion, go to confession, the whole business . . . and there was *loads* of guilt, by the pound. My mother took me to church for a while, but then she stopped going and I just went on my own because I was supposed to.

Id. at 41.

[119] MacKinnon, *Reflections on Sex Equality Under Law,* 100 Yale L.J. 1281, 1309–10 (1991) [hereinafter *Sex Equality*]; see also *Feminist Theory, supra* note 30, at 186: "On another level, men's issues of potency, of continuity as a compensation for mortality, of the thrust to embody themselves or their own image in the world, underlie their relation to babies (and much else)."

Racism is another reason for relating to and sympathizing with the unborn. Images of blue-eyed, smiling babies and infertile parents waiting to embrace them fire a lot of the pro-life momentum. Unfortunately, this is not the reality. The babies our teenagers give birth to are not healthy,[125] and although our society does not discriminate on the basis of race in drafting its parental involvement laws, we do discriminate when it comes to the babies we worry about.[126] I was encouraged to make this point by the words of Byllye Avery, founder of the National Black Women's Health Project:

> *Racism is also manifest in [the pro-life] movement in that they're talking about* white *babies, not black. There are so many white people who want to have babies but can't because of infertility due to sexually transmitted diseases, delayed pregnancy, and problems caused by poorly developed birth control technology like the IUD. But there ain't enough white babies around to adopt because the white girls are opting to either*

---

[120] *Sex Equality, supra* note 119, at 1326–27; *see also Feminist Theory, supra* note 30, at 190 (citation omitted): "The availability of abortion removes the one real consequence men could not easily ignore, the one remaining legitimate reason that women have had for refusing sex besides the headache. As Andrea Dworkin puts it, analyzing male ideology on abortion: 'Getting laid was at stake.' "

[121] In her contribution to the Yale Law Journal's Centennial Issue, Professor MacKinnon writes "when convenient to do away with the consequences of sexual intercourse (meaning children), women get abortion rights. Women can have abortions so men can have sex." *Sex Equality, supra* note 119, at 1300. She also writes that "[f]orced motherhood is sex inequality" and that "[i]f states wanted to protect the fetus, rather than discriminate against women, they would help the woman, not make her a criminal." *Id.* at 1319, 1320. I offer you a graphic illustration of this latter point:

> When [Pennsylvania] did not require that rape or incest be reported to appropriate authorities, an average of 36 rape-related abortions a month were paid for by the state. When reporting requirements took effect in 1988, that number went down to about three a month.

Carlson, *supra* note 80. Keep in mind that "rape is one of the most underreported crimes in America. The Senate Judiciary Committee estimates that a woman is raped every six minutes in the U.S." *Id.*

The duality of Professor MacKinnon's position—her opposition to forced motherhood as well as sexist society's institution of abortion—suggests that she should be distinguished from "pro-life" feminists. *See Sex Equality, supra* note 119, at 1300 n.93 ("Juli Loesch, a self-styled 'pro-life feminist' associated with Operation Rescue, says, 'the idea [of abortion] is that a man can use a woman, vacuum her out, and she's ready to be used again[.]' "). The position taken by pro-life feminists is reminiscent of the position taken by feminists who lived a few generations before:

> I never thought of telling my great-aunt, a suffragist who lived to the age of ninety-four. She had a somewhat Victorian viewpoint and would have been very disturbed at the idea of sex outside of marriage. To a lot of feminists of that era, that generation, who lived and died virgins, sex was something that men did to women. It was a mystery, a misery, but women went through it in order to have what she called "a nice baby."

Choices, supra note 10, at 64–65 (Nora Sayre's story).

[122] *Sex Equality, supra* note 119, at 1324: "Those who think that fetuses should not have to pay with their lives for their mothers' inequality might direct themselves to changing the conditions of sex inequality that make abortions necessary. They might find the problem largely withered away if they, too, opposed sex on demand."

[123] A. Rich, *Of Woman Born: Motherhood as Experience and Institution* 268–69 (1976) (emphasis added); *see also Choices, supra* note 10, at xxxi:

keep their babies or have abortions. So the anti-choice movement is trying to cut down on those white girls' abortions. It doesn't give a damn about black women and black babies. It just wants abortions stopped. Women of color and black women happen to be caught in the cross fire.[127]

Sexism and racism—it is often enlightening to push aside the positions we take and reach inside ourselves to find the honest reasons *why* we assume them. Following this approach, we may discover that our judgment is sheathed by layers of misconceptions. Aware of these misconceptions, we may then be able to peel them away.[128] Professor Tribe approaches abortion in a similar way on a societal level—that is, he focuses on our need for abortion and approaches the issue causally, proposing that we should leave the right of abortion alone and, instead, eliminate the need and desire to exercise that right.[129] More specifically, he suggests that we work on making people want children by providing affordable postnatal health care, mandatory maternity and paternity leave options, good child care and flexible time arrangements in the workplace.[130] Professor Tribe also encourages improving sex education and introducing new

---

> In spite of the fact that the United States leads all industrialized nations in teen pregnancy, our high schools offer a paltry six and a half hours of sex education per year—including less than two hours on sexually transmitted diseases and contraception—and studies show that parent-child communication about sex is limited at best.
>
> Most of the women kept their pregnancies and abortions a secret from their parents. Some feared physical retaliation, but most wanted to spare their parents stress, worry, or shame. These women kept the silence (some, to this day) so that their parents' dreams would not be dashed, dreams of daughters pure and innocent, asexual—and therefore not fully human. It was an impossible dream for most young women to live up to. It still is.

[124] *Feminist Theory, supra* note 30, at 185. Professor MacKinnon's observation is reflected in the stories of women who have had abortions, such as Polly Bergen's:

> I feel angry at the guy. I feel angry that guys were raised to believe that the most important thing was to get some girl in bed, girls were raised to believe that the most important thing was *not* to do it, and this conditioning created so much torture and hell for everybody, for boys as well as girls.

Choices, supra note 10, at 28.

[125] *See supra* notes 99 and 103 and accompanying text.

[126] *See supra* note 100 and accompanying text.

[127] *Choices, supra* note 10, at 152. Parental involvement laws will increasingly affect minorities disproportionately: The rates of abortion, birth, and pregnancy all declined between 1980 and 1987 for white adolescents aged 15–19, while, "[a]mong minority women aged 15–19, . . . the abortion rate increased 11 percent, from 66 abortions per 1,000 women in 1980 to 73 abortions per 1,000 women in 1987." *Characteristics, supra* note 3, at 79.

[128] *See supra* notes 98–99 and accompanying text.

[129] L. Tribe, *supra* note 27. For reviews of Tribe's book, see Compston, Book Review, The Christian Sci. Monitor, Apr. 10, 1991, at 13 (NEXIS, Papers source file) ("Persuaded not so much by constitutional arguments as by sociological evidence, Tribe in fact argues that the only 'reasonable' approach is to allow women to choose abortion. This bias, obvious in both tone and treatment, precludes his achieving his stated goal. Instead, he provides merely another prochoice polemic."); *and* Carter, Book Review, *supra* note 12 (criticizing "the tendency of the pro-choice perspective to dominate a book that strives to be even-handed").

[130] *See generally* L. Tribe, *supra* note 27. For a discussion of what single mothers do not have, based upon data compiled from the 1980 census, see R. Jiobu, *Ethnicity and Inequality* 79–80, 85–86 (1990); *id.* at 79 ("The present data show that over three times as many women as men are in the underclass (13% versus 4%) and that the underclass consists overwhelmingly of women (74%)."); *see also supra* note 103.

methods of birth control, including the (now illegal in the United States) abortion pill RU486.[131]

Professor Tribe has also directly addressed the parental involvement provisions that are the subject of this essay. To Professor Tribe, such statutes are cruelty in the guise of compromise:

> *The overarching problem with all these purported compromises is that they are not compromises at all. Many of the laws put forward to stake out what is supposedly a middle ground in the abortion debate, rather than meaningfully protecting either life or choice, randomly frustrate both and do not move us closer to a society of caring, responsible people.*
>
> *In the case of any given woman, these laws will either act as an absolute obstacle to abortion or will not stand in the way. . . . [These solutions] promise abortion rights in principle but deny them in practice*

---

[131] D. Meyers, *supra* note 23, at 46:

> It should perhaps be stated that the new French abortion pill RU-486, or discoveries similar to it, have the potential to radically change the practice of abortion. In use in France for about a year, where it is being used for one-third or more of all abortions, it apparently is more than 90 percent effective during the first seven weeks of pregnancy. It halts pregnancy by inhibiting delivery of progesterone essential to the embryo. Its importation and use in Britain or the United States, legally or illegally, could become a significant counter and to some extent moot abortion restrictions during the first trimester, if adopted by the courts or the legislatures.

Although the federal Food and Drug Administration has barred the import of RU486 into the United States since 1986, RU486 may in fact soon be licensed in Britain: "RU-486, or mifepristone, was developed by the French pharmaceutical company Roussel-Uclaf in 1980 and has been available in France since September 1988. It has been approved for use in China and is expected to be licensed in Britain later this year." *New Hampshire Lawmakers Mull Abortion Pill*, Worcester Sunday Telegram, May 5, 1991, at A12. For a timely account of RU486 and the efforts to keep it from us, see L. Lader, *RU486: The Pill that Could End the Abortion Wars and Why American Woman Don't Have It* (1991) (Lader's answer to the question posed by title is extremists in Congress and the White House who have blocked all testing—even for nonabortion uses). Lader predicts that efforts will be made to get RU486 to us through state legislatures. *Id.* at 129–30:

> [State] constitutions may assume a pivotal role in the introduction of RU 486 into the United States. The power of the federal bureaucracy and the Bush administration to ban RU 486 research at the National Institutes of Health extends only to the use of federal funds. If a state decided to allot its own money to RU 486 development, the White House would have little chance of intervening.

In fact, this is already happening:

> The New Hampshire state Legislature is moving toward approval of a resolution offering the state as a clinical test site for the French abortion pill RU-486. . . . [A] number of abortion-rights groups and politicians believe the Legislature's action may lead to similar action in other states and increase pressure on the Bush administration to allow testing of the pill.

New Hampshire Lawmakers, supra. This newspaper article also mentions similar efforts under way in California and Minnesota. *Id.* It also contains commentary on the power and efforts of antiabortionists:

> *to those who are least able to bear the burden of motherhood—particularly the young, the uneducated, the rural, and the nonwhite.*[132]

His message is that parental involvement provisions serve no useful purpose—an argument also made and substantiated by others.[133] Adding fangs to such provisions' cruelty, Professor Tribe also points out the hypocrisy of codifying parental involvement.[134]

I think we should follow the approach suggested by Professors MacKinnon and Tribe.[135] Rather than rationalizing parental involvement laws, let us ask ourselves why we are willing to vote for them. My suspicion is that, for most of us, the honest answer is not that we want to stop the pain of the unborn, believe the fetus is a person, or any such thing.[136] The primary reason is control. We, as concerned parents, want to control the sexual lives of our children. We do not want our teenage children to have sex, and we certainly do not want them to get pregnant and have abortions. We are afraid.[137]

Unfortunately, we cannot legislate away teenage sexuality. We may be able to

---

> Roussel-Uclaf has been reluctant to seek FDA approval to market [RU-486] here because of fears of boycotts by groups like the National Right to Life Committee. RU-486 works by inducing abortion in the first seven weeks of pregnancy.
>
> Some medical researchers in the United States believe the drug may also be useful in treating breast cancer, brain cancer, endometriosis and other diseases and have decried the federal government's ban on testing it as political interference in science.

Id.

[132] L. Tribe, *supra* note 27, at 208–09.

[133] First of all, minors often willingly tell their parents, and the younger the pregnant teen, the more likely that her parents know about/have suggested the abortion. *See generally Risking the Future, supra* note 103; Torres, Forrest & Eisman, *Telling Parents: Clinic Policies and Adolescents' Use of Family Planning and Abortion Services,* 12 Fam. Plan. Persp. 284, 288 (1980). Many minors are able to understand and reason about their health care alternatives and are therefore capable of making a decision without their parents. *See* Kaser-Boyd, Adelman & Taylor, *Minors' Ability to Identify Risks and Benefits of Therapy,* 16 Prof. Psychology: Res. and Prac. 411, 411 (1985) ("[E]ven young minors and those with no therapy experience were able to identify relevant and practical concerns that were appropriate to their situations and their developmental needs."); Kaser-Boyd, Adelman, Taylor & Nelson, *Children's Understanding of Risks and Benefits of Psychotherapy,* 15 J. Clin. Child Psychology 165, 165 (1986) ("Wide variability between minors at different ages, reading comprehension levels, and demographic characteristics suggest that determinations of competency to consent be based on the capacities of the individual child."); *see generally, Children's Competence to Consent,* G. Melton, G. Koocher, & M. Saks eds. (1983); Melton, *Developmental Psychology and the Law: The State of the Art,* 22 J. Fam. L. 445, 463–66 (1983–84). In fact, it is somewhat inevitable that parental involvement will either end in agreement or all out war, since adolescents have developed their own sense of conscience and morality by the age of 14. *See generally* L. Kohlberg, *The Psychology of Moral Development* (1984). And often, adolescents who choose not to tell a parent about their pregnancy or planned abortion often show an impressive degree of maturity and sensitivity in making their decision. My authority on this point is "Kathy," the first minor who appeared in an Alabama court to seek permission to have an abortion without her parents' consent: "Most of the time, kids will tell their parents if they're pregnant . . . it won't be in a situation like this. But I think kids know when they can tell their parents things and when they can't. Kids aren't totally stupid just because they're kids." *Choices, supra* note 10, at 177. Massachusetts' experience confirms that this is true:

> Sabino said that going to court made some teen-agers "feel like criminals." She said that the young women choose that route because they are afraid they will be thrown out of the house or abused in some way by their parents. Others do not want to tell their parents because the family has recently suffered a serious illness or death and they want to spare

parent some of it away—without raising frigid adults.[138] However, we have to accept the fact that, no matter what we do, many adolescents are going to have sex and some are going to get pregnant.[139] We should temper our craving to know by thinking about Spring.[140] If we try to make these adolescents ask their parents for legal abortions, whether it is because they are afraid of their parents or afraid of disappointing them, some of these minors are going to seek illegal abortions.[141] Most will get them, overcome the trauma and go on to live productive lives.[142] Some will give birth to unhealthy and/or unwanted children.[143] Others will die.[144]

One of Professor Tribe's major themes is that enlightened cultures adopt liberal abortion laws.[145] I would add that truly enlightened cultures maintain liberal abortion laws but few members of those cultures have the need to use them. This is the society we should strive to become. As the world seems to be recognizing,[146] we will not eliminate Becky's and Spring's need for abortions by taking away their access to them. Unfortunately, our society now appears to be spinning off in another direction.

---

their parents another trauma. . . . And others have problems communicating with their parents. . . .

Mitchell, *supra* note 64, at 4; *see also* Transcript of Record at 1143–44, Hodgson v. Minnesota, Civ. No. 3-81538 (D. Minn. January 23, 1985) (testimony of Dr. Gary Melton) (transcripts of trial testimony are on file with ACLU Reproductive Freedom Project); *id.* at 908–09 (testimony of Dr. Elissa Benedek).

[134] In the words of Professor Tribe "[T]he premises on which such consent requirements rest equally support parentally compelled abortions," but many of the pro-life advocates promoting parental involvement would cringe at this idea. *See* L. Tribe, *supra* note 27, at 199. This observation was also made by Polly Bergen in *Choices, supra* note 10, at 32: "Once you allow politicians to tell you you can't have [an abortion], those same politicians can turn around and say you must have one, or it can only be a boy, it can only have blue eyes, it can only be a girl, you can only have two, you can't have any."

Also consider that we limit the access of minors to abortion on the grounds that they are too immature; does it not follow that they are then too immature to raise a child? Moreover, remember what we let minors do in confidence: "All fifty states have enacted legislation protecting the confidentiality of the minor's decision to seek health care for medical problems related to sexual activity; all but one state allow minors to consent to medical treatment for sexually transmitted diseases." Brief for Petitioners, at 43 & Exhibit C, Hodgson v. Minnesota, 853 F.2d 1452 (8th Cir. 1988) (en banc), *aff'd,* 110 S. Ct. 2926 (1990) (discussed *supra* at Part II.B.6). Hypocrisy is also evidenced in the false distinctions we draw—such as the distinction between notification and consent. As a practical matter, there is no difference. *See* Benshoof & Pilpel, *supra* note 46, at 144. And, if these statutes are premised on the best interests of the minor, how can we justify requiring the involvement of two parents where there is, willingly, the involvement of one? Consider that 20 to 25% of Minnesota minors who went to court to avoid notification of both parents were accompanied by or had consulted one parent—mostly single mothers who had not seen their children's fathers in years. Hodgson v. Minnesota, 648 F. Supp. 756, 764 (D. Minn. 1986). Let me finish this point with the words of Linda Ellerbee:

> I think that one of the things that makes me angriest, as angry as the shame and pain I had to go through for the illegal abortion, is the lack of education, of sex education in the home, in the church, in the school, all of those places that didn't give me any information that got me into that place. The same people who don't want you to have an abortion don't want you to have sex education, and there is no question where this ignorance leads.

Choices, supra note 10, at 86.

[135] The conclusions reached by Professors Tribe and MacKinnon are supported by the Panel on Adolescent Pregnancy and Childbearing. This panel, after two years of review, analysis, and debate, has reached six general conclusions—conclusions that suggest our social policy should emphasize eliminating poverty,

Conclusion

This essay is my effort to summarize the existing law on minors and abortion and the ways in which that law is changing. In fact, as this article goes into print, the United States Supreme Court is deciding the constitutionality of Pennsylvania's restrictive abortion statute, and the nation waits to see what is left of *Roe v. Wade*.[147] The *Webster, Hodgson,* and *Ohio* trilogy is not difficult to interpret: Abortion access is an issue on its way down into the states, and the questions generated by this issue are eventually going to receive purely political answers. The poor and young, politically weak groups, are not likely to fair well when their mercy is at the feet of state legislatures. They were the first to have their access to abortion limited while the Court was protecting that right; the present trend among state legislatures—enacting, laws that mandate parental involvement and reduce the number of abortion providers—suggests that the young and poor are again the first targets.

---

strengthening family ties, and enhancing young people's perceptions of their futures. *See generally* Comment, *supra* note 3, at 119–20. I follow the panel's approach to this problem and agree with its conclusions:

- Our highest priority should be preventing adolescent pregnancy;
- We should encourage adolescents to delay sexual activity;
- Society must avoid treating adolescent sexuality as a problem peculiar to teenage girls;
- There must be flexibility to account for differences in values, attitudes, and experiences;
- In allocating limited resources, we should favor adolescents from socially and economically disadvantaged backgrounds, for they are the groups that have been shown to benefit most from such efforts; and
- Responsibility for dealing with adolescent sexuality should be shared among individuals and families, along with communities and governments; "Public policies should affirm the role and responsibility of families to teach human values. . . ."

Id.

Lists of ideals are easy to generate. Is it possible to transform this list of ideals into tangible, effective programs? I believe the answer is yes. Consider the controversial Dollar-a-Day program started in Denver, Colorado by Dr. Jeffrey Dolgan, Chief of Psychology in the Department of Psychiatry and Behavioral Sciences at Denver's Children's Hospital. The program encourages girls who have already had one baby to abstain from having another by paying them a dollar a day. This $7 per week subsidy is delivered with guidance and support. *See* Foley, *supra* note 4, at 18; Newcomer, *supra* note 103, at 7. And the program apparently works:

> After five years, 56 girls have successfully completed the Denver program by avoiding a second pregnancy before turning 18. This represents an 84 percent success rate. In more pragmatic terms, 56 girls broke the gripping cycle of having successive "stairstep babies" following their first child. National statistics show that in the two years following a girl's first pregnancy, there is a 30 to 50 percent likelihood that she will conceive again.

Foley, *supra* note 4, at 18. Especially important in these recessionary days, Dr. Dolgan has proven that our economy is no excuse for doing nothing: Creativity can, at least to some extent, serve as a substitute for money. It should be noted that "[e]ach teen pregnancy costs the state $19,000. The privately funded Dollar-A-Day program provides counseling for 15 girls for an entire year for just $10,000." *Id.* at 19.

[136] These reasons seem to immediately wilt away when reality is sprinkled on the misconceptions that support them—particularly misconceptions about the mother and her conception. For a bucket full of this reality, read *A Father's Story*, in *Choices, supra* note 10, at 179, 182, which is the story of a well-known journalist whose daughter was brutally gang-raped and became pregnant:

I have told you stories to help you understand the power of this law and the importance of the issue. My conclusion is theoretically simple: We should be honest about our motives, be realistic about our adolescents' sexuality, and recognize the danger of narrowing their access to safe, legal abortion. In practice, I ask for a great deal—that we as parents and teachers accept the reality of our adolescents' sexuality and raise them to make the "right" choices before and after mistakes happen, rather than trying to completely control and vote that reality away. Perhaps the most difficult thing I ask is that we be there *when* they make mistakes.

Becky has given us the means to accomplish what I ask. Just remember her story.[148]

> As soon as we knew, there was no question in my mind about what course to take. I didn't have any feelings about murder or innocent life. That's an argument that never went through my head. I never argued with myself or with my wife. We never raised the questions that all the right-to-life ethicists raise. The fetus didn't mean anything to me. I have no love for something that was brought about by horror, terror, and attack.

[137] Let us not forget how afraid our pregnant adolescents are. Consider how that fear almost took Rita Moreno's life:

> I went to my lover's doctor, reluctantly. He took one look and said, "You're going to the hospital . . . *now.*" I said, "Will they arrest me? Will I go to jail?" That's how scared I was. He told me not to worry about that. He admitted me to Cedars Sinai Hospital in Los Angeles and finished the procedure. When I came out of the anesthesia, he told me I had had an incomplete abortion [tissue fragments were left inside]. He hadn't told me earlier because he didn't want to scare me, but he told me afterwards: "You could have died."

Choices, supra note 10, at 48.

[138] I believe this is true. Actress Polly Bergen's explanation for why adolescents have sex confirms my belief, and may also explain why today's children—the "latch key," one-parent-family generation—are having more sex:

> Nobody ever took into consideration *feelings.* They never took into consideration wanting to be held or wanting to be loved or wanting to be cared for or wanting to not feel alone or frightened. I think even today there are so many young girls and so many young guys who get involved sexually because they need somebody to hold them. They put out . . . putting out seems like such a small price to pay for not being lonely.

Id. at 28. *See Our Children's Fate is our Nation's Future: Their Poverty and Neglect are More than "Family Issues,"* Los Angeles Times, May 17, 1991, at B6, col. 1 (NEXIS, Major Papers source file) ("America's children are growing up without their parents; even when parents are present, too often children are growing up without the benefit of parental wisdom and guidance.").

[139] I think Jill Clayburgh has said it best:

> There is an attitude that teenagers are wildly irresponsible and that making abortions illegal will affect their level of responsibility, which it won't. I mean, I'm a case in point. Abortion wasn't legal, but I was completely not careful. And they're saying that most teenagers don't use condoms. So what is that telling you? Teenagers don't use their brains! They're

not thinking. But I don't believe they should be punished for the rest of their lives because they have this mental derangement for a few years.

Choices, supra note 10, at 56.

[140] *See supra* Part IV. F.; *see also* Barbara Corday's story in *Choices, supra* note 10, at 78: "It's hard, but we know too many stories about rape and incest and alcoholic parents and violent parents to be comfortable saying that a girl has to tell. I am absolutely willing to risk not knowing in order to protect the girls who would suffer in the telling."

[141] *See supra* note 109 and accompanying text.

[142] *See generally Choices, supra* note 10.

[143] *See supra* notes 99, 103, and accompanying text.

[144] *See supra* note 109 and accompanying text. Women are sure to die if they are forced underground, and that is exactly what is going to happen . . . plans are already in the making. *See Some Women are Teaching Each Other How to Perform Early-Term Abortions,* San Antonio Express-News (Scripps Howard Service), Aug. 31, 1991, at 17A (discussing how network of feminist health-care workers is training women around the country to perform abortions); *id.:*

> Dr. Jane Hodgson of St. Paul, who's performed abortions for 20 years, strongly disapproves of menstrual extractions. Unsuspected complications can occur, she said, that call for immediate medical attention, problems such as infection because of lack of sterilization or excessive bleeding from an incomplete abortion.

[145] *See generally* L. Tribe, *supra* note 27.

[146] Data compiled during the 1980s shows an international trend towards liberalization of abortion in "industrialized" countries. Consider the following excerpt from a South African law journal:

> In the early 1980s, 38% of the population of the world lived in countries where abortion on request was permitted, while an additional 24% of the world's population lived in states that permitted abortion on request contingent upon liberal requirements, including a wide variety of social factors such as poverty and housing.
>
> Over the last 20 years at least 52 countries have liberalized their legislation pertaining to abortion while only four have limited the access. Many of these countries extending access have decriminalized abortion in the early stages of pregnancy and allow abortion at other times in accordance with specific criteria. Canada permits abortion on request up to 20 weeks while other countries such as Austria, Denmark, Greece, Greenland, Norway and Sweden allow a woman to request an abortion until approximately twelve weeks. Britain, Finland, France, the Federal Republic of Germany, Iceland, Italy, Luxembourg, the Netherlands and New Zealand allow abortion within the framework of certain liberal health and

social specifications, which in practice permit abortion upon request from the woman. . . .
Where abortion laws in various countries have been liberalized, there has been a dramatic
decrease in morbidity and mortality as a result of pregnancy termination.

Sarkin-Hughes, *supra* note 94, at 385 (citations omitted); *see also* C. Tietze & S. Henshaw, *A World
Review: 1986* 1 (6th ed. 1986) (Alan Guttmacher Institute):

The long-term worldwide trend toward liberalization of abortion laws, which began in northern
Europe in the 1930s, has continued in recent years. Since the previous edition of this fact
book appeared, in 1983, laws have undergone major liberalization in four countries with
populations of one million or more—Portugal, Taiwan, Turkey and Spain—and in a number
of less-populous areas. Only one country has significantly reduced access to legal abortion—Romania, in 1984—and Ireland amended its constitution to prevent future liberalization of its currently restrictive laws.

For another comparative approach to the abortion issue, see D. Meyers, *supra* note 23, at 23–46; *id.* at 45
("The U.S. is probably moving toward an unfortunate patchwork of laws on abortion. The likely result,
overall, will be a legal climate similar to Britain after the *Bourne* case, but before the Abortion Act [of]
1967. Only time, and some rather tumultuous political decisions, will tell.") (citation omitted); *see also*
Mitchell, *supra* note 64, at 4, which confirms that minors are already forum shopping:

Department of Public Health statistics indicate that the number of abortions obtained by 16-
and 17-year-old Massachusetts residents dropped markedly from 1980 to 1989. Although
this conclusion has been disputed by abortion opponents as overstated, abortion rights advocates are convinced that hundreds of teen-agers drive to clinics in New York, Connecticut, Maine and New Hampshire each year.

[147] *See supra* note 23.
[148] *See supra* Part IV.C.

Although no court has explicitly held that men have no rights with respect to abortion, the author states that "women's privacy interests usually lead courts to reject claims of male rights and to preclude judicial enforcement of men's interests." Also, in the cases of *Planned Parenthood of Central Missouri v. Danforth* and *Planned Parenthood of Southeastern Pennsylvania v. Casey,* the courts have thus far ruled that state requirements of spousal notification and spousal consent are both unconstitutional. Any rights of a partner that conflict with a woman's right to freely decide for or against abortion cannot be expected to withstand judicial review.

7 · Partners and the Abortion Decision

Susan M. Davies, J.D.

When the Supreme Court recognized a constitutional right to abortion in its landmark 1973 decisions in *Roe v. Wade*[1] and *Doe v. Bolton*,[2] it explicitly declined to consider men's interests. "Neither in this opinion nor in *[Doe]*," the *Roe* Court said in a footnote, "do we discuss the father's rights, if any exist in the constitutional context, in the abortion decision."[3] In the two decades since, the Court has not resolved the issue of men's rights; indeed, it still remains unclear whether any exist. This chapter considers briefly what involvement a man may have in the abortion decision of a woman he has impregnated.[4] States might try to regulate abortions in order to protect men's interests. Men might also have constitutional rights, independent of state regulation, with respect to their potential offspring. However, women's privacy interests usually lead courts to reject claims of male rights and to preclude judicial enforcement of men's interests. Although men have interests in their potential offspring and although the state may (under long-standing Supreme Court precedent) concern itself with protection of the family, neither of these interests is compelling enough to warrant interference with the woman's right to choose.

---

[1] 410 U.S. 113 (1973).

[2] 410 U.S. 179 (1973).

[3] 410 U.S. at 165 n.67.

[4] Of course, the impregnator of a married woman need not be her husband. *See* Roe v. Rampton, 535 F.2d 1219, 1221 (10th Cir. 1976) (noting ambiguity in statute requiring notification of husband: "whether under the statute the 'husband' means the 'father,' as it is apparent that the 'father' is the person who has an interest in the abortion"); Coe v. Gerstein, 376 F. Supp. 695, 697 n.5 (S.D. Fla. 1974) (recognizing possibility that husband and impregnator will not be same man).

Roe v. Wade established a legal regime strongly protective of a woman's right to obtain an abortion. The Supreme Court grounded its decision in the fundamental right of privacy guaranteed by the Constitution[5] and held that restrictions on abortions would be upheld only if they furthered compelling state interests. During the first trimester of pregnancy, *no* state interest is sufficient to restrict the decision made by a woman and her physician.[6] Second-trimester abortions may be regulated only to protect the woman's health, and during the third trimester the state may regulate abortions in the interest of fetal life but must still allow abortions to protect the woman's life or health.[7] The Court reaffirmed this framework in 1983, holding that only the health of the woman after the first trimester and the life of the fetus after viability can support state interference with the abortion decision.[8] Although subsequent decisions approving regulations restricting abortions have cast doubt upon the future of the right recognized in *Roe v. Wade,*[9] this chapter proceeds from the assumption that the *Roe v. Wade* compelling interest standard is the law of the land unless and until the Supreme Court declares otherwise.

In *Planned Parenthood of Central Missouri v. Danforth,*[10] the Court considered a state statute requiring a married woman to secure her husband's consent to obtain an abortion. The Court held that "the State may not constitutionally require the consent of the spouse . . . as a condition for abortion during the first twelve weeks of pregnancy."[11] Because the state itself could not prohibit abortions during the first trimester, the Court reasoned, the state could not "delegate authority to any particular person, even the spouse, to prevent abortion during the same period."[12] The state had asserted several justifications for the regulation, including the protection of marriage as an institution, the medical consequences of an abortion for later childbearing and other legislative limitations—such as consent requirements for adoption and disposition of real property—inherent in the marriage relationship, but the Court held that none of these was a compelling interest.[13]

The Supreme Court in *Danforth,* although invalidating the spousal consent provision, suggested that some lesser state recognition of male rights might pass constitutional muster: "This [spousal consent] section does much more than insure that the

---

[5] The majority opinion in Roe v. Wade grounded the privacy right in the fourteenth amendment, which provides that no state shall "deprive any person of life, liberty, or property, without due process of law." 410 U.S. at 163. The Supreme Court has since limited this privacy right to matters involving "family, marriage, or procreation." Bowers v. Hardwick, 478 U.S. 186 (1986).

[6] 410 U.S. at 163.

[7] *Id.* at 163–64.

[8] Akron v. Akron Center for Reproductive Health, 462 U.S. 416 (1983).

[9] *See* Rust v. Sullivan, 111 S. Ct. 1759 (1991); Hodgson v. Minnesota, 110 S. Ct. 2926 (1990); Webster v. Reproductive Health Services, 492 U.S. 490 (1989).

[10] 428 U.S. 52 (1976).

[11] *Id.* at 69.

[12] *Id.*

[13] Since spousal consent laws are unconstitutional, it follows that requiring the consent of the man who actually impregnated the woman is likewise unconstitutional. (*Danforth* involved a facial challenge to the statute, so the Court did not have to address the application of the spousal consent requirement in cases where the impregnator and the husband were not the same person.) In fact, the state justifications advanced in *Danforth* would be even less persuasive where the couple is not married, because most of those rationales were based on protecting the marital relationship. In either case, requiring male consent would give someone other than the pregnant woman a unilateral veto power over the abortion decision.

husband *participate* in the decision whether his wife should have an abortion."[14] Thus, some regulation short of a consent requirement, the Court implied, might be constitutional. An obvious such regulation would be a state requirement that a woman *notify* her partner before obtaining an abortion.[15]

The Court has already developed an extensive jurisprudence concerning state statutes that require minors to notify their parents before obtaining an abortion.[16] Parental notification requirements are constitutionally permissible if they provide judicial or administrative devices whereby parental notification is not required if the minor is sufficiently mature to make the abortion decision for herself or if it is in her best interests.[17] Proponents of partner notification statutes make similar arguments, attempting to draw analogies to the justifications for parental notification requirements. They suggest that, in both cases, a person other than the woman has an interest in the decision—the parents of the minor or the partner of the adult woman—and propose allowing the woman to circumvent the requirement when her interests substantially outweigh those of the man.[18]

But the analogy between adult women and minors is insupportable, because the two groups are differently situated with respect to the abortion decision. The parents of a minor have an interest in her abortion decision because she is their child, because of her presumptive vulnerability and lack of experience. The state may justify a parental notification requirement, for a minor's abortion decision implicates a societal interest in children already within a family, an interest perhaps rooted in a paternalistic conception of family deeply ingrained in our culture. An adult woman and her partner, on the other hand, are presumptively equally mature and capable of making significant decisions. But because only the woman is capable of pregnancy and only the woman must bear the consequences of childbirth or abortion, and because only the individual may control the destiny of her own body, the woman's right to choose between abortion and pregnancy is greater than the man's real, but ultimately lesser, personal interests.

Several lower federal courts have considered partner notification statutes, and they have reached conflicting results.[19] Most recently, a federal appellate court held, in *Planned Parenthood of Southeastern Pennsylvania v. Casey*,[20] that a spousal notification provision was unconstitutional "because it imposes an undue burden on a woman's abortion decision and does not serve a compelling state interest."[21] The provision required women seeking abortions to certify that they had notified their spouses; a false statement by a

---

[14] 428 U.S. at 70 (emphasis added).

[15] *See* Jones v. Smith, 474 F. Supp. 1160 (S.D. Fla. 1979).

[16] In *Hodgson*, 110 S. Ct. 2926, the Court held that a state law requiring minors to notify both parents was unconstitutional. The right of the father of a minor child to be notified before she obtains an abortion is conceptually different from the circumstance of the male partner. If a minor's father has such a right, it is because he is a parent, not because he is a man.

[17] *See, e.g.,* Bellotti v. Baird, 443 U.S. 622 (1979); Planned Parenthood Association of Kansas City v. Ashcroft, 462 U.S. 476 (1983). In H. L. v. Matheson, 450 U.S. 398 (1981), the Court upheld a Utah statute requiring physicians to "notify, if possible" the parents of a minor child before performing an abortion.

[18] *See, e.g.* 18 Pa. Cons. Stat. Ann. § 3209 (1983 & Supp. 1991); text at note 22, *infra*.

[19] *Compare* Scheinberg v. Smith, 659 F.2d 476 (5th Cir. 1981), and Jones v. Smith, 474 F. Supp. 1160 (S.D. Fla. 1979), *with* Planned Parenthood of Southeastern Pennsylvania v. Casey, 947 F.2d 682 (3d Cir. 1991), *cert. granted,* 60 U.S.L.W. 3498 (1992), and Planned Parenthood of Rhode Island v. Board of Medical Review, 598 F. Supp. 625 (D.R.I. 1984).

[20] 947 F.2d 683 (3d Cir. 1991).

[21] *Id.* at 715 (footnote omitted).

woman was a misdemeanor, and a doctor performing an abortion without spousal notification was subject to civil penalties.[22] The statute exempted a woman from the notification requirement in four situations: when her husband was not the impregnator, when her husband could not be located, when the pregnancy was the result of sexual assault by her husband (which had been reported to law enforcement officials) or when she reasonably believed that notification would result in the infliction of bodily injury by her spouse or someone else.[23]

The court in *Casey* scrutinized recent Supreme Court abortion opinions, most supported only by a plurality of the justices, and determined that *Roe v. Wade*'s "compelling interest" standard had been abandoned in favor of Justice O'Connor's "undue burden" test.[24] Under the undue burden approach, abortion regulations must pass only rational basis review unless they "unduly burden" a woman's right to choose, in which case they must survive strict scrutiny. Two of the three judges in *Casey* held that spousal notification imposes an undue burden on a woman's right to have an abortion, and they analyzed the provision under a *Roe*-like compellingness standard. Whether or not they impose a threshold "undue burden" test, the courts properly subject enforcement of men's rights to strict scrutiny: Any requirement purporting to recognize male rights to notification might deter some women from obtaining abortions and thus conflict with the constitutional requirement that abortion regulations "not interfere with the physician-patient consultation or with the woman's choice between abortion and childbirth."[25] The *Casey* court determined that notification was an undue burden on the woman's abortion decision. The Supreme Court has granted certiorari, and a decision is expected by July 1992.

As a practical matter, a notification requirement would have the same deterrent effect as the consent provision invalidated in *Danforth*. A man who is aware of his partner's desire to obtain an abortion may attempt to persuade her to change her mind, for example by presenting options previously ignored, such as financial support or adoption. Moreover, male involvement presents opportunities for abuse: A man might coerce his partner into giving birth when doing so is not in her best interests or might retaliate against her for choosing to have an abortion.[26] The primary justification for state regulations requiring women to notify their husbands is the state's interest in maintaining and protecting the traditional family unit. This interest in the family necessarily excludes unwed couples from the regulation: Where there is no marriage, the state recognizes no family to protect. But in the traditional, stable family, a woman will likely inform her husband of her decision to obtain an abortion anyway. It is only in those cases where the traditional structure is dysfunctional or where spousal communication or relationships are poor that the statute will have an effect on wife-husband communication, and there is no reason to think that forced disclosure will benefit the couple or the family.[27]

---

[22] *Id.* at 710.

[23] *Id.* at 709–10.

[24] *Id.* at 687–94. In contrast to *Casey, see* Guam Society of Obstetricians and Gynecologists v. Ada, 1992 U.S. App. LEXIS (9th Cir Apr. 16, 1992), explicitly declining to adopt the undue burden test and reaffirming Roe v. Wade's compelling interest standard.

[25] *Akron,* 462 U.S. at 430.

[26] For an extended discussion of the possibilities for physical, psychological and economic pressure that a husband could bring to bear against his pregnant wife in order to prevent her obtaining an abortion or to punish her for doing so, see *Casey,* 947 F.2d at 709–15.

[27] *See Casey,* 947 F.2d at 714.

It will simply interfere with—or penalize—the woman's exercise of her right to choose. The notification requirement is thus no less constitutionally infirm than a consent requirement, under either *Roe v. Wade*'s compelling state interest standard or Justice O'Connor's undue burden test.

Although the state's interest in protecting the traditional family structure is insufficient to justify restrictions on a woman's right to abortion, it may be argued that men have independent interests in their potential offspring and that the state may act to protect those interests. When a woman wishes to obtain an abortion, her partner might have reasons for wanting to participate in the decision. If the man and the woman are married or in an ongoing relationship, both partners have an interest in the procreative potential of that relationship. And if the woman decides to carry the fetus to term and ultimately give birth, the man who impregnated her has a legitimate interest in his offspring.[28] Although men cannot carry fetuses or give birth, a child, when born, is in a biological, moral, social and legal sense the father's as well as the mother's. Although the woman may have good reasons for wishing to abort the fetus, the man may have good reasons for wishing to see it carried to term and born. However, his *interests* can never outweigh her constitutional *right* to choose.[29]

Conn v. Conn,[30] decided by the Supreme Court of Indiana in 1988, provides an apt illustration. The couple involved was undergoing a divorce, and the wife was pregnant by her husband. She told him she would abort the fetus unless he agreed to put the child up for adoption and to relinquish any possible custody of the child. He sued to forestall the abortion, and the trial court granted a temporary injunction so the court could decide whose interest should prevail and whether the court should allow her to abort the fetus or should enjoin her from having an abortion and order her, in effect, to give birth to the child. The state court of appeals reversed and vacated the injunction,[31] and the state supreme court summarily affirmed. Both appellate courts held that the woman had the sole right to make the abortion decision and any recognition of the man's rights would run afoul of the Supreme Court's abortion opinions.[32]

---

[28] *See* Skinner v. Oklahoma, 316 U.S. 535, 541 (1942) (invalidating state statute authorizing sterilization of criminals: "Marriage and procreation are fundamental to the very existence and survival of the race.").

[29] *Cf.* Arnold v. Board of Education, 880 F.2d 305, 312 (11th Cir. 1989) (in action against school board for coercing minor to abort, man had no standing to sue: "As the boyfriend of Jane, John Doe's agreement or disagreement with Jane Doe's abortion decision does not enjoy constitutional protection.").

[30] 526 N.E.2d 958 (Ind. 1988), *cert. denied*, 488 U.S. 955 (1988).

[31] 525 N.E.2d 612 (Ind. App. 1988).

[32] *See also* Doe v. Doe, 314 N.E.2d 128 (Mass. 1974); *but see* Doe v. Smith, 486 U.S. 1309 (1988) (Stevens, J., sitting as circuit justice). In *Doe v. Smith,* a man sought to prevent the abortion of a fetus he had engendered. The state trial court had denied the injunction: "It would appear from the *Danforth* decision that in order to require the mother to carry a child to term against her wishes, the father must demonstrate clear and compelling reasons justifying such actions. In this case, the father has failed to do so. Reviewing the undisputed facts presented in this Cause, the Court is unable to find the interests of the [man] outweigh the interest of the [woman]." The trial judge concluded, "[E]ven if the *Danforth* decision permits the Court to balance the interest of the father of the unborn child against those of the mother, in this particular case the balancing would be in the mother's favor." The Indiana Supreme Court affirmed the trial court on the authority of its earlier disposition in *Conn.* The man brought an application in the United States Supreme Court for an emergency order restraining the woman from aborting the fetus. Justice Stevens, sitting as circuit justice, noted that the man argued only for a balancing of the relevant interests but concluded that the man's interest was insufficient to invoke the extraordinary jurisdiction of the Supreme Court "[s]ince such balancing has already been done by the trial court."

The Supreme Court in *Danforth,* by invalidating the spousal consent requirement, effectively protected women's unilateral control of the abortion decision and justified its decision by recognizing that when the man and the woman disagree, only one can prevail. "Inasmuch as it is the woman who physically bears the child and who is the more directly and immediately affected by the pregnancy, as between the two, the balance weighs in her favor."[33] Although the case is frequently cited as a forthright rejection of any assertion of a male role in the abortion decision,[34] the Court's reference to balancing implied that some interest short of consent might tip the scales the other way. Such reasoning suggests a shift toward a balancing test and away from a compelling state interest standard. That is, if enforcing the man's interests would not deprive the woman of her constitutional right to make the decision herself, the Court might uphold a law requiring that both partners be allowed to play a part.[35]

But this cannot be the case. The Supreme Court's decisions regarding other activities related to childbearing and childrearing, which are readily and necessarily distinguished from the decisions in abortion cases, suggest why. For the Court, whether intentionally or otherwise, appears to have divided the phases of procreation (potential and actual) into three parts, each of which involves different rights as between the male and the female.

First, there is sexual intercourse itself. Here, the right to use birth control[36] is premised on "the right of the *individual,* married or single, to be free from unwarranted governmental intrusion into matters so fundamentally affecting a person as the decision whether to bear or beget a child."[37] The right applies equally to men and women: Either partner in the sexual relationship can choose to use (or forgo) birth control devices.

Second, there is pregnancy and therefore the possibility of abortion. Unlike sexual activity, however, the abortion decision does not implicate both partners equally. Men certainly have some interest, but they simply cannot become pregnant; only women endure abortion operations or undergo pregnancy and childbirth. Precisely this fact underlies much of the Supreme Court's abortion jurisprudence: Because only the woman physically bears the consequences of pregnancy, only the woman may have a say in the abortion decision. Any judicial balancing that considers the man's interests could compel the woman to carry a fetus she wishes to abort. Such an order would constitute state action, blatantly violating the Constitution as interpreted in *Roe v. Wade* and cases following it. Thus, although the birth control cases recognize that sexual activity prior to, or not resulting in, conception involves purely individual rights and interests, conception—and the subsequent decision whether to carry the fetus or to abort it—of necessity and biology involves only the woman.[38]

Third, there are the cases concerning the rights to raise and care for one's children. Here, the interests of the man and the woman are basically equal, although now their

---

[33] 428 U.S. at 71.

[34] *See, e.g.,* Eubanks v. Brown, 604 F. Supp. 141 (W.D. Ky. 1984).

[35] *See, e.g.,* DiNatale v. Colonial Laboratory, Inc., 409 So.2d 512, 513 (Fla. App. 1982) ("Even though a father has no legally enforceable right to either compel or prevent an abortion, he has a right to participate in the decision").

[36] *See* Eisenstadt v. Baird, 405 U.S. 438 (1972); Griswold v. Connecticut, 381 U.S. 479 (1965).

[37] *Eisenstadt,* 405 U.S. at 543.

[38] The ability of modern science to preserve embryos cryogenically raises interesting questions in this context: Since *neither* the man nor the woman has contributed anything more than a single cell to the effort, which (if either) has the superior legal or ethical claim to control its ultimate disposition?

interest is shared (in the child) rather than purely individual (in contraception). Instructive in this context are the Supreme Court's cases concerning unwed fathers. The Court, in *Stanley v. Illinois,*[39] invalidated a state statute that conclusively presumed unwed fathers to be unfit parents and therefore without custody rights to their children. "The private interest here, that of a man and the children he has sired and raised, undeniably warrants deference and, absent a powerful countervailing interest, protection . . . Nor has the law refused to recognize those family relationships unlegitimized by a marriage ceremony."[40] The Supreme Court continued to treat the rights of unwed parents equally in *Caban v. Illinois,*[41] striking down a state statute granting unwed mothers, but not unwed fathers, a right to consent before their children could be adopted.

In *Quilloin v. Walcott,*[42] however, the Court upheld a state court's decision to allow adoption of the child by the natural mother's husband, based on the "best interests of the child," notwithstanding the assertion of the natural father—who had until then not contributed to the child's support nor participated in its upbringing—that he was a fit parent. "[T]his is not a case in which the unwed father at any time had, or sought, actual or legal custody of his child. Nor is this a case in which the proposed adoption would place the child with a new set of parents with whom the child has never before lived. Rather, the result of the adoption in this case is to give full recognition to a family unit already in existence."[43]

This line of Supreme Court decisions indicates that although fathers of illegitimate children cannot constitutionally be excluded from their upbringing, the rights of these men are largely contingent upon the exercise of parental responsibility.[44] In fact, the Court in *Caban* stated that "the special difficulties attendant upon locating and identifying unwed fathers at birth [might] justify a legislative distinction between mothers and fathers of newborns [as opposed to older children]."[45] The Supreme Court's recognition of a preexisting decisionmaking unit (the family) in *Quilloin,* notwithstanding the existence of the natural father, is somewhat like the situation of the pregnant woman and the man who impregnated her. The legal regime—protection of a stable family structure in the child's best interest in one case and *Roe v. Wade*'s near-total deference to the woman based on her constitutional rights in the other—excludes the man genetically related to the child or fetus in preference for a more important consideration.

In sum, it would be difficult to deny that a man who has impregnated a woman has an *interest* in the ensuing fetus. Nor should the state's historic interest in the family be treated lightly. But neither of these legitimate interests can permit a state-compelled intrusion on the woman's right to choose between abortion and pregnancy. The state's

---

[39] 405 U.S. 645 (1972).

[40] *Id.* at 651.

[41] 441 U.S. 380 (1979).

[42] 434 U.S. 246 (1978).

[43] *Id.* at 255.

[44] Note that the judicial rejection of state laws treating unwed parents inequitably by gender exemplified by *Stanley* and *Caban* does not extend so far as to invalidate state laws preferring married to unwed parents. In Michael H. v. Gerald D., 491 U.S. 110 (1989), the Supreme Court upheld a statute that provided that a child born into a marriage was presumed to be a product of that marriage. Relying on "the historic respect—indeed, sanctity would not be too strong a term—traditionally accorded to the relationships that develop within a unitary family," *id.* at 123, the Court refused to recognize a constitutional right of a putative father to establish his paternity of a child born into the marriage of its mother and her husband.

[45] *Id.* at 392. The Court declined to resolve the question, however, because it was not involved in the case. *Id.* at 392 n.11.

interest in promoting and maintaining stable family units is not served by coercing a woman to notify anyone of her decision to exercise her individual right. And whether the man's influence on the decision would be decisive (as in spousal consent statutes) or persuasive, or perhaps coercive (as in notification laws), any interference with the decision, appropriately assigned in *Roe v. Wade* to the woman and her physician, cannot pass constitutional muster.

The author traces the history of the tort action of wrongful birth-wrongful life and differentiates it from the tort action of wrongful conception. She shows that even though there have been landmark cases such as *Curlender v. Bio-Science Laboratories* and *Speak v. Finegold,* no case has been as influential as *Roe v. Wade.* The question must be asked, what happens if *Roe v. Wade* is overturned? The author suggests that the cause of action for wrongful birth and wrongful life may be severely limited. However, some state statutes such as Utah's contain language that *may*, somewhat paradoxically, further open up the torts of wrongful birth and wrongful life even while severely limiting the right to abortion.

8 • Wrongful Birth/Wrongful Life: The Tort Progeny of Legalized Abortion _____

Michele E. Beasley, J.D.

Where abortion is illegal, most pregnancies will conclude with a live birth,[1] whether or not the child is actually wanted. But where abortion on demand is legal, only children that are wanted should be born because unwanted pregnancies will be aborted. Therefore, when a child is born that it or its parents decide should not have been, either the parent(s) or child may have a cause of action in tort against a third person responsible for that birth, through negligence or misfeasance, under a theory of wrongful birth or wrongful life. Since the 1972 *Roe v. Wade*[2] U.S. Supreme Court decision, women in this country have had, at least in theory, a right to abortion on demand, limited only in time, for any reason—eugenics, economics, birth defects, parental handicap, inconvenience, birth control, age of the mother, marital status, stigma, etc. Certain kinds of interference in a woman's or couple's rights to terminate a pregnancy have been recognized as tortious by some courts. The duty of a medical care provider not to tortiously interfere in a pregnant patient's and/or her partner's decision whether to conceive or carry the pregnancy to term has come to be recognized, after more than 20 years of litigation, by at least 18 states and the District of Columbia, all of which give the parents a cause of action against the medical care provider.[3] The recognition of any cause of action by a child against a medical care provider has been more difficult. That is because the negligence complained of is simultaneously the cause of the harm, the child's painful or unwanted existence, and a benefit to the child, it's life. Only in 1982

---

[1] A pregnancy might also conclude with a natural miscarriage.
[2] 410 U.S. 113 (1973).
[3] *See infra* n. 62.

did a court first allow a child to sue for wrongful life and only two other states have followed its lead.

This chapter will explore the elements of the torts of wrongful birth and wrongful life and the theories by which courts have either rejected or accepted these causes of action. The chapter will address the interplay of tort and abortion law by looking at how the Supreme Court jurisprudence of *Roe v. Wade*[4] has allowed the wrongful birth and life causes of action to flourish. It will also discuss whether the recent *Webster v. Reproductive Health Services*[5] opinions or the possible overruling of *Roe* by challenges through laws such as Utah's recent "back alley abortion bill" may affect future cases in this area. Most importantly, however, it will discuss how the torts evolved in the wake of legalized abortion and how the controversy surrounding the legalization of abortion causes courts to treat wrongful birth and wrongful life differently, often in less coherently principled decisions, than ordinary medical malpractice torts.

I. Evolution of the Causes of Action

The terms wrongful birth and wrongful life are often used indiscriminately by courts or interchangeably with such phrases as wrongful pregnancy or wrongful conception. A cause of action for wrongful birth is brought by parents against a third party whose negligence caused them to have an "unwanted"[6] child. The child can be unwanted either because the parents did not wish to have *any* child or because the parents did not wish to have this *particular* child due to its impairment or birth defect. Contained within this group of cases is a subset in which the wrongful act of a third party, usually a physician or pharmacist, interfers with the parents' birth control, contraceptive measures, sterilization or abortion procedures. These suits are sometimes called wrongful conception or pregnancy[7] but are merely factually, rather than analytically, distinguishable from other wrongful birth cases because they too are suits by parents for the birth of an "unwanted" child. Courts and commentators differentiate further between wrongful conception and wrongful birth by looking at whether the child is healthy but unwanted (wrongful conception/pregnancy) or unhealthy and unwanted (wrongful birth).[8]

---

[4]410 U.S. 113 (1973).

[5]109 S. Ct. 3040 (1989).

[6]The use of the term "unwanted" in no way implies a lack of proper parental feeling on the part of parents who give birth to these children and sue on their behalf. Rather, it denotes the idea that these were unplanned children for whose birth their parents were unprepared.

[7]The terms appear to be used interchangeably. One commentator differentiates the terms on the basis of the child's health:

> [W]rongful life and wrongful birth claims . . . are attempts to recover for the birth of a planned child who was born with disabilities, while wrongful pregnancy or wrongful conception claims usually involve the birth of a healthy, but unplanned, child.

L. Hom, *Wrongful Conception: North Carolina's Newest Prenatal Tort Claim*—Jackson V. Bumgardner, 65 N. C. L. Rev. 1077, 1083 (1987).

[8]*See* Phillips v. United States, 508 F. Supp. 544, 545 n.1 (D.S.C. 1981) (action for wrongful birth similar to one for wrongful conception except that in wrongful birth action resulting child is unhealthy in some way).

Wrongful conception has been identified and accepted as a separate cause of action in at least 12 states.[9]

Wrongful life is a cause of action brought by a child against a third party whose negligence deprived the child's parents of the decision to abort or never conceive the child.[10] The children who bring these suits are generally severely handicapped. They claim that they should never have been born, and that the culpable third party at least should pay for the extraordinary expenses the child will incur as a result of living as a handicapped human being.[11]

Wrongful birth and wrongful life suits are not what are referred to as "prenatal tort" actions in which the child or its parents sue a third party for harming the child while it is in the womb. For example, a woman would bring a prenatal tort suit against a third party for beating her while pregnant, thereby causing the child to be born mentally retarded. In that situation, but for the tortious act of the third party, the child would have been born healthy or live. In a wrongful birth or life action, the third party did not cause the birth defect or impairment the child suffers but rather caused the parent(s) not to abort a child that would have been impaired anyway. Prenatal torts were first recognized in 1946 in *Bonbrest v. Kotz*[12] in which the court overturned the long-held common law view that "children were unable to recover for prenatal injuries because a duty could not be owed to someone as yet unborn."[13]

A. Wrongful Life

At present, the cause of action for wrongful life is only clearly recognized in three states;[14] two other states may allow it as well. The Louisiana Supreme Court, in dicta, said a duty exists toward an unconceived child and its parents when the physician knows or should know of the existence of an unreasonable risk the child will be born with a birth defect.[15] An Indiana appellate court also recognized a cause of action for wrongful life when the third party's negligent acts occurred prior to conception, despite the existence of a state statute prohibiting the cause of action

---

[9] **Alabama:** Boone v. Mullendore, 416 So. 2d 718 (Ala. 1982); **Connecticut:** Anonymous v. Hospital, 35 Conn. Supp. 112, 398 A.2d 312 (1979); **Florida:** Jackson v. Anderson, 230 So. 2d 503 (Fla. Dist. Ct. App. 1970); **Georgia:** Fulton-DeKalb Hosp. Auth. v. Graves, 252 Ga. 441, 314 S.E.2d 653 (1984); **Indiana:** Garrison v. Foy, 486 N.E.2d 5 (Ind. Ct. App. 1985); **Maine:** Macomber v. Dillman, 505 A.2d 810 (Me. 1986); **Maryland:** Jones v. Malinowski, 299 Md. 257, 473 A.2d 429 (1984); **Michigan:** Bushman v. Burns Clinic Medical Center, 83 Mich. App. 453, 268 N.W.2d 683 (1978); **New Jersey:** Betancourt v. Gaylor, 136 N.J. Super. 69, 344 A.2d 336 (1975); **North Carolina:** Jackson v. Bumgardner, 318 N.C. 172, 347 S.E.2d 743 (1986); **North Dakota:** Milde v. Leigh, 75 N.D. 418, 28 N.W.2d 530 (1947); **West Virginia:** James G. v. Caserta, 332 S.E.2d 872 (W. Va. 1985).

For a complete discussion of wrongful conception as a separate cause of action, *see generally* L. Hom, *supra* n. 7.

[10] For an in-depth discussion of the evolution and current status of wrongful life causes of action, *see* T. Dawe, *Wrongful Life: Time for a "Day in Court,"* 51 Ohio St. L.J. 473 (1990).

[11] *See, e.g.,* Harbeson v. Parke-Davis, 98 Wash. 2d 460, 656 P.2d 483, 494 (1983) and Section I.A. below.

[12] 65 F. Supp. 138 (D.D.C. 1946).

[13] Note, *Park v. Chessin: The Continuing Judicial Development of the Theory of "Wrongful Life",* 4 Am. J.L. & Med. 211, 219 (1978–79).

[14] **California:** Turpin v. Sortini, 31 Cal. 3d 220, 643 P. 2d 954, 182 Cal. Rptr. 337 (1982); **New Jersey:** Procanik v. Cillo, 97 N.J. 339, 478 A.2d 755 (1984); **Washington:** Harbeson v. Parke-Davis, Inc., 98 Wash. 2d 460, 656 P.2d 483 (1983).

[15] *See* Pitre v. Opelousas Gen'l Hospital, 530 So. 2d 1151, 1157 (La. 1988).

if the child claims that, but for the third party's negligence, it would have been aborted. It is not clear whether such a cause of action will survive state supreme court review.[16]

Six states have prohibited the cause of action by statute[17] and 20 states by operation of the common law.[18] Some courts have given reasons for rejecting the cause of action based on rights analysis, the speculative nature of damages or lack of authorization to recognize the cause of action.[19] Most courts assume, however, that existence, even if painful, impaired or deformed, is better than nonexistence, and even if not better, it is incapable of being compared to nonexistence since nonexistence is outside human comprehension.[20] Since no comparison can rationally be made, no damages can be assessed and there is therefore no harm that the law can recognize or compensate.

Zepeda v. Zepeda[21] is widely recognized[22] as the first case raising the claim of wrongful life. In *Zepeda* a minor male child, through his mother, brought suit against his natural father because the child had been born "an adulterine bastard.[23]

---

[16] *See* Cowe v. Forum Group Inc., 541 N.E.2d 962 (Ind. App. 1989), *citing* Ind. Code Ann. § 34-1-1-11 (Burns Supp. 1989).

[17] **Indiana:** Ind. Code Ann. § 34-1-1-11 (Burns Supp. 1989); **Maine:** Me. Rev. Stat. Ann. tit. 24, § 2931 (Supp. 1989); **Minnesota:** Minn. Stat. Ann. § 145.424 (West 1990); **Missouri:** Mo. Ann. Stat. § 188.130-1 (Vernon Supp. 1990); **North Dakota:** N.D. Cent. Code § 32-03-43 (Supp. 1989); **South Dakota:** S.D. Codified Laws § 21-55-1 (1987); **Utah:** Utah Code Ann. § 78-11-24 (1987 & Supp. 1989).

[18] **Alabama:** Elliott v. Brown, 361 So.2d 546 (Ala. 1978); **Arizona:** Walker v. Mart, 164 Ariz. 37, 790 P.2d 735 (Ariz. 1990); **Colorado:** Lininger v. Eisenbaum, 764 P.2d 1202 (Colo. 1988); **Delaware:** Garrison v. Medical Center of Del. Inc., 571 A.2d 786 (Del. Sup. Ct. 1989) (unpublished disposition); **Florida:** Moores v. Lucas, 405 So.2d 1022 (Fla. Dist. Ct. App. 1981); **Idaho:** Blake v. Cruz, 108 Idaho 253, 698 P. 2d 315 (1984); **Illinois:** Siemieniec v. Lutheran Gen. Hospital, 117 Ill. 2d 230, 512 N.E.2d 691 (1987); **Kansas:** Bruggeman v. Schimke, 239 Kan. 245, 718 P.2d 635 (1986); **Kentucky:** Schork v. Huber, 648 S.W.2d 861 (Ky. 1983) (dictum); **Massachusetts:** Viccaro v. Milunsky, 406 Mass. 777, 551 N.E.2d 8 (1990); **Michigan:** Proffitt v. Bartolo, 162 Mich. App. 35, 412 N.W.2d 232 (1987); **Missouri:** Wilson v. Kuenzi, 751 S.W.2d 741 (Mo. 1988); **New Hampshire:** Smith v. Cote, 128 N.H. 231, 513 A.2d 341 (1986); **New York:** Becker v. Schwartz, 46 N.Y.2d 401, 386 N.E.2d 807, 413 N.Y.S.2d 895 (1978); **North Carolina:** Azzolino v. Dingfelder, 315 N.C. 103, 337 S.E.2d 528 (1985), *cert. denied*, 479 U.S. 835 (1986); **South Carolina:** Phillips v. United States, 508 F. Supp. 537 (D.S.C. 1980); **Texas:** Nelson v. Krusen, 678 S.W.2d 918 (Tex. 1984); **West Virginia:** James G. v. Caserta, 332 S.E.2d 872 (W. Va. 1985); **Wisconsin:** Dumer v. St. Michael's Hospital, 69 Wis. 2d 766, 233 N.W.2d 372 (1975).

[19] *See, e.g.,* Becker v. Schwartz, 46 N.Y.2d 401, 386 N.E.2d 807, 413 N.Y.S.2d 895 (1978) (no right to be born healthy); Elliott v. Brown, 361 So. 2d 546 (Ala. 1978) (no right not to be born at all); Slawek v. Stroh, 62 Wis. 2d 295, 215 N.W.2d 9 (1974) (court should defer to legislature); *Gleitman*, 49 N.J. 22, 227 A.2d 689 (public policy against abortions means child never had a chance of not being born even if doctor had accurately informed pregnant woman of effects on fetus of contracting rubella); *cf. Zepeda*, 41 Ill. App. 2d 240, 190 N.E.2d 849 (1963) (potential scope of liability could be disastrously large so court should defer to legislature).

[20] *See, e.g.,* White v. United States, 510 F. Supp. 146 (D. Kan. 1981); Phillips v. United States, 508 F. Supp. 537 (D.S.C. 1980); Boone v. Mullendore, 416 So.2d 718 (Ala. 1982); Dinatale v. Lieberman, 409 So. 2d 512 (Fla. App. 1982); Beardsley v. Wierdsa, 650 P.2d 288 (Wyo. 1982); Dorlin v. Providence Hospital, 118 Mich. App. 831, 325 N.W.2d 600 (1982); Payton v. Abbott Labs, 386 Mass. 540, 437 N.E.2d 171 (1982); Maggard v. McKelvey, 627 S.W.2d 44 (Ky. App. 1981); Stribling v. deQuevedo, 288 Pa. Super. 436, 432 A.2d 239 (1980); Berman v. Allan, 80 N.J. 421, 404 A.2d 8 (1979); Speck v. Finegold, 268 Pa. Super. 342, 372, 408 A.2d 496, 512 (1979), *aff'd in part, rev'd in part,* 497 Pa. 77, 439 A.2d 110 (1981); Becker v. Schwartz, 46 N.Y.2d 401, 385 N.E.2d 807, 413 N.Y.S.2d 895 (1978); Sherlock v. Stillwater Clinic, 260 N.W.2d 169 (Minn. 1977); Dumer v. St. Michael's Hospital, 69 Wis. 2d 766, 233 N.W.2d 372 (1975); Jacobs v. Theimer, 519 S.W.2d 846 (Tex. 1975); Stewart v. Long Island College Hospital, 35 A.D.2d 531, 313 N.Y.S.2d 502 (1970), *aff'd,* 30 N.Y.2d 695, 283 N.E.2d 616, 332

The plaintiff child sought damages for

> *deprivation of his right to be a legitimate child, to have a normal home, to have a legal father, to inherit from his father, to inherit from his paternal ancestors and for being stigmatized as a bastard.*[24]

The Illinois appellate court rejected out of hand the plaintiff's due process and equal protection constitutional claims and a claim based on the child's position as a third party beneficiary to his parents' alleged contract to marry and focused on a tort claim as the plaintiff's only possible ground for recovery. Although the court found no theoretical or practical problems with recognizing prenatal torts in general,[25] the court stumbled on the step of characterizing the infant's claim for damages (it rejected "mental anguish" as being improperly pleaded[26]). Finally, after a lengthy discussion of the burdens and pain of being an illegitimate child, the court realized that it was of his "very birth" that the plaintiff was complaining and that "[r]ecognition of the plaintiff's claim [would] mean[] creation of a new tort: a cause of action for wrongful life." That court then framed the issue with which every court since has grappled:

> *[The plaintiff] protests not only the act which caused him to be born but birth itself. Love of life being what it is, one may conjecture whether, if he were older, he would feel the same way. As he grows from infancy to maturity the natural instinct to preserve life may cause him to cherish his existence as much as . . . he now deplores it. Be that as it may, the quintessence of his complaint is that he was born and that he is.*[27]

The court then gave a short homily on the dangers of creating a new tort in an area in which large amounts of litigation might occur and, leaving it to the legislature to recognize the new cause of action if it so chose, dismissed the case.[28]

Four years later, New Jersey faced an analogous situation in *Gleitman v. Cosgrove.*[29] In that case the parents of the child joined their offspring in suing the doctors

---

N.Y.S.2d 640 (1972); Gleitman v. Cosgrove, 49 N.J. 22, 227 A.2d 689 (1967), *overruled on other grounds sub nom.*, Berman v. Allan, *supra*; Zepeda v. Zepeda, 41 Ill. App. 2d 240, 190 N.E.2d 849 (1963), *cert. denied*, 379 U.S. 945 (1964).

[21] 41 Ill. App. 2d 240, 190 N.E.2d 849 (1963).

[22] *Cf.* Note: *Genetic Malpractice: Avoiding Liability*, 54 U. Cin. L. Rev. 857 (1986); Higgins, T., *Rethinking (M)otherhood: Feminist Theory and State Regulation of Pregnancy*, 103 Harv. L. Rev. 1325 (1990); Robertson, J., *Procreative Liberty and the Control of Conception, Pregnancy, and Childbirth*, 69 Va. L. Rev. 405 (1983); Schultz, M., *From Informed Consent to Patient Choice: A New Protected Interest*, 95 Yale L. J. 219 (1985); Stumpf, A., *Redefining Mother: A Legal Matrix for New Reproductive Technologies*, 96 Yale L. J. 187 (1986); Waslington, W., *THE LEGAL IMPLICATIONS OF HEALTH CARE COST CONTAINMENT: A SYMPOSIUM: Paying for Children's Medical Care: Interaction Between Family Law and Cost Containment*, 36 Case W. Res. 1190 (1986).

[23] 190 N.E.2d at 851.

[24] *Id.*

[25] *Id.* at 852–855.

[26] *Id.* at 856.

[27] *Id.* at 857.

[28] *Id.* at 859.

[29] 49 N.J. 22, 227 A.2d 689 (1967).

who failed to tell Mrs. Gleitman that the case of German measles she caught during her early pregnancy would very likely lead to birth defects. The infant, Jeffrey Gleitman, sued for his birth defects; his mother, Sandra, sued for the emotional distress caused by her son's birth defects, and his father, Irwin, sued for the costs that had been and would be incurred in caring for the handicapped child.[30] Although there was some contradiction in the testimony, the court accepted for the sake of the appeal that Dr. Cosgrove affirmatively misled Mrs. Gleitman when he told her German measles would have no effect on her fetus.[31]

Noting that the right of an infant to sue for prenatal torts had already been established in the state, the court began its analysis by stating that "a child has a legal right to begin life with a sound mind and body."[32] However, the court immediately rejected this idea because the doctor's conduct had not caused the birth defects, and therefore he could not be liable for them or sued on their basis. The court stated the core issue of the child's claim, for the first time tying the availability of the wrongful life cause of action to the question of abortion:

> *[t]he infant plaintiff is therefore required to say not that he should have been born without defects but that he should not have been born at all . . . but for the negligence of defendants, he would not have been born to suffer with an impaired body. In other words, he claims that the conduct of defendants prevented his mother from obtaining an abortion which would have terminated his existence, and that his very life is wrongful.*[33]

The court then looked to the *Zepeda* decision and a similar New York decision, *Williams v. State of New York*[34] and decided that it too would reject the wrongful life cause of action. But unlike the *Zepeda* court, the New Jersey high court did not reject wrongful life suits for policy reasons but because of the impossibility of measuring damages; it believed that it could not "measure the difference between [the plaintiff's] life with defects against the utter void of nonexistence . . . [or] weigh the value of life with impairments against the nonexistence of life itself."[35]

Curlender v. Bio-Science Laboratories[36] was the first decision to recognize wrongful life as a valid cause of action. In 1980 a California state appellate court held that "consistent with the applicable principles of the statutory and decisional tort law" of the state, an infant plaintiff born with Tay-Sachs disease was entitled to bring a cause of action against the third party whose negligence proximately caused its birth.[37] In reaching this revolutionary decision, the court rejected *Zepeda* as dispositive of the case

---

[30] 227 A.2d at 689.

[31] *Id.* at 691.

[32] *Id.* at 692. This concept has been reiterated in other important cases and continues to confuse the analysis as seen below in section II.

[33] *Id.*

[34] 18 N.Y.2d 481, 276 N.Y.S.2d 885, 223 N.E.2d 343 (Ct. App. 1966).

[35] 227 A.2d at 692. The court did *not* base its decision on the illegality of abortion in New Jersey, because it assumed that Mrs. Gleitman could have qualified for one of the exceptions to the New Jersey abortion ban in effect at the time. *Id. See generally* Berenson, M., *The Wrongful Life Claim—The Legal Dilemma of Existence Versus Nonexistence: "To Be Or Not To Be,"* 64 Tul. L. Rev. 895 (1990).

[36] 106 Cal. App. 3d 811, 165 Cal. Rptr. 477 (1980).

[37] 165 Cal. Rptr. at 489.

at bar and instead looked at the distinction between healthy and unhealthy unwanted children and then stated that *Roe v. Wade* was "of some significance to this question.":[38]

> *The nation's highest court determined that parents have a constitutionally protected right to obtain an abortion during the first trimester of pregnancy, free of state interference. We deem this decision to be of considerable importance in defining the parameters of "wrongful-life" litigation . . . "[t]o be denied the opportunity indeed, the right to apply one's own moral values in reaching that decision (concerning the child's future), is a serious, irreversible wrong."* [39]

Taking the "monumental implications of *Roe v. Wade*"[40] together with its own recognition of "the existence of a duty owed by medical laboratories engaged in genetic testing . . . to use ordinary care,"[41] the court found that a child could state a valid cause of action for wrongful life. The court dismissed the metaphysical difficulties encountered by prior judges who had grappled with the seeming contradiction between allowing a person to recover for having been born when the "harm" (life itself) was also an immeasurable benefit:

> *We need not be concerned with the fact that had defendants not been negligent, the plaintiff might not have come into existence at all . . . a reverent appreciation of life compels recognition that plaintiff, however impaired . . . has come into existence as a living person with certain rights.*[42]

It seems that the existence of legalized abortion took away the only significant barrier the court could see to granting some sort of recompense for the wrong done by the defendant, even if harm to the child-plaintiff was not necessarily obvious. Once the court discovered the presence of a duty,[43] it had no problem seeing the proximate cause link between the breach of that duty and the "reality" that the plaintiff "both exists and suffers, due to the negligence of others."[44] Without legalized abortion, the negligence of Bio-Science Laboratories would *not* have been the proximate legal (even if it was the factual) cause of the child's painful existence and, therefore, the lab not be liable. The *Curlender* court admitted as much when it noted that "[t]he real crux of the

---

[38] *Id.* at 483.

[39] *Id.*, *quoting* Allan v. Berman, 80 N.J. 421, 404 A.2d 8, 18 (1979) (dissent). The California appellate court was here approving of the *Berman* dissent that would have found a wrongful life cause of action for the child-plaintiff as well as the one the majority found for the parents.

[40] 165 Cal. Rptr. at 487.

[41] *Id.* at 488.

[42] *Id.*

[43] "In California, '(a)ll persons are required to use ordinary care to prevent others from being injured as a result of their conduct.' " 165 Cal. Rptr. at 487, *quoting* Rowland v. Christian, 69 Cal. 2d 108, 112, 70 Cal. Rptr. 97, 100, 443 P.2d 561, 564 (1968). From this general principle the court determined that there was "no difficulty in ascertaining and finding the existence of a duty [here] . . . ." 165 Cal. Rptr. at 488.

[44] 165 Cal. Rptr. at 488.

problem is whether the breach of duty was the proximate cause of *an injury cognizable at law*."[45]

Although the *Curlender* court limited the extent of the child's recovery,[46] it did recognize a cause of action by a child for wrongful life:

> *[W]e reject the notion that a "wrongful-life" cause of action involves any attempted evaluation of a claimed right not to be born. In essence, we construe the "wrongful-life" cause of action by the defective child as the right of such child to recover damages for the pain and suffering to be endured during the limited life span available to such a child and any special pecuniary loss resulting from the impaired condition.*[47]

Two years later, in *Turpin v. Sortini*,[48] another case involving an unwanted and unhealthy baby, the California Supreme Court, although it also held that the child could bring a cause of action for wrongful life,[49] decided that this portion of the *Curlender* court's reasoning was faulty and overruled it:

> *[T]he basic fallacy of the* Curlender *analysis is that it ignores the essential nature of the defendants' alleged wrong and obscures a critical difference between wrongful life actions and the ordinary prenatal injury cases . . . [where] if the defendant had not been negligent, the child would have been born healthy . . . In this case, by contrast, the obvious tragic fact is that plaintiff never had a chance "to be born whole . . .";* *if defendants had performed their jobs properly, she . . . would not have been born at all.*[50]

Although the state Supreme Court said that it "[could] not assert with confidence that in every situation there would be a societal consensus that life is preferable to never having been born at all,"[51] it agreed with other jurisdictions that found it impossible to measure the monetary difference between the value of impaired existence and the value of nonexistence.[52] The court framed this impossibility in terms of the "benefit" doctrine articulated in section 920 of the Restatement Second of Torts, which provides that "[w]hen the defendant's tortious conduct has caused harm . . . [*and*] has conferred a special benefit to the interest of the plaintiff that was harmed, the value of the benefit conferred is considered in mitigation of damages. . . ." The court decided that the benefit to the child was its physical existence, the value of which was incapable of monetary measure,

---

[45] *Id.* (emphasis added).

[46] The court decided that damages for the child's care could only be awarded once, to either the parents or the child. 165 Cal. Rptr. at 490.

[47] *Id.* at 489.

[48] 31 Cal. 3d 220, 182 Cal. Rptr. 337 (1982).

[49] 182 Cal. Rptr. at 348, 643 P.2d at 965.

[50] 182 Cal. Rptr. at 344, 643 P.2d at 961.

[51] 182 Cal. Rptr. at 346, 643 P.2d at 963.

[52] 182 Cal. Rptr. at 346, 643 P.2d at 963, *citing* Speck v. Finegold, 268 Pa. Super. 342, 408 A.2d 496, 512 (1979) (Spaeth J., concurring), *aff'd*, 439 A.2d 110 (1981); *Gleitman*, 49 N.J. 63, 227 A.2d at 711 (Weintraub, C. J., concurring); Becker v. at Schwartz, 46 N.Y.2d 401, 413 N.Y.S.2d 895, 386 N.E.2d 807, 812 (1978); Dumer v. St. Michael's Hospital, 69 Wis. 2d 766, 233 N.W.2d 372, 375–76 (1975).

and the benefit was therefore a complete mitigation of the harm caused by bringing the child into the world impaired and undesired.[53] In essence, the *Turpin* court appeared to agree with this part of the *Gleitman* court's reasoning.

Paradoxically, however, the California Supreme Court then went on to allow the child to recover special damages, reasoning that it was illogical to allow the parents to recover for the child's care but to bar the child from recovering for her own special needs.[54] This holding was immediately attacked as internally inconsistent by the dissenting justice[55] and in law review articles.[56] The inconsistency lies in the court's simultaneous denial of the maxim that all life is preferable to nonexistence, coupled with a refusal to weigh or decide *which* lives will be deemed better not lived. The *Turpin* majority's stance indicates a profound discomfort with the specific idea of eugenic abortion—that there are some children for whom life is not worth having. The court may also be implying discomfort with the general idea underlying abortion—that there are some pregnancies that women may choose not to carry to term for any number of reasons. This discomfort is shared by the other judges who have faced the issue and has its roots in the moral and political disagreement surrounding the *Roe v. Wade* decision itself. But that discomforting, problematic issue of abortion causes judges and courts to be less diffident than they ought about whether or not recovery should be allowed by 1) the parents, especially the mother to whom *Roe* shifted the decision about abortion, or 2) the child, who under *Roe* does not have an absolute right to existence. Although superficially it would seem obvious that *Roe* had decided the issue of whether or not recovery should be allowed in these cases, many judges still do not allow wrongful life recovery. The fact that they deny it because they cannot stomach *Roe*'s underpinnings—that there are some pregnancies that should not or may not be carried to term—proves that *Roe* was only the apparent last word in this area. Similar problems arise in wrongful birth cases.

B. Wrongful Birth

Along with a landmark wrongful life discussion, the New Jersey *Gleitman v. Cosgrove* decision in 1967 also marked the first appearance and rejection of a wrongful birth claim by a set of parents. Every common law decision since *Gleitman* has accepted wrongful birth as a valid cause of action. This is in part because no other cases were brought until after *Roe v. Wade* was decided in 1973[57] and thus the persuasive force of *Gleitman*'s abortion-based rationale for denial of the action dissipated. However, the "sanctity of life" issue still underlies wrongful life actions and influences courts' determinations of whether or not to recognize the child's cause of action, often brought for the same damages that its parents may now regularly claim in wrongful birth cases as discussed below.

Most courts have resolved their misgivings regarding abortion policy and allow wrongful birth as an unexceptionable cause of action in those states. Courts generally allow some recovery of traditional tort damages in wrongful birth actions: actual medical

---

[53] 182 Cal. Rptr. at 347, 643 P.2d at 964.

[54] 182 Cal. Rptr. at 348, 643 P.2d at 965.

[55] 182 Cal. Rptr. at 349–50, 643 P.2d at 966–67 (Mosk, J., dissenting).

[56] *See* Kearl K., Turpin v. Sortini: *Recognizing the Unsupportable Cause of Action for Wrongful Life*, 71 Calif. L. Rev. 1278 (1983); Milsteen, J., *Recovery of Childrearing Expenses in Wrongful Birth Cases: A Motivational Analysis*, 32 Emory L.J. 1167 (1983).

[57] *See infra* n. 62.

services, pregnancy and delivery-related expenses. A remaining controversial point is whether childrearing expenses ought also to be recoverable. Some courts deny all child-rearing expenses,[58] but others just allow them for the birth and childrearing of an impaired child.[59] The controversy centers around whether "the benefits of joy, companionship, and affection which a child can provide,"[60] even an unhealthy one, are outweighted by the pecuniary losses suffered by the parents and whether the benefits are capable of monetary measurement.[61] These are the same concerns underlying the widespread judicial reluctance to recognize wrongful life actions and the debate over whether a woman should have the right to abort her fetus for reasons other than preserving her own life (usually the only ground for obtaining a legal abortion before *Roe v. Wade* and the focus of restrictive legislation such as that just passed in Utah [discussed below in Section II.D.].

Wrongful birth has now been recognized at common law in at least 18 states and the District of Columbia.[62] One state has recognized the cause of action by statute;[63] five others have statutorily prohibited it.[64] It has been argued that such statutory prohibition of the cause of action is unconstitutional.[65]

The *Gleitman* court rejected the parents' wrongful birth claim largely because of a perceived inability to measure their damages. The *Gleitman* court's wrongful birth analysis was different from that on the wrongful life issue in that it did not attempt to measure the detriment to the parents (emotionally and financially) of having a handicapped child against the benefit of having a child at all. Rather, it chose to weigh "the right of [the

---

[58] *See, e.g.,* Terrell v. Garcia, 496 S.W.2d 124 (Tex. Civ. App. 1973), *cert. denied,* 415 U.S. 927 (1974); Rieck v. Medical Protective Co., 64 Wis. 2d 514, 219 N.W.2d 242 (1974).

[59] *See, e.g.,* Boone v. Mullendore, 416 So.2d 718 (Ala. 1982); Kingsbury v. Smith, 122 N.H. 237, 442 A.2d 1003 (1982); Mason v. Western Pennsylvania Hospital, 499 Pa. 484, 453 A.2d 974 (1982).

For a discussion of whether or not courts should award childrearing expenses as an element of damages, see Milsteen, *supra* n. 56; White, N., *District of Columbia Survey—Flowers v. District of Columbia: Another Court Refuses to Settle the Question of Damages in Wrongful Conception Cases,* 34 Cath. U.L. Rev. 1209 (1985).

[60] 439 A.2d at 117.

[61] *See* Restatement (Second) of Torts § 920 (1979); *cf.* White, *supra* n. 59.

[62] **Alabama:** Robak v. United States, 658 F.2d 471 (7th Cir. 1981); **California:** Andalon v. Superior Court, 162 Cal. App. 3d 600, 208 Cal. Rptr. 899 (1984); **District of Columbia:** Haymon v. Wilkerson, 535 A.2d 880 (D.C. 1987); **Florida:** Moores v. Lucas, 405 So. 2d 1022 (Fla. Dist. Ct. App. 1981); **Illinois:** Siemieniec v. Lutheran Gen. Hosp., 177 Ill. 2d 230, 512 N.E.2d 691 (1987); **Louisiana:** Pitre v. Opelousas Gen. Hosp., 530 So. 2d 1151 (La. 1988); **Maine:** Me. Rev. Stat. Ann. tit. 24, § 2931 (Supp. 1988); **Michigan:** Proffitt v. Bartolo, 162 Mich. App. 35, 412 N.W.2d 232 (1987); **New Hampshire:** Smith v. Cote, 128 N.H. 231, 513 A.2d 341 (1986); **New Jersey:** Procanik v. Cillo, 97 N.J. 339, 478 A.2d 755 (1984); **New York:** Becker v. Schwartz, 46 N.Y.2d 401, 386 N.E.2d 807, 413 N.Y.S.2d 895 (1978); **North Carolina:** Gallagher v. Duke Univ., 638 F.Supp. 979 (M.D.N.C. 1986), *aff'd in part, vacated in part,* 852 F.2d 773 (4th Cir. 1988); **Pennsylvania:** Speck v. Finegold, 497 Pa. 77, 439 A.2d 110 (1981); **South Carolina:** Phillips v. United States, 508 F. Supp. 544 (D.S.C. 1981); **Texas:** Jacobs v. Theimer, 519 S.W.2d 846 (Tex. 1975); **Virginia:** Naccash v. Burger, 223 Va. 406, 290 S.E. 2d 825 (1982); **Washington:** Harbeson v. Parke-Davis, 98 Wash. 2d 460, 656 P.2d 483 (1983); **West Virginia:** James G. v. Caserta, 332 S.E.2d 872 (W. Va. 1985); **Wisconsin:** Dumer v. St. Michael's Hosp., 69 Wis. 2d 766, 233 N.W.2d 372 (1975).

[63] Me. Rev. Stat. Ann. tit. 24 §. 2931 (1986).

[64] Idaho Code § 5-334 (Supp. 1986); Minn. Stat. § 145.424 (1987 Supp.); Mo. Ann. Stat. § 188.130 (Vernon Sup. 1987); South Dakota Codified Laws Ann. § 21-55-2 (Supp. 1986); Utah Code Ann. § 78-11-24 (1987 & Supp. 1989).

[65] Note, *Wrongful Birth Actions: The Case Against Legislative Curtailment,* 100 Harv. L. Rev. 2017 (1987).

Gleitman's] child to live'' against the parents ''right not to endure emotional and financial injury.''[66] It is interesting to observe that although the court explicitly stated that it did not need to consider whether the abortion of which the parent-plaintiffs were denied the opportunity would have been legal or not, its entire discussion of the parents' cause of action revolves around ''the sanctity'' and ''inalienability'' of the child's ''right to life.''[67] In fact, the core of the court's decision to reject the cause of action seemed to be their unwillingness to sanction eugenic abortions:

> *A court cannot say what defects should prevent an embryo from being allowed life such that denial of the opportunity to terminate the existence of a defective child in embryo can support a cause for action . . . A child need not be perfect to have a worthwhile life . . . The sanctity of the single human life is the decisive factor in this suit in tort. Eugenic considerations are not controlling.*[68]

The dissents pointed out that eugenic abortions were regularly performed in New Jersey even though the court decisions construing the state's abortion law held that only saving the life of the mother was a sufficient ''lawful justification'' to perform an abortion.[69] But the concurrence disagreed with this perspective:

> *I concur in the opinion of [the court], except that I prefer to deal more specifically with the problem of criminality of a eugenic abortion of the type involved in this case.*[70]

The judge then went on to explain that abortion was morally wrong and under the statutes and common law of New Jersey it was (or should) not be permitted except to save the life of the mother.[71] It is clear from these opinions that both the child's and the parents' causes of action were inextricably bound up in the minds of the court with the problem of abortion.[72] No other court has accepted *Gleitman's* rationale for disallowing wrongful birth suits.

The Pennsylvania case of *Speck v. Finegold,*[73] an oft-cited opinion, exemplifies the general reasoning given by courts in accepting wrongful birth suits. Mr. and Mrs. Speck had two children with neurofibromatosis, an incurable genetic disease. Desiring no fur-

---

[66] 227 A.2d at 693.

[67] *Id.*

[68] *Id. See also* New Jersey Statutes 2A.87—1, 2A:170—76, New Jersey Statutes Annotated (1955); State v. Shapiro, 89 N.J.L. 319, 98 A.2d 437 (1916); State v. Brandenburg, 137 N.J.L. 124, 58 A.2d 709 (Sup. Ct. 1948).

[69] 227 A.2d at 707–712 (Weintraub, C.J., dissenting); 227 A.2d at 703–707 (Jacobs, J., dissenting).

[70] 227 A.2d at 694 (Francis, J., concurring).

[71] 227 A.2d at 694–703.

[72] This was further made clear when in 1979, its abortion laws no longer valid, New Jersey overruled *Gleitman* and decided to allow wrongful birth causes of action by parents. Berman v. Allan, 80 N.J. 421, 404 A.2d 8 (1979). Although Mrs. Berman became pregnant in her late thirties, her doctor did not suggest amniocentesis to detect mongolism, a substantial risk for pregnant women of that age. Her child was born with Down's syndrome and the court found that she had stated a cause of action and allowed her to recover damages.

[73] 439 A.2d 110 (Pa. 1981).

ther children, Mr. Speck sought a vasectomy; nevertheless, Mrs. Speck subsequently became pregnant.[74] The court stated that it viewed the cause of action for wrongful birth

> *as merely requiring the extension of existing principles of tort law to new facts . . . It is fundamental that one may seek redress for every substantial wrong, and that a wrongdoer is responsible for the . . . consequences of his misconduct.*[75]

.   The court addressed Pennsylvania's public policy favoring birth over abortion and decided that recognition of wrongful birth would have no effect on whether or not abortions were performed in the state.[76] Furthermore, it realized that reliance on such state policy to defeat the cause of action "squarely conflict[ed]" with *Roe* and that the right to seek an abortion without the ability to seek a remedy at law for the negligent performance of that abortion "would be hollow indeed."[77] The court's third ground of decision rested on the usual tort rationales for victim compensation—deterrence of negligence and incentive for due care.[78] The courts of other states allowing wrongful birth echo some or all of these grounds of decision. What is not clear at present is what would happen if the second ground—the constitutional right to an abortion—were removed; it is not self-evident that state courts would be willing to bypass strong legislative policies disfavoring abortion if the federal Constitution were held no longer to guarantee the right to choose. That this might be a problem in the future is indicated by such comments as that of Pennsylvania Justice Kauffman:

> *Recognition of a cause of action for the negligent performance of lawful medical procedures certainly will not encourage or promote sterilization or abortion.*[79]

It is unknown what Justice Kauffman would have had to say if abortion had been unlawful at the time the Specks sued for recovery, especially if the procedure of which they complained was a negligently performed abortion instead of a vasectomy.

The inability to predict the future course of this area of law lies in the realization that courts do not treat wrongful birth, or its companion, wrongful life, as normal medical malpractice torts. Instead of focusing only on the negligence of the defendant, the "wrongful" behavior of which the plaintiff complains, courts trip over themselves in their haste to address the "birth" or "life" aspect of the problem; in no other area of medical malpractice is the patient's (here the potential parent's) decision to undergo a particular medical procedure subject to *post hoc* scrutiny by the court as to whether or not that decision was a "good" or socially desirable one. That is because there is an ongoing debate over whether abortion ought to be a choice for pregnant women and, if so, when, under what conditions and for what reasons it ought to be allowed.

---

[74] *Id.* at 113.

[75] *Id.* (emphasis added).

[76] *Id.* at 113–114.

[77] *Id.* at 114.

[78] *Id.*

[79] *Id.* at 118 (Kauffman J., concurring) (emphasis added).

II. Abortion Law and Wrongful Birth/Wrongful Life

A. *Roe v. Wade*

In 1973 the United States Supreme Court decision in *Roe v. Wade*[80] revolutionized the legal status of abortion in the United States. Virtually overnight, abortion went from a back-alley, largely criminal procedure to a legally sanctioned, elective medical procedure. In the process, courts such as the *Gleitman* majority lost their primary reason for denying recovery to parents who "suffered" the birth of a child due to the negligence of a third party. Before *Roe,* a doctor could have no postconception duty to respect or assist a parent's ability to choose abortion; now she does.

Even prior to the legalization of abortion there should have been no barrier to recognizing the duty of a physician to maintain a certain standard of care in counseling prospective parents regarding their potential offspring's chances of genetic impairment. Nevertheless, wholesale recognition of preconception negligence (what is now called wrongful conception) did not take place until the 1980s.[81] This could be because the idea that all children are always a "blessing" has lost some of its currency only since *Roe.* Although this may be in part attributed to *Roe* itself, it may also stem from the general evolution of tort concepts that has allowed courts to contemplate other new, equally problematic issues, such as the "right to die." Even if abortion becomes illegal again under some future Supreme Court case, wrongful birth or life claims could still rationally be allowed if the claims depend upon preconception negligence by the third party. Such actions would probably continue to be allowed now that courts have begun to be more conscious of the fine distinctions between the causes of action of wrongful birth, conception and pregnancy and the difference in the duties required of third parties in each situation.[82]

But even after *Roe* some states still prohibit parents from bringing wrongful birth suits,[83] and virtually all courts hold that wrongful life suits are not legally cognizable claims. This raises the specter that it is the values underlying the prohibition of abortion that are truly at the heart of courts' treatment of these two causes of action. The *Gleitman* case is a good example of this. The majority opinion "assumed," for purposes of its decision, that Mrs. Gleitman could have obtained a legal abortion "somehow or somewhere . . . that would not have subjected [the] participants to criminal sanctions."[84] But when it came to assessing whether or not Mrs. Gleitman had a valid claim, the majority specifically held that damages resulting from a violation of her right to obtain a "legal" abortion "would be precluded by the countervailing public policy supporting the preciousness of life."[85] Thus the majority made clear its belief as to the proper balance between the state's interest in preserving fetal life and the parents' right to choose an abortion (assumed for purposes of the decision to be legal). *Roe* did not disturb, and the Supreme Court has repeatedly emphasized that *Roe* does not even imply a limitation on, the states' ability to make value judgments disfavoring abortion.[86] In its

---

[80] 410 U.S. 113 (1973).

[81] *See supra* n. 9.

[82] *See, e.g.,* Phillips v. United States, 508 F. Supp. 544 (D.S.C. 1980) (explaining difference between wrongful birth and wrongful conception actions).

[83] *See supra* nn. 63–66.

[84] 49 N.J. at 27, 227 A.2d at 691.

[85] 49 N.J. at 31, 227 A.2d at 693.

[86] *See Webster,* 109 S. Ct at 3050, *citing* Maher v. Roe, 432 U.S. 464, 474 (1977).

1977 decision in *Maher v. Roe,* the Supreme Court, through Justice Powell, stated that "[*Roe*] implies no limitation on the authority of a State to make a value judgement favoring childbirth over abortion . . . ."[87] In a companion case decided the same day, Justice Powell, again writing for majority, reiterated and emphasized this point:

> [T]he State has a valid and important interest in encouraging childbirth. We expressly recognized in Roe the "important and legitimate interest [of the State] . . . in protecting the potentiality of human life" . . . it is a significant state interest existing throughout the course of a woman's pregnancy . . . [an] unquestionably strong and legitimate interest in encouraging normal childbirth.[88]

Roe v. Wade established a different balance from that in *Gleitman,* "plac[ing] abortion decisions during the first trimester of pregnancy within the constitutional right of privacy derived from the fifth and fourteenth amendments"[89] and it tipped the balance in favor of the parents' rights to choose. New Jersey acknowledged the new order in *Berman v. Allen* six years after *Roe:*

> [I]n light of changes in the law which have occurred in the 12 years since Gleitman was decided, the second ground relied upon by the Gleitman majority can no longer stand in the way of judicial recognition of a cause of action founded upon wrongful birth. The Supreme Court's ruling in Roe v. Wade . . . clearly establishes that a woman possesses a constitutional right to decide whether her fetus should be aborted . . . Public policy now supports, rather than militates against, the proposition that she not be impermissibly denied a meaningful opportunity to make that decision.[90]

Most other courts have also recognized that the antiabortion argument is no longer a valid one under *Roe,* at least with reference to wrongful birth actions. But this has not stopped most courts from relying upon the "sanctity of life" argument in their decisions disallowing wrongful life actions. This occurred in the *Berman* decision, which, like *Gleitman* before it, refused to recognize an action for wrongful life, but on slightly different grounds. Whereas in *Gleitman* the court denied recovery "solely because damages are [too] difficult to ascertain,"[91] the *Berman* majority refused to allow a wrongful life claim because the plaintiff had suffered no damages *cognizable at law.*[92] This change in rationale reveals that the court's bottom line was its preference for life, no matter how impaired, over nonlife.

Because states have taken the Court at its word, it appears likely that legislative and juridical valuations such as *Gleitman* will continue to hold wrongful life suits at

---

[87] *Id.*

[88] Beal v. Doe, 432 U.S. 438, 445–46 (1977), *quoting* Roe v. Wade, 410 U.S. 113, 162 (1973).

[89] Rogers, *Wrongful Life and Wrongful Birth: Medical Malpractice in Genetic Counseling and Prenatal Testing,* 33 S.C.L. Rev. 713, 722–23 (1981–82).

[90] 80 N.J. at 431–32, 404 A.2d at 14.

[91] *See Berman,* 80 N.J. at 429, 404 A.2d at 12.

[92] 80 N.J. at 428–29, 404 A.2d at 12.

bay, at least in states where those pronouncements prevail. If *Roe* becomes more limited than it already has been by *Webster v. Reproductive Health Services,* more states may return to the balancing done by the *Gleitman* majority and refuse to recognize wrongful birth actions on grounds similar to those now used to deny suits for wrongful life.[93] The prevalence of denying wrongful life recovery on a "sanctity of life" basis was noted by a federal court in *Phillips v. United States:*

> *Although these arguments are phrased in varying terminology—the "impossibiliity" of determining damages based on a comparison of defective existence with nonexistence . . . the absence of recongized damages . . . the metaphysical, theological, or philosophical nature of the issues . . . the lack of a "justiciable" issue . . . or the absence of a legally "cognizable" cause of action . . . [all] essentially focus on the "preciousness of human life."*[94]

The *Berman* court justified its use of this argument by gathering "concrete manifestations" of its belief in the sanctity of life[95] and ended by saying, "We cannot . . . say that [the child-plaintiff] would have been better off had she never been brought into the world."[96] One commentator has noted that the *Berman* majority misunderstood its judicial role in this instance:

> *[T]he court used its [presumption in favor of life] to determine, as a matter of law, that other reasonable persons could not find [for the child-plaintiff]. This proposition seems unlikely, given the fact that three of the seven justices dissented from some aspect of the majority's opinion in the case . . .*
> *[R]eversing the dismissal of plaintiff's cause of action would not necessarily have shown agreement with the plaintiff's ultimate assertion, but merely would have acknowledged that the matter was one on which reasonable persons could disagree, and thus should [have been] decided by the trier of fact.*[97]

It was not until the California cases, *Turpin* and *Curlender,* that a court finally decided that perhaps life was not always to be preferred over nonexistence, depending upon the nature of that existence. From *Curlender*'s focus on compensation for medical malpractice[98] (also a concern of one of the *Gleitman* dissents—that "a wrong with serious consequential injury [could] go wholly unredressed"[99]) and its refusal to con-

---

[93] For discussion of the current limitations of *Roe* in this area of law, *see generally* Such, S., *Note: Lifesaving Medical Treatment for the Nonviable Fetus: Limitations on State Authority Under Roe v. Wade,* 54 Fordham L. Rev. 961 (1986); Rush, C., *Genetic Screening, Eugenic Abortion, and Roe v. Wade: How Viable is Roe's Viability Standard?,* 50 Brooklyn L. Rev. 113 (1988).

[94] 508 F. Supp. 537, 543 (1980).

[95] The court took its evidence from such documents as the U.S. and New Jersey constitutions, the Declaration of Independence and criminal law. *See* 80 N.J. at 429–30, 404 A.2d at 12–13.

[96] 80 N.J. at 430, 404 A.2d at 13.

[97] Dawe, *supra* n. 9, at 493–94.

[98] *See supra* nn. 36–41.

[99] 49 N.J. at 49, 227 A.2d at 703 (Jacobs, J., dissenting).

template the "metaphysical" problems of existence versus nonexistence, it was a small step for the *Turpin* majority to oppose completely the *Berman* court's assessment and say "we *cannot* assert with confidence that in every situation there would be a societal consensus that life is preferable to never having been born at all."[100] But, with the exception of Washington and a later New Jersey majority, the *Turpin* court still stands alone. This is in no small part due to the currency and force of the beliefs expressed by the New Jersey high court and others, beliefs that are inching their way back into the United States Supreme Court's abortion jurisprudence.[101]

Most states today do not allow the wrongful life cause of action either because of the professed impossibility of establishing the existence of legally cognizable damages to the child-plaintiff or because of an overt state policy against abortion.[102] Given the recent trend of the U.S. Supreme Court's abortion jurisprudence, it seems likely that the growing movement to "sanctify" fetal life by always giving it precedence over the interests of already existing adults will continue. That means that the concern with remedying harm and compensating parents—who must foot the bill for the expensive, short and often painful life of a child parents would rather not have had and who herself may wish never to have been born—may give way to those values embodied in the denial of wrongful life actions. This trend in turn may spill over into wrongful birth and possibly even wrongful conception actions if *Roe* is overruled, leaving negligent medical personnel undeterred and significant personal, social and financial costs unremitted.

B. *Beal v. Doe* and *Maher v. Roe*

There is another aspect of the problem of obtaining tort recovery for medical malpractice in this area: poverty. It is a truism that those with the most need for legal services are often the ones least likely to obtain them, but that old maxim has new poignancy in the area of wrongful birth and wrongful life claims. In a recent AMA study it was shown that Americans without health insurance are less likely to be given routine diagnostic tests or to undergo key surgical procedures. Based on analysis of almost 600,000 patient records, the study found that the capacity of patients to pay or obtain insurance for their health care makes a difference in the quality of care they receive. Given these facts, it is correct to assume that poor women will not undergo amniocentesis testing for genetic defects as often as might be necessary; it is likely that poor women will receive more cursory and less accurate diagnoses and treatments for illnesses during pregnancy and will seldom receive prenatal care.

In a series of decisions beginning with *Maher v. Roe* and *Beal v. Doe,* the U.S. Supreme Court has repeatedly refused to require either the federal or state governments to use public funds to pay for "elective" or "non-therapeutic" abortions. Although scholars can debate whether or not the language of Title XIX of the Social Security Act (Medicaid) requires state funding of abortions, Justice Marshall in his dissent to the two cases was surely correct when he stated that "these regulations inevitably will have the practical effect of preventing nearly all poor women from obtaining safe and legal abor-

---

[100] 182 Cal. Rptr. at 346, 643 P.2d at 963 (emphasis added).

[101] *See infra* Section II.B.

[102] The five statutory prohibitions of the wrongful life cause of action only prohibit the suit where the child claims that but for the third party's negligence, it would have been aborted, and there are many states that have antiabortion policies expressed in other statutes. *See supra* n. 64.

tions."[103] Along with access to abortion itself, the fact of poverty and the denial of public funds for obtaining a legal abortion means that the class of women who would prefer to choose an abortion is divided into two groups: those who can afford one, and yet are prevented from obtaining one or realizing they want one through another's negligence, and those who cannot afford one and therefore will never be able to assert the claim that but for the medical provider's negligence, they would not have continued the pregnancy. The fact of poverty and the refusal of public resources eliminates the proximate cause link necessary to hold negligent medical personnel liable for their misconduct. But poverty also separates these two groups of women even farther back in the decision-making process. If Mrs. Gleitman had been without insurance or her family without an income, it is unlikely she would have sought prenatal care in the first place and thus Dr. Cosgrove would never have had the chance to give her faulty information about German measles. Conversely, being poor often means that a pregnant woman is more likely to contract an illness during pregnancy or come into contact with those hazardous substances that increase the likelihood of genetic defects. When poor women receive abortions, they may frequently be administered by illegal abortionists who will not be subject to suit for negligent performance because of the very illegality surrounding the procedure itself.

Ultimately, poverty practically negates the existence of *Roe;* poverty takes the decision to abort away from the pregnant woman since a right without the capacity to exercise it "is hollow indeed."[104] For the many women who do not have the practical capacity to exercise the right to choose granted them by *Roe,* the recognition of wrongful birth or life actions is a moot issue. The Supreme Court's abortion jurisprudence has not helped poor women, and maybe it cannot if the Court is bound to the statutes promulgated by a Congress and legislatures under political pressure not to fund abortions with public money. But it is important to recognize that even if *Roe* survives its challenges intact, and even if an increasing number of states recognize wrongful birth and life actions, that does not mean that all the women and families who receive negligent medical care or who have children born with devastating impairments will be able to receive compensation if a third party's negligence "caused" the birth. Nor does it mean that every child who wishes never to have been born because of a debilitating birth defect will have redress.

C. *Webster v. Reproductive Health Services*

But perhaps the most insistent question now is whether or not there will continue to be *any* recovery in this area at all. On July 3, 1989, the U.S. Supreme Court promulgated its decision in *Webster v. Reproductive Health Services.*[105] It was immediately proclaimed and decried as a partial retraction of *Roe,* not least by the dissenting justices. But aside from its implications for the continued existence of a constitutional right to privacy large enough to include the right to choose an abortion, *Webster* also dealt with a state statute that incorporated a strong fetal protection/antiabortion policy. The statute, which the appellees in *Webster* claimed unconstitutionally interfered with the right to an abortion, outlined the policy in the preamble:

---

[103] 432 U.S. at 455.
[104] *Speck,* 439 A.2d at 113.
[105] —U.S.—,109 S. Ct. 3040 (1989).

1. The general assembly of this state finds that:
    (1) The life of each human being begins at conception;
    (2) Unborn children have protectable interests in life, health, and well-being;
    (3) The natural parents of unborn children have protectable interest in the life, health, and well-being of their unborn child . . .[106]

Five justices, in deciding not to decide whether this preamble was constitutional,[107] stated that the preamble "[did] not by its terms regulate abortion"[108] but was instead a "value judgment" favoring childbirth over abortion, of the sort specifically left open to the states after *Roe*. Justice Rehnquist stated that

> *We think the extent to which the preamble's language might be used to interpret other state statutes or regulations is something that only the courts of Missouri can definitively decide. State law has offered protections to unborn children in tort and probate law . . . and § 1.205.2 can be interpreted to do no more than that.*[109]

In other words, the Court accepted the appellant's claim in the appellate court that "the preamble was 'abortion-neutral,' and 'merely determines when life begins in a nonabortion context, a traditional state prerogative.' "[110] Justice Blackmun, joined by Justices Brennan and Marshall, took umbrage with this position and could "not see how the preamble . . . realistically may be construed as 'abortion-neutral.' "[111] It appears that the state did not believe the preamble was abortion-neutral either. Along with this value judgment, the Missouri statute also mandated that state laws be interpreted to provide unborn children with extensive legal rights:

2. . . . the laws of this state shall be interpreted and construed to acknowledge on behalf of the unborn child at every stage of development, all the rights, privileges, and immunities available to other persons, citizens, and residents of this state . . .[112]

The gist of this value judgment, that human life is precious and that the state benefits from promoting a universal high regard for life, may posit a valid position, but the Missouri legislature, by enacting such a pronouncement, refuses to acknowledge the very real possibility that there are conditions under which a rational person might reasonably choose nonexistence or would have preferred never to have had existence at all. By foreclosing this possibility in its rush to regulate and discourage abortions, Missouri has created a nonrebuttable presumption in favor of existence that will surely operate to deny wrongful life suits and may cause courts in that state to retract whatever recognition of wrongful birth now exists there as well. In essence, Missouri is doing what the

---

[106] Mo. Rev. Stat. § 1.205(1) (1986).

[107] 109 S. Ct. at 3050.

[108] *Id.*

[109] *Id.*

[110] 851 F.2d 1071, 1076, *quoted at* 109 S. Ct. at 3049.

[111] 109 S. Ct. at 3068 n.1.

[112] Mo. Rev. Stat. Ann. § 1.205(2) (1986).

New Jersey court did—legally mandating its preference for life—only this time it does so with the blessing of the Supreme Court. In fact, the decision goes much further than *Gleitman*'s mere antiabortion value judgment, as noted by Justice Blackmun in his dissent:

> [B]ecause the preamble defines fetal life as beginning upon "the fertilization of the ovum" . . . [it] also unconstitutionally burdens the use of contraceptive devices . . . which [   ] operate to prevent pregnancy only after conception . . .[113]

If Justice Blackmun's reading of the preamble is correct, then it is conceivable that *Webster* heralds an era in which failure to properly insert an IUD or substitution of the wrong medication in place of a "morning after" pill would *not* be actionable because those actions would no longer constitute "preconception" negligence but would be statutorily defined as postconception and thus unavailable as the basis for a wrongful conception suit. *Webster* looms as an ominous cloud over the horizon of those who support pro-choice positions and implies a limited life span for the tort actions that evolved in the wake of *Roe*.

D. Utah Senate Bill No. 23

After the *Webster* decision, anti-choice forces in several states began to advocate passage of highly restrictive abortion laws that appear to herald a return to the status quo that existed before *Roe* was decided. The overt strategy of many of these legislators and activists is to pass a law that could be used to overturn *Roe v. Wade* as several Supreme Court justices stated they were willing to do. On Friday, February 1, 1991, Utah Governor Norman Bangerter signed into law S. B. No. 23, "An Act Relating to Abortion; Prohibiting Abortion Except Under Specified Circumstances." The act added several features to Utah's abortion laws:

(1) It defined abortion as the termination of a pregnancy "after implantation of a fertilized ovum,"[114] in effect defining implantation as the moment human life begins.
(2) It gave fetuses "inherent and inalienable" rights to life and liberty.
(3) It added a preamble containing the legislature's findings and policies that declared that a woman's right to an abortion only outweighed the child's right to life in cases of rape or incest that had been reported to law enforcement agencies, where the life or health of the mother was at risk of "grave damage" or if the child would be born with "irremediable physical or mental defects that are incompatible with sustained survival."[115]

---

[113] 109 S. Ct. at 3068 n.1.

[114] Utah Code Ann. § 76-7-3-1(1) (Supp. 1992).

[115] Utah Code Ann. § 76-7-301.1 (Supp. 1992) reads in its entirety:

> (1) It is the finding and policy of the Legislature, reflecting and reasserting the provisions of Article I, Secs. 1 and 7, Utah Constitution, which recognize that liberty and life founded on inherent and inalienable rights are entitled to protection of law and due process; and that unborn children have inherent and inalienable rights that are entitled

Unlike the statute in *Webster,* this preamble is not facially abortion-neutral. It explicitly links the state's clearly permissible legislative policy favoring childbirth over abortion with an arguably impermissible regulation of abortion in contravention of *Roe* and its progeny. Although it is anyone's guess whether the presently constituted Supreme Court will honor *Roe* as stare decisis, it is equally unclear how such a law will affect wrongful birth or life actions. Utah already prohibits wrongful birth and life actions by statute,[116] but if the United States Supreme Court finds this new statute or one like it constitutional, it could open the door for other states that currently recognize the wrongful birth or life causes of action to forbid them.

Paradoxically, the one area that the statute seems to open up is the possibility of recognizing wrongful life actions, the very cause of action so many courts and commentators, even pro-choice ones, have such grave problems with. By sanctioning eugenic abortions for physically or mentally impaired fetuses, the legislature appears to be echoing the *Turpin* court's assertion that it could not agree that *all* lives are worth living. Although the Utah statute arguably strikes a blow against the privacy right of pregnant women, it appears to defeat the presumption that the *Gleitman* court made that the intangible and usually inarticulable benefits of being alive always outweigh the pain and anguish of a particular life. This turns on its head the history and development of these causes of action and reverses the hierarchy of preferences, for wrongful birth and against wrongful life, that the common law and legislatures have developed over the past 20 years. Perhaps this anomalous result reflects the change in attitudes and technology regarding genetic birth defects and our ability to detect and treat them, coupled with an ongoing controversy over women's privacy rights. Or perhaps it is only a facial anomaly that will not fully come to pass because states that enact Utah-type laws will also find enough sweeping policy in them to prohibit both causes of action. Most probably no legislator has thought of the problems in this area and there will be no principled pattern to how states deal with the issues if they adopt similar laws.

---

to protection by the state of Utah pursuant to the provisions of the Utah Constitution.

(2) The State of Utah has a compelling interest in the protection of human life, including that of unborn children, and in the protection of each person's rights under the Utah Constitution, to exercise inalienable rights in accordance with the law.

(3) It is the intent of the Legislature to protect and guarantee to unborn children their inherent and inalienable right to life and liberty, as required by Article I, Secs. 1 and 7, Utah Constitution.

(4) It is also the policy of the Legislature and of the state that, in connection with abortion, a woman's liberty interest, in limited circumstances, may outweigh the unborn child's right to protection. These limited circumstances arise when the abortion is necessary to save the pregnant woman's life or prevent life-threatening damage to her physical health, and when pregnancy occurs as a result of rape or incest. It is recognized that, in cases of rape or incest, the fact that the woman has been an unwilling participant in the reproductive process may justify the preference of her rights over those of the unborn child. It is further the finding and policy of the Legislature and of the state that a woman may terminate the pregnancy if the unborn child would be born with grave and irremediable physical or mental defects that are incompatible with sustained survival.

[116]Utah Code Ann. § 78-11-24 (1987 & Supp. 1989).

III. Conclusion

It is difficult to say what long-term effect on tort law actions *Webster* will have, but several scenarios appear possible. As did one Pennsylvania justice, courts could continue to believe that "nothing about sterilization or abortion requires the application of legal principles different from those controlling in other medical malpractice actions."[117] That appears highly unlikely when statutes such as Missouri's, Pennsylvania's and Utah's express antiabortion policies more vehement and expansive than those at issue in *Gleitman v. Cosgrove*. It is more likely that a retraction of *Roe* would not only turn the clock back to 1967 but might also encompass wrongful conception actions, as Justice Blackmun's concerns imply. If a law such as Utah's is upheld, with its definition of abortion as terminating a pregnancy "after implantation of a fertilized ovum," wrongful conception cases would probably never get to the litigation stage due to the inexactness of medically determining at what point such implantation took place. Even if wrongful birth actions survived *Roe*'s overruling, it is far less likely that other courts will follow California and Washington in saying that sometimes life may not be preferable to nonexistence, if the assumption proves true that overruling *Roe* would cause wide-scale enactment of antiabortion legislation. Conversely, however, if overruling *Roe* merely sends the issue back to the states, then it is possible that some states will hold to their pro-choice principles, or at least limit their anti-choice legislation to direct regulation of abortion, as opposed to sweeping fetal protection statutes that define conception as the beginning of legally protectable human life. If *Webster* implies what Justice Blackmun fears, or if it heralds the beginning of the end of *Roe*, it is doubtful that this area of tort law will long survive to provide viable avenues of litigation for the remedy of medical mistakes that result in life for those who would rather not have been born and harm to parents who did not want a child only to have it live in painful sufferance.

---

[117] *Speck,* 439 A.2d at 116.

The author states that there have been two extremely different approaches taken to improving the health of newborns. The adversarial model uses punitive measures to impose special restrictions and duties on women solely because they are, or may become, pregnant. The facilitative model has as its premise that women who bear children share the government's objective of promoting healthy births. Throughout the article, the author contests one model against the other and shows how governmental coercion can actually be counterproductive to achieving the goal of promoting of healthy births.

9 · Shared Interests: Promoting Healthy Births Without Sacrificing Women's Liberty —

Dawn Johnsen, J.D.

I. Introduction

Although threats to a woman's fundamental right to decide whether to have an abortion have recently captured public attention, less-noticed legal and public policy developments also threaten American women's reproductive freedom and other fundamental liberties. During the last decade, courts, legislatures and other government entities increasingly have sought to impose special restrictions on women who decide to bear children. The government has attempted to use the force of law to compel women to behave in ways deemed likely to promote the birth of healthier babies. Special legal restrictions and requirements have been aimed at a wide variety of behaviors by women, ranging from failing to eat a balanced diet and being in automobile accidents to smoking, drinking alcohol and taking illegal drugs.

Restrictions on a women's right to choose abortion and a woman's behavior as it relates to bearing children both involve attempts by the government to interfere with women's liberty in making important personal decisions related to reproduction. Yet despite this significant similarity, there exists a difference between the two issues that is critical to the development of sound public policy. At the heart of the abortion debate lies a fundamental disagreement over the legitimacy of the government's goal in restricting abortion—namely, whether the government should adopt through law one answer to the moral, philosophical and religious question of when life begins. By contrast, there is strong agreement that once a woman has chosen to bear a child the government has an important interest in pursuing policies that will improve the likelihood that her baby will be healthy. There can be no serious dispute about the importance of this latter objective. The government has a responsibility to improve maternal health and reduce our nation's tragically high infant mortality and morbidity rates.

Therefore, unlike questions related to abortion restrictions, there is no dispute about the legitimacy of at least one objective that the government may be pursuing in imposing pregnancy-related restrictions on women's behavior. What is at issue are the specific means by which the government should seek to improve the health of children and pregnant women. How should the government pursue this important goal?

Assessing the merits of the possible governmental responses requires close attention to the profound policy and constitutional implications of these responses. Talk of protecting the rights and interests of the fetus masks the inescapable reality that, physically, a fetus is part of a woman's body. Once a woman is pregnant, the government can affect fetal development, and thus the health of the infant at birth, only through that woman's body and actions. This critical fact results in opportunities for the development of effective public policies, but it also creates the potential for conflict. If not formulated with care, governmental policies adopted to promote healthy births have a dangerous potential for inflicting significant intrusions on women's fundamental liberties and their ability to decide how to live their own lives.

During the last decade, legislatures, prosecutors and courts have in fact used many forms of coercive governmental power to force women to act in ways the government deemed optimal for fetal development. Courts have imposed civil penalties and have allowed children to sue their mothers for prenatal injuries attributed to the women's behavior while pregnant. Prosecutors have brought criminal charges ranging from prenatal child neglect to homicide. Women have been imprisoned and civilly committed for the duration of pregnancy. And courts have issued orders forcing pregnant women to submit to cesarean sections against their will. In at least one such case, the compelled surgery required physically tying the woman to the operating table; in a second case, it contributed to the woman's death.[1]

Overview

Coercive and punitive governmental policies that create conflicts between women's liberty and the promotion of healthy births are unnecessary. Indeed, this chapter will show that the most effective policies for improving the health of newborns are those that facilitate women's choices, not those that infringe on their liberty. This can be seen by analyzing two dramatically different approaches that the government has taken in addressing this important public policy issue. One approach is seen in the attempts made during the last decade to use punitive measures to impose special restrictions and duties on women solely because they are or may become pregnant. These governmental actions exemplify what can be categorized as the "adversarial model" of public policy. Adversarial policies approach the woman and the fetus she carries as distinct legal entities having adverse interests—the government's role being to protect the fetus from the woman.

The second approach, which historically and still today is far more common, can be described as the "facilitative model" of public policy. This approach is premised on

---

[1] See Gallagher, *Prenatal Invasions and Interventions: What's Wrong with Fetal Rights,* 10 Harv. Women's L.J. 9, 10 (1987) (quoting V. Kolder, *Women's Health Law: A Feminist Perspective,* 1–2 [Aug. 1985] [unpublished manuscript] [on file with the Harvard Women's Law Journal]); In re A.C., 573 A.2d 1235 (D.C. 1990) *(en banc).*

a recognition that women who bear children share the government's objective of promoting healthy births. The government's role is to help women achieve this common goal, to help women overcome the obstacles to healthy pregnancies that many of them face, by, for example, providing prenatal care, food, shelter and treatment for drug and alcohol dependency. Facilitative policies recognize that women inevitably must make numerous decisions that require them to balance varying and uncertain degrees of risk to fetal development against the many competing demands and interests in their lives. Rather than depriving women of their right to make these judgments or punishing women after the fact for making ''wrong'' choices, the facilitative approach seeks to expand women's options and enable women to make choices that will result in healthier pregnancies and births.

This chapter will explore the relative merits of the facilitative and adversarial models of governmental action. It concludes that the approach that best preserves women's liberty interests is also the most effective at promoting healthy pregnancies. The facilitative model—building on shared goals—offers opportunities for positive, effective and cost-efficient governmental policies. By contrast, the adversarial model—creating maternal-fetal conflict—is not only ineffective but often proves harmful to the governmental objective of increasing the likelihood of healthy births.

Following this introduction, this chapter will first describe the facilitative and adversarial models in more detail, focusing on how the underlying rationales and general effects differ. This will be followed by a brief review of the history of the legal status of the fetus, which reveals that the adversarial model is not supported by legal precedent.

The chapter will then discuss the ways in which governmental action premised on the adversarial model threatens women's fundamental liberties, including their rights to privacy and bodily integrity, protected under the fourteenth amendment of the U.S. Constitution and comparable provisions of state constitutions. The U.S. Supreme Court has held that these rights protect the individual from governmental interference with certain personal decisions that are critical to determing the course of one's life, particularly decisions concerning procreation and control of one's physical person. Due to the complete physical dependency of a fetus on a woman, a wide variety of highly personal decisions made by a woman during and before pregnancy—ranging from what to eat, where to work, when to sleep or exercise or have sexual intercourse—can significantly affect the fetus. Absent constitutional limitations on the government's use of criminal and civil sanctions to force women to act in the perceived best interests of fetal development, the government would have a justification for exerting unprecedented, sweeping control over women's lives.

The use of adversarial policies also implicate other constitutional guarantees, including federal and state constitutional protections against discrimination on the basis of sex or race. Adversarial policies employed to date have focused exclusively on restricting women's behavior, even though ample evidence exists that men can adversely affect fetal development through behavior that results in damage to sperm, including smoking, drinking alcohol, drug use and working in jobs that involve exposure to certain substances, such as lead. Moreover, women of color overwhelmingly have been the targets of the criminal prosecutions and court-ordered surgery premised on the adversarial model.

By examining in detail the four major types of coercive action that the government has employed under the adversarial model, this chapter will show that the resulting infringements on women's fundamental liberties are not justified by any countervailing concerns. Indeed, adversarial policies are ineffective in furthering their asserted purpose: the promotion of healthy births. There is overwhelming agreement among professional and advocacy groups that such policies are ineffective. Opposition to governmental attempts to impose special restrictions on pregnant or fertile women has come from medical groups such as the American Medical Association[2] and the American College of Obstetricians and Gynecologists,[3] organizations focusing on protecting children's interests, such as the National Association of Public Child Welfare Administrators,[4] and organizations concerned primarily with protecting individual rights, such as the National Abortion Rights Action League[5] and the American Civil Liberties Union.[6]

These groups and others who have studied the issue have recognized that adversial policies affect women's behavior in ways that are not only ineffective but actually harmful to fetal development and to the women themselves. Fear of prosecution, incarceration, civil liability and court-ordered surgery all work to deter women from obtaining the type of health care and the drug and alcohol treatment that are essential to promoting healthy births. Facilitative policies, on the other hand, work to make available to women the services they need to have healthy pregnancies.

These policy arguments against the adversarial model are also relevant to the constitutionality of adversarial policies. Governmental action that infringes on fundamental individual liberties—as adversarial policies do—will be upheld by the courts only if it can be shown to be necessary to further a compelling governmental interest. Because they do not further, and indeed often are counterproductive to, the governmental interest in promoting healthy births, adversarial policies cannot survive strict scrutiny by the courts and thus must fail on constitutional as well as public policy grounds.

II. Two Models of Governmental Action to Promote Maternal and Infant Health

A. The Facilitative Model

The core assumption underlying policies that follow the facilitative model is that the critical goal of improving maternal and infant health can best be achieved by building on the shared interests of women and the government. The facilitative model is premised on the view that women who decide to bear children wish to have healthy

---

[2] American Medical Association, Board of Trustees Report, *Legal Interventions During Pregnancy: Court-Ordered Medical Treatments and Legal Penalties for Potentially Harmful Behavior by Pregnant Women,* 264 JAMA 2663 (1990) (adopted by the AMA House of Delegates) [hereinafter AMA, *Legal Interventions During Pregnancy*]; American Medical Association, Board of Trustees Report, *Drug Abuse in the United States: The Next Generation* 12 (1989) (adopted by the AMA House of Delegates) [hereinafter AMA, *Drug Abuse in the United States*]; American Medical Association, *Treatment Versus Criminalization: Physician Role in Drug Addiction During Pregnancy,* Resolution 131 (1990) (adopted by the AMA House of Delegates) [hereinafter AMA, *Treatment Versus Criminalization*].

[3] American College of Obstetricians and Gynecologists, Committee on Ethics, ACOG Committee Opinion, No. 55 *Patient Choice: Maternal-Fetal Conflict* (Oct. 1987) [hereinafter ACOG Committee Opinion].

[4] National Association of Public Child Welfare Administrators, *Guiding Principles for Working with Substance-Abusing Families and Drug-Exposed Children: The Child Welfare Response* 3 (approved Jan. 1991).

[5] Coalition on Alcohol and Drug Dependent Women and their Children, *Statement Against Prosecution* (June 1990) (statement joined by over 20 organizations, including American Civil Liberties Union, American Nurses Association, National Abortion Rights Action League, National Association of Maternal and Child Health Programs, National Perinatal Association, Southern Regional Project on Infant Mortality [An Initiative of the Southern Governor's Association and the Southern Legislative Conference]).

[6] *Id.*

pregnancies and healthy babies and typically will go to great lengths to make this possible. In a statement opposing legal interference with women's decisions during pregnancy, the American Medical Association Board of Trustees noted:

> *Ordinarily, the pregnant woman, in consultation with her physician, acts in all reasonable ways to enhance the health of her fetus. Indeed, clinicians are frequently impressed with the amount of personal health risk undertaken and voluntary self-restraint exhibited by the pregnant woman for the sake of her fetus and to help ensure that her child will be as healthy as possible.[7]*

Rather than creating conflicts—as adversarial policies do—by transforming the sacrifices and choices women voluntarily make for the sake of the fetus into legally required standards of behavior for all women in all circumstances, facilitative policies support women's ability to make choices that promote healthy births.

Basic to the facilitative model is an understanding that women do not—indeed, could not—focus their every decision and action toward the sole goal of reducing any risk to fetal development in a current or future pregnancy. The unavoidable fact is that women must make countless decisions that, to varying degrees, affect the likelihood of optimal fetal development. Women must daily weight these risks against their desire to lead normal lives, to care for their children and other family members and to continue working in their jobs. How a particular woman's various decisions will combine to affect fetal development is far from certain. The facilitative model assumes that each woman—and not the government—is best situated ultimately to decide how to balance these different risks and moral factors in her life.

The facilitative model also, however, reflects an understanding that many women face obstacles to having the healthy pregnancies they desire. Such obstacles may include inadequate health care, illness, addiction, poor information and poverty. For example, one-third of pregnant women in the United States, or about three million pregnant women each year, currently receive inadequate prenatal care, which is closely linked to infant mortality and poor infant health.[8] The government's role under this model is to facilitate a woman's desire to bear a healthy child through policies that help women overcome such obstacles and provide women with the tools necessary to have the healthy pregnancies that are in the interests of all.

Facilitative policies need not be costly and indeed can save the government money, given the high costs associated with poor infant health. An example of an existing cost-effective program that takes a facilitative approach is the Special Supplemental Food Program for Women, Infants, and Children (WIC), which provides food supplementation, nutrition education and health care and social services referrals to low income women, infants and children. In operation since 1974, the WIC program is universally recognized as highly successful in reducing the incidence of low birthweight, infant

---

[7] AMA, *Legal Interventions During Pregnancy, supra* note 2, at 2663; *see also* ACOG Committee Opinion, *supra* note 3, at 2 ("The vast majority of pregnant women are willling to assume significant risk for the welfare of the fetus").

[8] *Panel Urges a Consolidation of Prenatal Care,* New York Times, Apr. 24, 1991, at A21 (citing study of National Commission to Prevent Infant Mortality).

mortality and other infant health problems. Yet the program is currently funded to allow only about 50% of the 8.7 million income-eligible women and children to participate. The WIC program is so successful in improving infant health that expanding funding for it would actually save the government substantial money in future health assistance to low income women and children. A recent study by the U.S. Department of Agriculture found that in just the first 60 days after birth, each dollar spent on the WIC program results in savings in Medicaid costs of between $1.77 and $3.13.[9] An analysis published by the National Bureau of Economic Research found that expenditures to improve prenatal care would be even more cost-effective than WIC.[10]

Policies that flow from the facilitative model employ a positive, cooperative approach even concerning behavior by women that both presents a relatively high risk of harm to fetal development and also is viewed by society as having little or no redeeming value. The facilitative model recognizes that the overwhelming majority of women who use substances such as cocaine, alcohol and tobacco during pregnancy do so because they suffer from strong physical and psychological dependencies that they developed prior to pregnancy and not because they desire to give birth to an unhealthy baby. In fact, providers of health care and drug and alcohol treatment find that women are highly motivated during pregnancy to seek help in overcoming their dependencies precisely because they want to minimize risks to fetal development.[11] The use of punitive adversarial approaches such as additional criminal penalties have the effect only of deterring women from seeking necessary treatment and prenatal care out of fear of prosecution and thus are counter to efforts to promote healthy births.

The facilitative approach instead provides treatment programs for the pregnant women dependent on drugs who are seeking help so that they may deliver healthy babies and become responsible parents. The vast majority of pregnant women seeking treatment find it impossible to obtain. Drug treatment programs routinely deny admission to pregnant women, and the few that will treat women during pregnancy typically have very long waiting lists.[12] Facilitative programs also include those designed to prevent people from forming dangerous dependencies in the first place, through, for example, public education about the harmful effects of drug and alcohol use by women during preg-

---

[9] Center on Budget and Policy Priorities, *Response to George Graham's Critique of the WIC Program* 4 (Apr. 1991) [hereinafter *Response to George Graham*]; Office of Analysis and Evaluation, Food and Nutrition Service, U.S. Department of Agriculture, *The Savings in Medicaid Costs for Newborns and their Mothers from Prenatal Participation in the WIC Program* xii (1990) [hereinafter Dept. Agriculture, *Savings in Medicaid Costs*]; Rich, *Mothers' Nutrition Program Is Effective, U.S. Study Finds,* Washington Post, Oct. 19, 1990, at A21; Center on Budget and Policy Priorities, *WIC: A Winning Strategy for Maternal and Child Health* (Jan. 1, 1990).

[10] Joyce, Corman and Grossman, *A Cost-Effectiveness Analysis of Strategies to Reduce Infant Mortality,* National Bureau of Economic Research (1988), *cited in Response to George Graham, supra* note 9, at 10 n.4; *see also* Social Services Program, National Governors' Association, *In Brief: NGA National Forum on Prevention Programs for Children* 1 (Sept. 21, 1990) (a study of North Carolina's program of expanded prenatal care services to Medicaid recipients disclosed that "the state Medicaid program saves an estimated $2.44 in newborn medical costs for each $1.00 spent for care coordination") [hereinafter NGA, *In Brief*]; Dept. of Agriculture, *Savings in Medicaid Costs, supra* note 9, at xiii.

[11] NGA, *In Brief, supra* note 10, at 2 ("Pregnancy is a motivating factor for most women to seek treatment because of concern for their soon-to-be-born child"); AMA, *Legal Interventions During Pregnancy, supra* note 2, at 2668; AMA, *Drug Abuse in the United States, supra* note 2, at 12.

[12] *See infra* notes 123–26 and accompanying text.

nancy. Prevention programs also target men for education about the dangers of damage to sperm from alcohol and drug use, which can result in fetal harm.[13]

B. The Adversarial Model

Most governmental responses to problems of poor infant health are premised on the facilitative model, but during the last decade governmental entities have increasingly employed approaches premised on the adversarial model. Under this model, a pregnant woman is viewed as two distinct entities—the woman and the fetus—each with separate and conflicting interests. Each of the countless decisions that a woman makes that could affect fetal development is viewed with suspicion. The government's role is to protect the fetus from the pregnant woman by using the force of law to compel women to act in ways that a court, legislature, physician or other appointed third party deems optimal for fetal health. Specifically, the government seeks to control women's behavior by second-guessing their decisions and subjecting them to special restrictions and obligations based solely on the fact that they are currently pregnant or may become pregnant in the future.

Courts, legislatures, prosecutors and other governmental officials have in recent years used adversarial approaches to police women's behavior with respect to a broad range of activities. Most sweeping have been attempts to define the fetus as a distinct legal "person" and then force women to comply with legally required standards of behavior that are broadly and vaguely defined.[14] In one of the first instances of the adversarial approach, a Michigan appellate court ruled in 1980 that a child could sue his mother for prenatal injuries if she failed to act, in the eyes of a court, as a "reasonable" pregnant woman. In the Michigan case, the child alleged that his mother's use of the antibiotic tetracycline during pregnancy caused him to be born with discolored teeth.[15] An Illinois appellate court—ultimately reversed by the Illinois Supreme Court—similarly allowed a girl in 1987 to sue her mother for prenatal injuries to her intestines allegedly caused when the woman was in an automobile accident during pregnancy.[16]

Women have also been criminally prosecuted under general child abuse statutes for "prenatal abuse" of their fetuses through their behavior during pregnancy. A California woman was criminally prosecuted in 1986 for allegedly causing her infant son to be born severely brain damaged as a result of her own loss of blood during delivery. The prosecution claimed that the woman could have avoided this tragedy if she had followed her doctor's advice and sought medical care as soon as she began bleeding vaginally, rather than waiting several hours. She was prosecuted under a statute that required parents to provide their children with "clothing, food, shelter [and] medical attendance," a statute that a judge ultimately ruled could not be used to prosecute a woman for her otherwise lawful behavior during pregnancy.[17]

---

[13] See infra note 138 and accompanying text.

[14] Numerous bills have been introduced in Congress and in state legislatures since Roe v. Wade, 410 U.S. 113 (1973), to grant fetuses sweeping rights as "persons" either through statute or amendment to the U.S. Constitution. See generally National Abortion Rights Action League, Who Decides? A State-by-State Review of Abortion Rights 1991 (Jan. 1991).

[15] Grodin v. Grodin, 102 Mich. App. 396, 301 N.W.2d 869 (1980).

[16] Stallman v. Youngquist, 52 Ill. App. 3d 683, 504 N.E.2d 920 (1st Dist. 1987), reversed, 125 Ill. 2d 267, 531 N.E.2d 355 (1988).

[17] People v. Stewart, No. M508197 (Cal. Mun. Ct. Feb. 26, 1987).

Since the California case, prosecutors across the country have argued that fetuses are distinct legal persons with interests adverse to those of pregnant women in attempts to prosecute women under statutes that clearly were never intended to criminalize women's conduct during pregnancy. A pregnant woman in Wyoming who went to a police station to report that her husband had physically assaulted her was herself arrested and charged with child abuse for drinking alcohol during pregnancy.[18] A woman in Massachusetts who suffered serious injuries in a car accident, including the loss of her pregnancy, was prosecuted for involuntry manslaughter because she allegedly caused the accident by driving while intoxicated.[19]

Citing adverse fetal interests, judges have overridden women's decisions regarding medical treatment and in at least 11 states and the District of Columbia have ordered women to give birth by cesarean section, rather than vaginal delivery, despite the greater risk and the severe bodily intrusion involved in the surgical procedure.[20] The District of Columbia Court of Appeals, sitting *en banc,* recently became the first court to address the full constitutional implications of this unprecedented bodily intrusion and ruled in 1990 that a court order forcing a woman to submit to a cesarean section violates her constitutional rights. Unfortunately, the court's ruling came after the surgery had already been performed: The fetus was not viable and did not survive, and the woman died two days after the forced surgery. The cesarean section was listed in her death certificate as a contributing factor to her death.

In addition to civil and criminal penalties and court-ordered medical interventions, states have attempted to deprive women of custody of their children based solely on their actions during pregnancy, rather than making the customary determination based on the current ability of the woman and other family members to care for the child. A Michigan woman in 1987 was charged with child abuse and temporarily lost custody of her infant because she has taken valium while pregnant to relieve pain from injuries she suffered in a car accident.[21] A woman in Iowa similarly lost custody of her son after being charged with prenatal child abuse based solely on her conduct during pregnancy. A news report described the testimony against the woman as including that she "paid no attention to the nutritional value of the food she ate during her pregnancy—she simply picked the foods that tasted good to her without considering whether they were good for her unborn child."[22]

The adversarial model has thus far been used most frequently in cases involving the use of already illegal substances by pregnant women. Obviously, a woman's pregnant status does not immunize her from prosecution under a generally applicable criminal statute that would otherwise prohibit her behavior. In the dozens of cases that have followed the adversarial model, however, women have been singled out for *special*

---

[18] Levendosky, *Turning Women Into 2-Legged Petri Dishes,* Star Tribune (Casper, Wyo.), Jan. 21, 1990, at A8; Levendosky, *Using the Law to Make Justice the Victim,* Star Tribune (Casper, Wyo.), Feb. 4, 1990 at A8.

[19] *See* Loth, *DA Sees No Politics in Fetal Death Case,* Boston Globe, Nov. 16, 1989, at 25; Daly, *Woman Charged in Death of Own Fetus in Accident,* Washington Post, Nov. 25, 1989, at A4.

[20] Kolder, Gallagher, & Parsons, *Court-Ordered Obstetrical Interventions,* 316 N. Eng. J. Med. 1192, 1194 (1987); In re A. C., 573 A.2d 1235 (D.C. 1990) *(en banc);* Jefferson v. Griffin Spalding County Hospital Authority, 274 Ga. 86, 274 S.E.2d 457 (1981) *(per curiam).*

[21] In re J. Jeffrey, No. 99851 (Mich. Ct. App. filed Apr. 9, 1987), *cited in* American Civil Liberties Union Reproductive Freedom Project, *Legal Docket* 140 (May 1987).

[22] *Baby Placed in Foster Home: Doctor Claims Prenatal Abuse,* Des Moines Register, Apr. 3, 1980, at 11A.

prosecutions and *additional* penalties solely because they were pregnant at the time of the drug use. Prosecutors bringing such actions have argued that fetuses were persons under statutes that were never intended to be used in that manner and that contained harsher penalties than those for simple possession.[23]

Although the overwhelming majority of these special prosecutions have failed, a woman in Florida was convicted in July 1989, and that conviction was upheld on appeal in March 1991, under a statute that prohibits the distribution of a controlled substance to a minor and imposes a penalty of up to 30 years imprisonment. The prosecution successfully argued that she delivered cocaine to her fetus (the "minor") through her umbilical cord during childbirth.[24] In a related context, a court ordered a Washington, D.C. woman imprisoned for the duration of her pregnancy following her arrest for forging checks. Although the prosecutor recommended probation, the judge sentenced the woman to imprisonment for 180 days—sufficient time to ensure she would give birth in jail—because she had tested positive for cocaine use and the judge wanted to prevent her from using cocaine again while pregnant.[25]

Women of course should not use cocaine during pregnancy, or indeed at any time. Ideally, women would be able to avoid using prescription drugs such as tetracycline and valium, and all women would obtain prompt and adequate prenatal care, eat balanced diets and avoid alcohol and smoking during pregnancy. Adversarial governmental policies transform these ideals—which are far from reality for many women living in poverty or with illness or addiction—into legally required behavior. The unprecedented legal obligations that increasingly have been imposed on pregnant and potentially pregnant women far surpass the legal obligations owed even by one person to another in our legal system. They create a new system of conflicting legal rights within a woman's body. Far from the facilitative model's positive approach to assisting women in making choices that will improve birth outcomes, the adversarial model perceives a woman's womb as a hostile environment from which the fetus must be protected. Using punitive and restrictive measures aimed only at women, adversarial policies reduce women to their role as childbearers and deny their right to balance competing demands and interests and make decisions that are critical to their ability to control the course of their lives.

C. Lack of Precedent for Adversarial Model

The adversarial approach has at times been defended as following a general trend in the law toward recognition of the fetus as a legal entity or "person," distinct from the pregnant woman. This description of the law is simplistic and misleading. In fact, before the very recent trend toward the adversarial approach, the law viewed the pregnant woman as a single legal entity and did not treat the fetus as a legal adversary of the woman.[26] As the U.S. Supreme Court stated in *Roe v. Wade,* "the unborn have never been recognized in the law as persons in the whole sense" and have not been

---

[23] American Civil Liberties Union, *Overview of ACLU National Survey of Criminal Prosecutions Brought Against Pregnant Women: 80% Brought Against Women of Color* (May 7, 1990) [hereinafter ACLU].

[24] Johnson v. State, No. 89-1765 (Fla. Dist. Ct. App. Apr. 18, 1991) (appeal pending before Supreme Court of Florida).

[25] United States v. Vaughn, 117 Daily Wash. L. Rptr. 441 (D.C. Super. Ct. Mar. 7, 1989).

[26] For a more extensive discussion of the legal status of the fetus, see Johnsen, *The Creation of Fetal Rights: Conflicts with Women's Constitutional Rights to Liberty, Privacy, and Equal Protection,* 95 Yale L.J. 599, 600–13 (1986).

recognized at all "except in narrowly defined situations and except when the rights are contingent upon live birth."[27]

Over the years, the law has developed to take into account the existence of the fetus prior to birth under certain circumstances, but this has occurred only for specific narrow purposes that promote the interests of born people—including women who bear children. Recognition of the fetus as a legal "person" in these instances in no way creates fetal interests assertable by the government or others against women. For example, the first context in which the definition of a legal "person" was expanded to include a fetus occurred in property law in the late 19th century. This status was conferred to protect not fetal interests but the interests of a deceased parent and was contingent upon the subsequent live birth of a child. The law presumed for purposes of inheritance that a man would desire to include among his heirs a child of his who was conceived but not yet born at the time of his death.[28]

Tort law also developed to recognize the existence of the fetus. In 1946, a court first allowed a child to maintain a cause of action against third parties such as physicians whose conduct toward a pregnant woman results in the subsequently born child suffering harm.[29] Allowing recovery for such prenatal injuries furthers the interests of women who bear children without creating conflicts with women's interests. It serves to compensate their children for injuries they suffer after birth, which helps women pay the costs associated with their children's care. It also serves to deter the acts inflicted upon pregnant women that cause the injuries.

Some states subsequently extended the law's recognition of the fetus as a legal entity for certain purposes under criminal and civil law without the traditional requirement of a subsequent live birth. Again, this development did not create maternal-fetal conflicts but actually served to further women's interests. For example, courts have explicitly noted that, when a woman is caused to suffer a miscarriage or a stillbirth, allowing a civil cause of action for wrongful death or a criminal prosecution for homicide serves to protect pregnant women from severe bodily intrusion, physical harm and the involuntary termination of wanted pregnancies.[30]

Thus, legal precedent does not support the adversarial approach to promoting maternal and fetal health. Traditionally the law did not treat the fetus as a separate entity

---

[27] Roe v. Wade, 410 U.S. 113 (1973).

[28] See, e.g., Christian v. Carter, 193 N.C. 537, 538, 137 S.E. 596, 597 (1927); Cowles v. Cowles, 56 Conn. 240, 13 A. 414 (1887); Medlock v. Brown, 163 Ga. 520, 136 S.E. 551 (1927); McLain v. Howald, 120 Mich. 274, 79 N.W. 182 (1899).

[29] Bonbrest v. Kotz, 65 F. Supp. 138 (D.D.C. 1946); see also W. P. Keeton, D. Dobbs, R. Keeton & D. Owen, Prosser & Keeton on the Law of Torts § 55, at 368 (5th ed. 1984).

[30] Some state courts have stated explicitly that the purpose behind recognizing a cause of action for wrongful death is to compensate parents. See, e.g., Volk v. Baldazo, 103 Idaho 570, 574, 651 P.2d 11, 15 (1982) ("[the wrongful death statute] confers upon parents a cause of action for the wrongful death of a 'child' and thus protects the rights and interests of the parents, and not those of the decedent child").

The Supreme Court has described wrongful death actions for the destruction of a fetus as providing compensation for the loss of a child: "[S]ome States permit the parents of a stillborn child to maintain an action for wrongful death because of prenatal injuries. Such an action, however, would appear to be one to vindicate the parents' interest and is thus consistent with the view that the fetus, at most, represents only the potentiality of life." Roe v. Wade, 410 U.S. 113, 162 (1973) (citation omitted).

Although most states that have used the criminal law in this manner have done so by amending the state homicide law to extend to fetuses, at least one state explicitly focused the law's protection on the pregnant woman rather than the fetus. See N.M. Stat. Ann. § 30-3-7 (Supp. 1989).

in contexts that would create an adversarial relationship between a pregnant woman and the fetus within her. Rather, the law recognized the fetus as a legal entity only for carefully defined purposes that sought to protect and promote the interests of women as well as their children.

III. Constitutional Limitations on the Adversarial Model

A. The Constitutional Framework: The Fundamental Right to Liberty

Governmental action based on the adversarial model is not only a sharp deviation from precedent, it also is at odds with the U.S. Constitution. The adversarial approach interferes with rights that the U.S. Constitution recognizes as so fundamental to individual liberty that they may be resticted by the government only under the most compelling circumstances.[31] Ordinarily, a duly enacted law or other governmental action is constitutional and enforceable as long as it can survive the easily satisfied "rational relation" standard of review by the courts, which requires only that the action be "rationally related" to a "legitimate" governmental interest. Courts use a much higher standard of review, however, for laws or other acts by the government that interfere with an individual right that is guaranteed as fundamental under the U.S. Constitution. Restrictions on fundamental rights must satisfy the demanding "strict scrutiny" standard of judicial review. Under this standard, a court will find a governmental action to be unconstitutional unless the interference is justified by and actually furthers a "compelling" governmental interest and is "narrowly tailored" to do so by the means that are the least restrictive of the fundamental right at stake.

Because the government's use of the adversarial approach is relatively recent and still atypical, no federal court and only a few state courts have had occasion to consider its implications for women's constitutional rights. Nonetheless, opinions of the U.S. Supreme Court in analogous areas suggest that governmental attempts to dictate women's behavior to further perceived fetal interests interfere with women's fundamental rights protected by the guarantee of "liberty" contained in the fourteenth amendment to the U.S. Constitution. Among the aspects of liberty that the Supreme Court has found to be fundamental, and thus deserving of heightened judicial protection, is the individual's autonomy in making certain personal decisions that are central to determining the course of his or her own life and in particular his or her own physical person. The Court has used various terms to describe these rights related to decision-making autonomy, most often referring to them as part of the "right to privacy."

A unanimous Supreme Court described one aspect of the fundamental right to privacy as the individual's right to "independence in making certain kinds of important decisions," in particular in "matters relating to marriage, procreation, contraception, family relationships, and child rearing and education."[32] The Court has also identified decisions related to procreation and pregnancy as being "at the very heart" of the "right

---

[31] As the Supreme Court has stated, "The very purpose of a Bill of Rights was to withdraw certain subjects from the vicissitudes of political controversy, to place them beyond the reach of majorities and officials and to establish them as legal principles to be applied by the courts. One's rights to life, liberty, and property, to free speech, a free press, freedom of worship and assembly, and other fundamental rights may not be submitted to vote; they depend on the outcome of no elections." West Virginia State Bd. of Educ. v. Barnette, 319 U.S. 624, 638 (1942).

[32] Whalen v. Roe, 429 U.S. 589, 599–600 (1977) (quoting Paul v. Davis, 424 U.S. 693, 713 [1976]).

of personal privacy'': ''The decision whether or not to beget or bear a child is at the very heart of this cluster of constitutionally protected choices.''[33]

Also fundamental is the right of the individual to privacy in decision-making in matters concerning his or her own physical body, which has been described by the Supreme Court and other courts as a right to bodily integrity.[34] As the Court explained in 1990, this principle of bodily integrity not only enjoys constitutional protection, but is also deeply embedded in our common law:

> *Before the turn of the century, this Court observed that ''[n]o right is held more sacred, or is more carefully guarded, by the common law, than the right of every individual to the possession and control of his own person, free from all restraint or interference of others, unless by clear and unquestionable authority of law.''*[35]

State constitutional guarantees of liberty and privacy may provide women with additional protection from the intrusions of adversarial policies. State courts are free to interpret state constitutional provisions as more protective of individual liberties than similar provisions of the federal Constitution. As former U.S. Supreme Court Justice William Brennan wrote: ''State constitutions, too, are a font of individual liberties, their protections often extending beyond those required by the Supreme Court's interpretation of federal law.''[36] State courts have, for example, interpreted privacy provisions in their state constitutions as more protective than the federal constitution of women's right to make their own decisions regarding abortion and on that basis have invalidated restrictions on minors' ability to obtain abortions without parental consent as well as discriminatory restrictions on funding for abortion.[37] Significantly, the Supreme Court of Florida is among the state courts that has interpreted a state constitutional guarantee of privacy as broader than the federal right. Currently pending before that court is the

---

[33] Carey v. Population Servs. Int'l, 431 U.S. 678, 684–85 (1977) (quoting *Whalen*, 429 U.S. at 599–600). This includes the right of the individual to choose to prevent a pregnancy through contraception, Griswold v. Connecticut, 381 U.S. 479 (1965), to terminate a pregnancy through abortion, Roe v. Wade, 410 U.S. 113 (1973), to continue a pregnancy through childbirth, Cleveland Bd. of Educ. v. LaFleur, 414 U.S. 632 (1974), and to remain fertile, Skinner v. Oklahoma, 316 U.S. 535 (1942). The Court has described the fundamental right to privacy as including the right of the individual ''to be free from unwarranted governmental intrusion into matters so fundamentally affecting a person as the decision whether to bear or beget a child.'' Eisenstadt v. Baird, 405 U.S. 438, 453 (1972).

[34] For example, citing a fourth amendment right to ''personal privacy and bodily integrity,'' the Supreme Court ruled that a state could not compel a criminal defendant to submit to the surgical removal of a bullet needed as evidence in the state's prosecution. Winston v. Lee, 470 U.S. 753, 761 (1985). In an earlier decision, the Court overturned as violative of the fourteenth amendment a conviction that was based on evidence obtained from what the Court described as a bodily invasion that ''shocks the conscience,'' consisting of the forced stomach pumping of a criminal suspect. Rochin v. California, 342 U.S. 165, 172 (1952).

[35] Cruzan v. Director, Missouri Dept. of Health, 110 S. Ct. 2841, 2846 (1990) (quoting Union Pacific R. Co. v. Botsford, 141 U.S. 250, 251 [1891]).

[36] Brennan, *State Constitutions and the Protection of Individual Rights,* 90 Harv. L. Rev. 489, 491 (1977).

[37] Doe v. Right to Life of Michigan, No. 116069 (Mich. Ct. App. Feb. 19, 1991); In re T. W., 551 So. 2d 1186 (Fla. 1989); American Academy of Pediatrics v. Van de Kamp, 214 Cal. App. 3d 831, 263 Cal. Rptr. 46 (Cal. Ct. App. 1989); Committee to Defend Reproductive Rights v. Myers, 29 Cal. 3d 252, 172 Cal. Rptr. 866, 625 P.2d 779 (1981); People v. Belous, 71 Cal. 2d 954, 80 Cal. Rptr. 354, 458 P.2d 194, *cert. denied,* 397 U.S. 915 (1969).

appeal in the first criminal conviction of a woman under a prosecution pursuant to the adversarial model.[38]

Although the constitutional right to choose abortion is currently at risk in the federal courts, even staunch opponents of this particular fundamental right have stated that the fourteenth amendment's guarantee of liberty protects individuals from physical intrusions such as being forced to undergo unwanted medical procedures. For example, in arguing on behalf of the Bush administration that the Supreme Court should overrule *Roe v. Wade* and rule that women do not possess a fundamental right to make their own decisions regarding abortion, Solicitor General Kenneth Starr sought to distinguish forced abortions as nonetheless unconstitutional: "A state law *mandating* abortions would present a starkly different question. Our Nation's history and traditions establish that a competent adult may generally refuse unwanted medical intrusion. This right would, we believe, extend to an unwanted abortion."[39]

B. The Need for Strict Scrutiny of Adversarial Policies

Laws and other governmental actions that follow the adversarial model by placing special restrictions on women's actions only as they relate to childbearing strike at the core of these rights recognized by the Supreme Court as fundamental. They deprive women of their fundamental right to privacy in decision-making regarding matters essential to controlling the course of their own lives, including decisions related to childbearing and bodily integrity. Courts, legislatures and prosecutors have already, under the adversarial model, second-guessed a wide array of decisions and actions by women that can be seen as posing risks or not maximizing benefits to fetal development. If courts were to fail to recognize adversarial policies as interfering with women's fundamental rights and therefore subject to strict scrutiny, the government would be free to override or penalize any decision by a woman upon a simple showing that the special

---

[38] Johnson v. State, No. 89-1765 (Fla. Dist. Ct. App. Apr. 18, 1991) (appeal pending before Supreme Court of Florida).

[39] Brief for the United States as Amicus Curaie Supporting Respondents in No. 88-1125 And Supporting Cross-Petitioners in No. 88-1309, at 14 n.7, *Hodgson v. Minnesota*, 110 S. Ct. 2926. During oral arguments in *Webster v. Reproductive Health Services*, then-Solicitor General Charles Fried similarly conceded that a forced abortion would be unconstitutional:

> JUSTICE O'CONNOR: Do you think the state has the right to, if in a future century we had a serious overpopulation problem, has a right to require women to have abortions after so many children?
> MR. FRIED: I surely do not. That would be a different matter.
> JUSTICE O'CONNOR: What do you rest that on?
> MR. FRIED: Because unlike abortion, which involves the purposeful termination of future life, that would involve not preventing an operation but violently taking hands on, laying hands on a woman and submitting her to an operation and a whole constellation—
> JUSTICE O'CONNOR: And you would rest that on substantive due process protection?
> MR. FRIED: Absolutely.

Transcript of Arguments Before Court on Abortion Case, New York Times, Apr. 27, 1989, at B12, B13, col. 2.

Both Fried and Starr failed to recognize that compelled pregnancy and childbirth also involve the government "violently taking hands on, laying hands on a woman," inconsistent with "our Nation's history and tradition."

regulation was rationally related to a legitimate interest in reducing a risk to fetal development.

Because the fetus is physically part of the woman's body, her every action has the potential to affect fetal development and thus could be viewed with suspicion under the adversarial approach. Government officials have already imposed or attempted to impose on women criminal and civil liability—including imprisonment, civil commitment and court-ordered surgery—for a broad range of behaviors during pregnancy that present some risks to fetal development, including failing to obtain adequate prenatal care,[40] failing to eat a balanced diet,[41] smoking cigarettes,[42] choosing vaginal delivery over cesarean section,[43] taking prescription drugs,[44] not following a doctor's advice,[45] engaging in sexual intercourse with a spouse,[46] drinking alcohol,[47] being injured in an automobile accident while driving negligently,[48] driving while under the influence of alcohol[49] and taking illegal drugs.[50]

Even greater restrictions on women's liberty have been proposed. One advocate of policies that follow the adversarial model, Dr. Margery Shaw, described a woman's "prenatal duties" necessary to avoid legal liability as including "regular prenatal check-ups, a balanced diet with vitamin, iron, and calcium supplementation, weight control, and judicious use of medications, tobacco, and caffeine."[51] Women's behavior prior to pregnancy that creates risks to future children could also be grounds for liability. Dr. Shaw writes, "parents may be found to have a duty to receive genetic counseling and carrier testing, to use contraceptives, to be sterilized, to reveal a genetic risk to a spouse or relative, to protect their gonads against adverse effects, and to consider whether they have a 'right' to knowingly pass on deleterious genes."[52] In support of creating a "duty not to conceive," she writes that parents "should be held accountable to their offspring for causing misery, pain, suffering, and death if it could have been avoided."[53]

Indeed, absent the protection of strict scrutiny, there is no logical stopping point for the kinds of personal decisions by women that could be second-guessed by zealous prosecutors, estranged husbands or judges examining an isolated decision with the benefit of hindsight. A legal framework that does not require strict scrutiny of adversarial policies could create a separate legal regime in which women—and not men—would be deprived of their right to make countless important judgments critical to personal auton-

---

[40] *Baby Placed in Foster Home: Doctor Claims Prenatal Abuse,* Des Moines Register, Apr. 3, 1980, at 11A.

[41] *Id.*

[42] *Id.*

[43] Kolder, Gallagher & Parsons, *supra* note 20, at 1192; Jefferson v. Griffin Spalding County Hospital Authority, 247 Ga. 86, 274 S.E.2d 457 (1981) *(per curiam)*; In re A.C., 573 A.2d 1235 (D.C. 1990) *(en banc).*

[44] Grodin v. Grodin, 102 Mich. App. 396, 301 N.W.2d 869 (1980).

[45] People v. Stewart, No. M508197 (Cal. Mun. Ct. Feb. 26, 1987).

[46] *Id.*

[47] *See* sources cited at *supra* note 18.

[48] Stallman v. Youngquist, 52 Ill. App. 3d 683, 504 N.E.2d 920 (1st Dist. 1987), *reversed,* 125 Ill. 2d 267, 531 N.E.2d 355 (1988).

[49] *See* Loth, *DA Sees No Politics in Fetal Death Case,* Boston Globe, Sep. 16, 1989, at 25; Daly, *Woman Charged in Death of Own Fetus in Accident,* Washington Post, Nov. 25, 1989.

[50] *Johnson,* No. 89-1765; *See also* ACLU, *supra* note 23.

[51] Margery Shaw, *Conditional Prospective Rights of the Fetus,* 5 J. of Legal Med. 63, 83 (1984).

[52] *Id.* at 93.

[53] *Id.*

omy with only the most minimal justifications. The burdens placed on women who choose to become pregnant, or simply to remain fertile, could even be sufficiently onerous to pressure some women to avoid or terminate otherwise wanted pregnancies. Women might also be coerced into submitting to unwanted sterilizations, as has resulted from policies of private employers that exclude fertile women from certain jobs involving exposure to substances that pose risks to fetal development.[54]

Thus, any imposition on a woman of a special restriction premised on the adversarial model must be strictly scrutinized even though the Constitution does not protect as fundamental the right to engage in all of the many activities potentially affected. To use an extreme example, the government certainly can—as it has—prohibit the use of cocaine by any individual. The fact that a woman is pregnant does not immunize her from prosecution under this type of criminal law of general application. Yet when the government prosecutes a woman for a crime not applicable to male users or imposes harsher penalties solely because the woman was pregnant when she used cocaine, the level of constitutional protection and judicial scrutiny increases because an essential element of the crime is the woman's pregnant status.

Under policies that follow the adversarial model by placing special restrictions on women solely based on their role in childbearing, it is the woman's pregnancy—or her ability to become pregnant—that is the impetus for the government's action, whether it be a court-ordered medical procedure or a criminal prosecution of a woman for delivering drugs to a ''minor'' (through the umbilical cord) or for ''prenatal child abuse.'' And it is this imposition of additional, special burdens aimed specifically at the procreative aspect of women's behavior that is deeply threatening to women's liberty and that therefore triggers strict scrutiny.

C. Unprecedented Intrusions on Women's Fundamental Liberties

Policies based on the adversarial model infringe on women's fundamental liberties to a greater extent than analogous governmental interferences that courts have found unconstitutional. This is most graphically illustrated in the cases in which women have been forced against their will to submit to cesarean sections. The bodily intrusion entailed in such a case—with the attendant risks of major surgery including greater risks of complications such as infection from the incision and higher rate of mortality— surpasses even those the Court has found unconstitutional in cases involving criminal defendants, over whom the government generally may exercise unusually far-reaching control. In one reported case, carrying out the court-ordered cesarean section required physically tying the woman to the hospital bed and forcibly removing her husband from the room.

> Confronted with the doctor's intentions, the woman and her husband became irate. The husband was asked to leave, refused, and was forcedly removed from the hospital by seven security officers. The woman became combative and was placed in full leathers, a term that refers to leather wrist and ankle cuffs that are attached to the four corners of a bed to prevent the patient from moving. Despite her restraints, the woman con-

---

[54] *See, e.g.*, International Union, UAW v. Johnson Controls, 59 U.S.L.W. 4209, 4210 (U.S. Mar. 20, 1991) (plaintiffs included woman who had been sterilized in order to retain her job).

tinued to scream for help and bit through her intravenous tubing in an attempt to get free.[55]

The bodily intrusion inflicted by ordering women to undergo cesarean sections in order to advance perceived fetal interests stands in sharp contrast with our legal system's typical refusal to force any person to help another. Our legal system so respects an individual's bodily integrity and freedom to make his or her own decisions that it generally does not require people to reach out to aid another person, even when doing so would save the other from grave injury or certain death at little or no personal sacrifice or risk to one's self. Attempts by the government to force people to assist others are so rare that relatively few courts have addressed the issue. Particularly instructive is *McFall v. Shimp,* in which a court ruled that a man could not be compelled to donate bone marrow necessary to save the life of his cousin. The court wrote:

> *The common law has consistently held to a rule which provides that one human being is under no legal compulsion to give aid or to take action to save that human being or to rescue . . . For our law to* compel *the Defendant to submit to an intrusion of his body would change every concept and principle upon which our society is founded. To do so would defeat the sanctity of the individual . . . and one could not imagine where the line would be drawn.*[56]

D. Judicial Responses to the Adversarial Model

Of the few courts that have as yet considered the legality of governmental action premised on the adversarial model, most have not acknowledged the implications for women's constitutionally protected interests. Courts instead have analyzed the governmental action in a narrow manner confined to the facts of the particular application. For example, although the overwhelming majority of special criminal prosecutions have been dismissed, they usually failed because charges were brought pursuant to criminal statutes that clearly were not enacted for the purpose of imposing special pregnancy-related penalties on the woman's behavior at issue.[57]

Since 1988 several courts have noted the broader implications of the adversarial model for women's liberty, both in cases that raised constitutional issues as well as in several that did not. For example, the Illinois Supreme Court ruled that a child could not sue her mother for causing the child to suffer injuries as a result of the woman's conduct during pregnancy. The Illinois court discussed the serious ramifications for women of recognizing, as the plaintiff requested, a legal right to begin life with a sound mind and body and stated "[m]other and child would be legal adversaries from the moment of conception until birth."[58]

---

[55] Gallagher, *supra* note 1, at 10; *see also* Kolder, Gallagher & Parsons, *supra* note 20 (citing instances of court-ordered cesarean sections in 11 states).

[56] McFall v. Shimp, 10 Pa. D. & C.3d 90 (Allegheny Cty. 1978) *(per curiam)* (emphasis in original) *(reprinted in,* 127 Pittsburgh Legal J. 14 [1979]; *see also* In re Pescinski, 67 Wis. 2d 4, 226 N.W.2d 180, 182 (1975) (court found it had no authority to order kidney transplant from incompetent mentally ill individual to his sister in dire need of transplant, "[i]n the absence of real consent on his part, and in a situation where no benefit to him has been established").

[57] *See, e.g.,* People v. Stewart, No. M508197 (Cal. Mun. Ct. Feb. 26, 1987); People v. Hardy, No. 128458 (Mich. Ct. App. Apr. 1, 1991).

[58] Stallman v. Youngquist, 125 Ill. 2d 267, 276, 531 N.E.2d 355, 359 (1988).

The most complete description of the dangers posed by interfering with a woman's ability to make her own decisions regarding childbearing came from Judge Frank Easterbrook of the U.S. Court of Appeals for the Seventh Circuit in *Johnson Controls,* a case that considered a company's policy of excluding women from jobs in which they were exposed to lead. Judge Easterbrook dissented and took the position ultimately adopted by the U.S. Supreme Court in March 1991: that in enacting the Pregnancy Discrimination Act to amend Title VII, which is the federal statute prohibiting sex discrimination in employment, Congress prohibited employers from excluding all fertile women from jobs based on potential harm to their fetuses.[59] Judge Easterbrook explained that to uphold the company's policy would set a sweeping precedent that could not easily be confined. He noted that ultimately 20 million jobs could be closed to women under the same rationale, just as women were excluded from public life less than a century ago based on the demands of their perceived role as childbearers. Judge Easterbrook observed:

> *The hazards created by occupational chemicals span many orders of magnitude: some are safer than the sweeteners we wolf down, some are dangerous indeed. Where does lead fit on that spectrum? I cannot believe that Johnson would be entitled to fire female employees who smoke or drink during pregnancy—let alone fire all female employees because some might smoke or drink—which makes it hard to exclude women to curtail risk from other substances.*

> *How does the risk attributable to lead compare, say, to the risk to the next generation created by driving a taxi? A female bus or taxi driver is exposed to noxious fumes and the risk of accidents, all hazardous to a child she carries. Would it follow that taxi and bus companies can decline to hire women? That an employer could forbid pregnant employees to drive cars, because of the risk accidents pose to fetuses?[60]*

In at least three contexts involving policies premised on the adversarial model, state courts have ruled that the restriction interfered with women's fundamental right to liberty and thus had to be reviewed under the strict scrutiny standard. The District of Columbia Court of Appeals ruled that a court order directing a woman to submit to a cesarean section against her will interfered with her fundamental right to bodily integrity: "[E]very person has the right, under the common law and the Constitution, to accept or refuse medical treatment." [61] In a particularly graphic description, the court focused on the violent bodily intrusion that would be necessary to enforce an order against a woman that refused to comply:

> *There are also practical consequences to consider. What if A.C. had refused to comply with a court order that she submit to a caesarean? . . . Enforcement could be accomplished only through physical force or*

---

[59] International Union, UAW v. Johnson Controls, 59 U.S.L.W. 4209 (U.S. Mar. 20, 1991), *reversing,* 886 F.2d 871 (7th Cir. 1989) *(en banc).*

[60] *Johnson Controls,* 886 F.2d at 915–16 (Easterbrook, J., dissenting).

[61] In re A.C., 573 A.2d 1235, 1247 (D.C. 1990) *(en banc).*

its equivalent. A.C. would have to be fastened with restraints to the operating table, or perhaps involuntarily rendered unconscious by forcibly injecting her with an anesthetic, and then subjected to unwanted major surgery. Such actions would surely give one pause in a civilized society, especially when A.C. had done no wrong.[62]

Courts in two states—Massachusetts and Michigan—have held that prosecuting a woman because she was pregnant at the time she used cocaine implicated her right to privacy.[63] The Massachusetts court in particular described the level of governmental intrusion into women's lives entailed by the prosecution: "In order to prosecute Ms. Pellegrini, the commonwealth must intrude into her most private areas, her inner body . . ."[64] The court noted that "the level of state intervention and control over a woman's body required by this prosecution" would set a dangerous precedent for numerous other pregnancy-related restrictions on women.[65]

Finally, a court in New York ruled that finding a woman guilty of child neglect based solely on her use of drugs while pregnant and without considering her fitness to parent after giving birth implicated her fundamental right to privacy. The court based its ruling on a recognition of the sweeping intrusions on women's liberty that could be justified on the basis of potential prenatal harm to a fetus:

> *[T]o carry the . . . argument to the logical extension, the State would be able to supersede a mother's custody right to her child if she smoked cigarettes during her pregnancy, or ate junk food, or did too much physical labor or did not exercise enough. The list of potential intrusions is long and constitute entirely unacceptable violations of the bodily integrity of women.*[66]

The court noted that "[b]y becoming pregnant, women do not waive the constitutional protection afforded other citizens."[67]

E. Application of Strict Judicial Scrutiny to Adversarial Policies

Although governmental action premised on the adversarial model interferes with women's fundamental right to liberty, it is not necessarily constitutionally prohibited in all instances. As is true for any governmental interference with a fundamental individual right, a legislature, court or other governmental entity may place special restrictions and additional penalties on women's actions as they relate to childbearing only if it can justify the constitutional infringement under the strict scrutiny standard of judicial re-

---

[62] *Id.* at 1244 n.12.

[63] The women in both cases were prosecuted under statutes that criminalized the distribution of cocaine to a minor, under the theory that during the seconds after birth, before the umbilical cord was cut, the baby was a "minor" and cocaine may have been transmitted. Commonwealth v. Pellegrini, No. 87970 (Mass. Super. Ct. Oct. 15, 1990); People v. Bremer, No. 90-32227-FH (Mich. Cir. Ct. Jan. 31, 1991).

[64] *Pellegrini*, No. 87970, at 6.

[65] *Id.* at 9.

[66] In re Fletcher, No. N-3968188 (N.Y. Fam. Ct., Bronx County, Oct. 7, 1958).

[67] *Id.* at 6.

view.[68] The U.S. Supreme Court has repeatedly ruled that to satisfy the standard of strict judicial scrutiny, the government must show that its interference with an individual fundamental right is both "necessary to serve a compelling state interest" and "narrowly drawn to achieve that end."[69] Although the Court has never articulated precise guidelines as to what these requirements entail—for example, how exactly an interest qualifies as "compelling"—the Court has provided some guidance.

A court may not simply accept the government's assertion that the interest it is pursuing is "compelling."[70] Rather, the court must carefully scrutinize even interests that appear compelling in the abstract to ensure that they justify the specific deprivation of the right at issue and are compelling in the particular context and way in which they are being asserted.[71] For a restriction to be considered "narrowly drawn" to achieve the compelling interest, it must be the "least restrictive alternative"—that is, the means of achieving the governmental goal that is least intrusive on the fundamental right at stake.[72]

Critical—and perhaps most basic—to the strict scrutiny standard, the restriction sought by the government must actually serve or promote the compelling interest. An adversarial policy that actually is harmful to the governmental interest being pursued obviously cannot be said to serve that interest and thus cannot survive strict scrutiny. In sum, to satisfy the demanding strict scrutiny standard, the government must convince the court that its infringement on a fundamental right is absolutely necessary to further an extraordinarily important public policy goal.

Because significant use of the adversarial model has emerged only in the last decade, no federal court and few state courts have considered the constitutional limitations on the adversarial model. To satisfy the compelling interest requirement when confronted with a legal challenge to an adversarial action, the government is likely to assert that the special restriction is necessary to serve its interest in promoting healthy births.

---

[68] For another discussion of the strict scrutiny standard as it applies to certain special restrictions on women's behavior that follow the adversarial model, see Johnsen, *From Driving to Drugs: Governmental Regulation of Pregnant Women's Lives After* Webster, 138 U. Pa. L. Rev. 179, 204–215 (1989).

[69] Boos v. Barry, 108 S. Ct. 1157, 1164 (1988) (quoting Perry Educ. Ass'n v. Perry Local Educs. Ass'n, 460 U.S. 37, 45 (1983) and citing Board of Airport Comm'rs of Los Angeles v. Jews for Jesus, 107 S. Ct. 2568, 2571 (1987); Cornelius v. NAACP Legal Defense & Educ. Fund, 473 U.S. 788, 800 (1985); United States v. Grace, 461 U.S. 171, 177 (1983)).

[70] For a comprehensive, thoughtful discussion of the compelling interest requirement as applied in the context of abortion restrictions, see Dellinger & Sperling, *Abortion and the Supreme Court: The Retreat From* Roe v. Wade, 138 U. Pa. L. Rev. 83 (1989); *see also* Brief of Seventy-Seven Organizations Committed to Women's Equality as *Amici Curiae* in Support of Appellees, Webster v. Reproductive Health Servs., 109 S. Ct. 3040 (1989).

[71] *Boos,* 108 S. Ct. at 1164–65 (though "[a]s a general proposition" the government "has a vital national interest" in protecting foreign diplomats in accordance with international law, that interest is not "automatically . . . 'compelling' " when its assertion infringes upon first amendment rights); *see also* Coy v. Iowa, 108 S. Ct. 2798, 2802 (1988) (criminal defendant's sixth amendment rights "outweighed" state's interest in "protecting victims of sexual abuse"); Korematsu v. United States, 323 U.S. 214, 244 (1944) (Jackson, J., dissenting) (arguing that courts may not "distort" the Constitution in order to approve all that the state may deem to be expedient and in the national interest when fundamental rights are at stake); City of Richmond v. J.A. Croson Co., 109 S. Ct. 706, 723 (1989) (governmental interest in redressing generalized societal discrimination deemed not to be sufficiently compelling to justify race-conscious remedies); Cohen v. California, 413 U.S. 15, 25 (1971) (governmental interest in preserving the public order not sufficiently weighty to justify restrictions on free expression because it is "inherently boundless").

[72] *Boos,* 108 S. Ct. at 1168.

This interest is undoubtedly an important one for the government to pursue, and, as discussed above in connection with the facilitative model, most means of achieving this goal actually further women's interests and raise no constitutional problems. But in those relatively rare instances when government chooses a response that infringes upon women's fundamental liberty, the role of the courts is to strictly scrutinize that action and determine whether it is justified.

This section will consider the application of the strict scrutiny standard to each of the four principal ways in which the adversarial model has thus far been used: (1) employment policies excluding women from certain jobs in the name of "fetal protection"; (2) the creation of special, broadly defined, required standards of behavior for women, such as a crime of "prenatal abuse" or civil liability for failing to act as a "reasonable" pregnant woman; (3) court orders compelling women to undergo cesarean sections against their will; and (4) the imposition of additional penalties on women for the use of illegal drugs based solely on the fact that they were pregnant at the time of use. Applying the requirements of strict scrutiny as outlined by the Supreme Court reveals that each of these types of adversarial actions will likely fail strict scrutiny. Though the precise reasons vary to some degree with the context, two constitutional shortcomings are common to the various governmental actions that follow the adversarial model.

First, the contexts in which adversarial policies typically have been employed have been fraught with uncertainty, undermining the government's justifications for second-guessing women's decisions and infringing upon women's fundamental rights. Women must continually make decisions—large and small—about how to balance fetal risks with other important interests and demands, such as having to care for and support themselves and their families. In making such judgments—where to work, when to take medication necessary for their own health, whether to spend limited resources on prenatal care or food for their already born children—women face significant uncertainty as to the cumulative effect on fetal development of their behavior during and even before pregnancy. As with all decisions people make, women must make these judgments without the benefit of being able to predict the future. Being able after the fact to imagine ways in which a woman could have improved the chances of a healthy birth clearly does not indicate that a woman's decision was "wrong" at the time she made it and thus worthy of punishment.

A policy premised on the adversarial model is in essence an attempt by the government to override the woman's judgment and substitute its own—or a third party's—decision about how to do this balancing. For an adversarial policy to pass strict scrutiny, the government must establish a compelling interest in substituting its judgments for those made by the woman herself. A court or legislature does not have an ability superior to that of the woman involved to make the complicated judgments that necessarily vary from case to case according to each woman's life circumstances. In light of the inherent uncertainties, constraints and complexities, and the unprecedented constitutional infringements that would result, the government typically will be unable to establish the existence of a compelling interest.

The second reason why most types of adversarial policies will fail to pass strict scrutiny is that their overall effect typically is not to advance the government's asserted interest in promoting healthy births; rather, it is to encourage behavior by women that will actually be counterproductive to that goal. In determining whether an adversarial policy actually serves the governmental interest, the court must examine not only the case at hand but also the more general effects of the policy at issue. If a governmental action may improve the chances of a healthy birth in one particular case, but only at the cost of causing a greater number of less healthy births in the long-run, then the action cannot be said to further the asserted governmental interest. The overwhelming consensus within the medical and public health community is that taking an adversarial approach is ineffective and even counterproductive. Adversarial policies fail to address the root causes of poor birth outcomes and often are damaging to the goal of improving maternal and infant health because the government's threat of punishment and interference will frighten away the women most in need of health care.

1.   EXCLUSIONARY EMPLOYMENT POLICIES   Although the federal courts have not had an opportunity to consider the constitutional limitations on governmental use of the adversarial model, the U.S. Supreme Court in March of 1991 addressed a related issue when it considered whether a private employer's implementation of an adversarial policy violated Title VII, the federal statute prohibiting employment discrimination. The employment policy at issue in *International Union, UAW v. Johnson Controls* excluded all women who had not proven that they were infertile from working in positions where they would be exposed to lead because of potential adverse effects on fetal development. The Supreme Court reversed the decision of the U.S. Court of Appeals for the Seventh Circuit and held that the policy violated Title VII. The Supreme Court's majority opinion and two dissenting opinions in the Seventh Circuit are instructive in explaining why even an adversarial policy aimed at a specific activity known to pose some risks to fetal development nonetheless involved the type of inherently complex judgments and unknowable outcomes that argued for leaving the decisions to the women whose lives and physical persons were directly affected.

Excluding all women who might be fertile from the company's highest-paying positions forces even women who are not sexually active or who do not plan to bear children to subordinate all other pursuits to the elimination of risks to a potential future fetus they have no intention of conceiving. A 40-year-old divorced woman struggling to raise three children on her own is denied the job along with a woman who is currently pregnant or attempting to conceive. Indeed, the plaintiffs in *Johnson Controls* included a 50-year-old divorced woman who had been transferred to a lower-paying job and a woman who had been sterilized in order to keep her job. Judge Richard Cudahy recognized in a dissent from the Seventh Circuit's *Johnson Controls* decision that it is far from clear that denying the job even to a pregnant woman is in the best interests of her future child: "What is the situation of the pregnant woman, unemployed or working for the minimum wage and unprotected by health insurance, in relation to her pregnant sister, exposed to an indeterminate lead risk but well-fed, housed and doctored? Whose fetus is at greater risk? Whose decision is this to make?"[73]

In a separate dissent, Judge Frank Easterbrook also addressed the difficulty in evaluating what is likely to be optimal for fetal development:

> *Excluding women from industrial jobs at Johnson may reduce risk attributable to lead at the cost of increasing other hazards. There is a strong correlation between the health of the infant and prenatal medical care; there is also a powerful link between the parents' income and infants'*

---

[73] International Union, UAW v. Johnson Controls, 886 F.2d 871, 902 (7th Cir. 1989) *(en banc)* (Cudahy, J., dissenting), *reversed,* 59 U.S.L.W. 4209 (U.S. Mar. 20, 1991).

health, for higher income means better nutrition, among other things. Removing women from well-paying jobs (and the attendant health insurance), or denying women access to these jobs, may reduce the risk from lead while also reducing levels of medical care and the quality of nutrition. The net effect of lower income and less medical care could be a reduction in infants' prospects.[74]

The U.S. Supreme Court agreed with Judge Cudahy and Judge Easterbrook that in enacting the Pregnancy Discrimination Act to amend Title VII Congress had determined that it is the woman's decision to make: "Employment late in pregnancy often imposes risks on the unborn child . . . but Congress made clear that the decision to become pregnant or to work while being either pregnant or capable of becoming pregnant was reserved for each individual woman to make for herself."[75] Although the ruling rested on an interpretation of the federal statute, the Court implied that Congress made the appropriate determination in leaving such decisions to the woman because she was most directly affected and it would be inappropriate for a court or employer to override her judgments about how to balance competing factors in her life:

Decisions about the welfare of future children must be left to the parents who conceive, bear, support, and raise them rather than to the employers who hire those parents. . . .

It is no more appropriate for the courts than it is for individual employers to decide whether a woman's reproductive role is more important to herself and her family than her economic role. Congress has left this choice to the woman as hers to make.[76]

These observations about the necessity for complicated balancing of uncertain probabilities of risks, costs and benefits would apply equally in a case involving a constitutional challenge to a governmental employer who excluded women from certain positions. The government would not be able to establish a compelling interest to justify taking those judgments from the woman who is best situated to make them.

2. BROADLY DEFINED STANDARDS OF MANDATORY BEHAVIOR: PRENATAL ABUSE AND THE "REASONABLE" PREGNANT WOMAN STANDARD   Of the various types of special restrictions premised on the adversarial model, those that require women to comply with broadly defined standards of behavior provide the clearest example of why the government does not have a compelling interest in substituting its judgments as to how women must weigh competing demands in the face of inherently uncertain outcomes. Women have been criminally prosecuted under child abuse and neglect statutes for behavior during pregnancy. In one case, a woman was prosecuted under a statute that required a parent "to furnish necessary clothing, food, shelter, medical attendance or other remedial care for his or her child."[77] In the civil context, a Michigan court ruled

---

[74]*Id.* at 917–18 (Easterbrook, J., dissenting).

[75]*Id.* at 4214.

[76]*Johnson Controls,* 59 U.S.L.W. at 4214, 4215.

[77]Cal. Penal Code § 270 (West Supp. 1986); People v. Stewart, No. M508197 (Cal. Mun. Ct. Feb. 26, 1987); *see also* People v. Hardy, No. 128458 (Mich. Ct. App. Apr. 1, 1991); Reyes v. Superior Court, 73 Cal. App. 3d 214, 41 Cal. Rptr. 912 (1977).

in 1980 that children can sue their mothers for injuries caused by any action during pregnancy that did not meet the "reasonable" pregnant woman standard.[78] Some legal commentators have advocated creating a "duty to bring the child into the world as healthy as is reasonably possible,"[79] "a fetal right to begin life with sound body and mind"[80] or a crime of "fetal abuse."[81] These legally mandated standards of required behavior share the characteristic that they allow any of a woman's countless decisions that pose any risk to fetal development to be second-guessed by a judge, state prosecutor, physician or family member who disagrees with the woman's decision after-the-fact when faced with a poor birth outcome.[82] The government cannot justify these sweeping, vaguely defined standards of legally mandated behavior as "necessary to serve a compelling state interest."[83]

The criminal prosecution in 1985 of a California woman named Pamela Rae Stewart—one of the first premised on the adversarial model—helps illustrate the government's lack of justification for taking these judgments away from women.[84] Ms. Stewart was prosecuted for allegedly causing the death of her son through her actions while pregnant, under a statute that requires a parent "to furnish necessary clothing, food, shelter or medical attendance, or other remedial care for his or her child." Although the court ultimately ruled that the statute did not apply to the conduct at issue, the circumstances of Ms. Stewart's life and pregnancy reveal the types of complex judgments women must make that could become the basis for criminal or civil liability under broad standards of governmentally mandated behavior.

Ms. Stewart gave birth in 1985 to her third child. Tragically, her son was born with severe brain damage and died six weeks later. Ms. Stewart was arrested—and jailed for six days before she could make bail—for allegedly causing his death through her failure to follow her doctor's advice and obtain prompt medical care while pregnant, which the prosecutor claimed constituted failure to provide the "medical attendance" to her fetus required by the statute. Ms. Stewart had a difficult pregnancy and suffered

---

[78] Grodin v. Grodin, 102 Mich. App. 396, 301 N.W.2d 869, 871 (1980).

[79] Robertson, *Procreative Liberty and the Control of Conception, Pregnancy, and Childbirth,* 69 Va. L. Rev. 405, 438 (1983).

[80] Dougherty, *The Right to Begin Life with Sound Body and Mind: Fetal Patients and Conflicts With Their Mothers,* 63 U. Det. L. Rev. 89, 89 (1985).

[81] Shaw, *supra* note 50, at 98.

[82] *Boos,* 108 S. Ct. at 1164. Moreover, subjecting women to a standard of legally required behavior that does not target only undesirable activities but also directly restricts and strongly deters constitutionally protected behavior that is socially and personally desirable cannot be said to be "narrowly tailored." Facilitative policies to promote maternal and infant health exist that could more effectively focus on promoting desirable behavior without unnecessarily restricting women's fundamental rights.

[83] The Supreme Court has rejected the assertion of interests that might otherwise be considered compelling where, as here, the resulting constitutional deprivations would be "inherently boundless," Cohen v. California, 403 U.S. 15, 25 (1971), and "essentially limitless in scope and duration," City of Richmond v. J.A. Croson Co., 109 S. Ct. 706, 723 (1989).

[84] Information about *People v. Stewart* is taken from the following sources: People v. Stewart, No. M508197 (Cal. Mun. Ct. Feb. 26, 1987); Defendant's Memorandum of Points and Authorities in Support of Motion to Dismiss, People v. Stewart; Brief Amici Curiae, People v. Stewart; Editorial, *Drop the Charges Against Stewart,* The Tribune, Nov. 11, 1986, at B6; *See Neighbors Cite Mother's Troubled Past,* Daily Californian, at 1A; *The Ordeal of Pamela Rae Stewart,* Ms. Magazine, July/Aug. 1987, at 92, 94; *Woman Charged in Fetal Neglect Did Not Abuse Drugs, Husband Says,* San Diego Union, Sept. 30, 1986, at B1. For further discussion of the *Stewart* case, see Johnsen, *A New Threat to Pregnant Women's Autonomy,* Hastings Center Report, at 33 (Aug. 1987).

from a dangerous condition known as placenta previa. This ultimately caused her to experience substantial blood loss as the result of vaginal hemorrhaging—threatening to her own life—that the prosecution claimed led to her son being born brain-damaged. The prosecutor argued that Ms. Stewart should be held criminally liable because she might have delivered a healthy baby if she had sought medical care as soon as she began bleeding vaginally, rather than allegedly waiting a number of hours.[85]

Ms. Stewart, like all women, made decisions about health care considering her resources and competing responsibilities. Like many women, she suffered significant obstacles to obtaining adequate medical care. She was very poor and had two small daughters to care for; while she was pregnant, the entire family lived first in a single hotel room and then in a mobile home they shared with her mother-in-law. Ms. Stewart also appears to have been the victim of physical abuse by her husband. The police were called between 10 and 15 times over the course of a year to intervene when Mr. Stewart was abusive. Despite these difficult circumstances, Ms. Stewart did obtain prenatal care. Although the prosecutor imprisoned her for allegedly waiting a number of hours before seeking medical assistance when she began bleeding, she had called her physician on two prior occasions specifically to tell him of vaginal bleeding, and she was told "everything was fine." Even if the tragedy of Ms. Stewart's loss of her son might have been avoided, the government does not have a compelling interest that supports criminally prosecuting her over a disagreement about the judgment she made about when to call her doctor. If this type of prosecution were constitutionally permissible, any woman who gave birth to a less than completely healthy baby would be vulnerable to a criminal investigation and prosecution, particularly if it were possible after the outcome is known to conceive of ways in which the chances of a healthy birth could have been improved.

Using this statute to prosecute Ms. Stewart also fails to pass strict scrutiny for the second reason common to many adversarial policies: The overall effect would be counterproductive to the asserted compelling goal of promoting healthy births. In a case in which the birth has already occurred, as in Ms. Stewart's prosecution, the only possible justification for the action is that it will promote healthy births for other women by causing them to obtain better medical care. Health care providers overwhelmingly agree that the effect of prosecutions like Ms. Stewart's would be just the opposite. They would deter—not encourage—women from seeking prenatal care and even proper medical care during the actual delivery. Women would fear subjecting their actions during pregnancy to official scrutiny and inviting accusations by prosecutors that they have failed to follow their doctors' advice. The women most likely to fear prosecution and therefore avoid health care are those most in need of it: Women at greater risk of having poor birth outcomes due to their illness, poverty or drug or alcohol addictions. As a result of even this single failed prosecution of Ms. Stewart, health care and drug treatment providers in the area reported that women were deterred from seeking care by fear of arrest and prosecution.

3. COURT-ORDERED CESAREAN SECTIONS   The issuance of court orders forcing women to give birth by cesarean section provides another context in which the government cannot establish a compelling interest to justify overriding women's decisions that involve balancing important interests and uncertain risks. A survey published in the *New*

---

[85]The prosecutor also cited other activities in which Ms. Stewart allegedly engaged against her doctor's advice, including having sexual intercourse with her husband and taking marijuana and amphetamines, but it was her loss of blood that the prosecutor alleged caused the injury.

England Journal of Medicine reported instances in 11 states in which courts issued orders forcing women to undergo cesarean sections against their will.[86] The purported justification for this extraordinary interference with women's liberty and bodily integrity is the well-being of the fetus. Yet even the medical judgment about the risk to the fetus is fraught with uncertainties that weaken any asserted governmental interest in overriding the woman's decision. The *New England Journal of Medicine* survey found anecdotal evidence of six cases in which the prediction of fetal harm proved to be inaccurate.[87] In one of these cases, the court based its decision on medical testimony that without the cesarean section, there was a "99 to 100 percent certainty" that the fetus would not survive, as well as a "50 percent chance" that the woman herself would die.[88] In fact, a few days after the court denied the stay of the order compelling the surgery, the woman had a safe vaginal delivery, without any harm to herself or the baby.

The District of Columbia Court of Appeals sitting *en banc,* in 1990 became the first appellate court to consider the full constitutional implications of a court-ordered cesarean section.[89] The court's opinion includes an extensive discussion of the fundamental rights at stake and concludes that there exists no governmental interest sufficiently "compelling" to override the woman's decision.[90] The *en banc* court reversed the three-judge panel of that court, which had upheld the issuance of the court order, and ruled that the right of the woman must be protected: "[I]n virtually all cases the question of what is to be done is to be decided by the patient—the pregnant woman—on behalf of herself and the fetus."[91]

The facts of *In re A.C.* provide tragic and compelling evidence that such decisions must be left to the woman. Twenty-seven-year-old Angela Carder (identified in the opinion by her initials "A.C.") was 26 weeks pregnant and ill with cancer, which she had successfully battled since age 13, when she was ordered by a court to give birth by cesarean section. The order was issued at the hospital's request over the unanimous objections of the woman, her husband, her parents and her physicians and despite evidence that the fetus might not be viable and that the surgery might cause Ms. Carder's death, given her poor health. A three-judge panel of the District of Columbia Court of Appeals refused to stay the order and the surgery was performed. The fetus, in fact, was not viable and did not survive. The woman died two days after the surgery, and the cesarean section was referred to on her death certificate as a contributing factor.

As is inevitably true in these cases, the court proceedings were held under tremendous time pressure with little opportunity for the woman to present her case. The entire process took only six hours, from the time the hospital first went to court to the time the surgery was performed. The judge never spoke to Ms. Carder, the attorney appointed to represent her had no opportunity to meet with her, review her medical records

---

[86] Kolder, Gallagher & Parsons, *supra* note 20, at 1193.

[87] Kolder, Gallagher & Parsons, *supra* note 20, at 1195.

[88] Jefferson v. Griffin Spalding County Hosp., 247 Ga. 86, 274 S.E.2d 457, 459 (1981) *(per curiam).*

[89] In re A.C., 573 A.2d 1235 (D.C. 1990) *(en banc), reversing* 533 A.2d 611 (D.C. 1987). Information about the case was also obtained from the briefs filed in the D.C. Court of Appeals and the transcript of the proceedings in the D.C. Superior Court, Transcript of Proceedings before the Superior Court of the District of Columbia Civil Division, June 16, 1987 [hereinafter Transcript].

[90] 573 A.2d at 1237.

[91] *Id.*

or prepare or call witnesses, and the physician who had the longest history of treating her was not even notified of the hearing. A lawyer was appointed to represent the fetus, and she argued "I think the potentiality of this fetus outweighs the imminent death of the patient." [92] In ordering the surgery, the judge stated: "It's not an easy decision to make, but given the choices, the Court is of the view the fetus should be given an opportunity to live." [93]

The opinion of the three-judge panel of the District of Columbia Court of Appeals issued after Ms. Carder's death provides a disturbing example of the dangers of allowing a court to substitute its own judgment for that of the woman affected. In explaining the way in which it balanced the interests involved, the court acknowledged "we well know that we may have shortened A.C.'s life span" but discounted the value of Ms. Carder's life because she was likely to die soon in any event: "The Caesarean section would not significantly affect A.C.'s condition because she had, at best, two days left of sedated life; the complications arising from the surgery would not significantly alter that prognosis." [94] In fact, this finding was disputed in an affidavit subsequently submitted by Ms. Carder's treating physician who stated that, had he been notified of the hearing, he would have testified that the surgery interfered with Ms. Carder's ability to receive potentially beneficial chemotherapy that could have allowed her to live longer. The court found that the value of Ms. Carder's life was outweighed by the admittedly "slim" chance that the fetus might survive: "The court based its decision to deny a stay on the medical judgment that A.C. would not survive for a significant time after the surgery and that the fetus had a better, though slim, chance if taken before A.C.'s imminent death." [95]

The trial court's willingness to discount the value of Ms. Carder's life, the profound intrusion on her bodily integrity, and the inherent medical uncertainties all powerfully illustrate why the government does not have a compelling interest in taking from the woman whose body will be subjected to surgery the ability to balance these competing factors for herself. Indeed, in this case, the only conflict of interests was the conflict created by the hospital in seeking the order and the court in issuing it: neither the woman nor the fetus benefitted from the surgery and Ms. Carder had been advised of the likelihood that the fetus was not yet viable. The decision of the *en banc* court striking down the order as an unjustified infringement of Ms. Carder's fundamental rights, while instructive for future cases, was obviously too late to protect Ms. Carder's rights and well-being.

The American Medical Association (AMA) has issued a comprehensive policy statement that concludes, as did the District of Columbia Court of Appeals sitting *en banc,* that physicians should not seek and courts should not issue orders overriding a pregnant woman's decision whether to have a cesarean section. Noting that "[p]erforming medical procedures against the pregnant woman's will violates her right to informed consent and her constitutional right to bodily integrity," the AMA statement stresses the inappropriateness of any party other than the woman herself deciding the necessary balancing of interests:

---

[92] Transcript, *supra* note 89, at 79.
[93] *Id.* at 84.
[94] 533 A.2d at 617.
[95] *Id.* at 613.

> *[D]ecisions that would result in health risks are properly made only by
> the individual who must bear the risk. Considerable uncertainty can sur-
> round medical evaluations of the risks and benefits of obstetrical inter-
> ventions. Through a court-ordered intervention, a physician deprives a
> pregnant woman of her right to reject personal risk and replaces it with
> the physician's evaluation of the amount of risk that is properly accept-
> able. This undermines the very concept of informed consent.*[96]

In addition, forcing a woman to have a cesarean section cannot survive strict scrutiny for the second reason common to adversarial policies: It does not serve—and indeed, is harmful to—the government's interest in promoting healthy births. The AMA
report discusses the adverse consequences of this practice, including the instillation of
general distrust of physicians in pregnant women:

> *[W]omen may withhold information from the physician that they feel might
> lead the physician to seek judicial intervention. Or they may reject med-
> ical or prenatal care altogether, seriously impairing a physician's ability
> to treat both the pregnant woman and her fetus.*[97]

The AMA concludes that "while the health of a few infants may be preserved by
overriding a pregnant woman's decision," the overall effect—which is the relevant issue
for constitutional analysis—is that "the health of a great many more may be sacrificed."[98] Thus, the government's objective is not served. In fact, the issuance of the
order may also endanger the health of the future child directly involved. In at least one
case, the woman against whom the order was directed left the hospital to avoid the
procedure.[99]

4. SPECIAL PENALTIES FOR DRUG USE DURING PREGNANCY   Courts, legislatures
and other governmental entities have most often taken an adversarial approach in addressing the use by pregnant women of harmful substances, such as cocaine and heroin,
that already have been criminalized for the general public. Dozens of women have been
criminally prosecuted, deprived of custody of their children, incarcerated or confined to
drug treatment centers during pregnancy because they were pregnant when they used

---

[96] AMA, *Legal Interventions During Pregnancy, supra* note 2, at 2665. Although the AMA declined to adopt
an absolute rule that no situation exists in which a physician should seek judicial intervention, it noted:

> [A] woman conceivably could refuse oral administration of a drug that would cause no ill
> effects in her own body but would almost certainly prevent a substantial and irreversible
> injury to her fetus. Given the current state of medical technology, it is unlikely that such a
> situation would occur. In addition, as a practical matter, it is unlikely that a woman would
> refuse treatment in that situation.

Id. at 2666; *see also* ACOG Committee Opinion, *supra* note 3, at 1 (noting "limitations and fallibility" of
obstetricians' assessments of medical risks and that a pregnant woman "evaluates the risks and benefits
presented to her from her own sense of values").

[97] AMA, *Legal Interventions During Pregnancy, supra* note 2, at 2666.

[98] *Id.*

[99] *Id.* at 2665; Gallagher, *supra* note 1, at 47.

drugs.[100] Most of these prosecutions ultimately were dismissed on the ground that the statute under which prosecution had been brought was being misused. For example, women have been prosecuted for distribution of cocaine to a "minor," a much more serious offense than possession, because they were pregnant at the time of use. Prosecutors have argued that the definition of "minor" under the statute was satisfied because cocaine may have been passed from the woman's body to her child's body after birth in the seconds before the umbilical cord was cut.

Courts in at least two states—Michigan and Massachusetts—have ruled not only that the statutes did not apply in the manner attempted by the prosecution but also that the prosecutions interfered with women's fundamental liberties. The courts therefore applied the strict scrutiny standard to determine if the liberty infringements were justified. Both courts concluded that they were not and dismissed the prosecutions.[101] A third court upheld the only successful criminal prosecution of this type to date with only a cursory discussion of the constitutional issues.[102] The conviction is being appealed to the Florida Supreme Court.

Women who use illegal drugs during pregnancy obviously can be prosecuted under laws that generally apply to all individuals. The factor that triggers constitutional protection and the need for strict judicial scrutiny—whether the activity involved is obtaining inadequate prenatal care, the woman's choice of method of childbirth or the use of already illegal drugs—is the imposition of special restrictions or obligations imposed only on women due to the fact they were pregnant, potentially pregnant or fertile when they engaged in the activity at issue. The government may not, however, increase the penalties or seriousness of the crime charged because the defendant is a woman who was pregnant or fertile at the time she used illegal substances unless the additional restriction is necessary and narrowly tailored to further a compelling interest.

It is in the context of drug use by pregnant women that the use of the adversarial model may initially appear to be the most justified and likely to survive strict scrutiny. The government's interest in reducing the use of illegal drugs by women during pregnancy is unquestionably strong. The risks posed to fetal development by a woman's use of substances such as cocaine have been widely publicized. In addition to its interest in protecting the health of infants and women, the government incurs high financial costs for the care and education of children born suffering from the effects of their mothers' drug use during pregnancy. What is at issue, however, is not the legitimacy of the governmental interest but whether the means chosen to effectuate that interest are appropriate and constitutionally permissible.

Evidence and opinion are overwhelmingly that special penalties directed only at women who use illegal drugs during pregnancy suffer from the second constitutional defect common to adversarial policies: They are counterproductive to the government's objective of promoting healthy births and therefore do not "serve a compelling state interest."[103] Recognizing the adverse consequences, a wide variety of professional and public interest organizations concerned with infant and maternal health have vigorously

---

[100] See ACLU, supra note 23.

[101] Pellegrini, No. 87970, at 1; Bremer, No. 90-32227-FH, at 12.

[102] Johnson v. State, No. 89-1765 (Fla. Dist. Ct. App. Apr. 18, 1991) (appeal pending before Supreme Court of Florida).

[103] Boos, 108 S. Ct. at 1164.

opposed governmental responses premised on the adversarial model. Among the organizations that oppose creating new penalties directed at drug use by pregnant women are the American Academy of Pediatrics,[104] the American Medical Association,[105] the American Public Health Association,[106] the American Society on Addiction Medicine,[107] the March of Dimes,[108] the National Association of Public Child Welfare Administrators[109] and the Southern Regional Project on Infant Mortality (an initiative of the Southern Governors' Association and the Southern Legislative Conference).[110]

The most commonly cited reason for opposition to adversarial policies is that they will deter women who use drugs from seeking drug treatment and prenatal care by causing women to fear that they will be arrested and prosecuted for a crime such as "prenatal abuse or neglect" or distribution to a "minor." Both the Massachusetts and Michigan courts cited this deterrent effect as a basis for their rulings that this type of prosecution fails strict scrutiny. The Massachusetts court wrote: "By imposing criminal sanctions, women may turn away from seeking prenatal care for fear of being discovered, thereby undermining the state's asserted interests."[111]

A 1990 report by the U.S. General Accounting Office, which included the results of a survey of health care providers and others, described fear of prosecution and loss of custody of their children as a "barrier to treatment" for pregnant women dependent on drugs:

---

[104] "The public must be assured of nonpunitive access to comprehensive care which will meet the needs of the substance abusing pregnant woman and her infant." American Academy of Pediatrics, Policy Statement, *Drug Exposed Infants,* at 2. "The AAP is concerned that such involuntary measures may discourage mothers and their infants from receiving the very medical care and social support systems that are crucial to their treatment." *Id* at 11.

[105] AMA, *Legal Interventions During Pregnancy, supra* note 2, at 2670 ("Criminal sanctions or civil liability for harmful behavior by the pregnant woman toward her fetus is inappropriate"); AMA, *Treatment Versus Criminalization, supra* note 2 ("[T]herefore be it . . . resolved that the AMA oppose legislation which criminalizes maternal drug addiction . . .").

[106] The American Public Health Association "recommends that no punitive measures be taken against pregnant women who are users of illicit drugs when no other illegal acts, including drug-related offenses, have been committed." American Public Health Association, Policy Statement, *9020: Illicit Drug Use by Pregnant Women,* Am. J. Pub. Health 253 (1990).

[107] "State and local governments should avoid any measures defining alcohol or other drug use during pregnancy as 'prenatal child abuse,' and should avoid prosecution, jail, or other punitive measures as a substitute for providing effective health services for these women." American Society on Addiction Medicine, Position Statement, *ASAM Policy Statement on Chemically Dependent Women and Pregnancy,* ASAM News, 6 (Sept./Oct. 1989) [hereinafter ASAM Policy Statement].

[108] "Punitive approaches to drug addiction may be harmful to pregnant women because they interfere with access to appropriate health care. Fear of punishment may cause women most in need of prenatal services to avoid health care professionals." March of Dimes, *Statement on Maternal Drug Abuse* 1.

[109] "Laws, regulations, or policies that respond to addiction in a primarily punitive nature, requiring human service workers and physicians to function as law enforcement agents are inappropriate." National Association of Public Child Welfare Administrators, *Guiding Principles for Working With Substance-Abusing Families and Drug-Exposed Children: The Child Welfare Response* 3 (approved Jan. 1991).

[110] "States should adopt, as preferred methods, prevention, intervention, and treatment alternatives rather than punitive actions to ameliorate the problems related to perinatal exposure to drugs and alcohol." Southern Regional Project on Infant Mortality (An Initiative of the Southern Governors' Association and the Southern Legislative Conference) Policy Statement, *Southern Legislative Summit on Healthy Infants and Families: An American Assembly* 8 (Oct. 4–7, 1990) [hereinafter Southern Regional Project on Infant Mortality].

[111] *Pellegrini,* No. 87970, at 9.

> *Drug treatment and prenatal care providers told us that the increasing*
> *fear of incarceration and losing children to foster care is discouraging*
> *pregnant women from seeking care. Women are reluctant to seek treat-*
> *ment if there is a possibility of punishment. They also fear that if their*
> *children are placed in foster care, they will never get the children back.*[112]

The report noted as particularly troubling criminal sanctions' effect of deterring women from seeking not only drug treatment but also prenatal care, which is particularly important for women who use drugs: "Prenatal care can help prevent or at least ameliorate many of the problems and costs associated with the births of drug-exposed infants." When prenatal care is provided, "the chances of an unhealthy infant are greatly reduced." In addition to being deterred from seeking drug treatment and prenatal care, women were also found to be giving birth at home without medical care because they feared detection.[113]

The American Medical Association expressed similar concerns about special prosecutions of women for drug use during their pregnancies and noted in particular that even if the health of a few children was promoted, the overall effect would be to sacrifice the well-being of many more children:

> *Pregnant women will be likely to avoid seeking prenatal or other medical*
> *care for fear that their physicians' knowledge of substance abuse or other*
> *potentially harmful behavior could result in a jail sentence rather than*
> *proper medical treatment. This fear is not unfounded . . . [T]he number*
> *of women who are convicted and incarcerated for potentially harmful*
> *behavior is likely to be relatively small in comparison with the number*
> *of women who would be prompted to avoid medical care altogether. As*
> *a result, the potential well-being of many infants may be sacrificed in*
> *order to preserve the health of a few.*[114]

Adversarial policies may also cause women who do seek prenatal care to withhold from their doctors and other health care providers information concerning their use of drugs and other potentially harmful substances such as alcohol, information critical to obtaining appropriate care.

Particularly counterproductive in this respect are statutes that require health care providers to report a patient to state authorities if they suspect she is using illegal drugs or other potentially harmful substances during pregnancy. Forcing doctors to betray their patients' confidences drives a wedge between pregnant women and their doctors and will deter the women who most need health care from obtaining it. Several organizations, in addition to opposing the creation of special crimes directed at drug use during

---

[112] United States General Accounting Office, *Drug-Exposed Infants: A Generation At Risk,* Report to the Chairman, Committee on Finance, U.S. Senate, June 1990.

[113] *Id.* at 9–10.

[114] AMA, *Legal Interventions During Pregnancy, supra* note 2, at 2667; *see also* ASAM Policy Statement, *supra* note 107, at 6. ("Criminal prosecution of chemically dependent women will have the overall result of deterring such women from seeking both prenatal care and chemical dependency treatment, thereby increasing, rather than preventing, harm to children and to society as a whole").

pregnancy, specifically oppose requiring doctors to report their pregnant patients whom they suspect of using drugs or alcohol. For example, the AMA has adopted a resolution stating that it opposes "legislation which criminalizes maternal drug addiction or requires physicians to function as agents of law enforcement—gathering evidence for prosecution . . . ."[115] The American Society on Addiction Medicine adopted the following policy: "No law or regulation should require physicians to violate confidentiality by reporting their pregnant patients to state or local authorities for 'prenatal child abuse.'"[116] The Southern Regional Project on Infant Mortality takes the position that states should "[b]ar[] pregnancy-related tests and care that reveal substance abuse from being used as evidence in criminal prosecutions."[117]

In addition to their effect of deterring pregnant women from seeking vital health care, adversarial approaches to the use of illegal drugs during pregnancy are ineffective at promoting healthy births for at least five reasons. First, incarcerating women for these special crimes while they are pregnant would likely be detrimental to fetal development due to the unhealthy conditions that exist in prisons. Litigation on behalf of pregnant female prisoners has documented shockingly dangerous conditions, including grossly deficient prenatal medical care and nutrition, exposure of pregnant women to contagious diseases, filthy and overcrowded living conditions and easy access to illegal drugs, which have resulted in high rates of miscarriage and infant mortality and morbidity.[118] Second, special penalties on already illegal activity are unlikely to be effective because any deterrent effect of criminalization on the activity should already exist. Third, imposing heavy criminal penalties on pregnant women may pressure some women to have unwanted abortions. As a Massachusetts court stated in dismissing a special prosecution, "The state's interest would be further undermined when women seek to terminate their pregnancies for fear of criminal sanctions."[119] Fourth, the Massachusetts court also expressed concern about the effect such prosecutions might have on women's attitudes toward their pregnancies: "There is no familiar bond more intimate or more fundamental than that between the mother and the fetus she carries in her womb. This court will not permit the destruction of this relationship by the prosecution. . . ."[120]

Finally, adversarial governmental actions are ineffective in reducing women's drug use during pregnancy because they fail to address the true problem: the strong physical and psychological dependencies from which the women suffer. As the AMA report states,

> In all but a few cases, taking a harmful substance such as cocaine is not meant to harm the fetus but to satisfy an acute psychological and physical need for that particular substance. If a pregnant woman suffers from a substance dependency, it is the physical impossibility of avoiding an im-

---

[115] AMA, *Treatment Versus Criminalization, supra* note 2.

[116] ASAM Policy Statement, *supra* note 107, at 6.

[117] Southern Regional Project on Infant Mortality, *supra* note 110, at 9.

[118] Barry, *Recent Developments: Pregnant Prisoners,* 12 Harv. Women's L.J. 189 (1989); Berrien, *Pregnancy & Drug Use: Incarceration is Not the Answer,* Women of Color Partnership, Religious Coalition for Abortion Rights Newsletter 7 (Aug. 1989); AMA, *Legal Interventions During Pregnancy, supra* note 2, at 2667.

[119] *Pellegrini,* No. 87970, at 9.

[120] *Id.* at 16.

pact on fetal health that causes severe damage to the fetus, not an intentional or malicious wish to cause harm.[121]

The same medical, children's welfare, women's rights and public policy groups that are unified in their opposition to the adversarial approach also agree that the effective policies are those that follow a facilitative model and help women overcome and avoid dependency on harmful substances.[122]

Today, however, the vast majority of pregnant women seeking assistance in overcoming a drug dependency cannot obtain the help they need.[123] The lack of drug treatment programs that serve pregnant women has been well-documented. Treatment programs routinely refuse to admit pregnant women, and programs that will typically have long waiting lists, often longer than the duration of the woman's pregnancy. A widely known survey of treatment programs in New York City found that 54% denied treatment to all pregnant women, and 87% said that they would not treat pregnant women on Medicaid who were dependent on cocaine.[124] The General Accounting Office's 1990 report also indicated a severe shortage of treatment programs.[125] Those few programs that do have space available rarely provide services that meet the needs of pregnant women, including prenatal care and child care. To be effective and accessible for pregnant women, treatment programs must provide comprehensive, community-based medical, educational, psychological and social services.[126] Education programs designed to prevent the initial use of harmful substances are particularly important because drug treatment often is not provided until after significant damage has been done to fetal development by the woman's drug use before she even knows that she is pregnant. Such programs are also useful in avoiding potential fetal harm attributable to men's drug use, which can alter sperm.

Although the cost of providing these needed services clearly is substantial, the cost of failing to do so is even greater. As the General Accounting Office's report concluded, the financial and other costs to society of drug-exposed infants come in many forms: extended and expensive hospital stays at birth for drug-exposed infants, subsequent need for special medical care, higher rates of foster care placement, special educational needs and limitations in employment possibilities later in life. If the government declines to provide funding for voluntary treatment programs necessary to avoid these costs and as a result women seeking help are turned away, it makes no sense for the government to then prosecute those same women, incarcerate them or place them in involuntary treatment programs. As the AMA states, "[I]t would be an injustice to punish a pregnant

---

[121] AMA, *Legal Interventions During Pregnancy, supra* note 2, at 2667–68.

[122] *See* sources cited at *supra* notes 104–110.

[123] *See generally Born Hooked: Confronting the Impact of Perinatal Substance Abuse: Hearing Before the House Select Committee on Children, Youth and Families,* 101st Cong., 1st Sess., 110, 112 (1989) (statement of Wendy Chavkin, M.D., M.P.H., Rockefeller Fellow, Sergievsky Center, Columbia University School of Public Health, New York, N.Y.) [hereinafter cited as Hearing]; McNulty, *Pregnancy Policy: The Health, Policy and Legal Implications of Punishing Pregnant Women for Harm to their Fetuses,* 16 N.Y.U. Rev. Law & Soc. Change 277 (1987–88); Mariner, Glantz & Annas, *Pregnancy, Drugs, and the Perils of Prosecution,* Crim. Just. Ethics, Winter/Spring 1990, at 36; Pollitt, *Fetal Rights—A New Assault on Feminism,* The Nation, Mar. 26, 1990, at 409; Brody, *Widespread Abuse of Drugs by Pregnant Women is Found,* New York Times, Aug. 30, 1988, at A1.

[124] Hearing, *supra* note 123.

[125] United States General Accounting Office, *Drug-Exposed Infants: A Generation At Risk,* 1990.

[126] *See* sources cited at *supra* notes 104–110.

woman for not receiving treatment for her substance abuse when treatment is not an available option to her.''[127]

Using adversarial approaches to the problem of drug use during pregnancy when facilitative approaches exist is also a basis for finding such policies unconstitutional because the government is not seeking to serve its interest in the manner least restrictive of the fundamental right at stake. As a Massachusetts court stated in dismissing a prosecution of a woman for ''distributing'' drugs through her use during pregnancy, ''The commonwealth may effectuate its stated interest in protecting viable fetuses through less restrictive means, such as education and making available medical care and drug treatment centers for pregnant women.''[128]

IV. Sex and Race Equality Concerns

A. Sex Equality

This chapter has focused on the threat posed by governmental policies premised on the adversarial approach to women's fundamental right to liberty. Yet because such policies burden the liberty only of women, and not men, adversarial policies also raise important sex equality concerns. The U.S. Supreme Court recently ruled in the *Johnson Controls* case that adversarial policies that exclude women from employment in jobs that present risks to fetal development violate Title VII's prohibition against sex discrimination in employment.[129] The U.S. Constitution's guarantee of equal protection of the laws and similar provisions of state constitutions that protect women from governmental action that discriminates on the basis of sex may provide women with additional protection from adversarial policies employed by the government.

Under the U.S. Supreme Court's current doctrine, the equal protection clause of the fourteenth amendment forbids governmental policies that discriminate on the basis of sex unless the distinction is ''substantially related'' to serving ''an important governmental interest.''[130] This test—sometimes referred to as middle-level scrutiny—is not as rigorous as the strict scrutiny reserved for race discrimination and policies burdening fundamental rights but nonetheless provides women with a heightened level of judicial protection. Several state courts have interpreted their state constitutions as providing women with higher levels of judicial protection from sex discrimination than under the federal Constitution.[131]

No state or federal court has yet considered whether an adversarial governmental policy that places on women special restrictions related to childbearing constitutes discrimination on the basis of sex for purposes of equal protection analysis. It is beyond the scope of this chapter to develop fully the constitutional theory for viewing adversar-

---

[127] AMA, *Legal Interventions During Pregnancy, supra* note 2, at 2669.

[128] *Pellegrini*, No. 87970, at 8.

[129] International Union, UAW v. Johnson Controls, 59 U.S.L.W. 4209 (U.S. Mar. 20, 1991).

[130] Craig v. Boren, 429 U.S. 190, 197 (1976); *see also* Mississippi Univ. for Women v. Hogan 458 U.S. 718, 724 n.9 (1982) (invalidating sex-based classification under strict scrutiny but stating ''we need not decide whether classifications based upon gender are inherently suspect,'' which would render them subject to strict scrutiny).

[131] *See, e.g.,* Doe v. Maher, 40 Conn. Super. 394, 515 A.2d 134, 157 (1986) (holding exclusion of funding for therapeutic abortions from state medicaid program violated state constitutional guarantee of equal protection and state equal rights amendment; discussing other state court decisions applying strict scrutiny and absolute scrutiny to sex discrimination).

ial policies as sex discrimination, but this section will briefly consider the principal arguments.

Heightened judicial review of the constitutionality of adversarial policies under the federal equal protection clause would require the Supreme Court to recognize distinctions based on pregnancy or the potential to become pregnant as sex-based. A 1974 Supreme Court case, *Geduldig v. Aiello,* touched on this issue.[132] The Court in *Geduldig* upheld California's disability insurance program despite its exclusion of health care related to pregnancy and childbirth from the program's coverage. The Court stated that not all pregnancy-related distinctions necessarily constituted discrimination based on sex and found that the disability program at issue distinguished not between men and women but between "pregnant women" and "nonpregnant persons."[133] Soon after, the Court in *General Electric v. Gilbert* applied the same strained reasoning in interpreting the scope of Title VII's prohibition on sex discrimination in employment.[134]

These opinions have been the subjects of harsh criticism and even ridicule[135] for their assertion that a distinction directly targeting a biological characteristic that only women possess and thus disadvantaging only women is not necessarily a sex-based distinction. The reasoning was directly and immediately rejected by Congress, which overturned *Gilbert* by amending Title VII to make clear that, for purposes of employment, discrimination on the basis of pregnancy is to be treated as discrimination on the basis of sex. For purposes of constitutional analysis, the question is whether the Supreme Court will adopt the logic of *Geduldig* or the Congress when considering whether adversarial policies constitute sex-based discrimination deserving of heightened scrutiny. There are at least five factors that suggest that the Court may not extend its logic in *Geduldig* to the adversarial policies discussed in this chapter.

First, when the Court decided *Geduldig* in 1974, it was just beginning to develop its constitutional jurisprudence concerning sex discrimination. Only one year before, the Court had, for the first time, ruled that women are a protected class under the equal protection clause.[136] The Court's discussion of distinctions based on pregnancy was brief, confined to a single footnote.

Second, even if *Geduldig* remains good law, the Court's distinction between "pregnant women" and "nonpregnant persons" is not applicable or appropriate in the context of adversarial policies that impose special restrictions on women related to both current and future childbearing. These adversarial policies threaten the liberty not only of pregnant women but of all women. This is clearly seen in the *Johnson Controls* case where a private employer excluded not only pregnant women but all potentially fertile women from working in high-paying jobs in which they would be exposed to lead.

Third, the notion that restrictions aimed at pregnancy do not constitute sex-based distinctions is clearly inappropriate in cases in which adversarial policies target only women even though the same behavior by men also increases the risk of fetal harm. In such cases, men and women are similarly situated, and governmental action that singles

---

[132] 417 U.S. 484 (1974).

[133] *Id.* at 496 n.20.

[134] 429 U.S. 125 (1976).

[135] *See* L. Tribe, *Constitutional Law* 1578 (2d ed. 1988) (describing the analysis in *Geduldig* as "so superficial as to approach farcical"); Law, *Rethinking Sex and the Constitution*, 132 U. Pa. L. Rev. 955, 983–84 nn.107–09 (1984) (citing numerous articles).

[136] Frontiero v. Richardson, 411 U.S. 677 (1973) (plurality).

out only women constitutes clear sex discrimination under current equal protection analysis. For example, the discriminatory employment policy at issue in the *Johnson Controls* case excluded only women from jobs in which they would be exposed to lead. Yet, as the Supreme Court noted in ruling that this policy violated Title VII by discriminating against women, men who are exposed to lead can also create risks to fetal development because of damage to their sperms.[137] In fact, one of the plaintiffs in that case was a man who had requested, but had been denied, a leave of absence that he sought because he wanted to become a father but first wanted to lower his lead level. In addition to lead exposure, other workplace toxins that may damage sperm and thus cause increased risks to men's future children include paints, pesticides, chemical solvents and radiation.[138] Adversarial governmental actions directed at women who use drugs and alcohol during pregnancy are another context in which only women have been penalized, despite evidence that alcohol and drug use—as well as smoking—by men can cause harm to their future children through the negative effect on sperm. The government's failure to date to focus on the role of men's behavior in determining the health of newborns may itself be a result of impermissible sex stereotypes about women's role in childbearing.

Fourth, Supreme Court precedent suggests that even if the Court upholds *Geduldig*, the Court will only apply it in the context of extending benefits and not to the type of affirmative penalties, burdens and obstacles employed by adversarial policies. When evaluating constitutional challenges to policies infringing on women's reproductive freedom, the Court has distinguished between laws that it views as placing obstacles and burdens on the exercise of fundamental rights and those that fail to extend benefits.[139] Indeed, despite the strong criticism this reasoning has received, as recently as May 1991 the Court relied on this distinction to uphold regulations that were challenged as interfering with the right to privacy and the right to freedom of expression.[140]

The Court's refusal to find impermissible sex discrimination in *Geduldig* can be seen as reflecting this benefit/burden distinction. Indeed, in *Geduldig*, the Court stated that the benefit at issue addressed "a risk that was outside the program's protection" and that women in the disability benefit program already in practice received a higher rate of benefit than men.[141] The Court explicitly relied on this benefit/burden distinction in the Title VII context and limited its ruling in *Gilbert* in *Nashville Gas Co. v. Satty*. The Court in *Satty* distinguished between a disability policy's failure "to extend to women a benefit that men cannot and do not receive" and the imposition on women of "a substantial burden that men need not suffer."[142] The Court held that although Title VII "did not require that greater economic benefits be paid to one sex or the other

---

[137] *Johnson Controls,* 59 U.S.L.W. at 4212.

[138] *Father's Exposure to Toxins Can Hurt Fetus, Too,* Indianapolis Star, Mar. 9, 1991, at A5; Davis, *Fathers and Fetuses,* New York Times, Mar. 1, 1991, at A27; *Father's Smoking May Damage Sperm,* Washington Post, Jan. 25, 1991, at A8; Blakeslee, *Research on Birth Defects Shifts to Flaws in Sperm,* New York Times, Jan. 1, 1991, at A1.

[139] *See, e.g.,* Webster v. Reproductive Health Servs., 109 S. Ct. 3040 (1989); Harris v. McRae, 448 U.S. 297 (1980).

[140] Rust v. Sullivan, Nos. 89-1391 & 89-1392 (U.S. May 23, 1991).

[141] 417 U.S. at 497 & n.21. The Court similarly based its ruling on the lack of evidence "that the selection of the risks insured by the program worked to discriminate against any definable group or class in terms of the aggregate risk protection derived by that group or class from the program." *Id.* at 496.

[142] 434 U.S. 136, 142 (1977). *But see* L. Tribe, *American Constitutional Law* 15–29, at 1579 (describing distinction as "at best problematic").

'because of their differing roles in the scheme of human existence' '' an employer could not ''burden female employees in such a way as to deprive them of employment opportunities because of their different role.'' [143] *Geduldig* therefore may be found inapplicable to adversarial policies that involve not the extension of benefits but affirmative burdens and special penalties placed on women.

Finally, adversarial policies that impose restrictions only on women's behavior because of their childbearing capacity should be subjected to heightened scrutiny because they constitute a government policy to create a separate regime of onerous legal restrictions and obligations only for women. As many people have argued, the core value behind the equal protection clause that necessitates heightened scrutiny of governmental distinctions on the basis of race or sex is a concern that the government not use its power to relegate any identifiable group to an inferior position in society. [144] Historically, the ''justification'' offered for the laws and policies that have been most insidious in relegating women to an inferior status in society has been that the limitations placed on women's actions and freedom served women's unique role in childbearing. The Supreme Court recently noted this in *Johnson Controls:* ''Concern for a woman's existing or potential offspring historically has been the excuse for denying women equal employment opportunities.'' [145] On this basis, women were restricted in the hours they could work in paid employment, [146] excluded from political and civic affairs [147] and excluded from certain professions such as the practice of the law. [148]

Although the current use of adversarial policies, such as those that exclude fertile women from high-paying jobs because of potential harm to potential fetuses, may be more subtle than the exclusionary policies of a century ago, the core of the justification is the same: Job opportunities and other liberties are restricted for women because someone other than the woman herself has decided that her childbearing role should be paramount. Indeed, it is difficult to distinguish between the rationale offered by proponents of adversarial policies today and the now-discredited 1908 Supreme Court opinion in which the Court upheld restrictions on women's ability to work in paid employment as necessary to promote the birth of healthy babies: ''[A]s healthy mothers are essential to vigorous offspring, the physical well-being of woman becomes an object of public interest and care in order to preserve the strength and vigor of the race.'' [149]

History should teach us that it is precisely when the government targets women for disadvantageous treatment because of their childbearing capacity that courts should be most suspicious and therefore apply heightened scrutiny to the governmental action. Unless required to provide a strong reason for disadvantageous treatment of women based on their childbearing capacity, not all legislatures, prosecutors and judges will adequately value the range of women's interests and needs and most important, women's right to make those value judgments themselves.

---

[143] 434 U.S. at 142.

[144] *See, e.g.,* Tribe, *supra* note 142; Dimond, *The Anti-Caste Principle—Toward a Constitutional Standard for Review of Race Cases,* 30 Wayne L. Rev. 1 (1983).

[145] *Johnson Controls,* 59 U.S.L.W. at 4215.

[146] *E.g.,* Muller v. Oregon, 208 U.S. 412 (1908).

[147] *E.g.,* Hoyt v. Florida, 368 U.S. 57 (1961) (women exempted from jury duty), *overruled,* Taylor v. Louisiana, 419 U.S. 522 (1975); Breedlove v. Suttles, 302 U.S. 277 (1937) (women who did not vote exempted from poll tax).

[148] *E.g.,* Bradwell v. Illinois, 83 U.S. (16 Wall.) 130 (1872).

[149] *Muller,* 208 U.S. at 421.

B. Racial Equality

The manner in which the government has pursued adversarial policies also raises serious concerns of racial injustice. The data that exist as to the race of the women against whom the government has taken adversarial action reveal that the vast majority of women targeted have been African-American women and other women of color. Although it is beyond the scope of this chapter to provide a thorough equal protection analysis of adversarial policies, the compelling evidence outlined below that such policies have been administered in a racially discriminatory manner hopefully will serve as an invitation to others to develop fully the constitutional and public policy analysis this critical issue deserves.

In 1987 the *New England Journal of Medicine* published the results of a national survey of obstetricians concerning the scope and circumstances of court-ordered obstetrical interventions during the preceding five years.[150] Among the information requested was the race of the woman against whom the court order was sought. The study uncovered 21 instances in which court orders were sought for cesarean sections, hospital detentions or intrauterine transfusions. Of the 21 women involved, 17, or 81%, were women of color. Court orders for cesarean sections were sought in 15 instances and obtained in 13. Eighty percent (12) of the women were African-American or Asian, and only 20% (three) were white. Two of the three cases in which hospital detentions were sought involved African-American women. Of the three women against whom court orders for intrauterine transfusions were sought, two were African-American and one was Hispanic.

Equally skewed on racial lines are the results found in the studies of women who have been the targets of special criminal prosecutions with harsher penalties because they were pregnant at the time they used illegal drugs. An article published in 1990, also in the *New England Journal of Medicine,* reported the results of a six-month study of women seeking prenatal care at five public health clinics and twelve private obstetrical offices in Pinellas County, Florida.[151] Florida is among the several states that require the reporting to health officials of the birth of infants to women suspected of using drugs or alcohol during pregnancy. The study found that 14.8% of women tested positive for drugs or alcohol and 13.3.% of women tested positive for illicit drugs. The rate of positive toxicologies for drug and alcohol use among white women was slightly higher, 15.4 percent, than it was for African-American women, 14.1 percent, with African-American women more likely to test positive for cocaine and white women more likely to test positive for marijuana. Despite the slightly higher rate for white women and the legal requirement that suspected drug and alcohol use be reported, the study found that the rate at which African-American women were reported to the health authorities was approximately 10 times the rate for white women. The proportion of white women reported was 1.1%, while the proportion of African-American women reported was 10.7%.

A 1990 national survey by the American Civil Liberties Union of women who have been criminally prosecuted for behavior during pregnancy found similar results.[152] The survey documented 50 criminal prosecutions, all but two of which were in the preceding

---

[150] Kolder, Gallagher & Parsons, *supra* note 20.

[151] Chasnoff, Landress & Barrett, *The Prevalence of Illicit-Drug or Alcohol Use During Pregnancy and Discrepancies in Mandatory Reporting in Pinellas County, Florida,* 322 N. Eng. J. Med. 1202 (1990).

[152] ACLU, *supra* note 23.

two years and the vast majority of which involved the use of illicit drugs during pregnancy. Of the 47 cases in which the race of the women could be identified, 80% of the prosecutions were against women of color.

V. Conclusion

One of the most harmful aspects of the recent use of adversarial policies is that it creates a societal impression that there exists an inherent conflict between promoting healthy births and protecting women's fundamental liberties. This may mislead policymakers and courts into believing that they must make tradeoffs between the important governmental objectives of protecting women's rights and reducing health problems for newborn children. Yet this apparent conflict is in fact no conflict at all. For although the punitive aspects of the adversarial model may create the impression that action is being taken to deter behavior by women that causes unhealthy births, in reality such policies have the effect not only of infringing on women's liberty but also of deterring the types of behavior necessary for healthy and safe pregnancies.

Policymakers who truly wish to foster healthy births must understand that government, women and their future children all have shared interests in taking the steps necessary to promote healthy births. They also must recognize that to further these shared interests the necessary steps are not special penalties that restrict the capacity of all women to control their lives but are positive steps to remove the obstacles that prevent women from receiving the health services, treatment and prenatal care they need. This is the core concept behind the facilitative model. Earnest policymakers must embrace it if we hope to ensure that every child has the best possible chance of being born healthy.

The authors begin with the traditional concept of fetal rights that was first promulgated by Justice Oliver Wendell Holmes in the *Dietrich* case—basically denying claims for prenatal injuries. This prevailing view lasted for 60 years until the *Bonbrest* case. The authors are careful to point out that even though it would be presumed that *Roe* would stem the tide of fetal rights, actually there has been an expansion of fetal rights through the state courts and legislatures. The problem really occurs when fetal rights run headlong into the privacy interests of the mother. The authors' solution is to treat fetal health as an adjunct to the health of the women who choose to carry the fetus to term.

10 · Fetal Rights: Sources and Implications of an Emerging Legal Concept

Christopher P. Yates, J.D.,* and
Corinne Beckwith Yates, J.D.**

In the landmark decision of *Roe v. Wade,*[1] the Supreme Court reasoned that a developing fetus[2] cannot be considered a "person" entitled to constitutional protection.[3] This premise served as the linchpin for the Supreme Court's ultimate conclusion that the constitutional right to privacy "encompass[es] a woman's decision whether or not to terminate her pregnancy."[4] The repudiation of fetal rights in *Roe* recently has given way to an emerging notion of the fetus as an independent entity vested with a broad array of rights. This portentous development has coincided with the erosion of the constitutional protection accorded pregnant women, thereby lending credence to the prop-

---

*Assistant United States Attorney for the Eastern District of Michigan; B.A., 1983, Kalamazoo College; J.D., M.B.A., 1987, University of Illinois. This work was improved immeasurably by the comments of my colleagues Patricia Blake, Julia Caroff and Stephen Hiyama. The views expressed in this article are not intended to represent the position of the Department of Justice or the United States Attorney's Office.

**Editor-in-Chief, Volume 90, Michigan Law Review; B.A., 1985, Kalamazoo College; M.S., 1987, University of Illinois; J.D., 1992, University of Michigan.

[1] 410 U.S. 113 (1973).

[2] The term "fetus" will be used to describe the developing human life form throughout the entire gestational period. Although the term "embryo" ordinarily denotes the human life form from the point of conception to the eighth week of development, *see* Note, *The Unborn Child and the Constitutional Conception of Life,* 56 Iowa L. Rev. 994, 995 n.9 (1971); *accord* State v. Merrill, 450 N.W.2d 318, 320 (Minn.), *cert. denied,* 110 S. Ct. 2633 (1990), courts generally have referred to prenatal protections as "fetal rights" regardless of the precise stage of human development. *E.g.,* International Union, UAW v. Johnson Controls, Inc., 111 S. Ct. 1196, 1199 (1991).

[3] *Roe,* 410 U.S. at 158.

[4] *Id.* at 153. The Supreme Court acknowledged that if fetal "personhood is established . . . the fetus' right to life would then be guaranteed specifically by the [Fourteenth] Amendment." *Id.* at 156–57.

osition that the expansion of fetal rights perforce imperils the basic liberties of pregnant women.[5]

Although federal courts have been loathe to identify fetal rights in the United States Constitution[6] and similarly have eschewed fetal interests when interpreting federal statutes,[7] many state courts and legislatures have become increasingly protective of fetal rights in a variety of contexts. This article examines the emerging concept of fetal rights, which has given rise to expanded tort liability for prenatal injuries, promulgation of fetal homicide statutes and criminal prosecution of pregnant women for their conduct during pregnancy. After reviewing the nature and sources of modern fetal rights, the article considers the impact upon women of such enhanced protections and analyzes the growing tension between fetal rights and the rights of women. The article ultimately criticizes the legal emphasis upon independent fetal rights and advocates a concept of derivative fetal rights designed to promote prenatal health through support and protection of all women who choose to bear children.

I. The Traditional Concept of Fetal Rights

Long before the abortion debate flared in the United States, Justice Oliver Wendell Holmes penned the first major fetal rights decision, *Dietrich v. Inhabitants of Northampton*,[8] which flatly rejected a claim for prenatal injuries. A woman "between four and five months advanced in pregnancy" had suffered a fall that resulted in a miscarriage.[9] Despite evidence that the resulting premature birth produced a child who "live[d] for ten or fifteen minutes,"[10] Justice Holmes ruled that an action for damages could not be maintained for the "benefit of the mother in part or in whole, as next of kin,"[11] because "the unborn child was a part of the mother at the time of the injury," and therefore "any damage to it which was not too remote to be recovered for at all was recoverable by [the mother]."[12]

From a historical standpoint, the impact of the *Dietrich* case was monumental. For more than 60 years, courts not only adhered to the seemingly unassailable proposition

---

[5] *See* Johnsen, *The Creation of Fetal Rights: Conflicts with Women's Constitutional Rights to Liberty, Privacy, and Equal Protection*, 95 Yale L.J. 599, 611 (1986) ("Given the physical reality of the fetus as part of the pregnant woman, there exists an inherent potential for conflict between the autonomy of pregnant women and any 'right' granted the fetus *qua* fetus").

[6] *See, e.g.*, *Roe*, 410 U.S. at 158; Keith v. Daley, 764 F.2d 1265, 1271 (7th Cir.) (denying intervention for the purpose of "the protection of 'unborn' children" because, *inter alia*, a fetus is not a "person" under the fourteenth amendment), *cert. denied*, 474 U.S. 980 (1985); McGarvey v. Magee-Womens Hosp., 340 F. Supp. 751 (W.D. Pa. 1972) (fetuses are not persons or citizens within the meaning of the fourteenth amendment), *aff'd*, 474 F.2d 1339 (3d Cir. 1973); *cf. also* Diamond v. Charles, 476 U.S. 54, 67 (1986) (rejecting claim of standing by individual who sought to "assert any constitutional rights of the unborn fetus").

[7] *See, e.g.*, International Union, UAW v. Johnson Controls, Inc., 111 S. Ct. 1196 (1991) (declaring fetal protection policy illegal under Title VII); Burns v. Alcala, 420 U.S. 575 (1975) (excluding the unborn from the definition of "dependent child" for AFDC eligibility); Arnold v. Board of Educ. of Escambia County, 880 F.2d 305, 312 n.9 (11th Cir. 1989) ("An unborn fetus is not a 'person' or a 'citizen' within the contemplation of [42 U.S.C.] § 1983").

[8] 138 Mass. 14 (1884).

[9] *Id.* at 14–15.

[10] *Id.* at 15.

[11] *Id.*

[12] *Id.* at 17.

that prenatal injuries could not form the basis for a civil action even if the prenatal injuries resulted in death after live birth [13] but also applied the logic of *Dietrich* to foreclose common law claims brought by living children who survived debilitating prenatal injuries. [14] The prevailing view, as defined by Justice Holmes, stemmed from the basic premise "[t]hat a child before birth is, in fact, a part of the mother and is only severed from her at birth[.]" [15]

The characterization of the developing fetus as a part of the mother, rather than an independent person, similarly led to minimal protection of fetuses under criminal laws. [16] The common law rule governing criminal prosecution mirrored the *Dietrich* holding: "[A]n infant could not be the subject of a homicide until it had achieved a completely free and independent existence with lung and heart action of its own." [17] Courts rigidly interpreted this requirement, overturning murder convictions that could have resulted from conjecture or suspicion concerning the independent nature of the child at the time of death. [18] Homicide statutes likewise tracked the logic of *Dietrich* by "treat[ing] the child as having no independent existence as a human being until it has been actually and completely born." [19]

In 1946, however, the United States District Court for the District of Columbia rejected the common law rule of *Dietrich* in *Bonbrest v. Kotz.* [20] The *Bonbrest* case was filed on behalf of an infant who suffered prenatal injuries due to the malpractice of two

---

[13] W. Keeton, D. Dobbs, R. Keeton & D. Owen, *Prosser and Keeton on the Law of Torts* § 55, at 367 (5th ed. 1984); Newman v. City of Detroit, 281 Mich. 60, 63–64, 274 N.W. 710, 711 (1937); Magnolia Coca Cola Bottling Co. v. Jordan, 124 Tex. 347, 78 S.W.2d 944 (1935); Stanford v. St. Louis-San Francisco Ry., 214 Ala. 611, 612, 108 So. 566, 566–67 (1926); Buel v. United Rys., 248 Mo. 126, 132–33, 154 S.W. 71, 73 (1913); Gorman v. Budlong, 23 R.I. 169, 177, 49 A. 704, 707 (1901).

[14] *E.g.*, Drobner v. Peters, 232 N.Y. 220, 224, 133 N.E. 567, 568 (1921) (holding that prenatal injuries "were, when inflicted, injuries to the mother"); Allaire v. St. Luke's Hosp., 184 Ill. 359, 56 N.E. 638 (1900); *see also Roe*, 410 U.S. at 161 ("[T]he traditional rule of tort law denied recovery for prenatal injuries even though the child was born alive").

[15] *Allaire*, 184 Ill. at 368, 56 N.E. at 640; *accord Drobner*, 232 N.Y. at 223, 133 N.E. at 568.

[16] Although abortion laws existed in many states at that time, they generally imposed only "minor penalties." *Cf.* Keeler v. Superior Court of Amador County, 2 Cal. 3d 619, 641, 470 P.2d 617, 631, 87 Cal. Rptr. 481, 495 (1970) (Burke, C.J., dissenting) (contrasting criminal sanctions for homicide and abortion and arguing for extension of homicide statute to "malicious slaying of a fully viable child").

[17] Note, *Criminal Law—Homicide—Subject of Infanticide*, 20 S. Cal. L. Rev. 357, 358 (1947); Jackson v. Commonwealth, 265 Ky. 295, 296, 96 S.W.2d 1014, 1014 (1936); *see also* People v. Hayner, 300 N.Y. 171, 174, 90 N.E.2d 23, 24 (1949) ("The true test of separate existence in the theory of the law (whatever it may be in medical science) is the answer to the question 'whether the child is carrying on its being without the help of the mother's circulation.' "); *see generally* Keeler v. Superior Court of Amador County, 2 Cal. 3d 619, 625–29, 470 P.2d 617, 620–22, 87 Cal. Rptr. 481, 484–86 (1970) (canvassing the "common law of abortional homicide").

[18] *E.g.*, Morgan v. State, 148 Tenn. 417, 420–21, 256 S.W. 433, 434 (1923) (noting the difficulty of proving murder under the rule that a child "cannot be the subject of a homicide until it has an existence independent of its mother"); State v. O'Neall, 79 S.C. 571, 573, 60 S.E. 1121, 1122 (1908) ("[H]owever painful and distressing child murder is felt to be, yet prudence requires, and humanity also demands, that a conviction of the poor mother is too dreadful to be rested alone upon suspicion"); State v. Winthrop, 43 Iowa 519, 523 (1876) (killing of a child cannot be murder "if actual independence was never established" because "[a]ny verdict based upon such finding would be the result of conjecture").

[19] Magnolia Coca Cola Bottling Co. v. Jordan, 124 Tex. 347, 357, 78 S.W.2d 944, 948 (1935); *accord Morgan*, 148 Tenn. at 420–21, 256 S.W. at 434 (discussing legal requirement of independence from mother).

[20] 65 F. Supp. 138 (D.D.C. 1946).

doctors who assisted in the child's birth.[21] The *Bonbrest* court challenged Justice Holmes's fundamental assumption that a viable child is not independent of its mother, arguing that "it is in the womb, but it is capable of extra-uterine life."[22] Once the prenatal independence—the personhood—of the surviving child was established, the *Bonbrest* court rhetorically asked "what right is more inherent, and more sacrosanct, than that of the individual in his possession and enjoyment of his life, his limbs and his body?"[23] The answer to this question, of course, was self-evident to the court, and the demise of the *Dietrich* rule began with the resulting denial of the doctors' summary judgment motion.

Decisions in the wake of *Bonbrest* refined its reasoning but adopted its basic holding that prenatal injuries could give rise to a cause of action.[24] In embracing *Bonbrest*, however, courts generally did not go so far as to recognize true fetal rights.[25] Most jurisdictions conditioned recovery for prenatal injuries upon live birth[26] and rejected claims on behalf of stillborn children who received prenatal injuries,[27] thereby linking the right of recovery in tort to traditional notions of personhood.

As tort law evolved, the criminal law of homicide similarly changed to accommodate the burgeoning legal status of fetuses.[28] The first major decision expanding the definition of homicide, *People v. Chavez*,[29] was handed down less than one year after the *Bonbrest* ruling. In affirming a manslaughter conviction of a woman whose child had died during birth, the *Chavez* court held that "a viable child in the process of being born is a human being within the meaning of the homicide statutes, whether or not the process has been fully completed."[30] This reading of the California homicide statute to include acts that were not deemed murderous at common law marked a subtle, yet inexorable, shift in the legal definition of homicide. Courts began to give greater deference to jury verdicts,[31] emphasizing the jury's role in applying the live birth require-

---

[21] *Id.* at 139.

[22] *Id.* at 140.

[23] *Id.* at 142.

[24] *E.g.*, Sinkler v. Kneale, 401 Pa. 267, 164 A.2d 93 (1960) (common law cause of action); Amann v. Faidy, 415 Ill. 422, 114 N.E.2d 412 (1953) (wrongful death claim); Woods v. Lancet, 303 N.Y. 349, 102 N.E.2d 691 (1951) (common law cause of action); Tucker v. Howard L. Carmichael & Sons, Inc., 208 Ga. 201, 65 S.E.2d 909 (1951) (common law); Damasiewicz v. Gorsuch, 197 Md. 417, 438–41, 79 A.2d 550, 560–61 (1951) (common law); Jasinsky v. Potts, 153 Ohio St. 529, 92 N.E.2d 809 (1950) (wrongful death); Williams v. Marion Rapid Transit, Inc., 152 Ohio St. 114, 87 N.E.2d 334 (1949) (common law).

[25] *See* Johnsen, *supra* note 5, at 602.

[26] *See, e.g.*, Amann v. Faidy, 415 Ill. 422, 432, 114 N.E.2d 412, 417–18 (1953) (limiting right of recovery to instances where the child "who suffered prenatal injuries . . . was thereafter born alive").

[27] *E.g.*, Endresz v. Friedberg, 24 N.Y.2d 478, 482–87, 248 N.E.2d 901, 902–05, 301 N.Y.S.2d 65, 67–71 (1969); Graf v. Taggert, 43 N.J. 303, 204 A.2d 140 (1964); Gordon, *The Unborn Plaintiff*, 63 Mich. L. Rev. 579, 591–95 (1965) (surveying relevant cases and advocating denial of wrongful death claim on behalf of stillborn fetus); *but see* Stidam v. Ashmore, 109 Ohio App. 431, 167 N.E.2d 106 (1959) (permitting recovery "for the wrongful death of a viable, unborn child which is subsequently stillborn").

[28] At least one commentator has expressly analogized the development of tort law to the evolution of the criminal law concerning infanticide. Meldman, *Legal Concepts of Human Life: The Infanticide Doctrines*, 52 Marq. L. Rev. 105, 111–12 (1968).

[29] 77 Cal. App. 2d 621, 176 P.2d 92 (1947).

[30] *Id.* at 626, 176 P.2d at 94.

[31] *E.g.*, Singleton v. State, 33 Ala. App. 536, 541, 35 So. 2d 375, 379 (1948) (quoting *Chavez* with approval).

ment.[32] Thus, when the Supreme Court decided *Roe* in 1973, the majority could accurately comment that "the law has been reluctant to endorse any theory that life, as we recognize it, begins before live birth or to accord legal rights to the unborn except in narrowly defined situations and except when the rights are contingent upon live birth."[33] This reluctance, however, was waning.

II. Fetal Rights in the Aftermath of *Roe v. Wade*

Although *Roe v. Wade* has spawned an ongoing debate over the constitutional protection of abortion rights, the Supreme Court's denial of personhood status to fetuses is more jurisprudentially significant than the Court's recognition of a woman's fundamental right to abortion.[34] Acceptance of the proposition that a fetus is not a person necessarily alters legal analysis of every facet of law dealing with prenatal rights. Not surprisingly, *Roe* has curtailed the development of fetal rights on the federal level.[35] Even the *Roe* decision, however, has done little to stem the tide of fetal protection under state law. Instead, the expansion of fetal rights by state courts and legislatures has advanced to the point of incompatibility with women's basic liberties.

A. Compensation of Prenatal Injuries under Modern Tort Law

In spite of the pronouncements in *Roe* denying constitutional "personhood" to fetuses, judicial acceptance of independent fetal rights in tort law proceeded with unwavering alacrity. By 1977, 25 jurisdictions had jettisoned the requirement of live birth in suits for prenatal injuries,[36] thus opening the courthouse doors to a wide range of claims filed on behalf of stillborn fetuses.[37] Almost invariably, decisions rejecting the live birth requirement rested upon the characterization of the fetus as a "person" for purposes of the pertinent wrongful death statute.[38]

Judicial abandonment of the live birth requirement, and the concomitant elevation of fetuses to personhood status, expanded the potential liability of pregnant women. The 1980 decision of *Grodin v. Grodin*[39] demonstrated the broad implications of fetal

---

[32] *E.g.*, Bennett v. State, 377 P.2d 634, 636 (Wyo. 1963) (citing *Chavez* with approval).

[33] Roe v. Wade, 410 U.S. 113, 161 (1973).

[34] Recognition of fetal "personhood" status would not only raise an insuperable due process barrier to abortion rights, *see Roe*, 410 U.S. at 156–57, but also modify analysis of criminal and civil issues involving fetuses.

[35] *See, e.g.*, International Union, UAW v. Johnson Controls, Inc., 111 S. Ct. 1196 (1991) (declaring fetal protection policy illegal under Title VII); Burns v. Alcala, 420 U.S. 575 (1975) (excluding the unborn from the definition of "dependent child" for AFDC eligibility); United States v. Spencer, 839 F.2d 1341 (9th Cir.) (adopting common law definition of fetal murder under 18 U.S.C. § 1111), *cert. denied*, 487 U.S. 1238 (1988).

[36] Justus v. Atchison, 19 Cal. 3d 564, 569–70 & n.4, 565 P.2d 122, 125 & n.4, 139 Cal. Rptr. 97, 100 & n.4 (1977). At least 32 jurisdictions now "recognize a cause of action on behalf of a fetus that sustains fatal injury in utero." Coveleski v. Bubnis, 391 Pa. Super. 409, 412–13 n.3, 571 A.2d 433, 435 n.3, *appeal granted*, 525 Pa. 656, 582 A.2d 323 (1990).

[37] *See, e.g.*, Carpenter v. Bishop, 290 Ark. 424, 720 S.W.2d 299 (1986) (negligence suit brought on behalf of stillborn fetus against mother was barred by parental immunity doctrine, but such a suit could be pursued if immunity were abrogated or if mother's conduct had been intentional); *see also* Johnsen, *supra* note 5, at 606–07.

[38] *E.g.*, Mone v. Greyhound Lines, Inc., 368 Mass. 354, 355, 331 N.E.2d 916, 917 (1975); Kwaterski v. State Farm Mut. Auto. Ins. Co., 34 Wis.2d 14, 148 N.W.2d 107 (1967).

[39] 102 Mich. App. 396, 301 N.W.2d 869 (1980).

"personhood." The *Grodin* court ruled that a mother who had taken tetracycline during her pregnancy was subject to suit for her surviving son's brown and discolored teeth.[40] Although the *Grodin* case did not involve true fetal rights because the plaintiff had been born alive and the claim against the mother was asserted for tactical reasons and with her consent,[41] the holding was a harbinger of increased maternal responsibility.

The Illinois Court of Appeals subsequently employed the rationale of *Grodin* to subject a mother to tort liability for negligently harming her fetus in an automobile collision.[42] The Illinois Supreme Court ultimately reversed this determination,[43] criticizing the *Grodin* decision that supported the lower court's ruling for failing "to address any of the profound implications which would result" from treating a pregnant woman as a "stranger to her developing fetus for purposes of tort liability."[44] The court explained that recognizing the "legal right of a fetus to begin life with a sound mind and body assertable against a mother would make a pregnant woman the guarantor of the mind and body of her child at birth."[45] Consequently, any conduct detrimental to the developing fetus would amount to a breach of the pregnant woman's duty to her fetus, thus positioning the woman and her fetus as "legal adversaries from the moment of conception until birth."[46]

The Illinois Supreme Court's carefully reasoned rejection of fetal independence as a basis for imposing a duty upon pregnant women wisely foreclosed tort actions brought by, or on behalf of, children against their mothers.[47] Nevertheless, as commentators have noted, principles of modern tort law offer ample support for claims against prospective mothers whose negligent actions harm their developing fetuses.[48] Although such a cause of action may not unnecessarily heighten maternal accountability when the suit is brought with the mother's consent,[49] the potential for abuse is manifest if a woman may be unwillingly held accountable for her behavior during pregnancy.

---

[40] *Id.* at 401–02, 301 N.W.2d at 871; *cf. also* Endo Labs., Inc. v. Hartford Ins. Group, 747 F.2d 1264 (9th Cir. 1984) (dispute over coverage for settlement of suit brought by child against mother for ingesting drug during pregnancy).

[41] *See* Robertson, *Procreative Liberty and the Control of Conception, Pregnancy, and Childbirth,* 69 Va. L. Rev. 405, 441–42 n.114 (1983) (summarizing telephone interview with counsel for the plaintiff).

[42] Stallman v. Youngquist, 152 Ill. App. 3d 683, 694, 504 N.E.2d 920, 927 (1987), *rev'd,* 125 Ill.2d 267, 531 N.E.2d 355 (1988).

[43] Stallman v. Youngquist, 125 Ill.2d 267, 531 N.E.2d 355 (1988).

[44] *Id.* at 274, 531 N.E.2d at 358.

[45] *Id.* at 276, 531 N.E.2d at 356. *E.g.,* Matter of Fathima Ashanti K.J., 147 Misc. 2d 551, 555, 558 N.Y.S. 2d 447, 449 (Fam. Ct. 1990) (finding mother's use of narcotics during pregnancy contravened her unborn child's "right to a gestation undisturbed by wrongful injury and the right to be born with a sound mind and body free from parentally inflicted abuse or neglect."); Matter of Baby X, 97 Mich. App. 111, 114–16, 293 N.W.2d 736, 738–39 (1980) (same).

[46] *Stallman,* 125 Ill.2d at 276, 531 N.E.2d at 359.

[47] *Id.* at 279–80, 531 N.E.2d at 360–61.

[48] *See, e.g.,* Annotation, *Right of Child to Action Against Mother for Infliction of Prenatal Injuries,* 78 A.L.R. 4th 1082, 1085 (1990); Note, *Setting the Standard: A Mother's Duty During the Prenatal Period,* 1989 U. Ill. L. Rev. 493, 503 & n.80.

[49] *See* Beal, *"Can I Sue Mommy?" An Analysis of a Woman's Tort Liability for Prenatal Injuries to Her*

B. Criminal Liability for Prenatal Harm

State tribunals, when interpreting criminal statutes, have exercised restraint in expanding fetal rights by limiting laws that proscribe the killing of a "person," an "individual" or a "human being" to the common law definition of homicide.[50] Courts specifically have applied the common law requirement of live birth to dismiss murder charges and overturn murder convictions predicated upon the intentional infliction of gruesome prenatal injuries that resulted in stillbirth.[51] Although the live birth requirement has thus retained its vitality, this phenomenon is not attributable to concern about the consequences of recognizing fetal rights in criminal laws. Rather, the courts' reluctance to abandon the requirement of live birth has stemmed from the belief that statutory crimes should not be altered by judicial fiat.[52]

This judicial restraint has prompted legislators to seize the initiative by aggressively modifying criminal statutes to outlaw the killing of fetuses. For example, in California and Minnesota, judicial adherence to the live birth requirement[53] precipitated statutory enactments that explicitly brought fetuses within the purview of state homicide laws.[54] While the statutes adopted in California and Minnesota granted enhanced status to fetuses for the beneficent purpose of safeguarding mothers and their fetuses against harmful acts committed by third persons,[55] subsequent legislative enactments broadening criminal laws to ensure prenatal protection have unnecessarily encumbered the rights of mothers for the sake of their developing fetuses.

The expansion of criminal neglect, child abuse and drug distribution statutes to facilitate prosecution of pregnant women,[56] like the modification of tort law to allow recovery for prenatal injuries, will inevitably bring pregnant women and their fetuses into direct and counterproductive conflict. Most new legislation presumes that fetal health

---

Child Born Alive, 21 San Diego L. Rev. 325, 358 (1984) (opining that most lawsuits brought by children against their mothers are pursued to obtain insurance proceeds).

[50] *See also* Reyes v. Superior Court, 75 Cal. App. 3d 214, 216, 141 Cal. Rptr. 912, 913 (1977) ("[T]he word 'child' as used in the [California child endangering statute] was not intended to refer to an unborn child and [the mother's] prenatal conduct does not constitute felonious child endangering within contemplation of the statute"); *but cf.* Matter of Baby X, 97 Mich. App. 111, 116, 293 N.W.2d 736, 739 (1980) ("[A] newborn suffering narcotics withdrawal symptoms as a consequence of prenatal maternal drug addiction may properly be considered a neglected child within the jurisdiction of the probate court").

[51] *E.g.,* State v. Soto, 378 N.W.2d 625 (Minn. 1985); People v. Greer, 79 Ill.2d 103, 110–16, 402 N.E.2d 203, 206–09 (1980); Keeler v. Superior Court of Amador County, 2 Cal. 3d 619, 470 P.2d 617, 87 Cal. Rptr. 481 (1970).

[52] *E.g.,* State v. Green, 245 Kan. 398, 402, 781 P.2d 678, 682 (1989); Hollis v. Commonwealth, 652 S.W.2d 61, 63–64 (Ky. 1983); People v. Guthrie, 97 Mich. App. 226, 232–33, 293 N.W.2d 775, 778 (1980).

[53] State v. Soto, 378 N.W.2d 625 (Minn. 1985); Keeler v. Superior Court of Amador County, 2 Cal. 3d 619, 470 P.2d 617, 87 Cal. Rptr. 481 (1970).

[54] Minn. Stat. § 609.2661 (1988) (prescribing "imprisonment for life" as the penalty for premeditated murder of an unborn child); *id.* § 609.2662 (specifying 40-year maximum prison term for "murder of an unborn child in the second degree"); Cal. Penal Code § 187(a) (West 1988) ("Murder is the unlawful killing of a human being, or a fetus, with malice aforethought").

[55] *See* People v. Apodaca, 76 Cal. App. 3d 479, 486, 142 Cal. Rptr. 830, 835 (1978) ("Section 187 gives all persons of common intelligence ample warning that an assault on a pregnant woman without her consent for the purpose of unlawfully killing her unborn child can constitute the crime of murder").

[56] *E.g.,* Ill. Rev. Stat. ch. 37, para. 802-3, § 2-3(1) (c) (1989) (defining neglected minor as "any newborn infant whose blood or urine contains any amount of a controlled substance . . . or a metabolite of a controlled substance . . ."); *see also* MINN. STAT. ANN § 626.5561 (West Supp. 1992) (allowing civil commitment of pregnant substance abusers).

can best be guaranteed by criminalizing an expectant mother's conduct that may adversely affect her developing fetus.[57] Such legislation discourages women from seeking prenatal care for fear of being prosecuted,[58] encourages abortion as an alternative to the risk of being jailed for impermissible behavior while carrying a fetus to term[59] and engenders an adversarial relationship between mother and child prior to birth.[60] In short, fetal protection through criminal law is evolving into a device that not only denigrates women by strictly regulating their behavior during pregnancy but also encourages conduct that threatens fetal welfare and even fetal life itself. Proper protection of fetal health and maternal autonomy cannot be achieved unless legislators pay closer attention to the full impact of criminalization before "transforming into a criminal act what is now essentially a moral obligation by the pregnant woman to her developing fetus."[61]

III. A Philosophy for Legislative Action

Through subtle accretions, the legal understanding of fetal rights has evolved toward an interpretation incompatible with women's privacy interests and bodily integrity. Moreover, recent and proposed legislation jeopardizes the fetal sanctity that such enactments are purportedly designed to ensure. In tort law, the recognition of fetuses as "persons" portends a legal regime that pits mother against fetus from the moment of conception.[62] Fetuses and pregnant women fare even worse under hastily devised modern criminal statutes, which proscribe broad categories of maternal activity and expose women to harsh sanctions for failure to abide by such prenatal codes of conduct.[63]

Attempts to define fetal rights in accordance with existing legal classifications founder upon an unworkable understanding of fetuses as entities wholly independent from their mothers. A third party who inflicts prenatal harm upon a fetus can be analogized to a tortfeasor or a criminal assailant who injures or kills a child, but a pregnant woman shares a legally unique and physically interdependent relationship with the fetus she carries. Thus, an analytically sound view of fetal rights must recognize that a fetus is neither a "person" nor an entity bereft of traditional legal rights but rather a developing individual whose rights should be safeguarded by concomitantly protecting the woman upon whom fetal well-being depends. Such an approach readily accommodates a cause of action against a third person who harms a fetus but avoids the specter—and, in some cases, the reality—of punishing women as fetal adversaries for the purpose of promoting adequate prenatal care. As the Illinois Supreme Court astutely reasoned:

The error that a fetus cannot be harmed in a legally cognizable way when the woman who is its mother is injured has been corrected; the law

---

[57] See Note, *The Prosecution of Maternal Fetal Abuse: Is This the Answer?*, 1991 U. Ill. L. Rev. 533, 538–39 (reviewing recent developments on the legislative front).

[58] Field, *Controlling the Woman to Protect the Fetus*, 17 Law, Med. & Health Care 114, 121 (1989).

[59] See Moss, *Substance Abuse During Pregnancy*, 13 Harv. Women's L.J. 278, 299 (1990) ("Some addicted women who recognize that they will not be able to obtain adequate prenatal care or drug treatment will be forced to turn to abortion to avoid prosecution").

[60] See Stallman v. Youngquist, 125 Ill.2d 267, 276, 531 N.E.2d 355, 359 (1988).

[61] People v. Hardy, 188 Mich. App. 305, 316, 469 N.W.2d 50, 55 (1991) (Reilly, P.J. concurring).

[62] See supra section II.A; *Stallman*, 125 Ill.2d at 276, 531 N.E.2d at 359 (recognizing the adversarial relationship between a pregnant woman and her fetus that results from allowing the fetus to assert legal rights against the woman).

[63] See supra section II.B.

will no longer treat the fetus as only a part of its mother. The law will not now make an error of a different sort, one with enormous implications for all women who have been, are, may be, or might become pregnant: the law will not treat a fetus as an entity which is entirely separate from its mother.[64]

The most dramatic and expedient legislative response to social problems often is simply to criminalize aberrant behavior or expand civil liability for such conduct.[65] Despite the allure of such purported solutions to the problem of prenatal injury, a coherent understanding of fetal interests neither warrants nor legitimizes the current legislative trend. If lawmakers are concerned with safeguarding fetal health, that worthy goal is not furthered by punishing the person most vital to the fetus's well-being but by channeling private and governmental resources into educational and rehabilitative programs that promote and provide prenatal care.[66] By treating fetal health as an adjunct to the bodily integrity of women who choose to carry fetuses to term, the law can resolve the seemingly intractable problem of prenatal damage in a less combative arena than the courts.[67]

---

[64] *Stallman,* 125 Ill.2d at 276–77, 531 N.E.2d at 359.

[65] The eighteenth amendment is a classic example of such a response to a call for stringent legislative measures.

[66] *Stallman,* 125 Ill.2d at 280, 531 N.E.2d at 361 ("The way to effectuate the birth of healthy babies is not . . . through after-the-fact civil liability in tort for individual mothers, but rather through before-the-fact education of all women and families about prenatal development"); *see also* Developments in the Law, *Medical Technology and the Law,* 103 Harv. L. Rev. 1519, 1564 (1990) (advocating the use of "drastically less restrictive alternatives for protecting fetal health, such as public education, free nutrition and prenatal care programs, and drug treatment centers designed for pregnant women").

[67] *See* Field, *supra* note 58, at 121.

Professor Kommers presents the law and history of abortion of six prominent countries. Each country decided whether to enact a time-frame test for abortion, an indication test for abortion or both. Even though the outcome for each country was different, they all struggled with the same issues presented in the *Roe* and *Doe* cases of 1973. This article shows that it did not matter if a country had a common law base or a statutory law base, it did not matter if the issue was resolved in the courts or in the legislature, it did not matter if fetal protection was predominant or the choice of the mother was predominant, all countries believed certain guidelines for abortion *had* to be made. The abortion conundrum in civilized nations is never easily solved, and each country, in its own way, is still struggling to enact a law that is both fair to the fetus and fair to the mother.

11 · Abortion in Six Countries: A Comparative Legal Analysis —

Donald P. Kommers, Ph.D.

I. Introduction

This chapter focuses on the abortion laws of Germany, Italy, France, Great Britain, New Zealand and Australia, each of which is an industrial society comparable to the United States in its commitment to individual liberty and political democracy. Since the 1960s, each of these countries, like the United States, has reformed its abortion laws, usually in the direction of greater leniency and often after bitter conflict in political or judicial arenas. The subject continues to inflame public debate in some of these countries as their legislatures and courts struggle to balance the state's interest in preserving unborn life against a woman's personal decision to terminate her pregnancy. Other equations entering this complex process of legal decision-making are the liberty interest of physicians and health care workers in freely practicing their professions as well as the stake that parents, husbands and nonmarital fathers have in the birth of their unborn children.

The six nations studied here now permit induced abortion in special circumstances, but the laws of these countries differ markedly from each other.[1] These abortion laws, in turn, differ from the rules laid down in the United States, although this chapter tries to steer clear of the American scene; for comparative purposes, however, it may be

---

[1] The legalization of abortion in the six countries under study is part of a world-wide trend toward the relaxation of restrictive laws on abortion. *See International Handbook on Abortion* (P. Sachden ed. 1988). For other comparative studies of abortion law, see M. Glendon, *Abortion and Divorce in Western Law* (1987) and M. Nijsten, *Abortion, Constitutional Law and Practice: A Comparative European-American Survey* (1985) (Ph.D. diss., European University Institute, Florence, Italy).

useful occasionally to point out where U.S. law converges with or diverges from the laws of these six nations. We would hasten to add that the legal status of abortion in these countries remains fluid. Their lawmakers, like those in the United States, are under constant pressure to change their policies by making abortion less or more easily accessible than at present. In any event, U.S. law is a convenient foil for marking the most important features of abortion policy outside of the United States.

Why is knowledge of foreign law important for Americans, especially on controversial topics like abortion? A standard answer is that such knowledge gives them a better grasp of their own law. Like astronauts whose appreciation of the earth's limits—and grandeur—is enhanced by viewing the globe from outer space, Americans who launch themselves into the orbit of foreign law get a better glimpse of their own legal system. An intellectual voyage into the domain of foreign law is useful for several reasons: First, the view from there may help expose the limits or failures of one's own laws or legal processes; second, it may provide interesting models for rethinking or reshaping these laws or processes; third, and alternatively, it may bolster or renew one's confidence in the practicality or adequacy—and even the moral superiority—of the home policy, particularly if after careful scrutiny other civilized nations have chosen a similar path toward the legal solution of a serious social problem.[2]

Finally, it might be asked why we have chosen to focus on the six named countries. One reason is that these countries are socioeconomically comparable to the United States in spite of notable differences in their cultural, religious, political and constitutional histories. All are modern pluralistic societies with developed economies; all are secular political cultures; all are liberal democracies driven by competitive party systems; and all subscribe to the rule of law reinforced by an independent judiciary. All have experienced accelerated social change of a similar nature, and all are faced with similar problems of governance. Moreover, all subscribe to a similar value system where the basic rights of human persons are concerned.

The six countries also represent a good mix of common law and civil jurisdictions, the two major legal families of the modern world. Germany, France and Italy are continental legal systems rooted in the civil or Roman law tradition, whereas the common law tradition prevails in Australia, New Zealand and Great Britain.[3] The two traditions differ from each other, especially in the way they distribute authority among branches of government, but they have experienced a number of converging trends in recent decades. One of these trends significant for our purposes is the establishment of constitutional courts in civil law jurisdictions.[4] All these features and developments—including the particular admixture of similarity and difference in the political and social struc-

---

[2] For further discussion of the uses of the comparative method in legal analysis, see Stein, *Uses, Misuses—and Nonuses of Comparative Law*, 72 Nw. U.L. Rev. 198 (1977); Kahn-Freund, *Comparative Law as an Academic Subject*, 82 L.Q. Rev. 40 (1966); and Kommers, *Comparative Constitutional Law: Casebooks for a Developing Discipline*, 57 Notre Dame L. Rev. 642 (1982). *See also Comparative Law and Its Teaching in Modern Society*, Proceedings of the Seventh International Symposium on Comparative Law, August 27–29, 1969 (1970). One of the best descriptions of the functions, aims, methods and history of comparative law is contained in 1 K. Zweigert & H. Koetz, *An Introduction to Comparative Law* 1–56 (2d ed. 1987).

[3] For a discussion of the differences in these traditions, see R. Schlesinger, H. Baade, M. Damaska & P. Herzog, *Comparative Law* 295–337 (5th ed. 1988).

[4] *See* M. Cappelletti, *The Judicial Process in Comparative Perspective* 117–149 (1989) and A. Brewer-Carias, *Judicial Review in Comparative Law* 125–270 (1989).

tures of advanced liberal democracies—make the six nations chosen for special attention here inviting candidates for comparative legal analysis.

II. Civil Law Jurisdictions

A. Germany

Abortion has long been a crime in Germany. The German Penal Code of 1871, the basis of Germany's present criminal law, made abortion a punishable act. The provision of the code banning abortion—the much-discussed section 218—dates back to the Prussian Penal Code of 1851. In its original version, section 218 imposed up to five years imprisonment upon any woman "who intentionally aborts her fetus or kills it in the womb." The same penalty applied to any person performing or assisting in an abortion.[5] In 1926 the code was amended to mitigate the punishment for self-induced abortions, but it imposed severe penalties, as before, upon abortionists.[6] One year later the Weimar Republic's Supreme Court ruled that a legal abortion could take place if necessary to save the life of a pregnant woman.[7] In spite of numerous efforts thereafter to reform and even to abolish section 218, abortion continued to be punished as a matter of principle. In due course, however, a woman could legally procure an abortion if her pregnancy resulted from an assault or if necessary to preserve her life or health. This is where the law stood before the 1974 Abortion Reform Act.[8]

The Abortion Reform Act emerged from a decade-long effort to recodify West Germany's criminal law. Two approaches marked the effort to revise section 218: One was an "indications," the other a "time-phase," solution. The first would allow abortions only in the presence of indications—that is, for serious reasons specified by law; the other would legalize abortion generally within a specified period. The Draft Penal Code of 1962, produced by the Justice Ministry's Grand Commission on Penal Reform, chose the indications solution. The draft would have continued to punish abortion, at all stages of pregnancy, but with less severity than previously.[9] Under a title labeled "Crimes Against Inchoate Life," abortion could be legally performed only if medically necessary to preserve a woman's life or to avoid "undue" or "serious injury" to her "body or health" and then only after certification by an advisory medical body.[10] The draft code also punished the procurement or advertising of abortifacients.[11]

An Alternative Draft of the Penal Code, proposed by a group of liberal legal scholars, preferred the time-phase rule. Under this draft, abortion would be legal if performed "within the first four weeks of pregnancy" or if, after visiting a counseling center, the pregnant woman would allow a licensed physician to abort her fetus before the end of

---

[5] Strafgesetzbuch [StGB] § 218. For an English translation of the criminal code, see *The German Penal Code of 1871* (G. Mueller & T. Buergenthal trans. 1961).

[6] 1926 Reichsgesetzblatt [RGBl] I, 239.

[7] Judgement of March 11, 1927, 61 Reichsgericht in Strafsachen [RGSt] 242.

[8] Abortion Reform Act, 1974 *Bundesgesetzblatt* [BGBl] I, 1297.

[9] The German Draft Penal Code of 1962 §§ 140–141. (N. Ross transl. 1966) [hereinafter Draft Penal Code]. For commentaries on the Draft Code, see Mueller, *The German Draft Criminal Code 1960—An Evaluation in Terms of American Criminal Law*, 1961 U. Ill. L. Forum 25 (1961); Schroder, *German Criminal Law and Its Reform*, 4 Duq. L. Rev. 97 (1965–66), and Draft Penal Code, *supra*, at 3.

[10] Draft Penal Code, *supra* note 9, § § 157–159.

[11] *Id.* § § 142–143.

the first trimester.[12] An abortion could be procured beyond this point only when necessary for medical or eugenic reasons after proper certification to that effect.[13] The Alternative Draft was "the first attempt in Germany to propose a substantial liberalization of the criminal law of abortion without at the same time abandoning all protection to the unborn child."[14] The time-phase rule was thought to be the best way to deal with the problem of illegal abortion, whereas compulsory counseling was thought to be an effective means of protecting fetal life. The majority of these framers believed that there would be far fewer abortions "if [women] had an adequate opportunity to obtain information."[15]

Neither of these drafts had enough political backing to win parliamentary approval, and by the end of the 1960s, the future of abortion reform looked bleak. The pressure for reform, however, started to build once again in the early 1970s. Groups within the medical and legal professions came out in favor of abortion reform, as did some religious groups. Parliament itself began to hold hearings on several bills to amend section 218. The Social Democratic Party (SPD) favored an abortion policy keyed to a time-phase rule, a policy the Free Democratic Party (FDP) was also prepared to support, but Christian Democrats (CDU/CSU) weighed in with proposals keyed to an indications solution. Finally, after months of legislative maneuvering, parliament passed the Abortion Reform Act of June 18, 1974 (The Fifth Statute to Reform the Penal Law).[16]

Backed by the SPD-FDP coalition government, the act made abortion legal during the first trimester of pregnancy if performed by a licensed physician and after counseling, but criminal penalties would continue to apply after this stage except where medical or genetic indications were present. (A bill rejected by parliament would have included "social hardship" among the conditions warranting a legal abortion.) The ink on the new statute had barely dried when five *Länder* (half of the German states), together with 193 Christian Democratic members of the Bundestag, filed petitions with the Federal Constitutional Court, challenging the act's validity under several provisions of the Basic Law.[17]

---

[12] Alternative Draft of a Penal Code for the Federal Republic of Germany § 105 (1977) [hereinafter Alternative Draft].

[13] *Id.* § 106 provides:

> Termination of pregnancy later than three months after conception shall be punished by imprisonment for up to three years or by fine, unless the pregnant woman has permitted a doctor to perform the act and:
>
> 1. in accordance with medical knowledge and experience, the termination was necessary in order to prevent a serious danger to the life or limb of the pregnant woman, or
> 2. the probability existed that the child would be seriously injured, either physically or mentally.
>
> The conditions set forth in subparagraphs 1 and 2 must be established by properly authorized medical attestation.

[14] *Id.* at 88.

[15] *Id.* at 89. A minority version of the Alternative Draft rejected counseling as unworkable, preferring instead to encourage the protection of fetal life through social welfare assistance. This version would also have permitted first trimester abortions for ethical (i.e., following rape or incest) and social reasons. After the first trimester, abortions would be permitted only in the presence of genetic or medical indications. *Id.* at 93–94.

[16] *Supra* note 8.

[17] The case was brought to the Federal Constitutional Court under a proceeding known as abstract judicial

By the time these actions were filed, the United States Supreme Court had already decided *Roe v. Wade*,[18] the landmark case upholding a woman's constitutional right to terminate her pregnancy. Some Germans might have wondered whether their highest court would follow the lead of the Supreme Court. The constitutional issue in the United States, however, was framed differently than in Germany. *Roe v. Wade* implicated the due process liberty clause of the fourteenth amendment under which no state "shall . . . deprive any person of life, liberty, or property without due process of law." Prior cases had established that the liberty referred to here protects personal privacy in matters relating to marital relations, procreation and birth control.[19] *Roe* held that "[t]his right of privacy . . . is broad enough to encompass a woman's decision whether or not to terminate her pregnancy."[20]

The language of Germany's constitution is more finely textured than the fourteenth amendment's terse reference to liberty. In assessing the validity of the Abortion Reform Act, the Constitutional Court considered three constitutional provisions, namely, the "human dignity," "personality" and "right to life" clauses of articles 1 and 2. Article 1, paragraph 1, proclaims: "The dignity of man shall be inviolable. To respect and protect it shall be the duty of all state authority." The other clauses are found in article 2: Paragraph 1 guarantees "[e]veryone . . . the right to the free development of his [or her] personality in so far as he [or she] does not violate the rights of others or offend against the constitutional order or the moral code," whereas paragraph 2 declares that "[e]veryone shall have the right to life and to the inviolability of his [or her] person." As commonly recognized, these two rights can be the source of incompatible liberty interests.

The human dignity clause of article 1 is the cornerstone of the constitution, and it casts a bright light on other guaranteed rights and liberties. Liberty, of course, is an essential component of dignity, as the Constitutional Court has underlined on many occasions. In German constitutional theory, however, liberty is not the whole of dignity; it may have to be restrained out of respect for human dignity. In addition, some liberties—or rights—may conflict, and when they do, the principle of dignity may be called upon to mediate the tension between them. This is what happened in the German abortion case.[21]

---

review. The Basic Law provides that the federal government, a state government or one-third of the Bundestag's members may petition the Federal Constitutional Court "in cases of differences of opinion or doubts on the formal and material compatibility of federal law or Land law with this Basic Law, or on the compatibility of Land law with other federal law." Even though such cases are not, as in the United States, raised within the context of a real case or controversy, decisions on abstract review have the force of law and are absolutely binding on all branches and levels of government. The discretionary jurisdiction of the Constitutional Court is also severely limited. The court is obligated to hear and decide cases meeting all jurisdictional requirements. For a discussion of abstract judicial review and other aspects of the Constitutional Court's jurisdiction see D. P. Kommers, *The Constitutional Jurisprudence of the Federal Republic of Germany* 11–17 (1989).

[18] 410 U.S. 113 (1973).

[19] *See especially* Loving v. Virginia, 388 U.S. 1 (1967); Skinner v. Oklahoma, 316 U.S. 535 (1942); Griswold v. Connecticut, 381 U.S. 479 (1965); and Eisenstadt v. Baird, 405 U.S. 453 (1972).

[20] Roe v. Wade, 410 U.S. 113, 153 (1973).

[21] Judgment of February 25, 1975, 39 Entscheidungen des Bundesverfassungsgerichts (hereafter cited as BVerfGE) 1 (1975). An English translation of this case appears in Jonas and Gorby, *West German Abortion Decision: A Contrast to* Roe v. Wade, 9 The John Marshall Journal of Practice & Procedure 605–684 (1976). For a partial translation, see Kommers, *supra* note 17, at 348–359.

The German case, which contrasts so sharply with *Roe v. Wade,* invalidated the Abortion Reform Act. In so doing, the Federal Constitutional Court, like the U.S. Supreme Court, laid down a binding national policy. Basing its argument on the framers' intent and recalling the disregard for human life during the Nazi period, the Constitutional Court ruled that unborn life is "life" within the meaning of the Basic Law.[22] The fetus, said the court, is "an independent legal value" that the state is obligated "to protect and foster" under article 1. In fact, this duty requires the state "to protect developing life" even against the wishes of the mother. In stark contrast to *Roe v. Wade,* the court held that "the protection of the child *en ventre sa mere* takes precedence as a matter of principle for the entire duration of pregnancy over the right of the pregnant woman to self-determination,"[23] a holding dictated by the court's declaration that life begins 14 days after conception.[24]

The right to life in this context, however, would not always prevail over a woman's right to self-determination under the personality clause. In balancing the two values in the light of the human dignity clause of article 1, the court conceded that in some situations a woman's interest would have to prevail over that of the fetus. The woman's interest would prevail, ruled the court, if an abortion is necessary to avert a serious threat to her life or health. In addition, said the court, parliament is free to legalize abortions in the presence of serious genetic, ethical or social indications. The reform statute, as noted, had already decriminalized abortion for medical or genetic reasons. By adding ethical (or juridical, i.e., rape or incest) and social reasons to the list, the court was inviting parliament to restore indications that it had earlier rejected. At all events, the court noted that some burdens go well "beyond that normally associated with pregnancy," as when pregnancy results from a sexual assault (ethical indication) or when a pregnant woman finds herself in a situation of severe hardship (social indication). In the matter of social distress, the court pointed out that a pregnant woman and her family may confront hardship the severity of which would make it unreasonable for the state to compel her to carry her fetus to term. When that point is reached, said the court, criminal law may not be used to compel the continuation of the pregnancy.[25]

The court then proceeded to point out the flaws in the reform statute. First, the time-phase rule violated the right to life. In practice, the court remarked, the rule permitted abortion for almost any reason within the first trimester of pregnancy, going far beyond the court's list of four permissible indications. Second, the law failed to make plain that abortion is "a wrong deserving punishment"[26]—aborting a fetus, said the court, is "an act of killing"[27]—because it subordinates the highest value of the legal order to the "unrestricted" decision of private parties. This legal order must champion the value of life as informed by the principle of human dignity. Third, and relatedly, the counseling system under section 218c was flawed because it failed to convey a strong pro-life message. Permitting the woman to seek the counsel of her physician was another flaw in the system. The court noted that a physician was unqualified to give

---

[22] *See* Jonas and Gorby, *supra* note 21, at 638.

[23] *Id.* at 643.

[24] The court declared: "Life, in the sense of the historical existence of a human individual, exists according to definite biological-physiological knowledge, in any case, from the 14th day after conception (nidation, individuation)." *Id.* at 638.

[25] *Id.* at 648.

[26] *Id.* at 649.

[27] *Id.* at 645.

advice on the nonmedical aspects of abortion, and even where the medical aspects are concerned, he is unlikely to be an objective counselor if he has a financial interest in performing the abortion.

Did the court's decision require the state to criminalize abortion at all stages of pregnancy? Or, to put the question another way, if the state is obligated to condemn abortion as a "wrong" or an "injustice," can it do this without punishing the wrong-doer under the penal code? "The decisive factor," said the court, "is whether the totality of the measures serving the protection of the unborn life, whether they be in civil law or in public law, especially of a social-legal or of a penal nature, guarantees an actual protection corresponding to the importance of the legal value to be secured."[28] In theory, comprehensive counseling—that is, noncriminal strategies—might possibly satisfy this requirement. Yet the Constitutional Court took the unusual step of restoring the criminal penalties of the old law, pending legislation to correct the flaws in the current statute.

The German parliament proceeded to amend section 218 in precisely the ways the court demanded. Under the newly revised statute, enacted into law on February 12, 1976,[29] abortion is a punishable offense. An abortion is legal, however, if performed by a physician with the woman's consent and if serious medical, genetic, ethical or social indications are present and certified by two medical practitioners. An abortion for medical reasons—that is, to protect the life or health of the mother—may be performed at any time; for genetic reasons, not more than 22 weeks after conception; and for ethical and social reasons, not more than 12 weeks after conception. Before terminating a pregnancy for any of these reasons, the woman is legally obligated to seek the advice of a counselor. The counselor must inform her of available assistance—including "those types of aids which make it easier to continue with the pregnancy and which ameliorate the conditions of mother and child."[30]

Despite these regulations, the statute tempers the crime of abortion with mercy, for even in the absence of the indications mentioned the pregnant woman herself is exempt from punishment if the abortion is performed by a licensed physician within the first 22 weeks of pregnancy provided she has sought medical and social counseling.[31] The burden of the law thus falls upon the physician, for the doctor is responsible for seeing that all the counseling requirements have been fulfilled.[32] The statute defines a counselor as a "counseling center recognized by a government agency or by a corporate body under public law" or "a physician [other than the one] performing the abortion." The physician must also be a "recognized member of a counseling center."[33]

Finally, the statute bans the commercial advertising of abortion services,[34] just as it bars commerce in abortifacients.[35] Abortions must be performed in hospitals or other authorized facilities. Since Germany has a federal system of government and since na-

---

[28] *Id.* at 646.

[29] The Fifteenth Criminal Law Amendment Act, Strafgesetzbuch [StGB] § 218. For a full English translation, see the appendix to *The Penal Code of the Federal Republic of Germany* (J. Darby transl. 1987). *See also* Eser, *Reform of German Abortion Law: First Experience,* 34 Am. J. Comp. L. 374–380 (1986).

[30] *StGB* at § 218b (1) 1.

[31] *Id.* at § 218 (3).

[32] *Id.* §§ 219b (2) 1 and 2 (a).

[33] *Id.* § 219b.

[34] *Id.* § 219b.

[35] *Id.* § 219 (c).

tional laws are carried out by the separate states, regulations on facilities differ from state to state. Abortions carried out in approved facilities are publicly funded by the national health service or the social security administration.[36] Pro-life advocates have challenged the constitutionality of abortion funding on the ground that the use of tax revenue for such a purpose violates freedom of conscience, but these efforts have failed.[37] The law does, however, respect the conscience of medical practitioners and their aides. They are not required to perform or assist in an abortion if their conscience so dictates unless the operation is necessary to save the life of the pregnant woman.

POSTSCRIPT   Sixteen years have passed since the West German parliament amended the criminal code to conform to the Constitutional Court's judgment. Despite ensuing changes in the political climate and in the court's membership, no constitutional challenge has been mounted against the existing policy. In 1976, however, two German citizens filed a petition with the European Commission on Human Rights, claiming that the Constitutional Court's decision and the Fifteenth Criminal Law Amendment Act contravened the European Convention on Human Rights. Their principal claim was based on article 8, which bars member states from interfering with a person's "private and family life."[38]

By a vote of 11 to 3, the commission found no violation of article 8. Echoing Justice Blackmun's observation in *Roe v. Wade* that a woman cannot be isolated in her pregnancy, the commission noted that "pregnancy cannot be said to pertain uniquely to the sphere of private life. Whenever a woman is pregnant her private life becomes closely connected with her developing fetus."[39] Having surveyed various national laws on abortion in Europe, the commission found that "certain interests related to pregnancy are legally protected,"[40] such as the right of the unborn child to inherit. Still, the commission could find no consensus on the legal or moral status of abortion within the Council of Europe and thus refused to regard abortion as a right under the convention. By the same token, the commission declined to decide whether the unborn child constitutes "life" within the meaning of article 2 of the convention.[41]

Germany's unification in 1990 reopened and intensified the debate over the legality of abortion. Since 1965 East Germany had permitted abortion on request during the first 12 weeks of pregnancy, a policy clearly unconstitutional in West Germany. East Germans agreed to national unity under West Germany's constitution, but they refused to be bound by the policy laid down by the Constitutional Court. The two sides compromised: Under the unification treaty, West Germany's abortion law shall not apply to the five eastern states of the old German Democratic Republic for a transitional period of

---

[36] *See* K. C. Horton, *Abortion Law Reform in the German Federal Republic,* 28 Int'l & Comp. L. Q. 288–296 (1979).

[37] *See* Abortion Finance Case, 67 BVerfGE 26 [1984].

[38] The petitioners also claimed that West Germany violated the convention's guarantee of religious freedom (Article 9) and association (Article 11); in addition, they challenged the court's assumption of legislative power in striking down the liberalized abortion statute of 1974. The European Commission on Human Rights unanimously rejected all of these claims. See Brüggemann and Scheuten v. Federal Republic of Germany, 3 E.H.R.R. 244 [1977].

[39] *Id.* at 253.

[40] *Id.*

[41] *See* John Gorby, *The West German Abortion Decision Before the European Commission on Human Rights,* in T. W. Hilgers *et al., New Perspectives on Human Abortion* 257–280 (1981).

two years, by which time an all-German parliament is expected to pass a new law applicable to the whole of Germany.

The new law, which will be enacted by the end of 1992, may very well duplicate the 1974 reform statute nullified by the Federal Constitutional Court. But any such statute is likely once again to be the subject of a constitutional challenge. In any event, the Federal Constitutional Court, given its powers of judicial review under the constitution, will have the last word on the validity of the new statute. And its judgment, should there be one, will bind the country as a whole.

B. France

The legal condemnation and punishment of abortion in France, as in Germany, reaches far into the past. Draconian measures inflicted upon abortionists in the 17th and 18th centuries—ranging from "20 years in irons" to the death penalty[42]—yielded to milder punishment under the Napoleonic Penal Code of 1810. The 1810 code nevertheless disallowed abortion by whatever means and punished abortion with imprisonment, whether performed by the woman or by an abortionist with her consent. As recently as 1959, any doctor, surgeon, medical assistant, pharmacist or other health officer assisting in or performing an abortion could be imprisoned up to five years.[43] Attempts to liberalize the law in the 1960s duplicated the strenuous debate that marked West Germany's effort to change its law. Finally, in 1975, the year of the German abortion case, the French parliament passed a reform statute of its own.

The French Abortion Act of 1975, as amended in 1979,[44] virtually permits abortion on demand during the first 10 weeks of pregnancy. The relevant portion of the statute reads: "A pregnant woman whose condition places her in a situation of distress may make a request to a physician for the termination of her pregnancy. The termination may be performed only before the end of the tenth week of pregnancy."[45] This time-phase rule treats abortion as a health problem; drawn up by the Ministry of Health, the statute also appears in the Code of Public Health (Code de la Sante Publique). At first glance, France's policy would seem to accord with Roe v. Wade, for a woman seeking an abortion early in pregnancy is usually able to have one. The French requirement of "distress" is no block to having an abortion since under the law the woman herself makes this determination.[46] To a large extent, therefore, the decision is left to the woman in consultation with her physician.

In other respects, however, French law seeks to circumscribe the abortion decision in ways that would be hard to reconcile with Roe v. Wade. The French have taken the pragmatic view that abortion should go unpunished in the early stages of pregnancy but that the community, through law, still has an obligation to remind citizens of their obligation to family, children and unborn life. Law in the French view need not act as

---

[42] Knoppers, Brault & Sloss, *Abortion Law in Francophone Countries*, 38 Am. J. Comp. L. 893 (1990).

[43] Code Penal [C. pen.] art. 317. For an English translation, see *The French Penal Code of 1810* § 317 (J. Moreau and G. Mueller, trans. 1960).

[44] Law No. 75-17 of January 17, 1975, as amended by Law No. 79-1204 of December 31, 1979 (J.O. January 18, 1975) [hereinafter *Law of January 17, 1975*]. A partial translation of the amended statute appears in M. Glendon, *Abortion and Divorce in Western Law* 155–157 (1987). Unless otherwise noted, quoted passages from the French Abortion Act are based on Glendon's translation.

[45] Code de la sante publique [C. san. pub.] art. 162-1.

[46] *Id.* art. 162-4.

a moral constabulary, as some might characterize the role of law as perceived by Germany's constitutional court, but it should subserve, even if it cannot enforce, the moral aspirations of a society. In a preambular statement, the French Abortion Act "guarantees the respect of every human being from the commencement of life."[47] In 1979, parliament added the following paragraph to this section:

> *The teaching of this principle and its consequences, the provision of information on the problems of life and of national and international demography, the education towards responsibility, the acceptance of the child in society, and family-oriented policy, are national obligations. The State, with the co-operation of local authorities, implements these obligations and supports initiatives towards these ends.*[48]

The statute seeks to minimize reliance on abortion through a vigorous program of public education on birth control and family planning. "The voluntary termination of pregnancy," declares the statute, "must under no circumstances constitute a means of birth control." Accordingly, the law directs government to "take all measures necessary to promote information on birth control on as wide a scale as possible, notably by the universal establishment, within maternal and child care centers, of family planning or education centers, and by the utilization of all communications media."[49] Since 1979 such measures have included instruction on the use of contraceptives in the practical training of doctors, nurses and midwives.

The French statute also contains a heavy emphasis on counseling. A pregnant woman wishing to terminate her pregnancy under the time-phase rule is legally required to consult with a physician of her choice. The physician in turn, on the woman's first visit, must inform her of the medical hazards associated with abortion and furnish her with detailed information concerning prenatal care, child-care assistance, family benefits provided by law, adoption possibilities and a list of where pregnant mothers are cared for and where voluntary abortions are carried out. After this formality she must go to a family counseling agency or other officially approved advisory center for "a certificate to the effect that the consultation has taken place." The counseling center provides the woman with additional information on her social situation with an eye to "enabling her to keep the child."[50] If at this stage she still wants an abortion she can go back to her physician and ask for it. She must, however, wait another seven days—a period presumably given over to serious thought and reflection about her decision—before the physician can legally accept her written consent. At this stage, if she signs the consent form, she is entitled to a legal abortion.

Therapeutic abortions are permissible at any stage of gestation when necessary for serious medical or genetic reasons. Two physicians are required to certify the presence of these indications before the abortion can legally be carried out.[51] All abortions, therapeutic or voluntary, must be carried out in an approved private or public hospital, a provision of the law designed to avoid the commercialization of abortion.[52] As a con-

---

[47] *Id.* art. 162-1.
[48] *Law of January 17, 1975, supra* note 37, art. 1.
[49] C. san. pub. art. 162-13.
[50] *Id.* art. 162-4.
[51] *Id.* art. 162-12.
[52] *See* Parliamentary Debates, Aseemblee Nationale, November 27–29, 1974, *Journal Officiel*, 7224 (1974).

sequence, the law bans abortion clinics as well as the advertising of abortion services,[53] a prohibition seemingly consistent with the goal of reducing the incidence of abortion for familial or socioeconomic reasons. On the other hand, in the interest of pregnant women who cling to their decision to have an abortion within the time-phase rule, the state regulates the cost of abortion and pays 75% of that cost out of public funds.[54]

There is yet another chapter to the French story. Before the 1974 statute became effective, 81 members of parliament who voted against the law contested its validity before the Constitutional Council *(Conseil Constitutionnel).*[55] They argued that the time-phase rule violated the Constitution's preamble as well as article 2 of the European Convention on Human Rights. The preamble to the French Constitution of 1958 incorporates the principles of liberty set forth in the 1789 Declaration of the Rights of Man as well as the preambular statements of the 1946 constitution, the relevant portion of which "guarantees to the infant the protection of his health." Article 2 of the European Convention declares: "Everyone's right to life shall be protected by law." Petitioners claimed that these provisions require the protection of the fetus at all stages of pregnancy.

The Constitutional Council rejected the first claim and declined to decide the second. In an unusually cautious and mercifully short opinion, the council ruled that it had no authority to review a statute in the light of a treaty (i.e., the European Convention). In answer to the argument that the voluntary termination of pregnancy violated French constitutional principles, the council simply concluded, without argument, that the "provisions of the law . . . are not contrary to the Constitution."[56]

C. Italy

The Italian legislature, like the German Bundestag and the French National Assembly, enacted a new abortion policy in the 1970s. As in Germany and the United States—but less so in France—the debate over abortion in Italy rooted itself initially in constitutional politics. The Italian Constitutional Court helped set the stage for the passage of the Italian Abortion Act of 1978.[57] In 1972 a Milan court that was called upon to apply the penal code to a woman who had procured an abortion referred the question of the law's validity to the Constitutional Court.[58]

---

[53] C. san. pub. art. 647.

[54] *See* Nijsten, *supra* note 1, at 199.

[55] Under Article 61 of the 1958 Constitution, laws passed by parliament may be submitted to the Constitutional Council prior to their promulgation. Parties eligible to submit petitions to the council for a review of the constitutionality of a law are the president of the republic, the premier, the president of the National Assembly, the president of the Senate or at least 60 members of the Assembly or the Senate. See M. Cappelletti and W. Cohen, *Comparative Constitutional Law* 68–69 (1979). For a discussion of the role and increasing importance of the Constitutional Council in France's system of constitutional review, see Davis, *The Law/Politics Distinction, the French Conseil Constitutionnel, and the U.S. Supreme Court,* 34 A.J.C.L. 45 (1986); Morton, *Judicial Review in France: A Comparative Analysis,* 36 Am. J. Comp. L. 89 (1988); and Alec Stone, *The Birth of Judicial Politics in France: The Constitutional Council in Comparative Perspective* (forthcoming).

[56] *See* Cappelletti and Cohen, *supra* note 55, at 579.

[57] Law No. 194 of May 22, 1978 [hereinafter Law No. 194]. The ensuing discussion of this law relies heavily on M. Nijsten, *supra* note 1, at 127ff. Quotations from the law are based on translated passages appearing in Bognetti, "Italy," 7 Comparative Law Yearbook 87–90 (1983).

[58] *See* Bognetti, *supra* note 57, at 86. Italy's Constitution of 1947 introduced judicial review, although on a scale less broad than in Germany. *See* Constitution of the Italian Republic of December 27, 1947, arts. 134–137.

The Italian Penal Code of 1889, like the Napoleonic Penal Code of 1810, had punished abortion with imprisonment. When the fascist government revised the penal code in 1930, the penalties were increased. Efforts to reform the code in the postwar years failed,[59] leaving the law as amended in 1930 intact. Under this law a woman could be imprisoned for one to four years for aborting herself;[60] persons performing the abortion, even with the woman's consent, could be jailed for two to five years.[61] Other provisions imposed penalties for ''instigating'' a pregnant woman to miscarry or for ''engag[ing] in propaganda in favor [of abortion].''[62] Although the code punished all abortions notwithstanding the reason and without regard for the stage of pregnancy, judicial decisions, according to one authoritative account, ''would excuse the woman [and those who helped her] if the abortion was committed to save the woman's life.''[63]

This then was the state of the law at the time of the constitutional challenge. The judge who referred the case to the Constitutional Court questioned the validity of the abortion ban under the constitution's ''right-to-health'' clause (article 32). Also implicated was article 2, which guarantees ''the inviolable rights of man'' and around which both sides could rally in defense of their respective positions. Actually, in a judgment one commentator described as ''Solomonic,''[64] the court managed to placate both sides. On the one hand, the court noted that the ''protection of conception . . . has [a] constitutional foundation,'' for ''article 31 . . . expressly imposes the 'protection of motherhood.' '' In addition, said the court, the inviolability clause of article 2 covers ''the legal situation of the fetus.''[65]

On the other hand, in language reminiscent of the 1975 German abortion case, the court observed that ''the constitutionally protected interest of the fetus may conflict with other values which are themselves constitutionally protected.''[66] The right of the unborn to life is not absolute, said the court, because in some situations the ban on abortion would not adequately protect the woman's physical or psychic health. The court acknowledged that under the penal code's general exemption clause (article 54) a woman could not be punished for having an abortion necessary to avoid a ''present danger of serious bodily harm,'' but the ''present necessity'' defense fell short of the constitutional protection a pregnant woman needs in certain circumstances.[67] Yet the court went on to say that even where an abortion may be necessary to safeguard the woman's health, ''the operation should [under present law] be performed in such a way as to save, when possible, the life of the fetus.''[68] At the conclusion of its opinion, the court reminded parliament of its obligation to amend the law to protect the interests of both fetus and mother.

When the struggle over abortion reform shifted to the parliamentary arena, Christian Democrats fought for the indications solution that the Constitutional Court appeared

---

[59] See the Italian Penal Code xli–xlii (E. Wise transl. 1978).

[60] *Id.* § 547.

[61] *Id.* § 546.

[62] *Id.* §§ 548 and 553.

[63] Bognetti, *supra* note 57, at 83.

[64] *Id.* at 86.

[65] Judgment of February 18, 1975, Corte Costituzionale, corte cost., 20 Guirisprudenza Italiana [Giur. Ital.] 117. An English translation of the case appears in Cappelletti and Cohen, *supra* note 55, at 612–614.

[66] Cappelletti and Cohen, *supra* note 55, at 613.

[67] *Id.* at 613.

[68] *Id.* at 614.

to prefer by its emphasis upon protecting the health of pregnant women. Opposition parties in the majority, however, enacted a statute similar to France's law. The 1978 statute begins by solemnly declaring that "the state guarantees the right to responsible procreation, recognizes the social value of maternity, and protects human life from its very beginning."[69] Like the French law, it also declares that voluntary "[a]bortion is not a means of birth control."[70] The Italians opted for a 90-day time-phase rule combined with extensive counseling and a seven-day waiting period designed to dissuade pregnant women from having an abortion.[71] A woman in the first trimester may request an abortion from a physician of her choice or a family counseling center if she claims that her pregnancy would seriously threaten her physical or psychological health owing to her economic or social situation, the "circumstances of conception" or "fear of malformation or abnormalities in the fetus."[72]

The statute reads as though it provides for an indications solution, allowing abortions, as in Germany, only for medical, genetic, ethical or social reasons. In reality, the time-phase rule prevails since the required certificate authorizing an abortion rests on the pregnant woman's own assessment that one of these "indications" is present. Although the law obligates the counseling center or the physician to furnish the woman with information as detailed as that required in France, the state does not attempt independently to ascertain whether a woman has met the statutory conditions for an abortion. In fact, the law specifies no criminal penalty for avoiding these conditions. A woman is subject to imprisonment of up to six months, however, is she fails to observe the procedures required for an abortion in the first trimester; for other actors involved in the abortion decision the penalty is from one to four years imprisonment.[73]

In the second trimester, abortion is legally permitted only for serious medical or genetic indications certified by a physician attached to an obstetrical unit of an approved hospital. Postviability abortions are permissible if the woman's life is threatened, but in such a case an effort must be made to preserve the life of the fetus.[74] As in France, the law respects the professional freedom of doctors to refuse to perform or participate in abortions. Whereas French doctors may refuse to do abortions for any reason, Italian doctors may refuse to do them only if they have registered as conscientious objectors with the health service or with the hospital that employs them.[75] (A similar rule applies to nurses and medical assistants.) In 1981, according to one report, at least 43% of Italy's gynecologists refused to perform abortions for moral reasons.[76]

In several respects, the Italian law is more permissive than the French. First, the time-phase rule is 12 rather than 10 weeks; second, the woman need not secure additional information from a counseling center if she has already consulted her physician and secured the required information from him or her; third, the abortion may be performed in a public hospital or in a private clinic licensed by regional health authorities. As in France, however, Italy seeks to avoid commercialized abortion by limiting the

---

[69] *See* Law No. 194, *supra* note 57, art. 1.1.

[70] *Id.* art. 1.2.

[71] *Id.* art 5.

[72] *Id.* art. 4.

[73] *Id.* art. 19.

[74] *Id.* art. 7.

[75] *See* Nijsten, *supra* note 1, at 188.

[76] *See* 17 Family Planning Perspectives 19 (January/February 1985).

number of abortions performed in private clinics;[77] finally, Italy's National Health Service fully funds abortions; those performed in private hospitals or clinics are reimbursed by the government.

The abortion debate entered a second constitutional phase after the passage of the 1978 act. Pursuant to article 75 of the constitution, pro-choice and pro-life forces sponsored referenda to amend the act, the former to remove all obstacles to freedom of choice at all stages of pregnancy, the latter to punish all abortions except those necessary to preserve the life or health of the mother. The Italian electorate overwhelmingly defeated both proposals. The Constitutional Court permitted the state to hold the referenda after finding that neither of them would offend the constitution.[78] In taking such a broad view, the court appeared to suggest that this was properly a legislative matter to be resolved in the light of evolving trends in public opinion. By finding no major constitutional flaw in the pro-choice position, the Court appeared to have backed away from its earlier *dicta* about the inviolable rights of the unborn. In a remarkable display of judicial self-restraint, the court appeared ready to follow the lead of public opinion.

III. Common Law Jurisdictions

A. England

English abortion law is the product of three major statutes: the Offenses Against the Person Act of 1869, the Life Preservation Act of 1929 and the Abortion Act of 1967. As these dates suggest, the law has evolved incrementally over a century and a half, representing a miscellany of statutory and common law rules. We need not tarry long over the status of abortion at common law. The common law treated abortion as an offense and punished the offense at the point of "quickening"—that is, the stage where a woman begins to feel the movement of the child *in utero*.[79] Punishment was rare, however, because most abortions took place before quickening. When it became a statutory offense in 1803, the quickening rule was abandoned. Abortion was now punished at any stage of pregnancy and, as at common law, aimed at abortionists or others helping women procure abortions.[80]

The modern period of abortion legislation in England begins with the 1861 Offenses Against the Person Act.[81] Section 58 punishes potional and instrumental abortions, whether self-induced or performed by other parties. Specifically, it covers the taking of "any poison or other noxious thing" or the use of any instrument. The offense occurs when these activities are performed "unlawfully" and with the *intention* of bringing

---

[77] *See* Law No. 194, *supra* note 57, art. 8.

[78] Judgment No. 26, 1981, corte cost., 26 Giur. Ital. 134 ff.

[79] The precise nature of the offense under the common law remains in dispute. Blackstone, like Sir Edward Coke, regarded abortion as a misdemeanor but only after quickening. The line drawn between before and after quickening corresponded to the distinction in canon law between the *embryo formatus* and the *embryo informatus*. Human life in this view began with the "animated" condition of the fully shaped fetus. The common law appeared to absorb this view. For a treatment of the link between canon and common law in the matter of abortion and for a fuller discussion of the dispute surrounding the precise nature of abortion as a crime, see Means, *The Phoenix of Abortional Freedom: Is a Penumbral or Ninth-Amendment Right About to Arise From the Nineteenth-Century Common-Law Liberty?* 17 N.Y.L.F. 335 (1971) and J. Keown, *Abortion, Doctors and the Law* 3–12 (1988). Another historical overview of the status of abortion at common law is B. Dickens, *Abortion and the Law* 20–28 (1966).

[80] This summary has been drawn from Dickens, *supra* note 79, at 20–28.

[81] *See* Offenses Against the Person Act, 1861, 9 Geo. IV ch. 31, §§ 58–60.

about an abortion. Section 58 also increases the offense beyond what it was at common law. For one thing, penalties now apply to a woman who aborts herself. For another, they apply to others who perform the abortion, whether the pregnancy is imagined or real. If convicted, a woman acting alone or her accessory is liable to the maximum penalty of life imprisonment. The act also punished, and for the first time, the activity of supplying another with an instrument or drug knowing that it would be used "unlawfully" to abort a fetus, "whether [the woman] be or be not with child."[82] The testimony of the medical profession appears to have had much to do with these new definitions of the crime.[83] Illegal abortions, although far from widespread, were becoming a problem in the early part of the 19th century. Although licensed physicians worried about the indiscriminate destruction of unborn children, they were equally concerned about the health of pregnant women and the unprofessional practice of medicine. Both altruism and self-interest combined to drive practicing physicians into the forefront of England's abortion reform movement. According to one study, "[t]here is substantial evidence that medical men were concerned not only for the welfare of the potential victims of abortion but also to further the process of establishing and consolidating their status as a profession."[84] The medical profession had mounted a massive assault on uncertified midwives, herbalists, drug dispensers and other quacks beginning to turn abortion into a profitable enterprise.

The medical profession also served as the driving force behind the 1929 Infant Life Preservation Act. This statute removed doubts over whether the 1861 act covered the killing of a child at birth.[85] As Nicolas Terry writes, the 1929 act made it easier for prosecutors to try "cases of child destruction at the time of birth where a murder charge could be met with the argument that the child had no life independent of the mother."[86] As interpreted, the statute now punished the destruction of an unborn child capable of being born alive. (The *de lege* fetal age, or point of viability, for this purpose was set at 28 weeks.) The act, however, contained the proviso that "no person shall be found guilty of an offense under this section unless it is proved that the act which caused the death of the child was not done in good faith for the purpose of preserving the life of the mother."[87] In the ensuing years, however, the courts seized on the language of this proviso to broaden the conditions under which therapeutic abortions could be "lawfully" performed. In short, common law was used to mitigate the severity of the statutory offense.[88]

England entered the present phase of abortion reform with the passage of the Abortion Act of 1967. Under this act, which replaced the common law entirely, the 1861 and 1929 statutes remain in force but they no longer apply to abortions performed for medical or genetic reasons, for criminalization gave way to medicalization. The physi-

---

[82] *Id.* § 59.

[83] *See* J. Keown, *supra* note 79, at 35–36.

[84] *Id.* at 40.

[85] For an excellent analysis of the 1929 act, see J. Keown, *The Scope of the Offense of Child Destruction,* 104 Law Quarterly Review 120 (1988).

[86] Terry, *England,* in *Abortion and Protection of the Human Fetus* 78 (S. Frankowski and G. Cole eds. 1987).

[87] Infant Life Preservation Act, 1929, 19 & 20 Geo. V ch. 34.

[88] The landmark case is *R v. Bourne,* decided in 1938. The law as expounded in *Bourne* still required a real threat to the woman's life or serious injury to her mental condition before an abortion would go unpunished. [1939] 1 K.B. 687, [1938] 3 A.E.R. 615. For a good discussion of *Bourne* and related cases see Dickens, *supra* note 80, at 38–91 and Keown, *supra* note 79, at 49–59.

cian rather than the constable plays the key role in carrying out England's present abortion policy. There are two conditions under which a woman may now "lawfully" procure an abortion under the 1861 statute: The first is when her continued pregnancy would pose a greater risk to her "physical or mental health" or to "any existing children of her family" than "if the pregnancy were terminated"[89]; the second is where "there is a substantial risk that if the child were to be born it would suffer from such physical or mental abnormalities as to be seriously handicapped."[90] Thus, under the literal terms of the statute, England appears to have opted, as in the case of Germany, for an indications solution to the problem of abortion.

Various technical and procedural standards govern the process of abortion decision-making. First, a physician is allowed to proceed with an abortion only after two other licensed physicians have certified that medical or genetic indications are present. Second, these physicians must form their opinion in "good faith." However, in determining whether there is a risk to the physical or mental health of the woman or to her existing children, doctors may consider "the pregnant woman's actual or reasonably foreseeable environment," a process of certification that does not apply if an abortion is necessary to save a mother's life.[91] For doctors who object to abortion on moral grounds, the act contains a conscience clause: Any person so opposed to abortion need not lend a hand in any treatment authorized by the act.[92] Finally, presumably to discourage commercialized abortion, the 1967 act requires abortions to be carried out in hospitals served by the National Health Service or in approved private facilities.[93] It also requires reports on all abortions.

The 1967 act fails to address the special problem of spousal or parental consent. Ordinary family law, however, would cover parental consent in the abortion context, for any invasive surgical or medical treatment performed on minors requires the consent of a parent or guardian.[94] *Paton v. Trustees of BPAS*,[95] on the other hand, appears to have resolved the issue of spousal consent. *Paton* involved a husband who sought to stop his wife from having an abortion authorized within the terms of the act. The court concluded that the act "gives no right to be consulted in respect of the termination of a pregnancy."[96] The law's silence on this matter ended the case. Two other defenses were possible: The father might have invoked the right of the fetus or challenged the "good faith" judgment of the physicians who certified the abortion. As to the first point, the court reasserted the common law view that the fetus is without rights until it

---

[89] Abortion Act, 1967, ch. 87, § 1(a).

[90] *Id.* § 1(b).

[91] *Id.* § 1 (4).

[92] *Id.* § 4.

[93] *Id.* § 1 (3).

[94] *See* Terry, *supra* note 86, at 91. Gillick v. West Norfolk Area Health Authority may have modified this rule. In this case—an action by a parent to revoke a health department order permitting doctors to give contraceptive advice and treatment to a girl under 16 without parental consent—England's highest court refused to recognize any rule of absolute parental authority until a fixed age. Parental control ebbs, said the court, as the child advances in age and maturity, and in the contraceptive context doctors may exercise their best clinical judgment if the patient is mature and intelligent enough to understand the proposed treatment. [1985] 3 All E.R. 402.

[95] [1978] 2 All E.R. 987.

[96] *Id.* at 991.

is born.[97] As to the second, it confessed a judicial inability to monitor the operation of the statute.[98] In fact, as the *Paton* court noted, the 1967 act places this "great social responsibility . . . firmly . . . on the shoulders of the medical profession."[99]

This judicial remark highlights the broad discretion the Abortion Act confers on the medical profession. The act does not sanction abortion on request, but in reality doctors authorize abortions in great numbers. In 1967, the year of the act's passage, 27,200 abortions were carried out in England and Wales; by 1973, the figure reached a high of 167,100.[100] These numbers suggest that doctors are certifying abortions without much attention to the "good faith" standard of judgment the law requires. But then the term "health" is elastic enough to authorize abortions based on humanitarian or socio-economic considerations.[101] In addition, women can usually find doctors who will agree with their view of the risk involved in carrying a pregnancy to term. The system as it exists lends credence to the view that the English rule is closer to France and Italy's time-phase than to Germany's indications solution.

Because the law has operated more permissively than originally expected, numerous attempts have been made to restrict the reach of the 1967 act. Proposals have ranged from permitting abortions only in cases of serious risk to the life or health of pregnant women to limiting the activities of abortion referral agencies.[102] The medical profession has strongly opposed these proposals, arguing that abuses under the present system are easily remedied by better administrative supervision. Yet, as a recent study concludes, the medical profession has become more tolerant of abortion, with some practitioners regarding it "as an integral part of fertility control."[103]

Any postscript to the story of abortion reform in England would have to mention certain amendments to existing abortion law contained in the Human Fertilization and Embryology Act of 1990, the full results of which are yet to be recorded. The new terms clarify the law by limiting "normal" abortions under the 1967 act to the first 24 weeks of pregnancy. (Under the 1929 Life Preservation Act, the 28-week rule prevailed.) Late abortions, however, can now be procured not only to save the mother's life but also to prevent the birth of an abnormal child or to avoid serious permanent injury to a woman's health.[104] But again, the "good faith" administration of these

---

[97] *Id.* at 989. For a similar ruling involving an illegitimate father, see *C v. S* [1987] 1 All E.R. 1230.

[98] [1978] 2 All E.R. 991. The husband in this case appealed to the European Commission of Human Rights, claiming that the Abortion Act of 1967 violated the "right to life" and "private and family life" clauses of Articles 2 and 8 respectively of the European Convention for the Protection of Human Rights and Fundamental Freedoms. The commission rejected both of these claims, holding that the "right to life" clause of Article 2 does not cover the fetus at "the initial stage of pregnancy." The commission also held that in early pregnancy, a woman's right to private and family life trumps that of the potential father. *See* Paton v. United Kingdom, 3 E.H.R.R. 408 (1980).

[99] [1978] 2 All E.R. 991.

[100] *See* Guttmacher Institute Report, *Induced Abortion: A World Review* 33 (6th ed. 1986). For an analysis of these figures, see A. Grubb, *Abortion Law—An English Perspective,* 20 N.M.L.R. 663–667 (1990).

[101] What the law requires, as already noted, is a good faith professional opinion that the woman would be at less risk by ending her pregnancy than by continuing it, a provision that lends itself easily to a pro-abortion decision since early abortions are on the whole less burdensome than complications or difficulties associated with childbirth.

[102] For a detailed discussion of these proposals, see Keown, *supra* note 79, at 138–158.

[103] *Id.* at 158.

[104] R. Hudson, *A Matter of Life and Death,* 140 New Law Journal 1499 (1990).

provisions will depend on the good will of medical practitioners. One observer concluded: "The intention of the Government in permitting amendments to the abortion law was, on the surface, to restrict the availability of abortion. In fact, quite the opposite has occurred and the law is now even more liberal than it was before."[105]

Notwithstanding these changes in the law, England's policy is more restrictive than U.S. law and less restrictive than German, French or Italian law. We might note that in England abortion is not a "right" in any constitutional sense; it is, as we have seen, a matter of social policy that has evolved over the years incrementally. England, like New Zealand, does not have a written constitution garnished with a bill of rights. On the other hand, U.S., German, French and Italian law implicate constitutional rights, either the right to life or the right to personality or the right to privacy or the right to respect for family life. Parliamentary supremacy is the hallmark of British constitutionalism. As a consequence, abortion law in England is a product mainly of statutory policy.

B. Australia

Australia has enjoyed two centuries of constitutional government.[106] She received her present constitution, however, in 1900.[107] This constitution guarantees freedom of religion and the rights of criminal defendants,[108] but it contains no comprehensive bill of rights and, therefore, as in England, there is no constitutional limitation rooted in the general notion of "liberty" that would protect women seeking to have abortions.[109] Yet Australia differs from England in that the former lacks a uniform abortion policy applicable to the nation as a whole. Australia's constitution, like that of the United States, establishes a federal system of government that grants the federal parliament express powers over certain matters but reserves all other powers to the states, including the authority to legislate in the field of criminal law. Abortion falls into this field. As a consequence, Australia allows each state to follow its own policy preferences with respect to abortion.[110]

Abortion is generally illegal under the criminal law of the Australian states, each of which has inherited the English law of 1861. Each state has also inherited the English rules of common law, especially those laid down in *R v. Bourne*, which mitigated the severity of the 1861 Act. Meanwhile, the Australian states, including the Northern Territory, have combined their own developing common law rules with statutory reforms that have added to the conditions under which a woman may lawfully procure an abortion. In terms of the extent to which they regulate abortion, the states and territory fall

---

[105] Grubb, *supra* note 100, at 673.

[106] See R. D. Lumb, *The Bicentenary of Australian Constitutionalism: The Evolution of Rules of Constitutional Change*, 15 U. Queensl. L. J. 3 (1988).

[107] Commonwealth of Australia Constitution Act (July 9, 1900).

[108] *Id.* §§ 116 and 80.

[109] Recent efforts to entrench a Declaration of Rights and Freedoms in the constitution have failed. Efforts to adopt a statutory bill of rights have also failed. *See* Campbell, *Changing the Constitution—Past and Future*, 17 Melb. U. L. Rev. 1 (1989); O'Neill, *Constitutional Human Rights in Australia*, 17 Fed. L. Rev. 85 (1987); and O'Neill, *The Australian Bill of Rights Bill 1985 and the Supremacy of Parliament*, 60 Aust. L. J. 139 (1986).

[110] Bills of rights are also absent from most state constitutions. Proposals to include a comprehensive list of rights in state constitutions have generated as much controversy at the state as at the federal level. *See*, for example, Alison Moran, *The Constitution (Declaration of Rights and Freedoms) Bill 1988 (Vic.)—A Doomed Proposal*, 17 Melb. L. Rev. 418 (1990).

into three categories: Victoria and New South Wales, which have followed the rules of common law;[111] Queensland, Tasmania, and Western Australia, which have adopted important statutory exemptions to the 1861 act;[112] and South Australia and the Northern Territory, which have enacted the most permissive laws.[113]

Since England's Offenses Against the Person Act of 1861 forms the essential core of Australian state abortion policy, let us recall its terms. First, it punishes with imprisonment any woman unlawfully using a drug or instrument to procure her own abortion. Second, it punishes in like fashion any person unlawfully using the same means "to procure the miscarriage of any woman," whether pregnant or not. Third, it punishes the suppliers of these means who know they are to be used unlawfully to abort a fetus. The offense may occur at any time during a pregnancy after the point of implantation.[114] *Rex v. Bourne*,[115] as we noted earlier, mitigated the severity of this policy by holding that an abortion is lawful when performed by a licensed medical practitioner acting *bona fide* to preserve the life of a pregnant woman. The term "life" in this context meant the woman's physical and mental health. Finally, Australian state law, in imitation of England's Child Destruction Act of 1929, prohibits the killing of any fetus capable of being born alive.[116]

There is no need here to discuss in detail each state's regulations on abortion. It is sufficient to say that with the exception of South Australia, the various states follow a similar policy. *Rex v. Bourne,* as just noted, is a major part of this policy. *Bourne* was followed by the Victorian case of *R v. Davidson*,[117] a decision followed later in New South Wales.[118] Queensland and Western Australia have incorporated the *Bourne* rule into their criminal codes.[119] Abortions, therefore, are generally unavailable in Australia unless necessary to preserve the life or health of the mother.[120] But as the Australian Medical Association has reported, "[t]he phrase 'preserve the life' has been given a

---

[111] *See* Crimes Act 1958 (Victoria) and Crimes Act 1900, §§ 82 & 83 (New South Wales).

[112] *See* Criminal Code Act 1899 (63 Vic. No. 9) (Queensland); Criminal Code Act 1924 (14 Geo. V No. 69) (Tasmania); and Criminal Code Act 1913 (Western Australia).

[113] *See, e.g.,* Criminal Law Consolidation Act 1935–66, amended by Crim. Law Consolid. Act Amend. Act 1969, § 82a (South Australia). For an overview of the legal status of abortion in Australia, *see* S. Siedlecky, *Australia* in *International Handbook, supra* note 1, at 22–33.

[114] *Supra* note 74.

[115] [1939] 1 K.B. 687.

[116] *See, e.g.,* Crimes Act 1958 (Vic.), § 10.

[117] [1969] VR 667. Judge Menhennit declared that "to establish that the use of an instrument with intent to procure a miscarriage was unlawful, the Crown must establish either (a) that the accused did not honestly believe on reasonable grounds that the act done by him was necessary to preserve the woman from a serious danger to her life or her physical or mental health (not being merely the normal dangers of pregnancy and childbirth) which the continuance of the pregnancy would entail; or (b) that the accused did not honestly believe on reasonable grounds that the act done by him was in the circumstances proportionate to the need to preserve the woman from a serious danger to her life or her physical or mental health (not being merely the normal dangers of pregnancy and childbirth) which the continuance of the pregnancy would entail." *Id.* at 672. More recently, a Queensland court handed down the same instruction. *See* K v. T [1983] 1 Qd. R. 396.

[118] R. v. Wald [1971] 3 D.C.R. (N.S.W.) 25.

[119] *See* Criminal Code (Qld.), § 282 and Criminal Code (W.A.), § 259.

[120] Tasmania has relaxed the *Bourne* rule to the extent that an abortion may be performed in the absence of a threat to the mother's life. An abortion need merely be "reasonable, having regard to all [of the patient's] circumstances. *See* Criminal Code (Tas.), § 51 (1).

wide meaning, where serious risk to mental or physical health is indicated on medical grounds."[121]

South Australia, on the other hand, has a much more liberal abortion law, one that closely tracks section 1 of England's Abortion Act of 1967. As amended in 1969, the law expands the definition of health to include all the circumstances surrounding a woman's condition. It also expands the discretion of medical practitioners: If physicians are reasonably certain that the risk to the woman, in the light of the surrounding circumstances, would be greater if she carried her pregnancy to term they may perform the abortion in the early stages of pregnancy.[122] For all practical purposes, abortion is lawful in South Australia for socioeconomic reasons. In the Northern Territory it is available virtually on request, for a physician may carry out an abortion within 14 weeks of pregnancy if he believes the abortion is necessary for reasons of health.

Australian state law contains no provisions on committee, spousal or parental authorization or procedural requirements dealing with abortion facilities or payment plans. Some of these issues, however, have been handled in the courts. For example, even though Australian—unlike English—courts have recognized actions for compensation growing out of prenatal injuries,[123] they have refused to recognize the legal standing of potential fathers (married or unmarried) suing to protect their unborn children, even in situations where fathers seek to invoke the criminal code to prevent the woman from having an illegal abortion.[124] By the same token, fathers have been prevented from invoking the unborn child's right to life. In *Attorney-General (Old) (Ex rel Kerr) v. T.*, the Australian High Court held that "a fetus has no right of its own until it is born and has a separate existence from its mother."[125]

Much of the public debate in Australia, as in the United States, has centered on abortion funding. Efforts to restrict the funding of lawful abortions in England, Italy and Germany have failed. These countries fund abortions within their national health insurance programs. In the United States, on the other hand, the federal and many state governments severely limit the funding of abortions. The most notable of these measures is the Hyde Amendment, which bars the use of federal Medicaid funds for abortion except where the life of the mother would be endangered if the fetus were carried to term. Under decisions of the Supreme Court, a woman retains the constitutional right to have an abortion, but government is under no obligation to pay for it.[126] And, in a recent and highly controverted case, the Court upheld regulations denying federal funds to family planning clinics that provide abortion counseling or referrals.[127]

Similar attempts to restrict abortion funding have been made in Australia, possibly in response to the opening in the mid-1970s of abortion clinics in New South Wales,

---

[121] See *Abortion Laws, A Survey of Current World Legislation* 67 (Geneva: World Health Organization, 1971) (sec. source).

[122] See Crim. Law Consolidation Act 1935 (S.A.), § 82a (2).

[123] See, e.g., Watt v. Rama [1972] V.R. 356.

[124] K v. T [1983] 1 Qd. R. 396.

[125] [1983] 46 A.L.R. 275, at 277.

[126] See Beal v. Doe, 432 U.S. 438 (1977) (upholding a state's refusal to fund abortions under a federal medicare program); Harris v. McRae, 448 U.S. 297 (1980) (upholding the Hyde Amendment's cutting off of federal funds); and Webster v. Reproductive Health Services, 492 U.S. 490 (1989) (upholding a ban on the use of public facilities and employees to perform or assist abortions not necessary to save the mother's life).

[127] Rust v. Sullivan, 111 S. Ct. 1759 (1991).

Victoria and Queensland. It is relevant to point out, however, that the Australian parliament has not explicitly approved of abortion funding. Under Medibank, Australia's national health insurance plan, the Australian Medical Association is empowered to list the medical services covered by federal funds. In 1973 it added abortion to the list, allowing funding for patients qualified to receive medical care under the federal program. In addition, the federal government funds a certain percentage of services provided by private medical clinics. Pursuant to a 1977 amendment to the federal health program these private facilities are no longer required to provide abortion services if they so decide.[128]

Later, in 1979, a parliamentary skirmish broke out over a proposal to stop the federal funding of abortion altogether unless performed ''to protect the life of the mother from a physical pathological condition and [provided] that the life could be protected in no other way.''[129] Certain members of parliament sharply objected to the proposal because in their view it cascaded into a debate less over abortion funding than over abortion *per se,* a matter the Australian constitution, as noted earlier, reserves to the states. As one commentator noted: ''Members generally opposed the [measure] either because they favoured abortion on request and saw the withdrawal of funds as inconsistent with that stance, or because they perceived the motion as interfering with the states' rights, or because they considered that it was unfair and discriminatory to deny less well-off women free access to medically safe abortions.''[130] The proposal failed to pass.

Finally, in 1989, in response to the large number of abortions funded by taxpayers,[131] the federal parliament witnessed the introduction of the Abortion Funding Abolition Bill. The bill's sponsor, Mr. Alasdair Webster, citing the U.S. experience under the Hyde Amendment, is reported to have said: ''Evidence from the U.S. is that withdrawal of subsidies will lower significantly the incidence of abortion. If women and their partners have to pay for their own decision, they are most likely to reconsider it.''[132] As of this date, no further action on the bill appears to have been taken in the Australian parliament.

C. New Zealand

New Zealand, unlike Australia, has a unitary system of government. As a consequence, its national parliament has sole authority to legislate for the country. The Statute of Westminster (1947), which granted independence to New Zealand, adheres to the principle of parliamentary supremacy. For this reason, particularly in the absence of a written constitution, the courts may not review the constitutionality of parliamentary acts. In the matter of abortion, therefore, as with other subjects of legislation, New Zealand has a national uniform policy, one that can be described briefly.

New Zealand's first abortion statute, enacted in 1866, substantially reproduced the English Act of 1861, which became part of the consolidated Criminal Code Act 1893.[133]

---

[128] K. A. Petersen, *The Public Funding of Abortion Services: Comparative Developments in the United States and Australia,* 33 Int'l & Comp. L. Q. 172 (1984). This summary of abortion funding in Australia relies heavily on Petersen's article.

[129] *Id.*

[130] *Id.* at 176.

[131] According to an unofficial report, 70,000 abortions were publicly funded in 1989–1990 at a cost of $7.8 million. *See Endeavour Forum,* Newsletter No. 59 (February 1991), p. 1.

[132] *Id.*

[133] Criminal Code Act 1893, §§ 200 and 201.

The code punished as a capital offense the willful act of carrying out an abortion at any stage of pregnancy after implantation unless necessary to preserve the life of the mother. In anticipation of England's Infant Life Preservation Act of 1929, New Zealand also made it a crime for anyone to cause "the death of any child that has not become a human being in such manner that he would have been guilty of murder if the child had become a human being."[134] The 1961 Crimes Act was the next major development on this front,[135] and it contains the heart of New Zealand's indications policy on abortion. Parliament had considered a more liberal measure that a committee of experts in criminal law examined in great detail, but the 1961 version that finally passed retained the form and wording of the 1893 act. Under this version, as just noted, abortions were permitted solely in the interest of maternal mortality. In a rare deviation from English law, New Zealand declined to pass a statute modeled on the Abortion Act of 1967.

England's Abortion Act, however, along with the passage of liberal abortion laws in other commonwealth nations, triggered a vigorous national debate in New Zealand. A Royal Commission of Inquiry looked into the current status of abortion law in the 1970s,[136] paving the way for several amendments to the 1961 Crimes Act. The inquiry was undertaken in large part because of growing uncertainty over the circumstances that would permit a lawful abortion within the meaning of the 1961 Act. Physicians were particularly at risk in determining whether under the act they were "unlawfully administer[ing]" any drug or "unlawfully us[ing]" any instrument intentionally to cause a miscarriage.[137] The risk is great because any violation of the act invites a penalty of up to 14 years imprisonment.[138] However, no person is guilty of any crime under the act "who before or during the birth of any child causes its death by means employed in good faith for the preservation of the life of the mother."[139]

The law's uncertainty was dramatically illustrated by the case of *R v. Woolnough*.[140] The Crown indicted a licensed doctor for terminating the pregnancy of 12 women in violation of the 1961 Act's "unlawful use" provision. In his defense, the doctor—James Woolnough—invoked the "good faith" clause of section 182 (2). Parliament provided no guidance in defining these standards, and the common law of New Zealand was equally unhelpful. So, in *Woolnough*, drawing inspiration from, but going beyond, the English case of *R v. Bourne*,[141] the court of appeals extended the statutory concept of "life" to include a *bona fide* intention to preserve the physical or mental *health* of the mother from serious harm, such harm being other than the normal dangers of pregnancy and child birth. The court sustained the validity of a jury instruction to that effect, over the objection of the solicitor-general that the 1961 act permitted an abortion only to protect a woman's *life*.

In deciding the case, the court also rejected the solicitor-general's argument that the act protected the fetus from the moment of conception. In his opinion, Judge Clif-

---

[134] *Id.* § 212.

[135] Crimes Act 1961, §§ 182–187.

[136] *See Royal Commission Inquiry into Contraception, Sterilisation, and Abortion in New Zealand* (Report 5, March 1977).

[137] *Id.* § 183(1)(a)(b).

[138] *Id.* § 182(1). The penalty applies to persons performing the abortion, not to the woman. Self-induced abortions are punished by a fine. *Id.* § 183(2).

[139] *Id.* § 182(2).

[140] [1977] 2 N.Z.L.R. 508.

[141] [1939] 1 K.B. 687.

ford P. Richmond rehearsed the history of the common law on this point, citing Justice Blackmun's recitation of this history in *Roe v. Wade,* and examined the purpose behind the New Zealand statute itself. That purpose, he found, was two-fold: "to protect the life, or potential for life, of the unborn child," and "to protect the life and health of the mother having regard to the grave dangers which, until comparatively recent times, were attendant upon induced abortions."[142] Since the abortions involved in this case took place in early pregnancy, the court attached priority to the life and health of the mother as reasonably ascertained by the attending physician.

As this case shows, the burden of laying down a modern abortion policy rested with the judiciary, and many judges complained that they were operating in uncharted waters. Critics feared that the courts were sanctioning a *de facto* policy of abortion on demand, while others chafed at the law's strictures. The long-festering problems mirrored in these complaints, along with the hue and cry associated with the opening of a private abortion clinic in 1974, prompted the establishment of the Royal Commission Inquiry into Contraception, Sterilisation, and Abortion. Having received "a large number of submissions from individuals and organizations, including the churches, women's groups, and professional bodies," the commission sought "to place the whole question of abortion within a broader context—the social, medical, and moral implications of fertility regulation—and to synthesize the varying viewpoints on what had become a deeply divisive issue."[143]

The commission's work resulted in several legislative measures, among them the Crimes acts of 1977 and 1978, which set forth three specific grounds for terminating a pregnancy. First, the law now permitted a lawful abortion in the first 20 weeks of pregnancy for medical reasons, that is, if performed to avert a serious danger to the woman's physical or mental health; an abortion is lawful after 20 weeks only if necessary to save the woman's life or to prevent serious permanent injury to her health.[144] Second, it legalized an abortion in the presence of indications that the child would be born seriously handicapped mentally or physically.[145] Third, it sanctioned an abortion caused by incest. Although rape was not included in this indication,[146] it could be considered as a factor in assessing the presence of a medical indication. Finally, the law repealed an earlier provision punishing a woman for attempting a self-induced abortion.[147]

The most significant legislation to emerge from the commission's report was the Contraception, Sterilisation, and Abortion Act of 1977. Its long title defines its purpose, which is "to provide for the circumstances and procedures under which abortions may be authorised after having full regard for the rights of the unborn child." A statute composed of 46 sections, it gives to New Zealand a set of procedural requirements more complex and detailed than the regulations of the other five nations discussed in this chapter. The medical profession strongly objected to certain features of its regulatory scheme, even to the point of threatening not to cooperate.[148] But as the court of appeals

---

[142] *Supra* note 140, at 517.

[143] *See* J. Sceats, *New Zealand* in *International Handbook, supra* note 1, at 349.

[144] Crimes Act 1977, § 187 A.

[145] Crimes Amendment Act 1978, § 2 (aa).

[146] *Supra* note 144.

[147] *Id.* § 5.

[148] This threat appears to have been implied in the parliamentary discussion of the bill. See 417 N.Z. Parl. Deb. (4th sess., 38th parl.) 517 (1978).

noted in 1982, "The Act itself reflects the very careful attempt made by Parliament to balance the deep philosophical and moral and social attitudes which surround this whole subject-matter."[149]

The Contraception, Sterilisation, and Abortion Act contains three sets of regulations. The first establishes an abortion supervisory committee charged with a wide variety of functions relating to the supervision of the new law.[150] The second set of regulations deal with the licensing of hospitals and clinics where abortions are to be performed.[151] Abortions are illegal if performed in an unlicensed institution. The third set, finally, lays down the procedures for certifying consultants and counselors as well as the guidelines they are legally obliged to follow.[152] After initial complaints that these regulations were unworkable, parliament passed additional amendments that physicians found more acceptable and other groups more tolerable.[153] For the most part, however, the detailed regulatory scheme remained firmly in place.

Two important cases have been reported under the statute: The first, *Re Brasted*,[154] challenged the abortion supervisory committee's refusal to license a private hospital for the performance of abortions, mainly on the ground of its "strong reservation about the ability of the medical staff employed at the hospital to correctly interpret the law and to carry it into effect in accordance with the tenor of the Act."[155] The supreme court held that the supervisory committee's discretion under the statute did not extend to the denial of a license to a hospital merely because of the personal views of its medical practitioners on the subject of abortion. The court also determined that if a woman meets the citeria for an abortion, she may have the operation performed in a licensed private facility as well as in a licensed public hospital.[156]

In *Wall v. Livingston*, the court of appeals made clear that the supervisory committee "is given no control or authority in respect of the individual decisions of consultants."[157] *Wall* involved a pediatrician who alleged bad faith on the part of two professional colleagues who authorized an abortion. Apart from the Court's statement separating the functions of the supervisory committee from the counseling procedure, the case held that the pediatrician had no standing to challenge the legality of the abortion since he was not one of the statutory participants in the procedure prescribed by the act.

The physician's invocation of the unborn child's right also failed. Although noting that the statute explicitly bars abortion on request and rejects the notion that the abortion decision is entirely a matter for the woman and her doctor to decide, the court declared that the act spells out no legal statutory right for the unborn child.[158] The court noted further that the statutory scheme would prove unworkable if outside parties were able to interfere in the abortion screening process in the absence of clear èvidence of bad faith. The act, said the Court, "provides an elaborate screening mechanism dependent

---

[149] Wall v. Livingston [1982] 1 N.Z.L.R. 734 at 737.
[150] Contraception, Sterilisation, and Abortion Act of 1977, §§ 10–17.
[151] *Id.* §§ 18–28.
[152] *Id.* §§ 29–36.
[153] *See International Handbook, supra* note 1, at 349–350.
[154] [1979] 1 N.Z.L.R. 400.
[155] *Id.* at 403.
[156] *Id.* at 407–408.
[157] *Supra* note 149, at 739.
[158] *Id.* at 740.

almost entirely on medical judgment [and] [i]t explicitly defines and prescribes the functions of those who have rights and responsibilities under the statutory scheme."[159]

IV. Concluding Remarks

As this survey shows, all six nations under study have liberalized their abortion laws since the mid-1960s. With the passage of its 1967 Abortion Act, England anticipated many of the changes that were to occur in other commonwealth countries and in western Europe within the next decade. *Roe v. Wade,* decided by the United States Supreme Court in 1973, may very well have accelerated this process of change. Most of the changes discussed in this article took place between 1975 and 1980. In the 1980s, each of the six countries witnessed pressures to amend their laws, either in a more liberal or a more restrictive direction. Very few of these efforts succeeded, but they are being renewed in the 1990s as pro-life and pro-choice forces regroup and recharge their arsenals.

The most significant change is likely to occur in Germany as a consequence of that country's reunification. But there is another reason, and it partly explains the intense controversy surrounding abortion in Germany. Germany's abortion policy sprang full-blown from the hands of the Federal Constitutional Court, just as American abortion policy erupted, and just as suddenly, out of the landmark case of *Roe v. Wade.* These judicial mandates, initiated pursuant to constitutional challenges to existing laws on abortion, did not allow for the kind of legislative compromises that marked the process of abortion reform in England, Australia and New Zealand, where change emerged incrementally over time. Constitutional decisions were also handed down in France and Italy, but these decisions sustained laws derived from long-negotiated legislative settlements preceded by royal commission inquiries. In the United States and Germany, by contrast, the courts seized the initiative from the legislature, in one case (United States) by striking down restrictive abortion laws and in the other (Germany) by nullifying a liberal abortion statute.

The future, however, is not of immediate concern here; nor are the empirical results of these abortion reform laws. The present reality shows that in all six countries the legality of abortion turns on whether the operation is performed by a licensed medical practitioner. All of the laws and policies under study appear to have been motivated primarily by the public's concern for the health and welfare of pregnant women. Except for the case of Germany, the preservation of the fetus turns out to have been a strong but clearly secondary motivation. In sharp contrast to United States policy, however— at least as represented by *Roe v. Wade*—this concern for the life of the unborn child takes on critical importance in the second trimester of pregnancy. Under *Roe,* the state develops a compelling interest in preserving potential life only in the last trimester.

On the basis of this study one notices a tendency in the civil law jurisdictions to adopt a time-phase rather than an indications solution to the abortion controversy. Again, of course, the exception is Germany, but it was the statutory 12-week time-phase rule that the constitutional court struck down. East Germany currently follows the same time-phase rule, a rule apparently preferred, given the nature of the political representation

---

[159] *Id.*

in the all-German parliament, by a majority of Germans but for the decision of the Federal Constitutional Court.

The common law jurisdictions, on the other hand, have preferred an indications solution. Legal indications for granting an abortion in New Zealand and Australia are, for the most part, medical and eugenic, although the medical indication includes both physical and mental health. In Victoria and New South Wales, however, a eugenic (i.e., fetal) or a juridical (i.e., rape or incest) indication may be interpreted as a risk to the woman's health. In South Australia and the Northern Territory, as in England, socio-economic indications have been added to the list. It needs to be recalled that with respect to each of these indications, a legal abortion can only be carried out in the early stages of pregnancy, after consultation and with proper certification. For physical and mental indications, the period within which an abortion can take place may run as high as 23 weeks of pregnancy, a limitation that does not apply if a pregnancy threatens the life of the mother.

Even where abortions are granted under the time-phase rule, as in France and Italy, counseling, certification and reflective waiting periods are required. France and Italy require a seven-day waiting period and Germany a three-day waiting period when an abortion is granted for juridical reasons or reasons of serious social hardship. In France, the abortion must take place within 10 weeks of pregnancy and in Italy within the first trimester. In Germany, it must take place within the first 12 weeks for juridical and social reasons. These regulations, incidentally, would not be permitted under the trimester rationale of *Roe v. Wade*. They would be clearly unconstitutional.

Roe v. Wade stressed that the state permissibly develops an interest in preserving the life of the fetus in the third trimester. None of the six nations under study accepts this broad, libertarian view. Two of the civil law countries—France and Italy—virtually grant abortions on request early in pregnancy, as the table in the appendix indicates; nevertheless, their laws reflect the view that the state has a legitimate interest in protecting the fetus *ab initio*. France's statute makes this explicit, and the 1974 German abortion case makes the protection of the fetus after the point of implantation a state duty. France and Italy opted for the time-phase rule in part *because* they felt that this solution, when combined with comprehensive counseling and waiting periods, was the most effective means of safeguarding the interests of *both* the unborn child and its mother, thereby resolving, however inadequately, the difficult social problem created by the illegal abortion trade. It is to be noted, too, that each of these civil law regimes, along with New Zealand and Australia, have sought either to limit or to ban commercialized abortion, another major departure from United States policy.

Still another noticeable difference between the abortion policies of the civil and common law countries is the tendency of the latter, including the United States, wholly to "medicalize" the abortion process. Here the courts have deferred to the expertise of medical practitioners and the ethos of professionalism that they exude. England's 1967 Abortion Act is the paradigmatic example of a law the effect of which is to insulate abortion decision-making from public scrutiny. The Abortion Act amounts to a strenuous defense of medical autonomy. This autonomy has been more circumscribed in Australia and New Zealand, but there judicial decisions have read broad discretionary medical authority into the "good faith" judgments physicians are legally obliged to make under the relevant statutes. This near reverential attitude toward medical practitioners is relatively absent from the policies of our civil law jurisdictions. The German abortion case, in sharp contrast to this policy as well as *Roe v. Wade,* went so far as to question the competence of medical practitioners to counsel women on anything other than the medical aspects of abortion. The constitutional court recommended that moral, social and general familial advice be rendered by counselors trained in these fields.

It is clear from this overview that our civil law countries perceive law's role with respect to the issue of abortion quite differently than does the United States. *Roe v. Wade* stands for the proposition that abortion is a liberty protected by the fundamental right of privacy, that freedom of choice in this domain is the paramount value to be defended and that the proper stance of the state—or law—is one of neutrality between competing moral positions or traditions.

The civil law jurisdictions, by contrast, do not speak of abortion as a right. It is rather a matter of social policy in which the state has a vital interest throughout the duration of pregnancy. Their laws reflect the view that law should play a role in affording moral guidance on the issue of abortion. French law, for example, declares that "law guarantees the respect of every human being from the commencement of life" and that "[t]here shall be no derogation from this principle except in cases of necessity and under conditions laid down by law." Here, as in Germany, law postulates an ideal of human behavior just as it tolerates in practice a lesser standard in order to avoid the social evil of back-alley abortions.

A short postscript may be warranted in the light of *Planned Parenthood of Southeastern Pennsylvania v. Casey,*[160] the Pennsylvania abortion case currently pending before the U.S. Supreme Court. *Casey* is being touted as a watershed case because it may signal a major retreat from the abortion liberty vindicated in *Roe v. Wade* and its progeny. When seen in comparative perspective, however, the statutory provisions under attack in *Casey* would cause little anxiety in the six nations whose abortion policies we have examined. Pennsylvania's informed consent and parental consent requirements, together with its compulsory 24-hour waiting period, would easily survive a constitutional challenge in France, Germany and Italy. Even in France, where abortions can be procured virtually on demand during the first 10 weeks of pregnancy, extensive counseling and a seven-day waiting period have been imposed. Consultation is also required, by definition, in those common law jurisdictions where abortion is permitted only in the presence of legally specified indications. Even in England, whose laws have been administered with indulgent permissiveness, two doctors other than the woman's personal physician must certify that relevant indications are present before an abortion can be authorized. Needless to say, all of the above regulations are in conflict with *Roe v. Wade.*

Pennsylvania's spousal notification requirement raises a more difficult issue. None of the countries under study requires women to notify their husbands before obtaining an abortion, although such a law, if adopted, would probably survive constitutional analysis in Germany in light of the state's duty under the Basic Law to extend its "special protection" to "marriage and the family." In England, on the other hand, as in the United States, courts have ruled that a husband has no right to be consulted with respect to the abortion decision of his wife. On the other hand, a simple notification statute, which in and of itself does not imply consultation, would probably pass muster

---

[160]947 F.2d 682 (3d Cir. 1991), *cert. granted,* 60 U.S.L.W. 3498 (1992).

Grounds for Abortion

| | Medical | | | | | |
	Narrow (life)	Broad (health)	Eugenic (fetal)	Juridical	Social	On request
Germany	—	x	x	x	x[a]	—
France	—	—	—	—	—	x[b]
Italy	—	—	—	—	—	x[c]
England	—	x	x	—	x[d]	—
Australia	—	x	x[c]	—	x[e]	—
New Zealand	—	x	x	—	—	—
United States	—	—	—	—	—	x[d]

Source: Drawn from Christopher Tietze and Stanley K. Henshaw, *Induced Abortion: A World Review 1986* 12–14 (6th ed.).

[a] 1st 3 months or 12 weeks from implantation

[b] first 10 weeks

[c] 1st 3 months

[d] prior to viability of fetus

[e] Northern Territory and South Australia
 • by legislation in South Australia
 • by judicial decision in Northern Territory and Victoria

in both France and Italy so long as it would not permit the spouse to veto his wife's decision.

Finally, Pennsylvania's reporting requirements are not dissimilar to those of other constitutional democracies. In this connection, it is relevant to point out that in most of the countries examined in this chapter, commercial advertising of abortion services is banned by law. The ban stems from a pervading belief, explicitly made clear in the laws of France, Italy and Germany, that abortion is not a choice to be equated with childbirth. Indeed, French law, despite its time-phase solution to the abortion problem, specifically declares that abortion is not a means of birth control. On the other hand, all of the countries under study, including Germany and France, allow abortions to be paid for under their national health insurance plans. Partly for this reason, as in England, abortions must be performed in hospitals or other state-approved health facilities, in which case, given the law's attempt to ban commercialized abortion facilities, public health departments may—and do—require confidential reports on each abortion performed.

This survey would appear to confirm Mary Ann Glendon's finding that the United States stands alone in the extent to which it has protected a woman's right to abort her fetus.[161] Most other nations have been able to adopt liberal abortion policies without going as far as the United States in rejecting values that conflict with a woman's freedom of choice. Of course, this does not mean that solutions or compromises reached in other liberal democracies with different constitutions, legal traditions and social policies can or should be adopted in the United States. Still, the experiences of these other democracies show that it is possible to sustain the constitutional validity of Pennsylvan-

---

[161] *Abortion and Divorce in Western Law* (1987).

ia's regulations and at the same time insure that the essential liberty secured by *Roe v. Wade* remains intact.

In Bonn, Germany, June 26, 1992, Germany gave women the right to choose abortion. After a fourteen-hour debate, the Bundestag (lower house of parliament) voted 357 to 284 to let a woman decide on an abortion in the first twelve weeks of pregnancy after submitting to a *non-binding* medical counseling session.

Upon reviewing the history of the abortion law in Canada, one is first struck by the similarities between the Canadian law and the U.S. law. Issues like right to privacy, fetal rights and compelling state interests are constantly interwoven through the Canadian law. There are, of course, important differences. The landmark *Morgentaler* case resulted from one of the longest and most successful campaigns of civil disobedience in Canadian history. In contradistinction to *Roe v. Wade*'s Roe, which was the fictitious name of the pregnant mother, Morgentaler was the name of a physician who actively sought to change the Canadian laws. One is also galvanized by the singularly powerful language of Justice Wilson of the Supreme Court of Canada where she states in the *Morgentaler* case, "This decision is one that will have profound psychological, economic and social consequences for the pregnant woman. The circumstances giving rise to it can be complex and varied and there may be, and usually are, powerful considerations militating in opposite directions. It is a decision that deeply reflects the way the woman thinks about herself and her relationship to others and to society at large. It is not just a medical decision: it is a profound social and ethical one as well. Her response to it will be the response of the whole person. It is probably impossible for a man to respond, even imaginatively, to such a dilemma, not just because it is outside the realm of his personal experience (although this is, of course, the case) but because he can relate to it only by objectifying it, thereby eliminating the subjective elements of the female psyche which are at the heart of the dilemma."

With this article Professor McLellan presents the interesting law and history of abortion in Canada.

12 · Abortion Law in Canada ⎯⎯⎯

A. Anne McLellan, LL.B., LL.M.

Introduction

In Canada, the legal context in which the issue of abortion is discussed has been fundamentally transformed since the adoption of the Charter of Rights and Freedoms.[1] Once considered to have a fairly restrictive abortion law, Canada currently has no law prohibiting a woman's right to an abortion.[2] The Supreme Court of Canada's decision declaring invalid section 251 of the Criminal Code of Canada,[3] which contained the prohibition against abortion, has created a significant change in the legal and political climate in which the contentious issue of abortion will be debated.

This chapter will briefly outline the history of the regulation of abortion in Canada before 1968, when significant changes were made to the Criminal Code prohibitions. Next will come an analysis of section 251 of the Criminal Code, followed by a discussion of the *Morgentaler* cases, including the 1988 case[4] in which the Supreme Court of Canada found that section 251 of the Criminal Code was unconstitutional. The decisions of the various members of the Supreme Court of Canada will be analyzed, their judgments reflecting deep divisions in relation to both the appropriate role for the Court in interpreting the *Charter* and in determining the extent of constitutional guarantees, if any, for a woman seeking an abortion.

---

[1] Enacted as schedule B of the *Canada Act 1982*, (U.K.) 1982, c.11.

[2] Some provinces have tried to place limitations upon a woman's right to an abortion, exercising their constitutional jurisdiction over health and hospitals. *See infra* ''The Aftermath of Morgentaler.''

[3] *See* Appendix I for the complete text of § 251.

[4] [1988] 1 S.C.R. 30.

Finally, the legal and political events in the post-*Morgentaler* period will be considered. This period has witnessed a marked increase in political activity for both anti- and pro-choice advocates; proposed new legislation from the federal government to recriminalize abortion[5], and attempts by provincial governments to regulate certain aspects of abortion through their constitutional jurisdiction over health care and hospitals. Although not discussed in the text, a noteworthy major report by the Law Reform Comission of Canada, *Crimes Against the Foetus*,[6] has been produced in the post-*Morgentaler* period also.

The History of Abortion in Canada Before 1968

The *Constitution Act, 1867,* gives the federal Parliament the exclusive jurisdiction over both criminal law and procedure.[7] It was by virtue of this power that Parliament enacted a criminal law in 1869, which prohibited abortion and punished it with a penalty of life imprisonment.[8] This law mirrored the laws of a number of provinces in pre-Confederation Canada, all of which were more or less modeled on Lord Ellenborough's Act.[9] Lord Ellenborough's Act criminalized abortion, whether procured before quickening or not, but continued to treat the fact of quickening as relevant in relation to the issue of penalty.[10] Those who procured abortions after quickening were subject to the penalty of death, and those who procured an abortion before quickening faced a lesser sentence. The basic structure of this legislation was adopted by the pre-Confederation provinces of Canada.[11] In the 1840s both Upper Canada[12] and New Brunswick[13] enacted legislation that abolished this distinction based upon quickening. Also, during this time, anti-abortion legislation was amended to make it clear that the prohibition against the procurement of an abortion applied to the pregnant woman herself.[14]

In 1892 the Canadian Parliament enacted the first Criminal Code,[15] which reflected the approach of earlier 19th century legislative attempts to criminalize abortion. Section

---

[5] Bill C-43, An Act Respecting Abortion, defeated in the Senate January 31, 1991. (*See* Appendix II for the text.)

[6] Working Paper 58, Law Reform Commission of Canada, 1989. The report recommended the creation of a general crime of causing fetal harm or destruction. However, acts done to save the mother's life, to protect the mother against serious physical injury and to protect the mother's physical and psychological health (if done before the twenty-second week of pregnancy) would not be caught by the prohibition. The report engendered fierce criticism and now appears to be largely forgotten.

[7] § 91(27).

[8] Offences Against the Person Act, 1869, 32–33 Vict., c.-20, § 60.

[9] 1803, 43 Geo. III, c.58. The act placed the offence of criminal abortion on a statutory basis for the first time. For a thorough history of English abortion laws, *see* B.M. Dickens *Abortion and the Law* (1966).

[10] Quickening has been defined as when a woman could feel the fetus move in her womb. Different times have been suggested as to when quickening occurs, but 14 weeks after conception is often suggested. Under common law, procuring an abortion before quickening was not a criminal offence.

[11] For an excellent history of the development of Canadian abortion laws in the 19th century, see Backhouse, *Involuntary Motherhood: Abortion, Birth Control and the Law in Nineteenth Century Canada* 3 Windsor Y.B. of Access to Just. 61 (1983).

[12] An Act for Consolidating . . . Offences Against the Person, 1841 (Upper Canada) 4&5 Vict., c.27, § 13.

[13] An Act Further to Amend the Law Relating to Offences Against the Person, 1842 (N.B.) 5 Vict., c.33, § 2.

[14] For example, New Brunswick passed such a law in 1849 and Nova Scotia did so in 1851.

[15] 1892, 55 Vict. c.29, §§ 272–274 (Can.).

273 made it possible to charge a woman with procuring her own abortion, whether or not pregnant. The Code also included section 179 dealing with obscenity, one of the provisions of which provided that everyone who "offers to sell, advertises, or publishes an advertisement of or has for sale or disposal, any medicine, drug or article intended or represented as a means of preventing contraception or causing abortion" was guilty of an indictable offence and liable to imprisonment for two years.[16] This was the first statutory prohibition against the sale, distribution and advertisement of contraceptives as well as abortifacients. It appears that this section was modeled upon the Comstock Act in the United States,[17] and it has been suggested that the net effect of the prohibitions in sections 273 and 179(c) was "to cover all aspects of fertility control—even the efforts of individual women who were unaided and not pregnant".[18]

The prohibition in section 273 of the Code continued in force until 1954 when an amendment made it plain that only a woman who was in fact pregnant could be found guilty of the crime of procuring her own miscarriage.[19] Another change in the legislation, seemingly a small one, was the removal of the word "unlawfully" from section 272(1), thereby calling into question the assumption of both the medical and legal professions that the defense of necessity was available in Canada to a physician accused of procuring an abortion.[20]

S.272:

> Every one is guilty of an indictable offence and liable to imprisonment for life who, with intent to procure the miscarriage of any woman, whether she is or is not with child, unlawfully administers to her or causes to be taken by her any drug or other noxious thing, or unlawfully uses any instrument or other means whatsoever with the like intent.

S.273:

> Every woman is guilty of an indictable offence and liable to seven years' imprisonment who, whether with child or not, unlawfully administers to herself or permits to be administered to her any drug or other noxious thing, or unlawfully uses on herself or permits to be used on her any instrument or other means whatsoever with intent to procure miscarriage.

S.274

> Every one is guilty of an indictable offence and liable to two years imprisonment who unlawfully supplies or procures any drug or other noxious thing, or any instrument or thing whatsoever, knowing that the same is intended to be unlawfully used or employed with intent to procure the miscarriage of any woman, whether she is or is not with child.

[16] Gavigan, *"On Bringing on the Menses": The Criminal Liability of Women and the Therapeutic Exception in Canadian Abortion Law*, 1 C.J.W.L. 279 at 296 (1986). It was only in 1969 that the Criminal Code was amended, making it legal to sell and advertise contraceptives.

[17] Backhouse, *supra* note 11, at 119–120.

[18] Gavigan, *supra* note 16, at 296. See generally A. McLaren & A.T. McLaren, *The Bedroom and the State* (1986) for a detailed discussion on birth control and abortion in Canada between 1880 and 1980.

[19] R.S.C. 1953–54, c.51. The amended section became 237(2).

[20] The amended section became 237(1) and read:

> (1) Every one who, with intent to procure the miscarriage of a female person, whether or not she is pregnant, uses any means for the purpose of carrying out his intention is guilty

The 1968 Amendments to the Criminal Code

There were no further changes in Canada's abortion law until 1968 when the Liberal government of Pierre Trudeau introduced significant amendments to the existing law.[21] The amendments created a therapeutic exception to the criminal prohibitions against doctors and women who procured abortions. The new law, in essence, legalized the procurement of an abortion in those circumstances in which a physician believed the life or health of a woman to be endangered. The legislation put in place a mechanism by which therapeutic abortion committees could be created in accredited or approved hospitals. Upon certification by such a committee, an abortion could be performed lawfully if, in the committee's opinion, the continuation of the pregnancy endangered the life or health of the woman.

Although the legislative reforms of 1968 were viewed by some as a liberalization of the existing criminal law,[22] practical problems immediately arose in relation to its implementation. It was believed that the new law created an unacceptable level of vagueness and uncertainty concerning the circumstances in which the therapeutic exception would be available. It must be remembered that the exception was only available when, in the opinion of a therapeutic abortion committee, the continuation of a pregnancy would, or would likely, endanger a woman's life or health. There was no definition of health contained in the legislation. Some had suggested that the definition of health should be that accepted by the World Health Organization, which defined the term as "a state of complete physical, mental, and social well being and not merely an absence of disease or infirmity".[23] Others suggested that, in spite of the wording of

---

of an indictable offence and is liable to imprisonment for life.

See Parker, *Bill C-150: Abortion Reform (1968–69)* 11 Crim. L.Q. 267 for a discussion of the possible implications of the removal of the word "unlawfully." The English case of *R v. Bourne*, [1939] 1 K.B. 687 appears to be the first case to consider the defense of necessity in the context of abortion. The prohibition against abortion, both under common law and by statute, was held to be subject to a common law defense based upon the necessity of saving the mother's life.

[21] *See* Appendix I for the text. Criminal Law Amendment Act S.C. 1968–69, c.38, § 18.

The abortion amendments were part of an omnibus criminal law reform package that included the legalization of homosexuality between consenting adults in private. It should be remembered that Trudeau, as minister of justice, had made the now-famous, if inaccurate, comment that "the state has no place in the bedrooms of the nation."

[22] This view was not shared by everyone. For example, then-Minister of Justice John Turner suggested in the House of Commons that the substance of the proposed amendments did no more than recognize what had actually been happening in a number of hospitals. House of Commons Debates, (1969) 28th Parl., 1st Sess. at 8058.

The Canadian Medical Association (C.M.A.) and the Canadian Bar Association (C.B.A.) were both instrumental in convincing the government to reform its abortion law. Both groups believed that the existing law put doctors in an untenable position, since it was not clear as to doctors' possible criminal liability when they performed abortions, believing in their medical opinion, that the life or health of a woman was endangered by the continuation of the pregnancy. All such abortions possibly were illegal under the existing law.

[23] Taken from the judgment of A.C.J. Parker in R. v. Morgentaler, Smoling and Scott (1984), 47 O.R. (2d) 353 at 377. In the House of Commons, the debate regarding the definition of the "health" had consumed considerable time and energy. Minister of Justice John Turner had offered the following comments in support of the government's decision not to include a definition of "health":

This is a question that is left to medical judgment. Certainly it has to be taken in a global sense. You cannot isolate physical from mental health; they interact and react each upon

section 251(4)(c) that referred to the endangerment of life or *health,* an abortion should only be performed where there was proof that the continuation of the pregnancy would endanger the life of the woman. It became clear that the definition of health could, and did, vary from province to province and between individual therapeutic abortion committees.[24]

Further, the therapeutic exception depended upon the establishment of abortion committees in accredited or approved hospitals.[25] No provision was made for the performance of therapeutic abortions in free-standing abortion clinics. The definition of accredited and approved hospitals was found in section 251(6) of the Criminal Code, and the effect thereof was to limit the number of hospitals in a position to create such committees.[26] It has been estimated that two out of five Canadians did not live in communities served by hospitals eligible to establish therapeutic abortion committees. Neither was there any requirement in the Criminal Code that approved or accredited hospitals establish committees, and therefore a significant number of hospital boards chose not to do so.[27]

---

the other. In that sense health is incapable of definition, and this will be left to the good professional judgment of medical practitioners to decide.

House of Commons Debates, (1969) 28th Parl., 1st Sess. at 8124.

[24] *See generally* on the differing and arbitrary definitions of health: Canada, *Report of the Committee on the Operation of the Abortion Law* (1977) (Badgley Report) [hereinafter Badgley Report]; *Report on Therapeutic Abortion Services in Ontario, A Study Commissioned by the Ministry of Health* (Toronto, 1987) (the Powell Report); and Smith & Wineberg, *A Survey of Therapeutic Abortion Committees (1968–70),* 12 Crim. L.Q. 279.

[25] Several conditions had to be complied with under § 251 before an abortion could be lawfully performed. They were:

1. The procedure must be done by a qualified medical practitioner, i.e., a person qualified to engage in the practice of medicine under the laws of the province.
2. The qualified medical practitioner must be a physician other than a member of a hospital's therapeutic abortion committee.
3. The abortion must be approved by a therapeutic abortion committee.
4. The therapeutic abortion committee for any hospital means a committee appointed by the board of that hospital for the purpose of considering and determining questions relating to the termination of pregnancy within that hospital.
5. The therapeutic abortion committee must be composed of not less than three members, each of whom is a qualified medical practitioner appointed by the board of that hospital.
6. The procedure must be done in an "accredited hospital" means a hospital accredited by the Canadian Council on Hospital Accreditation in which diagnostic services and medical, surgical and obstetrical treatment is provided. An approved hospital means a hospital in a province approved for the purposes of this section by the minister of health of that province.
7. Provincial statutes are operative as "nothing in subsection (4) shall be construed as making unnecessary the obtaining of any authorization or consent that is or may be required, otherwise than under this Act, before any means are used for the purpose of carrying out an intention to procure the miscarriage of a female person."

Badgley Report, *supra* note 24 at 85–86.

[26] Of a total of 1,348 civilian hospitals in Canada in 1976, 789, or 58.5%, were ineligible to establish committees. Badgley Report, *supra* note 24, at 105.

[27] In 1976, of the 559 general hospitals that met the conditions required for the establishment of a committee, 288, or 51.5%, did not have committees. *Id.*

The effect of the Criminal Code amendments was to require the involvement of a minimum of four doctors before a therapeutic abortion could be performed. The four doctors were the woman's physician and the three members of the therapeutic abortion committee, a majority of whom had to certify that the continuation of a woman's pregnancy would, or would be likely, to endanger her life or health. Of the 1,348 civilian hospitals in operation in Canada in 1976, at least 331, or 24%, of these hospitals had less than four physicians on their medical staffs.[28] Also, since the Code offered no guidance to hospital boards or committees as to whether the consent of a husband or father of the fetus was required or, in the case of an unmarried minor, the consent of a parent or guardian, considerable variation existed in practice between provinces and hospitals within provinces.[29]

The problems in relation to the availability, accessibility and terms on which therapeutic abortions could be procured were due almost entirely to the lack of legislative guidance from the federal Parliament. Parliament may have wished to leave such "details" to provincial legislative regulation, in a misguided attempt to respect provincial legislative jurisdiction over health care and the regulation of hospitals. The practical result for women seeking therapeutic abortions was uncertainty as to the availability of the procedure and the terms upon which an abortion would be performed. Not surprisingly, reports indicated that relatively well-off women, with a reasonably high level of education, living in urban centers, were those most likely to successfully procure therapeutic abortions.

The *Morgentaler* Cases

If there is one name, more than any other, that Canadians have associated with the issue of abortion over the past 20 years, it is that of Dr. Henry Morgentaler.[30] Dr. Morgentaler's importance to the issue of abortion in Canada operates on at least two levels—the first being strictly legal and the second, political. Dr. Morgentaler has been a ceaseless advocate for a woman's right to choose whether to terminate a pregnancy and lobbied unsuccessfully in 1967, as president of the Montréal Humanist Association, to have Parliament repeal its existing abortion law. Dr. Morgentaler established a free-standing abortion clinic in Montréal as early as 1968 to provide abortions to those women who requested them. Those abortions were in violation of existing Canadian criminal law. Dr. Morgentaler's political activities on behalf of women and their "right to choose" has continued for some 20 years. Viewed as a martyr by some and as a murderous villain by others, Dr. Morgentaler has kept the issue of abortion and a woman's right thereto at the forefront of the Canadian political and legal agenda.

Dr. Morgentaler's importance to the issue of abortion in Canada extends well beyond the political realm. He has been prosecuted four times for allegedly violating section 251 of the Criminal Code. He was charged first, in 1970, by the Attorney General of Québec.[31] Since that time, Dr. Morgentaler has been acquitted by four juries,

---

[28] Badgley Report, *supra* note 24 at 30.

[29] *Id.* at 32.

[30] Dr. Morgentaler emigrated to Canada in 1950, after surviving Auschwitz and Dachau. For a thorough, if uncritical, history of Dr. Morgentaler's life up to 1975, see E.W. Perline, *Morgentaler* (1975).

[31] For a detailed account of the numerous legal proceedings in which Dr. Morgentaler was involved from 1970 to 1976, see Dickens, *The Morgentaler Case: Criminal Process and Abortion Law* 14 Osgoode H.L.J. 229 (1976).

three in Québec and one in Ontario, and has proceeded with two appeals to the Supreme Court of Canada—the first of which he lost when the court rejected both his constitutional and criminal law arguments and upheld his conviction[32] and the second of which he won, when the Supreme Court of Canada declared section 251 of the Criminal Code unconstitutional, as being in violation of section 7 of the Charter of Rights and Freedoms.[33] However, to simply state these conclusions is to ignore the uniqueness and complexity of the litigation in which both the state and Dr. Morgentaler have been involved.

Dr. Morgentaler has waged one of the longest and most successful campaigns of civil disobedience in Canadian history.[34] As a humanist, Dr. Morgentaler has been deeply committed to the concepts of personal autonomy and equality and has consistently argued these beliefs in relation to a woman's right to choose whether to terminate a pregnancy.[35] To some extent, Dr. Morgentaler's subsequent treatment by the legal system was due to his openly defiant violation of Canada's existing criminal laws.[36] At no time did Dr. Morgentaler deny performing abortions in apparent violation of section 251 of the Criminal Code. He ignored the law because he believed it to be morally indefensible.[37] Since Dr. Morgentaler made no secret of his willingness to perform abortions in his private clinic in Montréal, the Attorney General of Québec soon concluded that he had no choice but to prosecute him.

Morgentaler (1975)

Dr. Morgentaler's clinic in Montréal was first raided in June 1970, and he was originally charged on a number of counts of conspiracy to commit abortion and procuring an abortion under section 251(1) of the Criminal Code. After numerous pretrial motions on the part of Dr. Morgentaler, the Attorney General preferred an indictment in relation to one count of unlawfully procuring the miscarriage of a female person.[38] Dr. Morgentaler was acquitted at trial in November 1973 but on appeal the Québec

---

[32] [1976] 1 S.C.R. 616. For convenience, I will refer to this decision throughout the chapter as *Morgentaler* (1975).

[33] *Supra* note 4. I will refer to this decision throughout the chapter as *Morgentaler* (1988).

[34] On Morgentaler and civil disobedience, see Wardhaugh, *Socratic Civil Disobedience: Some Reflections on Morgentaler* 2 Can. J. Law & Jurisprudence 91 (1989).

[35] These views informed the submission made by Dr. Morgentaler on behalf of the Humanist Fellowship of Montréal to the Parliamentary Committee on Health and Welfare in October 1967 when the committee was considering proposed reforms to Canada's abortion law. The brief affirmed the inherent dignity of the individual and suggested that "this ideal should be reflected in the laws governing our society which should provide equal justice and benefits to all, rich or poor, informed or uninformed, believer or non-believer, and be continually updated in accordance with new conditions and new knowledge." (Standing Committee on Health and Welfare, *Minutes of Proceedings and Evidence,* 1967/68).

[36] Perhaps most galling to Dr. Morgentaler's opponents was a nationwide television broadcast on Mother's Day 1973 in which Dr. Morgentaler permitted cameras into his clinic in Montréal and, with the consent of the patient involved, allowed the filming of an abortion being performed.

In addition, in the December 15, 1973, edition of the Canadian Medical Association Journal, Dr. Morgentaler published a report on 5,641 outpatient abortions by vacuum suction curettage. This frank disclosure of the number of abortions he had performed in his clinic surprised, and shocked, many.

[37] Throughout Dr. Morgentaler's numerous prosecutions by authorities, he maintained that the jury should acquit him because the law under which he was charged was "a bad law." In essence, Dr. Morgentaler was suggesting that a jury could ignore a law that it did not like.

[38] By preferring an indictment against Dr. Morgentaler, the Attorney General denied Dr. Morgentaler the opportunity of a preliminary inquiry.

Court of Appeal entered a conviction and returned the matter of the trial judge for sentencing. Dr. Morgentaler then applied for, and was granted, leave to appeal to the Supreme Court of Canada. Having admitted performing the act of abortion with which he was charged, Dr. Morgentaler argued the common law concept of necessity in his defense. In addition to this argument, Dr. Morgentaler attacked the constitutional validity of section 251 on a number of grounds, most of which related to the Canadian Bill of Rights.[39] His main arguments were based upon sections 1(a) and (b) of the Bill. Section 1(a) recognized and declared the right of an individual to life, liberty and security of the person and the right not to be deprived thereof except by due process of law, and section 1(b) spoke of the right of an individual to equality before the law and the protection of the law. Counsel for Dr. Morgentaler drew heavily upon the then-recently decided U.S. cases of *Roe v. Wade*[40] and *Doe v. Bolton*[41] for support for his claim that section 251 of the Criminal Code was unconstitutional. Counsel advanced the argument that the concept of liberty protected in section 1(a) of the Canadian Bill of Rights should be defined to include a right to privacy and the "qualified right" to terminate a pregnancy. In relation to Dr. Morgentaler's claim to security of his person, he argued that the standard established in section 251(4) under which an abortion could be performed lawfully was "so vague, so uncertain and so subjective as among different physicians and as among different therapeutic abortion committees as to deny due process of law".[42]

Dr. Morgentaler's equality argument under section 1(b) of the Bill of Rights was based on the operational effect of section 251(4). The section permitted, but did not compel, hospital boards to establish therapeutic abortion committees. In addition, the section specified the number of medical practitioners who were required to serve on such committees. Counsel for Dr. Morgentaler argued that such a requirement created inequality "in respect of women in rural areas and in areas where no such committee had been established."[43] Counsel further argued that the economic status of some women denied them the mobility necessary to avail themselves of therapeutic abortion committees, where they did exist. Finally, it was alleged that the vague standards to be applied by the committees led to varying applications and interpretations, having the effect of denying some women equal protection of the law.

Surprisingly, only in the minority judgment of the court is there any discussion of why these arguments, based on the Canadian Bill of Rights, were rejected.[44] Chief

---

[39] The Canadian Bill of Rights was enacted by the federal Parliament in 1960. It was an ordinary statutory enactment that could have been repealed by Parliament at any time. It applied only to the federal Parliament, federal government and businesses, agencies, etc., within federal legislative jurisdiction. Therefore, the Bill of Rights had no application to the provinces. The Bill has been described as having "quasi-constitutional" status only, and for this reason, and others, Canadian courts assumed a posture of some hostility toward the Bill, and therefore it was viewed as little more than an interpretive guide. The Supreme Court of Canada declared only one federal law invalid under the Canadian Bill of Rights in R. v. Drybones (1969) 9 D.L.R. (3d) 473 (S.C.C.).

[40] 410 U.S. 113 (1973).

[41] 410 U.S. 179 (1973). The legislative scheme struck down (in part) by the United States' Supreme Court in *Doe* was very similar to § 251 of the Criminal Code.

[42] *See supra* note 32, at 629.

[43] *Id.* at 630.

[44] At the conclusion of the submission by counsel for Dr. Morgentaler, the court announced that it did not need to hear from the respondent Crown on the applicability and effect of the Canadian Bill of Rights "because no case was made out on these matters which required an answer". (*Id.* at 624). Obviously, the

Justice Laskin provided the legal and historical context in which the Court considered these "rights" arguments. The Chief Justice commented:

> *How foreign to our constitutional traditions, to our constitutional law, and to our conceptions of judicial review was any interference by a Court with the substantive content of legislation.*[45]

Although recognizing the "quasi-constitutional" status of the Canadian Bill of Rights, the Chief Justice called for restraint in its application:

> *[I]t cannot be forgotten that it [the Bill of Rights] is a statutory instrument, illustrative of Parliament's primacy within the limits of its assigned legislative authority, and this is a relevant consideration in determining how far the language of the Canadian Bill of Rights should be taken in assessing the quality of federal enactments which are challenged under s.1(a). There is as much a temptation here as there is on the question of* ultra vires *to consider the wisdom of the legislation and I think it is our duty to resist it in the former connection as in the latter.*[46]

With these general comments to guide his approach to the interpretation of the Bill of Rights, it is not surprising that the Chief Justice rejected the approach adopted by the U.S. Supreme Court in *Roe v. Wade.*[47] Without clearly articulating why, he concluded that it would be unwarranted for the court to divide the normal period of pregnancy into zones of interest. The Chief Justice also rejected counsel's arguments based on the uncertainty and subjectivity of the standard upon which a lawful abortion could be performed under section 251(4) of the Code. The section required a finding on the part of a therapeutic abortion committee that the continuation of a pregnancy would, or would be likely, to endanger the life or health of the woman. Again, the Chief Justice cautioned restraint in relation to the doctrine of substantive due process and concluded:

> *It is enough to say that Parliament has fixed a manageable standard because it is addressed to a professional panel, the members of which would be expected to bring a practised judgment to the question whether "the continuation of the pregnancy . . . would or would be likely to endanger . . . health or life."*[48]

In relation to the appellant's arguments based on the concept of equal protection of the law, the Chief Justice concluded that section 1(b) of the Bill of Rights did not charge the courts with supervising the administrative efficiency of legislation or with evaluating the regional or national organization of its administration. The reality that economic or

---

court had concluded that Dr. Morgentaler's arguments in relation to the constitutionality of § 251 of the Criminal Code were without any legal basis whatsoever. However, Chief Justice Laskin, on behalf of himself and fellow Justices Judson and Spence, believed it was important to state why these arguments were being rejected.

[45] *See supra* note 32, at 632.

[46] *Id.* at 632–33

[47] *See supra* note 40.

[48] *See supra* note 32, at 634.

geographic circumstances precluded many women from sheltering under or taking advantage of the exculpatory provisions of section 251 was constitutionally irrelevant to the Chief Justice.[49] He concluded that any unevenness in the administration of section 251(4) was for Parliament to correct, not for the courts to monitor. In summary, in keeping with its restrained, if not completely ineffectual, approach to the interpretation and application of the Canadian Bill of Rights, the Court concluded that Parliament's legislative scheme in relation to abortion was constitutionally valid.[50]

The majority of the Supreme Court of Canada resolved the case on the basis of criminal law arguments only.[51] In relation to the common law defense of necessity, the Court was divided, with the majority expressing doubt as to the very existence of the defense but ultimately concluding that even if the defense was a "theoretical possibility" in the case, there was no evidence to support it.[52] Justice Dickson in reviewing the testimony of both Dr. Morgentaler and one of his patients, concluded that there was no evidence of urgency and no evidence that Dr. Morgentaler could not have complied with the law found in the Code, in relation to therapeutic abortions. Therefore, Justice Dickson concluded that the Québec Court of Appeal had not erred in deciding that "there was on the record little evidence of real and urgent medical need".[53]

In conclusion, the majority of the Supreme Court of Canada upheld the conviction against Dr. Morgentaler entered by the Québec Court of Appeal and sent the matter

---

[49]*Id.* at 636.

[50]Although it is only in the judgment of Chief Justice Laskin (concurred in by Justices Spence and Judson) that there is any discussion of the Bill of Rights, it can be presumed that the remaining justices of the Court concurred in his reasoning. The Chief Justice had earlier rejected Dr. Morgentaler's argument that § 251 exceeded the legislative jurisdiction of Parliament, being a law concerning hospitals and the regulation of the profession of medicine. Chief Justice Laskin concluded that § 251 was a valid exercise of the federal Parliament's criminal law power. He commented:

> Parliament has in its judgment decreed that interference by another, or even by the pregnant woman herself, with the ordinary course of conception is socially undesirable conduct subject to punishment. I need cite no authority for the proposition that Parliament may determine what is not criminal as well as what is, and may hence introduce dispensations or compensations in its criminal legislation.

Id. at 627.

[51]These arguments were primarily in relation to the common law defense of necessity and the appropriateness of the Québec Court of Appeal's actions in entering a verdict of guilty in place of the trial jury's acquittal.

[52]*See supra* note 32, at 681.

Chief Justice Laskin (with J.J. Spence and Judson concurring) considered the defense of necessity and concluded that there was evidence the trial judge could have left with the jury on the issue of necessity, and hence, they would have reinstated the verdict of acquittal.

[53]*Id.* at 685. Justice Dickson summarized the views of the majority of the Court on the defense of necessity in the following terms:

> On the authorities it is manifestly difficult to be categorical and state that there is a law of necessity, paramount over other laws, relieving obedience from the letter of the law. If it does exist it can go no further than to justify non-compliance in urgent situations of clear and imminent peril when compliance with the law is demonstrably impossible. No system of positive law can recognize any principle which would entitle a person to violate the law because on his view the law conflicted with some higher social value.

Id. at 678.

back to the trial judge for sentencing. Dr. Morgentaler was sentenced to 18 months in jail, of which he served 10 months, before being released on bail, pending retrial.[54]

Dr. Morgentaler had continued to operate his clinic during this protracted court process, and new charges were laid against him as a result of the continuation of his practice. Again he was tried and was acquitted. The Attorney General of Québec chose not to appeal this acquittal but to simply lay additional charges against Dr. Morgentaler for which he was again acquitted. After the election of the *Parti Québecois* in late 1976, the position of the Québec government in relation to the availability of abortion and the continued prosecution of Dr. Morgentaler changed dramatically. Due to the difficulty of obtaining a conviction from a jury under section 251(4), the government decided that no further charges would be laid against Dr. Morgentaler nor against any other doctor performing abortions in free-standing clinics within the province. Indeed, abortions have been regularly performed in government-sponsored community clinics in Québec since 1982. In essence, the government of Québec decided to ignore section 251 of the Criminal Code and by so doing offered to Canadian women the prospect of readily available abortion in private clinics.

Morgentaler (1988)

Dr. Morgentaler was not satisfied with this political victory in Québec. He believed that all women, wherever they lived in Canada, should have ready access to safe abortion procedures. His experiences had persuaded him that the requirements of section 251(4) of the Criminal Code limited or denied access to abortion for many Canadian women and that it was actually medically safer and psychologically less traumatic for women to have the procedure performed in free-standing clinics rather than in hospitals. Therefore, Dr. Morgentaler opened a new clinic in Toronto, Ontario in 1982.[55] The Attorney General of Ontario was not nearly as accommodating of Dr. Morgentaler's plans as was his counterpart in Québec. Dr. Morgentaler's clinic was raided by police in July 1982; he was charged and tried, before a judge and jury, and acquitted. The Attorney General appealed this acquittal, and the Ontario Court of Appeal ordered a new trial. This decision was appealed by Dr. Morgentaler to the Supreme Court of Canada, and in January 1988, a majority of the Court declared section 251 of the Criminal Code unconstitutional, as being in violation of section 7 of the Charter of Rights and Freedoms.

The Attorney General of Ontario charged Dr. Morgentaler with conspiring with fellow doctors, Smoling and Scott, who performed the majority of abortions at the Toronto clinic, to procure the miscarriage of female persons. Before entering a plea, counsel for Dr. Morgentaler and his alleged fellow conspirators moved to quash the indictment on the basis that section 251 was unconstitutional. Associate Chief Justice Parker of the Ontario High Court rejected the arguments of defense counsel as to the section's unconstitutionality.[56] The arguments advanced by the defendant closely resembled those raised in *Morgentaler* (1975), with the important addition of arguments based

---

[54] Dr. Morgentaler had applied for parole after serving six months, or one-third, of his sentence. However, his application was denied by the National Parole Board, apparently because he was viewed as a difficult prisoner and had spent some time in solitary. However, some suggest that the Parole Board's refusal of Dr. Morgentaler's application was politically motivated and an attempt to further punish him for his defiance.

[55] Dr. Morgentaler also opened a clinic in Winnipeg, Manitoba in 1982.

[56] *See supra,* note 23.

upon the Charter of Rights and Freedoms. In particular, counsel argued that section 251 of the Criminal Code violated section 7 of the Charter, which guarantees the right to life, liberty and security of the person, such rights not to be denied except in accordance with the principles of fundamental justice.

The importance of the Charter of Rights and Freedoms to the ultimate outcome in *Morgentaler* (1988) cannot be underestimated. Clearly, the only thing that had changed in Canadian law since the upholding of section 251 and the conviction of Dr. Morgentaler in 1976 was the adoption of an "entrenched" charter of rights.[57] The doctrine of parliamentary supremacy, which calls for judicial restraint in reviewing laws duly enacted by Parliament was no longer the paramount and fundamental value of the Canadian political order. The Charter of Rights guaranteed certain fundamental freedoms and rights to all Canadians that the government had to respect. For the first time in Canadian history, as part of the country's constitution, there were limitations placed upon lawmakers and government officials.

It is somewhat surprising, therefore, that Associate Chief Justice Parker drew so heavily from the Supreme Court of Canada's earlier decision in *Morgentaler* (1975). This is even more surprising in light of the fact that he recognized that "the Courts have entered a new age with the enactment of the *Charter*".[58] However, one senses in his language and approach an unease that is reflective of the long-standing judicial fear of overstepping the courts' appropriate role when asked to review legislative pronouncements.

The main argument, advanced by counsel for Dr. Morgentaler, claimed that the guarantee of "liberty and security of person" contained a right of privacy that would permit a woman to choose whether or not to have an abortion. Not surprisingly, U.S. jurisprudence was invoked to support this claim, but Associate Chief Justice Parker counseled caution in relation to the relevance of U.S. jurisprudence in the interpretation of the Charter:

> *Clearly, the entrenchment of the Constitution has brought our system of laws more closely in line with that of the United States. We now have constitutional limitations imposed upon our Legislatures which were formerly omnipotent within their respective spheres of power, with the modest exception of the federal limitations on Parliament due to the Canadian Bill of Rights. This transition does not, however, mean that we must accept an American interpretation whenever the wording of the Charter is similar to that of the American Bill of Rights. Differences in wording between the two documents, the use of headings, and our traditions will often be more powerful in construing a section of the Charter than the similarities between them.*[59]

In attempting to define the scope and content of the phrase "liberty and security of person," Associate Chief Justice Parker began with an inquiry into the legal rights

---

[57] In Canada, the concept of "entrenchment" is different than that in the United States. The Charter includes section 33, that permits the federal Parliament or provincial legislatures to "opt-out" of certain of the guaranteed fundamental rights and freedoms. In practice, what this means is that a province or the federal Parliament can insulate a legislative enactment from judicial review by simply including a section in the law indicating that it will operate "notwithstanding" the Charter of Rights and Freedoms.

[58] *See supra* note 23, at 366.

[59] *Id.* at 397.

Canadians have at common law or by statute. If the claimed right was not protected by the Canadian system of positive law, then it would be necessary to consider if it was "so deeply rooted in the traditions and conscience of our people as to be ranked as fundamental."[60] Since the claimed right to abortion was not recognized by either existing common law or statute law, Associate Chief Justice Parker focused his inquiry upon whether the asserted right was one rooted in our traditions. This analysis led him to conclude that certain elements of the right to privacy, for example the decision to marry and to have children, might be granted constitutional protection. However, he also decided that the right not to have children and the attendant right to terminate a pregnancy were not similarly "rooted in our traditions and conscience of this country."[61] He asserted this conclusion after a cursory and one might suggest, selective, historical review of the development of Canadian laws prohibiting abortion.

The interpretive approach of Associate Chief Justice Parker seemed to suggest that the definition of the guaranteed rights found in the Charter would be determined by a historical inquiry into the existing laws and morés of the country, thereby in reality providing scant recognition of the fact that the adoption of the Charter of Rights and Freedoms signaled a new constitutional order in Canada.[62] By concluding that section 7 of the Charter did not contain within it a right to privacy that extended to a woman's decision to terminate an unwanted pregnancy, he did not have to consider section 1 of the Charter, which explicitly calls upon the courts to balance the interests of the applicant, who is alleging a "rights" violation, against those of the state, in limiting the asserted right.[63] This task is, of course, one of assessing ends and means and calls upon the state to justify any limitation upon a guaranteed right. After finding that section 251 of the Criminal Code was constitutional, Associate Chief Justice Parker proceeded to trial, at the conclusion of which the jury acquitted Dr. Morgentaler and his fellow defendants. The Attorney General appealed this acquittal.

The Ontario Court of Appeal began its judgment by sounding the same note of caution expressed by Associate Chief Justice Parker in relation to the court's task—that task not being to express an opinion on the merits or demerits of abortion but on whether Parliament had the jurisdiction to enact section 251.[64] In essence, the Court of Appeal reiterated the approach taken by Parker in reviewing Canada's history in relation to abortion and concluded that the right to procure an abortion was not "so deeply rooted in our traditions and way of life as to be fundamental."[65] It would appear that upon this finding, the Court of Appeal needed to go no further. A woman's right to liberty

---

[60] *Id.* at 406.

[61] *Id.* at 408.

[62] It appears that Associate Chief Justice Parker is invoking a "frozen rights" concept in defining those rights guaranteed under the Charter. The content of Charter rights is to be determined by existing statutory and common law, such law reflecting the traditions and history of our country. Such a theory provides little flexibility or room for future expansion of the guaranteed rights. One presumes that the relevant date at which rights are "frozen" is April 1982, when the Charter was proclaimed in force.

[63] § 1 of the Charter states:

> The Canadian Charter of Rights and Freedoms guarantees the rights and freedoms set out in it subject only to such reasonable limits prescribed by law as can be demonstrably justified in a free and democratic society.

[64] (1985), 11 O.A.C. 81 at 85.

[65] *Id.* at 98.

and security did not include the right to choose to terminate her pregnancy; therefore, there should have been no necessity for the Court of Appeal to consider whether the right had been denied in such a way that the denial violated the principles of fundamental justice. However, the Court of Appeal offered a lengthy discussion of substantive and procedural due process, before concluding that the words of section 7 included both. The Court did caution, however, that "substantive reviews should take place only in exceptional circumstances where there has been a marked departure from the norm of civil or criminal liability resulting in the infringement of liberty or in some other injustice." [66] The Court concluded that section 251 did not contain any exceptional provision that would justify submitting it to substantive review. Indeed, the Court saw section 251 as relieving against the "somewhat Draconian provisions" of earlier legislative prohibitions. [67]

With this conclusion, the Ontario Court of Appeal avoided the application of section 1 of the Charter. After dismissing Dr. Morgentaler's constitutional arguments, the Court of Appeal concluded that the defense of necessity should not have been left with the jury because there was no evidence to support it. Due to this, and other "fundamental errors" in law at trial, the Court of Appeal set aside the verdict of acquittal and ordered a new trial. [68]

The Decision of the Supreme Court of Canada

In January 1988 the Supreme Court of Canada declared section 251 of the Criminal Code constitutionally invalid. [69] In a 5–2 decision, the Court determined that section 251 violated section 7 of the Charter of Rights and Freedoms and that it could not be justified under section 1. The decision surprised many in spite of the fact that the Court earlier had confessed to a lack of judicial will and enthusiasm in applying the Canadian Bill of Rights, a "mistake" the court indicated would not be repeated. [70] Further, the Court clearly felt emboldened by the fact that the Charter was part of the supreme law of the land and that Canada's latter day founding fathers had knowingly, if not exactly willingly, provided the courts with greater jurisdiction in resolving disputes between the individual and the state. However, based upon the traditions of judicial conservatism and restraint evident in the courts' earlier pronouncements on "rights issues," many presumed this deferential posture to legislative choice would continue. [71]

---

[66] Id. at 103.

[67] Id.

[68] Id. at 143. The Criminal Code had been amended after *Morgentaler* (1975) to prevent a court of appeal from entering a conviction after an acquittal by a jury. Therefore, the Ontario Court of Appeal had no choice but to order a new trial.

[69] See supra note 33.

[70] Singh v. Minister of Employment and Immigration [1985] 1 S.C.R. 177 at 209 per Wilson, J.:

> I do not think this kind of analysis is acceptable in relation to the Charter. It seems to me rather that the recent adoption of the Charter by Parliament and nine of the ten provinces as part of the Canadian constitutional framework has sent a clear message to the courts that the restrictive attitude which at times characterized their approach to the Canadian Bill of Rights ought to be re-examined.

[71] However, observers of the Court could have looked to the court's decisions in cases such as R. v. Big M. Drug Mart Ltd., [1985] 1 S.C.R. 295 and Re B.C. Motor Vehicle Act, [1985] 2 S.C.R. 486 for some indication of the court's new approach to rights issues.

If any further evidence was required that the Supreme Court of Canada believed, as of 1982, that a new constitutional order had been created in Canada, its decision in *Morgentaler* (1988) provided it. Many thought the Court would be reluctant to enter the contentious debate on abortion and would simply maintain the status quo, as reflected in section 251 of the Criminal Code. That was not to be the case.

It is not possible to speak of "the" decision of the Court in *Morgentaler*. Seven justices participated in the hearing, and there were four separate judgments written.[72] Although five of the seven justices found the law to be unconstitutional, they did so for remarkably different reasons and therefore the precedential value of *Morgentaler* is unclear. The following discussion will concentrate on the decisions of Chief Justice Dickson and Justice Wilson.[73]

THE JUDGMENT OF CHIEF JUSTICE DICKSON   A number of grounds for appeal were raised by counsel for Dr. Morgentaler, but the discussion that follows will deal only with the challenge to section 251 of the Criminal Code on the basis of section 7 of the Charter of Rights and Freedoms. It should be reiterated that section 7 is a somewhat complicated, two-part guarantee. The opening clause of the section guarantees to everyone the right to life, liberty and security of the person; the second clause requires that deprivations of those rights be in accordance with the principles of fundamental justice. Therefore, section 7 anticipates a two-stage analysis: first, prima facie proof of a violation of one or more of the three identified rights and second, proof that the alleged violation was not in accordance with the principles of fundamental justice. It is only after an applicant has convinced the court of both of these elements that the government will be called upon to justify a limitation under section 1 of the Charter.

Further, it should be noted that much controversy has surrounded the meaning of the phrase "the principles of fundamental justice." It appears that this phrase was deliberately chosen by the drafters of the Charter to avoid the jurisprudential quagmire created by the concept of "due process" in the United States.[74] It is clear that the drafters of the Charter had intended that "the principles of fundamental justice" refer only to issues of procedural justice or fairness and not to the possibility of substantive

[72] The four decisions were written by: (1) Chief Justice Dickson with whom Justice Lamer concurred, (2) Justice Beetz with whom Justice Estey concurred, (3) Justice Wilson and (4) dissenting, Justice McIntyre with whom Justice LaForest concurred.

[73] Justice Beetz (Justice Estey concurring) held § 251 unconstitutional but on narrower grounds than Chief Justice Dickson and Justice Wilson. However, like Chief Justice Dickson, Justice Beetz only deals with the right to security of the person, concluding that a "pregnant woman can not be said to be secure if, when her life or health is in danger, she is faced with a rule of criminal law which precludes her from obtaining efficient and timely medical treatment. If an act of Parliament makes a woman chose between the commission of a crime to obtain timely treatment and no treatment, that act is unconstitutional." *Morgentaler* (1988), *supra* note 33, at 90.

Justice Beetz did indicate that a legislative requirement for independent verification of a physician's medical opinion that a woman's life or health was endangered was reasonable but that the present requirement for therapeutic abortion committees was unreasonable and unconstitutional. He also concluded that the requirement that all abortions be performed in accredited or approved hospitals was unconstitutional.

He made one questionable comment in the course of his judgment to the effect that § 251(4) represented a constitutional minimum so that Parliament could not adopt a more restrictive abortion law. For him, it was as if that statutory provision was read into the definition of "security of the person," upon the proclamation of the Charter.

[74] *See, e.g.,* the comments of Barry Strayer, Assistant Deputy Minister of Justice for Canada in: Canada, Minister of Proceedings and Evidence of the Special Joint Committee of the Senate and House of Commons on the Constitution of Canada, 46: 32 (27 January 1981).

review of impugned legislation by the courts. However, the Supreme Court has stated that it is not bound by expressions of intention, whether made by government officials charged with the actual drafting of the Charter or by ministers of the Crown, such as the Attorney General of Canada.[75] Consequently, the court will interpret the necessarily general language of the Charter on the basis of a "purposive" approach, such approach being informed by the appropriate "linguistic, philosophical and historical contexts."[76] The Chief Justice, probably feeling some necessity to distinguish his approach and conclusions in *Morgentaler* (1988) from that which he had said and done in *Morgentaler* (1975), alluded to the additional responsibilities the Court had been given with the adoption of the Charter—to ensure "that the legislative initiatives pursued by our Parliament and legislatures conform to the democratic values expressed in the Charter."[77] This justified the Court taking "another look" at the validity of section 251 of the Criminal Code.

The Chief Justice concluded that "state interference with bodily integrity and serious state imposed psychological stress, at least in the criminal law context, constituted a breach of security of the person."[78] On the basis of this definition, the Chief Justice easily concluded that section 251 had violated the right to security of thousands of Canadian women who had made the decision to terminate a pregnancy. He went on to explain:

> At the most basic, physical and emotional level, every pregnant woman is told by the section that she cannot submit to a generally safe medical procedure that might be of clear benefit to her unless she meets criteria entirely unrelated to her own priorities and aspirations. Not only does the removal of decision-making power threaten women in a physical sense; the indecision of not knowing whether an abortion will be granted inflicts emotional stress. Section 251 clearly interferes with a woman's bodily integrity in both a physical and emotional sense. Forcing a woman, by threat of criminal sanction, to carry a foetus to term unless she meets certain criteria unrelated to her own priorities and aspirations, is a profound interference with a woman's body and thus a violation of security of the person.[79]

The Chief Justice identified additional violations of a woman's right to physical and psychological security in the documented delays caused by the procedures created by Parliament in section 251(4).[80] The requirement that lawful abortions be performed only in approved or accredited hospitals, after the granting of consent by a therapeutic abortion committee, led to delays that increased the health risks to women. Expert advice established that even short delays, for example, of a few weeks, led to a higher risk of complications and mortality. In addition, delay created greater psychological trauma;

---

[75] *See, e.g.,* the judgment of Justice Lamer in *Re B.C. Motor Vehicle Act, supra* note 71.

[76] *Big M. Drug Mart Ltd., supra* note 71.

[77] *See supra* note 33, at 46.

[78] *Id.* at 56.

[79] *Id.* at 56–57.

[80] The Chief Justice draws heavily upon two expert reports to provide evidence of both delay and variations in the definition of key concepts such as health. These two reports were the Badgley Report, *supra* note 24, and the Powell Report, *supra* note 24.

stress levels were increased because of the "red tape" created by section 251(4); and the committee structure created a high degree of uncertainty as to whether an abortion would be approved.

The Chief Justice went on to consider whether this violation denied the principles of fundamental justice. After documenting the limited, and uneven, accessability to the statutorily created procedures in section 251(4), he concluded that the subsection created a criminal defense that was, for many Canadian women, nothing more than an illusion. This illusory defense violated the principles of fundamental justice, those principles being found in "the basic tenets of our legal system."[81] He stated:

> One of the basic tenets of our system of criminal justice is that when Parliament creates a defence to a criminal charge, the defence should not be illusory or so difficult to attain as to be practically illusory . . .
>
> In the present case, the structure—the system regulating access to therapeutic abortions—is manifestly unfair. It contains so many potential barriers to its own operation that the defence it creates will in many circumstances be practically unavailable to women who would prima facie qualify for the defence, or at least would force such women to travel great distances at substantial expense and inconvenience in order to benefit from a defence that is held out to be generally available.[82]

After finding a violation of section 7, the Chief Justice had to consider the applicability of section 1 of the Charter, which can be used to save a legislative provision found to be in violation of a guaranteed right. In essence, the interpretive approach adopted by the Supreme Court to section 1 requires an ends and means analysis. For a limitation to be saved under section 1, it must be in pursuit of an objective "of sufficient importance to warrant overriding a constitutionally protected right or freedom."[83] The means chosen to achieve this sufficiently important objective must be proportional to the legislative ends. The means must be rational, fair and not arbitrary; they should impair as little as possible the right or freedom under consideration; and finally, the effects of the limitation upon the relevant right should not be out of proportion to the objectives sought to be achieved.[84]

The Chief Justice concluded that section 251 had been enacted in pursuit of an important government objective. He stated:

> I think the protection of the interests of pregnant women is a valid governmental objective, where life and health can be jeopardized by criminal sanctions . . . . I agree that protection of foetal interests by Parliament is also a valid governmental objective. It follows that balancing these interests, with the lives and health of women, a major factor, is clearly an important governmental objective.[85]

---

[81] See supra note 33, at 70.

[82] Id. at 70–73.

[83] Id. at 73. In R. v. Oakes, [1986] 1 S.C.R. 103, the Court articulated the test to be applied in the application of § 1.

[84] See supra note 33, at 74.

[85] Id. at 75.

However, the Chief Justice concluded that the means chosen by Parliament to achieve this objective were neither rational nor proportionate. He found that the procedures and administrative structures created by section 251 were often arbitrary and unfair. Further, the procedures established to implement the policy of section 251 impaired section 7 rights far more than was necessary because they held out an illusory defense to many women who would prima facie qualify under the exculpatory provisions. The effects of the limitation upon the section 7 rights of many pregnant women were disproportionate to the objective sought. He stated: "Indeed, to the extent that s.251(4) is designed to protect the life and health of women, the procedures it establishes may actually defeat that objective."[86]

The judgment of the chief justice provides Parliament with few clear guidelines as to what a new law on abortion should look like. Most importantly, he leaves unanswered the question of whether section 7 contains within it a right for women to control their reproductive capacity. He identifies only procedural deficiencies within section 251(4). Should we, therefore, conclude that if Parliament drafts a law that remedies these deficiencies, it will be immune from attack? He speaks of the security of the person being violated when laws force women to make choices unrelated to their own "priorities and aspirations". The sweeping implications of this statement must lead us to question its ultimate utility as a test for defining the concept of "security of the person". Further, the Chief Justice appears to suggest that his comments are limited to the criminal law context of section 251. Therefore, it is difficult to predict how his comments regarding "priorities and aspirations" will be applied in the context of provincial laws purporting to regulate the provision of health care and hospitals. He provides us with little indication as to how he would balance a claim that may be made by government on behalf of the fetus with that made on behalf of women to control their reproductive capacity. Finally, and perhaps most importantly, the Chief Justice does not inform us as to how he sees women's claims for equality within Canadian society enhancing or informing their claims for reproductive choice and control.

THE JUDGMENT OF JUSTICE WILSON   Justice Bertha Wilson took a dramatically different approach to the constitutional questions before her than did her fellow justices. For Justice Wilson, it was impossible to avoid answering the question of whether section 7 guaranteed to women at least a qualified right to terminate an unwanted pregnancy. The chief justice expressly refused to answer that question, finding it unnecessary because of his conclusion that the legislative procedures set out in section 251(4) were so arbitrary, unfair and vague that they could not be upheld. Justice Wilson refuses to take the "easy way out" in relation to this difficult issue and quite astutely comments:

> *A consideration as to whether or not the procedural requirements for obtaining or performing an abortion comport with fundamental justice is purely academic if such requirements cannot, as a constitutional matter, be imposed at all. If a pregnant woman cannot, as a constitutional matter, be compelled by law to carry the foetus to term against her will, a review of the procedural requirements by which she may be compelled to do so seems pointless.[87]*

---

[86]*Id.* at 75–76.
[87]*Id.* at 161–162.

Justice Wilson was the only member of the Court to consider the right to liberty protected by section 7. For her, the right to individual liberty was "inextricably tied to the concept of human dignity."[88] Respect for human dignity is given meaning, at least in part, by permitting individuals to make fundamental personal decisions without interference from the state. Justice Wilson drew heavily from U.S. case law in reaching her conclusion that the right to liberty guarantees to every individual a degree of personal autonomy over important decisions intimately affecting his or her private life.[89] She then considered whether the decision of a woman to terminate her pregnancy fell within this class of protected decisions and concluded that it did. In words of unusual sensitivity and insight she described this decision:

> *This decision is one that will have profound psychological, economic and social consequences for the pregnant woman. The circumstances giving rise to it can be complex and varied and there may be, and usually are, powerful considerations militating in opposite directions. It is a decision that deeply reflects the way the woman thinks about herself and her relationship to others and to society at large. It is not just a medical decision; it is a profound social and ethical one as well. Her response to it will be the response of the whole person.*
>
> *It is probably impossible for a man to respond, even imaginatively, to such a dilemma not just because it is outside the realm of his personal experience (although this is, of course, the case) but because he can relate to it only by objectifying it, thereby eliminating the subjective elements of the female psyche which are at the heart of the dilemma.*
>
> *. . . The more recent struggle for women's rights has been a struggle to eliminate discrimination, to achieve a place for women in a man's world, to develop a set of legislative reforms in order to place women in the same position as men. It has not been a struggle to define the rights of women in relation to their special place in the societal structure and in relation to the biological distinction between the two sexes. Thus, women's needs and aspirations are only now being translated into protected rights. The right to reproduce or not reproduce, which is an issue in this case, is one such right and is properly perceived as an integral part of a modern woman's struggle to assert her dignity and worth as a human being.[90]*

Based upon her definition of liberty, Justice Wilson concluded that section 251 of the Criminal Code violated a woman's right to choose for herself whether or not to terminate her pregnancy. She found particularly offensive the fact that section 251 left with a committee a decision she believed rightly belonged to the woman herself.

In defining the right to security of the person, Justice Wilson agreed with the Chief Justice that the guarantee protected both the physical and psychological integrity of a woman. However, she identified an additional and more fundamental concern with the

---

[88]*Id.* at 164.
[89]*Id.* at 166.
[90]*Id.* at 171–172.

legislative scheme established in section 251(4). For Justice Wilson, the effect of the section was to tell a woman that her capacity to reproduce was not to be subject to her own control. She chillingly described this reality:

> *She is truly being treated as a means—a means to an end which she does not desire, but over which she has not control. She is the passive recipient of a decision made by others as to whether her body is to be used to nurture a new life. Can there be anything that comports less with human dignity and self-respect? How can a woman in this position have any sense of security with respect to her person?*[91]

For Justice Wilson, the principles of fundamental justice included not only the concept of procedural fairness but also any infringement of other fundamental rights and freedoms set out elsewhere in the Charter. She believed that section 251 of the Criminal Code not only infringed section 7 of the Charter, but also section 2(a), which guaranteed to everyone freedom of conscience and religion. The decision whether or not to terminate a pregnancy was "essentially a moral decision, a matter of conscience. The question is: whose conscience? Is the conscience of the woman to be paramount or the conscience of the state?"[92] She ultimately concluded that for the state to take sides on the issue of abortion as it had done in the enactment of section 251(4) was to validate one conscientiously held view at the expense of another. "Legislation which treats some as a means to an end deprives them of their essential humanity and therefore violates freedom of conscience."[93] Such a violation could not be, according to Justice Wilson, in accordance with the principles of fundamental justice.

In the application of section 1, Justice Wilson disagreed with the Chief Justice as to the paramount legislative objective to be achieved by section 251. For Justice Wilson, the primary objective of the legislation was the protection of the fetus, which she considered to be a valid legislative objective. She would permit certain limitations to be placed upon a woman's right to terminate her pregnancy, depending upon the developmental stage of the fetus. She asked the question: "At what point does the state's interest in the protection of the foetus become compelling and justify state intervention in what is otherwise a matter of purely personal and private concern?"[94] Although Justice Wilson did allude to the viability test adopted by the U.S. Supreme Court in *Roe v. Wade*,[95] she did not expressly adopt it. Indeed, she was very careful to avoid the use of the concept of viability as the point at which the state's interest in the protection of the fetus becomes compelling.[96] She preferred to discuss this difficult and contentious issue of line-drawing or balancing in terms of a developmental progression. In

---

[91] *Id.* at 173–174. The language chosen by Justice Wilson in describing a woman merely as a means to an end evokes images of the bleak and repressive world so hauntingly described by Margaret Atwood in her novel *A Handmaid's Tale* (1985).

[92] *Id.* at 176.

[93] *Id.* at 179.

[94] *Id.* at 181.

[95] *See supra* note 40.

[96] This is undoubtedly because Justice Wilson was well aware of the advances in science and technology that make it more difficult to define this point and of the jurisprudential controversy surrounding it in the United States.

her opinion, a developmental view of the fetus supported a permissive approach to abortion in the early stages of pregnancy and a restrictive approach in the later stages:

> *In the early stages a woman's autonomy would be absolute; her decision reached in consultation with her physician, not to carry the foetus to term would be conclusive. . . . [H]er reasons for having an abortion would, however, be the proper subject of inquiry at the later stages of her pregnancy when the state's compelling interest in the protection of the foetus would justify it in prescribing conditions. The precise point in the development of the foetus at which the state's interest in its protection becomes "compelling," I leave to the informed judgment of the legislature which is in a position to receive guidance on the subject from all the relevant disciplines. It seems, however, that it might fall somewhere in the second trimester.*[97]

Justice Wilson astutely pointed out that section 251 of the Criminal Code took the decision away from a woman at all stages of her pregnancy and reposed it in a therapeutic abortion committee. The section worked as a complete denial of a woman's constitutionally protected right, not merely as a limitation upon it. Consequently, Justice Wilson concluded that it was impossible for section 251 to meet the proportionality test of *Oakes*.[98]

Therefore, for Parliament merely to remedy the procedural defects identified by the Chief Justice would not be sufficient to meet the concerns of Justice Wilson. Even if the facilities necessary to provide equal access to therapeutic abortions were available, Justice Wilson would continue to characterize the law as one that denied a woman the right to decide for herself whether or not to terminate her pregnancy. Although the state has the right to impose certain limitations upon a woman's right to an abortion, such limitations would only be constitutionally permissible later on in the "gestational process." Justice Wilson does not define the exact point in this "gestational process" at which Parliament could impose constitutionally valid limitations. Out of judicial deference to legislative choice, she leaves the definition of this crucial point to Parliament. One would presume, however, that had Justice Wilson believed it necessary to define this point, viability would be, for her, the determining factor.

The Aftermath of *Morgentaler*

Federal and Provincial Initiatives on Abortion

Predictably, the decision of the Supreme Court of Canada in *Morgentaler* (1988) did not end the debate surrounding abortion; if anything, the Court's decision has energized the competing sides on this divisive issue. There has been renewed political activity, with the anti-choice movement demanding a new federal criminal law that would clearly give supremacy to fetal rights; the pro-choice movement has argued against the recriminalization of abortion. After the defeat of Bill C-43 in the Senate in January

---

[97] *See supra* note 33, at 183.

[98] *Id.*

1991[99] and the federal government's pronouncement that there would be no new legislative initiatives from it in relation to abortion, political attention has shifted to the provinces. The provinces have constitutional jurisdiction over health care and hospitals, and the anti-choice movement has begun to lobby at the provincial level to have restrictions placed upon the medical procedure of abortion. Some of these restrictions include: (1) the "de-insuring" of the procedure of abortion under a province's health care system, thereby forcing women to pay for their abortions[100]; (2) requiring that the consent of at least two physicians be obtained before a provincial health care plan will authorize payment[101]; (3) requiring that abortions be performed only in hospitals[102]; and (4) requiring that doctors counsel women seeking abortions as to the stage of fetal development and alternatives to the procedure of abortion.[103] To date, these strategies have met with some political success but with no legal success.

For example, in Nova Scotia, the provincial Legislature passed an act to "prohibit the privatization of the provision of certain medical services in order to maintain a single high-quality health care delivery system for all Nova Scotians."[104] Doctors could perform "designated medical services" in approved hospitals only and anyone who performed such services outside an approved facility would not be reimbursed under the health insurance plan.[105] Under regulations passed by the Cabinet, abortion was one of a number of designated services that could be performed only in an approved hospital.[106]

Dr. Morgentaler is again at the center of this political and legal conflict. He opened a clinic in Halifax in 1989 and quickly was charged with 13 counts of performing abortions in contravention of section 4 of the Medical Services Act. Dr. Morgentaler's

---

[99] See Appendix II for the text of Bill C-43. The effect of the bill was to recriminalize abortion, making it punishable by up to two years in jail unless, in the opinion of a doctor, the physical, mental or psychological health of a woman was threatened. The impact of this proposed bill was felt immediately. It is estimated that between 60–100 doctors stopped performing abortions for fear of criminal prosecution (this was merely in anticipation of the bill becoming law) and that more than 275 doctors threatened to stop performing abortions if the bill was passed. Doctors particularly feared the prospect of third parties (e.g., anti-choice groups, disgruntled husbands, boyfriends, etc.) laying private prosecutions. While the federal Minister of Justice, Kim Campbell, tried to allay the fears of the Canadian Medical Association and individual doctors regarding this prospect, her efforts were met with hostility and disbelief.

The government's experience with Bill C-43 again proves that compromise on the issue of abortion is impossible. By requiring that the federal Cabinet support the government initiative in Bill C-43, its passage was assured in the House of Commons. However, when the bill was considered in the Senate there was no such government discipline imposed and pro-choice forces joined with anti-choice forces to defeat the bill. The vote was a tie, with the result that the bill failed.

[100] The government of British Columbia enacted such a provision on February 10, 1988, only 13 days after the Supreme Court's decision in *Morgentaler*. The government of Saskatchewan currently is considering such action.

[101] A number of provinces adopted this requirement, including Alberta and New Brunswick. However, Alberta dropped it in 1991, after receiving legal advice that such a requirement was likely unconstitutional.

[102] The Province of Nova Scotia has adopted this strategy. In addition, a number of provinces make it a condition of payment under their health care plans that an abortion be performed only in an approved hospital. These provinces are: New Brunswick, Prince Edward Island, Newfoundland, Nova Scotia, Manitoba and Saskatchewan.

[103] The Province of Saskatchewan has adopted this strategy.

[104] S.N.S. 1989, c.9, as quoted from *R. v. Morgentaler* (1991), 270 A.P.R. 293.

[105] In addition, anyone performing an abortion outside an approved facility was subject to a fine of not less than $10,000.00 and not more than $50,000.00. Medical Services Act, S.N.S. 1989, c.9 § 6(1).

[106] N.S. Reg. 152/89.

counsel argued that the legislation was unconstitutional on two main grounds: (1) that the legislation was criminal law, as it proported to prohibit abortions in all but approved hospitals, and legislative jurisdiction over criminal law is an exclusive federal matter; and (2) that the legislation violated sections 7 and 15 of the Charter of Rights and Freedoms. Provincial Court Judge Kennedy found it unnecessary to deal with the Charter arguments as he concluded that the legislation was a colorable attempt by the province to control and prohibit abortions, an objective beyond its legislative competence.[107] Therefore, the Court did not have to address the more difficult constitutional claims of Dr. Morgentaler that the law infringed women's rights under sections 7 and 15 of the Charter.

In British Columbia, the province with the highest per capita abortion rate in Canada, the provincial government chose to "de-insure" the medical procedure of abortion, unless there was a significant threat to a woman's life and the abortion was performed in an approved facility.[108] The former condition would preclude payment for most abortions performed in British Columbia. Chief Justice McEachern observed that this regulation was passed "almost upon delivery of judgment in *Morgentaler*."[109] As in Nova Scotia, this issue was decided without recourse to Charter arguments on the basis that the Cabinet had exceeded its delegated authority when it ordered that abortion was not to be considered a service that was medically required.

Due to the important questions left unanswered by the Supreme Court of Canada's decision in *Morgentaler* (1988), those provincial governments desirous of limiting access to abortion will continue to struggle with the challenge of developing policies that neither exceed their legislative jurisdiction in relation to health and hospitals nor violate the guaranteed rights of Canadian women under the Charter of Rights and Freedoms. Significant limitations may exist on provincial jurisdiction over the nature and delivery of health care in Canada, due to the federal government's cost-sharing arrangements, which are accompanied by federally imposed standards in relation to, among other things, accessibility. For a province to "de-insure" a procedure which is found to be "medically required" by a woman's physician or to limit its availability to only those circumstances in which the life of a woman is threatened, would call into question a province's

---

[107] *Supra* note 104 at 302–303. The provincial government claimed that the legislative purposes were: (1) a desire to prevent a two-tier system for the delivery of health care, one for the rich and one for the poor; (2) to provide high quality delivery of health care; and (3) to rationalize existing services to prevent duplication.

Judge Kennedy's decision has recently been upheld by a majority of the Nova Scotia Court of Appeal, (1992), 283 A.P.R. 361. Leave to appeal to the Supreme Court of Canada has been granted.

[108] B.C. Reg. 54/88, O.C. 221/88.

[109] B.C. Civil Liberties Assn. v. B.C. (A.G.), [1988] 4 W.W.R. 100 at 105. Chief Justice McEachern does suggest that the Cabinet might have been acting within its authority had it simply de-insured the procedure of abortion. However, he also notes the limitations upon a province in de-insuring medical procedures. Since the federal government pays for a percentage of provincial health care costs, it has created certain national standards or objectives, including universality and accessibility, that must be maintained by the provinces. The province could therefore run the risk of being disqualified from federal funding by de-insuring the medical procedure of abortion. Section 3 of the Canada Health Act, R.S.C. 1970, c.C-6 provides,

It is hereby declared that the primary objective in Canandian health care policy is to protect, promote and restore the physical and mental well-being of residents of Canada and to facilitate reasonable access to health services without financial or other barriers.

commitment to reasonably accessible health care. The federal government would probably, therefore, be justified in refusing further funding to such a province. In addition, any changes to provincial health care laws which appear to be "singling out" the medical procedure of abortion might be subject to challenge under section 15 of the Charter, which guarantees equal protection and equal benefit of the law discrimination on a list of nine proscribed grounds, one of which is sex.

Tremblay v. Daigle

Another recent development has been the attempted use of injunctive relief by disgruntled "boyfriends" to prevent women from terminating pregnancies. In the summer of 1990, two highly publicized incidents alerted Canadians to the possibility that this particularly traumatizing strategy might be employed by those opposed to choice.[110] The most troubling, and newsworthy, of these cases was that involving Chantal Daigle.

The story of Chantal Daigle is well known to everyone in Canada; her pregnancy, her failed relationship with her boyfriend, Jean-Guy Tremblay, her decision to terminate her pregnancy, Tremblay's attempts to stop the abortion, the Québec courts' granting Tremblay's request for an injunction,[111] her decision to have an abortion in defiance of the order of the Québec Court of Appeal[112] and finally, vindication from the Supreme Court of Canada when it allowed her appeal.[113]

The decision of the Supreme Court of Canada is an exercise in statutory interpretation, and in particular, the interpretation of the Québec Charter of Rights and Freedoms. The task of the Court was to determine if the phrase "human being," as used in Québec's Charter, included a fetus. In answering this question, the Supreme Court of Canada relied primarily upon the status of the fetus under the Civil Code of Québec.

Counsel for the respondent, Jean-Guy Tremblay, made three arguments to support the injunction: (1) that the fetus had a right to life under the Québec Charter; (2) that the appellant, Chantal Daigle, would violate this right by having an abortion: (3) that an injunction was an appropriate remedy by which to protect this right. The Supreme Court concluded that it needed to address only the first of these issues, since if there were no substantive rights of the fetus upon which to base an injunction, it would be vacated. The Court, exercising its characteristic judicial restraint,[114] simply declared that

---

[110] Murphy v. Dodd (1990), 63 D.L.R. (4th) 515; Tremblay v. Daigle [1989] 2 S.C.R. 530, *rev'g* [1989] R.J.Q. 1735, *aff'g.* [1989] R.J.Q. 1980.

[111] An interlocutory injunction was granted against Daigle by Justice Viens of the Québec Superior Court on July 17, 1989. An appeal from this decision was heard by the Québec Court of Appeal on July 20, 1989. It rendered its judgment on July 26 and, in a 3-2 decision, denied the request of the appellant to vacate the injunction.

[112] The Québec Court of Appeal upheld the interlocutory injunction issued by Justice Viens. The injunction stated, in part:

> . . . the Court grants the request for an interlocutory injunction, orders the Respondent to refrain, under threat of legal penalty, from having an abortion or taking recourse voluntarily to any method which directly or indirectly would lead to the death of the foetus which she is presently carrying.

[113] Although during the summer recess, due to the urgency of the matter, five justices of the Supreme Court of Canada heard the appellant's application for leave to appeal on August 1. Leave was granted the same day, and the appeal was heard on August 8 before the entire court.

[114] *See Morgentaler* (1988), *supra* note 33; Borowski v. Canada [1989] 1 S.C.R. 342.

it would answer no more questions than required to determine the appeal. Based on its decision that there were no substantive rights to justify the issuing of an injunction in the first place, the Court needed to go no further in its deliberations and, in particular, did not need to address the argument that the fetus had a constitutionally protected right to life independent of the woman carrying it.

The respondent argued that the substantive rights upon which an injunction could be based were: (1) that the fetus had a right to life, under the Québec Charter; (2) that the fetus had a right to life under the Canadian Charter of Rights and Freedoms; and (3) that the respondent, as "potential father," [115] had a right to be heard, in respect of decisions regarding his potential child. The Supreme Court devoted most of its judgment to the first of these three arguments. The Québec Charter guarantees that "[e]very human being has a right to life . . . he also possesses juridical personality." [116] There is no reference in the Québec Charter to the fetus or fetal rights.

Counsel for the respondent made much of the linguistic interpretation of the phrase "human being," seemingly basing his argument on something akin to the "plain meaning" rule. The Court made it plain that the question it was asked to resolve was a "legal" one, not a philosophical, theological, scientific or linguistic one, [117] although all might provide some assistance or background in resolving the "legal" issue. Indeed, the asserted linguistic approach would make strangely simple the most contentious of issues, that of the definition of a human being. Questions of when life begins, and when a "life form" becomes a human being, are deeply divisive and morally difficult issues that will not be resolved by reference to a dictionary.

Much was made of the differing uses of the words "human being" and "person" in the Québec Charter. It is only to human beings that the right to life is guaranteed. Persons are guaranteed other, and arguably, lesser rights, such as respect for their private life and peaceful enjoyment of their property. Although the Court made no final decision on this issue, it appears likely that the choice of words was dictated by a desire on the part of the Québec National Assembly to make clear that only natural persons or human beings possess the right to life, while artificial persons, such as corporate entities, might assert and enjoy the other rights guaranteed.

The Supreme Court of Canada quite reasonably concluded that the Québec Charter displayed no clear intent on the issue of who was to be included within the term "human being." Indeed, as the Court pointed out, one would expect that on such a controversial issue, if the National Assembly had intended to include protection for the fetus within this term, it would have said so explicitly.

Since the language of the Québec Charter displayed no clear intent on the meaning of the phrase "human being," the Court turned to the Civil Code to see if its provisions or its interpretation offered an answer to this definitional problem. The Court undertook a lengthy analysis of various provisions of the Code [118] and ultimately concluded that it

---

[115] The language of "potential father" is that used by the Supreme Court.

[116] § 1 of the Québec Charter of Rights and Freedoms, R.S.Q., c.C-12. In addition, § 2 of the Québec Charter states: "Every human being whose life is in peril has a right to assistance."

[117] The question the Supreme Court had to answer was whether the Québec legislature had accorded the fetus personhood. The Court suggests that classifying the fetus for the purpose of a particular law or for scientific or philosophical purposes may be fundamentally different tasks. The Court describes the ascribing of personhood to the fetus, in law, as a fundamentally normative task.

[118] In particular, Civil Code of Lower Canada, arts. 18, 338, 345, 608, 771, 838, 945, 2543.

"does not generally accord a foetus legal personality."[119] Indeed, the court suggested that a fetus is treated as a person under the civil code only where it is necessary to do so in order to protect its interests after it is born. The court found further confirmation for its interpretation of the civil code in Anglo-Canadian common law, in which it has been recognized generally that, to enjoy rights, a fetus must be born alive and have a separate existence from its mother.[120]

The Court quickly dealt with the remaining two "substantive rights" arguments of the respondent. The first of these was that the Charter of Rights and Freedoms provided the fetus with an independent right to life, under section 7. Again, the Supreme Court of Canada avoided the answering this question.[121] The Supreme Court invoked its decision in *Dolphin Delivery*,[122] in which it concluded that the Charter did not apply to private disputes. It should be remembered that the facts of this case involved Jean-Guy Tremblay seeking an injunction against his former girlfriend, Chantal Daigle, a matter the Court described as a private civil dispute. There was no law to which Tremblay could point nor any government action that created the asserted violation of section 7. The Court did not consider an argument based on government "inaction." The argument would be that, by not legislating to protect the rights of the unborn, both the Québec National Assembly and the federal Parliament were violating the right to life of the unborn.[123]

The Supreme Court concluded its assessment of the "substantive rights" arguments by briefly addressing the father's rights issue. The respondent argued that, since he had played an equal part in the conception of the potential child, he should have an equal say in what happened to it. The Court found no support for this proposition, the practical effect of which would be to provide a "potential father" with a veto over any decision made by a woman in relation to the fetus she was carrying.

The Supreme Court declined to answer many of the interesting Charter questions raised by this appeal. Some of them are: (1) the rights of the fetus, if any, under section 7 of the Canadian Charter of Rights and Freedoms; (2) the balance between a woman's right to liberty and security and governmental interest in the fetus; (3) the constitutional rights, if any, of potential fathers, and; (4) the possibility that the Charter may give rise to positive obligations upon government to act, at least in certain circumstances, to protect guaranteed rights.

Ultimately this was an "easy" case for the Supreme Court of Canada.[124] Undoubtedly, it was correct in its finding that the Québec National Assembly did not intend to

---

[119]*Supra* note 110 at 564.

[120]This view can be contrasted with that of Chief Justice Bernier of the Québec Court of Appeal [1989], R.J.Q. 1735:

> He (the foetus) is not an inanimate object nor anyone's property but a living human entity distinct from that of the mother who bears him . . . and who from the outset has the right to life and to the protection of those who conceived him.

[121]As it did in *Borowski*, *supra* note 114, and *Morgentaler* (1988), *supra* note 33.

[122]R.W.D.S.U. v. Dolphin Delivery Ltd., [1986] 2 S.C.R. 573. It must be presumed that the court-ordered injunctions do not constitute "government action" for the purpose of the application of the Charter.

[123]*See generally* Slattery, *A Theory of the Charter* 2 Osgoode H.L.J. 701 (1987). This raises an issue of major significance in the interpretation of the Charter, that of whether it can be construed as imposing positive obligations upon government to act.

[124]The reason offered by the Court for continuing the hearing, after Daigle's counsel announced that she had

extend protection to the fetus when it used the expression "human being" in section 1 of the Québec Charter. Therefore, if there is no right to life for the fetus recognized in either Québec human rights legislation or the Civil Code, then the only other source of such a right would be the Charter of Rights and Freedoms. The Court was able to deny the Charter's application to these facts by characterizing the dispute as a "private" one. Further, the right of the "potential father" to assert a claim to, or on behalf of, the fetus, over the objections of the woman carrying it, is one that has virtually no support in English, Canadian and U.S. law and was dismissed with even greater certainty.

Although in *Daigle* the Supreme Court avoided dealing with the claim that a fetus has a constitutionally protected right to life, the issue is one that has been before the courts in Canada, in one form or another, for some time.[125] These claims now usually involve an argument under section 7 of the Charter. Problematic for the proponents of this view is the question of to whom this right is granted. Section 7 rights are granted to "everyone," and although the Supreme Court of Canada has assiduously avoided ruling on this issue, it is predicted that the Court finally will conclude that the term "everyone" does not include a fetus.[126] It should be remembered that in *Morgentaler* (1988)[127] all members of the Court made a point of clearly stating that they were not deciding whether a fetus had constitutionally protected rights under section 7. In *Daigle*,[128] the Court avoided the issue by characterizing the dispute before it as a private one. Therefore, this important issue remains to be resolved by the Court.

Borowski v. Canada

Just as the name of Henry Morgentaler resonates with meaning for those who believe in choice, so does the name of Joe Borowski for many who support fetal rights. Mr. Borowski, a former cabinet minister in Manitoba, has championed the rights of the fetus for over 20 years. As has Dr. Morgentaler, Mr. Borowski has been involved in lengthy and legally significant litigation for the past 15 years. Ironically, Mr. Borowski also challenged the constitutional validity of section 251 of the Criminal Code on the basis of the Canadian Bill of Rights but did so on behalf of the fetus, arguing that the fetus was being denied the right to life guaranteed in section 1(a) of the Bill.

Because the federal Attorney General contested the "standing" of Mr. Borowski to challenge the constitutional validity of section 251 of the Code[129], by the time the merits of his claim were finally dealt with by the Saskatchewan Court of Queen's Bench, the Charter had come into force. Therefore Mr. Borowski's main constitutional argu-

---

obtained an abortion in defiance of the terms of the interlocutory injunction, was "so that the situation of women in the position in which Ms. Daigle found herself could be clarified." Technically, the issues raised in this appeal became moot upon Daigle obtaining an abortion.

[125] *See, e.g.* Dehler v. Ottawa Civic Hospital (1980), 117 D.L.R. (3d) 512 (Ont. C.A.); Medhurst v. Medhurst (1984), 9 D.L.R. (4th) 252.

[126] It is predicted that the Court will reach this conclusion on a number of grounds, including (1) the intention of the drafters of § 7 of the Charter, (2) existing statutory and case law and (3) the implications of such a conclusion for women.

[127] *See supra* note 33.

[128] *See supra* note 110.

[129] [1981] 2 S.C.R. 575. The Court granted Mr. Borowski standing on the basis that there was a serious issue as to the section's invalidity, that Mr. Borowski had a genuine interest as a citizen in the validity of the legislation and that there was no other reasonable and effective manner in which the issue might be brought before the Court. Martland J., speaking for the majority, at 598.

ments were based on section 7 of the Charter and not section 1(a) of the Canadian Bill of Rights.[130]

Borowski lost both at trial and on appeal.[131] Counsel for Mr. Borowski had presented extensive evidence in an attempt to convince the trial judge that the term "everyone" included the fetus. Although Justice Matheson clearly, and not surprisingly, accepted the fact that the fetus is a potential person, he rejected the argument that the term "everyone" was intended to include such potential persons. Historically the fetus had never been recognized in Canadian law as a legal person, and Justice Matheson concluded that "the Courts are not . . . endowed with the power to import into terms utilized in the *Charter* interpretations they cannot reasonably bear." [132]

The Saskatchewan Court of Appeal upheld the decision of Justice Matheson,[133] and on appeal to the Supreme Court of Canada, the Court declared Mr. Borowski's challenge moot.[134] The Court did so because Mr. Borowski's challenge to section 251 of the Code had been overtaken by the Court's decision in *Morgentaler* (1988)[135] in which section 251 had been declared null and void. Therefore, in the Court's opinion, the legal basis for Mr. Borowski's claim had disappeared.[136]

Sullivan and Lemay v. R.

The recent decision of the Supreme Court in *Sullivan and Lemay v. R.*[137] may provide a further indication as to the Court's thinking in relation to a constitutionally based right to life for the fetus. Sullivan and Lemay were two midwives charged under sections 203 and 204 of the Criminal Code[138] after a full term baby they were attempting to deliver died while in the birth canal. At trial, they were convinced of criminal negligence causing death to the baby but were acquitted of criminal negligence causing bodily harm to the mother. The case raised the question of whether a fetus in the birth canal is a "person" for the purposes of section 203 of the Code.[139] In reaching its conclusion that the word "person" in section 203 did not include a fetus, the Court considered section 206 (now section 223) of the Code, which stated that a child became a human being within the meaning of the Code when it had completely proceeded, in a living state, from the body of its mother. Much was made of the fact that section 203,

---

[130] However, Justice Matheson considered the arguments based on the Bill of Rights and for the reasons of Chief Justice Laskin, in *Morgentaler* (1975) dismissed them.

[131] [1984] 1 W.W.R. 15 (Sask. Q.B.); *aff'd.* [1987] 4 W.W.R. 385 (Sask. C.A.).

[132] *Id.* at 34.

[133] *See supra* note 131.

[134] [1989] 1 S.C.R. 342.

[135] *See supra* note 33.

[136] It might be argued that the issue was not moot on the basis that if the fetus does have a constitutional right to life, then "inaction" on the part of the federal Parliament in not legislating to protect fetal life constitutes government "action" in violation of § 7 of the Charter.

It was clear from the Court's comments that it did not wish to address the complex issue of fetal rights in the abstract, i.e., without a concrete legislative context in which the balancing of interests could take place.

[137] [1991] 1 S.C.R. 489.

[138] Now §§ 220 and 221.

[139] § 203 stated:

Everyone who by criminal negligence causes death of another person is guilty of an indictable offence and is liable to imprisonment for life.

under which Sullivan and Lemay were charged, did not use the term "human being" but used the term "person". It was argued that the two terms were not synonymous and that the term "person" was broader than that of "human being," and therefore could include a fetus. The Court commented that it was not persuaded by any of the textual arguments put forward and consequently it concluded that the terms "person" and "human being" were synonymous. Therefore, Sullivan and Lemay could not be convicted of criminal negligence in causing death to another person.[140]

This case, like *Daigle*,[141] involved the interpretation of existing statutory provisions. In neither case was the Court forced to consider the more fundamental question whether the fetus had a constitutional right to life. In all likelihood, the Court will not deal with this question unless the federal Parliament, or a provincial legislature, enacts a statutory provision that attempts to provide the fetus with rights. There would then be a concrete legislative context in which the Court could balance the state's interests in protecting fetal life with the interests of women in controlling their bodies and their reproductive capacity.[142].

---

[140] *See supra,* note 137 at 503.

L.E.A.F. (Legal Education and Action Fund), a national organization that promotes equality for women intervened in this case to argue that "the fetus should not be viewed as independent of a pregnant woman but as "in her" and "of her" in that it is interconnected with her in many intricate and intimate ways." Para. 43, p.22 of Factum of the Intervener, Women's Legal Education Action Fund. L.E.A.F. argued that the structuring of the legal issues in the appeal failed to place the pregnant woman, in whose body the fetus is, at the center of the legal analysis. *Id.* at para.27, p.15.

Clothing the foetus with independent legal and constitutional rights may lead to the foetus having a right to the use of a woman's body, or a right to medical treatment that overrides the welfare of the pregnant woman—rights to be asserted over the woman by the putative father, a doctor, a self-appointed foetal curator or an arm of the State. Id. at para.41, p.22.

L.E.A.F. was seeking on interpretation of the Criminal Code "that would enhance women's equality by ensuring that the status of the foetus was not considered apart from the woman who carries it." *Id.* at para.27, p.15.

Ultimately, the Court concluded that it did not have to deal with the equality arguments presented by L.E.A.F., although it recognized that the result it reached was consistent with L.E.A.F.'s "equality approach."

[141] *See supra* note 110.

[142] In a recent article entitled *Abortion & Democracy for Women: A Critique of* Tremblay v. Daigle (1989), 35 McGill L.R. 633 at 662, Donna Greschner offers the following explanation for the increasing demands to recognize and protect fetal rights:

The idea of foetal rights and personhood only entered political discourse when women began to achieve some control over our lives, when we gained a measure of freedom from the rule of fathers and husbands, when we could exercise some self-determination. With the rise of the women's movement has come, as a counter-attack, the concept of foetal personhood to guarantee women's traditional role in the patriarchal family. Abortion restrictions can no longer be overtly justified in order to ensure that women fulfil the function of mothers subject to the control of men. Hence laws are rhetorically justified as necessary to protect the foetus. Consider, for instance, that while all advocates of foetal rights state that someone must represent and speak for the foetus, they refuse to allow the mother to be that representative, proving the point that foetal rights are a method of controlling, not empowering or valuing, the women who create, nurture and deliver foetuses. Foetal personhood is the latest weapon in the battle to deny women's personhood . . .

Conclusion

This chapter has attempted to provide the reader with an overview of the historical development of Canadian law dealing with abortion. In Canada, as elsewhere, abortion will continue to be a highly emotional and divisive issue. It is an issue upon which compromise does not seem possible. Hence, a political solution is not likely.

For many women, the struggle for reproductive choice is an important part of their ongoing battle for equality. Reproductive choice is not only about abortion, it is about effective contraception, infertility, new reproductive technologies, medical practices surrounding birth and the development and control of all of these. The reproductive capacity of women provides a unique context within which women define themselves, their relationships and their role in society. Indeed, many others, including legislators, have defined women, and their appropriate roles, largely in terms of this capacity. Women have realized for a long time that control over reproduction is a starting point, from which they can take control over their lives, based on their priorities and aspirations. Therefore it is unthinkable that the control, so recently gained, over one small aspect of reproduction, that of deciding whether or not to terminate a pregnancy, will be relinquished without a struggle.[143]

In terms of the present situation regarding access to abortion, the Supreme Court's decision in *Morgentaler* (1988) appears to have changed little.[144] There are many hospitals that choose not to perform abortions at all and a growing number of doctors who also refuse to participate in the procedure. This perpetuates the inequality that existed under section 251 of the Code. Where a woman lives, both in terms of province of residence and the site of her residence within the province, will determine her accessibility to abortion services.

There continues to be resistance to the establishment of private clinics.[145] Even in communities where they exist, provincial health care plans usually only pay part of the

---

[143] Women have the support of the Canadian Medical Association in their efforts to prevent the recriminalization of abortion. In its *Brief to the House of Commons Legislative Committee on Bill C-43*, (Ottawa, February 6, 1990), it stated that the decision to perform an induced abortion is a medical decision made confidentially between the patient and her physician, within the context of a physician-patient relationship after conscientious examination of all other options.

[144] Although the number of abortions performed in 1989, the first full year after the *Morgentaler* (1988) decision, increased by 9.1% over 1988 for a total of 79,315 abortions, the increase may be explained, in part, by fewer women seeking abortions in the United States; 90% of all abortions were performed in the first 13 weeks of pregnancy. Taken from *Health Reports, Therapeutic Abortion, 1988*, Supp. No.9, Vol. 2, No.1, 1990, Minister of Supply and Services.

Statistics for 1990 indicate that 94,000 therapeutic abortions were performed in Canada during the year, an 18.6% increase over 1989. However, the actual increase over 1989 is hard to determine because 1990 numbers, for the first time, report abortions performed in private clinics. In 1990, 71,092 abortions were performed in hospitals and 21,443 in clinics. 87.7% of these abortions were performed in the first 13 weeks of pregnancy and 7.8% between 13–16 weeks.

[145] The number of private clinics performing abortions in Canada are as follows:

British Columbia	- 2 - both in Vancouver;
Alberta	- 2 - 1 in Edmonton and 1 in Calgary;
Manitoba	- 1 - in Winnipeg;
Ontario	- 4 - all in Toronto;
Quebec	- 4 - all in Montréal but there are also 3 Women's Health Centres and 12 Community Health Clinics that perform abortions;

actual cost of the procedure, the doctor's fee, thereby forcing doctors to bill directly their patients for an amount to underwrite the operating costs of the clinic. The effect of this practice is to discriminate against women in poor economic circumstances, particularly teenagers and women who already have large families and for whom another child will exacerbate conditions of poverty.

The battle lines are clearly drawn in the ongoing debate over abortion. The anti-choice forces will redouble their efforts to have the federal Parliament recriminalize abortion, and at the provincial level they will continue to lobby to prevent the establishment of private clinics and to have abortion de-insured under provincial health care plans. The pro-choice forces will continue to place the issue of abortion in the context of a larger struggle—the realization of equality for Canadian women.[146]

Appendix I

Sections of the Criminal Code Relating to Abortion as they existed up to January 1988

Procuring miscarriage	251(1) Everyone who, with intent to procure the miscarriage of a female person, whether or not she is pregnant, uses any means for the purpose of carrying out his intention is guilty of an indictable offence and is liable to imprisonment of life.
Woman procuring her own miscarriage	(2) Every female person who, being pregnant, with intent to procure her own miscarriage, uses any means or permits any means to be used for the purpose of carrying out her intention is guilty of an indictable offence and is liable to imprisonment for two years.
"Means"	(3) In this section, "means" includes (a) the administration of a drug or other noxious thing, (b) the use of an instrument, and (c) manipulation of any kind.
Exceptions	(4) Subsections (1) and (2) do not apply to (a) a qualified medical practitioner, other than a member of a therapeutic abortion committee for any hospital, who in good faith uses in an accredited or approved hospital any means for the purpose of carrying out his intention to procure the miscarriage of a female person, or

---

Nova Scotia   - 1 - in Halifax;
Newfoundland   - 1 - in St. John's.

[146] For a discussion of the political nature of the battle over abortion see: J. Brodie, S.A.M. Gavigan and J. Jenson, *The Politics of Abortion* (1992).

(b)   a female person who, being pregnant, permits a qualified medical practitioner to use in an accredited or approved hospital any means described in paragraph (a) for the purpose of carrying out her intention to procure her own miscarriage

if, before the use of those means, the therapeutic abortion committee for that accredited or approved hospital, by a majority of the members of the committee and at a meeting of the committee at which the case of such female person has been reviewed,

(c)   has by certificate in writing stated that in its opinion the continuation of the pregnancy of such female person would or would be likely to endanger her life or health, and

(d)   has caused a copy of such certificate to be given to the qualified medical practitioner.

Information requirement

(5)   The Minister of Health of a province may by order

(a)   require a therapeutic abortion committee for any hospital in that province, or any member thereof, to furnish to him a copy of any certificate described in paragraph (4)(c) issued by that committee, together with such other information relating to the circumstances surrounding the issuance of that certificate as he may require, or

(b)   require a medical practitioner who, in that province, has procured the miscarriage of any female person named in a certificate described in paragraph (4)(c), to furnish to him a copy of that certificate, together with such other information relating to the procuring of the miscarriage as he may require.

Definitions

(6)   For the purposes of subsections (4) and (5) and this subsection

• "accredited hospital" means a hospital accredited by the Canadian Council on Hospital Accreditation in which diagnostic services and medical, and surgical and obstetrical treatment are provided;

• "approved hospital" means a hospital in a province approved for the purposes of this section by the Minister of Health of that province;

• "board" means the board of governors, management or directors, or the trustees, commission or other person or group of persons having the control and management of an accredited or approved hospital;

• "Minister of Health" means

(a) in the Provinces of Ontario, Québec, New Brunswick, Manitoba, Alberta, Newfoundland and Prince Edward Island, the Minister of Health,

(b) in the Province of British Columbia, the Minister of Health Services and Hospital Insurance,

(c) in the provinces of Nova Scotia and Saskatchewan, the Minister of Public Health, and

(d) in the Yukon Territory and the Northwest Territories, the Minister of National Health and Welfare;

- "qualified medical practitioner" means a person entitled to engage in the practice of medicine under the laws of the province in which the hospital referred to in subsection (4) is situated;

- "therapeutic abortion committee" for any hospital means a committee, comprised of not less than three members each of whom is a qualified medical practitioner, appointed by the board of that hospital for the purpose of considering and determining questions relating to terminations of pregnancy within that hospital.

(7) Nothing in subsection (4) shall be construed as making unnecessary the obtaining of any authorization or consent that is or may be required, otherwise than under this Act, before any means are used for the purpose of carrying out an intention to procure the miscarriage of a female person. 1953–54 c.51, s.237; 1968–69, c.38, s.18.

252. Every one who unlawfully supplies or procures a drug or other noxious thing or an instrument or thing, knowing that it is intended to be used or employed to procure the miscarriage of a female person, whether or not she is pregnant, is guilty of an indictable offence and is liable to imprisonment for two years. 1953–54, c.51, s.238.

Appendix II

Bill C-43, An Act Respecting Abortion
(2nd Session, 34th Parliament 38
Elizabeth 11, 1989)
Introduced in the House of Commons November 3, 1989; defeated in the Senate, January 31, 1991

Inducing abortion

287.(1) Every person who induces an abortion on a female person is guilty of an indictable offence and liable to imprisonment for a term not exceeding two years, unless the abortion is induced by or under the direction of a medical practitioner who is of the opinion that, if the abortion were not induced, the health or life of the female person would be likely to be threatened.

Definitions

(2)   For the purposes of this section,
- ''health'' includes, for greater certainty, physical, mental and psychological health;
- ''medical practitioner,'' in respect of an abortion induced in a province, means a person who is entitled to practise medicine under the laws of that province;
- ''opinion'' means an opinion formed using general accepted standards of the medical profession.

Interpretation

(3)   For the purposes of this section and section 288, inducing an abortion does not include using a drug, device or other means on a female person that is likely to prevent implantation of a fertilized ovum.

Supplying noxious things

288.   Every one who unlawfully supplies or procures a drug or other noxious thing or an instrument or thing, knowing that it is intended to be used or employed to induce an abortion on a female person, is guilty of an indictable offence and liable to imprisonment for a term not exceeding two years.

Western European legal debate on abortion has had a character remarkably different from that in the United States—perhaps because the focal issue has been the nature and scope of the right to life rather than the nature and scope of any right to abortion. The typical procedural posture has been that a partial legislative depenalization of abortion is brought to court for unconstitutionally violating the right to life. The interests of the fetus tend to have more weight in the resulting judicial opinions than they do in *Roe v. Wade*.

One of the most recent examples of this sequence of events came to a head in 1985 when the Spanish Constitutional Court struck down a 1983 law for being insufficiently protective of the fetus. As subsequently amended, the Spanish Penal Code nevertheless depenalizes abortion where a second physician certifies that the abortion is necessary to avert "a serious risk to the physical or mental health" of the pregnant woman, or where the pregnancy is the result of rape and the abortion is performed during the first 12 weeks, or where two additional doctors (beside the aborting physician) certify that the fetus will probably be born with "serious physical or mental defects" and the abortion is performed during the first 22 weeks of pregnancy. (Spanish Penal Code Art. 417 *bis*.)

It is too soon to tell what impact, if any, Spain's 1985 high court opinion will have on Latin America or on the rest of the world. Professor Stith's commentary on it is reprinted here primarily because it captures a rich and nuanced European debate, the terms of which are largely unfamiliar to those on both sides of the abortion issue in the United States.

13 · New Constitutional and Penal Theory in Spanish Abortion Law

Richard Stith, J.D., Ph.D.*

The abortion debate in the United States is a clash of individualisms: the proponents of individual rights for putative unborn persons array themselves against the advocates of individual rights for women. Although the Left sides almost exclusively with the latter,[1] it is hard to discern anything more than a tactical nexus of abortion-related issues with the socialist goal of community-based decisionmaking.[2]

    Not so in European law. The important 1975 West German decision mandated laws *against* abortion from a dramatically communitarian perspective,[3] as has been so ably

*Richard Stith is Professor of Law, Valparaiso University. The author is indebted for assistance to Professors Antonio Carlos Pereira, Antonio Garcia Cuadrado, Cole Durham, Mary Ann Glendon, John Gorby, Donald Kommers and John Potts, as well as to Paige Cunningham.

[1] Mark Tushnet, a former coordinator and still a frequent speaker for the Critical Legal Studies movement, has called the right to reproductive choice "a leftish sort of right which, it is said, letists must recognize as *not* relative lest they lose their political credentials." Tushnet, *An Essay on Rights,* 62 Tex. L. Rev. 1363, 1365 (1984). Note, however, that Tushnet goes on to argue such a right would no longer make sense even to leftists in a society slightly different from our own. *See* also *infra* n. 21.

[2] Quintano Ripollés, in his historical analysis of abortion legislation, is puzzled by the fact that at the political level European socialists have long tended to favor more elective abortion, despite the "individualism" he sees represented by such a position. He theorizes that past explicit use of anti-abortion laws to increase the armies and labor forces of capitalist nations may have caused socialists to oppose such laws. It would add that Left commitments to sexual equality could also point in this direction. But neither demographic decline nor women's equality seems necessarily to further the development of socialism. 1 Tratado de Derecho Penal, Parte Especial, 504–05 (1962).

[3] Decision of 25 February 1975, [1975] 39 BVerfGE 1. Translated into English by Jonas & Gorby, *West German Abortion Decision: A Contrast to* Roe v. Wade—*with Commentaries,* 9 John Marshall J. of Prac., and Proc. 551 (1976).

pointed out by Donald Kommers.[4] The Spanish Constitutional Court decision of 11 April 1985,[5] which was strongly influenced by the German one,[6] is in many (but not all) ways even more communitarian than that prior opinion. Indeed, it may not be too much to say that social constitutional jurisprudence in the West may well find a landmark in this Spanish case. Socialism is relevant to abortion after all, but in a way quite different from that which might superficially have been expected.

The key point, to be developed below, is that the Spanish court considers the fetus neither a person possessing rights, as U.S. pro-life people argue, nor subject to a person possessing rights, as pro-choicers argue. Instead, unborn life is treated as a distinct constitutionally protected legal good. The nature of this Spanish status of the fetus as a public value will be elucidated in this commentary, and its status will be compared with that of unborn life according to the highest tribunals of Germany and the United States.

It will further be seen that the use of this value to require the prohibition of elective abortion is intimately linked in Spain, more explicitly than in Germany, with the communitarian ideal of the "Social State." U.S. constitutional doctrine, being much more individualist, might well not have required such a result even if the fetus had been recognized by our Supreme Court to have a very high public value.

Yet the Spanish and German decisions contain a surprise: At the same time that they base the protection of fetal life on the importance of public values, they withdraw that protection when continuation of a pregnancy is "too much to demand" or "nondemandable" (*"inexigible"* and *"unzumutbar,"* in the words of the Spanish and German courts respectively) of the individual pregnant women. I will point out that abortion in such hardship cases may come under a paradoxical category of penal theory in which individuals are legally justified (not merely excused) in doing that which from the standpoint of public legal values remains unjustified. This individualist doctrinal counterthrust may be just as important as the communitarian expansion occurring in the same Spanish abortion case. References to Germany and to the U.S. will again make this clear.

Before turning to case analysis, however, it would be well to define with greater precision the basic categories I have been and will be using: To the degree to which a "community" (or "socialism") exists, shared public values are effectively pursued by all. As long as those values inhere in states of being rather than in conduct considered right in itself, rules are unimportant. For example, if neighbors were to gather to build a common barn, it would be silly to set down rules granting individual claim rights to

---

[4] Kommers, *Abortion and Constitution: United States and West Germany,* 25 Am. J. Comp. L. 255, 280–284 (1977) and *Liberty and Community in Constitutional Law: The Abortion Cases in Constitutional Perspective,* 1985 Brigham Young U. L. Rev. 371, 391–399. For a quite useful critique from an individualist perspective, see Gerstein & Lowry, *Abortion, Abstract Norms, and Social Control: The Decision of the West German Federal Constitutional Court,* 25 Emory L. J. 849 (1976).

[5] Decision of 11 April 1985, STC 53/1985 (Pleno). The official version was first published in 119 Boletin Oficial dei Estado [hereinafter BOE] 10 (suplemento, 18 mayo 1985), but I have hereinafter cited the clearer and perhaps more accessible 1985–49 Boletin de Jurisprudencia Constitucional [hereafter BJC] 515.

[6] I do not believe this assertion to be controversial. The Spanish decision refers repeatedly to the German one in summarizing arguments of counsel. *Id.* at 521, 523, 526, 527. In the Comision de Justicia e Interior debates on 25 February 1983, opposition leader Ruiz Gallardón referred to the government's repeated statements that German law had been an inspiration for the present abortion depenalization proposal. The responding Justice Minister, Ledesma Bartret, did not dispute this assertion. Cortes Generales, Sesiones del Congreso de los Diputados, II Legislatura, Num. 18, 1983 at 6 ff. According to Ernst Benda, former President of the Constitutional Court of West Germany, the Spanish Court itself has been modeled on the German one. See *Constitutional Jurisdiction in West Germany,* 19 Colum. J. Transnat'l. L. 1 (1981).

hammers. There would no doubt be temporary rule-like guidelines provided, in order to aid coordination, but the common goal would be to use hammers wherever they are most needed. No individual would insist on getting his or her prescribed turn with a hammer, if a neighbor could use it better for their shared purpose.

By contrast, to the degree to which a society is "individualist," there are no public values. All goals are personal and private, and human beings interact only insofar as necessary in order for each to achieve his or her private values. Consequently, rules are very important. For example, if a number of individuals are constructing their own separate barns, and there is a scarcity of tools, they will surely set down a set of rules for sharing hammers. These rules will differ from the temporary guidelines used by the neighbors above not only in their substance but also in their lack of flexibility. Private planning requires certainty about rules, requires *rights*. This is particularly so if the others involved are competitors or even enemies, so that one is disinclined to relinquish a turn at the hammer even if one happens to have run out of nails.

At a constitutional level, a court might impose one or the other of these models. It might insist that the State require all to work together for a common goal (e.g., life), or it might insist that the State refrain from coordinating common pursuits in order to further the private values of individuals. Or, of course, it might do neither and let the whole matter remain in the hands of legislatures.

Chronology and Summary of the Decision

Prior to the bill here at issue, the Spanish Penal Code did not explicitly exempt any abortions from punishment.[7] However, the general defense of necessity includes an exemption for acts done to avoid harm equal to or greater than the harm caused,[8] which would make non-punishable at least those abortions necessary to preserve maternal life.[9]

Soon after the sweeping *Partido Socialista Obrero Espanol* (PSOE) electoral victory of 1982, which gave the party an absolute majority in the Spanish legislature, the new government proposed an addendum to prior abortion law,[10] declaring abortion unpunishable in certain circumstances. As approved by the Congress of Deputies on 6 October 1983, and by the Senate on 30 November 1983, the bill read:

> *Abortion will not be punishable if performed by a physician, with the consent of the woman, when any one of the following circumstances is present:*
> 1. That it is necessary in order to avoid a serious danger to the life or health of the pregnant woman.
> 2. That the pregnancy is the consequence of an act constituting the crime of rape under art. 429, provided that the abortion is performed within the first twelve weeks of gestation and that the aforementioned act has been reported.

---

[7] Codigo Penal arts. 411–417. Published as Codigo Penal y legislacion complementaria (1984).

[8] Codigo Penal art. 8(7).

[9] The supplemental brief of the anti-abortion petitioners (dated 3 January 1983[sic]) further states that in practice abortion was never punished when done for any of the reasons listed in the government's abortion depenalization bill, found *infra* note 11 and accompanying text. Therefore, the brief argues, statutory reform serves no purpose except to prepare the way for fully elective abortion.

[10] The addendum was to be inserted at the end of the existing sections on abortion and numbered "417 *bis*."

3. That it is probable that the fetus will be born with serious physical or mental defects, provided that the abortion is performed within the first twenty-two weeks of gestation and that the unfavorable prognosis is registered in an opinion issued by two medical specialists other than the one operating on the pregnant woman.[11]

The post-Franco Spanish Constitution of 1978 established for the first time a Constitutional Court with the power of judicial review of statutes.[12] Consistent with the Kelsenian European tradition, a petition alleging unconstitutionality may be interposed by certain authorized persons, without the need to await a concrete injury.[13] A 1979 sub-constitutional law, repealed in 1985, further established the right of these same persons to insist that the Court hear such a petition before certain allegedly unconstitutional bills could enter into effect.[14]

On 2 December 1983, the latter sort of petition was filed in the name of fifty-four Deputies led by the conservative *Alianza Popular* party. After receiving a series of supplements and responses during the first half of 1984, the Constitutional Court finally announced its decision on 11 April 1985. The abortion reform bill was declared in certain details to be an unconstitutional violation of article 15 of the Constitution, which reads "All have the right to life and to physical and moral integrity . . . ." ("todos tienen derecho a la vida y a la integridad física y moral . . ."). Although the twelve members of the Court were evenly divided for and against this declaration, Spanish practice in effect permitted a second and tie-breaking vote to be cast by the President of the Court, Dr. Manuel Garcia Pelayo y Alonso, an ex-soldier for the Spanish Republic who became an internationally-known scholar during his years outside of Spain.[15]

After a lengthy development of the arguments presented by the petitioners and by the governmental respondent, the Court built its position on twelve "Legal Foundations" *(Fundamentos Juridicos),* concluding with the holding of unconstitutionality. Five dissenting opinions, one of which is co-authored, follow.

The Court's argument in brief paraphrase is this: Human life is a superior constitutional value (Legal Foundation, hereinafter L.F., 3) and a Social State such as Spain has an affirmative duty to secure it by law (L.F. 4). This life is a reality distinct from the mother from the beginning of gestation and, therefore, the "one to be born" *(nas-*

---

[11] This is a translation of the bill as it appears in the Constitutional Court's opinion STC 53/1985, of 11 April, as published in the BJC, *supra* n. 5 at 531, which is slightly modified in capitalization and punctuation from the version earlier printed in the BOE, *supra* n. 5.

[12] The Court is made up of twelve members (four chosen by three-fifths of the Congress, four by three-fifths of the Senate, two by the current government, and two by the General Council of the Judicial Power), as authorized by art. 159(1) of the Constitution of 1978 [as found in Leyes politicas del Estado (1984)]. Members are elected for nine-year terms, which are staggered over three-year cycles. Art. 159(3).

[13] Art. 162(1)(a) of the Constitution of 1978.

[14] Organic Law of the Constitution Court (Ley Orgánica 2/1979, de 3 de octubre, del Tribunal Constitucional) art. 79(2). Repealed by Ley Orgánica 4/1985, de 7 de junio (BOE num. 137, de 8 de junio).

[15] The vote was not exactly along socialist vs. conservative lines. Of the six members of the "majority", two were those nominated by the General Council of the Judicial Power. The Court's president had been approved by the POSE. The remaining three were originally proposed by the old centrist party, the UCD, which virtually disappeared in the 1982 elections. The only woman on the court co-authored the resulting Court opinion. *El tribunal de los 12,* El Pais, 12 April 1985, p. 13. Additional chronological and biographical details may be found on the same page. See also *Asi votaron los doce magistrados,* Ya, 12 April 1985, p. 5, and *Diario 16,* 12 April 1985, pp. 6–7.

citurus)[16] must be considered a "legal good" *(bien juridico)* accorded protection by the Constitution. Legislative history indicates that the framers of the Constitution intended this result (L.F. 5), even though neither Spanish nor international law requires the conclusion that the one to be born possesses a personal subjective right to this protection (LL.FF. 5, 6, and 7). Such protection must be effective and, if necessary, include penal sanctions, although it need not be absolute (L.F. 7).

The Constitution also guarantees personal dignity, which includes rights such as free development of one's personality, physical and moral integrity, and personal and family intimacy (L.F. 8). When constitutional values collide, the legislator must weigh them and try to harmonize them or, if necessary, to specify the conditions under which one may prevail. He must also not forget the limits to what is reasonably demandable by the penal law. In carrying out his judgments, he need not turn only to the generalized exemptions from punishment found in article 8 of the Penal Code, but may use a different technique for certain crimes such as abortion (L.F. 9).

After disposing of statutory vagueness problems—by indicating, for example, that a "serious danger" is one which involves an important and permanent diminution of physical or mental health (L.F. 10)—the Court applies the foregoing principles to the bill in question. There is nothing unconstitutional in permitting the destruction of unborn life where the mother's life is at stake. Given a "serious danger" to her health, the mother's own right to life and to physical integrity is affected; not to punish abortion here is constitutional, especially in light of what is demandable by penal law. Rape violates personal dignity in the highest degree, and the law clearly cannot demand that the victim bear its consequences. As for the case of serious physical or mental fetal defects, recourse to penal sanctions against abortion would impose conduct beyond that which is normally demandable of a mother (L.F. 11).

The constitutionality of the non-punishment of abortion in such circumstances has thus been established, according to the Court. However, the State continues to have an obligation effectively to guarantee the life and health both of the woman and of the one to be born. It must, therefore, make sure that neither the former nor the latter is disprotected any more than may be required by those circumstances. For the protection of the woman, the State should provide that the abortion take place in public or private health centers authorized for this purpose. For the protection of the one to be born, in order to be certain that the first type of circumstance (serious maternal life or health danger) exists, the Constitution demands that the opinion of a medical specialist to be obtained prior to the abortion. Similarly, the opinions of the two specialists regarding any fetal disabilities must be obtained in advance of any abortion. Such changes, without excluding other possible ones, would permit the bill finally to be enacted into law (L.F. 12).[17]

---

[16]The Latin word *nasciturus* is here translated literally into English, despite the resultant oddity of speaking of the "one to be born" perhaps being aborted. "Fetus" would not be an acceptable alternative because the Spanish court had available, and elsewhere used, the equivalent *"feto."* Simply leaving the term untranslated would also not be appropriate, for the Latin word would not have the same feel in English as it would in Spanish. *"Nasciturus"* would connote a birth-related being to the educated Spanish reader, both because of its clear link to the Spanish *nacer* (to be born) and because of its most frequent use in civil law contexts where, in fact, the expectation of birth is uppermost in mind.

[17]The government did not delay in complying with the Court's demands. On 12 July 1985, a new enactment was published in BOE, *supra* n. 5 no. 166. (Ley Orgánica 9/1985, de 5 de julio, de reforma del articulo 417 bis del Codigo Penal.) The significant changes are as follows: The new law contains a preliminary paragraph requiring abortions to be done in an accredited health center, and requires a prior second medical

In the last two sections of its opinion, the Court declines to require paternal participation in the abortion decision (L.F. 13), or to enter into subsidiary civil law issues such as the relation of non-punishable abortion to social insurance. It does point out, though, that conscientious objection to abortion is protected by the Constitution (L.F. 14).

Prenatal Life as a Legal Value for the Community

The Constitutional Court of Spain finds that the one to be born has not been shown to possess any constitutional rights. At the same time, the fetus is protected by the Constitution, and indeed is protected by the sentence "All have the right to life . . ." Let us look more closely at the reasoning and results of these apparently contradictory findings by the Court.

The idea that our objective legal duties necessarily correspond to others' subjective rights is not universal,[18] being in the form we know it a development of late scholastic nominalism[19] and Enlightenment individualism. Some cultures apparently have no need to reify the benefits of the legal order and ascribe the ownership of these abstract benefits (primarily, the power to choose to make claims) to individual actors or subjects (whence "subjective"). Even today, we ordinarily think of the criminal law as a set of duties which do not respond to individual claims. I certainly have a duty not to steal from my neighbor, but only the State, not my neighbor, has the right to insist that I not do so under pain of criminal sanction. Analytically, the idea that duties need not entail rights is defended by a number of philosophers today.[20] The rise of socializing legal

---

opinion confirming that an abortion is necessary to avoid a serious danger to the life or health (which now explicitly includes mental health) of the pregnant woman. The law, however, does not require the second opinion (nor the woman's express consent) in an emergency. A new section indicates, in accordance with a remark of the Court, that the pregnant woman will not be punished even when an (otherwise non-punishable) abortion occurs in violation of the requirements of a health center or of confirming medical opinions.

Relations setting accreditation standards have become a focus of controversy under the new law.

[18] *See e.g.,* Lacruz Berdejo, *El Derechjo Subjetivo,* 3 Elementos de Derecho Civil, Parte General, 77–87 (1984). *See also* Benn, *Rights,* in 7 Encycl. Phil. 195 (1967), Benditt, *Rights* 3–8 (1982) and Hart, *Bentham on Legal Rights,* in Simpson (ejd.), *Oxford Essays on Jurisprudence* (second series) 171–202 (1973). The best short histories in English of the idea of a right may be Finnis, *Natural Law and Natural Rights* 205–210 (1980) and Golding, *The Concept of Rights: A Historical Sketch,* in Bandman & Bandman (eds.), *Bioethics and Human Rights,* (1978). *See also* Golding's more refined *Justice and Rights: A Study in Relationship,* Shelp (ed.), Justice and Health Care 23–35 (1981).

[19] The late Prof. Michel Villey has defended the thesis that William of Ockham was among the first fully to conceptualize subjective rights over property. Ockham did so, according to Villey, in order to permit the Franciscans more easily to renounce such rights and thus to fulfill their radical vows of poverty. At the same time that they renounced civil *claims* to property, they could continue to administer and to use it in a physical sense. *See* Villey, *Droit subjectif,* Seize essais de philosophie du droit 140 (1969).

[20] *See, e.g.,* the fine arguments and citations in Weiss, *The Perils of Personhood,* 89 Ethics 66 (October 1978), and in Hauerwas, *Truthfulness and Tragedy* 174 ff. and notes (1977). *See also* Feinberg, *Rights, Justice and the Bounds of Liberty* 135–39, 144 (1980). The inverse proposition, that the absence of rights need not entail the absence of duties has been well and relevantly put in Montague, *Two Concepts of Rights,* 9 Phil. and Pub. Aff. 372, 384 (1980):

> I suppose there is a sense in which I would deny that those incapable of acting intentionally have rights, but I do not see that doing so has any morally objectionable consequences. It isn't as if, for example, that by denying that infants have a right to self-defense

theory has also put pressure on the idea of individual claim rights as a foundation of the legal order.[21]

The received European legal protections accorded to the fetus cannot easily be squeezed into this modern subjective rights ideology.[22] Of the many nations following Continental traditions, apparently only Argentina has seen fit to acknowledge civil personality from the moment of conception.[23] The image of the person as a bargainer and a litigator indeed does not seem applicable to unborn life. Of course, children after birth likewise posses these traits of legal personality only *in potentia,* yet they are accorded personhood (through the exercise thereof is necessarily by a representative), so that the exclusion of fetuses remains problematic.[24] In any event, prior to 1985 many or most Spanish legal theorists granted the fetus a status lower than that of a person, perhaps even lower than that recognized in France or Italy.[25]

Anti-abortion strategy during the constitutional debates if anything reenforced the non-personhood of the fetus. Fearful that the sentence "All persons have the right to life . . ." could be read to protect only those who under the Civil Code had personality, i.e., those who had been born and were able to survive twenty-four hours,[26] opponents of abortion substituted the sentence "All have the right to life . . ," for the explicit purpose of protecting the unborn from abortion.[27] It became difficult for a court to say that a fetus is a constitutional person when the word "person" had been struck from the Constitution in order to ensure the inclusion of fetuses.

I am sanctioning infanticide; what I have said here implies only that the immorality of infanticide cannot be *grounded* on the rights of infants. Infanticide—as well as such things as cruelty to animals and non-therapeutic experimentation on the severely retarded—is immoral even if infants, animals, and the severely retarded have no (exercisable) rights.

[21] Lacruz Berdejo, *supra* n. 18 at 83. *See, e.g.,* Marx, *On the Jewish Question, Early Writings* 211, esp. 230–231 (1975) and Sandel, *Liberalism and the Limits of Justice* (1982). The socialist Mark Tushnet (*supra* n. 1) and Louis M. Seidman have explicitly argued for the permissibility of fetal protection on a non-rights basis in *A Comment on Tooley's "Abortion and Infanticide,"* 96 Ethics 350 (January 1986).

Mirjan Damaska's comprehensive new treatise contrasting the reactive and the activist state is a particularly rich theoretical context within which to understand the relative absence of rights in socialist law. *See The Faces of Justice and State Authority* 83 (1986).

[22] Lacruz Berdejo, *id.* at 93–94.

[23] Quintano Ripollés, *supra* n. 2 at 477. *But cf.* Jiménez de Asúa, arguing that the fetus still does not count as a "visible person" under Argentine law. 6 Tratado de derecho penal 988 n. 36 (2nd ed., 1962).

[24] The existence of infant persons can support the assertion that potentiality is sufficient for personhood and therefore that the unborn are likewise persons. *See Enciclopedia Juridica Espanola* 709. *See also* Rawls, *A Theory of Justice* 509 (1971), maintaining that potential rationality must be the basis for a non-arbitrary recognition of rights. *See also infra* n. 43 and accompanying text for the German high court's argument. Contrary resolutions are possible. It is common today for abortion-related philosophizing to end in approval of infanticide. *See, e.g.,* the authors Tooley and Warren cited by Weiss *supra* n. 20.

[25] Quintano Ripollés, *supra* n. 2 at 471 ff. *See also* Rodriguez Devesa, *Derecho penal espanol,* Parte Especial, 100 n. 42 (7th ed., 1979), arguing that feticide has never been considered homicide, *See generally* Cuello Calón, 2(2) *Derecho Penal* 522 (13th ed., 1972). Not all the juristic data are clear. For example, for civil purposes the prenatal child is conditionally considered born and the possessor of rights, provided that it eventually emerges viable from the womb. Codigo Civil art. 29. In criminal law, the Penal Code prohibits consensual abortion under the title "Crimes against Persons" ("Delitos contra las personas"), Codigo Penal, Titulo VIII.

[26] Codigo Civil, arts. 29–30.

[27] *Diario de Sesiones del Congreso,* Num. 105, 6 July 1978, at 3952 ff. *See also* the summary of these debates at L.F. 5 of the decision presently being considered.

The Constitutional Court in fact does not argue the issue of legal personality as such. Instead, it considers the closely related (if not ultimately identical in modern law) issue of whether fetuses are *titulares,* i.e., bearers or possessors, of a subjective constitutional right to life. It finds that they are not, a conclusion in accordance with the mainstream of Spanish legal tradition.

The Court nevertheless was faced with the apparently unanimous opinion of Spanish medical associations that the unborn child is a living human being.[28] From the materials available, the government does not appear to have disputed the physical fact of human life prior to birth. Instead, it approached the issue wholly formalistically, arguing that legal norms are independent of non-legal facts—a hard position to take when it comes to documents like constitutions which are meant to limit the legal order for the sake of a socially preferred physical reality. Moreover, the Court conceded that the substitution of "all" for "all persons" had been intended to protect nascent life. How could the Court conceptualize the legal status of living but unborn human beings?

Traditional Spanish legal doctrine may have provided some help. Not all legal goods in Spanish law have to pertain to individuals, or even to the State, in the manner of property ownership. Goods in the public domain and communal goods have long been recognized.[29] It has been argued that society, rather than the fetus or the mother, is the *titular* of the protection accorded to the unborn child.[30] Anti-abortion spokespersons had argued that even without a subjective right, the fetus may be protectable by an objective norm, as a "social good."[31] The Spanish Supreme Court (which does not have the power of judicial review nor of authoritative constitutional interpretation given to the Constitution Court) indeed asserted in its decision of 11 January 1984 that

> *Human life in formation is a good that constitutionally merits protection, is a constitutional legal good, a legal good of the community and not an individual legal good* . . .[32]

Even spokespersons for the right to abortion were willing to concede that the unborn are a legal good of the community.[33] Some interpreted such a concession to mean, however, that what the community possessed it could dispose of by its representatives

---

[28] The petitioners submitted statements from various medical associations to this effect, and the government submitted none to the contrary, or at least none the Court thought worth mentioning. See BJC, *supra* n. 5 at 525. See also *The Human Life Bill—S. 158, Report to the Committee on the Judiciary, United States Senate,* Subcommittee on Separation of Powers, 97th Congress (1981), arguing that there is a scientific consensus concerning the fact that life begins at conception but not concerning the value to be accorded to that life. The U.S. report was cited by the Spanish petitioners in their brief of amplification, dated 3 January 1983 [sic], at 7.

[29] Lacruz Berdejo, *supra* n. 18 at 42 ff., especially 51–55.

[30] Quintano Ripollés, *supra* n. 2 at 477, reports some support for all three possibilities.

[31] Diaz Fuentes calls the fetus a "social good", in *Diario de Sesiones del Congreso,* No. 105, 5 October 1983, at 2943. Oscar Alzaga is cited by Cerezo Mir, in n. 46 of his essay *La regulacion del aborto en el proyecto de nuevo Codigo Penal Espanol,* in La reforma penal (1982) to the effect that the fetus is protected by an objective norm even without a subjective right.

[32] TS 2a Sala 15 octubre 1983, reported in La Ley 11 enero 1984 at 1. Reversed (in effect) on other grounds by the Constitutional Court. TC 2a Sala 75/1984, 27 de junio, reported in La Ley, 24 octubre 1984 at 1.

[33] Sotillo Martí stated his agreement with the German high court that life in the womb is a legal good protected by the Constitution. *Diario de Sesiones del Congreso de los Diputados,* Sesiones informativas de Comisiones, No. 61, 7 septiembre 1983, at 2139.

in the legislature, and thus that the legislative depenalization of abortion was constitutionally permissible.[34] Perhaps for this reason, the anti-abortion briefs in this case resist the idea that the one to be born is only a legal good rather than a possessor of the right to life.[35]

Like the Spanish Supreme Court in the quotation above, the Constitutional Court in effect takes the traditional concept of the unborn as a protected legal good and inserts it into the constitutional "system of values." (LL.FF. 3, 4, 9). Since the Constitution emanates from the community, it would seem (though the Constitutional Court does not use these precise words) that the unborn are a legal good or value "of the community." But because of the superiority of the Constitution to ordinary legislation, the community has in effect made a commitment to the value of unborn life such that it no longer retains a right freely to dispose of that life by legislation. The community could also be seen to be simply acknowledging a preexisting and binding inherent value in such life. In either case, one might say that the one to be born has become not so much a good "of" the community, in a proprietary sense, but a good "for" the community, a good at whose furtherance the community is aiming.

It is worth pointing out that the very idea that there exists an objective order of values in a constitution is communitarian rather than individualist, because it makes the good, at least in part, public rather than private. Such an order (i.e., not only a list but also a *hierarchy*) of explicit and implicit values mandates not only a minimum set of formal rules which government and citizens must observe, but a set of goals they must aim at—particularly when combined with the idea of the Social State discussed later in this commentary.

Within this value order, life is not just any value, according to the Spanish Court, but is a "superior value" (L.F. 3), a "fundamental value" (L.F. 5), and a "central value" (L.F. 9). The Court reaches this conclusion by noting that life is a presupposition for all other rights, and by reflecting upon the placement of the right to life at the head of the list of constitutional protections (L.F. 3). The unborn are taken to "embody" (L.F. 5) this value, both because the framers of the Constitution apparently intended the unborn to be protected by the right to life clause of that document, and because of the fact, noted by the Court, that human life is a "reality from the beginning of gestation" (L.F. 5).

At the same time that the Court grants the fetus a high status as a "constitutionally protected legal good" (L.F. 7), it balances its conclusion by refusing to consider the unborn to "possess" the right to life, as discussed above, and by the curious and unexplained remark that at birth, not before or after, the fetus acquires "full human individuality" (L.F. 5). Moreover, a careful reading of the opinion will show that the Court

---

[34] The article by Luis Arroyo Zapatero discussed below at n. 69 develops the idea that what the community gives, the community can take away. Arroyo Zapatero, *Prohibicion del aborto y Constitucion,* Rev. Facultad de Derecho de la Universidad Complutense, no. 3, 195 (1980). The Constitutional Court's summary of the government arguments indicates that the latter admitted the existence of unborn life as a legal good, but claimed that the legislature had discretion over its protection. BJC, *supra* n. 5 at 526–28. Four of the dissenters to the final decision conceded that preborn life is or has some kind of legal value.

[35] *See e.g.,* the Court's summary, BJC, *id.* at 523, of petitioners' argument that life is a fundamental right or an absolute value rather than merely a legal good. Published anti-abortionist opinion had already rejected arguments like those of Arroyo Zapatero. *See* Federico Trillo-Figueroa (*La legalizacion del aborto en el derecho comparado,* at 113) and Fernando Diez Moreno (*El proyecto de Ley del Aborto desde la perspectiva constitucional,* at 181–89) in *En defensa de la vida* (1983).

never explicitly acknowledges that the fetus is among the "all" referred to in the protective phrase "All have the right to life . . ."

Let us try to understand this argument by means of an irreverent and slightly analogous hypothetical. Suppose the U.S. Constitution contained the following language: "All bald eagles, as the sacred symbol of the nation, have the right to life." Suppose further that the framers of this clause had inserted the word "all" for the precise purpose of protecting embryonic eagles as well as hatched eagles. Would we have to conclude that inside an egg is an eagle, or that a bird embryo has its own constitutional rights, in order to consider eagle eggs constitutionally protected? I think not. Such protection could be founded simply on our sense that an important meaning and purpose of the Constitution would be thwarted if eagle omelettes came into vogue.

The precise effort of the Court's elevation of fetal value is this: The Court affirms the superiority, or even the equality, of the mother's rights over the legal value of the fetus at most only in those situations covered in the first statutory depenalization, i.e., where the mother's life or health is seriously endangered, both of which values are found in the same Constitutional article held to protect the unborn (L.F. 12). In order to uphold the other two depenalizations, the Court turns instead to the doctrine of nondemandability discussed at the end of this article.

Perhaps even more importantly, the Court implicitly holds that *elective abortion is unconstitutional.* It does so by indicating that the obligation to protect the fetus requires the State to make sure beforehand (by means of a second medical opinion) that no abortions are done except where the mother is truly threatened. The exact content of the Court requirement is unimportant here. The point is this: If elective abortion were permissible, there would be no constitutional life-related value infringed upon even where an abortion were done outside the statutory provisions. By insisting that these provisions be strictly enforced *in order to protect the unborn,* the Court has clearly held the complete depenalization of abortion to be unconstitutional.[36] As a fundamental public value, developing human life cannot be converted into purely private property.

Not only did the Court manage to make this declaration in a case where elective abortion was not even an issue, but it did so in a manner highly likely to be acquiesced in by the government promoters of abortion depenalization. It asked only for tiny, technical additions to the bill, which were soon forthcoming. Had it done more, had it declared a broader right to life, the government might well have refused to go along, provoking a constitutional crisis.[37]

---

[36] The Spanish court may to a degree have been inspired by similar language in the 1975 Italian constitutional abortion decision, though the earlier phraseology would seem to appear in a procedural posture making it merely dictum: "[It] is the legislator's obligation . . . to forbid the procuring of an abortion without careful ascertainment of the reality and gravity of injury or danger which might happen to the mother as a result of the continuation of pregnancy: Therefore the lawfulness of abortion must be anchored to a preceding evaluation of the existence of the conditions which justify it." Carmosina et al., Corte Costituzionale. Decision of 18 February 1975, No. 27 [1975] 20 giur. Const. 117 as translated in Cappelletti & Cohen, *Comparative Constitutional Law* 612–14 (1979).

[37] Alfonso Guerra, vice-president of the PSOE government, in 26 March 1985 (sixteen days before the Court announced its decision) declared that if its bill were ruled invalid, the government would be forced to set up a "machinery for pardons" for those obtaining abortions. The Court itself, he said, would be placed in "a socially difficult situation," and he expressed regret that twelve non-elected persons should impede the will of 350 elected ones. He went on to oppose the separation of powers, calling it a relic of the epoch of Montesquieu, and promised to reform the norms governing the Court. These statements placed the justices

One essential element in the Court's argument above has not yet been fully explored—the idea that in a Social State constitutional values form not only negative limits to governmental action but also mold the required affirmative content of that action. This element has been postponed in order to develop more clearly the idea that the fetus has constitutional value in the first place, that the Spanish Constitution contains common public values (here unborn life) rather than only the rights of individuals. After a much briefer look at how Germany and the U.S. conceive the fetus, and some critical remarks of my own, we shall return to this postponed discussion of the interaction of fetal value and the Social State.

The 1975 West German Constitutional Court decision on abortion bears a striking resemblance to the 1985 Spanish ruling—not surprisingly since, as mentioned previously, the former served in many ways as a model for the latter.

Focusing upon the constitutional language "Everyone has the right to life . . . ," (*Jeder hat das Recht auf Leben . . .)*[38] the German Court finds it unnecessary to hold the unborn child to be a person, or a "bearer" of a subjective right,[39] in order to include it within the protection of the Basic Law. Note, however, that the Court does not shy away from referring to the unborn's "right to life." It avoids only the question of whether the child is the "bearer" (or "possessor") of this right. Perhaps the Court is thinking of analogous positive constitutional welfare "rights" for adults which need not necessarily give rise to individual claims presentable in a court. To return to our hypothetical, a similar analysis would find that bald eagles need not have civil law personality with access to courts in order to receive constitutional protection. Both this right-to-life guarantee and the explicit constitutional value of "human dignity"[40] lead the Court to rule that all human life, including prenatal life, is part of the "objective ordering of values" of the Basic Law.[41] Even the dissent agrees that the State has a constitutional duty to protect unborn life, and indeed states that the existence of this duty is "uncontested" (*unbestritten*)[42]—arguing further, however, that the duty need not be implemented by criminal sanctions.

The German decision is somewhat more "pro-life" in its reasoning than the Spanish. Like the Spanish, it notes that human life is a continuum, but unlike the Spanish it does not see "full human individuality" occurring at birth. It states

> The process of development . . . is a continuing process which exhibits no sharp demarcation and does not allow a precise division of the various steps of development of the human life. The process does not end even with birth; the phenomena of consciousness which are specific to the human personality, for example, appear for the first time a rather

---

under "intolerable pressure" according to the opposition parties. ABC 12 abril 1985 at 53. The Court's elegant self-defense reminds one of Marbury v. Madison, 5 U.S. (1 Cranch) 137 (1803).

[38] Basic Law (*Grundgesetz*) Art. 2, Sec. 2, Sentence 1.

[39] [1975] 39 BVerfGE 1, 41. See the full translation of the German decision by Jonas & Gorby, *supra* n. 3 at 641–42.

[40] Basic Law, Art. 1, Sec. 1, Sentence 1. Note that the Spanish constitutional equivalent here (Art. 10, Sec. 1, Sentence 1) refers to "the dignity of the person" rather than to "human dignity" and played only a minor role in the Madrid decision.

[41] [1975] 39 BVerfGE 1, 41; Jonas & Gorby translation, *supra* n. 3 at 642. For discussion, see Gerstein & Lowry, *supra* n. 4 at 862, 867 and materials there cited.

[42] [1975] 39 BVerfGE 1, 68 (abweichende Meinung); Jonas & Gorby, *id.* at 663 (dissent).

long time after birth. Therefore, the protection . . . of the Basic Law
cannot be limited either to the "completed" human being after birth or
to the child about to be born which is independently capable of living.[43]

Moreover, it specifically holds that the constitutional word "everyone" includes "everyone living"[44] and that no distinction can be made, with regard to the right to life, between various stages before birth, nor between unborn and born life.[45] Thus it could be argued that in Germany the fetus is in all but name constitutionally a person with rights, and so is closer than in Spain to being a full legal bearer of subjective rights. Or, put another way, Germany is more individualist and Spain more communitarian in their respective rationales for deference to unborn life.

Another way to understand the two decisions, however, would be to note that both call the one to be born a "legal value" or a "legal good" *(Rechtsgut, bien juridico)* rather than an individual possessing rights, although the German language is stronger concerning the high rank of that objective legal value. In both nations, unborn human life is an object more than a subject of constitutional protection, is a public value of the community rather than a private claim of the fetus or of the mother.[46] The German Court's further concern with government teaching and counseling in support of prenatal life also has a strongly communitarian ethos behind it.[47] The Court clearly hopes to build a common value commitment rather than only a balance of individual interests.

The explicit result of such fetal value recognition in Germany, like that implicit in Spain, is a holding that elective abortion is unconstitutional, even in the first three months of gestation.[48] New life, the next generation unborn, is the concern in some sense of the whole community, not only of individual pregnant women. Nevertheless, as in Madrid, the Court in Karlsruhe moderates the force of this conclusion by holding that there are limits to what the community can ask individuals to contribute to this

---

[43] [1975] 39 BVerfGE 1, 37; Jonas & Gorby, *id.* at 638. The Court appears to reason that as long as we protect newborn infants, whose human development is significantly incomplete, consistency requires protection prior to birth. Indeed, consistency requires a *theory* of protection which either values organic human life itself or else values the developing potentiality for higher "phenomena specific to the human personality"—for these are the only sources of inherent value which the infant possesses at birth. In other words, the Court argues that if we think newborns inherently worthy of protection, our normative theories require us also to protect life even in the early weeks of pregnancy. See further discussion *infra,* text accompanying n. 63–72.

[44] *Id.*

[45] *Id.*

[46] But note that the German court, despite its use of value terminology, insists that such value cannot be aggregated, that each particular life must be protected—even if the sacrifice of some could lead to the preservation of a greater number. [1975] 39 BVerfGE 1, 58–59; Jonas & Gorby, *id.* at 655–56. The refusal to aggregate is a departure from ordinary valuing and is more at home in discourse informed by rights.

Are there ways to avoid the ruthlessness of valuing, its common callousness toward particulars, without appealing to the selfishness of rights? I believe there are, in the ideas of respect or reverence (which perhaps may be the deep grounds of the German decision). See my critique of valuing, *Toward Freedom from Value,* 38 The Jurist 48 (1978), and my brief critique of rights in *Thinking about Ecology,* XLV(1) The Cresset 7 (1981).

[47] [1975] 39 BVerfGE 1, 50, 57–58, 61–64; Jonas & Gorby, *id.* at 649, 651–55, 657–60. For an excellent introduction to the German constitutional jurisprudence of values, *see* Benda, *New Tendencies in the Development of Fundamental Rights in the Federal Republic of Germany,* 11 John Marshall J. of Prac. and Proc. 1, 6–9 (1977). Dr. Benda at that time was president of the Constitutional Court.

[48] [1975] 39 BVerfGE 1, 68; Jonas & Gorby, *id.* at 662–63.

common value, and that as a result laws may permit abortion in various situations of relative hardship.[49] This individualist counterthrust will be examined further below.

The 1973 U.S. Supreme Court abortion decision, *Roe v. Wade,* is in surprisingly many ways similar to the Spanish and German decisions. Like them, although much more strongly, it refuses to acknowledge constitutional personhood or rights possessed by the unborn.[50] And just after its finding of non-personhood, in a largely unnoticed portion of its decision, our Court creates a legal category very similar to that into which the fetus is placed in those European opinions: non-personal human life. That is, the U.S. court indicates that its conclusion of non-personhood does not yet dispose of the contention that there is a compelling state interest in protecting life from the moment of conception. It does not respond to this contention by arguing that there would be no decisive state interest in protecting such non-personal life, should it exist, but rather by indicating the Court's doubts as to whether the fetus is actually human and alive in an extra-constitutional sense.[51] Presumably, had the Court been sure of the existence of a living human fetus, it would have found a strong public concern for fetal protection, similar to that found by the Spanish and German courts. In other words, the U.S. court creates the same category (non-personal life imbued with a high public value) brought forth by those other tribunals, but then fails to fill it.

It may well be this single difference, not a difference of constitutional categories but a disagreement about the face of actual human life, accounts for the tremendously disparate conclusions on abortion on the two sides of the Atlantic. For it is not only Spain and Germany which agree that human life exists prior to birth. The other four European constitutional courts which have considered the matter appear to have reached this same conclusion,[52] and none has subsequently seen fit to recognize a constitutional

---

[49] Very roughly speaking, the Court indicates that abortion need not be punished where the mother's life or health is at stake, or she has been raped, or the child will suffer from a serious health impairment, or she labors under some equivalent social hardship—inasmuch as each of these situations may make a continuation of pregnancy not demandable by means of the penal law. [1975] 39 BVerfGE 1, 48–50; Jonas & Gorby, *id.* at 647–49.

[50] Roe v. Wade, 410 U.S. 113, 156–58 (1973).

[51] *Id.* at 159–62. See also *infra* n. 53.

[52] The cryptic French opinion (permitting the legislature to leave most early abortions unpunished) contains the phrase "Considering that the law [permitting abortion] referred to this *Conseil Constitutionel* does not authorize any violation of the principle of respect for every human being from the very commencement of life except in case of necessity . . ." Decision of 15 January 1975, [1975] A.J.D.A. 134, as translated in Cappelletti & Cohen, *supra* n. 36, at 577–78. For a different interpretation of the French decision, see Glenn, *The Constitutional Validity of Abortion Legislation: A Comparative Note,* 21 McGill L. J. 673, 677 and accompanying notes (1975). The Italian decision referred to in n. 36 *supra* observes that Art. 2 of the Constitution guarantees the inviolable rights of man, "among which must be placed, although with the particular characteristics unique to it, the legal situation of the foetus [*'concepito'*]," at 613 of the translation, and later emphasizes obligatory protection for "the life of the foetus [*'feto'*]," at 614, even while declaring that an embryo is not yet a person, at 613, and that abortions for serious maternal health reasons must be permitted. Coret Costituzionale, Decision of 18 February 1978, n. 27 [1975] 98 *Foro It. I* (Giurisprudencia Costituzionale e Civile) 515, 516. Even the Austrian decision which alone holds that fully elective abortion in the first three months of pregnancy is constitutional, seems to concede "that throughout the whole duration of the pregnancy both the mother's life and the nascent human life constitute constant life," stating that the legislation is constitutionally free to protect the fetus by making abortion punishable, and is required to do so after viability if post-natal infanticide is punishable. Decision of 11 October 1974, Constitutional Court, [1974] *Erklärungen des Verfassungsgerichtshofs* 221, 234–35 G 8/74, as translated by Chappelletti & Cohen, *supra* n. 36 at 615, 620–21. The Portuguese decision of 19 March 1984 unanimously holds that the constitutional principle of the inviolability of human life embraces "intrauterine

right to abortion in any way as sweeping as that of *Roe v. Wade.* By and large, abortion has been left by them in the legislative domain.

Yet although the *Roe* majority does not consider the unborn child to be human and alive, it holds that the fetus does have some public value, not as life but as "potential life."[53] One might say that Europe considers the unborn child to be a *living human being,* albeit only a *potential legal person,* while the United States treats that same child as only a *potential life.* Nevertheless, there is some functional similarity to these two concepts, in that both recognize the fetus to be a value worthy of public concern, as a "legal good" and as a "state interest" respectively.

But let us not forget the Spanish and German decisions did not rest with the affirmation that the fetus is a "legal good." Those opinions tied unborn life to the order of constitutional values, while *Roe* did not. Perhaps the U.S. court could have done otherwise. While our constitutional doctrine does not acknowledge a full-blown hierarchy of values apparent or hidden in our Constitution,[54] the Supreme Court has gone beyond literal application of a set of unconnected rules. It has discerned the value of "privacy," for example, albeit linking this value to individual rights. Could our Court have looked at the various direct and indirect references to life in our fundamental law in order to give at least some attenuated *constitutional* status to what it calls "potential life"? Or would such a communitarian commitment to values be too alien to our focus on rights? In any event, in portions of Europe prenatal life has become something the State *must* respect, whereas in America it is only something the State *may* respect, even in the last moments before birth.[55]

Roe, then, treats the unborn as the object of no community commitment at the constitutional level, and as only the optional object of such a commitment at the legislative level. And even the latter option is sharply limited. The state interest in potential life without constitutional status fails entirely prior to viability, when confronted with a pregnant woman's right to privacy.[56] And even in the last period before birth, where

---

human life," even though it goes on to declare a limited disprotection of that life to be constitutional. 344 Boletim do Ministerio da Justiça 197, 216, 230 (March 1985). Thus all four other European national decisions appear to recognize actual rather than only potential human life in the unborn and to permit and even to require some measure of constitutional protection for that life, with the precise degree of protection left largely up to the legislature. *See generally,* Reis, *Das Lebensrecht des Ungeborenen Kindes als Verfassungsproblem* (1984).

Mary Ann Glendon's *Abortion and Divorce in Western Law* (1987) surveys the abortion laws of twenty Western nations and finds them all to be more sympathetic than *Roe* to fetal life.

[53] Roe v. Wade, 410 U.S. 113 calls the fetus, e.g., "potential life" (at 150, 154), "prenatal life" (at 151, 155), "potential human life" (at 159), "only the potentiality of life" (at 162), "fetal life" (at 163), and "the potentiality of human life" (at 162, 164)—the last referring to the period *after* viability. It also states "We need not resolve the difficult question of when life begins" (at 159), and ". . . a legitimate state interest need not stand or fall on the acceptance of the belief that life begins at conception or at some other point prior to live birth" (at 150). Putting all this together, one gathers that the Court does not know whether "life" (in the sense of "human" life) exists prior to birth but its potentiality does—in the form of "prenatal" or "fetal" life.

[54] *But cf.* Walter Murphy's attempt to construct such a system around the idea of "human dignity". *An Ordering of Constitutional Values,* 53 S. Cal. L. Rev. 703, 744 ff. (1980). Cf. also the works of Profs. Lawrence Tribe and Frank Michelman.

[55] Even after viability, the fetus need be protected by the State only "[if] the State is interested in protecting fetal life" (*Roe* at 163), and "if it chooses" (*Roe* at 164–65).

[56] Prior to viability, abortion can be limited only in the interest of maternal health, not in the interest of fetal life. *Id.* at 163–64.

the state's interest is nominally "compelling,"[57] it cannot compel much. Abortions destructive of the fetus must be permitted, even just before birth, if they promote what the Court calls "health"[58] but which it defines broadly to include virtually every significant reason a woman might have for a third trimester abortion.[59] Donald Kommers, in contrasting the American and German cases, has well described the outcome in our country:

> *A woman is thus entitled to separate herself from the community while the community is rendered powerless to act in its common defense for the purpose of safeguarding shared values.*[60]

The *Roe* result mandating elective abortion virtually throughout pregnancy could hardly be more at odds with the Spanish and German decisions forbidding elective abortion even in early pregnancy. And that result is likewise far from that reached by other European nations which, given the very great but nonpersonal public value of prenatal life, leave the matter of abortion almost entirely up to the legislature.[61]

How much likelihood is there that U.S. law on abortion might someday approach the mainstream of Western jurisprudence? Perhaps quite a bit. Justice O'Connor's dissent in the 1983 *Akron* case indicates a desire to find a compelling state interest in protecting the fetus *throughout* pregnancy, though there is no evidence she would recognize constitutional personhood prior to birth.[62] If she were to ground her position not merely on justices' sense of the weight of potentiality but on the fact and value of *actual* life or of the *constitutional* dignity even of potential life, then the two sides of the Atlantic would draw much nearer to each other.

Critique of Prenatal Life as a Legal Value

Individual rights for fetuses are not the only alternative to individual rights for pregnant women. Community concern for unborn human life provides another way to look at the

---

[57] *Id.*

[58] *Id.* at 165. The recent Supreme Court decision of Thornburgh v. A.C.O.G. 106 S. Ct. 2169, 90 L. Ed. 2d 779, 799 (1986) reemphasizes that even after viability, there cannot be "any 'trade-off' between the woman's health and additional percentage points of fetal survival" The holding in Webster v. Reproductive Health Services 109 S. Ct. 3040 (1989) has not yet produced any change here. *Webster* permits a new determination of viability but not new fetal protection after viability.

[59] *Roe's* companion case, which should be "read together" with the former (according to *Roe* at 165), defines "health" to be related to "all factors . . . relevant to the well-being of the patient." Doe v. Bolton, 410 U.S. 179, 192 (1973). The *Thornburgh* Supreme Court opinion, *id.*, does not refer to this definition, but the Court of Appeals did so in the decision under review. That decision states "It is clear from the Supreme Court cases that 'health' is to be broadly defined. As the Court stated in *Doe*, the factors relating to health include those that are 'physical, emotional, psychological, familial, [as well as] the woman's age' [quoting from *Doe*]." The court of appeals goes on to say that a law which punished postviability abortions which were done to avoid the "potential psychological or emotional impact on the mother of the unborn child's survival" would be clearly unconstitutional; 737 F.2d 283, 299 (1984).

[60] Kommers, *Abortion and Constitution, supra* n. 4 at 282.

[61] *See supra* n. 52.

[62] City of Akron v. Arkon Center for Reproductive Health, 462 U.S. 416, 459–466 (1983). She reaffirmed her position, again in dissent, in *Thornburgh*, 106 S. Ct. 2169 at 2214, 90 L. Ed. 2d 779 at 836–37. In the *Webster* case, *supra* n. 58, four other members of the U.S. Supreme Court affirmed the view which Justice O'Connor originally proclaimed in Akron. This time she herself refrained from taking a position on the matter.

abortion problem, a way which I personally find superior.[63] If you and I recognize someone's rights, we are not bound by love to him or her, nor do we feel between ourselves a bond of fellowship. By contrast, if we jointly commit ourselves to caring for another, the basis is laid both for affection for the object of our concern and for community among ourselves. The Spanish and German attitudes toward the unborn are much closer than the official rights-based positions of U.S. pro-lifers *or* pro-choicers to the actual feelings of parents for very young children. Parents feel infants neither to be their private property nor to be individuals negotiating their rights at arms' length. Instead and for many years, a baby is the shared value of a common life.

Yet this new perspective does not answer the question of how great a weight the child has before and after birth, in ordinary experience or in the law. And here I submit there is an antinomy for which there may well be no solution.

On the one hand, in early pregnancy, often the fetus is not sensed to be present as a separate entity, and abortion is not felt to be a kind of homicide.[64] On the other hand, a new born infant is considered a human being, and so is felt to possess what the German decision calls "inherent" *(selbtständig)* worth.[65] That is, the value of the newborn is perceived to be inherent in its being, and not in the eyes of the parental or juridical beholders.

How can these two perceptions be squared with each other? Obviously, by the assumption that the neonate is a different being from the preborn fetus. The change in being could be thought to come either from a qualitative biological leap or from the infusion of a spiritual soul, or from both.

Our modern quandary arises because we can no longer publicly affirm either basis for this assumption of discontinuity in being.[66] Human life, according to modern science, is a continuum and, as the German court notes, those traits (e.g., self-consciousness) for which many especially value our species do not arise until quite some time after birth. Neither can religion be the ground of a presumed change of being, in a pluralistic or secular society.

Thus the belief in and commitment to the inherent value of life *after* birth requires in our day (but did not require in that of our great-grandparents) significant protection for the child *before* birth[67]—because our law can no longer cogently proclaim that there is a difference in kind between the born and the unborn. To put the matter another way, if we as a legislating community permit relatively casual abortion we have rendered non-credible our commitment to the inherent value of every human being even after birth.

---

[63] So I have argued in *A Critique of Abortion Rights*, 3(4) democracy 60 (fall, 1983), and by implication in my broad attack on rights entitled *A Critique of Fairness*, 16 Valparaiso Univ. L. Rev. 459 (1982). *See also* my *Generosity: A Duty without a Right*, in which I further explore the nature of rightless relations among persons. 25.3 Journal of Value Inquiry (July 1991). *But cf.* my reservations concerning the "value" approach to human dignity in the article cited *supra* at the end of my n. 46. I am also troubled by the reemergence of an invidious separation between the concepts of "human being" and "legal person."

[64] Quintano Ripollés, *supra* n. 2 at 503, asserts that this is generally the case, at least as of 1962 (the year of that edition of this treatise).

[65] [1975] 39 BVerfGE 1, 67; Jonas & Gorby, *supra* n. 3 at 662.

[66] Justice Stevens' recent "pro-choice" concurrence in the *Thornburgh* case, 106 S. Ct. 2169 at 2188, demonstrates both the importance and the futility of such a claim of discontinuity. He there asserts that the permissibility of abortion hinges upon there being "a fundamental and well-recognized difference between a fetus and a human being" but fails even to hint at any grounds for such a distinction.

[67] And indeed throughout pregnancy, according to the argument of the German court, *supra* n. 43.

Yet at the same time, as private individuals involved with early pregnancies, we may continue not to *feel* the presence of another human life. Consequently, abortion may seem morally permissible, and our main concern with the law may be not getting caught.

There is one obvious way to cope with such dissonance: strong nominal legal protection for prenatal life coupled with large numbers of unlawful abortions.[68] Other solutions, which grant the fetus some kind of intermediate or compromise status, are trying to mix oil and water. They are in harmony neither with the intuition that the newborn's value is great and inherent nor with the intuition that early abortion concerns the pregnant woman alone.

A brilliant and influential article by Luis Arroyo Zapatero,[69] which appeared in Spain in 1980, attempts to cut this Gordian Knot. There he proposes that concern for unborn life, wherever and to the extent it exists, be treated as a kind of cultural value of the community.[70] Such life would receive protection not for its own sake, but for the sake of the community which cares about it—in a manner reminiscent of Lord Devlin's prohibition of homosexual activity in order to promote community moral solidarity,[71] and of the common suggestion that we prevent cruelty to animals not to protect them but to protect human society's sensibilities. In very early pregnancy, where such felt concern is minimal at best and important maternal rights are at stake, few if any prohibitions on abortion would be appropriate.[72] Under Arroyo's approach, we need not seek to harmonize pre- and post-natal intuitions about life, because only those intuitions (and not life itself) are being valued.

Arroyo's solution fails because we as legislators, as scholars, and as judges are not ourselves outside the community. We are not simply concerned with promoting some ethnic solidarity or sensibility which we do not share. We are members of the community which values human life, and as such are concerned with *truly* protecting that which we value—not with affirming the value of our irrational valuing. Someone from Mars might like us enough to want to preserve us in all our contradictory splendor, but we ourselves feel compelled by honesty to find ways to resolve rather than to uphold our contradictions.

Our belief in inherent postnatal human worth cannot logically coexist with lawful elective or nearly elective abortion, but neither can logic alone induce women in distress to avoid abortion. Perhaps that belief will disappear someday, or be pushed back to some point where a qualitative change (rather than only a change in location, as at birth) takes place in young human beings—say at self-consciousness, or at puberty. In that

---

[68] The model of nominal illegality can be seen as a version of "excuse" reasoning on abortion, which is discussed at greater length *infra* under the heading "The Doctrine of 'Too Much to Demand.'" Guido Calabresi's works emphasize the frequent usefulness of a difference between the law as ideal and the law in practice, e.g., *Ideals, Beliefs, Attitudes, and the Law* 88 (1985) where he contrasts the official prohibition of euthanasia with actual jury practice.

[69] Luis Arroyo Zapatero, *supra* n. 34. The abortion decision of the Audencia de Bilbao of 24 March 1982 treats fetal life as a cultural value of the community. According to Santiago Mir Puig (*Aborto, estado de necesidad y Constitucion*, 1982 Rev. Jur. Cataluna 1943, 1948, n. 1), this foundation for fetal protection entered Spain with Arroyo Zapatero's article and was then picked up by the Bilbao court. *See further supra* n. 35.

[70] *Supra* n. 34 at 209 ff.

[71] *See generally* Devlin, *The Enforcement of Morals* (1965).

[72] *Supra* n. 34 at 217 ff.

case, we could hold to the inherent value of the latter new kind of being but refuse to push that value forward to infantile or prenatal stages of life. Or technical developments such as ultrasound may in effect create windows in the womb, so that the intuition of inherent value can occur and have a moral effect on pregnant women even in the early months of pregnancy. But unless we evolve in one of these two ways, I cannot foresee a wholly satisfactory solution to the law's abortion dilemma.

The Court and the Social State

This commentary is presently concerned to understand the contrasting degrees of public value recognized in prenatal life in Spain, Germany, and the Untied States. We have analyzed and critiqued the various attempts to conceptualize the fetus as something other than a constitutional person or private property. We now turn to another important way in which Spain and Germany are more communitarian than the U.S. in their treatment of fetal life as a constitutional value.

The classical conception of fundamental constitutional rights is that of rights against the State. A right to free speech would mean, for example, that the State cannot punish an individual for the content of what he or she has said. But that right alone would not, say, give an employee a right not to be punished for speaking by an employer. A constitutional right which were construed to protect an employee in this circumstance, possibly via a civil damage action, would have *Drittwirkung,* efficacy against third parties.

The right to free speech might, however, be construed still more broadly. It, and other related constitutional provisions, could be found to be simply specifications of a deeper affirmative vision of the good society. In this hypothetical case, the value could be taken to be free and open discussion. From that value, new specific rights could be derived, e.g., the right to read as well as to speak whatever one wished, with or without *Drittwirkung.*

Even more, a court could hold that neither the old nor the new rights *qua* rules are what is essential. What really matters is that there be in the end an effective promotion of free and open discussion, that the whole community in all its legislation and activity work together for the sake of that shared ultimate value. So, for example, a state might be given the duty to subsidize small presses, or criminally to penalize private censorship, or to teach openmindedness, or otherwise to act affirmatively in ways which a constitutional court thought would be effective in promoting free and open discussion.

This latter communitarian vision is closely related in the Spanish decision to the constitutional demand for a "Social State."[73] Although the same ideas are clearly at work in the German court's insistence that the State affirmatively protect prenatal life, the Spanish opinion is noteworthy for the conciseness of its vision and the clarity of its "social" label and linkage. Legal Foundation 4 reads in part:

> *It is also pertinent to make . . . some references to the scope, meaning and function of fundamental rights in the constitutionalism of our day inspired by the social State of Law . . . [F]undamental rights do not include only subjective defense rights of individuals against the State . . .*

---

[73] Art. 1.1 reads in part "Spain is constituted as a social and democratic State of Law . . ." ("Espana se constituye en un Estado social y democratico de Derecho . . .") Other articles further this demand. Art. 9.2 emphasizes *effectiveness* as a constitutional requirement.

but also positive duties on the part of the latter (see in this respect arts 9.2, 17.4, 18.1 and 4, 20.3 and 27 of the Constitution). But, in addition, fundamental rights . . . are the legal expression of a system of values that, by decision of the framers, has to inform the whole legal and political organization . . . Consequently, from the obligation of all powers to submit to the Constitution, one deduces not only the negative obligation of the State not to injure the individual or institutional sphere protected by these fundamental rights, but also the positive obligation to contribute to the effectiveness of such rights, and of the values that they represent, even when a subjective claim does not exist . . .[74]

Such a conception is socialist rather than individualist because in it the State must take responsibility for the societal results of its laws, rather than simply setting down minimum rules of conduct and letting the strong work within those rules to exploit the weak for the sake of private interests.

It should not be forgotten that the issue in Spain was whether or not abortion *must* be penalized. Affirming the high constitutional value of unborn life, indeed even affirming fetal personhood, might not in itself do more than forbid State-sponsored abortions and, of course, allow (rather than *require*) anti-abortion legislation. The effective protection of this constitutional value had to become an affirmative duty of the State, and criminal sanctions had to be seen in empirical fact to be relatively effective, in order for the constitutional challenge to the Spanish government's partial depenalization of abortion to succeed.

The anti-abortion briefs in this case did not neglect to promote the Social State doctrine almost as prominently as the value of unborn life.[75] Somewhat amusingly, the briefs of the Socialist government argued instead for the classical individualist idea of constitutional rights, in which such rights are only limits to state action and do not require coercive penal acts of the State.[76]

Despite the latter ''socialist'' arguments, the Court affirmed a strong Social State doctrine in the abortion case and applied it to the fundamental constitutional value ''embodied'' in unborn life (L.F. 5), concluding:

On the basis of the considerations brought forward in Legal Foundation 4, [the] protection which the Constitution confers on the one to be born implies for the State two obligations of general character: that of abstaining from interrupting or obstructing the natural process of gestation and that of establishing a legal system for the defense of life which involves an effective protection of the same and that, given the fundamental character of life, includes also, as an ultimate guarantee, penal norms. (L.F. 7).

---

[74] BJC, *supra* n. 5 at 532.

[75] Brief of 2 December 1983, at 9, 16–18. Violation of art. 1.1, the Social State provision, is the second ground of unconstitutionality brought forward by petitioners, just after their discussion of art. 15, the right to life provision. At page 17 they wisely appeal to the authority of the works of Garcia Pelayo (then president of the Court) on the nature of the Social State. *Cf., e.g.,* his *Las transformaciones del Estado contemporaneo* (1977).

[76] BJC, *supra* n. 5 at 526. The German decision is strongly criticized.

Notice the *finesse* required by the constitutional value of life. While abortions for certain reasons may be permitted, under the curiously individualist rationale discussed below, other abortions must be criminally punished. But *ex post facto* punishment is not enough, as discussed above in the "Chronology and Summary of the Decision." In order to give adequate protection to unborn life, the penal laws must also require *ex ante* that a specialist physician certify that a particular reason exists before the abortion may take place.

The dissents in Spain, as one would expect, object to the Court acting as a legislature. But none argues clearly that it is the Court's expansive concept of the Social State which is at fault. Most object to the Court announcing in advance the kind of statutory protections it wants, rather than waiting to strike or uphold whatever may be the legislative response to a finding of unconstitutionality. They also reject the alleged constitutional requirement to use penal sanctions here and to perfect the protection given the fetus. The Court's attempt to discover and apply binding principles or abstract values latent in constitutional rules comes in for some criticism, but not the use of values to spell out affirmative duties of the State rather than only defense rights against the State.

The opinions of the German majority and dissent yield a fuller understanding of the interaction of the value of prenatal life and the ideas underlying the Social State. The Court there not only orders the government to punish elective abortion, in order to fulfill its affirmative duty effectively to protect the one to be born, but also requires that the State *teach* life's value in legislation and in individual counseling.[77] This pervasive emphasis on the pedagogical function of law is the most strikingly communitarian aspect of the German decision, while it is strangely absent from the Spanish. Surely public education is the ultimate difference between a communitarian law based on values and an individualist law based on rules. No matter how many constitutional or legislative rules are derived from public values, a community of shared values does not arise except to the extent that individuals come to aim at those values themselves rather than only at rule compliance. Otherwise even the most elaborate labyrinth of rules is only a complicated game played for the sake of the furtherance of private interests.

The German dissent well recognizes the difficulties inherent in court enforcement of constitutional values:

> As defense rights the fundamental rights have a comparatively clear recognizable content; in their interpretation and application, the judicial opinions have developed practicable, generally recognized criteria for the control of state encroachments—for example, the principle of proportionality. In the other hand, it is regularly a most complex question, how a value decision is to be realized through affirmative measures of the legislature. The necessarily generally held value decisions can be perhaps characterized as constitutional mandates which, to be sure, are assigned to point the direction for all state dealings but are directed necessarily toward a transposition of binding regulations. Based upon the determination of the actual circumstances, of the concrete setting of goals and their priority and of the suitability of conceivable means and ways, very different solutions are possible. The decision, which fre-

---

[77] *See* citations *supra* n. 47. Contrast *Thornburgh*, 106 S. Ct. 2169 at 2178–81, where counseling discouraging abortion is forbidden to the State.

> *quently presupposes compromises and takes place in the course of trial and error, belongs, according to the principle of division of powers and to the democratic principle, to the responsibility of the legislature directly legitimatized by the people.*[78]

The dissent's solution seems, however, largely to restate rather than to solve the problems it has raised. It urges the Court to "confront the legislature only when the latter has completely disregarded a value decision or when the nature and manner of its realization is obviously faulty."[79]

This last language reminds one a bit of the U.S. Supreme Court's "rational basis" and "state interest" tests. But note this important difference: Except for a very limited number of impermissible goals (such as the promotion of racism), U.S. legislation may aim at any state interest. Or, where equal protection or fundamental rights are involved, it may aim at any "compelling" state interest. There is not, except very broadly and by negative implication, an order of constitutional values which government must affirmatively promote. Indeed, our states may sometimes aim at values *opposite* to those underlying the Constitution as interpreted by the Court.

A glance at the U.S. abortion decisions of the last ten years will make clear the contrast between American and European doctrine here. The original *Roe* decision proclaimed the value of private choice with regard to abortion, and saw in that value a prohibition on state action interfering with abortion. Yet the government is under no obligation to use its funds[80] or its hospitals[81] neutrally to promote choice. Instead, it may favor childbirth over abortion, even where its motives are the very value philosophies condemned by *Roe* as a basis for penalizing abortion.[82] In later extrapolation upon this conclusion, the U.S. Court specifically appealed to the classic constitutionalism of defense rights only, rather than to the new communitarian emphasis on rights to affirmative state support.[83] In that later case, the Court ruled that even health abortions need not be funded by the State, despite the fact that in *Roe* maternal health broadly construed had been held to be constitutionally more important than fetal life even *after* viability.[84] The value decisions of our Constitution do not in themselves bind legislatures, and *a fortiori* need not be taught to citizens.

All this is not to say that there would be no possible way for an anti-abortion U.S. Supreme Court to require criminal laws against abortion. The Court could try to find some state action (e.g., financial) involved in depenalized private abortions, in order to forbid them. Or it could find state action in the enforcement of contracts related to abortion or of laws preventing sit-ins at abortion clinics, which would *de facto* make abortion unavailable. Or it could argue that equal protection, even if it were attenuated prior to birth, mandates some measure of protection for the unborn as long as the killing of neonates remains illegal. (Or it could go the other way and insist that equal protection for those who take human life requires that infanticide be unpunished as long as abortion

---

[78] [1975] 39 BVerfGE 1, 71–72; Jonas & Gorby, *supra* n. 3 at 665–66.

[79] [1975] 39 BVerfGE 1, 73; Jonas & Gorby, *id.* at 666.

[80] Maher v. Roe, 432 U.S. 464, 474 (1977).

[81] Poelker v. Doe, 432, U.S. 519, 521 (1977) and *Webstern, supra* n. 58.

[82] *Id.*

[83] Harris v. McRae, 448 U.S. 297, 317–18 (1980).

[84] *Id.* at 316, 325–26.

is unpunished.) But it could not, without a deep ideological shift, appeal to the social duty of the government to promote the constitutional value of respect for life.

Critique of the Court and the Social State

Though I am sympathetic both to socialism and to the protection of unborn life, I cannot agree with the approach taken by the Spanish and German high courts.

My problem is not with the idea of an order of principles implicit in legal rules and usable in deriving new rules. Such analogical reasoning, however indeterminate it may be, seems to me a necessary part of the honest and thoughtful evolution of public order. It accounts for the greatest achievements both of Anglo-American common law and of European legal science. Nor do I object to the affirmative quality of these values. I think life together is much more meaningful if we hold some, though not all, aims in common. I would like to think that there are common goods that many of our laws pursue and that are and ought to be taught to us all. Among these is the good of life, the foundation of nonviolence.

My problem is with the institution of judicial review. Even here I am less concerned where only defense rights are involved. As long as a high court can play only a negative role, it must at least work very hard to achieve institutional dominance. But when judicial review is combined with the vague values and affirmative duties of the Social State, then the power of judges may be overextended.

The rule of law *(Estado de Derecho)* itself may not survive, as the Spanish government argued in its brief.[85] The whole problem, in my view, lies in the word "effective" invoked both in Spain and in Germany. In order for values to be "effectively" promoted, empirical results rather than only rules must be scrutinized. Rules at the constitutional and at the legislative levels have to be changed whenever necessary in order to achieve results, even *ex post facto* in particular cases. That is how common barn builders would handle the rules for hammer use. It may even be unconstitutional *not* to change the rules whenever they produce results contrary to basic values.[86]

While I wish, with some trepidation, to affirm rule-less community (or, better, communities) as an ideal to be pursued, I am deeply concerned about placing virtually unlimited power over the development and content of such community in the potentially arbitrary discretion of any very small number of persons.

Judicial review and the Social State should not be combined. Perhaps judicial review should not exist even for defense rights. Such review implies a hostility between the legislating community and the individual which ideally should be overcome by education and by more participatory forms of democracy, rather than accommodated. But in any event judicial review should not extend to the positive and programmatic social duties stated or implied in a constitution. Those principles should be the starting points

---

[85] BJC, *supra* n. 5 at 527–28.

[86] Rule utilitarianism has no adequate response here, for it contains an antinomy. Even if we need rigid rules in order to preserve our values, why should those rules be followed when they seem certain to produce disvalue? A legal system wholly concerned about consequences could not avoid constantly rethinking its rules. It might avoid anarchy by disabling individual citizens or judges from ignoring rules, but it would have to make centralized review available in every case where one could plausibly argue that a revised rule would more efficiently promote the values at stake. For an excellent review of the proposed solutions to this general moral and legal quandary, see Alexander, *Pursuing the Good—Indirectly,* 95 Ethics 315 (January 1985).

for public reasoning by all citizens, not the privileged prerogative of a tiny group of jurists.[87]

The Doctrine of "Too Much to Demand"

Life is a "superior," "fundamental," and "central" constitutional value in Spain, and the fetus "embodies" this value. The government has an affirmative duty to protect unborn life by means of criminal penalties for its destruction. Yet the high court there goes on to permit abortion in all the circumstances listed in the bill under review: grave danger to maternal life or health, rape, and likelihood of severe disability in the child. How does the Court make such a turnaround?

One might have expected the Court, in line with its communitarian perspective elsewhere, to look to the common good and to argue that the protection of unborn life is not, or does not always result in, the highest constitutional value. But it nowhere asserts that other values are more important than fetal life. It mentions two theories by which the bill in question may be justified: legislative choice between conflicting values and the doctrine of non-demandability (L.F. 10). The latter, however, is the only clear referent in most of the situations considered. The Court appeals primarily to the idea that a continuation of pregnancy in such circumstances is just too much for the criminal law to demand of an individual. Even if such abortions do more harm than good to the values of the community, the State need not punish them because there is a limit to what individuals must sacrifice for constitutional values.

The doctrine of non-demandability in Spain has its origin in German legal thought, where it was originally conceived as an extrastatutory defense to crime from an individualist perspective.[88] It is felt in the Spanish Penal Code in various ways, particularly in Article 8, to which the Court specifically refers in its opinion.[89] That article permits the

---

[87] I do not think one should belittle a judicially unenforced constitutional social duty or right as "merely a platform plank elevated to constitutional status." *Cf.* the discussion of "programmatic" rather than "enforceable" constitutional provisions in Italy in Cappelletti, Merryman, & Perillo, *The Italian Legal System* 58 (1967). From the deliberations of juries to those of supreme courts we often rely upon non-enforceable good faith implementation of legally binding principles. I do not see why elected representatives should enjoy less confidence.

The Spanish constitution itself distinguishes between "rights" and "duties" (arts. 14–38) and "guiding principles of social and economic politics" (arts. 39–52), making the former "binding" (arts. 53.1 and 53.2) and the latter only "informing" (art. 53.3). Perhaps values (such as "life") latent in these rights and duties should be considered mere "guiding principles," though my own view is more that they should be considered binding in conscience upon the legislature but not enforceable by courts (at least not against statutes).

[88] One of the earliest uses of this concept in criminal law occurred in the famous 1897 *Leinenfanger* decision of the *Reichsgericht*. There the Court went beyond the penal code to reason that although the omission in question "considering the common good . . . could be demanded of the actor," one must also ask whether it could be demanded of the accused under the circumstances. 30 RGST 25–28, as quoted in Jiménez de Asúa, *supra* n. 23 at 935.

[89] Art. 8 of the Spanish Penal Code exempts various persons from criminal responsibility, including the insane and infants. Sec. 4 adds an exemption for "one who acts in defense of a person or rights, his own or alien *(propios o ajenos)*" as long as there has been illegitimate aggression, rational choice of means, and lack of provocation. The key sec. 7 exempts "one who, impelled by a state of necessity, in order to avoid an evil of his own or one alien to him *(mal propio o ajeno)*, injures a legal good *(bien juridico)* of another person . . . ," provided that the evil caused is not greater than that which he seeks to avoid, that he has not intentionally provoked the situation of necessity, and that he does not have a special obligation to

defense of necessity when an otherwise illegal act is done in order to avoid a greater *or an equal* harm. The doctrine of non-demandability is thought by the dominant opinion in Spain to account for the latter situation.[90] It is just too much to demand of a person that he or she sacrifice a personal interest simply for the sake of someone else's merely equal interest. A concrete example of the influence of this doctrine is found in Article 18 of the Penal Code, which exempts close family members from punishment for harboring a fugitive. Again, one might say that the penal law just cannot demand that a fugitive's spouse or parent refuse to take him or her in, despite the general prohibition of such an act.[91]

As will become evident later, it is very important to understand whether this doctrine is one of justification or of excuse. That is, does the personal burden under which the defendant labors serve to make an otherwise wrong act right, or does it only mean that the defendant is not to be blamed (or even simply not to be punished) for the still wrongful act?

The dominant theory[92] in Spain appears to treat the nondemandability doctrine as one of excuse. Under such an approach, no one is justified in preferring his or her own values, or own spouse, to the values established by the community, but nevertheless such antisocial acts are not punished where the subject in some sense could not act otherwise. An act which is wrongful but nonpreventable, or at least not preventable by means of the criminal law, is not to be punished. Note that if a mere excuse for an act is involved, legitimate defense against the act remains possible, and there are a number of other significant legal consequences to be explored later.

On the other hand, there are some Spanish doctrinal considerations which point to calling the non-demandability idea a justification.[93] And it can be argued that where no one, or no one except a hero, is in some sense able to comply with a certain legal

---

sacrifice himself. Sec. 9 covers those who act under "irresistible force" and sec. 10 those who act out of insuperable fear "of an equal or greater evil." Art. 8 thus incorporates ideas both of "excuse" (what might be called "necessity in the order of events") and of "justification" (what might be called "necessity in the order of ideas").

Luis Jiménez de Asúa, 7 *Tratado de Derecho Penal* 196 (2nd ed., 1962, 1977) considers fear and necessity under conflict of equal goods to be excuses originating in the non-demandability idea. He adds other examples from the Spanish Penal Code, including the harboring of a fugitive by near relations (art. 18) and the omission of non-demandable aid (art. 489).

Some Spanish opinion also supports non-demandability as a legal excuse existing outside the Penal Code, e.g. Ricardo de Angel Yaguez et al., *Ley del aborto* 100–01 (1985).

[90] Rodriguez Devesa, *Derecho penal español,* parte general at 556, 609–19 (1979).

[91] The rationale for this defense is disputed, but the dominant opinion today appears to be that non-demandability is its basis. *See* Jiménez de Asúa, *supra* n. 23 at 1014, and Rodriguez Devesa, *supra* n. 90 at 618–19.

[92] Both Jiménez de Asúa, *supra* n. 23 at 932 ff. and Rodriguez Devesa, *supra* n. 90 at 609 ff. treat non-demandability under the more general category of exculpation or non-blameworthiness, i.e., as a kind of excuse rather than of justification, and assert this to be the dominant view.

[93] Jiménez de Asúa, *supra* n. 23 at 967–69, discusses some penalists who consider non-demandability to be a justification. Rodriguez Devesa seems to use the non-demandability notion as a general concept containing all justifications and exculpations, as well as to use it as a specific concept involving non-blameworthiness, *supra* n. 90 at 609–11.

Note that the mere fact that an objective balancing of values may be involved is *not* necessarily a consideration leading us to classify non-demandability as justification. As George Fletcher has pointed out, *Rethinking Criminal Law* 804 (1978), we expect peopie to be *able* to make greater sacrifices when more is at stake. We may excuse someone who breaks another's leg under the threat of losing his own, but not someone who blows up a city under the same threat.

command, then acts or omissions in violation of that norm lose their wrongful character even though they do not avoid more harm than they cause. Furthermore, there are places in Spanish law where a theory of non-demandability seems to have resulted in a full statutory justification, in the sense of legal certification of the non-wrongfulness of the conduct in question. The penal law requirements to stop crime (Art. 338 *bis*), to rescue (Art. 489 *bis*), and to give assistance (Art. 586(2)) apply only where they can be observed without risk to the actor or to a third party. Note that the omission of risky acts is here justified, at least in the special sense that it is excluded from the definition *(tipo)* of these crimes, although Article 8 would not even excuse it—for the actor is refusing to risk a slight personal interest at the cost of greater harm to others. This contradiction can perhaps be overcome if we cannot demand and expect public spirited actions to the degree to which we exact public spirited omissions.

Legislators supporting the enactment of the new abortion statute appealed frequently to the non-demandability notion—often as an excuse.[94] Likewise the government brief in the constitutional case is written as though the issue of nondemandability is one of whether or not a woman having an abortion should be simply exculpated (i.e., excused) in the specified situations.[95] The only dissents which mention the matter in some detail link the idea of non-demandability to that of legal excuse.[96]

In some of the above arguments, however, there is an undercurrent of justificatory reasoning.[97] And on at least one occasion, spokespersons for the proposed legislation clearly insisted that the abortions at issue were to be treated as lawful, not simply unblameworthy.[98]

The Constitutional Court's own opinion, unfortunately, is far from clear. Neither in its general discussion of nondemandability (L.F. 9) nor in its specific applications of that idea (L.F. 11) does the Court label the notion "excuse" or "justification." The opinion does not, however, explicitly treat *any* abortion as justified in the sense that it is the best solution, the one which maximizes net resultant value. Except in the Court's treatment of abortion to save the mother's life and perhaps to avoid grave danger to her health (where it may possibly be treating the child as an aggressor against whom the

---

[94] The socialist Minister of Justice, Ledesma Bartret, argued on 25 February 1983 that the nondemandability of continued pregnancy in certain circumstances is a cause of excuse *("inculpabilidad")* for abortion. *Supra* n. 6 at 17. On 25 May that year, Saenz Coscullela, speaking "in the name of the Socialist Group", argued that the abortion bill does not "legalize." Indeed, it expresses a "generic disapprobation" of abortion, while establishing an "excuse" *("excusa")* for therapeutic abortion, and refuses to blame *("inculpar")* abortions occurring where further pregnancy is not demandable. *Diario de sesiones del Congreso de los Diputados,* II Legislatura, No. 40, at 1850. Again on 4 October 1983, the PSOE member Sotillo Martí argued, in favor of nonpunishment of some abortions, that where other conduct is not demandable, an act lacks blameworthiness, i.e., is excused. *Id.,* No. 61 at 2888.

[95] BJC, *supra* n. 5 at 529–30.

[96] Francisco Tomás y Valiente insists that the abortion bill contains neither a legalization nor a depenalization of abortion, but simply a declaration of non-punishment in certain situations, while maintaining intact the definition of the crime ("manteniendo intacto el tipo delictivo"). A judge, not a physician, thus should decide when those situational requirements have been met, since the acts regulated by art. 417 continue being criminal *("continuan siendo delictivas")*. He adds, however, that the basic rule prohibiting abortion appears to him of doubtful constitutionality. *Id.* at 539. See also the less clear linkage of nonculpability and excuse in the opinion of Jeronimo Arozamena Sierra. *Id.* at 537.

[97] Arozamena Sierra, *id.* Also Sotillo Martí, *supra* n. 94, and the government brief, *supra* n. 95.

[98] So argued bill supporters Lopez Riaño and Sotillo Martí on 7 September 1983, *supra* n. 33 at 2121 and 2140–41.

mother has a right of self-defense (L.F. 11(a)), the Court looks overtly to the idea (and only to the idea) that some pregnancy continuations are too much to demand of a woman. In considering rape pregnancies, the Court lists the constitutionally recognized values of the woman which have been harmed by that act of violence. But it does not suggest that denying her an abortion would have a further overall negative effect on the values at stake. Instead, it reasons that obligating her to put up with the consequences of rape is not demandable (L.F. 11(b)). In the case of abortion for probable grave disabilities in the child, the Court is even more straightforward. The basis for non-punishment of such abortions, according to the Court, is that to require continuation of pregnancy would be an imposition on the mother beyond that which is normally demandable. That parents put up with the inevitable insecurity attending such a pregnancy is too much to demand. It is hard even to imagine that avoiding such parental anxiety is constitutionally a fundamental value equal to life in Spanish law, so that the Court could in any event appeal only to nondemandability in order to uphold this portion of the law in question (L.F. 11(c)).[99]

Once again, the often unspoken background for all these Spanish arguments in German legal theory. It was in Germany that the idea of non-demandability first arose doctrinally.[100] It is there used to explain code-based "excusing necessity", which is structured differently from the necessity defense in Spain.[101] The German abortion de-penalization statute itself permitted post-twelve-week-gestation abortion where there was a danger to maternal life or health or of serious fetal defect such that no alternative to abortion could be demanded (*zumutbar* and *verlangt* respectively).[102]

Not surprisingly, the West German Constitutional Court likewise uses the non-demandability doctrine to deal with abortion. The Court indeed appears to base its ap-proval of hardship-case abortions *exclusively* upon this idea—even where continued pregnancy would threaten a woman's own life or health.[103] It applies the doctrine with-out further argument to the case of potentially grave disability abortions (which the Court calls "eugenic" abortions)[104] and to "social" abortions involving equivalent hardship

---

[99] Despite the Constitution's explicit directive, found in art. 49, that the State protect the disabled, the Court does not discuss the possible repercussions which the legalization of such abortions may have on future public and parental attitudes and actions with regard to those born with severe handicaps—but then this point is likewise ignored in the briefs. For research indicating a negative impact, see Fletcher, *Attitudes Toward Defective Newborns,* 2(1) Hastings Center Studies 21 (January 1974).

Nor does the Court anywhere suggest the now commonplace notion that life with severe disabilities may have relatively little value or even be a disvalue. Such a suggestion would obviously go a long way toward tipping the scales in favor of parental interests.

[100] For a discussion of the nature and context of the German (and, indirectly, the Spanish) concept of *"Un-zumutbarkeit,"* see Fletcher, *supra* n. 93 at 833 ff. and Albin Eser, *Justification and Excuse,* 24 Am. J. Comp. L. 624 (1976). See also Jiménez de Asúa, *supra* n. 23 at 930 ff.

[101] The German Penal Code separates necessity *(Notstand)* into two articles, 34 and 35, and titles the first "Justifying Necessity" and the second "Excusing Necessity." According to the latter, certain persons are excused when they must act illegally to avoid a danger to life, limb, or liberty, unless they could have been expected (demanded, *"zugemutet"*) to accept the risk involved. See e.g., Dreher & Tröndle, *Straf-gesetzbuch* 188, 196 (42nd ed. 1985).

[102] The actual statute was somewhat more complex than this summary. *See* [1975] 39 BVerfGE 1, 4–6, and Jonas & Gorby, *supra* n. 3 at 611–12.

[103] [1975] 39 BVerfGE 1, 48–50; Jonas & Gorby, id. at 647–48. *See also supra* n. 49.

[104] *Id.,* indicating approval of earlier governmental arguments in favor of nonpunishment of disability- and rape-based abortions.

because of the woman's life context. Unfortunately, the Court sends mixed signals on the issue of whether nondemandability makes all these abortions justified or merely excused.[105]

Spanish commentary upon the German constitutional settlement, prior to Spain's own proposed law reform, was generally critical. Commentators both opposing[106] and favoring[107] extensive abortion rights had difficulty understanding how non-demandability could permit abortion in the face of the German high court's strong affirmation of the duty of the State to protect unborn life. At most, it was argued, the Court's reasoning would lead to excusing such abortions, not to justifying them.

United States criminal law does not contain an explicit defense of non-demandability. Our "duress" or "coercion" defense, which is generally considered an excuse, is perhaps its closest analogue, but that defense is more limited than the Spanish Article 8 or German "excusing necessity".[108] It could not apply to abortion because no one is threatening harm to the mother unless she ends her pregnancy. There exists for us no comprehensive penal or constitutional principle which ensures that no one is punished for doing an act wherever not doing the act is "too much to demand".

Despite our restricted theory of excuses, however, it could be argued that something like non-demandability pervades our law, and does so often in the form of justification. After all, except in Vermont, we do not require rescues of strangers in the first place, not even where they involve no risk whatsoever. It has been suggested that it is too restrictive to impose on everyone that they be good samaritans.[109] Again, we sometimes permit a violent response to aggression, even where retreat is possible, and especially where retreat would involve some risk.[110] Are we perhaps saying that it is too much to ask of victims that they act against their own interests in order to protect the interests of aggressors, even when the net harm caused by resistance is much greater than that caused by retreat?

Roe v. Wade obviously did not need to draw upon anything like the above lines of reasoning; its denial of constitutional value in the unborn child meant that it did not have to search for a justification or excuse for abortion beyond the right of privacy. But there have been a number of scholars who have sought to justify the result in *Roe*, elective abortion, by appealing to our alleged tradition of "bad samaritanism."[111] The explicit thrust of these arguments is that even if the fetus were recognized to be a living human being, and even if it were seen to be a person possessing a constitutional right

---

[105] For example, the Court indicates that even where abortion is not punished, the State is expected to remind a woman of her "fundamental duty *(Pflicht)* to respect the right to life of the unborn, to encourage her to continue the pregnancy." *Id.* Yet the Court later insists that the law distinguish the justified *(gerechtfertigt)* cases of abortion from the reprehensible *(verwerflich)* ones. [1975] 39 BVerfGE 1, 58; Jonas & Gorby, *id.* at 654–55. Sorting out these remarks in light of the basic principles governing the decision, the Dreher & Tröndle commentary concludes that the Constitutional Court's decision points in the direction of an excuse understanding: *supra* n. 101, prenote 9 to § 218, at 999–1000.

[106] Rodriguez Devesa, *supra* n. 25, at 99. Rodriguez Devesa [later] joined in the book *En Defensa de la Vida, supra* n. 35, opposing the abortion depenalization bill.

[107] Arroyo Zapatero, *supra* n. 34 at 205.

[108] *Supra* n. 101. The German penal art. 35 is limited to excusing those who protect themselves or those near to them. But there remains some support for nondemandability as an extrastatutory defense.

[109] Calabresi, *supra* n. 68 at 102–03, reports and disagrees with this sentiment.

[110] *See e.g.*, the American Law Institute's Model Penal Code § 3.04(2)(b)(ii).

[111] *See e.g.*, Regan, *Rewriting* Roe v. Wade, 77 Mich. L. Rev. 1569 (1979) and Thomson, *A Defense of Abortion*, 1 Philos. & Pub. Affairs 47 (1971).

to life, elective abortion would be permissible because our law does not generally require individuals to aid others at substantial cost to themselves. Though I have not found these thoughts to coalesce around precisely the non-demandability doctrine of Europe, surely something similar is at work here. If elsewhere we are individualists believing in *laissez faire* and *laissez mourir,* it must seem to many of us "too much to demand" of a pregnant woman that she alone make great sacrifices—a point to which I return at the end of this commentary.

Critique of the "Too Much to Demand" Doctrine

There are three final points I would like to make at some length. The first is that the concept of non-demandability, even if accepted as a starting point for legal reasoning, is incapable of doing what its adherents want it to do, namely of giving at least some abortions the full support of the law. The second is that non-demandability is in fact unacceptable as a first principle of reason, for it obscures as much as it reveals. The third is that, despite its deficiencies, the doctrine remains extremely useful to show that the abortion dilemma is merely one manifestation of the tension between community and individual and that a solution to the dilemma depends, therefore, on a relaxation of the tension.

As we have seen, there are two ways to understand Spanish (and German) constitutional law on abortion—that the legislature may treat some abortions as excused or that it may treat them as justified. My argument is that under both hypotheses a tension results in the law, but only in the latter case does it approach a contradiction.

The first hypothesis—excuse—seems to me the most plausible interpretation of the Spanish court's opinion. The doctrine of non-demandability is ordinarily treated in Spain[112] and in Germany[113] as one involving excuse. Given both courts' refusal to affirm that the unborn child has substantially less legal value than the mother, it is hard to see how any abortion (except, perhaps, for the mother's life) could be justified without at least a great deal of argumentation, which is left unsupplied.[114] Moreover, the Spanish law in question bears a stronger resemblance to Penal Code Article 18 (excusing family members who harbor a fugitive) than it does to Article 489 bis (declaring a duty to rescue only where there is no risk to oneself). Like the former and unlike the latter, the abortion depenalization law does not expressly alter the definition (type) of the crime but only precludes the imposition of punishment in certain cases. This difference, I think, should be understood to be one of excuse vs. justification, as has been argued.

As excuse, non-demandability can be given a fairly precise meaning. Penalties are set according to what is ordinarily necessary for deterrence and must not be excessive in proportion to ultimate culpability. But then persons having to make unusually high sacrifices in order to comply with the law cannot be compelled to do so. Such persons are arguably both less culpable (because the *net* harm caused by the excused offense is less than that caused by an ordinary offense where no harm is at the same time avoided) and less deterrable (because again of the unusual personal harm resulting from failure to commit the offense). Thus, within the limits set by proportionality [See L.F. 10],

---

[112]*Supra* n. 92.

[113]Albin Eser, *supra* n. 10 at 627, 637. This essay is also a useful introduction to the basic structure of German (and of much of Spanish) penal theory.

[114]*See generally* the Dreher & Tröndle discussion cited, *supra* n. 105.

there may be no penalty adequate to deter individuals from acts necessary to avoid great personal hardship. Without an adequate deterrent motive, the "ideal type" rational self-interested individual may be literally unable to comply with the law. And where the threat of punishment can serve no purpose, it should not even be made. Acts involving great and unusual hardship cannot be exacted[115] by *ex post facto* penalties and should, therefore, be excused by law—even if those acts have a net negative effect on public values.

Excuse fits better than justification into the communitarian ethos of the Spanish decision. It is perhaps not logically inconsistent, but it certainly would be a shift in ideology for a court one moment to emphasize duties to pursue common values and the next moment to declare individuals to be legally justified in destroying those values. By contrast, there would be nothing strange about a fully developed socialist jurisprudence recognizing that human beings are not (or at least not yet) so constituted as to be *able* in all circumstances to give the same weight to others' interests as they do to their own. Where this is the case, proportionate punishment may serve little purpose. The penal law, at least, should excuse such unjustified self-preference.

But, for a number of reasons excuse thinking alone cannot fully legalize abortion. Excuse is considered to apply only to the person so burdened that he or she is unable to act rightly toward the fetus. It is not thought to apply to third parties. Specifically, it would seem not to apply to the doctor performing the abortion any more than the excuse of duress applies to bystanders who help a threatened person carry out some difficult crime. The government's strongest argument, non-demandability as excuse, in favor of its statute makes little sense, for that statute clearly exempts from punishment *all* parties to certain abortions, not just the mother. The difficulty of excusing the aborting physician had been noticed already in 1982, in a quite cogent Spanish law journal article.[116] If the anti-abortion brief had contained more than its one exceedingly short reference to this point,[117] perhaps the Court would not entirely have overlooked this stumbling block in its lengthy summary of the arguments.

At this time, of course, the non-punishment of the doctor has been approved. That is the Court's holding, regardless of whether or how that conclusion is supported by its reasoning (at least until fuller argument leads it to a different conclusion). The principle of legality, the principle of non-punishment without a prior statutory violation, would seem to preclude any penalty for a physician doing an abortion in one of the specified circumstances. But this does not entirely dispose of our problem. If abortion is only excused rather than justified under penal law, what is its status in civil law?[118] For

---

[115] "Exactability" is the word used by Jonas & Gorby, *supra* n. 3, to translate *Zumutbarkeit*. I have ordinarily preferred "demandability" because of its greater normative resonance in English, but here the more physically coercive feeling of the word "exacted" captures the point better.

[116] Cerezo Mir, *supra* n. 31.

[117] Petitoners' supplementary brief of 3 January 1983 [sic] at 16.

[118] The Spanish court opinion, in L.F. 14, explicitly avoids resolving the civil law issues raised by the non-punishment of abortion. BJC, *supra* n. 5 at 536. (Not all the issues I here raise were, however, brought forward in petitioners' briefs.) Rodriguez Devesa, *supra* n. 90 at 557, 616 points out that civil responsibility remains for excused criminal acts. *See also* Jiménez de Asúa, *supra* n. 89 at 201–02. Jonas & Gorby, in their commentary *supra* n. 3 at 591–92, raise the possibility of civil suits in Germany, and the Dreher & Tröndle discussion cited *supra* n. 105, makes clear that the legitimacy of social insurance payments for unpunished but possibly still unlawful abortions is a live issue in Germany. See also the excellent survey and argument by Kluth, who concludes that abortion remains illicit and therefore cannot be a duty in civil

example, could a father sue for damages because his unborn child has been aborted? (Or could he sue a physician for negligently *failing* to abort his handicapped infant?) Must, or even may, State social insurance programs pay for the commission of acts still considered unlawful? And what is the legal status of a contract to deliver abortifacients if abortion remains legally unjustified?[119]

Even more significantly, if abortion remains always wrongful albeit excused, could not third parties intervene to stop abortion of developmentally disabled fetuses, especially if they did so in some minimally intrusive non-violent way? The necessity defense in the United States has not been very successful in preventing the conviction of those who sit in at abortion clinics,[120] but Spanish law looks very different. Article 8's idea of necessity (preservation of the greater legal value) could be appealed to. Non-violent intervenors could argue ''legitimate defense''—just as a bank teller can defend himself or an associate against a robber acting non-culpably under duress.[121] Most precisely on point may be that in Spain a person is justified in preventing another from destroying something of his or her own which has social utility.[122]

---

law, *Zur Rechtsnatur der indizierten Abtreibung,* 5 Zf.ges.FamR 440 (1985), and the extensive and profound study by Reis, *supra* n. 52.

[119] *See* the Spanish Civil Code art. 1275, which deprives contracts for an illicit cause of any effect. An illicit cause is defined to be one opposed to laws or morals. Cf. the German Civil Code, art. 134. The perhaps leading Spanish scholar in favor of elective abortion appears to agree that the doctrine of non-demandability cannot in itself make abortion fully licit. Therefore, he wishes to change the basis of European constitutional treatment of abortion, which until now has rested on the idea of non-demandability. Luis Arroyo Zapatero, *supra* n. 34, *La indicacion eugenesica.* Revista de la Facultad de Derecho de la Universidad Complutense (1985).

[120] *See, e.g.,* Sigma Reproductive Health Center v. State, 297 Md. 660, 467 A.2d 483 (1983); City of St. Louis v. Klocker 637 S.W. 2d 174 (Mo. App. 1982); Cleveland v. Municipality of Anchorage, 631 P.2d 1073 (Alaska 1981); People v. Krizka, 92 Ill. App. 3d 288, 48 Ill. Dec. 141, 416 N.E.2d 36 (1980); Gaetano v. United States, 406, A.2d 1291 (D.C. App. 1979). These post-*Roe* lower courts have generally refused even to listen to necessity arguments concerning the fact and value of prenatal life. Their opinions are fascinating in the light of the constitutional models developed earlier in this article. One might have thought that American courts would construe *Roe's* constitutional right to abortion to be solely a *rule* against *state* intervention, particularly after the *Maher* and *Harris* cases (*see supra* n. 80 and 83 and accompanying text). *Private* intervention in abortion clinics (to protect what proffered evidence supposedly would show to be human life with significant ethical, statutory, or common law value) would remain unaffected by *Roe* and so possibly justified. But in fact virtually all lower court opinions treat *Roe* as imposing a negative *value* judgment, in regard to the fetus, on the whole legal order, quite analogous to the positive value imposed in Spain and Germany. The analogy is close: In those European nations the mandated high value of fetal life requires the State to *punish* conduct which destroys the fetus. In the U.S. the mandated low value of fetal life requires the State *not to refrain from punishing* conduct which prevents fetal destruction.

It could be argued that some of these lower courts have disallowed the necessity defense simply to prevent disorder at abortion clinics, without any sense of constitutional mandate. But the bare possibility of acquittal under necessity might not significantly increase the number of sitters willing to be arrested at abortion clinics. And even if clinic chaos were to result, a quick fix might be had in the form of a legislatively imposed abortion exception to the necessity defense. Judicial imposition of such an exception would not be required.

[121] Both Rodriguez Devesa, *supra* n. 90 at 557, 616 and Jiménez de Asúa, *supra* n. at 201–02 make clear that forcible defense is legitimate against acts which are merely excused. The former specifically applies this principle to the law excusing a parent who harbors a fugitive, at 619. The explicit wording of art. 8(4), referring to the defense ''of the person or [of] rights'' might not apply to the defense of the ''legal good'' of unborn life, but art. 8(7) would seem to offer obvious support for abortion clinic interventions. The latter permits actions against personal goods in order to avoid any ''alien'' evil. See the precise wording, *supra* n. 89. Of course, there would also have to be a weighing of the harm caused by the intervention against the value of any fetal life saved. In Spain this calculus is ordinarily based upon a comparison of

Nor are these arguments merely technical or sophistic. It is clearly one thing to say that someone does not deserve punishment for an act because she could not be expected to behave otherwise, and quite another for the State to support or even not to prevent that act. Remember that non-demandability is a *penal* law doctrine; there are some things which are supposedly too much to demand by means of *ex post facto* penalties. The Spanish court's own discussion of non-demandability theory (L.F. 10) emphasizes that penal punishment for failure to comply with a legal norm is sometimes "totally unsuitable," which does not entail that the norm itself is to be called into question. The Court also points out that the State's duty to protect the legal good of life continues to subsist in other areas. If the State allows civil suits against abortionists, denies insurance coverage, does not recognize contracts, and does not punish sit-ins in abortion clinics or the equivalent, it is not imposing punishment on women who have had abortions. There is nothing incoherent in a legal system which makes all abortions illegal, but excuses some women who have them with the thought that compliance with the law is too much to demand of persons in great distress. To the contrary, a system would be incoherent which punished justified acts (e.g., sit-ins)[123] in order to further excused ones (i.e., abortions).

That this is the present state of Spanish law is implied by a number of sources. Proponents of abortion depenalization, and at least one of the high court dissenters, argued that abortions were not being "legalized," as has been pointed out above.[124] Opponents of abortion now read the Court decision to say that abortion has not become "licit."[125] If such statements mean anything, they indicate a legal situation very close to that which has been described and very far from a legal right to abortion.

Can a case be made for a contrary interpretation of the Spanish decision, that it declares non-demandable abortions to be not excusable but justifiable and that the statute upheld is in fact one of justification? The most obvious argument in favor of this interpretation is not a legal but a political one. There might be little point in bringing about a legal situation which keeps women out of jail but which may well have very little

---

the usual criminal penalties for, say, trespass and abortion. Rodriguez Devesa, *supra* n. 90 at 546. The result of the balancing might well vary depending upon the means and consequences of the sit-in.

The wording of the German Penal Code is even more favorable to such defenses. In addition to the necessity arguments of arts. 34 and 35 of the Penal Code, *supra* n. 101 arts. 32 and 33 would seem to provide another justification and excuse argument for nonviolent clinic interventions. These *Notwehr* defenses are available to those who act to protect "another" against an unlawful attack, and the German court decision seems potentially open to an interpretation of the unborn child as "another." See *supra* n. 38–46 and accompanying text.

[122] Rodriguez Devesa, *id.* at 554.

[123] If non-violent clinic intervention were futile (in the sense that women wishing abortions will invariably simply postpone them if a particular clinic becomes unavailable for a time), the necessity justification for sit-ins would lose much of its force. But the mere fact that pregnancy continuation is too much to demand *by means of a posteriori punishment* does not, without more, prove that *prior* intervention to close clinics or to dissuade women might not be effective and normatively called for. Surely a legal system could appropriately abolish penalties for some or all (attempted) suicides, under nondemandability excuse thinking, without entailing the abolition of defenses to battery for those who intervene to prevent suicides.

[124] *Supra* n. 94 and 96. *But cf. supra* n. 98.

[125] So argues Federico Trillo-Figueroa in his early unpublished response to the Court entitled "En defensa de la vida" (the same title as that of the pre-decision book referred to *supra* n. 35 and to which he contributed). The anti-abortion commentary *Ley del aborto*, *supra* n. 89 at 91 ff., 327, also asserts and implies the continuing illicitude of almost all abortions.

effect on the actual availability of abortion. If abortion remains wholly illicit, clinics will be under burdens so great that they may find it unprofitable to operate. But an attempt at legal argumentation can also be made: Excuse reasoning is hard put to explain the Court's approval of the non-punishment of the aborting physician.[126] And the analogy of abortion law to fugitive law is not perfect. In the latter case, only certain actors (i.e., family members) are declared exempt from punishment. In the former, the act itself of abortion is declared non-punishable. From the point, of view of *penal* law, what can be made of a norm without a penalty? Perhaps the definition (type) of the crime of abortion has in effect been cut back after all, though not by the direct wording used in the Penal Code's article 489 *bis* requiring rescue.[127]

There is an undeniable appeal in the justification interpretation of non-demandability. Always to value the interests of others equally with one's own is a heroic or saintly ideal. To *demand* compliance with this ideal would clearly often be too much—whence the argument for excuse. But even to *ask* for heroic behavior may seem uncalled for. Don't we have a *right* not to be heroes, without incurring legal disapprobation? Quite a few spokespersons for abortion reform made just such an appeal, saying that to bear a child after rape or one likely to be gravely disabled is to be heroic, not just law-abiding. Analogies were made to self-defense law, which gives the victim's interest priority over that of the aggressor, and to the legal permission not to rescue others where any personal risk is involved.[128] In those situations, too, the law recognizes an apparent right not to sacrifice one's own lesser interests for the sake of others' greater interests. The communitarian principles of the necessity defense here give way to a deep individualism.

Such a politico-legal theory is quite evidently not in harmony with a spirit of dedication to common goals. Instead, it would seem to be founded on something like social contract reasoning. People with essentially private interests come together out of a limited need for mutual defense and cooperation. They agree to accept a certain burden,

---

[126] The Dreher & Tröndle commentary, however, has little problem treating the physician's exemption as based upon separable public health grounds. That is, in order for excused abortions to be performed in safety, physicians are permitted to perform them, without implying that the law favors or is even neutral on the question of whether abortions should occur. *Supra* n. 101, prenote 9e to art. 218, at 1001–02. Spanish law has a similar catch-all category of excuse, called the *excusa absolutoria,* which the law could use to understand the status of the aborting physician. *See* Jiménez de Asúa, *supra* n. 23 and 89. *But cf.* Nathanson, *Aborting America* 193–94 (1979), who argues that the advent of modern antibiotics, of the plastic suction curette, and of self-abortive drugs makes illegal abortion no longer a major public health problem even if the medical abortionist is held penally accountable.

[127] Despite its own conclusion that abortion is only excused, the Dreher-Tröndle commentary, *id.,* makes clear that the dominant legal opinion in Germany is that non-punished abortions are to be considered justified. *See generally* Eser, *Reform of German Abortion Law: First Experiences,* 34 Am. J. Comp. L. 359, 375 n. 40 and accompanying text (1986) and Gropp. *Der straflose Schwangerschaftsabbruch* (1981). The latter's arguments virtually ignore the need to integrate penal and constitutional theory, however, while the Dreher & Tröndle argument is built upon an attempt at such integration.

[128] On 25 May 1983, in the Congress of Deputies, the PSOE spokesperson Saenz Cosculluela argued that the law values one's own life more than that of another, and that the law cannot demand heroism of a pregnant woman, *supra* n. 94 at 1853, 1854. On 7 September 1983, Sotillo Martí argued for the abortion depenalization bill by appealing to the fact that the law does not always demand that we rescue others, even though it may be our moral duty to do so. Again on 5 October 1983, he argued that to require the continuation of pregnancy in the hardship conditions covered by the proposed law would be to demand heroism, which the Penal Code does not do when it comes to rescue. *Supra* n. 33 and 31 at 2138, 2946.

Cf. Sanford Kadish's important attempt to understand the interaction of the values of proportionality and autonomy: *Respect for Life and Regard for Rights in the Criminal Law,* 64 Cal. L. Rev. 871 (1976).

but no more, for the sake of their joint enterprise. Once they have made the maximum expected contribution, they have a right to refuse further payments. Where an act or omission is necessary in order to avoid an excess contribution to public values, that act or omission is legally justified.

It is a strange beast, this hybrid of Social State and social contract. From the point of view of community values, the act or omission is wrong. It results in a net value loss. Yet from the point of view of the individual, the act is right. The non-hero reasons that one should not have to give to the community anything more than one thinks one is likely to need from the community. Since he or she is certainly never going to be a fetus in need of maternal support, why should he or she feel obligated to give such support?[129]

The idea of non-demandability can in this way be thought to justify abortion (particularly in circumstances of unusual hardship) despite the fact that the values of the community, the values for the sake of which we have come together, thereby suffer. Abortion is somehow justified and not justified at the same time. The community permits abortions without saying that abortions ought to occur.

What legal concepts can express the permission to be nonheroic—in regard to abortion or to non-rescue or to other analogous situations? Surely not "claim" and "duty." The fact that someone violates no legal duty in refusing to maximize the common good of life does not mean that others violate a legal duty in striving by means other than penal law to further that good. In other words, any Spanish (or German) permission to abort should be labeled a "liberty"[130] rather than a "right." The State does not insist *sub poena* that a pregnancy continue, but neither may a pregnant woman insist upon support or protection for abortion. In this view, abortion would be objectively legal, not only excused, but it would be legalized only as a liberty and not as a claim upon the community. Such an understanding is similar to an old way of looking at the legal situation called "necessity"—that it returns all parties involved to a "state of nature," where legal duties and claims in the full sense do not yet exist.[131]

But if abortion is only a liberty, involves only the absence of penal prohibition, necessity doctrine might still justify intervention to *prevent* abortions.[132] Necessity always involves individual interference with what are otherwise legal rights of others. Even where one is not legally required to furnish his coat to a freezing child, the child may be excused and even justified in taking it. Or, better, suppose a nonswimmer bystander to be watching helplessly as an unknown child lies drowning at the bottom of a pool. A good swimmer walks by but refuses to help because he already has a cold and does not wish to risk making it worse. The bystander blocks the swimmer and grabs his hat, telling him will not get it back unless he rescues the child. Would a court convict the nonswimmer of battery or of theft? I suspect not. Thus even assuming

---

[129] Someone who thinks in this way puzzlingly overlooks the fact that he or she has *already* needed and received aid as a fetus. Yet such an analysis appears dominant in the decisions in question. Nowhere is the duty to support new life treated in these cases as a matter of simple reciprocity for benefits everyone has earlier received.

[130] The reference here is to the concept which Hohfeld calls "privilege." *See generally*, Hohfeld, *Fundamental Legal Conceptions* (1919).

[131] See discussion in Rodriguez Devesa, *supra* n. 90 at 555.

[132] And civil damages for abortion might still be recoverable by a father. Even an act that is justified under penal law may incur liability for civil damages. *See* Penal Code art. 20, and the commentaries thereon by Jiménez de Asúa, e.g., *supra* n. 89 at 198–99.

arguendo that we think the swimmer legally justified in refusing to help, we may also think the nonswimmer justified in forcing him to help. That we do not use the criminal law to coerce people into making sacrifices does not mean that we do not wish such sacrifices to be made, nor that we are willing to use criminal penalties to ensure that no sacrifices are made. If pregnancy is only like rescuing, and both are just sometimes too much to demand by means of criminal penalties, then abortion has not yet won the full support of the law. Particularly under a jurisprudence of ''effective'' community values, it would seem that courts ought to ignore rules wherever acts further the greater constitutional value. And, at least in the case of abortion to avoid bearing a disabled child, it would be very hard for a Spanish tribunal to find that prevention of such an abortion, by means of non-delivery of abortifacients or of a non-violent sit-in, is not in accord with the constitutional order of values. On the side of the fetus are the values of life and of protection for the handicapped, while the Court mentions no constitutional value at all on the side of abortion.

The theoretical and practical disadvantages of the conclusion reached here are obvious. Abortion, even if fully legal is in the sense that non-rescue in the face of risks is fully legal, may still not become easily available—because non-cooperation with, and even intervention against, the performance of abortion may be justified by the thinking at the base of the necessity defense. Conceptual and public order may thereby be threatened. These disadvantages do not often arise in the parallel case of non-rescue, because not rescuing another does not ordinarily require the participation of third parties, nor does the intervention of third parties ordinarily preclude not rescuing. By contrast, abortion necessarily implicates third parties and the judicial system which judges those parties.

If the idea of non-demandability were limited to excusing women who undergo abortions, it would lead to no such anomalous results and would probably find near universal support. Most states in the U.S., for example, *de facto* and even *de jure*,[133] did not punish women for abortion prior to *Roe v. Wade*. But they did prosecute abortionists. The values of life and order are compatible with excuses which are truly and merely excuses, with the desire not to use penal law against women, but not with more.

Alternatively, we can hold to a justificatory sense of the non-demandability of bearing a child, letting it mean community support for a right not to make undue sacrifices. But we can do so in an orderly fashion only at the cost of devaluing human life (or of somehow honestly separating fetal life from postnatal life). If unborn life has little value, abortion does little if any damage, and so contracts for it should be enforced and no one is justified in preventing it.

In other words, either abortion must remain a crime (though one for which many or even all women need not be punished), or it must be seen to promote the common good (because unborn human life hardly counts as part of that good). Only these two solutions are internally coherent in theory and practice.

Is the doctrine of non-demandability the best place to begin to think about which solution to seek? A good argument can be made that this doctrine is *not* a very helpful

---

[133] *See* Wohlers, *Women and Abortion*, published updated by the American Center for Bioethics. The author surveys pre-*Roe* statutory and case law and concludes that women were almost always exempted from punishment by one or the other. In the spring of 1989, the National Right to Life Committee (the most influential anti-abortion organization in the United States) took a stand officially opposing any and all punishment of women who have abortions.

starting point (anywhere in the world) because it is likely one-sidedly to obscure as much as it reveals of the legally significant dimensions of pregnancy and of abortion.

To ask whether a continuation of pregnancy in certain circumstances is demandable of a woman is to emphasize exclusively the affirmative and sacrificial character of pregnancy. In other words, it makes us think of pregnancy as an act of giving and of abortion as an omission or a ceasing so to give. But surely in many ways abortion is an act by the mother or by her agent, and continued pregnancy is an omission. Somehow this makes a difference. It is often worse legally, if not morally, to throw someone who has slipped into one's home out into the freezing cold than not to let her in to begin with. Abortion, at the least, is like that act of expulsion. And pregnancy, after conception, in an important sense requires no further acts. Gestation is automatic, one might say, as long as one omits to terminate it. This fact makes a difference at least psychologically. It is harder to pay taxes than to endure government withholding of them. To donate blood to a relative every day for nine months could easily *feel* like a much greater sacrifice than to have something similar occur by itself in the womb. The *power* of the non-demandability doctrine is precisely that, in all contexts (not just abortion), it makes us treat what could be seen as acts instead of omissions. We ask not "Should he have robbed the bank?" but "Can we demand that he have his legs be broken by those trying to force him to rob the bank?" I am not suggesting that pregnancy is wholly an omission and abortion is wholly an act, only that there are important considerations on both sides and the question of non-demandability tends to make us overlook one side.

This focus on omission to sacrifice also takes our eyes off immediate intentions and leads us loosely to speculate about ultimate motives—something we would be much less likely to do with regard to an act. In the abortion context, for example, many write as though avoiding the burdens of pregnancy were the main purpose of abortions,[134] though *Roe* itself emphasized post-natal burdens.[135] But the desire to separate oneself from the fetus, before or after birth, is not the sole aim of abortions, otherwise adoption would have been mentioned by *Roe* as an alternative way to avoid the burdens to which it points. Clearly, many people who have abortions aim not just at avoiding the burdens of pregnancy or of childcare, but at not being mothers at all. A decisive motive may be to avoid the burdensome adoption choice. The intent then comes to be to kill the fetus. A lethal act with a lethal intent is much harder to justify or excuse than a failure to be a hero. Non-demandability makes us forget the first way of looking at abortion and think only about the second.

Furthermore, just as non-demandability makes us turn away from the intent of an otherwise illegal act, it tends to make us forget the policy promoted by the particular law at issue. If we ask only "Can we force people to kill and risk being killed?", we may say "no." But if we ask whether national survival justifies the military draft, we may say "yes." If new life is to be treated as a fundamental public value, as the Spanish court asserts, it cannot be omitted from the question of how much can be demanded.[136] Yet this value is wholly left out of that court's demandability discussions.

Non-demandability also, it seems to me, tends to make us think in very general terms. Should one have to sacrifice one's legs? Should one be expected, under penalty,

---

[134] *See e.g.*, Regan & Thompson, *supra* n.111 and Calabresi, *supra* n. 68—though the latter at 114 notes that the purpose may also be to kill the fetus.

[135] Roe v. Wade, 410 U.S. 113, 153 (1973).

[136] See George Fletcher's argument that even excuse reasoning must involve value-balancing. *Supra* n. 93.

to put up with a handicapped child? The generic answer to these questions may be "no". But we should also refer to the various sources of a special duty to make sacrifices. Non-demandability does not in itself[137] allude to those sources.

Thus, U.S. commentators have sought to show that, even if the fetus were a person, the law should not impose the burden of supporting him or her on the mother, any more than one should have to support a famous violinist who needs transfusions for nine months.[138] But *if* the fetus is a person, it is not *only* a person. It is also *one's own child,* and that fact may make all the difference.

It is true that the Spanish high court uses the normal burdens of *parents* as a standard of what can be demanded,[139] which is no doubt higher than the standard for citizens in general. But are parents committed to putting up only with "normal" burdens? This question is never clearly addressed. Though the Spanish court uses article 8 necessity as a prop for its decision, it never discusses that portion of article 8 which denies the necessity defense to one who has a special obligation to sacrifice herself.

Nor are the many possible sources of the duties of parents explored. Is there a natural duty resulting from a biological relationship? Is there a duty resulting from causation, from the sexual creation of a situation in which the fetus is in peril? Or does the act of intercourse involve a tacit consent to care for life resulting from the act?[140] Does it matter that, if one were still a fetus, one would enter into a social contract to give birth, even under hardship, to other fetuses in order to be born oneself in like circumstances? Rather than careful analysis of the strengths of each such factor, non-demandability (at least as expounded by the Spanish and German Constitutional Courts) encourages a superficial global assessment.

Yet in the final analysis, despite all its flaws, the question of demandability should not be overlooked. Most of the myriad sources of obligation listed above end up with women carrying greater burdens than men. That is, the burdens even of ordinary pregnancy, not to speak of hardship pregnancy, are greater than our *law* places on non-pregnant people during most of their lives and those burdens fall unequally onto one sex.[141] Whether or not we consciously have recourse to a doctrine of non-demandability, we are bound to feel uneasy about demanding that women alone bear such burdens.

There are two ways, in my opinion, that this uneasiness can be overcome—and both bring us back to the Social State. As the Spanish court pointed out (L.F. 11) with regard to the burden of handicapped children, community aid can make the sacrifices entailed by pregnancy and parenthood much less—to the point where they may be demandable. If the legal community highly values unborn life, it ought to share the burden of bearing that life by means not only of social support services before and after birth, but even of special benefits and privileges for mothers[142]—including mothers who give

---

[137] But demandability as found in the German Penal Code art. 35 does require an inquiry into special legal relationships.

[138] *Supra* n. 111. The violinist is Thomson's creation.

[139] *See* L.F. 11, BJC, *supra* n. 5 at 535.

[140] Spanish law also creates another exception to art. 8's necessity defense for those who intentionally bring about the state of necessity.

[141] *See generally* Calabresi, *supra* n. 68 especially at 101 ff.

[142] Glendon, *supra* n. 52, indicates that almost all Western nations provide maternity benefits, child care, paid leaves, paternity support, family benefits and the like to a far greater degree than is done in the U.S. Perhaps it is partially for this reason that the burdens at least of normal pregnancy and parenthood seem not too much to demand in Germany and Spain.

up their children for adoption. That is what is often done in gratitude to young people who have been soldiers.

Secondly, the community must not refrain from asking for significant sacrifices from others beside women who have special abilities to contribute to what we value in common. From taxation and business regulation to zoning and blood donation, a high standard of expectation must be set—and backed up by some sort of penalty for unexcused failure to comply with that standard. Only then will the sacrifices of pregnancy seem obviously demandable. It is on some level bizarre, even if logically consistent, to take a stand both against abortion and for a *laissez-faire* economy and society.

This article by Dr. Henshaw goes well beyond the laws and policies of countries around the world. It looks at the incidents of abortion, abortion mortality, health issues, abortion services and demographic characteristics. These added elements only prove that there can be a great difference to a legal right to abortion and a right to abortion. Specifically, a country may allow abortion in the first trimester, but unless there are adequate medical services available, this may be a hollow privilege for the pregnant mother. Then, too, another country may be very restrictive as far as the abortion law and yet allow easy circumvention of this law by the mother or the physician. Finally, and tragically, a country may have restrictive medical and legal policies concerning abortion, yet maintain a significant number of illegal abortions. Nevertheless, Dr. Henshaw shows through his frequent uses of tables that a pattern is emerging among the civilized nations. He states, ''The continued improvement in the safety of abortion in developed countries is encouraging. Mortality is down to an average level of 0.6 deaths per 100,000 legal abortions, and declines are apparent in complication rates as well. . . . A number of a factors are working toward greater acceptance of abortion in developing areas: an increasing desire of a women and couples to control their fertility, a greater concern with women's roles and rights and population pressures. . . . Some countries may revise their laws in response to increased awareness of the adverse public health effects of illegal abortion. Others will undoubtedly follow the examples of Greece, the Netherlands, Turkey and other countries that liberalized their laws only after abortion had long been widely practiced.''

14 · Induced Abortion: A World Review, 1990

*Stanley K. Henshaw, Ph.D.**

The worldwide trend toward liberalization of abortion laws has continued in the last several years with changes in Canada, Czechoslovakia, Greece, Hungary, Romania, the Soviet Union and Vietnam. Forty percent of the world's population now lives in countries where induced abortion is permitted on request, and 25 percent now lives where it is allowed only if the woman's life is in danger.

In 1987, an estimated 26 to 31 million legal abortions and 10 to 22 million clandestine abortions were performed worldwide. Legal abortion rates ranged from a high of at least 112 abortions per 1,000 women of reproductive age in the Soviet Union to a low of five per 1,000 in the Netherlands. In recent years, abortion rates have been increasing in Czechoslovakia, England and Wales, New Zealand and Sweden and declining in China, France, Iceland, Italy, Japan and the Netherlands.

In most Western European and English-speaking countries, about half of abortions are obtained by young, unmarried women seeking to delay a first birth, while in Eastern Europe and the developing countries, abortion is most common among married women with two or more children.

Mortality from legal abortion averages 0.6 deaths per 100,000 procedures in developed countries with data. Abortion services are increasingly being provided outside of hospitals, and for those performed in hospitals, overnight stays are becoming less

*Stanley K. Henshaw is deputy director of research at The Alan Guttmacher Institute. The author thanks the Rockefeller Foundation for the funding that made this project possible, Evelyn Morrow for invaluable assistance in compiling data and constructing tables, Jacqueline Darroch Forrest and Henry David for helpful comments on earlier drafts of this article, and the many colleagues, too numerous to name here, in all parts of the world who took the time to provide information.

common. National health insurance covers abortions needed to preserve the health of a pregnant woman in all developed countries except the United States, where Medicaid and federal insurance programs do not cover abortion unless the woman's life is in danger.

Laws and Policies

Around the world, laws governing induced abortion range from those prohibiting abortion with no explicit exceptions to those establishing it as a right of pregnant women. In 1986, The Alan Guttmacher Institute (AGI) published *Induced Abortion: A World Review, 1986,* the sixth edition of a series created by Christopher Tietze of The Population Council. That work contained a summary of the legal status of abortion in all countries; statistics on the number and characteristics of women who obtain abortions in countries where such data are available; information about abortion procedures, related morbidity and mortality and the effects of policy changes; and a section on the statistical methods used. The present article updates the data presented in that earlier work and gives an overview of the subject, with an emphasis on the changes that have taken place since 1986.

Table 1 classifies all countries and dependent territories[1] with populations of one million or more according to the restrictiveness of their abortion laws. Some 53 countries of this size, containing 25 percent of the world's population, fall into the most restrictive category, where abortions are prohibited except when the woman's life would be endangered if the pregnancy were carried to term. In some of the countries in this category, statutes prohibit abortion without explicit exception—even if the life of the pregnant woman is in danger. But in most if not all cases, implicit provisions in the statutes or general principles of criminal law permit abortion to save the life of a pregnant woman.

Forty-two countries of at least one million people, comprising 12 percent of the world's population, have statutes authorizing abortion on broader medical grounds—to avert a threat to the woman's general health (not limited to the risk of losing her life) and sometimes for genetic or juridical indications, such as rape or incest—but not for social indications alone or on request. Some of the statutes permit abortion only when the woman's physical health is threatened, while others explicitly or by interpretation include her mental health as well.

Twenty-three percent of the world's population live in the 14 countries of one million or more people that allow abortions for social or social-medical indications; that is, adverse social conditions can either justify termination of a pregnancy or be considered in evaluating a threat to the woman's health. In many of these countries, including Australia, Finland, Great Britain, Japan and Taiwan, abortion is available virtually on request.

The least restrictive category includes the 23 countries where abortion is permitted on the request of the woman. Some of the world's most populous countries—China, the Soviet Union and the United States, as well as about half of the European countries—are in this category, which contains about 40 percent of the world's population. In Sweden, in the absence of medical contraindications, a woman has a right to have a

---

[1] In subsequent references, "countries" is used to refer to all areas for which data are presented. Tables with statistics for each country for all available years may be obtained from the author.

Table 1. Countries, by Restrictiveness of Abortion Law, According to Region, January 1, 1990

Law	Africa	Asia & Oceania	Europe	North America	South America
To save a woman's life	Angola Benin Botswana Burkina Faso Central Afr. Rep. Chad Côte d'Ivoire Gabon Libya Madagascar Malawi Mali Mauritania Mauritius Mozambique Niger Nigeria Senegal Somalia Sudan Zaire	Afghanistan Bangladesh Burma Indonesia Iran Iraq Laos Lebanon Oman Pakistan Philippines Sri Lanka Syria United Arab Emirates Yemen Arab Rep. Yemen, Peoples' Democratic Rep.	Belgium Ireland	Dominican Rep. El Salvador*,† Guatemala Haiti Honduras Mexico* Nicaragua Panama	Brazil* Chile Colombia Ecuador* Paraguay Venezuela
Other maternal health reasons	Algeria Cameroon* Congo Egypt† Ethiopia Ghana*,† Guinea Kenya Lesotho Liberia*,† Morocco Namibia*,† Rwanda Sierra Leone South Africa*,† Tanzania Uganda Zimbabwe*,†	Hong Kong*,† Israel*,† Jordan* Korea, Rep. of*,† Kuwait† Malaysia*,† Mongolia Nepal New Zealand*,† Papua New Guinea Saudi Arabia Thailand*	Albania Northern Ireland Portugal*,† Spain*,† Switzerland	Costa Rica Jamaica Trinidad & Tobago	Argentina* Bolivia* Guyana Peru

Social and social-medical reasons	Burundi
	Zambia†
		Australia†
		India*,†,**
		Japan*,†,§§
		Korea, Dem.
		   Rep.*,†
		Taiwan*,†
			Bulgaria*,†,‡,††
			Finland*,†,‡,‡‡
			German Fed
			   Rep.*,†,‡‡,*†
			Great Britain†
			Hungary*,†,‡,‡‡
			Poland*,§§,‡‡
					Uruguay*,§

On request	Togo Tunisia‡‡	China Singapore Turkey††	Austria‡‡,*† Czechoslovakia‡‡ Denmark‡‡	Canada Cuba†† Puerto Rico	

Law	Africa	Asia & Oceania	Europe	North America	South America
		Vietnam	France ‡‡	United States	
			German Dem. Rep.‡‡		
			Greece ‡‡		
			Italy ‡‡		
			Netherlands		
			Norway ‡‡		
			Romania ‡‡		
			Soviet Union ‡‡		
			Sweden *‡		
			Yugoslavia ††		

*Includes juridical grounds, such as rape and incest.   †Includes abortion for genetic defects.

‡Approval is automatic for women who meet certain age, marital and/or parity requirements.

§Not permitted for health reasons but may be permitted for serious economic difficulty.

**During the first 20 weeks.   ††During the first 10 weeks.

‡‡During the first three months or 12 weeks.

§§No formal authorization is required, and abortion is permitted in doctor's office; thus, abortion is de facto available on request.

*†Gestational limit is for interval since implantation.   *‡During the first 18 weeks.

Notes: Table does not include countries with fewer than one million inhabitants or those for which information on the legal status of abortion could not be located (e.g., Bhutan and Kampuchea). All abortions are permitted only prior to fetal viability unless otherwise indicated in footnotes.

legal abortion up to the end of the 18th week of gestation. In some of these countries—for example, Sweden and Yugoslavia—abortion is defined explicitly as a right of a pregnant woman.

Even where abortion is available on request, abortion services are generally subject to the restrictions that apply to other types of medical or surgical care. For example, in most if not all countries, abortion services may be provided only by licensed medical personnel and only with the consent of the woman. Many of the countries that permit abortion on request also have gestation limits (as shown in Table 1) beyond which health or other indications are required for the procedure to be permitted. In other countries, abortion is permitted through 24 weeks' gestation (Singapore) or up until viability (e.g., China, the Netherlands and the United States). In Great Britain, the legal gestation limit is 28 weeks, although administrative regulations have, in effect, lowered the limit to 24 weeks.

A variety of other restrictions exist throughout the world, the most common being parental notification or consent for minors, waiting periods, compulsory counseling and the prohibition of abortions in profit-making facilities. According to a recent analysis, spousal authorization requirements exist in several developing countries, including Kuwait, Taiwan and Turkey;[2] however, in countries without statutory provision for spousal consent, there have been no known cases in which "a husband's claim of veto [has] been judicially upheld."[3]

---

[2]R. J. Cook and B. M. Dickens, *International Developments in Abortion Laws: 1977–88,* American Journal of Public Health, **78**:1305, 1988.

[3]*Ibid.,* p. 1307.

It should be emphasized that the formal classification of the laws does not necessarily reflect their restrictiveness in actual practice. In most Muslim countries and in Latin America and Africa, few legal abortions are performed under the health exception, while in Israel, New Zealand and South Korea, the legal abortion rates are comparable to those in countries that allow abortion on request. Legal interpretations of the same law can even vary widely within a country, as in Switzerland, where the exception for medical reasons is interpreted very liberally in some cantons and very narrowly in others.

Restrictive laws do not necessarily mean that safe abortion services are unavailable. Services may exist despite legal constraints because laws are either interpreted with flexibility or not vigorously enforced or because physicians are willing to risk prosecution. Abortion is restricted in several countries that permit menstrual regulation (a procedure identical to an early abortion but performed without a pregnancy test). The government of Bangladesh, for example, supports clinics that provide menstrual regulations up to 10 or 12 weeks gestation as a public measure. Menstrual regulations are also performed in some areas of Indonesia[4] and Malaysia.[5]

Despite a highly restrictive law in Belgium,[6] abortions are provided through a network of nonhospital clinics as well as in a few hospitals and physicians' offices.[7] Similarly, in Latin America, although abortion providers are sometimes prosecuted, virtually all major cities have physicians who perform abortions and some have clinics that specialize in the procedure.

On the other hand, the absence of restrictions does not guarantee that services will be available. In India and Bangladesh, the overall shortage of medical facilities makes legal abortion and menstrual regulation unavailable to most women. Similarly, despite the relaxation of abortion restrictions in Ghana, and their elimination in Togo, the availability of services has changed little in those African nations. In Zambia, women commonly attempt illegal abortions and then go to a hospital for treatment of complications because few legal abortions can be done under current laws and resource limitations.

From the second half of the 19th century through World War II, abortion was highly restricted almost everywhere. Liberalization of abortion laws occurred in most of the countries of Eastern and Central Europe in the 1950s and in almost all the remaining developed countries during the 1960s and 1970s. A few developing countries also relaxed their restrictions on abortion during the same period, most notably China and India. By mid-1986, abortions could be legally obtained for health reasons in North America and in every European country except Belgium and the Republic of Ireland.

Since then, the trend toward abortion liberalization has continued with changes in seven countries of one million or more. In 1988, the Canadian Supreme Court voided the law allowing abortions only in hospitals and only on medical grounds, and abortions

---

[4]R. S. Samil, *Commentary on Menstrual Regulation as a Health Service: Challenges in Indonesia,* International Journal of Gynecology & Obstetrics, Supplement 3, p. 29, 1989.

[5]K. Pannikar, *The Karman Syringe in Family Practice: Techniques, Safety, and Usage,* in U. Landy and S. S. Ratnam, eds., *Prevention and Treatment of Contraceptive Failure,* New York, Plenum Press, 1986.

[6]Since this was written, the Belgian parliament has passed a law that permits abortions up to 14 weeks in approved facilities if the woman is "in distress," with a six-day wait between the first consultation and the abortion. After 14 weeks, abortions are permitted in cases of danger to the woman's health and fetal malformation.

[7]M. Vekemans and B. Verhaegen, *Enquête sur le nombre d'interruptions volontaires de grossesse pratiquées en Belgique en 1985,* Revue Medicale de Bruxelles, **8**:21, 1987.

are now legally permitted in that country on request. However, although abortions are easier to obtain in some hospitals that have eliminated their committee approval requirements, few nonhospital facilities have begun offering services, and some provinces have taken steps to discourage abortions by restricting insurance payments to those performed in hospitals or by prohibiting abortions outside of hospitals.

In 1986, the two republics that make up Czechoslovakia passed laws that eliminated the requirements that abortions be approved by a committee and be performed for medical or social reasons only.[8] Abortions are now available on request through 12 weeks of pregnancy and up to 24 weeks for fetal defects or if the woman's life would be threatened by continuing the pregnancy. Greece also revised its abortion law in 1986 and legalized first-trimester procedures on request.[9] Previously, abortions were technically illegal but had been readily available from physicians.

The abortion law in Hungary has been liberalized to permit abortions on request to married women with two living children (reduced from at least three children), and the approval of a committee is no longer needed. As before, abortion is permitted for women who have health, fetal defect or juridical indications, are unmarried, have been separated for at least six months, are older than 35 or have inadequate housing. Women not meeting the above conditions may apply for approval if they have another "social reason" for terminating the pregnancy.[10]

First-trimester abortions had been available on request in Romania from 1957 to 1966. Then in 1966, the government imposed severe restrictions on abortion, prohibited the importation of contraceptives and took other measures to encourage population growth; illegal abortions became increasingly common in succeeding years, reaching a higher rate than in any Western European country in which abortion was legal, according to official government statistics. In 1986, Romania renewed measures to suppress abortion and taxed both unmarried persons over age 25 and married couples who remained childless for more than two years without a medical reason.[11] According to press reports, the new Romanian government lifted the 1966 and 1985 restrictions on abortion as of January 1, 1990.[12]

In Vietnam, all reference to abortion was omitted from the criminal law in 1986, although abortion on request was already legal.[13] In addition, the grounds for second-trimester abortions have been broadened in the Soviet Union to include a number of social indications, reportedly to reduce the number of illegal procedures.[14]

In addition to the countries named above, all of which have populations of one million or more, several smaller states have liberalized their abortion laws, including Cape Verde, Cyprus, French Polynesia and Liechtenstein. Only the Philippines and the United States have passed restrictive measures at the national level since 1986: The Philippines incorporated a clause into its 1986 constitution stating that the state shall "protect the life of the mother and the life of the unborn from conception,"[15] and the

---

[8] Law 66/1986 in Czech Socialist Republic and Law 73/1986 in Slovak Socialist Republic.

[9] 1986 (28 Jun) Law 1609, § 2-5, Greece.

[10] Order No. 76/1988. /XL3./ MT of the Council of Ministers on the interruption of pregnancy, Hungary.

[11] H. P. David, *Romania Ends Compulsory Childbearing*, Population Today, Mar. 1990, p. 4.

[12] G. Lewthwaite, *Ceausescu Hit Hard at Abortion*, The Record, Hackensack, N.J., Jan. 14, 1990, p. A-37; and M. Dobbs, *Dictator's Dream Took Harsh Toll*, The Washington Post, Jan. 5, 1990, p. A1.

[13] *The 1986 Criminal Code of the Socialist Republic of Vietnam*, Review of Socialist Law 1987, **13**:121, 1987.

[14] *Abortion Research Notes*, Vol. 17, Nos. 1–2, July 1988, p. 5.

[15] Article II, Section 12.

United States Supreme Court weakened the constitutional guarantees of abortion rights in *Webster v. Reproductive Health Services* in 1989.[16]

Between 1986 and 1990, restrictions on abortion at the state level increased somewhat in the United States. The most important changes were the discontinuation of public funding (Medicaid) for poor women in Michigan and the District of Columbia (except in cases of life endangerment), leaving such funding available in only 13 states. Five more states have been added to the nine with parental notification or consent requirements (or, alternatively, a court order) for women under age 18; and abortions have been prohibited in government hospitals and clinics in Missouri and Pennsylvania (in addition to Kentucky and North Dakota, which already had such restrictions in place).

The full impact of the *Webster* decision has not yet been felt; some states are still considering new legislation, and some restrictions are temporarily enjoined while constitutional challenges are being debated. The Supreme Court's language suggests that more severe restrictions than those considered in the *Webster* case might now be upheld as constitutional. Even if the court overturns *Roe v. Wade,* thereby eliminating protection for abortion rights in the federal constitution, abortion will remain legal and available in many or most states because of the protection guaranteed under state constitutions or because of decisions made in state legislatures.

Incidence of Abortion

Table 2 shows the abortion numbers, rates and ratios among countries with populations of more than 300,000 for which official statistics could be obtained or for which estimates are available.[17] Not surprisingly, the most complete and accurate data available are those for developed countries and countries where abortion is legal. The first panel lists countries with data thought to be accurate within 20 percent of the true incidence, as well as a few countries for which there is limited evidence as to accuracy. The data were compiled primarily by government agencies and were obtained either from published reports or from persons with access to official statistics.

The middle of Table 2 contains official statistics that are probably low by at least 20 percent because of unreported legal abortions (in Bangladesh, France, the Federal Republic of Germany [West Germany], India, Italy,[18] Japan, Poland and the Soviet Union) or illegal abortions (in Bangladesh, India and probably the Soviet Union). The figures for Ireland include only those women who obtained an abortion in England and gave an Irish address; the number who gave an English address is unknown. The Romanian data reflect mainly illegal abortions and may either underestimate or overestimate true incidence; they exclude illegal abortions that did not require treatment but may include spontaneous abortions that were treated.

The data in the bottom panel, derived from a variety of sources, may be incomplete. Still, they indicate the magnitude of abortion incidence in a few populus countries and may be more accurate than the official statistics for Bangladesh, Japan and the

---

[16] Webster v. Reproductive Health Services, 57 U.S.L.W., No. 86-605, July 3, 1989.

[17] Scotland is included as a separate country because complete, accurate statistics are available and because its utilization of abortion differs from that of England and Wales.

[18] In Italy and possibly other countries, the unreported abortions are technically illegal even if performed by a physician, because reporting and other administrative requirements are not met.

Table 2. Number of Abortions, Abortion Rate per 1,000 Women Aged 15–44, Abortion Ratio per 100 Known Pregnancies* and Total Abortion Rate,† by Completeness and Reliability of Data and Country

Type of data and country	N‡	Rate	Ratio	Total rate
Statistics believed to be complete				
Australia (1988)	63,200	16.6	20.4	484
Belgium				
In Belgium§ (1985)	10,800	5.1	8.7	u
All** (1985)	15,900	7.5	12.2	u
Bulgaria (1987)	119,900	64.7	50.7	u
Canada				
In Canada (1987)	63,600	10.2	14.7	299
All†† (1985)	74,800	12.1	16.6	u
China (1987)	10,394,500	38.8	31.4	u
Cuba (1988)	155,300	58.0	45.3	u
Czechoslovakia (1987)	156,600	46.7	42.2	1,400
Denmark (1987)	20,800	18.3	27.0	548
England and Wales‡‡ (1987)	156,200	14.2	18.6	413
Finland (1987)	13,000	11.7	18.0	356
German Democratic Republic (1984)	96,200	26.6	29.7	u
Hungary (1987)	84,500	38.2	40.2	1,137
Iceland (1987)	700	12.0	14.0	336
Netherlands‡‡ (1986)	18,300	5.3	9.0	155
New Zealand (1987)	8,800	11.4	13.6	323
Norway (1987)	15,400	16.8	22.2	493
Scotland§§ (1987)	10,100	9.0	13.2	255
Singapore (1987)	21,200	30.1	32.7	840
Sweden (1987)	34,700	19.8	24.9	600
Tunisia (1988)	23,300	13.6	9.8	u
United States (1985)	1,588,600	28.0	29.7	797
Vietnam (1980)	170,600	14.6	8.2	u
Yugoslavia (1984)	358,300	70.5	48.8	u
Statistics that are incomplete				
Bangladesh (FY 1989)	77,800	3.4	1.6	u
France *† (1987)	161,000	13.3	17.3	406*‡
German Federal Republic				
In country (1987)	88,500	6.7	12.1	197
All** (1986)	92,200	7.0	12.8	u
Hong Kong (1987)	17,600	12.7	20.1	u
India (FY 1987)	588,400	3.0	2.2	u
Ireland*§ (1987)	3,700	4.8	5.9	139
Israel (1987)	15,500	16.2	13.5	u
Italy (1987)	191,500	15.3	25.7	460
Japan (1987)	497,800	18.6	27.0	564
Poland (1987)	122,600	14.9	16.8	u
Romania†* (1983)	421,400	90.9	56.7	u
Soviet Union (1987)	6,818,000	111.9	54.9	u
Estimates based on surveys or other data				
Bangladesh (FY 1986)	241,400	12	5	u
Japan (1975)	2,250,000	84	55	u
South Korea (1984)	528,000	53	43	u
Soviet Union (1982)	11,000,000	181	68	u
Spain (1987)	63,900	8	u	u

Type of data and country	N‡	Rate	Ratio	Total rate
Switzerland (1984)	13,500	9	15	u
Turkey (1987)	531,400	46	26	u

*Known pregnancies are defined as legal abortions plus live births. Births have not been lagged by six months because the necessary birth data are unavailable for most countries.

†The number of abortions that would be experienced by 1,000 women during their reproductive lifetimes, given present age-specific abortion rates.

‡Rounded to the nearest 100 abortions.

§Abortions performed in 17 hospitals and 20 nonhospital facilities, usually illegally.

**Including abortions obtained in the Netherlands and England.

††Including abortions obtained in Canadian clinics and in the United States.   ‡‡Residents only.

§§Including abortions obtained in England.   *†Provisional data.   *‡1986 data.

*§Based on Irish residents who obtained abortions in England.

†*Combining counts of illegal abortions with treated complications and of legal abortions.

Notes: Sources of country data for this table and subsequent tables available from author; u = unavailable.

Soviet Union. The figures for Bangladesh[19] and Spain[20] are derived from surveys of abortion providers and are probably fairly complete for legal abortions, but large numbers of illegal procedures are omitted, especially in the Bangladesh data. The Japanese data[21] are based on national projections for 1975 made from districts in which reporting was believed to be complete; the estimate of 2.3 million is about three times the official reported number for that year. The estimates for South Korea[22] and Turkey[23] are derived from population surveys that asked married women about their histories of legal and illegal abortions. The estimated abortion numbers and rates for these countries are thus conservative, since induced abortions tend to be underreported even in communities where the practice in widely accepted.[24] The estimates for the Soviet Union[25] may also have some downward bias because of underreporting, although the survey on which they are based was conducted only in the Russian Republic, which has a higher official abortion rate than the other Soviet republics. For Switzerland, 54 percent of the data are statistics from cantons that collect data, and the rest are estimates.[26]

Of the countries shown in Table 2, the Soviet Union has the highest abortion rate—112 per 1,000 women aged 15–44, as calculated from official data. That nation's abor-

[19]R. Amin et al., *Menstrual Regulation Training and Service Programs in Bangladesh: Results from a National Survey*, Studies in Family Planning, **20**:102, 1989.

[20]*Incidencia del Aborto Provocado en España*, Frederación de Planificaión Familiar de España, Madrid, 1989.

[21]M. Muramatsu, *Estimation of Induced Abortions, Japan, 1975*, Bulletin of the Institute of Public Health, **27**:93, 1978.

[22]*Fertility and Family Health Survey of 1985*, Korea Institute for Population and Health, Seoul, 1985.

[23]*1988 Turkish Population and Health Survey*, Hacettepe University Institute of Population Studies, Ankara, 1989.

[24]E. F. Jones and J. D. Forrest, *Contraceptive Failure in the United States: Revised Estimates from the 1982 National Survey of Family Growth*, Family Planning Perspectives, **21**:103, 1989.

[25]M. S. Bednii, *Demograficheskie Faktori Zdorovia*, Finansi i Statistika, Moscow, 1984.

[26]M. Dondénaz, *Avortement-Interruption de Grossesse: le Cas de la Suisse*, Réalités Sociales, Lausanne, 1987.

tion ratio is also high; officially, 55 percent of all known pregnancies are terminated by abortion, but because of illegal abortions and unreported legal abortions, the true rate is probably higher than the official figures indicate.[27] The survey results shown in Table 2 produce an estimate of 181 abortions per 1,000 women of reproductive age, suggesting that a significant proportion of abortions are performed outside the official system. Within the Soviet Union, the republics vary widely in abortion utilization; for example, in 1985, the abortion ratio calculated from official statistics ranged from 66 percent of pregnancies ending in abortion in the Russian Republic to 18 percent in Tadzhik.[28]

Abortion rates and ratios are relatively high in the Eastern and Central European countries as well, where rates range from 27 per 1,000 women of reproductive age in the German Democratic Republic (East Germany) to 71 per 1,000 in Yugoslavia. Except for East Germany, these countries have a history of reliance on abortion, which was legalized in the 1950s before modern contraceptive methods were fully developed. In addition, the full range of modern contraceptive methods is not readily available in most of Eastern and Central Europe and the Soviet Union. In Japan, hormonal methods have been approved for medical purposes (regulating menses) but not for contraception. The Japanese abortion rate is also estimated to be relatively high, although it has probably fallen below the rate of 84 per 1,000 women aged 15–44 estimated for 1975.

Abortion rates in most of the remaining developed countries range from 11 to 20 per 1,000 women of reproductive age, although the U.S. rate is higher (28 per 1,000). Italy's rate is probably well above this range also when unreported abortions are taken into account.[29] The rates for the Netherlands, Scotland and Switzerland are below the range found in most developed countries. Those reported for Belgium and Ireland— countries that have very restrictive laws—are also low, but are not significantly lower than the rate for the Netherlands, a country with one of the world's most liberal abortion laws. The low rate reported for Spain, where clinics have just begun to provide services, is based on a survey that might have missed some providers and that excludes illegal abortions.

Abortion rates tend to be higher in those developing countries with liberal abortion laws than in the developed countries, although there is a wide variation in rates. Cuba, South Korea and Turkey have rates of over 40 abortions per 1,000 women of reproductive age. Tunisia, on the other hand, has the relatively low rate of 14 per 1,000, in spite of a liberal law and government-supported services. (The Tunisian statistics, however, omit legal abortions performed in the private sector; in 1980, these were estimated to equal 15–20 percent of the reported abortions.[30]

The rate of legal abortion (or menstrual regulation) in Bangladesh is relatively low at 12 per 1,000 women or reproductive age because legal services are unavailable in many rural areas, and in others, women are unaware of existing services. Based on the assumption that one abortion death occurs for every 100 illegal abortions, one study used mortality data to estimate that 780,000 illegal abortions are performed each year.[31]

[27] M. S. Bednii, 1984, op. cit. (see reference 21).

[28] Academy of Sciences, State Committee of Labor, *Annual Demographic Report*, Moscow, 1988, p. 319.

[29] S. L. Tosi et al., *L'Interruzione voluntaria di gravidanza in Italia, 1983*, Istituto Superiore di Sanità, Rome, 1985.

[30] A. Charfeddine, *Evolution récente du Programme National de Planning Familial*, Revue Tunisienne des Etudes de Population, **1**:105, 1980.

[31] A. R. Measham, M. Obaidullah and M. H. Rosenberg, *Complications from Induced Abortion in Bangladesh Related to Types of Practitioner and Methods, and Impact on Fertility*, Lancet, **I**:199, 1981.

If this estimate is accurate, the illegal abortion rate in Bangladesh is three times the legal rate. Many clandestine abortions are performed in India as well because of a similar lack of medical services in rural areas. India's legal abortion rate is probably two to five times the reported rate of three abortions per 1,000 women, since only a fraction of the legal abortions, mainly those in government hospitals, are reported.

The total abortion rate given in Table 2 represents the number of abortions that 1,000 women could expect to have during their reproductive lifetimes, given present age-specific abortion rates. For example, at present rates of abortion in the United States, 1,000 women would have 797 abortions during their lifetime. Czechoslovakia and Hungary have rates over 1,000, meaning that the average woman in those countries would have more than one abortion during her lifetime. If accurate data were available, total abortion rates would probably be as high or higher in Cuba, Japan, South Korea, the Soviet Union, Turkey and Yugoslavia and perhaps other countries as well.

Among countries with complete data for a recent three-year period, usually 1984–1987, legal abortion rates have remained relatively stable in most, but significant changes have taken place in some. The largest increase in the legal abortion rate (35 percent) occurred in Czechoslovakia, and much of that may be attributable to the elimination of abortion approval committees. Legal rates also increased by more than 10 percent in England and Wales, New Zealand and Sweden. One source has suggested that the higher Swedish rate may be a result of an increased emphasis on AIDS prevention that has led to a greater use of condoms at the expense of more effective methods.[32]

Declines in abortion rates occurred in Iceland and the Netherlands. The drop in the Netherlands appears to represent a continuing recovery from the pill scare that caused an increase in abortions in 1980. The number of reported abortions in China fell markedly from 14.4 million in 1983 to 8.9 million in 1984, rose again to 11.6 million in 1986 and then fell to 10.4 million in 1987. While there are some reporting uncertainties, the decline in 1984 could be a consequence of a massive increase in the number of sterilizations and IUD insertions in 1983[33] and of a relaxation of the population control effort in 1984.[34] Declines in abortion rates have also been recorded in three countries with less complete data—France, Italy and Japan; although it is possible that the reporting itself has deteriorated in these countries, it seems more likely that the increased acceptance of modern contraceptive methods has caused real declines. Data from surveys in South Korea illustrate the relationship between abortion rates and contraceptive use. Between 1973 and 1979, both the abortion rate and the contraceptive prevalence rate rose rapidly, reflecting the increased desire of couples to reduce their fertility. But from 1979 to 1985, contraceptive prevalence especially sterilization, continued to increase, and the abortion rate fell back to its level of 1973.[35]

Since the widespread liberalization of abortion laws, illegal abortions have largely disappeared in most developed countries. However, physicians in Italy, Portugal, the Soviet Union and Spain still perform abortions that do not meet all the requirements of the law and, as such, are not counted as legal abortions. Further, traditional practitioners

---

[32] K. Holmgren *Sweden, an Open Society,* Planned Parenthood in Europe, Vol. 18, No. 1, 1989, p. 15.

[33] Renmin Weishen Chubanshe, *Zhengguo weisheng nianjian 1985,* Beijing, 1985.

[34] K. Hardee-Cleaveland and J. Bannister, *Fertility Policy and Implementation in China, 1986–88,* Population and Development Review, **14**:245, 1988.

[35] Korean Institute for Population and Health, *1985 Fertility and Family Health Survey,* Seoul, 1985.

may still be performing abortions in these countries and in Romania (before 1990) and Yugoslavia because of the persistence of restrictions, legal barriers and local customs.

In developing areas, abortions are commonly performed by both physicians and traditional practitioners whether or not the procedure is legal. In East Asian countries such as Indonesia and Malaysia, physicians provide menstrual regulations while traditional practitioners provide abortions by massage, insertion of objects into the uterus and other folk methods. In Latin America, abortion services are available from physicians in all major cities and in clinics in some areas. (In Rio de Janeiro, for example, there is a chain of abortion clinics that advertises in newspapers, without, however, using the word "abortion.") Nevertheless, because of the cost of these services and their scarcity outside of major cities, many or most abortions in Latin America are probably self-induced or performed by non medical practitioners. Cuba, where abortion is available on request, is a notable exception.

In Africa and parts of the Middle East, the desire for large families is still prevalent, and abortion is thought to be less common than in Latin America, where fertility rates have fallen rapidly. Nevertheless, hospital studies indicate that complications of illegal abortions are a major public health problem. For example, Jomo Kenyata Hospital in Nairobi, Kenya, treats 50 to 60 women a day for abortion complications.[36] A community-based study in Addis Ababa, Ethiopia, found that 24 percent of all maternal deaths and 54 percent of those directly related to pregnancy were attributable to complications of clandestine abortions.[37]

According to the numbers in Table 2, approximately 22 million legal abortions were reported in 1987 (or the closest year for which data were available for the countries listed). The number of unreported legal abortions can be estimated at six million—most of these accounted for by India, Japan, South Korea and the Soviet Union[38]—but this estimate is uncertain and could range from four to nine million. The estimated number of legal abortions performed worldwide in 1987 was approximately 28 million, but may have ranged from 26 million to 31 million. These estimates of the numbers of legal abortions are lower than those made in 1986 (33 million, with a range of 30–40 million) because reported abortions in China declined by four million and newly published abortion statistics for the Soviet Union resulted in a decrease in the maximum estimate for that country.

Information on clandestine abortions is too uncertain to know whether the worldwide total is increasing or decreasing, since few studies in developing countries have provided accurate measures even for small areas. Combining the estimates that other authors have generally used with guesses as to the probably rates of abortion results in rough estimates of clandestine abortions: 500,000 in Bangladesh, 600,000 in the rest of South Asia, 1.5 million in the rest of Asia, 400,000 for Romania, 1.5 million for Africa and approximately two million in the Soviet Union and four million each in India and

[36] F. M. Coeytaux, *Induced Abortion in Sub-Saharan Africa: What We Do and Do Not Know*, Studies in Family Planning, **19**:186, 1988.

[37] B. E. Kwast, R. W. Rochat and W. Kidane-Mariam, *Maternal Mortality in Addis Ababa, Ethiopia*, Studies in Family Planning, **17**:288, 1986.

[38] In making estimates for the Soviet Union, the difference between the seven million abortions reported and the 11 million estimated to have occurred (see Table 2) was assumed to be due half to unreported legal procedures and half to illegal abortions.

Latin America. This totals 15 million clandestine abortions, but, again, the uncertainty of the estimates suggests that the number could be as low as 10 million or as high as 22 million. The estimated worldwide total of abortions is therefore between 36 and 53 million, yielding an annual rate of 32–46 abortions per 1,000 women of reproductive age.

Abortion Mortality

The World Health Organization (WHO) has estimated that 99 percent of the 500,000 maternal deaths that occur worldwide annually take place in developing countries, of these, 115,000–204,000 result from complications of illegal abortions performed by unqualified practitioners.[39] A more conservative estimate may be derived from hospital studies that suggest that, on average, 20–25 percent of maternal mortality is attributable to abortion,[40] yielding totals of 100,000–125,000 deaths annually from illegal abortion. The WHO estimates that more than half of the deaths caused by induced abortion occur in South and Southeast Asia; the next largest proportion take place in Sub-Saharan Africa. The numbers are only approximate because of the difficulty in distinguishing between deaths from induced abortion and those from spontaneous abortion in countries where induced abortion is illegal, the problems of generalizing from studies done in particular hospitals and localities and the relatively small number of studies that have been reported. A literature review found that the highest reported mortality rate to be 2,400 deaths per 100,000 abortions in a rural area of Bangladesh.[41]

The provision of abortion under modern medical conditions has reduced abortion mortality to an extremely low level in developed countries that have legalized the procedure. Table 3 shows mortality rates in the 13 countries for which accurate numbers of deaths and abortions are known. While the rates range from zero to two deaths per 100,000 legal abortions, the differences between the countries are not statistically significant because the numbers of deaths are so small. The aggregate mortality rate of these countries is 0.6 deaths per 100,000 legal abortions; only in England and Wales is the rate statistically significantly higher, in part because of a relatively high proportion of abortions performed at later gestations.

The stage of pregnancy at which an abortion is performed affects the risk of mortality and complications; regardless of legal status and medical care, the risk of mortality rises with increasing gestation.[42] In 1981–1985 data for the United States, for example, deaths per 100,000 legal abortions rise from 0.2 at eight or fewer weeks since the last menstrual period to 0.3 at 9–10 weeks, 0.6 at 11–12 weeks, 3.7 at 16–20 weeks and 12.7 at 21 weeks or more.[43] In the developed countries, the risk of mortality from abortion has declined consistently since abortion was legalized; in all countries for which we have earlier data than those shown in Table 3, mortality rates were higher. In de-

[39] E. Royston and S. Armstrong, eds., *Preventing Maternal Deaths,* World Health Organization (WHO), Geneva, 1989.

[40] L. Liskin, *Complications of Abortion in Developing Countries,* Population Reports, Series F, No. 7, 1980.

[41] A. R. Kahn et al., *Induced Abortion in a Rural Area of Bangladesh,* Studies in Family Planning, **17**:95, 1986.

[42] E. Royston and S. Armstrong, eds., 1989, op. cit. (see reference 34).

[43] Special tabulations from data on deaths provided by The Centers for Disease Control; and S. K. Henshaw, J. Van Vort, eds., *Abortion Services in the United States, Each State and Metropolitan Area, 1984–1985,* The Alan Guttmacher Institute, New York, 1988, Detailed Table 4, updated to 1985.

Table 3. Number of Legal Abortions (in 000s), Number of Associated Deaths and Mortality Rate (95 Percent Confidence Intervals) per 100,000 Legal Abortions, by Country

Country	Abortions	Deaths	Mortality rate
Bulgaria	373.6	5	1.3
(1980, 1984, 1987)			(0.4–3.1)
Canada	511.0	1	0.2
(1980–1987)			(0.0–1.1)
Czechoslovakia	780.5	3	0.4
(1976–1983)			(0.1–1.1)
Denmark	269.3	2	0.7
(1976–1987)			(0.1–2.7)
England and Wales	1,094.8	14	1.3
(1980–1987)			(0.7–2.1)
Finland	154.1	2	1.3
(1976–1985)			(0.2–4.7)
Hungary	648.9	5	0.8
(1980–1987)			(0.2–1.8)
Netherlands	509.0	1	0.2
(1976–1983)			(0.0–1.1)
New Zealand	74.0	0	0.0
(1976–1987)			(0.0–5.0)
Norway	70.1	0	0.0
(1978–1982)			(0.0–5.3)
Scotland	101.0	2	2.0
(1976–1987)			(0.2–7.1)
Sweden	261.2	1	0.4
(1980–1987)			(0.0–2.1)
United States	9,445.9	54	0.6
(1980–1985)			(0.4–0.7)

Note: Deaths attributed to legal abortion on death certificate, except for England and Wales (where deaths are recorded on the form for abortion notification) and the United States (where deaths are associated with abortion after investigation by the Centers for Disease Control).

veloped countries where induced abortion is legal, the procedure is now safer than pregnancy and childbirth. During 1981–1985 in the United States, the maternal mortality rate excluding deaths from abortion and ectopic pregnancy was 6.6 deaths per 100,000 live births, a rate that is 11 times that associated with legal abortion.[44]

The possible effects on maternal mortality of the legal restrictions on abortion can be seen in Romania, where most abortions were prohibited in 1966. Between 1965 and 1984, abortion mortality rose from 21 deaths to 128 deaths per 100,000 live births. Over the same period, maternal mortality from other causes fell from 65 deaths to 21 deaths per 100,000 live births.[45] In 1984 alone, the WHO reports that there were 449 abortion deaths in Romania.[46]

---

[44] Special calculations using data on maternal deaths from U.S. National Center for Health Statistics (NCHS), *Vital Statistics of the United States, Volume II, Part A*, 1981 and succeeding years; and NCHS, *Advance Report of Final Natality Statistics, 1985*, Monthly Vital Statistics Report, Vol. 36, No. 4, Supplement, 1987.

[45] E. Royston and S. Armstrong, eds., 1989, op. cit. (see reference 34).

[46] WHO, *World Health Statistics Annual*, Geneva.

Other Health Issues

For first-trimester abortions in most Western developed countries, the traditional sharp curettage method (dilatation and curettage, or D&C) has been largely replaced by suction curettage (vacuum aspiration). The latter method requires less cervical dilatation and has less risk of uterine injury and retention of products of conception.[47] In the latest year for which data are available, more than 95 percent of curettage abortions were performed by suction in Denmark, England and Wales, Finland, France, the Netherlands, Sweden and the United States. By comparison, higher proportions of sharp curettage procedures were performed in Hungary (52 percent), Czechoslovakia (30 percent), West Germany (20 percent), Italy (18 percent) and Singapore (seven percent), and the use of sharp curettage is reportedly still common in the Soviet Union.

In developing countries where abortion is legally restricted, most physicians are not trained in suction curettage and do not have the necessary equipment, so office procedures are usually done by sharp curettage. Suction curettage is sometimes used, however, where large numbers of abortions are performed in clinics.

Second-trimester abortions may be performed by instrumental evacuation or by medical induction. In the 15 countries for which recent data are available, medical induction is used to perform more than eight percent of all abortions in only Scotland (14 percent) where a large number of second-trimester procedures are performed, and Finland (16 percent). Physicians in several countries—Canada, Denmark, England and Wales, New Zealand, Norway, Singapore, the United States and West Germany—reduced their reliance on medical induction by as much as 80 percent over the most recent five years for which data are available (1982 to 1987 for most countries). In Norway, for example, the proportion of abortions performed by medical induction fell from 2.1 percent to 0.4 percent. Even after 16 weeks' gestation, sharp curettage is sometimes used in Canada (16 percent of abortions at 17 weeks or more), Denmark (12 percent), England and Wales (44 percent of abortions at 20 weeks or more), Sweden (six percent) and the United States (61 percent of abortions at 16 weeks or later).

Abortion is occasionally performed by hysterectomy or hysterotomy, but these procedures now account for less than 0.1 percent of abortions in Czechoslovakia, Hungary, Italy, New Zealand, Norway and the United States. In other countries with recent data, uterine surgery is used in 0.1–0.3 percent of abortions in Canada, Denmark, England and Wales, Finland, France, Scotland, Singapore, Sweden and West Germany.

New compounds that block the effect of progesterone—a hormone that is needed for the successful implantation and maintenance of the embryo—are currently under development. One such compound, RU 486, is now being used to perform 25 percent of the abortions in France, and a 95 percent effectiveness rate has been reported when it is administered with a prostaglandin within 49 days of the last menstrual period and an effectiveness rate of up to 90 percent when it is administered without the prostaglandin.[48] The main complications reported are incomplete abortion, which increases sharply

---

[47] T. Van der Vlugt and P. Piotrow, *Uterine Aspiration Techniques,* Population Reports, Series F, No. 23, 1973, p. 25; E. Royco, *Cervical Dilatation: A Review,* Population Reports, Series F, No. 6, 1977, p. 85.

[48] M. Klitsch, *RU 486: The Science and the Politics,* The Alan Guttmacher Institute, New York, 1989; and D. Grimes et al., *Early Abortion with a Single Dose of the Antiprogestin RU 486,* American Journal of Obstetrics and Gynecology, **158**:1307, 1988.

Table 4. Percentage Distribution of Legal Abortions, by Weeks of Gestation, According to Country

Country	≤8	9–12	13–16	≥17	Total
Canada (1987)	33.2	55.3	8.0	3.5	100.0
Czechoslovakia (1987)	84.7	15.0	0.2	0.2	100.0
Denmark* (1988)	40.9	56.7	1.0	1.3	100.0
England and Wales					
Residents (1987)	34.5	52.5	8.5	4.5	100.0
Nonresidents (1987)	25.9	33.3	17.7	23.1	100.0
Finland (1987)	54.5	40.5	2.9	2.0	100.0
France (1986)	55.4	42.8	1.5	0.3	100.0
Hungary (1987)	67.8	30.7	0.8	0.7	100.0
India (FY 1983)	u	85.0†	15.0‡	u	100.0
Italy (1987)	49.5	49.8	0.7‡	u	100.0
Japan§ (1987)	52.4	41.1	3.3	3.2	100.0
Netherlands					
Residents** (1986)	69.8	21.5	6.0	2.7	100.0
Nonresidents** (1986)	42.8	29.4	17.6	10.2	100.0
New Zealand (1988)	23.0	69.8	5.9	1.3	100.0
Norway (1987)	45.0	52.5	2.0	0.5	100.0
Scotland†† (1987)	46.8	42.4	8.6	2.2	100.0
Singapore (1987)	72.4	24.0	2.5	1.1	100.0
Sweden (1987)	41.1	54.6	3.1	1.2	100.0
United States‡‡ (1985)	51.5	39.6	5.2	3.7	100.0

*Ordinal weeks.   †Distribution is for ≤12 weeks.   ‡Distribution is for ≥13 weeks.

§Distribution is for ≤7 weeks, 8–11 weeks, 12–15 weeks and ≥16 weeks.

**Abortions performed in clinics only.

††Distribution is for ≤9 weeks, 10–13 weeks, 14–17 weeks and ≥18 weeks.

‡‡Last two categories are 13–15 weeks and ≥16 weeks (see S. K. Henshaw and J. Van Vort [reference 36] for estimation methods).

Notes: In this and subsequent tables, abortions for which distribution data are unknown are assumed to have the same distribution as those for which data are known. Gestation is measured from the first day of the last menstrual period; u = unavailable.

with gestational age, and prolonged bleeding. Advantages of this nonsurgical method are the reduced risk of damage to the uterus and the elimination of any risk associated with the use of anesthesia. From the woman's point of view, the drug affords more of a sense of control, and the abortion is similar to a spontaneous miscarriage; however, the process takes longer than a surgical abortion.

A progesterone blocker does not solve the problem of providing safe abortion in developing countries without medical facilities, since medical backup is needed when the method fails and in the relatively rare cases of continued bleeding. Even when self-administered without the prostaglandin, however, RU 486 might be safer than some forms of nonmedical and self-induced abortion.

International comparison of the point in gestation at which abortions are performed are imperfect because of differences and uncertainties in the measurement of gestational age. Nevertheless, the data indicate significant differences among countries, as may be seen in Table 4. The proportion of abortions performed before nine weeks ranges from 23 percent in New Zealand to 85 percent in Czechoslovakia. The Czech government encourages women to have abortions as early as possible; women who have very early procedures avoid a four-day hospital stay and a fee that is charged for abortions performed beyond eight weeks.[49]

Among countries without legal restrictions on second-trimester abortions, the proportion of abortions done after 12 weeks' gestation ranges from four percent in Singapore to 15 percent in India. The relatively high proportion in India may be attributable to a scarcity of medical resources and to a disproportionate amount of data from government hospitals. The other countries with proportions larger than 10 percent—Canada, England and Wales, and Scotland—have approval procedures that cause delays, although this is no longer the case in Canada. In addition, women in Great Britain are often delayed by the National Health Service, which has difficulty meeting the demand for abortion services in some areas.

Fewer than five percent of abortions take place beyond 12 weeks' gestation in the countries that have restrictive gestational requirements. Some of the women from these countries who need later abortions travel to England and Wales (which provided 7,400 abortions past 12 weeks to foreign women in 1987) and the Netherlands (which provided 5,100 in 1986). Few abortions are performed after 20 weeks even in countries that have no specific restrictions on later abortions; the proportions of these late abortions range from a high of 0.9 percent among residents of England and Wales to a low of 0.1 percent in Czechoslovakia and Norway (not shown).

Overall, the proportion of abortions performed in the second trimester remained relatively stable in the most recent five years for which data are available. The proportion increased by 2.7 percentage points in New Zealand, by 0.7 percentage points in Japan and by 0.6 points in Finland. Declines of more than a percentage point occurred in Canada (1.6 points) and in England and Wales (1.3), the two areas (excluding India, for which the statistics are unreliable) that have the highest proportion of second-trimester abortions.

In all the countries for which age data are available, women younger than 20 have later abortions than do older women, and slightly more women over 40 experience delays than do women aged 35–39. Low levels of educational attainment are also associated with delays in obtaining abortions. Another reason that late second-trimester abortions are performed is suspicion or identification of a fetal defect late in pregnancy. A study in England and Wales found that in 1981–1982, 19 percent of abortions done at or after 20 weeks' gestation were performed for this reason.[50]

Surgical sterilization may be performed concurrently with an abortion. There is no agreement on whether complication rates for abortion and sterilization performed concurrently are greater than the aggregate risks from two separate procedures,[51] but the

---

[49] Jiři Šràček, personal communication, Feb. 12, 1989.

[50] C. Joseph, *Factors Related to Delay for Legal Abortions Performed at a Gestational Age of 20 Weeks or More*, Journal of Biosocial Science, **17**:327, 1985.

[51] M. C. E. Cheng, *Abdominal Sterilization*, in J. E. Hodgson, ed., *Abortion and Sterilization: Medical and Social Aspects*, Grune and Stratton, New York, and Academic Press, London, 1981, p. 395; W. M. Hern, *Abortion Practice*, Lippincott, Philadelphia, 1984; C. J. Levinson and H. B. Peterson, *Female Sterilization*, in S. L. Corson et al., eds., *Fertility Control*, Little Brown and Company, Boston, 1985; J. A. Ross et al., *Voluntary Sterilization: An International Fact Book*, Association for Voluntary Sterilization, New York, 1985, p. 89; A. A. Yuzpe and J. E. Rioux, *Pregnancy Termination Combined with Sterilization*, in G. I. Zatuchni et al., eds., *Pregnancy Termination: Procedures, Safety and New Developments*, Harper & Row, Hagerstown, Md., 1979, p. 312.

risk is generally believed to be greater than the risk associated with either procedure done alone. Among the 10 countries with the available data, the one with the highest proportion of abortions with concurrent sterilization is India (29 percent according to official statistics). Among developed countries, the proportion ranges from seven percent in Canada to 1.4 percent in the United States. Although no statistical data are available for Central and Eastern Europe, concurrent sterilization is known to be rare or nonexistent in those areas. The proportion of concurrent procedures has been decreasing in seven of the 10 countries; the exceptions are Finland, India and Sweden.

Serious postoperative complications are rare when abortions are performed in medical settings. For this reason, few extensive studies of complications have been published in recent years. The most comprehensive large-scale investigations of medical complications of legal abortions were undertaken in the United States by the Joint Program for the Study of Abortion. The last of these studies, undertaken from 1975 to 1978, found that 0.7 percent of abortions were associated with major complications (pelvic infection with fever of at least 38° C for three or more days, hemorrhage requiring blood transfusion and unintended major surgery).[52] The risk of developing complications was found to be strongly associated with gestational age.

Other studies have used different definitions of complications, which along with differences in medical practices and systems of care, make it difficult or impossible to compare the absolute level of complications that were found. A recent study in Denmark reported that six percent of abortion patients had complications requiring hospitalization.[53] Statistics kept by the National Abortion Federation on 68,828 abortions performed in U.S. clinics in 1988 show that 0.5 percent had complications that required hospitalization.[54]

Although direct comparisons between countries are risky because of differences in the definition and measurement of complications, the data show consistently lower complication rates for earlier abortions. Rates reported in four countries (Canada, Denmark, England and Wales, and West Germany) and New York State ranged from 0.4–3.4 percent for first-trimester abortions and from 1.1–8.7 percent for those in the second trimester. All of these areas experienced declines in complication rates in recent years, probably because of improved methods and the increasing technical skill of providers.

Adverse psychological sequelae to abortion have been studied by a WHO panel, which concluded that "there is now a substantial body of data, reported from many countries after careful and objective follow-up, suggesting frequent psychological benefit and a low incidence of adverse psychological sequelae."[55] A Danish study that compared women who had had abortions with those who had given birth found an increased rate of admissions to psychiatric hospitals among the separated, divorced and widowed women who had had abortions but not among the single and married women who had done so.[56] Studies based on the most appropriate comparison—that between

[52]C. Tietze and S. K. Henshaw, *Induced Abortion: A World Review, 1986,* The Alan Guttmacher Institute, New York, 1986, Table 16.

[53]L. Heisterberg and M. Kringelbach, *Early Complications After Induced First-Trimester Abortion,* Acta Obstetricia et Gynecologica Scandinavica, **66**:201, 1987.

[54]National Abortion Federation, *Summary of Annual Statistics, 1988,* Washington, D.C., 1989.

[55]WHO, *Induced Abortion,* Technical Report, No. 623, Geneva, 1978, p. 22.

[56]H. P. David et al., *Postpartum and Postabortion Psychotic Reactions,* Family Planning Perspectives, **13**:88, 1981.

Table 5. Percentage Distribution of Abortion Patients, by Type of Facility in which Abortion was Performed and Length of Hospital Stay (in nights), According to Country

Country	Nonhospital	Hospital							Total
		All	0	1	2	3	≥4		
Canada (1985)	14.5	85.5	65.8	12.9	4.5	1.3	0.9		100.0
Czechoslovakia (1987)	0.0	100.0	69.4	30.6*	u	u	u		100.0
Denmark (1987)	0.0	100.0	52.1	43.3†	u	u	4.7		100.0
England and Wales‡ (1987)	0.0	100.0	42.4	40.3	15.0	1.2	1.0		100.0
German Federal Republic (1988)	70.4	29.6	7.2	2.6	4.8	6.5	8.5		100.0
Hungary§ (1987)	0.0	100.0	0.0	81.7	14.6	1.8	1.9		100.0
Italy (1987)	66.1**	u	u	22.9	7.6	2.0	1.4		100.0
Netherlands†† (1986)	80.9	19.1	u	u	u	u	u		100.0
Norway (1987)	51.0	49.0	u	u	u	u	u		100.0
Poland‡‡ (1987)	53.8	46.2	u	u	u	u	u		100.0
Scotland (1983)	0.0	100.0	24.4	18.8	46.0	6.7	4.1		100.0
Sweden (1987)	0.0	100.0	86.7	13.3*	u	u	u		100.0
United States (1985)	86.9	13.1	10.3	2.8*	u	u	u		100.0

*Distribution is for ≥1 nights.   †Distribution is for 1–3 nights.

‡Residents only. Some hospitals provide mainly abortion services and are similar to nonhospital facilities in other countries.

§Hospitals include maternity homes.   **Includes hospital abortions with no overnight stay.

††Two nonhospital facilities allow patients to stay overnight, and one is located within a hospital. Data apply to residents only; almost all abortions provided to nonresidents are performed in nonhospital clinics.

‡‡Excluding unreported abortions performed in physicians' offices and nonhospital clinics.   Note: u = unavailable.

abortion patients and women giving birth after being unable to terminate an unwanted pregnancy—have not been attempted to date.

The possibility that induced abortion might impair future reproductive capacity has been a concern, but no new evidence has emerged in recent years to change earlier conclusions that any adverse effects of terminating a first pregnancy by suction curettage are at most quite small.[57]

Provision of Abortion Services

Abortions performed by instrumental evacuation may be provided safely in both hospital and nonhospital facilities.[58] Nevertheless, countries differ widely in their policies and practices regarding the settings in which abortions are performed, and for hospital abortions, the average length of stay. Among the countries for which data are available, the United States relies the least on hospitals, with 87 percent of abortions performed in nonhospital facilities in 1985 (Table 5, see above); this includes the 60 percent that were done in specialized abortion clinics. On average, abortion clinics in the United States perform 2,400 procedures a year; the largest have an annual caseload of over 10,000. The proportion of abortions performed in nonhospital facilities in the Netherlands (81 percent) is almost as high as that in the United States. Further, a majority of abortions are also provided outside of hospitals in West Germany (70 percent), Poland

---

[57]C. J. R. Hogue et al., *The Effects of Induced Abortion on Subsequent Reproduction*, Epidemiologic Reviews, **4**:66, 1982, Tables 2, 4–6.

[58]D. A. Grimes et al., *Abortion Facilities and the Risk of Death*, Family Planning Perspectives, **13**:30, 1981.

(54 percent, not including unreported abortions performed in physicians' offices) and Norway (51 percent).

At the other extreme are countries with laws or regulations requiring abortions to be performed only in hospitals. These countries include Czechoslovakia, Denmark, England and Wales, Hungary and Scotland, as well as Bulgaria, East Germany, Finland, France, New Zealand and Romania; the latter countries are not shown in Table 5 because of lack of information on the number of nights patients spend in the hospital. Bulgaria and Hungary have regulations specifying that abortion patients spend at least one night in the hospital, although physicians in Bulgaria may waive the rule in many cases. Although a hospital restriction existed in Canada until 1988, clinic abortions were provided in the province of Quebec, where the law was not enforced, and in Toronto, where the law was being challenged in court.

In some of the countries with in-hospital requirements, the term "hospital" is broadly interpreted to include facilities that closely resemble clinics. In England and France, for example, abortions are permitted in private facilities that resemble clinics in the United States. On the other hand, two of the abortion clinics in the Netherlands are like hospitals in that they have facilities for patients to stay overnight if necessary.

Nonhospital abortions have increased over time in all the countries where they are permitted. The most dramatic change has occurred in West Germany, where the proportion of abortions performed outside of hospitals rose from 15 percent in 1977 to 70 percent in 1988. In the United States, the proportion of nonhospital abortions went from 78 percent to 87 percent between 1980 and 1985. Increases have also been documented in Poland and are estimated to have occurred in the Netherlands.

A major advantage of nonhospital abortions is lower cost. In addition, the staffs of high-volume services, whether inside or outside of hospitals, have the technical skills and understanding of the needs of abortion patients that come from extensive experience. However, specialized abortion services may result in more fragmented follow-up care than would be the case when the woman's personal physician provides the abortion.[59]

For abortions performed in hospitals, large differences exist in the proportion of patients who stay overnight and in the number of days they remain in the hospital. In the United States in 1985, 79 percent of abortions performed in hospitals were outpatient procedures. Of all U.S. abortion patients, only about three percent stayed overnight in a hospital (excluding patients hospitalized for complications). Sweden and Canada also have relatively low rates of overnight hospitalization—13 percent and 20 percent, respectively. In England and Wales, 58 percent of abortions involve overnight hospitalization, and the corresponding proportion in Scotland is 76 percent. As mentioned earlier, all abortion patients in Bulgaria and Hungary are admitted for at least 24 hours, although some Bulgarian women leave early. In West Germany, 15 percent of abortions involve a hospital stay of three or more nights.

In all countries that have reliable data, there has been a trend over the most recent five years for which data were available toward much shorter hospital stays. For example, in England and Wales, the proportion of abortions involving an overnight stay decreased from 71 percent to 58 percent between 1982 and 1987, and in West Germany, the proportion of women staying three or more nights fell from 31 percent to 15 percent

---

[59] J. E. Hodgson, *Major Complications of 20,248 Consecutive First Trimester Abortions: Problems of Fragmented Care,* Advanced in Planned Parenthood, Vol. 9, No. 3-4, 1975, p. 52.

between 1983 and 1988. The principal reason for this trend is probably increased confidence among physicians and medical authorities that extended hospital care is usually unnecessary. However, other explanations may be the high cost of hospitalization, the declining use of instillation and the inconvenience to the patient of a hospital stay.

In most countries, abortion services are paid for by the same insurance or payment mechanism as other medical care. In 17 developed countries with populations of more than 300,000, abortion services are available without charge under national health insurance systems.[60] In a few of these countries, however, some women prefer to pay for private services. For example, the large majority of abortions in Spain and Greece are paid for privately. In England and Wales and in Poland, abortions obtained in private facilities are also common. Eleven countries require nominal payments from abortion patients,[61] although in most, no fee is charged for abortions needed for certain medical or other indications. One country, Austria, covers abortions through national health insurance only if they are medically necessary.

The United States is the only developed country where the health insurance programs mandated or funded by the national government exclude coverage for medically necessary abortions other than those needed to save the woman's life. However, 13 state governments do pay for abortion services for poor women—two less than did so in 1986.

In developing countries, legal abortions are usually provided in government health facilities in the same way as are other health services. Examples of such countries are Bangladesh (for menstrual regulations), China, India, Tunisia and Vietnam. Where abortion is legally restricted but nevertheless available from physicians, as in most of Latin America, women must pay privately for the service.

Demographic Characteristics

The incidence of abortion and the ratio of abortions to births vary between subgroups in a population for several reasons, most notably because of differing rates of and reactions to unintended pregnancy and differential access to legal abortion services. Although many unintended pregnancies are carried to term, the incidence of abortion can be used to identify the subgroups within a population with the greatest problem of unintended pregnancy and thus the greatest need for improved contraceptive services. Two of the most common groups who utilize abortion are unmarried women who wish to delay the birth of their first child and married women with children who want to space additional children or end childbearing.

Abortion is frequently used to delay childbearing in English-speaking developed countries (Australia, Canada, England and Wales, New Zealand, Scotland and the United States), where abortion is concentrated among young women. More than 50 percent of abortions are obtained by women younger than 25 in all of these countries except Australia, where the proportion is 47 percent (Table 6, page 427). The rate of abortion per 1,000 women peaks at age 18–19 in Canada, England and Wales, and the United States (and probably also in Australia and Scotland, where data on subgroups of teenagers are

---

[60] Canada, Cyprus, Czechoslovakia, Denmark, East Germany, England and Wales, Greece, Italy, Luxembourg, the Netherlands, New Zealand, Norway, Poland, Portugal, Scotland, Spain and West Germany.

[61] Australia, Bulgaria, Finland, France, Hungary, Japan, Romania, the Soviet Union, Switzerland, Sweden and Yugoslavia.

Table 6. Percentage Distribution of Legal Abortions, Abortion Rate and Abortion Ratio, by Woman's Age, According to Country

Measure	≤19				20–24	25–29	30–34	35–39	≥40	Total
	All	≤14	15–17	18–19						
% distribution										
Australia (1988)	19.1	u	u	u	28.1	23.3	16.8	9.4	3.3	100.0
Bulgaria (1987)	7.8	u	u	u	25.2	28.2	21.8	13.1	4.0	100.0
Canada (1987)	22.3	0.6	9.3	12.3	31.7	22.4	13.9	7.4	2.2	100.0
Czechoslovakia (1987)	7.7	0.0	2.4	5.3	23.5	24.3	23.4	15.5	5.5	100.0
Denmark (1988)	14.1	0.2	5.5	8.3	29.1	22.5	16.2	11.8	6.4	100.0
England and Wales* (1987)	24.9	0.6	11.1	13.2	31.5	20.0	12.1	8.1	3.3	100.0
Finland (1987)	18.9	0.2	7.0	11.7	26.6	17.3	14.3	13.3	9.6	100.0
France † (1986)	10.3	0.1	3.6	6.5	23.9	23.8	20.7	15.3	6.0	100.0
German Dem. Rep. (1976)	13.5	0.1	6.4	7.0	20.5	19.2	19.4	19.9	7.5	100.0
German Fed. Rep. (1988)	7.5	0.1	2.5	4.9	24.0	25.5	20.1	15.5	7.4	100.0
Hungary (1987)	11.0	0.1	4.2	6.6	16.7	18.8	24.5	19.8	9.2	100.0
India (FY1986)	5.1	u	u	u	26.0	33.0	23.2	10.2	2.6	100.0
Italy (1987)	7.5	0.1	2.0	5.4	20.5	22.5	21.7	18.3	9.6	100.0
Japan (1987)	5.5	u	u	u	16.3	17.4	23.7	26.4	10.6	100.0
Netherlands* (1986)	13.7	0.3	5.6	7.8	25.4	22.0	19.1	14.0	5.7	100.0
New Zealand (1988)	22.2	0.5	9.6	12.0	29.3	23.7	14.4	8.0	2.4	100.0
Norway (1987)	23.3	u	u	u	30.1	18.2	14.0	9.8	4.6	100.0
Scotland ‡ (1987)	28.1	u	u	u	31.9	18.6	11.6	7.2	2.7	100.0
Singapore (1987)	8.6	u	u	u	26.7	27.7	21.2	12.0	3.8	100.0
Sweden (1987)	17.1	0.4	7.1	9.5	26.9	19.3	15.4	13.8	7.5	100.0
Tunisia (1978)	2.5	u	u	u	16.5	25.2	25.3	20.0	10.5	100.0
United States (1985)	26.2	1.1	10.4	14.7	34.5	21.2	11.4	5.4	1.3	100.0
Rate §										
Australia (1986)	18.5	u	u	u	26.5	22.1	16.4	9.7	3.8	16.6
Canada (1987)	15.2	1.2	10.6	21.0	18.5	12.0	7.8	4.6	1.6	10.2
Czechoslovakia (1987)	22.5	0.3	11.4	40.4	68.4	73.1	60.2	39.4	16.3	46.7
Denmark (1987)	15.7	0.8	9.6	23.9	29.9	24.8	18.8	13.5	6.8	18.3
England and Wales* (1987)	20.9	1.4	15.9	26.8	23.8	16.4	11.3	7.2	3.0	14.2
Finland (1987)	15.4	0.4	9.9	22.4	19.0	12.2	9.5	8.2	7.0	11.7
German Dem. Rep. (1976)	16.9	0.4	12.8	23.0	26.2	31.3	31.3	24.4	11.4	23.3
Hungary (1987)	26.1	0.9	16.8	39.1	45.0	46.6	46.5	41.3	22.1	38.2
Italy** (1987)	6.4	u	u	u	16.4	20.2	21.3	17.7	10.1	15.3
Japan** (1987)	5.8	u	u	u	19.8	22.4	28.9	24.3	11.7	18.6
Netherlands* (1986)	4.2	0.2	2.9	5.9	7.4	6.7	6.2	4.4	2.2	5.3
New Zealand (1987)	13.2	0.9	9.6	18.0	18.3	14.9	10.1	5.5	2.6	11.4
Norway (1987)	22.1	u	u	u	29.0	18.3	14.2	10.2	4.9	16.8
Scotland ‡ (1987)	14.0	u	u	u	14.9	9.5	6.7	4.2	1.6	9.0
Singapore (1987)	16.7	u	u	u	43.1	40.8	33.8	22.6	10.9	30.1
Sweden (1987)	21.5	1.4	15.1	29.4	31.2	24.6	19.0	15.6	8.2	19.8
Tunisia (1977)	1.2	u	u	u	12.9	26.6	36.0	30.9	15.8	17.2
United States (1985)	45.7	4.8	30.7	63.0	52.3	30.9	17.8	9.7	2.9	28.0
Ratio ††										
Australia (1988)	40.4	u	u	u	22.6	13.2	16.0	27.4	52.0	20.4
Bulgaria (1987)	25.6	u	u	u	38.0	58.2	74.6	84.7	90.6	50.7
Canada (1987)	33.4	42.7	38.2	29.7	16.8	8.8	10.3	19.9	39.8	14.7
Czechoslovakia (1987)	26.1	43.0	32.4	23.6	27.5	43.3	63.2	78.9	91.7	42.2
Denmark (1987)	50.7	83.2	67.1	43.2	27.4	16.9	23.0	44.0	74.4	27.0
England and Wales* (1987)	34.6	62.9	40.9	29.5	19.0	11.6	13.4	24.7	44.2	18.6

Measure	≤19				20–24	25–29	30–34	35–39	≥40	Total
	All	≤14	15–17	18–19						
Finland (1986)	44.9	76.5	58.0	38.4	19.3	8.6	12.7	25.1	58.1	18.0
German Dem. Rep. (1975)	18.8	33.1	23.6	15.9	17.5	35.9	59.8	76.5	88.3	29.7
Hungary (1987)	30.7	26.6	34.3	28.6	23.3	32.1	54.6	77.8	91.2	40.2
Netherlands* (1986)	28.2	55.2	40.7	22.2	9.7	4.7	7.5	21.6	42.9	9.0
New Zealand (1987)	24.9	38.4	28.1	22.0	13.8	9.2	10.9	20.6	42.9	13.6
Norway (1987)	47.1	u	u	u	22.3	12.2	16.7	34.2	61.0	22.2
Scotland‡ (1987)	26.0	u	u	u	13.2	7.4	9.5	20.0	39.3	13.2
Singapore (1987)	57.8	u	u	u	38.0	24.2	28.2	45.5	73.1	32.7
Sweden (1986)	52.3	87.5	70.3	42.7	24.2	14.8	18.3	35.8	67.1	24.9
United States (1985)	42.1	45.7	43.2	41.0	31.5	22.0	21.8	32.2	49.4	29.7

*Residents only.

†Age attained during the year. By this measure, women are counted as one-half year older on average than when age is measured in completed years at time of abortion. For example, adjustment to age in completed years would increase the percentage of abortions obtained by women under age 20 in France in 1984 from 11.2 percent to 13.5 percent.

‡Including residents of Scotland who obtained abortions in England and Wales.

§For women under age 15, rate is computed per 1,000 women aged 13–14; for those under 20, rate is computed per 1,000 women 15–19; for 40 or more, rate is computed per 1,000 40–44.

**True rates are higher because many abortions are unreported.

††Ratio of abortions per 100 known pregnancies (defined as legal abortions plus live births, both adjusted to age of woman at time of conception). For the United States and the German Democratic Republic, live births six months later were used to match times of conception for pregnancies ending in birth and pregnancies ending in abortion; data needed for this adjustment were unavailable for other countries.

Note: u = unavailable.

unavailable). This is true also for Finland. In the remaining English-speaking and Scandinavian countries and in the Netherlands, the peak occurs at ages 20–24.

In Bulgaria, Czechoslovakia, Hungary, Japan and Tunisia, where fewer than one-third of abortions are obtained by women younger than 25 and 17–37 percent are obtained by women 35 and older, abortion is used predominantly for spacing and ending childbirth. In Central and Eastern Europe, young unmarried women often become pregnant but they commonly marry and carry the pregnancy to term. In Japan and Tunisia, premarital pregnancy is probably rare, so abortion to delay initial childbearing is also relatively rare. A relatively low contraceptive prevalence rate and limited use of sterilization in Bulgaria, Czechoslovakia, Hungary and Tunisia results in increased abortion among older, married women. Older married women are also the most frequent utilizers of abortion in Japan, where the pill has not been approved for contraceptive use and sterilization is also uncommon.

Over the most recent five-year period for which data are available, most countries experienced few changes in abortion patterns by age-group. In New Zealand, the abortion rate among teenagers was stable while that of other age-groups increased sharply. The rage among teenagers also declined in relation to that of other women in Canada, Denmark, Finland and Hungary. There has been a distinct decline in the abortion rate among women aged 35 and older in relation to the total abortion rate in seven of the countries that have data (Denmark, England and Wales, Finland, Norway, Scotland, Singapore and Sweden). In Norway, for example, the rate among women 40 and over fell 26 percent in five years, while the total abortion rate increased nine percent. The

**Table 7. Percentage Distribution of Women Who Obtain Legal Abortions,
by Marital Status, According to Country**

Country	Currently married	Previously married	Never-married	Total
Bulgaria*,† (1987)	78.3	21.7	u	100.0
Canada‡,§ (1987)	24.5	8.2	67.3	100.0
Czechoslovakia†,§ (1987)	77.6	7.9	14.4	100.0
Denmark† (1987)	33.6	7.4	59.0	100.0
England and Wales‡,** (1987)	24.8	9.8	65.4	100.0
Finland† (1987)	32.5	9.3	58.1	100.0
France‡ (1986)	42.2	9.2	48.6	100.0
German Federal Republic† (1988)	48.4	6.0	45.7	100.0
Hungary† (1987)	68.1	10.7	21.2	100.0
India‡ (1972–1975)	92.8	1.3	5.9	100.0
Italy‡ (1987)	67.6	3.5	28.9	100.0
Netherlands†,** (1986)	34.4	9.3	56.2	100.0
New Zealand‡ (1988)	27.7	13.2	59.1	100.0
Norway‡,§ (1987)	39.1	6.6	54.3	100.0
Scotland‡ (1987)	23.0	11.6	65.4	100.0
Singapore‡ (1987)	68.7	2.5	28.8	100.0
Sweden‡,†† (1974)	35.8	10.5	53.7	100.0
United States*,‡ (1985)	16.7	83.3	u	100.0

*Never-married included with previously married.

†Separated women are included with currently married.

‡Separated women are included with previously married.

§Women in informal unions are included with currently married.

**Residents only.

††Reporting by marital status was discontinued in 1975.

Note: u = unavailable.

increasing use of surgical sterilization undoubtedly contributed to the decline in some countries.

As Table 6 shows, the abortion ratio (the proportion of known pregnancies that end in abortion) is typically high among teenagers, falls to a low point at ages 25–29 and then increases with age to a high point among women 40 and older. Bulgaria and Czechoslovakia are exceptions in that women 19 and younger are less likely to terminate pregnancies by abortion than are older women. The United States is also unusual in that women aged 30–34 are no more likely to terminate pregnancies than women aged 25–29. In all countries, women 40 and older end a sizable proportion of their pregnancies, but the range varies from 39 percent in Scotland to 92 percent in Czechoslovakia.

As Table 7 indicates, 60 percent or more of women having abortions are unmarried in the United States (83 percent), the other English-speaking developed countries, the Netherlands (66 percent) and Scandinavia. In France and West Germany, slightly lower proportions of abortions occur among unmarried women (58 percent and 52 percent, respectively). In the remaining countries for which data are available, more than two-thirds of the women who obtain abortions are married.

The percentage of abortions obtained by unmarried women has been increasing in many countries. The increase was evident between 1982 and 1985 even in the United States, where the proportion was already high. This trend may be caused by an increasing desire among young people to delay marriage and childbearing and by increasing levels of marital dissolution. The percentage of abortions obtained by unmarried women has remained relatively stable in recent years only in Canada, Finland and New Zealand.

In India and Singapore, the two developing countries for which there are data, abortion is most commonly used by married women who want no more children or who want to space their children. This pattern is probably typical of Asian countries. A higher proportion of abortions in Africa is obtained by unmarried students, but the proportion is probably still less than half.[62] For Latin American, as well, the pattern probably falls somewhere between those in Asia and Europe.

The pattern of abortion utilization according to parity resembles that of marital status (Table 8). In English-speaking developed countries and in Finland, the Netherlands and Norway, 50–60 percent of women having abortions are childless. The proportion is almost as high in Denmark, West Germany and Sweden (46–48 percent). Among Western European countries, Italy has a uniquely low proportion of abortions obtained by childless women (29 percent). In contrast, fewer than one-fifth of women having abortions in Bulgaria, Czechoslovakia and Hungary have no children. In India and Tunisia, just 11 percent and seven percent, respectively, of abortion patients have had no children, but in Singapore, 41 percent are childless.

The proportion of abortions that are obtained by women who are childless has increased in most countries in recent years; Canada, Finland, Hungary, New Zealand and the United States are exceptions. During the 1970s, the proportion obtained by women with three or more children fell rapidly in almost all countries with data. In recent years, this proportion has continued to fall slowly in all countries except for Canada, Hungary and New Zealand, where the proportion has stabilized.

The abortion ratio dips for women with one child in all the countries shown in Table 8 except for Czechoslovakia and Hungary, where the ratio is lowest for women without children. The ratio of pregnancies that end in abortion is greater at parity two than at parity one, and in all countries except for the United States, it is greater among women who have had three children than among those who have had two. The ratio declines, however, after parity three in Canada, Czechoslovakia, Denmark, Hungary, Sweden and the United States, and after parity four in the remaining countries. This lower ratio reflects a concentration of higher parity women who avoid abortion for religious or other reasons and women who desire large families. In most countries, the abortion ratio has increased in recent years at parities zero and one and decreased among women who have four children or more.

The question of repeat abortion is detailed in Table 9, page 432 which shows that among industrialized countries, the proportion of abortions obtained by women who have had one or more prior induced abortions ranges from 17 percent in New Zealand to 49 percent in Hungary. In general, the proportion of all legal abortions that are repeat procedures is highest in countries that have high abortion rates.

In all countries, the proportion of abortions that are repeat legal procedures rose rapidly after legalization, because the proportion of women who had had a first legal abortion increased, and these women were at risk of another unintended pregnancy. This proportion continued to increase in the most recent five-year period for which data are available. Hungary is an exception because abortion has been legal long enough (since

---

[62] L. Liskin, 1980, op. cit. (see reference 35); and F. M. Coeytaux, 1988, op. cit. (see reference 32).

Table 8. Percentage Distribution of Women Who Obtain Legal Abortions and Abortion Ratio Per 100 Known Pregnancies, by Parity, According to Country

Measure and country	Parity						
	0	1	2	3	4	≥5	Total
% distribution							
Bulgaria* (1987)	16.1	83.9†	u	u	u	u	100.0
Canada‡ (1987)	58.4	19.9	15.2	4.9	1.2	0.4	100.0
Czechoslovakia* (1987)	12.4	19.9	47.8	15.8	2.9	1.1	100.0
Denmark§ (1987)	47.7	19.2	23.3	7.5	1.5	0.7	100.0
England and Wales**,†† (1987)	59.7	14.3	16.0	6.7	2.2	1.1	100.0
Finland‡ (1987)	50.1	17.0	20.5	9.3	2.5	0.6	100.0
German Fed. Rep.§ (1988)	47.4	20.3	20.9	7.5	2.4	1.4	100.0
Hungary§ (1987)	18.9	19.4	41.4	14.3	3.7	2.3	100.0
India* (1972–1975)	11.1	13.6	22.4	20.9	32.0‡‡	u	100.0
Italy‡ (1987)	28.9	19.6	31.7	13.1	6.7‡‡	u	100.0
Netherlands *,**,§§ (1986)	56.1	14.9	18.1	7.3	3.6‡‡	u	100.0
New Zealand§ (1987)	52.7	15.9	16.4	9.2	3.2	2.2	100.0
Norway§ (1987)	53.4	17.4	27.1*†	u	2.2‡‡	u	100.0
Scotland* (1987)	58.0	15.7	16.7	6.6	2.0	0.9	100.0
Singapore* (1987)	40.6	16.3	27.6	11.2	3.0	1.3	100.0
Sweden‡ (1987)	45.5	17.5	23.4	10.4	2.5	0.8	100.0
Tunisia* (1978)	7.1	10.4	15.2	14.7	16.9	35.7	100.0
United States§ (1985)	54.9	22.0	15.1	5.4	1.7	1.0	100.0
Ratio							
Canada‡ (1987)	18.9	8.7	15.1	16.5	14.6	8.1	14.7
Czechoslovakia* (1987)	16.9	28.3	73.3	75.7	63.9	45.4	42.2
Denmark§ (1987)	27.3	16.5	40.7	47.2	40.9	38.1	27.0
England and Wales**,†† (1979)	18.7	6.3	20.0	28.0	31.2	23.8	18.6
Finland‡ (1986)	21.9	9.5	21.3	28.3	29.6	8.7	18.0
Hungary§ (1987)	22.4	25.9	69.6	72.5	64.2	52.4	40.2
Netherlands*,**,§§ (1986)	11.2	3.9	11.4*†	u	13.8‡‡	u	9.0
Norway§ (1987)	26.0	12.3	28.3*†	u	u	u	22.2
Singapore* (1987)	30.9	16.1	43.5	57.8	59.5	50.8	32.7
Sweden‡ (1986)	25.5	14.2	31.3	41.0	37.9	31.3	24.9
United States§ (1985)	35.8	21.9	28.8	28.1	25.2	20.0	29.7

*Surviving children.   †Includes all parities.   ‡Prior deliveries.

§Prior live births.   **Residents only.   ††Prior live births and stillbirths.   ‡‡Includes parities of ≥4.

§§Based on clinic abortions; it is assumed that parity of women having abortions in hospitals is similar to those having clinic abortions.

*†Includes parities 2–3.   *‡Includes parities ≥2.   Note: u = unavailable.

1956) to allow the proportion of women who have had a first abortion to reach an equilibrium. Actually, the proportion of repeat abortions has fallen in that country because the overall abortion rate dropped sharply from 91 per 1,000 women of reproductive age in 1969 to the current rate of 38 per 1,000. In most other countries, if abortion rates do not change significantly, the proportion of abortions that are repeat procedures should stabilize in a few years.

Table 9. Percentage Distribution of Legal Abortions, by Number of Prior Induced Abortions, According to Country

Country	No. of prior abortions				
	0	1	2	≥3	Total
Canada (1987)	78.0	17.4	3.6	1.1	100.0
Czechoslovakia (1987)	57.8	27.9	10.3	4.1	100.0
Denmark (1987)	62.0	25.3	8.4	4.3	100.0
England and Wales* (1987)	82.3	17.7†	u	u	100.0
Finland (1987)	74.4	19.9	4.2	1.5	100.0
France (1987)	81.0	15.3	2.8	0.9	100.0
Hungary (1987)	51.1	27.8	12.0	9.0	100.0
India‡ (1975–1977)	93.5	5.8	0.7§	u	100.0
Italy (1987)	70.0	20.4	6.2	3.5	100.0
Netherlands*,** (1986)	78.4	17.2	3.2	1.2	100.0
New Zealand (1987)	82.6	14.6	2.4	0.5	100.0
Norway (1987)	73.2	21.0	5.8§	u	100.0
Singapore (1987)	58.2	28.3	9.2	4.3	100.0
Sweden (1987)	65.3	24.4	7.2	3.1	100.0
United States (1985)	59.5	26.2	9.4	5.0	100.0

*Residents only.   †Includes ≥1 prior abortions.

‡From Indian Council for Medical Research, Collaborative Study on Short Term Sequelae of Induced Abortion, New Delhi, 1981.

§Includes ≥2 prior abortions.   **Clinic abortions only.   Note: u = unavailable.

Discussion

Except in the United States, the trend in developed countries toward liberalization of abortion laws that began in the 1950s has continued, although at a slower rate in recent years. Aside from the possibility of a relaxation of the restrictive law in Belgium, little additional in the way of dramatic change can be expected.

Abortion rates in developed countries have been relatively stable in recent years. Some encouraging changes have occurred, however, such as a decline among women aged 35 and older, probably as a result of increased surgical sterilization and better contraceptive use. In a few countries, there have been decreases in the rates among teenagers in relation to those of other age-groups. A lurking question, however, is whether concern about AIDS will effect abortion rates either by encouraging contraceptive use or, conversely, by causing couples to switch to condoms from more effective methods.

In Scandinavia and English-speaking countries, especially the United States, the most important prerequisite for reducing unintended pregnancy and abortion is an improvement in contraceptive use among young, unmarried women. In most Central and Eastern Europe countries and probably the Soviet Union, on the other hand, the greatest need is to provide contraceptive services and supplies and encourage their use among married women with children.

The continued improvement in the safety of abortion in developed countries is encouraging. Mortality is down to an average level of 0.6 deaths per 100,000 legal abortions, and declines are apparent in complication rates as well. The improved safety record is in part attributable to the development and refinement of suction curettage, which has almost completely replaced the more difficult and hazardous sharp curettage for first trimester procedures in most developed countries. However, sharp curettage still predominates in some developed countries, where medical practitioners need training in suction curettage and equipment to do vacuum aspiration procedures. Similarly, sharp curettage has partially replaced instillation for second-trimester abortions, but there are still many instillation procedures in circumstances when curettage might be safer and less stressful for the woman.

At the same time that the safety of abortion has improved, the use of overnight hospitalization has been reduced. Outpatient care requires fewer medical resources and is preferred by many patients. In view of the positive results in areas where out-patient care is the norm, most countries can be expected to continue to reduce hospital stays. Along with the movement away from overnight hospitalization has been a shift to service outside of hospitals altogether. In the United States, 87 percent of abortions, including most of those in the second trimester, are now performed in clinics and doctors' offices. While hospitals may afford better integration of abortion services with other medical care, in some situations nonhospital clinics offer compensating advantages: lower costs, a staff that is more experienced and sympathetic in serving abortion patients, insulation of abortion patients from other obstetric and gynecology patients and from hospital staff hostile to abortion, easier access for women who cannot or prefer not to obtain abortions from their personal physicians and more timely service than in hospitals, where abortions must compete with other procedures for operating room time. Clinics are likely to continue to replace hospitals as the primary providers of abortion services in areas without legal barriers to their establishment.

A number of factors are working toward greater acceptance of abortion in developing areas: an increasing desire of women and couples to control their fertility, a greater concern with women's roles and rights and population pressures. While eventual relaxation of legal restrictions appears probable, the timing is difficult to predict. Some countries may revise their abortion laws in response to increased awareness of the adverse public health effects of illegal abortion.[63] Others will undoubtedly follow the examples of Greece, the Netherlands, Turkey and other countries that liberalized their laws only after abortion had long been widely practiced.

Changes in abortion rates are difficult to measure in developing areas, and patterns depend on the circumstances of the particular country. Probably typical of the long-term trend is South Korea, where the abortion rate increased sharply as fertility fell but has recently fallen back in response to more universal contraceptive use. In China, as well, the abortion rate is now significantly lower than its high point in 1983. As a country begins to reduce its fertility, it is common for the abortion rate to increase at the same time that contraceptive use increases. Eventually, contraceptive use becomes sufficiently widespread to cause the abortion rate to fall, but many developing countries have yet to reach this point.

Much needs to be done to improve the safety of abortion in developing areas. Where abortion and menstrual regulation are permitted, as in India and Bangladesh, physicians and other medical personnel are being trained in the procedures, but safe services are still not available to most women. Where abortion is restricted, clandestine procedures may be increasingly performed by physicians, as in some parts of Latin America, but outdated abortion methods are often used. Legal restrictions make it dif-

---

[63] E. Royston and S. Armstrong, eds., 1989, op. cit. (see reference 34).

ficult to train physicians; in addition, public services are usually not provided, and poor women are unable to pay the fees of private physicians.

An improvement in safety and a reduction in medical care costs can be made with a relatively small investment in suction equipment and training. Where electricity is unavailable or where more sophisticated equipment is too expensive, a simple hand syringe can be used for very early abortions. The same equipment and training are useful for treating incomplete spontaneous abortions and illegally induced abortions are, therefore, appropriate where abortion is legally restricted. Although progress is being made, greater awareness of the negative health consequences of unsafe abortions would speed the process.

2 · MEDICINE _____

Professor Flower's article describes prenatal human development as a process with four major transitions. He criticizes the idea of inherent personhood that can be scientifically discovered during the ontogenetic process. Human development is a continuum that moves from fertilization, through fetal motility, to human awareness. Since prenatal personhood cannot be validated empirically, we must *decide* when the prenatal human being becomes a person. The criteria for this is determined by morality, that is, what we consider human to be. Because the Constitution uses the word ''person,'' the scientific community has felt compelled to offer a definition of a person that is acceptable to both the legal community and the religious community. However, since any scientific definition of a ''person'' may be limited, one must also search beyond the realm of science.

15 · Coming into Being: The Prenatal Development of Humans

Michael J. Flower, Ph.D.

Introduction

Although the lives of women are the intimate ground of the struggle with the issue of abortion, more than pregnant women take an interest in emerging prenatal life. The once intimate couple—woman and preembryo/embryo/fetus—now stands at the center of a public gaze. Growing in size and complexity, prenatal life is the object of love, despair, litigation, philosophical argumentation, medical scrutiny, religious fervor and scientific interest. But in spite of much attention, the coming into being of a new human life is a process about which we know relatively little. A woman's life is visible to us; those about her can share in it. Prenatal life is secreted away, its gradual emergence most often an invisible affair—but not always. With the advent of in vitro fertilization, the first days of that life are available to us; ultrasonography allows us to visualize later stages in utero. Recently, the earliest hours, days and weeks of prenatal life have been chronicled photographically in dramatic pictures showing us the changing *form* of emergent human life.[1,2] Of course, there is more to know about prenatal human life beyond its emergent form—the rate of its development, appearance of various tissues and organs, the emergence of motility and (most importantly for some) the putting in place of

---

[1] *The First Days of Creation,* Life 26–46 (August 1990).

[2] An important corrective should be noted at this point. As Rosalind Petchesky has argued, the display of such photographs abstracts prenatal life from the body of the woman sustaining its development. Embryos and fetuses take on a life of their own in "isolation," suggesting an independence that simply does not exist. *See* R. Petchesky, *Fetal images: the power of visual culture in the politics of reproduction,* 13 (2) Feminist Studies 263–92 (1987).

the central nervous system. Furthermore, and perhaps most important of all, is the question of what all this information about prenatal human life might mean, that is, what is the *significance* of biological facts about prenatal human life? Asked differently, what ought we take to be significant about the development of prenatal life when we consider the many contexts in which such life is a matter of concern? After all, there are an increasing number of circumstances in which our knowledge of prenatal human life is of importance. In vitro fertilization presents us with preembryos that may be donated to ''adoptive'' parents, cryopreserved for later attempts at pregnancy, diagnosed for genetic defect or used in experimental investigations. Slightly older preembryos and embryos can be prevented from establishing stable, uterine implantation by the use of the contragestive chemical, RU486. Late-stage embryos and early fetuses can be examined for genetic defects using a relatively new diagnostic method known as chorionic villus sampling; while fetal abortuses have been used as the source of tissue for transplantation and late-stage fetuses have been helped surgically.

All of these interventions arise against the background of a central question about prenatal human life. What is the nature of its ''becoming''; what are the processes involved in coming into being as a human? This brief review will set out information about prenatal human life, placing that knowledge in the service of debates about abortion, as well as about the several reproductive and genetic technologies that heighten the presence of prenatal human life in our midst. The biological facts about this life do not determine moral status, but they can serve as points of reference for our individual and public deliberations about such status in abortion and other contexts.[3]

The Earliest Events of Prenatal Human Development[4]

We can begin our examination of prenatal development with the union of an egg and sperm. This joining, the process of *fertilization,* takes place in the upper reaches of the fallopian tube, the sperm having swum ''up'' the tube while the egg is swept toward the uterus. It has generally been thought that the likelihood of fertilization is high due to a presumably large number of sperm encountering the egg. However, there is recent laboratory evidence suggesting another mechanism that would enhance chances of fertilization, and that is the finding that an egg capable of being fertilized (or the ovarian follicle from which such an egg has been released) produces a substance to which sperm are attracted.[5] It may thus be the case that there is an initial ''communication'' between gametes.

Whatever the occasion of its beginning, fertilization is not a momentary event; it is a complex process lasting about 24 hours.[6] Upon reaching the egg surface, the first sperm to make contact moves into the egg itself, delivering a set of 23 chromosomes that contain the genetic information that will contribute the males's characteristics to a

---

[3] M. Flower, *Neuromaturation and the status of human fetal life,* in *Abortion Rights and Fetal ''Personhood''* 65–75 (E. Doerr and J. Prescot, eds., 2nd ed. 1989).

[4] A detailed but technical analysis of these events, accompanied by excellent illustrations, can be found in K. L. Moore, *The Developing Human: Clinically Oriented Embryology* (4th ed. 1988).

[5] D. Ralt, M. Goldenberg, P. Fetterolf, D. Thompson, J. Dor, S. Mashiach, D. L. Garbers & M. Eisenbach, *Sperm attraction to a follicular factor(s) correlates with human egg fertilizability,* 88 Proc. Natl. Acad. Sci. USA 2840–44 (1991).

[6] Thus, claims about life beginning at a ''moment'' of conception must be tempered in light of this extended period of time over which fertilization is accomplished.

Figure 1. The Preembryonic Human Blastocyst

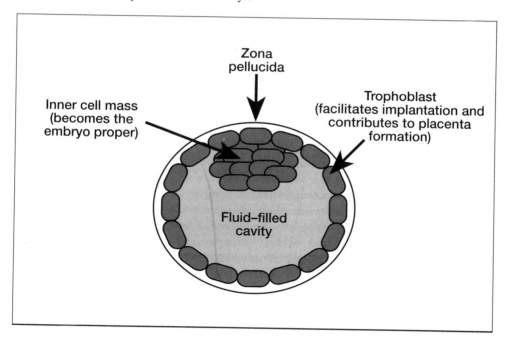

new individual. This first contact triggers the egg's completion of the process *(meiosis)* by which the female's contribution of 23 chromosomes is set aside, a process requiring about 12 hours. These two sets—together called a *genome*—constitute the unique genetic contribution of each parent to a cell (the fertilized egg) that now has the capacity to begin development. The fertilized egg is now called a *zygote*. The two sets of chromosomes are drawn together over the course of the next 12 hours, a process called *syngamy*. The zygote is then ready for the first cell division.

Soon afterward the zygote will begin dividing into smaller and smaller cells (the process of *cleavage*). Thus, the number of cells making up the zygote begins to increase in number. It is not until about 60 hours after egg and sperm first made contact that any new genetic information is expressed; this means that for about two and one-half days following initial egg/sperm contact, the molecular characteristics of the preembryo are maternally determined.[7] Following the third cell division, one or two of the seven or eight resulting cells are sequestered "inside" a space established by the remaining cells.[8] The cell membranes of these "outside" cells also undergo a change that allows them to adhere closely to one another, effectively sealing the "inside" of the zygote from the "outside." As cell division continues, producing more and more cells, the outer cells will form the "wall" of a fluid-filled, ball-like structure (figure 1) inside of which the

[7] This should lead one to conclude that, for a brief time at least, the possession of a unique set of paternal and maternal genes does not make the zygote similarly unique. None of the genes making up this unique combination have yet been expressed. Thus, the 50 to 60 hour preembryo has yet to exhibit any characteristics due to the unique joining of a particular sperm with a particular egg.

[8] The reason for the possible odd number of cells after three rounds of division is that the cells of mammalian zygotes do not necessarily divide in synchrony. Thus, three of the four cells of the four-celled stage may have divided, while the fourth has not—hence, seven cells instead of eight.

sequestered cells continue to proliferate to produce the *inner cell mass* (ICM). This whole structure—outer cells (the *trophoblast*) plus ICM—is referred to as a *blastocyst*. All this time the zygote is moving down the fallopian tube toward the uterus, reaching it four to five days after the first contact of egg and sperm. Also during this time the developing blastocyst has been enclosed by a membranous structure called the *zona pellucida*. As the blastocyst reaches the uterus, this outer structure disintegrates and exposes the trophoblast, the outer layer of cells whose function it is to interact with the cells of the uterus and facilitate the process of *implantation*—a process taking about a week and therefore completed by 12 to 14 days of development. The outer, trophoblast cells will later contribute to the formation of the placenta. The ICM, however, is of much greater interest. It is the cells of the ICM that will develop into the embryo and then the fetus.[9]

All of the stages of development up to this time have come to be referred to as *preembryonic,* for reasons that will become apparent in a moment. The cells of the inner cell mass continue to increase in number, producing a somewhat flattened disk of cells. As implantation comes to completion and as the third week of development commences, cells of this disk (which is about a millimeter—1/25th of an inch—in diameter) begin moving about in a process called *gastrulation.* What was once a disk of cells becomes an increasingly complex, three-dimensional *embryo* with a distinguishable anterior-posterior axis (i.e., one can identify the future head- and tail-ends). In addition, one can begin to make out the region of the embryo that will later develop into a functional central nervous system. The once rather amorphous mass of cells begins to take on a bodily shape inside and out; that is, the embryonic processes of *morphogenesis* and *organogenesis* have begun.

It is important to notice that we have applied two terms up to this point—preembryo and embryo. What is the reason for this distinction? At the time of implantation, there occurs a major transformation in the developmental nature of the ICM. Prior to the first indications of morphogenesis, the ICM is capable of splitting in two to yield twins, a capacity that is lost with the beginning of gastrulation.[10] The initiation of morphogenesis is somehow related to a change in the ICM that gives it the character of a unitary, unified collection of cells now beginning to produce human form. Because of this dramatic change, developmental biologists think there is good reason to coin the term preembryo to describe that period of time (the first two weeks of development) during which there is, at first, no ICM and then a growing ICM that is not yet determined to give rise to a single individual. This latter determination occurs with the initiation of morphogenesis and the formation of an embryo. This transformation from preembryo to embryo, from pluripotentiality to unipotentiality, is the *first integrative transition* (figure 2) in the course of what may now become a single and singular indi-

---

[9] As Buckle has pointed out, the newly fertilized egg has the potential to *produce* a human embryo, but only the inner cell mass has the potential to *become* such an embryo. This developmental distinction raises problems for those who wish to claim that a particular human being begins at conception. It is obvious that it is many days after fertilization before the cells are set aside that will continue to develop into an embryo. *See* S. Buckle, *Arguing from potential,* in *Embryo Experimentation* 90–108 (P. Singer, H. Kuhse, S. Buckle, K. Dawson & P. Kasimba eds. 1990).

[10] On rare occasion, two separately developing preembryos that would otherwise result in non-identical twins can fuse together to yield a single, chimeric individual. This capacity to fuse has been demonstrated with other mammalian preembryos (e.g., with those of mice). Thus, the preembryonic mammal has the capacity to produce "many from one" by splitting or "one from many" by fusion.

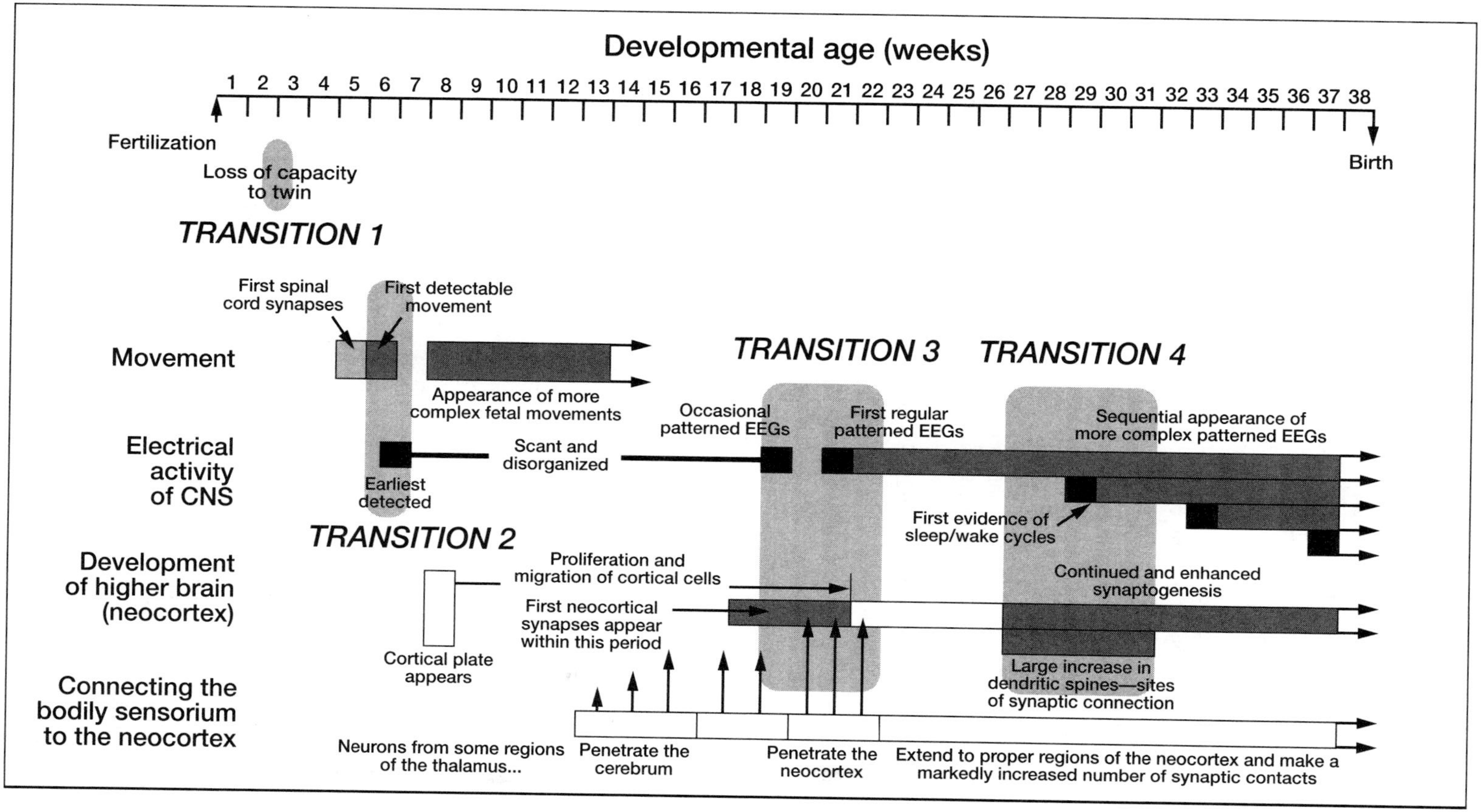

Figure 2. Key Developmental Transitions During Fetal Human Life

vidual.[11] Following this transition then, a once simple mass of cells gradually takes on a complex and increasingly recognizable human shape, with identifiable internal organs and organ systems.[12] The third through eighth weeks of development produce a rudimentary prenatal human (of about an inch in length) in which most of the tissues and organs are laid out in preliminary form. A period of rapid fetal growth, as well as further development of tissues and organs, will occur starting in the ninth week, with a much slower rate of growth beginning at about 20 weeks of development.

We might pause and reflect on what has been said to this point. The process of human development is generally described as a continuum, with the event of birth marking the only significant discontinuity subsequent to the initiating event of fertilization. In this view there are only two points that draw our special attention: a new life's beginning at fertilization and its separate existence begun at birth. However, we have already begun to erode the sharp edges of this view. First, we have seen that fertilization is not a momentary event but a process occurring over the course of nearly 24 hours. Furthermore, the new zygote is itself the product of two already living cells. Thus, life has not emerged where there was none before; rather it has continued on in new form. Second, we have seen that the ICM forming during the second week of development is not yet a unitary assembly of cells. Singularity is achieved only at the end of the second week with the onset of morphogenesis. Thus, we now have a third point of reference— the emergence of developmental individuality. To engage the second transition (of the four we will discuss), the transition from embryo to fetus, we must turn to the development of the central nervous system.[13]

Becoming Neural

It is important to note that we have in hand relatively little detail about the formation of the prenatal human nervous system. First, there is too little opportunity to study the prenatal human; second, the emergence of the nervous system is exceedingly complex. And yet, as we shall see, there are several noticeable developmental transitions that characterize this complex unfolding.

As noted above, we can readily identify the region of the early three week-old embryo that will later form the central nervous system (CNS). At this early developmental stage the progenitor cells of the CNS are said to be *presumptive;* that is, they will become the CNS but are not yet functioning as nerve cells (i.e., their future fate is known but they are as yet not present in their final numbers nor are they specialized). Once these cells are "set apart," further changes occur.[14] The presumptive neural cells proliferate, some move about, and others change their shape, the consequence being

---

[11] One must say "may" become rather than "will" because not every blastocyst that implants continues development.

[12] These organs and organ systems arise as a consequence of complex and poorly understood interactions among cells and tissues. What *is* known with certainty is that these interactions are subject to the disorganizing effects of various chemical substances, so-called teratogens, that produce congenital abnormalities. It is thus crucial that a woman avoid exposure to such substances during pregnancy, especially in this critical embryonic period.

[13] A fuller analysis of these four transitions and their significance can be found in C. Grobstein, *Science and the Unborn: Choosing Human Futures* (1988).

[14] These changes begin at different times and proceed at different rates in various parts of the CNS—a circumstance that makes it difficult to speak about neuromaturation of the fetal CNS as a whole.

that the CNS undergoes morphogenesis during the embryonic period. Various CNS regions become identifiable in broad outline; that is, the hind-, mid- and forebrain, as well as spinal cord, are "sketched in." Two other changes also occur. First, cells that earlier were presumptive now begin preparing to *function* as nerve cells; that is, they *differentiate* by changing their morphology and biosynthetic activities. As the cells differentiate, they begin to cooperate with one another. That is to say, the cells begin to *synapse* ("hook up") with one another or with other "targets" of innervation (e.g, muscles). The information-carrying circuits that result make possible the integrative function of the nervous system.

But let us return to the three-week-old embryo. If at this time there are only presumptive neural cells present in the rudimentary CNS, how long must we wait before we can see evidence of neural function (of some sort)? We can ask two simple questions: When do we first detect electrical activity? When does a complex function (such as motility) appear that we know is dependent on prior neural maturation? The answer to both questions is the same: about the sixth-to-seventh week (figure 2). The *first neuro-integrative process* is preceded, in the fifth week, by the appearance of interconnected cells in the spinal cord,[15] cells that can detect a stimulus, send the "message" to the cord and then deliver a signal to body or limb muscles that contract and produce movement (thus constituting a simple "reflex arc" not unlike that which underpins the automatic "knee jerk" with which we are all familiar). Even though motility is manifest, it does not require higher brain (neocortical) function; at this time there is no neocortex, not even in rudimentary form. Thus, even though electrical activity has been observed[16] at this time (figure 2), it does not indicate neocortical function (though it may be a manifestation of early embryonic brainstem function).

What more can we say about the newly emergent motility? When observed ultrasonigraphically, the late-stage embryo of six weeks can be seen to exhibit occasional and "just discernible movement." Because the emergence of motility is such a dramatic event, and one that results from a new level of integration between CNS and developing musculature, Grobstein has argued that we ought to take this first motor activity as an indicator of the transition from embryo to fetus.[17] About a week later, a "startle" response emerges. Over the next six to seven weeks, a relatively complex repertoire of spontaneous motor activities appears; the fetal limbs and head move about, breathing movements occur, and swallowing and sucking are observed.[18,19] Because there is not

---

[15] N. Okado, *Onset of synapse formation in the human spinal cord,* 201 Journal of Comparative Neurology 211–19 (1981).

[16] W. J. Borkowski & R. L. Bernstine, *Electroencephalography of the fetus,* 5 Neurology 362–65 (1955).

[17] Grobstein, *supra* note 13, at 99.

[18] J. I. P. de Vries, G. H. A. Visser & H. F. R. Prechtl, *The emergence of fetal behaviour. I. Qualitative aspects,* 7 Early Human Development 301–22 (1982).

[19] M. Flower, *Neuromaturation of the human fetus,* 10 Journal of Medicine and Philosophy 237–51 (1985). The "control" of this activity might conceivably reside in the relatively simple neural circuitry of the spinal cord. However, as the development of younger fetuses proceeds, the various motor activities exhibit temporal patterns of expression that differ one from the other (*see* J. I. P. de Vries, G. H. A. Visser & H. F. R. Prechtl, *The emergence of fetal behaviour. II. Quantitative aspects,* 12 Early Human Development 99–120 [1985]), possibly indicative of some measure of modulatory influence "higher" than the spinal cord. I have suggested (*supra*, at 242) that the earliest modulator of such activity is the brainstem (serving, for example, to integrate rudimentary sensory input from such sources as fetal muscle "stretch receptors," small "sensors" embedded in muscle tissue and triggered by muscle contractile activity to send electrical impulses to the CNS).

yet a functional neocortex (and will not be for another several months), we can be certain that the patterned changes in fetal motility are not the result of intention; they are not indicative of any sort of conscious direction. With the transition by the emergence of motility we have in hand yet another marker event (Transition 2).

As just noted, neocortical development requires many months. Beginning at about 52 to 54 days of development, neocortical cells are produced by a zone of proliferative cells located some distance from the site of neocortex formation (the latter, a region called the cortical plate); thus, the "newly minted" cells must spend some time migrating to their final position.[20,21] This process or cell proliferation and migration continues for about three months, producing a neocortex with "layers" of cells differently specialized to process neural information. Such processing, of course, can only occur once neocortical cells are connected to one another and (eventually) to cells sending information "in" and cells receiving the information that is sent "out" from the neocortex. The first of these connections are thought to be formed some time between 19 and 22 weeks of development.[22] This connective event is taken as an indicator of a third transition (figure 2).

The greatest degree of neocortical interconnection occurs over several weeks beginning rather abruptly at about week 28 (figure 2).[23] During this latter period, the dendritic extensions of neocortical cells (the dendrites being a part of the nerve cell that receives a large proportion of the "input" from other neurons) become covered with a vastly increased number of tiny surface projections of "spines" that serve as "targets" for synaptic contact. As a consequence of this sharp change (Transition 4, figure 2), the potential for neocortical circuitry increases dramatically (at least in the region of the neocortex that will process "visual information"). Thus, at least one region of the neocortex exhibits a sharply-bounded developmental leap in synaptic connectivity. Whether this transition is characteristic of other neocortical regions remains to be determined.[24]

This fourth transition appears significant for an additional reason. Normal postnatal brain function is characterized by *continuous* electrical activity as displayed by an electroencephalogram (EEG). Only discontinuous EEG activity occurs at about the time neocortical cells first begin making synaptic contact; the change to continuous EEG activity occurs at about 30 weeks of gestation. In addition, this time periods marks the appearance of fetal wakefulness and sleep.[25] Thus, Transition 4 may represent a functional maturation of the neocortex resulting from the greatly enhanced connectivity occurring between 28 and 32 weeks of development. This transition period is significant

---

[20]M. E. Molliver, I. Kostovic & H. Van Der Loos, *The development of synapses in cerebral cortex of the human fetus*, 50 Brain Research 403–07 (1973).

[21]M. Marin-Padilla, *Structural organization of the human cerebral cortex prior to the appearance of the cortical plate*, 168 Anatomy and Embryology 21–40 (1983).

[22]Molliver et al., *supra* note 20 at 404.

[23]D. P. Purpura, *Morphogenesis of visual cortex in the preterm infant*, in Growth and Development of the Brain (M. A. B. Brazier ed. 1975).

[24]P. Rakic, J.-P. Bourgeois, M. F. Eckenhoff, N. Zecevic & P. S. Goldman-Rakic, *Concurrent overproduction of synapses in diverse regions of the primate cerebral cortex*, 232 Science 232–35 (1986). Rakic and his colleagues have observed simultaneous or *isosynchronous* synapse production in *diverse* regions of the cortex of nonhuman primates at a stage of neuromaturation comparable to that of Transition 4, suggesting the possibility of a similar process in humans. If fetal humans exhibit this self-same isosynchronous synaptic transition, then we might expect that Transition 4 leads to a fetus exhibiting capacities *significantly* different from those of just a few weeks before.

[25]R. Spehlmann, *EEG Primer* (1981).

in yet another way. Premature fetal-infants of this age are described as "loosely articulated and flaccid mannikins"; if stimulated, they are limp and torporous. It is still
several weeks before such torpor will be replaced by a genuine wakefulness when the
newborn is stirred to activity.

But what of Transition 3? For there to be any possibility of fetal awareness (unless
there is a form of awareness dependent on parts of the lower brain) the neocortex must
be composed of cells that are in synaptic contact with one another and must receive
input from those cells of the body that constitute what might be termed the sensorium—
cells that detect externally and internally derived stimuli and pass signals to the CNS.
On the way to the sensory information-processing regions of the neocortex, these signals
pass through the thalamus, a multi-component structure that modulates the different
"types" of sensory signals (e.g., visual, auditory and such) before passing them to the
neocortex. What this means, of course, is that the higher brain will be isolated from
"sensations" originating in the body until the thalamus is connected to the neocortex.
The evidence in hand suggests that at least some regions of the thalamus make input-
connection with the neocortex by week 22 or 23.[26,27] Although other thalamic regions
may contain neurons whose axons have reached the neocortex at earlier times, it is
unlikely that they will have made synaptic contact with neocortical cells, for there appeared to be no synapses in the neocortex earlier than 19 weeks.

It may thus be the case that it is only after Transition 3 is well underway that the
human fetus is potentially sentient. It must be said, however, that we cannot yet define
what degree and kind of neocortical synaptogenesis is necessary and sufficient to enable
awareness. All we know at present is that Transition 3 probably represents a significant
shift in CNS function; it is a time during which the neocortex first exhibits connectivity,
receives sensory information and shows patterned electrical activity. The two-month
period from Transition 3 to Transition 4 is a time of marked change—from a collection
of individual neurons to an interconnected collective exhibiting continuous electrical
activity and participating in cycles of fetal sleep and wakefulness.

The Significance of Developmental Transitions During Prenatal Life

It has been argued that, in addition to the commonly recognized events of fertilization
and birth, there are at least four significant transitions during the continuous course of
prenatal human development (figure 3). They can be recounted briefly. Two weeks
following fertilization the inner cell mass of the human preembryo undergoes a dramatic
developmental change (Transition 1), one that results in the emergence of an embryo
that can now give rise to only a single individual if development proceeds without
interruption. About four to five weeks later, development of nerve cells and muscles is
sufficient to enable motility, and we can begin to speak of the developing human as a
fetus (Transition 2). Around midgestation, the rudimentary neocortex is in place (Transition 3). It contains many cells, but only a few of these are synapsed to others, with
most of the process of neocortical synaptogenesis yet to follow. Also around this time

---

[26] I. Kostovic & P. S. Goldman-Rakic, *Transient cholinesterase staining in the mediodorsal nucleus of the
thalamus and its connections in the developing human and monkey brain,* 219 Journal of Comparative
Neurology 413–47 (1983).

[27] I. Kostovic & P. Rakic, *Development of prestriate visual projections in the monkey and human fetal cerebrum revealed by transient cholinesterase staining,* 4 Journal of Neuroscience 25–42 (1984).

Figure 3. Integrative Developmental Transitions

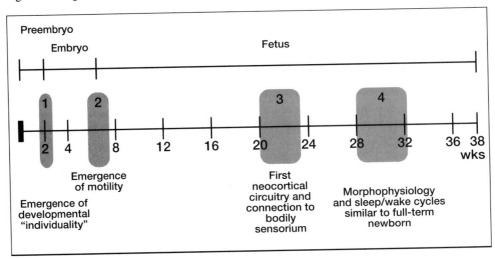

there is evidence that rudimentary input from bodily "sensors" (if, indeed, there is any such input at this time) could reach the neocortex after the cells from the thalamus have sent their first axonal extensions into the higher brain. Finally, there appears to be a time in the eighth lunar month of development during which neocortical circuitry is dramatically increased, perhaps coupled with the appearance of brain activity that resembles the wake/sleep cycles of newborns (Transition 4).

What is a reasonable way to think about these transitions? In what way are they important; what role do they play in our moral thinking about prenatal human life? One way to argue for their (indirect) utility is as follows:

> The question "When does human life begin?" has become the well-known and controversial encapsulation of a central issue in the conflict over abortion—the moral status of embryonic/fetal life. From one perspective the question as put is thought to frame the issue adequately. In this view personhood is a matter of natural objectivity; we are simply presented with the fact of full humanness or personhood—an intrinsic and scientifically discoverable property emerging during the course of a continuous ontogenetic process. However, there is a problem with this notion of intrinsic personhood, and it is deciding which of several different suggested properties is the one "real" answer to when a particular and personal human life has begun. Is it possession of the unique human genome achieved after fertilization, loss of embryonic ability to twin (i.e. developmental individuality) roughly two weeks later, appearance of fetal motility at 6 to 7 weeks of gestation, emergence of unmistakably human form a few weeks later still, first awareness, or birth? In deciding, one must give reasons for one's choice and thereby necessarily introduce "extra-biological" dimensions as part of the choosing. As a result, the biological indicators come to serve as little more than the material referents for these reasons. The recognition that reasoned choices among contending properties must be made has led many to focus precisely on those

reasons, and to claim that the properties whereby we understand and value prenatal personhood are not those discoverable by science but those constituted within a social fabric.

Harrison,[28] for example, claims that our evaluation of embryonic and fetal human life is a complex exercise of moral agency in the face of a precise moral question: "When shall we predicate full human value to developing fetal life?" Such predication or attribution is clearly a socially constitutive act extrinsic to the fetus. It is not, however, an act unconcerned with the changing nature of the fetus or its intimate and dependent relation to the woman nurturing it. Thus, as we exercise this moral agency we are counselled to take into account "developmental criteria for stipulating the degree of similarity to existing human beings required for counting fetal life as a human life" while attending to "the moral reasons for and against viewing prenatal life as morally continuous or discontinuous with existent humanity" (pp. 208–209). That is, we are to look for developmental differences which make a moral difference. Given the view expressed by Harrison, how do we engage in the process of predication? If we cannot begin with scientific facts about prenatal ontogenesis, if the meaning or definition of personhood is simply not something arrived at empirically, then it must be decided upon. The justification for a choice of developmental criterion must originate elsewhere and earlier, within our moral communities. Thus, we look toward the embryo or fetus from the vantage point of existent humanity, having already chosen one or more criteria—about ourselves—as anchors of a possible moral continuity with the developing fetus. These prior choices of criteria thereby condition the nature of our moral gaze. If, for example, we are persuaded that the functional capacities of our neocortex set us apart, then our moral sensibilities will turn our gaze to a collection of important, neurally-enabled capacities warranting attention. We will look for a nervous system of sufficient material complexity to embody those neural capacities we have (already) judged as morally pertinent.[29]

The position taken is quite simple. Biological marker events do not carry the day with respect to ethically difficult situations; they have no morally determining force. They can, however, be useful as reference points for our ethical thinking and public policy discussions.

There is not space here to join the controversy about prenatal personhood, but it is obvious that the transitions spoken of would inform that debate. If a physically unitary being is necessary before one can speak of personhood, then such talk makes sense (if it does then) only after Transition 1. If one is moved to a moral attachment with the fetus in virtue of its capacity for movement and its recognizable human likeness, then Transition 2 constitutes a significant developmental passage. If, alternatively, one is moved to privilege the emergence of rudimentary higher brain function, then Transition 3 looms large. In this last case, for example, one might argue (as in the article excerpted above) that it is rudimentary neocortical function that first makes possible the emergence

---

[28] B. W. Harrison, *Our Right To Choose: Toward a New Ethic of Abortion* (1983).
[29] M. Flower, *supra* note 3, at 65–66.

of a particular, personal life. If it is the case (as it surely is) that the process of neocortical synaptogenesis occurring through and after Transition 3 is stochastic (i.e., not strictly determined by genetic information but in part the consequence of the unique influences of mid- to full-term development in utero), then one's "neocortical embodiment" (one's importantly particular emergence) is a matter for the second half of gestation (and beyond). As Coughlan has recently put it (in a quite different context), before the critical events that underpin personhood[30] are attained

> the life of the embryo or fetus is not the bodily life of the person to be, but the life of the body of the person to be. *That is to say, the life of the embryo from which I grew was not a stage of* my *life, but a stage in the life of* my body. *I am not my body; I am a person, and* my *life began when the person I am came to be. The life of the embryo was a stage in the life of the body which* came to be my body *when I came to be.*[31]

Using the form of Coughlan's argument, one can imagine making the claim that prior to the emergence of the neocortex a personal human life has not yet begun, that what underpins my emergence is not the "bodily embodiment" that begins with Transition 1 and extends through Transition 2, but the neocortical *neuro*embodiment begun with Transition 3. However, it is not the intent of this article to pursue such an argument or alternatives to it; rather, the intent is to suggest, however sketchily, ways in which one can think about the transitions just summarized.

Before turning to some closing thoughts, it might be useful to put the argued transitions to further use. With respect to the timing of abortions, we can set recent data on abortion in the context of Transitions 1 through 3 (figure 4).[32] As one can see, perhaps a quarter of abortions are performed during the embryonic period (prior to the emergence of motility) with nearly all remaining abortions being done prior to Transition 3 and the emergence of rudimentary neocortical function. Such a display gives no solace to those who are firmly convinced that an inviolate human life emerges at conception, but it makes clear that more than 99% of abortions are performed before higher brain activity is likely. Although we have no good way to judge fetal sentience (awareness), if such awareness depends on neocortical function (as most think it does) then concern about terminating a sentient life is something we may well be able to set aside so long as earlier abortions are at issue.

Although abortion is the central topic of this collection of papers, our concerns about prenatal life emerge in other contexts, key ones of which are displayed in figure 5. It is quite clear here, as it is in figure 4, that most of our interventions in prenatal life occur in the first half of gestation (the exception being those rare cases of surgery that are directed at fetuses past midgestation). Thus, for example, a growing dimension of infertility practice entails work with prenatal human life in its first week. Eggs are fertilized in the laboratory, undergo the first few cleavages in laboratory incubators and are then transferred to a woman's uterus or cryopreserved (frozen) for later transfer or

---

[30] It is not at all clear that it makes any sense to talk of prenatal personhood. *See* E. Doerr & J. Prescott, *Abortion Rights and Fetal "Personhood"* (2nd ed. 1989).

[31] M. Coughlan, *The Vatican, the Law and the Human Embryo* 110 (1990).

[32] Centers for Disease Control, *Abortion surveillance: preliminary analysis—United States, 1984, 1985,* 260 J. A. M. A. 3410–11 (December 16, 1988).

Figure 4. Abortion and Prenatal Transitions

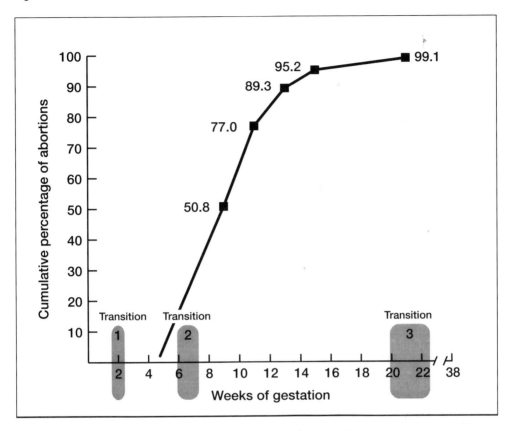

other use (including investigative study). Only just beginning is the sample of single cells from (for example) eight-celled human preembryos for purposes of genetic diagnosis.[33] During the embryonic period of development, other interventions and concerns come into play. There is considerable debate, for example, about the use of RU486 as a contragestive abortifacient during the first few weeks of the embryonic period (see the article by Etienne-Emile Baulieu in this volume). The embryonic period is a time of great sensitivity to noxious chemicals, viral agents and such. Thus, this period of prenatal life is one about which great care must be taken if one is to avoid the production of congenital birth defects. One can also imagine the possibility of aborted late-stage embryos (but more often fetuses) being used as donors of tissue or organs (see the article by Kenneth Ryan in this volume). Finally, there are two diagnostic procedures utilized during the period following Transition 2: chorionic villus sampling and amniocentesis.

---

[33] Because the cells of the human preembryo are pluripotential at this time (i.e., each of the cells is capable of becoming any part of the future embryo), the diagnostic "loss" of a single cell is not even "missed." The remaining cells are able to constitute a complete and normal human being as development proceeds.

Figure 5. Interventions into Prenatal Human Life

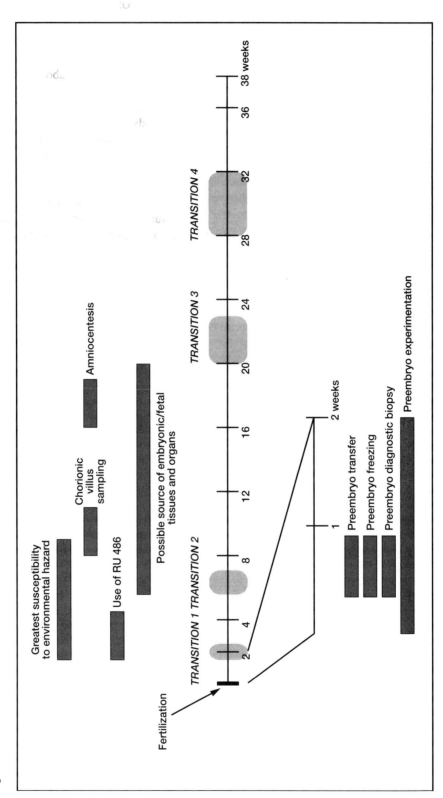

Final Thoughts

Although it would certainly be of value to know more than we do about prenatal human life, it appears clear that what we do know can help us be more precise about just what sort of being a prenatal human is during the course of its coming into being. It is clearly changing in rapid fashion; it is what Clifford Grobstein has called "a moving target" in our deliberations about it. On the other hand, if one finds persuasive the evidence for the transitions outlined in this survey, then an admittedly continuous process has been shown to exhibit several periods of distinctive emergence. Whether additional information will require a modification of the four transitions set forth here remains to be seen. What additional "meaning" is made of these transitions also remains to be seen. One hopes, in any case, that greater biological knowledge of prenatal human life will permit those who must make difficult decisions concerning such actions as abortion, prenatal diagnosis and infertility treatment to do so in a way that takes fuller account of the nature of prenatal life.

Some claim that a person is created at the moment of conception. However, medical research shows that this may not be true. The thrust of Dr. Gardner's argument is that at the early stages of development the individual has not been determined; although the fertilized egg contains all the DNA information, it is not an automatic blueprint of an individual. DNA is not the whole answer but provides only part of the information necessary for the ultimate formation of the embryo. And once the embryo is fully developed, it must undergo additional changes to reach the state of being human.

16 · Is an Embryo a Person? _____

Charles A. Gardner, Ph.D.

In the familiar polemics on the subject of abortion one side argues in support of women's rights, the other in support of babies' rights. But so far only one side of the debate has attempted to engage a question that should be intrinsic to the abortion issue: What is the embryo?

To Dr. Jack Willke, president of the National Right to Life Committee, the embryo is a human being from the moment of conception. His definition of a human being depends upon the forty-six chromosomes first present in the fertilized egg. "Contained within the single cell who I once was," he says, "was the totality of everything I am today."

Judges and state legislators across the United States seem inclined to accept this argument about chromosomes and totality. In *Webster v. Reproductive Health Services* the Supreme Court upheld a Missouri fetal rights law that asserts "life begins at conception." In September a Tennessee court ruled that seven frozen embryos at the center of a bitter divorce suit are children, that they are "human beings existing as embryos." Judge W. Dale Young gave "custody" of the embryos to their "mother," and, basing his decision entirely upon the testimony of one geneticist, concluded that "a man is a man; that upon fertilization, the entire constitution of the man is clearly, unequivocally spelled-out, including arms, legs, nervous systems and the like; that upon inspection via DNA manipulation, one can see the life codes for each of these otherwise unobservable elements of the unique individual."

The "biological" argument that a human being is created at fertilization is increasingly used by antiabortion forces in their effort to back up religious arguments based on church tradition. This purportedly scientific argument comes as a surprise to most embryologists, however, for it contradicts all that they have learned in the past few decades. The benefit of that knowledge, more sophisticated, subtle and complete than ever before, has been notably missing from most public discussions of abortion and from all the legal decisions that have created so much recent publicity.

The embryo exists utterly beyond our normal means of understanding. We are accustomed to trust our eyes. A thing has bark around a thick column, limbs, branches and bunches of green leaves. It must be a tree. While the early embryo bears no physical resemblance to anything we think of as human, later, at three months, it has fingers, legs, a nose and eyes. But the first conclusions that one draws from even those appearances may have to be revised.

The fertilized egg knows nothing about how to make a finger, a nose or eyes. It knows only how to divide into two cells, which then know how to divide to make four. How, then, does the fertilized egg give rise to a baby?

The fertilized egg contains all the DNA necessary for the embryo to develop. Half the DNA has been supplied by the egg and the other half by a single sperm cell. We often read in textbooks and the press that this DNA is the "blueprint of life." But an analogy between a blueprint and the DNA is misleading. If a human being were a house, then the DNA would specify doorknobs, hinges, lumber and nails, window panes, wires, switches, fuses and a thousand other individual parts. But it would not tell how to put all those parts together in the right order and at the right time. It is unfortunate that biologists have contributed to the belief that DNA represents some sort of essence of "life force." Rather, it is only part of the information necessary for the correct formation of the embryo.

In fact there does not seem to be any blueprint for embryonic development. Each step toward greater complexity depends instead upon the pattern of cells and molecules just reached in the preceding step. The information required to make an eye or a finger does not exist in the fertilized egg. It exists in the positions and interactions of cells and molecules that will be formed only at a later time.

But if the individual does not arise out of the DNA then from where does he or she come? The fertilized egg clearly has potential. Perhaps if we consider the fertilized egg as a whole, poised as it seems to be to follow a preset pathway (blueprint or no), then we can discern the incipient individual.

We must ask, Is there a preset pathway? Is there only one road for the fertilized egg to travel? Embryologists have always been impressed by the ability of the embryo to adjust to alterations in its normal path of development. They have studied the embryos of fish, frogs, chickens and mice because these closely resemble human embryos. In fact, when early human and mouse embryos are compared, the process of development is so similar that these embryos are not distinguishable from each other in any significant way. Let us, therefore, consider one experiment.

If a fertilized mouse egg from two white-furred parents goes through four cell divisions, the embryo will have reached the sixteen-cell stage. If this embryo is then brought together with a sixteen-cell embryo from two black-furred parents, a ball of thirty-two cells is formed. This ball of cells will go on to make a single individual with mixed black and white fur: one mouse with four parents, two white and two black. Any particular cell of its body has come from either the one set of parents or the other. A similar event sometimes occurs naturally in humans when two sibling embryos combine into one. The resultant person may be completely normal.

If the two original embryos were determined to become particular individuals, such a thing could not happen. The embryos would recognize themselves to be different mice, or different people, and would not unite. But here the cells seem unaware of any distinction between themselves. They seem to recognize each other as early embryonic cells and nothing more. The only explanation is that the individual is not fixed or determined at this early stage. In fact the body pattern has not even begun to form.

The early human embryo, like the mouse, is a ball of cells. The body pattern of the embryo will be established only very gradually by these cells, and not in a way that one might intuitively expect. The fertilized egg does not divide into one cell destined to make the head, one to make an arm, another a leg. There is no program to specify the fate of each cell. Rather, a cell's behavior is influenced at each stage by its location within the developing body pattern of the embryo. Each stage brings new information, information that will change as the body pattern changes. And each cell will respond to this new information in a somewhat random way. For example, one cell of the sixteen-cell embryo may contribute randomly to the formation of many different organs or structures of the body. Later on a descendant of that cell may find itself restricted to the brain but will still be able to contribute to a wide variety of cell types there. It may make different types of nerve cells or non-nerve cells. And because of the extremely complex cell migrations that take place during the development of the brain, the cell's progeny may function in many regions of the brain.

With this layering of chance event upon chance event the embryo gradually evolves its form. The mixture of chance and planning that goes into every step of the process is what makes each person unique. Even the distinct pattern of ridges and swirls that make up a fingerprint is not preset in the fertilized egg. Identical twins grow from the same egg, have exactly the same DNA and develop in the same maternal environment, yet they have different fingerprints. If something so relatively simple and superficial as a fingerprint arises out of chance events, then what of an organ as complex as the human brain?

The fertilized egg is clearly not a prepackaged human being. There is no body plan, no blueprint, no tiny being pre-formed and waiting to unfold. It is not ''complete'' or ''the totality'' of a person. The fertilized egg may follow many different paths; the route will be penned in only as the paths are taken; the particular person that it might become is not yet there. Our genes give us a propensity for certain characteristics, but it is the enactment of the complex process of development that gives us our individual characteristics. So how can an embryo be a human being?

Of course, the embryo is always human; it is of human origin, but so is every egg and every sperm cell. The problem is in the definition of the word ''human.'' It may be either an adjective or a noun. As an adjective it carries no particular moral weight. We have human hair, human fingernails; the human cells in our saliva all have forty-six chromosomes, but they have no special significance. The noun, however, does have a moral dimension. Its synonym ''human being'' connotes individuality or personhood. It may also be associated with human thoughts and feelings. With respect to the embryo, then, its use may relate to the development of the brain.

In the early embryo a structure forms that biologists call the neural tube. It is a hollow cord of cells that runs along the central axis of the body, complete from head to tail after the first month (human embryos have tails for a while). One end of this tube bulges like the far tip of a long thin balloon being inflated. This area is called the brain, although until the second month of development the cells there do not become nerves; there are no special connections among them and there can be no thoughts. During the third and fourth months, nerve cells appear. Simple reflexes form first. The largest and most complex area of the brain, the cerebrum, develops last of all. In its decision in the *Webster* case the Supreme Court majority took up the issue of "viability"—the point at which the fetus can survive outside the womb—and suggested that this stage might be reached as early as the twentieth week. Apart from the question of whether the lungs could function at this point, which in itself is doubtful, there is the more compelling matter of the brain, whose qualities ultimately distinguish us as human beings. In the cerebrum, the mature brain cell pattern is not seen until the sixth or seventh month.

The conscious mind is dauntingly complex, and its workings are just now beginning to be understood. We do know that the structure of the brain—the types and locations of its nerve cells and their interconnections—is intimately related to the function of the brain. The higher faculties must develop very late. Thoughts and feelings must arise very gradually. Thus, an embryo may have fingers, hands, a nose and eyes, even reflex movements, but still have no mind.

The early embryo, before the development of the mature human brain, has only one quality to distinguish it from all other living things: It has the potential to become a human being. But it is a strange kind of potential, having no determined path or blueprint to follow. The fertilized egg cell does not contain its fate, just as a grape seed does not contain wine.

Of course we know the potential of the fertilized egg and the early embryo because we have awareness, thoughts and feelings. But the early embryo has none of these things. This group of cells cannot know its fate or want to become anything. Still, each of us must struggle with the philosophical and moral implications of this type of potential. It may help to remember that potential here is very tenuous and dependent upon the influence of many extrinsic factors. And the very question of potential presents us with a "chicken or the egg" kind of problem. Every egg and every sperm cell in our bodies could contribute to the formation of a human being. Obviously, an egg or sperm cell is not a "complete" human being, but then neither is the fertilized egg. Fertilization, the injections of sperm DNA into the egg, is just one of the many small steps toward full human potential. It seems arbitrary to invest this biological event with any special moral significance. As we have seen, we are more than the sum of our chromosomes; DNA is not destiny.

There will always be arguments based on spiritual or ethical beliefs to convince an individual of the rightness or wrongness of abortion, but each person should first understand the biology to which those beliefs refer. State-imposed restrictions on abortion would clearly take away individual choice in the matter. But the state may not act on the basis of religious tradition. It must recognize the fundamental difference between an embryo and a human being. The nature of embryonic development makes it impossible to think of an egg or a cluster of cells as a person. Time itself must be woven into the fabric of the embryo before it becomes a baby. And most abortions in the United States are performed well before the pattern of the weave is recognizable. Ninety-one percent are performed within three months of fertilization. It would be a great tragedy if, in ignorance of the *process* that is the embryo, state legislators pass laws restricting individual freedom of choice and press them upon the people. The embryo is not a child. It is not a baby. It is not yet a human being.

The article states that since 1980 the number of legal abortions reported to the national Centers for Disease Control (CDC) has remained fairly stable. Women undergoing legally induced abortions tended (1) to be young, white and unmarried, (2) to live in a metropolitan area, (3) to have had no previous live births and (4) to be having the procedure for the first time. Approximately half of all abortions were performed before the eighth week of gestation, and greater than 85% were performed during the first trimester of pregnancy. This article by the CDC presents a very accurate statistical study of abortions in the United States for the year 1988.

17 · Abortion Surveillance, United States, 1988*

Lisa M. Koonin**
Kenneth D. Kochanek, M.A.
Jack C. Smith, M.S.
Merrell Ramick

Summary

Since 1980, the number of legal abortions reported to CDC has remained fairly stable, varying each year by <3%. In 1988, 1,371,285 abortions were reported—a 1.3% increase from 1987. The abortion ratio for 1988 was 352 legally induced abortions/1,000 live births, and the abortion rate was 24/1,000 women ages 15–44 years. The abortion ratio was higher for black women and women of other minority races and for women <15 years of age. However, the abortion ratio for women <15 years was lower in 1988 than in any previous year since 1972. Women undergoing legally induced abortions tended 1) to be young, white, and unmarried, 2) to live in a metropolitan area, 3) to have had no previous live births, and 4) to be having the procedure for the first time. Approximately half of all abortions were performed before the eighth week of gestation, and >85% were performed during the first trimester of pregnancy (<13 weeks of gestation). Black women and women of other minority races tended to obtain abortions later in pregnancy than did white women; however, age was a more dominant influence than race. Younger women tended to obtain abortions later than older women. Educational

*This report was originally published by CDC in 1991. Only tables 1, 3, 4, 5, 6, 7, 13 and 14 and Figures 1, 2, 3 and 4 are included here.
**M.N., M.P.H., Statistics and Computer Resources Branch, Division of Reproductive Health, National Center for Chronic Disease Prevention and Health Promotion

level strongly influenced when an abortion was performed; better educated women had an abortion earlier in gestation.

Introduction

In 1969, CDC [national Centers for Disease Control] began abortion surveillance to document the number and characteristics of women obtaining legally induced abortions and to assist efforts to eliminate preventable causes of morbidity and mortality associated with abortions. This report, as in past years, is based primarily on abortion data provided to the Division of Reproductive Health (DRH), National Center for Chronic Disease Prevention and Health Promotion (NCCDPHP), CDC. For the first time, this report incorporates additional abortion data reported to the Division of Vital Statistics (DVS), National Center for Health Statistics (NCHS), CDC.

Methods

For 1988, the DRH received data from 52 reporting areas: 50 states, New York City, and the District of Columbia. The total number of legally induced abortions was available from all reporting areas, most of which provided information on the characteristics of women obtaining abortions. Central health agencies [1] reported data for 45 areas; hospitals and other medical facilities reported data for seven areas. Data are reported by the state in which the abortion occurred, unless otherwise noted.

In addition to abortion data provided to DRH, data are reported to the DVS of NCHS. NCHS abortion data for 1988 represent approximately 22% of all abortions reported to the DRH. The data were collected at the state/registration-area level for each induced abortion and were provided to NCHS on magnetic tape as a part of the Vital Statistics Cooperative Program. The NCHS data contain information on two demographic characteristics not collected by DRH: educational level and area of residence (metropolitan or nonmetropolitan). The NCHS data system enables detailed cross-classification of these and other characteristics.

Data on induced abortions from NCHS (except for education) were reported from New York City and 14 states: Colorado, Indiana, Kansas, Maine, Missouri, Montana, New York, Oregon, Rhode Island, South Carolina, Tennessee, Utah, Vermont, and Virginia. [2] Data on education were reported from New York City and 11 states (Indiana, Kansas, Maine, Missouri, Montana, Oregon, South Carolina, Tennessee, Utah, Vermont, and Virginia) . . .

Age was classified in 5-year intervals. Race was classified as white or black/other races.

Abortion statistics for 1988 and selected previous years are presented in a summary table (Table 1) . . . Percentage distributions in Table 1 include data from all areas reporting a given characteristic and exclude all unknown values unless otherwise noted. Information about education and area of residence from NCHS was available for 1980

[1] Includes state health departments and health departments from New York City and the District of Columbia.
[2] Kochanek KD. *Induced terminations of pregnancy: reporting states, 1988.* Monthly vital statistics report 1991; 39(suppl): 12. Hyattsville, Maryland: US Department of Health and Human Services, Public Health Service, National Center for Health Statistics; DHHS publication no. (PHS)91-1120.

through 1988 only; a different number of states reported each characteristic for different years . . .

State-specific characteristics of women obtaining abortions in 1988 are also presented (Tables 3 through 7), and tabulations of selected characteristics are given (Tables 8 through 18).

Results

In 1988, 1,371,285 legal abortions were reported to the DRH—an 1.3% increase over the number reported for the preceding year.[3] The national abortion rate increased from 23 abortions/1,000 women ages 15–44 years in 1986 to 24/1,000 in 1987 and remained at that rate in 1988. The abortion ratio rose slightly from 354 abortions/1,000 live births in 1986 to 356/1,000 in 1987 and then declined to 352/1,000 in 1988 (Table 1, Figure 1).

In 1988, as in previous years, most abortions were performed in California, New York City, and Texas; the fewest were performed in Wyoming, South Dakota, and Alaska.[4] For women whose state of residence was known, approximately 92% had the abortion done within their state of residence. The percentage of abortions obtained by out-of-state residents ranged from approximately 50% in the District of Columbia to <1% in Hawaii (Table 3). Data on the percentage of abortions obtained by out-of-state residents were not available for 12 reporting areas in 1988.

In 1988, 40 states, the District of Columbia, and New York City reported legal abortions by age. Women 20–24 years of age had approximately 33% of all abortions, whereas women <15 years of age had approximately 1% (Table 4). The abortion ratio was highest for the youngest women (949 abortions/1,000 live births for women <15 years of age and 624/1,000 for women 15–19 years of age) and for women of the oldest age category (514/1,000 for women ≥40 years); the ratio was lowest for women ages 30–34 years (188/1,000) (Figure 2). Although the abortion ratio was highest for teenagers, the proportion of abortions they obtained decreased slightly—from 26% of all legal abortions in 1987 to 25% in 1988. Among teenagers, the abortion ratio was highest for those <15 years of age and lowest for 19-year-olds (Table 5).

In 1988, approximately 48% of reported legal abortions were performed at or before 8 weeks of gestation, and 87% were done at or before 12 weeks of gestation (Table 6). Four percent of the abortions were performed at 16–20 weeks of gestation, and approximately 1% were performed ≥21 weeks of gestation.

Approximately 98% of legal abortions were performed by curettage (Table 7) and approximately 1% by intrauterine saline or prostaglandin instillation. Hysterectomy and hysterotomy were rarely used; <1% of abortions were performed by these methods.

Almost two-thirds of women obtaining legal abortions were white; this finding continued a previously noted trend[5]. The abortion ratio, however, was 1.9 times higher for black women and women of other minority races (489 abortions/1,000 live births) than for white women (259 abortions/1,000 live births).

---

[3]CDC. *Abortion surveillance, 1986–1987*. In: *CDC Surveillance Summaries*, June 1990. MMWR 1990; 39(no. SS-2): 23–56.

[4]CDC. *Abortion surveillance, United States, 1984–1985*. In: *CDC Surveillance Summaries*, September 1989. MMWR 1989; 38(no. SS-2): 11–45. Also, *supra* note 3.

[5]*Id.*

Figure 1. Legal Abortions, Ratio, and Rate, by Year, United States, 1970–1988

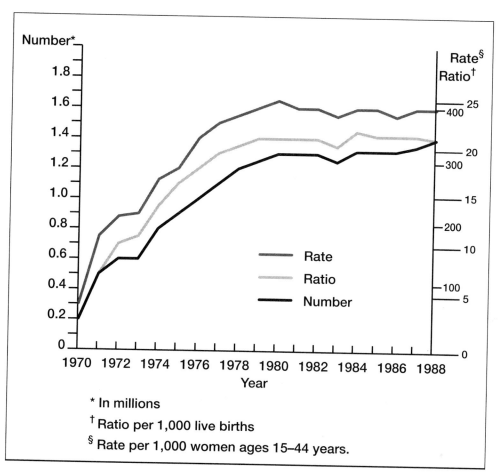

The percentage of women undergoing legal abortions who were unmarried increased from 76% in 1986 and 1987[6] to almost 78% in 1988. The abortion ratio was 11.7 times higher for unmarried women than for married women: 1,027 abortions/1,000 live births versus 88 abortions/1,000 live births.

Fifty-one percent of the women obtaining legal abortions had had no previous live births, and approximately 89% had had two or fewer live births. The abortion ratio was highest for women who had had no live births and lowest for women who had had one live birth. Approximately 56% of women obtaining abortions had the procedure for the first time, whereas 15% had had at least two previous abortions.

For the 15 reporting areas of the NCHS data system, most women (approximately 88%) who obtained abortions lived in metropolitan areas. For these women, the abortion ratio was approximately 2.2 times greater than that of women who lived in nonmetropolitan areas (373 versus 168 abortions/1,000 live births). The difference by place of

---

[6] These findings update previously published data on marital status for 1986 and 1987.

Table 1. Characteristics of Women Who Obtained Legal Abortions—United States, Selected Years, 1972–1988*

Characteristic	Year									
	1972	1973	1976	1978	1980	1982	1984	1986	1987	1988
Reported number of legal abortions	586,760	615,831	988,267	1,157,776	1,297,606	1,303,980	1,333,521	1,328,112	1,353,671	1,371,285
Abortion ratio[†]	180	196	312	347	359	354	364	354	356	352
Abortion rate[§]	13	14	21	23	25	24	24	23	24	24
Percentage distribution[¶],[**]										
Residence										
Abortion in-state	56.2	74.8	90.0	89.3	92.6	92.9	92.0	92.4	91.7	91.4
Abortion out-of-state	43.8	25.2	10.0	10.7	7.4	7.1	8.0	7.6	8.3	8.6
Geographic area[††,§§]										
Metropolitan	—	—	—	—	85.3	86.7	86.9	86.7	86.9	86.3
Nonmetropolitan	—	—	—	—	14.7	13.3	13.1	13.3	13.1	13.7
Age (years)										
≤19	32.6	32.7	32.1	30.0	29.2	27.1	26.4	25.3	25.8	25.3
20–24	32.5	32.0	33.3	35.0	35.5	35.1	35.3	34.0	33.4	32.8
≥25	34.9	35.3	34.6	34.9	35.3	37.8	38.3	40.7	40.8	41.9
Race										
White	77.0	72.5	66.6	67.0	69.9	68.5	67.4	67.0	66.4	64.4
Black and other	23.0	27.5	33.4	33.0	30.1	31.5	32.6	33.0	33.6	35.6
Marital status										
Married	29.7	27.4	24.6	26.4	23.1	22.0	20.5	20.2[¶¶]	20.8[¶¶]	20.3
Unmarried	70.3	72.6	75.4	73.6	76.9	78.0	79.5	79.8[¶¶]	79.2[¶¶]	79.7
Education (years of school completed)[††]										
0–8	—	—	—	—	3.3	2.8	2.5	2.5	2.3	1.6
9–11	—	—	—	—	20.3	19.4	18.1	18.2	18.1	13.0
12	—	—	—	—	44.7	44.5	46.4	47.1	49.9	54.1
13–15	—	—	—	—	21.3	22.5	21.8	21.4	19.6	16.9
≥16	—	—	—	—	10.4	11.0	11.2	10.8	10.1	14.4

Year

Characteristic	1972	1973	1976	1978	1980	1982	1984	1986	1987	1988
Number of live births***										
0	49.4	48.6	47.7	56.6	58.4	57.8	57.0	55.1	53.6	52.4
1	18.2	18.8	20.7	19.2	19.5	20.3	20.9	22.1	22.8	23.4
2	13.3	14.2	15.4	14.1	13.7	13.9	14.4	14.9	15.5	16.0
3	8.7	8.7	8.3	5.9	5.3	5.1	5.1	5.3	5.5	5.6
≥4	10.4	9.7	7.9	4.2	3.2	2.9	2.6	2.6	2.6	2.6
Type of procedure										
Curettage	88.6	88.4	92.8	94.6	95.5	96.4	96.8	97.0	97.2	98.6
Suction	65.2	74.9	82.6	90.2	89.8	90.6	93.1	94.5	93.3	95.1
Sharp	23.4	13.5	10.2	4.4	5.7	5.8	3.7	2.5	3.7	3.5
Intrauterine instillation	10.4	10.4	6.0	3.9	3.1	2.5	1.9	1.4	1.3	1.1
Hysterotomy/ hysterectomy	0.6	0.7	0.2	0.1	0.1	0.0†††	0.0†††	0.0†††	0.0†††	0.0††
Other	0.5	0.6	0.9	1.4	1.3	1.0	1.3	1.6	1.5	0.3
Weeks of gestation										
≤8	34.0	36.1	47.0	52.2	51.7	50.6	50.5	51.0	50.4	48.7
9–10	30.7	29.4	28.0	26.9	26.2	26.7	26.4	25.8	26.0	26.4
11–12	17.5	17.9	14.4	12.3	12.2	12.4	12.6	12.2	12.4	12.7
13–15	8.4	6.9	4.5	4.0	5.2	5.3	5.8	6.1	6.2	6.6
16–20	8.2	8.0	5.1	3.7	3.9	3.9	3.9	4.1	4.2	4.5
≥21	1.3	1.7	0.9	0.9	0.9	1.1	0.8	0.8	0.8	1.1

*Based on data reported to the Division of Reproductive Health, National Center for Chronic Disease Prevention and Health Promotion, unless otherwise noted.

†Number of abortions per 1,000 live births.

§Number of abortions per 1,000 women 15–44 years of age.

¶Excludes unknown values, unless otherwise noted.

**Because the number of states that reported each characteristic varies from year to year, temporal comparisons should be made with caution.

††Reported to the Division of Vital Statistics, National Center for Health Statistics.

§§Unknowns have been redistributed, based on known values.

¶¶Updates data previously published.

***For years 1972–1976, data indicate number of living children.

†††<0.05%.

— Not reported.

Figure 2. Abortion Ratio, by Age Group, United States, 1988

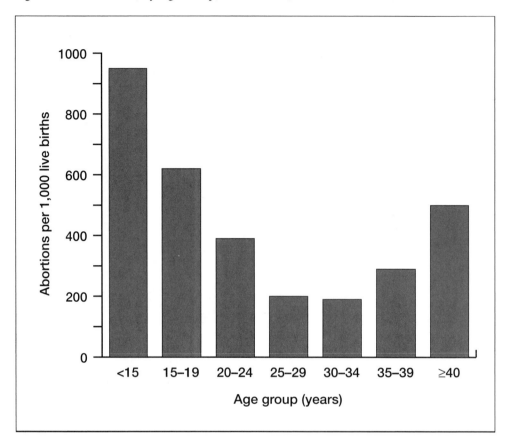

residence was greater for black women and women of other minority races than for white women. The abortion ratio for minority women living in a metropolitan area was 2.8 times that for those living in a nonmetropolitan area (599 versus 210 abortions/1,000). In contrast, the abortion ratio for white women living in a metropolitan area was 1.9 times that of white women living in a nonmetropolitan area (302 versus 162 abortions/1,000).

When the proportion of women undergoing legal abortions was analyzed by age group, few differences were found between white women and minority women (Table 13). However, the proportion of minority women < 15 years old who had abortions was over twice that of white women in this age group. In addition, a slightly higher proportion of minority women who had abortions were unmarried.

Most women obtained abortions during the first 12 weeks of pregnancy. However, women < 15 years of age obtained abortions later in pregnancy than did older women (Table 14). Minority women tended to obtain abortions later in pregnancy than did white women. However, age was a more dominant influence than race, particularly for women who obtained abortions at ≥ 16 weeks of gestation . . . For all races, the proportion of women obtaining an early abortion (≤ 8 weeks) increased with age, and the proportion obtaining a late abortion (≥ 16 weeks) decreased with age (Figure 3).

Table 3. Reported Number of Legal Abortions, Abortion Ratio and Rate, and Percentage of Abortions Obtained by Out-of-State Residents, by State of Occurrence, 1988

State	Number of abortions*	Ratio†	Rate§	Percentage of abortions obtained by out-of-state residents¶
Alabama	14,746**	243	16	—
Alaska	1,463**	132	11	—
Arizona	15,922	243	20	8.3
Arkansas	5,439	155	10	2.0
California	334,887††	628	49	—
Colorado	12,425	233	16	7.4
Connecticut	20,219	421	28	4.3
Delaware	5,458	525	36	—
Dist. of Col.	20,822	§§	¶¶	50.4
Florida	65,153	356	23	—
Georgia	35,213	335	23	8.9
Hawaii	6,040	319	26	0.6
Idaho	1,650	105	8	7.8
Illinois	50,478	273	18	2.7
Indiana	13,003	160	10	4.6
Iowa	6,405**	168	10	—
Kansas	7,534	195	13	4.2
Kentucky	11,631	228	13	3.2
Louisiana	15,367	208	15	—
Maine	4,723	275	18	1.9
Maryland	23,707	310	20	1.2
Massachusetts	38,841	441	26	6.8
Michigan	46,747	335	21	—
Minnesota	17,975	269	17	10.2
Mississippi	5,170	123	9	15.2
Missouri	17,382	228	14	11.3
Montana	2,866	245	16	25.0
Nebraska	6,006	251	17	21.0
Nevada	6,936	377	28	11.9
New Hampshire	4,156**	239	15	—
New Jersey	35,987	306	19	3.2
New Mexico	5,126	190	15	4.2
New York	142,862	519	34	5.9
(City)	90,137***	733	—	7.6
(Upstate)	52,725	346	—	3.2
N. Carolina	37,629	386	25	7.7
N. Dakota	2,221	220	15	44.1
Ohio	34,543	215	14	7.0
Oklahoma	11,073**	262	15	—
Oregon	13,309	334	21	9.2
Pennsylvania	50,786	307	19	5.9
Rhode Island	7,615	537	33	—
S. Carolina	14,133	257	17	5.5
S. Dakota	898	80	5	13.1
Tennessee	21,589	305	20	17.8
Texas	81,474	269	20	4.6
Utah	4,732	131	13	14.5
Vermont	3,309	408	26	29.1
Virginia	34,029	367	24	5.9
Washington	29,802	411	27	5.8

State	Number of abortions *	Ratio†	Rate §	Percentage of abortions obtained by out-of-state residents¶
West Virginia	3,467**	159	8	—
Wisconsin	17,986	254	16	7.1
Wyoming	351	49	3	12.1
Total	**1,371,285**	**352**	**24**	**8.6**

*Abortion data from central health agency unless otherwise noted.

†Abortions per 1,000 live births (live-birth data from central health agency).

§Abortions per 1,000 women ages 15–44 (number of women ages 15–44 from Bureau of the Census, Current Population Survey, March 1988, Tape Technical Documentation, Washington, DC).

¶Based on number of abortions for which residence status of woman was known.

**Reported from hospitals and/or other medical facilities in state.

††CDC estimate.

§§>1,000 abortions per 1,000 live births.

¶¶>100 abortions per 1,000 women ages 15–44.

***Reported from New York City Health Department.

— Not reported.

When analyzed by gestational age, approximately 99% of abortions at ≤12 weeks of gestation were performed by curettage (primarily suction procedures) . . . Beyond 12 weeks of gestation, the most common procedure was curettage, which was usually reported as dilation and evacuation (D & E). Most intrauterine instillations involved the use of saline and were performed at ≥16 weeks of gestation.

For all racial groups, education level (years of school completed) strongly influenced when an abortion was performed . . . For example, for white women who obtained an abortion, 60% of the college-educated women (≥16 years of school completed) had an early abortion (≤8 weeks), compared with 46% of the women who completed high school (12 years) only. For minority women who obtained an abortion, approximately 53% of college-educated women had an early abortion, compared with 42% of women who completed high school only.

Abortion ratios were calculated by race, age, and educational level . . . Patterns were different between whites and minorities. Among white women ≥25 years, the abortion ratio rose with increasing levels of education for women with less than a high school education, was highest for high school graduates, and declined for women with higher educational levels (Figure 4). For minority women ≥25 years, the abortion ratio was also highest for high school graduates; it declined for women with some college (13–15 years completed), and then rose for college graduates (≥16 years).

Discussion

From 1970 to 1982, the reported number of legal abortions in the United States increased every year (Figure 1); the largest percentage increase occurred during the period 1970–1972. From 1976 to 1982, this annual increase declined continuously, reaching a low of 0.2% for the period 1981–1982. Since 1983, the number of abortions has remained relatively stable, with only small (<3%) year-to-year fluctuations.

The abortion ratio increased each year from 1970 to 1980 and has remained relatively stable since 1980 (Figure 1). The abortion rate also increased each year through 1980, when it reached 25 abortions/1,000 women ages 15–44 years. Since that time, the rate has remained stable, fluctuating from 23 to 24 abortions/1,000 women ages 15–44 years (Figure 1).

The number of legal abortions reported to CDC in 1988 was probably lower than the number actually performed. Totals provided by central health agencies are often lower than those obtained by direct surveys of abortion providers.[7] For example, in 1988, the total number of abortions reported by DRH was approximately 16% lower than that reported by the Alan Guttmacher Institute, a private organization that obtains information on the number of abortions performed directly from abortion providers.[8]

Since 1972, the abortion ratio has declined for all age groups, particularly for women ages ≥30 years. Higher rates of childbearing among women ages 30–39 years may account for some of this decline.[9] The abortion ratio for teens has also steadily declined since 1972. In 1988, the abortion ratio for women <15 years was lower than in any other year since 1972.

Several other trends were observed—not necessarily related to each other—for women who obtained abortions between 1972 and 1988 (Table 1). During that period, the proportion of women obtaining an abortion in their state of residence-increased from 56% to 93% and has remained at approximately 92% since 1984 (Table 1). From 1972 through 1985, the proportion of women who were unmarried obtaining abortions increased steadily—from 70% to 81%.[10] In 1986, the proportion of unmarried women obtaining abortions decreased slightly to 80% and remained at that level in 1988. The percentage of abortions among minority women increased from 23% in 1972 to 36% in 1988, and the number of women with one or no previous live births increased from 68% to 76% during the same period. The percent distribution of abortions by gestational age has been relatively stable since 1977.

From 1974 to 1988, the trend of a smaller proportion of women obtaining abortions for the first time—75% of women in 1974 and 56% in 1988—continued. During this 15-year period, the percentage of women who had previously had one induced abortion increased from 10% to 26%, the percentage who had had two increased from about 1% to 10%, and the percentage who had had three or more increased from 0.4% to approximately 5%. These increases probably reflect the increasing number of women at risk of having more than one abortion and the fact that women who have had an abortion are more likely to have another one than are women who have never had one.[11, 12]

[7] Atrash HK, Lawson HW, Smith JC. *Legal abortion in the US: trends and mortality.* Contemp OB GYN 1990; 35: 58–69.

[8] Henshaw SK, Forrest JD, Van Vort J. *Abortion services in the United States, 1987 and 1988.* Fam Plann Perspect 1990; 22: 102–8.

[9] NCHS. *Advance report of final natality statistics, 1988. Monthly vital statistics report* 1990; 39(suppl): 4. Hyattsville, Maryland: US Department of Health and Human Services, Public Health Service, National Center for Health Statistics; DHHS Pub. No. (PHS) 90–1120.

[10] *Supra* note 4.

[11] Tietze C, Jain A. *The mathematics of repeat abortion: explaining the increase.* Stud Fam Plann 1978; 9: 294–9.

[12] Tietze C, Bougaarts J. *Repeat abortion in the United States: new insights.* Stud Fam Plann 1982; 13: 373–9.

Table 4. Reported Legal Abortions, by Age Group and State of Occurrence, Selected States,* 1988

State	<15 No.	%	15–19 No.	%	20–24 No.	%	25–29 No.	%	30–34 No.	%	35–39 No.	%	≥40 No.	%	Unknown No.	%	Total No.	%
Arizona	87	0.5	3,493	21.9	5,113	32.1	3,655	23.0	1,965	12.3	858	5.4	184	1.2	567	3.6	15,922	100.0
Arkansas	62	1.1	1,690	31.1	1,714	31.5	1,025	18.8	563	10.4	288	5.3	96	1.8	1	0.0	5,439	100.0
Colorado	76	0.6	3,106	25.0	3,851	31.0	2,636	21.2	1,608	12.9	820	6.6	213	1.7	115	0.9	12,425	100.0
Connecticut	159	0.8	5,183	25.6	6,684	33.1	4,248	21.0	2,270	11.2	1,059	5.2	309	1.5	307	1.5	20,219	100.0
Dist. of Col.	357	1.7	3,746	18.0	6,622	31.8	4,942	23.7	2,871	13.8	1,280	6.1	254	1.2	750	3.6	20,822	100.0
Georgia	393	1.1	8,824	25.1	11,644	33.1	7,665	21.8	4,226	12.0	1,960	5.6	493	1.4	8	0.0	35,213	100.0
Hawaii	38	0.6	1,288	21.3	1,840	30.5	1,412	23.4	842	13.9	485	8.0	133	2.2	2	0.0	6,040	100.0
Idaho	11	0.7	411	24.9	506	30.7	333	20.2	229	13.9	109	6.6	44	2.7	7	0.4	1,650	100.0
Indiana	135	1.1	3,079	24.8	4,176	33.6	2,492	20.1	1,431	11.5	718	5.8	180	1.5	200	1.6	12,411†	100.0
Kansas	69	0.9	2,405	31.9	2,361	31.3	1,438	19.1	776	10.3	385	5.1	99	1.3	1	0.0	7,534	100.0
Kentucky	155	1.3	3,568	30.7	3,838	33.0	2,030	17.5	1,186	10.2	593	5.1	146	1.3	115	1.0	11,631	100.0
Louisiana	187	1.2	3,577	23.3	4,815	31.3	3,325	21.6	2,056	13.4	1,075	7.0	267	1.7	65	0.4	15,367	100.0
Maine	29	0.6	1,460	30.9	1,480	31.3	872	18.5	474	10.0	231	4.9	68	1.4	109	2.3	4,723	100.0
Maryland	285	1.2	5,572	23.5	8,055	34.0	5,435	22.9	2,882	12.2	1,165	4.9	313	1.3	0	0.0	23,707	100.0
Massachusetts	186	0.5	9,827	25.3	11,473	29.5	8,455	21.8	4,695	12.1	2,601	6.7	843	2.2	761	2.0	38,841	100.0
Michigan	—§	0.0	12,900	28.4	14,895	32.8	9,391	20.7	5,196	11.4	2,392	5.3	570	1.3	94	0.2	45,438†	100.0
Minnesota	92	0.5	4,533	25.2	6,012	33.4	3,804	21.2	2,091	11.6	1,039	5.8	281	1.6	123	0.7	17,975	100.0
Mississippi	103	2.0	1,441	27.9	1,616	31.3	1,003	19.4	620	12.0	297	5.7	84	1.6	6	0.1	5,170	100.0
Missouri	194	1.1	4,022	23.1	5,855	33.7	3,795	21.8	2,149	12.4	1,072	6.2	291	1.7	4	0.0	17,382	100.0
Montana	18	0.6	833	29.1	847	29.6	555	19.4	350	12.2	195	6.8	62	2.2	6	0.2	2,866	100.0
Nebraska	34	0.6	1,725	28.7	1,937	32.3	1,233	20.5	616	10.3	362	6.0	99	1.6	0	0.0	6,006	100.0
Nevada	39	0.6	1,439	20.7	2,067	29.8	1,703	24.6	1,046	15.1	494	7.1	107	1.5	41	0.6	6,936	100.0
New Jersey	333	0.9	8,393	23.3	12,199	33.9	7,869	21.9	4,259	11.8	2,212	6.1	694	1.9	28	0.1	35,987	100.0
New Mexico	30	0.6	1,233	24.1	1,559	30.4	1,098	21.4	692	13.5	366	7.1	117	2.3	31	0.6	5,126	100.0
New York	1,092	0.8	30,110	21.1	46,052	32.2	32,199	22.5	18,295	12.8	9,109	6.4	2,608	1.8	3,397	2.4	142,862	100.0
(City)	785	0.9	16,728	18.6	27,959	31.0	21,555	23.9	12,646	14.0	6,162	6.8	1,750	1.9	2,552	2.8	90,137	100.0
(Upstate)	307	0.6	13,382	25.4	18,093	34.3	10,644	20.2	5,649	10.7	2,947	5.6	858	1.6	845	1.6	52,725	100.0
N. Carolina	482	1.3	10,672	28.4	12,473	33.1	7,294	19.4	3,962	10.5	1,835	4.9	449	1.2	462	1.2	37,629	100.0
N. Dakota	13	0.6	653	29.4	737	33.2	422	19.0	232	10.4	133	6.0	31	1.4	0	0.0	2,221	100.0

Age group (years)

State	<15		15–19		20–24		25–29		30–34		35–39		≥40		Unknown		Total	
	No.	%	No.	%	No.	%	No.	%	No.	%	No.	%	No.	%	No.	%	No.	%
Ohio	190	0.6	8,195	23.7	11,500	33.3	6,945	20.1	4,022	11.6	1,942	5.6	584	1.7	1,165	3.4	34,543	100.0
Oregon	69	0.5	3,586	26.9	4,192	31.5	2,727	20.5	1,649	12.4	849	6.4	187	1.4	50	0.4	13,309	100.0
Pennsylvania	511	1.0	13,595	26.8	16,173	31.8	10,464	20.6	6,201	12.2	2,997	5.9	826	1.6	19	0.0	50,786	100.0
Rhode Island	27	0.4	1,754	23.0	2,697	35.4	1,643	21.6	939	12.3	427	5.6	128	1.7	0	0.0	7,615	100.0
S. Carolina	137	1.0	3,880	27.5	4,651	32.9	2,891	20.5	1,670	11.8	711	5.0	192	1.4	1	0.0	14,133	100.0
South Dakota	7	0.8	245	27.3	292	32.5	184	20.5	99	11.0	50	5.6	21	2.3	0	0.0	898	100.0
Tennessee	202	0.9	5,946	27.5	6,990	32.4	4,424	20.5	2,418	11.2	1,261	5.8	329	1.5	19	0.1	21,589	100.0
Texas	398	0.5	16,564	20.3	26,772	32.9	19,518	24.0	11,227	13.8	5,413	6.6	1,568	1.9	14	0.0	81,474	100.0
Utah	35	0.7	1,154	24.4	1,539	32.5	1,052	22.2	594	12.6	268	5.7	76	1.6	14	0.3	4,732	100.0
Vermont	11	0.3	897	27.1	1,088	32.9	662	20.0	384	11.6	203	6.1	64	1.9	0	0.0	3,309	100.0
Virginia	297	0.9	8,442	24.8	11,191	32.9	7,316	21.5	4,190	12.3	2,003	5.9	537	1.6	53	0.2	34,029	100.0
Washington	187	0.6	7,073	23.7	9,527	32.0	6,692	22.5	3,834	12.9	1,977	6.6	497	1.7	15	0.1	29,802	100.0
Wisconsin	118	0.7	4,522	27.1	5,733	34.3	3,381	20.2	1,842	11.0	871	5.2	222	1.3	15	0.1	16,704†	100.0
Wyoming	9	2.6	102	29.1	97	27.6	66	18.8	38	10.8	32	9.1	4	1.1	3	0.9	351	100.0
Total	**6,857**	**0.8**	**211,138**	**24.2**	**282,863**	**32.5**	**188,294**	**21.6**	**106,689**	**12.3**	**52,137**	**6.0**	**14,270**	**1.6**	**8,568**	**1.0**	**870,816**	**100.0**
Abortion ratio¶	949		624		374		214		188		280		514				312	

* All states for which data were available (40), the District of Columbia, and New York City.

† Includes residents only.

§ Women <15 years were included with the 15–19 age group.

¶ Calculated as the number of legal abortions obtained by women in a given age group per 1,000 live births to women in the same age group for these states. For each state, women with unknown age are distributed according to known age distribution for that state. Excludes states reporting age unknown for >15% of women having abortions.

Table 5. Reported Legal Abortions Obtained by Teenagers, by Age, Selected States,* 1988

State	<15		15		16		17		18		19		Total	
	No.	%	No.	%	No.	%	No.	%	No.	%	No.	%	No.	%
Arizona	87	2.4	168	4.7	403	11.3	653	18.2	1,157	32.3	1,112	31.1	3,580	100.0
Arkansas	62	3.5	116	6.6	219	12.5	373	21.3	489	27.9	493	28.1	1,752	100.0
Colorado	76	2.4	199	6.3	421	13.2	707	22.2	900	28.3	879	27.6	3,182	100.0
Connecticut	159	3.0	276	5.2	756	14.2	1,272	23.8	1,463	27.4	1,416	26.5	5,342	100.0
Georgia	393	4.3	717	7.8	1,294	14.0	1,892	20.5	2,439	26.5	2,482	26.9	9,217	100.0
Hawaii	38	2.9	82	6.2	167	12.6	265	20.0	405	30.5	369	27.8	1,326	100.0
Idaho	11	2.6	26	6.2	50	11.8	62	14.7	135	32.0	138	32.7	422	100.0
Kansas	69	2.8	178	7.2	393	15.9	560	22.6	649	26.2	625	25.3	2,474	100.0
Kentucky	155	4.2	292	7.8	549	14.7	813	21.8	984	26.4	930	25.0	3,723	100.0
Louisiana	187	5.0	311	8.3	458	12.2	514	13.7	1,199	31.9	1,095	29.1	3,764	100.0
Maine	29	1.9	93	6.2	246	16.5	382	25.7	361	24.2	378	25.4	1,489	100.0
Maryland	285	4.9	423	7.2	801	13.7	1,160	19.8	1,521	26.0	1,667	28.5	5,857	100.0
Massachusetts	186	1.9	630	6.3	1,175	11.7	1,740	17.4	3,057	30.5	3,225	32.2	10,013	100.0
Minnesota	92	2.0	240	5.2	567	12.3	935	20.2	1,405	30.4	1,386	30.0	4,625	100.0
Mississippi	103	6.7	134	8.7	215	13.9	320	20.7	386	25.0	386	25.0	1,544	100.0
Missouri	194	4.6	300	7.1	497	11.8	593	14.1	1,322	31.4	1,310	31.1	4,216	100.0
Montana	18	2.1	50	5.9	134	15.7	210	24.7	242	28.4	197	23.1	851	100.0
Nebraska	34	1.9	95	5.4	221	12.6	377	21.4	498	28.3	534	30.4	1,759	100.0
Nevada	39	2.6	64	4.3	176	11.9	310	21.0	468	31.7	421	28.5	1,478	100.0
New Mexico	30	2.4	80	6.3	186	14.7	287	22.7	348	27.6	332	26.3	1,263	100.0
New York (City)	1,092	3.5	1,826	5.9	3,950	12.7	6,411	20.5	8,787	28.2	9,136	29.3	31,202	100.0
(Upstate)	785	4.5	1,179	6.7	2,314	13.2	3,582	20.5	4,612	26.3	5,041	28.8	17,513	100.0
N. Carolina	307	2.2	647	4.7	1,636	12.0	2,829	20.7	4,175	30.5	4,095	29.9	13,689	100.0
N. Dakota	482	4.3	750	6.7	1,574	14.1	2,350	21.1	3,028	27.1	2,970	26.6	11,154	100.0
Oregon	13	2.0	24	3.6	43	6.5	103	15.5	262	39.3	221	33.2	666	100.0
Pennsylvania	69	1.9	219	6.0	500	13.7	763	20.9	1,098	30.0	1,006	27.5	3,655	100.0
Rhode Island	511	3.6	855	6.1	1,702	12.1	2,820	20.0	4,174	29.6	4,044	28.7	14,106	100.0
S. Carolina	27	1.5	70	3.9	154	8.6	252	14.1	637	35.8	641	36.0	1,781	100.0
	137	3.4	270	6.7	580	14.4	870	21.7	1,057	26.3	1,103	27.5	4,017	100.0

Age (years)

	Age (years)													
	<15		15		16		17		18		19		Total	
State	No.	%	No.	%	No.	%	No.	%	No.	%	No.	%	No.	%
South Dakota	7	2.8	17	6.7	33	13.1	56	22.2	70	27.8	69	27.4	252	100.0
Tennessee	202	3.3	406	6.6	778	12.7	1,244	20.2	1,847	30.0	1,671	27.2	6,148	100.0
Texas	398	2.3	829	4.9	1,881	11.1	3,333	19.6	4,876	28.7	5,645	33.3	16,962	100.0
Utah	35	2.9	72	6.1	141	11.9	208	17.5	387	32.5	346	29.1	1,189	100.0
Vermont	11	1.2	54	5.9	114	12.6	188	20.7	262	28.9	279	30.7	908	100.0
Virginia	297	3.4	580	6.6	1,138	13.0	1,776	20.3	2,536	29.0	2,412	27.6	8,739	100.0
Washington	187	2.6	403	5.6	891	12.3	1,540	21.2	2,116	29.1	2,123	29.2	7,260	100.0
Wisconsin	118	2.5	276	5.9	601	13.0	966	20.8	1,330	28.7	1,349	29.1	4,640†	100.0
Wyoming	9	8.1	9	8.1	15	13.5	23	20.7	31	27.9	24	21.6	111	100.0
Total	**5,842**	**3.2**	**11,134**	**6.2**	**23,023**	**12.7**	**36,328**	**20.1**	**51,926**	**28.7**	**52,414**	**29.0**	**180,667**	**100.0**
Abortion ratio¶	978		767		728		654		666		535		637	

* All states for which data were available (36) and New York City.

† Includes residents only.

¶ Calculated as the number of legal abortions obtained by women in a given age per 1,000 live births to women in the same age for these states. For each state, women with unknown age are distributed according to known age distribution for that state. Excludes states reporting age unknown for >15% of women having abortions.

Table 6. Reported Legal Abortions, by Weeks of Gestation and State of Occurrence, Selected States,* 1988

| | Weeks of gestation | | | | | | | | | | | | | | | |
| State | <8 | | 9–10 | | 11–12 | | 13–15 | | 16–20 | | ≥21 | | Unknown | | Total | |
	No.	%	No.	%	No.	%	No.	%	No.	%	No.	%	No.	%	No.	%
Arizona†	6,905	43.4	4,759	29.9	2,400	15.1	1,026	6.4	613	3.9	55	0.3	164	1.0	15,922	100.0
Arkansas	2,891	53.2	1,568	28.8	551	10.1	269	4.9	104	1.9	6	0.1	50	0.9	5,439	100.0
Colorado	4,528	36.4	4,194	33.8	2,144	17.3	926	7.5	490	3.9	110	0.9	33	0.3	12,425	100.0
Connecticut†	9,146	45.2	7,060	34.9	2,046	10.1	1,365	6.8	221	1.1	11	0.1	370	1.8	20,219	100.0
Dist. of Col.	9,919	47.6	4,713	22.6	2,592	12.4	1,589	7.6	987	4.7	47	0.2	975	4.7	20,822	100.0
Georgia	12,463	35.4	9,835	27.9	5,899	16.8	3,030	8.6	1,734	4.9	674	1.9	1,578	4.5	35,213	100.0
Hawaii	3,326	55.1	1,340	22.2	653	10.8	327	5.4	350	5.8	31	0.5	13	0.2	6,040	100.0
Idaho	568	34.4	690	41.8	334	20.2	12	0.7	8	0.5	1	0.1	37	2.2	1,650	100.0
Kansas	2,763	36.7	2,013	26.7	1,376	18.3	477	6.3	572	7.6	308	4.1	25	0.3	7,534	100.0
Kentucky	5,100	43.8	2,245	19.3	1,225	10.5	1,203	10.3	1,382	11.9	393	3.4	83	0.7	11,631	100.0
Louisiana	7,566	49.2	3,883	25.3	1,693	11.0	960	6.2	970	6.3	172	1.1	123	0.8	15,367	100.0
Maine†	1,956	41.4	1,364	28.9	715	15.1	455	9.6	143	3.0	0	0.0	90	1.9	4,723	100.0
Maryland†	11,779	49.7	6,516	27.5	2,998	12.6	1,283	5.4	1,054	4.4	49	0.2	28	0.1	23,707	100.0
Minnesota	9,242	51.4	4,175	23.2	2,256	12.6	1,259	7.0	853	4.7	162	0.9	28	0.2	17,975	100.0
Mississippi	2,424	46.9	1,375	26.6	740	14.3	377	7.3	112	2.2	10	0.2	132	2.6	5,170	100.0
Missouri	6,852	39.4	5,237	30.1	2,922	16.8	1,152	6.6	558	3.2	75	0.4	586	3.4	17,382	100.0
Montana†	1,665	58.1	583	20.3	407	14.2	128	4.5	75	2.6	0	0.0	8	0.3	2,866	100.0
Nevada	4,334	62.5	1,477	21.3	576	8.3	333	4.8	170	2.5	12	0.2	34	0.5	6,936	100.0
New Jersey	18,559	51.6	7,652	21.3	3,197	8.9	3,321	9.2	2,981	8.3	277	0.8	0	0.0	35,987	100.0
New Mexico	2,656	51.8	1,274	24.9	544	10.6	319	6.2	280	5.5	15	0.3	38	0.7	5,126	100.0
New York	67,439	47.2	35,068	24.5	17,126	12.0	9,934	7.0	7,316	5.1	2,534	1.8	3,445	2.4	142,862	100.0
(City)	41,198	45.7	21,215	23.5	10,957	12.2	6,813	7.6	5,816	6.5	2,272	2.5	1,866	2.1	90,137	100.0
(Upstate)	26,241	49.8	13,853	26.3	6,169	11.7	3,121	5.9	1,500	2.8	262	0.5	1,579	3.0	52,725	100.0
N. Carolina	17,049	45.3	9,323	24.8	5,314	14.1	3,129	8.3	1,252	3.3	115	0.3	1,447	3.8	37,629	100.0
N. Dakota	1,360	61.2	457	20.6	255	11.5	142	6.4	5	0.2	0	0.0	2	0.1	2,221	100.0
Oregon	6,385	48.0	3,754	28.2	1,692	12.7	721	5.4	461	3.5	211	1.6	85	0.6	13,309	100.0
Rhode Island	3,242	42.6	2,677	35.2	1,117	14.7	457	6.0	114	1.5	8	0.1	0	0.0	7,615	100.0
S. Carolina†	8,598	60.8	3,732	26.4	1,724	12.2	30	0.2	26	0.2	21	0.1	2	0.0	14,133	100.0
S. Dakota	473	52.7	381	42.4	40	4.5	4	0.4	0	0.0	0	0.0	0	0.0	898	100.0

Weeks of gestation

State	<8		9–10		11–12		13–15		16–20		≥21		Unknown		Total	
	No.	%	No.	%	No.	%	No.	%	No.	%	No.	%	No.	%	No.	%
Tennessee	8,035	37.2	7,379	34.2	4,045	18.7	1,485	6.9	180	0.8	57	0.3	408	1.9	21,589	100.0
Texas	39,871	48.9	20,796	25.5	9,757	12.0	5,216	6.4	4,387	5.4	1,391	1.7	56	0.1	81,474	100.0
Utah	3,180	67.2	757	16.0	350	7.4	236	5.0	165	3.5	0	0.0	44	0.9	4,732	100.0
Vermont†	1,820	55.0	947	28.6	411	12.4	112	3.4	13	0.4	5	0.2	1	0.0	3,309	100.0
Virginia†	19,450	57.2	8,899	26.2	4,141	12.2	560	1.6	792	2.3	138	0.4	49	0.1	34,029	100.0
Washington†	17,350	58.2	6,993	23.5	2,548	8.5	1,335	4.5	1,164	3.9	396	1.3	16	0.1	29,802	100.0
Wisconsin†	8,388	50.2	4,366	26.1	1,870	11.2	1,173	7.0	734	4.4	173	1.0	0	0.0	16,704§	100.0
Wyoming†	187	53.3	138	39.3	22	6.3	1	0.3	0	0.0	0	0.0	3	0.9	351	100.0
Total	**327,469**	**48.0**	**177,620**	**26.0**	**85,680**	**12.5**	**44,346**	**6.5**	**30,266**	**4.4**	**7,457**	**1.1**	**9,953**	**1.5**	**682,791**	**100.0**

* All states for which data were available (34), the District of Columbia, and New York City.

† Weeks of gestation is physician's estimate.

§ Includes residents only.

Table 7. Reported Legal Abortions, by Type of Procedure and State of Occurrence, Selected States,* 1988

					Procedure												
	Suction curettage		Sharp curettage		All curettage		Intrauterine saline instillation		Intrauterine prostaglandin instillation		Hysterotomy/ hysterectomy		Other†		Unknown		Total	
State	No.	%	No.	%	No.	%	No.	%	No.	%	No.	%	No.	%	No.	%	No.	%
Arizona	15,621	98.1	5	0.0	15,626	98.1	1	0.0	0	0.0	0	0.0	3	0.0	292	1.8	15,922	100.0
Arkansas	3,031	55.7	2,359	43.4	5,390	99.1	0	0.0	6	0.1	2	0.0	5	0.1	36	0.7	5,439	100.0
Colorado	11,887	95.7	27	0.2	11,914	95.9	9	0.1	90	0.7	4	0.0	392	3.2	16	0.1	12,425	100.0
Connecticut	19,952§	98.7	2	0.0	19,954	98.7	2	0.0	—	—	0	0.0	14	0.1	249	1.2	20,219	100.0
Dist. of Col.	19,709	94.7	81	0.4	19,790	95.0	295	1.4	0	0.0	0	0.0	2	0.0	735	3.5	20,822	100.0
Georgia	30,564	86.8	3,586	10.2	34,150	97.0	141	0.4	775	2.2	22	0.1	103	0.3	22	0.1	35,213	100.0
Hawaii	5,939	98.3	14	0.2	5,953	98.6	0	0.0	50	0.8	1	0.0	31	0.5	5	0.1	6,040	100.0
Idaho	1,648	99.9	0	0.0	1,648	99.9	0	0.0	1	0.1	0	0.0	1	0.1	0	0.0	1,650	100.0
Indiana	11,864	95.6	33	0.3	11,897	95.9	22	0.2	1	0.0	—	—	337¶	2.7	154	1.2	12,411**	100.0
Kansas	7,521	99.8	6	0.1	7,527	99.9	0	0.0	2	0.0	1	0.0	3	0.0	1	0.0	7,534	100.0
Kentucky	11,327††	97.4	222	1.9	11,549	99.3	4	0.0	0	0.0	0	0.0	2	0.0	76	0.7	11,631	100.0
Louisiana	14,496††	94.3	45	0.3	14,541	94.6	1	0.0	0	0.0	1	0.0	32	0.2	792	5.2	15,367	100.0
Maine	4,651††	98.5	44	0.9	4,695	99.4	0	0.0	0	0.0	0	0.0	28	0.6	0	0.0	4,723	100.0
Maryland	22,612	95.4	125	0.5	22,737	95.9	160	0.7	448	1.9	7	0.0	352	1.5	3	0.0	23,707	100.0
Massachusetts	37,726	97.1	182	0.5	37,908	97.6	393	1.0	520	1.3	0	0.0	20	0.1	0	0.0	38,841	100.0
Michigan	44,994	96.3	379	0.8	45,373	97.1	1,350	2.9	23	0.0	0	0.0	1	0.0	0	0.0	46,747	100.0
Minnesota	17,972††	100.0	2	0.0	17,974	100.0	0	0.0	0	0.0	0	0.0	1	0.0	0	0.0	17,975	100.0
Mississippi	5,138	99.4	6	0.1	5,144	99.5	0	0.0	21	0.4	4	0.1	1	0.0	0	0.0	5,170	100.0
Missouri	17,218	99.1	10	0.1	17,228	99.1	0	0.0	3	0.0	0	0.0	17	0.1	134	0.8	17,382	100.0
Montana	2,802	97.8	1	0.0	2,803	97.8	0	0.0	0	0.0	0	0.0	63	2.2	0	0.0	2,866	100.0
Nebraska	5,992	99.7	6	0.1	5,998	99.8	0	0.0	0	0.0	0	0.0	4	0.1	11	0.2	6,013§§	100.0
Nevada	6,616	95.4	7	0.1	6,623	95.5	64	0.9	2	0.0	0	0.0	2	0.0	245	3.5	6,936	100.0
New Jersey	28,062	78.0	7,375	20.5	35,437	98.5	421	1.2	83	0.2	12	0.0	27	0.1	7	0.0	35,987	100.0
New Mexico	5,102	99.5	3	0.1	5,105	99.6	0	0.0	0	0.0	0	0.0	0	0.0	21	0.4	5,126	100.0
New York	135,947	91.9	5,925	4.0	141,872	95.9	2,062	1.4	491	0.3	8	0.0	260	0.2	3,204	2.2	147,897	100.0
(City)	83,638††	92.8	2,131	2.4	85,769	95.2	1,345	1.5	209	0.2	2	0.0	32	0.0	2,780	3.1	90,137	100.0
(Upstate)	52,309††	90.6	3,794	6.6	56,103	97.1	717	1.2	282	0.5	6	0.0	228	0.4	424	0.7	57,760§§	100.0

Procedure

State	Suction curettage No.	Suction curettage %	Sharp curettage No.	Sharp curettage %	All curettage No.	All curettage %	Intrauterine saline instillation No.	Intrauterine saline instillation %	Intrauterine prostaglandin instillation No.	Intrauterine prostaglandin instillation %	Hysterotomy/ hysterectomy No.	Hysterotomy/ hysterectomy %	Other† No.	Other† %	Unknown No.	Unknown %	Total No.	Total %
N. Carolina	36,206	96.2	114	0.3	36,320	96.5	406	1.1	322	0.9	7	0.0	513	1.4	61	0.2	37,629	100.0
N. Dakota	2,220	100.0	0	0.0	2,220	100.0	0	0.0	0	0.0	0	0.0	0	0.0	1	0.0	2,221	100.0
Ohio	31,885	77.2	9,429	22.8	41,314	100.0	0	0.0	0	0.0	0	0.0	0	0.0	0	0.0	41,314	100.0
Oregon	13,121††	98.6	1	0.0	13,122	98.6	1	0.0	0	0.0	0	0.0	47	0.4	139	1.0	13,309	100.0
Pennsylvania	50,188††	98.8	68	0.1	50,256	99.0	471	0.9	41	0.1	1	0.0	17	0.0	0	0.0	50,786	100.0
Rhode Island	7,593	99.7	8	0.1	7,601	99.8	1	0.0	5	0.1	0	0.0	3	0.0	5	0.1	7,615	100.0
S. Carolina	14,070	99.6	7	0.0	14,077	99.6	11	0.1	32	0.2	4	0.0	9	0.1	0	0.0	14,133	100.0
S. Dakota	897	99.9	0	0.0	897	99.9	0	0.0	0	0.0	0	0.0	1	0.1	0	0.0	898	100.0
Tennessee	21,514	99.7	15	0.1	21,529	99.7	7	0.0	42	0.2	5	0.0	0	0.0	6	0.0	21,589	100.0
Texas	81,087††	99.5	0	0.0	81,087	99.5	344	0.4	0	0.0	5	0.0	0	0.0	38	0.0	81,474	100.0
Utah	4,726††	99.9	3	0.1	4,729	99.9	0	0.0	0	0.0	2	0.0	0	0.0	1	0.0	4,732	100.0
Vermont	3,290	99.4	1	0.0	3,291	99.5	1	0.0	0	0.0	0	0.0	17	0.5	0	0.0	3,309	100.0
Virginia	33,109	97.3	34	0.1	33,143	97.4	57	0.2	38	0.1	18	0.1	170	0.5	603	1.8	34,029	100.0
Washington	29,593††	99.3	12	0.0	29,605	99.3	94	0.3	91	0.3	4	0.0	4	0.0	4	0.0	29,802	100.0
Wyoming	348	99.1	0	0.0	348	99.1	0	0.0	0	0.0	0	0.0	0	0.0	3	0.9	351	100.0
Total	**818,238**	**94.4**	**30,137**	**3.5**	**848,375**	**97.8**	**6,318**	**0.7**	**3,087**	**0.4**	**108**	**0.0**	**2,482**	**0.3**	**6,846**	**0.8**	**867,234**	**100.0**

*All states for which data were available (39), the District of Columbia, and New York City.

†Includes instillation procedures not reported as a specific category and procedures reported as "other."

§Includes abortions performed by both suction and sharp curettage.

¶Reported as "all other procedures."

**Includes residents only.

††Includes dilatation and evacuation procedures.

§§Does not add to total abortions because of some reported combination procedures.

— Not reported.

Table 13. Number and Percentage of Reported Legal Abortions, by Race, Age Group, and Marital Status, 1988

Age group and marital status*	Race					
	White		Black/other		Total	
	No.	%	No.	%	No.	%
Age group (years)						
<15	2,328	0.6	2,922	1.4	5,250	0.8
15–19	103,835	25.0	46,372	22.2	150,207	24.1
20–24	135,931	32.7	69,905	33.5	205,836	33.0
25–29	89,314	21.5	47,894	22.9	137,208	22.0
30–34	50,795	12.2	26,814	12.8	77,609	12.4
35–39	25,777	6.2	12,076	5.8	37,853	6.1
⩾40	7,432	1.8	2,941	1.4	10,373	1.7
Total†	**415,412**	**100.0**	**208,924**	**100.0**	**624,336**	**100.0**
Marital status						
Married	80,596	20.9	36,694	18.6	117,290	20.1
Unmarried	305,784	79.1	160,619	81.4	466,403	79.9
Total§	**386,380**	**100.0**	**197,313**	**100.0**	**583,693**	**100.0**

*Excludes unknowns.

†Reported by 32 states and New York City.

§Reported by 31 states and New York City.

Between 1972 and 1988, the percentage of abortions performed by curettage increased from 89% to almost 99%. Surveillance during the same period showed a sharp decline in the percentage of abortions performed by intrauterine instillation (from 10% to 1%) and by hysterectomy and hysterotomy (from 0.6% to 0.01%).

Between 1975 and 1988, the percentage of second-trimester abortions performed by D&E increased from 33% to 88%, whereas the percentage of second-trimester abortions that were performed by intrauterine instillation decreased from 57% to 9%. The increasing use of D&E may result from the improved technology and the lower risk of complications associated with the procedure.[13,14]

For the first time, this report analyzes women having abortions by age, race, and weeks of gestation and includes data on residence and educational status from data reported to NCHS. The abortion data collected through the NCHS data system in selected states may not be representative of all women who obtained abortions in 1988. However, the information on residence and educational status provides an additional characterization of women who use abortion services in certain states.

[13] Cates W Jr, Schulz KF, Grimes DA, et al. *Dilatation and evacuation procedures and second-trimester abortion: the role of physician skill and hospital setting.* JAMA 1982; 248: 559–63.

[14] Grimes DA. *Second-trimester abortions in the United States.* Fam Plann Perspect 1984; 16: 260–6.

Table 14. Number and Percentage of Reported Legal Abortions, by Weeks of Gestation, Age Group, and Race, 1988

Age group and race*	Weeks of gestation																		
	≤8		9–10		11–12		13–15		16–20		≥21		Total	
	No.	%	No.	%	No.	%	No.	%	No.	%	No.	%	No.	%
Age group (years)														
<15	1,679	31.7	1,365	25.8	832	15.7	640	12.1	590	11.1	190	3.6	5,296	100.0
15–19	63,599	40.8	42,609	27.3	23,620	15.1	13,519	8.7	9,877	6.3	2,684	1.7	155,908	100.0
20–24	100,271	47.0	57,901	27.1	28,354	13.3	14,698	6.9	9,701	4.5	2,400	1.1	213,325	100.0
25–29	74,621	52.4	37,354	26.2	16,616	11.7	7,822	5.5	4,950	3.5	1,132	0.8	142,495	100.0
30–34	45,409	56.3	20,213	25.1	8,334	10.3	3,684	4.6	2,410	3.0	553	0.7	80,603	100.0
35–39	23,106	58.8	9,472	24.1	3,672	9.3	1,576	4.0	1,180	3.0	278	0.7	39,284	100.0
≥40	6,332	58.9	2,573	23.9	985	9.2	445	4.1	324	3.0	95	0.9	10,754	100.0
Total†	**315,017**	**48.6**	**171,487**	**26.5**	**82,413**	**12.7**	**42,384**	**6.5**	**29,032**	**4.5**	**7,332**	**1.1**	**647,665**	**100.0**
Race														
White	205,975	51.0	105,703	26.2	48,454	12.0	23,566	5.8	16,158	4.0	4,349	1.1	404,205	100.0
Black/other	90,272	44.0	53,728	26.2	29,815	14.5	16,326	8.0	12,095	5.9	2,843	1.4	205,079	100.0
Total§	**296,247**	**48.6**	**159,431**	**26.2**	**78,269**	**12.8**	**39,892**	**6.5**	**28,253**	**4.6**	**7,192**	**1.2**	**609,284**	**100.0**

*Excludes unknowns.

† Reported by 34 states and New York City.

§ Reported by 32 states and New York City.

Figure 3. Percentage of Women Having Early and Late Abortions,* by Age Group and Race, United States, 1988

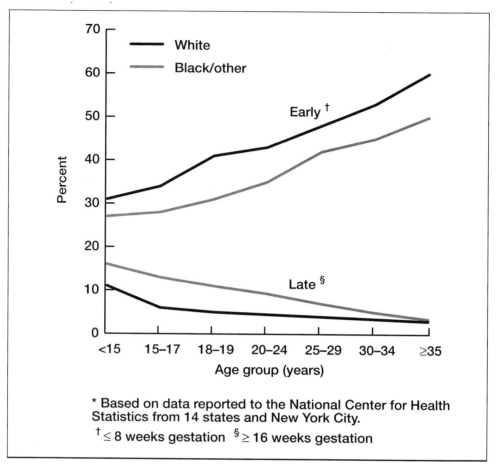

* Based on data reported to the National Center for Health Statistics from 14 states and New York City.

[†] ≤ 8 weeks gestation   [§] ≥ 16 weeks gestation

Previous reports have found, as did this study, that age is inversely correlated with the timing of abortion.[15] Moreover, other studies have found that black women have abortions later than white women do.[16]

The abortion ratio was higher for women residing in metropolitan areas than in nonmetropolitan areas. This difference was especially marked for minority women. Other studies have consistently found higher use of abortion services among metropolitan women.[17–19] Access to local abortion services varies widely by geographic area of the

[15] Tietze C, Henshaw SK. *Induced abortion: a world review*. 6th ed. New York: The Alan Guttmacher Institute, 1986.

[16] Kochanek, KD. *Induced terminations of pregnancy: reporting states, 1987. Monthly vital statistics report* 1989; 38(suppl): 9. Hyattsville, Maryland: US Department of Health and Human Services, Public Health Service, National Center for Health Statistics; DHHS publication no. (PHS)90-1120.

[17] Id.

Figure 4. Abortion Ratio* among Women Ages ≥25 Years, by Education and Race, United States, 1988

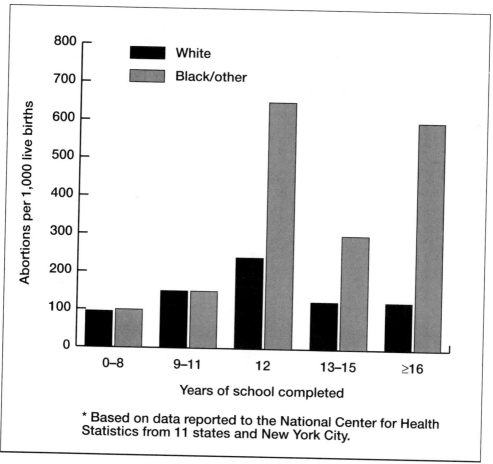

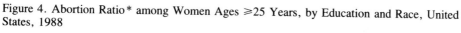

*Based on data reported to the National Center for Health Statistics from 11 states and New York City.

country. In 1988, only 17% of women ages 15–44 years residing in nonmetropolitan counties lived in a county where there was an abortion provider, whereas 84% of women residing in metropolitan counties had such access.[20] Distance needed to travel to seek an abortion provider may affect use of such services.

Other studies have found, as did this study, that women with 12 years of education were more likely to have an abortion than were women with < 12 years of education.[21] This relation was true for women of all races and was previously found for women

[18] Griner-Powell E, Trent K. *Sociodemographic determinants of abortion in the United States.* Demography 1987; 24: 553–61.

[19] Henshaw SK, Silverman J. *The characteristics and prior contraceptive use of U.S. abortion patients.* Fam Plann Perspect 1988; 20: 158–68.

[20] *Supra* note 8.

[21] *Supra* note 18.

residing in the NCHS reporting areas.[22] However, minority women who completed college had an abortion ratio substantially higher than that of women who had some college (13–15 years); this unexplained finding has not been previously observed and may have resulted from population trends in the limited number of states reporting this information. As shown in this and in previous studies, better-educated women had abortions earlier in gestation than did women with limited education.[23,24] Future studies that examine educational level and other socioeconomic factors can provide an increased understanding of the characteristics of women obtaining abortions in the United States.

---

[22] Kochanek KD. *Induced terminations of pregnancy: reporting states, 1985 and 1986. Monthly vital statistics report* 1989; 37(suppl): 12. Hyattsville, Maryland: US Department of Health and Human Services, Public Health Service, National Center for Health Statistics; DHHS publication no. (PHS)89-1120. Also, *supra* note 16.

[23] Burr WA, Schultz KF. *Delayed abortion in an area of easy accessibility.* JAMA 1980; 244: 44–8.

[24] Fielding WL, Sachtleben MR, Friedman LM, Friedman EA. *Comparison of women seeking early and late abortion.* Am J Obstet Gynecol 1978; 131: 304–10.

Between 1973 and 1976, the number of abortions performed in the United States rose drastically as a result of the legalization of abortion. Between 1976 and 1980, the number of abortions continued to rise gradually, and between 1980 and 1988, the number has been relatively stable, with slight fluctuations. Approximately 1.6 million abortions are performed each year, and almost all of them are performed in metropolitan areas. In 1988, 90% of all abortion providers were located in metropolitan counties, making it difficult for women living in rural communities to gain access to these services. In 1977, 1,654 hospitals offered abortion services, in contrast to the 1988 figure of 1,040 hospitals offering these services. This decline has had a particularly detrimental effect on women who do not live in cities because hospitals are the predominant places offering abortion services in nonmetropolitan areas.

18 · Abortion Services in the United States, 1987 and 1988

Stanley K. Henshaw, Ph.D.* and Jennifer Van Vort

Introduction

Although induced abortion was legalized nationally in the United States by the Supreme Court decisions of 1973, abortion services did not automatically become available in all parts of the country. In many areas, physicians were slow to offer the services, and most hospitals either prohibited the procedures or had no affiliated physicians who chose to perform them. In 1974, in response to concerns about the availability of abortion services, The Alan Guttmacher Institute (AGI) conducted the first of a series of periodic surveys of all identifiable abortion providers in the country. These Abortion Provider Surveys were designed to obtain information about abortion service providers as well as the number of procedures performed. The last published report is based on the 1986 survey and covers the years 1984 and 1985.[1]

The AGI surveys have shown that gaps in service caused by the unwillingness of most hospitals and physicians to perform abortions have been partly filled by free-standing clinics and by a few private physicians who perform the procedure in their offices, but that in many geographic areas, women live dozens or even hundreds of miles from the nearest abortion provider. Information from the surveys on the extent to which

---

*Stanley K. Henshaw is deputy director of research. Coauthor Jennifer Van Vort is senior research assistant at The Alan Guttmacher Institute. The authors would like to thank senior research assistant Theresa Camelo for her invaluable assistance with this project. The research on which this article is based was funded in large part by The Robert Sterling Clark Foundation, The David and Lucile Packard Foundation and an anonymous foundation. .

[1] S. K. Henshaw, J. D. Forrest and J. Van Vort, *Abortion Services in the United States, 1984 and 1985*, Family Planning Perspectives, 19: 63, 1987.

American women have recourse to abortion has proved useful in assessing teenage pregnancy rates[2] and calculating contraceptive failure probabilities.[3] Presented here are the results of the tenth survey, including new information on service availability and utilization for 1987 and 1988.

Methodology

In June 1989, questionnaires were mailed to all hospitals, clinics and physicians' offices where abortions were believed to have been performed in 1987 or 1988. The mailing list included all facilities surveyed in 1986, except those that did not perform abortions in 1985 or were known to have closed before 1987, as well as possible new providers. The latter were suggested by affiliates of Planned Parenthood and the National Abortion Rights Action League, which supplied names of additional doctors and facilities in their areas believed to offer abortion services. Others were identified through the Yellow Pages of major cities and the membership directory of the National Abortion Federation, and from newspaper articles. These methods yielded 3,422 possible providers.

The questionnaire asked, among other questions, if these facilities provided abortions, and if so, the number of induced abortions (including endometrial aspirations and menstrual regulations) performed in 1987 and 1988. Facilities that did not respond to the first mailing were sent as many as three additional questionnaires. State health department data were used, when available, to provide missing information on the numbers of abortions performed in individual facilities. The remaining nonrespondents were contacted by telephone; in some cases, a dozen or more calls were necessary before data were obtained or a final refusal received. Because antiabortion harassment has made some providers increasingly reluctant to release data pertaining to abortion, efforts were more intensive than in previous surveys. Health departments provided information on an additional 76 providers that had not previously been identified, bringing the total to 3,498 known or possible providers.

Information about the availability and number of abortions was obtained from the providers themselves or from the state health departments for 3,169 facilities. The remaining 329 facilities either did not respond to requests for data (265) or had closed or moved and could not be located (64). For 97 of these providers, estimates of the number of abortions performed in 1987 and 1988 were obtained from knowledgeable sources in the community. These tended to be smaller providers, and together they represent only 1.1 percent of the abortions counted. We estimated data for an additional 70 facilities that did not respond but which we were sure provided abortions, including a large organization with 22 locations mainly in Southern California, and 48 other providers. Because of the large number of abortions involved and because some earlier data on these providers were available, we projected the number of abortions performed, using data from previous years and taking into account trends over time. Estimations for these 70 providers represent 8.2 percent of all abortions in 1988.

The remaining 162 facilities for which no data or estimates are available had provided about 9,000 abortions in 1985, although some of these facilities had not responded

[2]S. K. Henshaw et. al., *Teenage Pregnancy in the United States: The Scope of the Problem and State Responses,* The Alan Guttmacher Institute, New York, 1989.

[3]E. F. Jones and J. D. Forrest, *Contraceptive Failure in the United States: Revised Estimates from the 1982 National Survey of Family Growth,* Family Planning Perspectives, 21: 115, 1989.

that year either. No projections were made for these facilities and they were not counted as providers in 1987–1988. Some additional providers were undoubtedly missed because they were not identified. Most of the overlooked providers are probably small ones, since facilities where large numbers of abortions are performed are generally known to those in the area who are involved in issues related to women's health and abortion. In an earlier study comparing results from the AGI's Abortion Provider Survey with an independent survey of private physicians, we estimated that the provider survey may have missed some 110,000 abortions performed in physicians' offices in 1982, for an overall undercount of 6.5 percent.[4] The undercount in the current survey is likely to be similar.[5] (Such undercounts may be partly offset, however, by two factors: Overcounting may occur when abortion facilities are listed under two different names and counted twice; and, according to previous surveys, physicians tend to overestimate the number of abortions they provide.)

Over the years, the number of abortions reported to the AGI has been higher in every survey than the number reported by the Centers for Disease Control (CDC), the other source of national data on abortion.[6] The amount by which the AGI national abortion counts exceed those of the CDC ranges from 18 percent in 1977 and 1978 to 13 percent in 1987. The CDC data for most states are obtained from state health departments, some of which do not receive information from all providers and may receive incomplete information from others. The AGI figures for most states and for the nation as a whole are therefore believed to be more accurate.

Trends in U.S. Abortion Statistics

From 1973 to 1976, the number of abortions performed in the United States rose sharply as legal abortion services became available, thereby supplanting the numbers of both illegal abortions and unplanned births (Table 1). Between 1976 and 1980, the number of abortions continued to rise gradually, probably reflecting an increase in the number of unplanned pregnancies. However, the annual number of abortions has been remarkably stable since 1980; year-to-year fluctuations between 1980 and 1988 were small enough to be within the margin of error of the surveys. Results of the latest survey show that in 1988, as in each of the previous eight years, approximately 1.6 million abortions were performed. From the late 1960s, when states began to liberalize their laws, through 1988, 23.6 million legal abortions have been performed; 22.3 million of these occurred since *Roe v. Wade* was decided in 1973.

Almost all abortions in the United States occur in metropolitan areas. In 1988, only 27,000 or 1.7 percent, took place in nonmetropolitan counties; this represents a continued decrease from a peak of 67,000 (4.5 percent) in 1979. The abortion rate in 1988 was 27 per 1,000 women aged 15–44, slightly lower than the rate in 1985 (28 per

---

[4] S. K. Henshaw, J. D. Forrest and E. Blaine, *Abortion Services in the United States, 1981 and 1982*, Family Planning Perspectives, 16: 119, 1984.

[5] For a more detailed explanation of the survey methodology, which was essentially the same as that used in 1986, and for state and national statistics for previous years, see S. K. Henshaw and J. Van Vort, eds., *Abortion Services in the United States, Each State and Metropolitan Area, 1984–1985*, The Alan Guttmacher Institute, New York, 1988, pp. 71–118.

[6] Centers for Disease Control, *Abortion Surveillance: Preliminary Analysis—United States, 1986 and 1987*, Morbidity and Mortality Weekly Report, 38: 662, 1989; and H. W. Lawson et al., *Abortion Surveillance—United States, 1984–1985*, CDC Surveillance Summaries, Vol. 38, No. SS-2, Sept. 1989, p. 11.

Table 1. Number of Reported Abortions, by Metropolitan Status; Rate of Abortions per 1,000 Women Aged 15–44; and Ratio of Abortions per 100 Pregnancies Ending in Abortions or Live Births; United States, 1973–1988

Year	No. of abortions (in 000s)			Rate	Ratio*
	Total	Metro†	Nonmetro		
1973	744.6	720.2	24.4	16.3	19.3
1974	898.6	860.7	37.9	19.3	22.0
1975	1,034.2	985.7	48.5	21.7	24.9
1976	1,179.3	1,123.3	56.0	24.2	26.5
1977	1,316.7	1,258.0	58.7	26.4	28.6
1978	1,409.6	1,345.2	64.4	27.7	29.2
1979	1,497.7	1,430.9	66.8	28.8	29.6
1980	1,553.9	1,507.7	46.2	29.3	30.0
1981	1,577.3	1,538.3	39.0	29.3	30.1
1982	1,573.9	1,537.3	36.6	28.8	30.3
1983	(1,575.0)	u	u	(28.5)	(30.4)
1984	1,577.2	1,543.9	33.3	28.1	29.7
1985	1,588.6	1,556.4	32.2	28.0	29.7
1986	(1,574.0)	u	u	(27.4)	(29.4)
1987	1,559.1	1,532.0	27.1	26.9	28.9
1988	1,590.8	1,563.4	27.4	27.3	28.8

*For each year, the ratio is based on births occurring during the 12-month period starting in July of that year (to match times of conception for pregnancies ending in births with those for pregnancies ending in abortions).

†For 1973–1979, metropolitan status has been defined according to criteria published by the Office of Management and Budget (OMB), Oct. 1975. For 1980–1988, definitions by the OMB based on the 1980 census have been used.

Notes: Figures in parentheses are estimated by interpolation of numbers of abortions; u = unavailable.

Sources: **Abortion by metropolitan status**—1973–1985: see reference 1, Table 1. 1987–1988; AGI Abortion Provider Survey. **Population data**—1973–1985: see reference 1, Table 1. 1986–1988: U.S. Bureau of the Census, *State Population and Household Estimates with Age, Sex, and Components of Change: 1981–88*, Current Population Reports, Series P–25, No. 1044, 1989, Tables 7–8. **Birth data**—1973–1984: see reference 1, Table 1. 1985–1987: Natural Center for Health Statistics (NCHS), *Advance Report of Final Natality Statistics*, Monthly Vital Statistics Report, Vol. 36, No. 4, Supplement, 1987 [for 1985]; Vol. 37, No. 3, Supplement, 1988 [for 1986]; Vol. 38, No. 3, Supplement, 1989 [for 1987]. 1988–1989: NCHS *Births, Marriages, Divorces, and Deaths for June 1989*, Monthly Vital Statistics Report, Vol. 38, No. 6, 1989.

1,000) and 1980 (29 per 1,000). The abortion ratio has also fallen slightly since 1980—from 30 to 29 per 100 pregnancies that result in births or abortions—because of an increase in the number of births during the period.[7] The abortion ratio of 29 means that about 29 percent of pregnancies not ending in miscarriage or stillbirth were terminated

[7]National Center for Health Statistics (NCHS), *Advance Report of Final Natality Statistics, 1987*, Monthly Vital Statistics Report, Vol. 38, No. 3, Supplement, 1989.

by abortion. When miscarriages and stillbirths are included, the proportion is 25 percent.

One of the survey questions asked the number of abortions performed during the first quarters of 1988 and 1989; this allowed us to calculate the trend in the number of abortions performed by continuing providers. The question was answered only by providers who returned the original questionnaire and had access to this information; no such data were obtained for those who responded to telephone queries, those who returned a special short form of the questionnaire, or those whose data came from state health departments. The providers answering the question, who provided 56 percent of all 1988 abortions, indicated that collectively they performed three percent more abortions in the first quarter of 1989 than in the same period of 1988, which suggests that the number of abortions may have increased slightly in 1989.[8]

Abortion rates by state of occurrence vary dramatically (Table 2, page 487). Variations between the states may result from a number of factors, including differences in the availability of abortion services, the proportion of the population that is nonwhite or Hispanic (characteristics that are associated with above-average abortion rates), the degree of urbanization (rates tend to be higher in large cities) and state policies, especially public payment for abortion services for low-income women. The highest rate in 1988, 46 abortions per 1,000 women of childbearing age in California, was nine times that of Wyoming, which had the lowest rate (5 per 1,000). The other states with rates of 40 or higher were New York (43), Hawaii (43) and Nevada (40). Like other large cities, the District of Columbia has a higher rate (163) than any state. At the other extreme are states with rates below 10 abortions per 1,000 women: Wyoming (5), South Dakota (6), West Virginia (8), Idaho (8), and Mississippi (8). These are rural states with relatively few places where women can obtain abortion services.

In general, rates are highest on the East and West Coasts (not shown). The Pacific and mid-Atlantic census divisions had the highest rates in 1988 (42 and 34 abortions per 1,000 women aged 15–44, respectively), followed by the New England and South Atlantic regions (both 28 per 1,000). The lowest rates occurred in the East South Central and West North Central census divisions (16 and 17 per 1,000).

Table 2 shows the changes in the abortion rates between 1985 and 1988, but because such changes can be strongly influenced by small errors in the data, they should be interpreted with caution. Errors can be introduced by incomplete or inconsistent reporting of abortions by the providers and by inaccurate estimates of the size of the female population aged 15–44. Sharp drops in state abortion rates of 25 percent or more occurred between 1985 and 1988 in six states, all of which already had relatively low rates in 1985: South Dakota (46 percent drop), New Hampshire (40 percent), Wyoming, (36 percent), Alaska (34 percent), Idaho (26 percent), and West Virginia (25 percent). In all these states, physicians or clinics that had been providing a large proportion of the abortions in 1985 either retired or discontinued their services. In South Dakota, for example, one of the two physicians who had been performing abortions retired, leaving women in the western and central parts of the state as far as 200 miles from the nearest provider. North Dakota has also been left with only one provider of abortion services since the retirement of a physician in February 1990. The decline in abortions performed

---

[8]This conclusion assumes that the number of large-scale providers did not decrease between 1988 and 1989. This assumption seems reasonable, since there was a small increase in these providers between 1987 and 1988.

Table 2. Number of Reported Abortions, Rate per 1,000 Women Aged 15–44, and Absolute Change in Rate, by State of Occurrence, 1985, 1987 and 1988

State	No. of abortions			Abortion rate			Rate change 1985–1988
	1985	1987	1988	1985	1987	1988	
Total	**1,588,550**	**1,559,110**	**1,590,750**	**28.0**	**26.9**	**27.3**	**−0.7**
Alabama	19,380	19,630	18,220	20.2	20.2	18.7	−1.5
Alaska	3,450	2,560	2,390	27.7	19.7	18.2	−9.5
Arizona	22,330	22,130	23,070	29.9	28.2	28.8	−1.1
Arkansas	5,420	7,030	6,250	10.1	13.1	11.6	1.5
California	304,130	300,830	311,720	47.9	45.0	45.9	−2.1
Colorado	24,350	18,850	18,740	28.8	22.4	22.4	−6.4
Connecticut	21,850	22,380	23,630	29.3	29.4	31.2	−1.8
Delaware	4,590	5,680	5,710	30.9	35.9	35.7	4.8
District of Columbia	23,910	25,840	26,120	145.9	158.5	163.3	17.4
Florida	76,650	80,560	82,850	31.8	31.2	31.5	−0.3
Georgia	38,340	36,030	36,720	26.1	23.3	23.5	−2.6
Hawaii	11,160	11,290	11,170	43.7	44.1	43.0	−0.7
Idaho	2,660	1,980	1,920	11.1	8.5	8.2	−2.8
Illinois	64,960	72,180	72,570	23.8	26.2	26.4	2.6
Indiana	16,090	14,750	15,760	12.2	11.2	11.9	−0.2
Iowa	9,930	8,900	9,420	15.0	13.8	14.6	−0.4
Kansas	10,150	11,430	11,440	18.2	20.2	20.1	2.0
Kentucky	9,820	11,550	11,520	11.0	13.1	13.0	2.0
Louisiana	19,240	16,550	17,340	17.4	15.4	16.3	−1.1
Maine	4,960	4,950	4,620	18.6	17.7	16.2	−2.4
Maryland	29,480	31,240	32,670	26.9	27.6	28.6	1.7
Massachusetts	40,310	41,490	43,720	29.3	28.7	30.2	0.9
Michigan	64,390	61,060	63,410	28.7	27.3	28.5	−0.3
Minnesota	16,850	17,810	18,580	16.6	17.5	18.2	1.6
Mississippi	5,890	5,430	5,120	9.7	8.9	8.4	−1.3
Missouri	20,100	20,190	19,490	17.3	17.0	16.4	−0.9
Montana	3,710	3,280	3,050	19.0	17.7	16.5	−2.5
Nebraska	6,680	6,580	6,490	18.2	18.0	17.7	−0.4
Nevada	9,910	10,710	10,190	40.5	43.9	40.3	−0.2
New Hampshire	7,030	4,680	4,710	29.0	17.8	17.5	−11.5
New Jersey	69,190	63,570	63,900	39.6	34.9	35.1	−4.5
New Mexico	6,110	6,650	6,810	17.4	18.6	19.1	1.8
New York	195,120	184,420	183,980	47.4	43.3	43.3	−4.0
North Carolina	34,180	37,630	39,720	22.6	24.2	25.4	2.8
North Dakota	2,850	2,560	2,230	18.5	17.0	14.9	−3.6
Ohio	57,360	51,490	53,400	22.4	20.2	21.0	−1.4
Oklahoma	13,100	11,000	12,120	17.1	14.5	16.2	−0.9
Oregon	15,230	14,370	15,960	22.3	21.8	23.9	1.7
Pennsylvania	57,370	51,800	51,830	21.3	18.9	18.9	−2.4
Rhode Island	7,770	7,390	7,190	35.5	31.3	30.6	−4.9
South Carolina	11,200	12,770	14,160	13.7	15.2	16.7	3.1
South Dakota	1,650	860	900	10.6	5.5	5.7	−4.9
Tennessee	22,350	22,050	22,090	19.1	18.9	18.9	−0.2
Texas	100,820	100,210	100,690	25.5	24.7	24.8	0.7
Utah	4,440	4,830	5,030	11.1	12.4	12.8	1.7

State	No. of abortions			Abortion rate			Rate change 1985–1988
	1985	1987	1988	1985	1987	1988	
Vermont	3,430	3,690	3,580	26.2	26.9	25.8	−0.5
Virginia	34,180	34,410	35,420	24.0	23.3	23.7	−0.3
Washington	30,990	29,840	31,220	28.0	26.9	27.6	−0.4
West Virginia	4,590	2,990	3,270	10.1	6.8	7.5	−2.6
Wisconsin	17,830	18,330	18,040	15.7	16.3	16.0	0.2
Wyoming	1,070	680	600	7.9	5.7	5.1	−2.8

Note: In this and subsequent tables, numbers of abortions are rounded to the nearest 10.

Sources: **1985**—see reference 1. **1987–1988**—See sources to Table 1.

in these states may lead to an overestimation of the decline in the number of residents obtaining abortions, since more women may be traveling out of state for abortion services.

The only abortion rate increases of 15 percent or more from 1985 to 1988 occurred in Delaware (16 percent), Kentucky (18 percent) and South Carolina (22 percent). In Delaware and South Carolina, new providers began offering abortion services during this period and established providers increased their caseloads. The increase from 146 to 163 abortions per 1,000 women aged 15–44 in the District of Columbia represents a partial return to a higher rate of 170 abortions reported in 1982; the drop had been caused by the closing of a major clinic. Among the census divisions, the largest changes in abortion rates were declines of nine percent in the mid-Atlantic states and seven percent in the Mountain states (not shown). Changes in other census divisions were minor.

The data collected by the Abortion Provider Survey are recorded according to the state where the abortions were performed and reflect the presence of services (Table 3). When analyzing abortion utilization, however, it is more appropriate to compare rates of abortions obtained by residents of the states rather than the rates of abortions occurring in the states. For each state, the percentage distribution of abortions performed according to the women's state of residence has been obtained from the CDC or estimated from AGI sample surveys of providers. This information has been used to estimate the abortion rates among residents of each state in 1985, the most recent year for which the data are available.

In Arkansas, Indiana, Maryland, Mississippi and Wyoming, the abortion rates among residents (shown in Table 3) are substantially higher than the rates of abortions occurring in those states in 1985 (shown in Table 2) because many residents travel to other states for abortion services. Low occurrence rates by state often reflect a lack of services: In the 10 states where fewer than 15 abortions per 1,000 women were performed in 1985 (Arkansas, Idaho, Indiana, Kentucky, Mississippi, South Carolina, South Dakota, Utah, West Virginia and Wyoming), an average of 26 percent of the residents who obtained abortions went to other states for the services.

In the District of Columbia, on the other hand, the 1985 resident rate of 75 abortions per 1,000 women is much lower than the rate of 146 abortions performed per 1,000 women shown in Table 2 because many women from Maryland and Virginia go to Washington, D.C., for abortions. Delaware, Kansas, North Dakota, New Hampshire,

Table 3. Total Number of Abortions and Number and Percentage Provided to Nonresidents, by State; Total Number of Abortions and Number and Percentage Obtained Out of State, by Woman's State of Residence; and Resident Abortion Rate per 1,000 Women 15–44; 1985

State	Abortions provided (by state)			Abortions obtained (by residents)			Resident abortion rate
	Total	To nonresidents		Total	Out of state		
		N	%		N	%	
Total	**1,588,550**	**98,570**	**6**	**1,578,800***	**88,820***	**6**	**27.8**
Alabama	19,380	1,170	6	19,620	1,410	7	20.5
Alaska	3,450	0	0	3,780	330	9	30.4
Arizona	22,330	600	3	22,590	860	4	30.2
Arkansas	5,420	190	4	7,050	1,820	26	13.2
California	304,130	1,440	†	304,120	1,430	†	47.9
Colorado	24,350	1,450	6	23,120	220	1	27.4
Connecticut	21,850	580	3	22,780	1,510	7	30.6
Delaware	4,590	1,490	32	3,490	390	11	23.5
District of Columbia	23,910	12,280	51	12,340	710	6	75.3
Florida	76,650	6,910	9	70,750	1,010	1	29.4
Georgia	38,340	3,090	8	37,860	2,610	7	25.7
Hawaii	11,160	140	1	11,030	10	†	43.2
Idaho	2,660	210	8	3,060	610	20	12.7
Illinois	64,960	1,360	2	67,490	3,890	6	24.7
Indiana	16,090	540	3	20,970	5,420	26	15.9
Iowa	9,930	750	8	10,870	1,690	16	16.4
Kansas	10,150	3,850	38	7,190	890	12	12.9
Kentucky	9,820	3,730	38	8,690	2,600	30	9.7
Louisiana	19,240	2,230	12	19,000	1,990	10	17.2
Maine	4,960	730	15	5,190	960	18	19.5
Maryland	29,480	1,650	6	37,940	10,110	27	34.7
Massachusetts	40,310	1,410	3	42,180	3,280	8	30.6
Michigan	64,390	1,890	3	63,390	890	1	28.3
Minnesota	16,850	1,580	9	16,030	760	5	15.8
Mississippi	5,890	370	6	7,570	2,050	27	12.4
Missouri	20,100	2,800	14	21,800	4,500	21	18.8
Montana	3,710	650	18	3,210	150	5	16.4
Nebraska	6,680	1,350	20	5,780	450	8	15.7
Nevada	9,910	1,230	12	9,100	420	5	37.2
New Hampshire	7,030	1,990	28	5,960	920	15	24.6
New Jersey	69,190	1,980	3	71,940	4,730	7	41.2
New Mexico	6,110	200	3	7,160	1,250	17	20.4
New York	195,120	7,790	4	189,840	2,510	1	46.1
North Carolina	34,180	1,810	5	33,880	1,510	4	22.4
North Dakota	2,850	1,390	49	1,610	150	9	10.4
Ohio	57,360	3,260	6	55,720	1,620	3	21.8
Oklahoma	13,100	690	5	13,380	970	7	17.5
Oregon	15,230	1,260	8	14,520	550	4	21.2
Pennsylvania	57,370	2,580	4	59,360	4,570	8	22.1
Rhode Island	7,770	1,870	24	6,170	270	4	28.2

State	Abortions provided (by state)			Abortions obtained (by residents)			Resident abortion rate
	Total	To nonresidents		Total	Out of state		
		N	%		N	%	
South Carolina	11,200	610	5	12,700	2,110	17	15.5
South Dakota	1,650	400	24	1,630	380	23	10.5
Tennessee	22,350	3,850	17	20,090	1,590	8	17.1
Texas	100,820	5,890	6	96,620	1,690	2	24.5
Utah	4,440	340	8	4,440	340	8	11.1
Vermont	3,430	990	29	2,820	380	13	21.6
Virginia	34,180	2,000	6	37,470	5,290	14	26.4
Washington	30,990	1,890	6	30,370	1,270	4	27.4
West Virginia	4,590	830	18	5,200	1,440	28	11.4
Wisconsin	17,830	1,270	7	17,740	1,180	7	15.7
Wyoming	1,070	10	1	2,190	1,130	52	16.2

*Excludes an estimated 9,750 nonresidents of the United States who obtained abortions in the United States. About 3,500 of these are Canadian, 1,900 Mexican, and most of the remainder are from the Caribbean area.

†Fewer than 0.5 percent.

Sources: **Number of abortions**—AGI survey and unpublished data compiled by the Centers for Disease Control. **Number of women**—see sources to Table 1.

Rhode Island and Vermont also have lower resident rates than occurrence rates because of the numbers of out-of-state women served.

Geographic Availability

The distance a woman has to travel for abortion services can be an important determinant of whether she is able to obtain the services when she needs them. Lack of local services makes it harder for women to obtain information about facilities, and, if they do, they may face other difficulties: prohibitive travel expenses, the need for overnight lodging and the loss of pay due to absence from work. In addition, rapid diagnosis and treatment of postabortion complications are more difficult, and privacy is jeopardized by the need to be away from home and work for a longer period. Research has shown that the greater the distance from an abortion provider, the less likely a woman is to gain access to the service.[9]

The proportion of women who obtain abortions outside their home states is an indicator of the lack of local services. Table 3 shows that in Wyoming, more than half the residents who obtained abortions in 1985 did so in other states, as did 20 percent or more of the women residing in Arkansas, Idaho, Indiana, Kentucky, Maryland, Missouri, Mississippi, South Dakota and West Virginia who had abortions. Except for Maryland, many of whose residents use health services in the District of Columbia, all these states have resident abortion rates under 20 per 1,000. While distance from providers may not be the only cause of low rates in these states, it may be preventing some women from obtaining needed services. In the same year, 20 percent or more of abor-

[9] J. D. Shelton, E. A. Brann and K. F. Schulz, *Abortion Utilization: Does Travel Distance Matter?* Family Planning Perspectives, 8: 260, 1976.

Table 4. Number of Counties, Number and Percentage with an Abortion Provider and Number with a Large-Scale Provider,* by State, 1988

State	No. of counties	Counties with		Large-scale provider
		Any provider		
		N	%	N
U.S. total	**3,135**	**536**	**17**	**261**
Alabama	67	6	9	5
Alaska	23	6	26	1
Arizona	14	3	21	2
Arkansas	75	3	4	2
California	58	40	69	26
Colorado	63	16	25	6
Connecticut	8	7	88	4
Delaware	3	3	100	2
Dist. of Col.	1	1	100	1
Florida	67	20	30	18
Georgia	159	21	13	5
Hawaii	4	4	100	2
Idaho	44	4	9	1
Illinois	102	9	9	8
Indiana	92	12	13	4
Iowa	99	7	7	2
Kansas	105	10	10	3
Kentucky	120	2	2	2
Louisiana	64	5	8	5
Maine	16	10	63	1
Maryland	24	15	63	6
Massachusetts	14	12	86	7
Michigan	83	21	25	12
Minnesota	87	5	6	3
Mississippi	82	3	4	3
Missouri	115	7	6	6
Montana	56	6	11	3
Nebraska	93	2	2	2
Nevada	17	2	12	2
New Hampshire	10	4	40	2
New Jersey	21	16	76	11
New Mexico	32	8	25	2
New York	62	48	77	18
North Carolina	100	42	42	10
North Dakota	53	3	6	3
Ohio	88	11	13	7
Oklahoma	77	4	5	3
Oregon	36	12	33	5
Pennsylvania	67	19	28	8
Rhode Island	5	2	40	1

State	No. of counties	Counties with		Large-scale provider
		Any provider		
		N	%	N
South Carolina	46	6	13	3
South Dakota	66	1	2	1
Tennessee	95	11	12	5
Texas	254	22	9	15
Utah	29	2	7	1
Vermont	14	7	50	2
Virginia	136	29	21	8
Washington	39	14	36	7
West Virginia	55	3	5	1
Wisconsin	72	6	8	4
Wyoming	23	4	17	0

*A provider of 400 or more abortions in 1988.

tions in nine states (Delaware, Kansas, Kentucky, Nebraska, New Hampshire, North Dakota, Rhode Island, South Dakota and Vermont) and the District of Columbia were provided to out-of-state residents. Nationally, six percent of all abortions in 1985 were obtained out of state.

Other indicators of the availability of abortion services are the proportion of counties that have a provider and the proportion that have a large-scale provider (Table 4). The proportion of U.S. counties that have abortion providers has been decreasing since the late 1970s. This decline has been concentrated among counties with only small facilities; the proportion of counties with providers of 400 or more abortions per year has remained stable or increased slightly in recent years (not shown). Only about half as many nonmetropolitan counties had services in 1988 as in 1977 (seven and 14 percent, respectively).

The proportion of counties with abortion services varies widely by state and is associated with state abortion rates. As shown in Table 4, one state, South Dakota, had only one county with an abortion provider in 1988, and in 17 other states fewer than 10 percent of the counties had a provider. The resident abortion rate is below 20 per 1,000 women in all but three of these states. In 10 states, at least half of the counties have abortion services, and seven of the 10 have resident rates above 30. It should be noted, of course, that a causal connection between the availability of services and abortion rates is not proven by these associations, since abortion services may gravitate towards areas with greater demand and other factors may contribute to low rates in states with few services.

As shown in Table 5, 83 percent of U.S. counties have no identified abortion services; 31 percent of women of reproductive age live in these counties. An additional four percent of counties where four percent of women live have facilities that reported 10 or fewer abortions in 1988; such facilities are usually hospitals that perform abortions in rare emergency cases or private physicians who serve established patients only. Only eight percent of counties, where 58 percent of women live, have a large-scale facility

Table 5. Percentage of Counties with No Abortion Providers and with No Providers Reporting 400 or more Abortions, and Percentage of Women aged 15–44 Living in Those Counties, by Metropolitan Status,* 1988

Measure	Total	Metro	Non-metro
Counties (N = 3,135)			
With no provider	83	51	93
With no provider reporting ⩾400 abortions	92	67	99
Women 15–44 (N = 58,192,000)			
Living in counties with no providers	31	16	83
Living in counties with no provider reporting ⩾400 abortions	42	26	97

*Defined according to criteria published by the OMB after the 1980 census.

(one that provides 400 or more abortions per year). Women in nonmetropolitan counties are more likely than those in metropolitan counties to have to cross county lines to obtain abortion services. Eighty-three percent of nonmetropolitan women live in the 93 percent of nonmetropolitan counties without a provider. In contrast, just 16 percent of metropolitan women live in the 51 percent of metropolitan counties that have no provider.

According to the 1985 survey, 81 of the country's 305 standard metropolitan statistical areas (SMSAs) [10] either had no provider or had providers reporting a total of fewer than 50 abortions. At least 400 abortions would have been performed per year in each of these SMSAs if their abortion rates met the national average. In 1988, nine additional SMSAs joined this underserved category. These 90 SMSAs include 70 that have no identified provider and 20 with providers that together reported fewer than 50 procedures.[11] They are located in 33 different states in all parts of the country except New England; Indiana, Ohio, Pennsylvania, Texas and Wisconsin each have six or more.

---

[10] An SMSA consists of a county containing a city of 50,000 or more people, plus any surrounding metropolitan counties. All metropolitan counties are included in SMSAs. We have used the definitions of SMSAs published by the Office of Management and Budget after the 1980 census.

[11] The 90 SMSAs that have no abortion provider or that reported fewer than 50 abortions (shown in italics) in 1988 are: Alabama—Anniston, *Florence,* Gadsden; Arkansas—*Fort Smith,* Pine Bluff, Texarkana; California—*Visalia, Yuba City;* Colorado—Pueblo; Florida—Bradenton, Panama City; Georgia—*Albany,* Athens; Illinois—Bloomington, Decatur, Kankakee, Springfield; Indiana—Anderson, Elkhart, *Evansville,* Kokomo, Muncie, Terre Haute; Iowa—Davenport, Dubuque, Sioux City; Kansas—*Topeka;* Kentucky—Owensboro; Louisiana—Alexandria, Lafayette, Lake Charles, Monroe; Maine—Lewiston; Maryland—*Cumberland;* Michigan—Battle Creek, *Bay City;* Minnesota—St. Cloud; Mississippi—Pascagoula; Missouri—Joplin, St. Joseph; New Jersey—Vineland; New Mexico—*Las Cruces;* North Carolina—*Burlington;* North Dakota—Bismarck; Ohio—*Canton, Hamilton,* Lima, Lorain, Mansfield, Newark, Springfield, Steubenville; Oklahoma—Enid, Lawton; Pennsylvania—*Altoona,* Erie, Johnstown, Lancaster, Sharon, State College, Williamsport; South Carolina—Anderson, Florence, Rock Hill; Tennessee—Clarksville; Texas—*Abilene,* Amarillo, Bryan, *Galveston,* Longview, Midland, San Angelo, Sherman, Victoria, Waco; Utah—Provo; Virginia—*Danville, Lynchberg;* Washington—Bremerton, Richland; West Virginia—Huntington, Parkersburg, *Wheeling;* Wisconsin—Eau Claire, Janesville, Kenosha, *La Crosse,* Racine, Sheboygan, Wausau.

Abortion Providers

Abortions are performed in hospitals, as inpatient services and in outpatient departments; in nonhospital clinics, including specialized abortion clinics, surgical centers, group practices, health maintenance organizations and other types of clinics; and in private physicians' offices. It is difficult to distinguish between clinics and physicians' offices where large numbers of abortions are performed, and in this analysis all nonhospital facilities reporting 400 or more abortions per year are classified as clinics. Clinics are further subdivided into "abortion clinics" and "other clinics." Abortion clinics are those in which at least 50 percent of patient visits are reported to be for abortion services.[12]

The number of abortion providers identified in AGI surveys increased throughout the 1970s and reached 2,908 in 1982. It has since fallen steadily to 2,618 in 1987 and 2,582 in 1988, a decline of 11 percent. Providers have always been concentrated in urban areas, but the concentration has become more pronounced in recent years. The number of nonmetropolitan providers is now 51 percent below the peak figure in 1977, while the number of providers in metropolitan counties has dropped only six percent from its peak in 1982. In 1988, 2,315 (90 percent of all providers) were in metropolitan counties, slightly less than the 2,331 (89 percent) in 1987.

The decline in the number of providers has occurred entirely among hospitals. In 1977, there were 1,654 hospitals offering abortion services; the number fell to 1,405 in 1982, to 1,191 in 1985 and to 1,040 in 1988. Because a disproportionate number of the abortion providers in nonmetropolitan areas are hospitals, a decline in the number of these providers especially affects women not living near major cities.

Between 1985 and 1988, 91 new hospital abortion providers were identified, 230 hospitals discontinued their services, and 12 others did not respond to the survey, for a net reduction of 151, or 13 percent in the number of hospitals that offer abortion services. As shown in Table 6, more than half of the reduction (87) occurred among voluntary nonchurch hospitals. The percentage reduction was greatest among county hospitals (22 percent), those run by hospital district organizations (18 percent) and proprietary hospitals (16 percent).

Of the country's 5,533 short-term general hospitals,[13] only 19 percent provided abortions in 1988, down from 21 percent in 1985 (not shown). Excluding Catholic hospitals,[14] the proportion is 21 percent, down from 23 percent. Private general hospitals offer the service more often than public ones—24 percent (excluding Catholic hospitals) compared with 15 percent.

The number of nonhospital facilities where abortions are performed increased four percent between 1985 and 1988, as shown in Table 6. The number of clinics reporting 400 or more abortions per year rose two percent, with 16 additional facilities. Between 1982 and 1985, the number of clinics this size had increased by 32, or five percent. Because several new group practices are classified as small clinics, the number of clinics

---

[12] Clinics that did not provide information about the percentage of patient visits made for abortion were classified as abortion clinics if they reported 1,000 or more abortions during 1988. However, if their self-definition is physician's office (i.e., if they have not adopted a clinic name), the cutoff is 1,500 abortions.

[13] American Hospital Association, *Hospital Statistics, 1989–90 Edition*, Chicago, 1989, Table 5A, p. 20.

[14] Catholic Health Association of the United States, personal communication with Mark Unger, Mar. 22, 1990.

Table 6. Number of Abortion Providers in 1985 and 1988, and Change Between 1985 and 1988, by Type of Facility

Type of facility	1985	1988	Change 1985–1988	
			N	%
Total	**2,680**	**2,582**	**−98**	**−4**
Hospital	**1,191**	**1,040**	**−151**	**−13**
Public	265	230	−35	−13
Federal	0	1	1	*
State	40	39	−1	−3
Hospital district	100	82	−18	−18
County	74	58	−16	−22
City; city/county	51	50	−1	−2
Private	926	810	−116	−13
Voluntary, church	50	48	−2	−4
Voluntary, other	702	615	−87	−12
Proprietary	174	147	−27	−16
Nonhospital facility	**1,489**	**1,542**	**53**	**4**
Clinics	837	885	48	6
<30 abortions	16	33	17	106
30–390 abortions	132	147	15	11
400–990 abortions	228	233	5	2
≥1,000 abortions	461	472	11	2
Physicians' offices	652	657	5	1
<30 abortions	154	181	27	18
30–390 abortions	498	476	−22	−4

*Cannot be calculated.

performing fewer than 30 abortions annually more than doubled in the most recent period; this size clinic also increased in number between 1982 and 1985. The number of physicians offering abortion services in their offices stayed fairly constant, with a decline in the number performing 30 or more abortions balanced by an increase in those performing fewer than 30.

Since 1973, there has been a major shift in the proportion of abortions performed by hospitals and nonhospital facilities, especially abortion clinics. In 1973, slightly more than half of all abortions were performed in hospitals, compared with 46 percent in clinics. However, the proportion of abortions performed in hospitals has declined steadily to just 10 percent in 1988, while the proportion handled by clinics increased each year, to 86 percent in 1988. This shift reflects reductions both in the number of hospitals performing abortions and in the average number of abortions per hospital (among those that provide the service). The percentage of abortions performed by physicians in their own offices has always been low, representing 3–5 percent of all abortions.

Hospitals tend to have small abortion caseloads, with 45 percent of the hospital providers reporting fewer than 30 abortions. As Table 7, page 496 indicates, only 30 hospitals performed 1,000 or more abortions. The average number of abortions per hospital provider fell from 175 in 1985 to 153 in 1988. As has been noted in earlier

Table 7. Number and Percentage Distribution of Abortions and Abortion Providers by Type of Facility, According to Caseload, 1988

Caseload	Total		Hospitals		Abortion		Other clinics		MD's offices	
	N	%	N	%	N	%	N	%	N	%
Abortions	**1,590,750**	**100**	**159,170**	**10**	**1,015,400**	**64**	**355,020**	**22**	**61,160**	**4**
<30	6,260	*	3,600	*	0	0	370	*	2,290	*
30–390	136,690	9	53,930	3	1,480	*	22,410	1	58,870	4
400–990	182,680	11	33,580	2	38,390	2	110,710	7	na	na
1,000–4,990	948,100	60	50,190	3	676,380	43	221,530	14	na	na
≥5,000	317,020	20	17,870	1	299,150	19	0	0	na	na
Providers	**2,582**	**100**	**1,040**	**40**	**409**	**16**	**476**	**18**	**657**	**25**
<30	678	26	464	18	0	0	33	1	181	7
30–390	1,116	43	493	19	7	*	140	5	476	18
400–990	286	11	53	2	53	2	180	7	na	na
1,000–4,990	459	18	27	1	309	12	123	5	na	na
≥5,000	43	2	3	*	40	2	0	0	na	na

*Fewer than 0.5 percent.   Note: na = not applicable.

surveys, hospital abortions are increasingly being performed as outpatient procedures. In 1988, only 14.6 percent of hospital abortions, or 1.5 percent of all abortions, involved hospitalization. In 1985, 2.7 percent of all abortions were performed as hospital inpatient procedures.

Most abortions are performed in specialized abortion clinics; the proportion has increased to 64 percent, up from 60 percent in 1985. The number of abortions performed in abortion clinics grew six percent between 1985 and 1988, while the number in each of the other types of facilities declined. Similarly, the proportion of abortions in the largest facilities, those reporting 1,000 or more procedures, was higher in 1988 (80 percent) than in 1985 (77 percent). Doctors' offices constitute 25 percent of the abortion providers but reported only four percent of all abortions. Thus, abortion services are becoming increasingly concentrated in the largest, most specialized facilities.

Discussion

The annual number of abortions has remained nearly stable since 1980, even though several factors could have affected it in either direction. Although the number of women of reproductive age in the population increased, the age distribution changed: More are over 30 years old, and abortion rates for such women are low. Specifically, the number of women aged 20–24 fell 10 percent between 1980 and 1988.[15] If age-specific abortion rates had remained at their 1980 levels, the number of abortions in 1988 would have been four percent lower than the observed number. Changes in the marital status of the population, on the other hand, should have increased the age-specific abortion rates, since a lower proportion of women in each age-group are now married, and unmarried women are much more likely than married ones to have abortions.[16] In addition, the

[15] Bureau of the Census, *United States Population Estimates, by Age, Sex, Race, and Hispanic Origin: 1980 to 1988,* Current Population Reports, Series P-25, No. 1045, 1990, Table 2.

[16] S. K. Henshaw and J. Silverman, *The Characteristics and Prior Contraceptive Use of U.S. Abortion Patients,* Family Planning Perspectives, 20: 158, 1988.

proportion of unmarried teenagers who are sexually active increased during the 1980s.[17] The direction and extent of these influences and the impact of changes in use of the various contraceptive methods will be better understood when the 1988 National Survey of Family Growth has been analyzed.

The basic trends in abortion service delivery that were observed in 1985 have continued through 1988. The concentration of abortion services in specialized abortion clinics has continued to increase as a result of growth in the number of such providers and higher caseloads per provider. Conversely, abortion services in hospitals have been declining as a result of lower caseloads and discontinuation of abortion services altogether. The number of physicians providing small numbers of abortions in their offices has stabilized, but their average caseload is smaller than before.

The shift of abortions from hospitals to clinics is probably due in large part to the cost advantage of clinics, as well as to the increasing ability of clinics to provide abortions at later gestations. In addition, clinics offer other advantages for women: their medical and support staffs understand the problems faced by abortion patients; they have the competence that comes from extensive experience; and they are relatively easy to find, especially if they advertise. However, services provided by physicians in their offices and by hospitals are also needed. Some women prefer the care of their personal physicians, and the continuity such care offers may be advantageous. Hospital services are needed for women with health conditions that put them at high risk for complications, as well as for women requiring concurrent surgery or abortion by instillation procedures.

It is equally important that physician and hospital services be available in sparsely populated areas where it is not economical to establish clinics. The loss of hospital abortion services has left increasing numbers of women without any provider in their local areas. It is surprising, however, that the loss of providers has been limited to hospitals, considering the problems confronting private physicians and clinics; antiabortion harassment and violence have most often been directed at nonhospital providers. In addition, private physicians and clinics may have difficulties in obtaining insurance, paying legal and security expenses, and stretching income based on fees that have not kept up with inflation.[18]

The net decrease in the number of hospitals that perform abortions has had the unfortunate effect of reducing abortion services in states and counties where they were already scarce. Extreme inequality of access to such services already exists, even without new state restrictions that may result from the decision in *Webster v. Reproductive Health Services*. Women in many parts of the country have to travel long distances to obtain abortions, and those who manage to overcome such obstacles are likely to have their abortions later in pregnancy, when the health risks are greater.

---

[17]F. L. Sonenstein, J. H. Pleck and L. C. Ku, *Sexual Activity, Condom Use and AIDS Awareness Among Adolescent Males,* Family Planning Perspectives, 21: 152, 1989.

[18]S. K. Henshaw, J. D. Forrest and J. Van Vort, 1987, *op cit.* (see reference 1).

RU486 upsets the normal balance between progesterone and prostaglandin in pregnancy and leads to a disruption of the implantation of the embryo. Over 50,000 women in France have used RU486/PG (prostaglandin) instead of abortive surgery, with a success rate of 95.4%. Evidence suggests that when RU486/PF is administered the risk of fetomaternal hemorrhage is less than in surgical abortions, and the drug may be more effective than vacuum aspiration in pregnancies of less than six weeks. It is not, however, without problems. The use of RU486/PG is not advisable in some cases, such as insulin-dependent diabetes, renal and hepatic insufficiency and malnutrition. This method of abortion requires strict medical supervision to spot cases where blood loss might be excessive. The use of RU486 appears, in some studies with animals, to inhibit follicle maturation, ovulation and egg implantation, so the drug may also be used as a form of contraception. However, administering RU486 as a contraceptive measure has a 20% failure rate. RU486 is also utilized in pregnancy management, as well as in the treatment of endometriosis and breast cancer.

The article is divided into four sections: (1) cellular and molecular mechanism of RU486 action, (2) clinical applications, (3) what's next with voluntary pregnancy interruption and (4) contragestion. The first section on the cellular and molecular mechanism of RU486 presupposes that the reader has a strong foundation in molecular and cellular biology, physiology and chemistry. To assist the reader, Professor Baulieu included six graphics with legends. Even with these visual aids, the first section of Professor Baulieu's article can present a formidable task for the nonscientist; therefore, one might prefer to begin with the second section on clinical applications.

19 · The Biology and Clinical Uses of the Antisteroid Hormone RU486

Etienne-Emile Baulieu, Ph.D., and
Thanh-Van Ngoc Nguyen

RU486* is a steroid hormone antagonist. Principally, it opposes the action of two types of hormones: progesterone, the hormone necessary for initiation and continuation of pregnancy, and glucocorticosteroids, cortisone-like hormones involved in most metabolic processes, stress, inflammatory lesions and immunity.[1-8]

---

*Full number in Roussel-Uclaf list of products: 36,486; Generic name: mifepristone; Formula: 11β-(4-di-methyl-amino phenyl)-17β-hydroxy-17α-(prop-1-ynyl)-estra-4,9-dien-3-one.

[1] W. Hermann, R. Wyss, A. Riondel, D. Philibert, G. Teutsch, E. Sakiz & E. E. Baulieu, *Effet d'un stéroïde anti-progestérone chez la femme: interruption du cycle menstruel et de la grossesse au début.* 294 C. R. Acad. Sci. Paris 933–938 (1982).

[2] *The Antiprogestin Steroid RU486 and Human Fertility Control.* (E. E. Baulieu & S. J. Segal eds. 1985).

[3] D. L. Healy, *Clinical status of antiprogesteorne steroids.* 3 Clin. Reprod. Fert. 277–296 (1985).

[4] P. F. A. Van Look & M. Bygdeman, *Antiprogestational steroids: a new dimension in human fertility regulation,* in 11 Oxford Reviews of Reproductive Biology 1–60 (S. R. Milligan ed. 1989).

[5] I. T. Cameron & D. T. Baird, *Early pregnancy termination: a comparison between vacuum aspiration and medical abortion using prostaglandin (16,16 dimethyl-trans-Δ_2-PGE$_1$ methyl ester) or the antiprogestogen RU486,* 95 Br. J. Obst. Gynecol. 271–276 (1988).

[6] L. Silvestre, C. Dubois, M. Renault, Y. Rezvani, E. E. Baulieu & A. Ulman, *Voluntary interruption of pregnancy with mifepristone (RU486) and a prostaglandin analogue,* 322 New Engl. J. Med. 645–648 (1990).

[7] D. Philibert, *RU38486: an original multifaceted antihormone in vivo,* in Adrenal Steroid Antagonism 77–101 (M. K. Agarwal, ed. 1984).

[8] G. P. Chrousos, L. Laue, L. K. Nieman, R. Udelsman, S. Kawai & D. L. Loriaux, *Clinical applications of RU486, a prototype glucocorticoid and progestin antagonist,* in 57 Adrenal and Hypertension: From Cloning to Clinic 273–284 (F. Mantero, B. A. Scoggins, R. Takeda, E. G. Biglieri & J. W. Funder, eds. 1989).

Figure 1. Steroid hormones (progesterone and estradiol), synthetic agonists (norethindrone and diethylstilbestrol) and antagonists (RU486 and 4-hydroxytamoxifen). Note on ''profiles'' the extra-cycle of the antagonists, branching out of the flat molecule.

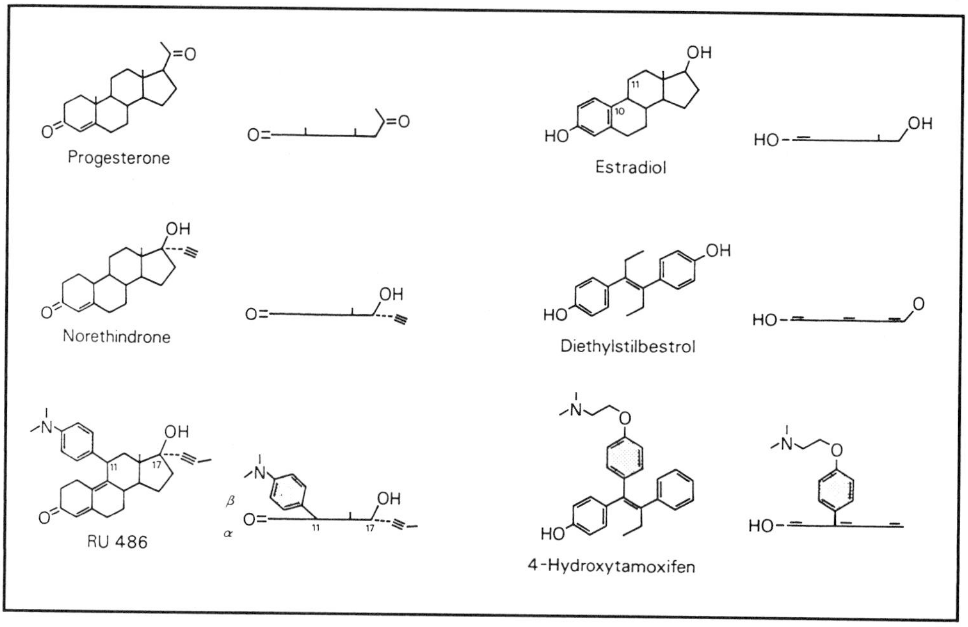

The work on steroid receptors and antihormones, the progress in understanding progesterone action in the human menstrual cycle and pregnancy, the concern for insufficient fertility control methods and the talent of the Roussel-Uclaf chemists and pharmacologists have merged to produce the first efficient, acceptable nonsurgical method of ''contragestion.''[9] The controversies around pregnancy interruption have generated much attention toward the compound and have created a unique situation where the development of a medical product may be jeopardized by nonmedical considerations related to socioeconomic, religious and political problems.

I. Cellular and Molecular Mechanism of RU486 Action

1. RU486: An Antagonist at the Receptor

Binding experiments have indicated that RU486 has high affinity for both human progesterone (P) and glucocorticosteroid (G) receptors (R). It is the first antisteroid of affinity superior or equal to that of natural agonist hormones used clinically (the antiestrogen tamoxifen, the antiandrogens flutamid and anandron, and the antimineralocorticosteroids spironolactones have lower affinity than estradiol, dihydrotestosterone and aldosterone for their respective receptors). The powerful antiestrogen 4-hydroxytamoxifen (figure 1) has higher affinity than estradiol for the estradiol receptor but is not used

---

[9]E. E. Baulieu, *RU486 as an antiprogesterone steroid; from receptor to contragestion and beyond*, 262 J. Am. Med. Assoc. 1808–14 (1989).

therapeutically; however, it provided the first experimental example[10,11] contradicting the concept that antihormone should be of lower affinity than the agonist.[12] This was clearly demonstrated in the studies of chick oviduct and liver where the 4-hydroxyta-moxifen is a "pure" antiestrogen (in contrast to some agonistic activity found in rodents and human beings).[13] Therefore, it is now accepted that binding parameters do not predict whether a ligand will be agonistic or antagonistic. RU486 also binds weakly to the androgen receptor (AR) and is a feeble antiandrogen. It does not bind to the miner-alocorticosteroid and estrogen receptors. It does not bind to specific steroid binding plasma proteins such as CBG (transcortin) and SBP (sex steroid binding plasma protein) but has high affinity ($K_D \approx 10^{-7}$ M) for human α_1-mucoprotein.[14,15]

As far as the chemical structure of RU486,[16] it has been surprising that the large 11β-branched additional aminophenyl group binds with high affinity to PR, which already binds tightly the flat progesterone molecule (figure 1). This suggests that this receptor, like GR and the androgen receptor, may have a large "pocket" capable of accommodating the extra-substituent. However, things are not simple because, despite the amino acid sequence homology between the ligand binding domains (LBD) of chick and mammalian PRs,[17-20] the former does not bind RU486.[21] Recently, this result has been attributed to a single amino acid difference in the LBD (T. Garcia at Roussel-Uclaf, Paris and H. Gronemeyer at INSERM U184, Strasbourg, in preparation). The detailed modalities of interaction of agonist and antagonist ligands with PR LBD await X-ray crystallography studies. These studies will be particularly interesting because of the many functions of LBD (discussed later in this chapter).

[10] V. C. Jordan, C. J. Dix, K. E. Naylor, G. Prestwich & L. Rowsby, *Nonsteroidal antiestrogens: their biological effects and potential mechanisms of action*, 4 J. Toxicol. Environ. Health 363–90 (1978).

[11] H. Rochefort, M. Garcia & J. L. Borgna, *Absence of correlation between antiestrogenic activity and binding affinity for the estrogen receptor*, 88 Biochem. Biophys. Res. Commun. 351–57 (1979).

[12] J. P. Raynaud, M. M. Bouton & T. Ojasoo, *The use of interaction kinetics to distinguish potential antagonists from agonists*, 1 TIPS 324–27 (1975).

[13] N. Binart, M. G. Catelli, C. Geynet, V. Puri, R. Hahnel, J. Mester & E. E. Baulieu, *Monohydroxytamoxifen: an antioestrogen with high affinity for the chick oviduct oestrogen receptor*, 91 Biochem. Biophys. Res. Commun. 812–18 (1979).

[14] E. E. Baulieu, *Contragestion and other clinical applications of RU486, an antiprogesterone at the receptor*. 245 Science 1351–57 (1989).

[15] M. Moguilewski & D. Philibert, *Biochemical profile of RU486*, in The Antiprogestin Steroid RU486 and Human Fertility Control 87–97 (E. E. Baulieu & S. J. Segal eds. 1985).

[16] G. Teutsch, *Analogues of RU486 for the mapping of the progestin receptor: synthetic and structural aspects*, in The Antiprogestin Steroid RU486 and Human Fertility Control 27–47 (E. E. Baulieu & S. J. Segal, eds. 1985).

[17] R. M. Evans, *The steroid and thyroid hormone receptor family*, 240 Science 889–95 (1988).

[18] H. Gronemeyer, S. Green, J. M. Jeltsch, V. Kumar, A. Krutz & P. Chambon, *The nuclear receptor family: cloning, structure and function*, in Affinity Labelling and Cloning of Steroid and Thyroid Hormone Receptors 252–297 (H. Gronemeyer ed. 1988).

[19] M. Misrahi, M. Atger, L. D'Auriol, H. Loosfelt, C. Meriel, F. Fridlansky, A. Guiochon-Mantel, F. Galibert & E. Milgrom, *Complete amino acid sequence of the human progesterone receptor deduced from cloned cDNA*, 143 Biochem. Biophys. Res. Commun. 740–48 (1987).

[20] O. M. Conneely, A. D. W. Dobson, M. J. Tsai, W. G. Beattie, D. O. Toft, C. S. Huckaby, T. Zarucki, W. R. Schrader & B. W. O'Malley, *Sequence and expression of a functional chicken progesterone receptor*, 1 Mol. Endocrinol. 517–25 (1987).

[21] A. Groyer, Y. Le Bouc, I. Joab, C. Radanyi, J. M. Renoir, P. Robel & E. E. Baulieu, *Chick oviduct glucocorticosteroid receptor. Specific binding of RU486 and immunological studies with antibodies to chick oviduct progesterone receptor*. 149 Eur. J. Biochem 445–51 (1985).

A number of classical pharmacological and physiological experiments have demonstrated strong antihormonal activities of RU486. That it acts at the receptor has been clearly shown in primates by the endometrium bleeding occurring when RU486 is given during an artificial cycle established in castrated animals receiving estrogen and progesterone,[22] or during pseudo-pregnancy after gonadotropin administration provoking corpus luteum survival and thus continuing progesterone secretion.[23] Similarly, both antagonism of administered glucocorticosteroids and suppression of the negative feedback of endogenous cortisol have demonstrated convincingly antiglucocorticosteroid activity in vivo.[24,25] Effect at the level of the production, secretion or transport of progesterone is improbable, even though in vitro experiments with high concentration of RU486 have indicated a decrease of progesterone formation by granulosa cells[26] and cited references. Therefore, RU486 appears to be an effective antisteroid hormone acting at the receptor. Unpredicted side-effects resulting from extra-receptor activity have not been observed.

Here, we shall not review problems posed by the use of RU486 at different doses and variable periods of time, nor the management of its anticorticosteroid effects. We are not studying the mechanisms of RU activity in diseases such as endometriosis and breast cancer, in pregnancy interruption (which includes prostaglandin release and increased contractile sensitivity to prostaglandin of uterine smooth muscle[27]), in the initiation of labor nor in luteolysis (indirectly) during the menstrual cycle. Instead, we will try to dissect some molecular and cellular events that may explain not only the "simple" antagonist effects related above but also some complexity that has been revealed clinically and in in vivo experiments. Before going into details, note that an antagonist at the receptor level, like RU486, competitively excludes the agonist from binding and replaces it at the same site. A "pure" antagonist will not lead to any agonist effect and will be a "null" ligand in terms of hormonal response. This does not mean that following antihormone binding to receptor, there is not some molecular modifications provoked by RU486 in the cellular machinery.

Structures of Steroid Receptors and Hormone Response Elements

PR and GR, as other members of the superfamily of DNA-binding receptors, have been cloned in different species. The primary sequence of amino acids deduced from cDNA analysis indicates four main domains (Figure 2).

The DNA binding domain (DBD) is characteristic of all these receptors. It is the most homologous domain ($\approx 50\%-95\%$ among different steroid hormone receptors) and

---

[22] D. L. Healy, E. E. Baulieu & G. D. Hodgen, *Induction of menstruation by anti-progesterone steroid (RU486) in primates: site of action, dose-response relationships and hormonal effects* 40 Fert. Ster. 253–257 (1983).

[23] H. B. Croxatto, I. M. Spitz, A. M. Salvatierra & C. W. Bardin, *The demonstration of the antiprogestin effects of RU486 when administered to the human during hCG-stimulated pseudopregnancy,* in *The Antiprogestin Steroid RU486 and Human Fertility Control* 263–69 (E. E. Baulieu & S. J. Segal eds. 1985).

[24] R. C. Gaillard, A. Riondel, A. F. Muller, W. Herrmann & E. E. Baulieu, *RU486: studies of its antiglucocorticosteroid activity in man,* in *The Antiprogestin Steroid RU486 and Human Fertility Control* 331–37 (E. E. Baulieu & S. J. Segal eds. 1985).

[25] X. Bertagna, C. Bertagna, J. P. Luton, J. M. Husson & F. Girard, *The new steroid analog RU486 inhibits glucocorticoid action in man,* 59 J. Clin. Endocrinol. Metab. 25–38 (1984).

[26] J. Parinaud, B. Perret, H. Ribbes, G. Vieitez & E. E. Baulieu, *Effects of RU486 on progesterone secretion by human preovulatory granulosa cells in culture,* 70 J. Clin. Endocrinol. Metab. 1534–37 (1990).

[27] M. Bygdeman & M. L. Swahn, *Progesterone receptor blockage. Effect on uterine contractility and early pregnancy,* 32 Contraception 45–51 (1985).

Figure 2. Steroid hormone receptors. Consensus structure and interactions with hsp90. The representation relates to notions described in the text and is structurally arbitrary.

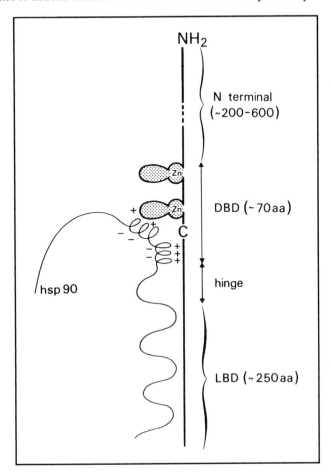

includes approximately 70 amino acids that make up two "Zn-fingers." DBDs of PR, GR, AR and the mineralococorticosteroid receptor (MR) contain much similarity, and the four proteins form a subgroup of steroid receptors that can interact with the same hormone response elements (HREs) of DNA (discussed later).

The LBD comprises approximately 250 amino acids at the C-terminal extremity of the molecule. Again the LBDs of PR, GR, AR and MR show more homology ($\approx 50\%$) than do ER ($\approx 30\%$), calcitriol receptors, thyroid receptors and retinoic acid receptors ($\approx 15\%$). It is known that there is some cross-binding affinity for steroids between the former four receptors. An LBD should have a very specific three-dimensional structure, responsible not only for hormone binding but also for other functions more recently demonstrated: interaction with heat shock protein of molecular weight 90,000 da (hsp90), hormone-dependent transactivation and dimerization.

Between DBD and LBD lies a hinge region, with poor amino acid homology among receptors. However, there is a charged 8-amino acid region, with more than 4 lysines or arginines, which starts 10 (11 for ER) amino acids after the last (C-terminal) cystein of the DBD. Such a positively charged sequence, found in all steroid receptors, has been demonstrated to be involved in the nuclear localization of GR, PR and ER.[28-30]

The fourth region, located at the N-terminal of the molecule, is hypervariable in size and amino acid composition among steroid receptors. Its detailed function(s) is unknown, but preliminary results have indicated that, at least for GR, ER and PR, it has a transactivation property that increases gene transcription regardless of hormone binding. However, this transactivation function appears specific in terms of particular regulated genes and cells, depending on precise amino acid sequences.

Experiments utilizing hybrid proteins constructed with different regions of different receptors, based on the knowledge of their primary sequences, have built up the notion of modular structure, which states that each domain of a receptor can demonstrate independently most, if not all, characteristic functions of its own.

PR is actually found in human and chick in two forms, B and A.[31] The A form is an N-terminal truncated version of the B form (minus ≈ 130 aa). In spite of apparently identical hormone and DNA binding properties, the two forms demonstrate different cell and gene specificities in their transcriptional activities, making the progesterone system rather complex. The A and B forms are coded by a single gene and their concentration in target cells appears developmentally regulated. Three mechanisms—differential RNA processing, alternate translation initiation and specific proteolysis—have been invoked to explain their synthesis.

Steroid receptors are proteins that transactivate transcription of target genes which are therefore hormone-regulated. In many cases, the segment(s) of DNA (HREs) with which receptors interact has been described (reviews in[32-34]). These HREs are called PRE (progesterone response element), GRE (glucocorticosteroid response element) and so on. They share most properties of enhancers. They may be inverted and may be found near or far upstream from the 5'-start site of transcription, occasionally in an intron, or even furtherdown. They include fifteen base pairs that form an imperfect palindrome (two half-sides of 6bp plus 3bp in between) (Figure 3). Most PREs have in common the same six bp in one half-site but varied sequences in the other half-site. Interestingly, PR binds all GREs and inversely all PREs can be bound by GR. Certain genes have several HREs, including one or several half-HREs.

It has been shown for PR, GR and ER that two receptor molecules bind to a palindromic HRE, forming a functional dimer. PRs can form homodimers (BB or AA)

[28] D. Picard, & K. R. Yamamoto, *Two signals mediate hormone-dependent nuclear localization of the glucocorticoid receptor*, 6. Embo J. 3333–40 (1987).

[29] D. Picard, V. Kumar, P. Chambon & K. R. Yamamoto, *Signal transduction by steroid hormones: nuclear localization is differentially regulated in estrogen and glucocorticoid receptors*, 1 Cell Reg. 291–99 (1990).

[30] A. Guiochon-Mantel, H. Lossfelt, P. Lescop, S. Sar, M. Atger, M. Perrot-Applanat & E. Milgrom, *Mechanisms of nuclear localization of the progesterone receptor: evidence for interaction between monomers*, 57 Cell 1147–54 (1989).

[31] M. R. Sherman, P. L. Corvol & B. W. O'Malley, *Progesterone-binding components of chick oviduct*, 245 J. Biol. Chem. 6085–96 (1970).

[32] S. Green & P. Chambon, *Nuclear-receptors enhance our understanding of transcription regulation*, 4 Trends Genet. 309–14 (1988).

[33] M. Beato, *Gene regulation by steroid hormones*, 56 Cell 335–44 (1989).

[34] J. Ham & M. G. Parker, *Regulation of gene expression by nuclear hormone receptors*, 1 Curr. Op. Cell Biol. 503–11 (1989).

Figure 3. Hormone response elements (HREs). Consensus sequences for progesterone (P) and glucocorticosteroid (G) receptors and estrogen (E) receptors.

PRE/GRE	ERE
G	A
G	G
T	G
A	T
C	C
A	A
n	n
n	n
n	n
T	T
G	G
T	A
T	C
C	C
T	T

or heterodimers (AB),[35] but heterodimers of receptors of different hormones have not been observed. It is probably that PR dimerization is mostly a property of the LBD, as already demonstrated for ER[36,37] and GR.[38]

PR (as ER) is a nuclear protein. Whether detected in absence of hormone by immunocytochemical methods[39–42] or after binding of hormone by radioactive labeling,

[35] M. E. Meyer, A. Pornon, J. Ji, M. T. Bocquel, P. Chambon & H. Gronemeyer, *Agonist and antagonist activities of RU486 on the functions of human progesterone receptor* (1990 submitted for publication).

[36] V. Kumar & P. Chambon, *The estrogen receptor binds tightly to its responsive element as a ligand-induced homodimer*, 55 Cell 145–56 (1988).

[37] M. Sabbah, G. Redeuilh & E. E. Baulieu, *Subunit composition of the estrogen receptor. Involvement of the hormone-binding domain the dimeric state*, 264 J. Biol. Chem. 2397–400 (1989).

[38] O. Wrange, P. Eriksson & T. Perlmann, *The purified activated glucocorticoid receptor is a homodimer*, 264 J. Biol. Chem. 5253–59 (1989).

[39] J. M. Gasc, B. W. Ennis, E. E. Baulieu & W. E. Stumpf, *Récepteur de la progestérone dans l'oviducte*

the receptor is distinctly nuclear (not present in the nucleolus). GR also is in part a nuclear protein in absence of hormone.[43] The significance of cytoplasmic immunoreactive GR has not been elucidated. We believe that in absence of hormone, the receptor is loosely bound in the nucleus and may be in part cytoplasmic, while after in vivo hormone binding, all receptors are tightly attached to nuclear elements. More importantly than its subcellular localization, as indicated by available techniques (which are imperfect), is the receptor's structure, which appears to be modified according to absence or presence of hormone binding.

It was believed for a long time that the unliganded receptors were cytoplasmic, since after homogenization of cells not exposed to progesterone, they are obtained in the cytosoluble fraction of the homogenate (cytosol). In fact, receptors in absence of hormone are heterooligomers loosely bound to nuclear structure and "extracted" into cytosol during homogenization. PR was detected in the nucleus in absence of hormone. The cytosol PR and thereafter GR were found to be associated with a "90 k protein" rapidly identified as hsp90.[44-46] The same was found for ER, MR and AR. Although most hsp90 molecules are cytoplasmic, experiments have demonstrated the presence of some hsp90 in the nucleus[47] and the nuclear localization of the non-transformed, hsp90 containing, unliganded receptor complex.[48] Very likely, the linkage between hsp90 and the receptor occurs just after synthesis of the latter in the cytoplasm.[49] The mode of transport into the nucleus is unknown. The binding to hsp90 may play a role in protecting the unliganded receptor against chemical/enzymatic degradation.[50] This binding may

de poulet: double révélation par immunohistochimie avec des anticorps antirécepteur et par autoradiographie à l'aide d'un progestagène tritié. 297 C. R. Acad. Sci. Paris 477–82 (1983).

[40] J. M. Gasc, J. M. Renoir, C. Radanyi, I. Joab, P. Tuohimaa & E. E. Baulieu, *Progesterone receptor in the chick oviduct: an immunohistochemical study with antibodies to distinct receptor components,* 99 J. Cell Biol. 1193–201 (1984).

[41] W. J. King & G. L. Greene, *Monoclonal antibodies localize oestrogen receptor in the nuclei of target cells,* 307 Nature 745–47 (1984).

[42] W. Welshons, M. E. Lieberman & J. Gorski, *Nuclear localization of unoccupied oestrogen receptors,* 307 Nature 747–49 (1984).

[43] J. M. Gasc, F. Delahaye & E. E. Baulieu, *Compared intracellular localization of the glucocorticoid and progesterone receptors: an immunocytochemical study,* 181 Exp. Cell Res. 492–504 (1989).

[44] I. Joab, C. Radanyi, J. M. Renoir, T. Buchou, M. G. Catelli, N. Binart, J. Mester & E. E. Baulieu, *Immunological evidence for a common non hormone-binding component in "non-transformed" chick oviduct receptors of four steroid hormones,* 308 Nature 850–53 (1984).

[45] M. G. Catelli, N. Binart, I. Jung-Testas, J. M. Renoir, E. E. Baulieu, J. R. Feramisco & W. J. Welch, *The common 90-kd protein component of non-transformed "8S" steroid receptors is a heat-shock protein,* 4 Embo J. 3131–35 (1985).

[46] E. R. Sanchez, D. O. Toft, M. J. Schlesinger & W. B. Pratt, *Evidence that the 90-kDa phosphoprotein associated with the untransformed L-cell glucocorticoid receptor is a murine heat-shock protein,* 260 J. Biol. Chem. (1985).

[47] J. M. Gasc, J. M. Renoir, L. E. Faber, F. Delahaye & E. E. Baulieu, *Nuclear localization of two steroid receptor-associated proteins, hsp90 and p59,* 186 Exp. Cell Res. 362–67 (1990).

[48] J. M. Renoir, C. Radanyi, I. Jung-Testas, L. E. Faber & E. E. Baulieu, *The nonactivated progesterone receptor is a nuclear heterooligomer,* 265 J. Biol. Chem. in press (1990).

[49] F. C. Dalman, E. H. Bresnick, P. D. Patel, G. H. Perdew, S. J. Watson & W. B. Pratt, *Direct evidence that the glucocorticoid receptor binds to hsp90 at or near the termination of receptor translation in vitro,* 264 J. Biol. Chem. 19815–21 (1989).

[50] J. Mester, J. M. Gasc, T. Buchou, J. M Renoir, I. Joab, C. Radanyi, N. Binart, M. G. Catelli & E. E. Baulieu, *Structure properties and subcellular localization of the chick oviduct progesterone receptor,* in *Molecular Mechanism of Steroid Hormone Action* 36–60 (V. K. Moudgil ed. 1985).

also help LBD to remain susceptible to bind the incoming hormone instead of taking an unfavorable conformation (this appears to be the case for the glucocorticosteroid receptor, which does not bind the hormone in absence of hsp90[51]).

Molecular genetics and biochemical experiments have indicated that the non-covalent interaction of hsp90 with the receptor is two-fold. First, LBD binds hsp90[52-56] in a multipoint process. There is evidence for at least three sections, each sufficient but not necessary for the binding of hsp90 by the GR LBD.[57] Second, we have suggested that the charged amino acids in the C-terminal Zn-finger (and certainly with ER[58]) and the charged sequence in the hinge region of the receptor interact with a predominantly negatively charged so-called region A of hsp90.[59] Since hsp90 does not bind DNA nor does the heterooligomeric form of the receptor (so-called "8S" according to the sedimentation coefficient), it has been proposed that hsp90, fastened in an appropriate disposition by binding to LBD, precludes the binding of the receptor to DNA by electrostatic mechanism and by steric hindrance.[60,61]

Apparently hsp90 is always in dimeric form. The dimers may be homo- or heterodimers since there are two very similar isoforms ("α" and "β"), both of which can interact with receptors. Unlike with ER, whose 8S-form contains two ER molecules and two hsp90 molecules,[62] the 8S-PR and 8S-GR may contain only one receptor molecule and two hsp90 molecules.[63,64]

[51] E. H. Bresnick, F. C. Dalman, E. R. Sanchez & W. B. Pratt, *Evidence that the 90-kDa heat shock protein is necessary for the steroid binding conformation of the L cell glucocorticoid receptor*, 264 J. Biol. Chem. 4992–97 (1989).

[52] U. Gehring & H. Arndt, *Heteromeric nature of glucocorticoid receptors*, 179 Febs Lett. 138–42 (1985).

[53] W. B. Pratt, D. J. Jolly, D. V. Pratt, S. M. Hollenberg, V. Giguere, F. Cadepond, G. Schweizer-Groyer, M. G. Catelli, R. M. Evans & E. E. Baulieu, *A region in the steroid binding domain determines formation of the non-DNA-binding,9S glucocorticoid receptor complex*, 263 J. Biol. Chem. 267–73 (1988).

[54] M. Denis, J. A. Gustafsson & A. C. Wikstrom, *Interaction of the Mr = 90,000 heat shock protein with the steroid-binding domain of the glucocorticoid receptor*, 263 J. Biol. Chem. 18520–23 (1988).

[55] M. A. Carson-Jurica, A. T. Lee, A. W. Dobson, O. M. Conneely, W. T. Schrader & B. W. O'Malley, *Interaction of the chicken progesterone receptor with heat shock protein (hsp) 90*, 34 J. Steroid Biochem. 1–9 (1989).

[56] K. J. Howard, S. J. Holley, K. R. Yamamoto & C. W. Distelhorst, *Mapping the hsp90 binding region of the glucocorticoid receptor*, 265 J. Biol. Chem. 11928–35 (1990).

[57] F. Cadepond, G. Schweizer-Groyer, I. Segard-Maurel, N. Jibard, V. Giguere, R. M. Evans & E. E. Baulieu, *Three regions in the ligand binding domain of the human glucocorticosteroid receptor can determine 8S-heterooligomer formation and repress transcriptional activity* (1990, submitted for publication).

[58] B. Chambraud, M. Berry, G. Redeuilh, P. Chambon & E. E. Baulieu, *Several regions of human estrogen receptor are involved in the formation of receptor-hsp90 complexes*, J. Biol. Chem. (1990).

[59] N. Binart, B. Chambraud, B. Dumas, D. A. Rowlands, C. Bigogne, J. M. Levin, J. Garnier, E. E. Baulieu & M. G. Catelli, *The cDNA-derived amino acid sequence of chick heat shock protein Mr 90,000 (hsp90) reveals a "DNA like" structure, potential site of interaction with steroid receptors*, 159 Biochem. Biophys. Res. Commun. 140–47 (1989).

[60] E. E. Baulieu, *Steroid hormone antagonists at the receptor level. A role for the heat-shock protein MW 90,000 (hsp90)*, 35 J. Cell Biochem. 161–74 (1987).

[61] E. E. Baulieu, N. Binart, F. Cadepond, M. G. Catelli, B. Chambraud, J. Garnier, J. M. Gasc, G. Groyer-Schweizer, M. E. Oblin, C. Radanyi, G. Redeuilh, J. M. Renoir & M. Sabbah, *Do receptor-associated nuclear proteins explain earliest steps of steroid hormone function?* in The Steroid/Thyroid Hormone Receptor Family and Gene Regulation 301–18 (J. Carlstedt-Duke, H. Eriksson & J. A. Gustafsson eds. 1990).

[62] G. Redeuilh, B. Moncharmont, C. Secco & E. E. Baulieu, *Subunit composition of the molybdate-stabilized "8-9S" non-transformed estradiol receptor purified from calf uterus*, 262 J. Biol. Chem. 6969–75 (1987).

Figure 4. Mechanism of action of steroid hormone at the receptor (H: hormone; R: receptor; hsp: heat shock protein, MW 90,000; p59: see text; -,*: symbols for transconformations of the receptor protein).

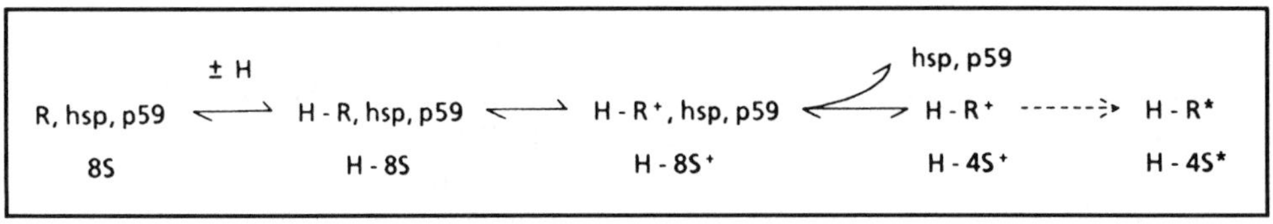

$$R, hsp, p59 \underset{}{\overset{\pm H}{\longleftrightarrow}} H\text{-}R, hsp, p59 \longleftrightarrow H\text{-}R^+, hsp, p59 \overset{hsp, p59}{\underset{}{\rightleftharpoons}} H\text{-}R^+ \cdots\cdots\!\!\!\dashrightarrow H\text{-}R^*$$

$$8S \qquad\qquad\qquad H\text{-}8S \qquad\qquad\qquad H\text{-}8S^+ \qquad\qquad\qquad H\text{-}4S^+ \qquad\qquad H\text{-}4S^*$$

Recently, a third nuclear protein (p59)—MW $\approx$ 59,000 Da—has been identified as being part of the 8S-PR (and other steroid receptors).[65,66] It binds to hsp90. Cloned recently, it does not resemble any known protein (M. C. Lebeau, N. Massol and J. Herrick, in preparation). Preliminary investigations ascribe one molecule of p59 to one 8S-PR complex. One possibility is that p59 sequesters part of hsp90 in the nucleus and then anchors the receptor complex to a nuclear structure in the absence of hormone.

The physiological significance of the binding of several proteins to receptors (including a heat shock protein of MW $\approx$ 70,000 family[67]) has not been established.

3. Hormone Action: Three Steps (figures 4 and 5)

After steroid hormone has entered the target cell and reached the receptor, the hormone-receptor complex binds tightly to DNA. After homogenization, it is not found in the cytosol but attached to the nuclear fraction.

a.   TRANSFORMATION   The receptor's high affinity for the nucleus is correlated to a physical transformation[68]: the receptor becomes smaller (so-called ''4S'') and separates from the hsp90 and p59 present in the 8S-heterooligomeric form (figure 4). The most likely hypothesis is that transconformation of the LBD upon hormone binding leads to the release of hsp90 (and p59 attached to it). It is not known whether only the release of hsp90, and/or a hormone-induced transconformation by itself, and/or the subsequent binding of receptor to palindromic DNA is (are) operational in receptor dimerization.

b.   DNA BINDING   Steroid receptors bind to HRE by their DBD. Experiments using purified PR and GR with PRE, GRE or nonspecific-DNA have indicated that, provided hsp90 is removed, PR will bind to DNA identically in the presence or absence of hormone. The preventive effect of hsp90 may explain the lack of receptor activity in

[63] J. M. Renoir, T. Buchou & E. E. Baulieu, *Involvement of a non-hormone binding 90kDa protein in the non-transformed 8S form of the rabbit uterus progesterone receptor,* 25 Biochemistry 6405–13 (1986).

[64] J. A. Gustafsson, J. Carlstedt-Duke, L. Poellinger, S. Okret, A. C. Wikstrom, M. Bronnegard, M. Gillner, Y. Dong, K. Fuxe, A. Cintra, A. Harfstrand & L. Agnati, *Biochemistry, molecular biology and physiology of the glucocorticoid receptor,* 8 End. Rev. 185–234 (1987).

[65] P. K. K. Tai, Y. Maeda, K. Nakao, N. G. Wakin, J. L. Duhring & L. E. Faber, *A 59-kilodalton protein associated with progestin, estrogen, androgen, and glucocorticoid receptors,* 25 Biochem. 5269–75 (1986).

[66] J. M. Renoir, C. Radanyi, L. E. Faber & E. E. Baulieu, *The non-DNA binding heterooligomeric form of mammalian steroid hormone receptors contains a hsp90-bound 59-Kilodalton protein,* 265 J. Biol. Chem. 10740–45 (1990).

[67] D. F. Smith, L. E. Faber & D. O. Toft, *Purification of unactivated progesterone receptor and identification of novel receptor-associated proteins,* 265 J. Biol. Chem. 3996–4403 (1990).

[68] E. V. Jensen & E. R. De Sombre, *Mechanism of action of the female sex hormones,* 41 Ann. Rev. Biochem. 203–30 (1972).

Figure 5. Cellular and molecular mechanism of action of steroid hormone (H) and antihormone (RU, RU486). In absence of hormone, the ligand binding domain of the receptor (R) is bound to hsp90, and the DNA binding domain is capped by the negatively charged A region of hsp90 (see text). The nuclear p59 protein binds hsp90. After H binding, R is released and binds to a hormone response element (HRE) of the DNA, present in the promoter of a regulated gene; a change of nucleosome structure and the binding of a transcription factor (TF) are represented; transcription can then start. After RU binding, the interaction of R to hsp90 is reinforced, and there is no interaction of R with DNA (a), and/or hsp is released secondarily and, although R may bind to DNA, its new form hinders the function of transcription factors (see text).

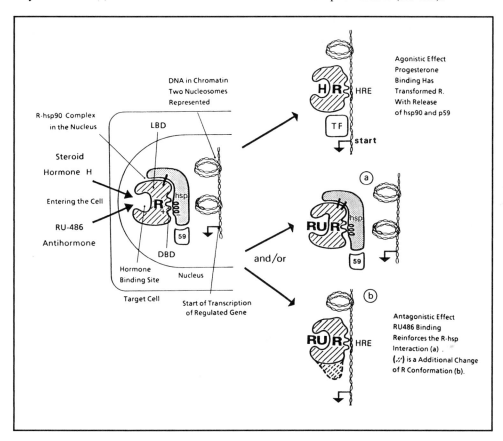

vivo in absence of hormone, in spite of the intrinsic capacity of the receptor molecule itself to bind to DNA. Several recent publications have indicated the possible role of yet poorly defined nonreceptor proteins in the achievement of high affinity specific binding to HREs. Two receptors as PR and GR can bind to the same HRE. However, small differences in the contacts between the receptors and DNA may be responsible in part for dissimilar potency and kinetics of the hormone responses.[69]

c.   AFTER DNA BINDING   Two main consequences of the receptor-hormone complex binding to DNA have been studied. The first is a chromatin effect. With the mouse

---

[69] D. Von Der Ahe, J. M. Renoir, T. Buchou, E. E. Baulieu & M. Beato, *Receptors for glucocorticosteroid and progesterone recognize distinct features of a DNA regulatory element,* 83 Proc. Natl. Acad. Sci. USA 2817–21 (1986).

mammary tumor virus (MMTV) system, the binding of the corticosteroid-GR complexes alters chromatin structure, specifically altering a GRE-bearing nucleosome in the long terminal repeat (LTR)-promoter region.[70,71] Such change, represented arbitrarily on figure 5, may modify the access to DNA of transcription factors (TF) involved in transactivation. This model has recently been extended to a regulatory region of the tyrosine amino transferase gene.[72] Hormone-induced changes of chromatin structure and function is a very important sector of current research.

Secondly, the consequence of receptor binding on TFs' activity cannot be overstated. TFs not only differ according to the DNA cis-transactivation elements to which they bind (thus activate or block transcription), they also differ qualitatively and/or quantitatively according to cell types. Their role as limiting factors for receptor activity may be critical for the steroid-induced responses.[73] Binding of receptor to DNA may facilitate the binding of TFs to their own DNA targets, whether or not there is direct interaction between receptor and TFs. Conversely, receptor binding to HRE may impede the function of a TF, by steric hindrance or by competition with TF binding to DNA or to another protein; in this case, the hormone-induced response will be inhibitory to transcription.

Other molecular changes may accompany hormone effects at the receptor-DNA-chromatin-TF level. For example, a protein kinase follows PR closely during its purification.[74,75] A change in phosphorylation of the receptor or nonreceptor protein(s) may be involved in the early steps of hormone action and/or, as suggested by experiments in absence of ATP supply, in the recycling of the receptor.[76]

In summary, the very first step following hormone binding to PR is a change of receptor conformation, releasing hsp90. This change occurs in the LBD which may then become an active transcriptional activator, probably via interaction with the function of transcription factors. There is no evidence that a change in conformation is required for DBD to bind to specific PRE(s) after hsp90 release. Binding of DBD to DNA may provoke changes in chromatin structure and in TF function.

Whether the hormone-receptor complexes interact directly with RNA processing, mRNA stabilization and translation and other steps of protein synthesis is unknown; however, indirect effects may occur via a change in synthesis of important proteins involved in RNA and protein metabolism.

---

[70] T. K. Archer, M. G. Cordingley, V. Marsaud, H. Richard-Foy & G. L. Harger, *Steroid transactivation at a promoter organized in a specifically-positioned array of nucleosomes,* in The Steroid/Thyroid Hormone Receptor Family and Gene Regulation 221–38 (J. Carlstedt-Duke, H. Eriksson & J. A. Gustafsson eds. 1989).

[71] T. Perlmann & O. Wrange, *Specific glucocorticoid receptor binding to DNA reconstituted in a nucleosome,* 7 Embo. J. 3073–79 (1988).

[72] K. D. Carr & H. Richard-Foy, *Glucocorticoids locally disrupt an array of positioned nucleosomes on the rat tyrosine amino transferase promoter in hepatoma cells,* Proc. Natl. Acad. Sci. USA (1990, in press).

[73] M. E. Meyer, H. Gronemeyer, B. Turcotte, M. T. Bocquel, D. Tasset & P. Chambon, *Steroid hormone receptors compete for factors that mediate their enhancer function,* 57 Cell 433–42 (1989).

[74] T. Garcia, T. Buchou, J. M. Renoir, J. Mester & E. E. Baulieu, *A protein kinase copurified with chick oviduct progesterone receptor,* 25 Biochemistry 7937–42 (1986).

[75] F. Logeat, M. Le Cunff, M. Rauch, S. Brailly & E. Milgrom, *Characterization of a casein kinase which interacts with the rabbit progesterone receptor,* 661 Eur. J. Biochem. 51–57 (1987).

[76] D. B. Mendel, J. E. Bodwell & A. Munck, *Glucocorticoid receptors lacking hormone-binding activity are bound in nuclei of ATP-depleted cells,* 324 Nature 478–80 (1986).

4. Mode of Action of RU486

RU486 has high affinity for the receptor and a long metabolic half-life. Thus, it can effectively exclude the corresponding agonist from receptor binding, and itself binds to the receptor. The agonist is then eliminated from the target cells or metabolized in situ.

Why the RU486-receptor complexes are inactive and thus in effect oppose progesterone action, and why they occasionally exert agonist activity may be explained by examining the three levels discussed above.

a. DECREASED RATE OF TRANSFORMATION   In vitro experiments have indicated that the binding of RU486 to 8S-PR or GR increases the stability of the heterooligomer when it is exposed to temperature increase as a function of time.[77,78] The significance of these cell-free experiments is reinforced by observations made in intact cells. Some researchers have looked at the 8S-form of the receptor itself; others have demonstrated that there is no protection of GRE against artificial methylation if the cells have been exposed to RU486, in contrast to when the cells have been exposed to a glucocorticosteroid agonist that provokes receptor binding to the GRE.[79] The logical interpretation is that the non-DNA binding heterooligomer has been stabilized by RU486, in contrast to the effect of the agonist. The relatively slow kinetics of RU486-induced transformation of the receptor contributes to antihormone action. Experiments performed with different biological systems under various conditions have shown that RU486-receptor complexes do behave dynamically differently from agonist-receptor complexes.[80,81]

b. DNA BINDING   From the preceding section, one may think that the mechanism of antagonistic action of RU486, via stabilization of hsp90-receptor interaction, is to prevent DNA binding. However, in a number of experiments, transformation of the receptor and tight binding to the nucleus of antagonist-receptor complex have been observed. The binding parameters of RU486-receptor to PRE are indistinguishable from that of agonist-receptor in in vitro experiments (receptor separated from hsp90). However, RU486-receptor-PRE complexes behave electrophoretically differently from agonist-receptor-PRE complexes. This is probably due to change of conformation of the receptor when binding RU486 as compared to agonist and may be due to "abnormal" DNA bending. Therefore, although differential effects at the DNA level are still possible, it is likely that RU486's lack of agonist activity is due to the RU486-induced LBD transconformation, which is then not able to insure transcriptional activity, even if DBD binds to DNA.

The agonistic activities of RU486 almost certainly depend on binding of RU486-receptor complex to PRE.

---

[77] A. Groyer, G. Schweizer-Groyer, F. Cadepond, M. Mariller & E. E. Baulieu, *Antiglucocorticosteroid effects suggest why steroid hormone is required for receptors to bind DNA in vivo but not in vitro*, 328 Nature 624–26 (1987).

[78] B. Segnitz & U. Gehring, *Mechanism of action of a steroidal antiglucocorticoid in lymphoid cells*, 265 J. Biol. Chem. 2789–96 (1990).

[79] P. B. Becker, B. Gloss, W. Schmid, U. Strahle & G. Schutz, *In vivo protein-DNA interactions in a glucocorticoid response element require the presence of the hormone*, 324 Nature 686–88 (1986).

[80] M. Moguilewski & D. Philibert, *RU38486: potent antiglucocorticoid activity correlated with strong binding to the cytosolic glucocorticoid receptor followed by an impaired activation*, 20 J. Steroid Biochem. 271–76 (1984).

[81] S. Bourgeois, M. Pfahl & E. E. Baulieu, *DNA binding properties of glucocorticoseroid receptors bound to the steroid antagonist RU486*, 3 Embo J. 751–55 (1984).

In conclusion, slow-down of the transformation rate described in the previous section does not exclude binding of RU486-receptor complex to DNA, whether the ultimate effect is antagonistic or agonistic.

c. PRE-, AT- OR POST-DNA BINDING EFFECT(S)   It is important to note that in experiments with intact cells or performed in vivo, the agonistic effect of RU486 is always much inferior to that of the corresponding agonist. In addition, there are many systems where RU486 does not display any agonistic action. Indeed, RU486 is essentially an antagonist.

The reasons for differences according to the observed systems may be found at different levels. We have seen that before DNA binding, the transformation of the receptor by RU486 can be slow and minimal. We have also suggested that the binding to DNA of RU486-receptor complexes may differ qualitatively from the binding of agonist-receptor complexes, although there is no available data to support this hypothesis.

Importantly, RU486-receptor complexes, more specifically RU486-LBD complexes, differ conformationally from agonist-LBD complexes. This seems indicated by the following observations: PR A or PR B can make a heterodimer if both bind either an agonist or RU486; however, if one binds an agonist and the other RU486, they cannot form a heterodimer, as if their surfaces of interaction have become incompatible. The "abnormal" conformation of the receptor complexed with antihormone may interfere with receptor-TF interaction and thus prevent TF from activating transcription. When heated (and thus presumably transformed and rid of protective hsp90) RU486-GR complexes are particularly unstable, and this may be involved in the antihormonal property of RU486.

There is also a transactivation function in the N-terminal domain of the receptor, independent of hormone binding, that may or may not work according to the cell system. Therefore, although RU486 antagonizes transcriptional activity of the LBD, this N-terminal activating function may or may not be active according to the cell system and can be responsible for the occasional agonist activity of RU486.

d. RECEPTOR REGULATION   Besides direct effects of ligand binding on receptor molecular structure and function, hormone and antihormone molecules can change the concentration of the receptor, a process that may be critical to explaining hormonal and antihormonal activities. In most mammalian systems, progestins have a down-regulation effect on PR activity[82]; this was demonstrated independently at the same time as the down-regulation of insulin receptor.[83] The decrease of PR concentration suggested by radioligand binding assay was confirmed immunohistologically,[84] indicating an effect on receptor protein synthesis responsible for the functional deficit of hormone binding. RU486 antagonizes the progestin down-regulation effect, but the detailed mechanism by which the down regulation occurs (at the transcriptional, post-transcriptional or receptor half-life level) remains unknown. Regulatory aspects of PR concentration may be even

---

[82] E. Milgrom, M. Luu Thi, M. Atger & E. E. Baulieu, *Mechanisms regulating the concentration and the conformation of progesterone receptor(s) in the uterus,* 248 J. Biol. Chem. 6366–74 (1973).

[83] J. Roth, C. R. Kahn, M. A. Lesniak, P. Gorden, P. De Meyts, K. Megyesi, D. M. Neville, J. R. Gavin, A. H. Soll, P. Freychet, I. D. Goldfine, R. S. Bar & J. A. Archer, *Receptors for insulin, NSILA-s and growth hormone: applications to disease states in man,* 31 Rec. Progr. Hormone Res. 95–139 (1975).

[84] E. J. Rajpert, F. P. Lemaigre, P. H. Eliard, M. Place, D. A. Lafontaine, I. V. Economidis, A. Belayew, J. A. Martial & G. G. Rousseau, *Glucocorticoid receptors bound to the antagonist RU486 are not down-regulated despite their capacity to interact in vitro with defined gene regions,* 26 J. Steroid Biochem. 513–20 (1987).

more complex; for example, in the young chick oviduct system, progestin causes an increase of PR concentration.[85] More research should be done in this area, considering that the concentration of progesterone receptor is decisive in determining the amplitude of hormone effect. Even less well established, down regulation of other steroid receptors by their own hormones seems also to occur.

5. Conclusions

In summary, that RU486 can bind to LBD of PR and GR is certain. It is logical that LBD changes conformation and that the produced transconformations are different when agonist or antagonist binds to it. Like GR and ER, PR binds hsp90, very likely at the LBD level. Hormone-induced transformation with release of hsp90 permits binding to the corresponding PRE/GRE. The weak agonist property of RU486 does not provide an obstacle clinically when RU486 is suppressing progesterone or cortisol action. However, the limited progestin-like activity, especially significant in the absence of progesterone, could be of pharmacological interest (see above). In molecular terms, the antagonistic activity of RU486 may be due principally to the stabilization of LBD-hsp90 binding and to the specific LBD transconformation that makes it inactive. Slow transformation thus is followed by the formation of a receptor with inactive LBD transactivation function but with still an N-terminal domain that may be responsible for some agonistic activity.

LBD, binding hormone or antihormone, thus appears to play a critical role in receptor function. Its ligand-induced transconformation involved in hsp90 release appears to occur independently from transconformation involved in transactivation.

Detailed studies in different cell types and different hormonal environments are required to apply these concepts to clinical and physiological situations.

II. Clinical Applications

1. Pregnancy Interruption

Since the first publication, the story of RU486 has been dominated by the abortion issue. The use of RU486 as an abortifacient has been the subject of a number of recent reviews. Briefly, RU486 upsets the normal balance between progesterone (P) and prostaglandin (PG) in pregnancy: RU486 exerts an antiprogesterone effect, sensitizes the uterus to PG and increases endogenous PG level (by provoking PG production by endometrial decidual cells and inhibiting PG catabolism). Decreased P bioactivity prevents or disrupts implantation of the embryo. Increased PG bioactivity stimulates uterine contractility and dilates and softens the cervix. RU486 thus both directly and indirectly creates an environment unfavorable for the establishment and maintenance of pregnancy.

A short interruption of progesterone activity appears sufficient to stop early pregnancy[86] and the luteal phase of a nonfertile cycle. Therefore, only a brief period of toxicology studies in animals was required before clinically testing the antiprogesterone

[85] T. Ylikomi, J. Isola, J. Ratia, T. Vaha-Tahlo & P. Tuohimaa, *Augmentation of progesterone receptor concentration by progesterone and estrogen treatments in the chick oviduct*, 20 J. Steroid Biochem. 445–47 (1984).

[86] A. I. Csapo & T. Erdos, *The critical control of progesterone levels and pregnancy by anti-progesterone*, 126 Am. J. Obstet. Gynecol. 598 (1976).

activity of RU486. The success rate for a single dose of 600 mg of RU486 alone[87,88] is 80% in pregnancies of less than 42 days of amenorrhea, but this percentage decreases significantly in longer pregnancies. However, RU486 plus a small dose of prostaglandin (PG),[89] given 36–48 hours later,[90-92] would raise the efficiency rate to equal to or greater than 95% up to 49 days of amenorrhea.[93] The delay allows time for the reversal of transcription-dependent P activity. Of failures, 4% are due to incomplete abortions and/or bleeding, indicating instrumental intervention. In 1%, RU486 exerts no effect; with reference to the case of the chick receptor (see above), the reason may be of genetic origin. As expected, an ovulatory cycle is restored after abortion; there are no long-term effects, and several women have subsequently brought pregnancies to term successfully.

Over 50,000 women in France have chosen RU486/PG over surgery for abortion. A study from May 1988 to November 1989 of 10,244 cases in 246 centers in France yielded an efficacy rate of 95.4% (95% CI 95.0–95.8%) (unpublished international report by Roussel-Uclaf) for pregnancies $\leq$ 49 days of amenorrhea. In Great Britain, a study by 13 hospital units from August 1987 to June 1988 involving 588 pregnant women with $\leq$ 63 days of amenorrhea yielded 94% efficacy (95% CI 92–96%).[94] Incidentally, the difference between France and Great Britain in the maximum number of days of amenorrhea arises from the fact that a doctor appointment requires a longer delay in Great Britain. Studies conducted in China from May 1986 to July 1988 that included 422 pregnancies $\leq$ 49 days of amenorrhea gave 94.1% efficacy.[95] The evidence for the safety and efficacy of the RU486/PG method is compelling.

The success rate of this method is thus comparable to vacuum aspiration minus the complications of surgical and anesthetic techniques.[96] Fetomaternal hemorrhage has been shown to occur less often during medical than surgical abortion, reducing the risk of isoimmunization with benefit for the woman and for future pregnancies.[97] In addition,

---

[87] A. Ulmann, *Uses of RU486 for contragestion: an update,* 36 Contraception 27–31 (1987).

[88] B. Couzinet, N. Le Strat, A. Ulmann, E. E. Baulieu & G. Schaison, *Termination of early pregnancy by the progesterone antagonist RU486 (mifepristone),* 315 New Engl. J. Med. 1565–70 (1986).

[89] S. Bergström, E. Diczfaluzy, U. Borell, S. Karim, B. Samuelsson, B. Uvnas, N. Wiqvist & M. Bygdeman, *Prostaglandins in fertility control* 175 Science 1280–87 (1972).

[90] M. Bygdeman & M. L. Swahn, *Progesterone receptor blockage: effect on uterine contractility and early pregnancy,* 32 Contraception 45–51 (1985).

[91] M. W. Rodger & D. T. Baird, *Induction of therapeutic abortion in early pregnancy with Mifepristone in combination with prostaglandin pessary,* 2 Lancet 1415–16 (1987).

[92] C. Dubois, A. Ulmann, E. Aubeny, D. Elia, M. C. Jourdan, M. C. Van Den Bosch, M. Leton & E. E. Baulieu, *Contragestion par le RU486: intérêt de l'association à un dérivé prostaglandine,* 306 C.R. Acad. Sci. Paris 57–61 (1988).

[93] L. Silvestre, C. Dubois, M. Renault, Y. Rezvani, E. E. Baulieu & A. Ulmann, *Voluntary interruption of pregnancy with mifepristone (RU486) and a prostaglandin analogue,* 322 New Engl. J. Med. 645–48 (1990).

[94] UK Multicentre Trial, *The efficacy and tolerance of mifepristone and prostaglandin in first trimester termination of pregnancy,* 97 Br. J. Obstet. Gynaecol. 480–86 (1990).

[95] Z. Shu-Rong, *RU486 (mifepristone): clinical trials in China,* suppl. 149 Acta Obstet. Gynecol Scand. 19–23 (1989).

[96] I. T. Cameron & D. T. Baird, *Early pregnancy termination: a comparison between vacuum aspiration and medical abortion using prostaglandin (16,16 dimethyl-trans-Δ_2-PGE$_1$ methyl ester) or the antiprogestogen RU486,* 95 Br. J. Obstet. Gynaecol. 271–76 (1988).

[97] D. R. Urquhart & A. Templeton, *Reduced risk of isoimmunisation in medical abortion,* 335 Lancet 914 (1990).

Table 1. Practical Developments of the Method in France

Day 1: The first consultation
- Ask for a voluntary interruption of pregnancy (VIP)
- Confirm the diagnosis and determine the age of pregnancy (dosage of β-hCG, eventually ultrasound)
- Choose the method
- Listen to explanation of information concerning the method and sign the consent form
- Make appointments for interview with social worker and for administration of RU486 after one week of reflection

Day 8: The second consultation
- Confirm your wish for a VIP
- Take 3 tablets of RU486 in the presence of the doctor who countersigns the consent form
- Determine the blood type
- Make appointment for administration of prostagladin

Day 10: The third consultation
- Prostaglandin is administered (by intramuscular injection or by vaginal pessary)
- Rest under the supervision of staff members of the center for 3–4 hours
- Immunize against Rh factor in case the mother is Rh negative (anti-D gamma globulin)
- Make appointment for the last visit

Day 16–20: The fourth consultation
- Verify that bleeding has ceased
- Verify that expulsion is complete (if necessary β-hCG and/or ultrasound)
- Decide on a contraceptive method

it has been argued that vacuum aspiration proves less effective in pregnancies of less than six weeks. Physicians have had to ask their patients to wait until the six to eight week period to perform aspiration despite the psychological hardship involving such a delay. Thus RU486/PG may be the preferred method in terminating pregnancies earlier than 42 days of amenorrhea.

Table 1 outlines the practical procedures of this method. According to Roussel-Uclaf, expulsion can take place before (3.4%), within 4 hours after (53.1%) or in the 24 hours following (43.5%) PG administration. Gestational age and/or dosage may explain the discrepancy in expulsion times, although the literature to date on predictors is limited.

The contraindications as listed by Roussel-Uclaf are still undergoing revision as more studies are performed. Pregnancies not confirmed biologically or by ultrasound top this list. The limit of 50 days of amenorrhea has been chosen because it is feared that after this date a more completely vascularized placenta would cause excessive bleeding. Suspicion of an ectopic pregnancy would preclude this method since antiprogesterone is not an efficient treatment in this case. Since RU486 is also an antiglucocorticosteriod, patients with adrenal insufficiency and those on long-term corticotherapy should not use this method. Anemia and hemostatic troubles also make the contraindication list since bleeding begins 2 or 3 days after intake of RU486 and continues for a mean duration of 10 days. Imperative contraindications against the use of prostaglandin include pulmonary troubles such as asthma and spasmodic bronchitis as well as cardiovascular problems including thoracic angina, arhythmia, and hypertension. As a measure of precaution due to absence of specific studies, the utilization of RU486/PG is also not advisable in the following cases: insulin-dependent diabetes, renal and hepatic insufficiency and malnutrition.

Despite its relatively few complications compared to the complications of vacuum aspiration, this method is not without problems. Ten percent of women require opioid analgesia. As mentioned above, bleeding lasts 10 days with individual variations between 4 and 40 days. This is slightly longer than after aspiration. The total measured blood loss is about 70–80 ml (range 14–400 ml), not significantly different from what is observed with RU486 or PG (large dose) alone, after vacuum aspiration or during heavy menstruation.[98] Since PG induces constriction of blood vessels, a higher dose of PG would be expected to help control bleeding; instead, clinically it is found that uterine bleeding increases with an increase in PG dosage. In an out-patient setting, this method requires strict medical supervision in order to monitor cases of excessive blood loss; ≦ 1% of cases require dilation and curettage (D & C); approximately 0.1 % of RU486-treated patients require blood transfusion. Nevertheless, although the method is highly effective, pregnancies continue in 1% of cases. Under these circumstances, termination of pregnancy by aspiration or D & C is recommended since RU486 crosses the fetoplacental barrier. As use of RU486/PG increases, so too can we expect an increase in the small number of incomplete abortions. Several studies have tested the teratogenic effects in embryos exposed to RU486. In mice and rats, no fetotoxicity has been observed. The weight and morphological characteristics of surviving fetuses appear normal. A limited trial with 16 female cynomolgus monkeys has indicated the tolerance of perinidatory embryos to RU486 exposure in vitro and in vivo.[99] However, some malformations mainly affecting the cranium were observed in rabbits.[100] Teratogenic effects of RU486 may have been associated with a malformed fetus aborted in the second trimester after the mother had taken the drug and the pregnancy had continued.[101] A recent report on the outcome of the pregnancies of three women who decided to continue to term before administration of PG shows that postnatal examination of the three infants revealed no abnormality and that each presently continues to develop normally six, nine and 15 months later, respectively.[102] Although these limited findings offer some comfort that human fetuses that have been exposed to RU486 continue to develop normally, extreme caution is recommended until more conclusive results are obtained with RU486 plus PG.

2. Contraception

Besides the successful clinical use of RU486 for early abortion, this compound appears, from experimental studies in animals, to inhibit follicle maturation, ovulation and egg implantation.

Much work has been done on interruption of the cycle at midluteal phase[103–105] with 50–200 mg RU486/d administered two to four times. However this method would

---

[98] D. T. Baird, M. Rodger, I. T. Cameron & I. Roberts, *Prostaglandins and antigestagens for the interruption of early pregnancy*, Suppl. 36 J. Reprod. Fertil. 173–79 (1988).

[99] J. P. Wolf, C. L. Chillik, C. Dubois, A. Ulmann, E. E. Baulieu & G. D. Hodgen, *Tolerance of perinidatory primate embryos to RU486 exposure in vitro and in vivo*, 41 Contraception 85–92 (1990).

[100] A. Jost, *Animal reproduction—New data on the hormonal requirement of the pregnant rabbit; partial pregnancies and fetal anomalies resulting from treatment with a hormonal antagonist given at a sub-abortive dosage*, 7 C.R. Acad. Sci. Paris. 281–84 (1986).

[101] R. Henrion, *RU486 abortions*, 338 Nature 110 (1989).

[102] B. H. Lim, D. A. R. Lees, S. Bjornsson, C. B. Lunan, M. R. Cohn, P. Stewart & A. Davey, *Normal development after exposure to mifepristone in early pregnancy*, 336 Lancet 257–58 (1990).

[103] W. Hermann et al., *supra* note 1.

be extremely unreliable since it often leads to changing the time of the next ovulation even in the absence of fertilization.

The use of RU486 *late in the cycle,* specifically on the last two days, 100–400 mg/d administered twice induces earlier menses in the nonpregnant women with no change in the next cycle.[106,107] A woman with a regular sex life has a 20% chance of being pregnant if she goes unprotected. This contraceptive method has a 20% failure rate.[108,109] Thus, the overall 4% (20% × 20%) failure rate of "late luteal contraception" leads to one pregnancy in two years. This result is insufficient. It may be improved with the addition of a small dose of PG or anti-GnRH; however, trials have not been conducted.

Periovulatory, and more precisely *2–3 days after the LH peak,* administration of RU486 at very low dose does not modify the luteal function and LH output. It provokes endometrium alteration[110,111] that may then prevent implantation (midcycle). Although this method works post-ovulatorily, it fits the definition of contraception by most societies of obstetrics and gynecology.

Finally, *conventional contraception* by prevention of fertilization could be obtained with RU486 since, administered during the follicular phase, it delays and eventually suppresses ovulation.[112,113] Croxatto has proposed a succession of RU486-progestin-RU486,[114] which may insure anovulation and cyclic "menses." However, even if this appealing estrogen-free contraception proves to have high efficacy, it probably will not be available in the near future. The problem lies in finding a drug company that would be willing to spend money on safety testing and development of a new contraceptive pill when several already exist.

But the fact remains that U486 may offer new methods of contraception in the near future.

---

[104] G. Schaison, M. George, N. Lestrat, M. Reinberg & E. E. Baulieu, *Effects of the antiprogesterone steroid RU486 during mid-luteal phase in normal women,* 61 J. Clin. Endocrinol. Metab. 484–89 (1985).

[105] V. G. Garzo, J. Liu, A. Ulmann, E. E. Baulieu & S. S. C. Yen, *Effects of an antiprogesterone (RU486) on the hypothalamic-hypophyseal-ovarian-endometrial axis during the luteal phase of the menstrual cycle,* 66 J. Clin. Endocrinol. Metab. 508–17 (1988).

[106] *Id.*

[107] H. B. Croxatto, A. M. Salvatierra, C. Romero, I. M. Spitz, *Late luteal phase administration of RU486 for three successive cycles does not disrupt bleeding patterns or ovulation,* 65 J. Clin. Endocrinol. Metab. 1272–77 (1987).

[108] P. Lähteenmäki, T. Rapeli, M. Kääriäinen, H. Alfthan & O. Ylikorkala, *Late postcoital treatment against pregnancy with antiprogesterone RU486,* 50 Fertil. Steril. 36–38 (1988).

[109] C. Dubois, A. Ulmann & E. E. Baulieu, *Contragestion with late luteal administration of RU486 (Mifepristone),* 50 Fertil. Steril. 593–96 (1988).

[110] T. C. Li, P. Dockery, P. Thomas, A. W. Rogers, E. A. Lenton, I. D. Cooke, *The effect of progesterone receptor blockade in the luteal phase of normal fertile women,* 50 Fertil. Steril. 732–42 (1988).

[111] M. L. Swahn, E. Johannisson, V. Daniore, B. de la Torre & M. Bygdeman, *The effect of RU486 administered during the proliferative and secretory phase of the cycle on the bleeding pattern, hormonal parameters and the endometrium,* 3 Hum. Reprod. 915–821 (1988).

[112] J. H. Liu & S. C. C. Yen, *Induction of midcycle gonadotropin surge by ovarian steroids in women: a critical evaluation,* 57 J. Clin. Endocrinol. Metab. 797–802 (1983).

[113] R. L. Collins & G. D. Hodgen, *Blockade of the spontaneous midcycle gonadotropin surge in monkeys by RU486: a progesterone antagonist or agonist,* 63 J. Clin. Endocrinol. Metab. 1270–76 (1986).

[114] H. B. Croxatto & A. M. Salvatierra, *Cyclic use of antigestagens for fertility control,* Ann. N.Y. Acad. Sci. (1990, in press).

3. Other Uses of RU486 as an Antiprogestin

A number of studies have shown the efficacy of RU486 as an abortive agent in the first trimester of pregnancy. Late in pregnancy, placental production of progesterone increases to a much higher level than that present during early pregnancy, and part of it may reach the uterine tissues directly (in contrast to progesterone of luteal origin). RU486 can also be a safe and useful adjunct in second-trimester prostaglandin-induced abortion.[115–117] Pretreatment with RU486 significantly reduces the dose of PG required and the interval between induction and abortion. In addition, RU486 can facilitate endouterine maneuvers that require opening and softening of the cervix. Since all vacuum aspirations require prior dilatation of the cervix with rigid or soft dilators, complications such as uterine perforation, cervical laceration or rupture can occur. Administration of RU486 has demonstrated significant cervical dilatation and ripening before aspiration.[118] RU486 may also have a role in therapeutic abortions. A fetus dying in the second or third trimester may be retained in utero for several weeks. This is distressing for the woman and carries a time-related risk of disseminated intravascular coagulation. Results from preliminary clinical trials have suggested the effectiveness of RU486 in combination with prostaglandin or oxytocin in the induction of labor after intrauterine fetal death.[119]

At delivery time, when the aim is to deliver a healthy child, RU486 may trigger labor in cases of undue delay. Experiments in monkeys have indicated its effectiveness.[120] Incidentally, the antiprogesterone effect of RU486 also facilitates early milk secretion. Thus, the findings above suggest that priming the uterus and cervix with RU486 would have wide application in spontaneous and induced labor it if can be shown to be without hazard to the fetus.

Beyond pregnancy management, RU486 may have a role in the treatment of endometriosis and breast cancer. Roussel-Uclaf clinical coordinators, André Ulmann and Louise Silvestre, are currently establishing multicenter programs to conduct appropriate studies. Trials are also performed in progesterone receptor-containing neurological tumors (e.g., meningiomas). The depressing effect of RU486 on LH and FSH output, including after menopause,[121] may be of therapeutical importance. In any case, for long-

[115] D. R. Urquhart, C. Bahzad & A. A. Templeton, *Efficacy of the antiprogestin mifepristone (RU486) prior to prostaglandin termination of pregnancy*, 4 Human Reprod. 202–3 (1989).

[116] M. W. Rodger & D. T. Baird, *Pretreatment with mifepristone (RU486) reduces interval between prostaglandin administration and expulsion in second trimester abortion*, 97 Br. J. Obstet. Gynaecol. 41–45 (1990).

[117] N. C. W. Hill, M. Selinger, J. Ferguson, A. Lopez-Bernal, I. Z. Mackenzie, *The physiological and clinical effects of progesterone inhibition with mifepristone (RU486) in the second trimester*, 97 Br. J. Obstet. Gynaecol. 487–92 (1990).

[118] Y. Lefebvre, L. Proulx, R. Elie, O. Poulin & E. Lanza, *The effects of RU-38486 on cervical ripening*, 162 Am. J. Obstet. Gynecol. 61–65 (1990).

[119] D. Cabrol, M. Bouvier-D'Yvoire, E. Mermet, L. Cedard, C. Sureau, E. E. Baulieu, *Induction of labour with mifepristone after intrauterine fetal death*, 8462 Lancet 1019 (1985).

[120] J. P. Wolf, M. Sinosich, T. L. Anderson, A. Ulmann, E. E. Baulieu & G. D. Hodgen, *Progesterone antagonist (RU486) for cervical dilation, labor induction, and delivery in monkeys: effectiveness in combination with oxytocin*, 160 Am. J. Obstet. Gynecol. 45–47 (1989).

[121] A. Gravanis, G. Schaison, M. George, J. De Brux, P. G. Satyaswaroop, E. E. Baulieu & P. Robel, *Endometrial and pituitary responses to the steroidal antiprogestin RU486 in postmenopausal women*, 60 J. Clin. Endocrinol. Metab 156–63 (1985).

term administration of RU486, evaluation of the safety of the drug will be necessary, particularly with reference to the glucocorticosteroid system.

4. Uses of RU486 as an Antiglucocorticosteroid

Originally, RU486 was found to be an anticorticosteroid[122] and indeed it binds with high affinity to the glucocorticosteroid receptor. The counteraction of RU486 on the negative feedback activity of corticosteroids provokes an increase of ACTH, endorphin and cortisol in humans.[123,124] Thus, large doses of RU486 are needed to overcome this reaction in order to obtain a state of hypocorticism.

Four categories of use may be envisaged:

1. Exploration of the hypothalamus-pituitary-adrenals (HPA) system, thus providing a new way to test this important axis implied in stressful conditions, immunological reactions and so forth.
2. Therapeutical intervention on the functioning of the HPA regulation in some states of depression, immunological abnormalities and stressful conditions. Much work will be necessary to establish useful therapeutical protocols.
3. Intervention on cortisol excess independent of the CNS-pituitary regulatory mechanism, as in inoperable adrenal cancers or ACTH-producing ectopic tumors. These rare cases have clearly demonstrated the antiglucocorticosteroid effect of RU486. Surgical removal of a tumor has occasionally become possible with this treatment.
4. Local administration of RU486, permitting a circumscribed antiglucocorticosteroid effect without interference with the HPA system. This could be the case for treating glaucoma or favoring/accelerating the healing of wounds or burns.

III. What's Next with Voluntary Pregnancy Interruption (VPI)?

Although 96% is a high rate of efficiency, it may still be possible to improve the method. RU486 doses lower than 600 mg (e.g. 200 mg) may yield the same results in the combined treatment but may necessitate uncomfortably higher doses of PG. The search for an active PG that would cause less uterine cramps should have high priority. Furthermore, an oral PG would render the process of VPI less intimidating to patients; presently, injections and vaginal pessaries are used. If a PG derivation could exert a delayed effect and could be administered at the same time as RU486, then one less visit would be required.

In France, all voluntary pregnancy interruptions done with RU486/PG respect the obligations of the law, which was originally conceived for instrumental techniques: consultation at a registered center, medical supervision during administration of RU486 and PG and a follow-up visit. In fact, provided that medical surveillance is established, the

[122] D. Philibert, R. Deraedt & G. Teutsch, *RU486 a potent antiglucocorticoid in vivo*, Program of the 8th International Congress of Pharmacology, Tokyo, Japan 1463, Abstract (1981).

[123] R. C. Gaillard, A. Riondel, W. Herrman, A. F. Muller, & E. E. Baulieu, *RU486: a steroid with antiglucocorticosteroid activity that only disinhibits the human pituitary-adrenal system at a specific time of day*, 81 Proc. Natl. Acad. Sci. 3879–82 (1984).

[124] X. Bertagna, C. Bertagna, J. P. Luton, J. M. Husson & F. Girard, *The new steroid analog RU486 inhibits glucocorticoid action in man*, 59 J. Clin. Endocrinol. Metab. 25–38 (1984).

RU486/PG treatment should not necessarily be performed in a medical center and thus the privacy of a woman would be better insured. However, medical supervision will remain necessary for detection of ectopic pregnancy (not affected by RU486) and for prevention and treatment of complications such as hemorrhages, incomplete evacuation and cardiovascular effects of PG. In addition, the French abortion law imposes a delay of reflection of one week. To make this delay period optional would be desirable medically (earlier treatment with RU486/PG would result in easier evacuation and less pain and bleeding) and psychologically (given that the woman has clearly made up her mind).

In all other European countries (except Ireland), although different laws regulating abortion exist, RU486 should become available to women in the next few years. The registration process is starting currently in Great Britain and hopefully soon in Holland and the Scandinavian countries.

In the United States, there is no law preventing the use of RU486, but it is important to consider several points. First, the current climate of uncertainty over the legal status of abortion has discouraged the major drug companies, including Hoescht-Roussel Product Incorporated (HRPI), from even applying for licensing RU486. Women should not remain prisoners of the feminine physiology when science can help liberate them from biological constraints. Second, and probably more important, product liability concerns and the prospect of expensive litigation have deterred companies from any involvement in fertility control research in the United States (and consequently in the rest of the world). An urgent change in the legal practice is needed for the survival of reproductive medicine as well as many other therapeutic innovations. A third difficulty is the lack of PG for pregnancy interruption in the United States; this problem must be resolved together with RU486 registration. Globally, the situation in the United States is critical, not only to American women but also to women of developing countries because U.S. financial support is needed by the World Health Organization (WHO) and by other important groups involved in trying to solve population problems.

In the developing countries, although each has a different situation, all share one common problem: the deficit in medical manpower and health systems. Surgery for appendicitis in any country of the developing world involves more risk than in the United States or in France. With RU486, we shall see misuses and accidents. However, compared to the present tragic situation of 150,000 deaths yearly due to abortion in addition to grave infections, countless cervical and uterine traumatisms and perforations, a nonsurgical method cannot be but a progress toward solving a major health problem. It has to be combined with the education of physicians and medical personnel as well as of women (to consult medical personnel early). We do not agree with those who are preventing the introduction of RU486 into the developing world. We believe that research such as that conducted by WHO and PATH (Program for Appropriate Technology in Health) is of extreme value.

Abortion has been a fact of humanity for centuries. In the next generation, the inefficiency of contraceptive methods, which unfortunately will remain in spite of scientific progress, should be backed up by a safe and dignified means to interrupt early pregnancies.

IV. Contragestion

Contraception is an abbreviation for *contra-conception*. Despite the broad meaning of the word conception, contraception, for the majority of people, is synonymous with

Figure 6. Fertile cycle (d indicates the number of days after the first day of the last menstrual period) and methods of fertility control. Differences between various methods tend to be minimized when the mechanisms of action are considered (full-line frames indicate when the primary mode of action takes place; and dotted-line frames, periods at which the secondary mode of action may work). hCG indicates human chorionic gonadotropin.

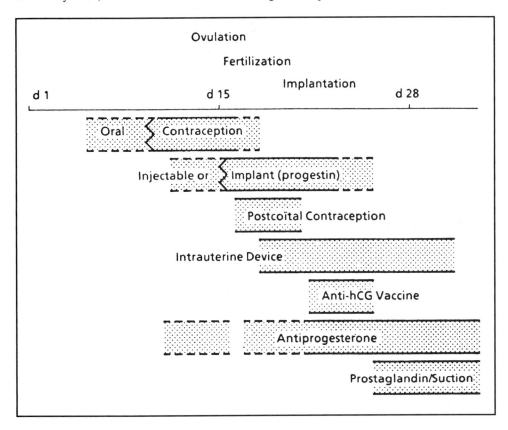

prevention of fertilization. However, fertilization is not the unique determining event in the conception of a new human being. It is preceded by meiosis (for the preparation of functional female and male gametes fundamental to the determination of genetic uniqueness) and followed by the several-day process of implantation and several steps that are critical for the proper development of the embryo. Thus, the generation of life, and human life specifically, is a continuous process that involves interdependent, sequential events and that cannot be attributed uniquely to fertilization. Nature, in the absence of any human intervention and apparently according to mechanisms selected to ensure the continuation of the species, eliminates the vast majority of potentially unique individuals: This is the fate of non-fertilized haploid oocytes, millions of spermatozoa and the majority of fertilized eggs that do not implant or that are aborted spontaneously (often because of chromosomal abnormalities) or that subsequently become chorioepitheliomas and so on.

In fact, many methods of fertility control are not contraceptive in the acquired sense of the term. As indicated in figure 6, this is the case for intrauterine devices, hormonal contraception based on progestin and postcoital contraception. Indeed, post-fertilization interruption, which might be considered an "abortion," is an everyday process. Almost all women have had or will have abortion(s) (although they may not be aware of it) or *"miscarriage"*, terminology for an event that is considered more "natural" than abortion. The concept of abortion has a violent and controversial connotation, as if collectively, consciously or not, we were preoccupied only by the occurrence of fertilization and forgetful of the multitude of steps that must occur for the development of a human being. Considering the process of generating life, in its globality and continuity, and the natural, selective mechanisms that determine existence, the use of the terms "murder" and "killing" in relation to abortion cloud the real issues pertaining to an existing health problem. We have proposed the word *"contragestion"* for this reason, a contraction of contra-gestation, inclusive of most methods of fertility control, that, it is hoped, will be helpful in "containing" the debate.

Other antiprogestins and antiglucocorticosteroids, possibly "better" than RU486, will appear in the near future. However, considering the time and money necessary for developing new compounds, it is advisable to continue further studies with RU486, treating it as a representative of a new class of useful drugs. Besides being used in human fertility control, RU486 may help the treatment of several serious conditions. Despite the controversy surrounding this compound, further research needs to be done not only for medical and humanitarian reasons but also for the preservation of scientific integrity.

Prenatal diagnosis is an area in which advanced technology is constantly expanding our knowledge of the diseases of the pregnant woman and the fetus. From radiographic pictures we have gone to ultrasound and computerized axial tomography (CAT) scans; from amniotic testing we have gone to chorionic testing and fetoscopes. In the future, it may be possible to obtain blood from the mother and the fetus in order to check for flaws in selected genes. Once such information is obtained, the parents may be faced with unusually difficult decisions concerning the future life of their child. Professor Macintyre also brings to the fore another focus, that of counseling individuals and families affected by the various problems associated with actual or potential defects.

20 · The Impact of an Abnormal Fetus or Child on the Choice for Prenatal Diagnosis and Selective Abortion ─────────

M. Neil Macintyre, Ph.D.
Llew Keltner, M.D., Ph.D.
and Dorothy A. Kovacevich, Ph.D.*

I. Introduction

Years ago in the 2nd edition of this book, the introduction to this chapter by the then sole author (Macintyre) opened with this paragraph:

> In the burgeoning debate on the subject of therapeutic abortion and proposed changes in the state abortion laws, numerous situations have been proposed as valid indications for interrupting a pregnancy. Of these, the one which ordinarily has received the least attention has been the risk that the child would be born with grave physical or mental defects.

During the intervening period, numerous significant changes have occurred. As usual, changes in the laws have resulted from changes in societal attitudes, which in turn have come about because of increased awareness and sensitivity regarding existing areas of human need or human suffering as well as the acquisition of new knowledge.

In the last decade there has been a tremendous amount of new knowledge gained concerning the principles and techniques of human genetics in general and prenatal diagnosis specifically. Much of this recent learning is of obvious importance to certain aspects of the abortion issue.

There are glimmers of change in public awareness of the nature and intensity of human suffering resulting from the birth of an abnormal child. Health care professionals

*We wish to express our gratitude to Leila Hocking-Keltner for her assistance in the construction and preparation of this article.

are showing signs of slowly learning that effective handling of such situations requires a special degree of understanding, empathy, and demonstrated caring toward the parents. Traditionally, these professionals have avoided the issue by being very clinical and appearing aloof in their presentation of data, thereby protecting themselves from becoming emotionally involved and at the same time setting up communication barriers between themselves and their patients.

II. Prenatal Diagnosis

The diagnosis of fetal disease is no longer an unusual or speculative event. Advances in medical diagnostic technology have been quickly and successfully applied to the prenatal period. A great many fetal diseases may now be detected, and the potential exists for the rapid development of diagnostic techniques for detection of many more. At present, amniocentesis and ultrasound definitely predominate in fetal diagnosis, but several other techniques either provide excellent information in specific circumstances or show great promise for future development.

A. Amniocentesis

Amniocentesis is but one of a number of techniques used in medical diagnosis for obtaining fluid from internal body cavities. Cardiocentesis consists of withdrawing fluid from around the heart, thoracentesis from the space outside the lungs, and amniocentesis from the amniotic space surrounding the growing fetus. A needle of the appropriate length and diameter is introduced into the body cavity, and fluid is withdrawn through the hollow core of the needle.

The amniocentesis needle is inserted, under sterile conditions, through the abdominal and uterine walls. Although anticipation of the procedure may produce considerable anxiety, little discomfort is involved. For example, in most cases discomfort certainly is subjectively less than in a routine pelvic examination.

The fluid in the amniotic cavity is principally fetal urine and filtered fluid from the natural bloodstream. Cells sloughed from fetal tissues populate the fluid. Current technology allows biochemical examination of the fluid for abnormalities indicating fetal disease. Also possible are isolation, growth and examination of living fetal cells to determine both their chromosomal and their biochemical composition.

The timing of fetal amniotic fluid constituent secretion critically affects the use of amniocentesis as a diagnostic technique. A common use of amniocentesis is for determination of fetal maturity, which is accomplished by comparing the ratio of amounts of two proteins secreted by the fetal lungs. The first use of amniocentesis was for the estimation of the severity of damage to fetal red blood cells in Rh disease, requiring measurement of breakdown products from those cells. In neither of these cases are the necessary substances present in sufficient quantity in the amniotic fluid for measurement before the 24th week of pregnancy.[1]

The same is true for many substances that require the maturation of various fetal physiological systems before secretion occurs. Fetal cells are sloughed into the amniotic fluid from early in gestation. Only at the eighth week, however, is there enough fluid

---

[1]D. P. Cruikshank, *Amniocentesis for Determination of Fetal Maturity*, 25 Clin. Obstet. & Gynecol. 773 (1982).

present for a sample to be obtained, and until about 12 weeks the number of fetal cells obtained may not be sufficient to allow successful culture.

By far the most important of the substances directly assayed from amniotic fluid is alpha-fetoprotein (AFP), a protein made by the fetal liver and a normal constituent of the fluid. The level of AFP changes very predictably with the progress of pregnancy. Abnormally high levels of AFP usually indicate leakage from fetal tissues into the fluid. Fetal diseases that allow such exposure of tissues include anencephaly (an incomplete skull with absence of much of the brain), encephalocele (herniation of the brain through the skull), spina bifida (incomplete closure of the bony spine with exposure of the spinal cord) and omphalocele (abdominal contents on the outside of the abdominal wall).[2] Intrauterine fetal death will also yield abnormally high AFP levels. Unlike many other prenatal diagnostic techniques, assessment of amniotic fluid AFP levels never can provide a specific diagnosis; an abnormally high level must always be followed with other tests—usually more expensive and time-consuming than an AFP assay—to arrive at a specific diagnosis.

Lack of certain crucial enzymes in fetal cells can lead to the buildup of metabolic products in the amniotic fluid to the point where the products can be detected. In most cases, however, the diagnoses are much more accurately made from analysis of the activity of fetal cells in culture. Direct testing of amniotic fluid for diagnosis of fetal disease in the first two trimesters of pregnancy is thus at present limited primarily to AFP assay.

The one technological breakthrough that gave the greatest stimulus to the development of prenatal diagnosis was the discovery in 1965 by Klinger and Macintyre[3] of techniques allowing fetal cells derived from amniocentesis to be cultured in the laboratory. Fetal cell cultures are used today for both chromosome and biochemical analyses.

Individuality in structure and physiological function of each person is determined to a very large extent at the cellular level. The formation of each unique chemical part of a cell is governed by one or more templates called genes. These genes are strung together end to end in microscopically visible entities, the chromosomes. The genes in each human cell are arranged on 23 matched pairs of chromosomes; one of each pair is inherited from the individual's mother, the other from the father. In males, one pair of chromosomes, the sex chromosomes, is unevenly matched. The genes inherited from the father on the Y chromosome do not match the genes inherited from the mother on the X chromosome. If a fertilized human egg contains anything other than this critical amount of genetic material, development of the fetus will be altered. Duplication or deletion of all or part of any one of the chromosomes results in birth defects of varying severity.

To assess the status of the chromosome complement of fetal cells, the cells present in the amniotic fluid sample obtained from amniocentesis are first isolated and placed in a nutrient medium. Ten to 28 days are required for the growth of sufficient numbers of fetal cells in these cultures. At maturity, the cultures are concentrated and the cells prepared for microscopic examination. The process of preparing cells has become extremely sophisticated. A combination of techniques is now routinely used that results in

[2]W. F. Rayburn, *Surveillance Techniques Other Than Ultrasonography for Detecting Fetal Malformations,* 27 J. Repro. Med. 565 (1982).
[3]Personal Communication.

the production of microscope slides containing groups of chromosomes that are easily visible to the trained examiner. The chromosomes can be individually counted and identified, and chromosomes with added or missing parts may be recognized.[4] Chromosomes from a number of cells are examined to ensure consistency of the diagnostic conclusion.

Diagnoses resulting from chromosome analysis are surprisingly specific. Most often encountered is the diagnosis of Down Syndrome, or trisomy 21, which occurs where there are three rather than two 21st chromosomes in each cell. Although each person born with Down's Syndrome is different, there are striking similarities resulting from the redundancy of specific genetic material. The facial appearance of children and adults with Down's Syndrome, which led to the unfortunate and inappropriate 'mongoloid' label, is quite consistent. Equally typical is the accompanying mental retardation. As with most syndromes resulting from chromosomal imbalance, internal organ systems are malformed in cases of Down Syndrome. With the exception of the 21st chromosome and the sex chromosomes, three copies of an entire chromosome almost invariably results in death, even though in rare instances affected fetuses may maintain respiration a short time after delivery. When only one copy of any of the chromosomes exists, again with the exception of the sex chromosomes, malformations are always fatal, with death usually occurring early in gestation.

Current techniques in cultured fetal cell preparation allow the identification of quite small missing or redundant parts of individual chromosomes as well. Several hundred specific syndromes have been described, each with very consistent presentation in the affected individual, involving particular deletions or duplications of chromosomal material.[5] Although defects in organ systems vary greatly from syndrome to syndrome, mental retardation is an alarmingly common finding when chromosomal imbalance exists.

The startling advances in biochemical technology of the last two decades have allowed analyses of many enzyme systems within cultured fetal cells. In many inheritable diseases a single gene, far too small to be visualized by the techniques of chromosome analysis, is altered. The cellular chemical coded for by that gene will then be defective, usually causing serious alterations in the function of most if not all the cells in the body. One example of such a metabolic disease is Tay-Sachs disease, which results in progressive degeneration of the nervous system and in death early in childhood. Many other serious metabolic genetic diseases have been prenatally diagnosed by simple assays of enzyme levels in amniotic fluid cell cultures.

More sophisticated techniques are also being used to directly identify altered genes. For example, specialized enzymes are used in the laboratory to break up DNA that has been isolated from cell cultures of fetuses suspected of having sickle-cell anemia. The fragments of DNA are processed and compared to similarly processed fragments of DNA from normal individuals. The existence of an altered gene for hemoglobin, the defective protein in sickle-cell anemia, can be easily demonstrated in affected fetuses.[6]

---

[4] A. Daniel et al., *Prenatal Diagnosis in 2000 Women for Chromosome, X-Linked, and Metabolic Disorders*, 11 Am. J. Med. Genetics. 61 (1982).

[5] S. R. Stephenson & D. D. Weaver, *Prenatal Diagnosis—A Compilation of Diagnosed Conditions*, 141 Am. J. Obstet. Gynecol. 319 (1981).

[6] M. S. Golbus, *Prenatal Diagnosis*, 19 Birth Defects: Orig. Art Series. 121 (1983).

B. Ultrasound

Many areas of modern medicine have been remarkably influenced in the past decade by the advent of the noninvasive and apparently nondestructive technique of diagnostic ultrasonography. Prenatal diagnosis is certainly no exception.

To obtain an image of fetal structures, high-frequency sound waves are projected into the abdomen from a small hand-held transducer. Time differences in returning echoes reflect varying densities of internal organs, and are thus translated into a visual image.

The fetal structural defects detectable by ultrasound may be isolated defects resulting from maldevelopment of single organs. Alternatively, they may be part of syndromes occurring as a result of chromosomal anomalies, disease processes during pregnancy, exposure to teratogens (external agents causing maldevelopment) or inheritable genetic diseases. As a general rule, large defects are more easily seen than smaller ones at a given stage of fetal development. Anencephaly, encephalocele, myelomeningocele and omphalocele are diagnosed routinely in the second trimester. Small defects such as polydactyly (more than five fingers per hand) and cardiac hypertrophy (enlarged heart) may not be visible until well into the third trimester, and detection even then is greatly dependent on the ultrasonographer's skill and on the fetal position.

Other fetal defects detectable by ultrasound examination include dwarfism, cardiac valvular defects, hydrocephaly, microcephaly, fetal tumors, and polycystic kidneys.[7] As equipment and methods become more sophisticated, more exact images of the pregnant uterus and its contents become available. Relatively small defects, like cleft lip, have been noted.[8]

Echocardiography is an offshoot of ultrasonography and has also been used in fetal diagnosis. Ultrasound equipment is used to obtain detailed information about cardiac rhythms from analysis of the movements of the fetal heart.[9] Fetal cardiac rhythm disturbances of several types have been detected using echocardiography, and cardiac structural anomalies have also been identified.[10]

Using Doppler flow studies, there have been recent advancements detecting fetal cerebral arteries, umbilical arteries and maternal uterine arteries.

C. Other Techniques

1. DIRECT VISUALIZATION   Fiber-optic technology now allows insertion of very thin light-conducting flexible tubes through large diameter needles into the amniotic cavity. The image of the fetus or placenta obtained is used either directly in reaching diagnostic conclusions or as a guide for the placement of blood or tissue sampling devices.

Between 8 and 20 weeks of fetal development, the amniotic fluid surrounding the fetus is very transparent and the fetus is still quite small. Through a one- to two-millimeter wide fiber-optic fetoscope, an area of two to three square centimeters of the fetal

---

[7]P. A. Smith, P. Chudleigh & S. Campbell, *Prenatal Diagnosis: Ultrasound,* 6 Br. J. Hosp. Med. 421 (1984).

[8]R. A. Bowerman, *Using Ultrasonography to Diagnose Fetal Malformations,* 27 J. Repro. Med. 560 (1982).

[9]C. S. Kleinman et al., *Fetal Echocardiography for Evaluation of In Utero Congestive Heart Failure,* 306 N.E.S. Med. 568 (1982).

[10]K. L. Reed, *Fetal Echocardiography: New Horizons in Ultrasound,* 6 Br. J. Hosp. Med. 600 (1984).

surface may be seen. Positioning of the fetus is critical in determining which fetal structures may be visualized. Several otherwise difficult syndromes have been diagnosed by visualization in the fetoscope of small structural anomalies not identifiable on ultrasound.

The most important current use of the fiber-optic fetoscope is to guide the placement of tools for obtaining fetal blood samples. After 18 weeks, the fetal blood volume is great enough to tolerate the loss of one to two milliliters of blood, which is obtained from a placental vessel punctured by a sampling needle carried in a tube next to the scope. Blood samples thus obtained have been used to diagnose sickle cell anemia, thalassemia, hemophilia, immunodeficiencies, viral infections and metabolic disorders. Culturing cells from blood samples takes only two or three days rather than the 10 to 28 days required for the culture of amniotic cells.

Fiber-optic scopes have also been used to guide instruments for obtaining biopsies of the fetal skin on scalp or flank. Skin samples have been used to diagnose several inheritable disorders that include skin changes as part of their pathology.[11] Samples of the fetal liver have also been obtained to aid in the diagnosis of metabolic disorders specific to that organ.[12]

2. BIOPSY OF CHORIONIC VILLI   One of the tissue layers surrounding the fetus is the chorion, which is also made up of cells originating from the fertilized egg. Between the 8th and 12th weeks of gestation, it is possible to insert a small tube through the cervical opening and to aspirate a small piece of the chorion. Many cells may be obtained (allowing rapid culture) and analysis proceeds in the same manner as with cells from amniotic fluid. The chorionic villi cells are dividing very rapidly unlike amniotic fluid cells so that results of the chromosome analysis may be obtained in as short a time as 24 hours. The striking advantage of the technique is that since chorionic villi sampling can take place during the first trimester and since culture results are available much more rapidly than with amniotic cell cultures, results may be obtained as much as three months earlier in the pregnancy. The technique is very new, however, and further study is needed to determine the associated risks and complications. Chorionic villi biopsy does have immense potential as an early prenatal diagnostic technique.[13]

3. RADIOGRAPHY   The use of X-ray fetal analysis is limited by the certain but difficult to quantify carcinogenic or other risk to the fetus. Although radiographic information could be used in the diagnosis of many conditions identifiable by ultrasound, its use is limited primarily to situations involving skeletal maldevelopment. Relatively rare syndromes like osteogenesis imperfecta (a disease involving incomplete calcification of developing bones) are difficult to diagnose with other techniques.[14] However, ultrasonography techniques are rapidly attaining a degree of sophistication that may soon eliminate the necessity for use of fetal radiography.

4. AMNIOGRAPHY   A water soluble X-ray opaque contrast material may be injected into the amniotic fluid followed by radiographic examination. The outline of the

---

[11] M. J. Mahoney & J. C. Hobbins, *Fetoscopy and Fetal Blood Sampling,* in *Genetic Disorders and the Fetus* 501 (A. Milunsky, ed. 1980).

[12] K. Nicolaides & C. H. Rodeck, *Prenatal Diagnosis: Fetoscopy,* 6 Br. J. Hosp. Med. 396 (1984).

[13] V. Cowart, *NIH Considers Large-scale Study to Evaluate Chorionic Villi Sampling,* 252 J.A.M.A. 11 (1984).

[14] Stephenson & Weaver, *supra* note 5.

fetus is made visible by this technique, which offers diagnostic possibilities of conditions where the fetal shape has been altered, such as teratoma (a soft tissue tumor) and omphalocele.[15]

As the fetus swallows the contrast material, the fetal gastrointestinal tract can be visualized radiographically, allowing diagnosis of conditions where the course of the tract is altered. Duodenal atresia (constriction of the tract just below the stomach) and diaphragmatic hernia (protrusion of the stomach up through the diaphragm) are examples of conditions diagnosable with amniography.[16]

5.   FETOGRAPHY   A variation of amniography, this technique uses an oil soluble contrast material which is obsorbed by the waxy covering of the fetus. Radiography then shows the outline of the fetus, providing diagnostic information about outline altering conditions.[17]

6.   MATERNAL SERUM ALPHA-FETOPROTEIN DETERMINATION   Some fetal proteins cross the placenta and enter the maternal circulation. Among these is alpha-fetoprotein (AFP). The AFP level in the maternal circulation is a reflection of the amniotic fluid AFP level, albeit at a much lower concentration. Measuring levels of AFP in the maternal serum offers increasingly accurate information about fetal status. When AFP is sufficiently elevated over successive samples, an indication of fetal tissue exposure or distress is possible just as in amniotic fluid AFP evaluation. An association has been suggested between lower than normal AFP levels and chromosomal anomalies such as Down Syndrome.[18] The technique is as nonspecific as amniotic fluid AFP measurement but does offer valuable initial information.[19]

D. The Future of Prenatal Diagnostic Techniques

Prenatal diagnosis is unquestionably in its infancy. The catalog of available techniques will undoubtedly increase by the addition of new methods. On the immediate horizon are enhancements of present techniques to increase the scope and accuracy of diagnostic possibility.

Chromosome analysis continues to improve steadily in terms of the resolution with which details on a given chromosome can be seen, which allows diagnosis of additional syndromes. Improvement is likely to continue for some time, with potential breakthroughs resulting from new microscopic techniques.[20]

Recombinant DNA technology will undoubtedly allow definition of many more inheritable genetic diseases through the production of specific endonuclei. These will allow, as with sickle cell anemia at present, diagnosis of the disease from uncultured amniotic fluid.[21]

Better biochemical analysis techniques are already allowing the detection of more substances in amniotic fluid which, like AFP, are indicators of fetal disease. Some of these indicators will probably be much more specific than AFP.

---

[15] S. Semchyshyn et al., *Fetal Tumor: Antenatal Diagnosis and Its Implications*, 27 J. Repro. Med. 231 (1982).

[16] Rayburn, *supra* note 2; Stephenson & Weaver, *supra* note 5.

[17] *Id.*

[18] A. Tabor et al., *Low Maternal Serum AFP and Down Syndrome*, 2 Lancet. 161 (1984).

[19] Rayburn, *supra* note 2.

[20] Daniel et al., *supra* note 4.

[21] Colbus, *supra* note 6.

Methods are under development that will allow the separation of fetal cells in the maternal circulation. In theory this technique may provide a mass screening tool for indicating the potential presence of chromosomal anomalies or metabolic disorders, but the methods remain impractical and unreliable.[22]

As ultrasound equipment becomes more sophisticated, structural defects will be more easily and thus more frequently resolved. Computer enhanced ultrasound images, perhaps similar to those provided now by computerized axial tomography (CAT scan) will very probably also be available.[23]

Nuclear magnetic reasonance scanning, a technique that can produce cross-sectional images of internal body structures similar to those produced by computerized axial tomography, is now being applied experimentally to fetal diagnosis. The technique is new but is gaining rapid acceptance as an apparently nondamaging alternative to computerized axial tomography.[24]

Use of direct fetal biopsies via the fetoscope will probably increase. Teratogenic fetal infections and toxin levels will be measured via such biopsies, and cells obtained will more frequently be used for biochemical studies and rapid chromosome analysis. Diagnostic biopsy of internal fetal organs will become more common as the already developing techniques of fetal surgery improve. Presently available diagnostic aids, such as the electrocardiogram and electroencephalogram, will be used with direct visual guidance as fiber-optic systems improve.[25]

Although prenatal diagnostic techniques offer information now about many fetal diseases, there is great room for improvement. For example, there is not today a good technique for the prenatal diagnosis of cystic fibrosis, the most common serious inheritable disease, in spite of enormous research efforts.[26]

E. Risks of Prenatal Diagnosis

The risks involved in prenatal diagnostic techniques follow very logically from the descriptions of the methods involved. Degree of invasiveness is the most obvious factor influencing fetal risk.

Ultrasound is now so widely used largely because of its apparently benign nature. Many analyses have been made of the outcomes of pregnancies involving ultrasound diagnosis and no harmful effects have been conclusively demonstrated.[27] Deleterious fetal effects from diagnostic radiology are almost equally difficult to demonstrate, but the harmful effects of ionizing radiation are so well known that it is safe to assume the existence of a definite level of carcinogenic risk to the exposed fetus.

Introduction of sharp foreign bodies into the uterine cavity during pregnancy, inherently carries the risk of damage to the fetus, the fetal blood supply or the placenta. In one large series of amniocenteses, the rate of spontaneous abortions was found to

---

[22] Daniel et al., *supra* note 4.

[23] J. C. Hobbins et al., *Stage II Ultrasound Examination for the Diagnosis of Fetal Abnormalities With an Elevated Amniotic Fluid Alpha-Fetoprotein Concentration*, 142 Am. J. Obstet. Gynecol. 1026 (1982).

[24] S. McCarthy et al., *Obstetrical Magnetic Resonance Imaging: Fetal Anatomy*, 154 Radiology, 427 (1985).

[25] Mahoney & Hobbins, *supra* note 11.

[26] H. Travers, M. Shwartzman & P. J. Benke, *False Positive Prenatal Diagnosis of Cystic Fibrosis by Protease Activity*, 146 Am. J. Obstet. Gynecol. 338 (1983).

[27] Bowerman, *supra* note 8.

increase by 1.6% following the procedure. Fetal damage not resulting in abortion was suspected in 0.3% of cases.[28]

The fiber-optic scope is much larger and requires more manipulation than the amniocentesis needle. It is thus not surprising that a fetal death rate of 3% occurred (from infection of the amniotic fluid and membranes) in one series of fetoscopic procedures. Worldwide experience shows a fetal loss of 5.6% following biopsy of chorionic villi.[29]

Maternal risks from prenatal diagnostic procedures are very difficult to assess. The reports of large series of amniocenteses, fetoscopies and placental aspirations do not reveal maternal complications, but neither do the reports carefully analyze maternal sequelae.[30]

The risk of diagnostic error is particularly important in prenatal evaluation. When prenatal diagnostic techniques are applied to obtain information to be used in a decision about elective abortion, the results have obviously far-reaching consequences. False positive results from a test can lead to abortion of fetuses unaffected by the disease in question. False negative results would probably cause continuation of a pregnancy on the supposition that the fetus was normal with serious possible consequences.

Diagnostic accuracy in chromosomal analysis from cultured amniotic fluid cells has been reported from 99.53% to 99.93% (true positive plus true negative).[31] False positive results make up the majority of the diagnostic errors. It should be noted that follow-up is very difficult in studies of this kind, and the actual rates may be higher. Due primarily to the lower frequency of use of other fetal diagnostic methods, carefully compiled failure rates are not yet available. Methods such as ultrasound which are dependent on fetal position, maternal obesity and other difficult to control variables are likely to have relatively high false negative rates, particularly since many anomalies are very difficult if not impossible to visualize before the time when abortion decisions must be made.

F. The Process of Prenatal Diagnosis

The course of the prenatal diagnostic process will be different for each individual pregnancy. Reasons for obtaining prenatal diagnostic services, results of tests, use of multiple tests and response of the pregnant woman will all influence the diagnostic outcome.

1. REASONS FOR DIAGNOSTIC TESTS   Pregnant women have procedures performed to obtain information about fetal disease either because they have a specific concern about the health of the fetus or simply to obtain general information about the pregnancy. The diagnostic process is quite different in these two situations.

When any member of a family, including very distant relatives, is known to have been born with a birth defect, to be mentally retarded or to have been affected with a disease perceived by the family to have a heritable component, the pregnant woman or other family members normally have a need to know if the fetus is affected with the same condition. The perception of risk to the fetus may be quite different from person to person. Many factors have an impact on the level of concern in a given individual. Depth of exposure to a family member with a particular disease may have a tremendous effect on efforts to obtain prenatal diagnosis. For example, a woman who has a sibling

---

[28] Daniel et al, *supra* note 4.
[29] Cowart, *supra* note 13.
[30] Daniel et al., *supra* note 4; Mahoney & Hobbins, *supra* note 11.
[31] Daniel et al., *supra* note 4.

with Down Syndrome is very likely to seek diagnosis, while a man with a second cousin born with an extra digit is much less likely to encourage his pregnant partner to do so. A greater occurrence risk of specific conditions within population groups leads to a greater demand for a diagnostic procedure as in the frequent consultations obtained by families of European Jewish descent to rule out Tay-Sachs disease.[32] Increased public awareness about risk factors for fetal disease also affects the level of concern. For example, maternal age greater than 35 years is a common reason for obtaining amniocentesis due to the well known and publicized increased chromosomal defects risk with increasing maternal age.[33]

In rare cases, one of the parents will know that their cells contain a chromosome consisting of two normal chromosomes fused together end to end—a chromosome translocation—and that any fetus is at high risk for serious disease. About 5% of Down Syndrome cases are the result of translocations, and parents who know they carry such a translocation usually seek amniocentesis for fetal chromosome analysis.

Information about fetal disease is very often obtained incidentally. Ultrasound is routinely used to determine fetal size and thus stage of pregnancy, and fetal defects are sometimes clearly visualized or suspected. Since maternal serum AFP is a relatively inexpensive, easily done and virtually harmless test, it is being performed more and more often even when there are no specific indications.[34] Both ultrasound and maternal serum AFP testing are thus beginning to be used as general fetal health screening tools for the population.

Maternal conditions that have potentially harmful fetal effects are often detected by screening methods. Routine health histories may reveal maternal alcohol abuse, toxin or radiation exposure or diabetes, all yielding increased risks of birth defects. Testing of maternal blood may reveal increased levels of antibodies to rubella and other viruses, indicating recent exposure and possible consequent fetal damage. Glucose tolerance tests are used to determine the existence of gestational diabetes.

2.   RESULTS OF TESTS   The unique characteristics of a diagnostic technique, and thus the nature of the diagnostic outcome, determine to a great extent the progression of the diagnostic process. Since ultrasound provides only a rough visualization of the fetus, an ultrasound done early in the pregnancy to determine fetal size that shows no specific structural defects is not at all definitive in ruling out fetal disease. On the other hand, an amniocentesis providing a negative chromosome analysis for Down Syndrome is very conclusive and may be a result sufficient to terminate the diagnostic process.

Positive results are usually less equivocal and either provide a diagnosis or suggest further study. Amniocentesis demonstrating a chromosomal defect provides very specific information about the probable fetal condition. Elevated alpha-fetoprotein—either in maternal serum or in amniotic fluid—usually requires repeat testing with continued positive results followed by chromosome analysis, ultrasound or other diagnostic techniques to locate the specific defect present.

3.   USE OF MULTIPLE TESTS   As noted above, few of the techniques available for fetal diagnosis are used in isolation. With the increasing use of screening techniques such as ultrasound and maternal serum AFP determination, less expensive and less in-

[32] J. R. Rucquoi, *Genetic Counseling and Prenatal Genetic Evaluation,* 36 Med. North. Am. 3359 (1983).

[33] S. P. Rubin, J. Malin & J. Maidman, *Genetic Counseling Before Prenatal Diagnosis for Advanced Maternal Age: An Important Medical Safeguard,* 62 Obstet. Gynecol. 155 (1983).

[34] C. Marwick, *Controversy Surrounds Use of Test for Open Spina Bifida,* 250 J.A.M.A. 575 (1983).

vasive techniques are followed by more elaborate procedures if positive results are obtained. The number and type of diagnostic techniques used are determined primarily by the degree of specificity at the time of referral for diagnosis. Suspected chromosomal abnormalities may require only amniocentesis for definitive diagnosis, while a chance finding of elevated maternal serum AFP may require follow-up with ultrasound and amniocentesis. The very elaborate techniques such as fetoscopy and fetal blood sampling are suggested only when earlier tests create very high suspicion of diseases amenable to diagnosis by the more complex methods.

Research has been done in the area of detection of fetal cells in maternal circulation. Using DNA techniques, chromosomal abnormalities have been diagnosed.

4. RESPONSE OF THE PREGNANT WOMAN   As in any diagnostic process, the most important element is the response of the patient to the information provided by the techniques used. Because of the great emotional overlay involved in the production of new human life, the process of fetal diagnosis is subject completely to the pregnant woman's interpretation and use of diagnostic information. Termination of the diagnostic process at the first sign of positive test results is a common occurrence. Successful diagnosis of fetal disease requires that an emotional environment be provided that allows for the complex of attitudes and feelings brought to the diagnostic practitioner by the client. Careful and thoughtful planning and explanation of the diagnostic process is of great benefit to the pregnant woman and to her family.

5. EXPLAINING THE DIAGNOSTIC PROCESS   This explanation might also be labeled "information counseling" because it can and should be more than a giving of information. In fact, explaining this procedure is often done by listing the steps in writing and then using the face-to-face time to clarify, explain and answer questions about the procedures. Professionals usually have little difficulty doing this.

It is also necessary to explain the possible hazards and risks in a realistic manner. This is not so easy. The line between frightening, cold, hard facts about the risks and the reassurance needed to undergo the relatively safe procedure is not clear. It is possible to err in either direction. One must bear in mind that the woman is frightened to begin with or she would not be seeking prenatal diagnosis. Because of age, family history or a variety of other reasons, she fears that her child may be abnormal. What she desires most is the assurance that the fetus is normal. When confronted with the possibility that the procedure may harm the baby, which in the vast majority of cases will prove to be normal, the anxiety may be overwhelming. At this point some women choose not to undergo the procedures.

For those who do undergo the procedures, particularly amniocentesis, which requires a relatively long period of suspenseful waiting before results are available, some reassurance or means of support is necessary. This could be something as simple as a phone number to call to see how the tests are coming along or to get reassurance that the process is progressing according to schedule.

During the initial visit, the patient should be made aware of all the services available in the area if advice, assistance or counseling is needed. In that way, if the results of the tests indicate problems, the parents have had time to consider or investigate possible resources and to consider the possibility of using such services.

Some people need counseling, support and assistance whether the results are positive or negative because they frequently have other problems that brought them in the first place. For example, having a normal child the second time does not automatically resolve the problems of having an abnormal sibling at home or in the family.

If the available resources have been mentioned in the first meeting, it will be easier to refer back to them when the diagnostic results are presented to the parents. If the fetus is found to be abnormal, the need for further counseling or referral seems more obvious to the physician even though it is not always pursued. What must not be overlooked is the need that may underlie the fear that brought them initially. No one expects the physician to do the counseling, but it is important to develop an awareness of the possible needs and to be familiar with the resources that are available in the community. Parent groups, agencies, schools and individual counselors are becoming increasingly available, and often the families are not aware of their existence. Becoming an informed member of the developing network of resources is a duty incumbent upon every professional who works with these families.

III. Emotional Effects of the Birth of an Abnormal Child on the Parents

With the development of human cytogenetics (chromosome analysis) techniques beginning in the late 1950s, the need for effective counseling for the prospective parents became evident. At that time, genetic counseling consisted essentially of providing factual information relative to the genetics of the problem and an explanation of the techniques to be used in gathering additional data. Little attention was paid to the emotional effects that may accompany the fear of producing an abnormal child or the experience of actually giving birth to such a child.

In time it became clear that the approach used in genetic counseling was actually preventing the communication that the parents needed most, namely, an opportunity to discuss their fears and other distressing feelings. Once these parents were given the opportunity and the freedom to speak openly and honestly, in marked contrast to the limited interchange they had experienced with most health professionals, they literally overflowed with information. These parents represent a population of deeply distressed individuals who are very misunderstood and hence are inadequately ministered to.

Gradually we began to provide extended counseling for some of these families where the need appeared critical. Counseling sessions were audiotaped with the knowledge and permission of the individuals involved. These tapes contain thousands of hours of statements made by emotionally affected individuals in an environment that has allowed them free and trusting disclosure.

Both the counseling and the subsequent study of the tapes has brought out some vitally important basic information. Obviously, no two individuals react exactly the same to stressful situations, and no two of the cases are identical in all respects. However, there are certain patterns that recur so often from case to case that they are predictable. Some were also unexpected. For example, despite differences in intensity of the impact and ways in which the pain is handled, the loss of an expected child results in the same basic reaction patterns when the actual child is abnormal, whether or not the child: (1) is wanted and planned for; (2) is lost through miscarriage or after birth; (3) dies early or lives for an extended period; or (4) has relatively minor or severe structural or mental abnormalities.

Five different individuals worked in developing categories and listing recurrent patterns in the tapes. There was such a high degree of correlation among the separate evaluations of the most critical reactions that the validity of the conclusions appears certain, and those conclusions are the basis on which the following descriptions of reaction patterns have been formulated.

Most individuals never have the opportunity to gain an insight into the true nature and complexity of the emotional pain suffered by parents who produce an abnormal child. Regardless of personally held attitudes about such an emotionally charged issue as abortion, the intelligent and honest person will want to judge the behavior of those who are trapped in such a tragic situation on the basis of informed insight rather than on uninformed emotional bias or condemnation.

A. The Impact on the Individual Parent

1. INITIAL SHOCK, DENIAL, REALITY AND ANGER   For most couples during pregnancy, certain changes in feelings and awareness ordinarily occur, whether or not they are all consciously recognized at the time. These changes include a maturing sense of responsibility, increased appreciation for each other, awe, excitement at the marvel of creating a new life and, above all, a sense of personal pride and feeling ''special.'' There are few if any more ego-involving phenomena than being part of producing a child. Furthermore, the need for some sense of immortality seems inherent in human existence. Producing an offspring, literally a part of yourself, to continue your existence beyond your corporal lifetime probably represents the most palpable essence of immortality available. The expected child becomes a representation of the best in you and your spouse, to be eventually presented to the world with ultimate pride, and it is natural to feel that there is no way that the child will be anything but perfect and beautiful. With these feelings to buoy them up, a couple reaches a special emotional high. If the expected child is lost to death or is born with abnormalities, the plunge to an emotional low is immediate and devastating.

The initial reaction is a state of shock so overwhelming and confusing that the individual appears to be living in a nightmare, a dream world, out of touch with reality. Reality is often too painful to bear, and the reaction is one of denial as a protection from the pain, a feeling that when the nightmare is over everything will somehow be all right. Some individuals avoid recognizing the full truth of reality by viewing the tragic event as a complete blessing, thereby prolonging the avoidance of reality. The majority of individuals soon find that they cannot avoid facing the reality of the shattering event that has so upset their lives, and at that point the predominant reactions tend to be a vacillating mixture of depression, anger and mistrust. ''Why me?'' ''Why us?'' ''What have I done to deserve this?'' are the big questions. The utter unfairness of the situation gives rise to overwhelming anger, anger at everything and everyone connected with the unfortunate event; in effect, anger at the world. Religious faith tends to crumble under the impact of the question: '''What kind of a God would do this to me?''

From a legal standpoint, the intensity of the parental anger reaction is important to understand because even individuals who would not be likely to bring suit against physicians, staff and the hospital involved may and do sue when they produce an abnormal child. Often such suits are based on the parents' belief that they were not adequately informed of their risk or of the availability of certain prenatal diagnostic tests, or anything else that seems plausible in their situation.

2. THE DAMAGED SELF-IMAGE   When the anticipation of a wished-for child with all its ego-boosting effects terminates in reproductive failure, a severe blow to an individual's self-image is inevitable. There is an unavoidable feeling of failure and inadequacy leading to periods of despair and depression.

In our society, in which such great emphasis is placed on being a winner, to be a loser in such a vital and personal event as producing a child has a particularly threatening effect on a parent's self-esteem and raises the common question: "What will people think?" The answer to the question is usually clear and negative in a society that generally views a birth-defective child as a fearsome object and tends to shun it, stigmatizing both the child and parents, thereby adding to the feelings of isolation, despair and personal worthlessness.

One might assume that this feeling of being rejected by society would bring the parents closer together in an effort to achieve mutual support, and ideally this could be; but in most cases, because husband and wife tend to react very differently in handling their emotional pain, they withdraw from each other. This phenomenon will be discussed in greater detail later in this chapter.

3.   GUILT AND THE DEATH-WISH FOR THE CHILD   We live in a culture in which the predominant method of raising children for generations has been through the use of conditional love or conditional acceptance by parents or parent figures, such as church and school. The message has been clear: Your parents won't love you if you don't do things exactly their way; God won't love you and will punish you if you deviate from the laws of the Church; the teacher will give you bad grades if you don't conform and pay strict attention, etc.

With that kind of a background so prevalent in our culture, it is inevitable that guilt becomes a significant and destructive part of the picture when a couple produces an imperfect offspring. There is generalized guilt for being a part of a major failure, disappointing not only one's own expectations but those of one's parents and family and, in effect, of society as a whole.

In addition to the generalized guilt reaction described above, specific sources of self-directed guilt results from the parent's own thinking or behavior. The most frequently occurring and probably the most frightening of these is the death-wish for the child: "I am glad the child died" or "I wish the child would die." In counseling, over 90% of parents admit that they are plagued with the recurring thought of wanting their child to die, and when they learn that such a thought is entirely normal under the circumstances, the depth of their relief is obvious. The death-wish for the child is so powerful that many parents have mentally considered methods of causing the child's death; some have caught themselves in the process of acting it out, and a few have probably gone further. No one recommends or condones such behavior as the appropriate solution, but it must be recognized, understood and accepted as part of the tragic evidence of the potentially destructive effect of producing a defective child.

Guilt plays such an important part in the individual parent's loss of self-esteem that before anything else of real substance can be accomplished toward rehabilitating the individual and the couple, the self-esteem of each person must be helped to improve at least enough for him or her to be able to face other issues with some confidence and clear thinking.

One of the most harmful and cruel things that anyone, professional or otherwise, can do is to criticize or condemn the hurting and confused parent, either directly or by implication. Genuine acceptance and support are the essentials for assisting the parent.

4.   MOURNING THE LOSS OF THE WISHED-FOR CHILD   When an abnormal child is born, the expected and wished-for normal child dies in that it ceases to exist as a viable possibility, and one component of the resulting mourning process is equivalent to that following the death of an apparently normal child.

Mourning the loss of a loved one at any age results in sadness and some diminution of one's normal level of effectiveness. The process is usually least painful and protracted if the beloved individual is elderly and has had a chance to live a full life. If a child dies, the sadness lasts much longer and is far more intense, partly due to the prevention of the parental desire and expectation to savor the child's growth and development and to be an essential part of it. When an abnormal child is born, the entire reaction pattern of parents is so much more complex that it is virtually impossible for them to cope with it in a truly rational fashion. Not only are they faced with the intensely saddening ''death'' of the wished-for normal child, but they are simultaneously smitten with the additional and more destructive emotions described earlier. In a very real sense, such parents are faced with the almost intolerable task of going through two mourning processes, different in some respects, yet overlapping and intertwined.

Mourning at best is a difficult, confusing and often lengthy process. The amount of time required to complete the process successfully varies with the nature of the initial event, the total personality structure of the principal individual or individuals involved, and, to a significant extent, the behavior of people with whom the grieving individual is in contact. If a person is denied understanding, support and the time required to complete the grieving process, it may continue unresolved throughout an entire lifetime.

Cultural attitudes are usually not helpful in our dealing with grieving parents. In our efforts to protect ourselves from accepting the personal discomfort that goes with watching another person mourn, we urge them to be strong, to know that in a very short time everything will be fine, *etc.*, at a time when it is impossible for the parent actually to be strong or in any way to feel optimistic. We often add to their feeling of inadequacy and worthlessness, forcing them to deny the full reality of their child's abnormality and of their own sadness. We virtually demand that they prove their worthiness by coping well. In short, we fail to provide the environment that would allow completion of the grieving process. The result is that such parents are forced to pretend that they are coping well when it is highly unlikely that they are able to do so. What passes as coping often is the equivalent of lying convincingly, and many parents become so adept at it that they fool not only those around them but themselves as well. They share their pain with no one, bearing it as it lies festering as an ongoing source of anger, despair and deep chronic sadness.

B. Religion as a Source of Spiritual Strength or Destructive Guilt

One of the most predominant initial parental reactions to the knowledge that their child is abnormal is questioning the nature or even the existence of God. At this point members of the clergy are in a crucial position either to significantly aid or to severely impair the parents' rehabilitation process.

There is no question about the potential value of religious faith in the emotional healing process if faith can survive the severe questioning period, and if religious concepts are carefully interpreted and presented by sensitive and understanding individuals. Unfortunately, members of the clergy often suffer from the same lack of accurate information, the same lack of awareness, as health care professionals concerning the true feelings of the parents. As a result, they often inadvertently deepen the guilt and anger.

In the population we have studied and from which we have learned so much, the cases in which contact with the clergy has been harmful, particularly in the early stages of grieving, greatly outnumber those in which it has been proven to be genuinely supportive. The obvious miscarriage of what is generally considered an important source of uplifting support and spiritual strength needs to be changed.

Increased guilt is the predominant result of the misuse or inappropriate use of certain traditional and dogmatic religious statements. The classic statement that "It's God's will" almost invariably gives rise in the grieving parent to the question: "If it's God's will, what kind of a God would will this much pain on anybody?" The resulting anger at God gives rise to further guilt in an already guilt-ridden person. Our culture tells us we are not supposed to question God, much less be angry at God. Even more potently destructive is the guilt generated in the parent by being told by a religious authority that the abnormal child is in fact a beautiful gift from God at a time when the parent is desperately wrestling with the conflicting emotions of wanting to love the child and not being able to love it, or, worse, wanting it to die.

Our data indicate that there is a correlation between the degree to which a religion is fundamentalist, authoritarian, rigid and dogmatic and its likelihood of producing guilt, anger and a feeling of worthlessness in the grieving parent.

The type of approach required to reverse this tragic situation was clearly stated a couple of years ago at a program entitled "Mourning the Loss of the Wished-for Child." One of the speakers was a gentle, soft-spoken and courageous priest who is a chaplain at one of our hospitals. His opening remark was: "When I became a hospital chaplain, I quickly learned that in order to be effective I had to kill my God and find another one." There was an absolute hush in the audience in response to this seemingly blasphemous statement. Then that remarkable and perceptive man went on to explain that much of what had been drilled into him in seminary in the classic fashion resulted in turning most frightened and hurting hospital patients away from him. "It was at that point," he continued, "that I realized that rather than preaching to them as I had been taught to, and telling them what they ought to be feeling and thinking when they were in no condition to do so, I needed to learn to listen, to learn where they were coming from, to accept their feelings without direct or implied condemnation, and to move carefully and supportingly from there."

In a society that espouses religions that proclaim the importance of faith, trust, forgiveness, the joy of giving and, above all, the nature and importance of genuine love as the keystone of all religion, it is saddening to recognize a dearth of these qualities expressed in actual behavior, even among the official dispensers of the faith. Religion, mishandled, can cause guilt feelings instead of spiritual growth, and it can cause permanent harm.

True spiritual belief can be of inestimable value in working with grieving parents. True understanding, acceptance, compassion and love, and the development of genuine trust, can pave the way for proper guidance, effective and permanent emotional healing and spiritual growth. The awesome power of genuine love in operation can be witnessed, but it is not easily explained.

What does all this have to do with abortion? Consider, if you will, the impact of all the pain and turmoil suffered by the parents of an abnormal child as described earlier, and identify with it if you can. Then consider the absolute horror of going through it again. Now recognize the shattering fact of being faced with a choice between two virtually intolerable courses of action. Consider the couple under such horrendous pressure who might choose to terminate a pregnancy as being the least destructive course for them. How would you react to them? Would you join that segment of society which would willfully heap rejection, condemnation, insults and accusation on two such vulnerable and devastated souls, or would you be supportive?

C. The Impact on the Couple's Marital Relationship

As a part of a routine review of the records of children enrolled in two large county facilities for the mentally retarded in Northeasten Ohio in 1976, one of the authors was struck by the fact that so many of the older children (age 18 through 21) had parents who were divorced or separated.[35] The actual percentage was approximately 75%. A further investigation of the records indicated that the figures were lower for the parents of younger children but increased steadily as the ages of the children increased. As the first author has traveled and lectured to other professionals in the field, quoting the 75% figure, comments from members of the audiences have indicated a widespread acceptance of the data. This figure is about twice the national average of separation and divorce for all reasons. Since the national average includes the couples studied, the significance of the abnormal child is, if anything, understated by the quoted statistic.

In our population of couples, a large number have reached the state of seriously considering divorce before reaching out for professional help; yet less than 5% have ended up in separation or divorce, and most have found that by working through the effects of the tragedy with proper guidance and support and by better understanding themselves individually and collectively as a couple, they have ended with a stronger relationship than they had before the unhappy event of their abnormal child's birth.

Several things are clear: (1) parents who suffer from the effects of producing a defective child need a great deal of help; (2) most couples either do not seek help or receive inappropriate and ineffective advice; and (3) the marital relationship suffers to the point of dissolution in most cases in which the right kind of help is not forthcoming from professionals and from society in general.

There are multiple reasons for the breakup of marriage in these cases, but the study of our tapes indicates that the following three categories encompass most of them.

1.   BREAKDOWN OF COMMUNICATION   In an increasingly mistrustful society, psychologists, sociologists and specialists in related fields have long recognized that the degree of openness and honesty in communication is directly related to the level of trust existing between the individuals involved. In an increasingly untrusting and complicated world, then, it is no wonder that in terms of open communication and genuine sharing, the average marriage, even without the impact of major tragedies, is far less rewarding than it could be. Furthermore, trust and open communication are essential ingredients in the establishment of genuine love, as differentiated from purely romantic love. This is not to say that genuine love cannot be romantic but rather to point out that "falling in love," that fantastic but unrealistic state of emotional confusion, is far different from genuine, growing and lasting love. The difference is well described by Peck.[36]

To repeat two well-established truisms: You cannot trust others if you do not trust yourself, and you cannot love others if you do not first love yourself. Loving oneself in this sense translates to self-respect and feeling good about oneself—having a good self-image. Thus the steps in breakdown of communication are the development of a damaged self-image, leading to a loss of trust and love, followed by a retreat from open communication.

Communication takes many forms, from nonverbal awareness of body language, to verbalization, to tactile reaching out, to the joy of physical closeness, to the potential

---

[35] Personal Communication.

[36] S. M. Peck, The Road Less Traveled, in *Love* (1978).

fulfillment of genuine and total sexual sharing. All are impaired as a result of producing a defective child.

The effects on a couple's sexual relationship is of special significance and should be dealt with at least briefly. In our culture it is extremely difficult for most individuals to reach the point of totally accepting their sexuality as a vital, powerful and positive force that is truly a part of them, uncontaminated by guilt, ugliness and fear. In less than a century we experienced everything from the straitlaced denial of mid-Victorianism and the guilt-producing impact of unloving religious condemnations to a rebellious and equally unfulfilling attitude of so-called sexual liberation, which in most cases has meant sex without love. Ignored has been the uniquely human capacity to accept and rejoice in sexuality and sexual sharing as the ultimate in intimate communication between two genuinely loving individuals.

Considering this kind of an insecure base, it is not difficult to understand why the sexual relationship between a husband and wife so often ceases to exist as a potential means of intimate and effective communication under the impact of all the other pain and confusion produced when a defective child is born to them. Not infrequently sexual union entirely ceases to occur or is undertaken only rarely, and then only as an outlet for purely physical need, or even anger.

2. PROJECTION OF GUILT AND ANGER   Guilt and anger have been discussed in some detail and are inevitable problems for the individual parents of an abnormal child and also a threat to the marital relationship. As already noted, both parents suffer the effects of guilt and anger, but there are significant differences between the initial reactions of the husband and wife.

For a woman, the entire pregnancy and childbirth experience is far more personal than for a man, both physically and emotionally for many reasons, some obvious, some more subtle. Guilt in the woman is likely to be self-directed initially in the form of searching for what she has done wrong with respect to nutrition, medication, activities, *etc.*, which might have caused damage to the child. Historically, our culture has directed blame and condemnation toward the woman as being responsible for all reproductive problems, from sterility to the birth of an abnormal child, and women have been expected to carry the burden of guilt. Therefore, the woman is less likely to think of blaming her spouse initially.

The husband, being less personally involved in the reproductive process, and with traditional thinking firmly on his side, is in a position to move more directly to including his wife among those whom he seeks to blame for his disappointment and pain and resulting anger. The attack on the wife may be subtle, by innuendo or the withdrawing of demonstrated affection, or it can be outspoken and more patently cruel. It is not unusual for a confused, angry and irrational husband openly to blame his wife for infidelity, claiming that the child is not his, thereby avoiding the stigma associated with the child's being abnormal. The wife, of course, has no such avenue of escape. Regardless of the wife's greater willingness to accept the reality of personal involvement in the problem, ultimately, as communication breaks down and support for her is withdrawn in favor of blame and stigmatization, the utter unfairness of the situation generates her frustration and anger.

Guilt is a difficult burden to carry, even for normally rational people. Rather than facing up to the fact of one's shortcomings or hurtful errors in judgment and action and taking steps to correct the errors, the typical behavior, one learned early in life, is to deny the guilt of hurtful behavior and, if that is not possible, to blame some other individual or situation, reinforcing the action by anger expressed toward the target of the projected blame. For the parents we are considering, the target most readily available is the spouse, and as guilt is projected as blame and anger, neither parent is likely to recognize that the anger actually is at themselves for their own inability to handle their guilt rationally.

3. DIFFERENCES BETWEEN HUSBAND AND WIFE IN HOW EMOTIONAL PAIN IS HANDLED Of all the personality patterns we have recognized and studied in our patient population, the one that emerges as the greatest threat to the marital relationship, as well as to the individual parent, is based on the difference in what our culture approves of in males as compared with females in the expression of the basic emotions of pain, tenderness, warmth, affection and genuine love.

From the first day of our birth we begin to receive the imprint of what society envisions we should become as a boy or a girl, as a man or a woman. Just listen to the manner in which nurses in a newborn nursery speak to infants they hold, and recognize that there are marked differences depending on whether the infant comes from a bassinet with a pink card or a blue card on it. When the child is presented to doting parents and relatives, it is as a bouncing, vigorous baby boy or as a beautiful, sweet, little girl.

Later, the male youngster will receive the dictate "little boys don't cry," probably even before he is out of diapers, and the attitude will continue, despite the fact that little boys, and men as well, have every bit as much need to cry as females. On the other hand, little girls are allowed to cry because it is accepted as female behavior in our society. If a man cries, it is a source of extreme uneasiness to those around him, whereas tears in a female are part of society's expectations. We overlook the well-documented fact that tears, whether they be of pain, joy or other feelings, are a biologically natural and normal response to emotion, and that the continued repression of natural emotions is hazardous to one's mental health.

Up to the age of about five years or so, the average child of either sex is comfortable in the embrace of its parents, but the little boy then begins to learn to shake his daddy's hand instead of hugging him, and even resists the embraces and kisses of his mother because such things are only for "little girls." He, by watching his role models, is on his way to becoming a man. Tenderness and uninhibited demonstration of affection and love will brand him as a sissy among his peers.

To sociologists, psychologists and other who study the evolution of male versus female behavior in our culture, it has become increasingly clear that a major deterrent to genuinely happy and fulfilling marriages is the fact that our culture inhibits in the male the development of freedom to express emotion openly, while fostering that freedom in females. Anger is perhaps the one emotion in which the reverse tends to be true. It has also become clear that the same basic need to express emotions exists equally in both sexes. Both need to be able not only to express tenderness, affection and love, but also to receive it. Therefore, both men and women are plagued by an underlying sense of unfulfillment and frustration, often without recognizing the basis for it.

In the last few years there has been encouraging movement toward societal acceptance of the open expression of emotions such as affection, warmth, tenderness, grief, etc. by males; however, it is our belief that there is still a great deal of room for improvement.

When a couple faces the overwhelming emotions associated with the birth of an abnormal child, the disparity between a husband's and a wife's ability to express emotions openly becomes a critical issue. Characteristically, the husband, raised to feel that he should be capable of being strong and not show evidence of deep hurt, confusion or despair, tries to hide his pain, fearful that if he lets himself go he will fall apart emotionally. He attempts to solve his dilemma by showing anger, by not wanting to talk about the child, and as much as possible by physically avoiding contact with the situation—staying longer hours at the office or getting involved with other time-consuming activities away from home.

The wife recognizes her need to talk about her feelings but finds access to her husband blocked. His behavior causes her to feel that she is weak and inadequate. Above all, she desperately needs to be reassured that she is still loved and wanted despite what she feels she has done in producing the abnormal child, and her husband's actions seem to indicate to her that she is neither loved nor wanted. Furthermore, his increased time away from home makes her feel abandoned, and her anger at him mounts.

A couple in this difficult situation need help, both as individuals and for the sake of the marriage: yet they are in no position to help each other. The husband, in his continuing attempt to solve his problems by denying them, pretends that there is little or nothing seriously wrong with him or the relationship and implies that everything would improve if his wife would only show some strength of character. She, on the other hand, is far more realistic about the fact that both she and the marital relationship are in trouble. Our data show that in almost all cases it is the wife who makes the first contact asking for professional help. The admission of needing help, particularly in the area of emotional problems, seems to be too threatening to the male ego.

Professional help is needed and is of great value providing it is of the right sort, but we have not yet trained enough professional counselors who specialize in the area of helping parents of an abnormal child. Beyond the need for professional help, and every bit as important to the rehabilitation process for the parents we have discussed, is the need for greater knowledge, awareness, acceptance and compassion on the part of society in general. In this area, we have an even greater distance to go.

D. Siblings and Other Family Members

We have focused on parents of a birth-defective child for the purpose of this book because the decision to terminate a pregnancy when the unborn child is proven to be abnormal is primarily a parental decision. However, our efforts to help our readers take a realistic look at a complex and heartrending facet of human existence would be incomplete if we failed to point out that the event of an abnormal child's birth has an impact that extends considerably beyond the parents to those with whom they are associated, particularly the immediate family and relatives.

When an abnormal child is born, a question arises in the minds of any blood-relative individual as to the possibility of some heretofore hidden hereditary trait that might be present in them, and at least some of the effects that we have discussed in foregoing statements are bound to come into play. The child's grandparents are literally parents in a genetic sense and unwillingly feel a responsibility for the problem. For them, as for the child's immediate parents, the tendency is to try to get off the hook of responsibility, and the easiest and most obvious way is to focus the blame on the son-in-law or daughter-in-law. The classic remark that "nothing like that ever happened in our family" is a very likely one.

For the parents of the abnormal child, their own parents and parents-in-law can be an extremely important source of understanding and support, but, unfortunately they become an additional problem more often than not. The same can be said for the distressed parents' siblings, aunts and uncles of the problem child.

The siblings of a child born with an abnormality, particularly that of mental retardation, face very special problems. They suffer in an insidiously destructive way from the feeling that something must be wrong with them also. Beyond that, they are forced in many ways into a life-style that is so different from that of their peers that they often develop a pervasive feeling of resentment and anger which, in many cases, they are required to hide. The effects are likely to be lifelong in duration. In many ways, the normal siblings of an abnormal child suffer more than anyone in the long run, particularly if that child continues to live in the household.

Approximately 7% of all children born suffer from some problem severe enough to warrant medical intervention, thereby triggering some if not all of the effects we have discussed. If we assume as a very conservative figure for the number of living relatives that the child will have one sibling, two parents, four grandparents, two uncles or aunts, and four cousins, we recognize that at least 13 individuals are immediately and directly involved to a greater or lesser degree. Based on 1980 census figures of more than 3.2 million children under one year of age, and using the 7% figure for abnormal births, each such birth having an emotional impact on at least 13 people, the number of individuals just beginning to experience the effects of each abnormal birth is in excess of 3 million every year. The total number of persons suffering some emotional ill effects from this cause at any time in this country alone is inestimable.

We are faced with a very significant medical, psychological and sociological problem in severe human suffering that has for the most part been ignored, partly through lack of information and partly through unwillingness to face the reality of the problem honestly.

Dr. Alan F. Guttmacher was a giant in the area of family planning and reproductive health. Here, he gives a history of his involvement with the abortion issue from the 1920s to the 1970s and explains how his personal experience in medicine began to shape his opinions on abortion laws. Dr. Kaiser discusses the many abortion techniques along with the dangers inherent in any medical or surgical procedure.

The irony of Dr. Guttmacher's article is that the history he presents before *Roe* could become an everyday occurrence in some states if *Roe* is overturned. At one time, the state of Maryland prohibited abortion except when necessary to preserve the life of the mother. Dr. Guttmacher writes, "Such a restrictive policy could only lead to reliance on those who would go outside the law to provide the desired services." It is quite obvious that the strength of this article is not only that it provides a historical perspective but also that it acts as a warning to what the future might hold.

21 · The Genesis of Liberalized Abortion in New York: A Personal Insight* _____

Alan F. Guttmacher, M.D.
Update by Irwin H. Kaiser, M.D.

I. Prelude to Liberalized Abortion Statutes

Since my debut as an Aesculapian antedates those of other physician contributors to this volume, I thought it valuable to relate medical practices and attitudes toward induced abortion three-quarters of a century ago and to analyze the genesis, direction, and magnitude of the change in those attitudes and practices and its reflection in the legal position on abortion.

I was taught obstetrics at the Johns Hopkins Medical School by Dr. J. Whitridge Williams, one of the great medical figures of the 1920s. He was forceful, confident and didactic. To him, and therefore to us, induced abortion was either therapeutic or "criminal." He told us therapeutic abortion was performed to save the life of the pregnant woman and that the primary threats involved dysfunction by three organs: the heart, the lung, and the kidney. To these hazards he begrudgingly added toxic vomiting of pregnancy. I say "begrudgingly" because I remember full well the drastic treatment meted out to hyperemetic gravidae: isolation, submammary infusions, rectal clyses, and feeding by stomach tube. To resort to therapeutic abortion in these cases was admission of medical failure. No medical sanction was then given to abortion on socioeconomic or psychological grounds.

The experiences I encountered during my residency from 1925 to 1929 made me question the wisdom of such a restrictive medical policy. In a short period I witnessed three deaths from illegal abortions: a 16-year-old with a multiperforated uterus, a mother of four who died of sepsis rejecting another child, and a patient in early menopause

---

who fatally misinterpreted amenorrhea. My skepticism of the wisdom of existing abortion laws was further reinforced by an incident involving Dr. Williams. A social worker came to me seeking abortion services for a 12-year-old black child who had been impregnated by her father. Dr. Williams was a court of one to validate abortion requests, so I sought his permission to perform the operation. He was sympathetic but reminded me that Maryland prohibited abortion except where necessary to preserve the life of the mother,[1] and he did not believe that continuation of pregnancy in this case would endanger the girl's life. When I brought up the social injustice of compelling a child to bear her father's bastard, Dr. Williams compromised, saying that if I could obtain a letter from the district attorney granting special permission to the Johns Hopkins Hospital, then I could perform the abortion.[2] I failed to get this permission and delivered the baby seven months later. At about the same time, one of the residents at a neighboring hospital showed me a child, the daughter of an army colonel, who had been hysterotomized to eliminate pregnancy conceived through "rape." Experiences such as this made me question the possibilities for social injustice and disparate treatment, ever present under a restrictive policy which gave one man the sole power to determine the validity and permissibility of abortion services.

Such a restrictive policy could lead to reliance on those who would go outside the law to provide the desired services. Indeed, during the same period there were two competent physician-abortionists in Baltimore who practiced for many years relatively unmolested by the police. They were so well-known that an inquiry addressed to either a traffic policeman or a salesgirl would have elicited their names with equal ease. They were not partners, but close collaborators, occasionally preparing death certificates for each other. One, while attending a public national meeting in Washington, rose to defend the service provided by illegal medical abortionists who had been defamed by a speaker. He stated openly that there had been but four deaths in the 7,000 abortions with which he had been associated. This was before the first use of antibiotics, "salting out," and other precautionary procedures. Finally, years later when a complaint was filed, the district attorney was compelled to take official cognizance of the existence of one of the two abortionists. At the trial, the abortionist offered to produce, in his defense, a list of 300 reputable physicians who had referred cases to him. I assume my name was among them.

On one occasion, the nestor of American gynecologists, Dr. Robert L. Dickinson, called me from New York requesting that I arrange a meeting in Baltimore with Dr. T. We lunched at a hotel, and Dr. T. produced a roster of his patients, duration of pregnancy, parity, city of residence, fees, source of referral, *etc.* On another occasion Dr. T met with a few of the senior medical faculty of Johns Hopkins to disclose his technique. To minimize infection, he had invented a boilable rubber perineal shield with a rubber sleeve that fitted into the vagina and through which he worked. His technique was to pack one-inch gauze strips into the cervix and lower uterine segment the night before he was to evacuate the conceptas. After 12 hours of packing, the cervix was

---

[1] *Cf.* Md. Ann. Code art. 43. § 137(a) (1971). The present statute is patterned after the Model Penal Code. *See* note 10 *infra* and accompanying text.

[2] Presently, California follows a similar procedure in cases of incest. Cal. Health & Safety Code § 25952 (West Supp. 1971) (permitting abortion where the district attorney is satisfied that there is probable cause to believe that the pregnancy resulted from rape or incest and this validation is transmitted to the Committee of the Medical Staff).

wide open, and he was able to empty the uterus with an ovum forceps, followed by curettage without anesthesia. In advanced pregnancies he inserted intrauterine bougies, held in place by a vaginal pack until strong contractions commenced, which not infrequently took several days.

These early medical experiences with the unavailability of abortions in reputable hospitals and the incidence of illegal abortion convinced me that permitting abortion only "to preserve the life of the mother"[3] was undesirable and unenforceable. I thus sought changes which would both curb the morbidity and mortality of illegal abortion and eliminate the ethnic and social discrimination which was inherent to all induced abortions, whether legal or illegal.

I found in my hospital contacts that obstetricians and gynecologists were the most conservative medical group in regard to abortion. Internists and psychiatrists were constantly berating us for our low incidence of legal pregnancy terminations. Indeed, there had developed a feeling of prideful accomplishment among the obs-gyn staff if one's hospital had a low therapeutic abortion rate and a feeling of disgrace if the rate was relatively high compared to similar institutions. I shared this viewpoint, no doubt swayed by the writings and addresses of obstetrical leaders such as Drs. George Kosmak and Samuel Cosgrove. My sentiment was that as long as the law was as restrictive as it was, doctors should not breach it, but work to change the law—a position which I forthrightly espoused in the classroom. Despite the fact that it was not a radical notion, this position had few adherents. Members of the medical profession were content to leave things as they were; they would frequently perform a therapeutic abortion for a favored patient because of her important social position, or at least refer her to a safe, illegal medical operator. But acceptance of generally available legal abortion was still far in the future. In the early 1930s, I was invited to present a paper on abortion reform before the New Jersey Obstetrical and Gynecological Society. One participant, Dr. Cosgrove, tore into me like a tank. I can still recall my discomfiture and frustration at the unyielding establishment.

Until 1940, the decision to permit or to deny therapeutic abortion in the individual case was made solely by the chief of the obstetrical service. The physician handling the case presented the patient's history, physical examination, and laboratory findings to the chief who, in turn, made an immediate decision. Through personal observations, I learned that it was impossible to predict how the chief would decide, for such decisions seemed to turn on his mood and on the latest article he had read on the subject.

It was in recognition of the inadequacies of such a procedure that, when I became chief of obstetrics at Baltimore's Sinai Hospital in 1942, I decided to have a staff committee of five make decisions about abortion.[4] This committee consisted of representatives from medicine, surgery, pediatrics, psychiatry, and obstetrics, with the obstetrician as chairman. As far as I knew, such a plan had never been tried, although I have since learned that it had been in force in a few other hospitals. The abortion committee system functioned well. Among other things it added medical expertise in special areas

---

[3] *See, e.g.,* Tenn. Code Ann. § 39–301 (1955), which restricted abortions to such cases of necessity.

[4] The committee method of decisions regarding abortions is prevalent and is codified in many states. Cal. Health & Safety Code § 25951 (b) (West Supp. 1971), for example, requires the consent of an approved hospital committee before an abortion can be performed. The statute requires that the committee be composed of not less than three licensed physicians and requires that the decision to permit an abortion be unanimous.

beyond obstetrics. Moreover, greater consistency was attained through adherence to guidelines adopted in cases with similar factual patterns. I do not believe that the committee system significantly affected the hospital's incidence of legal abortion, but at least all applicants were treated on an equal basis.

When I became director of obstetrics and gynecology at the Mount Sinai Hospital in New York in 1952, I learned that the department of gynecology (there had been no department of obstetrics previous to my arrival) had performed 30 abortions in the previous six months. I was told that if a private patient was denied abortion in another institution, she frequently sought abortion at Mount Sinai because of its well-known, relatively liberal policy. I recall resenting this reputation. Forthwith we introduced the committee system, the results of which have been reported in three publications.[5] The committee met each Wednesday afternoon if any case was to be heard. Forty-eight hours prior to that meeting, the staff obstetrician who wished to carry out an abortion would have provided each member a summary of the case together with recommendations from consultants, if any had examined the patient. The staff obstetrician and frequently a consultant from a medical discipline germane to the problem (for example, a cardiologist for a cardiac case or a neurologist for the mother who had borne a child with muscular dystrophy) presented their findings or views. The committee always voted in executive session, and a unanimous vote was required to authorize abortion. This requirement was not as forbidding as it sounds, for in almost every instance the other members of the committee would agree with the opinion of the member within whose discipline the problem lay.

Statistics on the number of abortions performed at Mount Sinai and at other New York hospitals over generally contemporaneous time periods are illuminating. At Mount Sinai Hospital, 207 therapeutic abortions were performed between 1953 and 1960, yielding an incidence of 5.7 abortions per 1,000 live births. Partly because of my efforts to eliminate discrimination, the rate was 6.3 per 1,000 live births on the private service and 4.6 per 1,000 births on the ward service.[6] One commentator, in reporting figures from another large New York voluntary hospital for the years 1951 to 1954, showed an incidence of 8.1 abortions per 1,000 live births on the private service and a rate of 2.4 on the ward service.[7] Statistics were also available for two New York municipal hospitals: Metropolitan Hospital (1959–61) and Kings County Hospital (1958–60). In the former, the abortion incidence was 0.077 per 1,000 live births, and in the latter the incidence was 0.37 per 1,000 live births.[8] Gold published a study of abortion incidence for all New York hospitals for the period 1960–62.[9] The incidence in proprietary institutions was shown to be 3.9 per 1,000 live births; and in the voluntary hospitals the incidence was 2.4 on the private services and 0.7 on the ward services. Municipal hospitals showed a rate of 0.1 per 1,000 live births. There was also a marked ethnic

---

[5] Guttmacher, *Therapeutic Abortion: The Doctor's Dilemma*, 21 J. Mt. Sinai Hospital 111 (1954); Guttmacher, *Therapeutic Abortion in a Large General Hospital*, 37 Surgical Clinics of North America 459 (April 1957); Guttmacher, *The Legal and Moral Status of Therapeutic Abortion*, in *Progress in Gynecology* IV 279 (J. Meigs & S. Sturgis eds. 1963).

[6] Guttmacher, *The Legal and Moral Status of Therapeutic Abortion*, in *Progress in Gynecology* IV 289 (J. Meigs & S. Sturgis eds. 1963).

[7] C. McLane, *Abortion in the United States* (Calderone ed. 1958).

[8] Guttmacher, *supra* note 6.

[9] Gold, Erhardt, Jacobziner & Nelson, *Therapeutic Abortions in New York City: A 20 Year Review*, 55 Am. J. of Public Health 964 (1965).

differential: the ratio of therapeutic abortions per 1,000 live births was 2.6 for whites, 0.5 for Negroes, and 0.1 for Puerto Ricans.

Not only was there great disparity in the incidence rates among various hospitals but, in addition, the abortion policies and rules established by hospitals were confusingly different. Mount Sinai, for example, validated abortion for well-documented rubella (German measles), whereas Columbia-Presbyterian did not. Mount Sinai did not permit abortion for rape, whereas St. Johns in Brooklyn did. The marked differences among hospitals in regard to incidence and standards as well as patient discrimination—discrimination between ward and private patients and between ethnic groups—served to aggravate my dissatisfaction with the status quo and led to my desire for the enactment of a new law.

The question was, what should be the content of an ideal law? Because my twin brother, the late Dr. Manfred Guttmacher, a forensic psychiatrist, was a member of the American Law Institute (ALI), which was then engaged in writing a revised penal code, I was present on a Sunday afternoon in December 1959 when Mr. Herbert Wechsler (professor of law at Columbia) unveiled his model abortion statute now called the ALI bill.[10] The recommended statute provided that a doctor would be permitted to perform an abortion: (1) if continuation of pregnancy "would gravely impair the physical or mental health of the mother"; (2) if the doctor believed "that the child would be born with grave physical or mental defects"; or (3) if the pregnancy resulted from rape or incest.[11]

When Professor Wechsler had finished presenting his suggested statute, an elderly gentleman sitting at the large, felt-covered table inaudibly mumbled some comment. Mr. Wechsler said, "What did you say, Judge Hand?" The eminent federal jurist, Learned Hand said, "It is a rotten law." Mr. Wechsler asked why, and Judge Hand responded, "It's too damned conservative." How right he was. Yet most of those present, including myself, disagreed with him. The Wechsler abortion bill was passed by the institute as part of the total revised penal code revealed to the public in 1962. Many, including myself, hailed it as the answer to the legal problems surrounding abortion, which had always been the doctor's dilemma.

Even though the ALI Code had not yet been adopted by any state, its mere promulgation opened the medical profession's eyes to the preservation of health as being a justification for abortion. The most difficult health hazard to document (but equally difficult to refute) was significant trauma to the psychic stability of the pregnant individual. "Psychiatric" indications for abortion rapidly increased in importance. Tietze's figures demonstrate that in 1963 psychiatric indications accounted for 0.57 legal abortions per 1,000 live births in the United States; in 1965 the rate was 0.76 per 1,000, and in 1967 it was 1.50 per 1,000.[12] The increasing frequency of psychiatric justifications for abortion caused concern for many. Because the psychiatric indications were so ill-defined and pliable, it was feared that they might become an upperclass ticket for legal abortion, thus increasing discrimination and doing little to lower the morbidity and mortality rates in the population at large. In 1967, Colorado, California, and North

---

[10] Model Penal Code § 230.3(2) (Proposed Official Draft, 1962).

[11] *Id.*

[12] Tietze, *United States: Therapeutic Abortions, 1963 to 1968*, 59 Studies in Family Planning 5 (1970). Tietze's figures were based on hospitals reporting to The Professional Activities Survey in Ann Arbor, Michigan.

Carolina,[13] and in 1968, Maryland and Georgia,[14] all modified their respective statues, using the ALI bill as the prototype. Between 1967 and 1968 the incidence of legal abortions in the United States increased from 2.59 to 5.19 per 1,000 live births, and abortions for psychiatric indications increased from 1.50 to 3.61 per 1,000 live births.[15]

In December 1968, I was appointed to Governor Rockefeller's 11-member commission which had been formed to examine the abortion statute of New York State and to make recommendations for change. When the governor convened the commission, he said, "I am not asking whether New York's abortion law should be changed. I am asking how it should be changed." The commission was made up of a minister, a priest, a rabbi, three professors of law, three physicians, a poetess, and the president of a large black woman's organization. There were four Catholics, four Protestants, and three Jews. The commission met every two weeks for more than three months. It was apparent that three members wanted no change in the old law despite the governor's charge, two wished abortion removed entirely from the criminal code, and six advocated the enactment of the ALI model with further liberalization: the majority report—approved 8–3—added legal abortion on request for any mother of four children. My proposal of adding a clause to permit abortion on request for any woman 40 years or older was voted down—this was April 1969.

The more I studied early results from the five states which had been the first to liberalize their laws, the more I began to espouse the opinion that abortion statutes should be entirely removed from the criminal code. The number of legal abortions being undertaken under the new liberalized laws, when contrasted with the figures for the previously undertaken illegal abortions, was far too low. In 1968, for example, California reported only about 5,000 abortions under the new law.[16] It is true that this number has steadily increased to a present rate of over 100,000 per year, but that increase stems in large part from an increase in the number of abortions legitimized on psychiatric grounds: Over 90 percent of current abortions are performed on that ground.[17] In actuality it places the psychiatrist in the untenable situation of being an authority in socioeconomics. I examined the situation personally in Colorado and discovered that two Denver hospitals were doing virtually all of the pregnancy interruptions and these were being performed primarily on the private sector. This clearly implied that the state-imposed requirement of two psychiatric consultations was causing an effective discrimination against ward patients: private consultations were too expensive as to be available only to the wealthier patients, and psychiatric appointments in public facilities were booked solid for three months—far beyond the time limitation on obtaining an abortion. From these experiences, I reluctantly concluded that abortion on request—necessitating

[13] See Colo. Rev. Stat. Ann. § 40-6-101(3)(a)(1971); Cal. Health & Safety Code § 25951 (West Supp. 1971); N.C. Gen. Stat. § 14-45.1 (supp. 1971).

[14] See Md. Ann. Code art. 43, § 137(a) (1971); Ga. Code Ann. § 26-1202 (1971). See also Ga. Code Ann. § 26-9925a(a) (1971) (worded identically to section 26-1202) (a prefatory note preceding section 26-9921a indicates that there is some doubt as to which statute is in effect).

[15] Tietze, supra note 12, at 7.

[16] California's Therapeutic Abortion Act became operative November 8, 1967. During the first calendar year under the new law, legal abortions reported from the entire state were 5,030. See Overstreet, California's Abortion Law—A Second Look, in Abortion and the Unwanted Child, 16 (C. Reiterman ed. 1971).

[17] See Bureau of Maternal and Child Health, 4th Annual Report on the Implementation of the California Therapeutic Abortion Act (1971).

removal of "abortion" from the penal codes—was the only way to truly democratize legal abortion and to sufficiently increase the numbers performed so as to decrease the incidence of illegal abortions. I came to this conclusion in 1969, 47 years after abortion first came to my medical attention when I was a third-year medical student. Abortion on request, a position which I now support after having been converted by years of medical practice and observation, was soon to have its trial in New York, the state in which I reside. This gave me the opportunity to observe firsthand how effectively it would function. The three criteria to be used for evaluation were straightforward. Did abortion on request save lives? Did it minimize socioethnic discrimination? Did it reduce the incidence of illegal abortion?

Update
Irvin H. Kaiser, M.D.

It is difficult to remember the excitement and confusion that surrounded the dramatic changes in public attitude and in the law concerning abortion that descended on the unprepared medical and legal professions in 1970. Alan F. Guttmacher in his chapter in the second edition of the present work captured this in the section which was headed "The New York Situation," the opening paragraphs of which read as follows:

> *On April 10, 1970, the New York State Legislature amended the State Penal Code, permitting licensed physicians to provide abortion services for any consenting woman less than 24 weeks pregnant. The law specifies no restrictions on place of residence, age, marital status, or consent of spouse, if married, and it makes no restrictions as to the type of facility where abortions might be performed. After 142 years of one of the most restrictive abortion statues—allowing abortions only when necessary to preserve the life of the mother—New York suddenly had the most liberal abortion law in the world.*
>
> *The New York State Legislature in 1969 had flatly rejected the bill produced by the Governor's Commission—basically the ALI model plus permissible abortion on request for any woman with four or more children. Those of us in favor of reform hoped in 1970 that we could somehow put through a modified ALI bill. We knew of the "radical" bill sponsored by Constance Cook, an upstate legislator, but had no hope for passage. Much to everyone's surprise, however, it passed the House by a modest majority. When it came before the Senate there was a tie vote and an expectation that the speaker would break the tie with his negative vote since he was a strong opponent of abortion reform. However, a senator from an upstate Catholic county broke the tie by changing his negative vote to an affirmative one. The bill was to become law July 1, less than 3 months later.*
>
> *The medical community was in a state of shock, not from opposition, but from total surprise. There were dire prophecies that all existing medical facilities would be dangerously overtaxed by a nationwide demand for abortion. But the New York City Department of Health began to ready the facilities of the 15 municipal hospitals, and the mayor appropriated an extra 3 million dollars to fund the new abortion service. In recognition*

of the financial potential, several proprietary hospitals were converted into abortoria. The voluntary hospitals agreed to do their part and some arranged to perform abortions on both an inpatient and an outpatient basis. Some physicians began to prepare their private offices for abortions, and others advocated free-standing clinics with built-in safety factors such as blood available for transfusion, cardiac arrest equipment, quick access to a back-up hospital, counselling before and after the operation and performance of abortion only by specialists in obstetrics and gynecology.

When July 1 arrived, the City Board of Health had not yet established its own standards for abortion services, and it did not do so until September 17. On that day the New York City Board of Health issued regulations outlawing private office abortions within New York City. They agreed that abortions could be performed in accredited hospitals and their outpatient departments. Also permitted were abortions in licensed free-standing abortion clinics which could meet certain enunciated standards regarding factors such as the size of the operating room, the availability of resuscitating equipment, and the availability of blood: furthermore, abortion of a pregnancy beyond 12 weeks could not be performed in such a free-standing clinic.

The next act in the drama took place in 1973 in the form of the Supreme Court decision in *Roe v. Wade*[18] and *Doe v. Bolton*.[19] Based on the Supreme Court's concept of a woman's right to privacy, *Roe* established her right to terminate an unwanted pregnancy in consultation with her physician. The second case established, in view of the medical difficulties of abortion in the second trimester, that the state had a right to make regulations governing the way in which abortion would be provided at that trimester, provided that these regulations did not interfere with a woman's access to pregnancy termination. One remarkable aspect of these decisions was the extent to which the Court relied on social and medical expert advice in formulating its rules.

The opponents of abortion have been organized and extraordinarily well-financed. Soon after *Roe* they began a campaign to undo these Supreme Court decisions. In the Congress, amendments to appropriations bills have gradually withdrawn federal funds from the support of abortions, principally affecting those women dependent on welfare. The campaign also took the form of ordinances and statutes at the community and state level intended to restrict access to abortion services. In a long string of court decisions, the federal judiciary struck down one after another of these restrictive regulations until finally a group of such cases had accumulated on appeal on the docket of the Supreme Court.

In 1983, in a very firmly enunciated decision, the Supreme Court once again asserted the right of women to have access to abortion.[20] The Court declared unconstitutional a series of restrictive regulations that had been enacted in Akron, Ohio, with the explicit purpose of limiting the availability of abortion services. In addition, in related decisions announced at the same time, the Court pointed out that the greatly improved

---

[18] 410 U.S. 113 (1973).
[19] 410 U.S. 179 (1973).
[20] Akron v. Akron Center for Reproductive Health, 103 S. C. 2481 (1983).

safety of techniques for abortion in the second trimester of pregnancy now made it possible to provide such abortion services on an ambulatory basis. The denial of access to this constitutes an interference with the availability of such services. The Court thereby acknowledged the evidence, accumulated over the last decade, of the safety of second-trimester pregnancy interruption by contemporary techniques.

At the present time the best estimate is that 1.6 million abortions are performed in the United States annually.[21] Approximately 90 percent of these were completed in the first trimester in 1987. The overwhelming proportion is accomplished by minimal dilatation of the crevix and suction evacuation of the products of conception, prior to the 13th week of pregnancy. The safety of this procedure, particularly if it is undertaken under local anesthesia or without anesthesia at all, is such that the best estimate of the risk of maternal death is three deaths or less per 1 million abortions.[22] The lowest rate is observed at the seventh week. Indeed, abortion of early pregnancies by this technique is so safe that Tietze has argued that the use of a barrier method of contraception such as the condom and diaphragm, in combination with abortion for the failures of these methods, results in an overall decreased risk of contraception when compared with the use of oral contraceptives or IUDs.[23] It is not necessary to accept Tietze's hypothesis entirely to recognize that interruption of pregnancy in the first trimester is an extremely safe procedure, with probably the lowest risk of any commonly undertaken surgical intervention, with the possible exception of circumcision in the newborn and cutting of the umbilical cord.[24]

The interruption of pregnancy in the second trimester results in mortality and morbidity substantially greater than that due to interruption in the first trimester, regardless of the technique employed.[25] At this duration too, however, there has been a dramatic improvement in available methods. Of the procedures commonly undertaken in the United States for abortion in the second trimester in the 1970s, almost all involved the induction of labor by the introduction into the amniotic sac of chemicals whose purpose is to kill the fetus and the placenta and thereby indirectly induce labor. In addition, some of these at the same time stimulate uterine activity. This technique results in a substantial number of complications. The earliest material used for this purpose was concentrated salt solution, which was highly efficient in inducing fetal death, but also had the hazards of salt intoxication and disseminated intravascular coagulation (DIC).[26] In some instances, labor of some violence, induced by this technique, resulted in injury to the cervix. The method therefore incurred both early and late morbidity. The replacement of concentrated saline solutions with prostaglandins and with urea, and with varying combinations of these, has markedly cut down the incidence of intoxication and DIC but has not reduced these accidents to zero. Injuries to the cervix have been minimized by the use

---

[21] S. K. Henshaw and L. Koonin, *Characteristics of U.S. Women Having Abortions, 1987*, 23 Fam. Plann. Perspect. 75 (1991).

[22] Centers for Disease Control, U.S. Public Health Service, *Abortion Surveillance, United States, 1988* (July 1991); W. Cates Jr., *Abortion Myths and Realities: Who Is Misleading Whom?* 142 Am. J. Obstet. Gynecol. 954 (1982).

[23] C. J. R. Hogue, W. Cates Jr. & C. Tietze, *Impact of Vacuum Aspiration Abortion on Future Childbearing: A Review*, 15 Fam. Plann. Perspect. 119 (1983).

[24] Centers for Disease Control, U.S. Public Health Service, *Vital Statistics of the United States—1987* (1990) [hereinafter cited as *Vital Statistics*].

[25] Centers for Disease Control, *supra* note 22; *Vital Statistics*, *supra* note 24.

[26] S. Neubardt & H. Schulman, *Techniques of Abortion* (2d ed. 1977).

of materials to dilate the cervix prior to or simultaneous with the intra-amniotic instillation. It is nevertheless necessary for all these patients to experience labor, and, although there are no particular limitations on the administration of drugs for pain relief, the patient's experience is nonetheless dismal.

Some special mention needs to be made of the use of ethacridine (Rivanol) for second-trimester abortion. There have been reports from the Netherlands, Sweden, Germany, and Japan of its efficacy and safety when injected by catheter in an extraamniotic position. There has also been a report from the People's Republic of China (PRC).[27] A remarkably low incidence of complications is described as compared to the use of hypertonic saline and various other methods in use in the PRC. There is no comparable study of the United States experience.

Evacuation of the uterus in the second trimester by what is commonly called dilatation and evacuation (D&E) appears to be safer than these methods for the induction of labor.[28] There is no question that D&E demands a considerable degree of experience and surgical skill. It can, however, be carried out rapidly, with the use of modest amounts of analgesia and local anesthesia. Bleeding is minimal in most patients. Ideally, the patients are prepared for the evacuation, after screening by pelvic sonography, with the use of devices for dilating the cervix. These devices can be put in one, two, or even three days prior to the evacuation of the uterus, depending on the duration of pregnancy. The evacuation is therefore carried out through a prepared, dilated cervix. The evacuation itself is accomplished by forceps and suction of the fragmented fetus and the placenta. The safety of this procedure was acknowledged in the 1983 Supreme Court decisions,[29] which agreed that in properly regulated clinics, abortion in the second trimester could appropriately be performed on an ambulatory basis, provided that hospital backup was readily available.

It would be a mistake to assume that the opponents of abortion will abandon their efforts simply because the Supreme Court has not overruled *Roe v. Wade*.[30] A substantial proportion of the movement consists of those who are stimulated to greater effort by the defeats they have experienced and by their basic awareness that approximately 85 percent of the adult population of the United States supports the availability of abortion. That a well-concerted effort to amend the Constitution was defeated in the United States Senate shortly after the 1983 decisions does not alter the fact that some 49 senators voted for it. This vote is looked upon as an encouraging development by some of the opponents of abortion. We can expect to have to go back to court repeatedly in actions against local legislation, enacted in the face of its obvious unconstitutionality.

II. The Outcomes of Abortion

Abortion has probably been studied in greater detail than any other surgical procedure in the history of medicine. Fortunately, in the early 1970s, the Centers for Disease Control (CDC) perceived the necessity of a careful national study of abortion services

---

[27] K.-H. Tien, *Intraamniotic Injection of Ethacridine for Second Trimester Induction of Labor,* 61 Obstet. Gynecol. 733 (1983).

[28] W. M. Hern, *Midtrimester Abortion,* 10 Obstet. & Gynecol. Ann. 375 (1981); W. F. Peterson, F. N. Berry, M. R. Grace & C. L. Gulbranson, *Second Trimester Abortion by Dilatation and Evacuation: An Analysis of 11,747 Cases.* 62 Obstet. Gynecol. 185 (1983).

[29] Akron v. Akron Center for Reproductive Health, 103 S. Ct. 2481 (1983).

[30] 410 U.S. 113 (1973).

and initiated the steps to gather data prior to the 1973 Supreme Court decisions. The CDC statistics are based on reports to governmental bodies. A large number of abortions are provided in doctors' offices, and these are not necessarily reported to health departments. The Alan Guttmacher Institute (AGI) has therefore compiled its own statistics, based upon reports from abortion providers in addition to those reported to the CDC. Both the CDC and the AGI have published remarkably detailed reports on abortion. The last annual summary published from the Public Health Service is that for 1988, issued in July 1991.[31] The Public Health Service has also reported a preliminary analysis of abortions in 1987 in its *Vital Statistics of the United States*.[32] The most recent report from the AGI was published in Family Planning Perspectives for January/February 1987 and also records data up to 1987.[33] The following statistics are based on these documents.

In 1987 some 1,559,110 abortions were performed in the United States.[34] Some 51 percent of these were carried out at eight weeks of gestation or less; 26.6 percent in the ninth and 10th weeks; 13 percent in the 11th and 12th weeks; and the remainder at the 13th week and beyond. Only 0.9 percent of all the abortions were carried out past the 21st week. Of these abortions, 95 percent were done by instrumental evacuation, which includes suction and sharp curettage in early pregnancy and dilatation and evacuation at 13 weeks' gestation and later. Only 3.8 percent were done by intrauterine instillation, prostaglandin, urea, and some combination procedures. Fortunately, only 0.1 percent of the abortions were done by hysterotomy and hysterectomy.

Nationally, approximately 27 percent of pregnancies were terminated by abortion in 1987. The highest percentage of pregnancies so terminated is found among women aged 18 to 19 at the rate of 61.8. However, the next highest rate is 52.3 among women up to the age of 24.[35]

The number of deaths associated with abortion has decreased steadily since the CDC began to collect its statistics. The fewest deaths were achieved in 1987 which is the most recent year for which statistics are available.[36] In 1987 there were only eight deaths associated with legal abortion. In addition 5 deaths were reported to the CDC as following spontaneous abortion, and no deaths from illegally induced abortion were reported in that year. These figures have to be contrasted with those of 1972. In that year 88 women died of abortion-related deaths, 24 of them from legal abortion, 39 from illegally induced abortion and 25 following spontaneous abortion. The most spectacular figure, of course, is the virtual disappearance of death due to illegal abortion, there have actually been none at all in 1987.

There has now been adequate follow-up of women who have had a first-trimester suction abortion of their first pregnancy to indicate that there is no adverse effect on carrying the next pregnancy to term.[37] The incidence of mid-trimester spontaneous abortion and low-birthweight infants is not increased. However, the protective effect that a

---

[31] Centers for Disease Control, *supra* note 22.

[32] *Vital Statistics, supra* note 24.

[33] Henshaw and Koonin, *supra* note 21.

[34] *Id.*

[35] *Id.*

[36] *Vital Statistics, supra* note 24.

[37] Hogue, Cates & Tietze, *supra* note 23.

first live birth has on a subsequent birth is not observed with a prior abortion. Abortion does not appear to result in infertility. There is no clear effect of multiple abortions.

There have not been enough pregnancies studied following D&Es in the second trimester on which to base any conclusions as to later effects.

III. Techniques of Abortion in the United States

Attention has been directed over the years to developing methods of "medical" abortion, which is to say interruption of pregnancy by a nonsurgical means. Four techniques are worthy of some attention, although unfortunately all have sufficient drawbacks as that they do not adequately meet the need for a simple noninvasive abortion method.

High-dose estrogen therapy of brief duration has been employed to prevent an unimplanted pregnancy from implanting, a therapy commonly referred to as the morning-after pill. It is not really known how frequently it prevents the successful implantation of a fertilized ovum and how frequently it simply produces sufficient hormone interference to prevent fertilization from taking place. The rate of pregnancy is nevertheless markedly reduced. There is very little question, in view of the DES experience, that estrogens are teratogenic and therefore probably not to be recommended except to patients who will certainly accept pregnancy interruption should estrogen prophylaxis fail.

Insertion of an intrauterine device is also done to prevent implantation of an unwanted pregnancy after unprotected coitus.

Considerably more attention has been directed to the use of prostaglandins for abortion, and several large study programs in this respect have been completed over the course of the last decade. The earliest hope was that the oral administration of prostaglandins could interfere with the development of the corpus luteum sufficiently to result in its degeneration and consequent abortion, because of failure of hormonal support of the early implanted pregnancy. That expectation has not been realized because luteolytic doses also result in an unacceptable incidence of side effects, particularly nausea, vomiting, and diarrhea. Administration of other prostaglandin preparations in the form of vaginal suppositories has also been attempted, but once again the success rate is not sufficiently high to justify this technique in preference to the simplicity and safety of suction evacuation. Extraamniotic instillation of prostaglandin has a substantially higher success rate than suppositories but is not a modality that can be self-administered. In sum, then, the hope of a decade ago for simple, do-it-yourself abortion techniques has not been realized.[38]

Finally, there is RU486. (See Etienne-Emile Baulieu's chapter in this book.)

A. Suction Curettage in the First Trimester

This technique can be employed for patients on an ambulatory basis, under local anesthesia with paracervical block, occasionally supplemented with modest doses of tranquilizers and analgesics. In patients whose cervices are prepared for the procedure either by previous vaginal delivery or by the preparatory insertion of laminaria, the procedure can be carried out without any anesthesia. Clearly it also can be accomplished

---

[38] It should be noted that a procedure called "menstrual extraction" has been used at home up to eight weeks of pregnancy. *In Health* (November 1991).

under conduction or general anesthesia, but these are more than are required for the successful performance of the abortion.

In the very earliest days of pregnancy the hormonal changes have not as yet begun to soften the cervix; this is most noteworthy among patients who have never had a previous vaginal delivery. It is therefore preferable to wait to abort until approximately the seventh menstrual week of pregnancy, by which time the cervix has already begun to soften.

Laminaria is a dehydrated seaweed that can be gas sterilized and that swells up notably when moist. If on examination the cervix seems to be unusually resistant, one or more of these laminaria can be inserted into the cervix and allowed to remain for four or more hours. During this period their outer diameter enlarges as they draw water from the tissues and gradually open the cervix. Synthetic materials with similar properties are now becoming available.

The procedure is best carried out with the patient lying supine and a speculum in the vagina exposing the cervix. The cervix is stabilized with one of several grasping instruments and may or may not be cleaned off with one of a number of standard antiseptics. The operator is then obligated to test the cervix to be certain that it is sufficiently open to allow the passage of the suction curette. At present these curettes are made of transparent or translucent plastic. Some are completely rigid and others somewhat pliable. They all have blunt ends and one or two openings on either side just near the uterine end of the curette. There is a rough correlation between the diameter of the curette in millimeters and the duration of pregnancy to be interrupted, such that at the seventh menstrual week, six- or seven-millimeter curettes are sufficient, whereas at the 10th or 11th week, a 10- or 11-millimeter curette is ordinarily to be preferred. The smaller curettes will almost certainly go through the cervix of a patient who has had a previous dilatation of the cervix. With pregnancies of greater duration some dilatation is needed. This is facilitated by administration of a paracervical block with a local anesthetic agent.

Once the cervix is adequately prepared and dilated, the suction curette is inserted and then connected with a negative pressure device. The electric pumps which have become virtually standard throughout the United States generate negative pressures up to 50 to 60 centimeters of mercury. The intrauterine curette is rotated in place. Since the products of conception are less firmly attached than the endometrium itself, they come away differentially. It is possible, in view of the translucency of the curettes, to see that the abortion is being completed. It is necessary to inspect the tissue removed to identify ectopic pregnancies. With later abortions all the fetal parts should be identified.

The greater the duration of pregnancy the longer the procedure, but ordinarily the suction evacuation can be completed in a matter of a few minutes. The operator must then inspect the material that has been evacuated to see that it includes placenta. It is also possible for the operator to note immediately when the procedure has not been successful. It is standard procedure and generally required by law that this material be submitted for pathological examination.

Anatomical variations, such as the presence of uterine fibroids or double uteri, on occasion interfere mechanically with the efficient evacuation of the uterus. It is important for the operator to be aware of these possibilities.

There is not complete agreement on whether to carry out uterine sharp curettage following the evacuation of the products of conception by suction curette.

The use of antibiotic therapy prophylactically appears to reduce the incidence of infection, particularly in those patients in whom laminaria have been used. Routine use of antibiotics with suction at the seventh week is directed at a very low risk, and so its efficacy is difficult to confirm.

At the completion of the suction procedure the patient can be released to ambulatory care. The subsequent self-care differs in no particular respect from what the patient would ordinarily do at the time of a menstrual period. The evidence at the present time is that there are no immediate or late sequelae of an abortion of this sort which have any adverse impact on a patients' long-term reproductive career. There is a very low, probably less than 3 percent incidence of endometritis and, since the cervix is open and the products of conception have been efficiently cleaned out, this ordinarily responds well to antibiotic therapy and repeat curettage.

There is a curious syndrome in which clotted blood blocks the internal cervical os and additional bleeding into the uterine fundus causes severe uterine distention. This can be suspected when a patient who has had an abortion within the previous 18 hours returns for care complaining of very severe, cramping uterine pain with minimal bleeding. The syndrome can be rapidly alleviated by repeat evacuation to remove the obstructing blood clots and establish drainage.

The incidence of uterine perforation is extraordinarily low. Probably in the hands of experienced operators it should be substantially less than 1 percent. The largest proportion of perforations are the result of difficult dilatation of the cervix, which can be minimized by the laminaria techniques suggested above. Other complications are missed abortion and unidentified ectopic pregnancy.

B. Dilatation and Evacuation in the Second Trimester

There is a clear consensus that safety in the performance of D&E depends on the accurate determination of the size of the fetus by ultrasound examination. The most serious error is to undertake the abortion of a patient in the second trimester through an inadequately dilated cervix or with inadequate instrumentation. When the patient is more than 12 weeks pregnant (in this procedure the fetus must be delivered by dismemberment) the most critical single step consists of crushing the calvarium to reduce its volume. It is therefore essential to know the biparietal diameter (BPD) before initiating any procedure. Sonographic scanning of the pregnancy has therefore become an essential part of this undertaking.

At 11 to 12 weeks fetal (not menstrual) age (FA), the BPD is 20 to 26 millimeter. Therefore, dilatation to about 13 or 14 millimeters is desirable, and a 12-millimeter cannula curette is used. At 13 weeks FA, the BPD is 30 millimeters, and at 14 weeks, 36. Since some of the forceps used to deliver the fetus are as wide as 20 millimeters, dilatation to nearly that diameter is desirable.

At 14 to 15 weeks, BPDs range from 33 to 37 millimeters, and by 20 weeks has reached 50 millimeters. At the later durations difficulty in extraction can be encountered from the fetal pelvis, and special instruments are needed.

The first step in D&E is the preliminary dilatation of the cervix with gradual dilators such as laminaria. A few operators of considerable experience still use tapered metal dilators. When the pregnancy is of greater duration, the laminaria have to be left in for longer periods of time, and larger numbers of laminaria are necessary. It is entirely possible to dilate the cervix to a diameter as much as 30 millimeters by the use of multiple laminaria insertions over a span of 48 hours, increasing the number of laminaria with each successive insertion. Graduated tapered (Pratt) dilators are now available up to 89 French—or almost 30 millimeters.

As has been noted, D&E can be carried out with modest systemic sedation, making use of analgesics and tranquilizers and then employing a paracervical block to anesthetize the cervix. The procedure can also be done under general anesthesia, which allows the various maneuvers to be done more rapidly but confers no other advantage and unfortunately incurs the unavoidable risks of general anesthesia.

As with the interruptions in the first trimester, the cervix is visualized with a speculum and stabilized with a tenaculum. The adequacy of the dilatation of the cervix is then confirmed, and if necessary the cervix can be even further dilated by graduated Pratt dilators. When access to the uterine cavity is demonstrated, an appropriate suction cannula is then passed through the cervical canal into the lower uterine segment. No effort is made to introduce it to the fundus. Negative pressure is then made. With pregnancies up to 15 weeks, ordinarily the amniotic fluid is obtained and emptied out first, and then the uterus begins to contract. Some operators prefer to employ parenteral administration of 200 micrograms of Methergine at this point to enhance uterine contractility, but there is no clear consensus as to the necessity for this. Suction continues to be exerted through the curettes, which ordinarily are either 12 or 14 millimeters in diameter when the abortion to be undertaken is less than 16 weeks. Once some placenta and umbilical cord is obtained, the suction is discontinued and a grasping forceps is introduced into the fundus. The tissue that has been brought down into the lower uterine segment by the suction is then removed with the forceps until no more can be obtained. The curette is then reintroduced and negative pressure again made. By alternating from suction to removal of tissue with forceps, the products of conception can gradually be extracted. For abortion beyond 15 weeks' duration, suction is of little help except to remove amniotic fluid and thereby reduce uterine volume. The fetus must be removed with appropriate forceps.

It is essential to the procedure to be certain that the spinal column, thorax, and particularly the skull of the fetus be identified in the tissue removal, for assurance of the completeness of the evacuation. It is important after termination of the procedure to identify the long bones as well.

Bleeding during this procedure is ordinarily minimal, in all likelihood because the evacuation of the placenta takes place relatively early in the course of the procedure and uterine contraction achieves hemostasis. Extraordinary bleeding is suggestive of an inadvertent perforation or loss of normal blood coagulability rather than uterine atony, particularly if the bleeding does not respond to administration of Methergine or oxytocin.

D&E can been done as late as the 24th week of pregnancy. It would be wise to limit these late procedures to situations with urgent indication. Certainly up to the 16th week D&E appears, on the basis of several large series from careful observers, to be a feasible and a safe procedure.

The death-to-case ratio is about 7.7 per 100,000 D&Es and can be expected to fall as techniques improve. This rate, although at least an order of magnitude greater than that for suction abortion in the first trimester, is nonetheless substantially less than that for other methods of second-trimester abortion. There is agreement that prophylactic administration of tetracycline should be prescribed.

Follow-up care for D&E is essentially the same as it is for abortion in the first trimester, and the complications are essentially the same. There are occasional instances of endometritis but the incidence of this is no greater than 1 percent. On unusual occasions fragments of the fetus are left in the uterus; these ordinarily pass uneventfully in the course of the next few days. Late bleeding is unusual, and the incidence of DIC is much lower than with intraamniotic instillations. Suitable sonographic study prior to the abortion will avoid the difficulties that can occur with unrecognized multiple pregnancy, myomata, and ovarian cysts.

C. Induction of Labor in the Second Trimester

Abortion in the second trimester can be accomplished by injecting into the uterus materials that will stimulate uterine contractility and induce a premature labor. This same effect can be accomplished by the injection of corrosive materials that will kill the fetus and placenta by one of several modes of action. With the death of the placenta, labor ordinarily follows in a reasonable period of time. This period can be shortened by the administration of oxytocin and can be curtailed even further by the preliminary dilatation of the cervix with laminaria.

The first material to be used successfully in this technique was hypertonic saline solution, introduced into the amniotic cavity. This is ordinarily done after the 16th week of pregnancy. A suitable needle is inserted into the amniotic sac. Amniotic fluid may or may not be withdrawn, and a volume of 20 to 23 percent salt solution, but not more than 200 milliliters, injected into the amniotic sac. A number of techniques for doing this have been described. The essential feature of all of them is that inadvertent intravenous administration must be avoided. A patient who is conscious will ordinarily report to the operator sensations of pain and extreme thirst if the hypertonic saline is being injected into either the uterine wall or a uterine blood vessel. The procedure must be promptly terminated under such circumstances. If the saline is put into the amniotic sac, the patient ordinarily has no sensations at all. The fetal heart ceases within a half-hour of the instillation, and patients fall into labor for the most part anywhere between 12 and 36 hours later. An occasional patient experiences missed abortion.

Because of the early experience with complications of the injection of intraamniotic saline, including several deaths from hypernatremia, attention has been directed to a number of other drugs for abortion. These include the intrauterine instillation of prostaglandin F2 alpha, generally in amounts of 30 and 40 milligrams; hyperosmolar glucose, which has generally been abandoned because of problems with chorioamnionitis; urea solutions; and combinations of these. As mentioned, in some series the cervix has been prepared with laminaria and a number of regimes of additional uterine stimulation with oxytocin have also been described, to shorten induction to abortion time.

In most institutions, it is desirable that whatever is undertaken to accomplish abortion also accomplishes fetal death so that neither the patient nor the staff has the unpleasant experience of witnessing the birth of a live abortus. Indeed, one of the disadvantages of this technique of abortion is that the patient experiences labor, which in many instances is substantially more uncomfortable than normal labor at term. This has to be taken into consideration in view of the fact that a very high proportion of our patients who present for abortion in the second trimester are young adolescents with inadequate support systems.

A common complication is retained placenta, defined as failure to pass the placenta spontaneously within one hour, which may occur in as many as 50 percent of all cases. A possible exception is the use of ethacridine (Rivanol), which in the reports from the People's Republic of China has a very low incidence of placental retention when compared with prostaglandin, urea, and saline instillation. Placental retention is associated with excessive loss of blood. Therefore, a number of regimes to speed the birth of the placenta have been described, most of which involve relatively early surgical intervention, either with the use of forceps to grasp the placenta and deliver it or the employment of an intrauterine suction curette.

All of the modalities for intraamniotic instillation have resulted in episodes of disseminated intravascular coagulation, the commonest association being with saline instillation. Because of this and because of the discomforts of this form of abortion, abortion by this technique has been limited to the care of hospitalized patients. This has put a premium on abbreviating the delay from injection to abortion and the duration of the labor that ensues. A number of regimes directed toward these ends have been described. Despite this, abortion by this technique ordinarily requires a hospitalization of at least two days and, in the presence of complications, it can be substantially longer than that. Since some of the labors that ensue are rather rapid, there have resulted injuries to the cervix, producing cervico-uterine tears and subsequent cervical uterine fistulas. Uterine rupture has also been observed with extrusion of the fetus into intraperitoneal or retroperitoneal sites. The administration of intravenous oxytocin therefore has to be undertaken with care, and probably should not be done prior to the rupture of membranes.

Several techniques for induction of labor by the insertion of dilating materials in the cervix, supplemented by the instillation of oxytocic materials in an extraamniotic location, have also been described. The two preparations principally used for this purpose have been prostaglandin F2alpha and ethacridine. At the present time, it does not appear that this route of induction of abortion confers any particular advantages.

Abortion has also been induced by the intravaginal application of prostaglandin E2 and the 15 methyl form. On the average this modality results in a substantially longer delay than intraamniotic infusion and does not appear to confer any advantage except in those circumstances where intraamniotic instillation presents anatomic problems.

The advantage of these techniques for the induction of labor is that they do not require forcible dilatation of the cervix, and they do not require dismemberment of the fetus. Such follow-up studies as are available do not, however, indicate that they do not reduce the likelihood of subsequent pregnancy loss, due to injury of the cervix, as compared with D&E.

D. Abortion by Hysterotomy and Hysterectomy

As mentioned above, these major surgical procedures accounted for 0.1 percent of all abortions done in 1987. There is probably only the rarest indication for doing them, and they carry a prohibitively high morbidity and mortality rate.[39] When a patient re-

---

[39] Third-trimester abortions remain very rare, representing just 0.1% of all abortions in the United States. Because of the size and the age of the fetus involved, these third-trimester abortions push the limits of what many people are willing to accept. Specifically, in *Roe v. Wade* the Supreme Court stated that abortions during the third trimester of pregnancy could only be performed when the woman's life or health was in danger. It is also noted that abortions in the third trimester involve fetuses that are potentially viable, and therefore we have a balancing problem between the rights of the fetus and the rights of the mother. Doctors

quests sterilization as well as abortion, risk is minimized by doing them as separate procedures. The risk of hysterectomy done solely for sterilization is excessive even in the nonpregnant state.

---

who perform third-trimester abortions are uncomfortable doing late abortions unless the fetus is abnormal or the woman's physical or mental health is in danger. Many women who have been able to procure late abortions say that it is only through tremendous effort that they even learned that an abortion was possible. A typical case is as follows:

> Anne Elfant, a 36-year-old New York woman, learned when she was seven months pregnant that her fetus had severe problems. The fetus had 4 holes in the heart, was missing a kidney, had a defective esophagus, a cleft lip and palate, and was extremely small. Her doctors said it was unclear whether the fetus would live, but, they told her, they would do their best to 'patch him up'.

> Mrs. Elfant said her doctor told her that he felt very sorry for her, but added that there was no guarantee that the fetus would die after he was born. He added that maybe she would be lucky and the fetus would die inside of her. "He told me, 'If the baby stops kicking, don't call me for a week and then come in and I'll do a delivery,' " Mrs. Elfant recalled.

> Concerned about the sort of life the baby would have and about the effects on her, her husband and their 4-year-old son, Mrs. Elfant tried first to see if she could guarantee that the baby would have a 'do-not-resuscitate order' after he was born. She learned that that was impossible and, in addition, says she was told that she would have to have the baby at a hospital with the most sophisticated newborn intensive care unit to assure his survival.

> "A very big part of me just wanted to have the baby and hold him until he died," Mrs. Elfant said. But she envisioned instead a long, lingering hospital death or a long and rocky medical course that would impoverish her family and leave them with a child with severe handicaps. "The medical profession leaves everyone high and dry," she said. "As parents, you have no rights."

> Mrs. Elfant spent weeks trying to induce a miscarriage, jogging and smoking cigarettes. She tried to get an abortion from a clinic by misrepresenting the date of her pregnancy, but she was turned away when the clinic did a sonogram and discovered her ruse. She hid in her house during the day, trying not to reveal her pregnancy to outsiders so that if she did somehow obtain an abortion, no one would know and judge her. And she frantically called doctors and lawyers, asking whether anyone, anywhere, could do an abortion for her.

Finally, she learned about a group of doctors at the Boulder Abortion Clinic in Colorado.

Techniques used in third-trimester abortions vary. Some doctors inject digoxin into the chest of the fetus to stop its heart from beating. Then, over a period of days, laminaria are used to enlarge the woman's cervix. Several days later, labor is induced.

Another technique involves a small tube that is pressed into the fetal head to remove the spinal fluid. Later the fetus is delivered. The advantage of this technique is that the fetus is intact and can therefore be autopsied to determine the extent and cause of the abnormalities.

It should be noted that third-trimester abortions can be emotionally devastating and are not easy decisions for either the woman or the doctor involved.

(Footnote information source—Kolata, *In Late Abortions, Decisions are Painful and Options Few, The New York Times National* Sunday, January 5, 1992, p. 16.)

This article by Doctors Niswander and Porto focuses on the medical indications for therapeutic abortions. Because of the discovery of new diseases, along with better treatment for older ones, the list for medical indications for abortion changes with the advancement of technology. An example of a new disease entity is the HIV-pregnant female. On February 2, 1991, in volume 337 of the *Lancet,* a European Collaborative Study (ECS) titled "A Perspective Study of Children Born to HIV Infected Mothers" revealed that of 600 such children born by June 15, 1990, more than 10% became infected with the HIV virus. As many as 83% of the infected children present with clinical or immunological symptoms by the age six months. It is understandable, then, that abortion is considered an option for the HIV-positive pregnant female. However, it should be noted that in an additional study (volume 338, July 27, 1991, of the *Lancet*) an article by A. Hernst titled "HIV in Pregnant Women and Their Offspring: Evidence for Late Transmission" showed that there is no consistent spread of HIV across the placenta during maternal viremia; most cases show transmission close to or at delivery.

It might appear then that the abortion option should be somewhat controversial for the HIV-positive mother. However, equally controversial is the *treatment* for the HIV-positive mother. The *New York Times* (August 25, 1991, p. 20) in "U.S. Rule on Fetal Studies Hampers Research on AZD," revealed

> [r]esearchers studying ways to treat pregnant women infected with the AIDS virus are running up against a Federal regulation devised in the 1970s to protect the fetus. And many of the researchers, highly critical of the regulation, are quietly finding ways to circumvent it . . . The regulation says that whenever the Federal government pays for fetal research, the fathers—if they are available—as well as the mothers, must give written permission. Until now, the regulation had gone unnoticed by most researchers and ethicists.

The committee that developed the regulation was appointed in 1973, the year the Supreme Court legalized abortion. One branch of government said that women could terminate their pregnancies for any reason whatever, and another branch of government said that women could not consent to even trivial research on their fetuses without the father's permission.

(continued)

Just as there have been new diseases that have indications for therapeutic abortions, medical breakthroughs for older conditions are just around the corner. Consider the *Washington Post* article of Thursday, August 22, 1991, titled "Experimental Treatment Could End Deaths From Cystic Fibrosis," by William Booth:

> Researchers for the first time have developed a treatment that promises to clear the mucous-clogged lungs of cystic fibrosis patients, offering hope that the most common inherited disease in the United States may no longer be fatal . . . If cystic fibrosis were no longer the deadly disease it is today, it is thought that many couples might feel less compelled to seek the test, or to abort their fetus if the test showed it would have the disease.

In Leon Jaroff's new book, *The New Genetics, the Human Genome Project and Its Impact on the Practice of Medicine,*

> "Molecular biologist Leroy Hood expects enormous predictive value from the anticipated ability to take a blood sample from every newborn infant and subject it to automatic analysis of perhaps one hundred selected genes for flaws known to be prediagnostic for certain diseases."

We are only one step away from analyzing the blood of both parents and fetus to see if the selected genes are flawed. This information would certainly be important to any couple contemplating a reproductive decision.

The article presented by Drs. Niswander and Porto details a history of abortion practices in the United States along with contemporary indications for therapeutic abortions. They conclude by stating, "Prenatal diagnostic centers can detect nearly 200 fetal abnormalities for which abortion services must be available. While not a total solution, legalized abortion has improved the morbidity and mortality for pregnant women and has had a beneficial impact on the quality of life."

22 · Abortion Practices in the United States: A Medical Viewpoint

Kenneth R. Niswander, M.D., and
Manual Porto, M.D.

Just 28 years ago, Alan F. Guttmacher stated, "Illegal or criminal abortion is the only great pandemic disease which remains unrecognized and untreated by modern medicine."[1] During 1965, in fact, 235 deaths, or 20% of all deaths related to pregnancy and childbirth, were attributed to abortion.[2] As recently as 1972, the Centers for Disease Control reported 39 maternal deaths associated with illegal abortion in the United States, this in spite of the fact that liberalized abortion legislation in many states, most notably New York and California, accounted for some 587,000 legal abortions reported nationally that year.

Since the Supreme Court decisions in 1973, the number of maternal deaths related to abortion has decreased precipitously, and in 1979 there were *no* deaths resulting from illegal or self-induced abortion procedures in the United States.[3] The overall abortion-related maternal mortality, including spontaneous (miscarriage), legal and illegal procedures decreased from 90 women in 1972 to 8 in 1987. These figures are all the more impressive in light of the procedures performed (nearly 1.6 million in 1987).[4] Overall maternal mortality in the United States declined by 50% during the last decade.[5] Although contraceptive and sterilization practices have been major contributors to the overall decrease, clearly, legal abortion has also had a significant impact. As Cates so elo-

---

[1] Guttmacher, *Induced Abortion,* 63 N.Y.J. Med. 2334 (1963) (editorial).

[2] E. C. Moore-Cavar, *International Inventory of Information on Induced Abortion,* New York (1974), 520, 593–95, 603–06, 642.

[3] Cates, *Legal Abortion: The Public Health Record,* 215 Science 1587 (1982).

[4] Henshaw et al., 23 Fam. Plann. Perspect. 75 (1991).

[5] Rochat, 34 World Health Stat. Q. 2 (1981). CDC, *Vital Statistics* (1990).

quently wrote, "[T]he data clearly indicate that legalization of abortion has had a definite impact on the health of American women faced with unwanted pregnancies, by providing them with a safer option than the alternative of either illegal abortion or continuing the pregnancy to term."[6]

The widespread prevalence of abortion has never been seriously questioned, nor is it a new issue. In order to fully comprehend this most controversial subject, it is important to study the historical background of abortion, the contemporary indications for therapeutic abortion, and the current legal abortion practices in the United States.

I. History

Abortion is an ancient practice. The records of almost every civilization indicate knowledge of abortifacients and abortive techniques. Among primitive peoples these were gruesome when practiced in the extreme, and remain so among certain primitive tribes today. In one tribal rite, for example, large ants were encouraged to bite the woman's body, and on occasion, the insects were taken internally.[7] Gross traumatization of the pregnant abdomen was a popular method of attempting to induce abortion and is still used by some primitive groups. The early Hebrews knew abortive techniques, although they strongly disapproved of the practice. The Greeks, on the other hand, advocated abortion in order to control population size and ensure good social and economic conditions. Hippocrates advised abortion in certain situations but as a general rule condemned the practice because it so often resulted in the mother's injury or death.[8]

Christian belief in the immortality of the viable fetus' soul has largely been responsible for the Roman Catholic church's condemnation of abortion. Doctrine has placed abortion in the same category as infanticide, and the unbaptized soul of the fetus, like that of the infant, was considered in limbo. Many early canonists, however, did not feel that the soul entered the fetus at the time of conception; rather, the belief was prevalent that while the soul entered the body of a female fetus at 90 days gestation, the soul of the male fetus was present after the 40th day of gestation. Because of this belief, interruption of the pregnancy before the 40th day was punished only by a fine, whereas abortion when the soul was present was regarded as murder and was punished accordingly. In 1869, Pope Pius IX made this distinction become unimportant, since abortion before the soul entered the fetus became "anticipated homicide."[9] In spite of the church's opposition, abortion *was* practiced, and not infrequently resulted in the mother's death.

According to English common law, legal existence of the fetus was not recognized in criminal cases until quickening (the first perception of fetal motion), which usually occurs after the fourth month of pregnancy.[10] As American jurisprudence was firmly based on English common law, it is not surprising that in 1821 a Connecticut statute (followed by similar ones in 10 other states), made abortion illegal only after quickening. Indeed, abortions were quite common in early America, being performed for the most part by poorly trained practioners. It was not until 1845 that Massachusetts became

[6]Cates, *Abortion Myths and Realities: Who Is misleading whom?*, 142 Am. J. Obstet. & Gynecol. 954 (1982).

[7]*See generally* Devereux, *A Typological Study of Abortion in 350 Primitive, Ancient and Pre-industrial Societies*, 97 Therapeutic Abortion 121.

[8]*See generally* F. Taussig, *Abortion, Spontaneous and Induced: Medical and Social Aspects* 31 (1936).

[9]G. Williams, *The Sanctity of Life and the Criminal Law, passim* (1957).

[10]*Issues in Brief*, Alan Guttmacher Institute, vol. II (no. 4) 1 (January 1982).

the first state to make abortion, or attempted abortion, at any point in pregnancy a criminal offense. Dr. Horatio Robinson-Storer, an obstetrician-gynecologist, launched an antiabortion crusade in 1857 with the support of the American Medical Association. By 1880, antiabortion legislation had been adopted in 40 states and territories.[11] Into the early 1960s, abortion was prohibited throughout the United States unless the life of the pregnant woman would be endangered should the pregnancy be carried to term. Yet in the 1950s, the number of illegal abortions in the United States was conservatively estimated at 300,000 annually.[12] Kinsey noted that 22% of the married women he interviewed had had one or more abortions *in marriage* by the age of 45.[13] Nearly 95% of the premarital pregnancies in his survey were resolved by abortion.[14] Obviously, society found a frequent need for pregnancy interruption.

The punishment for the poor Renaissance woman who induced abortion was death by crucifixion, whereas her rich sister might buy her way out of such punishment. So, too, in the United States, poor women, especially those from minority groups, were the principal victims of our restrictive abortion laws. The data clearly show that a disproportionate number of women who obtained the few therapeutic abortions done in the past were both affluent and white. A report on abortions in New York City covering a 20-year period indicated that 90% of the therapeutic abortions were performed on white women[15]; and the review of the abortions in two Buffalo, New York hospitals attests to the paucity of therapeutic abortions among nonwhite patients.[16] Although the indications for abortion may have changed over the centuries, discrimination against poor and minority women, and the very real dangers of criminal abortion, remained until the early 1970s. In 1972, the second year of New York state's free-choice statute, the ratio of abortions to live births was 366 to 1,000 for white women, in contrast to 736 to 1,000 for nonwhite women.[17]

In 1976, some 46.5% of pregnancies among Medicaid-eligible women in New York state were terminated by abortion, as compared to 36% of pregnancies for more affluent women.[18] In California, 57% of the total number of induced abortions reported in 1978 were funded by Medi-Cal.[19]

Taussig, in his classic book on abortion, gives a good historical account of the medical indications for abortion and discusses some of the early authorities who referred to abortion.[20] Plato and Aristotle clearly encouraged abortion on social or economic grounds. In Rome, especially during the era of the Roman empire, abortion was approved for social indications. The influence of Christianity, although not actually diminishing the practice of abortion, did make it socially unacceptable.

---

[11]*The Abortion Quandary: No Truce in Sight,* M.D. Magazine 154 (January 1982).

[12]Fisher, *Criminal Abortion,* in *Therapeutic Abortion: Medical, Psychiatric, Legal, Anthropological, and Religious Considerations* 3,6 (H. Rosen, ed. 1954).

[13]*Abortion in the United States* 55 (M. Calderone ed., 1958).

[14]*Id.*

[15]Gold et al., *Therapeutic Abortions in New York City: A 20 Year Review,* Am. J. Pub. Health 966 (1965).

[16]Niswander, Klein, & Randall, *Changing Attitudes Toward Therapeutic Abortion,* 196 J.A.M.A. 1141, 1143 (1966).

[17]*Abortion: Public Issue Private Decision,* New York, Public Affairs Pamphlet No. 527:16 (1975).

[18]*Safe and Legal: 10 Years' Experience With Legal Abortion in New York State* 31 (1980).

[19]*Induced Abortion in California: A Biennial Report to the 1980 Legislature,* State of California, Office of Family Planning 7.

[20]*See generally,* Taussig, *supra* note 8, at 31–45.

Early in the Christian era, Priscianus, a physician, recommended abortion to save the life of the mother; but writings about therapeutic abortion are scarce and the ramifications of the abortion issue do not seem to have been reconsidered until 1772.[21] At that time, William Cooper suggested therapeutic abortion for cases of contracted pelvis, in order to prevent the horrors of attempted delivery through a malformed bony structure. Dewees, Velpeau, Hodge and other prominent physicians continued to encourage abortion in cases of contracted pelvis. This suggestion was accepted by many obstetricians in Europe, and during the latter half of the 19th century "the indications, especially in Germany, were extended to include tuberculosis, heat disease, nephritis, and certain forms of psychosis."[22] These indications became more prevalent. In the year preceding liberalized abortion legislation, there was a growing tendency to abort for psychiatric or socioeconomic reasons. While these factors undoubtedly continue to exert significant influence on the decision to terminate pregnancy, there is no longer the need to label these as truly medical, or "therapeutic," abortions.

II. Contemporary Indications for Therapeutic Abortion

"The most astute medical minds could not possibly devise a predetermined list of conditions completely including each individual patient for whom a procedure is medically necessary and excluding all others . . . The final decision as to performing the abortion must be left to the medical judgment of the pregnant woman's attending physician, in consultation with the patient. That responsibility is the physician's, both ethically and by reason of his experience."[23]

While the term "therapeutic abortion" is commonly used today to describe interruptions of early pregnancy by licensed medical personnel, the vast majority of pregnancy terminations should be classified as induced abortions. "Therapeutic abortion" is a term that should be reserved for those few instances when abortion is indicated for medical or fetal reasons. Few of these medical indications are absolute, and the decision to terminate the pregnancy frequently is based not only on the risk to the gravida's health, but also on such factors as the patient's inability to care for a child after birth. In deciding on therapeutic abortion, a couple may not wish to assume certain risks, such as those involved in pregnancy, or in the child care required thereafter. Many of the former medical and fetal indications for therapeutic abortion represented justification for abortion at the patient's request. Similarly, the vast majority of psychiatric and socioeconomic indications for therapeutic abortion have been replaced by a unilateral patient decision to terminate an unwanted gestation for personal reasons. There remain, however, numerous medical and fetal conditions for which a therapeutic abortion is warranted.

A. Medical Indications

This summary is not intended to be the definitive list of medical indications for therapeutic abortion. However, the vast majority can be included in one of the following

---

[21] *Id.* at 277.

[22] *Id.* at 278.

[23] American College of Obstetricians and Gynecologists, 13671 Congr. Rec. (August 4 1977).

categories of disease: cardiovascular, gastrointestinal, renal, neurologic, pulmonary, endocrine and malignant. Each will be briefly considered. The paucity of papers in the medical literature recommending abortion for medical disease undoubtedly reflects the infrequency with which medical illnesses are currently thought to require abortion.

1. CARDIOVASCULAR DISEASE   Cardiovascular disease has long been implicated as a risk factor for maternal death during pregnancy. However, with recent advances in cardiac surgery, cardiology and maternal-fetal medicine, the majority of pregnant cardiac patients can successfully complete a pregnancy with little risk of maternal death. Patients with unusual congenital heart disorders, such as tetralogy of Fallot, Eisenmenger's syndrome, Marfan's syndrome and primary pulmonary hypertension have such high maternal mortality, up to 50%,[24] that pregnancy termination is recommended. In patients with severe heart valvular disease, rheumatic or otherwise, and in patients with debilitating heart disease, abortion is also advisable. The unusual syndrome of peripartum cardiomyopathy, seen almost exclusively in multiparous black women, carries a poor prognosis for both mother and fetus in a subsequent pregnancy.[25]

While special precautions must be taken in pregnancy for patients with prosthetic heart valves, including anticoagulation and antibiotics to prevent valve infection, many such patients are delivered without complications. Hence, the majority of pregnant cardiac patients face the difficult decision of weighing some increased maternal and fetal risk against their desire for a new baby. Not infrequently, a major influence in the decision to interrupt the pregnancy is the appreciation of the difficult situation that could eventually face the disabled cardiac patient who must attempt to care for her newborn.

2. GASTROINTESTINAL DISEASES   Few if any of these disorders can be considered absolute indications for therapeutic abortion. However, patients with inflammatory bowel disease, such as Crohn's disease and ulcerative colitis, have a 50% risk of disease exacerbation during pregnancy.[26] These recurrences tend to be most frequent during the first trimester and the postpartum period. Ulcerative colitis seems to have little effect on pregnancy outcome.[27] While higher spontaneous abortion rates have been documented in Crohn's disease patients (up to 25%),[28] the fetus that is carried to term has no greater risk of malformation, stillbirth or other pregnancy complication.

Unfortunately, a patient's previous pregnancy history provides little guidance for patient and physician in making an intelligent decision as to whether to carry or terminate a given pregnancy.[29] It appears that successive pregnancies can have varying effects on inflammatory bowel disease, and the physician cannot be certain what that effect will be.[30] Overall, as in so many other disease states, the decision to abort or continue a pregnancy in inflammatory bowel diseases must be left to the woman and her partner.

---

[24] Metcalfe & Ueland, *Heart Disease and Pregnancy in Cardiac Diagnosis and Treatment* 1047–48 (Fowler ed. 3d ed. 1976).

[25] Demakis & Rahimtoola, *Peripartum Cardiomyopathy*, 44 Circulation 964 (1971).

[26] Dobbins & Spiro, *Gastrointestinal Complications*, in *Medical Complications During Pregnancy* 272 (Burrow & Ferris eds. 2d ed. 1982).

[27] *Id.*

[28] *Id.*

[29] MacDougall, *Ulcerative Colitis in Pregnancy*, 2 Lancet 641 (1956).

[30] Vender & Spiro, *Inflammatory Bowel Disease in Pregnancy: A Review of the Literature*, J. Clin. Gastroenterol. (in press).

3. RENAL DISEASE [31]   Patients in this category are likely to be victims of chronic glomerulonephritis,[32] or hypertension of renal origin.[33] While the widely available dialysis therapy for chronic renal failure is effective, it is only palliative in nature. Dialysis in pregnancy is extremely risky to both mother and fetus, and such patients are usually offered therapeutic abortion. Patients with chronic nephritis [34] (whose lives will actually be shortened by the effects of a pregnancy), women with severe chronic hypertension, and especially those with previous hypertensive exacerbations in pregnancy, are at extremely high risk for both maternal and fetal morbidity and mortality in a subsequent pregnancy.

Now that kidney transplantation has become almost commonplace, literally hundreds of women have successfully conceived after transplantation. While the vast majority of these pregnancies succeed, they are truly high-risk pregnancies, requiring close supervision and precautionary medicine.[35] Kidney transplantation prior to an attempt at pregnancy appears to be preferable to such an attempt in a patient on chronic dialysis for end stage renal failure.

Some other renal conditions which might seem to indicate therapeutic abortion, however, do not significantly affect the risk of maternal death. Often, if one kidney has been removed, there will be little increased risk for the pregnant patient as long as the remaining kidney functions well. The risk of nephrolithiasis cannot be minimized, but the instances when it might actually increase the risk of death in a pregnant patient seem remote.

4. NEUROLOGIC DISEASE   Diseases such as multiple sclerosis,[36] myasthenia gravis,[37] post-poliomyelitis, paralysis, epilepsy and various congenital neurologic diseases form the bulk of the neurologic conditions for which therapeutic abortion may be contemplated. It is unusual for a patient with multiple sclerosis to be made worse by pregnancy, but the effect of pregnancy on the disease is unpredictable.[38] Several investigators have

---

[31] This is a disease pertaining to, or involving, the kidneys. J. Schmidt, *Attorneys' Dictionary of Medicine and Word Finder* 691 (1969).

[32] Chronic glomerulonephritis is a variety of kidney disease in mild form in which the tufts formed by the tiny blood vessels are inflamed. It leads to hypertension (high blood pressure) and eventually to uremia, a poisoning of the body due to failure of the kidneys to eliminate the toxic substances. Schmidt, *supra* note 31, at 365.

[33] *Id.*

[34] This is a prolonged and progressive form of nephritis (inflammation of the kidney or a deterioration of the tissue forming its delicate structure) that may follow an acute attack or may result from other diseases of the body, poisons, alcohol, germs, etc. The fine and delicate structure of the kidney becomes distorted; the fine blood vessels become thicker; the supporting tissue (the nonfunctional part) begins to overgrow the functional parts; and even the heart is affected. *Id.* at 544.

[35] Lindheimer & Katz, 18 Kidney International 149 (1980).

[36] Multiple sclerosis is a disease of the brain and spinal cord. In this condition, various parts of the brain and spinal cord are subjected to a type of deterioration called sclerosis. Sclerosis in this instance is a hardening of the nerve tissue and its displacement by overgrowing connective (supporting) tissue. Basically functional nerve tissue gives way to supporting, nonfunctional tissue. The disease progresses slowly but is incurable. Schmidt, *supra* note 31, at 534.101.

[37] Myasthenia gravis is a syndrome of fatigue and exhaustion of the muscular system marked by progressive paralysis of muscles without sensory disturbance or atrophy. It may affect any muscle of the body but especially those of the face, lips, tongue, throat and neck. *Dorland's Medical Dictionary* 1004 (25th ed. 1974).

[38] Cohen & Kreuger, *Multiple Sclerosis and Pregnancy: Report of a Case,* 6 Obstet. & Gynecol. 144, 145 (1955).

found no justifiable indication for pregnancy interruption in patients with multiple sclerosis.[39] However, given the unpredictable course of the disease, and the likelihood of progressive deterioration of neurologic function in the mother, patients with active MS should probably be dissuaded from becoming pregnant.[40]

A patient with myasthenia gravis in pregnancy undertakes an increased risk for both herself and her offspring. According to Plauche, there is a 40% incidence of exacerbation of myasthenia during pregnancy and 30% in the postpartum period.[41] Maternal mortality is 3.4 per 100 live births, and perinatal mortality is at least five times that of uncomplicated pregnancies. While a successful outcome is likely with intensive high-risk obstetrical prenatal surveillance and treatment for myasthenic crises, it is appropriate to offer therapeutic abortion for patients suffering this condition.

Although epileptics have a twofold increase in the incidence of maternal complications during pregnancy, there appears to be no increased risk of maternal mortality. Such pregnancies are at higher risk for toxemia, labor complications, prematurity, as well as increased neonatal morbidity and mortality.[42] The major risk in pregnancies in epileptics seems to relate to the drugs used for seizure control. These will be detailed in the section dealing with drug effects on the fetus.

5.   PULMONARY DISEASE   In previous years pregnancy was believed to adversely affect the tubercular patient, and in some instances, actually to increase the risk of death from tuberculosis. With the advent of drug therapy, tuberculosis has essentially disappeared as an indication of therapeutic abortion. Patients with a previous history of a documented pulmonary embolism, occurring during pregnancy, are at high risk for a potential life-threatening recurrence in a subsequent pregnancy. Patients who would prefer to avoid such risk, and the need to self-inject anticoagulants during a subsequent pregnancy, have a justifiable indication for therapeutic abortion.

6.   DIABETES MELLITUS[43]   Diabetes, in varying degrees of severity, has often been an indication for therapeutic abortion. While there is no doubt that pregnancy exaggerates the metabolic defect in diabetes, there is less evidence available concerning pregnancy's effect on the complications of the disease, including arteriosclerosis, retinal disease and renal disease. Felig and Coustan reviewed the recent literature in this regard, noting that pregnancy does not increase the risk to the mother for progression of retinal changes or visual loss.[44] They further cited a Joslin Clinic study of 144 diabetic women with preexisting nephropathy and found that none developed renal failure following delivery.[45] They concluded that no general recommendations can be made regarding the desirability of pregnancy termination because of the presence of retinopathy or nephropathy.

---

[39] Riva, Carpenter & O'Grady, *Pregnancy Associated With Multiple Sclerosis,* 66 Am. J. Obstet. & Gynecol. 403, 407 (1953).

[40] Dalessio, *Neurologic Diseases,* in *Medical Complications: During Pregnancy,* 458 (Burrow & Ferris eds. 2d ed. 1982).

[41] Plauche, *Myasthenia Gravis,* 26 Clin. Obstet. & Gynecol. 594 (1983).

[42] Bjerkedal & Bahna, *The Course and Outcome of Pregnancy in Women With Epilepsy,* 52 Acta Obstet. Gynecol. Scand. 245 (1973).

[43] Diabetes mellitus is a disease in which the metabolism (body utilization) of sugars is greatly impaired due to the faulty secretion of insulin by the pancreas. Schmidt, *supra* note 31, at 248.21.

[44] Felig & Coustan, *Diabetes Mellitus,* in *Medical Complications During Pregnancy* 56–57 (Burrow & Ferris eds. 2d ed. 1982).

[45] White, *Pregnancy and Diabetes,* in *Joselyn's Diabetes Mellitus* (Marbel, et al., eds. 11th ed. 1971).

With current medical and obstetrical management of diabetes, the maternal mortality rate is now essentially the same among diabetic patients as in the overall pregnant population. While fetal risk, particularly from congenital anomalies, is distinctly increased in the diabetic patient, this would seem to have little to do with the "health" or "life" of the mother. Therapeutic abortion should be offered to the brittle diabetic who has recurrent bouts of diabetic coma in pregnancy despite appropriate medical therapy. For most advanced diabetics, the decision to undertake the intensive therapy and monitoring for a successful pregnancy must be weighed individually, taking into consideration the extent of the disease, the degree of metabolic control, and of course, ultimately, the patient's desires.

7. MALIGNANCY   Many physicians have long felt that pregnancy will adversely affect a patient's medical course when a prior malignancy has been treated. However, Mitchell and Capizzi, in their review of neoplastic diseases in pregnancy, clearly state that pregnancy does not alter the course of a coexistent tumor.[46] Despite past suggestions to the contrary, even with a malignancy that is frequently affected by changes in female hormones, such as carcinoma of the breast, the course of the disease is unchanged by pregnancy. Patients with acute leukemia, Hodgkin's disease and lymphomas show similar five-year survival rates in pregnant and nonpregnant groups. Majury says that "no convincing evidence has been produced which shows that subsequent pregnancy affects adversely the prognosis in extrauterine malignancy."[47] In the case of invasive carcinoma of the uterine cervix discovered in the first or second trimester, the pregnancy should be aborted immediately and therapy instituted. If detected in the third trimester, the fetus should be allowed to come almost to term, then should be delivered by cesarean section prior to initiating therapy. Similarly, ovarian carcinoma detected in the first two trimesters of pregnancy should be treated without regard to the gestation. Hence, for disease beyond stage one (disease involving more than one ovary), total abdominal hysterectomy, bilateral salpingo-oopherectomy with pregnancy in situ or preceded by therapeutic abortion, should be accomplished.

Therapeutic abortion is indicated in a select few malignant diseases where the nature of the tumor and the necessity for rapid treatment so dictate.

B. Fetal Indications

Abortion for fetal indications may be recommended in five situations: (1) where there has been an ingestion of certain harmful drugs during pregnancy; (2) where certain viral infections, especially rubella, have been contracted by the mother; (3) where the mother's abdomen has been exposed to radiation during pregnancy; (4) where there is substantial risk of fetal malformation due to genetic or congenital factors; and (5) where there is a sensitization to the Rh factor in the bloodstream.

1. DRUGS   The tragedy that occurred following the ingestion of thalidomide by pregnant women, both in Europe and in the United States is well-known to everyone. However, thalidomide is not the first drug known to cause severe fetal abnormalities. Folic acid antagonists (methotrexate and aminopterin) employed in the treatment of leu-

---

[46] Mitchell & Capizzi, *Neoplastic Diseases,* in *Medical Complications During Pregnancy* 510–11 (Burrow & Ferris eds. 2d ed. 1982).

[47] Majury, *Therapeutic Abortion in the Winnipeg General Hospital,* 82 Am. J. Obstet. & Gynecol. 10, 13 (1961).

kemia and other neoplasms are proven teratogens[48] producing severe anomalies with a prevalence of about 70%.

Certain anticonvulsant drugs used in the treatment of seizure disorders have been clearly implicated to have teratogenic risk. Trimethodione (tridione), a drug used in the treatment of petit mal epilepsy, has a greater than 80% fetal risk for a spectrum of abnormalities, including abnormal facies, growth deficiency, mental retardation, skeletal malformations, cleft lip or palate, congenital heart disease and abnormalities of the trachea and the esophagus.[49] Diphenylhydantoin (dilantin), the most commonly used drug in the treatment of grand mal epilepsy, carries a significant risk: 10% for serious defects and 30% for one or more less serious defects. This hydantoin syndrome consists of growth deficiency, mental deficiency, abnormal facies, cleft lip or palate, cardiac defects and abnormal genitalia.[50] Patients who have taken these drugs during the embryogenic period of the first trimester of pregnancy should be counseled and offered therapeutic abortion if desired.

The anticoagulant coumadin (warfarin, bishydroxicoumarin) has been associated with a 25% to 50% risk of congenital anomalies in fetuses exposed during the first trimester of pregnancy. The syndrome includes hypoplastic nose, bony abnormalities, eye problems, including optic atrophy and cataracts, as well as mental retardation.[51]

The teratogenicity of alcohol abuse during pregnancy was first reported in 1973.[52] This fetal alcohol syndrome, with microcephaly, micrognathia, microphthalmia, cardiac defects and growth retardation has been well-documented. The risk to heavy drinkers is reportedly about 30%.[53]

Masculinization of female fetuses, as well as cardiac anomalies, limb reduction anomalies and esophageal anomalies have been reported with the use of synthetic sex steroid preparations (such as those in birth control pills) in the first trimester.[54] The frequency of these abnormalities in patients exposed to sex hormones in early pregnancy is not clear; hence, patients and their physicians must make a qualified decision on the basis of the patient's desire for pregnancy at the time. Diethylstilbesterol (DES), a synthetic estrogen once believed to prevent spontaneous abortion, was later implicated as a cause for an otherwise rare vaginal cancer in female offspring.[55]

Lithium, a drug commonly used in the treatment of manic-depressive illness, has been found to produce an 11% incidence of birth defects, primarily serious cardiac anomalies.[56] Patients exposed to this drug during early pregnancy should be offered the possibility of therapeutic abortion.

---

[48] A teratogen is an agent or factor that causes the production of physical defects in the developing embryo. *Dorland's Illustrated Medical Dictionary, supra* note 37.

[49] Howard & Hill, *Drugs in Pregnancy,* 34 Obstet. & Gynecol. Survey 646, 647 (1979).

[50] *Id.* at 647.

[51] *Id.* at 648.

[52] *Id.* at 647.

[53] Ouellett, Rosett, Rosman & Weiner, *Adverse Effects on Offspring of Maternal Alcohol Abuse During Pregnancy,* 297 N.E.J. of Med. 528 (1977).

[54] Janerick, Piper, & Glebatis, *Oral Contraceptives and Congenital Limb Reduction Defects,* 291 N.E.J. of Med. 697 (1974).

[55] Herbst, *Diethylstilbestrol and Other Sex Hormones During Pregnancy,* 58 Obstet. & Gynecol. (supplement) 35S (1981).

[56] Briggs et al., *Drugs in Pregnancy and Lactation* 198 (1983).

As the rapid expansion of developmental pharmacology continues, there seems little doubt that other drugs will soon be implicated as having significant teratogenic potential. The drugs listed above comprise those with definite risk, justifying thoughtful consideration of therapeutic abortion. The risk of many other drugs remains uncertain at this time.

2.   VIRAL INFECTIONS   It is estimated that some 30,000 affected children were conceived during the rubella (German measles) epidemic in the United States in 1964 and 1965. Unfortunately many parents desperately sought, but failed to find, a physician who would abort these pregnancies, in spite of the relatively high likelihood that such a child would be the victim of the rubella syndrome. The most common manifestations of this syndrome include cataracts, cardiovascular abnormalities and hearing impairment. Growth retardation is a prominent feature of the syndrome, with birthweights less than the 10th percentile being quite common. While the above abnormalities are the most frequent, virtually every organ system has been affected in some patients.

Since the introduction of rubella vaccine in the United States in 1969, the disease has had a sharp and steady decline, reaching an all-time low of approximately 2,000 cases in 1981.[57] The risk of a permanently disabled infant is inversely related to the gestational age at which the disease is contracted. With maternal exposure in the first month of pregnancy, 50% of the infants will be permanently disabled. There remains a 6% risk at four and five months of gestation. Previously, gamma globulin was commonly used to reduce the risk for pregnant women exposed to rubella. However, the results were quite unsatisfactory, and gamma globulin is rarely recommended today.[58] In light of the foregoing discussion, a confirmed diagnosis of naturally acquired rubella infection in the first trimester of pregnancy is recognized as an indication for termination of the pregnancy.[59]

Cytomegalovirus (CMV), a herpes-type virus, can cause similar permanent disabilities and is actually far more common than rubella. It is estimated that 1% of all newborn infants are born with some manifestation of CMV infection.[60] Unfortunately, at this writing, our understanding of the manifestations of maternal CMV infections is still quite limited. Consequently, confirmed exposure in the first and early second trimester must be dealt with individually; for it would seem that primary CMV infection in early pregnancy would warrant consideration of therapeutic abortion.

3.   RADIATION   It is generally agreed that when radiation is given in therapeutic doses to the mother in the first few months of pregnancy, malformation or death of the fetus may result.[61] According to Parlee, "[I]t appears that ionizing radiation in therapeutic doses in the early months of pregnancy are grounds for the termination of the pregnancy."[62] Doses of radiation in therapeutic quantities are usually reserved for the treatment of malignant neoplastic disease, such as carcinoma of the cervix. Fetal death and spontaneous abortion of the products of conception are the usual, but not inevitable, result of such radiation exposure.

---

[57] Horstmann, *Rubella,* 25(3) Clin. Obstet. & Gynecol. 593 (1982).

[58] *Id.* at 592.

[59] *Id.*

[60] Stagno, Pass, Dworsky & Alford, *Maternal Cytomegalovirus Infection and Perinatal Transmission,* 25 Clin. Obstet. & Gynecol. 563 (1982).

[61] Parlee, *Radiation Hazards in Obstetrics and Gynecology,* 75 Am. J. Obstet. & Gynecol. 327, 328 (1958).

[62] *Id.* at 332.

The exposure of the human fetus to diagnostic radiation less than five rads has not been observed to cause congenital malformations or growth retardation.[63] When extensive diagnostic X-ray procedures that equal or exceed the five-rad level are used during the early weeks of pregnancy, therapeutic abortion should be offered. With modern low-dose X-ray equipment, however, such a level is rarely achieved with routine diagnostic procedures. The fact that doses of one to three rads can produce cellular effects on the fetus and that diagnostic exposure during pregnancy has been associated with malignancy in childhood makes appropriate patient counseling in this "gray zone" (between one and five rads), difficult for health care professionals.[64] In general, the radiation risk to the embryo or fetus should not be the predominating factor in arriving at a decision to terminate pregnancy unless exposure is in the five rad or greater range.

4.   GENETICS   Great scientific advances in the field of genetics, coupled with the safety of amniocentesis,[65] have provided an opportunity to make the firm diagnosis of nearly 200 chromosomal and congenital malformations prenatally. Indeed, genetic counseling in prenatal diagnostic centers is available nationwide to all women over the age of 35 and with a previous history of genetic or congenital problem in the patient or her spouse. Examples of disorders that can be diagnosed by amniocentesis include Down's syndrome, other trisomies (13 and 18), Tay-Sachs disease, neural tube defects and sickle-cell anemia. Sex-linked abnormalities such as hemophilia and muscular dystrophy (Duchenne's) either can be ruled out or the appropriate risk can be assessed.[66]

Revolutionary improvements in ultrasonic technology have recently provided the opportunity to diagnose major congenital anomalies with confidence. Such disorders, including anencephaly, spina bifida and other neural tube defects, as well as hydrocephalus, to mention but a few, can be identified early enough in the second trimester to provide an opportunity for therapeutic abortion.

Recent work using the still experimental technique of chorionic biopsy in the first trimester may provide the opportunity for earlier diagnosis, and therefore earlier and safer first-trimester therapeutic pregnancy termination. It is this area of genetic and congenital anomalies that currently accounts for the bulk of true therapeutic abortions performed in the United States.

5.   ERYTHROBLASTOSIS FETALIS[67]   The primary hazard to the fetus affected by Rh or other antibodies produced by the maternal immune system, is anemia or lack of red blood cells. This anemia can often be corrected by intrauterine fetal transfusion at pe-

---

[63] Tabuchi et al., *Fetal Hazards Due to X-Ray Diagnosis During Pregnancy*, 16 Hiroshima J. MEDSCI. 49 (1967); Kinlen & Acheson, *Diagnostic Irradiation, Congenital Malformations and Spontaneous Abortion*, 41 Brit. J. of Radiol. 648 (1968).

[64] Brent, *The Effects of Embryonic and Fetal Exposure to X-Ray, Microwaves and Ultrasound*, 26 Clin. Obstet. & Gynecol., No. 493 (1983).

[65] This involves perforating or tapping the amnion (the inner of the two bags containing the fetus) with the use of a needle. The procedure is used to remove and study part of the amniotic fluid. Schmidt, *supra* note 31, at 83.

[66] Centerwall & Tennant, *Genetic Diseases*, in *Manual of Obstetrics, Diagnosis and Therapy* 277–79 (Niswander ed. 2d ed. 1983).

[67] This is a hemolytic anemia of the fetus or newborn infant, caused by the transplacental transmission of maternally formed antibodies, usually secondary to an incompatability between the blood group of the mother and that of her offspring (usually an incompatability of the Rh factor). Schmidt, *supra* note 31, at 294.701.

riodic intervals.[68] As a result, the baby may be born alive and maintain good health with the aid of exchange transfusion. Hence, abortion for fetal hemolytic disease, once a rather common indication for therapeutic abortion, is rarely indicated in contemporary medical practice.

The routine administration of the Rh antibody (RhoGAM) to the unsensitized gravida immediately following the delivery of an Rh positive infant prevents the formation of maternal antibodies and thereby minimizes the risk of fetal sensitization during a subsequent pregnancy. More recently, the prophylactic administration of RhoGAM to unsensitized Rh negative women early in the third trimester reduces the risk even further.[69] Since the introduction of RhoGAM into everyday medical practice, erythroblastosis fetalis has become a most uncommon clinical entity that should become even rarer in the future.

III. Current Legal Abortion Practices in the United States

A. Changes in the Indications

In 1936 Taussig called tuberculosis "the most significant indication for therapeutic abortion in point of frequency."[70] This disease is virtually unheard of as a reason for abortion today. In the same volume, he pointed out that psychiatric indications accounted for only a small percentage of therapeutic abortions but that such procedures were occurring more frequently. In one study, for example, psychiatric indications increased in a linear fashion from about 10% in 1943 to about 80% in 1963.[71] Perhaps at the peak of this trend, the state of California reported that during 1970 over 98% of the legal abortions performed in that state were indicated for reasons of mental health.[72] These "therapeutic" abortions occurred while many psychiatrists maintained that rarely is psychiatric disease an absolute indication for therapeutic abortion.[73] Until 1973 many states required a true suicidal risk to be present in the psychiatric patient legally to permit abortion. Psychiatrists were in the forefront of the fight to expand the grounds for legal pregnancy termination. They were frequently willing to find that the patient desiring abortion suffered from psychiatric disease severe enough to threaten her life. It was suggested by Rosenberg and Silver that a psychiatrist recommending therapeutic abortion was likely to be considering the socioeconomic factors at least as much as the psychiatric indications.[74] It is clear from the foregoing information that social factors had become a the prime consideration in the decision to terminate pregnancy long before liberalized abortion legislation took effect. Physicians performing these abortions maintained that the patient had a right to make her own decision concerning a given pregnancy.

Other interesting trends regarding the maternal age, parity and marital status of women securing legal abortion should be noted. In one study in the 1940s, no women

[68] Larkin, Knochel & Lee, *Intrauterine Transfusions: New Techniques and Results,* 25 Clin. Obstet. & Gynecol. 309 (1982).

[69] Kochenour & Beeson, *The Use of Rh-Immune Globulin,* 25 Clin. Obstet. & Gynecol. 286 (1982).

[70] Taussig, *supra* note 8, at 292.

[71] Niswander, Klein & Randall, *supra* note 16, at 1142.

[72] Bureau of Maternal and Child Health, 4th Annual Report on the Implementation of the California Therapeutic Abortion Act, Table I (1971).

[73] Sim, *Abortion and the Psychiatrist,* II Brit. Med. J. 148 (1963).

[74] Rosenberg & Silver, *Suicide, Psychiatrists and Therapeutic Abortion,* 102 Cal. Med. 407, 410 (1965).

under 20 years of age were aborted. During the 1950s, approximately 7% of the patients were under 20, and from 1960 to 1964 nearly 15% of the patients were in this teenage group.[75] A 17% decline in the birthrates of New York state adolescents was experienced in the three years following legalization of abortion, in contrast to the preceding three-year period.[76] More recent data from New York reveal that more than 60% of unmarried teenagers terminated their pregnancy by abortion in 1978. In addition, approximately 25% of married pregnant teenagers also chose to terminate their pregnancy by abortion.[77] Nationally, according to the Centers for Disease Control, approximately 31% of women obtaining abortions in 1977 were age 19 or younger. In that same report, young teenagers were followed by women 40 years of age and above with the second highest ratio of legal abortions to live births (about 725 to 1,000).[78] The proportion of nullipara[79] undergoing abortion increased from about 20% during the 1940s to 36% during the early 1960s. By 1977, a consistent inverse relationship existed between the number of living children a woman had and the percentage of abortions obtained. Fifty-two percent of abortions that year were for nulliparous women, and only 3% were performed for grand multiparous (five or more children) women.[80] The percentage of married patients seeking pregnancy termination has declined steadily in the last 40 years. During the 1940s, over 93% of abortion patients were married; this had dropped to nearly 59% during the 1960s.[81] By 1977, more than three of four women obtaining abortions in the United States were unmarried at the time of the procedure.[82]

It should not be surprising that since the legalization of abortion nationwide, a substantial increase in the number of repeat procedures has occurred each year. This is primarily the result of the continually increasing pool of women who have undergone their first pregnancy termination. In 1972, 14% of all abortions performed in New York City were repeat procedures; by 1978, 40% of women obtaining abortion had undergone a previous procedure.[83] Statistics from the Centers for Disease Control, however, note that only 22% of abortions performed in 1977 were repeat procedures.[84]

Perhaps the most encouraging trend in abortion practices in the United States since 1973 has been the steady increase in the percentage of procedures performed in the first 12 weeks of gestation. In fact, during 1977 nearly half of all reported legal abortions were performed in the first eight weeks of gestation.[85] Data from New York state indicate that more than 90% of abortions in 1978 were performed during the first 12 weeks of pregnancy,[86] when the procedure involves the least danger. This is in sharp contrast to the data from 1970, the first year of legalization in New York, when 30% of their abortions were performed beyond 12 weeks, 18% greater than 16 weeks.[87] This trend

---

[75] Niswander, Klein & Randall, *supra* note 16, at 1141.

[76] Safe and Legal, *supra* note 18, at 28.

[77] *Id.*

[78] *Abortion Surveillance, Annual Summary* (1977), Centers for Disease Control, U.S. Department of Health, Education and Welfare, 3.

[79] A nullipara is a woman who has never given birth to a child. Schmidt, *supra* note 31, at 567.

[80] Safe and Legal, *supra* note 18, at 4.

[81] Niswander, Klein & Randall, *supra* note 16, at 1141.

[82] Safe and Legal, *supra* note 18, at 3–4.

[83] *Id.* at 35.

[84] *Id.* at 5.

[85] *Id.* at 4.

[86] *Id.* at 18.

[87] *Id.*

will be further elaborated upon in the context of the medical procedures used at various gestational ages for pregnancy termination, as well as the inherent hazard in the various types of operations performed.

B. Hazards of Induced Abortion

As we stated at the outset, the number of maternal deaths related to abortion has decreased precipitously in the last decade. This is even more impressive in light of the fact that induced abortion is the most commonly performed operation on adults in the United States.[88] Prior to the legalization of abortion, the reported experience of various investigators concerning the frequency of complications with abortion was so varied that it was difficult, if not impossible, to make any generalizations regarding the safety of induced abortion. However, as a rule of thumb, the safety of a particular procedure varies directly with the technical ease and the experience of the physician performing the operation.

One of the beneficial byproducts of the legalization of abortion has been the marked improvement in surgical expertise in the performance of the procedure. In 1971, a study of first-trimester abortions at England's Oxford University Hospital reported the complications among 830 patients undergoing vacuum aspiration (786 patients) or D&C (44 patients).[89] Seventeen percent of the patients experienced hemorrhage of at least 500 cc's of blood, 8.5% suffered a traumatic cervical laceration, 15% experienced endometritis, and nearly 2% suffered a perforated uterus (two patients required hysterectomies as a result of perforation). Such a report would be appalling by today's standards, as the incidence of major complications for first-trimester abortion by suction curettage is 0.4% or less.[90]

One reason for the dramatic improvements in abortion complications in the first trimester is the avoidance of general anesthesia in the vast majority of cases. Hemorrhage, perforation of the uterus and cervical injury are more common with general than with local anesthesia.[91]

More common complications of first-trimester abortion include endometritis (0.75%), excessive bleeding and retained products of conception (0.61%).[92] Antibiotic therapy and/or reaspiration will suffice in most of these cases, many times without the need for inpatient hospitalization. The risk of uterine perforation is only 0.2%,[93] and can often be managed by close in-hospital observation without surgery. Menstrual extraction results in failure to interrupt the pregnancy in approximately 1% of patients and requires reaspiration for completion in an addition 2%.[94]

The effect of induced abortion on future fertility and childbearing capacity has long been a major concern. A recent study covering five years at the Boston Hospital for

---

[88] *Abortion Surveillance, 1979–1980,* Centers for Disease Control (issued January 1983).

[89] Stallworthy, Moolgaoker & Walsh, *Legal Abortion: A Critical Assessment of Its Risks,* Lancet 1246 (1971).

[90] Grimes & Cates, *Complications From Legally-Induced Abortion: A Review,* 34 (3) Obstet. & Gynecol. Survey 178 (1979).

[91] Grimes, Schulz, Cates & Tyler, *The Comparative Safety of Local vs. General Anesthesia for Suction Curettage Abortion.* An Analysis of 54,155 Cases, Presented at the 11th Annual Meeting of the Society for Epidemiologic Research, Iowa City, Iowa (June 14, 1978).

[92] Grimes & Cates, *supra* note 91, at 183.

[93] *Id.* at 179.

[94] Niswander, *Contraception, Abortion and Sterilization,* in *Manual of Obstetrics, Diagnosis and Therapy* 21–22 (Niswander ed. 2d ed. 1983).

Women found no evidence that a single induced abortion had any effect on a woman's ability to carry a subsequent pregnancy to term. However, there was some evidence that with two or more abortions, an increased risk of miscarriage in subsequent pregnancies exists.[95] These data remain controversial.

While the complication rates for mid-trimester abortion far exceed those for first-trimester procedures, the introduction of the D&E has had a major impact on the reduction of morbidity and mortality for mid-trimester procedures, especially those less than 16 weeks. In fact, the mortality from induced abortion during the first 15 weeks of pregnancy is one-seventh the risk of dying from pregnancy and childbirth.[96] Prior to the introduction of the D&E, virtually all mid-trimester abortions were performed by the instillation techniques outlined above. These procedures are generally performed in the latter half of the mid-trimester (greater than 16 weeks) when sufficient amniotic fluid is available within the uterus.

Trauma to the cervix, including laceration and fistula formation, can occur with all mid-trimester abortion techniques. However, this problem has been markedly reduced by the widespread use of laminaria tents (sterilized dehydrated Japanese seaweed). These devices are safe, effective cervical dilators as a result of their intense higroscopic properties. A detailed account of the complications of mid-trimester abortion can be found in Drs. Guttmacher and Kaiser's chapter in this text.

IV. Conclusion

Legalized abortion on request has essentially removed criminal abortion as a major health problem in the United States. By-products of this legislation have included widespread availability of contraceptive, family planning and abortion services, as well as improved medical expertise, and the consequent reduction in the morbidity and mortality of pregnancy termination. The safety of legal abortion cannot be questioned: indeed, the mortality rate for abortion is far less than that for tonsillectomy.[97] The majority of abortion procedures can be safely carried out in an outpatient or clinic setting, with a significant reduction in the cost of medical care.[98]

We must never return to the dark ages of the back-alley abortionist, a threat that seemed quite real in some states after the Hyde Amendments restricted federal funds for abortion in 1977.[99] It is most unlikely that human nature, or society as a whole, will ever completely avoid all unsafe or unwanted pregnancies. Prenatal diagnostic centers can detect nearly 200 fetal abnormalities for which abortion services must be available. While not a total solution, legalized abortion has improved the morbidity and mortality for pregnant women and has had a beneficial impact on the quality of life.

---

[95] *Issues in Brief,* Alan Guttmacher Institute, vol. 1, no. 9, 3 (October 1981).

[96] LeBolt, Grimes & Cates, *Mortality From Abortion and Childbirth: Are the Populations Comparable?*, 248 J.A.M.A. 188 (1982).

[97] National Center for Health Statistics, DHHS, *Final Mortality Statistics, 1975, and Commission on Professional and Hospital Activities* (1974–75), PAS Hospital mortality data, CDC, *Vital Statistics,* 1990.

[98] Grimes, Cates & Selik, *Abortion Facilities and the Risk of Death,* 13 Fam. Plann. Perspect. 30 (1981).

[99] Gold et al., *A Cluster of Septic Complications Associated With Illegal Induced Abortions,* 56 Obstet. & Gynecol. 311 (1980). Harris v. McRae, 448 U.S. 297 (1980). This confirmed the Hyde Amendment when funds could not be used for abortion unless the life of the mother is endangered if the fetus is carried to term.

Research using human fetal tissue in combating disease is a highly charged issue. Dr. Ryan's article details the numerous diseases that transplantation of fetal tissue can possibly treat. However, because much fetal tissue research is conducted after induced abortions and abortion is now as much an issue as the research itself, a moratorium was placed on fetal research in 1974. Since 1974 we have had congressional debates, a set of general requirements for fetal research, additional panels studying the issue of fetal research and then finally another moratorium. The end result, as shown by Dr. Ryan, is the loss of precious years of important research. The moratorium is still in effect, and the issue of fetal research has not been resolved; other countries, and even private groups in the United States, have shown the benefits of fetal transplantation.

23 · The Medical and Research Uses of Human Fetal Tissues

Kenneth J. Ryan, M.D.

Research and Transplantation Involving Human Fetal Tissue

Human fetal tissue has been used in research studies to advance general biological knowledge and for specific application to human medical needs. In the most notable case, kidney tissue obtained from a human fetal source was used to culture the polio virus in the development of the polio vaccine. Since some viruses infect only human cells, human fetal cells in culture provide a way to study viruses outside the body. Human fetal tissue also allows detailed study of the factors controlling the normal growth and development of the fetus as well as those factors causing fetal disease and disability. Actually, the bulk of research performed with fetal tissue is for the ultimate benefit of the fetus as a class in terms of better management of normal pregnancy and better diagnostics and therapy for problem cases. Amniocentesis to determine fetal lung maturity as a marker of the ability to survive outside the womb is a good case in point. Study of fetal lung cells and their excretory products provided the basis for this life-saving diagnostic test.[1]

Another form of research has involved the use of fetal tissue for transplantation to human recipients to correct a disease process. In the most promising cases, the human subject has a disease caused by the absence of a substance that the fetal tissue can provide after transplantation. An example is a diabetic lacking insulin who is now treated by daily injections of the hormone. That individual might benefit from a transplant of

---

[1] Association of American Medical Colleges, *Summary, Fetal Research and Fetal Tissue Research* (June 1988).

583

pancreatic cells that could produce insulin. If the transplant is successful, the diabetic would essentially be cured of the disease.

The diseases and conditions for which fetal tissue transplantation is being considered include not only diabetes but Parkinson's disease, immune deficiency diseases, disorders of the blood cells including leukemia, Alzheimer's disease, spinal cord injuries and a range of other conditions.[2]

Clinical Experience with Fetal Tissue Transplantation

Human deficiency diseases have been treated since the early part of the 20th century with extracts of animal organs, as in the case of thyroid extract for hypothyroidism and pancreatic extracts of insulin for diabetes. In each case the animal hormone is similar or identical to the human form and can make up for the body's inability to secrete the hormone. With modern science, human hormones are synthesized chemically or by recombinant technology as, for example, insulin of recombinant DNA origin. In any case, rather than inject hormone extracts or pure hormones, it is preferable to substitute the diseased hormonal tissue with tissue transplants and thus "cure" the deficiency. Animal tissues (xenografts) cannot ordinarily be transplanted to humans because of the body's immune rejection response. Even tissue of human origin is rejected as a transplant unless immune suppressive drugs are used or the tissue is typed for compatibility. Some of these problems can be overcome by the use of fetal tissue, which may elicit less of an immune rejection response and which contains fewer cells that can attack the tissue recipient with a graft versus host reaction.

Fetal Transplants to Replace the Thymus

Transplantation of the thymus is perhaps the only example in which fetal transplantation might reasonably be considered a form of therapy rather than simply a research maneuver. One defect of the relatively rare congentital disease called DiGeorge's Syndrome is an inadequate immune system due to the absence of the thymus gland. Without a thymus the infant cannot fight off infections and generally dies in the first year of life from overwhelming sepsis. More than 20 years ago, the first successful fetal thymus transplant was performed, followed by at least 27 more cases with nine infants surviving. The fetal thymus has been obtained from fetuses at 12 to 20 weeks gestation with the earlier tissue being more immunologically compatible. An alternative to thymus transplantation is donation of bone marrow cells from compatible tissue of a sibling. Otherwise fetal tissue transplantation is the only life-saving option for infants with DiGeorge's syndrome.[3]

Transplantation of Fetal Pancreatic Tissue

Diabetes is a common disease affecting at least one million juvenile diabetics in the United States who require insulin for most of their lives. The disease results in the inability to metabolize sugar unless insulin is provided and, if inadequately treated, is

---

[2]Council Report, *Medical Applications of Fetal Tissue Transplantation.* 263 J. Am. Med. Assn. 565–570 (1990).

[3]R. H. Buckley, *Fetal Thymus Transplantation for the Correction of Congenital Absence of the Thymus (DiGeorge's Syndrome),* 2 Report of the Human Fetal Transplantation Research Panel D50–D57 (December 1988).

complicated by shortened life span, risks of blindness, heart and kidney disease as well as loss of limbs from poor circulation. The use of pancreatic transplants for this condition is still largely experimental and has yet to be perfected. Such questions as the ideal tissue preparation for transplantation, the mode and site of transplanting, the regulation of the grafted tissue and its survival all need to be worked out. Human fetal pancreatic tissue has been injected into animals with experimental diabetes and has reversed the metabolic defect. Fetal pancreatic tissue can be transplanted under the capsule of the kidney in conjunction with an otherwise needed kidney transplant. Under these circumstances the fetal pancreatic graft will grow, differentiate and secrete insulin. The use of fetal tissue is generally more successful than tissue obtained from adult cadavers. Although very promising, much work remains to be done to perfect the transplanting of fetal pancreatic cells in treating the diabetic.[4]

Transplantation of Fetal Neural Tissue

The use of fetal transplants to treat neurological conditions such as Alzheimer's disease, Huntington's chorea, spinal cord injury and Parkinson's disease has been proposed but only in the case of Parkinson's disease have promising results recently been obtained. Parkinson's disease is a chronic human ailment that afflicts about 400,000 patients in the United States. It is typified by uncontrollable tremors, loss of posture, muscle rigidity and extreme slowness and difficulty with purposeful motion. It is a progressive and crippling disease. The cause of the disease is believed to be the loss of cells from the central nervous system that secrete a neurotransmitter substance, dopamine, that is responsible for normal function. The loss of cells is believed to be due to a combination of genetic predisposition and environmental toxins. The objective of transplantation is to replace those cells and their secretory product. Current forms of therapy are limited. The disease can be treated with the drug L-Dopa, but the response is variable, the drug has side effects and its beneficial action may be lost over time.

Transplantation of fetal nerve cells in animals such as rats and the rhesus monkey has been successful. The cells divide, undergo differentiation and integrate themselves into existing nerve networks. In addition, there are drugs that can artificially induce a Parkinson-like disease in animals that can in turn be ameliorated by fetal tissue grafts. Fetal tissue transplantation into the brains of patients with Parkinsonism has occurred worldwide, but there have been few carefully documented studies to demonstrate its true efficacy. In 1990 two very promising reports from Stockholm and Denver demonstrated that the fetal nerve cells transferred to the brain of patients actually function to produce the missing substance, dopamine. The patients demonstrated measurable and documented improvement.[5,6] Much remains to be learned in terms of the wider applicability of the technique and of course whether the improvement is permanent or transient.

---

[4] K. J. Lafferty, *Diabetic Islet Cell Transplant Research: Basic Science,* 2 Report of the Human Fetal Tissue Transplantation Research Panel D142–D144 (December 1988).

[5] O. Lindval, P. Brundin, & H. Widner et al., *Grafts of fetal dopamine neurons survive and improve motor function in Parkinson's Disease,* 247 Science 574–577 (1990).

[6] C. R. Freed, R. E. Breeze, N. L. Rosenberg, S. A. Schneck, T.H. Wells, J. N. Barrett, S. T. Grafton, S. C. Huang, D. Eidelberg & E. A. Rottenberg, *Transplantation of Human Fetal Dopamine Cells for Parkinson's Disease: Results at one year,* 47 Archives Neurology 505–512 (1990).

Special Properties, Advantages and Alternatives to the Use of Fetal Tissue

Fetal tissue has special properties that make its transplantation advantageous. In contrast to completely differentiated adult cells, fetal cells have "plasticity," which allows them to adapt to new environments, to change in shape and migrate and to integrate functionally in the transplant recipient. Fetal cells also "proliferate" more readily than adult cells, dividing more rapidly through cell cycles. Fetal cells can induce an "angiogenic" response inducing new blood vessel growth and vascularization. Fetal cells are more immunologically compatible because they are less inherently antigenic than adult cells and have fewer immune attack cells among them to attack the host.[7] Fetal tissue research allows access to human cells to study conditions peculiar to the human. Fetal cells behave metabolically like cancer cells, making the study of them applicable to the vexing problem of malignancy. Fetal tissue is available after pregnancy terminations and would under other circumstances simply be discarded. The association of fetal tissue with induced abortion makes fetal research unacceptable to many who oppose abortion. As noted below, the use of fetal material from spontaneous abortion does not arouse as much controversy but it is much less suitable for research and medical use. Alternatives to the use of fetal tissue are to immortalize cells by tissue culture, to try to research the problems with adult or animal grafts or to seek alternative drug delivery systems and therapies.

Other Research Involving the Fetus

Research on the living fetus ex utero was the type of investigation that first prompted societal concern. The controversial studies involved perfusion of the intact fetus in order to study metabolic pathways or to develop perfusion apparatus that would allow extrauterine development and help treat extreme prematurity at the margins of viability. The living previable fetuses for these studies were obtained at abortion and were kept functioning by perfusion during the course of studies which were terminated by discontinuation of the perfusion apparatus. There were objections to the research technique itself and not just to the association with abortion.[8] These types of ex utero studies are noteworthy in that they represented the exception to most fetal research, which was and is performed on the living fetus in utero on desired pregnancies going to term. Such in utero studies are largely observational and involve potential diagnostic and therapeutic modalities intended to develop improved care of the pregnant woman and fetuses for conditions such as diabetes, pregnancy-induced hypertension, blood group incompatability, use of anesthetic agents, inducing or stopping labor, fetal diagnosis and fetal surgery. The importance of this research required that ethically and socially acceptable methods be developed to allow them to continue. In most instances of fetal research, abortion is not involved, and the concerns about the protection of research subjects could focus on the similarity of the fetus with that of the newborn in terms of matters of risk and parental consent.

---

[7] R. Auerbach, *Qualities of Fetal Cells and Tissues,* 2 Report of the Human Fetal Tissue Transplantation Research Panel D27–D31, December 1988.

[8] M. J. Mahoney, *Research on the Fetus, The Nature and Extent of Research Involving Living Human Fetuses, Appendix,* National Commission for the Protection of Human Subjects of Biomedical and Behavioral Research 1–1 to 1–48 (1975).

Social and Political Issues in Fetal Tissue Research

Use of the human fetus or fetal tissues for research is fraught with controversy largely because of the common association of the fetus as a product of an induced abortion. In fact, abortion is now a more contentious issue than the research itself. Human fetal tissue was not available to any significant degree for medical or research purposes until pregnancy terminations became openly practiced in the middle of the 20th century. This availability and use of fetal tissue from induced abortion took place first in Scandinavia and England before becoming common in the United States, since abortion laws were liberalized in Europe before similar changes in abortion law crossed the Atlantic Ocean. On the other hand, there is essentially no controversy over the use of fetal material from a spontaneous abortion for research. However, tissue from this source has limitations. With a spontaneous loss the fetus is often not recovered, and when it is, the event is sporadic and unpredictable and the infectious, genetic and other causes of the spontaneous loss of pregnancy could confound experimental observations.

Fetal tissue from pregnancy terminations also became available for research in the 1960s and thereafter, when rapid progress was being made in the biological sciences. As a consequence, major medical advances have been made from research using fetal tissue that can be applied for human benefit.

The National Commission and The First Fetal Research Moratorium, 1974

With the *Roe v. Wade* Supreme Court decision in 1973 that legalized abortion, some states responded with restrictions on fetal research, and the matter of research on the live fetus became a matter of congressional debate. A moratorium on fetal research before or after induced abortion was imposed in the National Research Act, which established the National Commission for the Protection of Human Subjects of Biomedical and Behavioral Research in 1974. Although the mandate to the commission covered a wide array of research issues, its first tasks were a study of the practice and ethics of fetal research and a determination of whether federal regulations could be proposed that would allow the moratorium to be lifted. The commission concluded that ethically acceptable fetal research was possible with attention to certain general requirements:

1. Appropriate prior investigations using animal models and nonpregnant humans must have been completed.
2. The knowledge to be gained must be important and obtainable by no reasonable alternate means.
3. Risks and benefits to both the mother and the fetus must be fully evaluated and described.
4. Informed consent must be sought and granted under proper conditions.
5. Subjects must be selected so that risks and benefits will not fall inequitably among economic, racial and social classes.

The commission went on to stipulate the risk and type of research that would be acceptable and prevailed in having the congressional moratorium lifted for certain types of nonrisky, noncontroversial research. The commission also asked that a proposed successor body, the Ethics Advisory Board, be empowered to consider waivers on a national level for risky or controversial fetal research where the social and medical need was compelling. The commission voted unanimously with one abstention that research on the dead fetus and on fetal tissue be permitted consistent with local law, the Uniform Anatomical Gift Act and commonly held convictions about respect for the dead. Between 1969 and 1973 essentially all 50 states adopted the Uniform Anatomical Gift Act, which authorizes the gift of all or part of a human body after death for specified purposes, including research. The commission recommended that no inducements should be offered to procure an abortion for research purposes and that the research should in no way determine the advisability, timing or method of abortion.[9]

The Ethics Advisory Board and the De Facto Moratorium on Research of the Fertilized Egg

A ban on research funding similar to that involving fetal research existed from 1975 for research with human in vitro fertilization. In vitro fertilization involves the fertilized human egg, pre-embryo and embryo before the fetus is formed. The commission recommended that the deliberations on this matter be referred to an ethics advisory board reporting to the secretary of health, education and welfare. On July 25, 1978, Louise Brown, the first human product of in vitro fertilization was born in England. Since research on in vitro fertilization had been stopped due to the ban on research funding noted above, the technique was introduced into clinical practice in the United States without the usual careful investigation that precedes widespread application. Two months later, the Ethics Advisory Board was formed to investigate the matter and concluded that the government should support such research with the proviso that no material should be sustained in vitro beyond 14 days after fertilization.[10] The issues that aroused controversy were that risks to offspring might not be foreseen before it was too late and that in the process of research some early stages of human life would be discarded. Since the findings of the Ethics Advisory Board, there have been over 85 statements and at least 15 extended reports on the ethics and public policy related to reproductive technology. These reports came from Australia, the European community and the United States. In at least 10 reports, research with or without some restrictions was allowed as long as the duration of the embryo culture in vitro prior to discard was 14 days, one report limited culture to 7 days.[11]

In spite of the Ethics Advisory Board's findings, a de facto moratorium on in vitro studies has remained in the United States since no research was ever approved while the board existed and its charter expired in 1980.

A New Moratorium on Granting Waivers on ''Risky'' Fetal Research

Under the recommendation of the original National Commission, a fetal research project with some risk could be considered for funding if approved by the Ethical Advisory Board. In 1979, the Board granted a waiver to obtain fetal blood samples in utero to study sickle cell anemia. In spite of the fact that no other waiver had been granted and no waiver could be granted because the charter for the Ethics Advisory Board had expired, the Congress in 1984 decided to impose a three-year ban on granting any waivers while a new Biomedical Ethics Commission studied the matter further.[12] The

---

[9]*Research on the Fetus, Report and Recommendations,* National Commission for the Protection of Human Subjects of Biomedical and Behavioral Research (1975).

[10]M. Steinfels, *In Vitro Fertilization: Ethically Acceptable Research,* 9 Hastings Report 3–11 (1979).

[11]LeRoy Walters, personal communication.

[12]*Moratorium Imposed on Rare Fetal Research,* Cong. Q. 2633 (Oct. 13, 1984).

debate in Congress centered around the needs to advance knowledge to care for fetuses versus the question of misuse of fetal tissues, strange experiments and objectional research as well as any association with abortion.

The Fetal Tissue Transplantation Advisory Committee and a New Moratorium

In 1988, the director of the National Institutes of Health asked the assistant secretary of health for approval of a research protocol to study the transplantation of human fetal tissue into the brain of a patient with Parkinson's Disease. The request was denied, a moratorium was imposed on federal funding of any similar study, and an advisory panel was created to study the matter and make recommendations. The assistant secretary of health, Robert Windom, revealed the political and ethical concerns behind the moratorium by the specific questions he posed to the panel as paraphrased below:

1. Is an induced abortion of moral relevance to the decision to use human fetal tissue for research?
2. Does the use of fetal tissue in research encourage women to have abortions that they might otherwise not undertake?
3. Does the very process of obtaining informed consent from the pregnant woman constitute a prohibited inducement to terminate the pregnancy?
4. Is maternal consent sufficient for the use of fetal tissue?
5. Should there be a prohibition on donation of fetal tissue between family members, friends and aquaintances?
6. Would the research or its clinical application affect the timing or conduct of abortions?
7. Are payments involved in obtaining fetal tissue and would they fall inside the scope of the Hyde amendment on funding of abortions?
8. Would there be conflicts with state laws?
9. Have enough animal studies been done?
10. Could fetal cell cultures ultimately replace the need for fresh tissue transplantation?

These questions clarified the politics behind the issue and made induced abortion the central issue rather than any other aspect of the research itself. The Human Fetal Tissue Transplantation Research Panel was first assembled in September 1988. After several meetings and public hearings, their report was conveyed to the advisory committee to the director of the National Institutes of Health, which in turn also made recommendations to the director for final presentation to Assistant Secretary of Health Robert Windom.[13] Although the panel and the advisory committee voted overwhelmingly to lift the moratorium and fund such research, no action was taken for several months during the installation of a new government and a change in administration. Ultimately, the secretary of health and human services extended the moratorium indefinitely. The new assistant secretary of health, Dr. James Mason, in testimony before a congressional committee hearing, justified the moratorium arguing that to do otherwise might encourage women to have abortions.

---

[13] *Report of the Advisory Committee to the Director, National Institutes of Health,* Report of the Human Fetal Tissue Transplantation Research Panel (December 1988).

The panel was carefully selected so that its members came from lists drawn up by the White House and conservative legislators. The attorney for the National Right to Life Committee, James Bopp, was appointed as well as Father James Burtchaell, professor of theology at Notre Dame University. A majority of the panel were believed to be against abortion on demand, and some were more extreme in their positions. It must have come as somewhat of a shock for the conservative administration that the panel voted to lift the moratorium. Most votes on issues were 19 to 2 with the two dissenters being Bopp and Burtchaell. The deliberations of the panel were carried out in open hearings and are a matter of public record. Many on the panel do not favor abortion (including the chairman, Judge Arlin Adams), but they believed that the issue of abortion could be separated from the research use of the fetus. They recommended that safeguards be put in place to separate the abortion decision and the subsequent research use. A prohibition on the designation of fetal tissue to relatives and friends was proposed. It was also recommended that the process be handled much like the national organ donation program, which includes a prohibition on the sale of organs. The majority of the panel did not believe that supporting such research would affect women's decisions on abortion. The panel accepted the scientific judgment that sufficient animal research had been done to justify involving the human at this time.

The dissent rested on three major points:

1. There is complicity between everyone connected with the research effort and the abortion itself. Evoking the Holocaust analogy, the dissenters created a good deal of ill will, offended many people and provoked an angry rebuttal by one of the panelists who was outranged by this inspiration to intolerance and extremism. The rebuttal letter by Professor Aaron Mascona went on to say: "The Holocaust was not a medical research project to help Parkinson patients and rescue infants from fatal diseases. It was not scrutinized by peer-reviews, examined by NIH panels, publicized by the media, open to public questioning, debated in Congress, challenged by the Administration." Mascona quoted Julian Bond: "Such comparisons are at best disingenuous and misleading attempts to capture someone else's history in a tactical maneuver to deny women constitutional rights."

2. There is no one to give consent since, by requesting the abortion, the pregnant woman revokes any claim to kinship. This proved an interesting point of discussion. The panel concluded that disputes about the morality of abortion should not deprive the woman of the legal authority to dispose of fetal remains. She still has a special connection with the fetus, and she has a legitimate interest in its disposition and use. Any other mode of transfer appeared to raise more serious ethical concerns.

3. Use of the aborted fetus would be an incentive to future abortions. This proved to be the argument that the administration used to justify siding with the dissent. There is, however, no credible evidence for this in countries that allow such research on transplantation or even in the Untied States over the past 30-odd years of fetal research. The argument was extended to include a likelihood of a traffic in fetuses if the research was successful and the demand for clinical practice outstripped the supply.[14]

---

[14] 1 Report of the Human Fetal Tissue Transplantation Research Panel (December 1988).

In April 1990, Congressman Henry Waxman held hearings on the moratorium. LeRoy Walters testified that between 1972 and 1989, 14 committee or parliamentary reports had been issued on the ethics of fetal tissue research from the United States, Canada, Australia, the United Kingdom, Sweden, France, the Netherlands and the Council of Europe. All 14 agreed that research involving the study of the transplantation of human fetal tissue was ethical in principle. They all recommended use of only cadaveric tissue and that the use be insulated from the abortion decision and be kept from the commercial sphere. The concensus and agreement with the panel recommendations are quite remarkable. I testified that the moratoria had unfortunate consequences:

1. Moratoria impede progress toward the amelioration and cure of chronic diseases such as parkinsonism and diabetes. It withdraws hope from the victims, a point made most eloquently by the public testimony.

2. Moratoria create a siege state of mind for the scientists and discourage research beyond the kinds in question. It even affects recruitment of students into science. It is a form of government repression for very limited political goals.

3. The moratorium creates a "moral vacuum" for the oversight of transplantation as it moves into clinical use. Although there are federal regulations for government funding of medical research, the practice of medicine is a state-by-state affair. This moral vacuum already occurred with in vitro fertilization, as discussed above, when research stopped due to lack of government funding and in vitro fertilization entered into wide medical use that has since been criticized by the very Congress that wanted to finesse the moral debate.[15]

Filling a Moral Vacuum

On January 7, 1991, the American College of Obstetricians and Gynecologists and the American Fertility Society announced that they would sponsor a National Advisory Board in Ethics of Reproduction to oversee both fetal transplantation research and studies in reproductive technologies on a voluntary basis. Congressman Waxman commented that private initiatives are welcome, but they cannot substitute for federal activity. "The Federal Government should be conducting this life-saving research, not ignoring it. Additionally, the Federal Government should be leading the way in the establishment of ethical guidelines."[16] Meanwhile, the promising reports on the outcome of fetal brain transplants into patients with Parkinson's disease will make keeping up with medical application difficult, and the technological imperative will have the last word.

---

[15] House Committee on Energy and Commerce, *Hearing before the Subcommittee on Health and the Environment, Fetal Tissue Transplantation Research* (1990).

[16] Hilts, *P. J. Groups Set Up Panel on Use of Fetal Tissue*, New York Times C3 (January 8, 1991).

Professor Russo's article explains the effects of unwanted child-bearing by exploring the negative physical, psychological, social and socioeconomic factors associated with unwanted pregnancies. In the United States 45% of women ages 15 to 44 have had at least one unintended pregnancy; 54% of pregnancies each year are unwanted, and over half of them are terminated. With statistics such as these, it is necessary to explore the ramifications of unintended pregnancies and unwanted childbearing. Many children of unwanted pregnancies are victims of abuse and criminal behavior. Additionally, about one million teenagers become pregnant each year, and five out of six of these pregnancies are unwanted. The children of these teenage mothers are at a much higher risk of neonatal death, mental retardation and low birth weight. Teenage parenthood is also correlated to "economic disadvantage," and many teenage mothers are single parents, which is linked to lower educational achievement in their children. Marital violence is also seen to increase during unintended pregnancy. Certainly, the risks of unwanted pregnancies to both the mother and child deserve careful examination. But, as Professor Russo details, so should we carefully examine the "psychological risk" of abortion compared to adoption.

24 · Psychological Aspects of Unwanted Pregnancy and Its Resolution _____

Nancy Felipe Russo, Ph.D.

Bearing and raising a child is a personal decision that requires a deep, long-lasting commitment. When that commitment is not made and a child is unwanted, there are substantial health, psychological, social and economic implications for the child, the mother, the family and society. There is no simple way to predict the reasons that a particular pregnancy may be unwanted or what a woman's psychological response may be after an unwanted pregnancy is resolved. This fact holds whether resolution comes through bearing and keeping the child, terminating the pregnancy or giving the child up for adoption.

Unwanted Childbearing

Although modern contraceptive methods are available, about 45% of U. S. women aged 15 to 44 have experienced at least one unintended pregnancy, that is, a pregnancy that was not wanted at the time it was conceived. An estimated 54% of pregnancies that occur each year are unintended; approximately half of them are terminated by legal abortion.[1]

A substantial proportion of unintended pregnancies become unwanted births, that is, births that are not wanted at the time or at any future time. Taking all pregnancies during the five years preceeding 1982, 37% of births to women ages 15 to 44 were unintended; of that number, 27% were unwanted (10% of all births).[2]

---

[1] Forrest, *Unintended pregnancy among American women,* 19, no. 2 Fam. Plan. Persp. 76–77 (1987).
[2] Forrest, *supra* note 1.

Women at greater risk for a variety of social problems—poor women, single women, young women and women of color—are overrepresented among women who have unintended pregnancies and unwanted births. Sixty-four percent of unintended pregnancies are to unmarried women, 32% to teenagers, 26% to black women.[3]

The proportion of unwanted births was higher before the legalization of abortion.[4] It is estimated that during the 1950s and 1960s, one in five births to married women was unwanted.[5] In the mid-1960s, these children began bearing children themselves. For the last two decades they have been in their childbearing years and will continue to be so over the coming decades.

Estimates of the numbers of unwanted children born in the United States will vary depending on the definitions used. Definitions of unwantedness, when applied to pregnancy and childbearing, are extremely complex. People change their minds—sometimes an unwanted pregnancy results in a wanted child, and vice-versa. It is possible to avoid becoming immersed in such complexities, however, by sticking to the question of whether or not being unwanted during pregnancy predicts a higher risk for psychological and social disadvantage for the parties involved.[6] The evidence suggests that it does.[7]

Correlates of Unwanted Childbearing

As seen in table 1, unwanted childbearing has a host of negative physical, psychological and social risks that will vary with the health, age and personality of the mother, her marital status, her relationship with others and her socioeconomic circumstances, among other factors. Health problems include increased risk for illness and death for both mother and child. The few available studies of women denied abortion suggest unwanted childbearing can have a profound and long-lasting psychological impact. In one investigation, one out of three women still actively resented the baby at a one-year follow-up.[8] Similarly, in another study of 95 women, one-third of the sample had not adjusted at a two-year follow-up; 6% of the women in that study had attempted suicide.[9]

In one study of 249 women interviewed seven years after they were denied a request for abortion, 11% of the sample had aborted the pregnancy illegally. Of the women who had given birth, 27% had not adjusted to the child at the time of the interview. The proportion not adjusting was higher for women who had not married the child's father: 58%.[10]

---

[3] Westoff, *Contraceptive paths toward the reduction of unintended pregnancy and abortion*, 20, no. 1 Fam. Plan. Persp. 4–13 (1988).

[4] Challenges to restrictive U.S. abortion laws intensified in the 1960s. In 1967, 13 states liberalized their abortion laws. By 1970, Alaska, Hawaii, New York and Washington in effect had abortion on request. In 1973, *Roe v. Wade* was decided, and abortion became legal, albeit not always accessible, throughout the nation. C. Tietze & S. K. Henshaw, *Induced abortion: A world review—1986* (6th ed. 1986).

[5] H. P. David, Z. Dytrych, Z. Matejcek & V. Schuller, *Born unwanted: Developmental effects of denied abortion* (1988).

[6] David et al., *supra* note 5, provides a detailed discussion of issues related to the definition of unintended, unplanned and unwanted pregnancies.

[7] David et al., *supra* note 5.

[8] Pare & Raven, *Follow-up of patients referred for termination*, 1 The Lancet 653–658 (1970).

[9] Visram, *A follow-up study of 95 women who were refused abortions on psychiatric grounds*, in *Proceedings of the Third International Congress of Psychosomatic Medicine in Obstetrics and Gynaecology, London* (N. Morris ed. 1971).

[10] Study described in David et al. *supra* note 5, at 47–48.

Table 1. A Portrait of Unwanted Childbearing

Correlates of unwanted childbearing
- Immaturity
- Poverty
- Social and educational disadvantage
- Marital conflict and instability
- Teenage childbearing
- Single parenthood
- Psychological and social disadvantage for mother and child

Unwanted children are more likely to
- Have chaotic and insecure family lives
- Suffer child abuse and neglect
- Be seen as anger prone and irritable by their teachers
- Be involved with drugs and alcohol as teenagers and display delinquent and criminal behavior
- Exhibit psychological distress and psychopathology and receive psychiatric services
- Have problems in educational achievement and job satisfaction
- Have earlier initial sexual experiences
- Have marital problems
- Be welfare recipients

Correlates of unwanted childbearing include poverty, forced marriage, teenage childbearing, single parenthood and marital conflict and disruption. Unwanted children are more likely to have chaotic and insecure family lives, perform more poorly in school, exhibit delinquent behavior and require treatment for symptoms of psychological distress and psychopathology. As adults, unwanted children have been found to be more likely to engage in criminal behavior, be welfare recipients and receive psychiatric services.[11–14]

Many of the most devastating effects associated with unwanted childbearing in both teenagers and adults reflect the fact that unwanted childbearing in the United States is associated with immaturity, poverty and marital instability. But even in intact families with good economic circumstances, unwanted children are at higher risk for psychological and social problems.

A classic, longitudinal study in Czechoslovakia[15] documented differences between children born to women after they were twice denied a request to abort the pregnancy and a matched control group at ages 9, 14–15 and 21–23. The unwanted children were found to be at higher risk for problems in educational achievement and job satisfaction. They were more likely to have poorer grades in school, be less liked by other children and be regarded by teachers and parents as more anger-prone and irritable. They were also more likely to be involved with drugs, alcohol and criminal behavior, have earlier initial sexual experiences and, if married, have marital problems.

---

[11] David et al., *supra* note 5.

[12] Forssman & Thuwe, *One hundred and twenty children born after application for therapeutic abortion refused,* 64 Acta Psychiatrica Scandinavica 142–146 (1966).

[13] Blomberg, *Influence of maternal distress during pregnancy on postnatal development,* 62 Acta Psychiatrica Scandinavica 405–417 (1980).

[14] Terhune, *A review of the actual and expected consequences of family size,* Calspan Report NO. DP-5333-G-1, USGPO (1975).

[15] David et al., *supra* note 5.

At age 21, compared to control children, these unwanted children were 1.5 times as likely to be registered for drunken misconduct, 1.9 times as likely to have experienced psychiatric consultation and hospitalization, 3.3 times more likely to be registered for a crime on a panel register and 2.2 times as likely to be registered for delinquency at a children's aid bureau. They were 5.7 times as likely to have received public assistance between the ages of 16 and 21. More than 1 out of 10 of the unwanted children were described as of "subnormal educability or ineducability," a figure double that for controls.[16]

CHILD ABUSE AND NEGLECT   In 1985, the Surgeon General's Workshop on Violence and the Public Health concluded that "the starting point for effective child abuse prevention is pregnancy planning."[17] Child maltreatment, including child abuse and neglect, has been conclusively and prospectively linked to unplanned and unwanted childbearing,[18–21] but the causal relationships are complex. Factors associated with reports of child maltreatment embrace psychological, sociological and environmental influences, including history of abuse, parental rigidity, unhappiness, loneliness, unrealistic expectations for children and the characteristics of the child, such as disabilities or ill health. Other correlates include poverty, marital conflict, spouse abandonment, single parenthood, illness, poor education and inadequate housing, transportation and health services.[22,23]

Researchers have found mothers of abused and neglected children to be more likely than controls to (1) have unplanned pregnancies; (2) have first births at a younger age; (3) have more births, (4) space their first two children more closely and (5) have more children by different fathers.[24,25]

Two of the strongest predictors of future child abuse are having two or more children under age five and less than a 12-month spacing between the first two births. Others include frequent changes in residency, a disturbed childhood, low self-image, unemployment, crowding and large family size.[26]

[16] David et al., *supra* note 5.

[17] Cron, *The Surgeon General's workshop on violence and public health: Review of the recommendations*, 101 Pub. Health Rep. 10, 8–14 (1986).

[18] Altemeier, O'Connor, Vietze, Sandler, & Sherrod, *Antecedents of child abuse*, 100 Behavioral Pediatrics 823–829 (1982).

[19] Egeland & Brunquell, *An at-risk approach to the study of child abuse*, 18 J. of the Am. Acad. of Child Psychiatry 219–235 (1979).

[20] Hunter, Kilstrom, Kraybill & Loda, *Antecedents of child abuse and neglect in premature infants: A prospective study in a newborn intensive care unit*, 61 Pediatrics 629–635 (1978).

[21] Murphy, Orkow & Nicola, *Prediction of child abuse and neglect: A prospective study*, 9 Child Abuse and Neglect 225–235 (1985).

[22] For a review of this literature, see Smith, *Significant research findings in the etiology of child abuse*, Soc. Casework 337–346 (June 1984).

[23] Williams, *Child abuse reconsidered: The urgency of authentic prevention*, 12, no. 3 J. of Clin. Child Psychology 312–319 (1983).

[24] For a summary of these studies, see Zuravin, *Unplanned pregnancies, family planning programs, and child maltreatment*, Fam. Relations 135–139 (April 1987).

[25] Zuravin, *Fertility patterns: Their relationship to child physical abuse and child neglect*, 50 J. of Marriage and the Fam. 983–993 (November 1988).

[26] Altemeier, O'Connor, Vietze, Sandler, & Sherrod, *Prediction of child abuse: A prospective study of feasibility*, 8 Child Abuse and Neglect 393–400 (1984).

Table 2. The Link Between Unwanted Childbearing and Child Maltreatment

Fertility-related predictors of child abuse and neglect
- Unplanned pregnancy
- Ambivalence toward pregnancy
- Younger age at first birth
- Two or more children under age five
- Large family size
- Close spacing (less than 12 months) between first two births
- More children by different fathers
- Crowding

Some factors are more predictive for neglect; others, for abuse. Among single mothers on public assistance, the number of unplanned pregnancies appears to be a better predictor of neglect, close spacing a better predictor of abuse.[27]

Unwanted pregnancy's contribution to risk for child maltreatment is significant. One study found that 80% of parents at high risk for abusing and neglecting their children had been ambivalent toward them during pregnancy, compared to 29% of parents not at high risk for abuse.[28] Nonetheless, as G.J.R. Williams has pointed out, "[W]hile not wanting the pregnancy or the child is a parental attitude related to child abuse, wanting the pregnancy and the child is insufficient to prevent abuse."[29] Abusive mothers can view pregnancy and motherhood as ways to define their identity and of providing the security they themselves were denied during their own childhoods.[30]

Child maltreatment occurs in all racial and ethnic groups and at all levels of socio-economic circumstance. No one factor is necessary or sufficient to determine abuse or neglect. It is a combination of negative life events and circumstances, including a chaotic lifestyle, severe crises, a history of abuse during the parent's childhood, ambivalence toward the pregnancy and social isolation that predicts higher risk for child maltreatment.[31]

Consequences of abuse   Physically abused children are more likely to exhibit chronic aggressive behavior, attribute negative hostile intentions to others and be unable to solve interpersonal problems.[32] What happens to abused and neglected children when they grow up and become parents themselves? Again, it is important to recognize diversity in this population and avoid stereotyping. However, one study found that white low-income mothers who reported a childhood history of child maltreatment were more likely to report feeling unwanted and unloved as children. Such mothers also were more likely to have lower self-images, more feelings of isolation and aggressive tendencies and more problems with interpersonal relationships at home and at work than control low-income mothers.[33]

These mothers were asked if they had ever become so angry that they had lashed out and done things they were sorry about, and if so, what? Forty-one percent reported

---

[27] For a discussion of this literature, see Zuravin, *supra* note 25.

[28] Murphy et al., *supra* note 21.

[29] Williams, *supra* note 23, at 316.

[30] Williams, *supra* note 23.

[31] Murphy et al., *supra* note 21.

[32] Dodge, Bates & Petit, *Mechanisms in the cycle of violence,* 250 Science 1678–83 (December 21, 1990).

[33] Altemeier, O'Connor, Sherrod, Tucker & Vietze, *Outcome of abuse during childhood among pregnant low income women,* 10 Child Abuse and Neglect 319–30 (1986).

they regretted hitting their children with their hand or object somewhere other than on legs, buttock or hands. This figure is 2½ times the figure of 17% for the control mothers.[34]

Severe abuse during childhood underlies many kinds of dysfunction in youth as well as in adulthood. As Fontana has observed:

> *The teenage delinquents, alcoholics, drug addicts, and prostitutes on our streets are for the most part products of multiproblem homes where they suffered abuse and neglect. They are throwaway, runaway, kicked-out children. They are children who commit suicide. They are children who assault, rob, and murder . . .*[35]

About one in ten homicide arrests are of juveniles. In 1989, 2,208 murders were committed by minors, most of them by boys. Recent research has confirmed that juvenile murderers are more likely than other children to have either witnessed domestic violence or to have themselves experienced child abuse.[36]

People who were abused and neglected as children are overrepresented in psychiatric populations. One study found approximately half of psychiatric inpatients in their sample to have indications of physical or sexual abuse in their charts.[37,38] Another study involving in-depth structured interviews with 100 inpatients found 81 of them to have experienced some kind of physical or sexual assault during childhood; 49% of these patients experienced more than 20 episodes of assault.[39]

Children who were unwanted at birth in the 1950s and 1960s have now grown up and are becoming parents themselves. What kind of parents are they? Research to date has been insufficient to answer that question. Although some of the work on child abuse is relevant, thorough and systematic scientific study of the intergenerational consequences of unwanted childbearing continues to be needed. Society's rising rates of psychological and social problems that have been correlated with increasing numbers of unwanted children entering their teens and then adulthood lends urgency to such research.

TEENAGE PREGNANCY AND CHILDBEARING   One out of ten U. S. women aged 15 to 19 experiences pregnancy each year—about a million teenagers annually. About five out of six of these pregnancies are unintended. The proportion of unintended pregnancy is higher for black teenagers—nine out of ten of such pregnancies are unintended.[40,41]

The gap between white and minority teenagers' rates of unwanted pregnancy is of particular concern, for it is increasing. For white teenagers above age 15, both abortion and birth rates declined between 1980 and 1987. In contrast, both abortion and birth rates for ethnic minority teenagers increased during that period. In 1987, 62% of preg-

---

[34] Altemeier et al., *supra* note 33.

[35] Fontana, *Child abuse, past, present, and future,* Human Ecology Forum 5–7, (n.d.).

[36] Ewing, *Kids who kill* (1990).

[37] Carmen, Reiker & Mills, *Victims of violence and psychiatric illness,* 141, no. 3 Am. J. of Psychiatry 378–382 (1984).

[38] Jacobson & Richardson, *Assault experiences of 100 psychiatric inpatients,* 144 Am. J. of Psychiatry 908–913 (1987).

[39] Jacobson & Richardson, *supra* note 38.

[40] Henshaw & Van Vort, 21 Fam. Plan. Persp. 85–88 (1989).

[41] Trussell, *Teenage pregnancy in the United States,* 20, no. 6 Fam. Plan. Persp. 262–272 (1988).

Table 3. A Portrait of Teenage Childbearing

Correlates of teenage childbearing
- Enduring poverty
- Social and educational disadvantage
- Inadequate prenatal care
- Health problems, including pregnancy-induced hypertension for the mother and low birth weight and higher risk of death in infancy for the child
- Limited educational and employment achievement
- Early marriage and marital disruption
- Larger family sizes

Children of teenage mothers are more likely to
- Experience child neglect
- Display lower intelligence and repeat a grade
- Show poorer adjustment to school and exhibit delinquent behavior
- Live in homes not headed by their biological parents
- Live with a single parent
- Have social and emotional problems, including problems relating to peers
- Smoke, drink and use drugs as teenagers
- Become teenage parents themselves

nancies to white teenagers resulted in abortion, compared to 50% of pregnancies to minority teenagers.[42]

Consequences to teenage mothers   Teenage pregnancy is correlated with inadequate prenatal care and nutrition, poverty and lack of education. As a result, teenage mothers are at risk for a host of health, psychological, social and economic problems.[43] Such mothers are more likely than older mothers to experience pregnancy-induced hypertension, preeclampsia and perinatal death.[44,45] Although high quality medical care can greatly reduce health risks to mother and child,[46] such care is not accessible to all teenagers, particularly black teenagers who live in poverty.

Educational attainment predicts welfare dependency and enduring poverty. Teenage mothers are more likely than older mothers to experience limited educational and employment achievements. The younger the mother, the greater the decrement.[47,48] Teenage childbearing, whether or not it ends in keeping the child or placing it for adoption, is associated with a subsequent deterioration of self-esteem and quality of life for the teenage mother.[49] Teenage childbearing is also associated with early marriage, with its subsequent higher risk for marital disruption,[50] and larger family sizes.[51]

[42] Henshaw, Koonin & Smith, *Characteristics of U.S. women having abortions, 1987*, 23, no. 2 Fam. Plan. Persp. 75–81 (1991).

[43] *Risking the future: Adolescent sexuality, pregnancy, and childbearing*, Vols. 1–2 (Hofferth & Hayes eds. 1987).

[44] Strobino, *The health and medical consequences of adolescent sexuality and pregnancy: A review of the literature*, in Hofferth & Hayes, *supra* note 43, at 93–122.

[45] Hofferth, *The children of teen childbearers*, in Hofferth & Hayes, *supra* note 43, 174–206.

[46] Makinson, *The health consequences of teenage fertility*, 17, no. 3 Fam. Plan. Persp. 132–39 (1985).

[47] Hofferth & Hayes, *supra* note 43.

[48] Baldwin & Cain, *The children of teenaged parents*, 12, no. 1 Fam. Plan. Persp. 34–43 (1980).

[49] McLaughlin, Manninen & Winges, *Do adolescents who relinquish their children fare better or worse than those who raise them?* 20, no. 1 Fam. Plan. Persp. 25–32 (1988).

Many women do overcome the disadvantages associated with adolescent mother-hood, and it is important to avoid stereotypes that may impede that recovery—but a large proportion do not. Further, even if a mother works to overcome such disadvantages, her children are still at risk for a variety of problems. One study found that second-generation teenage mothers appear less likely to escape poverty than first-generation teenage mothers.[52] In that study, nearly half of the first-born female offspring of teenage mothers became pregnant before the age of 19, and about one-third of first-born male offspring reported impregnating someone before that age.

Children of teenage mothers Babies born to teenage mothers are more likely to be of low birth weight and to experience birth injury, mental retardation and neonatal death. Twice as many infants of mothers 10 to 14 years of age are low birth weight than infants of mothers aged 20 to 24. Infants of teenage mothers, particularly if they are not the first infant, are more likely to die in infancy than are babies of older mothers and are at greater risk for a fatal accident before age one.[53–55]

Although teenage mothers do not appear to be more likely to physically abuse their children than mothers in their twenties, they are more likely to exhibit various types of child neglect, such as inadequate nutrition and lack of attention to health care.[56]

In addition to health risks, children born to teenage mothers have psychological and social risks, partially because of lack of education and employment opportunities for their mothers.[57] On average, such children have lower intelligence and academic achievement, as well as poorer adjustment to school (including suspension, running away, being stopped by police and inflicting a serious injury on someone else).[58,59] These children are also more likely to live in homes not headed by their biological parents, and this is associated with lower intelligence test scores.[60] Children of teenage mothers are at higher risk for living with a single parent, repeating a grade, having social and emotional problems, smoking, drinking and using drugs and becoming teenage parents themselves.[61–63]

The effects on social behavior of having a teenage mother are greater for boys than girls, especially among black children, and such effects appear to increase over time. On average, male offspring of black teenage mothers appear more openly hostile and

---

[50] Card & Wise, *Teenage mothers and teenage fathers: The impact of early childbearing on the parents' personal and professional lives,* 10, no. 4 Fam. Plan. Persp. 199–207 (1978).

[51] Furstenberg Jr., Brooks-Gunn & Morgan, *Adolescent mothers and their children in later life,* 19, no. 4 Fam. Plan. Persp. 142–151 (1987).

[52] Furstenberg Jr., Levine & Brooks-Gunn, *The children of teenage mothers: Patterns of early childbearing in two generations,* 22, no. 2 Fam. Plan. Persp. 54–61 (1990).

[53] Strobino, *supra* note 44.

[54] Makinson, *supra* note 46.

[55] Hofferth, *supra* note 45.

[56] Miller, *The relationship between adolescent childbearing and child maltreatment,* 63, no. 6 Child Welfare 553–557 (1984).

[57] Hofferth, *Social and economic consequences of teenage childbearing,* in Hofferth & Hayes, *supra* note 43 at 123–44 (1987).

[58] Furstenberg & Brooks-Gunn, *Adolescent fertility: Causes, consequences, and remedies,* in *Applications of social science to clinical medicine and health policy* (Aiken & Mechanic eds. 1985).

[59] Hofferth, *supra* note 57.

[60] *Id.*

[61] Baldwin & Cain, *supra* note 48.

[62] Hofferth, *supra* note 57.

[63] Furstenberg & Brooks-Gunn, *supra* note 58.

Table 4. The Deleterious Effects of Too Many Children

Correlates of larger family size
- Social, educational and economic disadvantage on the part of parents
- Lower marital satisfaction on the part of parents
- Single parenthood
- Child maltreatment
- Antisocial behavior, delinquency and criminality on the part of the child
- Lowered intelligence and limited academic achievement

aggressive and have greater difficulty relating to peers than male offspring of older black mothers. In contrast, female children of black adolescent mothers are more likely to express more fearfulness and other symptoms of psychological distress than the female children of older black mothers.[64]

Teenage parenthood is linked to economic disadvantage. Mothers receiving Aid for Dependent Children are more likely to have borne children when they were in adolescence than U.S. women in general. An estimated 56%–60% of the public assistance caseload is attributable to families begun by a first birth to an adolescent. It is estimated that in 1985, public outlays attributable to families begun by teenage mothers totaled between $15.7 to $18.84 billion.[65]

FAMILY SIZE   In addition to their association with unwanted pregnancy and child abuse, larger family sizes have been linked to other social, educational and economic disadvantages, including antisocial behavior, delinquency and criminality. Intelligence and academic achievement of children is inversely correlated with family size, and these effects appear to hold even when social class is controlled.[66] These findings reflect effects of number of children as well as later birth orders.[67,68] Also, larger family sizes are associated with lower marital satisfaction, an important predictor of marital disruption.[69]

Family size is as important as socioeconomic and marital status in promoting educational attainment and achievement. After a major review of five large data sets encompassing information on 22,950 individuals, J. Blake concluded: "On average, children from large families have less ability, lower grades, and apparently receive less academic encouragement from their parents, even when parental background and 'advantages' in the home are controlled. Large families are considerably more deleterious to child's educational attainment than are broken [sic] homes . . ."[70]

On average, the larger the family size, the lower the education of the parents and the lower the income.[71] Furthermore, the economic disadvantage associated with larger family size is greater for women of color. For example, in 1988, among married couple

---

[64] Hofferth, *supra* note 45, at 193.

[65] Burt & Levy, *Estimates of public costs for teenage childbearing: A review of recent studies and estimates of 1985 public costs,* in Hofferth & Hayes, *supra* note 43, at 264–93 (1987).

[66] Terhune, *supra* note 14.

[67] Belmont & Marolla, *Birth order, family size, and intelligence,* 182 Science 1096–1101 (1973).

[68] Terhune, *supra* note 14.

[69] Anderson, Russell & Schumm, *Perceived marital quality and family life-cycle categories: A further analysis,* J. of Marriage and the Fam. 127–39 (February 1983).

[70] Blake, *Family size and the quality of children,* 18, no. 4 Demography 441, 421–442 (1981).

[71] U. S. Bureau of the Census (1989).

Table 5. A Portrait of Single Parenthood

Correlates of single parenthood
* Poverty
* Social and educational disadvantage
* Larger family size
* More sources of life stress
* Higher rates of psychological distress for the mother, including depression and anxiety

Children of single parents are more likely to
* Be of lower birth weight
* Have lower educational and economic achievement
* Have sexual intercourse, smoke cigarettes and use marijuana at younger ages
* Have their first child at a younger age
* Become single parents themselves

families where husbands are the sole wage earners, whites had $14,600 to spend per child. Comparable black couples had 61% of that amount to spend per child, Hispanic couples, 55%.

SINGLE PARENTHOOD   Family structure has changed, and the number of single-parent households has increased rapidly over the last decade. Of the 9.4 million single-parent families in 1988, 87% were headed by women. Of these women, 57% were separated or divorced, 33% had never married.[72,73]

Births to unmarried women of all ages have increased since 1970, with the fastest rate of increase among births to white women. Birth rates are higher for black unmarried women: 85 per 1,000 compared to 17 per 1,000 for comparable white women.

In 1988, 24% of the 63.2 million children in the United States lived with a single parent—54% of black children and 30% of Hispanic children, compared to 19% of white children. Among children under 6 years of age, 61% of black children were living with one parent, compared to 17% of white children.[74]

Cross-sectional statistics involving family structure can be misleading. Over time children may spend part of their lives in both types of family structure. White women are more likely to maintain a female-headed household because of divorce than black women, who are more likely to be never married and come to head a family through teenage childbearing. As a consequence, black children spend more of their lives in single-parent families than white children.[75] Seventy percent of white children have spent all of their first 15 years in two-parent households, compared to 22% of black children.[76]

Unfortunately, much of the research on the effects of single parenthood does not make distinctions between the paths to single parenthood (nonmarital pregnancy vs. marital dissolution), nor does it take into account timing and spacing of childbirth.

[72] Saluter, *Singleness in America,* Stud. in Marriage and the Fam. 1–12, Current Population Reports, Series P-23, No. 162, USGPO (1989).

[73] Rawlings, *Single parents and their children,* Stud. in Marriage and the Fam. 13–25, Current Population Reports, Series P-23, No. 162, USGPO (1989).

[74] Saluter, *supra* note 72.

[75] Krein & Beller, *Educational attainment of children from single-parent families: Differences by exposure, gender, and race,* 25, no. 2 Demography 221–32 (1988).

[76] Duncan & Rodgers, *Single-parent families: Are their economic problems transitory or persistent?* 19, no. 4 Fam. Plan. Persp. 178, 171–76 (1987).

Whatever the path to single parenthood, the economic problems of single-parent families can be persistent and severe. The lower the education and income of a family, the greater their likelihood of marital instability.[77] One out of two single mothers lives below the poverty line. The low educational attainment and low earning capacity of single mothers, lack of child support from fathers and inadequate public assistance combine to mire single-mother families in economic disadvantage.[78] Poverty rates are higher for black single-parent families. In 1983, more than 40% of black children in such families lived in poverty; for white children the figure was 23%. In contrast, 22% of black children and 5% percent of white children in two-parent households lived in poverty.[79,80]

Among single mothers, average family size is larger for blacks than for whites; the likelihood of such black mothers having three or more children is double that of comparable white mothers.[81,82]

Compared to married mothers, divorced single mothers have been found to report more sources of life stress related to economic, family and personal health problems and more symptoms of depression and anxiety, even after controlling for income.[83] Changes in residence, shown to be risk factors for child abuse, are a common source of instability in single-parent households. One study found that about 38% of mothers experienced a move during their first year after divorce. After that first year, residential shifts continued to be about 20% higher than those of two-parent families.[84]

Many single-parent families are characterized by positive adjustment and well-being.[85] However, as a group, women and children in single-parent families are at greater risk for the health, psychological, social and environmental problems associated with teenage childbearing, larger family sizes and poverty status, including higher rates of psychopathology and violent and antisocial behavior.[86,87]

Children of single mothers   Births to single mothers, especially black single mothers, are more likely to entail low birth-weight babies, with the higher risk for the health, psychological and social problems that low birth weight implies.[88] In 1983, the risk of having a very low birth weight baby (under 1,500 g) was 11.1 per 1,000 live births for unmarried white women; the comparable figure for married white women was 6.9 per

---

[77] Staples, *Social structure in black female life,* 17 J. of Black Stud. 267–86 (1987).

[78] McLanahan & Booth, *Mother-only families: Problems, prospects, and politics* 51 J. of Marriage and the Fam. 557–580 (August 1989).

[79] Bumpass & Sweet, *Children's experience in single-parent families: Implications of cohabitation and marital transitions,* 21, no. 6 Fam. Plan. Persp. 256–260 (1989).

[80] Duncan, & Rodgers, *supra* note 76.

[81] Krein & Beller, *supra* note 75.

[82] U. S. Bureau of the Census, Current Population Reports, series P-20. No. 437 (1988).

[83] Compas & Williams, *Stress, coping, and adjustment in mothers and young adolescents in single- and two-parent families,* 18, no. 4 Am. J. of Community Psychology 525–45 (1990).

[84] McLanahan, *Family structure and stress: A longitudinal comparison of two-parent and female-headed families,* 45 J. of Marriage and the Fam. 347–57 (1983).

[85] Green & Crooks, *Family member adjustment and family dynamics in established single-parent and two-parent families,* Social Service Review 600–613 (December 1988).

[86] Moilanen & Rantakallio, *The single parent family and the child's mental health,* 27, no. 2 Soc. Sci. Med. 181–86, (1988).

[87] Dornbusch, Carlsmith, Bushwall, Ritter, Leiderman, Hastorf & Gross, *Single parents, extended households, and the control of adolescents,* 56 Child Development 326–41 (1985).

[88] See Hofferth & Hayes, *supra* note 43, for a discussion.

1,000. Among blacks, the comparable figures were 23.6 and 17.5 per 1,000 for unmarried and married women, respectively.[89]

Living in a single-parent family is correlated with lower educational achievement of children. This effect is stronger the longer one lives in a single-parent family, is greatest during the preschool years and is larger for boys than girls.[90] Research has also found teenagers in one-parent households are more likely than those in two-parent households to have sexual intercourse, smoke cigarettes and use marijuana.[91] As adults, children born in mother-only families are more likely to be poor, to have their first child at a younger age and to become single parents themselves.[92,93]

In conclusion, in the United States, adverse circumstances associated with unwanted childbearing are disproportionately experienced by women who are poor, ethnic minority, single or young—that is, those who are least likely to have access to effective contraception or a voice in the making of the laws and policies affecting their reproductive alternatives.

The Experience of Pregnancy

Unwanted pregnancy is a stressful event no matter how it is resolved. The idea that pregnancy is always a beautiful and fulfilling experience for women is one of our culture's most pervasive myths. However, the reality of the experience is different for many women. A woman's response to her pregnancy and its method of resolution will reflect the resources—physical, psychological, social and financial—she has for dealing with negative life events. It will also reflect the pregnancy's meaning to the woman and her comfort with her decision-making process.[94]

Pregnancy—whether it is wanted or unwanted—is a stressful life event. As such, it can exacerbate problems for women with histories of mental disorder.[95] Psychological problems during and after pregnancy most often occur in women who have a history of such disorders, regardless of the method of resolution.[96]

The stress of unwanted pregnancy can be compounded by many other sources of stress in the woman's familial and social context. As Schwartz has pointed out, a pregnant woman may realize she is already stretching her and her family's coping resources to the limit in dealing with a host of pressures and problems and be unable to add the additional burden of another child.[97] Researchers have typically failed to separate wanted

---

[89] Kleinman & Kessel, *Racial differences in low birth weight: Trends and risk factors* 317 New Eng. J. of Med. 749–53 (1987).

[90] Krein & Beller, *supra* note 75.

[91] Flewelling & Bauman, *Family structure as a predictor of initial substance use and sexual intercourse in early adolescence,* 52 J. of Marriage and the Fam. 171–181 (1990).

[92] McLanahan & Booth, *supra* note 78.

[93] Mueller & Cooper, *Children of single parent families: How they fare as young adults,* 35 Fam. Rel. 169–76 (January 1986).

[94] Adler, David, Major, Roth, Russo & Wyatt, *Psychological responses after abortion,* 248 Science 41–44 (1990).

[95] Schwartz, *Abortion on request: The psychiatric implications,* in *Abortion, Medicine, and the Law* 323–340 (Butler & Walbert, eds. 3rd ed. 1986).

[96] Hamilton, Parry & Blumenthal, *The menstrual cycle in context: I. Affective syndromes associated with reproductive hormonal changes,* 49 J. of Clin. Psychology 474–80 (1988).

[97] Schwartz, *supra* note 95.

from unwanted pregnancies in examining the effects of these factors on pregnant women. Given the correlates of unwanted childbearing, women with unwanted pregnancies would be expected to have greater exposure to stressful negative life events than other pregnant women, including exposure to marital violence, drugs and AIDS.

Marital Quality and Intimate Violence

Marital quality has an impact on the mental health of both women and their children.[98] Conflict between parents has been connected to psychopathology in children, including acting out in boys and withdrawal in girls. In particular, the parents' ability to handle negative emotions is a central cause of marital distress that directly affects child functioning.[99] One reflection of the inability to deal with anger and other negative emotions is intimate violence, which is pervasive in the United States. Best estimates suggest that about 31% of married women report violence in their recent relationships.[100]

The phenomenon of violence during pregnancy has been recognized for more than a decade.[101] A national study found that about 17% of pregnant women experienced violence during the previous year compared to 12% of nonpregnant women. The difference appears to reflect the fact that women are most likely to become pregnant during ages when they are at highest risk for experiencing violence.[102] In another study, 23% of "healthy" women attending prenatal clinics were found to have been battered before or during the pregnancy; 10.3% of these battered women reported that the battering increased during pregnancy.[103]

Other research suggests an estimated 42% of women entering battered women shelters have been battered during pregnancy, with injuries including slaps, kicks and punches to genitals and abdomen. More than one in four (29%) of these battered women reported that violence increased during their pregnancy, violence that was directed toward their fetuses as well as towards themselves.[104]

CHILDREN OF BATTERED WOMEN   Children born to battered women are more likely to be of low birth weight, even after controlling for race, smoking, alcohol consumption, prenatal care and maternal complications.[105] In one study of women delivering at public and private hospitals, an estimated 12% to 18% of battered women delivered low birth-weight babies.[106] In addition to the obvious physical effects on the woman and her

---

[98] E.McGrath, G. P. Keita, B. R. Strickland & N. F. Russo, *Women and depression: Risk factors and treatment issues* (1990).

[99] *See* Howes & Markman, *Marital quality and child functioning: A longitudinal investigation,* 60 Child Dev. 1044–51 (1989), for a summary of these findings.

[100] Koss, *The women's mental health research agenda: Violence against women,* 45 Am. Psychologist 375, 374–80 (1990).

[101] Gelles, *Violence and pregnancy: A note on the extent of the problem and needed services,* 24 Fam. Coordinator 81–86 (1975).

[102] Gelles, *Violence and pregnancy: Are pregnant women at greater risk of abuse?* 6 J. of Marriage and the Fam. 841–47 (August 1988).

[103] Helton, McFarlane & Anderson, *Battered and pregnant: A prevalence study,* 77, no. 10 Am. J. of Pub. Health 1337–39 (1987).

[104] McFarlane, *Battering during pregnancy: Tip of an iceberg revealed,* 15, no. 3 Women & Health 69–83 (1989).

[105] McFarlane, *supra* note 104.

[106] Described in McFarlane, *supra* note 104.

fetus, violence has both immediate and long-term psychological effects.[107] And as we have seen, a history of violence is "a strong risk factor for the development of . . . lifetime mental health problems."[108]

Drug Abuse and AIDS

Physical abuse during pregnancy is correlated with drug abuse and alcohol abuse during pregnancy.[109] One study of adolescent mothers found that those who used illicit drugs during pregnancy were more than 2½ times as likely to be exposed to physical abuse as were pregnant adolescents who did not use drugs (24% compared with 9%). Pregnant adolescent drug users were also more likely to be African-Americans, report more negative life events (violent and nonviolent) and have histories of venereal disease and of elective abortion.[110]

The link between pregnancy and intravenous (IV) drug abuse means that AIDS has become a source of chronic reproductive-related stress, particularly among ethnic minority women. Women are 7% of individuals diagnosed with AIDS; 70% of those women are ethnic minority (black, white and Hispanic women comprise 49%, 30% and 20% of women with AIDS, respectively).[111] In 1988, 80%, 74% and 52% of AIDS cases among Hispanic, black and white women, respectively, were IV drug-related. That year black and Hispanic children accounted for 55% and 20% of pediatric AIDS cases, respectively.[112] Meanwhile, the proportions of black and Hispanic children in the U.S. population that year were only 15% and 11%. Intravenous drug use by pregnant women was implicated in 72%, 62% and 31% of pediatric AIDS cases among Hispanic, black and white children, respectively.[113]

Abortion

Unintended pregnancies are often unwanted pregnancies but not necessarily so. As we have seen, it is possible to define "unwanted pregnancy" in a variety of ways. One clear way is to define it behaviorally, that is, pregnancies are defined as unwanted when women seek to abort them.

Reasons Pregnancies are Unwanted

Understanding why a particular woman's pregnancy may be unwanted requires looking at her pregnancy in her particular psychological, social and economic context.

---

[107] Koss, *supra* note 100.

[108] D. G. Kilpatrick, L. J. Veronen, B. E. Saunders, C. L. Best, A. Amick-McMullan & J. Paduhovich, *The psychological impact of crime: A study of randomly surveyed crime victims* (Final report on grant No. 84–IJ–CX–0039) (1987) (cited in Koss, *supra* note 100).

[109] Amaro, Fried, Cabral & Zuckerman, *Violence during pregnancy and substance abuse*, 80, no. 5 Am. J. of Pub. Health 575–79 (1990).

[110] Amaro, Zuckerman & Cabral, *Drug use among adolescent mothers: Profile of risk*, 84, no. 1 Pediatrics 144–51 (1989).

[111] Fullilove, *Ethnic minority women and AIDS*, 2, no. 2 Multicultural Inquiry and Research on AIDS (MIRA) Newsletter 4–5 (1988).

[112] R. M. Selik, K. G. Castro & M. Pappaioanou, *Distribution of AIDS Cases, by Racial/Ethnic Group and Exposure Category, United States, June 1, 1981–July 4, 1988,* MMWR CDC (1988).

[113] Selik et al. *supra* note 112.

Research on women who seek abortions suggests that pregnancy decision-making involves weighing multiple factors: More than 9 out of 10 women (93 percent) give more than one reason for their decision to terminate their pregnancy. On average, women give four different reasons.[114]

As Lemkau has observed, ''abortion decisions emerge within the complex web of a women's relationships and life choices.'' [115] These decisions typically reflect women's roles and circumstances, including life stage (one out of four U.S. abortion patients is a teenager), lack of stability in relationships (six out of ten are unmarried), commitments to others (nearly one out of two are mothers) and economic circumstances (one out of three have incomes of less than $11,000 per year).[116]

Overall, not being ready for how a baby would change their lives (76%), not being able to afford a baby (68%) and wanting to avoid single parenthood or having problems with partner relationships (51%) are reasons most often given by U.S. women for seeking abortions.[117]

Such summary statistics fail to communicate the diversity of circumstances for women who decide that their pregnancy is unwanted. Yet recognizing women's diversity is the key to informed discussion of the possible effects of abortion, adoption and unwanted childbearing.

WOMEN WHO SEEK ABORTION AND WHY   Race, ethnicity and socioeconomic status are all related to seeking abortion. Henshaw provides a more detailed description of the characteristics of U.S. abortion patients.[118] Several aspects of those characteristics with particular implications for understanding outcomes of unwanted pregnancy are mentioned below.

Minors   More than one out of ten abortion patients are minors, and most of these minors are unmarried (99%). Many issues related to informed consent and reproductive outcome differ for unmarried minors, so that it is important to separate them from older age groups in discussions of effects of abortion.[119]

Unmarried minors who seek abortion are more likely to be white (64%), enrolled in school (86%), with no previous births (91%). When asked their most important reasons for seeking abortion, most minors say they are not ready for childrearing (76%), are not mature enough to raise a child (61%), need to stay in school (37%) and cannot afford a baby (28%). The abortion decision of such minors thus can be understood in the context of avoiding the negative outcomes of teenage pregnancy and preparing themselves to be able to provide a home for their future children.

Such a portrait of the minor abortion patient, which reflects the ''average'' patient, hides substantial variation in the role obligations and life circumstances of these young women, however. For many teenagers, it appears to take the actual experience of unplanned childbearing to bring home the difficulties of single parenthood. Research has found that unmarried pregnant teenagers are least likely to choose abortion if they have

---

[114]Torres & Forrest, *Why do women have abortions?* 20, no. 4 Fam. Plan. Persp. 169–76 (1988).

[115]Lemkau, *Emotional sequelae of abortion: Implications for clinical practice,* 12 Psychology of Women Q. 461–72 (1988).

[116]Torres & Forrest, *supra* note 114.

[117]Torres & Forrest, *supra* note 114.

[118]See Henshaw, *Abortion Services in the United States, 1987 and 1988* in this volume.

[119]Russo, *Adolescent abortion: The epidemiological context,* in *Adolescent abortion: Psychological and legal issues* 40–73 (G. B. Melton ed. 1986).

no previous births or abortions, are poor and have low levels of education.[120] Thus, nearly one out of ten unmarried minor abortion patients is already a mother; more than 15% of these patients (who have yet to reach their 18th birthday) have two or more children. Their decision to terminate their pregnancy must be understood in the context of their responsibilities and commitments to their current children.

The opportunities and resources for these unmarried minors who are mothers are also more limited than for those who are nonmothers. Compared to nonmothers, they are more likely to be black (62% vs. 25%) or Hispanic (17% vs. 8%) and have family incomes of less than $11,000 a year (53% vs. 30%). Such mothers are also less likely to be enrolled in school (62% vs. 89%) than nonmothers.

Thus, restrictive abortion policies would clearly have an effect on all pregnant unmarried minors but would have a disproportionate impact on the ability of teenage mothers of color to manage their stresses and their struggles against their social and economic disadvantages. The finding that unmarried teenagers are more likely to abort their second pregnancy than their first underscores the importance of educational programs that will fully inform teenagers about the realities of teenage parenthood. It should not be necessary to experience the realities before learning to avoid them.

Adults   There are also substantial variations in opportunities, resources and responsibilities among adult women who seek abortion depending on whether they are unmarried or married, mothers or nonmothers. Unmarried women (who comprise 79% of adult abortion patients) have more role commitments and fewer opportunities and resources than married women: They are more likely to be students (27% vs. 8%), be employed outside the home (74% vs. 66%) and have family incomes of less than $11,000 per year (37% vs. 20%). One out of five unmarried adult abortion patients (21%) cite the desire to avoid single parenthood among their most important reasons for seeking abortion.[121]

More than one out of two adult abortion patients (52%) are mothers. Marriage and motherhood do not necessarily go together for women who seek abortion. Of the mothers who seek abortion, more than two out of three (67%) are not married, and their seeking of abortion must be considered in the context of their seeking to avoid compounding consequences of single parenthood for their current children in addition to themselves. Unmarried mothers are more likely to be black or Hispanic than unmarried nonmothers—in fact, although black women are 28% of adult abortion patients, they are 40% of unmarried mothers who seek abortion.[122]

Some of the reasons mothers seek abortion overlap with those of nonmothers, whether or not they are married. When the four groups are compared—unmarried mothers and nonmothers, married mothers and nonmothers—economic issues and relationship problems cross all four groups. The proportion of women reporting not being able to afford a baby ranges from 34% for married mothers to 44% for unmarried nonmothers. Similarly, the proportion mentioning problems with their partners ranges from 17% for married mothers to 28% for married nonmothers.[123]

---

[120] Joyce, *The social and economic correlates of pregnancy resolution among adolescents in New York City, by race and ethnicity: A multivariate analysis,* 78, no. 6 Am. J. of Pub. Health 626–31 (1988).

[121] Russo, Horn & Schwartz, *U.S. abortion in context: Selected characteristics and motivations of women seeking abortions, Journal of Social Issues,* 48 (1982).

[122] *Id.*

[123] *Id.*

Fetus-related health reasons for abortion (including effects of prescription medicine or other toxins and diagnosed fetal defect) are more often mentioned by married non-mothers—24% mention this reason, a figure more than double that of women in the other three groups. One out of ten married mothers seeks abortion due to her own health problems, compared to 3% to 7% percent of women in the other groups.[124]

Unmarried nonmothers are eight times more likely to say they are not mature enough to raise a child than members of the other groups.[125] As one woman described on learning of her pregnancy:

> *I knew that my responsibility now extended beyond just myself. I was not financially or emotionally capable of providing a child with the kind of life it deserved, and I could not in good conscience bring such a child into the world.*[126]

Mothers in general are more likely to say they are seeking abortions to meet responsibilities to others, whether they are married (17%) or unmarried (19%).[127] Motivations of mothers who seek abortion have thus not substantially changed from those so eloquently expressed in a woman's letter to her brother prior to her death from an illegal abortion in 1934. She bled to death when her family doctor, a Catholic, refused to treat her when he realized the cause of her hemorrhaging:

> *Last week I realized that I am going to have another baby. Maybe I'm happy; but mostly I'm scared . . . Is it fair to have children we can't feed properly; can't keep decently warm, or give them medical attention when they become critically ill? . . . Must I keep having children whether we want them or not? I find myself constantly day-dreaming of a way to give my children the things I always wanted both you and Jane [her siblings] to have, like a Mama and a Papa, and a home and the love that children need. Children are so wonderful. I think only those should be born who will have a fair chance at life.*[128]

Black unmarried mothers who seek abortion bear substantial childrearing responsibilities with few financial resources: 49% of them already have two or more children, and 46% of them have family incomes less than $11,000 a year.[129] Without access to legal abortion, the childbearing burdens of these mothers would be even greater: nearly two out of three black unmarried mothers have had at least one abortion.

In the words of a 37-year-old black woman with four children whose husband was killed by a hit-and-run driver when she was 8 weeks pregnant:

> *. . . after much soul searching and suffering, I decided to abort the pregnancy because I could not get anyone to agree to knock on my door*

---

[124] *Id.*

[125] *Id.*

[126] Anonymous, *The voices of women. Abortion: In their own words* 15 (n.d.).

[127] Russo et al., *supra* note 121.

[128] Sis, *The voices of women. Abortion: In their own words,* 126 (n.d.).

[129] Russo et al., *supra* note 121.

> *once a week and say . . . "Ms. Evans, let me give you $25 per month*
> *to add to your food bill at the grocery store, let me go with you to the*
> *electric company and pay that final notice before they turn off your lights*
> *and heat." I felt I had enough responsibility to my children who were*
> *already here.*[130]

In considering the circumstances of the more than one out of three adult abortion patients who are women of color (black or Hispanic),[131] it should be remembered that women in ethnic minority families have both greater sources of stress and fewer resources to deal with that stress than white women.[132,133] They suffer effects of poverty, which include poor housing, lack of access to health care and greater exposure to violence and death.[134,135] Black families must also endure "the continuing stress of perpetual and pervasive racism," including discrimination, harassment and personal humiliation.[136]

The large role that abortion plays in the timing and spacing of childbearing for both minor and adult women has important health implications. More than one out of four mothers who seek abortion have a youngest child less than two years of age; for 12% of mothers who seek abortion, their youngest child is less than 12 months old.[137]

Childspacing intervals of less than two years are associated with prematurity and neonatal death and are predictive of child abuse. It is estimated that avoiding birth intervals of less than two years would reduce the risk of low birth weight and neonatal death from 5% to 10% below its current level.[138] Small intervals are also physically hard on the woman:

> *. . . what is seldom addressed in these discussions is what child-*
> *bearing does to a woman's body. The old expression "worn out by child-*
> *bearing" was literally true . . . by the second [pregnancy] I . . . had*
> *a prolapsed uterus . . . What would a third pregnancy have done? I*
> *had, in addition, terrible varicose veins with both pregnancies. By the*
> *third month I could barely stand 20 minutes at a time. What if I'd had*
> *three or four pregnancies?*[139]

In summary, unwanted pregnancies are experienced by women of diverse circumstances, with a wide range of developmental levels, health conditions, competing role obligations, access to coping resources and exposure to stressful life events. Their mo-

---

[130] Barbara, *The voices of women. Abortion: In their own words* 14 (n.d.).

[131] Russo et al., *supra* note 121.

[132] Amaro & Russo, *Hispanic women and mental health: An overview of contemporary issues in research and practice*, 11 Psychology of Women Q. 393–407 (1987).

[133] Staples, *supra* note 77.

[134] Belle, *Poverty and women's mental health*, 45 Am. Psychologist 385–89 (1990).

[135] McGrath et al., *supra* note 98.

[136] Peters & Massey, *Mundane extreme environmental stress in family stress theories: The case of black families in white America*, 6, no. 1–2 *Marriage and Fam. Rev.* 193–218 (1983).

[137] Russo et al, *supra* note 121.

[138] Miller, *Birth intervals and perinatal health: An investigation of three hypotheses*, 23, no. 2 Fam. Plan. Persp. 62–70 (1991).

[139] Judy, *The voices of women. Abortion: In their own words* 12–13 (n.d.).

tivations for terminating their pregnancies reflect those circumstances. They are seeking a balance between stress and coping resources and are acting on their responsibilities to avoid or postpone childbearing due to lack of physical, psychological, social and financial resources to continue the pregnancy and bear the child.

Women who seek abortion are minors and adults, married and unmarried, mothers and nonmothers. They are diverse in physical health, race/ethnicity, religion, education and income. These are but a few of the ways that such women differ, and all are factors related to a woman's emotional responses after an unwanted pregnancy, however it is resolved.

Postabortion emotional responses

A woman's response after an unwanted pregnancy is terminated by an abortion is influenced by her personal characteristics and reasons for abortion and by the social and societal context of the abortion. In evaluating research on postabortion emotional responses, a number of problems must be kept in mind. First, it is important to know whether or not the abortion was legal or illegal and the type of abortion procedure under discussion.[140]

> My mother had an abortion in 1931. She had two small children whose births had been bracketed by the deaths of her parents and the loss of my father's job. There was no way, physically, emotionally or economically, that she could have another baby. But the necessity to go furtively to a criminal abortionist seriously traumatized her. I think she never fully recovered.[141]

Two features of the medical environment are especially important to consider: type of procedure and attitudes of medical staff. Type of procedure used is associated with gestational stage at which the abortion is performed. The greater the delay, the more likely inducing labor is involved, and the greater the risk for negative medical and psychological effects of abortion.[142]; Such abortions may also be more likely to affect the emotions of medical staff.[143] Both the emotional sensitivity of staff and their technical expertise have been found to relate to postabortion emotional responses.[144,145]

More than 90% of all abortions are performed in the first trimester of pregnancy, during the first 12 weeks of gestation. Fewer than 1% of abortions occur after 20 weeks of pregnancy. The median duration of gestation for U. S. abortion patients is about 9.2 weeks. Early abortion is associated with the enhanced coping resources that come with education, maturity and stable relationships.[146] Women who are more educated (more

---

[140] In the post *Roe v. Wade* context of legal abortion, most U.S. abortions (97%) fall into the category of "instrumental evacuation": vacuum curettage, surgical curettage and dilation and evacuation. Approximately 3% are classified as "medical induction": hypertonic saline, prostaglandin, urea and combinations; about .1% are uterine surgery: hysterotomy and hysterectomy. *See* Tietze & Henshaw, *supra* note 4.

[141] Judy, *supra* note 139.

[142] Adler et al., *supra* note 94.

[143] Adler, *Abortion: A psychological perspective*, 45 J. of Soc. Issues 446–54 (1979).

[144] Lemkau, *supra* note 115.

[145] Adler, *Psychosocial issues of therapeutic abortion*, in *Psychosomatic obstetrics and gynecology* 159–177 (D. Youngs & A. Ehrhardt eds. 1980).

[146] Bracken & Kasl, *Delay in seeking induced abortion: A review and theoretical analysis*, 121, no. 7 Am. J. of Obstetrics and Gynecology 1008–19 (1975).

than 12 years of education) and older (over age 35) have earlier abortions (8.6–8.7 weeks median length of gestation).

There are various reasons for women's delay in having an abortion until the second trimester, when psychological and physical risks are greater, including factors related to economic status and the health care system.[147–150] Women who are likely to be economically and socially disadvantaged because of their race or immaturity are more likely to delay in seeking abortions. Women who delay until the second trimester were more likely to be black, less educated, nonmothers, younger and in relatively unstable relationships compared to women having first trimester abortions.[151,152] In general, the younger the teenager, the later the abortion. In 1980, more than 12% of pregnancies to adolescents aged 14 years or under were terminated at 16 weeks or above, compared to 2.2% to 2.5% for women above age 25.[153]

Abortions are typically available in the third trimester only when a women's life is in danger. Such late abortions are the most physically and psychologically stressful. Some of these abortions may even be outcomes of planned or previously wanted pregnancies that are discovered to involve birth defects. Although their number is small (approximately 1,500–3,750 per year),[154] women who desire a child but find the fetus they are carrying is defective are at particular risk for psychological distress after abortion.[155–157] Despite high levels of distress, however, most families report they would repeat their course of action and choose abortion rather than bear a child suffering serious birth defects.[158]

In any case, the experience of these women should not be generalized to other women who obtain abortions. Macintyre and his colleagues provide a detailed discussion of the emotional aftermath of such a pregnancy in the chapter on prenatal diagnosis and selective abortion that is included in this volume.[159]

THE SCIENTIFIC EVIDENCE   Emotional responses after abortion have been the subject of investigation by countless researchers. R. A. Schwartz reported that a 1981 review of the literature identified more than 1,000 articles on psychological and social consequences of abortion in the English language alone.[160] Unfortunately, much of the

---

[147] Bracken & Kasl, *supra* note 146.

[148] Bracken & Swigar, *Factors associated with delay in seeking induced abortion*, 113, no. 3 Am. J. of Obstetrics and Gynecology 301–309 (1972).

[149] Mallory, Robenstein, Drosness, Kleiner & Sidel, *Factors responsible for delay in obtaining interruption of pregnancy*, 40 Obstetrics and Gynecology 556 (1972).

[150] Torres & Forrest, *supra* note 114.

[151] Bracken & Kasl, *supra* note 146.

[152] Torres & Forrest, *supra* note 114.

[153] Tietze, Forrest & Henshaw, *United States of America*, in *International handbook on abortion* 473–94 (P. Sachdev ed. 1988).

[154] Grimes, *Second-trimester abortions in the United States*, 16, no. 6 Fam. Plan. Persp. 260–66 (1984).

[155] Ashton, *The psychosocial outcome of induced abortion*, 87 Brit. J. of Obstetrics and Gynecology 1115–22 (1980).

[156] Blumberg, Golbus & Hanson, *Psychological sequelae of abortions performed for a genetic indication*, 122, no. 7 Am. J. of Obstetrics and Gynecology 799–808 (1975).

[157] Friedman, Greenspan & Mittleman, *The decision-making process and the outcome of therapeutic abortion*, 131 Am. J. of Psychiatry 1332–37 (1974).

[158] Blumberg et al., *supra* note 156.

[159] Macintyre, Keltner, & Kovacevich, *The impact of an abnormal fetus or child on the choice for prenatal diagnosis and selective abortion*, chapter 20 this volume (1992).

[160] Schwartz, *supra* note 95.

research on emotional consequences of abortion has been conducted with inadequate methodology. Flaws in research on effects of abortion include use of individual case studies, clinical populations or otherwise unrepresentative samples; lack of appropriate control groups and failure to use scientifically sound measurements; failure to control for other stressful life events, such as marital conflict or disruption or health problems; failure to control for history of mental disorder, low self-esteem or other sources of coping impairment associated with unwanted pregnancy, whether or not it is terminated by abortion; and failure to follow a woman's psychological status over time to separate chronic conditions from temporary, acute responses.[161] Research on abortion has also been selective in focus, failing to examine positive as well as negative consequences.

Several reviews of the scientific literature have been conducted over the last two decades. In 1975, a panel of experts commissioned by the Institute of Medicine of the National Academy of Sciences issued a report, *Legalized Abortion and the Public Health,* that concluded ''the mild depression or guilt feelings experienced by some women after an abortion appear to be only temporary, although for women with a previous psychiatric history, abortion may be more upsetting and stressful.''[162]

Schwartz identified 32 systematic and scientifically sound studies on the psychological consequences of abortion. He concluded psychiatric problems were rare (1%–2% in most studies where preexisting history was controlled). When serious psychiatric responses did occur, psychiatric history and pressure to have an abortion were found to be risk factors for them.[163] It appears, however, that the great majority of women, whether or not they have a history of psychiatric disturbance, recover within three months after an abortion.[164] As Lemkau points out, even among psychiatric populations, post-abortion emotional responses are ''as likely to be positive as negative.''[165]

In 1988 the American Psychological Association (APA) commissioned a panel of abortion research experts[166] to review the most scientifically rigorous studies published in the United States since abortion was legalized nationwide by the 1973 Supreme Court decision in *Roe v. Wade.* The panel found that although each individual study may have specific flaws, the overwhelming body of findings, which consists of diverse samples, methods and measurements, was nonetheless consistent: Legal abortion did not have severe or lasting negative effects on most women, especially when the abortion was conducted during the first trimester of pregnancy.

That review revealed that women often feel mixed emotions—positive and negative—after an abortion. But typically the positive feelings (relief and happiness) far exceed the negative (shame, guilt, regret, anxiety and depression). Typically such negative feelings are mild and transitory and do not affect general functioning.[167] The predominant response to a legal abortion, particularly in the first trimester, is relief.[168]

---

[161] Public Interest Directorate, *Testimony on the psychological sequelae of abortion,* Presented to the Office of the U. S. Surgeon General (December 2, 1987).

[162] National Academy of Sciences, *Legalized Abortion and the Public Health* (1975).

[163] Schwartz, *supra* note 95.

[164] Belsey, Greer, Lal, Lewis & Beard, *Predictive factors in emotional response to abortion: King's termination study: IV.,* 11 Soc. Sci. & Med. 71–82 (January 1977).

[165] Lemkau, *supra* note 115, at 466.

[166] The panel of experts included Nancy E. Adler, Henry P. David, Brenda N. Major, Susan H. Roth, Nancy Felipe Russo and Gail E. Wyatt.

[167] Adler et al., *supra* note 94.

[168] Adler et al., *supra* note 94.

Most women's distress levels drop immediately after an abortion and are lower several weeks later than they were before the abortion.[169–171] One study found that women retrospectively reported both positive and negative aspects of their adjustment after abortion. However, positive aspects, such as improved outlook on life, higher energy level, reduced tension and anxiety and better relations with partner as well as with other people were mentioned more often than negative aspects. Some women reported difficulties after abortion, including increased depression, anxiety, tension, sleep problems, decreased enjoyment of sexual relations and lowered energy level.[172] Unfortunately, most studies do not make comparisons with other alternatives, so it is impossible to separate effects of the abortion experience from those stemming from the experience of unwanted pregnancy and its correlates.

Studies that have compared postabortion and postpartum responses after unwanted pregnancy find few differences. One investigation of satisfaction with pregnancy decision-making in teenagers found that the majority of teenagers were satisfied with their decisions and would choose the same options again, whether abortion, single parenthood or married motherhood.[173] (The option of adoption was not included in this study.)

Another longitudinal study carefully controlled for age, race, number of children, marital status and socioeconomic status while comparing adolescents who experienced either a birth at term, first-trimester abortion by suction curettage or a second-trimester abortion by saline induction. At 16 months follow-up, the pre- and post-procedure scores for all three groups were found to be strikingly similar. Only two significant differences out of many comparisons were found. First, compared to the other two groups, women carrying to term scored higher on the paranoia scale of the Minnesota Multiphasic Personality Inventory. Second, first-trimester abortion patients reported fewer physical complaints than the other two groups.[174]

A more recent study followed low-income adolescents who sought pregnancy tests. Three groups were compared—those with negative tests, those who were pregnant and carried to term and those who were pregnant and had an abortion. Two years after testing, transient anxiety had declined for all three groups and was not significantly different across groups. The abortion group showed the most positive mental health profile, with lower scores on trait anxiety than members of both other groups and a greater sense of internal control than the childbearing group. The abortion group also had higher self-esteem scores than the negative pregnancy group.[175]

Adler found that emotions after abortion fall into three clusters. One cluster is based on positive emotions (e.g., relief and happiness). The other two are based on negative emotions, one internally-based, one socially-based. Anger, anxiety, depres-

---

[169] Cohen & Roth, *Coping with abortion,* 10, no. 3 J. of Human Stress 140–145 (1984).

[170] Major, Mueller & Hildebrandt, *Attributions, expectations, and coping with abortion,* 48, no. 3 J. of Personality and Soc. Psychology 585–99 (1985).

[171] Zabin, Hirsch & Emerson, *When urban adolescents choose abortion: Effects on education, psychological status, and subsequent pregnancy,* 21 Fam. Plan. Persp. 248–55 (1989).

[172] Burnell & Norfleet, *Women's self-reported responses to abortion* 121, no. 1 J. of Psychology 71–76 (1987).

[173] Eisen & Zellman, *Factors predicting pregnancy resolution decision satisfaction of unmarried adolescents,* 145 J. of Genetic Psychology 231–39 (1984).

[174] Athanasiou, Pooel, Michelson, Unger & Yager, *Psychiatric sequelae to term birth and induced early and late abortion: A longitudinal study,* 5 Fam. Plan. Persp. 227–31 (1973).

[175] Zabin et al, *supra* note 171.

sion, doubt and regret represent internally-based emotions and were related to the meaning of the pregnancy for the woman. Fear of disapproval, guilt and shame represent socially-based emotions and were related to the woman's social environment. In Adler's study, the positive emotions were experienced much more strongly than the negative emotions (3.96 on a 4-point scale for positive emotions, compared to 2.26 and 1.81 for internally-based and socially-based emotions, respectively).

The more difficulty a woman had in choosing abortion, the stronger her internally-based negative emotions after abortion. Marital status was associated with strength of socially-based negative emotions, with unmarried women experiencing such emotions more strongly than married women after controlling for age. Similarly, attending church more frequently (an indicator of religiosity) was associated with stronger socially-based negative emotions.

Most empirical abortion research is based on ratings of emotional distress, not on measures of severe psychological disorder. When rate of actual mental disorder is examined, the risk for severe negative response after abortion is low. For example, Brewer found the risk of postabortion psychosis and postpartum psychosis in England to be 0.3 psychoses per 1,000 legal abortions compared to 1.7 postpartum psychoses per 1,000 deliveries.[176]

A nationwide study of more than a million women in Denmark controlled for previous psychiatric history by examining only first admissions to psychiatric hospitals three months postpartum or postabortion for all women under 50 years of age. The risk for psychosis after pregnancy was even lower than that found in the English sample— 1.2 per 1,000 abortions and .7 per 1,000 deliveries, respectively). The difference between rates for abortions and deliveries is not statistically significant.[177]

These studies have established that the abortion experience *per se* is not an important risk factor for severe psychopathology in women. Nonetheless, some women are at higher risk for negative postabortion emotional responses than other women. In addition to a history of emotional disturbance and termination of a pregnancy that was originally wanted, other risk factors for negative emotional responses after abortion include difficulty in deciding to have an abortion, abortion in the second trimester of pregnancy, feeling coerced to have the abortion, not expecting to cope well with the abortion and limited or no social support for the abortion decision.[178]

The finding of that perceived choice in pregnancy decision-making is a critical determinant of subsequent psychological sequelae, was illustrated in a small retrospective study of 30 white women who reported having high stress (including grief, regret, sadness and a sense of loss) as a result of their abortion experience. More than nine out of 10 (92%) of the women in the study reported feelings of anger, hostility or rage toward individuals (including partner, medical professionals and significant others) who were perceived as being coercive in the pregnancy decision-making process.[179]

This study has been widely cited as evidence for a "postabortion syndrome." However, due to methodological problems it can tell us little about the normative ex-

---

[176] Brewer, *Incidence of post-abortion psychosis: A prospective study,* 1 Brit. Med. J. 476–77 (1977).

[177] David, *Post-abortion and post-partum psychiatric hospitalization,* in *Abortion: Medical progress and social implications* 150–61 (R. Porter and M. O'Connor eds. 1985).

[178] Adler et al., *supra* note 94.

[179] A. C. Speckhard, *The psycho-social aspects of stress following an abortion,* unpublished Ph.D. diss., University of Minnesota (1985).

perience of abortion patients and cannot separate the effects of abortion *per se* from the coercive, punitive social context in which it was experienced for these women. Causal statements and generalizations based on this study are inappropriate. Time between the retrospective account and the most recent abortion varied from one to 25 years and both legal and illegal abortions were included. Forty-six percent of the women had abortions in their second trimester; 4% in their third.[180] Further, most measures used in the study were psychometrically weak.

The involvement of women in pro-life groups who had programmed their thinking about their abortion experience was evident:

> *In these social systems [pro-life and fundamental religious groups] subjects found members who allowed them to freely discuss their feelings of grief, guilt, loneliness, anger, and despair . . . members of these systems were not adverse to discussing the details of the abortion experience with particular reference to concern over pain that the fetus may have experienced and damage that may have occurred to the subjects' reproductive organs.*[181]

As a result of their interactions with pro-life groups, the women in this sample increasingly came to view abortion as the taking of a life:

> *They became increasingly angry about the way abortion had been explained to them . . . Many learned a great deal from pro-life groups about fetal development which initially increased their guilt, grief, and anger.*[182]

Whether or not these women would feel differently had they obtained the services of a qualified and sensitive mental health professional upon having difficulties with their abortion is unknown.

Women who are under greater stress during unwanted pregnancy and afterward are at higher risk for subsequent negative emotional responses, and the context under which abortion takes place is critical. Thus, the Denmark study mentioned above found that risk for first admissions within 3 months after abortion for separated, divorced and widowed women was more than five times greater than that for all women. The higher risk for abortion under conditions of marital disruption may reflect the fact that pregnancy for such women may have been wanted originally.

The relatively lower rates of mental disorder after pregnancy must be interpreted in Denmark's context of accessible health care. In Denmark reliable pregnancy testing is available in any pharmacy, with confidential results provided within 24 hours. If pregnant, a woman is encouraged to see a physician, who can make all arrangements for prenatal care and delivery or for early pregnancy termination. There is no charge for these services. After resolution of the pregnancy, follow-up care is also free.[183]

---

[180] *Id.* at 71.

[181] *Id.* at 139–40.

[182] *Id.* at 140–41.

[183] David, *supra* note 177.

Thus, in Denmark's modern society, which has both access to health care and social services and tolerance for sexuality and reproductive choices, neither abortion nor childbirth poses substantial risk for severe psychopathology, even under the stressful conditions of marital disruption. What happens in countries where unwanted pregnancy and childbearing rates are high, abortion is socially disapproved and health care and social services to poor families are inadequate is another matter.

Women appear to manage the stress of unwanted pregnancy by selecting alternatives perceived as less stressful and that more closely fit with their coping resources. Social disapproval is stressful. Research has found that women who tell close others about their abortion and perceive them as unsupportive have poorer psychological adjustment after the abortion than women who do not tell others or women who tell others and receive support. It appears that when women perceive others as nonsupportive they attempt to avoid stress by not telling them about their decision.[184] A woman's desire to keep her abortion decision private may thus be an important strategy for managing the stress of an unwanted pregnancy. If so, policies that force a woman to inform others about her abortion decision without regard to whether or not she will receive support could have negative mental health consequences.

Social support affects postabortion adjustment indirectly by increasing a woman's belief in her ability to cope after the abortion. Belief in one's ability to cope is *causally* linked to postabortion emotional responses. An important experimental study of counseling interventions revealed that enhancing self-efficacy for coping, combined with a regular counseling session, was more effective at lowering women's risk for depressive symptoms after abortion than receiving the standard abortion counseling alone.[185]

Research has typically sought to identify negative abortion outcomes. Positive psychological outcomes have not been fully assessed, although they might have implications for understanding women's lack of psychopathology after abortion despite experiencing the stress of an unwanted pregnancy. One study found that after an abortion women reported feeling more self-directed and instrumental, suggesting that the experience may enhance women's personal coping resources.[186] Abortion may also indirectly enhance women's mental health by maintaining a smaller family size. Larger family size has been associated with feelings of powerlessness among women. The association between female powerlessness and family size remains after controlling for use of contraception, age, education, husband's occupation and family income.[187] Close spacing of children has psychological implications as well, in addition to those associated with the health issues noted above.

THE MYTH OF POSTABORTION SYNDROME   Antiabortion activists have engaged in efforts to define women's response to abortion as a clinical diagnosis. They have characterized emotional response after abortion as a postabortion syndrome, allegedly a type of post-traumatic stress disorder (PTSD). There is no scientific basis for such a category, however. Further, it is not an officially recognized diagnosis, and is not included in the

---

[184] Major, Cozzarelli, Sciacchitano, Cooper, Testa & Mueller, *Perceived social support, self-efficacy, and adjustment to abortion,* 59 J. of Personality and Soc. Psychology 452–63 (1990).

[185] Mueller & Major, *Self-blame, self-efficacy, and adjustment after abortion,* 57 J. of Personality and Soc. Psychology 1059–68 (1989).

[186] Freeman, *Influence of personality attributes on abortion experiences,* 47 Am. J. of Orthopsychiatry 503–13 (1977).

[187] Morris & Sison, *Correlates of female powerlessness: Parity, methods of birth control, pregnancy,* J. of Marriage and the Fam. 708–12 (November 1974).

1987 American Psychiatric Association's *Diagnostic and Statistical Manual,* the diagnostic "bible" for the mental health professions.

There is no indication that a legal, noncoercive abortion leads to women suffering PTSD, for the pattern of women's responses during and after legal abortion do not fit a PTSD profile. Women do not typically exhibit negative responses after abortion—in fact the point of highest distress is *before* the abortion. Distress levels begin to drop after the abortion and continue doing so for several months. Studies of other life stressors suggest that women who show no evidence of severe negative responses after a stressful event are unlikely to develop significant psychological problems in the future in conjunction with that event.[188]

Although unwanted pregnancy and its resolution is a potential source of stress, under what conditions an abortion might compound, relieve or otherwise affect such stress has yet to be fully determined. Given that a history of mental disorder and expectancies for coping are associated with emotional problems after an abortion, however, focusing on the abortion itself rather than exploring the problems that preceded the pregnancy could impede the therapeutic process.

It is important to recognize that people do continually reconstruct and reinterpret past events in the light of subsequent experiences. Under stressful and tragic circumstances ideas of punishment and retribution surface, even among people who do not consider themselves especially religious. As Lemkau has noted, under stressful conditions such as infertility, infant death or catastrophic illness, which are associated with depressed mood and cognitive distortions, it is possible for a woman to make highly idiosyncratic causal connections to an earlier abortion as well as other events in her life history.[189]

Such connections and their associated feelings need to be explored in therapy without prejudging their underlying causality. All people can experience sadness or depressed mood at times. But if a woman is severely anxious or depressed or has other symptoms of psychological distress it is important that she see a qualified, licensed mental health professional.[190]

Due to their psychological, social and environmental circumstances, women are at higher risk for depression than men.[191] One of the many factors that contributes to that higher risk is that women are more likely to ruminate about things that bother them rather than to take instrumental action. Self-help groups have many useful benefits. However, when a woman is clinically depressed, merely talking to others who are sympathetic may only serve to perpetuate her depression. It is thus possible for support groups that are not monitored by a qualified professional to contribute to prolonging clinical depression.[192]

The inaccurate portrayal of abortion as having widespread severe negative psychological effects could also subvert women's mental health by undermining the positive coping expectancies that are associated with beneficial mental health outcomes after abortion. Social ostracism and harassment of women seeking abortion could also have

---

[188] Adler et al., *supra* note 94.

[189] Lemkau, *supra* note 115, at 469.

[190] Lemkau, *supra* note 115, provides a thoughtful review of clinical issues and therapeutic approaches for women who exhibit psychological distress after abortion.

[191] McGrath et al., *supra* note 98.

[192] S. Nolen-Hoeksema, *Sex differences in depression* (1987).

harmful mental health effects, through inducing negative socially-based emotions, undermining social support and encouraging unwanted childbearing.

From 1980 to 1987 the abortion rate declined 6% after controlling for effects of changes in age, race and marital status during that period. Since 1982 the rate of unintended pregnancy has not changed, but the proportion terminated by abortion has declined—from 54% to 50%.[193] The exact reasons for the decline are unclear—it could reflect changed attitudes toward abortion, changed attitudes toward carrying a pregnancy to term or decreased access to abortion services.[194] All three of these alternatives, however, reflect success in attempts to socially control women's reproductive decision-making.

Conclusion

In conclusion, after two decades of scientific research on the effects of abortion, the results of reviews of the scientific literature on postabortion responses are captured in the 1963 conclusions of Kummer, who wrote:

> [A]bortion, as a precipitating stress toward moderate to severe psychiatric illness, is of only very minor significance, probably similar to any of a number of non-specific factors, such as a disappointment in love, an accident, loss of job . . .[195]

Alternatively, in the words of Surgeon General C. Everett Koop:

> [T]he people who would like to see a report that the health effects of abortion are so devastating that abortion should be stopped, use as one of their weapons the fact that there is such a thing as a postabortion syndrome . . . As we have talked to various groups, there is no doubt that there are people who experience a postabortion syndrome, but there are people who have a post-death-of-my-child syndrome, post-death-of-my-mother syndrome, post-lost-my-job syndrome . . .[196]

A full discussion of psychological responses related to abortion would include the psychological effects of a woman's death from abortion on her family. In the context of legal abortion the risk of death is minimal—less than that from an injection of penicillin—and at less than 1 per 100,000 procedures, this is a rare occurrence.[197] Should abortion become illegal, however, the situation may change. Although there is little

---

[193] Henshaw, Koonin & Smith, *Characteristics of U.S. women having abortions, 1987*, 23, no. 2 Fam. Plan. Persp. 75–81 (1991).

[194] In 1987–88, 51% of metropolitan counties and 93% percent of nonmetropolitan counties had no identified abortion service provider. From 1985–1987, there was a 13% reduction in the number of hospitals providing abortion services in nonmetropolitan areas. Henshaw & Van Vort, *Abortion services in the United States, 1987 and 1988*, 22, no. 3 Fam. Plan. Persp. 102–108, 142 (1990) (reprinted in this volume, chapter 18).

[195] Kummer, *Post-abortion psychiatric illness: A myth?* 119 Am. J. of Orthopsychiatry 982, 980–83 (1963).

[196] Author, *More on Koop's Study of Abortion*, 22, no. 1 Fam. Plan. Persp. 37, 36–39 [Excerpts from *The Federal Role in Determining the Medical and Psychological Impact of Abortion on Women*, report of the Subcommittee on Human Resources and Governmental Operations, 1987–88].

[197] Author, *supra* note 196.

empirical work on the subject, individual reports of relatives of women who have died from abortions suggest that the event has long-lasting impact:[198]

> *My earliest recollection is of my father standing at the head of [the dining room] table. I must have been four years old; my sister was two . . . I can still see him [my father] standing there, and a woman with her dress on the floor . . . That was my mother's death scene . . .*
>
> *What makes me angriest about what happened to me is that everybody ignores the orphans. They don't even try to figure out how many children are orphaned by abortion, neither side, pro-life or pro-choice, not even a wild guess . . .*
>
> *When we get into it now . . . something will hit me and I get so emotional. I can't believe how strongly I feel . . . It just tears me up. It never ceases to amaze me that, when you talk about certain aspects of it, bang! It hits me. I'm not able to control it. But I'm sixty-six and a retired marine. I don't have to control anymore.*[199]

Adoption

Adoption has been advocated as an alternative to abortion for resolution of an unwanted pregnancy, but there has been little scientific research on the psychological and social consequences of adoption. There is no national system for collecting data on adoptions or on the characteristics of women who surrender their children for adoption. It is likely, however, that the psychological risks for adoption are higher for women than those for abortion because they reflect different types of stress. Stress associated with abortion is acute stress, typically ending with the procedure. With adoption, as with unwanted childbearing, however, the stress may be chronic for women who continue to worry about the fate of the child, resulting in a process of searching for offspring.

Effects on the Biological Mother

As in the case of abortion, clinical and case studies suggest that giving up a child for adoption may pose some psychological and interpersonal risks for some women. For some people, such risks persist over long periods of time.[200] As one woman said, 17 years after surrendering her child:

> *I don't think there is a woman alive who has been through this, as I have, who doesn't wonder what happened to her child. It doesn't make any difference how many other children you have, they never take the place of that one you 'put out' for adoption. I would like to know if my first boy is happy and healthy, and if he forgives me . . . I don't even know if he is alive or dead.*[201]

---

[198] Friedl, in *The choices we made: twenty-five women and men speak out about abortion* (A. Bonavoglia ed. 1991).

[199] *Id.* at 35–39.

[200] A. Sorosky, A. Baran & R. Pannor, *The adoption triangle: The effects of the sealed record on adoptees, birth parents, and adoptive parents* (1978).

[201] Baran, Pannor & Sorosky, *The lingering pain of surrendering a child,* Psychology Today 58 (June, 1977).

Studies of postadoption and postabortion experiences have similar methodological limitations, including reliance on clinical samples and a focus on negative experiences. Unfortunately, there are few scientific investigations of psychological consequences of adoption for the woman who relinquishes her child.

Lessons from scientific research on postabortion emotional responses would suggest that some postadoption women would be at higher risk than others. Individual coping resources and social support would be expected to affect postadoption emotional responses. Characteristics of the adoption experience would have effects as well. As adoption procedures change, findings from earlier studies may not apply, so generalizations must be made with caution.

A study of adults belonging to a national organization that began as an initial support group for people dealing with postadoption emotional responses found such individuals to perceive adoption as having a long-lasting negative impact in the areas of marriage, childbearing and parenting.[202] These individuals, who had relinquished their children when closed adoption records were the standard practice, had not adjusted to their decision. They reported that their decision-making process was characterized by lack of social support in the form of family opposition to their decision, pressure by physicians or social workers and a lack of financial resources.

This is not a random sample of parents who surrender children for adoption, and the experience of these parents may not be typical. It is notable, however, that the risk factors are similar to those for emotional responses after abortion. Sixty-five percent of the sample had initiated a search for the relinquished child. These searchers, who were more highly distressed than nonsearchers, were more likely to report external pressure on their adoption decision than internal reasons such as lack of preparation for parenthood. Childlessness was not a predictor of search activity; the majority of searching parents had other children.

Negative attitudes toward adoption and low coping expectancies may also predict negative mental health outcomes of people who relinquish their children. Thus, the experience of adoption in the context of legal abortion may differ from that of earlier adoption because individuals who perceive themselves least able to cope with postadoption stress may currently choose the abortion alternative.

Indeed, one 1980 study found higher proportions of searchers among individuals who relinquished their children before legal abortion began to become accessible. For the seven year interval after *Roe* was decided, this percentage of searchers was 37%. For the five years before *Roe* was decided, the figure was 43%. The figures for the next two previous five-year intervals were 69% and 81%, respectively.[203] (Reminder: Although *Roe v. Wade* was decided in 1973, many states had begun to make abortion more accessible in the late 1960s.)

It may be that under conditions of legal abortion pregnant women are able to choose the alternative that will be least stressful to them. Thus, the link between length of time since adoption and search activity might reflect the difference between adoption when the alternative of legal abortion was not available and adoption under conditions of legal abortion. These findings may also suggest that the chronic stress of adoption increases rather than dissipates over time. Research on change in risk for psychological stress

---

[202] Deykin, Campbell & Patti, *The postadoption experience of surrendering parents*, 54, no. 2 Am. J. of Orthopsychiatry 271–80 (1984).

[203] Deykin et al., *supra* note 201.

over time that controls for access to legal abortion is needed. In any case, it appears that if coercion is used to encourage women to use adoption as an alternative to abortion, the risk for psychological distress after adoption may increase.

The legalization of abortion in 1973 has enabled women to select abortion versus childbirth based on a host of psychological, social and economic factors. Because ability to manage stress through selecting alternatives that match coping resources should promote mental health, the mental health of all women able to exercise their reproductive choices (whatever their specific choice) would be expected to improve.

For example, studies of teenage mothers have found that an increasing proportion of them now keep their babies rather than give them up for adoption. This change in proportion reflects the fact that many women who did not wish to keep a child but also did not wish to give it up for adoption are no longer in such study populations—they now have abortions. In the words of Jill Clayburgh when describing her abortion:

> *I think adoption for me [at 14 years of age] would have been so traumatic. To go through pregnancy, the hormonal changes, the growth of a child within you, leaving school, the social stigma . . . and childbirth, and then suddenly to have that baby taken away would have been the most cruel form of punishment. I really don't see how a child—and I consider myself at that time a child—could incorporate that into their understanding of life.*[204]

The removal of such women from the childbirth population can help partially explain the increased well-being and reduction of psychopathology seen in teenage mothers in studies after 1973.[205]

There are marked ethnic and cultural differences in the use of adoption as an alternative to keeping the child or having an abortion. For example, white teenagers are more likely to use adoption than black teenagers. Before 1973, 19.5% of white babies born to unmarried teenage mothers were placed for adoption; after 1973, this figure dropped to 8%. Only a small proportion of comparable black babies are placed for adoption: .7% before 1973 and .1% thereafter.[206] A black woman described her visit to an adoption agency before choosing abortion:

> *Next option was to visit an adoption facility . . . I had volunteered in one when I was younger and I wanted to see if the conditions had changed much since then. Unfortunately, they hadn't, minority children sadly waiting for someone to adopt them. I realized that it was not an option for me and my minority child.*[207]

---

[204] Clayburgh, *The choices we made: twenty-five women and men speak out about abortion* 51–58 (A. Bonavoglia ed. 1991).

[205] Barth, Schinke & Maxwell, *Psychological correlates of teenage motherhood,* 12 J. of Youth and Adolescence 471–87 (1983).

[206] Bachrach, *Adoptive plans, adopted children, and adopted mothers,* 48 J. of Marriage and the Fam. 243–53 (May 1986).

[207] Barbara, *supra* note 130, at 14.

Although some individuals view adoption as a preferred moral alternative to abortion,[208] this position is not universally held. There are people who believe that allowing a child to be born and abandoning its fate to others is irresponsible and immoral:

> . . . *notions of mature middle class women with families bearing a child to give out for adoption may be the* most *pernicious cruelty perpetrated by so-called "right-to-life." There is no way I will not rear and take responsibility for any child I bring into the world.*[209]

It will be important for discussions on the moral and ethical issues involved in adoption to include such perspectives.

If those discussions are to be informed, more research on the outcomes of adoption must be undertaken. Recent research suggests that adolescents who relinquish their children in an open adoption process are generally satisfied with their decision when compared to teenage mothers who bear and keep their babies, at least if satisfaction is retrospectively measured in a group varying from six months to seven years after experiencing an open adoption. As procedures change and open adoption becomes more widespread, longitudinal research on outcomes to mother and child will be critical. The research on searching after adoption described above, however, suggests that time intervals longer than seven years need to be included.

The feasibility of adoption as a strategy to reduce abortion also needs more thoughtful discussion. In addition to ethnic and cultural differences in attitudes toward adoption and preferences for adopting children of one's own race, there is a resistance to adopting unhealthy children. The fact that births to unmarried women are at higher risk for low birth weight and other health problems has significant implications for adoption programs, as do the increasing rates of drug and alcohol abuse and AIDS among pregnant women.

Effects on Adopted Children

As described above, research has documented negative and long-lasting effects of being unwanted during pregnancy for children who are subsequently born and raised with their biological parents. More needs to be known, however, about the psychological and social risks for such children who are relinquished for adoption. Much of the research has consisted of clinical samples and lacked appropriate comparison groups.

Nonetheless, there are several methodologically rigorous studies that identify adoptees as at higher risk for psychological and academic problems, particularly during elementary- and high-school years.[210] One study found that at five years of age, adopted children were rated by researchers (but not by parents) as less confident, more fearful and less task motivated than nonadopted children.[211] Adopted children have also been

---

[208] Callahan, *Changing motivation,* 19, no. 2 Fam. Plan. Persp. 124–125 (1987).

[209] Judy, *supra* note 139, at 12.

[210] A more detailed discussion of this literature can be found in Brodzinsky, *Looking at adoption through rose-colored glasses: A critique of Marquis and Detweiler's "Does Adoption Mean Different? An Attributional Analysis,"* 52 J. of Pers. and Soc. Psychology 394–98 (1987).

[211] J. L. Hoopes, *Prediction in child development: A longitudinal study of adoptive and nonadoptive families* (1982).

found to be more likely to be viewed by teachers but not by parents as having more personality problems, conduct disorders and delinquency than nonadopted children.[212] Other research suggests that between the ages of 7 and 12, adopted boys may be at higher risk for poorer school adjustment and emotional problems than nonadopted boys, although at 15 years of age these differences are no longer statistically significant.[213,214] A national health survey found that adopted children were more likely to have higher scores on a behavior problem index and be more likely to have been treated by a psychologist or psychiatrist than nonadopted children (13% vs. 5%).[215]

Brodzinsky has provided an eloquent summary of the findings in the scientific adoption literature:

> *As a substitute form of child care for children whose parents cannot or will not provide for them, the practice of adoption has proved to be an unqualified success. Children placed in adoptive homes . . . fare much better than children who live with birthparents who are ambivalent about raising them . . . Still . . . it would be inappropriate and unjustified to disregard what is becoming increasingly clear to adoption caseworkers, mental health professionals, and researchers alike: namely, that certain genetic and prenatal vulnerabilities . . . as well as intrapersonal, familial, and sociocultural stresses associated with adoption render adoptees more vulnerable to a host of emotional and school-related problems than their nonadopted counterparts. To ignore or distort this situation . . . is to look at adoption through rose-colored glasses.[216]*

Not all adoptive children have problems. It appears that a perception that adoption made one feel "different" and a traumatic adoption revelation both contribute to problems with identity development within the adoptive family.[217] Infertile parents, in particular, may have difficulty in disclosing the child's adoptive status, and it has been suggested that infertility is the critical variable in explaining the success or failure of adoption.[218] Societal attitudes that make distinctions between adoptive children and biological children are a source of stress for adoptive families and compound their difficulties in adjustment. One study reported:

---

[212] Lindholm & Touliatos, *Psychological adjustment of adopted and nonadopted children*, 46 Psychological Reports 307–310 (1980).

[213] M. Bohman, *Adopted children and their families: A follow-up study of adopted children, their background environment, and adjustment* (1970).

[214] J. Seglow, M. K. Pringle & P. Wedge, *Growing up adopted* (1972).

[215] Zill, *Behavior and learning problems among adopted children: Findings from a U.S. national survey of child health,* Paper presented at the meeting of the Society for Research in Child Development, Toronto, Canada (April 1985).

[216] Brodzinsky, *supra* note 187, at 391–398.

[217] Sobol & Cardiff, *A sociopsychological investigation of adult adoptees' search for birth parents,* 32 Fam. Rel. 477–83 (1983).

[218] For a brief summary of this literature, see Miali, *The stigma of adoptive parent status: Perceptions of community attitudes toward adoption and the experience of informal social sanctioning,* 36 Fam. Rel. 34–39 (January 1987).

*[T]he emotions experienced, the value of the children, and the validity of
the parenting experience within the adoptive family were all perceived by
the larger society to be less authentic.*[219]

In considering the full mental health impact of reproductive choices, it will be
important to examine psychological and social risks for all family members. In one
study[220] 80% of the sample said that surrendering a child had powerful effects on their
parenting practices, including overprotectiveness and difficulty in dealing with children's independence. This was not a random sample, however.

In assessing the effects of alternative means of resolving an unwanted pregnancy,
the most remarkable feature of the literature is the similarity in the factors affecting
postpregnancy pathology, whatever the specific outcome of the pregnancy. A history of
psychiatric disorder, lack of access to psychological, social and economic resources,
low expectations for coping, level of stress from other life events and powerlessness
and feelings of coercion all appear linked to postpregnancy psychopathology in women,
whatever the means for resolving the pregnancy.

Assessing Reproductive Alternatives: Some Societal Implications

The decision to bear and raise a child—or to avoid doing so through abortion or adoption—is complex and personal. It is unclear where a state's interest might lie in interfering with such decision-making. In thinking about the State's interest in the outcomes
of a woman's pregnancy, it is instructive to consider how the United States might be
different if women who sought abortions over the last decade had not been able to attain
them.[221]

Given that characteristics of abortion patients have not changed substantially over
the past 10 years, they can be used to roughly project the impact of denying abortion
on various groups in society at high risk for many of the psychological and social
problems linked to unwanted childbearing described above. In this alternative future, if
abortion had been denied over the past 10 years, the subsequent children born would
include an estimated:

- 15 million children born unwanted at some time during pregnancy
- 5 million children born below the poverty line
- 12.2 million children born in single parent households
- 4.8 million children born to women who were unemployed
- 1.7 million children born to minors
- 4 million children born into families who already had 2 or more children
- 3.8 million children born to women whose youngest child was less than 2 years of
  age
- 2.25 million children born to women abused during pregnancy

Although these are rough estimates, the size of the numbers leaves a large margin
for error. They are sufficient to raise the question of the state's interest in restricting

---

[219] Miali, *supra* note 217, at 38.
[220] Deykin et al., *supra* note 201.
[221] This discussion is adapted from Russo et al., *supra* note 121.

access to abortion based on a concern with the integrity of the institutions of marriage and the family.

In the final analysis, existence of contraceptive technology is not sufficient to ensure avoidance of unwanted pregnancy. Unwanted childbearing both contributes to and reflects social and economic disadvantage and will not be eliminated until inequities among disadvantaged groups in our society are eliminated.

Further, unintended pregnancy and unwanted childbearing must be understood in the context of women's roles and status in society. Studies of the differences between women who have experienced unwanted pregnancy and those who have avoided it have consistently found that a sense of self-competence and control is positively correlated with the effectiveness of contraceptive protection.[222] Lack of self-esteem and passivity with regard to one's partner have been related to engaging in intercourse and failure to use contraception, particularly by adolescents.[223,224]

Yet responsible childbearing also comes from the female's ability to say "no" to males who engage her in sexual intercourse counter to her self-interest; it involves having goals and aspirations that make planning one's life meaningful; it involves developing a sense of independence and competence in women so that if they do develop an intimate relationship they will have the knowledge and ability to participate equally with their partner in responsible decision-making on issues of sexuality and childbearing. Unfortunately, traditional sex role socialization has contributed to the incidence of unintended and unwanted pregnancy by socializing females to be unassertive with men, to have low self-esteem and to hold limited aspirations.[225]

In addition, sex role expectations have emphasized male prerogatives that interfere with the mutual communication and respect needed for the development of nonexploitive sexual relationships. Such mutual communication is critical for effective contraceptive use. All of these things must be kept in mind in the development of laws, policies and programs to prevent unintended pregnancy.

In conclusion, the circumstances surrounding a woman's pregnancy decision-making are complex, and her decision is multidimensional. There is a discrepancy between the focus of the public debate on abortion, which emphasizes rights, and a woman's reasons for abortion, which reflect an evaluation of her ability to care for a child in the context of her responsibilities to herself, to her children (current and future) and to others. This discrepancy undermines policymakers' understanding of the full implications of restricting abortion policies for women, families and society. Policymakers and the public must learn to appreciate the meaning of abortion from the point of view of the pregnant woman if they are to fully appreciate what they are doing when they seek to restrict a women's right to use abortion to avoid having an unwanted child.

---

[222] Adler, *Sex roles and unwanted pregnancy in adolescent and adult women,* 12, no. 1 Prof. Psychology 56–66 (1981).

[223] Goldsmith, Gabrielson, Gabrielson, Mathews & Potts, *Teenagers, sex, and contraception,* 4, no. 1 Fam. Plan. Persp. 32–38 (1972).

[224] Steinhoff, *Premarital pregnancy and the first birth,* in *The first child and family formation* (W. B. Miller & L. F. Newman eds. 1978).

[225] Cvetkovich, Grote, Lieberman & Miller, *Sex role development and teenage fertility-related behavior,* 13, no. 50 Adolescence 231–36 (1978).

3 · ETHICS _____

Senator Bob Packwood of Oregon, longtime champion of reproductive freedom and equal rights for women, presents a 10-year history of the abortion issue in Congress. As early as 1973, some 18 constitutional amendments on the topic had been proposed, but often the many groups proposing the amendments disagreed. The amendments took several focuses: states' rights to decide the legality of abortion; conception as the beginning of recognition of the unborn persons within the meaning of the fifth and fourteenth amendments. The article also discusses the issues of fetal research, abortion funding and the ''Baby Doe'' legislation. This history ends in 1983, but when coupled with the following article by Sharon Block, a clear picture emerges concerning two decades of activity in Congress.

25 · The Rise and Fall of the Right-to-Life Movement in Congress: Response to the *Roe* Decision, 1973–83 *

Senator Bob Packwood **

It has been 10 years since the historic *Roe*[1] decision, 10 years of legislative and judicial skirmishes to guarantee a woman's right to reproductive freedom. During this decade, the right-to-life movement has grown into a singularly effective single-issue grass roots organization. But not effective enough. The right-to-lifers have tried repeatedly during the past 10 years to reverse *Roe*. They have tried to pass constitutional amendments; they have tried to enact laws; they have tried to limit the availability of abortions by restricting funding; they have tried to change the philosophical orientation of the Senate by promoting the election of candidates whose primary platform is an opposition to abortion rights; and they have tried to get courts to reverse or qualify *Roe*. In a few of these efforts they have succeeded. But they lost the big ones in 1983.

June 1983 may come to be viewed as a pivotal month in the battle to guarantee a woman's right to choose. In two weeks' time, the right-to-life movement suffered as many major defeats. The first was the Supreme Court's decision in *Akron v. Akron Center for Reproductive Health*,[2] a strong reaffirmation of *Roe*. Thirteen days later, the Republican-controlled Senate overwhelmingly rejected a proposed constitutional amendment that stated: "A right to abortion is not secured by this Constitution."[3] This 49–50 defeat is particularly significant for several reasons: First, in addition to falling far

---

*This article was completed for publication in December, 1983.

**I am grateful for assistance in preparing this chapter from two of my legislative assistants, Jill Beimdiek and Eleanor Wenner, and from my administrative assistant, Sana F. Shtasel.

[1] Roe v. Wade 410 U.S. 113 (1973).

[2] 462 U.S., 416 (1983).

[3] S.J. Res. 3, 98th Cong., 1st Sess. (1983).

short of the two-thirds vote (67 votes) required to approve a constitutional amendment, the right-to-life movement failed to convince even a simple majority of the Senate. The margin of defeat was greater than anyone on either side of the issue had imagined. Second, this vote was taken in the Republican-controlled Senate. In light of the jubilance of the right-to-life movement following the 1980 elections in which the Republicans gained a Senate majority, this is particularly noteworthy since the right-to-life movement had targeted a number of pro-choice senators and claimed responsibility for the Republican gains. Finally, the simple text of the defeated amendment, "A right to abortion is not secured by this Constitution," was a watered-down proposal, one that was deemed the most likely to pass of all the proposed constitutional amendments. The right-to-life movement's best hope for victory was in the 97th Congress (1981–82) and in the first session of the 98th Congress (1983), and that victory was soundly denied.

A discussion of the right-to-life movement logically begins in 1973 with the *Roe* decision. A few brief comments about the years preceding that decision, however, are necessary. The right-to-life movement originated in the Catholic church in the early 1960s, when several states began to consider liberalizing restrictive anti-abortion laws. Tentative reform of abortion laws began when the American Law Institute (ALI) proposed a Model Penal Code in 1959. State-level opposition intensified in the late 1960s and early 1970s when many states adopted more liberal abortion laws, 13 of which were based on the ALI Model Code.[4] However, a nationwide right-to-life effort did not coalesce until after *Roe*.[5]

Congressional consideration of the abortion issue also began before *Roe*. The question of federal funding was addressed in the Family Planning Services and Population Research Act of 1970:

> *Section: 1008. Prohibition of Abortion.*
>   *None of the funds appropriated under this title shall be used in programs where abortion is a method of family planning.*[6]

This was watershed legislation, because restricting the use of federal funds in specified programs was to become one of the right-to-life movement's chief activities and, to date, its only successful one.

I, too, attempted pre-*Roe* statutory involvement by introducing legislation in the 91st (1969–70) and 92nd (1971–72) Congresses to *legalize* abortions both in the District of Columbia and in the entire Unites States.[7] No action was taken on these bills; the right to reproductive freedom was not yet a controversial question on the national level.

---

[4] Ark. Stat. Ann. § 41-304 to 41-310 (Supp. 1971); Cal. Health & Safety Code § 25950 to 25955.5 (Supp. 1972); Colo. Rev. Stat. Ann. § 40-2-50 to 40-2-53 (Cum. Supp. 1967); Del. Code. Ann. tit. 24, § 1790–1793 (Supp. 1972); Fla. Law of April 13, 1972, C. 72–196; Ga. Code § 26-1201 to 1203; Kan. Stat. Ann. § 21-3407 (Supp. 1971); Md. Ann. Code art. 43 § 137-139 (1971); N.M. Stat. § 40A-5-1 to 40A-5-3 (1972); N.C. Gen. Stat. § 14045.1 (Supp. 1971); Ore. Rev. Stat § 435.405 to 435.495 (1971); S.C. Code Ann. § 16-82 to 16-89 (1962 and Supp. 1971); Va. Code Ann. § 18.1-62 to 18.1-62.3 (Supp. 1972).

[5] A. A. Merton, *Enemies of Choice: The Right-to-Life Movement and Its Threat to Abortion* at 7 (1981).

[6] Pub. L. No. 91-572 § 1008, 84 Stat. 1504 (1970).

[7] S. 3501, 91st Cong., 2d Sess. (1970); S. 3746, 91st Cong., 2d Sess. (1970); S. 1750, 92d Cong., 1st Sess. (1971); S. 1751, 92d Cong., 1st Sess. (1971).

It was soon to become one. On January 22, 1973, the U.S. Supreme Court handed down its landmark decisions in *Roe v. Wade*[8] and *Doe v. Bolton*.[9] In *Wade*, the Court held that the decision of a woman to terminate her pregnancy is protected by the right to privacy. The Court said a woman's right to choose is a "fundamental right," guaranteed by the privacy component of the due process clause. In *Doe*, the Court bolstered *Roe* by ruling that a state may not unduly burden the exercise of that fundamental right by regulations that prohibit or substantially limit access to abortions.

Congressional reaction to the *Roe* decision was swift. The right-to-life movement, led primarily by the Catholic church, pushed Congress to consider proposed constitutional amendments that would effectively overturn *Roe*. No fewer than 18 proposed constitutional amendments were introduced before the end of September 1973. The right-to-lifers knew then, as they know now, that the only way to overturn the *Roe* decision was by enacting a constitutional amendment, but they did not limit their legislative initiatives accordingly. There were also attempts to reverse *Roe* by a simple statute and to limit federal involvement in and funding of abortions. By the end of the year, nearly 10% of the membership of the House of Representatives had co-sponsored some form of anti-abortion legislation.

It is important to note both that the involvement of religious groups in the abortion rights issue predates the *Roe* decision and that there has never been consensus on the issue among them. No fewer than 27 religious groups endorsed the pro-choice position before the 1973 Supreme Court decisions. A 1972 statement by the United Methodist Church is representative:

> *Our belief in the sanctity of unborn human life makes us reluctant to approve abortion. But we are equally bound to respect the sacredness of the life and well-being of the mother for whom devastating damage may result from an unacceptable pregnancy.*
>
> *In continuity with past Christian teaching, we recognize tragic conflicts of life with life that may justify abortion . . . We support removal of abortion from the criminal code, placing it instead under laws relating to other procedures of medical practice. A decision concerning abortion should be made after thorough and thoughtful consideration by the parties involved, with medical and pastoral counsel.*[10]

In 1973, three distinct types of constitutional amendments were introduced in Congress. The first was the "right-to-life" amendment. H.J. Res. 261,[11] for example, sponsored by Congressman Lawrence Hogan (R-Maryland),[12] sought to ensure that due process and equal protection under the fourteenth amendment be extended to all individuals "from the moment of conception."[13]

---

[8] 410 U.S. 113 (1973).

[9] 410 U.S. 170 (1973).

[10] B. Packwood, *The Wisdom of the Supreme Court Decision on Abortion*, 121 Cong. Rec. 6085 (March 11, 1975).

[11] 93d Cong., 1st Sess. (1973).

[12] "R" designates a member of the Republican Party and "D" designates a member of the Democratic Party.

[13] On July 10, 1973, Congressman Hogan filed a "discharge petition," a device used as an alternative to regular legislative procedures in the House. When a specific bill or resolution is delayed in a committee

The second type of amendment was a "states' rights" amendment, such as H.J. Res. 468, sponsored by Congressman William Whitehurst (R-Virginia).[14] This amendment stated that nothing in the Constitution shall bar any state "from allowing, regulating or prohibiting the practice of abortions." Such amendments sought to allow each of the 50 states to regulate abortion one way or another, as they had before the *Roe* decision.

The third type of constitutional amendment is typified by the one proposed by Senator James Buckley (Conservative-New York), S.J. Res. 119.[15] This amendment sought to extend the definition of the word "person" within the meaning of the fifth and fourteenth amendments to "all human beings, including their unborn offspring at every stage of biological development." This "personhood" amendment displeased many purists in the right-to-life movement because it included an exception for women whose lives would be threatened by continued pregnancy. These purists argued that they must remain consistent and seek to protect the absolute right to life of the unborn with no exceptions allowed.[16]

Many in the right-to-life movement contended that Congress should correct the Court's decision in *Roe* through enactment of a simple statute, holding that the Court erred in its *Roe* decision, and a number of bills to accomplish this were introduced. Congressman Frank Denholm (D-South Dakota) introduced H.R. 7752, which defined the word "person" to include the fetus or "viable human cells."[17] Congressman Harold Froehlich (R-Wisconsin) introduced a bill, H.R. 8682, which extended power to the states to regulate abortion under the fourteenth amendment (this bill included the exception for danger to the life of the woman).[18]

Congressman Froelich also offered an amendment to the 1973 Legal Services Corporation Bill that would have prohibited Legal Services lawyers from assisting women to obtain nontherapeutic abortions or from forcing medical facilities or personnel to participate in abortions.[19] This amendment was approved by a vote of 316-52, but the bill stalled in the Senate and was not enacted until 1974.

The issue of compelling a medical facility or its personnel to perform abortions or sterilizations as a condition to receive federal aid was also addressed in the Health Programs Extension Act.[20] A so-called conscience clause that prohibited coercion was included in the act. Many similarly restrictive provisions were attached to other bills, including some not directly related to health programs. The Foreign Assistance Act of 1973, for example, provided that:

---

and a member of the House wishes to bring it before the full House immediately, he or she may file a discharge petition. If more than half the House members sign the petition, the committee to which the legislation has been referred can be discharged from consideration of the measure and the measure can be brought before the full House. Hogan failed to obtain the necessary signatures on his discharge petition, and the resolution was never considered by the full House.

[14] 93d Cong., 1st Sess. (1973).

[15] *Id.*

[16] A. Schardt, *Saving Abortion,* American Civil Liberties Union (1973).

[17] 93d Cong., 1st Sess. (1973).

[18] *Id.*

[19] Pub. L. No. 93-335 § 1007, 88 Stat. 378 (1973).

[20] Pub. L. No. 93-45 § 401, 87 Stat. 91 (1973).

None of the funds made available to carry out this part shall be used to pay for the performance of abortions as a method of family planning or to motivate or coerce any person to practice abortions.[21]

The abundance of proposals introduced in 1973 on the abortion issue clearly shows a growing interest in the right-to-life movement, but, with the exceptions noted above, little congressional activity occurred. This inactivity prompted Congressmen Froelich, William Keating (R-Ohio), and Angelo Roncallo (R-New York) to introduce H. Res. 585, which would have created a special congressional committee to address the abortion issue and to hold hearings on it.[22] No action was taken on this proposal, however.

In the 1973 legislative attempts to restrict abortion rights, we can see the beginnings of the initiatives introduced in 1983—the proposed constitutional amendments and bills to overturn *Roe* are still around 10 years later, although in different forms. Although funding restrictions were spotty in 1973, this was to become an increasingly important focus of the right-to-life movement in the late 1970s and the 1980s.

January 24, 1974 was the beginning of some new traditions on Capitol Hill. The right-to-life movement held what was to become an annual March for Life, in which participants delivered red roses to each congressional office. This practice grew from the original 6,000 marchers to a reported 26,000 in 1983. The pro-choice movement also made its presence felt, however. Pro-choice speeches were made in the House and the Senate, and pro-choice activists demonstrated their support for reproductive freedom around Capitol Hill. In my remarks to the Senate, I listed more than 60 religious, medical, and miscellaneous groups including the American Bar Association and the YWCA that had publicly declared pro-choice positions.[23] Support for reproductive freedom seemed to be the position of the majority of Americans, but the efforts of the right-to-life movement continued unabated.

The pro-life movement in 1974 extended its fight to protect the unborn by seeking to prohibit fetal research particularly in connection with abortion. *In utero* research on fetuses and testing with fetal tissue have provided many advances in the areas of maternal and child health and much of the medical information on fetal development and pregnancy. In the early 1970s, however, concern had grown over human experimentation in general, especially on live subjects in prisons and mental institutions, as well as on aborted fetuses.

The right-to-life movement made fetal research one of its primary battlegrounds, and they won several victories. The National Science Foundation Authorization Act of 1974 prohibited the use of federal funds for fetal research.[24] The National Research Service Award Act of 1974 authorized the National Commission for the Protection of Human Subjects of Biomedical and Behavioral Research and placed a moratorium on fetal research.[25]

---

[21] Pub. L. No. 93-189 § 2, 87 Stat. 714 (1973).

[22] 93d Cong., 1st Sess. (1973).

[23] B. Packwood, *Supreme Court Abortion Decision and Freedom of Conscience*, 120 Cong. Rec. 214–15 (January 22, 1974).

[24] Pub. L. No. 93-96 § 10, 87 Stat. 315 (1973).

[25] Pub. L. No. 93-348 § 213, 88 Stat. 342 (1973).

In 1974 and 1975, the Department of Health, Education and Welfare (HEW) issued regulations on research on pregnant women and fetuses, and the commission completed its study on fetal research, resulting in the lifting of the moratorium.[26] Since then it has been generally acknowledged that there has been little, if any, abuse of the 1974 regulations, and that any further restrictions could endanger research projects for improved maternal and child health.[27]

The fiscal year 1975 budget for the Department of Labor and HEW[28] was the next major battle site. Attempts to restrict the use of any Labor-HEW funds to pay for abortions were made in both the House and the Senate. Congressman Roncallo offered the amendment in the House, which rejected it by a vote of 123-247. Congressman David Obey (D-Wisc.), a Catholic who personally opposed abortion, was among those speaking against the Roncallo amendment:

> *I will be damned if I, a male legislator, will vote to prohibit a woman from having a therapeutic abortion necessary to save her life by any action I take tonight. I am going to vote against this and you should too.[29]*

Senator Dewey Bartlett (R-Oklahoma) offered in the Senate language similar to that rejected by the House. The debate was impassioned, and a motion to table the Bartlett amendment was offered by Senator William Hathaway (D-Maine), who said:

> *As Members of Congress, we do not have the right to deny constitutional rights to people because they are poor, and that is what we would be doing with this amendment. Constitutional rights should be equally available to all, and until the Constitution itself is changed in this regard, this right should not be available to some, but not to others.[30]*

Senator Hathaway's words and those of other pro-choice senators failed to persuade a majority in the Senate; the tabling motion was defeated and the Bartlett amendment was then accepted by a voice vote.

A House-Senate conference committee, formed to work out the differences between the two versions of the Labor-HEW bill, deleted the Bartlett amendment. The conference report included a specific comment on the funding questions:

> *Nevertheless [the conferees] are persuaded that an annual appropriations bill is an improper vehicle for such a controversial and far-reaching legislative provision whose implications and ramifications are not clear, whose*

---

[26] 45 C.F.R. § 46, subpart B.

[27] In 1982 and 1983, there have been attempts to ban fetal research under legislation to reauthorize the National Institutes of Health (NIH). In 1982, I prevented final passage of the FY83 NIH bill because of restrictive language proposed by Representative William Dannemeyer (R-California) and passed by the House.

[28] Pub. L. No. 93-517, 88 Stat. 1634 (1974).

[29] D. Obey, 120 Cong. Rec. 21693 (June 27, 1974).

[30] W. Hathaway, 120 Cong. Rec. 31456 (September 17, 1974).

constitutionality has been challenged and on which no hearings have been held.[31]

The right-to-life movement ignored this comment about the appropriateness of using annual appropriations bills as vehicles to block federal funding of abortions. The battle on the Labor-HEW bill became an annual protracted one.

Hearings on the abortion issue were held intermittently during 1974, but no further action was taken on any of the bills or proposed constitutional amendments.

However, in 1975, the Senate Judiciary Subcommittee on Constitutional Amendments, chaired by Senator Birch Bayh (D-Indiana), held extensive hearings on the various proposed amendments. All sides of the issue—pro-choice, right-to-life religious groups, the medical profession, constitutional lawyers—were represented. In my March 10 testimony before Senator Bayh's committee, I maintained that the Supreme Court's decision in *Roe* was precisely correct:

> *The abortion issue is highly complex and emotional, and one on which there is no consensus among theologians and others who deal with values in our society. The Supreme Court importantly recognized this fact, and the broad range of values in our pluralistic society, and wisely placed the state in a neutral stand on the theological questions. At the same time, the Court acted appropriately to protect the health and welfare of our citizens, their right to privacy, and the right of physicians to make medical decisions according to their best judgments.*[32]

I included in my testimony a statement made by the America Lutheran Church (ALC). The ALC asserts that its pro-choice position is a ''pro-life'' one, but that in some cases it is preferable to choose to obtain an abortion. The statement concludes:

> *We have no need to itemize a list of circumstances under which abortion is acceptable or is forbidden. We have the responsibility to make the best possible decision we are capable of making in light of the information available to us and our sense of accountability to God, neighbor and self.*[33]

Senator Bayh summed up the beliefs of many who opposed the constitutional amendments considered by his subcommittee:

> *The question of whether we, as elected representatives, feel that amending the Constitution to impose one conception of life on all our citizens is indeed the most responsible course of action. I have concluded it is*

---

[31] Making appropriations for the Department of Labor, Health, Education and Welfare and Related Agencies, Conf. Rep. 93-89 to accompany H.R. 15580, 93d Cong., 2d Sess. at 20 (1974).

[32] *Hearings Before the Senate Judiciary Committee on S.J. Res. 6, S.J. Res. 10 and 11, and S.J. Res. 91,* 94th Cong., 1st Sess., Part 4 at 7 (1975).

[33] *Id.* at 13.

not . . . Each of us must make that important choice for himself or herself.[34]

Six months later the subcommittee voted not to report a number of the proposed constitutional amendments to the full Judiciary Committee for its consideration. The subcommittee session was not open to the public, but it is reported that one of the states' rights amendments failed by a 4-4 tie vote.

The House Judiciary Subcommittee on Constitutional Rights also held hearings on proposed constitutional amendments to limit reproductive freedom. Subcommittee Chairman Don Edwards (D-California) held seven days of hearings in 1976, but no further action was taken.[35]

No additional hearings were held on proposed constitutional amendments on the abortion issue until 1981. Senator Jesse Helms (R-North Carolina), however, insisted in 1976 that the full Senate consider his resolution, S.J. Res. 178,[36] a proposed amendment that would grant personhood to every human being from the moment of fertilization. On April 28, 1976, he called for consideration of his resolution even though identical language in another of his resolutions, S.J. Res. 6, had earlier been rejected by the Constitutional Amendments Subcommittee by a 5-2 vote.[37] Senator Bayh moved to table Senator Helms's motion to proceed[38] to his resolution, and the tabling motion was agreed to by a 47-40 vote. This was the last formal consideration of constitutional amendments to overturn the *Roe* decision until 1983.

When the right-to-life movement realized that they could muster neither the votes in subcommittees nor those in the full Senate to approve a constitutional amendment, they changed their focus. Proposed amendments were still introduced in each Congress, but no particular effort was made to move them. The new focus was funding: The goal was to eliminate all federal funding for the performance of abortions, counseling about abortions, even a study about abortions by the Civil Rights Commission.

In 1975, both the Senate and the House defeated amendments barring the use of Medicaid funds for abortions under the FY76 Labor-HEW appropriations bill.[39] In the House, an amendment offered by Congressman Robert Bauman (R-Maryland) was defeated by voice vote. In the Senate a similar amendment offered by Senator Bartlett was tabled by a vote of 77-14 after a heated floor debate.

The annual battle on the Labor-HEW appropriations was even more prolonged on the FY77 bill[40]—the House and Senate engaged in an 11-week stare-down over the disputed abortion funding language. The House version included a prohibition against all funding for abortions with no exceptions. The Senate deleted that language and neither body budged. The eventual compromise language has come to be known as the

---

[34] B. Bayh, *Constitutional Amendments Relating to Abortion,* 121 Cong. Rec. 29058 (September 17, 1975).

[35] *Hearings Before the House Judiciary Committee on Proposed Constitutional Amendments on Abortion,* 94th Cong., 2d Sess., Sev. 46 (1976).

[36] 94th Cong., 2d Sess. (1976).

[37] S.J. Res. 6, 94th Cong., 1st Sess. (1975).

[38] A motion to proceed is a parliamentary procedure than can be used to compel the Senate to consider a particular measure. The majority leader, in conjunction with the committee chairmen and the minority leader, sets the schedule for bringing legislation before the Senate; a motion to proceed is used when the measure desired to be considered is not on the schedule.

[39] Pub. L. No. 94-206, 90 Stat. 3 (1975).

[40] Pub. L. No. 94-439 § 209, 90 Stat. 1418 (1976).

Hyde Amendment after Congressman Henry J. Hyde (R-Illinois) even though the actual compromise language was offered by Congressman Silvio O. Conte (R-Massachusetts):

> *None of the funds contained in this Act shall be used to perform abortions except where the life of the mother would be endangered if the fetus were carried to term.*[41]

Lawsuits against the abortion funding language were filed immediately after it was enacted, and a federal judge in New York held that the language was unconstitutional. The issue was finally decided by the Supreme Court on June 20, 1977. In *Maher v. Roe*[42] and *Beal v. Doe,*[43] the Court ruled that the states, and by implication the federal government, are not required to fund nontherapeutic abortions.[44] The injunction against the Hyde Amendment was lifted on August 20, 1977, and the language in the Labor-HEW appropriations was put into effect. To this date, we have not been able to rid ourselves of it, although it has been liberalized from time to time.

By the time the Hyde language went into effect, however, we were back in battle on the FY78 Labor-HEW appropriations.[45] After a five-month struggle, the pro-choice forces gained a significant victory: The House retreated and voted 181-167 to agree to the Senate language that allowed abortion funding in cases of rape and incest, where continuing the pregnancy would result in "severe and long-lasting physical damage" to the woman as determined by two physicians, for the termination of an ectopic pregnancy, and where carrying the pregnancy to term would threaten the life of the woman.

Although the right-to-life movement had been dealt a setback, they were not dismayed. William Cox, executive director of the National Committee for a Human Life Amendment, remarked in 1977 after the enactment of the 1978 Labor-HEW appropriations:

> *The most important aspect of this entire thing is that the pro-life movement established itself as a major political force in this Congress. We'll come back much wiser and better prepared to get a narrower provision in 1978.*[46]

The right-to-life movement did flex its growing muscle in the political arena in 1978, claiming victory in and responsibility for defeating two pro-choice senators, Dick

---

[41] *Id.*

[42] 432 U.S. 464 (1977).

[43] 432 U.S. 438 (1977).

[44] In Harris v. McRae, 448 U.S. 297 (1980), and William v. Zbaraz, 448 U.S. 358 (1980), the Supreme Court upheld both federal—the Hyde Amendment—and state laws prohibiting governmental funding of therapeutic abortions.

[45] H.R. 7555, 95th Cong., 1st Sess. (1977). Regular Labor-HEW/HHS appropriations bills were not enacted from fiscal years 1978 through 1983. During these years, funding for these agencies was included under continuing appropriations bills (continuing resolutions). All departmental appropriations that have not been enacted by the beginning of the new fiscal year are funded under a single appropriation, known as a continuing resolution. Many continuing resolutions have specific expiration dates. If the designated date is reached and a departmental appropriations bill still has not been enacted, an additional continuing resolution known as a further continuing resolution is enacted. Labor-HEW appropriations for FY78 were included in Pub. L. No. 95-205 § 101, 91 Stat. 1460 (1977).

[46] Congressional Quarterly Almanac, 1977, at 296.

Clark (D-Iowa) and Thomas J. McIntyre (D-New Hampshire). Losing Clark and Mc-Intyre was a blow to pro-choice efforts in the Senate, but the biggest strategic loss was the defeat of Edward Brooke of Massachusetts, a pro-choice Republican. While we did not lose a pro-choice vote, we did lose a senator who held a key position. Brooke had been a ranking minority member of the Senate Appropriations Subcommittee on Labor-HEW, and in that role he was fundamental in ensuring liberal Senate language on abortion funding.

Some important victories ensued in 1978 in restricting federal funding of abortions outside the Labor-HEW programs. Funding restrictions were successfully attached to the FY79 Department of Defense appropriations,[47] which affected military personnel and their dependents, and the foreign assistance appropriations,[48] which affected members of the Peace Corps. The exceptions in both of these bills, as well as in the FY79 Labor-HEW appropriations[49] included the same exceptions as in the FY78 Labor-HEW bill. The inclusion of restrictive language in the defense and foreign assistance bills was a first, however.

A nonfunding victory by the right-to-life movement was achieved in the 1978 bill to extend the Civil Rights Commission.[50] The House accepted an amendment by Congressmen David Treen (R-Mississippi) and Tom Hagedorn (R-Minnesota) to bar the commission from studying or recommending any action on abortion or federal laws, policies, or other government authorities affecting it. The commission had only addressed the abortion issue once during its 21-year history, a study entitled "Constitutional Aspects of the Right to Limit Childbearing," and there had been no accusations that the commission had exceeded its jurisdiction in this study. Congressman Treen maintained that this amendment was necessary because abortion was not, in his view, a civil rights issue. This is an ironic position in light of the *Roe* decision, in which the Supreme Court declared that the right to abortion was encompassed in the constitutionally protected right to privacy.

The absence of Senator Brooke and his pro-choice influence from the Senate Appropriations Committee was evident during the committee's consideration of the FY80 Labor-HEW bill.[51] Members could not agree among themselves about abortion funding language, so they decided to incorporate the House-approved, more restrictive language in the Senate bill. Brooke had consistently argued for the "medically necessary" exception in Senate appropriations language; it was not included in the FY80 bill. As appropriated under a continuing resolution, the Labor-HEW funding allowed exceptions for the life of the woman, rape and incest victims, and termination of ectopic pregnancies. The growing influence of the right-to-life movement can be seen in the Senate's reluctance to insist on the more liberal language it had previously approved. While the end result may not have differed, the Senate would at least have had a bargaining point with the House conferees.

---

[47] Pub. L. No. 95-457, § 863, 92 Stat. 1254 (1978).

[48] Pub. L. No. 95–481, tit. 111, 92 Stat. 1597–1599 (1978).

[49] H.R. 12929, 95th Cong. 2d Sess. (1978). Funding appropriated under Pub. L. No. 95-480 § 210, 92 Stat. 1586 (1978). *See* note 45 *supra*.

[50] Pub. L. No. 95-444 § 3 (a), 92 Stat. 1067 (1978).

[51] H.R. 4389, 96th Cong., 1st Sess. (1979). Funding appropriated under Pub. L. No. 96-123 § 109, Stat. 126 (1979). The Department of Health, Education, and Welfare (HEW) was redesignated the Department of Health and Human Services (HHS) when a separate Department of Education was created in 1979. Pub. L. No. 96-88, 93 Stat. 668 (1979).

Other funding battles won by the right-to-life movement during 1979 included the FY80 Department of Defense[52] and District of Columbia appropriations,[53] which included language essentially the same as that in the Labor-HEW bill. A new twist on the "conscience clause" was enacted in the 1979 Nurse Training Amendments.[54] The prohibition against coercing a health professional to participate in or perform abortions or to discriminate against students because of their religious or moral convictions concerning abortions or sterilizations was broadened to include all programs or institutions that received federal grants, loans, or other subsidies under the Health Programs Extension Act of 1973.[55]

If June 1983 is viewed as a pivotal month for the pro-choice forces, November 1980 may be seen as the apex for the right-to-life movement. The Republican Party regained control of the Senate after 25 years of Democratic control. With that change in control came a change in emphasis, a move away from developing social programs toward more controversial social issues such as allowing prayer in schools and restricting abortion rights. Leaders of the right-to-life movement were quick to claim a large share of credit for the GOP gains. Nine senators had been targeted by the right-to-life organizations in 1980; pro-choice senators Frank Church (D-Idaho), John Culver (D-Iowa), Birch Bayh (D-Indiana), Gaylord Nelson (D-Wisconsin), Jacob Javits (R-New York) and George McGovern (D-South Dakota) were all defeated by candidates whose platforms included opposition to abortion rights. I was among the three targeted senators who were reelected in 1980; the others were Alan Cranston (D-California) and Patrick Leahy (D-Vermont). In addition, four other candidates who were strongly opposed to abortion rights won Senate seats: Don Nickles (R-Oklahoma), Jeremiah Denton (R-Alabama), John East (R-North Carolina), and Paula Hawkins (R-Florida).[56]

In 1981, prospects for a big right-to-life victory in the Senate looked very promising indeed. Opponents of reproductive freedom chaired key committees and subcommittees. The new freshman class was eager to make good on their campaign promises to abolish abortion. But what the right-to-life movement did not anticipate was the divisiveness within its ranks. Put simply, the various players in the movement could not agree on how to proceed. Some held out for a "perfect" constitutional amendment, an absolute prohibition on abortions. Others offered amendments that included exceptions for the life of the woman. Still others argued that ratification of a constitutional amendment was too far in the future and that a simple statute declaring the beginning of life and the establishment of personhood for fetuses was the logical—and necessary—first step.

The first hearings on abortion legislation in this changed environment were held in the Senate Judiciary Subcommittee on the Separation of Powers, chaired by Senator John East (R-North Carolina), on S. 158, Senator Jesse Helms's Human Life Bill.[57] The bill would have "provided that human life shall be deemed to exist from concep-

---

[52] Pub. L. No. 96-154 § 762, 93 Stat. 1162 (1979).

[53] Pub. L. No. 96-93 § 220, 93 Stat. 719 (1979).

[54] Pub. L. No. 96-76 § 208, 93 Stat. 583–584 (1979).

[55] Pub. L. No. 93-45 § 101, 87 Stat. 91 (1973).

[56] A strong opponent of abortion rights was elected to the presidency in 1980. Candidate Ronald Reagan voiced strong opposition to reproductive freedom throughout his campaign. He has reiterated that position throughout his presidency.

[57] 97th Cong., 1st Sess. (1981).

tion'' and held that ''the Congress finds that present day scientific evidence indicates a significant likelihood that actual human life exists from conception.'' Senator East had planned to hold brief hearings only on the narrow medical issue of when life begins, but vociferous protests from pro-choice groups and the subcommittee's ranking Democrat, Senator Max Baucus of Montana, forced him to broaden the scope of the hearings.

During the hearings Senator Baucus introduced into the record numerous letters he had received from constitutional and medical scholars.[58] Baucus also received a letter from six former attorneys general which he inserted into the *Congressional Record*.[59] The disagreement among the attorneys general on the abortion issue was admitted— some were pro-choice, some anti-abortion; some agreed with the Supreme Court's decision in *Roe,* some believed the Court was in error. But there was unanimous agreement that S. 158 was unconstitutional.

I never believed that S. 158 was simply a declaration of the beginning of life. It was really an attempt to ban abortions in the United States until a constitutional amendment could be passed by the Congress and ratified by the states. This was the focus of my testimony before the Separation of Powers Subcommittee on May 21.[60] I also tried to establish historical precedent for *not* restricting abortions. Our founders had wisely chosen not to extend the fifth and fourteenth amendment protection to fetuses. English common law, on which we patterned our Constitution, did not hold abortion to be a crime. I argued against making it a crime in the 1980s.

The Separation of Powers Subcommittee held a total of eight days of hearings on S. 158 and then voted favorably to send it to the full Judiciary Committee for consideration. The 3-2 vote was strictly along party lines, but the unanimous Republican vote was not reflective of unanimous support for the bill among the leaders of the right-to-life movement. An agreement was reached in an attempt to bring the factions of the right-to-life movement together: before the full Judiciary Committee would consider S. 158, the Constitution Subcommittee would hold hearings on proposed constitutional amendments.

The Constitution Subcommittee did not begin its hearings on the abortion issue until fall. Senator Hatch's proposed amendment, S.J. Res. 110, a compromise among anti-abortion amendments, was the focus of attention:

> *A right to abortion is not secured by this Constitution. The Congress and the several States shall have the concurrent power to restrict and prohibit abortions:* Provided, *That a law of a State which is more restrictive than a law of Congress shall govern.*[61]

I testified on October 5 against the proposed amendment, arguing again that abortion had been around when our founders drafted our Constitution, and they had wisely

---

[58] *Hearings Before the Senate Judiciary Committee on S. 158, a Bill to Provide That Human Life Shall Be Deemed to Exist From Conception,* 97th Cong., 1st Sess. § J-97-16 at 260–962 (1981).

[59] M. Baucus, 128 Cong. Rec. 10579 (August 16, 1982). This letter, dated May 1, 1981, stated that S. 158 and its House companion bill, H.R. 900, were unconstitutional. Former attorneys general signing the letter were Herbert Brownell, Jr. (1953–57), Nicholas Katzenbach (1965–66), Ramsey Clark (1967–68), Elliott L. Richardson (1973), William B. Saxbe (1973–74), and Benjamin R. Civiletti (1979–81).

[60] *Hearings on S. 158, supra* note 58, at 155.

[61] 97th Cong., 1st Sess. (1981).

chosen not to address it in the document.[62] I firmly believe that our Constitution was written to protect liberties, not to restrain them. I believe that an amendment which imposes a single moral view on abortion—or any issue—has no place in our Constitution.

Nine days of hearings were held on S.J. Res. 110, and diverse opinions were expressed by many interested groups and individuals. The National Conference of Catholic Bishops, a group that had previously supported only absolute bans of abortions, endorsed the Hatch amendment in November, claiming it was the only proposal with a realistic chance of passing. Some of the major right-to-life groups, however, withheld their support. For some, the only legislation worth supporting was that which would ban all abortions without exception. This fragmentation among right-to-life groups was a major contributing factor to their inability to move any legislation to the Senate floor.

The Constitution Subcommittee voted on S.J. Res. 110 only one hour after the hearings concluded on December 16. The vote was 4-0, but pro-choice Senator Leahy withheld his vote, asserting that the vote was taken too soon, that the intent of hearings was to present views which would be carefully considered before a vote was taken.

The right-to-life movement may have been successful in obtaining a constitutional amendment approved by a subcommittee, but they couldn't move it to the floor for full Senate consideration. In 1982, the focus of the right-to-life movement, therefore, shifted to two bills that sought to overturn *Roe* by means of a simple statute.

S. 2148,[63] introduced in March by Senator Helms, was an expanded version of his Human Life Bill, S. 158.[64] Like S. 158, the new bill declared that life begins at conception, and it extended "personhood" and protection under the fourteenth amendment to fetuses. The bill also contained a provision that would have *permanently* prohibited almost all federal funding of abortions, allowing exceptions only when the life of the woman was jeopardized. The congressional procedure regarding abortion funding at that time—which has not been changed—was an annual review; restrictions on funding were enacted on departmental appropriations bills each year. Senator Helms's bill would have also restricted abortion coverage under federal employees' health insurance policies, referrals for abortion and training in abortion techniques.

Senator Mark Hatfield (R-Oregon) introduced S. 2372 in April.[65] While it was similar to the Helms bill in its funding restrictions, it differed in its findings of "personhood." S. 2372 found, "Unborn children who are subjected to abortion are living members of the human species." The Hatfield bill stopped short of conferring "personhood" to fetuses; instead, it encouraged states to enact legislation more restrictive than that allowed by *Roe*, based on the finding quoted above.

Both the Hatfield and Helms bills would also have provided a direct appeal to the Supreme Court if restrictive abortion language were enacted by a state and subsequently invalidated by a lower court. The intent of the expedited appeal process was to bombard

---

[62]*Hearings Before the Senate Judiciary Committee on S.J. Res. 17, S.J. Res. 18, S.J. Res. 19, and S.J. Res. 110, Bills Proposing a Constitutional Amendment with Respect to Abortion*, 97th Cong., 1st Sess. § J-97-62 at 24 (1981).

[63]97th Cong., 2d Sess. (1982).

[64]97th Cong., 1st Sess. (1981).

[65]97th Cong., 2d Sess. (1982).

the Supreme Court with new anti-choice cases and try to force the Court to reconsider its *Roe* decision. No action was taken on either bill.

Action did occur, however, in 1982—big action. I filibustered the abortion amendment that Senator Helms sought to attach to the resolution to extend the debt ceiling, H.J. Res. 520.[66] Senator Helms had been dangling the possibility of attaching amendments on abortion and other controversial social issues to the "must pass" debt ceiling extension, legislation that had to be passed if the government were to continue to borrow money.[67] Twelve senators joined me in writing to our Senate colleagues, announcing our intention to filibuster if any abortion amendment were offered.[68] We believed it was inappropriate—as well as unconstitutional—to try to overturn a Supreme Court decision by a simple statute.

Let me explain a bit about filibusters and why we threatened one. The Senate basically operates on the principle of unfettered debate. There are few restrictions on germaneness of amendments,[69] and it is a common practice to offer amendments unrelated to the bill under consideration in order to circumvent standing procedures. For example, a senator can offer as an amendment the substance of a bill that is held up in committee. Since there was no way to prevent Senator Helms from offering his amendment, we announced in advance our intention to filibuster, which would inevitably delay progress on the "must pass" debt ceiling extension. We hoped either that Senator Helms would choose to withhold his amendment or that Senate leadership would convince him that the full Senate would address the substance of his amendment, essentially the same as S.2148[70] except that "personhood" and fourteenth amendment protection was not extended to the fetus in the amendment, at another time. If Senator Helms proceeded to offer his amendment, we planned to tie up the Senate proceedings by filibustering for as long as necessary.

Senator Helms offered his amendment on August 16.[71] We began our filibuster shortly thereafter. Once a filibuster begins, it can only be cut off if the senator loses his or her right to the floor or if cloture is invoked. Invoking cloture requires 60 votes, and once invoked, limits are placed on the debate: each senator is entitled to one hour of debate, a germaneness requirement is imposed on amendments, and an overall 100-hour cap is placed on the consideration of the cloture provision. It is important to remember that cloture can be invoked on a single amendment as well as on a bill or resolution.

In preparation for the filibuster, pro-choice senators coordinated a strategy, each assuming responsibility for a particular argument. Extensive materials were accumulated which could be read as part of the debate. My staff prepared more than 700 amendments to offer if we needed to stall further. I gained recognition by the presiding officer and

---

[66] Pub. L. No. 97-270, 96 Stat. 1156 (1982).

[67] The government is prohibited from exceeding the debt limit as established by law. When the public debt approaches the limit, Congress must approve and the president must sign legislation to raise the limit.

[68] Senators Max Baucus (D-Montana), Alan Cranston (D-California), Gary Hart (D-Colorado), Nancy Landon Kassebaum (R-Kansas), Edward Kennedy (D-Massachusetts), Patrick Leahy (D-Vermont), Howard Metzenbaum (D-Ohio), George Mitchell (D-Maine), Daniel Patrick Moynihan (D-New York), Arlen Specter (R-Pennsylvania), Paul Tsongas (D-Massachusetts), and Lowell Weicker (R-Connecticut) signed the letter.

[69] Germaneness restrictions can only be imposed in very limited circumstances, including by unanimous consent, during consideration of budget resolutions, and when cloture is invoked.

[70] 97th Cong., 2d Sess. (1982).

[71] This was an unprinted, unnumbered amendment. For the text of this amendment, *see* 128 Cong. Rec. 10736 (August 18, 1982).

made some initial remarks. Then I began to read from *Abortion in America,* a history of abortion by University of Maryland professor James C. Mohr.[72] Our filibuster was under way.

The filibuster continued for almost a month. Several unsuccessful attempts to invoke cloture were made, and on September 13 Majority Leader Howard Baker (R-Tennessee) announced his intention to bring S.J. Res. 110,[73] Senator Hatch's proposed constitutional amendment, to the floor for consideration by the full Senate on the following day. Senator Hatch was absent the next day, so Senator Baker chose not to bring up S.J. Res. 110. Debate continued on the debt ceiling extension amendments.

On September 15, Senator Hatch withdrew S.J. Res. 110 from consideration. He believed its chances for passage were nearly nonexistent. Senator Baker agreed to bring up a constitutional amendment early in 1983. That afternoon the third attempt to invoke cloture was voted on and rejected. Senator S. I. Hayakawa (R-California) then moved to table the Helms abortion amendment. The tabling motion was approved by a one-vote margin, 47-46. Our filibuster was more successful than anticipated: in addition to blocking Senator Helms's abortion amendment on the debt ceiling extension, we had laid the constitutional amendment to rest until 1983.

Additional action on abortion during 1982 was confined to sporadic attempts to restrict abortion funding. Several of these attempts were successful, but the enacted language was no more restrictive than what had been approved in prior appropriations bills.

With the beginning of the 98th Congress in January 1983, both pro-choice and right-to-life forces knew the agenda: the full Senate debate of Senator Hatch's constitutional amendment, numbered S.J. Res. 3 in the new Congress.[74] No one could have anticipated the defeats the right-to-life movement would experience.

Two days of hearings were held on S.J. Res. 3. Senator Hatch had reintroduced language identical to his proposal in the 97th Congress, S.J. Res. 110.[75] In the Constitution Subcommittee hearings, which were chaired by Senator Hatch, an amendment was offered by Senator Thomas Eagleton (D-Missouri) to delete all the language except for the first 10 words: "A right to abortion is not secured by this Constitution." This amendment was approved, after Senator Eagleton pointed out that this was the only form of constitutional amendment that had any chance of passing. Ten years had passed since *Roe,* and Senator Eagleton was convinced that a simple 10-word amendment was the only hope for the right-to-life movement. The subcommittee approved S.J. Res. 3 as amended, and the full Judiciary Committee reported it to the Senate without recommendation after a tie 9-9 vote was taken on the proposal.[76]

The rest of the story on S.J. Res. 3 is well-known: on June 28, after two days of debate in the Senate, the measure was defeated soundly, 49-50, failing even to get a majority of the votes cast. The right-to-life movement had had its "day in court"—and

---

[72] J. Mohr, *Abortion in America: The Origins and Evolution of National Policy* (1978).

[73] 97th Cong., 1st Sess. (1981).

[74] 98th Cong., 1st Sess. (1983).

[75] 97th Cong., 1st Sess. (1981).

[76] On April 19, 1983 the Judiciary Committee debated a motion to favorably report S.J. Res. 3 to the Senate. After the 9–9 tie vote, there was a motion to report S.J. Res. 3 *without* recommendation. This subsequent motion was approved by voice vote without objection.

the jury had come in against it. This was the first time abortion legislation had been debated on its merits by either the House or the Senate and a vote had been cast on substance, not procedure.[77]

But two weeks earlier, on June 15, the Supreme Court had also spoken, handing down decisions in *Akron v. Akron Center for Reproductive Health,*[78] *Planned Parenthood Association of Kansas City v. Ashcroft,*[79] and *Simopoulos v. Virginia.*[80] These decisions strongly reaffirmed and strengthened the *Roe* decision by ruling that government may not interfere with a woman's fundamental right to choose abortion unless it is clearly justified by accepted medical practice and by striking state statutes that sought to impede. The Court ruled that state abortion requirements for second-trimester hospitalization, 24-hour waiting periods and "informed" consent place significant obstacles in the path of women seeking abortions.

The right-to-life movement was stunned by the two defeats it suffered, but its attempts to restrict abortion funding have only intensified since June 1983.

During its consideration of the FY84 Labor-Health and Human Services (HHS) appropriations bill in the fall of 1983, the House approved an outright ban on abortion funding.[81] The Senate insisted on an exception for cases in which the life of the woman would be threatened, and that language was included in the signed appropriation.[82]

The right-to-life movement did win a new one, however: A restriction on abortion funding under the Federal Employees Health Benefits Program, the umbrella program of more than 120 health insurance plans available to federal workers as an employee benefit, was enacted.[83] This restriction is known as the Ashbrook amendment, after the late Congressman John M. Ashbrook (R-Ohio), who had tried repeatedly until his death in 1982 to enact such restrictive provisions. The House had approved the Ashbrook amendment as part of the FY81 and FY82 Treasury, Postal Service, and general government appropriations bills, but the language was never enacted.[84] The Ashbrook language was approved in a continuing resolution in 1982 that expired on December 17.[85] The further continuing resolution approved that December did not include the Ashbrook language.[86]

During Senate consideration of the continuing resolution in December 1982, the Ashbrook language was deleted by the Senate from the House-passed bill by a one-vote margin, 49-48. In November 1983, we were not so lucky: The Senate approved the

---

[77] Previous votes on the abortion issue had been taken when the issue was linked (or when attempts were made to link the issue) to other legislation (e.g., appropriations bills, foreign aid). S.J. Res. 3 was the first abortion measure to be considered in either the House or Senate on the merits of abortion per se. The previous votes were not votes solely on abortion; for example, when attempts were made to add abortion amendments to appropriations bills, some senators who support restrictions on abortion funding voted against those amendments because they believed the vehicle (the appropriations bill) was an inappropriate one to carry the abortion amendment. This is an example of a procedural, not substantive, vote.

[78] 462 U.S. 416 (1983).

[79] 103 S. Ct. 2517 (1983), 462 U.S. 476 (1983).

[80] 462 U.S. 506 (1983).

[81] H.R. 3913, 98th Cong., 1st Sess. (1983).

[82] Pub. L. No. 98-139 § 204, 97 Stat. 871 (1983).

[83] Pub. L. No. 98-151 § 101(f), 97 Stat. 964 (1983).

[84] H.R. 7584, 96th Cong., 2d Sess. (1980); H.R. 4121, 97th Cong., 1st Sess. (1981).

[85] Pub. L. No. 97-276 § 101(a) (1), 96 Stat. 1186 (1982).

[86] Pub. L. No. 97-377, 97 Stat. 1830 (1982).

Ashbrook language by a 44-43 vote as part of the continuing resolution.[87] These one-vote margins reflect the continuing vitality of the abortion funding fight—and the strength of the commitment on both sides.

No sooner had the Ashbrook language been approved than we faced another abortion amendment, this time a resurrected form of Senator Helms's Human Life Bill. Senator Roger Jepsen (R-Iowa) offered an amendment[88] to the Civil Rights Commission Reauthorization Bill[89] that was similar to the amendment Senator Helms offered on the debt ceiling extension in 1982.[90] The Jepsen amendment was essentially the same as his Respect Human Life Bill, S. 467,[91] which would declare that life begins at conception, impose a permanent ban on most abortion funding and allow expedited review to the Supreme Court for restrictive state language on abortion that is overturned by a lower court. The Jepsen bill also addresses one of the peripheral issues that has been adopted by the right-to-life movement, the "Baby Doe" issue.

The Baby Doe issue arose during the spring of 1982 when a Bloomington, Indiana couple refused to allow an operation and medical intervention on their newborn baby who was born with Down's syndrome and several other serious medical problems. The infant died when nutritional sustenance was not provided, and an Indiana court upheld the parents' right to decide how their child should be treated. In response to this decision, HHS issued regulations on March 7, 1983.[92] The regulations have not been finalized yet because of numerous legal conflicts.[93] The right-to-life movement has also seized "Baby Doe" as one of its issues.

Senator Jepsen's Respect Human Life Bill addresses the Baby Doe issue by denying federal financial assistance to any institution that withholds nutritional sustenance or medical or surgical treatment to handicapped infants. This provision was also included in the amendment he offered to the Civil Rights Commission Reauthorization Bill.

We got off easy on the Jepsen amendment this time: The Civil Rights Commission Bill was a carefully designed compromise among the Congress, the White House, and civil rights groups. The Jepsen amendment was simply too controversial, and its inclusion in the bill would have resulted in unacceptable delays. When Senator Jepsen offered his amendment, I threatened to filibuster for six weeks until Christmas. The amendment was subsequently tabled, the last of the abortion skirmishes in the first session of the 98th Congress.

The right-to-life movement has been dealt a couple of big defeats in the *Akron* decision and the Senate's defeat of Senator Hatch's proposed constitutional amendment,

---

[87] Pub. L. No. 98-151 § 101(f), 97 Stat. 964 (1983).

[88] Senate Amendment Nos. 2607 and 2608, 98th Cong., 1st Sess. (1983).

[89] Pub. L. No. 98-183, 97 Stat. 1301 (1983).

[90] Pub. L. No. 97-270, 96 Stat. 1156 (1982).

[91] 98th Cong., 1st Sess. (1983).

[92] 48 Fed. Reg. 9630 (March 7, 1983).

[93] In American Academy of Pediatrics v. Heckler, 561 F. Supp. 395 (D.D.C. 1983), the D.C. District Court struck down these regulations on the procedural grounds that they failed to follow the requirements of the Administrative Procedures Act (APA) concerning notice and comment. This decision is presently being appealed. On July 5, 1983, HHS issued proposed rules (48 Fed. Reg. 30846) that are very similar to the March rules, although they followed relevant APA procedure. In fall 1984 Congress created a new grant requirement for states to qualify for Federal grants on child abuse programs (48 Fed. Reg. 1340, 1985 Federal Register 14878–14893).

but they are far from ready to send white roses instead of red. The Jepsen amendment will certainly resurface on other legislation; Baby Doe provisions are included in several bills that are awaiting consideration by the full House and Senate.[94] Comprehensive funding restrictions have been approved by a Senate committee as part of a bill to provide health insurance for unemployed Americans.[95]

Clearly, battles with the right-to-life movement remain to be fought. And I will fight. I am convinced that victories in the funding area are the only ones the right-to-life movement can even hope to attain; someday we will win those, too. The constitutionally protected right to reproductive freedom has been unquestionably upheld. The right-to-life movement's chiseling efforts reflect their knowledge that they simply cannot overturn *Roe*. In that sense, they have been defeated.

---

[94] Sections dealing with the Baby Doe issue were added to both the House and Senate bills concerning the reauthorization of the Child Abuse Prevention and Treatment Act. Both bills, H.R. 1904 and S. 1003, 98th Cong., 1st Sess., were reported out of their respective committees on May 16, 1983.

[95] S. 242, 98th Cong., 1st Sess. (1983).

Congressional action on abortion has centered on three areas: federal funding, foreign aid and funding for the District of Columbia. In the arena of federal funding, there has been an ongoing conflict over the labor and health and human services appropriations bill, which prohibits the use of Medicaid funds for abortion except when the mother's life is in danger. The bill bans the use of Medicaid funds for abortion even in cases of rape or incest. Since 1984 the House and Senate have debated whether funds could be used in cases of rape or incest and each year have dropped a provision to allocate funds in such cases.

Furthermore, the United States prohibits foreign aid to countries who support involuntary abortions, such as China. Additionally, Peace Corps funds cannot be utilized for abortions or abortion-related services. In 1985 the House passed a bill that gave the president the right to deny funds to any organization if he disagreed with its family planning methods.

Since 1980 the District of Columbia Appropriations Bill has prohibited the distribution of federal funds for abortion within the district, except in cases in maternal danger or in cases of rape and incest. In 1989 Congress passed a bill that would allow local funds to be used in Washington for abortion, but the president vetoed it.

This article, coupled with the one by Senator Bob Packwood, reveals the decades-long struggle that Congress has had with the abortion issue.

26 · Congressional Action on Abortion: 1984–1991 _____

Sharon Block, J.D.

I. Introduction

For at least the past 20 years, abortion has been a constant topic in our national dialogue. This dialogue has been conducted in our homes, schools and houses of worship as well as in our political institutions. The subject has been approached as a political issue, a medical issue and a moral issue. Although the issue often provokes intolerance and raised voices, there is just as often calm and reasoned exchange on the subject. The power of the two sides to the abortion issue has remained in a relative balance, with one side or the other occasionally gaining greater momentum only to have the pendulum shift back again. However, as we enter the 1990s, people on both sides of the dialogue appear to agree that a turning point is near.

The dialogue on abortion conducted in the Congress of the United States has closely mirrored the dialogue in the nation as a whole during the period from 1984 to 1991. The issue has been a recurrent important subject in Congress. Legislation concerning the issue has addressed it from all sides: political, fiscal, medical, moral and even diplomatic. The debates on the floors of the House and Senate over abortion-related legislation have often been filled with insults and invective, but the backroom bargaining has been more reasoned and collegial. As in the nation-at-large, the balance between those Congresspeople who suppport abortion rights and those that oppose them has remained relatively static throughout this period. However, increasing pressure is building on Capitol Hill for the deadlock to break.

In dealing with the issue of abortion and related issues, Congress has established a pattern for itself that is dominated by the perennial appropriations process. Most congressional action on abortion arises in three areas: federal funding of abortion and abortion counseling services, restrictions on foreign aid and spending of government revenue on abortion in the District of Columbia. However, Congress has not limited itself to these areas. Abortion-related legislation has been linked to a wide variety of issues including tax reform, the Peace Corps, constitutional amendments and criminal law. In recent years abortion has also been prominent in the Senate's mind when debating the confirmation of high ranking government officials, especially the confirmation of Supreme Court justices and Cabinet-level officials.

Congressional action from 1984 to 1991 provides a necessary backdrop for any predictions as to what the future of abortion may be in Congress and in the country. This chapter will examine this recent history and draw from it clues as to what is likely to happen next.

II. The Legislation: 1984–1991

The question of federal funding of abortion is addressed primarily in the appropriation of funds for the departments of Labor and Health and Human Services (HHS), which administer the disbursement of Medicaid funds. The battle in this area is over whether to allow federal funds spent through Medicaid to be used to pay for abortions for poor women and whether family planning programs receiving federal funds can counsel clients as to abortion-related services. In the foreign aid arena, the principal abortion-related question in the late 1980s has emerged as whether to appropriate money for international family planning organizations that operate in countries that have abortion policies in conflict with those of Congress. Finally, the Congress, in debating the appropriation of funds for the District of Columbia, perennially debates whether the District of Columbia can use federal funds or its own funds to pay for abortions.

A. Federal Funding

Federal funding for abortion and abortion-related services appears to be at the core of both sides of the debate on congressional action on abortion. The pro-life side finds federal funding of abortion to be the ultimate corruption of their tax dollars. The pro-choice movement sees it as the key for providing access to abortion services for those who most desperately need it. This fierce conflict is played out primarily in two arenas: the fight over the Labor and Health and Human Services appropriations bill and the appropriations for Title X of the Public Health Services Act, which governs family planning programs receiving federal funds. Since 1984 Congress has been deadlocked on these issues, relying on presidential vetoes to break the stalemate.

1. LABOR/HEALTH AND HUMAN SERVICES APPROPRIATIONS   In 1984 the issue of federally funded abortions arose in the form of an omnibus continuing resolution appropriating funds for the continuation of government services.[1] In the section devoted to the departments of Labor and Human Services, a restriction on Medicaid funding is traditionally included to prohibit Medicaid recipients from using federal funds for abortion services. The issue in the 1984 bill, as it is every year, was the scope of the prohibition. The Senate initially approved a version of the bill that allowed Medicaid-funded abortion in cases of rape or incest in addition to those abortions necessary to save the life of the mother. However, the House passed a version of the bill that contin-

---

[1] See HJ Res. 648; Congressional Quarterly Almanac [hereinafter CQA] 1984, pp. 444–47.

ued the traditional practice of only allowing Medicaid funds to be used when the life of the mother was endangered.[2] The pressure of the dire need to continue to finance the government led the Senate to adopt the House version of the legislation instead of forcing a drawn-out conflict between the two houses while the entire federal government ran dry of money.

The traditional ban on the use of Medicaid funds for abortions except where the life of the mother is endangered was continued in 1985.[3] Again, a conflict arose between the House and the Senate, and again the House prevailed. In this round, however, the more liberal restriction favored by the Senate was approved by the House Appropriations Committee only to be stripped from the bill before it reached the floor. The language allowing Medicaid-funded abortions in the cases of rape and incest was removed from the bill by the House Rules Committee, which is responsible for setting guidelines for the debate of all bills before they reach the floor of the House for debate, at the request of one of the authors of the bill, Rep. Richard Durbin (D, Ill.).[4]

The Senate was the site of the abortion-related action during the debate over the 1986 Labor/HHS appropriations bill for fiscal year 1987. The Senate Appropriations Committee adopted the more liberal restriction on Medicaid funding that they had supported for several years.[5] However, when the bill reached the Senate floor, Sen. Jesse Helms (R, N.C.) objected to the bill's allowance of federal funds for abortions in cases of rape or incest.[6] Sen. Lowell Weicker (R, Conn.), the primary supporter of the liberalized provision, negotiated a compromise with Senator Helms in order to avert a filibuster and enable the bill to move on. Senator Weicker agreed to allow the rape and incest provisions to be dropped from the bill in exchange for Senator Helms' promise not to fight the appropriation of $145,000,000.00 in federal funds for family planning programs also proposed for fiscal year 1987.[7] Because the House version of the appropriations bill matched the version that ultimately came out of the Senate, the bill proceeded on to become law without any further hurdles.

The Senate continued to be the site of heated debate in 1988. As it had done repeatedly, the House voted to keep its traditional exception that only allowed Medicaid funding for abortions where the life of the mother was endangered.[8] The Senate, however, dealt with the problem much more creatively than it had in the past. The Appropriations Subcommittee on Labor/HHS voted out the bill with an amendment, offered by Senator Weicker, that included funding for abortions in the cases of rape or incest.[9] The full Appropriations Committee approved the bill as presented to them by the subcommittee after defeating an attempt by Senator Mark Hatfield (R, Ore.) to have the Weicker amendment deleted.[10] On the Senate floor, the bill was subjected to many substantive amendments. An amendment offered by Sen. Jim Exon (D, Neb.) requiring

---

[2] This practice began in 1976 with the passage of the first amendment, known as the Hyde Amendment for its sponsor Representative Henry Hyde (R, Ill.) which prohibited Medicaid funds for abortion except when the mother's life is endangered. CQA 1980 pp. 467–68.

[3] See HJ Res. 465.

[4] Daily Report for Executives, Dec. 3, 1985.

[5] H.R. 5233.

[6] CQA 1986, p. 198.

[7] Id.

[8] H.R. 4783.

[9] CQA 1988, pp. 706–13.

[10] Id.

the prompt reporting by the victim to the police of any incidents of rape or incest in order to qualify for a Medicaid-funded abortion was approved by the full Senate.[11] An amendment by Sen. Gordon Humphrey (R, N.H.) asserting that no person would be forced to have an abortion also received approval.[12] However, an amendment offered by Senator Helms to defund the federal program that supports family planning programs and to prohibit abortion referrals and contraceptives in public schools was narrowly defeated, 48-45. In its place, an amendment offered by Sen. Don Nickles (R, Okla.) prohibiting abortion services in public schools passed easily.[13]

The conference committee on the Labor/HHS appropriations bill was unable to reconcile the positions of the House and Senate and instead decided to agree to disagree. The bills then went back to the floor where the House promptly reapproved their original version. As the Senate was preparing to open their discussion again, the administration warned of a veto if the Senate version of the bill was sent to the president. After a long debate, the Senate dropped the Weicker amendment and once again sent the president a restriction on federally funded abortion with an exception only when the mother's life is endangered.[14]

The 1989 Labor/HHS appropriations bill[15] took a slightly different route to enactment than its predecessors, primarily due to the Supreme Court's decision in *Webster v. Reproductive Health Services*.[16] The House followed the same routine it had for the past few years, with the full House approving the House Appropriation Committee's recommendation that the exception on the ban for Medicaid-funded abortions cover only cases where the mother's life is endangered.[17] The Senate Appropriations Committee repeated its previous year's performance by reporting out a bill with exceptions for cases of promptly reported rape or incest and when the mother's life is endangered. The Senate also specifically exempted from the ban contraceptive devices that prevent implantation of fertilized ovum or necessary medical procedures used to terminate ectopic pregnancies.[18] The full Senate approved the committee's version of the bill without debate.[19] Once again, the conferees, unable to reconcile the two versions, agreed to disagree. However, between the conference committee's action and the House's taking up of the bill again, the Supreme Court issued its opinion in *Webster* allowing states more leeway to restrict abortion rights. With the impact of *Webster* fresh in their minds, the House of Representatives reversed its earlier action and, along with the Senate, approved the Senate version of the bill.[20]

The president, as he had promised, vetoed the bill that came to his desk specifically because the bill would allow federal funding for abortions in cases of promptly reported rape or incest. The bill went back to the House for a vote on overriding the veto. Although the Senate version of the bill had only passed by 10 votes, the vote on the veto override gave a much greater margin to the pro-choice position, with 23 represen-

---

[11] S.2699.
[12] S.2658.
[13] S.2701.
[14] CQA 1988, pp. 706–13; Pub. L. No. 100-436.
[15] H.R. 2990.
[16] 109 S. Ct. 3040 (1989).
[17] CQA 1989, p. 708.
[18] CQA 1989, p. 709.
[19] CQA 1989, p. 711.
[20] CQA 1989, p. 713.

tatives changing their votes. Still, the tally was 51 votes short of the supermajority necessary to override the president's veto.[21] Three weeks later both houses approved a bill[22] identical to the earlier one, except that the provision allowing for Medicaid funding for abortions in the cases of rape and incest was dropped. The president immediately signed this version into law.[23]

In 1990 the House and Senate squared off again over the scope of the exception for Medicaid-funded abortions with the House only allowing funding when the mother's life was endangered and the Senate broadening the exception to include cases of rape and incest.[24] However, the Senate version of the bill also included a parental notification requirement for any minors receiving abortion services. When the two versions of the bill got to the conference committee, a compromise was struck wherein both the provision broadening the exception for cases of rape and incest and the parental notification provision were dropped.[25] The modified bill passed both houses, leaving the 1990 version of the exception exactly the same as it was in 1984 despite the attempts over the intervening years to alter it.

2.   APPROPRIATIONS FOR TITLE X OF THE PUBLIC HEALTH SERVICES ACT   The funding of family planning clinics and counseling services has been the other main focus of the debate over federal funding of abortion and abortion-related services. Federal funds are distributed to family planning clinics through two major programs, Title X of the Public Health Services Act (PHSA) and the Adolescent Family Life Program. Title X of PHSA was first enacted in 1971 for the purpose of supporting family planning clinics and disseminating family planning information. The Adolescent Family Life Program was the brainchild of Sen. Jeremiah Denton (R, Ala.) who devised the program in 1981 to be a source of support for community groups counseling young adults on family-related issues.[26]

In 1984 both Title X and the Adolescent Family Life Program were reauthorized for one year.[27] In 1985, the programs were again refunded but only after attempted alterations in both houses. In the House Appropriations Committee, Rep. Jack Kemp (R, N.Y.) introduced an amendment to Title X that would have barred any abortion referrals by recipients of Title X monies. The committee rejected the Kemp amendment and instead adopted a substitute amendment offered by Representative Durbin that barred recipients from providing or advocating abortions. However, the House Rules Committee deleted the Durbin amendment and prohibited the Kemp amendment from being reintroduced on the floor.[28] Sen. Orrin Hatch tried to revive the Kemp amendment in the Senate Labor/Human Resources Committee but then renounced the amendment in return for the committee's approval of an allowance for Utah state recipients of Title X monies to require parental consent before minors in Utah could receive any services from Title X clinics.[29] The final reauthorization for Title X remained unchanged from previous years and kept funding at the same 1984 level.[30]

---

[21] CQA 1989, pp. 713–14.
[22] H.R. 3566.
[23] Pub. Law No. 101-166.
[24] H.R. 5257.
[25] CQ, Oct. 20, 1990, No. 42, p. 3513.
[26] For the background of these programs, see CQA 1984, pp. 467–69.
[27] S. 2616.
[28] CQA 1985, p. 300.
[29] Id. at 301.

Although the two programs continued to exist, they did so without being officially refunded by Congress. Congress did not even formally address the issue of reauthorizing the programs from 1985 to 1988. However, in 1987 Congress did turn its attention to the program in response to regulations that were proposed that year by the administration. The proposed regulations would bar Title X providers from making abortion referrals, mentioning abortion as an option or using money raised independently by the grant recipient for abortions or abortion-related services in any facility not physically and financially separate from the facility receiving Title X monies.[31] In the Labor/HHS Committee, Senator Weicker got approval of an amendment barring the administration from changing the operation of Title X through regulations.[32] The administration threatened to veto any bill restricting its ability to set regulations for the program. The conference committee on the bill deleted the Weicker amendment and reported the bill out with a warning to the administration that it should not try to change the law through unconstitutional means.[33] The regulations, however, were published in 1988, and their constitutionality was quickly challenged. The Supreme Court upheld the regulations in a 5–4 decision in the spring of 1991.[34]

The Senate flirted briefly in 1988 with renewing the debate over the restrictions on the family planning programs. Following the Supreme Court's affirmance of the constitutionality of the administration's restrictions on recipients of money under the Adolescent Family Life Program,[35] a bill was introduced to lift the ban on abortion counseling and referrals.[36] The bill, however, made it no further than the Senate Labor and Human Resources committee.[37]

Both Title X and the Adolescent Family Life Program met a similar fate in 1990. A reauthorization bill was introduced in both houses.[38] The Senate, in considering the bill, approved two amendments: One sought to overturn the Reagan administration's 1988 regulations covering Title X and thereby return the program to its original mandate of providing nondirective information, and the other proposed to require parental notification for any abortion performed in a Title X facility.[39] When the bill's sponsor, Sen. Edward Kennedy (D, Mass.), couldn't get enough votes to invoke cloture for a vote on the bill as a whole, he withdrew the bill from the floor and, thereby, left both programs unauthorized for another year.[40] Meanwhile, in the House, the bill met the same fate, being reported out of committee after defeat of an amendment requiring parental notification for any family planning services, only to fail to get to the House floor.[41]

---

[30] Id.

[31] CQA 1987, p. 454.

[32] H.R. 3058.

[33] CQA 1987, pp. 538–40. The conference committee was suggesting that the administration's regulations changed the legislative character of Title X and, thereby, constituted legislation. This type of legislating through the regulatory power would be unconstitutional as a violation of the separation of powers doctrine and as a violation of the Constitution's requirement of bicameral approval for all legislation.

[34] Rust v. Sullivan, 111 S. Ct. 1759 (1991).

[35] Bowen v. Kendrick, 487 U.S. 589 (1988).

[36] S. 1950.

[37] CQA 1988, p. 325.

[38] S. 110; H.R. 5693.

[39] CQ, Sept. 29, 1990, No. 48, p. 3124.

[40] Id.

[41] Id. at 3126.

3. OTHER APPROPRIATION BILLS   Restrictions on the use of federal funds for abortion sometimes appear in appropriations bills that seem to be wholly unrelated to the abortion issue. For example, in both the 1986 and 1987 appropriations bills for the departments of Commerce, Justice and State, amendments were offered and adopted to prohibit the use of any funds appropriated therein for performing abortions, providing abortion-related services or requiring anyone to perform an abortion against his or her will. The 1985 Justice Department appropriations bill also included a prohibition on the use of any funds authorized for the Legal Services Corporation to be used to fund any abortion-related litigation.[42] The House Judiciary Subcommittee on Administrative Law tried to lift that ban in 1990 but could not get the matter raised before the whole committee.[43]

Even the Treasury Department appropriations bill in 1984 included an abortion-related provision. The Treasury bill prohibited federal employees from using their health benefits to pay for abortions.[44] An amendment offered by Rep. Barbara Boxer (D, Calif.) to delete the provision was defeated on the floor of the House. Senator Packwood reportedly declined to bring up a similar amendment in the Senate because he knew it would be defeated there as well.[45] The bill was signed into law with the restriction intact.[46]

In addition, supporters of abortion rights in Congress introduce bills every year to amend various laws to ensure that services related to abortion are made available in the same manner as are all other pregnancy-related services under federally funded programs. These proposed bills do not go anywhere in the legislative process but are a testament to their sponsors' efforts to change this area of the law.

Despite a number of dramatic battles in federal funding for abortion and abortion-related services, the landscape of this area thus looks much the same at the end of 1990 as it did at the beginning of 1984. Medicaid still will only pay for abortions if the life of the mother is endangered. Family planning programs that receive federal funds still cannot perform abortions, nor can they counsel their clients as to the availability of abortion services. Legal Services Corporation attorneys still cannot litigate abortion-related cases for their indigent clients.

B. Restrictions on Foreign Aid

Congress in 1984 made two stabs at passing a foreign aid appropriations bill. The first effort only got as far as the floor of the House. Before abandoning their effort to pass a bill, the House had agreed to an amendment that prohibited the use of funds to carry out population planning programs in the People's Republic of China or to support any organization that carries out any population planning program in China that includes forced or coerced abortion.[47] The bill also prohibited the use of any funds appropriated for the Peace Corps to be used for abortions.

---

[42] H.R. 2965.
[43] H.R. 5271.
[44] H.R. 5798; S. 2853.
[45] CQA 1984, pp. 426–27.
[46] Pub. Law No. 98-473.
[47] H.R. 5119.

Congress' second attempt at passing a foreign aid bill came in the form of an omnibus continuing resolution bill in which both houses approved an appropriation of $290 billion in aid for population planning programs that did not support involuntary abortions overseas.[48] The only essential difference between the first draft and second draft of the bill was the change from prohibiting support for "forced or coerced" abortions to "involuntary" abortions.[49] The only major skirmish that developed during the process of passing this legislation occurred in the Senate. Senator Packwood introduced a controversial amendment stating opposition to the Reagan administration's position on the funding of family planning programs in overpopulated countries. He withdrew his amendment, however, when a vote to table an amendment offered by Senator Helms in praise of the administration failed.[50] The final version of the omnibus resolution relating to foreign aid included the restriction on the family planning funds and on the Peace Corp's use of its funds.[51]

After much debate on the issue in 1985, Congress failed to take any decisive steps towards reconciling their conflicting views on restricting aid to population control organizations. The House Foreign Affairs Committee rejected a proposal by the administration to cut off funding to the International Planned Parenthood Foundation (IPPF) and the United Nations Fund for Population Control because of their involvement in providing abortion services abroad and adopted an amendment barring U.S. money to any agency that supported family planning programs in countries that coerce abortions.[52] However, on the floor of the House, the administration ban on funds for the two groups mentioned above passed. The House gave the president the power to deny funds to any organization because of his disagreement with their family planning methods, even if the methods in question are not carried out with the help of U.S. money.[53]

The Senate Foreign Relations Committee and the full Senate approved a bill that essentially mirrored the bill approved by the House Foreign Affairs Committee.[54] This created a problem for the conference committee, which was presented with irreconcilable bills from the House and Senate. The conferees decided to kill all provisions that either endorsed or restricted administration actions, leaving the $290 billion appropriation intact.[55] The final version of the bill gave no directive as to how the money should be spent, other than to specify that it is to support family planning programs.[56]

In the following years, Congress failed to act decisively on the issue of funding family planning organizations abroad generally and the IPPF and the UN Population Fund specifically. For example, in 1986 the Foreign Aid Appropriations bill included a provision barring aid to any group that participates in management of a program of coercive abortion without mentioning the status of the two most prominent groups in

[48] H.R.J. Res. 648.
[49] CQA 1984, p. 398.
[50] CQA 1984, p. 443.
[51] Pub. Law No. 98-473, 98 Stat. (1888).
[52] CQA 1985, pp. 45–47.
[53] CQA 1985, p. 53.
[54] S. 960.
[55] CQA 1985, pp. 60–61.
[56] Pub. Law No. 99-83.

the field.[57] The 1987 foreign aid appropriations bill did not include any new approach to the issue, although it did again specifically prohibit the use of Peace Corps funds to pay for abortions.[58]

The issue was revisited with greater vigor in the 1989 debate over the foreign aid appropriations bill. The Senate Appropriations Committee approved an amendment requiring a $15 million disbursement to the UN Population Fund with the stipulation that the money not be spent in China.[59] The full Senate approved the bill narrowly.[60] The House version did not contain a similar expenditure requirement.[61] Before the conference committee met to resolve the differences between the two bills, the president threatened to veto the bill if it came to him with the Population Fund appropriation.[62] The conferees, nonetheless, approved the Senate version of the bill. It took the House three floor votes to make a final decision on the matter, but it finally joined the Senate in approving the original Senate version requiring the money for the UN organization.[63] The president kept his word and vetoed the bill, forcing the Congress to delete the requirement.[64]

Abortion as it relates to foreign affairs arose in another context in 1989. During its consideration of the bill protecting Chinese students in the wake of the Tiananmen Square tragedy, the Senate adopted an amendment to the bill requiring that the Immigration and Naturalization Service give extra consideration to Chinese nationals whose reason for applying for refugee status is related to fear about having violated the Chinese government's policy of "one couple, one child."[65] The House rejected the Senate's amendment, and the bill went into conference.[66] The bill as reported out of conference moderated the Senate's language, stating only that violation of China's population policy by an applicant for refugee status could be a basis for the granting of such status.[67] Although both houses approved the conference's version of the bill, the bill was vetoed by the president for reasons wholly unrelated to the abortion issue.[68]

The latest action taken by Congress is completely consistent with their frustrated efforts of the past six years to define policy in this area. The House recently rejected a bill appropriating aid for family planning efforts in Romania to be administered by the IPPF and the UN Population Fund.[69] As can be seen in congressional action every year since 1984, Congress has mired itself in an inconclusive position. It continues to appropriate money for family planning programs but is unable to decide whether to entrust money to two of the major players in the area, the International Planned Parenthood Foundation and the United Nations Population Fund. Congress' indecision has its roots in its ambivalence about abortion in general.

---

[57] CQA 1986, p. 165.
[58] H.R. 3100, H.R. 471.
[59] CQA 1989, p. 791.
[60] CQA 1989, p. 793.
[61] H.R. 2655.
[62] CQA 1989, p. 795.
[63] CQA 1989, pp. 799–800.
[64] H.R. 2939; CQA 1989, pp. 799–800.
[65] H.R. 2712.
[66] CQA 1989, pp. 280–81.
[67] CQA 1989, pp. 281–82.
[68] Id.
[69] H.R. 5114.

C. District of Columbia Appropriations

Although most of the country does not consider the debate over appropriations for the District of Columbia to be of great significance, those involved on both sides of the abortion issue have made this otherwise little-watched process a rallying point for their movements. Since 1980, the District of Columbia appropriations bill has included a ban on the use of federal funds for abortions in the District of Columbia except when the life of the mother is endangered or in the cases of rape or incest.[70] Since 1980 Congress has fought within itself both to expand and to restrict this amendment.

In 1985 amendments were introduced in both the House and the Senate to expand the ban on the use of government funds for abortion in the District to cover monies raised by the local District government as well as money given to the District by the federal government.[71] The amendment, sponsored by Rep. Chris Smith (R, N.J.), was adopted in the House but was rejected by the Senate after being offered by Sen. Gordon Humphrey (R, N.H.).[72] The conferees decided to drop the House amendment, and the bill passed with the Hyde amendment in its traditional form.[73] This same scenario was repeated in 1986 and 1987.[74]

Although in 1988 the scenario began in the same manner as it had the previous three years, the result was dramatically different. The House again passed a version of the District of Columbia appropriations bill that included a ban on the use of all government funds, federal and local, for abortion-related services.[75] Likewise, the Senate continued its practice of passing a bill that only restricted the use of federal funds. Again, the conference reported the bill out of its committee with the Senate's less restrictive language. However, this time the House refused to acquiesce to the Senate's version of the bill and voted to recommit the bill to conference with instructions that the House language be put back in the bill. The Senate eventually adopted the House's language, altering the restrictions on the District of Columbia for the first time in years.[76]

The battle over the precise limits of the abortion funding restriction for the District in 1988 was only a prelude to the much more drawn out debate that took place in 1989. The House Appropriations Committee approved a bill that only limited the use of federal funds for abortion in the District.[77] On the floor of the House, in its first post-*Webster* abortion vote, the House rejected an amendment banning the use of federal and local funds for abortion. Twenty-three house members who had supported an identical amendment in 1988 opposed the amendment in 1989.[78] For the first time in years, the House sent to conference a bill without a ban on local District funds. The Senate approved the House version of the bill, the conferees made no change in the abortion funding provision, and both houses voted to send the bill to the president as it stood.[79] The president, as he had warned, vetoed the bill because of the absence of the ban on local funds. Congress took up the bill again, altering it slightly by taking out the excep-

[70] Pub. Law No. 96–530; CQA 1980, p. 217.
[71] H.R. 3067.
[72] CQA 1985, p. 249.
[73] CQA 1985, pp. 359–60.
[74] Pub. Law No. 99–591 (H.R.J. Res. 738); Pub. Law No. 100-202 (H.R. 2713).
[75] H.R. 4776.
[76] CQA 1988, pp. 713–15.
[77] H.R. 3026.
[78] CQA 1989, pp. 757–58.
[79] CQA 1989, pp. 758–59.

tion to the ban on federal funds for abortions in cases of rape or incest but continuing to keep silent on the District's right to use its own funds for abortion. Once again, the president vetoed the bill because of the absence of the ban on the use of local funds for abortion. Acknowledging that they did not have the votes to override the president's veto, Congress finally approved an appropriations bill for the District that included a ban on the District's use of its locally raised revenue for abortion-related services.[80]

The following year the House repeated itself and approved an appropriations bill limiting the restriction on the use of government funds for abortion to the use of federal funds with an exception for cases where the mothers life is endangered and in cases of rape or incest.[81] The House's version of the abortion restriction made it through the Senate and conference committee before being defeated on the floor of the House when it rejected the conference committee bill.[82] The liberalized language was removed from the bill, and it was passed by both houses.[83]

The fierce debate over the District of Columbia's appropriation bill from 1984 to 90 did yield a dramatic change in the law governing the District. The change was a step in the direction of a decrease in the availability of abortion services in the District. However, this change could not be said to accurately represent the Congress' will. The change was only achieved with an exertion of great power on the part of the president as exhibited by his two vetoes of the District's appropriations bill in 1989. Although it is not reflected in the law as it appears on the books, the Congress for the past two years has voted to liberalize its control over the District's abortion policy.

D. Other Areas of Legislation

Congressional action on abortion has not been limited to the three areas discussed above. Congress has dabbled in many aspects of the abortion issue. Legislation has been introduced on such subjects as the tax implications of failed abortions, the availability of abortions in military hospitals overseas and proposed criminal sanctions for performing abortions. Although most of these efforts are symbolic, an examination of them yields an interesting insight into the scope of the abortion question.

1. MEDICAL ASPECTS OF ABORTION   The use of fetal tissue in medical research emerged at the end of the 1980s as one of the most pressing and controversial aspects of the abortion issue. Congress dealt with this issue in 1984 in a bill that sought to set restrictions on research funded by the National Institutes of Health.[84] The restriction covered the use of nonviable living human fetuses and required that (1) the research must enhance the well being of fetuses; (2) it must increase the fetuses' chances for survival; or (3) it must develop important biomedical information that cannot be obtained any other way and be done in a manner that does not make the fetus suffer unnecessarily. President Reagan vetoed the bill because he believed that the funding provisions of the bill were unnecessary.[85]

This issue received renewed attention in 1990. Rep. Henry Waxman (D, Calif.) sponsored a bill to overturn the existing prohibition on funding for research into trans-

---

[80] CQA 1989, p. 760.
[81] CQ, July 28, 1990, No. 30, p. 2409
[82] CQ, Oct. 27, 1990, No. 43, p. 3600.
[83] Id.
[84] S. 540.
[85] CQA 1984, p. 474.

plants of fetal tissue obtained from abortions.[86] Though still in experimental stages, it is hoped that these transplants will help victims of juvenile diabetes and Parkinson's disease. Rep. Waxman held hearings on the issue but was unable to get action on his bill before the Congress adjourned.[87]

Many bills have also been introduced to require individuals who perform abortions to obtain an informed consent from the patient before the procedure.[88] In 1986 Rep. Mark Siljander (R, Mich.) introduced a bill to require that women upon whom abortions were to be performed be informed about the use of anesthetics and analgesics in cases where there is reasonable medical certainty that organic fetal pain will occur.[89] Senator Humphrey introduced a similar bill in the Senate that session.[90] None of these bills progressed in the legislative process past their introduction.

2.   TAX-RELATED LEGISLATION   Every year from 1984 to 1989 legislation has been introduced in Congress to deny tax-exempt status for nonprofit organizations that perform or finance abortions or abortion-related services.[91] In 1986 Senators Humphrey (R, N.H.) and Armstrong (R, Colo.) first tried to attach an amendment to the tax overhaul bill denying tax-exempt status to organizations than perform and finance abortion other than when the mother's life is endangered.[92] When President Reagan asked them not to encourage a move to laden the bill with amendments, the senators withdrew their amendment.[93] They resurrected the amendment later in the year and attached it to a continuing appropriations resolution.[94] Their strategy was defeated, however, when Sen. Bill Bradley (D, N.J.) stated during the debate on the amendment that if Senators Humphrey and Armstrong's amendment was ruled germane, he would offer an amendment to deny tax deductions for cigarette advertising. The Senate ruled the Humphrey/Armstrong amendment not germane.[95] Senator Humphrey raised this issue during the confirmation hearing of Lawrence Gibbs, nominee for the job of Commissioner of the Internal Revenue Service.[96] Humphrey delayed the confirmation of the nomination while he investigated Mr. Gibbs' position on the issue.[97]

Bills are also often introduced, although none have been acted upon, seeking to disallow a personal income tax exemption for any child born alive after an induced abortion.[98] Another bill was introduced in 1987 to deny an income tax deduction for any medical expenses incurred for most abortions; this bill also was not acted upon.[99] In 1990 legislation was again introduced and not acted upon that sought to prohibit the use of tax-exempt bonds to finance a health care facility that performs abortions.[100]

---

[86]H.R. 5456.

[87]CQ Aug. 25, 1990, No. 34, p. 2719.

[88]S. 272 (1987); S. 2791 (1986); H.R. 5303 (1986).

[89]H.R. 203.

[90]S. J. Res. 163.

[91]S. 1513 (1989); H.R. 624 (1989); S. 2238 (1988); S. 264 (1987); H.R. 719 (1987); H.R.J. Res. 738 (1986); H.R. 2897 (1985).

[92]CQA 1986, p. 512.

[93]Id.

[94]H.R.J. Res. 738.

[95]Daily Report for Executives, Oct. 6, 1986.

[96]Daily Report for Executives, July 31, 1986.

[97]Id.

[98]S. 2088 (1986); H.R. 4041 (1986); H.R. 786 (1987); S. 162 (1989).

[99]H.R. 1591.

[100]H.R. 4922.

Finally, one pro-choice member of Congress also tried to use the tax system to advance her cause, albeit unsuccessfully. Rep. Patricia Schroeder (D, Colo.) introduced a bill in 1985 to establish a national indigent women's trust fund that would be funded through a $1 check-off option on the federal income tax form.[101] The trust fund would have provided financial support for indigent women seeking to have abortions.

3. CRIMINAL LAWS   The 101st Congress saw the introduction of three bills linking abortion and criminal activity. A number of senators introduced a bill to make it illegal to perform an abortion with the knowledge that the purpose of the abortion is sex selection.[102] On the House side, a bill was introduced to make the performance of an abortion in the District of Columbia a criminal offense.[103] Finally, Senator Alan Cranston (D, Calif.) introduced a bill to create a federal criminal offense for interfering with access to and egress from a medical facility.[104] It seems obvious that the introduction of all three of these bills was motivated more by a desire to make a symbolic statement about an aspect of the abortion issue than by an expectation that the bill would mature into law.

4. CONSTITUTIONAL AMENDMENTS AND CIVIL RIGHTS LEGISLATION   Numerous bills have been introduced in Congress since 1984 to amend the Constitution to prohibit abortions. In fact, in the 101st Congress alone, 10 separate proposals for constitutional amendments were introduced. Some of the bills seek to guarantee the right to life, others seek to protect unborn children, and one sought to declare that the preborn are entitled to the protections of the fifth, thirteenth and fourteenth amendments to the Constitution. Rep. Bill Emerson (R, Mo.) and Sen. Orrin Hatch (R, Utah) took a different approach. They introduced a bill to remove control over the abortion issue from the exclusive domain of the judicial branch. Their bill sought to amend the Constitution to establish legislative authority in Congress and states with respect to abortion.[105]

The pro-choice movement introduced its version of an abortion civil rights bill in 1990.[106] The Freedom of Choice Act would prohibit states from restricting the right of women to terminate a pregnancy before fetal viability or if the woman's life is endangered.[107] The bill would also prohibit parental notification requirements and other conditions on the performance of an abortion.[108] Before Congress recessed, the Senate Labor and Human Resources Committee held hearings on the proposed legislation, but no further action was taken.[109]

5. CONFIRMATION HEARINGS   The issue of abortion has played an important role in many confirmation hearings since 1984. The importance of the abortion issue has become especially acute in the confirmation of Supreme Court justices. Judge Robert Bork's views on abortion were a central focus of his testimony before the Senate Judiciary Committee during his confirmation hearings. Most of the abortion-related controversy over the Bork nomination centered on a statement he made in congressional tes-

---

[101] H.R. 608.

[102] S. 1681. The bill's sponsors were Senators Humphrey, Armstrong, Coats, Grassley and Helms.

[103] H.R. 2752. The bill's sponsors were Representatives Dornan, Hyde, Smith (N.J.), Hunter, Holloway, Sensenbrenner, Dannemeyer, Shumway and Herger.

[104] S. 2321.

[105] H.R.J. Res. 59; S.J. Res. 3.

[106] H.R. 3700; S. 1912.

[107] CQ, Aug. 25, 1990, No. 34, p. 2717.

[108] Id.

[109] Id at 2719.

timony in 1981. At that time, Judge Bork told the Congress that he believed that *Roe v. Wade* was "an unconstitutional decision, a serious and wholly unjustifiable usurpation of state legislative authority."[110] In his confirmation hearings, Judge Bork told the committee that his 1981 testimony did not mean that he had already decided that he would vote to overrule *Roe v. Wade*.[111]

Abortion has continued to play a role in the confirmation of Supreme Court justices subsequent to the rejection of Judge Bork's nomination. Justice Kennedy was asked numerous questions about his views on abortion and the existence of a constitutional right to privacy during his confirmation hearings. He claimed to have no hidden agenda or "fixed view" on the abortion issue.[112] Senators Biden and DeConcini especially pressed the nominee on his views on abortion before voting in favor of his confirmation.[113] Justice Souter was questioned about his views on abortion but declined to give much insight into his position. He testified in his confirmation hearings that he had not decided whether or not he would vote to overturn *Roe v. Wade* if the issue was before him and that he would not reveal his personal feelings on abortion, which he believed to be irrelevant to his legal analysis of the issue.[114] Not only did abortion play a role in the senators' questioning of Souter, it was also raised by a number of witnesses testifying both for and against the Souter nomination. A number of pro-choice groups testified against the nomination because of Justice Souter's refusal to reveal his views on abortion since he testified as to his views on other issues that may come before the Court.[115] Howard Phillips of the Conservative Caucus also testified against the nomination, but for a very different reason. He opposed the Souter nomination because Souter, when he was trustee of a hospital, voted to allow doctors to perform abortions in the hospital.[116] Despite finding his testimony on the abortion issue frustrating, the Senate voted to confirm Justice Souter's nomination overwhelmingly.[117]

This exact scenario was replayed with the Clarence Thomas hearings, where the nominee refused to discuss his opinion of *Roe* and, in fact, stated that he had not reached an opinion on this landmark case. However, his opinion of *Roe* for confirmation purposes eventually took a backseat to other issues presented in the Thomas-Hill hearings.

Abortion also played a major role in the confirmation hearings of at least one Cabinet member. When Leon Sullivan testified before the Finance and Labor and Human Resources Committees on his nomination to the post of Secretary of Health and Human Services, he was asked repeatedly to clarify his position on abortion. He testified that his views on abortion were the same as the president's views: He is opposed to abortion except when the mother's life is endangered or in the cases of rape or incest, he favors the overturning of *Roe v. Wade,* and he supports adoption and other alternatives to abortion. Senator Armstrong also pressed Secretary Sullivan on his views on fetal tissue research. The nominee refused to endorse a complete ban on federal funding of fetal tissue research, claiming that he needed more information on the subject. De-

[110] CQA 1987, p. 272.

[111] *Id.*

[112] A. Kamen, *Kennedy: No "Fixed View" on Abortion,* Washington Post, Dec. 15, 1987, at A1.

[113] *Id.*

[114] R. Marcus, *Souter: "I Have Not Made Up My Mind" on ROE,* Washington Post, Sept. 15, 1990, at A1.

[115] R. Marcus, *Liberal Organizations Split over Souter Nomination,* Washington Post, Sept. 19, 1990, at A6.

[116] *Id.*

[117] H. DeWar, *Souter Wins Approval in Senate 90–9,* Washington Post, Oct. 3, 1990, at A1.

spite some controversy over the consistency between his views as expressed in his hearings and his prenomination positions, Secretary Sullivan was confirmed by the Senate.

In 1985 abortion was even raised in the confirmation hearings of an ambassador. Senator Helms delayed the nomination of Winston Lord to be the United States ambassador to China for the purpose of putting pressure on the administration to take a harder line on the funding of international population control programs.[118] Senator Helms sought assurance from the administration that it would not support aid for the UN Fund for Population (UNFPC) Control because of its involvement in countries, such as China, that encourage abortion.[119] As mentioned above, in 1985 the administration made a request to Congress that UNFPC not be funded, and Senator Helms eventually allowed the nomination of Ambassador Lord to proceed successfully.

6. MISCELLANEOUS LEGISLATION   Abortion is raised in such a wide variety of congressional contexts that some legislation defies categorization. The miscellaneous abortion-related legislation includes:

- The Non-Discrimination in Insurance Act—The purpose of this legislation was to bar insurance companies from using gender as an actuarial factor for computing insurance rates and benefits.[120] The original version of the bill also included a provision requiring all health plans to provide maternity and abortion coverage.[121] However, in the committee process, the bill was amended—the maternity and abortion coverage provision became voluntary, and a provision was added requiring any insurer who offered abortion coverage to provide the same plan at a lower cost without the abortion coverage.[122] The bill was approved by the House Energy and Commerce Committee, but no further action was taken.[123]
- Prison funding—Senator Helms introduced an amendment to the 1985 Commerce, Justice and State Department appropriations bill that sought to bar the performance of abortions in federal prisons.[124] Senator Helms withdrew the amendment when Sen. Howard Metzenbaum (D, Ohio) threatened to filibuster.[125] However, when Senator Helms brought the amendment up for a second time, the Senate voted their belief that the amendment was unconstitutional.[126]
- Overseas military hospital services—Despite garnering a majority of votes in the Senate, the fight to overturn the ban on abortions performed in military hospitals overseas failed in 1990.[127]

III. The Future

As the preceding chronicle of congressional action on abortion demonstrates, the landscape of federal abortion legislation has not changed much since 1984. Restrictions on

---

[118]CQA 1985, p. 419.
[119]Id.
[120]H.R. 100.
[121]CQA 1984, p. 280.
[122]Id.
[123]Id.
[124]H.R. 2965.
[125]CQA 1985, p. 249.
[126]Id.
[127]S. 2884; H.R. 4739.

the use of Medicaid funds for abortion were identical in 1990 to the restrictions that Congress allowed in 1984. Congress became completely inert regarding the funding of Title X of the Public Health Services Act, failing to respond in any definite manner to the administration's co-optation of the congressionally created program. In the area of foreign affairs, Congress failed to take decisive action on the issue of funding international family planning programs, leaving the administration to execute the final version as it sees fit. No abortion-related alteration of the Internal Revenue Code has been adopted by Congress. Neither has Congress issued a definitive statement on the use of fetal tissue in federally funded medical research, considered by many to be one of the most controversial abortion-related issues today. Perhaps the most dramatic change in Congress' stand on abortion can be found in the expansion of the restriction on government-funded abortions in the District of Columbia. However, Congress' decision to prohibit the use of locally raised funds for abortions speaks more dramatically to the issue of home rule for the District of Columbia than to the abortion issue.

One method employed by Congress in recent years to ensure the preservation of the status quo in the abortion area is the legislative poison pill. When faced with a credible threat in the direction of change, those opposed to the change have offered companion amendments that make the price of change higher than its proponents are willing to pay. For example, in 1990 Senators Tim Wirth (D, Colo.) and John Glenn (D, Ohio) introduced an amendment to the defense authorization bill to lift the ban on abortions in military hospitals overseas when paid for by the patient herself.[128] During the debate on the amendment, Senator Humphrey threatened to add an amendment to the Wirth/Glenn amendment to allow sex change operations and cosmetic breast surgery at military hospitals.[129] Although the Wirth/Glenn amendment on its own garnered majority support, Senator Wirth withdrew the amendment after failing to invoke cloture.[130] This approach was also used successfully by Sen. Phil Gramm (R, Tex.) in the 1990 debate over a supplemental appropriations bill. In considering the bill, which primarily concerned emergency aid to Nicaragua and Panama, the Senate Appropriations Committee voted to remove the ban on the use of District of Columbia local funds for abortion.[131] When the bill reached the floor, Senator Gramm added an amendment authorizing capital punishment for drug-related murders in the District of Columbia.[132] Both amendments were approved by the Senate, and both were dropped in the conference.[133] Pro-choice members of Congress have also used the poison pill method to block legislation counter to their objectives.[134]

There are indications that this trend will continue. As the Supreme Court continues to take the judicial system out of the abortion debate by allowing control over abortion to return to the states, abortion is quickly becoming a legislative issue, not a constitutional/judicial one. Although most of the legislative action on abortion has taken place thus far on the state level, if the Supreme Court removes itself even further from the

---

[128] S. 2884; H.R. 4739.
[129] CQ, Aug. 25, 1990, No. 34, p. 2718.
[130] Id.
[131] H.R. 4404.
[132] CQ, May 5, 1990, No. 18, p. 1361.
[133] CQ, May 19, 1990, No. 20, p. 1532.
[134] Daily Report for Executives, Oct. 6, 1986.

abortion rights arena, the pressure to pick up the issue will fall eventually on the national legislature.

Evidence of this increasing pressure on Congress to deal with abortion in a serious and meaningful manner can already be seen. The most immediate evidence of the increasing importance of abortion as a congressional issue is the role it has played in election politics. Abortion has flourished as a campaign issue, and activists on both sides have flourished as a source of campaign funds. Since 1983 abortion-related political action committees have donated almost $5 million dollars to federal candidates.[135]

Abortion was a major campaign issue in the 1990 elections. Although its influence was most forcefully felt on the state level, it was a key issue in a number of congressional contests. Senator Tom Harkin's support for abortion rights figured prominately in his reelection campaign against Rep. Tom Tauke, an opponent of abortion rights.[136] The National Abortion Rights Action League spent $250,000.00 on an independent effort to support Harkin's campaign, and the candidates devoted one of their seven scheduled debates to the issue of abortion.[137] Abortion also became a key issue in Mayor Jim Moran's defeat of Rep. Stan Parris in Virginia's Eighth Congressional District. Both candidates ran controversial commercials during their campaigns explaining their position on abortion and trying to undermine their opponent's position. Parris spent a good portion of his campaign trying to define his stand on federal funding of abortion, which he was accused of moderating as the campaign progressed.[138] The focus on abortion as a national issue in these off-year elections was somewhat dampened by the emergence over the summer of critical issues such as the savings and loan crisis and the impending war in the Middle East.

As voters increasingly consider a candidate's views on abortion before pulling the lever for the candidate, voters will begin to expect candidates to deliver on their abortion-related campaign promises. Pressure will mount on Capitol Hill to engage in meaningful debate on abortion. During the years surveyed here, congressional action on abortion has impacted most forcefully on the women most removed from the political process: poor women on Medicaid, women in foreign countries who rely on international family planning programs, adolescents seeking counseling and women in the District of Columbia who don't even have a congressperson for whom to vote. As abortion becomes more of a mainstream political issue, voters from the mainstream of America who consider the abortion issue when making their election choices may expect Congress to act on the issue in a broader context. Supporters of openly pro-life candidates may expect their representatives to take more decisive action to restrict the access of all women to abortion, not just the poor. Supporters of pro-choice candidates may expect their representatives to turn their commitment to choice into action as well, enacting the protections of *Roe v. Wade* into law if the Supreme Court abandons the existing constitutional protections.

Until one side of the debate garners enough support to be able to invoke cloture or override a presidential veto, it is unlikely that Congress will be able to deliver on their promises in the form of new laws. Abortion seems to be the one issue on which even

---

[135] S. Heilbronner, *Antiabortion PAC Donations Trail Pro Choice Contributions 10–1*, UPI, Sept. 26, 1990. Washington news section.

[136] M. Hall, *In Most Cases, Abortion Is Only a Marginal Issue*, USA Today, Nov. 5, 1990, at 7A.

[137] CQ Apr. 7, 1990, No. 14, pp. 1090–91. Senator Harkin was reelected.

[138] K. Jenkins, Jr., *Parris Renounces Abortion Opposition*, Washington Post, Sept. 26, 1990 at D5.

Congress cannot compromise. It is more likely that individual congresspeople, feeling the need to have something to report home, will continue to make individual stands by introducing legislation that is quickly abandoned and to administer dramatic poison pills to legislation that is contrary to their interests. In turn, voter frustration over the inability of Congress to act in a meaningful manner will grow with unknown, but inevitably divisive, results.[139]

---

[139] As the year 1991 drew to a close, several bills on abortion reached their final conclusion without making any significant changes in the antiabortion position of the Bush administration.

In the most highly disputed issue, Congress approved legislation to lift the administration's ban on abortion counseling at federally funded family planning clinics. The Bush administration had approved the ban, which was also upheld by the Supreme Court case, *Rust v. Sullivan*. After President Bush vetoed congressional legislation to remove the ban, the House voted 276 to 156 to override the president's veto. However, this fell 12 votes short of the necessary two-thirds. In 1992 the "gag rule" was lifted for physicians, but not for medical personnel.

The house included in its Defense Authorization bill a provision to allow military personnel and dependents to obtain abortions at military hospitals overseas. The provision was eliminated in a House-Senate conference because it was feared that President Bush would veto the whole defense bill if this abortion provision was included.

Proposals to overturn the policy that denies funds to international organizations that promote abortions and to resume U.S. payments to the U.N. family planning fund were both approved by Congress. However, these proposals eventually reached a roadblock when the foreign aid authorization bill, which contained these provisions, died in the House.

The House voted to include in its National Institutes of Health bill a provision allowing fetal tissue research. The bill did not pass the House by enough votes to overcome a presidential veto, and the Senate will not act on this measure until 1992.

The Senate once again voted to allow Medicaid-funded abortions for victims of rape and incest. However, this bill was not passed by the House.

Both the House and the Senate voted to repeal the law barring the District of Columbia from using funds from local tax sources to finance abortions for Medicaid recipients. President Bush vetoed this bill, and Congress did not have enough votes to override this veto.

The Senate also debated the issue of parental notification for minors seeking abortions. The outcome of this issue is unknown because the House had not acted on the bill before the end of the year 1991.

Finally, both the executive and the legislative branches of the government are watching the Supreme Court and the several cases that will challenge *Roe v. Wade*. It is generally acknowledged that any Supreme Court decision on abortion in 1992 will have a profound impact on the 1992 elections. The legislative branch is also considering a Freedom of Choice Act that will protect abortion rights for all women throughout the United States.

This article argues that one has to look beyond the cases of *Roe* and *Griswold* in order to understand the right to privacy. A survey of Western civilization demonstrates that an increased concern with privacy as a cultural and legal value distinguishes the modern world from ancient and medieval societies. Thus while the famous legal article by Samuel B. Warren and Louis D. Brandeis in 1890 may have been the first to explicitly identify the right to privacy in the legal realm, it was not the first expression in the cultural realm. Ironically, women's rights were not originally linked to privacy because 19th-century feminists were trying to escape from the central focus of privacy concerns: the home. Mid-20th-century Americans turned increasingly to privacy as a legal and cultural value in the face of new technologies that seemed to threaten them with totalitarianism. Contemporary Americans' general valuing of privacy and the particular evocation of a right to privacy in the abortion debates are both products of these varied historical developments.

27 · The Right to Privacy: A Historical Perspective _____

Linda Przybyszewski, Ph.D.

The purpose of considering history when making present policy is to find out what people have done in an earlier time and what the consequences of their choices were. Also, by learning how our society has come to take the shape it has, we know better how to make decisions about the shape we want it to be.

In order to write a history of the right to privacy, it is necessary to investigate more than the history of the laws that legislatures have passed and the decisions that courts have made. Historians go on to ask what actual practices were. Did a certain court decision change how people behaved, or was it ignored? What were the cultural assumptions and political loyalties of the various people—lawyers, litigants, judges, legislators, voters—involved in a controversy? To the legal historian, legal events must be placed against a broad background of private and public life. Without an understanding of what the people making those decisions thought they were doing, without an understanding of the cultural assumptions that informed their decision-making, we cannot understand the nature of what we have inherited and of what we are.

One chapter in the previous edition of this book, entitled "The Law and History of Abortion: The Supreme Court Refuted," written by Stephen M. Krason and William B. Holberg, is an example of a limited historical search because it considers only legal precedent. Most historians would consider incomplete, for example, their citation to a passage in Sir William Blackstone's *Commentaries on the Laws of England* that declares abortion a crime because they make it without any reference to the other passages in Blackstone that affected women and without any reference to the status of women in 18th-century English society. Historical method assumes that a passage in Blackstone has meaning only within the specific context in which it was written. The same is true of our understanding of the passage of a law by a legislature or of a decision of a court or a public speech about the legal system. In each of these instances, what the historian should be doing is offering information on the significance of actions and statements made by legal authorities so that later generations may understand them as the products of a certain time and place.

In other words, it is not enough to say that we as a society or we in Western culture passed a law criminalizing abortion before, therefore we can do it again. Such evidence of legal precedents are insufficient. We must also ask how and why and what exactly we did do before. What is the cultural web of which these laws were a part? How has that web changed in shape over time? And what shape are we now dealing with and what are its consequences?

In the case of Blackstone, for instance, there are several passages relevant to women's status. The passage on abortion declares that "if a woman is quick with child, and by a potion or otherwise, kills it in her womb . . . this though not murder, was by the ancient law homicide or manslaughter."[1] Other passages make clear the subordinate position women held in English society and within marriage. Blackstone writes, "By marriage, the husband and wife are one person in law; that is, the very being or legal existence of the woman is suspended during the marriage . . ." and also, "The husband, by the old law, might give his wife moderate correction. For as he is to answer for her misbehavior, the law thought it reasonable to intrust him with this power of restraining her, by domestic chastisement, in the same moderation that a man is allowed to correct his apprentices or children . . ."[2] Putting the passage on abortion in Blackstone along side these other passages makes it difficult to accept the simplistic argument that if something was the law before, so it should be the law again.

The placement of Blackstone against a historical background highlights the particular package of beliefs and practices of which the illegality of abortion in 18th-century England were a part. Women's subordination to men was another piece of that package. That is undeniable. What other packages may be possible now or in the future is a different question.[3]

A full history of the right to privacy also demands the placement of laws and case decisions in a cultural web of practices and beliefs. It would be wrong to begin a history of the right to privacy by starting from decisions on the Supreme Court involving contraception and abortion and working our way backward along legal precedent to the Bill of Rights. So, too, it would be wrong to work our way forward from an article written in 1890 by Louis D. Brandeis, later Justice Brandeis, and Samuel D. Warren where the two lawyers made the first explicit attempt to introduce a right to privacy into American tort law.[4] Looking at the legal world alone is unsufficient for telling the story because the history of the right to privacy is intertwined with the history of privacy itself as a cultural value.

Privacy, its shape and its limits, is at the heart of any social order because it is the point of intersection between the individual and the community. Because the topic is so

---

[1] Sir William Blackstone, *Commentaries on the Law of England* 101 (Robert Malcom Kerr ed. 1876).

[2] Blackstone, *supra* note 1, at 418–420.

[3] Thus John T. Noonan's piece "An Almost Absolute Value in History," which is an account of Catholic ethicists' discussion of abortion, provokes the feminist concern that the subordination of women to men has also been an almost absolute value in history. *The Morality of Abortion: Legal and Historical Perspectives* 1–59 (J. Noonan ed. 1970).

[4] Samuel D. Warren and Louis D. Brandeis, *The Right to Privacy,* 4 Harv. L. Rev. 193–220 (December 1890).

broad and because this article is one part of a larger project, we will be looking here at only some of the ways in which our society has construed what is public and what is private.[5] It is a preliminary effort at considering both legal precedents that are well-known and at the same time their relatively neglected cultural surroundings.

The argument made here is that the right to privacy as used in 20th-century Supreme Court decisions is the result of a number of far-flung cultural and legal traditions and practices. We will be looking at a select set of interconnected phenomena dating back to the premodern era. Privacy will be analyzed in reference to the withdrawal of the family into the home and the rise of manners that put a premium on the creation of distance between individuals and between the individual and the community. Related but distinguishable from this privatization of the home is the idea of the individual having rights against the community and against state power. Similarly connected is the notion of the individual having bodily integrity; this can be referred to as a source or a result of privacy rights. The gradual evolution of these practices and values have bestowed upon late 20th-century American society a variety of means for valuing privacy in and of itself.

This explanation for the use of the right to privacy first in *Griswold v. Connecticut* and eventually in *Roe v. Wade* differs from some of the contentions of renowned feminist theorists. Rosaline Pollack Petchesky has argued that it was the combination of fears of overpopulation and the efforts of women's rights advocates that explain how the Supreme Court came to legalize abortions.[6] This piece would add that the historical weight of beliefs about the public and the private, which were first formulated without reference to those two concerns, shaped the particular way in which legalization occurred. A second important feminist scholar Catharine MacKinnon has criticized the right to privacy as a male-centered idea that implicitly allows men their free reign in the private sphere where women remain subordinate to them. Abortion is made available under the right to privacy so that men do not have to take responsibility for their active sexual domination over women.[7] But this article will show that there has been more to the creation of the distinction between public and private than the purposeful oppression of women. The maintenance of a protective distance between the citizen and the state has come to be especially valued. This brings me to a last point—about reconstructing the evolution of privacy as a cultural value.

By looking at earlier periods when privacy and the right to privacy did not exist as we know them, we will be acknowledging that the construction of what is private and what is public are cultural conventions. The innate truth of any particular practice cannot be proven through history. However, that historical knowledge does not make privacy into a relative value of shape so varying that it does not matter what shape it takes today. These are the cultural conventions of our society and these values are ones that

[5] There are several useful bibliographies: D. Siepp, *Privacy and Disclosure Regulation of Information Systems: A Bibliographic Survey* (1975), *The Right of Privacy—Its Constitutional and Social Dimensions: A Comprehensive Bibliography* (D.M. O'Brien ed. 1980); A. G. White, *Privacy, Confidentiality: A Selected Bibliography* (1982); H. A. Latin, *Privacy: A Selected Bibliography and Topical Index of Social Science Materials* (1976). Paul L. Murphy has edited a collection of essays, *The Right to Privacy and the Ninth Amendment* 2 vols. (1989); and on cultural understandings of the public and private split, see *Public and Private in Social Life* (S. I. Benn and G. F. Gaus eds. 1983).

[6] R. P. Petchesky, *Abortion and Woman's Choice: The State, Sexuality, and Reproductive Freedom* 101–138 (rev. ed. 1984).

[7] C. A. MacKinnon, *Feminism Unmodified: Discourses on Life and Law* 93–102 (1987).

we have inherited. That makes them important, not relative. And that makes it necessary for us to consider how women's right to choose abortions is intertwined with the long history of the cultural ascendancy of privacy. In making decisions about abortion policy, we must remember how a whole web of beliefs and practices are affected by them.

To better understand the specific 20th-century American form of privacy that we have inherited, we have to begin much earlier by considering the premodern world of western Europe, a world one historian called "a world without intimacy" and thus without privacy.[8]

Social historians of medieval Europe depict a world where the physical possibilities for privacy were few, and the accompanying estimation of its worth was low. Philippe Ariès, the foremost among these scholars, wrote that "until the end of the seventeenth century, nobody was ever left alone."[9] Whether individuals were rich or poor, they lived in crowds of people. The household and not the biological family was thought of as the basic social unit. A household consisted of servants or apprentices as well as parents and children.

Peasants usually had only one room to their house, so everything from cooking to sleeping happened in it. Often several people slept in the same room and in the same bed. Although the rich lived in larger houses, such houses contained many people and served as a sort of public meeting place. Thus, human density was still high.[10] Because of the difficulty of heating such poorly insulated buildings, even a wealthy man would eat in the kitchen.[11] Most rooms opened onto other rooms so that one had to pass through each room to get to the other end of a house. Again, beds and rooms were shared. Perhaps a curtain surrounded a bed, but that was the only concession to privacy.

The physical arrangements of life were of a piece with the customs and values of the people. Jacob Burckhardt, a 19th-century historian, observed of the medieval Italians: "Man was conscious of himself only as a member of a race, people, party, family, or corporation—only through some general category."[12] One was less an individual than a member of a family bloodline or a practitioner of a trade or an inhabitant of a village.[13] Writing of the dependent members of the traditional English household before the onset of industrialization, historian Peter Laslett argued that "such men and women,

[8] J. Amato, *A World Without Intimacy: A Portrait of a Time Before We were Intimate Individuals and lovers*, 61, no. 4 Int'l. Soc. Sci. Rev. 155–168 (1986). For a useful historical sketch of cultural privacy, see J. Bensman and R. Lilienfeld, *Between Public and Private: The Lost Boundaries of the Self* 28–53 (1979).

[9] Philippe Ariès, *Centuries of Childhood: A Social History of Family Life* 398 (R. Baldick trans. 1969) (originally published in 1960 in French with the less poetic title *L'Enfant and La Vie Familiale sous L'Ancien Régime*).

[10] Ariès, *supra* note 9, at 391ff.

[11] Amato, *supra* note 8, at 156.

[12] J. Burckhardt, *The Civilization of the Renaissance in Italy* 100 (1954). Although Natalie Zemon Davis has argued in contrast that such people found various strategies for asserting the self, an emphasis on what she calls embeddedness is more suitable for comparative purposes. See her piece *Boundaries and the Sense of Self in Sixteenth-Century France*, in *Reconstructing Individualism: Autonomy, Individuality, and the Self in Western Thought* 53–63 (T.C. Heller ed. 1986).

[13] The ancients appear to have shared this understanding of the self. Paul Veyne writes, "no ancient, not even the poets, is capable of talking about himself. Nothing is more misleading than the use of 'I' in Greco-Roman Poetry." Emotions were either personified or generalized, never personalized. *A History of Private Life: From Pagan Rome to Byzantium* 231ff. (P. Veyne ed. 1987).

boys and girls, were caught up, so to speak, 'subsumed' is the ugly word we shall use, into the personalities of their fathers and masters.''[14]

Besides being displayed in personal dependency, this embeddedness, as Natalie Zemon Davis has called it, was made visible in community practices. The marriage of a couple was accompanied by the blessing of their bed, the visiting by family and friends when they were already in bed, as well as general rowdiness throughout the night.[15] The event was a public one that members of the community felt they should oversee. If some group did not approve of the marriage because of the disparate ages or ranks of the two partners, then they felt it their right or duty to make a public display (called a *charvari*) to mock the couple.[16] Such practices were not written in law books but were part of the community's notions of correct and legitimate customs. In general in the Middle Ages, as Ariès wrote, ''[P]rivate was confounded with public.''[17] Notice, however, that the general realm of action was local and that it was the community that affected people's lives. The state as we know it, an organized and centralized authority, had yet to be invented.

Then by the end of the 17th century, historians begin to see changes in the construction of social and family life in Europe and England. The houses of the rich acquired the hallways that we are all familiar with; one no longer had to pass through one room to get to another. Builders moved bedrooms to the upper floors and out of the general pattern of traffic. The French language now distinguished between the words *chambre* (meaning bedroom) and *salle* (meaning a room of any other kind). The wealthy kept their servants at a distance by using dumbwaiters, which made their presence superfluous, and by using bells to call them.[18] The changes were not distributed evenly, of course, partly because they cost money. Also, those who lived in cities gained more privacy as did those whose work necessitated solitude, for example, artists or religious authorities. Peasants were still living crammed together and would for centuries to come.[19]

These changes in the physical layout in houses reflected a new valuing of privacy for the individual and for the family.[20] As servants and friends and business acquaintances were pushed out of the house, the family turned in on itself. Parents began to conceive of their children as distinct individuals who were worth cherishing more than ever. They put a greater value on their children's health and education.[21] The nature of courtship was also changing: Although the familial alliances that a marriage created

---

[14] P. Laslett, *The World We Have Lost: England Before the Industrial Age* 21 (1965).

[15] Ariès, *supra* note 9, at 405.

[16] Daniel Fabre, in *A History of Private Life: Passions of the Renaissance* 533 (R. Chartier ed., A. Goldhammer trans. 1989) [hereinafter Chartier ed.].

[17] Philippe Ariès, *Introduction*, in Chartier ed., *supra* note 16, at 1.

[18] L. Stone, *The Family, Sex and Marriage in England, 1500–1800* 169, 245 (abridged ed. 1977, 1979); Ariès *supra* note 9, at 399. Stone has been criticized for his generalizations, but on privacy he is in line with many others.

[19] Stone, *supra* note 18, at 170, 384; Ariès *supra* note 9, at 404.

[20] For a useful if dated survey of the literature, see B. Laslett, *The Family as a Public and Private Institution: An Historical Perspective*, 35 J. of Marriage and the Fam. 480–492 (1973). For the latest historiographical survey, see T. K. Hareven, *The History of the Family and the Complexity of Change*, 96 Am. Hist. Rev. 96–124 (1991).

[21] Ariès, *supra* note 9, at 399–402; also J. Gélis, *The Child: From Anonymity to Individuality*, in Chartier ed., *supra* note 16, at 320ff.

were far from neglected, people began to speak of the paramount importance of affection and love for a couple.[22] Courtship took on its romantic and intimate coloring.

The community's power to punish and correct, in effect a legal power, was challenged by these changes. Roger Chartier has written of pre-modern France that its

> *collective surveillance gradually was repudiated, discredited, and denounced as an intolerable violation of individuals' freedom of choice or the family's sovereign right, an invasion of what came to be considered as privacy, the private sphere being that which was not subject to the jurisdiction of the community.*[23]

The ritualized disapproval of the *charvari* was now condemned as illegitimate and disorderly. Its victims appealed successfully to state authorities and local religious authorities for relief.[24] In fact, one of the best known historians of the creation of centralized state authority in France, Norbert Elias, emphasized its connection with the code of behavior that put distance between people.[25] As though the rise of a powerful and remote state necessitated the withdrawal of the individual personality into its own shelter, a withdrawal that would not have been countenanced by traditional community standards.

The interaction of the family and other members of the community became formalized, as did the manners all people were supposed to display before others. Jacques Revel has written of France between 1500 and 1800 that manners evolved in two contradictory ways:

> *Public behavior was subject to strict regulation through education and various physical and spiritual disciplines [while] . . . extracommunal refuges proliferated, the family foremost among them.*[26]

One was no longer supposed to drop in unannounced at a great house; instead one left a card, and the family decided whether or not it was "at home." Special days might be set aside when guests would be welcome, but otherwise they took their chances.[27] Guests were no longer welcomed in rooms containing beds but were restricted to public downstairs rooms. The notion of civility, a code of manners that were necessary to proper public life, arose. Etiquette books became the handbooks for civilized behavior. Their rules were all designed to put distance—physical and psychological—between individuals and between the family and the community.[28] Practices that had been accepted in medieval life as normal were now rejected.

The first European colonists came to the American continent after these changes had already begun in their homelands. However, the idea of civility and its accompany-

[22] *See* O. Ranum, *The Refuges of Intimacy,* in Chartier ed., *supra* note 16, at 297ff.

[23] R. Chartier, in Chartier, ed., *supra* note 16, at 401.

[24] Fabre, *supra* note 16, at 555ff.

[25] N. Elias, *The Civilizing Process: The Development of Manners: Changes in the Code of Conduct and Feeling in Early Modern Times* (E. Jephcott trans. 1939, 1978).

[26] J. Revel, *The Uses of Civility,* in Chartier ed., *supra* note 16, at 167–8.

[27] Ariès, *supra* note 9, at 399.

[28] Elias, *supra* note 25.

ing valuation of privacy made uneven progress at first. In Puritan New England, ideo-logical pressures placed privacy lower than other values. In other areas of the colonies too, the physical difficulty of settling meant privacy was sacrificed out of necessity. But once these twin forces—the ideological and the physical—lost their primacy, privacy grew in cultural and legal importance.

The Puritans brought with them to New England the mixed legacy of early modern England where traditional community and family practices were being reshaped by peo-ple's new concern for the integrity of the individual. Puritan religion, an all-pervasive force at first, affected privacy in contradictory ways.

On the one hand, Puritanism stressed the importance of each worshiper's personal experience with God. Each member of the church was supposed to open his or her soul and mind to direct communication with the divine. The mediating role Catholic priests had played between God and the communities in which they served was absent in this Protestant religion. One's communication with the Lord became a private and sacred act that required that others stay out of it.

On the other hand, the Puritans were very concerned with correct behavior in their community. Everyone was supposed to remain watchful of sinful behavior in others and report it; no one was allowed to settle in a town until his or her good character was proven. As historian David Flaherty, the author of a volume examining privacy among the Puritans, has written, "A deeply held conviction 'Not to Suffer Sin in My Fellow Creature or Neighbor' " undermined what privacy could be found.[29] The Puritans' was a communal venture of "saints" from the first.

Flaherty contends that the Puritans were thus torn between "introspection" and "watchfulness."[30] Privacy was valued but ambivalently. Other historians have empha-sized how often watchfulness reigned supreme. Michael Zuckerman wrote of the 18th-century, "In the little towns of Massachusetts . . . there was no place of privacy, no time of a man's life when he could rest secure from scrutiny."[31] By turning to the practices of the Puritans in their homes and towns, we can see how much they shared with their medieval ancestors and how the circumstances of life in the colonies changed.

Like the rural peasants of England and Europe, the Puritans at first lived in homes of high density and physical proximity. Perhaps no more striking expression of how privacy was sacrificed to social control can be found than in the fact that it was illegal for a person to live alone.[32] Towns were laid out so that houses were built closely together and the first homes were simple with one central fireplace.[33] But as the colo-nists became more settled and prosperous, they built larger homes and added hallways.[34] They also moved their homes away from the central town in order to lessen the distance from their houses to their fields. Geographically, the Puritan settlements were resem-bling those compact rural villages of the old country less and less. One historian has described the affect the movement of these outlanders had: "No one could disregard the

---

[29] D. Flaherty, *Privacy in Colonial New England* 94 (1972). Flaherty's contribution is important, yet it is flawed by a tendency to search for precedent and an adoption of the ahistorical notion of a balance of privacy, a concept first used by Alan Westin.

[30] *Id.* at viii.

[31] M. Zuckerman, *Peaceable Kingdoms: New England Towns in the 18th Century* (1970).

[32] Flaherty, *supra* note 29, at 175–179.

[33] *See* J. Demos, *A Little Commonwealth: Family Life in Plymouth Colony* 46 (1970).

[34] Flaherty, *supra* note 29, at 26ff.

overtones of disorder and sin attached to removal from the protecting village.''[35] Beyond the eyes of the church and neighbors, individuals and families might be doing things both immoral and illegal.

As with the medieval peasants who confounded public and private, the Puritans confounded immoral and illegal.[36] Their treatment of evidence against alleged criminals makes particularly clear how they stood at midpoint between medieval and modern legal worlds. One incident has particularly drawn the attention of historians: the interception of a packet of letters by the governor of Plymouth Colony in 1624.

Governor William Bradford and his allies suspected two men, named Lyford and Oldham, of plotting "a reformation in church and commonwealth," that is, an overthrow of Bradford's government. So Bradford intercepted and copied letters that the two men had written to England containing "slanders and false accusations" against the government of the colony. Bradford gathered the whole community together in a court (a traditional way of doing justice) and denounced Lyford and Oldham for their treachery. When they denied any guilt, Bradford produced and read the letters outloud. Lyford was cowed by proof of his crime, but Oldham, in the words of Bradford himself, "began to rage furiously because they had intercepted and opened his letters, threatening them in a very high language, and in a most audacious and mutinous manner stood up and called upon the people" to join in open rebellion since they had much to complain of at the hands of the authorities for what they had done. When Bradford asked him rhetorically "if he thought they had done evil to open his letters," the implication being that the letters contained an evil that needed to be exposed, Lyford fell quiet. Bradford then emphasized how he was acting in a magisterial capacity when he got his hands on the letters, and the community appears to have been satisfied with him. Lyford and Oldham were expelled from the colony.[37]

Obviously, in the Puritan world, private letters were not supposed to be intercepted and handed about for amusement, but they became fair game in the event of a crime. Bradford argued that he had gotten hold of the letters to stop the two men from making trouble, so he felt that he must justify his actions, as Flaherty has pointed out in his comments on the incident. But Bradford's actions were in effect justified by what he had found, not merely by why he had acted. And one gets the impression from other incidents that the technical requirements practiced by modern criminal courts were either less important (the rules for warrants were laxer in Puritan New England) or nonexistent (the reading of rights, the exclusionary rule) in the Puritan legal system.[38] One can hardly imagine the Puritans adopting the exclusionary rule of the 20th-century Supreme Court that because evidence was gathered in an improper way a criminal must go free.

True, the Puritans punished eavesdropping and spying, but if a nosy person found proof of wrongdoing, then his or her effort was considered legitimate. The court records

---

[35] R. L. Bushman, *From Puritan to Yankee: Character and the Social Order in Connecticut, 1690–1765* 56 (1967).

[36] *See* Flaherty, *Law and the Enforcement of Morals in Early America,* in *Law in American History* 203–253 (D. Fleming and B. Bailyn eds. 1971).

[37] William Bradford, *Of Plymouth Plantation, 1620–1647* 149–163 (Samuel Eliot Morison ed. 1952). This incident is cited for entirely different purposes by Flaherty, *supra* note 29, at 124–125, and by T. H. O'Connor, *The Right to Privacy in Historical Perspective,* 53 Mass. L. Q. 101–115 (1969). O'Connor's is a generally undistinguished piece, but he appears more cognizant of the lack of limits on legal authorities than Flaherty.

[38] *See* Flaherty on warrants, *supra* note 29, at 192–3.

contain numerous tales of prosecuting witnesses banging unannounced through doors, peeping through knotholes or keeping a close ear out and thus discovering adulterers.[39] These efforts to watch family and neighbors became more difficult physically as houses grew larger and further from one another and became less appealing to the less religious members of younger generations.

Early settlers in the southern colonies also built small and compact houses so that privacy within the home was hard to come by. (And for slaves and indentured servants, there could especially be little or no claim to privacy.) Unlike in New England, these dwellings were from the first scattered, and there were no towns. People separated themselves by great tracts of land. They practiced a kind of generous hospitality, however, that bridged isolation.[40] The high death rates in the first generations meant that few parents were around to raise their children and control them.[41] This meant that larger kin networks had to take over looking after the interests of large numbers of orphans and step-children. With time, however, the death rates decreased and longevity increased.

Nuclear families thus became far more durable, and their members began in the 18th century a process that would mark the 19th century particularly: the privatization of the family, also seen in Europe and New England. Southern colonial families already lived like the New England outlanders physically; they increased their exclusivity by turning inward emotionally and devaluing the large kin networks that had been so necessary earlier.[42] Refinements of manners, as historian Rhys Isaac has written, "expressed an increasingly felt need to shield individuals from close interaction with an enveloping social world, a world that was now held to be impure and vulgar."[43] Southern hospitality became a legend rather than a practice.

So, as the 18th century drew to a close, social life in the colonies was growing increasingly privatized. Richard Lyman Bushman noticed the connection in colonial society between privacy and political thought when he wrote of the New England outlanders: "They would themselves be rulers."[44] Outlander farmers valued distance between themselves and the community in both physical and emotional terms. By moving out, they simultaneously defied the community's physical ability and its political authority to control them.

A similar defiance appeared in the colonists on a broader scale as the imperial government of England tried to reassert its control over its colonies. Long neglected imperially and thus habituated to self-rule, many colonists balked when the English administration tried to reintegrate them into the empire by making them submit to taxation to pay for the armies that protected their western boundaries. The ensuing political disputes over self-rule and representation finally escalated into violence and revolution. Still, the founding generation expressed a vision of the individual and the polity that was a mixture of the traditional and the modern.

---

[39] *Id.* at 42–3, 54.

[40] Rhys Isaac, *The Transformation of Virginia, 1740–1790* 71 (1982, 1988).

[41] Lorena Walsh, " 'Til Death Us do Part'': Marriage and Family in Seventeenth Century Maryland in *The Chesapeake in the Seventeenth Century: Essays on Anglo-American Society* 126–152 (T.W. Tate and D. L. Ammerman eds. 1979).

[42] D. B. Smith, *Inside the Great House: Planter Family Life in 18th-Century Chesapeake Society* 22, 175, 229 (1980).

[43] Isaac, *supra* note 40, at 303.

[44] Bushman, *supra* note 35, at 64.

The republican ideology professed and practiced by the revolutionary generation contained much of the traditional confounding of public and private and was consciously drawn from classical political examples. The revolutionaries' political ideas demanded that personal self-interest be sacrificed to the common good.[45] The characteristic that impelled such a sacrifice was called civic virtue, and as its two-part name suggests, it was both political and personal in nature.

We may think of virtue as a strictly personal characteristic, but our nation's founders were of an age that used the words "manners" and "politeness" to denote attitudes and behavior that necessarily spilled over into the civil realm. They believed in a reciprocal relationship between manners and public institutions: The structure of government was supposed to instill certain characteristics in the people, yet any structurally sound institution might be undermined by the corruptive nature of the people.[46] A most striking example of this phenomenon is Thomas Jefferson's chapter in his *Notes on the State of Virginia* where he laments how the institution of slavery corrupts the democratic character of white men by versing them in tyranny over blacks; the chapter is entitled "Manners." Since many of the elite of the founding generation had received classical education, they must have known of the origins of the word individual: that its root was the Greek word for a private (i.e., non-civic) person, "idios," from which came also the word idiot.[47] Established colonial rituals and institutions, especially the mob in the streets, made it clear that the community as a whole would act to keep individuals in line.

So if the *charvari* had been quieted in Europe, it acted out in different form in the colonial mob. By intimidating customs agents or exposing a loyalist to public humiliation through tarring and feathering, the revolutionary mobs made it clear that individual beliefs and behavior would be punished by the community, that men would be made to sacrifice their self-interests, to their civic virtue, by force if necessary. Ironically, this revolution gave a constitutional impetus to the individualism that was in turn linked to the rise of privacy.

Still, the revolutionaries' concern with individual rights was set upon an older ideological base. The social evolution of privacy in England and its coexistence with the rise of a powerful centralized state should be remembered when considering the traditions upon which the founders drew. The English had already begun to put limits on their sovereign mirroring that proper distance now espoused between the individual family and the community. These changes were in part the result of the religious wars that had begun in the 16th century all over Europe with the Reformation. The instability such fighting created for state-building prompted theoretical and practical responses that would legitimate freedom of conscience as a natural right born of one's relation with God. Also, unhappily for the English who wished to keep the colonies part of the Empire, they had set an example for overturning an unjust king in 1688 with the Glo-

---

[45]The literature on American republicanism is vast; it began with B. Bailyn, *Ideological Origins of the American Revolution* (1967) and G. Wood, *The Creation of the American Republic, 1776–1787* (1969). That the idea is starting to collapse under its own explanatory weight is demonstrated unintentionally in R. E. Shalhope, *Republicanism and Early American Historiography*, Ser. 3, 39 Wm. & Mary L. Q. 334–356 (1982).

[46]*See also* 1 *The Founders' Constitution* 654 (P. B. Kurland and R. Lerner eds. 1987); and S. A. Conrad, *Polite Foundation: Citizenship and Common Sense in James Wilson's Republican Theory*, Sup. Ct. Rev. 359–388 (1984).

[47]B. Moore Jr., *Privacy: Studies in Social and Cultural History* 82 (1984).

rious Revolution when William of Orange was invited to take the English throne. Such incidents threw into question the divine legitimacy of any given monarchy.

When the revolutionaries fought the imperial forces, they were trying to preserve what they considered their traditional rights as free-born Englishmen who had previously defied a king. (The men is literal here, for as our reading of Blackstone earlier has indicated, women were still subsumed into the male heads of household even while male citizenship was being defined and redefined.) For example, the prohibition on unreasonable search and seizure found in the United States Constitution was rooted in the English understanding of the limits even the sovereign must respect when faced with a private dwelling. William Pitt, the 18th century English statesman, declared in an oft-quoted passage:

> *The poorest man may in his cottage bid defiance to all the forces of the Crown. It may be frail—its roof may shake—the wind may blow through it—the storm may enter—the rain may enter—but the King of England cannot enter—all his forces dare not cross the threshold of the ruined tenement!*

Which is a poetic exaggeration of course, because with a warrant, the King could go wherever he liked. Still the purport of the quote is most important. Both Pitt and the revolutionaries were arguing for explicit limits on government action; they were setting off a portion of individual behavior and being that could not be interfered with. Liberty versus power was the leitmotif of the new scheme of government; privacy was necessarily protected when liberty gained over power. This is how advocates of the right to privacy in the 20th century managed to find it as part of the "penumbra" emanating from the Constitution's general purpose as a shield against arbitrary governmental power.

The word privacy is not in the Constitution, of course, but a whole set of concerns about the citizen's ability to keep government officials at a physical distance are in the Bill of Rights. The Bill of Rights itself was a kind of redundancy since the explicit enumeration of the powers that the national government could have should have theoretically been sufficient to indicate that it could not go beyond those powers and invade individual rights. But those who feared the potential power of the new national government succeeded in having the first amendments added to the document.[48] These guarantees were expressions of the fear that the national government might try to abuse its power as the imperial English government had. Among the numerous complaints that the colonists had had about their imperial governors were the searching of property without proper warrants and the quartering of soldiers in private homes.[49] Both practices were aimed at keeping the colonists in line, and both were targeted in the Bill of Rights as practices that must be prohibited to ensure the liberties of the people. Both could be called invasions of privacy.

In addition to the limitations on the quartering of soldiers and the use of warrants, other rights in the Constitution promoted privacy as an aspect of personal liberty. The first amendment with its right of free speech and the fifth amendment with its protection

---

[48] R. A. Rutland, *The Birth of the Bill of Rights, 1776–1791* (1955). For a collection of articles, see *The Historic Background of the Bill of Rights* (P. L. Murphy, ed. 1989).

[49] David M. O'Brien gives a brief account of the historical origins of the first, fourth and fifth amendments in his book, *Privacy, Law and Public Policy* (1979).

against self-incrimination worked to protect the individual's private thoughts and public expressions of them. Also the first amendment's nonestablishment clause concerning religion shielded the individual conscience from state oppression. Although the purpose of the first eight amendments in the Bill of Rights was to limit national governmental power, the founders added the ninth and tenth amendments to ensure that no right had been inadvertently left open to government attack.

It is the ninth amendment that has played an important role in constitutionalizing the right to privacy. The ninth amendment made it clear that the enumeration of certain rights in the other amendments "shall not be construed to deny or disparage others retained by the people." The tenth amendment declared that the states or the people retained any powers not explicitly granted to the national government. Both summed up the overall purpose of the Constitution: to give the federal government only limited powers so that the citizenry would remain free and ultimately control that government. The ninth amendment has natural law implications. As legal scholar Leslie Dunbar wrote, "[I]t instructs the court to act on the principle that rights are not created by law, and do not require legal recognition for their exercise."[50] This notion of limits on national government is essential to understanding the historical basis for mid-20th century demands for a right to privacy. Of equal importance is an awareness of how privacy in social life continued to change and grow in importance.

Both the mob and republican ideology lost some of their legitimacy in the post-war years. Once the community was free from imperial supervision, the legitimacy of the mob fell into question. If the people ruled in the legislature, the reasoning went, what need had they to rule in the streets?[51] At the same time, the republican vision, which demanded that the individual sacrifice personal interests (one's salary paid by the imperial government, for example) for the common good of the community, suffered a decline in the face of economic change and the privatization of the family. The distance between the family and the community that had begun growing long before the war would accelerate in the 19th century, especially as the population began to concentrate in cities.

The frontier communities that would become the towns of the mid-19th century resembled the Puritan ideal at first. In a phrase that echoes Ariès, Mary P. Ryan writes of Baptist and Presbyterian communities in the years 1790 to 1820 that "the first generation on the New York frontier seemed careless of the distinction between family and church and society."[52] This confusion (in the non-pejorative sense of the word) lessened as the family lost its public role and retreated into the household. The status of women altered as they were designated as primarily private, familial beings whose lives should be based within the household. These changes in the nature of the household were possible because of changes in the economy.

On a farm, a woman's role was necessarily productive and partially public despite her subordinate political and social status; she was a lesser partner in the running of the operations. Even in the cities, when production was organized in the households of artisans, women had an economic, semi-public role. But at the beginning of the 19th century, the small cities of the northeast saw the kind of industrial organization that had

---

[50] L. W. Dunbar, *James Madison and the Ninth Amendment*, 42 Va. L. Rev. 627–643, 641 (1956).

[51] P. Maier, *Popular Uprisings and Civil Authority in Eighteenth-Century America*, Ser. 3, 27 Wm. & Mary Q. 3–35 (1970).

[52] M. P. Ryan, *Cradle of the Middle Class: The Family in Oneida County, New York, 1790–1865* 41 (1981).

been typical since medieval times give way to modern forms. Originally, artisanal households had been organized in the traditional form of family plus servants and apprentices. Wage-earners lived and ate with the masters who employed them and were included in their definition of their "family."[53] Masters were able and desirous of controlling their workers' private lives for financial and moral reasons. Wives and daughters might take part in some stage of production or sale.

But as the scale of production increased and the successful shops grew larger until they reached small-factory size, close supervision and intrusion into dependents' privacy was no longer possible.[54] The master-servant hierarchy began to be replaced by more impersonal power structures. At the same time, prosperity and new middle-class notions of propriety pushed women deeper inside the house just as workers were pushed outside it. The historical paradox for feminists, of course, is that it is the right to privacy that has been invoked by the Supreme Court to protect reproductive choices yet the privatization of the family prescribed for women a restrictive sphere of action with childbearing as a primary responsibility.

Historians have ascribed the privatization of the family to the anxieties middle-class people felt in the face of the numerous changes that urban and economic growth produced.[55] The city now contained new immigrants who seemed dangerously different and unsettled to older inhabitants. No longer able to control their communities, the middle-class families began to see their homes as a kind of sacred refuge from the dangers of the world. As cultural historian Karen Haltunnun has written of 19th-century fiction, the underlying premise was "that private experience was morally superior to public life."[56]

There in the house the women would wait, making a safe and comfortable place for men to return to after a difficult day fighting in the marketplace. Women's nature was defined as particularly suited for this quiet, supportive role and men's for their aggressive, public one.[57] The reality was far more complicated than this ideal, of course. Any family too poor to allow the wife to escape wage labor could not comply. Some women of all classes challenged the strictures laid against their public activities as abolitionists and feminists. Feminists also objected to the inefficiency and isolation produced by segregating women in homes divided from one another.[58] But in the main, Victorian thought equated woman with the home and the home with privacy.

And the middle-class Victorians constructed their homes with the preservation of privacy in mind. As one expert on the social history of American housing has written, "although the differentiation between public and private spaces in the house had been

---

[53] P. E. Johnson, *A Shopkeeper's Millennium: Society and Revivals in Rochester, New York, 1815–1837* 43 (1978).

[54] S. M. Blumin, *The Urban Threshold: Growth and Change in a 19th-Century American Community* 86–7 (1976).

[55] Ryan, *supra* note 52, at 153–154; Johnson, *supra* note 53, at 136–141.

[56] K. Haltunnen, *Confidence Men and Painted Women: A Study of Middle-Class Culture in America, 1830–1870* 56–7 (1982). At the same time, physical privacy could facilitate immorality: one British writer speaking of the villa suburbia of London in 1853 admitted, "St. John's Wood was once resorted to by dissipated men of affluence for the indulgence of one of their worse vices," quoted in D. J. Olsen, *Victorian London: Specialization, Segregation, and Privacy,* 17 Victorian Studies 273 (1974).

[57] B. Welter, *The Cult of True-Womanhood, 1820–1860,* 18 Am. Q. 151–74 (1966).

[58] D. Hayden, *The Grand Domestic Revolution: A History of Feminist Designs for American Homes, Neighborhoods and Cities* (1981).

well underway by the end of the 18th century, by the middle of the 19th century such divisions had become an obsession."[59]

The 18th century had found Americans adopting the hallway, but the 19th century witnessed a slew of innovations that treated the hallway as a place requiring its own accessories and furniture. Kenneth L. Ames has described how front hallways—the place where public and private life were mediated—acquired their own kind of furniture.[60] Special stands, chairs and card-receivers were all placed in new, enlarged halls where servants sorted out the visitors according to the family's opinion of their status. As in the earlier European example, the members of the household made themselves available to their visitors only if they wished.

The spatial construction of the rest of the house continued this effective physical control over the community's intrusion into family life. Lawns and side porches were semi-private areas, like the hall, where outsiders could be received on the family's terms.[61] The availability of the members of the family to servants, as well as to each other was also limited. Back stairs were built for the movement of servants; doors slid to divide spaces.[62] If once colonists had shared beds uncomplainingly even with strangers if necessary, now husband and wife had their own bedrooms and accompanying dressing rooms.[63] Bodily functions, which had been regulated by the earliest codes of etiquette, became unmentionable in social settings.[64] Houseguests were never supposed to make themselves "at home" even when told to; instead they were to take care not to disturb their hosts and discreetly ignore the accidental viewing of private acts.[65]

This description, of course, applies to the middle and upper classes in the United States for this restructuring of the house cost money. There is evidence from the complaints of middle-class reformers and philanthropists that poverty and preference stopped the working class from adopting this high valuing of privacy. Impoverished immigrants who were crammed into tenements lived much as peasants of centuries earlier, in one room with shared beds, as the photos of Jacob Riis remind us.[66] Yet the social historians of the poor immigrants have noted that even when forced to share apartments, immigrant families divided the space and respected each other's territory.[67]

Despite evidence of those efforts, Progressive reformers at the turn of the century worried that working-class families sacrificed privacy and its accompanying morality for financial gain. Boarding houses produced what they called "the lodger evil."[68] By

---

[59] C. E. Clark Jr., *The American Family Home: 1800–1960* 42ff. (1986). On Europe see C. Hall, *The Sweet Delights of Home*, and M. Perrot *The Family Triumphant*, in *A History of Private Life: From The Fires of the Revolution to the Great War* (M. Perrot ed., A. Goldhammer trans. 1990) [hereinafter Perrot ed.].

[60] K. L. Ames, *"Meanings in Artifacts: Hall Furnishings in Victorian America*, 9 J. of Interdisciplinary Hist. 19–46 (Summer 1978).

[61] K. T. Jackson, *Crabgrass Frontier: The Suburbanization of the United States* 58 (1985).

[62] C. McDannell, *The Christian Home in Victorian America, 1840–1900* 47 (1986).

[63] R. Lynes, *The Domesticated Americans* 217 (1957, 1963).

[64] J. F. Kasson, *Rudeness and Civility: Manners in Nineteenth-Century Urban America* 34–69, 112–146 (1990).

[65] Haltunnen, *supra* note 56, at 107–8.

[66] *See generally*, J. F. Sutherland, *Housing for the Poor in the City of Homes: Philadelphia at the Turn of the Century*, in *The People of Philadelphia: A History of Ethnic Groups and Lower-Class Life* 175–201 (A. F. Davis and M. H. Haller eds. 1973).

[67] D. R. Gabaccia, *From Sicily to Elizabeth Street: Housing and Social Change Among Italian Immigrants, 1880–1930* 73ff (1984).

[68] J. Modell and T. K. Hareven, *Urbanization and the Malleable Household: An Examination of Boarding*

allowing outsiders into its very heart, its home, the family exposed its members to all the corruption of the outside world.

To the reformers, the privacy of the family in its house was absolutely necessary to preserve its moral character. One reformer wrote in 1919:

> *The twin sister of the boarding house is the rooming house which pro-*
> *fesses to cater to families . . . . This institution paves the way for many*
> *social evils. It destroys in one blow the very basis of a home—i.e. privacy*
> *. . . too great familiarity grows up among the different ages, parental*
> *authority is weakened and held in contempt . . . and by the indiscrimi-*
> *nate association of the sexes of all ages undue familiarity and immodesty*
> *pave the way for subsequent [im]morality.*[69]

The comparison with the Puritans is striking. While the New Englanders assumed that the household had the power to hold individuals in line, the Progressives conceived of the household as highly vulnerable in its attempts to hold evil at bay. Privacy was a valued but precarious thing.

The complaints of the middle-class reformers signal as well their willingness to investigate the homes of their socioeconomic inferiors, which of course led to invasions of that group's privacy. We should also notice that women were active in these investigations despite their supposedly private nature because they were successfully defining such efforts as "municipal housekeeping."[70] Historian Donald J. Olsen has noted of Londoners "what the Victorians desired was privacy for the middle classes, publicity for the working classes, and segregation for both."[71] Although privacy was supposed to be essential to the family's ability to cope with the immoral conditions of modern society, the family could be investigated to see if it was doing the job in the first place.

One of the most relevant examples for us of intrusions into privacy in the name of morality is that of the social purity reformers who condemned the use of contraceptives even by married couples. Anti-vice activists such as Anthony Comstock argued that contraception degraded sexual intercourse because it could then be indulged in for pleasure and not for its natural and Christian purpose of reproduction. Feminist activists of the late 19th century argued for the availability of contraception under the slogan of voluntary motherhood.[72] Notice that a general call for the right to privacy would have made little sense when women's rights activists were trying to gain a freedom of women to engage in public activity. The privatization of the home was what segregated women from political centers of power and what left individual women at the mercy of their male relatives.[73] Also, most feminists steered clear of radical demands for sexual free-

---

and Lodging in American Families, in *The American Family in Social-Historical Perspective* 52 (M. Gordon ed. 2d. ed. 1979). On the British experience, see D. J. Olsen, *Victorian London: Specialization, Segregation, and Privacy,* 17 Victorian Studies 265–78 (1974).

[69] Quoted in Lynes, *supra* note 63, at 46. *See also* Arthur W. Calhoun, 3 *The Social History of the American Family: From Colonial Times to the Present* 72–3 (1919). *See also* R.-H. Guerrand, *Private Spaces,* in Perrot ed., *supra* note 59, at 422–23.

[70] Jane Addams, the settlement worker, was a particularly articulate exponent of this rationale. *See also* M. S. Wortman, *Domesticating the Nineteenth-Century City,* 3 Prospects 531–71 (1977).

[71] Olsen, *supra* note 68, at 271.

[72] L. Gordon, *Woman's Body, Woman's Right: A Social History of Birth Control in America* 95–115 (1976).

[73] On women's public activities in the 19th century, see C. N. Degler, *At Odds: Women and the Family in America from the Revolution to the Present* 298–361 (1980).

dom and instead insisted upon women's control over their reproduction within the traditional boundaries of married family life. In short, women's rights activists of varying types demanded empowerment as members of the polity instead of asking for privacy per se.

The campaign for voluntary motherhood even as part of married life was shocking to many. In 1873, Congress passed a law named after Anthony Comstock that declared contraceptive devices and information about them to be obscene and that prohibited their transportation through the U.S. mail.[74] Individual states followed suit, and it was such a law that the Supreme Court struck down in 1965 on the grounds that it violated a married couple's right to privacy. As contradictory as it may seem, a high value on the privacy of the home and family and the social purity campaign that necessarily intruded into that privacy coexisted within a 19th-century moral framework of respectability.[75]

We can now place into this social and cultural web of information one of the most famous legal articles of the late 19th century: Samuel D. Warren's and Louis D. Brandeis's 1890 *Harvard Law Review* piece entitled "The Right to Privacy." Their specific complaint about the press reporting on the private lives of prominent citizens is as much an expression of their identification with a genteel social class as it is a legal innovation. In fact, the phrase "the right to privacy" already existed in cultural terms. Thus, Brandeis and Warren were the last leg of a dialectical borrowing wherein first constitutional language had affected social practices and then such practices were blended back into the legal realm.

Decades before Warren and Brandeis wrote, when the legal periodicals contained no references to the right to privacy, the etiquette manuals already "intoned repeatedly" that "the right to privacy is sacred, and should always be respected."[76] Obviously, these writers were not using the term as though it were a right they could call upon the lawful authorities to protect. Still, they had been influenced, as Americans have continued to be, by the explicit legal rights found in the Constitution. Historians have long noticed how rife our society has been with talk of rights.[77] The etiquette writers who borrowed constitutional vocabulary to make social rules about privacy are but one example. It appears that they in turn influenced Warren and Brandeis who, in criticizing the newspaper reporters, were in effect asking them to act like gentleman. A houseguest who carried tales out of a house was disqualified from good society. The reporters had not been invited in the first place, so their metaphorical intrusion into the home was even worse. And according to Warren and Brandeis, it should also be punishable by law through suits brought against the inhabitants of the house.

Warren and Brandeis accounted for their concern for privacy by explicit reference to historical change. They argued that civilization's advance and the evolution of the common law demanded an increased protection of privacy:

---

[74]See J. Reed, *From Private Vice to Public Virtue: The Birth Control Movement and American Society Since 1830* 34–45, especially note 1 (1978). Also D. M. Kennedy, *Birth Control in America: The Career of Margaret Sanger* 218–71 (1970).

[75]For an example of this phenemenon in a different culture, see A. Marcus, *Privacy in 18th-Century Aleppo [Syria]: The Limits of Cultural Ideas*, 18 Int'l. J. of Middle Eastern Stud. 165–83 (1986).

[76]Quoted in Haltunnen, *supra* note 56, at 109.

[77]See T. L. Haskell, *The Curious Persistence of Rights Talk in the "Age of Interpretation,"* and H. Hartog, *The Constitution of Aspiration and "The Rights That Belong to Us All,"* 74 J. of Am. Hist. 984–1012 and 1013–34 (1987).

*The intensity and complexity of life, attendant upon advancing civiliza-
tion, have rendered necessary some retreat from the world, and man,
under the refining influence of culture, has become more sensitive to publicity, so that solitude and privacy have become more essential to the
individual.*[78]

Technological changes had made the individual vulnerable; instantaneous photography
made possible the taking of pictures without permission, for example. Also, the publication of personal gossip in the newspapers, the physical proof of invasions of privacy,
lowered the tone of the community as a whole, they argued. As one modern legal critic
has commented of the article, there is a certain note of "injured gentility" about such
descriptions of the effects of sensationalistic journalism as

*Triviality destroys at once robustness of thought and delicacy of feeling.
No enthusiasm can flourish, no generous impulse can survive under its
blighting influence.*[79]

Although such phrases carry the image of a respectable Victorian, brow stern with
disapproval, they also expressed that idea shared with our nation's founders that the
character (in the moral sense) of the people is formed in part by the character (the
nature) of their public institutions.

Warren and Brandeis tried to root their right to privacy in the common law by
drawing analogies from other legal rights. They cited as a general point of reference the
contention of Judge Thomas F. Cooley, who defined the right to one's person as "the
right to be left alone."[80] The evolution of legal protections was from physical to intangibles, Warren and Brandeis further argued. Freedom from assault was extended to
mean freedom from fear of assault; to do the physical act and to threaten were both
made into crimes. So physical liberty should be extended to cover the intangible of
privacy.

Warren and Brandeis threaded their way through tort law showing how the wrong
done against privacy might be compared to other wrongs for which the law had already
devised remedies. Defamation was punished under the laws of libel and slander, but it
required the declaring of an untruth. The authors wanted someone to be able to sue the
papers for publishing a truth, but one which they had no business publishing. So Warren
and Brandeis borrowed from "the common law right to intellectual and artistic property" that "secures to each individual the right of determining, ordinarily, to what
extent his thoughts, sentiments, and emotions shall be communicated to others."[81] To
avoid the logical rap some courts had fallen into of punishing publications of such
information only if they appeared to have sufficient artistic merit, Warren and Brandeis
acknowledged that privacy differed from this kind of property. They argued that the

---

[78] Warren and Brandeis, *supra* note 4, at 196.

[79] H. Kalven Jr., *Privacy in Tort Law—Were Warren and Brandeis Wrong?* 31 Law & Contemp. Probs. 329
(1966). He answers yes.

[80] Thomas F. Cooley, *A Treatise on the Law of Torts, or the Wrongs which arise Independent of Contract* 29
(1879).

[81] Warren and Brandeis, *supra* note 4, at 198.

best way to interpret the tendency of courts to protect private letters from publication
was to think of such decisions as "in reality not [upholding] the principle of private
property, but that of an inviolate personality."[82]

In support of their arguments, they cited, among others, the English case of *Prince
Albert v. Strange*, which is a fitting example of the Victorian period's concern with
family privacy since at issue were the public dissemination of etchings Queen Victoria
and Prince Albert had made among friends for their own private amusement.[83] The
English courts announced that the royal couple had property rights in their etchings and
forbade Strange from selling those he had somehow gotten hold of. What Warren and
Brandeis were at pains to emphasize was that the couple was not arguing for their
artistic property rights in order to keep the profits from their labors to themselves but to
keep the etchings and information about them out of the public eye altogether.

Thus the authors ended by objecting to the mere dissemination of information about
private life to the public at large. Although they made exceptions for public figures who
were necessarily subject to public scrutiny, Warren and Brandeis demanded this privacy
as a right for the violation of which one could be sued in court under tort law:

> the right of one who has remained a private individual, to prevent his
> public portraiture . . . the right to protect one's self from pen portrai-
> ture, from a discussion by the press of one's private affairs.[84]

Notice that they were not objecting to governmental actions (the usual second half in
the political battle between liberty and power) but to the behavior of the press that they
considered a new source of public power. Making clear this analogy, they concluded
their piece with the following passage and its final rhetorical question:

> The common law has always recognized a man's house as his castle,
> impregnable, often, even to its own officers engaged in the execution of
> its commands. Shall the courts thus close the front entrance to constituted
> authority, and open wide the back door to idle or purient curiosity?[85]

Thus the first important, explicit, legal reference to the right to privacy is not about
control of governmental power but about a new kind of power that threatens liberty.[86]
The right emerges in reference to private family life but without any to the contraceptive
and abortion issues that the 20th-century jurists would struggle with.

Warren and Brandeis received early fulsome praise for their article, which has since
been quieted by historians and legal scholars of a more critical bent.[87] The idea that the
two authors had been reacting to indefensible actions of a sensationalistic press has been
refuted by the work of Don T. Pember who surveyed the surviving runs of the Boston
newspapers (Warren and Brandeis lived in Boston) and found that keyhole journalism

---

[82] *Id.* at 205.
[83] *Prince Albert v. Strange,* 2 De Gex & Sm. 652 (1849) and on appeal 1 McN. & G. 25 (1849).
[84] Warren and Brandeis, *supra* note 4, at 213.
[85] *Id.* at 220.
[86] There was a rare case dealing with the right to privacy previously. *See* W. L. Prosser, *Privacy,* 48 Calif.
   L. Rev. 383–423 (August 1969). Although a valuable review of the right to privacy cases, Prosser incor-
   rectly describes the origins of the article.
[87] W. Zelermyer, *Invasion of Privacy* 25 (1959) calls the article "brilliant."

was the rare exception rather than the rule.[88] Only the very sensitive could have been offended by the kind of mentions made of Warren's family in the papers: mere notices of their hosting a wedding reception or leaving town for the season. Warren *was* "hypersensitive" according to legal scholar James H. Barron, and he convinced an ambivalent Brandeis into coauthoring the piece in order to give the fledgling *Harvard Law Review* something to print.[89] Thus, when the particular circumstances of the article's genesis are laid out, its claim to be responding to unsupportable press activity and the acceptance by some later writers of that claim are thrown into question.[90]

Those legal scholars who had uncritically praised the Warren and Brandeis piece had also ignored other historical issues. The idea that the sensationalistic press needed to be controlled carried with it a set of class assumptions that should be examined as well. If society so needed the controls, why was society so eagerly buying these nasty newspapers? Legal scholars who praised Warren and Brandeis did not make clear just who made up this historical "society." But evidently it could be divided into sensitive and vulgar parts.[91] Also those who praised the authors for responding to a social need for privacy in the face of technological change failed to notice that the social need for privacy in any particular form is not a given but a historical artifact.

At the same time, we should keep in mind that new technology and the increased interdependency of economic networks were indeed changing the fundamental character of social life. The telegraph, for example, linked cities instantaneously. It also created a concern for the privacy of its communications, which resulted in the passage of federal laws.[92] Regional economies were being meshed into a national economy. The mass press was reaching ever more people and covering ever more territory. The changes that had frightened the middle-class northeasterners in the early 19th century into retreating into their homes were now affecting a greater and greater part of the population as the country was becoming industrialized and urbanized. The late 19th century witnessed an information revolution as governmental bureaucracy first began collecting data for statistical analysis.[93] Extended census questionnaires, for example, affected everyone. In such a context, privacy was more than a middle-class issue; most Americans were having to deal with it in deciding what shape their communities and lives would take.

Despite the effort of Brandeis and Warren to remove the property component from their version of the right to privacy, the judicial decisions and legislation that followed their effort clung to the idea of property. The most famous decision was one made by the New York Court of Appeals in 1902 in a suit brought on behalf of a girl whose photo was used as a advertisement by a flour milling company without her consent.[94]

---

[88] D. T. Pember, *Privacy and the Press, The Law, Mass Media, and the First Amendment* 20–57 (1972).

[89] J. H. Barron, *Warren and Brandeis, "The Right to Privacy," 4 Harv. L. Rev. 193 (1890): Demystifying a Landmark Citation*, 13 Suffolk U.L. Rev. 907–910 (Summer 1979).

[90] *See, e.g.,* Dorothy Glancey's misguided piece, *The Invention of the Right to Privacy*, 21 Ariz. L. Rev. 1–39 (1979); or the lavish praise of the two authors by M. L. Ernst and A. U. Schwartz, *Privacy: The Right to Be Left Alone* 45ff. (1962). On the legal scholars' debate over the Warren-Brandeis piece, see P. A. Dionisopoulos and C. R. Ducat, *The Right to Privacy: Essays and Cases* 15–30 (1979).

[91] *See especially* Glancey, *supra* note 90, who used James Fenimore Cooper, an antebellum critic of democracy, and Henry James, the novelist, to illustrate "society's" needs.

[92] *See* D. J. Siepp, *The Right to Privacy in Nineteenth-Century America*, 94 Harv. L. Rev. 1902. (1981).

[93] *See* M. F. Steig, *The 19th-Century Information Revolution*, 15 J. of Libr. Hist. 22–52 (1980).

[94] Roberson v. Rochester Folding Box Co., 171 N.Y. 538 (1902). For a popular listing of cases, see Ernst and Schwartz, *supra* note 90, and for a casebook, see Dionisopoulos and Ducat, *supra* note 90.

She objected to the humiliation and embarassment she suffered from having her face plastered all over town. The majority of the court suggested that, since the right to privacy did not exist at common law, what was needed was a new law. The dissenting minority insisted that the girl had had her property rights violated.

The New York state legislature obliged both judicial opinions by passing a law in 1903 that prohibited the use of a person's image for trade or advertisement purposes without his or her consent. Subsequent amendments in 1911 and 1921 allowed for releases to be signed and for photographs of a creator to accompany the sale of the creation.[95] Because this right to privacy could be bargained away through release or sale of an artistic creation, the idea of the right as a kind of property persisted within this law.[96] The intangibility that Brandeis and Warren were after was neglected.

The state courts worked out various strategies for dealing with the appropriation of images for advertising purposes; they also invoked the right to privacy in a range of dissimilar cases. Unlike the New York courts, the Georgia Supreme Court in 1904 found a right to privacy in common law and therefore did not call for legislative action.[97] Over the decades other states came to adopt the right to privacy either through statutes or case decisions, so that 28 had the right by 1960.[98] By that time the state courts had figured out rules to distinguish, as had Warren and Brandeis, between public figures and ordinary individuals and between advertisements and news.[99] The press usually won cases where individuals complained that their private business was not of public interest because of the judiciary's deference to constitutional protection of freedom of the press.[100]

If the intrusions of the press and the appropriation of images for advertisements had been the primary way in which writers and legal scholars discussed privacy and the right to privacy in the 20th century, then indeed the critic who marveled at the "pettiness of the tort" Warren and Brandeis described would have had the last word.[101] Instead, legal writers and political commentators began to speak of privacy in terms of the fundamental conflict between liberty and power, either governmental or corporate. They spoke less of the family than people of the 19th century and more of the individual. The new technology of wiretapping and recording phone lines put the intangibility of an intrusion into privacy at the forefront of legal debate in the early 20th century. The clumsiness with which the Supreme Court dealt with its early cases on the subject

---

[95] The law remains to this day: New York Civil Rights Law, §§ 50–41.

[96] The propertied character of the right to privacy as connected to legislation that protects its exploitation for trade purposes led to the eventual creation of a right to publicity, a perverse-sounding right created by judges who wanted to acknowledge that people such as entertainers made money by surrendering their privacy voluntarily. See F. Davis, *What Do We Mean by "Right to Privacy"?* 4 S.D.L. Rev. 17–81 (Spring 1959).

[97] Pavesich v. New England Life Insurance Co, 122 Ga. 190 (1904).

[98] See Pember, *supra* note 88, at chapter openings for statistics.

[99] Prosser's article, *supra* note 86, contains a list of the various state cases; he also discerned in the decisions a breakdown of the tort of privacy into four types: intrusion, public disclosure of private facts, one's presentation in a false light in the public eye and image appropriation. His article met with a heated (over)reaction from E. J. Bloustein in *Privacy as an Aspect of Human Dignity: An Answer to Dean Prosser*, 39 N.Y.U. L. Rev. 962–1007 (1964). For an earlier piece with a different breakdown of the common-law cases, see L. Nizer, *The Right To Privacy: a Half-Century's Development*, 39 Mich. L. Rev. 526–560 (Feb. 1941).

[100] Pember argues that only in "outrageous" cases did the press lose, *supra* note 88, at 145.

[101] Kalven, *supra* note 79, at 328.

would be one of many provocations that produced the pro-privacy writers of the mid-20th century.

In one of the first important cases, *Olmstead v. United States* in 1928, Louis D. Brandeis, now a justice of the Supreme Court, dissented when his brethren refused to define wiretapping as a search and seizure needing a warrant under the fourth amendment.[102] The courts had always defined searches as happening in a place and resulting in the gathering of physical evidence, but the evidence here was a conversation that had been tape-recorded. Brandeis insisted that the physicality of search and seizure was a historical necessity in earlier days that technology now made unnecessary. Still, the nature of the intrusion by government into the sanctity of homes and conversations was the same. He asked his brethren to extend the fourth amendment's protections to include tangible but pernicious violations of privacy. Otherwise governmental investigators would evade the constitutional limitations on their powers.

Using language very similar to that found in his earlier article on the right to privacy, Justice Brandeis stressed the historical and continuing importance of the protection of the intangibles of human life. He wrote of the Constitution's writers:

> *They recognized the significance of a man's' spiritual nature, of his feelings and of his intellect. They knew that only a part of the pain, pleasure and satisfactions of life are to be found in material things. They sought to protect Americans in their beliefs, their emotions and their sensations.*[103]

He then summed up the founders' attempt to ensure the people's freedoms as their conferral through the Constitution of, "as against government, the right to be left alone— the most comprehensive of rights and the right most valued by civilized man."[104] Brandeis failed to convince his brethren, however, who suggested that Congress take action in this field,[105] action that proved to be largely ineffective according to the pro-privacy writers of later decades.

These writers were dealing in sweeping terms with what Brandeis had criticized in *Olmstead*. They were responding to new technology and giving it meaning through their contemporary political setting. Computer data banks and wiretapping were the two most criticized innovations. Their abuse whether real or potential was examined in light of World War II and the fascist regimes of Germany and Italy, as well as the authoritarian communism of the Soviet Union. The Cold War between the United States and the Soviet Union threatened to bring authoritarianism home according to the pro-privacy writers. An American police state was being constructed in the name of national security; the destruction of the American system was being effected in the name of saving it.

All of these authors made references to George Orwell's novel *1984* and its depictions of a society where government, in the name of order and security, went so far as to monitor the private thoughts of its citizens. The corporate surveillance of employees

---

[102] Olmstead v. United States, 277 U.S. 438 (1928).

[103] Olmstead v. United States, 277 U.S. 438, 478 (1928).

[104] *Id.*

[105] For the evolution of the Court's response, see also Goldman v. U.S., 316 U.S. 129 (1942); Lee v. U.S., 342 U.S. 747 (1952); Silverman v. U.S. 505 (1961); Katz v. U.S., 389 U.S. 347 (1967). *See also* Dionisopoulos and Ducat's case book, *supra* note 90.

also smacked of Orwell's fictional "thought police." Private corporations as well as governmental practices were establishing "the pre-conditions for totalitarianism," as popular writer Vance Packard put it in 1964.[106]

Concerned that doctrines of constitutional rights were being outpaced by technological change, the Bar of the City of New York organized a Special Commission on Science and the Law, which in 1959 began the first large-scale systematic inquiry into privacy, the new technology and legal protections. Its efforts, according to chairman Oscar Ruebhausen, resulted in "symposia, conferences, keynote addresses, and panels on privacy . . . blossoming all over the cultural landscape."[107] The committee sponsored political scientist Alan F. Westin's important volume *Privacy and Freedom* published in 1967. Westin took note of the 1965 *Griswold* decision, but he devoted the bulk of the book to technological intrusions into privacy by government and the ways in which they upset what he called the "balance" among "privacy, disclosure, and surveillance" that the framers of the Constitution had constructed.[108]

Westin's notion of a set, constitutional balance came from his reading of history. The balance the Constitution put forth by limiting governmental power and protecting individual rights had been "based on the technological realities of eighteenth century life."[109] The balance was upset with 20th century technologies such as tagging devices, hidden mirrors and cameras, microphones, bugs, tape-recorders, record-keeping and data banks.[110] Our survey of the cultural history of privacy made above should make clear that more than technology had changed, without requiring that we reject Westin's generalization that "the effort to limit official surveillance over man's thoughts, speech, private acts, confidential communications, and group participation has for centuries been a central part of the struggle for liberty in Western society."[111] This message was an essential component of the work of the pro-privacy advocates.

Vance Packard wrote one of the most popular pro-privacy books aimed at a lay audience, *The Naked Society*, in 1964. Full of anecdotes, some humorous in their exposure of the stupidity of authorities and others chilling in their effects, Packard's book opened with the image of a whole family under seige: A television camera spied on Mom while she shopped; a private investigator posing as a fellow employee chatted with Dad; son John was taking a lie-detector test as part of a job application; and daughter Mary was being asked to fill out a highly personal questionnaire by her teacher to measure her psychological adjustment. Packard, like other pro-privacy writers, pointed to the Cold War mentality that fueled the investigations of the House Un-American

---

[106] V. Packard, *The Naked Society* 4 (1964). Similar books include M. Brenton, *The Privacy Invaders* (1964) on private institutions and J. M. Rosenberg, *The Death of Privacy* (1969). A modern version of the same kind of book is D. F. Linowes, *Privacy in America: Is Your Private Life in the Public Eye* (1989).

[107] Foreward to A. Westin, *Privacy and Freedom* xi (1967) [hereinafter *Privacy and Freedom*]; the committee also produced several historical reports that are available at the Columbia Law School in manuscript form: Norman Cantor, *Privacy in Rome* (1964); Marvin E. Gettleman, *Privacy in the Perspective of U.S. History* (1964); Alan F. Westin, *Privacy in Western History: From the Age of Pericles to the American Republic* (1965).

[108] *Privacy and Freedom, supra* note 107, at 67; a similarly brief treatment of *Griswold* is found in Sen. Edward V. Long's *The Intruders: The Invasion of Privacy by Government and Industry* 35 (1967).

[109] *Privacy and Freedom, supra* note 107, at 67.

[110] Westin and others opposed the plan for a national data bank based on census returns. H. Alterman, *Counting People: The Census in History* 257–59 (1969). *See also Census, Surveys and Privacy* (M. Blumer ed. 1979).

[111] *Privacy and Freedom, supra* note 107, at 67.

Activities Committee as the impetus for modern invasions of privacy.[112] Although willing to concede that "the combination of Soviet and Red Chinese ambitions and the ghastly potency of atomic weapons have produced a hazardous situation," he argued that thoughtful citizens agreed with him that "the continuing vigilance" necessary to control the situation "can be achieved within the framework of personal freedom and privacy enunciated by the Bill of Rights."[113] Packard suggested, as one of his chapters was entitled, that free, republican government conferred "The Right To Have Unfashionable Opinions."

What most of these writers failed to notice was that although the privacy they treasured was confronted with new technologies, their concern for privacy took a particular historical shape. True, there were new kinds of intrusions into privacy, but an increased cultural demand for privacy made some of those instrusions seem more invidious than they would have at earlier periods in history.

For example, one pro-privacy author criticized a manager who explained why he had prospective employees investigated: "We can't afford to take chances on hiring somebody who could embarrass us—not in a small community like this . . . What an employee does—what he is—reflects on the company."[114] Such a statement would have been unquestioned in early 19th-century artisanal households where masters felt a moral responsibility for their apprentices and journeymen. The physical possibility of privacy had been further advanced by the post-World War II federal housing programs that made the detached suburban home, once available only to better-off Victorians, the norm for middle- and even working-class housing.[115] Similarly, pro-privacy writers of the 1950s and 1960s who complained that bank records demonstrating that a man supported an unmarried woman financially were nobody's business were displaying a 20th-century belief (obviously not unchallenged) that sexual relations between consenting adults should not be the subject of community scrutiny or punishment. The sexual revolution of the 1920s divided such writers from their 18th- and 19th-century ancestors.[116]

That the pro-privacy writers of the 1950s and 1960s were often unaware of the complicated cultural history of their topic does not undermine the compelling arguments they made for privacy as an integral part of a republican system of government, nor should it make us neglect the important technological innovations that concerned them.

These fears of governmental and corporate power are the context of the *Griswold* and *Roe* decisions. As early as 1958, Supreme Court Justice William O. Douglas had published a set of lectures that adopted Cooley's phrase "the right to be let alone" and that contained a section on the right to privacy. He objected there to governmental investigations into Communist subversion. In 1962, legal scholar William M. Beany already felt able to argue that "decisions of the Supreme Court involving the right to privacy or containing extensive references to that right have been part of the staple fare of constitutional litigation for many decades."[117] During this period, the Warren Court

---

[112] *See* Zelermyer, *supra* note 87, at 1; and E. Shils, *Privacy: Its Constitution and Vicissitudes,* 31 Law & Contemp. Probs. 297 (1966) (this entire issue of the journal is devoted to the privacy issue).

[113] Packard, 233.

[114] Quoted in Brenton, *supra* note 106, at 64.

[115] Jackson, *supra* note 61, at 190–239.

[116] John D'Emilio and Estelle B. Freedman write of the 1920s: "[T]wo changes stand out as emblematic of this new sexual order: the redefinition of womanhood to include eroticism, and the decline of public reticence about sex." *Intimate Matters: A History of Sexuality in America* 233, also 239–74 (1988).

[117] W. M. Beany, *The Constitutional Right to Privacy in the Supreme Court,* Sup. Ct. Rev. 212 (1962).

extended constitutional protections in criminal procedure to state investigations, thus forwarding individual privacy at the expense of the estate's powers.[118] Throughout the 1960s congressional committees in the House and Senate held hearings on privacy, and more were held in the 1970s, resulting in the passage of the Fair Credit Reporting Act of 1970, the Privacy Act of 1974 and the Right to Financial Privacy Act of 1978.[119]

Thus, the activities of the pro-privacy writers, political activists, scholars and judges amounted to a legal and cultural ferment that produced works and testimony on privacy in a variety of contexts. All this was done by people who, usually without knowing it, lived in houses whose structures and communities whose manners demonstrated a historically distinctive valuation of personal privacy.

It is against this broad background of cultural beliefs, constitutional understandings and social practices, that *Griswold* and *Roe* were decided. The pattern of this history left its impression on those decisions. The Supreme Court's decisions brought the specific concerns of women's rights advocates into the constitutional dialogue, thus redoubling the heatedness of the debate, yet worries about other governmental intrusion into individual life continued to be expressed in terms of a right to privacy. Set against this background, the contraception and abortion decisions appear surrounded by a host of similar concerns understood under the rubric of privacy.[120]

What appears most striking in the history of privacy as a cultural and legal value is how little it has explicitly referred to women's civil rights. Privacy was early on equated with the home into which the male citizen could retreat, and in his home that male citizen held sway over his dependent wife, children and servants. In the name of his privacy and liberty, he controlled their privacy and liberty as he wished. Women were left out of the social contract in theory and in practice.[121] Thus, when women's rights activists demanded empowerment, they had to break out of the home and into the public sphere.[122] In their calls for suffrage, they were demanding a place in the polity, that is, direct contact with the state by participation in it as full citizens.

So women's rights demands were not made in the name of privacy per se, although someone like Margaret Sanger, the crusader for access to birth control, could argue that "it is none of Society's business what a woman shall do with her body," and in so doing echo that statement of Judge Cooley later taken up by Warren and Brandeis that all Americans have a constitutional right to be left alone.[123] But largely, women's rights activists used phrases such as voluntary motherhood in the 19th century and reproductive choice in the 20th century, which indicate their greater concern with specific female

---

Beany greeted the *Griswold* case in *The* Griswold *Case and the Expanding Right to Privacy,* 1966 Wis. L. Rev. 979–95 (1966).

[118] *See, e.g.,* Mapp v. Ohio 367 U.S., 63 (1961) on search and seizure and Malloy v. Hogan 378 U.S. 1 (1964) on self-incrimination. For full lists of cases, see O'Brien, *supra* note 49.

[119] *See* R. F. Hixson, *Privacy in a Public Society: Human Rights in Conflict* 207–29 (1987); Also *Uncle Sam Is Watching You: Highlights from the Hearings of the Senate Subcommittee on Constitutional Rights* (1971).

[120] For a list of major privacy cases before and after *Griswold* and *Roe,* see S. F. VanBurkleo, *The Right to Privacy,* in *By The People, For The People: Constitutional Rights in American History* 131–132 (K. Hall ed. 1991).

[121] For recent efforts to rethink women's position in the polity, see C. Pateman, *The Sexual Contract* (1988) and *The Family in Political Thought* (J. B. Elshstain ed. 1982).

[122] On the suffragists' examination of woman and the home, see A. S. Kraditor, *The Ideas of the Suffrage Movement, 1890–1920* 96–122 (1965, 1981).

[123] D'Emilio and Freedman, *supra* note 116, at 232.

empowerment than with a general right to privacy. That the constitutional protection for women's ability to have legal abortions was rooted in the right to privacy in *Roe* in 1973 is something of a paradox on one level.

On another level, *Roe* appears eminently a product of the cultural history, both recent and far, both of women and of citizenship. Without the efforts of 19th-century reformers who wanted legalized access to contraceptives, without the sexual revolution of the 1920s that made sexual matters discussable in public and without the women's movement of 1960s and 1970s that made an explicit political demand for women's freedom to choose abortion, no one would have been bringing court cases against state laws that criminalized abortion.[124] That a majority of the Supreme Court Justices opted to use the right to privacy to protect women's decisions to abort is coherent as history, whatever questions its critics may have as to its coherence as constitutional doctrine.[125]

Privacy in its various forms has a long history in the United States as both a cultural and legal value. Women's entrance into the political arena is of much more recent date, as were demands for the decriminalization of abortion. In some ways, in *Griswold* and *Roe,* the justices were acknowledging a new status for women through a more familiar idea. The right to privacy in this specific context was part of the long genesis of privacy as a cultural ideal and the reciprocal relationship between explicitly legal concepts and societal practices. The majority justices could draw a right to privacy as an "emanation" or "penumbras" from the Bill of Rights because of the other shadows that surrounded their culture. The outlander farmer seeking peace on his own domain, the Victorian who attended to the rules of the etiquette, the mid-20th century opponents of a national data bank and numerous other figures offered to those who came after a set of beliefs that gave the word "privacy" value.

The general American cultural preference for privacy is thus an essential component in the struggles over the legality of abortion. Those legal scholars who have criticized the Court for its decisions have stressed the illogic of its constitutional reasoning. Some of the justices have taken the ninth amendment with its implication about unenumerated rights, found in it a right to privacy and applied it to the states. How, the critics ask, can a constitutional provision aimed against the national government be used against the states? The idea of unenumerated rights is especially dangerous to some critics. Judges can make up such rights according to their own political preferences. The people's ability to rule through their state legislatures is undermined by an appointed judiciary that invents things like the right to privacy.[126]

From the cultural historians' point of view, of course, there is irony to the complaint that the right to privacy is an undemocratic creation. This cultural and social history has offered enough of a sketch to show that a popular belief in a right to privacy pre-dates any legal articles or decisions on the subject. More recently, Alan Westin continued his studies of privacy by supervising a 1973 survey that showed that some 75% of those questioned were willing to add privacy to a list of fundamental U.S. rights

---

[124] On the sexual revolution of the late 20th century and its connection to a renewed women's rights movement, see D'Emilio and Freedman, *supra* note 116, at 300–25.

[125] Among the best known is John Hart Ely's *The Wages of Crying Wolf: A Comment on* Roe v. Wade, 82 Yale L. J. 920–49 (1973), which was foreshadowed by P. Kauper, *Penumbras, Peripheries, Emanations, Things Fundamental and Things Forgotten: The* Griswold *Case,* 64 Mich. L. Rev. 235–68 (December 1965).

[126] *See, e.g.* R. Berger, *The Ninth Amendment* in *The Rights Retained by the People: The History and Meaning of the Ninth Amendment* 191–218 (R. Barnett ed. 1989).

along with life, liberty and the pursuit of happiness.[127] The percentage dropped, yet remained over a majority, when a specific question about abortion rights was asked. More recent polls show that although ambivalence about the morality of abortion continues, large majorities believe that government interference is illegitimate.[128]

If the historical ascendancy of privacy as a cultural value is any indicator of the future, the anti-abortion activists are right to fear the availability of the French abortion pill (RU486). There has been, of course, much feminist criticism of the private/public split as defined by the Court, yet this new medical technology may alter the terms of the debate about privacy just as other innovations did earlier in history.[129] Since most abortions occur during the first trimester, many women could opt for the abortion pill and have no need for medical help outside of a doctor's visit. The abortion clinic, the site of public protest, would become less important. Ironically, women would be retreating into the privacy of their homes in order to gain the reproductive control that was so much a part of their first battles to act outside of the home.

One of the advertisment run by Planned Parenthood during the 1980s demonstrated that organization's canny recognition of the cultural symbolism of the home. In it a woman is facing two men in hats and coats whose features cannot be seen. Her expression seems to be turning from greeting to a mix of shock and fear. The rhetorical question the advertisement asks is whether we would want a world in which the police investigate miscarriages.[130] The question hits hard, of course, on the experiential subjectivity of pregnancy and the tragedy of women who want to be pregnant instead of those who do not.

But of as much importance, and doubtlessly carefully chosen, is the setting for this confrontation. The woman has opened the door of her home to find these men standing on her front step. The picture demonstrates the symbolic weight the threshold carries. It implicitly asks us whether we could tolerate having it breached. Those who offered the image believed that the weight of history would have us answer no.

---

[127] Louis Harris & Associates and A. F. Westin, *The Dimensions of Privacy: A National Opinion Research Survey of Attitudes Toward Privacy* 15 (1973).

[128] Petchesky, *supra* note 6, at xxvii.

[129] The public/private split is responsible for the Court's willingness to allow federal funding for abortions to be withheld. *See Maher v. Roe* 432 U.S. 464 (1977) and *Harris v. McRae* 448 U.S. 297 (1980).

[130] Considering how callously and unconstitutionally (by present-day standards) the police treated women who had abortions when it was illegal—because the police found it impossible to get information of this secret act in any other way—probably few of us now could tolerate effective investigations. *See* L. J. Reagan, *"About to Meet Her Maker": Women, Doctors, Dying Declarations and the State's Investigation of Abortion, Chicago, 1867–1940*, 77 J. of Am. Hist. 1240–1264 (March 1991).

This article by Daniel Callahan was written in 1973, but it illuminates the central conflicts of the abortion issue of the 1990s. Special note should be taken of section II. D., which discusses the question of when human life begins. The author mentions that collateral issues—such as when life requires protection or respect—are just as important as when life begins. Clearly, Daniel Callahan anticipated the difficulty Congress would have with the Human Life Bill, namely, reaching moral conclusions from scientific facts.

28 · Abortion: Some Ethical Issues

Daniel Callahan, Ph.D.

I. Introduction

Abortion is a peculiarly passionate topic, largely because many people invest their positions with a symbolic weight that transcends immediate social and legal issues. The most obvious examples of this tendency can be found in some segments of the women's liberation movement, on the one hand, and in some factions of those opposed to abortion, on the other. For each the way society solves the abortion problem will be taken to show just what its deepest values are. And those values have implications that extend far beyond abortion.

The women's liberation movement sees abortion as the most significant liberation of all, from the body and from male domination. The most effective solution to unwanted pregnancy, it removes the final block to full control of reproduction. Unless reproduction can be fully controlled, women will remain in bondage not only to their sexuality but, even more, to those legions of male chauvinists who use female sexuality to their own domineering ends.

By contrast, many of those opposed to abortion see the issue as indicating the kind of respect society will show the most defenseless beings in our midst. If the life of a defenseless fetus is not respected, then there is good reason to believe that the most fundamental of all human rights—the right to life—will have been subverted at its core. The test of the humane society is not the respect it pays to the strongest and most articulate, but that which it accords to the weakest and least articulate.

Of course, these arguments and the symbolic weight they carry simply bypass one another. The opposition seems so fundamental, and the starting premises so different, that any meaningful debate—the kind that leads to give-and-take, concession and adaptation—is ruled out from the start. Moreover, the very charges each side hurls at the other are of a psychologically intolerable nature. No vigorous proponents of abortion are likely to admit, either privately or publicly, that they sanction "murder"; nor are opponents of abortion likely to admit that they sanction the suppression of women. I am using the word "admit" here in a serious sense which implies that one is willing to ponder seriously the possibility that the worst things said about oneself are true. Given that possibility, there remain only two choices: change one's views and confess the errors of one's old ways or violently and aggressively deny the charges.

There is, of course, a third possibility: Concede that there may be a grain of truth in what one's opponent says and then undertake the development of a position that tries to meet and integrate the objection in some new position. But this may be the most distasteful solution of all for most people, since it entails a long, drawn-out wrestling with oneself. Abortion is a painful issue, and for just that reason people seemed impelled to proceed in all haste to the comfort of "Here I stand," which ends the self-wrestling.

My comments here are not drawn from any hard evidence. They are meant only as reflections on years of trying to discuss abortion in a reasonably calm, rational way, both in public and private. My own professional training is in philosophy, a discipline which (to the despair of many nonphilosophers) places a heavy premium on precision of argument, careful distinctions, developed justifications of ethical positions, methodological elegance, and a cool, temperate mode of discourse. These traits have, to be sure, led to more than one accusation that philosophers are prone to fiddle while the city is burning; and there is probably some truth in this. Nonetheless, I think these traits are still somewhat useful, especially when discussing a topic like abortion, which many take as an invitation to express their unbridled feelings and convictions. Worse still, the politics of abortion seems to pay handsome dividends for such a stance. It can, and has, pushed many an abortion reform bill through reluctant legislatures, just as it has, in different hands, killed many a bill. When argument fails, what better tactic is there than to bring out the fetus-in-a-bottle ("See what you are doing to innocent life!") or the raped mongoloid mother of 10 with the drunken husband ("See what you are doing to her!")?

In discussing the quality and weight of ethical arguments here, I hope to achieve the most minimal kind of goal—simply to make plausible the radical notion that there remain some unresolved questions, some hazy areas, and some further points to be thought about. Before proceeding, let me state something for the record about my "position." (Experience has taught me the painful lesson that abortion politicians of either persuasion usually care not at all about one's arguments, but only about one's final "position.") My position is that abortion should be legally available on request up to the 12th week of pregnancy; that abortion is morally justifiable under a variety of circumstances, but should always be undertaken reluctantly and with a strong sense of tragedy; and that the humane society would be one in which women were neither coerced to go through with pregnancies they do not want nor coerced by social, economic, or psychological circumstances into abortion. I cannot accept the position of those who would deny all respect to the fetus. Nor can I accept the position of those who hold that the right to life of the fetus is sufficient in all cases to override the right of women to choose an abortion. On the contrary, I accord the right of women to control their procreation a high status, as a crucial ingredient of the sanctity or dignity of life.

I will not try to defend or fully explain this position here. My intent is, resolutely, to talk about what seem to me good and bad arguments. But I want to note, no less resolutely, that it is perfectly possible for those with bad arguments to come nevertheless to good conclusions. This happens all the time, even if it is a process which does some violence to logic. (Or, as is more likely the case, people begin with good intuitions and then defend them with bad reasons.) Let me begin by laying out what seem to me bad or at least incomplete arguments. For convenience, I shall set them out as propositions, most of which should be readily recognizable to anyone even faintly acquainted with the abortion literature.

II. Nine Inadequate Arguments

A. Abortion is a religious or philosophical issue, best left to the private conscience rather than to public legislation

This argument rarely makes much sense. If it means that for some churches and some religious believers their positions are the direct results of religious teachings, this hardly entails the conclusion that the issue is thus intrinsically religious. One might as well say that the Vietnamese war was a religious issue, not subject to legislation because there are some churches which declare that war immoral on religious grounds. Religious groups have taken religious stands on many social issues, including war, race, poverty, population, and ecology, without exempting those problems from public legislation or turning them into "theology."

Nor is it enough to argue "sociologically" that religion plays a large role in what people feel and think about abortion, and that, somehow, this shows the religious issue to be paramount. If that were the case (and the sociological facts are, in any event, more complicated), then everyone, regardless of position, is implicated: for virtually everyone can be identified (if only culturally) with one or another religious heritage. Why is it, however, that the person who comes out of a religious heritage (e.g., Roman Catholicism) that condemns abortion is said to be acting on "religious" grounds, while a person from a heritage which does not condemn abortion is not (particularly when the latter tradition has *theological* reasons for not condemning abortion, as with some branches of Judaism and Protestantism)?

The claim that abortion is not a religious but a "philosophical" issue is surely true. But, then, every serious social question is philosophical. What is justice? What is freedom? Those questions arise all the time, and they are philosophical (and legal) in nature. The answers to them shape legislation in a very decisive way. It is inconsistent to argue that the right of the fetus is exclusively a philosophical problem, to be left to individual conscience, while the right of women is a matter to be protected or implemented legislatively. If it is legitimate to legislate on the latter (which it is), then it should be equally legitimate to legislate on the former.

B. To remove restrictive abortion laws from the books passes no judgment on the substantive ethical issues; it merely allows individuals to make up their own minds

That an absence of legislation allows freedom of individual choice is undoubtedly true. But it would be highly surprising if a social decision to remove restrictive laws did not reflect a significant shift in public moral thinking about the issue at hand. Civil libertarians, for instance, would be outraged if it were proposed to repeal all legislation designed to protect the civil rights of blacks on the ground that this would maximize individual freedom of choice: they would accurately discern any such trend as both moral and constitutional regression.

In the instance of abortion, a public decision to leave the question up to individuals reflects at least three premises of a highly philosophical sort: (1) that private abortion decisions have few if any social implications or consequences; (2) that there are no normative standards whatever for determining the rights of fetuses, except the standard that individuals are free to use or create any standard they see fit; and (3) that changes in law have no effect one way or another on individual moral judgments. My point here is not to judge these premises (though obviously much could be said about them), but only to point out that each involves a philosophical judgment and has philosophical implications. A decision to remove abortion laws from the books is no more ethically neutral than a decision to put such laws on the books or keep them there.

C. Any liberalization of abortion laws, or a repeal of such laws, will lead in the long run to a disrespect for all human life

This is a fundamental premise of those opposed to abortion. There is no evidence to support such a judgment, however, and evidence rather than speculation is what is required.

In the first place, it is exceedingly difficult to correlate abortion attitudes throughout the world with any trend toward disrespect for nonfetal life. On the contrary, insofar as liberal abortion laws are designed to promote free choice for women, there is a prima facie case that their intent is to enhance respect for the lives of women.

Secondly, there is no evidence to support a "domino theory" of the kind that predicts a quick move from liberalization of abortion laws to the killing of the defective, the elderly, and the undesirable. This has certainly not happened in Japan or the eastern European countries, which have had liberal abortion laws for a number of years.

Finally, since most of those who support liberal abortion laws either do not believe that fetal life is human life or do not believe that it is life which has reached a stage requiring social protection, it is unfair to accuse them of harboring attitudes which inevitably lead to atrocities against all forms of human life. This kind of judgment reflects more the moral logic of the group leveling such charges than the moral principles of those at whom the charge is leveled.

D. Scientific evidence, particularly modern genetics, has shown beyond a shadow of a doubt that human life begins at conception, or at least at the time of implantation

Scientific evidence does not, as such, tell us when human life begins. The concept "human" is essentially philosophical, requiring both a philosophical and an ethical judgment. Even if it could be shown that human life begins at conception, that finding would not entail the further moral judgment that life at that stage ethically merits full protection. When human life begins and when human life, once begun, merits or requires full respect are two different questions.

It is, I think, reasonable to contend that human life begins at conception. But this is as much a philosophical and ethical position as it is scientific. At the same time, however, it is capricious to ignore all scientific evidence. As any elementary textbook in genetics shows, the fusion of sperm and egg marks a decisive first step in the life of any individual. It is only in abortion arguments that one hears vague protestations that life is just one great continuum, with no decisive, significant changes from one stage or condition to another. But if it is bad science to talk that way, it is equally bad science to say that science dictates in some normative manner when human life begins.

E. The fetus is nothing more than "tissue" or a "blob of protoplasm" or a "blueprint"

Definitions of this kind can only be called self-serving. This is not the way a fetus is defined in any dictionary or any embryological text. All life is tissue and protoplasm: that fact alone tells us nothing whatever. Would it be acceptable for a student in a college biology course to define "fetus" with a one-word term "tissue" or "protoplasm"?

It is no less unscientific to call an embryo or a fetus a mere "blueprint." Blueprints of buildings are not ordinarily mixed into the mortar; they remain in the hands of the architects. Moreover, once a building has been constructed, the blueprint can be thrown away, and the building will continue to stand. The genetic blueprint operates in an entirely different way: it exerts a directly causal action in morphological development; as an intrinsic part of the physiological structure, it can at no point be thrown away or taken out.

F. All abortions are selfish, ego-centered actions

This reflects a strain of thought which runs very deep among those violently opposed to abortion. But the argument manages to ignore the decisions of those who choose abortion out of a sense of responsibility to their living children. It also manages to beg the question of whether individuals have some rights to determine what is in their own welfare, and to choose in favor of themselves some of the time.

Most broadly, this contention typifies the widespread tendency on all sides of the abortion debate to indulge in amateur psychologizing and *ad hominem* argumentation. Those opposed to abortion are adept at reducing all pro-abortion arguments to their psychological ingredients: homicidal impulses, selfishness, the baneful effects of a decadent culture, genocidal aspirations, a hatred of children, and the like. Those favorable to abortion are no mean masters of the art themselves: since it is well-known that all opposed to abortion are dogma-ridden, male chauvinists (or females brainwashed by male chauvinists), insensitive to the quality of life, sadists, and/or fascists. In short, don't listen to anyone's arguments; it is more profitable to hunt out hidden pathologies. And don't credit anyone with a mistake in reasoning, too small and human a flaw for propaganda purposes, when it is far more emotively effective, to convict them of general crimes against humanity.

G. Abortions are "therapeutic," and abortion decisions are "medical" decisions

Abortion is not notably therapeutic for the fetus—an observation I presume will elicit little disagreement. Even in the instance of a fetus with a grave defect, abortion is not therapeutic. It may be merciful and it may be wise, but, unless I am mistaken, the medical profession does not classify procedures with a 100 percent mortality rate as therapeutic.

Perhaps, then, abortion is therapeutic for the woman who receives it. That it is beneficial to her in some ways seems undeniable; she is relieved of an unwanted social, economic, or psychological burden. But is it proper to employ language which has a very concrete meaning in medicine—the correction or amelioration of a physical or psychological defect—in a case where there is usually no physical pathology at all? Except in the now-rare instances of a direct threat to a woman's life, an abortion cures no known disease and relieves no medically classifiable illness.

Thomas Szasz has been an especially eloquent spokesman for two positions. The first is that abortion should be available on request in the name of individual freedom. The second is that essentially nonmedical decisions should not be dressed in the mantle of "medical" language simply because they require medical technology for their execution. "To be sure," he has written, "the procedure is surgical; but this makes abortion no more a medical problem than the use of the electric chair makes capital punishment a problem of electrical engineering."[1]

Szasz's point seems undeniable, yet it is still common to hear abortion spoken of as a medical problem, which should be worked out between the woman and her physician. Even if that is the proper way to handle abortion, that does not make it a medical solution. The reason for this obfuscation is not far to be sought, and Szasz has stressed it as a constant theme in a number of his writings: the predilection in our society to translate value judgments into medical terms, giving them the aura of settled "scientific" judgments and the socially impregnable status of medical legitimation.

H. In a just society there would be no abortion problem, since there the social and economic pressures that drive women to abortion would not exist

This proposition is usually part of a broader political argument which sees abortion as no more than a symptom of unjust, repressive societies. To concentrate on abortion as a response to poverty, poor housing, puritanical attitudes toward illegitimacy, and racism is a cheap and evasive solution. It achieves no more than reinforcement of unjust political and social structures and institutions.

Up to a point there is some merit in this kind of argument, and that is why I believe that (as in the Scandinavian and eastern European countries) abortion should be handled in a context of full maternal and child care welfare programs. A woman who wishes to have a child but is not socially and economically free to do so is not a free woman. Her freedom is only superficially enhanced by allowing her, in that kind of repressive context, to choose abortion as a way out. She is not even being given half the loaf of freedom, which requires the existence of a full range of viable options.

At the same time, however, there are some serious limitations to the notion that abortion is nothing but a symptom of an unjust society. It utterly ignores the fact, common enough in affluent countries, that large numbers of women choose abortion because they have decided they want no children at all, or at least no more children than they already have. They are acting not out of social or economic coercion but out of a positive desire to shape and live a life of their own choosing, not dominated by unexpected pregnancies and unwanted children. In addition, it neglects the reality of contraceptive failure, which can and does occur independently of economic and social conditions (though it may of course be influenced by them). Short of the perfect contraceptive perfectly used, some portion of women, against their intentions, will become pregnant.

---

[1] Szasz, *The Ethics of Abortion,* Humanist 148 (September-October 1966).

I. Abortion is exclusively a women's issue to be decided by women

The underpinning of this argument seems to consist of three assumptions. First, that there is no role for male judgment, intervention, or interference because it is women who get pregnant and who have to live with the pregnancies. Second, that abortion laws are repressive because they have been established by male legislators. And, third, that that fetus is a part of a woman's body and is thus exclusively subject to her judgments and desires.

While I am fully prepared to agree that approval of a male, whether husband and/or father, should not be a legal condition for a woman to receive an abortion, this should not be construed to mean that nothing is owed, in justice, to the male. Even ignoring the well-known fact that women do not get pregnant by themselves, a few other considerations remain. At the least, there is an injustice in giving males no rights prior to birth but then imposing upon them a full range of obligations after birth. If the obligations toward a child are mutual after birth, why should there not be a corresponding parity of rights prior to birth? I have not seen a satisfactory answer to that question. Moreover, if—to accept the feminist premise—women have been forced to carry through unwanted pregnancies because of male domination, the sexist shoe is put on the other foot if all the rights involved in having a child are ceded exclusively to women. One injustice is corrected at the expense of creating another, and sexism is still triumphant.

That legislatures are dominated by males is an obvious fact. That the history of abortion legislation would have been different had there been legislative equality or even a female majority, however, has not been demonstrated. Indeed, it has been a consistent survey finding that women are less willing than men to approve permissive abortion laws. There have of course been attempts to explain these rather awkward findings, since they are inconsistent on their face with claims that resistance to abortion is a male phenomenon. These efforts usually take the form of speculations designed to show that the resistant women were culturally brainwashed into adopting repressive male attitudes. This is a plausible theory, but one for which there unfortunately is no evidence whatever. And, apart from these speculations, there is no evidence that the thinking of women on abortion must, of biological and experiential necessity, be utterly different from that of men. But that is exactly the premise necessary if the contention is to be sustained that an exclusively female domination of abortion legislation would produce a different result from either a male domination or legislative equality.

In this context, it should be mentioned that childbearing and childrearing have consequences for everyone in a society, both men and women. To imply that women alone should have all the rights, even though the consequences involve the lives of both sexes, is an unfair conclusion. Or are we to overthrow, as the price of abortion reform, the long-honored principle that all of those who will have to bear the consequences of decisions have a right to be consulted? I find that price too high. Yet, since I agree that abortion decisions should not legally require the consent of husband and/or father—for I see no way to include such a requirement in the law without opening the way for a further abuse of women—I am left with the (perhaps pious) hope that there will be some recognition that problems of justice toward the male are real (however new!) and that an ethical resolution will be found.

Finally, a quick word about the contention that a fetus is ''part'' of a woman's body. That a fetus is *in* a woman's body is an evident biological datum. That it is thereby a *part* of her body, in much the same way that her heart, arm, liver, or leg is part of her body, is biologically false. The separate genetic constitution of the fetus, its rate of growth and development, and its separate organ system clearly distinguish the body of the fetus from the body of the mother.

Some clarity would be brought to the language of the abortion debate if this distinction were admitted. It could still be argued that, because the fetus is in the mother's body, she should have full rights in determining its fate. But that argument is different from likening the fetus to say any other part of a woman's body and then transposing the rules concerning the exercise of rights over one's body. Here is a clear instance where, in order to find a constitutional precedent for women's right to control procreation, violence is often done to some elementary facts of biology.

III. Some Valid Conclusions

I have tried to show, using nine different propositions, that some bad, or at least incompletely developed, arguments are too much in currency to be allowed to go by default. Would the abortion debate be significantly altered if these arguments were no longer used by the contending sides? This is a moot question, as there seems to be little likelihood that they will cease being employed. They are too powerful to be set aside, for both good and bad reasons—the good being that they are able to elicit responses which build upon some pervasive feelings about abortion, feelings which are decisive in shaping thought and behavior, even if they are poorly articulated.

The great strength of the general movement for abortion on request (apart from the questionable validity of particular arguments brought to bear in support of it) is that it perceives and seeks to correct two elementary realities, one social and the other biological. The social reality is that women have not had the freedom to make their own choice in a matter critical to their development as persons. Society, through the medium of male domination, has forced its choice upon them. The biological reality is that it is women who become pregnant and bear children; nature gave them no choice. Unless they are given a means to control the biological facts—and abortion is one very effective means—they will be dominated by them.

Without such control, which must be total if it is to have any decisive meaning, women are fated to accept Freud's principle that "anatomy is destiny." That kind of rigid biological determinism is increasingly unacceptable, not only to women in the case of procreation, but to most human beings confronted with the involuntary rigidities of nature. The deepest philosophical issue beneath the abortion question is the extent to which, in the name of freely chosen ends, biological realities can be manipulated, controlled, and set aside. This is a very old problem, and the trend toward abortion on request reflects the most recent tendency in modern thought—namely, the attempt to subordinate biology to reason, to bring it under control, to master it. It remains to be seen whether procreation can be so easily mastered. That question may take centuries to resolve.

The great strength of the movement against abortion is that it seeks to protect one defenseless category of human or potentially human life; furthermore, it strives to resist the introduction into society of forms of value judgments that would discriminate among the worth of individual lives. In almost any other civil rights context, the cogency of this line of reasoning would be quickly respected. Indeed, it has been at the heart of efforts to correct racial injustices, to improve health care, to eradicate poverty, and to provide better care for the aged. The history of mankind has shown too many instances of systematic efforts to exclude certain races or classes of persons from the human community to allow us to view with equanimity the declaration that fetuses are "not human." Historically, the proposition that all human beings are equal, however "inchoate" they may be, is not conservative but radical. It is constantly threatened in theory and subverted in practice.

Although the contending sides in the abortion debate commonly ignore, or systematically deride, the essentially positive impulses lying behind their opponents' positions, the conflict is nonetheless best seen as the pitting of essentially valuable impulses against one another. The possibility of a society which did allow women the right and the freedom to control their own lives is a lofty goal. No less lofty is that of a society which, with no exceptions, treated all forms of human life as equally valuable. In the best of all possible worlds, it might be possible to reconcile these goals. In the real world, however, the first goal requires the right of abortion, and the second goal excludes that right. This, I believe, is a genuine and deep dilemma. That so few are willing to recognize the dilemma, or even to admit that any choice must be less than perfect, is the most disturbing element in the whole debate.

The bad reason why the arguments I have analyzed will endure is that they readily lend themselves to legal use. Nothing in our society has so muddied the ethical issues as its tendency to turn ethical problems into legal matters. The great prize, sought by all sides, is a favorable court decision. Toward that end, the best tactic is to find a way of bringing one's own ethical case under one or more constitutional protections or exclusions. If one can succeed in convincing the courts that abortion is a religious issue (which it is not), then there is a good chance that they will favor private choice and rule against legislation. The same tactic is evident in efforts to show that abortion decisions come under the constitutional protections afforded to "privacy" (which begs the question of the rights of the fetus), or, on the other side, to show that abortion violates the equal protection and due process requirements of the Constitution (which also begs the question of the rights of the fetus). Since the possibility of a legal victory is an irresistible goal, there seems to be no limit to the bad arguments which will be brought to bear to gain it.

In this article Dr. Murray carefully examines the many arguments both for and against the use of fetal tissue. First, he looks at the issue of the value of fetal tissue. Is it really beneficial to mankind? Second, he looks at the relationship between fetal tissue and abortion. Is it always related? Third, he looks at the solution other countries have reached with fetal tissue. Is it possible to avoid the ethical dilemma posed by the use of fetal tissue? This article, coupled with the one by Daniel Callahan, reveals why the abortion issue extends much further than the confines of a medical, legal and religious debate.

29 · Human Fetal Tissue Transplantation Research: Conflict in Ethics and Public Policy

Thomas H. Murray, Ph.D.

In a wide variety of human diseases, the cause can be traced to a group of cells that do not function properly. In diabetes the islet cells of the pancreas fail to secrete insulin as needed; in Parkinson's disease certain brain cells appear to die; in inherited diseases of the immune system, cells essential to fighting infection do not develop as they should. In the treatment of these diseases, fetal tissue has properties that may allow it to be transplanted into children or adults where it could substitute for the cells that have failed.

The prospect of an effective treatment—or cure—for diabetes, Parkinson's and several other debilitating or deadly diseases has aroused great interest in experiments using tissue from aborted fetuses. Researchers proposed such an experiment to the U.S. National Institutes of Health (NIH). Recognizing that the proposed study touched a sensitive political nerve, NIH requested guidance from its parent agency, the Department of Health and Human Services. On March 22, 1988, Dr. Robert Windom, assistant secretary for health, wrote to NIH's director and declared a moratorium on NIH research involving human fetal tissue transplantation. The letter also instructed NIH to establish a panel to answer 10 questions about ethical, legal and scientific issues raised by such research.

The Human Fetal Tissue Transplantation Research Panel (as it was officially known) submitted its official report to NIH on December 14, 1988. The panel recommended that, with appropriate safeguards, research should proceed.[1] Nevertheless, in November

---

[1] *Report of the Advisory Committee to the Director, National Institutes of Health: Human Fetal Tissue Transplantation Research* (December 14, 1988) [hereinafter Report of Human Fetal Tissue Transplantation Research Panel].

1989, the Department of Health and Human Services announced that its moratorium on fetal tissue transplantation research would remain in effect indefinitely.

This bare bones description of events only hints at the ethical and political complexities of the controversy. Research on human fetal tissue transplantation, like other issues such as decisions at the end of life, had become hostage to perhaps the most politically divisive and morally intractable issue in all of bioethics—abortion. What has happened with this issue can be interpreted as a case study of how a dispute over the ethics of one social practice can infect moral debate and hamstring policymaking in other areas. The controversy raises interesting issues in its own right; it also illuminates some of the complex connections between ethics and public policy.

Factors that Caused the Argument

Several factors coalesced to bring the conflict to this juncture. First, fetal tissue transplantation research on animal models looked very promising for several diseases, creating pressure to begin experiments in humans. Second, certain characteristics of fetal tissue gave it advantages, at least in theory, over other sources of healthy cells. Fetal tissue grows and proliferates easily, is relatively "plastic," that is, differentiates into a variety of tissue types, produces growth factors affecting the development of itself *and* neighboring cells and in some cases does not prompt rejection as foreign tissue from the body into which it is transplanted.[2]

Third, problems exist with other potential sources of fetal tissue. The most desirable fetal tissue for transplantation is fresh or well-preserved, sterile and not abnormal. Spontaneous abortions rarely occur under conditions that allow fresh, sterile tissue to be recovered. Furthermore, scientists believe that when fetuses are spontaneously aborted it is often because they were abnormal. Few people would welcome the transplantation of possibly decaying, contaminated, abnormal tissue into their bodies.

One commentator has suggested using tissue from ectopic pregnancies—fetuses developing outside the womb.[3] Ectopic fetuses may develop normally for a brief time, but they are not viable and must be removed to protect the health of the woman. Like elective abortuses, ectopic fetuses can be removed under relatively controlled sterile conditions; because they are not viable at all, their removal does not prompt the moral objections some have against elective abortions. Whether this is a practical alternative is uncertain, but researchers do not appear to have embraced the suggestion.

Another potential source of fetal tissue is fetal cell cultures: tissue originally derived from fetuses and grown in culture medium. Too little is known about how such tissue behaves after transplantation for it to be an acceptable alternative at the moment, though it might become so in the future.

A fourth factor was at least as important as the scientific and clinical reasons in making fetal tissue transplantation research politically controversial—the political clout of abortion opponents. In the 1980s, antiabortion activists supported successful presidential candidates who were sympathetic to their cause. Their concerns frequently found a friendly reception in the administration. They took on fetal tissue transplantation research as a major issue and apparently succeeded in bringing federal support for it to a

---

[2] Council on Scientific Affairs and Council on Ethical and Judicial Affairs, American Medical Association, *Medical Applications of Fetal Tissue Transplantation,* 263, no. 4 JAMA 565–570 (January 26, 1990).

[3] Kathleen Nolan, Hastings Center.

complete halt. This controversy is noteworthy because the people on the other side of the dispute—those in favor of the research—are not the usual pro-choice groups but rather organizations of people suffering from the diseases for which fetal tissue transplantation holds some promise.

What Does the Ethics of Abortion Have to Do with Fetal Tissue?

Opponents of fetal tissue transplantation research have fought it as a surrogate for the abortion issue. But it is far from obvious that the ethics of the use of fetal tissue is inextricably bound up with the ethics of abortion. One issue is clear: Proponents of the research are not urging the killing of fetuses. Their interest is in recovering tissue from fetuses that are already dead. In broad terms, they argue that to recover such tissue does no harm to the fetus and might do others a great deal of good (if the therapy turns out to work). Proponents suggest an analogy with recovering organs and tissues from the bodies of adults and children—practices we clearly accept. The analogy is worth examining more closely.

Suppose a U.S. senator proposed a new law that would raise the speed limit on interstate highways to 120 miles per hour. As the principal rationale for the change, she cites the shortage of transplantable organs. Raising the speed limit would result in more fatal accidents and more organs to save other lives. The beauty of the law is that most of the people killed would be those who chose to drive fast, so they can be said to have perished by their own choice.

The senator can accept amendments to her bill that would forbid, say, people over the age of 40 from driving so fast (their organs have suffered more wear and tear and are less desirable). But let us say that she is correct about the result: more fatal accidents by young people and many more organs recovered. Let us even say, though this is implausible, that since several organs can be recovered from each cadaver, the net balance of lives saved over lives lost is positive. Is her bill a good idea? Or does it miss the point about the relationship of highway speed limits and organs for transplantation?

Many considerations are relevant to setting highway speed limits. The most prominent considerations balance values: On the side of higher speeds are liberty (to choose whatever risks one is willing to accept) and efficiency (getting where we want to go as quickly as possible); on the side of lower limits are safety (preventing injuries and deaths) and, more recently, energy conservation. Most people, I think, would throw some other considerations out as morally inappropriate. Higher speed limits would lead to more wrecks, which could lead to greater demand for new cars, hence more jobs for auto workers and bigger profits for auto manufacturers. Or, as the senator suggested, more organs for transplantation. These may well be consequences of higher speed limits, even consequences most of us would judge were good on the whole. But that does not mean that they ought to be counted as good reasons for raising the speed limit. When a direct consequence of a public policy is an evil, such as untimely deaths, the fact that indirect but desirable consequences flow from the evil does not legitimate their consideration in the public policy debate.

My conclusion from this is that if fetal tissue ever did emerge as an effective therapy, it could not legitimately be used as a reason for changing public policy to encourage elective abortions. But, of course, this is not what proponents of fetal tissue transplantation research are asking for at all.

The hypothetical senator's problem was that she failed to understand the relation between the unfortunate, direct consequence and the desirable, indirect and secondary consequence. The latter cannot serve as a moral justification for the former. Recovering organs from highway accident victims is no more than an effort to salvage some good from an evil that occurred completely independently. Similarly, recovering tissue from electively aborted fetuses, if the recovery effort is not allowed to affect the decision to have an abortion, cannot be said to approve of or partake in whatever moral judgment is attached to abortion. It must also be said that, whereas untimely deaths from traffic accidents are regarded universally as bad, there is much less agreement that abortions are always morally undesirable or unjustified. If anything, general sentiment appears to be that the killing of a fetus is a regrettable but sometimes morally defensible act.

Does the ethics of abortion make a difference in any case? It makes less of a difference than one might think. Consider organs for transplantation again. Some highway deaths result from bad weather or bad luck and cannot be said to be someone's fault. Other deaths are caused by careless driving, faulty maintenance or faulty engineering. Still others are the direct result of driving while impaired by alcohol or other drugs, or fleeing in a stolen car. The extent or nature of human culpability for the death simply does not matter when it comes to recovering organs from highway accident victims. The same is true for deaths from other causes. As horrible as it is to contemplate, organs are recovered from victims of homicide and child abuse. The act of recovery in no way is a sign that we condone any of these acts, from faulty car design to drunken driving to murder. We do not believe that organ recovery and the good that may come from it makes any of these death-causing actions an iota less wrong. Imagine a driver charged with negligent homicide arguing that he ought to be congratulated, not prosecuted: Because of his actions three lives were saved and only one lost! No sensible person would take him seriously (except perhaps our hypothetical senator).

The connection between the morality of abortion and the moral acceptability of fetal tissue transplantation research is far from straightforward. Abortion opponents argue that, even if the ties are indirect, fetal tissue transplantation research may help legitimate abortion or make those who use the tissue complicit in what abortion opponents regard as the frank evil of abortion.

The Case Against Fetal Tissue Transplantation Research

People who claim that fetal tissue transplantation research is immoral typically claim that it will, directly or indirectly, result in more abortions or that it makes one complicit in the evil of abortion. It must be emphasized that these arguments are premised on two assumptions: that abortion *is* a grave evil and that our laws permitting abortion should have no bearing on what our public policy toward fetal tissue transplantation research ought to be. The latter assumption has not been scrutinized carefully. It will be reexamined later.

The first claim is that fetal tissue transplantation research will lead directly to more abortions. Women, it is said, will become pregnant in order to provide fetal tissue for themselves or a relative. Or perhaps a woman who has become pregnant will be pressured to have an abortion in order to make fetal tissue available to a family member. These two scenarios, "custom pregnancies" and "directed donations" of fetal tissue, if they were permitted, would link abortion directly to fetal tissue transplantation. Other incentives to abort are likewise possible. A commercial market in fetal tissue could be developed, and women could be paid for fetal tissue. Every agency that has addressed fetal tissue transplantation research has rejected these scenarios as morally unacceptable.

More subtle effects have been suggested. Suppose a woman were undecided whether to have an abortion. Critics of fetal tissue transplantation research argue that women who would not otherwise have abortions would have them because the tissue might help someone else. Given the gravity of most abortion decisions, this seems very unlikely, though it is impossible to say that such considerations will never tip the balance in any individual decision.

If fetal tissue transplantation should become a proven therapy, abortion opponents fear that it could influence public sentiment toward abortion. People might view abortion more favorably if they knew some good might come to others—or themselves—from it.

This is like arguing that attitudes toward highway safety will become lax because we recover organs from victims of fatal accidents. It has not happened in the case of speed limits. This is not proof that it would not happen with fetal tissue transplants and abortion, but there is nothing in our comparable experiences to suggest it would.

The arguments against proceeding with fetal tissue transplantation research just considered all have important empirical premises—that custom pregnancies or directed donations will be permitted by law, that compensation will be offered, that more women will have abortions for altruistic reasons or that public sentiment will change, followed by public policy. In each case, either the premise's plausibility is questionable, or the possibility of safeguards preventing the unwanted consequences is ignored. Another criticism does not depend on such empirical premises—the claim that anyone who benefits from fetal tissue from elective abortions is in complicity with the evil of abortion.

The accusation of complicity depends, like the earlier complaints, on the assumption that abortion is a grave moral evil. It makes no sense to say that someone was "complicit" in an action that was not itself wrong. But even assuming that one regarded elective abortion as immoral, does using tissue from elective abortions necessarily make one complicit with them? The organ recovery teams, surgeons and patients who receive organs from victims of drunk drivers, or even murderers, cannot fairly be said to be complicit in those wrongs. If you asked them, you would expect them to say that these acts that resulted in deaths were horrible wrongs, and you would not think they were being inconsistent in saying so.

Minority Moral Beliefs and Public Policy

There is a difference worth exploring. Public policy and public moral sentiment are clearly opposed to driving while intoxicated and to murder. People who benefit from the organs of accident and murder victims can say that they are participants in a society that is in general, at least, trying to prevent wrongs from happening. Abortion opponents, in contrast, might say that our current laws protect a grossly immoral practice and that anyone who participates in or benefits, however indirectly, from that practice is in complicity with it. They frequently refer to the evils done by the Nazis as an analogy. Anyone who would benefit from such evil, they claim, shares in the wrong.[4] But this raises an interesting question: How should society act when the moral beliefs of a segment of society would be offended?

[4] James Burtchaell, *University Policy on Experimental Use of Aborted Fetal Tissue*, 10, no. 4 IRB 7–11 (1988).

Take the case where, for religious reasons, a group regards a particular form of tissue transplantation as morally wrong. What should we do as a pluralistic political community?

It appears clear that we should not force the transplanted tissue on individuals who believe that it is immoral, nor should we compel them to participate in the gathering, distribution or transplantation of that tissue. We should not, that is, force people to violate their conscience or religious beliefs.

Suppose that a clear majority of thoughtful and decent people believed that the practice rejected by some was nonetheless morally acceptable and had placed into civil law permission to do that thing or to refuse it according to one's conscience. Is this an unreasonable way to construct public policy? Or is it a constructive response to moral and religious pluralism?

The tissue referred to in this example, by the way, is blood; the people believing that the transplantation (transfusion) of blood is morally evil are members of the Jehova's Witness religion. Witnesses believe that "eating" blood, of which transfusion is an instance, is a grave sin and a direct contravention of a Biblical injunction.

In this case, the beliefs of a religious minority are respected by not imposing the majority's beliefs directly on individuals who oppose the transfer of blood into their bodies. But these minority beliefs are not permitted to dictate public policy for all others. The practice of transfusing blood continues, despite the belief of some that it is wrong.

Fetal tissue transplantation is not blood transfusion, of course. But it differs in ways that weaken, rather than strengthen, the case against it. Jehovah's Witnesses oppose blood transfusion because they believe the act of transfusion itself is sinful. People opposed to elective abortion oppose fetal tissue transplantation not because they think that such transplantation in itself is immoral but because of what they claim are its links to abortion. The various proposals for fetal tissue transplantation research go a long way toward severing that link.

Proposals for Fetal Tissue Transplantation Research

The Human Fetal Tissue Transplantation Research Panel of the U.S. National Institutes of Health—the panel whose recommendations were ignored by the Department of Health and Human Services—affirmed the desirability of severing the decision to have an elective abortion from the use of fetal tissue. It suggested several ways to do this.[5] The report states that "the decision to terminate a pregnancy and the procedures of abortion should be kept independent from the retrieval and use of fetal tissue."[6] They urge that women not be informed about the possibility of donating fetal tissue or asked to donate until after they have made their decision to have an abortion. Clinics or other institutions processing fetal tissue should not receive any remuneration for their efforts, except "for reasonable expenses occasioned by the actual retrieval, storage, preparation, and transportation of the tissues."[7] The panel dealt with the threats of directed donations and custom pregnancies by stating that "the pregnant woman should be prohibited from

---

[5] Report of Human Fetal Tissue Transplantation Research Panel, *supra* note 1, at volume 1.
[6] *Id.* at 1.
[7] *Id.*

designating the transplant-recipient of the fetal tissue.''[8] The panel also urged that anonymity between donor and recipient be maintained and that "the timing and method of abortion should not be influenced by the potential uses of fetal tissue for transplantation or medical research.''[9] Finally, they concluded that the woman's consent is always necessary and usually sufficient, except in cases in which the father of the fetus objects (unless the fetus is a result of rape or incest).[10] The NIH panel's recommendations were endorsed by the great majority of its members, but they were not unanimous.

The United Kingdom had its own commission of fetal tissue transplantation research. Their conclusions were remarkably similar to those of the NIH panel, with one addition. The Polkinghorn Commission, as it was known, recommended that an agency be established in the United Kingdom to which all requests for fetal tissue for transplantation should be submitted and all offers of donated tissue be directed. This agency, serving as a buffer between potential sources of tissue and those who would use the tissue, minimizes even further the likelihood that any pressure will be exerted on women to donate at the same time that it assures such tissue will not become the subject of for-profit companies.

Conclusion

The controversy over fetal tissue transplantation research reveals some of the complexities in the relationship of ethics and public policy. That a certain practice is judged morally reprehensible by a portion of the community does not mean that banning it for all is justified. It remains to be seen if it is possible in practice, as it appears to be in principle, to separate elective abortions from the recovery of fetal tissue from those same abortions. Some useful information on that question may come from other nations where such research is permitted. Even in the United States, most states do not prohibit research with tissue from dead fetuses. Indeed, at least one major study is in progress at this writing—without federal support.

---

[8] *Id.* at 3
[9] *Id.* at 4.
[10] *Id.* at 6.

Professor Simmons' article is an overview of the major religious views on abortion. He deals most extensively with the pro-life Roman Catholic views on the subject as they have been central to U.S. policy-making. However, other religious groups have had a moral impact on the abortion issue as well. For example, where Presbyterian, Baptists and Jews are pro-choice, they often emphasize a personal responsibility for a moral decision. Here lies the strength of this article: The author shows the delicate balancing act of strict religious rules versus individual freedom. It should also be noted that religious pluralism in the United States has been placated by *Roe v. Wade* because no group is forced to live by another's beliefs or standards and each religion is free to teach its own particular morality to its followers.

30 · Religious Approaches to Abortion _____

Paul D. Simmons, Th.M., Ph.D.

Few issues generate such profound divisions within and among the various religious groups as that of abortion. The power of the topic to generate debate is related to its profundity as a human issue. Abortion is related to life and death, sexuality and pro-creation—all of which are integrally related in the human psyche. Public policy questions are raised by questions about the power of the state to regulate matters that relate to population growth and personal well-being. The legal question as to the relation between religious and/or moral issues and the government powers of coercion and enforcement is also posed.

Religious concerns in the abortion debate relate to theological questions at issue, moral rules and principles based on distinctively religious traditions or teachings and ecclesiastical prerogatives over the private lives of believers. Theological issues are raised as to the nature of personhood, the relation of God to the generative process, the place of conscience in fertility control, male-female relations in matters of authority or power and the proper relation of morality to law. These are arguably the primary variables to be found in the debate among religious leaders as to the moral acceptability of abortion and the proper role of government in regulating this intensely private and deeply personal matter.

The purpose of this essay is to indicate the various answers given the central questions concerning abortion by various religious groups. Major denominational or religious traditions will be considered in order to understand better the variety of perspectives that exist. The complexity of the debate makes generalizations and categorizations both problematic and misleading, of course. Even official statements may conceal as much as they reveal. Where possible, qualifications will be made to indicate sources of division and disagreement.

Understanding the reasons behind the differences among people of intelligence and good faith is perhaps more important than simply listing or citing statements that have been made by the various groups. Even so, the primary emphasis will fall upon the statements themselves. Each group does not receive equal time or space, in part because some have more complex approaches. The Roman Catholic response is treated first and covered in greater detail because it has arguably set the agenda for the abortion debate in America. Others are treated in particular groupings and in alphabetical order.

Roman Catholics and Abortion

Roman Catholics are deeply divided over the issue of abortion because of profound differences over the issues involved in theological/ethical reasoning about the moral acceptability of terminating a pregnancy. The official teaching of the church is that abortion is a moral and social evil. The church heirarchy regards its ban on abortion as the basis for Catholic orthodoxy on the issue. The point was stated emphatically by Pope Paul VI:

> . . . *the direct interruption of the generative process already begun, and, above all, directly willed and procured abortion, even if for therapeutic reasons, are to be absolutely excluded as licit means of regulating birth.*

The prohibition of abortion stems from the Catholic ban on any type of contraception. Every act of sexual intercourse is to be open to conception as the moral justification for an act that is inevitably and inescapably tainted with sin. The belief that abortion is forbidden as the murder of a human being is actually an inference drawn from statements such as that of Pius XII who indicated that "Innocent human life . . . is withdrawn, from the very first moment of its existence, from any direct deliberate attack."[1] The church has not reached an official position as to when the fetus becomes a person.[2]

The first legislation applying to the Western church was in *The Decretals* of Pope Gregory IX in 1234 A.D. and was based on the notion of delayed hominization. Pius IX eliminated the distinction between the formed (ensouled) and unformed fetus in 1869 following Mendellian genetics. Since that time, a succession of popes has held that the direct killing of a fetus at any time after conception is a mortal sin and carries an automatic penalty of excommunication. The *indirect* killing of a fetus as a consequence of surgery for cancer or an ectopic pregnancy is morally justifiable.[3] The principle of double effect allows lifesaving surgery for the woman even if it has the (unintended) effect of destroying the conceptus.

Abortion as the taking of innocent human life is regarded as a principle of the natural law—the right to life of innocent persons. It is thus held to be true for all people; it is not simply sectarian doctrine. The strict moral rule should thus be implemented by restrictive civil law.

---

[1] Pope Pius XII, *Acta Apostolicae Sedis* 43 (1951).
[2] F. Kissling, *Introduction,* in *Guide for Prochoice Catholics: The Church, the State and Abortion Politics* 2 (1990).
[3] D. Callahan, *Abortion, Law, Choice and Morality* (1970).

Politics and the NCCB

The National Council of Catholic Bishops (NCCB) is committed to implementing this church position as law in the United States. In its 1975 "Pastoral Plan for Pro-Life Activities," it declared its opposition to *Roe v. Wade* and set in motion an organized effort to have Congress pass a human life amendment. Both educational and political structures were established in every diocese and congressional district. The aim was to persuade the public and members of Congress to ban abortion.[4]

The U.S. Catholic Conference 1985 "Statement on Abortion" declared that "abortion (is) a grave moral evil" and that the church's "teaching expresses the objective demands placed on all of us by the inherent dignity of human life."[5]

The NCCB is probably the most significant and powerful antiabortion force in America. Along with the United States Catholic Conference (USCC), it is the source of policy decisions for Catholics in America. Two recent events have encouraged the bishops to intensify their efforts. The first was the Supreme Court's *Webster* decision in 1989, permitting states to impose limitations on a woman's access to abortion services. The second was the dismissal of a 1980 suit filed by a coalition of clergy and pro-choice groups who thought the Internal Revenue Service should revoke the church's tax exempt status because of its overt and extensive political activity on behalf of anti-choice politicians.[6] The intensity of these efforts will likely increase.[7] In March 1990, the NCCB hired Hill & Knowlton, the nation's largest public relations firm, to run a five million dollar campaign against legal abortion. The antiabortion campaign has the unqualified support of the Vatican and is widely funded by local parish churches.

At another level, bishops and priests have used coercive measures against Catholic politicians, theologians and others in an attempt to consolidate the church's witness. Legislators have been threatened with excommunication and professors have been fired for advocating choice or dissenting from the "official" position. Other Catholics whose work reveals support for choice have been refused holy communion. These measures are traditional levers for enforcing conformity to church teachings, but they are a source of controversy within that communion.

Understanding the Catholic Position

The Catholic position on abortion is not a matter of papal infallibility. On this issue, no pope has claimed to speak *ex cathedra,* even though the uncompromising nature of papal opposition to legalized abortion would appear to imply that it had.

Opposition to restrictive abortion laws has strong support among American catholics. The most vocal and organized group is Catholics for Free Choice (CFFC) based in Washington, D.C. A large number of prominent Roman Catholic theologians have also questioned the efficacy of the absolutist position claiming that pluralism is the Catholic norm. Those who support the legal availability of abortion appeal to several points: (1) the lack of uniformity in historical teachings about the human status of the fetus; (2) the perception that the moral status of the woman is made secondary to that of a zygote; (3) the centrality of personal conscience; and (4) ecumenical concerns.[8]

---

[4] *The Churches Speak On: Abortion* 8–15 (J. G. Melton ed. 1990) [hereinafter *The Churches Speak*].

[5] *Id.* at 17.

[6] F. Kissling, *supra* note 2, at 1.

[7] *Abortion and the Constitution* (D. J. Horan et al. 1987).

[8] D. C. Maquire, *Catholic Options in the Abortion Debate,* in *Guide for Prochoice Catholics: The Church, the State and Abortion Politics* 16 (1990).

Three additional points deserve elaboration. The first is the Catholic moral principle of probabilism, which holds that "a doubtful moral obligation may not be imposed as though it were certain."[9] Certainly there is no metaphysical certainty regarding fetal personhood, though one could hardly dismiss the moral claims of the woman as person. Dissent is allowed when following reasonable and sufficiently cogent reasons and when there are a significant number of theologians or reputable experts who agree with the dissenting view. That certainly is the case with abortion, as a survey of historical opinion and the contemporary scene reveals. Thus individual conscience (with community support) becomes the forum for decision-making rather than extrinsic authority. Catholic legislators can support choice at law even though they may believe it personally immoral.

Another appeal for choice is made by pointing to the inconsistencies in canon law. Although the strong condemnations are typically emphasized, there are a significant number of "excusing causes" and "mitigating circumstances" that are seldom mentioned. The rule of excommunication for abortion does not apply to women under 17, those ignorant of the penalty, those under duress, those who are in fear and those who act in self-defense. Further, those who act with imputability, that is, the conscientious conviction that abortion is permissible in certain circumstances are also excused.[10] The canon law is aimed at those *directly* involved in the procurement of abortion—women and physicians. It does not apply to persons indirectly involved as in cases of legislators supporting choice.

The third basis Catholics use to argue for choice is religious liberty. Pro-choice Catholics follow two Vatican II documents, *Declaration of Religious Liberty* and the *Pastoral Constitution on the Church in the Modern World,* which affirmed religious freedom as an intrinsic human right. These documents reflected the thought of Jesuit theologian John C. Murray who argued that religious liberty and church-state separation left Catholics free to worship and did not require assent to error. The church is free to promote human rights and dignity and should not promote its own political agenda. He had argued strongly that Catholic teachings on human dignity, justice and freedom were consistent with the political values of equality and inalienable rights. He also helpfully distinguished between spiritual/moral and temporal/legal matters. Catholics could be faithful to religious convictions without trying to impose those upon others through law.[11]

Such distinctions are vital to those Catholics committed both to religious fidelity and to American diversity. Pope John Paul XXIII embraced the principle of pluralism in *Pacem in Terris,* declaring that even the erroneous conscience of the nonbeliever was to be respected. Significant numbers of U.S. Roman Catholics are thus supportive of choice, that is, of keeping abortion legal, even while personally opposing abortion as a matter of religious convictions. That posture is found among politicians as well as priests and activists.

---

[9] *The Churches Speak, supra* note 4, at 16.

[10] F. Kissling, *supra* note 2, at 23.

[11] M. C. Segers, *American Catholicism: The Search for a Public Voice in a Pluralistic Society,* in *Guide for Prochoice Catholics: The Church, the State and Abortion Politics* 6 (1990).

Division of Opinion among Catholics

A majority of Catholics in the United States appear to disagree with the political posture of the NCCB. A 1989 poll of Catholics conducted by Greenberg-Lake found that 58% said the Catholic church has no right to tell its members how to vote for candidates for political office.[12] According to a 1987 CBS/*New York Times* poll, eighty-five percent of Catholics believe that women can both have an abortion and be a good Catholic. A 1989 poll found that 70% of Catholic respondents expressed stong disapproval of the use of pastoral sanctions against Catholic politicians.[13]

Opposition to abortion is primarily within the heirarchy of the church.[14] Papal pronunciations and the political efforts of the NCCB notwithstanding, the great majority of American Roman Catholics do not favor making abortion illegal. A 1988 Hickman Maslin poll indicated that 81% of Catholics agreed that "abortion is a private decision mainly up to the woman and her doctor." A CBS/*New York Times* poll in 1989 found that only 15% of Catholics believe that abortion should not be legally permitted under any circumstance. In cases of rape, 84% supported legal abortion; 68% in cases of genetic defects; 51% for economic hardship, 48% for unmarried women; and 45% if pregnancy threatened to cause dropping out of school. The Alan Guttmacher Institute found that Catholic women constitute 30% of those who have abortions in the United States and that they have 30% more abortions than Protestants or Jews.[15]

Profound divisions concerning the morality of elective abortion and its relation to civil law clearly exist among Roman Catholics.

Abortion and Protestant Christianity

Protestants are understandably and predictably deeply divided about the moral and legal acceptability of abortion. Such divisions grow out of the nature of Protestantism, which turns to Scripture as authority in matters of faith and practice, and also tends to emphasize personal responsibility in moral decision making as a corollary to active obedience to the living Christ. Some groups have heirarchical structures for matters of polity, but none govern the beliefs and actions of all constituents. Great variety in doctrinal and moral beliefs is allowed within the general parameters of common religious commitments.

Baptists

There are many Baptist denominations in the United States. They are characterized by belief in the authority of Scripture, local church autonomy and moral conservatism. Their enormous differences of opinion on questions pertaining to abortion stems from emphases on religious liberty, personal responsibility for actions and the leadership of the Holy Spirit.

AMERICAN BAPTIST CONVENTION (ABC)   A 1988 statement of the General Board of the ABC recognized the genuine diversity of opinion among members both on the issue

---

[12] D. Shannon, *Outside the Chancery: Catholics Take Issue*, in *Guide for Prochoice Catholics: The Church, the State and Abortion Politics* 28 (1990).

[13] F. Kissling, *supra* note 2, at 3.

[14] *Abortion and the Constitution*, *supra* note 7; *Abortion and Catholicism: The American Debate* (P. B. Jung and T. A. Shannon eds., 1988).

[15] D. Shannon, *supra* note 12, at 25, 26.

of the morality of abortion and the proper approach to state control. Support was given to all members to voice their opinion consistent with personal convictions. The board registered opposition to abortion as a primary means of birth control and to the violence and harassment against women seeking abortion. Supportive ministries to women and responsible sex education materials were advocated. Until 1985, the Board of Social Ministries was a sponsor of the Religious Coalition for Abortion Rights.

SOUTHERN BAPTIST CONVENTION   The largest Protestant body in the United States, the SBC supported resolutions during the 1970s that were generally supportive of legalized abortions. Since 1980 resolutions have strongly condemned abortion and called for "legislation and/or a constitutional amendment prohibiting abortion except to save the life of the mother."[16] The shift represents the ascension to power of a conservative faction deeply influenced by and involved with the new political right, which has a legal ban on abortion as a major goal. This transition has also involved a virtual retraction of the SBC commitment to religious liberty and first amendment rights, which has been a hallmark of the Baptist witness. Convention literature as well as the activities of the Christian Life Commission now reflect views that are not dissimilar to those of the National Council of Catholic Bishops.

The fetus is regarded as a person from the moment of conception, making abortion a matter of sacrificing the right to life of a human being. The image of God is interpreted as a unique genetic code and the "harm" done in the Exodus 21 passage is interpreted as applying both to the fetus and the woman. Passages such as Jeremiah 1:5 and Psalm 139 are used to argue that God causes each pregnancy and knows each fetus as a person from conception. The fact that efforts to pass a constitutional ban on abortion rest on such a distinctively sectarian belief is dismissed as moral insincerity.

Even so, convention resolutions are not binding on local churches or on individual members. Polls show most Southern Baptists support legal abortion—certainly for therapeutic reasons. Pro-choice Baptists stress the personhood of the woman as *imago dei,* the competency of each believer to make moral judgments based on the guidance of Scripture and the Holy Spirit, and the problem of attempting to camouflage doctrine as law.[17]

BAPTIST GENERAL CONFERENCE   The Baptist General Conference has taken no definitive stand on abortion and public policy. It has affirmed the sacredness of life and criticized abortion on demand while recognizing the complexity of the issue.

CONSERVATIVE BAPTIST ASSOCIATION   This denomination has declared its opposition to abortion as the taking of innocent human life. In strong language it called upon all member medical personnel to refuse to take part in any abortion procedure and supported legal efforts "to curb this monstrous evil."[18]

Christian Church

CHRISTIAN CHURCH (DISCIPLES OF CHRIST)   The Christian Church has affirmed freedom of conscience and individual moral responsibility regarding abortion. It also strongly opposes any legislative regulation based upon a specific religious belief. Its

---

[16]*Annual of the Southern Baptist Convention* (1971), *The Churches Speak On: Abortion, supra* note 4, at 153–156.

[17]P. D. Simmons, *Birth and Death: Bioethical Decision Making* (1983); P. D. Simmons, *Religious Liberty and the Abortion Debate,* 32 J. of Church and State 567–584 (Summer 1990).

[18]*The Churches Speak, supra* note 4, at 47.

resolution understands sacredness of life in terms of freedom and responsibility in matters involving religious faith.

UNITED CHURCH OF CHRIST (UCC)   In 1987 the UCC saw abortion as a social justice issue and upheld the right to legal abortions. It expressed support for adequately funded services for those who choose to raise children as well as those who abort. Leaders at every level of the church were encouraged to oppose legislative efforts to revoke or limit access to abortion.

CHRISTIAN AND MISSIONARY ALLIANCE AND CHRISTIAN REFORMED CHURCH IN NORTH AMERICA   These denominations approve abortion only when the woman's life is threatened. The Alliance, in its 1981 statement, equated "abortion on demand" with "moral relativism and sexual permissiveness" and said that all lives were equally sacred. The Reformed statement counsels nonjudgmental compassion for those who have chosen to abort and material support for those who choose to bring a burdensome pregnancy to term.

Episcopal Church

In 1967 the House of Deputies of the Episcopal Church supported the American Law Institute suggestion of establishing at law four causes for which abortion might be induced. They are (1) threat to the physical health of the woman; (2) pregnancy from rape or incest; (3) fetal deformity; and (4) emotional burden to the woman or family. A 1988 resolution supported choice but opposed abortion as "a means of birth control, family planning, sex selection, or any reason of mere convenience." It also called for educational materials on human sexuality to include discussions of abortion both in the church and the public schools.[19]

Evangelical Churches

The term "evangelical" is used descriptively by many denominations other than those with the name in the title. As a rule, evangelical churches have been very active in their opposition to legalized abortion.[20] During the 1980s, a number of political action groups were founded by evangelical church leaders. Moral Majority, led by Jerry Falwell, American Coalition for Traditional Values, led by Tim LaHaye, Billy Graham's Christian Action Council, James Dobson's Focus on the Family and Pat Robertson's 700 Club formed a coalition with other antiabortion groups. They combined moral fervor with sophisticated political strategies and the goal of passing a Human Life Amendment.[21] The most extreme evangelical antiabortion group is "Operation Rescue," which engages in tactics of civil disobedience and other efforts to harass and hinder women seeking abortions.[22] Most responsible evangelical leaders have disassociated themselves from this group.

Evangelicals for Social Action[23] and the magazine, *Sojourners,*[24] the left wing of evangelicalism, extend the notion of sanctity of life to include issues such as capital

---

[19] *Id.* at 22.

[20] P. B. Fowler, *Abortion: Toward an Evangelical Consensus* (1987); *Applying the Scriptures* (K. Kantzler ed. 1987); J. J. Davis, *Abortion and the Christian* (1984).

[21] R. J. Neuhaus, *The Naked Public Square* (2nd ed. 1984).

[22] R. Terry, *Accessory to Murder: The Enemies, Allies and Accomplices to the Death of Our Culture* (1990).

[23] R. J. Sider, *Completely Pro-Life* (1987).

[24] R. Terry, *supra* note 22.

punishment, poverty and war. Thus, opinion varies widely among evangelicals as to the proper witness to render regarding the morality and legality of abortion. Some of the representative groups and their positions can be noted.

EVANGELICAL CONGREGATIONAL CHURCH   This group sees abortion not as a matter of reproductive freedom but a question of when a human being may be morally permitted to take the life of another. It condemned abortion on demand but recognized that it may be morally justified "on rare occasions" (1983).

EVANGELICAL FREE CHURCH OF AMERICA   In a 1977 statement, the Evangelical Free Church called upon the state to guarantee the rights of the unborn child and condemned abortion as a way to handle unwanted pregnancies. It also feared for the "aged and infirm" and that the "eclectic morality" upheld by the courts would have dire consequences for the future of the nation.

EVANGELICAL MENNONITE CONFERENCE   In response to the *Roe v. Wade* decision, this group declared its opposition to induced abortion as a violation of God's will citing Psalm 139:13–16.

FUNDAMENTALIST BIBLE TABERNACLE   The Fundamentalist Bible Tabernacle issued a statement celebrating the retirement of Justice Burger and praying for the repentance, retirement or removal by death of other justices of the Supreme Court who supported *Roe v. Wade*. It disavowed any advocacy of violence against any person or abortion clinic.

Pentecostalist Churches

ASSEMBLIES OF GOD   In 1985 the Assemblies of God called upon Christians to support pro-life legislation and work for pro-life politicians. Only in those extreme cases where the woman's life is endangered by pregnancy would abortion be morally justified, believing as they do that the Bible considers abortion the killing of innocent persons. Even so, compassion should be demonstrated for those who show remorse for in any way having been identified with abortions.

CHURCH OF THE NAZARENE   A more moderate statement was made by the Church of the Nazarene in 1985 that supported therapeutic abortions while opposing laws that permit abortion on demand. Programs of support and care for mothers and children were also supported.

CHURCH OF GOD (JERUSALEM ACRES)   This church declared, in a 1968 statement, that abortion could in no case be called murder. If the woman's health is endangered, terminating a pregnancy is similar to removing any other diseased part of the body. One is a human being only with birth and breath. Even so, nontherapeutic abortions are an offense to God. The final decision is to be by the believer who is not to be judged by anyone else.

CHURCH OF GOD AT ANDERSON, INDIANA   This group approved a resolution in 1981 calling the unborn fetus a living human being and thus opposing abortion on demand and calling for laws to protect the rights of the unborn. It also called for care for all persons and supported sex education to reduce both the causes and the consequences of unwanted pregnancies.

INTERNATIONAL PENTECOSTAL CHURCH OF CHRIST   An undated resolution by this denomination condemned abortion on demand and opposed any legalization of abortion except for reasons of maternal health and perhaps in cases of rape and incest.[25]

---

[25] *The Churches Speak, supra* note 4, at 57.

UNITED PENTECOSTAL CHURCH INTERNATIONAL   This church passed a resolution in 1988 relating abortion to sexual permissiveness and condemning abortion on demand morally and legally. Compassion was expressed for those suffering from the "trauma" of abortion.

Lutherans

EVANGELICAL LUTHERAN CHURCH OF AMERICA   The ELCA was formed in 1988 with the merger of the American Lutheran Church and the Lutheran Church in America. The 1991 assembly passed a social teaching statement acknowledging that its member constituency holds different opinions about the legal regulation of abortion. Some advocate prohibitions for any abortion except to save the life of the woman, others oppose regulations on the basis of freedom of conscience and religious liberty guarantees of the first amendment. Even so, the assembly statement held that regulating abortion is a legitimate role of government, both to protect prenatal life and to protect the dignity of women and their "freedom to make responsible decisions in difficult situations." The fetus does not have an absolute right to be born, it said, nor does the woman have an absolute right to terminate a pregnancy. Abortion for reasons of maternal health, rape or incest and where fetal abnormalities are incompatible with life are morally justifiable. These should be legally available as should funding for low-income women. Abortion after fetal viability should be legally prohibited except when the woman's life is threatened or the fetus has life-threatening abnormalities.[26]

LUTHERAN CHURCH-MISSOURI SYNOD   This Lutheran group accepts the premise that the unborn child is a human being and seeks a constitutional amendment to prohibit abortions. It recognizes the permissibility of abortion in cases where the woman is threatened by death but not in cases of rape or incest. It condemns the pro-choice approach on the analogy to those who wanted "choice" regarding slavery. Organized efforts are encouraged to support pro-life activities, including care for unwed mothers.[27]

Methodists

METHODIST CONFERENCE (ENGLAND)   This denomination focuses on both the value of fetal life and the place of conscience in decisions regarding abortion. In general, it supported the 1967 law in England that made abortion legal only under certain circumstances. The Methodist Conference advocates limiting elective abortions to the first 20 weeks of pregnancy. It believes that abortion as birth control is immoral and that it should never be available on demand. Responsible sexual relations in marriage are advocated while acknowledging that, in an imperfect world, "abortion may be seen as a necessary way of mitigating the results of . . . failures."[28]

UNITED METHODISTS   The third largest religious group in the United States, United Methodists dealt with abortion in statements on responsible parenthood. In 1968 support was given to liberalizing U.S. abortion laws. They supported laws that would require the recommendation of a panel of physicians taking into account the health needs of the woman, deformity of the fetus and whether rape or incest caused the pregnancy. They also advocated making contraceptives and abortion available at public expense. Their 1976 statement (which was reaffirmed in 1988) supported *Roe v. Wade* while emphasiz-

---

[26] Evangelical Lutheran Church in America, *A Social Statement on Abortion* 9, 10 (pamphlet) (1991).

[27] R. J. Neuhaus, *supra* note 21; *The Churches Speak, supra* note 4, at 69–70.

[28] *The Churches Speak, supra* note 4, at 82–84.

ing moral responsibility in sexual relations. They rejected both the "abortion as murder" argument and the notion that there is no moral significance in pregnancy termination. A comprehensive approach to responsible family planning was recommended as was support for safe, legal abortions and further research and development of more effective contraceptives.[29]

Not all United Methodists are happy with the official pro-choice position. In September 1990, "The Durham Declaration" was drafted for use by churches in teaching "a more theologically positive stand on abortion." The signees affirmed that the unborn child is created in the image of God and it is sin to take its life. It also calls for the church's agencies to end their pro-choice political advocacy and for Methodist hospitals to protect the unborn child.[30]

WESLEYAN CHURCH   The Wesleyan Church is opposed to induced abortion except for grave medical conditions threatening the life of the woman. It has encouraged its members to work for "appropriate legislation" to protect unborn children.[31]

Orthodox

The official position of the Greek Orthodox Church and Russian Orthodox Church is that life begins at conception. The Annunciation to Mary (Luke 1:31) is a biblical passage of importance to both. Appeal is also made to tradition, such as the teaching of St. Basil in A.D. 375 that forbade potions for the destruction of the child in the womb. Current Greek Orthodox canons regard abortion as the unjust killing of a person, justifiable only to save the life of the woman. Even so, the penalty is not excommunication; she is forgiven with repentance.[32] The *Russian Orthodox* resolution of 1986 called for a human life amendment to ban abortion.[33]

Presbyterians

PRESBYTERIAN CHURCH (U.S.A.)   This church of approximately 3 million members has been a strong voice on behalf of reproductive choice and the decriminalization of abortion decisions since 1970. Its position is based theologically on individual freedom and responsibility. The lordship of Christ and the stewardship of sexual powers are also important concepts. Fetal life is thought inviolable only after viability. Commitments to religious liberty form the major reason for rejecting legal prohibitions, since each theological tradition is to be respected and none is to be imposed as law. Abortion decisions should be regulated by health concerns for the woman and the moral reflections of those most intimately involved. Strong moral reservations are thus held about abortion after the first trimester as well as abortion for gender selection. In successive general assemblies during the 1980s, Presbyterians have supported *Roe v. Wade* and caring ministries for women who face problem pregnancies. In 1989 the church voiced strong support for the Religious Coalition for Abortion Rights and "Operation Respect," the counter

---

[29] *Id.* at 162–164.

[30] *The Durham Declaration,* in *Christians and Society Today* (March 1991).

[31] *The Churches Speak, supra* note 4, at 165–166.

[32] M. Weston, *Faith and Abortion: Where the World's Major Religions Disagree,* Washington Post Health 14 (Jan. 23, 1990).

[33] *The Churches Speak, supra* note 4, at 88.

movement to "Operation Rescue,"[34] and, in 1991, condemned the Supreme Court decision in *Rust v. Sullivan* as both bad morals and bad medicine.

PRESBYTERIAN CHURCH IN AMERICA   This group has condemned abortion as a violation of the sixth commandment based on the sanctity and inviolability of human life from conception. Even in those extreme cases in which the life of the woman is threatened, every effort is to be made to save the fetus. Its 1978 statement claimed God's authority for addressing the state and that the sixth commandment was universally valid as the basis for laws prohibiting abortion.[35]

REFORMED PRESBYTERIAN CHURCH OF NORTH AMERICA   The Reformed Presbyterian Church expressed its outrage at "the wickedness of abortion" and proposed to make picketing against abortion clinics part of its annual meetings. It invited all other Christian denominations to engage in such protests at their convention meetings as well.[36]

Other Protestant Perspectives

REFORMED CHURCH IN AMERICA   This church strongly objected to *Roe v. Wade* in 1973, believing that "abortion performed for personal reasons . . . ought not be permitted." A year's study of the issue by its Christian Action Commission and the Theological Commission concluded that the Scripture does not directly address the issue. Caution against biased exegesis of Scripture was advised, as was hasty condemnation of others who act in good conscience. Support was given for "conscience clauses" for medical personnel as well as for assistance with alternatives to abortion.[37]

THE SALVATION ARMY   The Salvation Army is opposed to abortion on demand or as a means of birth control but believes it may be justified for reasons such as a threat to woman's health, fetal deformity and rape or incest. It has no specific statement with regard to legal protections of the unborn, preferring to offer support and counsel to all people and to promote social systems that are conducive to personal wholeness and health.[38]

CHURCH OF THE BRETHREN   The Brethren stress both the belief that all of life is from God and that the commandment to love is a universal norm. Fetal life is not equal to that of the woman, however, and abortion may be justified where other alternatives are more destructive. The Brethren oppose abortion for their membership but refuse to support legal or coercive attitudes toward others. Not condemnation but Christlike compassion is needed to find creative alternatives to abortion. Laws should protect human life, freedom of moral choice and make available good medical care.[39]

Jewish Views on Abortion

The Jewish tradition appeals to the Hebrew Scriptures, Talmudic interpretations and rabbinic law for authoritative guidance in matters pertaining to abortion.[40]

---

[34] *The Churches Speak, supra* note 4, at 88–131; *We Affirm: National Religious Organizations' Statements on Abortion Rights* (1990); *Covenant and Creation: Theological Reflections on Contraception and Abortion* (1983); *Resolutions of the General Assembly* 1035 (1989, 1991).

[35] *The Churches Speak, supra* note 4, at 131–149.

[36] *Id.* at 152.

[37] *Id.* at 150–151.

[38] *Id.* at 152.

[39] *Id.* at 41–46.

[40] D. M. Feldman, *Jewish Views on Abortion* (1984). D. M. Feldman, *Marital Relations, Birth Control and Abortion in Jewish Law* 3–18 (1974).

Personhood and the Fetus

Talmudic law deems the fetus "part of its mother," rather than a person or an independent entity. Thus, abortion is not considered murder, which is the killing of a human person, a *nephesh adam*. The fetus is not a person until it comes into the world. A clear distinction in value between the fetus and the woman is expressed in Exodus 21:22 where harm to the woman is punished by the rule of injury for injury, life for life. On the other hand, only a monetary fine is imposed for injury to or loss of the fetus.

Maternal indications are the primary concerns in decisions about abortion. The biblical mandate to "choose life" means that the health and well-being of the woman is to be protected. The *Mishnah* requires the dismemberment of a fetus in the womb if the woman's life is threatened. The life of the woman always takes precedence over that of the fetus, which means that mental as well as physical health risks qualify for abortion.

Morality and Abortion

Therapeutic abortions are therefore explicitly supportable and permissible under Jewish religious law. Elective abortions are morally problematic. Reasons of convenience or economics usually do not suffice for rabbinic support. Thus, Orthodox Jews tend to discourage abortions for all but the most serious threats to the woman. Rabbi Issar Unterman labeled abortion "akin to murder" to underscore the gravity of the action. The most conservative Jewish approaches to abortion begin with the assumption and then develop exceptions for life-threatening situations.

Reform, Conservative and Reconstruction Jewish approaches begin with the assumption that the fetus is not a person and that there is no real prohibition to abortion. They then develop safeguards against the indiscriminate or unjustified thwarting of potential life. Thus, in case of rape, which causes "great pain" to the woman, abortion may be justified. She may properly "uproot" seed implanted in her against her will. In case of adultery, however, abortion may not be approved as a safeguard against immorality.

The Jewish approach to abortion is that it is always to be a last resort. Procreation is a moral obligation, and casual abortion is morally abhorrent. There is a pro-natalist respect for life and a belief in the sanctity of life from the moment of birth. The religious and moral dimensions of the decision to abort place it beyond legal regulations, however. There is therefore a strong commitment to pluralism and individual liberty on this matter.

Judaism and Civil Law

Strong support for abortion law reform was expressed by Reform Jews in the United States long before the *Roe v. Wade* decision of 1973. In 1965 the National Federation of Temple Sisterhoods urged the liberalization of state laws on abortion based on humane concerns for women in unfortunate circumstances. In a 1967 Statement, the Central Conference of American Rabbis said that liberalized abortion laws were "religiously valid and humane." It urged all states to permit abortions for the emotional and physical well-being of the woman and in those cases involving sexual crimes. Its 1977 statement firmly supported *Roe v. Wade*. Saying that "the proper locus for . . . this decision must be the individual family or woman, and not the state or other external agency," it opposed any legislation that would abridge access to abortion.

The National Council of Jewish Women expressed strong support for *Roe v. Wade* in 1989, calling abortion a constitutional right.

A resolution by the Rabbinical Assembly of Conservative Jews indicated in 1985 that abortion is not only permitted but *mandated* by Jewish law when the woman's life or well-being is threatened. The same point was made in a 1981 statement by the Reconstructionist Rabbinical Association. It saw antiabortion legislation and efforts to pass a Human Life Amendment as threats to both establishment and free exercise guarantees of the first amendment.[41]

The Jewish approach to abortion is carefully nuanced. It is not murder, but aborting a fetus is a serious matter and a diminishment of the image of God. Under certain circumstances, abortion is morally justified and even religiously mandated. In every case, it is a matter of such sacredness that it is best left to the woman, who decides based upon her own religious commitments. It should not be legally prohibited.

Other Religious Approaches

That abortion is a human dilemma is illustrated by the fact that almost every religious group deals with it in the context of cultural norms and politics. The sources of moral authority may differ from those already considered, but the options are very similar. The following are simply listed alphabetically.

Buddhism

Various opinions regarding abortion can be found among Buddhists, who number more than 300 million worldwide. It is not a divisive issue, however, because there is neither an ecclesiastical heirarchy nor an official dogma to establish orthodox belief and behavior. Buddhism also emphasizes a belief in rebirth, which mitigates the notion of killing a life. Some Buddhists believe that consciousness arises at the moment of conception. Thus, abortion is morally wrong and should be prohibited at law. Others accept the notion that all killing is evil but place the abortion decision with the woman. In Japan, abortion is extremely common and is not opposed by any political party. The Buddhist clergy have created a rite to relieve the anxiety of women who have had abortion called "Mizuko Kuyo."[42]

Hinduism

Hinduism teaches that the soul enters the fetus at the moment of conception. Thus, abortion is prohibited except in cases of rape, incest and material burden. Even so, abortion is widely practiced in India without opposition from Hindu priests. There are two reasons for the concession. First, the rapid growth of the population has made birth control necessary. Second, the Hindu belief in *karma,* or rebirth, mitigates the gravity of the action against life.[43]

Mormon

CHURCH OF JESUS CHRIST OF LATTER DAY SAINTS   This Mormon group strongly opposes abortion and supports legislative restrictions. A 1986 statement by Russell M.

---

[41] *The Churches Speak, supra* note 4, at 167–172.
[42] M. Weston, *supra* note 32, at 15.
[43] *Id.*

Nelson, M.D. regarded abortion as the killing of defenseless persons and said that it should be legally prohibited. He dismissed justifying abortions because of rape and incest since they constitute less than 3% of all cases. The logic of abortion for fetal deformity would require terminating all handicapped persons, he said. Women are free to abstain from intercourse, but they are not free to abort once they are pregnant.[44] The recent passage of restrictive abortion legislation in Utah, Idaho and other western states shows the political strength of the Mormon church, which has no discernible commitment to religious liberty.

REORGANIZED CHURCH OF JESUS CHRIST OF LATTER DAY SAINTS   Responsible parenthood is stressed by this church as the proper context for abortion decisions. Its 1974 statement on abortion affirmed a profound regard for the woman as well as concern for the potential life of the fetus. It rejected the notion that abortion is murder and the idea that it has no moral significance as "simplistic" and thus unacceptable. It affirmed the right of the woman to decide the continuation or termination of a problem pregnancy, hopefully with the counsel of family and skilled counselors.[45]

Islam

The 860 million followers of Muhammad constitute the largest single religion in the world, 2.6 million of whom live in North America. Muslims permit abortion for any reason in the first 40 days of pregnancy, since the Hadith, the sayings of Muhammad, described the fetus as being "40 days in the form of a seed."[46]

The Koran says nothing about abortion. Even so, abortion is typically regarded as a heinous crime, according to W. D. Muhammad, chief minister of the American Muslim Mission, who gives guidance on this and other matters for the faithful. Women should not abort without permission from husbands. Abortion is not justified for reasons of economic hardship, sex selection or to avoid social disgrace. But in cases where the woman's life is at stake, it is up to her to decide whether to abort or sacrifice her own life.

Considerable lattitude in opinion and action is allowed among American Muslims. Contraception is approved and recommended for the faithful, but those who believe it to be immoral are equally respected. The same attitude governs the abortion decision on the principle that the believer is to pray to Allah and then do what conscience dictates. W. D. Muhammad nowhere suggests that abortion should be regulated by civil or criminal law.[47]

Unitarian Universalist Association

Unitarians have given solid and consistent support for legalized abortion. A resolution was adopted in 1977 opposing the Supreme Court's decision that denied Medicaid funding to poor women and ruled that public hospitals were not required to offer abortion services. A more comprehensive statement in 1987 acknowledged the complexity

---

[44]*The Churches Speak, supra* note 4, at 180ff.
[45]*Id.* at 187.
[46]M. Weston, *supra* note 32, at 15.
[47]W. D. Mohammad, *The Man and the Woman in Islam* (1976); *The Churches Speak On: Abortion, supra* note 4, at 173–176.

of the abortion decision; affirmed individual rights of conscience and abortion as a matter of privacy; opposed all legislative and regulatory procedures that circumvented or contradicted *Roe v. Wade;* supported government funding for abortions; and called upon members to expose and oppose bogus clinics. The Association believes antiabortion legislation violates the separation of church and state, to which it is committed. Tolerance for differences of religious opinion is advocated as is freedom in personal decision-making.[48]

Reflection and Assessment

The profoundly different approaches to abortion by the various religious groups are easier to discern than to resolve. Several things are noticeable:

1. The "official" statements of the various groups mean and represent different things. For Catholics, the document or statement is an effort to establish orthodox belief and behavior. Resolutions passed by Baptists express a sentiment supported by a majority in an annual meeting but not required for all members. For Presbyterians and Methodists, they are the recommendations of an official committee supported by the leaders of the church but not necessarily by a majority of members.

2. Both choice and anti-choice proponents can be found in almost every denomination or major religious group. Even those with the most centralized and heirarchical ecclesiastical structures are unable to achieve general compliance to harsh antiabortion rules. Women and their families who face problem pregnancies are likely to disregard absolutist teachings that permit no reasonable lattitude under circumstances of duress. Their obedience is often governed by conscience, not religious mandates.

3. Attitudes toward abortion are linked to beliefs about human sexuality, contraception, the equality of the sexes, the relation of morals to law, moral authority, God's relation to natural processes (e.g., conception, deformity), the meaning of human freedom and religious liberty or separation of church and state. An adequate understanding of any religious approach to abortion would have to explore the fuller theological/moral context of thought in which it is treated.[49]

4. The issue of authority in religion and morality is variously stated. Roman Catholics, Orthodox and Mormons, for instance, turn to the authority of the church's teaching and ecclesiastical leaders. Most Protestants stress the authority of the Bible; Moslems turn to the Koran; Jews depend upon Scripture and tradition. Conscience or personal convictions are primary for moral authority for Quakers, Unitarians and many Baptists.

    Regardless of the source or authority to which their appeal is made, variations in belief will emerge. People will reach different interpretations of Scripture and tradition. Theologians seldom fully agree on substantive matters. Social and sexual circumstances and private convictions will always be uniquely personal and there-

---

[48] *The Churches Speak, supra* note 4, at 188–189.

[49] B. W. Harrison, *Our Right to Choose* (1983); P. D. Simmons, *Birth and Death: Bioethical Decision Making* (1983).

fore will differ among members of the same religious group. The result is that moral opinion will vary tremendously but in each ease will shape the religious beliefs or conscientious convictions of the believer.

5. Beliefs about fetal personhood appear the single most important variable concerning the *moral* acceptability of abortion. Typically, those who believe it to be wrong reason that it is the killing of a human being made in God's image. Even so, many believe the fetus is a person but do not support legal prohibitions, believing either that law is impotent to resolve the issue or that the moral issue should be separated from legal penalties.

6. Those supporting choice on religious grounds do not dismiss the moral gravity of the decision to abort. Being legally available does not settle the moral question. Rather, the *moral* issue is to be dealt with in terms of one's religious beliefs, moral principles and personal convictions. Factors concerning the pregnancy (age and health of the woman, fetal condition, circumstances of impregnation) are also to be considered. The stage of gestation is a vital concern: The moral gravity of abortion increases as the pregnancy progresses. Extremely grave health risks to the woman are necessary to justify abortion in the later stages of pregnancy. Thus, no one answer will be appropriate for all problem pregnancies.

7. Attitudes toward religious liberty are the single most important variable in whether a group advocates the *legal* prohibition of abortion.[50] A legal ban based on a human life amendment would require finding that a conceptus (zygote) is a person. But that notion is not persuasive to a majority of Americans on either logical or religious grounds. It is based on metaphysical speculation, not scientific facts that are available or convincing to a majority. Metaphysics is the work of religion but is a poor basis for legislation.

In politics, metaphysics assumes an ideological posture. Claims to special knowledge or superior moral insight accompany the harshest forms of restrictive legislation. The efforts to ban abortion in Louisiana, Utah, Guam and elsewhere are the outcomes of political processes without regard for first amendment protections. In each case, the presupposition of the law is that a conceptus is a person with constitutional protections. The Supreme Court's *Webster* decision allowed such language to stand in the preamble to the Missouri law regulating abortion. That seems to violate the social contract of mutual respect and tolerance that are to be accorded various religious traditions. Whether the Court's review of certain facets of the Pennsylvania law portends a further erosion of the protections against government intrusion into matters belonging properly to the prerogatives of conscience is a matter of intense concern.

Those who champion religious liberty object strongly to laws based upon the belief that a zygote is a person on both establishment and free exercise grounds. The Religious Coalition for Abortion Rights counts 35 member organizations, all of whom are united around the one theme of religious liberty. The enormous variety of theological beliefs about abortion found among religious groups is evidence of the pluralism in American life. The genius of *Roe v. Wade* in the view of church-state separationists was that no group was coerced to live by any other group's religious beliefs. Each tradition is free to teach its membership according to its own

---

[50] Simmons, *Religious Liberty and the Abortion Debate,* 32 J. of Church and State 567–584 (Summer 1990).

understandings. Those who object to abortion will not abort; those whose religious beliefs emphasize individual responsibility have the legal option of acting accordingly. Such latitude at law seems a minimal requirement for a society that prides itself on enhancing liberties and protecting politics from the pervasive influence of sectarian belief systems.

APPENDIXES

Appendix I

The U.S. Surgeon General's Report on the Health Effects of Abortion

Letter to the President

The Surgeon General of the
Public Health Service
Washington DC 20201

January 9, 1989

Mr. Ronald Reagan
The President of the United States
The White House
1600 Pennsylvania Avenue, NW
Washington, DC 20500

Dear Mr. President:

On July 30, 1987, in remarks at a briefing for Right to Life leaders, you directed the Surgeon General to prepare a comprehensive report on the health effects of abortion on women. It was clear from those remarks that such a report was to cover the mental, as well as the physical, effects of abortion. A review of the scientific literature, the expertise of the Public Health Service, and the experience of national organizations with an interest in this issue form the basis for my conclusions.

The health effects of abortion on women are not easily separated from the hotly debated social issues that surround the practice of abortion. Therefore, every effort had been made to eliminate the bias which so easily intrudes even into the accumulation of scientific data. In this study I have purposely avoided any personal value judgement vis-a-vis abortion as a social issue.

I have approached this task as I did in writing the AIDS report which you requested in 1986. Scientific, medical, psychological, and public health experts were consulted. I met privately with 27 different groups which had philosophical, social, medical, or other professional interests in the abortion issue. The process involved groups such as the Right to Life National Committee, Planned Parenthood Federation of America, the U.S. Conference of Catholic Bishops, the American College of Obstetricians and Gynecologists, and women who had had abortions.

In summary of the situation, each year approximately 6 million women become pregnant; of that number 54 percent or 3.3 million of those pregnancies are unplanned. Over 1.5 million women, or 25 percent of those pregnant, elect abortion each year. Since the legalization of abortion in 1973, over 20 million abortions have been performed. Even among groups committed to confirming a woman's right to legal abortion there was consensus that any abortion represented a failure in some part of society's support system,—individual, family, church, public health, economic, or social.

At the time the report was requested, there were those advising you and intimately involved with the social issues of abortion who truly believed that such a report could be put together readily. In the minds of some of them, it was a foregone conclusion that the negative health effects of abortion on women were so overwhelming that the evidence would force the reversal of Roe v. Wade.

There were also others who truly believed differently. While they acknowledge that any surgical procedure done 1.5 million times a year may have some negative health effects on women, in their minds the positive effects of abortion—release from the unwanted pregnancy—far outweighed the perceived negative results.

It is difficult to label the opposing groups in the abortion controversy. Those against abortion call themselves pro-life. On the other hand, those who are not pro-life say they are not pro-abortion; rather, they refer to themselves as pro-choice and supporters of a woman's right to choose abortion.

It is also true that some who are pro-choice are personally opposed to abortion. It is not clear to them where the lines should be drawn between the right of the fetus and the right of the mother. So the pro-choice forces are not monolithic.

Nor are the pro-life forces monolithic. Many ardent pro-life individuals who are dedicated to perserving the life of the fetus do not consider contraception to be ethically, morally, or religiously wrong. But others in the pro-life camp do; indeed, some equate contraception with abortion.

I believe that the issue of abortion is so emotionally charged that it is possible that many who might read this letter would not understand it because I have not arrived at conclusions they can accept. But I have concluded in my review of this issue that, at this time, the available scientific evidence about the psychological sequelae of abortion simply cannot support either the preconceived beliefs of those pro-life or of those pro-choice.

Today considerable attention is being paid to possible mental health effects of abortion. For example, there are almost 250 studies reported in the scientific literature which deal with the psychological aspects of abortion. All of these studies were reviewed and the more significant studies were evaluated by staff in several of the Agencies of the Public Health Service against appropriate criteria and were found to be flawed methodologically. In their view and mine, the data do not support the premise that abortion does or does not cause or contribute to psychological problems. Anecdotal reports abound on both sides. However, individual cases cannot be used to reach scientifically sound conclusions. It is to be noted that when pregnancy, whether wanted or unwanted, comes to full term and delivery, there is a well documented, low incidence of adverse mental health effects.

For the physical situation, data have been gathered on some women after abortions. It has been documented that after abortion there can be infertility, a damaged cervix, miscarriage, premature birth, low birth weight babies, etc. But, I further conclude that these events are difficult to quantify and difficult to prove as abortion sequelae for two reasons. First, these events are difficult to quantify because approximately half of abortions are done in free-standing abortion clinics where records which might have been helpful in this regard, have not been kept. Second, when compared with the number of abortions performed annually, 50 percent of women who have had an abortion apparently deny having had one when questioned. Further, these events are difficult to *prove*, as sequelae of abortion because all of these same problems can and do follow pregnancy carried to term or not carried to term,—indeed can occur in women who have never been pregnant previously. Clearly, however, the incidence of physical injury is greater in instances where abortions are performed or attempted by those not qualified to do them or under less than sterile conditions.

I have consulted with the National Center for Health Statistics and Centers for Disease Control about the design of appropriate studies which could answer the questions dealing with the physical and psychological effects of abortion.

There has never been a prospective study on a cohort of women of childbearing age in reference to the variable outcomes of mating. Such a study should include the psychological effects of failure to conceive, as well as the physical and mental sequelae of pregnancy,—planned and unplanned, wanted and unwanted—whether carried to delivery, miscarried, or terminated by abortion. To do such a study that would be above criticism would consume a great deal of time. The most desirable prospective study could be conducted for approximately $100 million over the next five years. A less expensive yet satisfactory study could be conducted for approximately $10 million over the same period of time. This $10 million study could start yielding data after the first year.

There is a major design problem which must be solved before undertaking any study. It is imperative that any survey instrument be designed to eliminate the discrepancy between the number of abortions on record and the number of women who admit having an abortion on survey. It is critical that this problem of "denial" be dealt with before proceeding with further investigations.

This is where things stand at this moment. I regret, Mr. President, that in spite of a diligent review on the part of many in the Public Health Service and in the private sector, the scientific studies do not provide conclusive data about the health effects of abortion on women. I recommend that consideration be given to going forward with an appropriate prospective study.

Sincerely,

C. Everett Koop, M.D., Sc.D.
Surgeon General, U.S.P.H.S.

Final Draft

Foreword

This is my report to the people of the United States about the health effects, physical and psychological, of abortion on women. It is most difficult to look at the health aspects of abortion in isolation from the many other issues that surround it. As I stated in my July 31, 1987, press statement, the health effects of abortion are public health issues that require an objective analysis. This report considered all points of view; they were fairly and extensively heard.

Before accepting the position of Surgeon General, I was very outspoken against abortion. In fact, my nomination to the position of Surgeon General was adamantly opposed, in large part, because of my convictions. In preparation for this report, I have made every effort to separate my long-standing personal views about abortion from those of experts on all sides of this issue.

The health effects of abortion on women are not easily separated from the emotionally debated social issues that surround the practice of abortion. In this report, careful attention has been given to eliminate the biases that so easily intrude even into the accumulation and review of scientific data.

Labeling the opposing groups involved in the abortion debate is not easily done. Those against abortion call themselves pro-life.

On the other hand, those who would permit abortion say they are not pro-abortion; rather, they refer to themselves as pro-choice, as supporters of a woman's right to choose abortion.

It is also true that some who are pro-choice are personally opposed to abortion. It is not clear to them where or when the lines should be drawn between the rights of the unborn child and the rights of the pregnant woman.

But if the pro-choice forces are not uniform, neither are the pro-life forces. Although many ardent pro-life individuals who are dedicated to preserving the life of the unborn do not consider contraception to be ethically wrong, others in the pro-life side do.

I have approached this task as I did when writing the AIDS Report. My staff and I reviewed the available literature on the health effects of abortion and consulted experts in the fields of science, medicine, psychology, and public health. I met privately with 27 different groups that had medical, philosophical, or psychosocial expertise or other professional interests in abortion. The process involved groups such as the Alan Guttmacher Institute, the American Public Health Association, the American College of Obstetricians and Gynecologists, the National Right-to-Life Committee, the Planned Parenthood Federation of America, the Southern Baptist Convention, and the U.S. Conference of Catholic Bishops, as well as groups for women who have had psychological and social difficulties that were directly related to abortions.

In all of my discussions, I did not find any individual or group that thought abortion per se was a good idea. No matter how anyone felt philosophically, all agreed that an abortion represented a failure of some part of our society—be it the individual, the family, a religious group, a public health service, or any other social support system.

Each year, approximately 6 million American women conceive; about 54% or 3.3 million of these pregnancies are unplanned. Over 1.5 million women a year elect to have an abortion. Since the legalization of abortion in 1973, over 20 million of these operations have taken place in the United States. Regardless of one's view of abortion, this tragic figure represents a failure that has many dimensions.

The ultimate goal should be to eliminate the need for abortions. I think we can all agree, however, that a critical first step in addressing this problem is to set a national goal of reducing the annual number of abortions each year. This reduction can only be achieved by instituting strong prevention programs, strengthening incentives for alternatives to abortion, educating ourselves about our sexuality and responsibilities, and educating ourselves about pregnancy, contraception, and abortion. Only when we all look for acceptable ways to eliminate unwanted pregnancies can America progress toward offering a more healthful welcome for children and a more effective support for those parents who bear and rear them.

I have tried to give a fair and balanced presentation of key points that emerged during the consultations. I have also tried to articulate these key points in language that is both free from scientific jargon and free from any generality or vagueness that would compromise the scientific integrity of this report. I now present what I have learned so that you, the American people, can weigh the information and make up your own mind about the best course of action for you and your family.

In my opinion, it is time for all of us to engage in positive efforts to solve this major problem that encompasses both public health and social mores.

C. Everett Koop, M.D., ScD.
Surgeon General

The Surgeon General's Report: The Public Health Effects of Abortion

THE PRESIDENT'S REQUEST   On July 30, 1987, at a White House speech to right-to-life leaders, President Reagan directed the Surgeon General to assemble a body of public health information on the health effects of abortion on women.

THE SUPREME COURT DECISIONS   On January 22, 1973, the Supreme Court issued its landmark decisions on abortion (*Roe* v. *Wade* and *Doe* v. *Bolton).* These judgments drew the Nation's attention to an issue that has been argued in each generation since the time of the Persian Empire. The Court determined that a woman's rights under the Constitution include the right to have an abortion. This decision, based on the Court's interpretation of the Fourteenth Amendment to the Constitution, held that the fetus is not a person and is therefore not entitled to the same protection guaranteed to women by the Constitution.

HUMAN DEVELOPMENT   There is considerable controversy about when life begins, and when that life becomes human. It is a question about which sincere, learned people differ, and as such is a question that cannot yet be answered with scientific certainty.

At conception, the female's egg and the male's sperm unit to form a single cell with 46 chromosomes—23 from the female and 23 from the male. In these 46 chromosomes, the human embryo contains genetic information that will direct fetal development, infant growth, child development, adolescent transformation, and adult maturation. From conception until death, human growth is a continuing and maturing process—physically and, eventually, mentally and emotionally.

ABORTIONS   Induced abortions are to be distinguished from spontaneous abortions or miscarriages. The term abortion in this report will mean the intentional termination of pregnancy to prevent a live birth. Abortions resulting from rape or incest or from genetic defects or other health-related reasons are not considered in the context of this report. Although abortions are performed on women, this report throughout recognizes the male partner's joint responsibility for preventing unwanted pregnancies.

TYPES OF ABORTIONS   The following are the most common types of abortion performed in the United States:

Suction Curettage (performed up to 12th week): The canal of the uterine cervix is mechanically dilated until the opening is large enough to allow the passage of a tube into the uterine cavity. The fetus and placenta are sucked out by means of a powerful vacuum pump attached to the inserted tube. The uterus is then examined to ensure complete removal of the fetus.

Dilation and Curettage (performed up to 12th week): The cervix is mechanically dilated, and the fetus and placenta are scraped out of the uterus with a sharp curette, which resembles a small spoon.

Dilation and Evacuation (performed after 12th week): The cervix is mechanically dilated, and the membranes and fetus are dismembered inside the womb and then removed with forceps.

Saline Abortion (performed after 12th to 14th week): Amniotic fluid is removed through the abdominal wall. This fluid is replaced with a concentrated saline solution that induces labor and results in the expulsion of a dead fetus within 24 to 48 hours.

Prostaglandin (performed after 12th to 14th week): A type of prostaglandin that causes strong muscular contraction is injected in milligram doses into the uterine cavity without withdrawing amniotic fluid. The period between injection and expulsion of the fetus is of a shorter duration than with saline solution.

DATA AND INFORMATION   No comprehensive system exists for collecting data on abortion in the United States. The Centers for Disease Control (CDC) operates an abortion surveillance program that gathers information from approximately forty state health departments and from individual hospitals and clinics within the ten remaining states. The Alan Guttmacher Institute (AGI) also publishes abortion statistics. Their findings supplement the CDC data with information obtained from service providers who do not report to state health departments. The AGI statistics generally report 15%–20% more abortions than do the CDC's findings.

There is also no comprehensive system for data collection of morbidity related to pregnancy outcomes—that is, for medical and psychological complications resulting from pregnancy, delivery, or abortion. In addition, there has never been a reproductive health study in the United States that compared pregnancy outcomes over time. Most of the information we use as national data is collected in special surveys, such as the ongoing National Survey of Family Growth.

OUTCOMES OF SEXUAL ACTIVITY   In the United States, approximately 55 million women are of childbearing age (15–44 years of age), of whom 32 million are sexually active and able to bear children. Among the sexually active women who are not sterile, an estimated 11 million do not intend to have any more births, and an estimated 12 million more are practicing contraception to postpone a birth. At any given time, then, approximately 23 million women are at risk of an unintended pregnancy. Of the more than 6 million pregnancies annually, approximately 54% are unintended, and over 1.5 million of all pregnancies ended in abortion.

WHY SO MANY UNINTENDED PREGNANCIES?   Generally, one of three situations leads to an unintended pregnancy: failure to use a contraceptive method, improper use of a contraceptive method, or failure of a contraceptive method.

Contraceptive and sexual responsibility require constant vigilance during the lifetime of a sexually active person. Eighty-eight percent of sexually active women who are able to but do not want to become pregnant use contraceptives; 12% do not. (Women in the 1982 Nation Survey of Family Growth were categorized as nonusers if they were not using contraceptives for at least one month before conception.) Some women, however, do not consistently or properly use contraceptives, some switch to less effective methods or may be unprotected for a time, and occasionally others become pregnant despite careful and proper use of effective contraceptives.

Not enough is known about why women and men who have decided to become sexually active are willing to risk unintended pregnancy—and the possibility of resolution by abortion—when safe and effective family planning methods are available. We need to learn much more about what is keeping so many couples from translating their knowledge of contraceptive methods into effective and consistent contraceptive practice.

WHO HAS AN ABORTION?   Abortions are not just a phenomenon of the adolescent, the poor, or the uneducated; they are neither a class, a religious nor an age phenomenon. Rather, the population involved in abortions mirrors the sexually active population as a whole.

Although 81% of abortions are performed on single women, adolescents make up only a fraction of these. Although approximately 50% of teen pregnancies end in abortion, approximately 90% of all abortions occur among women 18 years of age and older. The median age at which women have abortions is 23.1 years for white women and 23.7 years for black women. This median age is comparable to that of women giving birth, as is the median amount of education attained (about twelve and a half years).

If we break down all abortions by age groups, we find that 25% occur among women younger than 20 years of age, 35% occur among the 20–24 age group, and the remaining 40% occur among the 25–44 age group. The age differentials reflect patterns of sexual activity, contraceptive practice, desire for children at a particular time in these women's lives, marital status, and other characteristics of sexually active women.

A sexually active woman who is at risk of an unintended pregnancy and who is using no contraceptive method is 14 times more likely to have an abortion than is a woman using the pill . . . Couples who are nonusers of contraceptives during the time the pregnancy occurs account for more than 50% of all abortions.

WHEN?   Before the legalization of abortion, women were having abortions later in their pregnancies when they are less safe. Today, approximately 90% of women who have had abortions had them during the safer first trimester of pregnancy (12 weeks); 47% of the pregnancies were terminated in the first eight weeks and 43% between the ninth and twelfth week. Approximately 10% of abortions occurred after the 12th week. Less than 1% of all abortions occurred after the 20th week.

THE REALITY   Abortions have been performed in the U.S. since colonial times. Although it is difficult to estimate the number that were illegally performed in the United States before the *Roe v. Wade* decision, a reasonable annual estimate would be 200,000 to 1,200,000. Today, as in the past, a woman with an unwanted pregnancy is faced with difficult choices: delivering and rearing an infant; placing the child for adoption; or having an abortion. For a single woman, the situation creates additional economic and social hardships. The decision process in choosing to deliver or to abort is complex and is influenced by a woman's values, her relationships with her parents and with the father of the child, the support structures available to her, the strength of her personality (ego resilience), her available finances, and her ability to cope with these factors.

HEALTH ASPECTS OF ABORTION   Valid scientific studies have documented that, after abortion, physical health sequelae (including infertility, incompetent cervix, miscarriage, premature birth, and low birth weight) are no more frequent among women who experienced abortion than they are among the general population of women. The major medical and public health associations thus consider abortion a safe surgical procedure when performed by a licensed physician in a good clinical setting. The fact that abortion imposes a relatively low physical risk to maternal health does not imply, however, that it is the appropriate decision for a woman or for the fetus; it means only that there is not a significant risk of physical complications for the woman.

The earlier in gestation that a woman has an abortion, the safer it is for her medically. Because the fetus will be much smaller and less developed, the procedure will be easier to perform and will have less of a risk for medical complications. Abortion in the first trimester is much safer than in the second trimester, and a second-trimester abortion is safer than a third-trimester abortion. If complications do occur, they may be serious, particularly in the second and third trimesters when a hemorrhage, a bowel injury, or a perforated uterus may occur. The risk of the procedure and the potential for complications increase with the length of pregnancy.

DOES ABORTION CAUSE PSYCHOLOGICAL PROBLEMS? The psychological outcomes of pregnancy-related events have been exceedingly difficult to assess for at least two reasons: the lack of consensus on what variables are to be investigated, and the need for the psychological history of women who have had abortions.

The physiological evaluation falls neatly into the realm of physicians. However, psychological problems are in the domain of many types of counsellors, including family physicians, psychiatrists, clinical psychologists, marriage and family therapists, social workers, pastoral counselors, and the clergy. A general consensus is that the psychological consequences of abortion are dealt with either by the woman alone or by the woman together with the sexual partner, with her family, or with her friends.

The American Psychiatric Association has identified abortion as a "psychosocial stressor." Some clinicians and researchers consider abortion a psychosocial stressor capable of causing what they call a postabortion syndrome, which they consider a form of post-traumatic stress disorder. Other equally well-qualified scientists refute this assertion because an abortion seldom constitutes an event that is outside the range of usual human experiences, the essential feature of the post-traumatic stress disorder as defined by the American Psychiatric Association.

Of the more than 250 studies in the international literature that discuss the psychological outcomes of abortion, most have major methodological flaws. Although numerous case histories attest to immediate or delayed psychological problems following abortions, the actual number of women who have suffered in this way is unknown.

Inconclusiveness regarding the psychological outcomes of abortion stems from the lack of consensus regarding the symptoms, severity, and duration of mental disorder; from the problem of controlling for psychological symptoms associated with life events experienced before or after the abortion; and from the methodological difficulties related to sampling for an appropriate study group, establishing appropriate control groups, and finding a technique that can surmount the statistical absence of as many as half of the women who have undergone abortion but are likely to deny having done so; and from the logistics of managing a longer-term prospective study more than 5 to 10 years. Hence, it is neither reasonable nor advisable to rely on prevailing opinions, based on flawed studies, to conclude whether or not psychological risks are associated with abortion.

Even though presently available studies conducted in the United States do not provide conclusive evidence, it appears likely that certain factors combine to make deciding to have an abortion and coping with its aftermath more difficult for some women than for others. These factors include strongly held personal values, an ambivalence about abortion, excessive pressure from others, the termination of an originally desired conception, a decision made late into the second trimester, or the lack of partner or family support.

As I have alluded, the factors related to the decision of whether or not to have an abortion becomes increasingly complex as one analyzes it. The beliefs that some women hold about the sanctity of life versus the freedom to choose an abortion and about the ethical circumstances under which the decision to abort is made can elevate abortion into a third area—the spiritual, which extends beyond the bounds of the medical and psychological professions and beyond the bounds of this report.

From a public health perspective, there is a need to assess the following: the incidence and prevalence of the psychological outcomes of pregnancy-related events; the onset and severity of these events over time; and comparisons between women who have terminated an unwanted pregnancy, carried to term, or experienced a miscarriage. Longer-term prospective studies in the United States should be encouraged. Knowledge may also be derived from methodologically sound research conducted in culturally comparable countries that have computerized national health registration systems. Such studies would lend themselves to large-scale statistical assessment and to follow-up, over time, of the psychological outcomes of pregnancy-related events.

CONSULTING THE PRINCIPAL PARTIES   Two well-known outcomes are discussed in the abortion debates. At one end of the continuum are women who have had abortions and who state that the health and psychological effects have been beneficial. At the other end are those women who have had abortions and who state that the operation has left them grieving for their lost infant and has caused them anxiety, depression, and guilt. For some women these feelings may not be triggered until years after the event. However, there is a third group about which little is said and who say little. Those are the women who have had an abortion but who, for whatever reason, deny that they have done so. Their feelings remain private and unknown.

I would not like to *SUMMARIZE* what was presented to me by those who had abortions and others who consulted with me. Some of them believe abortions can be beneficial and others believe abortions contribute to long-term psychological problems:

Schools of Thought: Beneficial Effects
According to this school of thought, unwanted births have a known risk of postpartum depression and psychosis that poses a greater threat to the mental health of a woman than does a legal abortion. The major positive benefit of terminating an unwanted pregnancy is the feeling of relief, of having successfully dealt with a problem pregnancy.

The emotional, financial, or vocational consequences of an unwanted birth on the mother, her family, and her other children could lead to long-lasting life distress and disability.

Further, well-conducted studies document that children born as a result of an unwanted pregnancy are more likely to experience detrimental psychosocial development, emotional adjustment problems, and a poorer quality of life than are children born to women who desired or otherwise accepted their pregnancies.

Compelling a woman to carry a child to term has societal as well as personal consequences. Children who cannot be cared for by the mother or by her parents place demands on the state for welfare services and financial support. Not all children unwanted by the mother will be placed for adoption, nor will all children placed for adoption be adopted.

Schools of Thought: Negative Effects
This school of thought views abortion as a stressful experience that overwhelms the coping abilities of some women. As previously noted, this condition has been

characterized as postabortion syndrome. The symptoms include (1) exposure to the violence of intentionally destroying one's unborn child; (2) uncontrolled and involuntary negative reexperiencing of the abortion death; (3) attempts to avoid or deny abortion pain or grief, which can result in reduced responsiveness toward one's environment; and (4) experiencing associated symptoms, including sleep disorders, depression, secondary substance abuse, intense hostility, and guilt about surviving. The course of this disorder may be acute (30 days or less), or chronic (6 months or longer), or may be delayed, occurring 5–10 years or more after the operation.

Clinicians who hold this position believe that abortion is a human death experience that women and men need help in resolving. This school believes that the specific diagnosis of postabortion syndrome provides validation to those women and men who suffer, in silence and isolation, the pain, depression, and unresolved grief that has resulted from the loss of their unborn child in abortion. The resolution of postabortion syndrome for men and women requires the individual to acknowledge what an abortion is, that he or she has participated in a death experience, that a loss has occurred, and that grieving and forgiveness are necessary.

SUPPORT AND COUNSELLING   The abortion decision is seldom made quickly or easily. Deciding to terminate a pregnancy often involves considerable personal ambivalence and emotional cost.

Women who have had an abortion and later regret it have told me that they often recall their compulsion, at the time of counselling, to be rid of the problems resulting from the pregnancy; they also recall that they felt relief after the abortion.

In retrospect, however, they say that they wish they had been better informed about the procedure, about alternatives to abortion, and about fetal development. It is possible that some of them were presented such information but their receptivity to that information may have been very much affected by the dilemma they faced.

A point that was made a number of times by the groups we consulted was that preabortion counselling offers an opportunity to present unbiased, accurate information. However, such counselling can also offer an opportunity—either for those who oppose abortion or for those who favor it as a choice—to misrepresent information to those who are in dire need of unbiased counselling. It can be a difficult task for a counselor to objectively present facts when the counselor has strong convictions about the subject.

Women seriously distressed over their pregnancies need access to competent and sympathetic counselling about the availability of legally, medically, ethically, and socially unencumbered alternatives. If these women carry their babies to term, they need affordable prenatal, obstetrical, and pediatric care. This need is even greater if they decide to bear their children while continuing to resent them, since children born from unwanted pregnancies require help to surmount the greater risk they have of experiencing detrimental psychosocial development, emotional adjustment problems, and a poorer quality of life than do children of accepting mothers. On the other hand, those parents who wish to place their child for adoption require extensive information about what that will mean for the child, for the adoptive parents, and for themselves. And if abortion is the alternative they end up choosing, they require unbiased information beforehand.

THE REAL FAILURE   The *public* issue of abortion is not primarily a debate about health but is about morality and law. But because the *personal* issue of abortion is about an unintended pregnancy and an unwanted fetus, even a nationwide accord concerning the moral aspects of this issue would not prevent an unplanned pregnancy.

Most women who have an abortion because of an unintended conception know about contraceptive methods. Some are using methods properly but become pregnant because even effective contraceptives occasionally fail to prevent pregnancy. Many women may have used effective contraceptives at some point but have chosen, consciously or unconsciously, to switch to less effective methods or to practice no contraception—in either case, thereby risking an unwanted pregnancy. On the other hand, all too many men understand male contraceptive methods but choose to ignore their own responsibility in the sexual act. These men feel comfortable letting women take the risk of becoming pregnant and resolving an unplanned pregnancy.

Those men and women who, though unwilling to welcome a child or to have a child adopted, choose to act in a sexually irresponsible way are, in effect, relying on abortion to prevent the birth of an unwanted child. When viewed in this light, abortion is difficult for society as a whole to accept as a solution to the failure of some to deal responsibly and honestly with individual and societal sexuality.

ALTERNATIVES TO ABORTION   Women who have unintended pregnancies need practicable alternatives to abortion. Three major alternatives that would eliminate or decrease the number of abortions performed in the United States are to bear and raise the child, to place the child for adoption, and to prevent unintended pregnancy in the first place.

Birth and Adoption   To give birth and raise a child demands a long-term commitment to placing someone else's welfare above one's own. To give birth and to place a child for adoption is an unselfish act that requires great emotional strength and courage. In this self-sacrificing respect for the life and welfare of the child, the birth parents may be able to give a beautiful gift to a couple who want a child but cannot have their own.

As a nation, we must be willing to help those women who wish to see their unintended pregnancy to term. The woman who chooses to have an unintended baby rather than an abortion will take on a great social and financial burden. If our society wants fewer abortions, it must be willing to support not only those children who are so born but also the women who make that choice. As a society, we must make a commitment to provide loving families for all children placed for adoption. When women decide to bear their own child, rather than stigmatize them, we must sustain them by ensuring subsidized prenatal and delivery costs, foster care, day care benefits for the working mother, and educational and job guarantees during maternity leave.

The sexual partners of such women should be held jointly responsible for the mother and child's medical care and for child support. Otherwise, society must carry the financial liability.

Prevention   As long as there are unwanted and unaccepted pregnancies, some women will find a way to have an abortion. Since there is consensus that abortion is a tragedy and represents the failure of individuals, of some part of our society, or of both, it would seem that here, as in other health issues subject to personal control, we must deliver prevention messages to the population at risk. The vast majority of the groups that consulted with me agreed that prevention of an unintended pregnancy is the best approach for reducing the need for abortion.

America must invest in a long-term program that aggressively markets prevention to the various populations at risk for unintended pregnancy. We must:

- Recommend successful family life programs that teach postponement of sexual involvement and responsible decision making. We cannot rely on programs that limit sex education to biology and birth control;
- Structure family life courses so that parents, civic groups and church groups can participate and reinforce behaviors based on communal values and on respect and love for oneself and others;
- Educate the public about methods to prevent unwanted pregnancies. Such education must be honest in its appraisal of the methods and must dispel myths, so that an informed decision can be made;
- Initiate programs that attempt to modify the behavior of those sexually active men and women who do not always use contraceptives or who practice ineffective contraception;
- Teach men that they are as responsible as their sexual partners for preventing unwanted pregnancies;
- Support behavioral research to identify and modify the risk factors of those women most likely to have unintended pregnancies;
- Promote a national commitment to contraceptive research for both men and women. The objective should be a method that is 100% effective, has minimal side effects, and is safe and easy to use;
- Encourage family physicians to actively convey information and to teach sexuality in reference to family planning, as they have for AIDS.

CONCLUSION   While issuing this report as the chief public health officer of the United States Government, I am fully aware that the skills of the medical, psychological, and public health professions serve but a few areas within the full band of human need. Health is only one element of our overall welfare, personal or public. The commitments of childbearing and the sequelae of abortion are realities more profound and complex than can be addressed through the perspective and the programs of public health. Health professionals should not be deterred by the small role we play in human lives. Instead, we have to realize that although public health policies, at their best, can provide only part of an answer to the problem of abortion, the part they can provide is essential.

Even though abortion has by judicial decision been made the free choice of any pregnant woman, all those with whom I have consulted agree that this freedom is not entirely without consequences for the mothers, their children, and society. A primary task of a public health officer is to inform the citizenry about how some of their free choices can incur harm. I have endeavored to report, to the limits of present information, the effects that abortion seems to have upon maternal health and well-being.

The limited nature of this information has pointed out a need to increase the level and quality of information about the reproductive health of women. I recommend that the Federal Government undertake a carefully considered, prospective longitudinal study of women. To obtain an adequate baseline for assessing psychological and physical status and changes over time, that study should begin to follow women from a point that would precede the conception of their children (intended or not).

Insofar as the public health resources of this country can make a difference, I conclude that the following must be done:

- Men and women should be helped and encouraged, as a matter of national public health policy, to conceive children only when they are ready and able to welcome and care for them;
- When children *are* conceived unintentionally, we must remove the stigma from this very human event;
- We must support those parents who bear their children and either keep them or place them for adoption, just as our laws support those who resort to abortion as the only feasible personal alternative.

To realize these goals, we as a Nation must provide better choices. How can we be less resourceful in supporting parents who decide to bear their children than we are in protecting other parents' freedom not to bear unwanted children?

Appendix II _____
Report of the Human Fetal Tissue
Transplantation Research Panel

Letter to the Director of the National Institutes of Health

Arlin M. Adams
1600 Market Street
Philadelphia, Pennsylvania 19103

December 12, 1988

James B. Wyngaarden, M.D.
Director
National Institutes of Health
Shannon Building, Room 124
Bethesda, MD 20892

Dear Dr. Wyngaarden:

The Assistant Secretary for Health, Dr. Robert Windom, posed a series of questions concerning the use of fetal tissue in medical research. You convened a panel to assist you in answering these questions. I am pleased to forward to you the answers to the questions as formulated by the panel; the considerations underlying the answers; and a number of dissenting and concurring opinions regarding the work of the panel.

Many members of the panel hold deep reservations about abortion. Yet, the United States Supreme Court has declared that a woman has a constitutional right in the first and second trimester of pregnancy to proceed with an abortion. Whatever doubt any of the panel members may have regarding the Supreme Court opinion, it still constitutes the law of the land. Thus, until the Supreme Court decision is reversed, all citizens are bound by it. Nonetheless, any activity which would serve as an inducement to women to have abortions must be dealt with extremely carefully and circumscribed to the extent possible.

Counterbalancing these concerns is the evidence brought to the panel's attention that a series of maladies might be substantially ameliorated by the prudent use of fetal tissue. Although complete proof that fetal tissue will be clinically useful has not been obtained, current evidence indicates that the use of such tissue might be beneficial in treating Parkinson's disease, childhood diabetes, Huntington's disease, and perhaps Alzheimer's disease.

The panel has carefully weighed concerns over abortion against concerns for medical research that could improve the lot of thousands of Americans. Certain precautions are paramount if such research is to be permitted. Prevention of any commercialization in obtaining the fetal tissue would seem an absolute requirement. Also, the need to separate completely the abortion procedure and the use of fetal tissue seems essential. Furthermore, Federal funding should be limited to situations that employ the most careful scientific approaches and the highest professional standards. As an additional condition for approval of this research, it is recommended that the NIH conduct periodic reviews to ensure that the concerns expressed in this report, as well as other concerns that arise as research progresses, are carefully safeguarded.

Without Federal funding, other efforts to continue research with human fetal tissue would undoubtedly proceed without Federal supervision. Thus, if the NIH proceeds cautiously, and with carefully articulated safeguards, and a program of periodic review, there would be much greater assurance that the research will be undertaken with adherence to carefully crafted guidelines. Such an arrangement would protect pregnant women and fetuses in a far more thoughtful and intelligent manner than if the NIH did not participate. Based on available evidence, various safeguards can be instituted.

It has been a high honor to serve the National Institutes of Health and the Department of Health and Human Services, and I am confident that the members of the panel stand ready to continue to assist in any way that is deemed appropriate.

Respectfully yours,

Arlin M. Adams
Chairman, Human Fetal Tissue
Transplantation Research Panel

Panel Members

Chairman
The Honorable Arlin M. Adams
U.S. Court of Appeals Judge (Ret.)
Schnader, Harrison, Segal and Lewis
Philadelphia, PA

Chairman, Scientific Issues
Kenneth J. Ryan, M.D.
Chairman, Department of Obstetrics and
Gynecology
Brigham and Women's Hospital
Boston, MA

Chairman, Ethical and Legal Issues
LeRoy Walters, Ph.D.
Director
Center for Bioethics
Georgetown University—Kennedy Institute
of Ethics
Washington, DC

Members
Rabbi J. David Bleich
Professor of Law
Cardozo Law School
New York, NY

James Bopp Jr., Esquire
Brames, McCormick, Bopp, and Abel
Terre Haute, IN

Father James T. Burtchaell
Professor of Theology
Department of Theology
University of Notre Dame
Notre Dame, IN

Robert C. Cefalo, M.D., Ph.D.
University of North Carolina School of
Medicine
Chapel Hill, NC

James F. Childress, Ph.D.
Chairman
Department of Religious Studies
University of Virginia
Charlottesville, VA

K. Danner Clouser, Ph.D.
Professor, Hershey Medical Center
Pennsylvania State University
Hershey, PA

Dale Cowan, M.D., J.D.
Hematologist/Oncologist
Marymount Hospital
Garfield Heights, OH

Jane L. Delgado, Ph.D.
President and Chief Executive Officer
National Coalition of Hispanic and Human
Services Organizations
Washington, DC

Bernadine Healy, M.D.
Chairman, Research Institute
Cleveland Clinic Foundation
Cleveland, OH

Dorothy I. Height, Ph.D.
President
National Council of Negro Women
Alexandria, VA

Barry J. Hoffer, M.D., Ph.D.
Professor of Pharmacology
University of Colorado
Denver, CO

Patricia A. King, J.D.
Professor of Law
Georgetown University Law Center
Washington, DC

Paul Lacy, M.D., Ph.D.
Professor of Pathology
Washington University School of Medicine
St. Louis, MO

Joseph B. Martin, M.D., Ph.D.
Chief, Neurology Service
Massachusetts General Hospital
Boston, MA

Aron A. Moscona, Ph.D.
Professor
Department of Molecular Genetics and Cell
Biology
University of Chicago
Chicago, IL

John A. Robertson, J.D.
Baker & Botts Professor of Law
University of Texas School of Law
Austin, TX

Daniel N. Robinson, Ph.D.
Chair
Department of Psychology
Georgetown University
Washington, DC

Reverend Charles Swezey, Ph.D.
Annie Scales Professor of Christian Ethics
Union Theological Seminary
Richmond, VA

PANEL REPORT

Question 1

Is an induced abortion of moral relevance to the decision to use human fetal tissue for research? Would the answer to this question provide any insight on whether and how this research should proceed?

Response to Question 1

It is of moral relevance that human fetal tissue for research has been obtained from induced abortions. However, in light of the fact that abortion is legal and that the research in question is intended to achieve significant medical goals, the panel concludes that the use of such tissue is acceptable public policy.

This position must not obscure the profound moral dimensions of the issue of abortion, nor the principled positions that divide scholars, scientists, and the public at large. It is not the charge of this panel to attempt to settle the issue of abortion or to weigh the worthiness of competing principled perspectives on abortion itself. The panel notes that induced abortion creates a set of morally relevant considerations, but notes further that the possibility of relieving suffering and saving life cannot be a matter of moral indifference to those who shape and guide public policy.

Recognizing the moral convictions deeply held in our society, the panel concludes that appropriate guidelines are required even as the research proceeds. Accordingly, the following points are noted:

1. The decision to terminate a pregnancy and the procedures of abortion should be kept independent from the retrieval and use of fetal tissue.
2. Payments and other forms of remuneration and compensation associated with the procurement of fetal tissue should be prohibited, except payment for reasonable expenses occasioned by the actual retrieval, storage, preparation, and transportation of the tissues.
3. Potential recipients of such tissues, as well as research and health care participants, should be properly informed as to the source of the tissues in question.
4. Procedures must be adopted that accord human fetal tissue the same respect accorded other cadaveric human tissues entitled to respect.

(Panel Vote: 18 Yes, 3 No, 0 Abstain)

Considerations for Question 1

In reaching its answer to the first question, the panel weighed the proposition that the morality of abortion could be separated in principle from the morality of the uses to which fetal tissue from induced abortions might be put. It was noted that fetal tissue would be obtained as a result of lawful, constitutionally protected decisions and actions to terminate unwanted pregnancy, and that use of cadaveric fetal tissue from induced abortions for research or therapy was generally legal. But it was also noted that the lawfulness of decisions and actions can be distinguished from their morality.

On the morality of research use of fetal tissue from induced abortion, three positions were discussed during the panel's deliberations.

1. Abortion is morally acceptable, and thus the research and therapeutic use of fetal tissue derived from induced abortion is also morally acceptable.
2. Abortion is immoral and so is the use of fetal tissue obtained thereby. No amount of good achieved in research or therapy could erase institutional complicity in the immorality of abortion itself or in encouragement of future abortions. No efforts at separating the procurement and use of fetal tissue from the abortion decision and procedure could make the use of fetal tissue from induced abortion morally acceptable.
3. Abortion is immoral or undesirable, but as abortion is a legal procedure in our society and with appropriate safeguards can be separated from the subsequent research use of tissue derived therefrom, the use of fetal tissue in research and therapy is not seen as complicitous with the immorality of abortion.

A decisive majority of the panel found that it was acceptable public policy to support transplant research with fetal tissue either because the source of the tissue posed no moral problem or because the immorality of its source could be ethically isolated from the morality of its use in research. Considerations supporting this decision were the fact that these abortions would occur regardless of their use in research, that neither the researcher nor the recipient would have any role in inducing or performing the abortion, and that a woman's abortion decision would be insulated from inducements to abort to provide tissue for transplant research and therapy. Accordingly, the panel found it essential that abortion decisions and procedures be kept separate from considerations of fetal tissue procurement and use in research and therapy. In keeping with that separation, it is essential that there be no offer of financial incentives or personal gain to encourage abortion or donation of fetal tissue.

Because some persons opposed to abortion would not accept the use of fetal tissue from induced abortions regardless of these insulating measures, the interests of those persons in neither participating in the research nor in receiving fetal tissue transplants should be protected by informing them of the source of such tissue.

The majority's approval of the research use of tissue from elective abortions is not to be construed as a majority vote for the moral acceptability of elective abortion.

Question 2

Does the use of the fetal tissue in research encourage women to have an abortion that they might otherwise not undertake? If so, are there ways to minimize such encouragement?

Response to Question 2

Research using fetal tissue has been conducted and publicized for over 30 years. There is no evidence that this use of fetal tissue for research has had a material effect on the reasons for seeking an abortion in the past. Some panel members were concerned that a more publicized and promising research program might have such an effect in the future. To minimize any encouragement for abortion as might arise from the use of fetal tissue in research, we recommend that the measures outlined above under Question 1 be implemented, as well as the following:

- The decision and consent to abort must precede discussion of the possible use of the fetal tissue and any request for such consent as might be required for that use.

- The pregnant woman should be prohibited from designating the transplant-recipient of the fetal tissue.

The foregoing recommendations are not to be construed as denying or in any way impeding a pregnant woman's access to information regarding the use of fetal tissue in research should she request this information.

(Panel Vote: 19 Yes, 1 No, 1 Abstain)

Considerations for Question 2

The panel noted that the reasons for terminating a pregnancy are complex, varied, and deeply personal. The panel regarded it highly unlikely that a woman would be encouraged to make this decision because of the knowledge that the fetal remains might be used in research.

The panel concluded further that it was sound public policy to separate as much as possible the deliberations and decisions about the abortion from any discussion of the disposition of the fetal remains.

Question 3

As a legal matter, does the very process of obtaining informed consent from the pregnant woman constitute a prohibited ''inducement'' to terminate the pregnancy for the purposes of the research—thus precluding research of this sort, under HHS [Department of Health and Human Services] regulations?

Response to Question 3

The panel agrees that a pregnant woman should not be induced to terminate pregnancy in order to furnish fetal tissue for transplantation or medical research.

The process for obtaining informed consent from a pregnant woman for fetal tissue research does not by itself constitute a prohibited inducement to terminate the pregnancy for the purposes of research. However, knowledge of the possibility for using fetal tissue in research and transplantation might constitute motivation, reason, or incentive for a pregnant woman to have an abortion. This would not constitute a prohibited ''inducement,'' since it is not a promise of financial reward or personal gain, nor is it coercive.

However, because the panel believes strongly that we should keep transplantation and research on fetal tissue from encouraging abortion, the panel recommends that informed consent for an abortion should precede informed consent or even the provision of preliminary information for tissue donation.

Moreover, anonymity between donor and recipient shall be maintained, so that the donor does not know who will receive the tissue, and the identity of the donor is concealed from the recipient and transplant team.

Further, the timing and method of abortion should not be influenced by the potential uses of fetal tissue for transplantation or medical research.

In the long term, the problem alluded to by this question may be able to be addressed by deferring the discussion of possible tissue donation until after the abortion procedure has been performed. The feasibility of this approach to fetal tissue procurement should be reviewed on a regular basis by the Department.

(Panel Vote: 20 Yes, 0 No, 1 Abstain)

Considerations for Question 3

As a preliminary matter, we assume that the informed consent mentioned in the question refers to the consent sought for the purpose of using the fetal tissue in research—as distinguished from the informed consent for the abortion itself. As we have emphasized in several places, in the consent process for termination of pregnancy, we believe there should be no mention at all of the possibility of fetal tissue use in transplantation and research. The one exception might be if the pregnant woman were to ask a direct question. And even then only general information should be given; there should be no promise that her fetal tissue either could or would be so used. Panel members individually take this stand either because they do not want to do anything that might encourage abortion or as a concession to those who do not want to risk encouraging abortion.

The heart of the question pivots on the meaning of "prohibited 'inducement.' " It is not clear which inducements are in fact prohibited by Department of Health and Human Services (HHS) regulations nor is it clear exactly what an inducement is. Therefore, some clarifications are in order to determine what would be a reasonable and defensible position in the matter.

An inducement could be a coercion, an incentive, or a reason. (1) Coercion is in any case unacceptable and would surely be prohibited. In order for consent to be valid it must at least be free, voluntary, and informed. (2) We would also find incentives to be unacceptable inasmuch as our panel recommends at every turn that we should (for reasons articulated elsewhere) keep fetal tissue transplantation and research from encouraging abortion. Also, incentives to terminate a pregnancy would probably be prohibited under HHS regulations, though it might turn on how strong, i.e., how irresistible, the incentive was. (3) However, with respect to reasons, it would be unrealistic not to consider the possibility that transplantation and research with fetal tissue may enter the balance of considerations of a pregnant woman in deciding whether to have an abortion. It would be unrealistic because transplantation and research with fetal tissue will become general knowledge; it will not be possible to keep the populace from knowing about it.

By no reasonable interpretation can sheer information constitute a "prohibited 'inducement.' " The point of labeling some inducements as prohibited is to avoid manipulation of persons by coercion (a threat of harm) or by incentives (the promise of personal gain) unrelated to the risks, harms, and benefits of the act itself. Thus, that fetal tissue could benefit others might be one of many reasons to be weighed in deciding whether to terminate a pregnancy. We clearly would be unable to keep such knowledge from functioning as a reason, and in any case it does not and should not be construed to constitute a "prohibited 'inducement.' "

Question 4

Is maternal consent a sufficient condition for the use of the tissue, or should additional consent be obtained? If so, what should be the substance and who should be the source(s) of the consent, and what procedures should be implemented to obtain it?

Response to Question 4

Fetal tissue from induced abortions should not be used in medical research without the prior consent of the pregnant woman. Her decision to donate fetal remains is sufficient for the use of tissue, unless the father objects (except in cases of incest or rape).

The consent should be obtained in compliance with State law and with the Uniform Anatomical Gift Act.

Customary review procedures should apply to research involving transplantation of tissue from induced abortions.

(Panel Vote: 17 Yes, 3 No, 1 Abstain)

Considerations for Question 4

There are several possible ways to transfer or acquire any human tissue: donation (express or presumed), abandonment, sales, and expropriation. Although each method of transfer has been used for some human biological materials in some contexts in the United States, our society has largely adopted express donation—by the decedent while alive or by the next of kin after his or her death—as the method of transfer of cadaver organs and tissues. In cases where the decedent while alive could not or did not express his or her wishes about donation, the Uniform Anatomical Gift Act (UAGA) allows express donation by the next of kin. Presumed donation (or presumed consent) is used in 12 States for the removal of corneas; the donation of corneas by the decedent and next of kin is presumed to have been made if there is no express objection. The panel believes that express donation by the pregnant woman after the abortion decision is the most appropriate mode of transfer of fetal tissues because it is the most congruent with our society's traditions, laws, policies, and practices, including the Uniform Anatomical Gift Act and current Federal research regulations.

When a woman chooses a legal abortion for her own reasons, that act does not legally disqualify her—and should not disqualify her—as the primary decisionmaker about the disposition of fetal remains, including the donation of fetal tissue for research. Objections to this conclusion are grounded in the assumption that the decision to abort severs kinship in any but the biological sense. Nonetheless, the panel concludes that disputes about the morality of her decision to have an abortion should not deprive the woman of the legal authority to dispose of fetal remains. She still has a special connection with the fetus, and she has a legitimate interest in its disposition and use. Furthermore, the dead fetus has no interests that the pregnant woman's donation would violate. In the final analysis, any mode of transfer of fetal tissue other than maternal donation appears to raise more serious ethical problems. For all these reasons, the pregnant woman's consent, or decision to donate, should be sufficient (within the limits identified below). The panel heard no compelling reasons why federally funded transplantation research should depart from ordinary and legal practice in the disposition and use of cadaver tissues, including fetal cadaver tissues.

However, questions have been raised about whether additional consent is needed from other parties, such as the father or a hospital ethics committee or an institutional review board. We believe that the structure provided by the UAGA (revised 1987) is generally adequate but that a modification in policy is needed for the donation of fetal tissue. Where the decedent did not express his or her wishes, the UAGA authorizes "either parent of the decedent" to make a donation, unless there is a known objection to such a donation from the other parent (or from the decedent's spouse or adult children). As applied to the donation of fetal tissue, the UAGA provides that either parent may donate unless there is a known objection by the other parent. In the panel's view, the pregnant woman's consent should be *necessary* for donation—that is, the father should not be able to authorize the donation by himself, and the mother should always be asked before the fetal tissue is used. In addition, her consent or donation should be *sufficient,* except where the procurement team knows of the father's objection to such donation. There is no legal or ethical obligation to seek the father's permission, but there is a legal and ethical obligation not to use the tissue if it is known that he objects (unless the pregnancy resulted from rape or incest).

Review procedures have been developed for federally funded research involving human subjects. These review procedures would also apply to fetal tissue transplantation research, which must be reviewed and approved by Institutional Review Boards (IRBs) before it can proceed. Such research would fall under the purview of IRBs because human subjects would receive experimental transplants of fetal tissue in a research protocol. In addition, IRBs will need to consider the adequacy of the information disclosed to the pregnant woman who is considering whether to consent to tests (e.g., for antibody to the human immunodeficiency virus) to determine the acceptability of the fetal tissue for transplantation research. Nevertheless, the pregnant woman's consent to donate the tissue is legally sufficient and should be sufficient in federally funded transplantation research, as long as there is no known objection from the father (except in cases of rape or incest).

Question 5

Should there be and could there be a prohibition on the donation of fetal tissue between family members, or friends and acquaintances? Would a prohibition on donation between family members jeopardize the likelihood of clinical success?

Response to Question 5

There should be no Federal funding of experimental transplants performed with fetal tissue from induced abortions provided by a family member, friend, or acquaintance. Absent such prohibition, the potential benefits to friends and family members might encourage abortion or encourage pregnancy for the purpose of abortion—encouragements that the panel strongly opposed.

Concerns regarding maternal welfare as well as the moral status of the human fetus and, therefore, the morality of abortion itself, militate against Federal practices or policies that could have the effect of in any way encouraging abortions for the purpose of benefiting family members or acquaintances.

There is no evidence now that a prohibition against the intrafamilial use of fetal tissue would affect the attainment of valid clinical objectives. Given the current state of scientific knowledge, the treatment of diabetes with intrafamilial transplants would be contraindicated. For other conditions that are considered to be candidates for fetal tissue transplantation, currently available scientific evidence allows no definitive conclusions to be drawn with respect to this question.

(Panel Vote: 19 Yes, 0 No, 1 Abstain [Note: One panel member was out of the room when this vote was taken.])

Considerations for Question 5

There was no plea from the scientists for doing intrafamilial transplantation. In fact, the experts gave testimony that there ought to be a prohibition. If circumstances change, however, there may be reasons to modify the prohibition.

The panel did not hear any compelling evidence that suggests that a relationship between the donor and the fetus would improve the likelihood of success. Repeatedly, testimony of the experts emphasized the lack of scientific justification for intrafamilial donation by reason of current state of knowledge of immunology and disease pathophysiology. In fact, some argued that relatedness may induce the potential for disease recurrence, e.g., diabetes mellitus. It was strongly urged that the Secretary for Health and Human Services review these recommendations at regular intervals.

Question 6

If transplantation using fetal tissue from induced abortions becomes more common, what impact is likely to occur on activities and procedures employed by abortion clinics? In particular, is the optimal or safest way to perform an abortion likely to be in conflict with preservation of the fetal tissue? Is there any way to ensure that induced abortions are not intentionally delayed in order to have a second trimester fetus for research and transplantation?

Response to Question 6

If fetal tissue transplants become more common, the impact on the activities and procedures of abortion clinics will depend upon the demand for tissue and the regulations and safeguards that restrict tissue procurement. To minimize this impact, it is essential that requests to donate tissue be separated from consent to the abortion, and that no fees be paid to the woman to donate, or to the clinic for its efforts in procuring fetal tissue (other than expenses incurred in retrieving fetal tissue).

The most certain impact if fetal tissue transplants become more common is that abortion facilities will more frequently—perhaps even routinely—ask women to donate fetal remains for research and therapy after they have decided to abort the fetus. The abortion clinic will also coordinate retrieval and temporary storage of fetal remains with tissue procurement organizations, either retrieving the tissue themselves or permitting procurement agency personnel to do so.

The greatest pressure for change in abortion clinic practices beyond requesting women to donate fetal tissue would occur if abortion clinics and women could profit financially from procuring fetal tissue. Current Federal law and the law of many States prohibit the buying and selling of fetal tissue, though they do permit payment of expenses incurred in procuring tissue for transplantation. Enforcement of these laws, including clear guidelines about what constitutes procurement expenses, is essential to prevent pressure to abort and to donate fetal tissue.

One could contemplate a scenario in which demand outstripped the supply of fetal tissue from abortions to end unwanted pregnancies. More effective contraception, greater acceptance of pharmacologically induced abortions, and great success in treating major diseases (such as Parkinson's and diabetes) could make the demand greater than the supply. To accommodate this scarcity, mechanisms for distributing fetal tissue to the larger number of patients demanding it would have to be devised, such as now exist for distributing the scarce supply of hearts, livers, and kidneys to patients on waiting lists for transplants.

However, this situation alone would not change the activities and practices of abortion clinics. Pressures to conceive and abort for transplantation purposes would arise outside of or apart from the activities of such clinics. Adherence to rules that specify when the request to donate tissue is made and that ban sales of fetal tissue would also limit the impact of such demand on abortion clinics.

The future medical possibilities cannot be foreseen with clarity. If, however, presently unexpected conflicts arise in the future, the choice of the abortion procedure should always be dictated by the health considerations of the woman.

(Panel Vote: 19 Yes, 2 No, 0 Abstain)

Considerations for Question 6

Predicting the impact on abortion clinics of a greater frequency of fetal tissue transplants is difficult and necessarily speculative at this time. The impact will depend upon many factors, including the extent of the demand for tissue, the number of abortions, the time at which viable fetal tissue may be obtained, the rules for obtaining consent, and rules against buying and selling fetal tissue. History, of course, will supply the most accurate answers, for no one can tell just how successful the research under consideration will be.

Ideally, permission to use tissues from the aborted fetus would not even be sought until the abortion itself had been performed. The timing of and the procedures associated with the abortion would be set and the abortion would be performed before the question of tissue donations was even raised. However, post mortem tissue quickly deteriorates, and, in most instances, (e.g., transplantation of neural tissue) cryogenic storage is not a scientifically effective alternative. Thus, the pregnant woman must be consulted before the abortion is actually performed. In such instances, it is always possible for the woman herself to consider procedural options that might render the fetal tissue more useful for research or therapy; possible, but, according to experienced persons, entirely unlikely.

It was the judgment of the panel that the concerns behind Question 6 are best addressed by strict adoption of a number of safeguards; safeguards that would eliminate or at least radically reduce profit motives and tendencies toward commercialization, and safeguards that would ensure the greatest possible separation between abortion procedures, facilities, and personnel on the one hand, and fetal-tissue research procedures, facilities and personnel on the other.

Where the panel was divided was on the question of which "scenario" to adopt in framing recommendations; a so-called "worst-case" situation in which demand so outstrips supply as to exert great financial and altruistic pressures, or a so-called "reasonable-case" situation in which modest medical objectives are met only over a long period. The energetic support of research by the NIH would, of course, affect the rate of progress in this area. The strictest principles of separation would be necessary in the "worst case" and would not be untoward in their effects even under current conditions.

Question 7

What actual steps are involved in procuring the tissue from the source to the researcher? Are there any payments involved? What types of payments in this situation, if any, would fall inside or outside the scope of the Hyde Amendment?

Response to Question 7

Past experience with fetal tissue research usually has had the medical researcher directly requesting fetal remains for research from physicians performing abortions, usually in the same institution. Occasionally, medical researchers have requested fetal tissue from freestanding abortion clinics in the same city.

In these instances, it is assumed that the woman aborting has consented to donation of fetal remains, though it is possible that in some instances the tissue, which would otherwise be discarded, has been treated as abandoned and used without maternal consent. If consent was obtained, it would ordinarily have been obtained before the abortion occurred but after the decision to abort had been made.

More recently, agencies or organizations have developed to provide tissue, including fetal tissue, to researchers. These have been nonprofit agencies that have solicited fetal tissue from abortion facilities and paid them a small fee for each fetal tissue retrieved to cover the costs of retrieval, including time of staff and rental of space. They have then distributed the tissue to previously identified and approved researchers conducting legitimate medical research. These agencies have usually charged the researchers the cost they have incurred in procuring the tissue.

There sometimes have been payments made to abortion facilities and physicians who have provided fetal tissue for research. These payments are intended to cover the costs to the abortion facility of providing access to the procurement agency, including staff time in requesting consent and retrieving tissue, and use of the clinic space by employees of the procurement agency.

If Federal research funds were used to pay the cost of the abortion procedure that makes fetal tissue available for research, such payment would violate the Hyde Amendment. On the other hand, the use of Federal research funds to pay tissue retrieval agencies for the costs of retrieving fetal tissue after the abortion has occurred would not violate the Amendment. Those funds would not be used "to perform abortions," but to obtain fetal tissue from abortions that would otherwise be occurring. Similarly, Federal support of fetal tissue research activities other than the cost of fetal tissue retrieval would also not violate the Hyde Amendment.

(Panel Vote: 19 Yes, 2 No, 0 Abstain)

Considerations for Question 7

The description of fetal tissue procurement procedures described here is based on information presented to the panel concerning past experience in obtaining fetal tissue and on information about new organizations that have arisen to provide fetal tissue for research and therapy. Some further development along these lines may be expected, with a strong emphasis on nonprofit retrieval agencies and no payments for tissue procurement beyond expenses.

There is no evidence that women who abort are paid money or other consideration to donate fetal tissue. Payments to abortion facilities have purported to cover expenses involved in collecting tissue and making it available. To prevent abortion clinics from making profits from fetal tissue donation, specific rules for what counts as a reasonable payment for retrieval expenses may be required.

The Hyde Amendment prohibits the use of designated Federal funds "to perform abortions except where the life of the pregnant woman would be endangered if the fetus were carried to term." It would appear, therefore, that the Hyde Amendment is not violated by support of research with fetal tissue or payment of costs incurred in retrieving that tissue because those funds would not be paid "to perform abortions."

Question 8

According to HHS regulations, research on dead fetuses must be conducted in compliance with State and local laws. A few States' enacted version of the Uniform Anatomical Gift Act contains restrictions on the research applications of dead fetal tissue after an induced abortion. In those States, do these restrictions apply to therapeutic transplantation of dead fetal tissue after an induced abortion? If so, what are the consequences for NIH-funded researchers in those States?

Response to Question 8

While the Uniform Anatomical Gift Act in every State permits donations of fetal remains with maternal consent (as long as the father does not object), the panel is aware of eight States (Arkansas, Arizona, Illinois, Indiana, Ohio, Louisiana, New Mexico, and Oklahoma) that have statutes that prohibit the experimental use of cadaveric fetal tissue from induced abortions. Provisions of one statute (that in Louisiana) have been struck down on constitutional grounds.

Six of the eight States prohibit experimentation on fetuses from induced abortion. By their terms, these statutes do not apply to *nonexperimental* therapeutic transplants, but arguably would apply only to *experimental* therapeutic transplants. However, if the subject of the research is deemed to be the recipient of the fetal tissue transplant, then it may be that these statutes do not apply to experimental therapeutic transplants because they are experiments on the recipient and not on the aborted fetus.

Two of the six States would ban any use of fetal tissue from induced abortions, whether experimental or not.

Several States also have laws requiring that maternal consent be obtained before fetal tissue may be used, and ban payments for fetal tissue or providing the abortion free as an inducement to obtain fetal tissue for research.

The consequences for NIH researchers in those States depend upon the meaning of the term "experimentation" in the statutes at issue. In at least two of the States no use could be made of aborted fetal tissue. In the other six they could be used for *nonexperimental* therapeutic transplants or for experimental therapeutic transplants that are reasonably viewed as experiments on the recipient of the transplant and not on the fetal tissue itself.

Researchers in States with statutes appearing to ban fetal tissue transplants may seek clarification of the law.

(Panel Vote: 20 Yes, 0 No, 1 Abstain)

Considerations for Question 8

Research using tissue from dead fetuses is permitted in most States, because these States have statutes modeled on the Uniform Anatomical Gift Act, which treats fetal tissue like other cadaveric remains. The panel knows of only two States that prohibit all use of fetal remains from induced abortion. In six other States known to the panel, whether tissue from induced abortions may be used is dependent upon clarification of the statutory meaning of the term "experimental."

Question 9

For those diseases for which transplantation using fetal tissue has been proposed, have enough animal studies been performed to justify proceeding to human transplants? Because induced abortions during the first trimester are less risky to the woman, have there been enough animal studies for each of those diseases to justify the reliance on the equivalent of the second trimester human fetus?

Response to Question 9

There is sufficient evidence from animal experimentation to justify proceeding with human clinical trials in Parkinson's disease and juvenile diabetes. Although fetal tissue of diverse ages may be scientifically and clinically advantageous for transplantation to relieve various pathologies, no abortion should be scheduled or otherwise accommodated to suit the requirements of research.

In terms of Parkinson's disease there is a wealth of positive data on graft efficacy from animal models. Extensive research has been conducted in rodents and in nonhuman primates. Additional testimony from some scientists suggested that further animal studies would be helpful. It is not known, for example, if there are any long-term adverse immunological effects of the grafts. It was also pointed out that the same disease processes that caused the initial dopamine neuron degeneration could also produce degeneration of grafted neurons. Testimony stressed the need for additional research, especially in terms of developing cell lines, as discussed in Question 10, below.

In terms of diabetes, there was presented a considerable body of data with animal models of diabetes supporting the efficacy of fetal islet transplants in man and suggesting that human clinical trials were timely and appropriate. Such trials are now in progress and are currently being evaluated.

Experts testified that in other disease states, such as Alzheimer's disease, Huntington's disease, spinal cord injury, and neuroendocrine deficiencies, promising results have derived from experiments using allografts in animal disease models. In these latter diseases, experts urged further animal studies before using human fetal tissue. Acceptable preliminary data would then need to be presented to an appropriate Institutional Review Board, NIH Initial Review Group, and National Advisory Council before Public Health Service funds would be obtained.

Research in diabetes, Parkinson's disease, and neural regeneration has found that first trimester fetal tissue is not only more apt, but optimal, for transplantation, since it survives better and contains cells at a stage of differentiation which is more appropriate for the therapeutic goals. Animal studies on other disorders have not revealed a transplantation protocol that would require the use of more mature fetal tissue.

Should that possibility arise and not be restricted by law, then tissue available from abortions that have already occurred during the second trimester may be used. But, to the extent that Federal sponsorship or funding is involved, no abortion should be put off to a later date nor should any abortion be performed by an alternate method entailing greater risk to the pregnant woman in order to supply more useful fetal materials for research.

(Panel Vote: 18 Yes, 2 No, 1 Abstain)

Considerations for Question 9

A summary of current literature underlying this response is to be found in the Addendum. The scientific testimony presented to the panel is provided in the appendices.

Question 10

What is the likelihood that transplantation using fetal cell cultures will be successful? Will this obviate the need for fresh fetal tissue? In what time frame might this occur?

Response to Question 10

In terms of alternatives to the use of fetal tissue for transplantation, an option that was presented to the panel was the use of established lines of cells that are maintained in culture. The scientific testimony was optimistic that transplantation using cell cultures may ultimately be successful. This use of cultured cells might obviate the need for tissue directly obtained from the fetus for some purposes of research and therapy. The time frame for use of defined cell lines for transplantation is estimated to be at least 10 years, given the problems of genetic engineering to have the cells synthesize chemical messengers and differentiate after grafting.

(Panel Vote: 21 Yes, 0 No, 0 Abstain)

Considerations for Question 10

The evidence in the field and expert testimony indicate that an established cell line for transplantation in diabetes must be able to synthesize, store, and release appropriate amounts of insulin when the blood sugar exceeds normal limits. At the present time, it is possible to construct cell lines by genetic engineering which synthesize insulin, but the newly formed insulin is released immediately regardless of the level of blood sugar. The genetic information for the storage and controlled release of insulin is not available at the moment and thus cannot be inserted into these cells.

A second problem may occur even if a cell line could be developed which would synthesize, store and release insulin upon demand. A normal insulin-producing cell in the pancreas is surrounded by other cells which secrete hormones that control and modulate the secretion of insulin. Thus, it may require the development of additional cell lines to release these hormones and permit the normal secretion of insulin from an insulin-producing cell line.

In regard to Parkinson's disease, it is unknown whether the transplanted neural cells will be needed only to release a specific chemical messenger or whether the transplanted cells must contact other neural cells. If both properties are required, then these two different types of genetic information would have to be inserted into the cell line.

A final problem for the development of cell lines for transplantation into patients with either diabetes or Parkinson's disease is that genetic information would have to be inserted to permit the multiplication of the cells before transplantation and then stop multiplying after transplantation. If cell multiplication could not be stopped after transplantation, the cell line would form a tumor in the patient.

PARTIAL ADDENDUM TO REPORT

Summary of Current Literature Underlying the Response to Question 9

Prepared by Dr. Barry J. Hoffer

In terms of Parkinson's disease (PD), there is a wealth of positive data on graft efficacy from animal models. The possible clinical application of neural grafting in patients with PD was first suggested a decade ago when it was reported that striatal implants of dopamine-(DA)-rich ventral mesencephalic tissue from rat fetuses could improve the symptoms of a 6-hydroxydopamine-induced Parkinsonian syndrome in rats (Björklund and Stenevi, 1979; Perlow et al., 1979). It has since then been convincingly demonstrated that the functional recovery is dependent on graft survival and DA fiber ingrowth into the denervated striatum (Björklund and Stenevi, 1979; Björklund et al., 1980). The growth of the grafted DA neurons exhibits a high degree of specificity and the distributional pattern of the outgrowing fibers is reminiscent of that found in the normal brain (Björklund et al., 1983). The ingrowing graft-derived DA fibers form abundant synaptic contacts with host striatal neurons (Freund et al., 1985). The grafts are metabolically, physiologically, and biochemically active (Zetterström et al., 1986; Strecker et al., 1987; Rose et al., 1985) in that they exhibit transmitter synthesis, normal firing patterns, and organotypic DA release. Successful grafting of DA-rich ventral mesencephalic tissue from fetuses to the striatum has also been reported in nonhuman primates with MPTP-induced Parkinsonism. Survival of implanted DA neurons in the caudate nucleus or the putamen has been demonstrated microscopically in rhesus monkeys (Bakay et al., 1985), african green monkeys (Redmond et al., 1986) and common marmosets. Biochemical data have indicated a near-normal ratio of homovanillic acid (a major DA metabolite) to DA in the vicinity of the grafted cells indicating that in nonhuman primates as well, grafted dopaminergic neurons are able to normalize DA turnover in DA depleted areas of CNS. Such animals have shown a permanent reduction of both drug-induced motor abnormalities and of hypokinesia, rigidity and tremor.

A key finding supporting the recent clinical trials is that human fetal DA neurons are able to survive transplantation into the DA-denervated rat striatum, reinnervate the host brain and counteract Parkinsonian symptoms (Brundin et al., 1986, 1988; Strömberg et al., 1986, 1988).

The experiments with human donor to rat host ventral mesencephalic grafts indicate that the optimal donor age is 8 to 10 weeks. About 15,000 DA cells from each human fetus were found to survive grafting to the striatum of cyclosporin A treated rats (Brundin et al., 1988). Since it has been estimated (Lindvall et al., 1987) that the human putamen is normally innervated by about 60,000 DA neurons, grafting of ventral mesencephalic tissue from one fetus into this structure should be able to restore approximately 25 percent of the normal number of cells. Further estimates, taking into account the growth capacity of each individual human DA neuron, indicate that the DA innervation provided by mesencephalic tissue from one fetus would be able to reach 40 to 80 percent of the volume of the human putamen. The symptoms of PD do not appear until more than 70 percent of the DA neurons have degenerated (Berheimer et al., 1973); until this stage is reached, DA transmission is maintained through hyperactivity of remaining neurons and postsynaptic receptor supersensitivity (Ungerstedt, 1971). It is therefore realistic to believe that tissue from human fetuses implanted into the putamen, caudate nucleus, or both, would elicit a symptomatic improvement for a patient with PD.

Transplantation has also been considered as a possible "cure" for type I diabetes. In animal models, it has been known since the early sixties that it was possible to reverse the metabolic problems of diabetes by either whole pancreas or pancreatic islet transplantation (Lacy, 1984). Islet grafting was also shown to either prevent or arrest the development of diabetic complications, seen in animals with long lasting poorly controlled diabetes (Lacy, 1984).

Animal studies show that we are now in a position to isolate islets from the rodent pancreas and transplant them to unrelated animals without the need of recipient immunosuppression (Lafferty et al., 1983). Fetal pancreas can also be used as a source of tissue for transplantation (Lafferty et al., 1983). This tissue does not contain mature islets but does contain cells which give rise to islets. Grafts of fetal pancreas are relatively slow to reverse diabetes because the islet tissue must grow and differentiate before it can function.

Fetal pancreatic tissue, with appropriate treatment, can also be grafted without the need for recipient immunosuppression (Lafferty et al., 1983). The development of technology which provides the ability to graft without the need for immunosuppressive therapy, or at least using limited immunosuppressive therapy, makes islet or fetal pancreas transplantation a potential treatment for type I diabetes.

Studies have been carried out to determine whether human fetal pancreas, obtained from cadaveric donors, has the capacity to grow, differentiate and function in animals (Hullett et al., 1987; Tuch et al., 1988). These studies have involved the grafting of human fetal pancreas to animals with no functioning immune system (i.e., "nude" mice). The fetal pancreas does grow and develop insulin containing islets. The tissue also has the capacity to reverse a diabetic condition in these animals.

Since experimental studies have reached the stage of demonstrating that human fetal pancreas can grow, differentiate, and function in animals, it now seems scientifically justified to move to experimental studies in man, while continuing with research in animals.

References

Bakay, R.A.E., Fiandaca, M.S., Barrow, D.I., Schiff, A., and Colins, D.C. Preliminary report on the use of fetal tissue transplantation to correct MPTP-induced Parkinson-like syndrome in primates. Appl. Neurophysiol., 48: 358–361, 1985.

Berheimer, H., Birkmayer, W., Hornykiewicz, O., Jellinger, K., and Seitelberger, F. Brain dopamine and the syndromes of Parkinson and Huntington. J. Neurol. Sci., 20: 415–455, 1973.

Björklund, A., Dunnett, S.B., Stenevi, U., Lewis, M.E., and Iversen, S.D. Reinnervation of the denervated striatum by substantia nigra transplants. Functional consequences as revealed by pharmacological and sensorimotor testing. Brain Res., 199: 307–333, 1980.

Björklund, A., Schmidt, R.H., and Stenevi, U. Functional reinnervation of the neostriatum in the adult rat by use of intraparenchymal grafting of dissociated cell suspensions from the substantia nigra. Cell Tissue Res., 212: 39–45, 1983.

Björklund, A., and Stenevi, U. Reconstruction of the nigrostriatal dopamine pathway by intracerebral nigral transplants. Brain Res., 177: 555–560, 1979.

Brundin, P., Nilsson, O.G., Strecker, R. E., Lindvall, O., Pstedt, B., and Björklund, A. Behavioral effects of human fetal dopamine neurons grafted in a rat model of Parkinson's disease. Exp. Brain Res., 65: 235–240, 1986.

Brundin, P., Strecker, R.E., Widner, H., Clarke, D.J., Nilsson, O.G., Pstedt, B., Lindvall, O., and Björklund, A. Human fetal dopamine neurons grafted in a rat model of Parkinson's disease: Immunological aspects, spontaneous and drug-induced behavior, and dopamine release. Exp. Brain Res., 70: 192–208, 1988.

Freund, T.F., Bolam, J.P., Björklund, A., Stenevi, U., Dunnett, S.B., Powell, J.F., and Smith, A.D. Efferent synaptic connections of grafted dopaminergic neurons reinnervating the host neostriatum: A tyrosine hydroxylase immunocytochemical study. J. Neurosci., 5: 603–616, 1985.

Hullett, D.S., Falany, J.L., Love, R.B., Burlingham, W.J., Pan, M., Sollinger, H.W. Human fetal pancreas: A potential source for transplantation. Transplantation, 43: 18, 1987.

Lindvall, O., Backlund, E.-O., Farde, L., Sedvall, G., Freedman, R., Hoffer, B., Nobin, A., Seiger, P., and Olson, L. Transplantation in Parkinson's disease: Two cases of adrenal medullary grafts to the putamen. Ann. Neurol., 22: 457–468, 1987.

Lacy, P. E. Transplantation of pancreatic islets. Ann. Rev. Immunol., 2: 183–198, 1984.

Lafferty, K.J., Prowse, S.J., and Simeonovic, C.J. Immunobiology of tissue transplantation: A return to the passenger leukocyte concept. Ann. Rev. Immunol., 1: 143–173, 1983.

Perlow, M., Freed, W., Hoffer, B., Sieger, P., Olson, L., and Wyatt, R. Brain grafts reduce motor abnormalities produced by destruction of nigrostrial dopamine system. Science, 204: 643–647, 1979.

Redmond, D.E., Sladek, J.R., Roth, R.H., Collier, T.J., Elsworth, J.D., Deutch, A.Y., and Haber, S. Fetal neuronal grafts in monkeys given methylphenyltetrahydropyridine. Lancet, 8490: 1125–1127, 1986.

Rose, G., Gerhardt, G., Strömberg, I., Olson, L., and Hoffer, B. Monoamine release from dopamine-depleted rat caudate nucleus reinnervated by substantia nigra transplants: An in vivo electrochemical study. Brain Res., 341: 92–100, 1985.

Strecker, R.E., Sharp, T., Brundin, P., Zetterström, T., Ungerstedt, U., and Björklund, A. Autoregulation of dopamine release and metabolism by intrastriatal nigral grafts as revealed by intracerebral dialysis. Neuroscience, 22: 169–178, 1987.

Strömberg, et al. Human fetal substantia nigra grafted to the dopamine denervated striatum of immunosuppressed rats. Neurosci Lett., 71: 271–276, 1986.

Strömberg, et al. Intracerebral xenografts of human mesencephalic tissue into athymic rats. Proc. Natl. Acad. Sci. U.S., 85: 8331–8334, 1988.

Tuch, B.E., Osgerby, K.J., and Turtle, J.R. Normalization of blood glucose levels in nondiabetic nude mice by human fetal pancreas after induction of diabetes. Transplantation, 46: 608–611, 1988.

Ungerstedt, U. Postsynaptic supersensitivity after 6-hydroxy-dopamine induced degeneration of the nigro-striatal dopamine system. Acta Physiol. Scand., 367: 69–93, 1971.

Zetterström, T., Brundin, P., Gage, F.H., Sharp, T., Isacson, O., Dunnett, S.B., Ungerstedt, U., and Björklund, A. *In vivo* measurement of spontaneous release and metabolism of dopamine from intrastriatal nigral grafts using intracerebral dialysis. Brain Res., 362: 344–349, 1986.

Executive Summary

Although clinical transplantation efforts involving fetal tissues are at an early stage of development, they may lead to new therapies to treat diseases, particularly diabetes and Parkinson's disease, affecting millions of Americans of all ages. Because of its biological plasticity, fetal tissue carries distinctive advantages for transplantation. Thus, for instance, fetal pancreatic tissue can make insulin and also can, under appropriate circumstances after transplantation, develop a response to biochemical feedback signals that control the body's energy metabolism. Similarly, fetal brain tissues can produce specific neurotransmitter substances such as dopamine, which is missing or in low supply in the brains of individuals with Parkinson's disease. Already, some limited clinical experiments of this type have begun in Sweden, Great Britain, Mexico, China, and the United States.

In October 1987, NIH submitted a request to Assistant Secretary for Health Robert Windom, asking his approval for a clinical experiment at NIH that involved transplantation of human fetal tissue into the brain of a patient suffering with Parkinson's disease. This protocol proposed the use of fetal tissue obtained after induced abortions. The current debate about the ethics of using fetal tissue in biomedical research stems in large part from profound differences in opinion over abortion. Although abortions are legal, opinion is deeply divided over whether they are moral and/or ethical.

In his response to the NIH request, Assistant Secretary Windom asked NIH to convene a special outside advisory panel to examine policy issues arising from such contemplated experiments, and his staff submitted a series of ten questions to guide the panel's deliberations. In the meantime, he withheld approval of the experiment proposed at NIH, and also of "future experiments [involving] transplantation of human tissue from induced abortions" pending the mandated assessment.

Accordingly, NIH convened an *ad hoc* panel of consultants with diverse expertise in scientific, legal, and ethical matters to consider whether clinical experiments involving the transplantation of human fetal tissues should be approved. The panel met on several occasions in late 1988—first to hear the views held by a wide variety of experts and public witnesses, and then to respond to the specific questions raised by Assistant Secretary Windom. The panel subsequently submitted its report on December 14, 1988, to the NIH Director's Advisory Committee, which meets periodically to counsel NIH on policy matters.

Despite the diversity of views held by members of the *ad hoc* panel, the group steadfastly tried to follow a consensual approach during its deliberations. Although consensus was difficult to achieve, the panel members consistently tried to accommodate one another's respective positions. Thus, in most cases, very disparate philosophical positions were melded into a coherent stance that was deemed acceptable by a substantial majority of the panel. However, neither of these observations should be taken to suggest that the debate within the panel was somehow constrained by the majority viewpoint, as indeed it was not.

After a great deal of careful consideration, a majority group of the panel members concluded that, although it is of moral relevance that fetal tissues may derive from induced abortions, use of such tissue for research "is acceptable public policy" in this pluralistic society. In answering Dr. Windom's questions, the panel members also outlined principles for safeguarding such use against potential abuses and for protecting the sensitivities of individuals who do not believe that such research should be conducted. Included among the panel's conclusions are the following key points, some of which are already addressed in existing Federal and state regulations:

- The timing of abortions must not be linked with the research use of fetal tissues,
- A woman's decision to donate fetal tissue remains is a "sufficient condition for their use" (that is, under most circumstances, no other consent is necessary),
- "Profiteering" in , or "valuable consideration" for, donations of fetal tissue should be strictly prohibited,
- General knowledge of potential biomedical research uses for fetal tissue should not be considered a "prohibited inducement" for a woman's decision to have an abortion, and
- Because current research leading to fetal tissue transplant experiments in humans is showing promise, the ethical questions it poses should be addressed now.

A minority within the panel did not agree with these conclusions, and three separate dissenting statements were submitted outlining specific objections. In addition, several Panelists who concurred with the conclusions of the report submitted statements elucidating their thoughts in arriving at those conclusions.

Concurring Statements

Judge Arlin M. Adams

The questions posed by Dr. Windom to the panel and the concerns underlying those questions raise a number of difficult and indeed anguishing issues for me.

I have been opposed to abortion except in very limited situations for a very long time. Yet, I recognize that the Supreme Court of the United States has declared that a woman has a constitutional right in the first and second trimester to proceed with an abortion. Although I have serious reservations regarding the Supreme Court opinion, both in its reasoning and in its ultimate result, I recognize that Supreme Court decisions in matters of this type constitute the law of the land. Thus, until those decisions are reversed, all citizens are bound by them.

Nonetheless, any activity which would serve as an inducement to women to have abortions must, in my view, be dealt with in a most cautious fashion, and to the extent possible be carefully circumscribed.

Counterpoised against the concerns set forth above is the evidence produced during the hearings which indicate that there are a series of illnesses that might be substantially ameliorated by the prudent use of fetal tissue. Although proof of the efficacious use of such tissue is not yet established beyond all peradventure, every indication is that research in maladies such as Parkinson's disease, Huntington's disease, childhood diabetes, and perhaps Alzheimer's disease, can be considerably improved by the use of such tissue.

Consequently, at least for me, the problem has been weighing one major concern, my objections to abortions, against another major concern, making it possible to do medical research that could improve the lot of thousands of our citizens, in a sensible and rational fashion.

Certainly the prevention of any commercialization of this process would seem to me to be an absolute requirement. Also, the need to separate completely the abortion procedure and the use of the fetal tissue would seem to be an essential step, assuming that such a separation is possible. Further, it must be mandatory that any funding by the government be limited to situations which employ the most careful scientific approaches as well as the highest professional standards.

Based on the evidence that has been made available, I believe, at least preliminarily, that these various safeguards are possible in today's environment. Accordingly, I would insist as a condition to providing for any approval that the National Institutes for Health commit itself to conduct periodic reviews, from time to time and with great care, to insure that the concerns expressed herein, as well as concerns that may be uncovered as medical research proceeds, are carefully safeguarded.

One other element has tipped the balance so far as my vote is concerned in proceeding even with carefully crafted guidelines and on a periodic review basis only: I am troubled that without government funding there undoubtedly would be many efforts to use fetal tissue for medical research that would be completely unsupervised and not governed by any guidelines. Thus if the National Institutes of Health proceeds cautiously, and with carefully articulated safeguards and a program of periodic reviews, there would be much greater assurance that carefully crafted guidelines will be put in place as an absolute condition to any research procedures. Such an arrangement would protect pregnant women and fetuses in a far more circumspect and intelligent manner than if the NIH did not participate in any way.

Dr. Aron A. Moscona

joined by: Professor John A. Robertson and Dr. LeRoy Walters

I wish to comment on the Statement of Dissent by Mr. James Bopp, Jr. and Professor James T. Burtchaell, distributed to the NIH Panel on Human Fetal Tissue Transplantation Research on October 21, 1988. This Statement refers to ''instructive similarities'' between Holocaust atrocities of the Nazis and elective abortions and transplantation research; it argues that transplantation research represents complicity in abortion and is, thus, ''a perversion of both the scholar's and the healer's work'' similar to the crimes of the Nazis and the Nazi ''doctors.''

Although voluntary elected abortion is within the pregnant woman's lawful right of choice and decision, this issue has become polarized by extremist views and beliefs.

However, this panel was not convened to offer opinion on the abortion issue. Its task—specified by Dr. Windom's set of questions—was to evaluate research on fetal tissue transplantation in the context of laws, scientific-medical knowledge, and ethical and societal standards. It was the panel's majority opinion that existing medical knowledge justified funding of this research and that it could be lawfully and ethically conducted. The recommendations included complete insulation of the woman's choice and decision from influence by possible use of fetal cells in transplantation research and rigorous separation of the researchers from this process. As I see it, the essence of these recommendations was in accord with protection of individual freedom under the law and with uncompromising insistence that ethical-moral principles would be safeguarded in the pursuit of this new medical knowledge.

Dissent can make a positive contribution to our process. However, this Statement of Dissent is detached from reality in implying that the panel's majority position embraces moral complicity in deeds analogous to the Holocaust atrocities. Perhaps such a speculative analogy requires no comment. However, since it neglects the root causes which inspired and unleashed the atrocities of the Holocaust, this analogy not only is invalid, but is ethically repugnant and might be seriously misleading.

In a *New York Times* article (November 2, 1988), Julian Bond, the veteran of the 1960s civil rights struggle, comments on how the anti-abortion demonstrators compare themselves with the fight for black equality, claiming solidarity with the civil rights movement. Such comparisons, he says, are, at best, disingenuous and misleading attempts to "capture someone else's history" in a tactical maneuver to deny women constitutional rights. The attempt to bracket transplantation research in one context with the Nazi dictatorship's crusade to exterminate a people because of religion or creed is even more shockingly misleading: it closes its eyes to the "ideological" dogmas that, by denying human rights to one class of citizens, unlocked oppression and provided the warrant for genocide; and it exploits deeply lacerated memories and emotions in the service of an extremist position.

The Holocaust was not a medical research project to help Parkinson patients and rescue infants from fatal diseases. It was not scrutinized by peer reviews, examined by NIH panels, publicized by media, open to public questioning, debated in Congress, challenged by the Administration. The Holocaust victims did not board trains out of free will and choice; there were no clergymen, lawyers, ethicists, and social activists urging them to reconsider; they were not advised of constitutional rights or offered adoption as an alternative. They had no contraceptives against rape by racial prejudice and intolerance. At the gates of Auschwitz, no one asked for "informed consent." Gas chambers were not a freely elected option to donate skin and hair to make lamp shades and mattresses for the Third Reich. The "medical experiments" did not involve freely surrendered clumps of embryonic cells lacking neural mechanisms for consciousness and pain. The "experimental" cruelties were not a main objective of the annihilation enterprise; they were just an incidental, opportunistic sideline of an obsessive "ideology" that denied human freedom and enslaved it to medieval hatreds in the name of world conquest. It was this unshakable "ideology," spawned of dogmatic religious intolerance, tribal feuds, and dark prejudices against one class of people that was the root cause and the sanction for the "final solution." This "ideology," above all the unspeakable deeds which followed, is the never-again-to-be-forgotten lesson and legacy of the Holocaust.

But this cardinal lesson is side-stepped by the Statement of Dissent in its use of the Holocaust to oppose transplantation research and elective abortions. Women do not choose abortion in the cause of racial extermination and fanatical nationalistic dogmas. They are dissuaded from contraception and family planning by beliefs and taboos. And equating freely surrendered abortus cells with tormented people poisoned with lethal insecticides defies reason and outrages morality. Is it negligence or a different frame of priorities that inspire such analogies? Or, are they meant to deny individual rights and freedoms in the name of preformed convictions. Is the Holocaust to be taken hostage in an assault on transplantation research? This is not constructive dissent. This might only feed ignorance, inflame passions, and inspire intolerance and extremism.

I trust that this was not the intent of the authors of the Statement of Dissent. But, in attempting to stigmatize the panel with "moral complicity," have they not strayed and lost sight of ethical and societal responsibilities?

Professor John A. Robertson

joined by: Dr. Robert C. Cefalo, Dr. James F. Childress, Dr. K. Danner Clouser, Dr. Dale Cowan, Dr. Barry Hoffer, Professor Patricia A. King, Dr. Paul Lacy, Dr. Joseph B. Martin, Dr. Aron A. Moscona, and Dr. Leroy Walters (Note: Dr. Walters does not accede to the final section, "Aborting to Obtain Tissue for Transplant.")

I concur in the panel's Report to the Assistant Secretary of Health. I write to provide a more complete rationale for some of the panel's positions and to address some issues not directly covered therein.

Clarifying the Issues

At the outset it is essential to separate out several issues that have become entangled in public, press, and scholarly commentary about fetal tissue transplant research.

The proposed research to be funded by NIH would make use of fetal remains from abortions that occur independently of tissue transplant research. Fetuses would not be kept alive or killed to obtain tissue. Nor would abortions be performed solely or primarily to get tissue for transplant. No fees would be paid to women to abort or to donate tissue, nor fees beyond actual expenses paid to abortion clinics to provide the tissue.

The main question before the panel is whether the NIH should support transplant research with fetal remains from the 1.5 million abortions performed annually to end unwanted pregnancies. If fetal remains may be used, the circumstances and procedures by which fetal tissue will be retrieved and distributed must then be addressed.

The Case for Funding Fetal Tissue Research

Transplantation research using fetal tissue from induced abortion should be funded because of its great clinical potential, and the ethically acceptable ways in which such tissue may be obtained.

Ample evidence was presented to the panel to justify proceeding with clinical research with fetal tissue transplants. Extensive animal studies have shown that clinical applications in humans are now justified for Parkinson's disease, and possibly diabetes. Promising results with fetal thymus transplants have also been shown. Given these clinical possibilities, there is an important role for the NIH to play in supporting such research so that progress in treating diseases affecting millions of persons may occur.

Fetal tissue research is permitted by current Federal research regulations and applicable law. Federal regulations permit research "involving the dead fetus, macerated fetal material, or cells, tissue, or organs excised from a dead fetus . . . in accordance with any applicable State or local laws regarding such activities."[1] The Uniform Anatomical Gift Act in all States treats fetal remains like other cadaveric remains and allows next of kin to donate the tissue.[2] While eight States have laws banning experimental use of aborted fetuses, these statutes are of doubtful constitutionality.[3] One law has already been invalidated, and the others are vulnerable to challenge.[4] Advisory and review bodies in Great Britain, Sweden, Australia, and France have also approved such research when conducted under certain guidelines.[5]

Fetal tissue for clinical research may be made available in ethically acceptable ways. As noted, fetal tissue transplant research would use tissue retrieved from the 1.5 million legal abortions performed annually in the United States to end unwanted pregnancies. No need now or in the foreseeable future exists to have a woman conceive and abort to produce fetal tissue.

Given that these abortions will occur regardless of the needs of researchers, the research use of fetal remains from induced abortions performed to end unwanted pregnancies is ethically acceptable.[6] The researchers and recipients will have no role in the decision to abort or the abortion itself. The abortions at issue will occur regardless of research needs. If not used in research, fetal remains will be discarded. It is reasonable to conclude that the NIH may ethically fund transplant research with such tissue.

It should be emphasized that this conclusion is not determined solely by one's views about the morality of induced abortion. Because the abortion and subsequent research use occur independently, views about the immorality of abortion do not necessarily determine the morality of research with tissue from aborted fetuses. As evidenced by several members of the panel, persons opposed to abortion might reasonably view the research use of fetal remains as so separate and independent of the abortion as to be acceptable even if they disapprove of the abortion that makes the tissue available.

Similarly, the Catholic Church is not against all use of fetal tissue from induced abortions. A representative of the Bishop's Committee for Pro-Life Activities of the

---

[1] 45 CFR 46.210. These recommendations resulted from the 1976 study of fetal research conducted by the National Commission for the Protection of Human Subjects of Biomedical and Behavioral Science Research.

[2] Unif. Anatomical Gift Act, 8A U.L.A. 15–16 (West 1983 & Supp. 1987) (Table of Jurisdictions Wherein Act Has Been Adopted); 45 CFR 46.207(b).

[3] For an analysis of these laws, see King and Areen, Legal Regulation of Fetal Tissue Transplantation, 36 Clinical Research 205–209 (1988); Robertson, Fetal Tissue Transplants, 66 Washington Univ. Law Quarterly 1–65 (1988).

[4] *Margaret S. v. Edwards*, 794 F.2d 944 (5th Cir. 1986).

[5] Peel Committee on the Use of Fetuses and Fetal Material for Research (1972); British Medical Association, Interim Guidelines on the Use of Fetal Tissue in Transplantation Therapy (1988); National Health and Medical Research Council, Ethics in Medical Research Involving the Human Fetus and Human Fetal Tissue (1984); National Ethics Consultative Committee for Life and Health Sciences (France, 1984); Parliamentary Assembly of the Council of Europe (1986).

[6] While this claim is justified on utilitarian grounds, it also would not violate deontological concerns, because the abortion and subsequent use are so clearly independent. The question of whether such research would be acceptable if tissue could be obtained only from abortions performed for the purpose of providing fetal tissue raises issues that do not arise if the supply of tissue from family planning abortions is adequate. For discussion of those issues, see Robertson, Fetal Tissue Transplants, note 3 *supra*.

National Conference of Catholic Bishops testified that "It may not be wrong in principle for someone unconnected with an abortion to make use of a fetal organ from an unborn child who died as a result of an abortion. . . ."[7] The Vatican Instruction on Respect for Human Life in Its Origin and on the Dignity of Procreation forbids use of deliberately aborted fetuses only if they are not dead and the consent of the mother has not been obtained.[8]

The Case Against Research With Tissue From Induced Abortions

Some—but not all—persons opposed to abortion object to research with fetal remains from the million plus abortions that occur annually for reasons unrelated to fetal tissue procurement. They make three arguments, none of which withstand scrutiny as reasons not to proceed with fetal tissue transplants at this time.

EXPLOITATION OF THE FETUS   Several of the right-to-life groups that testified before the panel argued that to use fetal remains in experimentation after an abortion had taken the fetus' life would be further "exploitation" of the fetus.[9] This objection is misguided. The abortion that makes tissue available occurs independently of the need for tissue. Also, fetuses are dead when tissue is retrieved for transplant. However one views the pre-abortion status of the fetus, once dead the fetus clearly lacks interests and can no more be exploited or harmed than can any cadaver.

COMPLICITY IN ABORTION   A main argument of opponents of fetal tissue transplant research is that it will necessarily create complicity in past abortions.[10] But their account of complicity does not withstand scrutiny, and does not provide a sufficient basis for rejecting the benefits of research with fetal tissue obtained from elective family planning abortions.

The charge of complicity can appeal only to persons who think that family planning abortions are a moral evil. But even if one accepts that premise, it does not follow that use of fetal remains makes one morally responsible for or an accomplice in abortions that occur prior to and independent of later uses of fetal remains.

A researcher using fetal tissue from an elective abortion is not complicitous with the abortionist and woman choosing abortion. The researcher and patient will have no role in the abortion process.[11] They will not have requested it, and may have no knowledge of who performed the abortion or where it occurred. A third party intermediary will procure the tissue for the researcher. They may be morally opposed to abortion, and surely are not corrupted because they choose to salvage some good from an abortion that will occur regardless of their research or therapeutic goals.

A useful analogy is transplant of organs and tissue from homicide and accident victims. Families of murder and accident victims are often asked to donate organs and bodies for research, therapy and education. If they consent, organ procurement agencies

---

[7] Testimony of Richard Doerflinger, September 15, 1988, *Panel Transcript,* 240–41. However, he was concerned that use of fetal tissue could not "be institutionalized without threatening a morally unacceptable collaboration with the abortion industry." *Id.* at 241.

[8] Vatican Congregation for the Doctrine of the Faith, Replies to Certain Questions of the Day, p. 18 (St. Paul Editions, 1988).

[9] Testimony of Ms. Kay James, *Panel Transcript* at pp. 485–86.

[10] Dissenting statement of Rev. James Burtchaell and James Bopp, Esq.

[11] Note that the complicity objection as framed by the opponents is a claim of complicity in abortions that have occurred in the past independent of research, and not a claim that fetal tissue research will lead to future abortions. That argument is treated separately.

retrieve the organs and distribute them to recipients unconnected with organ retrieval. No one would seriously argue that the surgeon who transplants the homicide or accident victim's kidneys, heart, liver, or corneas or the recipient who receives it become accomplices in the homicide or accident that made the organs available. Nor is the medical student who uses the cadaver of a murder victim to study anatomy an accomplice in that murder.

James Burtchaell's approach to the problem of complicity assumes that researchers necessarily applaud the underlying act of abortion, thereby allying themselves with it.[12] But one may benefit from another's evil act without applauding or approving of that evil. A may disapprove of B's murder of C, even though A gains an inheritance or a promotion as a result. The willingness to derive benefit from another's wrongful death does not create complicity in that death when the beneficiary has played no role in causing the death.[13]

Burtchaell and others try to shore up their complicity argument by drawing upon revulsion toward the unethical experiments that Nazi physicians carried out on concentration camp victims, which led to promulgation of the Nuremberg Code of human experimentation. But this analogy is inapposite. The Nazi experiments that were so revolting were carried out on live patients and clearly harmed them. Fetal tissue transplant research will be carried out with material from dead fetuses that have been lawfully aborted for reasons unrelated to the research. Unlike the Nazi experiments, the research in question does not harm fetuses. They are not aborted to advance research, and are dead when the research occurs.

These references to the Nazi experiences are inapposite for two other reasons. One is that no doctors were tried or convicted at the Nuremberg war trials who had not directly researched on live persons before their death.[14] No one was prosecuted merely for making use of cadaveric remains from unethical experiments carried out by other physicians. Thus Nuremberg is no precedent for condemning the use of fetal remains made possible by independently occurring abortions.

The second reason is that reasonable persons clearly differ over whether benefits may ethically be drawn from the unethical experiments conducted on live persons in concentration camps under the Nazis. One could rely on Nazi-generated data while decrying the horrendous acts of Nazi doctors that produced the data without dishonoring those unfortunate victims.[15] Indeed, reliance on this data to save others could reasonably

---

[12] Burtchaell, Case Study: University Policy on Experimental Use of Aborted Fetal Tissue, 10 IRB: A Review of Human Subjects Research 7, 8 (1988). See also Robertson, Response to Burtchaell: Fetal Tissue Transplant Research Is Ethical, 10 IRB (forthcoming, 1988).

[13] The dissent also claims that use of tissue from aborted fetuses would "institutionalize a collaboration with the abortion industry," and create "an institutional partnership, federally sponsored and funded, whereby the bodily remains of abortion victims become a regularly supplied medical commodity." The terms "partnership" and "collaboration" imply active or intentional agreement and participation, and thus are a misleading way to describe a relationship in which independent tissue agencies will make fetal tissue that will otherwise be discarded available for research and therapy.

[14] See, e.g., Trials of War Criminals Before the Nuremberg Military Tribunals Under Control Council Law No. 10, vols. 1&2 (Washington, D.C.: U.S. Government Printing Office, 1949); Leo Alexander, Medical Science Under Dictatorship, 241 New Eng. J. Med. 39 (1949).

[15] For example, scientists and officials at the EPA were divided over whether Nazi studies of certain gases could be cited in a proceeding related to a certain gas. Phillip Shabecoff, Head of E.P.A., Bars Nazi Data in Study in Gas, New York Times, March 23, 1988, p. 1. On the other hand, a University of Minnesota researcher has relied heavily on and would cite Nazi studies of hypothermia in his own studies of ways to

be viewed as retrospectively honoring the victims without justifying the horrors that produced the data. The Jewish doctors who made systematic studies of starvation in the Warsaw ghetto in order to reap some good from the evil being done to their brethren were not accomplices in that evil, nor are doctors and patients who now benefit from their studies.[16] Indeed, Burtchaell himself accepts that a physician may use a drug that has been produced by lethal experiments once the drug has been developed, despite the unethical process of developing it.[17]

If the complicity claim is doubtful when the underlying immorality of the act is clear, as with Nazi experiments and murder, it is considerably weakened when the act making the benefit possible is legal and its immorality is vigorously debated, as is the case with abortion. Given the range of views on this subject, perceptions of complicity with abortions that will occur regardless of tissue research should not determine policy on fetal tissue transplants.

LEGITIMATING AND ENCOURAGING ABORTIONS   The dissent asserts that if fetal tissue transplants become common, "the incidence of abortion can reasonably be expected to increase from a combination of beneficent reasons motivating pregnant women who are ambivalent about abortion, and financial incentives motivating abortion clinics."[18] To support this claim the dissent cites studies about women who are ambivalent about abortion and the motivations that influence the abortion decision.

Although the main appeal of this argument is to persons opposed to elective abortions, there are several reasons why this argument is not persuasive even to opponents of abortion. One is that the predicted impact on abortion practices is highly speculative, particularly at a time when few fetal transplants have yet occurred. There is no way to predict with certainty how fast the success of clinical research or the future demand for fetal tissue will progress. Judged by the progress of other research, it may take several years for effective clinical techniques for even a subgroup of seriously ill patients to be developed. Moreover, the research may lead to the development of cultured cells and other substances for transplant that minimize the need for fetal tissue in the future.

Nor is it clear that even successful use of fetal tissue will change individual or social practices concerning abortion. It is just as reasonable to think that successful fetal tissue transplants will have little effect on the incidence of family planning abortions, as that they will substantially increase them. The chief motivation for abortion is the desire to avoid the burdens of an unwanted pregnancy. As several physicians testified, even if fetal tissue transplants are successful, they will have no appreciable impact on the incidence of abortion.[19] A physician member of the panel noted that improving sex education and access to contraception would reduce abortion rates much more than banning fetal tissue transplants.[20]

---

save persons swept into icy seas. Minnesota Scientist Plans to Publish a Nazi Study, New York Times, May 12, 1988, p. 9.

[16] Leonard Tushnet, *The Uses of Adversity: Studies of Starvation in the Warsaw Ghetto* (New York: Thomas Yoseloff, 1966).

[17] Burtchaell, see note 12, *supra*. Yet Burtchaell finds that research use of cadaveric remains from those lethal experiments would not be acceptable, e.g., would create complicity. He makes no attempt to justify this distinction.

[18] Dissenting statement [of James Bopp and Rev. James Burtchaell].

[19] Statement of Ezra Davidson, M.D., *Panel Transcript* at p. 420.

[20] Statement of Kenneth Ryan, M.D., *Panel Transcript* at p. 701.

The willingness of women to donate fetal tissue after abortion does not prove otherwise. Having decided to abort, a woman may feel better if she then donates the fetal remains. But this willingness does not show that tissue donation will lead to a termination decision that would not otherwise have occurred. Even if women consider donation before deciding to abort, the chance to donate will not necessarily lead to abortions that would not otherwise have occurred to any significant extent. One may acknowledge the ambivalence some women have about abortion, and still reasonably conclude that the desire to avoid the burdens of unwanted pregnancy and childrearing will continue to be the primary motivation to abort.

Yet even if *some* increase in the number of family planning abortions due to tissue donation occurred, it would not follow that fetal tissue transplants should not be supported. Surely it does not follow that *any* increase in the number of abortions makes fetal tissue transplants unacceptable. Automobile design, highway engineering, bridge building, drug licensing, and gun sales will lead to *some* loss of life as a result of the activity (in the case of gun sales, the deaths may even be intentionally caused). The risk that *some* lives will be lost, however, is not sufficient to stop those projects when the number of deaths is not substantial, when the activity serves worthy goals and when reasonable steps to minimize the loss have been taken. A more stringent policy is not justified for fetal tissue transplants just because the risk is to prenatal life from *some* increase in the number of legal abortions.

The dissent does not address the question of magnitude of impact. It asserts that "an increase" in the number of abortions will occur, but provides no convincing reasons to think that the increase will be substantial. Furthermore, it assumes that even a marginal increase in abortion should bar fetal tissue transplant research. As a result, the dissent would deny thousands of patients potentially important benefits to prevent a potentially marginal or insignificant increase in the number of abortions. Its stance would also bar fetal tissue research that could lead to developing cultured cells or direct chemical substitutes out of a speculative fear that "some" increase in abortions would occur.[21]

Other aspects of the concern about encouraging or legitimizing abortion are also unpersuasive. For example, the dissent's claim that abortion clinics would have financial incentives to persuade women who are ambivalent to abort is unconvincing because of the clear preference of the panel and existing law for prohibiting payments (other than reasonable retrieval expenses) for fetal tissue.[22] Nor would the use of fetal remains for transplant mean that a public otherwise ready to outlaw abortion would refrain from doing so. The continuing legal acceptance of abortion flows from the wide disagreement that exists over fetal status. If a majority were agreed that fetuses should be respected as persons despite the burdens placed on pregnant women, secondary benefits from induced abortion such as fetal tissue transplants would not prevent a change in the

---

[21] If there were a substantial increase in the number of abortions, it still would not follow that fetal tissue transplant research and therapy should not occur. Given the rudimentary development of early fetuses, the potentially great benefit to recipients, and the legality of abortion, such transplants might still be ethically and legally acceptable.

[22] The panel has clearly recommended against buying and selling fetal tissue from women undergoing abortions and abortion clinics. See *Panel Report,* Responses to Question 1 and Question 6. Yet the dissent inaccurately states that the panel "has refused to recommend" such a restriction [dissenting statement of Rev. James Burtchaell and James Bopp, Esq.].

legality of abortion. Speculation about the legitimizing effect of tissue transplants should not stop the great good that fetal tissue transplants may provide.[23]

Maternal Consent for Fetal Tissue Donation

The acceptability of fetal tissue transplant research rests on the assumption that the tissue will be legally obtained for transplant. In the context of tissue and organ transplantation, this means that the consent of the woman (unless the father objects) be obtained. Maternal consent is a legal requirement for use of fetal remains under the Uniform Anatomical Gift Act and current Federal research regulations.[24] The previously cited Vatican Instruction also recognizes the importance of maternal consent to use of fetal remains from induced abortions.[25]

These rules should apply to donation of fetal remains for transplant research. A woman who aborts a pregnancy does not lose or forfeit all interest in an aborted fetus. She may care deeply about whether fetal remains—a product of her body and potential heir that she has for her own personal reasons chosen to abort—are contributed to research or therapy to help others. Given that interest, there is good reason to respect her wishes, as current law presently does. Her consent to donation of fetal tissue should be routinely sought.

The argument of some ethicists that her decision to abort disqualifies her from playing any role in disposition of fetal remains is not persuasive.[26] It overlooks her continuing interest in what happens to fetal tissue that results from her abortion. It also mistakenly assumes that a person who disposes of cadaveric remains acts as a guardian or proxy for the deceased, who has no interests, rather than as a protector of their own interests in what happens to those remains. Finally, it would lead to a policy of using fetal remains without parental consent or to a total ban on fetal transplants.[27]

Fetal Tissue Procurement Practices

The conclusion that fetal remains from family planning abortions may be ethically used in transplant research assumes that fetal tissue can be obtained and distributed for research use without close involvement in the abortion process. Current Federal regulations and solid organ procurement practices provide sufficient guidance here and should be followed for fetal procurement.

A central feature of these rules is that the researcher has nothing to do with the decision to make the tissue available, including the decision to abort and determination of fetal death.

Another important feature is that consent to donate tissue be requested after the decision to abort has occurred. This will assure that tissue donation is not a prerequisite

---

[23] It could also be said that the willingness to use organs from homicide, suicide, and accident victims might encourage or legitimate such deaths, or at least make it harder to enact lower speed limits, seatbelt, gun control, and drunk driving laws to prevent them. After all, the need to prevent fatal accidents, murder and suicide becomes less pressing if some good to others might come from use of victim organs for transplant. But the connection is too tenuous and speculative to ban organ transplants on that basis. It is similarly speculative and tenuous as a ground for banning fetal tissue transplants.

[24] See note 2 *supra*.

[25] See note 8 *supra*.

[26] Dissent at 2–5; Burtchaell, note 12 *supra* at p. 8.; Mary Mahowald, Placing Wedges Along a Slippery Slope: Use of Fetal Neural Tissue for Transplantation, 36 Clinical Research 220 (1988).

[27] Robertson, Fetal Tissue Transplants, note 3 *supra*.

to having the abortion performed. Also, it will prevent the prospect of donating fetal remains from influencing the decision to abort, a clearly preferable policy when an adequate supply of fetal tissue is available from elective family planning abortions. Of course, there will be situations in which women may know of the possibility of tissue donation prior to being asked. In some cases, women considering abortion may inquire about donation of fetal remains. In those cases women should be informed of donation possibilities. As a general rule, however, requests to donate fetal tissue should wait until the woman has clearly indicated her decision to abort.[28]

Laws and policies against paying women to abort or to provide fetal tissue for transplant, and against paying abortion facilities for fetal tissue, are desirable to remove any taint of commercialization or profit from the enterprise. The National Organ Transplant Act now makes payment of "valuable consideration" for the donation or distribution of specific fetal organs and "any subparts thereof" (which arguably includes tissue and cells) a Federal crime, as do many States.[29] Such laws are thought necessary to protect human dignity and to prevent exploitation. They will also allay fears that women are paid to conceive and abort to obtain fetal tissue.

Current bans on buying and selling fetal tissue do not—and should not—prohibit making reasonable payments to recover the costs of retrieving fetal tissue.[30] Tissue procurement agencies should be free to pay the costs of personnel directly involved in tissue retrieval, whether employees of the procurement agency or of the facility performing the abortion. For example, a tissue retrieval agency may reimburse the abortion clinic for using its space and staff to obtain consent for tissue donations and to retrieve tissue from aborted fetuses. However, the abortion facility should not charge the agency a fee beyond reasonable expenses incurred in retrieving fetal tissue at their facility.

For-profit firms that prepare, process, and distribute fetal tissue for research or therapy should be free to recoup their costs, including some "profit" to cover the costs of obtaining the capital that makes their services possible. Such payments are consistent with the role of for-profit physicians, hospitals, drug companies, air transport, and other services in solid organ transplantation, all of which also depend upon altruistic donation of cadaveric human remains.

---

[28]This does not mean that it would be unethical to abort after having been made aware of donation options. See note 6 *supra*.

[29]42 U.S.C.A. #274e (West Supp. 1985); ARK. STAT. ANN § 82-439 (Supp. 1985); ILL. ANN. STAT. ch. 38, § 81.54(7) (Smith-Hurd 1983); LA. CIV. CODE ANN. art. 9:122 (Supp. 1987); OHIO REV. CODE ANN. § 2919.14 (Page 1985); OKLA. STAT. tit. 63, § 1-735 (1987); FLA. STAT. ANN. § 873.05 (West Supp. 1987); MASS. GEN. LAWS ANN. ch. 112, § 1593 (1964); ME. REV. STAT. ANN. tit. 22, § 1593 (1964); MICH. COMP. LAWS ANN. § 333.2690 (West); MINN. STAT. ANN. § 145.422 (West Supp. 1986); N.D. CENT. CODE § 14-02.2-02 (1981); NEV. REV. STAT. § 451.015 (1985); R.I. GEN. LAWS § 11-54-1(f) (Supp. 1987); TENN. CODE ANN. § 39-4-208 (Supp. 1987); TEX. PENAL CODE ANN. §§ 42.10, 48.02 (Vernon 1974 and Supp. 1988); and WYO. STAT. § 35-6-115 (1986); 18 PA. CONS. STAT. § 3216 (Purdon 1983). See also Note, Regulating the Sale of Human Organs, 71 Va. L. Rev. 1015 (1985).

[30]The National Organ Transplant Act, for example, allows "reasonable payments associated with the removal, transportation, implantation, processing, preservation, quality control, and storage of the organs and tissue covered by that act. 42 U.S.C.A. #274 (e). Many state laws have similar exceptions.

Aborting to Obtain Tissue for Transplant

Central to the argument for NIH funding of fetal tissue transplant research has been the assumption that such transplants will not necessitate pregnancy and abortion to produce fetal tissue.

No need now or in the foreseeable future will exist to have a woman conceive and abort to produce fetal tissue. With 1.5 million abortions occurring annually to end unwanted pregnancies, the supply of fetal tissue for research and therapeutic needs appears to be adequate for many years to come. Nor is there presently any indication that fetal tissue antigenicity will be so important that a close genetic match between source and recipient will be necessary, which could lead family members to conceive and abort to obtain tissue for transplant.

In light of these supply considerations, at the present time a policy against aborting solely to obtain tissue for transplant, against donor designation of tissue recipients, and against fetal tissue donations to family or friends is desirable. It will not prevent needy patients from receiving fetal tissue transplants, and will quiet fears that women will be coerced or pressured into conceiving and aborting for transplant purposes, or that abortions solely to produce tissue for transplant will occur.

If the situation changes so that the supply of fetal tissue from family planning abortions proves inadequate, the ban on donor designation of recipients and aborting for transplant purposes should be re-examined. The ethical and legal arguments in favor of and against such a policy would then need careful scrutiny to determine whether such a policy remains justified.[31] In the meantime the fear that fetal tissue transplants will lead to abortions to obtain tissue for transplant should not prevent use of tissue from abortions not performed for that purpose.

---

[31] When another person's life or health depends on it, the argument in favor of abortions to obtain tissue is much stronger than has generally been thought. See Robertson, note 3 *supra*.

Dissenting Statements

Fetal Tissue Research and Public Policy   *(Rabbi J. David Bleich)*

Questions focusing upon the morality of abortion are among the most emotion-laden and divisive issues of our time. The Supreme Court has ruled that, as a matter of law, the constraints that society may place upon performance of abortions are severely limited. Although the judiciary is empowered to declare the law, it does not function as an arbiter of morality. The morality of induced termination of pregnancy remains a contentious issue in our society.

The decision of the Supreme Court in *Roe v. Wade* serves to curtail legislative initiative designed to hamper a woman's right to make her own determination regarding the morality of induced abortion. There is, however, nothing in our law or in the mores of our society that argues for governmental action designed to support or to facilitate abortion. Quite to the contrary, it behooves all branches of government to maintain strict neutrality with regard to matters of controversy judicially declared to fall within the realm of private morality. Thus governmental agencies should neither grant their imprimatur—nor allow themselves to be perceived as granting their imprimatur—to the voluntary termination of pregnancy even when such a procedure is undertaken for the most noble of reasons. Support or encouragement of abortion by any Federal agency is *ipso facto* governmental endorsement of the moral nature of such procedures.

It has been tacitly assumed by the Advisory Panel from the very outset of its deliberations that our society should not lend its sanction to the performance of an abortion when the decision to induce an abortion is motivated solely by a desire to further scientific knowledge. Societal support of a woman's decision to conceive so that the fetus may be aborted for such purposes has been viewed by the Advisory Panel as equally repugnant. Moreover, although the goal may be realizable only to a greater or a lesser degree, the report of the Human Fetal Tissue Transplantation Research Panel is clearly predicated on the acknowledged, albeit unenunciated, premise that NIH-funded fetal tissue transplantation should not be conducted in a manner that might encourage the performance of any abortion that would otherwise not occur. To that end, the participants in the majority report of the Advisory Panel have unanimously recommended that there be no Federal funding of programs involving experimental transplants performed with fetal tissue derived from an abortion provided by a family member, friend, or acquaintance; that solicitation of consent for use of such tissue and even preliminary discussion of tissue donation be delayed until after a consent to the abortion has been signed; that anonymity between donor and recipient be maintained; and that the identity of the donor be concealed from the transplant team.

These mitigating safeguards notwithstanding, intellectual integrity compels recognition that the goal of preventing an increment in the total number of abortions performed is not totally attainable. The research proposals under discussion, if successful, will yield therapies designed to cure or to prolong the lives of countless numbers of individuals afflicted with life-threatening illnesses. Generation of the potential for preservation of life through the intermediacy of abortion must perforce diminish the odium associated with that procedure. As an instrument for good, the act of abortion cannot be perceived as an unmitigated evil. A torn, tormented and guilt-ridden young lady struggling with the moral dilemma associated with a resolution of the question of whether "to abort or not to abort" will now have forced upon her one additional consideration to be added to the potpourii of social, economic, and moral forces pushing and tugging in opposite directions. Moreover, involvement of prestigious institutions and respected members of the scientific community coupled with implied governmental approval, as evidenced by the NIH funding of research in which utilization of the aborted fetus is crucial, combine to endow the abortion procedure with an aura of moral acceptability. Surely, in at least some instances, those factors will tip the decisionmaker's scales against preservation of the fetus.[1]

The Advisory Panel has endeavored to formulate recommendations designed both to safeguard fetal life and to permit support of potentially life-saving scientific research. The conclusions of the Advisory Panel reflect a balancing of those interests expressed through a policy of damage containment. Those conclusion[s] represent an attempt to discourage abortion to the fullest extent possible short of an outright ban on fetal tissue transplantation. The goal of nonenhancement of abortion is illusory; the attempt at approximation is laudable.[2]

Opposition to Federal funding of research projects involving use of fetal tissue obtained by means of induced abortions focuses upon three considerations:

1) No benefit may be derived from an act of such inherent immorality; the benefit itself constitutes a *malum per se.*

2) Federal funding constitutes complicity and collusion in the antecedent abortion even if the abortion would have been performed in the absence of a research program for which utilization of the abortus is required. Since the implication of endorsement is a necessary concomitant of funding, funding may be eschewed in order to avoid the collusion inherent in the funding relationship.

3) Research of this nature will inevitably effect an increment in the total number of abortions performed. Hence governmental funding is, in effect, application of societal resources to activities that will result in loss of additional fetal lives.

---

[1] It is certainly not uncommon for women generally disposed against abortion to decide to terminate an unwanted pregnancy. Such women are reported to experience a significant degree of cognitive dissonance. See Michael B. Brachen, "The Stability of the Decision to Seek Induced Abortion," *Research on the Fetus: Appendix,* HEW Publication No. (OS) 76-128, p. 16-15. Thus it is not surprising that conflict during decisionmaking is reported as being quite prevalent. *Ibid.,* p. 16-16. The percentage of women who undergo at least one change of decision with regard to abortion is reported to be approximately one third. *Ibid.,* pp. 16-2 and 16-16. Given the vacillation which is known to exist, any relevant factor may become decisive in reaching a decision. Although, in the absence of statistical data, it is impossible to predict the percentage of women to whom beneficial aspects of participation in fetal tissue transplantation projects may become the factor in the absence of which a final determination to abort would not occur, it is certain that for at least some women this will be the case.

[2] Regrettably, the recommendations of the Advisory Panel fall short of maximum approximation of this goal. Federal funding conveys an unintended message of moral approval for every aspect of the research program. The distinction between moral approval of use of the product of an already completed abortion and the abortion itself is extremely subtle and, even if expressly formulated, unlikely to be fully appreciated. Nevertheless, if left unarticulated, many more women will be left with the erroneous impression that induced abortion is condoned by the Federal Government as acceptable. For at least some of those women, this erroneous impression will have a decided effect upon their determination to undergo an abortion. The NIH should certainly take appropriate measures to counteract any such misimpression. Meaningful measures should be taken to assure that literature describing fetal transplant programs, press releases, and public information programs spell out this point with utmost clarity. The method most effective in assuring that this information is actually received by women involved in fetal tissue donation is to include a legend or notice to this effect in the consent form signed by the donor. The consent form might simply state that solicitation of the consent does not necessarily signify that any person, institution, or agency involved in the transplant procedure, or in its funding, approves the abortion procedure by means of which the tissue has become available.

It must be emphasized that these objections would not necessarily obtain in a situation involving organ tissue obtained from a homicide victim. Homicide is recognized by all, and commonly by the perpetrator himself, as a heinous offense and as a crime against society. From the societal perspective, homicide is aberrant behavior. Homicide is a crime and, if apprehended, the murderer will be prosecuted to the fullest extent of the law. Utilization of the body of the victim for scientific purposes could not conceivably be construed as an endorsement of the antecedent homicide. Nor could such utilization, or the contemplation of such utilization, possibly lead to an increase in the incidence of homicide. Abortion, on the other hand, is regarded in some sectors of our society as innocuous and condoned as a morally neutral act. Those who regard feticide as akin to homicide perforce view abortion, as presently performed, as socially sanctioned homicide. The wanton nature of the destruction of fetal life with societal approval imbues the moral offense with a gravity that greatly exceeds that of aberrant, socially condemned acts of homicide. Moreover, the sheer number of abortions required to sustain such research programs serves to magnify the immoral nature of the offense. We are confronted, not by isolated, individual acts of immorality in which the product of the act can be isolated from the act itself, but with programs and policies predicated upon the assumption that such acts are performed in inordinately large numbers, as a matter of course.

Each of the earlier enumerated objections is founded upon a cogent moral concern. *Ceteris paribus* each of those considerations may well be of sufficient moral gravity, in and of itself, to compel withholding of support for such research. However, the problem is rendered more complex by virtue of the fact that the lives of countless numbers of patients might be saved or prolonged by utilization of tissue derived from fetuses that would have been aborted regardless of whether or not such transplantation will take place subsequently. In this context, the question is not whether the procedure is or is not morally acceptable because of one or more of the previously enumerated considerations, but whether those considerations are of sufficient gravity to prevail over the moral imperative associated with the preservation of human life. Stated somewhat differently, the issue is whether policies designed to preserve human lives may be put into place with the knowledge that the inexorable effect will be the snuffing out of an undeterminable number of fetal lives.

Resolution of this dilemma will, in part, hinge upon the weight to be given preservation of human life as a value within a system of values. If rescue of an endangered human life is to be accepted as the dominant value to which all others are subservient, and if the immediacy of danger is regarded as establishing an immediate duty taking precedence over duties less immediate in nature, a compelling case can be made for utilization of an abortus for the rescue of a life at risk here and now on the grounds that the duty of preserving that life is immediate whereas the obligation to prevent the taking of fetal life is less compelling since, at the present moment, no fetal life is as yet at risk.

If, however, a system of values is posited in which preservation of human life is not the dominant value, an entirely different moral calculus emerges. In such a system homicide remains an unparalleled evil. Nonfeasance and malfeasance may well be regarded as occupying entirely disparate moral planes; acts of commission may indeed be regarded as entirely different in nature from acts of omission. In such a system, prevention of homicide—and of feticide—may well occupy a dominant position. Thus, society's duty to prevent destruction of fetal lives—a duty to prevent grave evil—may indeed become a far more weighty concern than the duty to enhance longevity anticipation.

A system of ethics which does not recognize an obligation to employ extraordinary means in the preservation of human life does not posit preservation of human life as the paramount moral value. Renunciation of an obligation to employ extraordinary means is nought but a tacit acknowledgement that other values are at least equal to the value of human life. Inordinate expense, pain, loss of limb, separation from family and familiar surroundings have all been held to constitute extraordinary means. Those considerations reflect values that, in such a value system, need not be sacrificed for prolongation of life. It may well be contended that utilization of an abortus for such purpose is "extraordinary" if for no other reason than that it will lead to an increase in loss of fetal life or, to state the same proposition in different terms, because prevention of feticide constitutes a value at least equal to and, arguably, greater than prolongation of life.

Our society, in its institutions, mores, and public policies, certainly regards enhancement of longevity anticipation as but one value among many—an important value, to be sure, but hardly as the paramount value to which all others are subordinated. Failure to regard prevention of wanton destruction of nascent life as a value at least on par with much lesser concerns that are permitted to interfere with and to negate the value inherent in prolongation of human life can only be the product of either a failure to appreciate the sanctity of fetal life or of a certain inconsistency in moral reasoning.

Moreover, the duty of preservation of life is rendered far less compelling by virtue of the fact that the projects for which funding is presently sought are experimental in nature. The procedures, as applied to humans, are essentially untried and untested; therapeutic benefit is, as yet, undetermined. The cost in terms of fetal life is far more certain than the therapeutic benefit. Furthermore, the benefit to prospective patients cannot be regarded as immediate. Assuming that the contemplated research is fruitful and will lead to development of therapies for various life-threatening illnesses, the benefits will be eventual rather than immediate. Procedures must be perfected and techniques honed before significant benefits can be anticipated.

To the extent that the duty to preserve life is compelling and takes precedence over other duties because the demand for rescue is present here and now, responsive action in the form of allocating societal resources for research programs cannot be subsumed under that imperative; scientific research cannot be regarded as commanded by virtue of the immediacy of the compelling demand to rescue human life.

The duty to embark upon such projects because of their lifesaving potential is thus diminished for two reasons: 1) the therapeutic efficacy of the procedure is unknown, and 2) the benefits will not accrue immediately but will become available only to future patients. The moral harm, on the contrary, is 1) known with a conviction approaching certainty, and 2) immediately attending upon, and triggered by, implementation of the social policy under consideration. On balance, the duty to refrain from a course of action that will have the effect of increasing instances of feticide must be regarded as the more compelling moral imperative.

Statement of Dissent *James Bopp Jr., Esq., and James Tunstead Burtchaell,*
C.S.C., Ph.D.

The report of this panel is essentially a series of answers to ten questions posed to the National Institutes of Health by the Assistant Secretary for Health. With the other panelists we have participated in the discussions and the drafting process, and have cast our votes for or against the various answers.

In a larger sense, however, the sum of it all is a single question: whether transplantation research using human fetal tissue derived from induced abortions is an acceptable act for sponsorship by an agency of the Federal Government. That great issue has not been dealt with adequately by the Report. Indeed, we believe it has been avoided. Hence the need to file this Dissent.

The Assistant Secretary for Health has ranked the questions he set before us, in order of significance, as ethical, legal, and scientific.

To begin with the matter of last priority, the hasty and unmethodical nature of our scientific inquiry[1] accredits us to do little more than report: 1) that compassionate advocates of those afflicted by various handicaps, diseases, and injuries ardently champion the resumption of transplantation research; 2) that scientists and clinicians are more cautious in their hope than are the advocates, at this early stage of research, about the therapeutic results it might yield; and 3) that we might all be disposed towards the proposed research were there no ethical objection to the source of the fetal tissue. That this research might be scientifically promising has not been at issue among us, though our collegial competence to make such a judgment at this time is incomplete.

Indeed, it was obvious that the scientists elected by the NIH to give testimony were long-term NIH beneficiaries, and they did little to spread before us any of the serious opposition being raised in the scientific literature to such research. For instance, we heard little of the more cautionary view held among scientists and clinicians, that in many applications there have not been adequate animal research trials using subhuman primates.[2]

---

[1] This panel has been asked to resolve matters of great import with much less time and resources than its two antecedent bodies, the Peel Commission in Great Britain (*The Use of Fetuses and Fetal Material for Research:* Report of the Advisory Group to the Department of Health and Social Security, Scottish Home and Health Department and the Welsh Office, 1972) and the DHEW Commission in the United States (*Report and Recommendations on Research on the Fetus:* The National Commission for the Protection of Human Subjects of Biomedical and Behavioral Research, 1975). Of the former, Peter J. McCullagh writes: "The Peel Report . . . was the product of six meetings. Its reading provides no grounds to disbelieve this. . . . My advice to the reader who remains unconvinced of its superficiality is that, to paraphrase the Report's comments on fetal tissue use, 'there is no substitute' for reading the original in its entirety. No attempt was made, in writing the Report, to attribute sources to any of the categorical statements it contains." (*The Fetus as Transplant Donor: Scientific, Social and Ethical Perspectives* [New York: Wiley/ Liss, 1987], 197). As for the latter report, Paul Ramsey has recounted how attempted evasions of the Freedom of Information Act and active disinformation by the NIH promoted its arrival at desired conclusions (*The Ethics of Fetal Research* [New Haven: Yale University Press, 1975], ch. 1).

[2] See, for instance, R. J. Joynt & Donald M. Gash, "Neural Transplants: Are We Ready?" *Annals of Neurology* 22 (1987): 455–56; John R. Sladek, Jr. & I. Shoulson, "Neural Transplantation: A Call for Patience Rather than Patients," *Science* 240 (1988): 1386–88; Roy A. E. Bakay & Daniel L. Barrow, "Neural Transplantation for Parkinson's Disease," *Journal of Neurosurgery* 69 (1988): 807–810. In this regard, Dr. Thomas Gill was one of only two experts to address the panel that expressed this view. He gave four cogent reasons why further animal studies might be needed before human trials were begun. Statement of Thomas J. Gill, *Panel Transcript*, 15 September 1988, 40–41. The reasons to postpone human fetal transplant research were neither refuted nor discussed by the swarm of experts who urged no delay.

Ascending to the next level of concern: the legal questions put to the panel should probably be answered by a group that can address them more rigorously than we have. What we do find is a pattern of State legislation which suggests substantial support for prohibiting or restricting the use of aborted fetal tissue in research.

But since the panel's advice is asked about Federal sponsorship through funding, not just about criminal statutes, larger public policy concerns must also claim our attention. It is true, as advocates reminded the panel repeatedly, that abortion is currently legal. But it is also true that for over a decade it has been the policy of the Federal Government not to allow taxpayers' money to subsidize abortions—by the Hyde Amendment. With the action of the 100th Congress, there is no longer any direct Federal subsidization of abortion. Moreover, the 1988 presidential proclamation affirming the personhood and right to life of the unborn,[3] the Title X family planning regulations which separate family planning programs from symbiotic relationships with abortion providers, the repeated attempts of the several States to reinstate some of the restrictions on abortion struck down by the *Wade* and *Bolton* decisions, and the consistent rejection of abortion on demand by public opinion during the past thirty years[4] all cast a very dark shadow over any government proposal to institutionalize a collaboration with the abortion industry.

Further reflection on the panel's responses and the Assistant Secretary's concerns makes it clear that both proponents and opponents understand that whether or not fetal tissue transplantation is scientifically plausible or legally permissible and/or well intentioned is beside the point if the procedure is ethically unacceptable to begin with. We cannot conclude, as the panel does, that because abortion and research that profits from abortion are legal and because the research is conducted with therapeutic intentions, it is therefore acceptable public policy for the government to sponsor it. This entirely sidesteps the ethical issue, or else it assumes that what is legal and well intentioned must be morally acceptable.

The question of overriding importance is whether the beneficial prospect of transplantation research is subverted by its association with elective abortion. For example, is the source of the fetal tissue inseparably linked to any uses subsequently made? Will fetal tissue transplants increase the probability that women who are ambivalent about

---

[3] Presidential Proclamation of 14 January 1988.

[4] Public opinion polls for nearly thirty years now manifest a stable ethical appraisal of abortion. One fifth of all adult Americans reject abortion except to spare the life of the mother. At the other end of the opinion spectrum, one fourth of the public accepts abortion on demand. The large population between those polar groups accepts abortion in the rare and difficult cases when pregnancy results from felonious intercourse (rape or incest). Abortion to avert the birth of a handicapped child usually receives less than a clear majority of affirmative opinion. These polls are frequently interpreted as showing that about 80% of all Americans accept abortion for some reasons. This is true but misleading, because the reasons they accept account for only perhaps 1% of all abortions performed. It is more accurate to read in the polls that 75% of the public considers about 99% of all present abortions to be unacceptable. This consistency of public opinion as manifest in Gallup, Harris, NORC, Yankelovich, *Newsweek,* and other polls has been chronicled by Professor Judith Blake of UCLA and Professor Raymond Adamek of Kent State University, the most capable analysts of opinion surveys on abortion in the 1960s and 1970s, and in the 1980s, respectively. See Blake and Jorge del Pinal, ''Predicting Polar Attitudes toward Abortion in the United States,'' in *Abortion Parley,* ed. James Tunstead Burtchaell (Kansas City: Andrews & McMeel, 1980), 27–56; Adamek, ''Abortion Policy: Time for Reassessment,'' *ibid.,* 1–26; *Abortion and Public Opinion in the United States* (Washington: NRL Educational Trust Fund, 1986). See also Burtchaell, *Rachel Weeping* (Kansas City: Andrews & McMeel, 1982), 96–105.

carrying their pregnancies to term will abort? Even assuming that direct involvement or close cooperation between the transplant team and the abortion industry were avoidable, is there a more moral complicity between them? These are only a few of the questions which must all be answered satisfactorily in order for this research to the considered ethically acceptable.

1)   First Argument: Lack of Rightful Consent[5]

Who can grant authentic consent for the use of electively aborted fetal remains? The panel proposes that the mother can do so. The usual understanding is that she would be acting as the parent/protector of her offspring, after she agrees to consent to the abortion. But when a parent resolves to destroy her unborn, she has abdicated her office and duty as the guardian of her offspring, and thereby forfeits her tutelary powers. She abandons her parental capacity to authorize research on that offspring and on his or her remains.

The late Paul Ramsey considered the plausibility of an aborting mother giving consent to have her unborn offspring's body used for research:

> *The fundamental model for legitimate parental consent in place of a child's is . . . proxy consent that is medically* on behalf of the child . . . *Parental consent is sought and is believed valid because parents are presumed to be "caretakers" for their infant children. Care is the attribute or virtue that qualifies parents as proxies, not strong or weak feelings, or strong or mild "interest"* . . . *It would be odd if we do not rescue from the deputyship of parents abortuses who have been abandoned by them as we would children abandoned in institutions.*[6]

He concludes that it is "morally outrageous," "a charade," to give to an aborting woman any legitimate standing to act as a protective proxy for that child's body. Though he was speaking of research on a still-living fetus, the moral force of his comments applies as well to permission to use aborted fetal remains.

This same point was made clearly by the President of the United States only a week ago in his letter to the spokesman for the group of more than 800 signatories of an appeal not to permit fetal transplantation research from aborted remains:

> *The use of any aborted child for these purposes raises the most profound ethical issues, especially because the person who would ordinarily authorize such use—the parent—deliberately renounces parenthood by choosing an abortion.*[7]

---

[5] Our remarks here are thus offered as primarily ethical, not legal. The Uniform Anatomical Gift Act appears to categorize unborn humans as subjects for research only if they are living. Consent for use of cadaverous fetal tissue is not treated under the ordinary legal norms for informed consent, but under those for disposition of human remains. But there are ethical obligations that restrict us from arbitrary seizure of another's bodies or property *post mortem*. For what follows on the subject of consent, see Burtchaell, "University Policy on Experimental Use of Fetal Tissue," *IRB: A Review of Human Subjects Research* 10,4 (July/August 1988): 7–11.

[6] Paul Ramsey, *The Ethics of Fetal Research* (New Haven: Yale University Press, 1975), 89–99 (emphasis in original).

[7] President Ronald Reagan, in a letter to Joseph R. Stanton, M.D., Brighton, Massachusetts, of the Value of Life Committee.

Ours is an ancient obligation to treat human remains—body and property—with deference. The body may be a mere corpse and the estate mere chattels, but our treatment of them—insofar as they are identifiable with the person who left them behind— takes on the color of our relationship to that person. "If the body is indivisible from that which makes up personhood, the same respect is due the body that is due persons."[8]

How we treat human remains is both a function and a cause of our bond with human persons. No one who remembers Mussolini's body hanging by the heels from a Milan lamppost could doubt it. The partisans were dishonoring his person, and enacting defiance against any future tyrant. Creon's insistence that Polyneice's corpse lie exposed and Antigone's determination to bury her brother at peril of her own life, are both quite personal actions: towards the dead youth and towards all whose spirits crave rest. John Kennedy's funeral and the disposal of Adolph Eichmann's remains both illustrate how our treatment of bodies is, in a powerful way, our definitive treatment of those they embodied.

If we honor a fellow human while she is living we have no choice but to honor her body after death. To confiscate it discredits all ostensible dignity we accorded that person *in vivo* and orients us to treat still other persons with contempt. Stephen Toulmin mentions the importance and the moral relevance of the "fear that any relaxation in the general feelings of reverence towards the tissues and remains of the dead and dying could give the color of extenuation to other forms of callousness, violence and human indifferences."[9] If my property is the extension of my person, then my body is my surrogate. Especially if one has had an ambiguous association with someone's death, to seize the dead person's remains for one's own purposes is the act that dissolves all ambiguity. When we forcibly requisition someone's body we are treating that person— not just his or her corpse—as of negligible dignity, or none.

There is nothing inherently unethical in research or experimentation upon the remains of humans who are victims of homicide, provided that consent is given, as is normally required, by the surviving guardian or next-of-kin and that the experiment does not enact indignity upon the deceased. But the very agents of someone's death are surely disqualified to act on the behalf or in the stead of the victim—disqualified as a man who has killed his wife is morally disqualified from acting as her executor. And in the case of a human abortus, it is the very guardians of the unborn who have collaborated in his or her destruction.

We must note one further point in this matter of maternal consent. The panel attempts to avoid this objection by proposing that the mother decides to donate her to-be-aborted offspring's remains for research in the way that a surviving relative can bury or otherwise dispose of a cadaver after death. Yet the panel recalls that tissue donation

---

[8] U.S. Congress, Office of Technology Assessment, *New Developments in Biotechnology: Ownership of Human Tissues and Cells—Special Report,* OTA-BA-337 (Washington, DC: U.S. Government Printing Office, 1987), 130. This study, which enjoyed the consultancy of four members of our panel, stated that if the Congress were to be guided by the view quoted, it should incline to the policy that commercialized sale and purchase of body parts ought to be prohibited. *Ibid.,* 15. This did prove to be the choice of the present Congress whose bill to that effect, the Organ Transplant Amendments Act of 1988, P.L. 100-607, was signed on 4 November 1988, during our panel's term of service; see also 42 U.S.C., sec. 274e.

[9] Stephen Toulmin, "Fetal Experimentation: Moral Issues and Institutional Controls," *Research on the Fetus: Appendix,* 10-11.

is commonly made either "by the decedent while alive or by the next of kin after his or her death." [10] As is well known, during one's lifetime no one but the person himself or herself can consent to donation of remains (unless empowered by protectorship of minor children or power of attorney or court-assigned wardship). To avoid the thrust of our argument about the abrogation of parental authority the panel treats the mother as one acting, not as a protector or proxy for her child, but as "next-of-kin." And since the scientific requirements for fetal tissue preservation practically require the consent to be made *ante mortem,* the panel's position associates itself with an ominous innovation: that within one's lifetime another person be legally permitted to assume authority, not as a protector exercising protective care, but as a survivor acting in her own interests. We can think of no sound precedent for putting a living human into the power of such an estranged person, not for his or her own welfare, but for the "interests" of the one in power.

IS THIS RESEARCH DISSOCIABLE FROM ABORTION?   We were presented with four distinct ethical defenses of the use of tissue obtained through induced abortion. Firstly, objections to scientific use of abortion-supplied body parts have repeatedly been characterized as strongly felt sentiment, "deeply charged with emotion." "Emotivism" is the name for this kind of moral reflection, if it can be called reflection at all, which "understands" the warrants for serious moral judgments to rest ultimately upon rationally undiscussible and irreconcilable desires or feelings. Thus the measure of rightness for any moral claim is not its coherence with a rationally defensible set of practical principles or their position relative to some objective "good," but the degree of emotional vehemence behind it. "Good will" replaces the good; "sincerity" displaces rational argument. In the discussion of fetal transplantation research, determined and disciplined moral discourse has been so regularly confused with emotion that one may fairly ask whether some advocates of this research believe that all ethical conviction is nothing more than passionate and irrational feeling.[11]

Another vindication of fetal research with aborted tissue was grounded on the assumption that our inward dispositions alone determine the ethical value of our behavior. Several senior research sponsors expressed to the panel their indignation that the work to which they had dedicated years of goodwill could be considered exploitative. They resented having their integrity appraised by reference to anything but their good intentions.[12]

A third ethical stance dealt with the abortion/transplantation matter as one devoid of morally relevant considerations. Its advocates behold the prospect of relieving handicap and affliction as so incomparably beneficial that any moral deficits are irrelevant. As the director of the American Parkinson Association has been quoted as saying, "The

---

[10] *Panel Report.* Answer to Question 4, Considerations.

[11] Dean Samuel Gorovitz, of Syracuse University, in his remarks to the panel, characterized those who oppose the use of fetal tissue from induced abortions for transplantation as "driven by a naive passion for simplicity . . . whose capacity to reason simply shuts down when they hear the word 'fetus'." Statement of Samuel Gorovitz, *Panel Transcript,* 15 September 1988, 479. Dr. Kenneth Ryan, the panel's chairman of scientific issues, is quoted in an article about the panel's deliberations as describing the antiabortion lobby as appealing to "a form of fundamentalism" that "foments hatred and violence." *The Washington Post: Health,* 18 October 1988, 4/19.

[12] See, e.g., Statement of Robert Stevenson, *Panel Transcript.* 15 September 1988, 543. One is reminded that it is not the goodness of the decisionmaker but the goodness of the decision that is morally relevant.

majority of people with the disease couldn't care less about the ethical questions—they just want something that works."[13]

These two approaches—which focus exclusively on the actor's motives or on the benefits to be derived from the therapy—take little account of the reason why we were called to consider these matters at Bethesda in the first place. The history of the abuse of human research subjects, from Tuskegee to Dachau to Willowbrook to Helsinki, cries out unambiguously that neither the goodwill of the researcher nor the prospective yield in beneficial knowledge has the slightest fingerhold on any moral right to relieve one human's affliction by exploiting another. That same abuse-marked history shows well that when scientists or therapists set out to exploit one group to benefit another, it is invariably the disadvantaged who suffer for the powerful.

It was the fourth defense of transplantation research that was most thoughtfully argued and the one which the panel adopted. After conceding that "(i)t is of moral relevance that human fetal tissue for research has been obtained from induced abortions," the panel endorsed the use of aborted fetal remains for transplantation based upon a utilitarian calculus[14] of the "significant medical goals" which the research seeks to achieve.[15] The panel thus sought to dissociate the research from abortion in numerous ways: informed consent for the research must be distinct from and subsequent to consent for the abortion; even preliminary information about tissue donation should be withheld from the pregnant woman before she consents to the abortion; the procedures of abortion should be kept independent from the retrieval and use of fetal tissue: no financial compensation should be offered to parents or providers for aborted remains; parents must not be permitted to designate or to know the identity of the beneficiaries of their aborted children's tissue; no abortion and donation should be permitted between relatives, lest a child be conceived for this purpose; and abortion procedures should not be altered to accommodate the transplantation.

The panel thus attempts to evade the ethical issue by sequestering fetal tissue research from the broader matter concerning abortion. The research problem is thereby reduced to a legal or scientific one, and the only moral problems left are procedural ones. Indeed, in its central recommendation, it reaches an ethical conclusion on legal and scientific grounds:

> *It is of moral relevance that human fetal tissue for research has been obtained from induced abortions. However, in light of the fact that abortion is legal and that the research in question is intended to achieve significant medical goals, the panel concludes that the use of such tissue is acceptable public policy.*[16]

---

[13] In Richard John Neuhaus, "The Return of Eugenics," *Commentary* 85,4 (April 1988): 18.

[14] Inexplicably missing from this utilitarian calculation are the morbidity and mortality risks to the recipient of the transplant, which are reported as "high." Rick Weiss (quoting Donald M. Gash of the University of Rochester), "Fetal-Cell Transplants Show Few Benefits," *Science News* 134 (1988): 324.

[15] That fetal tissue transplantation may be longer on promise than on results was reported at the annual meeting of the Society for Neuroscience (18 November 1988) where researchers conceded that few of the patients who have received fetal tissue transplants for Parkinson's disease have shown defined clinical improvement. In the case of those who have shown some improvement it was difficult to resolve whether the transplants were responsible. As a result, more animal studies were called for. *Ibid.*

[16] *Panel Report,* Answer to Question 1. In several of its segments the report reaches ethical conclusions grounded on considerations that are exclusively legal or scientific.

The only signifiant ethical claim propounded in the *Panel Report* is a negative one: that human fetal tissue transplantation research is ethically so isolated from the abortion which delivers up its supplies that there is no moral connection between the two. It is that claim, which is stated but not argued, that we undertake here to discredit.

Advocates of this use of fetal tissue have acknowledged that induced abortion is a "tragedy," that they regret or even deplore it, but that the use of human flesh supplied by induced abortion implies no moral agency in that abortion. Research can then draw some benefit for medical science from what might otherwise have been an unrelieved tragedy. Death was not the scientists' doing. Indeed it was they who turned one victim's death into another victim's recovery. And by establishing various barriers between abortion and tissue use, they imply that a sort of moral autoclave will sterilize the tissue ethically so that it can be used without contamination by association with its method of supply.[17]

We contend that this attempt is futile, and that the appropriation of aborted human fetal remains for transplantation research effectively allies itself to the abortion industry in two distinct ways. We note that our argument runs in close concurrence with the dissenting statement of Rabbi J. David Bleich, a member of the panel.

2) Second Argument: An Incentive for Future Abortions

We must now ask whether the institutionalized use of aborted human remains will foreseeably constitute an endorsement that will effectively increase the incidence of abortion in our land.

This could happen in two ways. First, fetal tissue transplantation would further entrench the abortion industry by the symbiotic relationship which would arise between it, the medical community, and the beneficiaries of fetal tissue transplants.[18] Second, the widespread use of fetal tissue transplantation could reasonably be expected to increase abortions, since knowledge of transplantation will induce some women to have abortions, who would otherwise not do so. In other words, this research may constitute complicity with abortion before the fact.

Successful fetal transplantation therapies will require the systematic acquisition of fetal tissue from abortion clinics and hospitals. To ensure that fetal tissues are fresh, the process of tissue acquisition must be integrated into the procedures of the abortion clinic, so that the woman's consent to the use of fetal tissue would be obtained before the abortion and the fetal remains collected and processed immediately afterwards. If this process is conducted by tissue acquisition personnel who are not abortion clinic employees, their presence on site at the clinic would be required.[19]

---

[17] The panel makes its recommendations in the belief "that these abortions would occur regardless of their use in research, that neither the researcher nor the recipient would have any role in inducing or performing the abortion, and that a woman's abortion decision would be insulated from inducements to abort to provide tissue for transplant research and therapy." *Panel Report,* Answer to Question 1, Considerations. The panel however provides no evidence or analysis to support the belief that the guidelines will actually have such an effect. It thus assumes that which is most seriously contested.

[18] One witness before the panel predicted that "as various interest groups become accustomed to and dependent upon supplies of fetal tissue they will inevitably seek to enforce their right to this material." *Idem* (quoting Stuart A. Newman of the New York Medical College), "Forbidding Fruits of Fetal-Cell Research," *Ibid.* 134 (1988): 297.

[19] The intimate relationship between tissue acquisition personnel and the abortion clinic was illustrated in the first fetal tissue transplant for Parkinson's disease by Dr. Curt Freed of the University of Colorado in

There would arise, therefore, a symbiotic relationship between the abortion indus-try and fetal tissue transplantation therapy. Transplants and transplant research could not proceed without the assurance that the abortion industry will continue to produce suffi-cient fetal tissue in the future. The nation's medical establishment would thereby rec-oncile itself with the abortionists it has so far disdained, and some of the most enter-prising intellectuals in medical research and practice would enter into partnership with the abortion industry as the supplier of preference for one of their most venturesome, and perhaps promising, endeavors. The dignity and prestige this relationship confers upon the abortion trade should not be underestimated.

Beyond the institutional respectability which would be conferred upon the abortion industry is the effect of fetal tissue acquisition upon the practice and incidence of abor-tion. If fetal tissue transplantation from induced abortion becomes common, the inci-dence of abortion can reasonably be expected to increase from a combination of benef-icent reasons motivating pregnant women who are ambivalent about abortion and financial incentives motivating abortion clinics.

Ambivalence toward abortion is a well documented reaction of many women when confronted with a problem pregnancy.[20] A period of intense anxiety and ambivalence is often experienced during the 24 hours preceding an abortion.[21] This ambivalence is reflected in the fact that from one-fourth[22] to approximately one-half[23] of women abort-ing find the decision difficult to make. In addition, in studies of pregnant women who chose to abort and others who chose to deliver their children, approximately one-third[24] to 40 percent of the women, whatever their ultimate decision, were reported to have changed their decision at least once, with women who aborted being significantly more likely to report their decision as a relatively difficult one, to rethink their initial choice, and to regret having to have made that decision.[25] Some women who have made an initial decision to abort will change their minds at the last minute, with approximately five percent changing their minds after making an appointment to have an abortion[26]

November 1988. In order to obtain desirable fetal neural tissue, Freed spent four days at the abortion clinic "drinking coffee all day and looking at tissue that was unacceptable." Thomas H. Maugh II (quoting Freed), "Doctor Who Broke Restriction on Fetal Tests Under Attack," *Los Angeles Times,* 21 November 1988, I/3. During his time at the clinic, Freed was not only looking for the presence of "a portion of the brain tissue that hasn't been destroyed that is potentially useful," but also examining the fetal remains to ensure that the abortions were complete, a procedure normally performed by an abortion clinic employee. Leslie Bond (quoting Freed), "First U.S. Fetal Brain Tissue Transplant Performed," *NRL News,* 5 Decem-ber 1988, 1.

[20] David C. Reardon, *Aborted Women* (Westchester, IL: Crossway, 1987), 71; Joyce L. Dunlop, "Counselling of Patients Requesting an Abortion," *The Practitioner* 220 (1978): 847; Michael B. Bracken & Stanislav V. Kasl, "Delay in Seeking Induced Abortion: A Review and Theoretical Analysis," *American Journal of Obstetrics and Gynecology* 121 (1975): 1008.

[21] Carol Nadleson, "Abortion Counseling: Focus on Adolescent Pregnancy," *Pediatrics* 54 (1974): 768.

[22] Thomas D. Kerenyi, Ellen L. Glascock, and Marjorie L. Horowitz, "Reasons for Delayed Abortion: Results of Four Hundred Interviews," *American Journal of Obstetrics & Gynecology* 117 (1973): 307.

[23] Michael B. Bracken, "The Stability of the Decision to Seek Induced Abortion," *Research on the Fetus: Appendix,* 16–3.

[24] *Ibid.,* 16–16.

[25] Michael B. Bracken, Lorraine V. Klerman, and Mary Ann Bracken, "Abortion, Adoption, or Motherhood: An Empirical Study of Decision-Making During Pregnancy," *American Journal of Obstetrics & Gynecol-ogy* 130 (1978): 256–57.

[26] Editor's Note, *Obstetrics & Gynecological Survey* (1977), 97.

and approximately one percent changing their minds at the abortion clinic itself.[27] Significantly, studies reveal that from 24 percent[28] to 37 percent[29] of women who abort do not make up their minds until just before the procedure.

Women's decision to abort is influenced by multiple reasons: four, on the average.[30] For those women who are ambivalent about abortion—that is, the 40 percent of the pregnant women who have changed their minds at least once and who have found the abortion decision difficult—"the pros and cons of the decision were somewhat evenly balanced" regardless of which decision is made.[31] Most women who decide to abort are uncertain about and uncommitted to their abortion decision. For them, abortion is a "marginal good," at best.[32]

In the abortion decision, there are two important motives which may influence the choice: concern for self and concern for others. The most common motivation for abortion is self-centered concerns. In the most recent study of specific reasons which contributed to the decision to abort, a majority of women reported that they were influenced to have an abortion because they were concerned about how having a baby could change their lives, they could not afford a baby now, and they were having problems with a relationship or wanted to avoid single parenthood.[33] Some women also felt that they were unready for responsibility, or not mature enough, or had all the children they wanted.[34]

Concern for others is reflected in the decision of those women who said that others' wishes figured in their decision. More than one in five women chose to have an abortion at least in part because their husband or partner wanted them to.[35] About one-quarter of married women were influenced by their husband's desire for an abortion and more than one-quarter of those under 18 were influenced by their parents' wishes.[36] Thus women seeking abortion are influenced by a number of reasons, often in combination, that reflect both concern for self and concern for others.[37]

---

[27] Bracken, "Stability," 16–16.

[28] M. Diamond, P. G. Steinhoff, J. A. Palmore, et al., "Sexuality, Birth Control and Abortion: A Decision-Making Sequence," *Journal of Biosocial Science* 5 (1973): 347.

[29] Reardon, 15.

[30] Aida Torres and Jacqueline D. Forrest, "Why Do Women Have Abortions?" *Family Planning Perspectives* 20,4 (1988): 175.

[31] Bracken et al., "Abortion, Adoption or Motherhood," 256.

[32] Reardon, 15.

[33] Torres and Forrest, 170.

[34] *Ibid.*

[35] *Ibid.*, 176.

[36] *Ibid.*

[37] Recent court cases indicate that some women may also be motivated by malice. In *Conn v. Conn,* a court found that a pregnant woman was willing to carry the child to term if she could be sure that her husband, against whom she had filed a marriage dissolution action, could not gain custody of the child when born. She said she would carry the child to term if her husband would agree to put the child up for adoption by a third party, foreign to the marriage. *Conn v. Conn,* No 73C01-8806-DR-127, slip op. at 4 (Shelby County [Ind] Cir. Ct. June 27, 1988), *rev'd,* 525 N.E.2d 612 (Ind. Ct. App. 1988), *aff'd and opinion of app. ct. adopted by order,* No. 73S01-8807-CV-631 (Ind. July 15, 1988).

In addition, the self-centered reasons of some pregnant women are immature and even frivolous. In a court case where an unwed father attempted to prevent his girlfriend from having an abortion, the court found that the reasons why she sought an abortion included the desire not to be pregnant in the summertime so as to look good in a bathing suit and not have an impaired social life, and a desire not to share the father

Fetal tissue transplantation from induced abortions is possessed of strong potential to increase abortions by providing both selfish and selfless reasons for abortion.

The American Bar Foundation's Lori B. Andrews, a witness before the panel, has argued that a woman should be able to sell the tissue of the fetus she has agreed to abort,[38] in part because this will make more body parts available.[39] The sale of human embryos for cosmetic production has already been reported and kidneys for transplantation from live donors in Brazil and India have been advertised for sale to physicians in Germany.[40] One bioethicist who addressed the panel has acknowledged that "poor women in nations where markets are permitted in organs and tissues might seek abortion for financial gain."[41] Thus if more fetal tissue is needed, "policies aimed at maximizing the utilization of infants as donors could lead to increases in the number of elective abortions."[42]

Selfless motivation can also lead to an increased incidence of abortion. A person is motivated by concern for others when the person cares for the welfare of others, as a matter of genuine concern.[43] Concern for others is manifested when the person views her own welfare as bound up in the welfare of others, when the welfare of others is of positive concern to her in its own right, and when she gives so much weight to the welfare of others that she is prepared in principle to subordinate her own welfare to that of others.[44] In each of these cases, the person is motivated by concern for others, *"because their welfare is at issue."*[45] The motivation comes into operation when the person has "internaliz(ed) the welfare of another by way of prizing it on the basis of the relationship that subsists between them—a relationship that may be as tenuous as mere common humanity."[46]

It is reasonable to expect that this selfless motivation, when placed in the balance with all other reasons, will tip the balance in favor of abortion for some women who are ambivalent. Advocates for fetal tissue transplantation have themselves argued that this will provide "some solace" to those having abortions, since it will enable them "to help others with whose plight they can well empathize."[47] One physician who testified before the panel reported that women who are to abort consent to fetal tissue transplantation because they are "glad something positive could come out of it."[48] Indeed, one bioethicist claims that "There's a strong argument that intending to use tissue to relieve someone else's disease is a better ethical act than having an abortion just because you forgot to use a diaphragm."[49] Thus, a powerful human motivation will

---

with anyone, including their baby. *In the Matter of Unborn Child H*, No. 84C01-8804-HP-185, slip op. at 2 (Vigo County [Ind] Cir. Ct., Apr. 8, 1988), *rev'd sub nom. Doe v. Smith*, No. 84A01-8804-CV-00112 (Ind. Ct. App. 1988).

[38] Lori B. Andrews, "My Body, My Property," *Hastings Center Report*, Oct. 1986, 28.

[39] Rorie Sherman, "The Selling of Body Parts," *National Law Journal*, Oct. 7, 1987, 32.

[40] Alan Fine, "The Ethics of Fetal Tissue Transplants," *Hastings Center Report*, June/July 1988, 7.

[41] Arthur Caplan, "Should Fetuses or Infants be Utilized as Organ Donors?" *Bioethics* 1 (1987): 135.

[42] *Ibid.*

[43] Nicholas Rescher, *Unselfishness* (London: Feffer & Simons, 1975), 9.

[44] *Ibid.*

[45] *Ibid.*, 6 (emphasis in original).

[46] *Ibid.*, 7.

[47] Caplan, 128.

[48] Statement of Lars Olson, *Panel Transcript.* 14 September 1988, 58.

[49] Karen Matthews (quoting Prof. Marjorie Schultz), "Fetal Cell Research Under Fire," *Alameda Times*, 27 March 1988, 1.

be thrown into the balance for women considering abortion: concern for others. The decision to abort, once difficult and troubling, becomes, for some, a noble and selfless act of "doing good for humanity."

In addition to concern for humanity in general there is concern for a family member. Reports have surfaced concerning women who considered getting pregnant to provide tissue to treat themselves or a family member,[50] and prominent bioethicists have argued that this is ethical.[51] This has led one proponent to conclude that a concern that "the use of fetal tissue for transplantation in such cases could become an incentive for abortion . . . appears well grounded,"[52] and another called it "a serious concern that ought to give us pause."[53]

The panel acknowledges that "knowledge of the possibility for using fetal tissue in research and transplantation might constitute motivation, reason, or incentive for a pregnant woman to have an abortion." As a result, the panel recommends that "even the provision of preliminary information for tissue donation" should not be volunteered to the pregnant woman.[54] This recommendation does not address the problem, however, as the panel itself inadvertently acknowledges. Proponents of fetal tissue transplantation from induced abortion claim that it holds "the promise of becoming a revolutionary therapy for millions of people suffering from a number of diseases."[55] Thus the panel admits that "transplantation and research with fetal tissue will become general knowledge." Even the relatively rare occurrence of infant organ transplant is now well enough known through reports in the media. As a result, many parents of dying infants are reported to request on their own that their child serve as an organ donor.[56] If many are helped by fetal tissue transplantation from induced abortions, the knowledge of it would be even more widespread, and thus, as the panel finds, "might be one of many reasons to be weighed in deciding whether to terminate a pregnancy."[57]

For those few woman seeking abortion who are unaware of fetal tissue transplantation, current abortion practice suggests that they will be informed by abortion clinic personnel, reinforcing the abortion decision previously made and decreasing the number of those women who would change their minds. The vast majority of first trimester abortions are performed in free-standing clinics, many for profit, which offer no alternative solutions for an unintended pregnancy. Abortion clinic patients are counseled by abortion clinic employees, not physicians. The patient does not meet the physician until she is on the operating table, prepared for an abortion. Under current law, the pregnant

---

[50] "A Balancing Act of Life and Death," *Time*, Feb. 1, 1988, 49; Tamar Lewin, "Medical Use of Fetal Tissue Spurs New Abortion Debate," *New York Times*, Aug. 16, 1987, 1.

[51] Mary Anne Warren, Daniel C. Maguire, and Carol Levine, "Can the Fetus Be an Organ Farm?" *Hastings Center Report*, Oct. 1978, 23–25.

[52] Fine, 6.

[53] Rick Weiss (quoting Kathleen Nolan of the Hastings Center), "Forbidding Fruits of Fetal-Cell Research," *Science News* 134 (1988): 297.

[54] *Panel Report*, Answer to Question 3.

[55] Statement of H. Fred Voss, 14 September 1988, *Panel Transcript*, 173.

[56] Caplan, 128.

[57] *Panel Report*. Answer to Question 3, Considerations. Ironically, while acknowledging that this information will serve to motivate some to abort, the panel thought it should be provided to her before the decision to abort, if she asked. Indeed, one panel witness argued that if a pregnant woman asks about fetal tissue transplantation there is a moral obligation to provide such information—"even when one knows in advance that it will sway [her into an abortion]." Statement of Alan Meisel, *Panel Transcript*, 15 September 1988, 463.

woman can consent to abortion for any reason and this consent is obtained by abortion clinic employees.[58] The role of the abortion clinic counselor is to "support the patient and the [abortion] decision she has made"; counselors are admonished not to open "new issues of conflict, or to reawaken . . . ambivalence."[59] Thus abortion counselors act as "facilitators" who are not to "inform" their clients, but only to help them "make the choice for abortion with the least amount of pain and doubt."[60] The prospect of fetal tissue transplantation, therefore, offers a powerful argument in the hands of abortion clinic counselors: "doing good for humanity" is a powerful additional reason to go through with the abortion.

The actions by the Supreme Court are generally believed to have increased abortions in this country by legalizing them. A reasonable reckoning is that there are perhaps about five times as many abortions annually after *Wade* and *Bolton* as before.[61] We are persuaded, however, that the Court unwittingly had as much ethical influence as it did legal. The action which decriminalized abortion also drew the cloak of powerful moral approbation over a practice that had been inhibited even more by shame than by criminal penalty.

It is willful fantasy to imagine that young pregnant women estranged from their families and their sexual partners and torn by the knowledge that they are with child but do not want that child, will not be powerfully relieved at the prospect that the sad act of violence they are reluctant to accept can now have redemptive value. Governmental sponsorship of research with tissue supplied by the abortion industry is likely to be the most persuasive, implicitly moral, accolade given to abortion since *Roe v. Wade*.

Fetal tissue transplantation can also be reasonably expected to increase abortions due to financial incentives motivating abortion clinics. If fetal tissue transplants are successful, the supply would not begin to meet the demand. For the transplant of fetal pancreatic tissue as a treatment for diabetes, for example, only 10,000 tissue recipients[62] could be benefited, based upon current abortion rates, whereas over 2,000,000 diabetic patients[63] might desire such transplants if the technique proved successful. For the transplant of fetal neural tissue for the treatment of Parkinson's disease, only 10,280 fetal transplants[64] could be expected from aborted fetal tissue compared with 300,000 to

---

[58] Some institutions now obtain consent from the woman to use the fetal tissues at the same time the consent to the abortion is obtained. Statement of Robert J. Levine, *Panel Transcript,* 15 September 1988, 421.

[59] Nadleson, 768.

[60] Reardon, 270.

[61] Burtchaell, *Rachel Weeping,* 90–96.

[62] The fetal pancreas most suitable for transplantation is retrieved from fetuses of 16 to 20 weeks gestation. Statement of Kevin Lafferty, *Panel Transcript,* 14 September 1988, 83. Approximately 50,000 abortions are performed during this period under current practices. Centers for Disease Control, *Morbidity and Mortality Weekly Report,* Feb. 1987, 12ss–13ss. Assuming a consent rate of 80 to 90 percent (Voss, 204), and a retrieval rate of 90 percent, then approximately 40,000 fetal pancreata from induced abortion in the United States would be available for transplant. Assuming four fetal pancreata are needed for one successful transplant (estimates range from one to two [Olson, 107–8] to 25 [Thomas H. Maugh II, quoting Brent Formby of the Sansum Medical Research Center, Santa Barbara, CA, "Use of Fetal Tissue Stirs Hot Debate," *Los Angeles Times,* Apr. 16, 1988, 28]), then only 10,000 transplants could take place yearly under current practices.

[63] Statement of Hans Sollinger, *Panel Transcript,* 14 September 1988, 100.

[64] The optimal fetal neural tissue for transplantation is of 7 to 10 weeks gestation. Olson, 65. Approximately 635,000 abortions are performed during this period. Stanley K. Henshaw, "Characteristics of U.S. Women Having Abortions, 1982–1983," *Family Planning Perspective* 19 (Jan./Feb. 1987): 6. Assuming a consent rate of 80 to 90 percent (Voss, 204) and a retrieval rate of nine percent (as experienced by the British

500,000 patients who could potentially demand the benefits of such transplants.[65] Thus a dramatic disparity would exist between supply and demand: only .5 percent of diabetes patients could be treated with fetal transplants, and only 2.5 percent of those with Parkinson's disease.

If tissue supplied by abortion is adequate and if transplantation should be successful, it is expected to become big business. Hana Biologics estimates that the total potential market in treating diabetes and Parkinson's disease, using fetal tissue from induced abortions, exceeds $6 billion. Hana anticipates sales of insulin-producing cells in 1989 at a price of $5,000 per treatment.[66] Thus an extremely lucrative market would be created for fetal tissue from induced abortion which currently does not exist.

Abortion clinics gross perhaps $250 million annually from first-trimester abortions.[67] Currently, nonprofit fetal organ acquisition organizations offer $25 per fetal organ.[68] Since at least four fetal organs are currently being actively procured, the fetal pancreas, brain, adrenal gland, and liver,[69] abortion clinics stand to reap a substantial increase in revenue from each abortion.

The effect of these financial incentives, even at the current low price for fetal organs, would be dramatic and direct. With demand constant and overwhelming, the incentive to increase the supply of aborted fetal tissue will be great.[70] In this respect, transplants of fetal organs differ dramatically from transplants of organs from deceased adults. The number of dead adults is not likely to increase because there is a need for organ transplants. Homicides are not likely to be committed to gain access to human organs since society condemns and severely punishes such homicides. Abortions, however, are legal and, some claim, ethical. Some women who would otherwise decide not to have an abortion can be persuaded to do so. Abortion clinics will have substantial financial incentives to do so. Even some advocates of fetal tissue transplants from induced abortion admit that "successful therapeutic use of fetal brain tissue, once widely available, may indeed influence a woman's abortion decision," but they argue that "it would be improvident to legislate against them," since it is impractical to ascertain motives.[71] Indeed, under the current state of the law, States could not prohibit abortion clinic personnel from discussing fetal tissue transplants when obtaining consent to

---

Medical Research Council Tissue Bank, Written Statement of Leslie Wong, 12), approximately 51,400 fetal brains from induced abortions would be available for transplantation. If five to ten fetal brains are needed for sufficient neural tissue for one successful transplant (Statement of Thomas J. Gill, *Panel Transcript*, 14 September 1988, 46), sufficient fetal tissue would be available yearly for, at most, only 10,280 transplants.

[65] Statement of Harold Klawans, *Panel Transcript*, 14 September 1988, 278.

[66] Karen Southwick, "Fetal Tissue Market Draws Profits, Rebuke," *Health Week*, Oct. 12, 1987, 1.

[67] Based on approximately 1,426,000 abortions a year at $175 per procedure. Henshaw, 6.

[68] Statement of Leatrice Ducat, *Panel Transcript*, 14 September 1988, 188.

[69] Voss, *ibid.*, 190.

[70] Harvey Cohen, representing the American Academy of Pediatrics, recognized that "successful fetal transplantation therapies may lead to the demand for such tissue exceeding supply, as has occurred with other organ transplantation." His solution to the problem is the development of methods for growing fetal cells in the laboratory which could reduce the need for donors. Statement of Harvey Cohen, *Panel Transcript*, 15 September 1988, 547–48. Since fetal transplant therapy and therapy from cell cultures are both predicted to be available in a decade, and since therapies from cell cultures present no ethical concerns and can provide sufficient supply to meet an unlimited need for such tissue, there is no need to pursue fetal tissue transplants, which are ethically dubious, at best.

[71] Fine, 7.

abortion[72] and the reasons for abortion are not subject to State regulation. Unless abortion clinics themselves are prohibited from purveying fetal organs, a restriction which this panel has refused to recommend,[73] substantial financial incentives will exist for abortion clinics to encourage abortions. Abortions, therefore, are bound to increase.[74]

A final troubling tissue raised by fetal issue transplantation from induced abortion is the potential for obtaining tissue from live fetuses. Fetal tissue degenerates as soon as it is without oxygen.[75] Therefore, fetal research using animals has involved removing tissues directly from living animal fetuses or abortuses. Some bioethicists argue that the use of organs or tissues from nonviable but live fetuses "is morally defensible if dead fetuses are not available or are not conducive to successful transplants."[76] In support of this view, other bioethicists, including some members of this panel, have suggested that a new definition of death—and of life—should be crafted: one based upon the degree of neocortical function of the child, particularly if post-mortem donation of tissue will not yield viable organs.[77]

Some researchers in the field have already accepted this new definition of fetal life. One physician involved in fetal research expressed his view to the panel that fetal life does not exist until the three conditions of human personhood exist: cognition, volition, and sensation of pain, which are determined in the neocortex of the brain.[78] Thus he objected to the use of the word "life" to refer to fetal existence until viability.[79] During nonviability the fetus is not "alive" and thus fetal tissue could be taken from the fetus as if it were "dead."[80] With a need for fetal tissue "the fresher the better," these

---

[72] *Akron v. Akron Center for Reproductive Health,* 462 U.S. 416, 442–445 (1983).

[73] While the panel recommends that "payments . . . associated with the procurement of fetal tissue should be prohibited," abortion clinics could be paid "reasonable expenses occasioned by the actual retrieval, storage, preparation and transportation of the tissues." *Panel Report,* Response to Question 1. Based upon current practices, the $25 fee per organ, which the panel characterized as "a small fee for each fetal tissue retrieved to cover the costs of retrieval, including time of staff and rental of space," *ibid.,* Answer to Question 7, could amount to an additional fee of $100 per abortion, a potential increase in revenue of 57 percent to the abortion clinic.

[74] Several members of the panel claim that this predicted impact "is highly speculative" but then argue that it will not occur "to any significant extent." John A. Robertson et al., Concurring Statement, 36. That they consider a prospective increase in abortions, however, to be of negligible concern in the final analysis is revealed when they say that even "if there were a substantial increase in the number of abortions . . . such transplants might still be ethically and legally acceptable" (footnote 21). Since one principal effort of the panel was to ensure that fetal tissue transplantation did not encourage induced abortion, because, in part, of "the morality of abortion itself," a reasonably foreseeable increase in induced abortions, of whatever magnitude, should render the practice of fetal tissue transplantation morally unacceptable. With 40 percent of pregnant women at risk, however, there is likely to be a significant effect.

[75] Statement of Kevin Lafferty, *Panel Transcript,* 14 September 1988, 104–5.

[76] Mary B. Mahowald, Jerry Silver, and Robert A. Ratcheson, "The Ethical Options in Transplanting Fetal Tissue," *Hastings Center Report,* Feb, 1987, 12.

[77] John C. Fletcher, John A. Robertson, and Michael R. Harrison, "Primates and Anencephalics as Sources for Pediatric Organ Transplants," *Fetal Therapy* 1 (1986): 158; LeRoy Walters, "Ethical Issues in Fetal Research: A Look Back and A Look Forward," *Clinical Research* 36 (1988): 213. While these proposals are often suggested in the context of taking tissues from anencephalic infants, it would also be applied to "anencephalic fetuses—with the result that tissue or organ transplantation from such intact fetuses would become feasible." Walters, *ibid.*

[78] Statement of William Lyman, *Panel Transcript,* 15 September 1988, 428–29.

[79] *Ibid.,* 430.

[80] Some would take this even farther, by applying "non-viable" "not only to anencephalic infants, but also

views provide a justification for taking tissues from live fetuses. When tissue procurement is to be conducted by abortion practitioners already committed to the destruction of these live fetuses, the potential for abuse becomes overwhelming.

The majority of the panel implies that fetal tissue transplants, if successful, could have the effect of encouraging abortion, since it recommends various "guidelines" by which it hopes to "minimize" such risk. This is a vain hope. Support for fetal tissue transplantation using aborted fetuses is premised upon the hope that fetal tissue transplantations will be successful, in large part due to NIH sponsorship, and thus will move from research to applied therapies. Whether it can then be conducted in an ethically appropriate manner is a critical question. NIH must consider not only the conduct of its sponsored research but the reasonably foreseeable consequences if its sponsored research leads to useful therapies.

In this case, the guidelines proposed by the panel will be irrelevant to the actual practice of fetal transplant therapy, since NIH regulations apply only to entities receiving NIH grant funds. Most abortion clinics receive no NIH funds and are not subject to its requirements. Nor is it reasonable to expect that most abortion clinics will voluntarily comply with NIH recommended guidelines; the market forces previously described, supported by the justifications already provided by those who favor such practices, provide powerful incentives to increase the supply of fetal tissue. Only the enactment of new laws, in all fifty States and the District of Columbia, could compel compliance with the guidelines recommended by this panel, an unlikely prospect and certainly one beyond the NIH's power.[81]

Even for those bound by NIH regulations, two of the most significant guidelines recommended by this panel are either unenforceable or irrelevant. The panel recommends that the process of obtaining consent to the use of fetal tissue be deferred until after the decision to terminate the pregnancy has been made. Enforcement of this requirement would require NIH personnel to monitor counseling sessions in the abortion clinic, an unlikely and problematic process. In addition, the panel has recommended that the pregnant woman not be offered any financial incentive for consenting to the use of fetal tissue. This requirement is simply unenforceable. If an abortion clinic has agreed to sell fetal organs, it could reduce its price for abortion services, in effect splitting the proceeds from the sale of fetal organs with its patients. This lower price for abortion services, offered to all clients (but with the expectation that 80 to 90 percent would consent to the use of fetal tissues), would be a financial incentive for abortion, but one

---

to fetuses or individuals whose imminent death is unavoidable." Mahowald et al., "Ethical Options," 13. Since the imminent death of fetuses destined for induced abortion is, under current law, "unavoidable," then all live fetuses would be non-viable—thus dead—and subject to removal of their organs.

[81] The assumption that there will be any "voluntary" compliance with NIH guidelines by those not bound by them was discredited on 9 November 1988 when Dr. Curt Freed of the University of Colorado performed a fetal tissue transplant from an aborted fetus into a patient suffering from Parkinson's disease. Thomas H. Maugh II, "Doctor Who Broke Restriction on Fetal Tests Under Attack," *Los Angeles Times,* 21 November 1988, I/3. Dr. Freed, using private funds, ignored the NIH moratorium during which this panel was to develop guidelines for research. Freed is reported to have performed the transplant "strictly for scientific reasons." The transplant was praised by the chairman of the medical advisory board of the American Parkinson Disease Association as "courageous." "First Brain-to-Brain Transplant Patient Goes Home," UPI wire story, 24 November 1988. That there will be many "courageous" entrepreneurs prepared to ignore NIH guidelines if fetal transplantation should become successful, cannot be disputed.

which could not be regulated. In addition, this recommendation is irrelevant. As noted above, it is the financial incentives to abortion clinics, not pregnant women, which are the larger problem.[82]

Thus the proposed procedural mechanisms will not ensure that the use of fetal tissue after induced abortions does not affect the decision to abort. One can reasonably expect that more induced abortions will result from the decision to use aborted fetal tissues[83] for transplantation.

3) Third Argument: Complicity with Abortions Already Performed

It is the assumption of the panel that transplantation research with fetal tissue from induced abortions neither implies nor fortifies a moral acquiescence in or complicity with the prerequisite abortions because the research occurs after the fact and cannot play any role in having caused them to occur. We cannot join the panel in this act of faith.

> *For a scientist to claim that the ethical status of any experiment can be assessed in splendid isolation from its antecedents is as myopic as to maintain that its consequences are irrelevant.*[84]

In its drift and its dimensions that claim yields instructive comparisons with the War Crimes Trial in Nuremberg known as "The Medical Case." There is a special irony in this for it was that Tribunal's "medical" trial which produced the Nuremberg Code of 1946, the great charter that initiated formal protection for human subjects of research. It inspired the Declarations of Helsinki in 1964 and 1975 that in turn begot virtually all of our present ethical norms for protecting human subjects in experimentation. Without Nuremberg and its judgment the world's conscience might never have gazed head-on at the intrinsic depravity of the doctors' defense.

In some respects the savagery and the genocidal ideology of the Nazi Holocaust defy any rational attempt at comparison with other instances of massive annihilation. Since, however, the Nuremberg Code stands as the inspiration and the progenitor of virtually every moral safeguard for human subjects of research, the world's conscience inevitably refers to the Nazi crimes as the explanatory context for construing and applying these ethical norms.

One lawyer who had taken part in prosecuting Nazis for war crimes explained how the German nation could have acted so savagely: "There is only one step to take. You may not think it possible to take it; but I assure you that men I thought decent men did take it. You have only to decide that one group of human beings have lost human rights."[85]

---

[82] A further likelihood, when demand exceeds the supply of fetal tissue, is that fetal tissue will be imported from foreign countries. William Regelson, "A Wise Fetal Tissue Policy," *The New York Times,* 14 November 1988, A19. Voluntary NIH guidelines can be expected to play no part in abortion practices abroad.

[83] Indeed, some would argue that when the supply of fetal tissue is overcome by the demand for it, some of the guidelines recommended by the panel should be reconsidered with an eye towards deletion. John A. Robertson et al. Concurring Statement, p. 40. Thus some members of the panel seem to agree to certain guidelines only when they are irrelevant; they are prepared to revise them as soon as they might effectively restrict transplantation. That position is clearly grounded on expediency, not on any moral principle.

[84] McCullagh, 146.

[85] R. J. V. Pulvertaft, "The Individual and the Group in Modern Medicine," *The Lancet* 2 (1952): 841; cited in Jay Katz, *Experimentation with Human Beings* (New York: Russell Sage Foundation, 1972), 292.

The insight of Nuremberg taught us that when we take possession of others, when their bodies are forcibly delivered up to be used as we wish, then no antecedent good will and no subsequent scientific yield will absolve us from having been confederates in their oppression.

The device of conscience whereby the Nazi physicians absolved themselves from moral association with the torment and abuse of their human subjects was a belief that they had had no say in how those subjects were delivered into their hands. The Nazi doctors had learned the ethic of their profession: that a physician may not relieve one human being's affliction at the cost of another fellow human's suffering. But they contrived to believe that if an associate had already done the subjugating and they then did the healing-oriented research, they could divide the responsibility down the middle. The Tribunal and the world judged otherwise—and condemned the researchers for it all.[86]

The arguments of the physicians in defense of their experiments upon prisoners and patients are exemplified by the chief defendant, Dr. Karl Brandt. It was in the "interests of the community" confronted with "hard necessity," when many lives had to be protected from death and epidemics, that he and his colleagues were given leave by the State to experiment on human subjects put at their disposal. "There is no prohibition against daring to progress."

The traditional restrictions that protected human subjects from harm had to yield to this urgent community need. "In all countries experiments on human beings have been performed by doctors, certainly not because they took pleasure in killing or tormenting, but only at the instigation and under the protection of the State, and in accordance with their own conviction of the necessity of these experiments in the struggle for the existence of the people." This apparently inhumane treatment of their helpless fellow humans for the sake of research was admittedly brutalizing, but as Brandt's lawyer Dr. Robert Servatius (who would later appear as attorney for Adolph Eichmann) explained: "a measure may be as unavoidable as war and yet be abhorred in the same way."[87]

Most of the Nazi research subjects, of course, were still living, though their lives were forfeit, when they fell into the doctors' hands.[88] But there were many experiments that employed organs and tissue from cadavers: human muscle for culture media at the Hygienic Institute in Auschwitz; livers, spleens and pancreata for Dr. Kremer's experi-

---

[86] After elaborating its code of ethics for medical experiments the Tribunal proceeded to condemn defendants, not only for having acted as principals in criminal experiments, but even for having "taken a consenting part" in these and other atrocities. "Permissible Medical Experiments," *ibid.*, 2:181–84.

[87] *Trials of War Criminals before the Nuremberg Military Tribunals under Control Council Law No. 10*, vols. 1&2 (Washington, DC: U.S. Government Printing Office, 1949). For the quotations given in our text above, see "Final Plea for Defendant Karl Brandt by Dr. Servatius," 2:123–138; "Final Statement of Defendant Karl Brandt," 2:138–140.

[88] This type of research on doomed, living subjects may be compared to the research project presented to the panel by Dr. Ezra Davidson of UCLA as a model for incorporating ethical concerns into research protocols. With Federal funding in 1979 Dr. Davidson tested a diagnostic procedure, fetoscopy, on the unborn offspring of a series of black and Hispanic women intending to undergo elective abortions, to see how often it would cause a miscarriage; his defense was that the fetuses were already slated for death. Congress regarded this experiment as so unethical that in 1985 it banned for 3 years any use by DHHS of the regulation that had allowed it. Lifton's remark is apposite: "If one felt Hippocratic twinges of conscience, one could usually reassure oneself that, since all of these people were condemned to death in any case, one was not really harming them. Ethics aside, and apart from a few other inconveniences, it would have been hard to find so ideal a surgical laboratory." Robert Jay Lifton, *The Nazi Doctors: Medical Killing and the Psychology of Genocide* (New York: Basic, 1896), 295.

ments on site; hearts, brains, and other organs provided by Dr. Mengele for research in Berlin; testicles and heads sent to Dr. Hirt in Strassburg for study, and brains for the work of Dr. Hallervorden.[89]

One sees, however, instructive similarities in the ways the Nazi researchers dealt with both live subjects and cadaverous remains:

> There was also a scramble for bodies and bones. When anatomy profes-
> sor August Hirt set about assembling a collection of body casts for his
> institute, he requested that captured Russian Jews, both men and women,
> be brought to Strassburg alive so that he might arrange for a "subse-
> quently induced death" in such fashion "that the heads not be dam-
> aged." They were not; the U.S Army arrived unexpectedly to find 150
> bodies still floating in formaldehyde.
>
> Some German laboratory people also harbored a scientific curiosity
> about the Polish intelligentsia. When Dr. Witasek of Poznan and a group
> of his comrades in the resistance movement were executed, their heads
> were removed and sent in gunnysacks to Germany for study. Professor
> Julius Hallervorden, who was shipped six hundred preserved brains of
> "mercy death" victims for his research in neuropathology, testified after
> the war: "There was wonderful material among those brains: beautiful
> mental defectives, malformations and early infantile diseases. I accepted
> these brains, of course [he had requested them]. Where they came from
> and how they came to me was really none of my business." [One Amer-
> ican professor commented that Hallervorden "merely took advantage of
> an opportunity."][90]

For both research groups, what lies within their grasp is anonymous "tissue," brains, pancreata, spleens. To an unblinded world those are the remains of Jewish, Gypsy, mentally handicapped, or unborn children: fellow victims sent nameless to destruction. It is the flesh of victims.

The carry-over in the analogy is the naive and vain belief that both groups of researchers and those they benefit are not pulled into the gravity field of responsibility for the violent act which supplies them with vanquished human bodies for study. The Nazi physicians were generally careful to keep the medical personnel involved in research separate from those responsible for killing.[91] They were much more explicit in their insistence that their experiments were going to bring some good out of tragedy. Dr. Hallervorden explained: "If you are going to kill all these people, at least take the brains out so that the material could be utilized." Dr. Hirt was of a similar mind: "These condemned men will at least make themselves useful. Wouldn't it be ridiculous

---

[89] Lifton, 285–295; William Brennan, *The Abortion Holocaust: Today's Final Solution* (St. Louis: Landmark, 1983), 58–61.

[90] Leo Alexander, "Medical Science Under Dictatorship," *New England Journal of Medicine* 241 (1949): 40; Burtchaell, *Rachel Weeping*, 182–83.

[91] As Dr. Hallervorden noted, there was a strict division of labor: "I gave them the fixatives, jars and boxes, and instructions for removing and fixing the brains, and then they came bringing them in like the delivery van from the furniture store." Bernhard Schreiber, *The Men Behind Hitler: A German Warning to the World*, trans. H. R. Martindale (Les Mureaux: La Haye-Mureaux, n.d.), 56. See also Lifton, 285, 292.

to execute them and send their bodies to the crematory oven without giving them an opportunity to contribute to the progress of the society?'' Likewise Dr. Rose: ''The victims of this Buchenwald typhus test did not suffer in vain and did not die in vain.'' Countless numbers of people ''were saved by these experiments.''[92]

One perceives this same justification at work among researchers who derive their materials from induced abortion. Dr. Martti Kekomäki, whose experiments on the severed heads of late-abortion fetuses are widely known, has said: ''An aborted baby is just garbage and that's where it ends up. Why not make use of it for society?''[93] Dr. Lawrence Lawn, of Cambridge University: ''We are simply using something which is destined for the incinerator to benefit mankind.''[94] And Drs. Willard Gaylin and Marc Lappé, associated with the Hastings Center, believe that the death of the ''doomed fetus'' ''can be ennobled'' through experimentation because the scientific results can be used for ''the saving of the lives (or the reduction of defects) of other, wanted fetuses.''[95]

''Abortion is a tragedy,'' says one transplant researcher. ''But as long as it occurs, I believe it is immoral to let tissue and materials go to waste if it can cure people who are suffering and dying.''[96] To compensate for the obvious lack of informed consent, both groups of doctors have supported that those who gave their victims over to destruction should, by some grotesque contortion of human rights, be acknowledged as their protectors and empowered to hand over their remains. ''All of us that work in fetal research feel that if someone has decided to have an abortion and gives permission, it is all right to use that tissue to help someone else.''[97]

What this line of thinking does not wish to recognize is that we can associate ourselves with others' moral agency after the fact. Consider a banker who judges narcotics use to be a tragedy, but agrees to accept the proceeds from the local drug network in order to make more capital available for home-owners and small businesses in the area. Who would or should believe that his readiness to accept those funds is not an act of acquiescent association—indeed, of partnership—in the human wastage and abuse that those moneys have already purchased? The banker has become a party to destruction even though it was complete before his subsequent involvement.

Elie Wiesel has said: ''If we forget, we are guilty, we are accomplices . . . I swore never to be silent whenever and wherever human beings endure suffering and humiliation. We must always take sides. Neutrality helps the oppressor, never the victim.''[98] Wiesel is saying that even by acquiescent silence after the fact we can sign on as parties to a deed already done. But what we are considering here is no mere *post mortem* silence, no simple averting of the gaze after the fact. We are considering an

---

[92] Brennan, 62.

[93] Naomi Wade, ''Aborted Babies Kept Alive for Bizarre Experiments,'' *National Examiner,* 19 August 1980, 20–21.

[94] J. and B. Willke, *Handbook on Abortion* (Cincinnati, Hayes, 1975 [2nd ed.]), 131.

[95] Willard Gaylin and Marc Lappé, ''Fetal Politics: The Debate on Experimenting with the Unborn,'' *Atlantic,* May 1975, 69–70.

[96] D. Eugene Redmond, Jr., director of Yale Medical School's neurobehavioral laboratory, in *The New York Times,* 15 March 1988. This was the theme of some lay advocates who testified before the panel. See, e.g., Statement of Leatrice Ducat, *Panel Transcript,* 15 September 1988, 175–80.

[97] Dr. Robert Gale of UCLA, in *The New York Times,* 16 August 1987.

[98] Excerpted from his 1986 Nobel Prize acceptance speech.

institutional partnership, federally sponsored and financed, whereby the bodily remains of abortion victims become a regularly supplied medical commodity.[99]

The validity of our concern was suggested in 1974 by the chairman for ethical issues of this panel:

> *Ought one to make experimental use of the products of an abortion system, when one would object on ethical grounds to many or most of the abortions performed within that system? . . . If a particular hospital became the beneficiary of an organized homicide-system which provided a regular supply of fresh cadavers, one would be justified in raising questions about the moral appropriateness of the hospital's continuing cooperation with the suppliers.*[100]

Our objections are congruent with the concern of 18 staff members at the Environmental Protection Agency who called for a halt in the application of Nazi research data from experiments with phosgene gas on prisoners of war. Their moral misgiving was that "to use such data debases us all as a society, gives such experiments legitimacy, and implicitly encourages others, perhaps in less exacting societies, to perform unethical human experiments."[101] When Dr. Robert Pozos of the University of Minnesota proposed to use the findings of the Dachau experiments in freezing prisoners alive, it was because "it could advance my work in that it takes human subjects farther than we're willing." Reaction was prompt. Daniel Callahan said, "We should under no circumstances use the information. It was gained in an immoral way." Abraham Foxman, national director of the Anti-Defamation League, added, "I think it goes to legitimizing the evil done. I think the findings are tainted by the horror and misery."[102]

The Nazi atrocities are now nearly a half-century behind us, and they are universally condemned, yet any impression of nonchalance about them is taken still today to be morally alarming. When the affliction is still underway in our own time, and has received only ambivalent repudiation in our society, any act of association speaks with much louder significance.

If, for the refining of his healing art, today's physician goes for his authorization to a mother who has abandoned her offspring to destruction, takes delivery of an insulted and mutilated body from the practitioner who dispatched the offspring, undertakes sponsored research upon those remains, publishes his results in professional journals, and then turns those findings to the resulting benefit of patients in pain—with all this

---

[99] Several members of the panel claim that a more apt analogy is the transplantation of organs from homicide or accident victims, whence they argue that "no one would seriously argue that the surgeon who transplants" becomes an accomplice "in the homicide or accident that made the organs available." John A. Robertson et al., Concurring Statement, p. 10. Such a serious argument could be made, however, if the surgeon contracted with the murderer to provide him organs for transplantation, to tell him when and where the organs would be made available, to arrange for the surgeon or his agents to be present to harvest the organs in "fresh" condition, and to reimburse the murderer for any expenses incurred in making the organs available. These are the types of arrangements that are routinely made to obtain fetal tissue.

[100] LeRoy Walters, "Ethical Issues in Experimentation on the Human Fetus," *Journal of Religious Ethics* 2 (Spring 1974): 41,48.

[101] Letter to Lee Thomas, Administrator of the Environmental Protection Agency, 15 March 1988. See also the letter to *The New York Times*, 19 April 1988, by Howard M. Spiro of Yale University.

[102] Chicago *Sun-Times*, 12 May 1988.

being held together by a network of accounts payable and receivable—then he becomes party, even though after the fact, to all that it took to put that research subject's body at his disposal. He has effectively acquiesced in it all.

Is it possible, as the panel has apparently proposed, to fend off moral complicity by some sort of disclaimer, simply by asserting aloud that one's use of this tissue for research implies no approbation of the antecedent abortion? There is little to encourage such a hope. Consider that most explicit of disclaimers composed by Mr. Justice Blackmun fifteen years ago on behalf of the U.S. Supreme Court. The Court acknowledged in *Roe v. Wade* that the entire ethical and legal reality of abortion pivots on whether the unborn is a live human being entitled to the protections promised to all persons by the Constitution.[103] It then proceeded to strip the unborn of those protections. "We need not resolve," Justice Blackmun wrote, "the difficult question of when life begins."[104] But they did. The public disallowed the Court's disclaimer and saw it had indeed resolved that, being disposable at the will of another, the unborn was no fellow human. That was the confident inference we heard in so many testimonies presented to our panel: abortion is the law of the land, so it must be ethical.[105] So much for disclaimers when actions prevail over words. The commercial partnership between the abortion industry and fetal transplant therapy which this panel proposes will make equally implausible any disclaimer that they take no position on abortion.

Our argument, then, is that whatever the researcher's intentions may be, by entering into an institutionalized partnership with the abortion industry as a supplier of preference, he or she becomes complicit, though after the fact, with the abortions that have expropriated the tissue for his or her purposes. It is obvious that if research is sponsored by the National Institutes of Health, the Federal Government also enters into this same complicity.

Conclusion

An attentive reader of the *Panel Report* will note in it an unresolved inconsistency. It purports to address and resolve the question of primary ethical concern: Is the use of aborted fetal remains subverted by ethical complicity with elective abortion? This implies: first, that the panel considers elective abortion to be ethically suspect; and second, that the panel is as concerned as the Assistant Secretary for Health that its recommendations be governed by ethical inquiry and judgment.

A majority of the panelists who voted to approve this *Report* have asserted that even "if there were a substantial increase in the number of abortions, it still would not follow that fetal tissue transplant research and therapy should not occur. Given the rudimentary development of early fetuses [up to 6 months old], the potentially great benefits to recipients, and the legality of abortion, such transplants might still be ethically and legally acceptable."[106] A causative effect upon abortion increase is thus considered no obstacle to medical prospects. The same majority, in proposing a guideline to prohibit research on fetuses conceived in order to be aborted for their useful tissues, explains openly that the restriction is proposed because there appears to be no present

---

[103] *Roe v. Wade,* 410 U.S. 113, 156–7 (1973).

[104] *Ibid.,* 159.

[105] See, e.g., Statement of Lynn Phillips, *Panel Transcript,* 14 September 1988, 288.

[106] John A. Robertson et al., Concurring Statement, note 21. A majority of those who support the *Report* have concurred in this Statement.

market need for such a resource. "In light of these supply considerations," the restriction is accepted. But, "if the situation changes so that the supply of fetal tissue from family planning abortions proves inadequate, the ban . . . should be reexamined."[107]

The controlling convictions within this *Report* do not, as often implied, consider complicity with elective abortion to be significantly objectionable because they do not consider abortion to be objectionable. Nor do they reach their conclusion on grounds of ethical principle. The recommendation to proceed with this use of aborted fetal remains in research is grounded on a raw and ruthless determination "to achieve significant medical goals" no matter what the moral consequences.

Our conclusion is different because our grounds for judgment are different. Though there are scientific reasons for caution and though there are legal prohibitions in some States, it is not primarily on these grounds that the proposed research and experimental therapy could most clearly be judged unacceptable. It is on ethical grounds that it must be disapproved.

Research employing the remains of electively aborted fetuses is, in our judgment, ethically compromised

1)   by the absence of authentic informed consent,
2)   by the incentives it will offer for yet more abortions, and
3)   by complicity with the abortions that supply the tissues.

It is additionally objectionable because of its dissonance from other elements of public policy.

For these reasons we consider it a perversion of both the scholar's and the healer's work, and we must respectfully dissent from the panel's principal conclusion.

---

[107] *Ibid.*, p.30.

PARTIAL APPENDIX TO REPORT

Qualities of Fetal Cells and Tissues
Presented by Robert Auerbach, Ph.D., Harold R. Wolfe Professor and Director,
Center for Developmental Biology, University of Wisconsin-Madison

Introduction
I have been asked to address in a general way the unique properties of fetal cells and tissues that lead to their proposed use in transplantation.

When one thinks about embryonic and fetal development, two basic properties immediately come to mind: the extensive changes—differentiations—that the fetus undergoes during its embryogenesis or, for mammals, during its intrauterine existence, and the rapid growth that occurs in the short period between the establishment of the fertilized egg and the parturition of the newborn. In addition to these two properties, I will discuss briefly several additional qualities: the fact that fetal tissues are not as readily recognized as foreign when transplanted, that they contain no cells that can mount an immune attack against the recipient, that they are generally free of pathogens or pathology, and that their growth properties make them amenable to various technical procedures such as in vitro maintenance or storage.

I. Plasticity

Embryonic and fetal cells can adapt to their environment

Cells can change in shape

Cells are capable of extensive movement to assume correct location and orientation

Cells become functionally integrated with their surroundings

The fertilized egg has the potential to form every cell and tissue type found in the adult. During early development, major lines of differentiation are established: cells destined to be neural tissue; hematopoietic cells such as lymphocytes and red blood cells; endothelial cells that will line the capillaries and larger blood vessels; mesenchymal lineages destined to form muscle and cartilage; gonadal tissues and germ cells; tissues that will form the various regions of the digestive tracts; respiratory tissue; and so on. Within this broad compartmentalization there is still much flexibility: in the eye, neural and pigmented retinal cells may still be flexible enough to be interchangeable; there is still much room for alteration of structures within the developing skeletal system (e.g. wing vs. leg in chicken embryos; number of digits and shape of the limb in mammals). Cells can migrate from one site to another within the embryo and reorganize by cell movement within developing structures. They can stretch to cover underlying membranes or contract and compact as they become organized into nodules or vessels or fibers. As development proceeds, however, more and more cell types become more rigidly defined and no longer capable of redifferentiation. Plasticity gradually becomes more and more limited, finally restricted to only a few modulations such as can occur in the hematopoietic system.

An exciting example of the plasticity of embryonic cells and tissues were published this week in SCIENCE. Nicole LeDouarin and her colleagues in Nogent-sur-Marne near Paris showed that they could replace a large region of the chick embryo early brain with a similar region from quail embryos. After hatching, the birds could be stimulated by testosterone to make crowing sounds, and the sounds made by these chick embryos were frequently of typical quail type, rather than chick type. Thus the transplanted embryonic brain tissue had not only become established, but had demonstrated its ability to function in accord to both its own genetic constitution and coordinately in the environment in which it had been place. Immediately following this report was one which demonstrated that extreme plasticity also exists in the brain cells from a developing rat embryo. It is worth noting that the stage of development was a 2-day chick and 13-day rat, representing human gestational age of about 3–7 weeks.

II. Proliferative Capacity

Fetal cells can divide more frequently

A higher percentage of cells retain the capacity to divide

Fetal cells have a capacity to divide for more generations

At certain times during the period of organ formation an embryo may roughly double its size in a single day. When one examines the number of cells undergoing cell division one may find as many as 25–50% of a given organ in active proliferation. This contrasts to the less than 1% found in more mature tissues. Clearly, the ability to divide is an important attribute when considering the requirements placed on cells and tissues used in transplantation protocols, for cell division both assures growth to the appropriate size (subject to regulation), and the means for repairing the extensive cell death that of necessity accompanies most surgical manipulations.

The ability to divide is particularly crucial when we are dealing with hematopoietic cells, since these must be replaced frequently during the life of an individual. Moore and Metcalf many years ago carried out incisive studies in mice: Using X-irradiation, they destroyed an adult animal's capacity to replace its own blood cells. They then injected hematopoietic cells either from the embryonic yolk sac, from the fetal liver, from newborn bone marrow or from adult bone marrow. They found that by far the greatest number of cell replications could be achieved from the cells obtained from the embryonic yolk sac. It was fewer for fetal liver, still fewer for newborn bone marrow, and least for bone marrow from adults.

There is a biological calendar clock: as cells mature and age their ability to continue to multiply is gradually reduced. In addition, the rate at which cell division occurs is slower, and this is a regularly observed adjunct of the aging process that occurs in all tissues that have been studied to date. It is a developmental reality that the best growth rate and growth potential are achieved early in development, and that these decline during the process of maturation and differentiation.

III. Angiogenetic Ability

Ability to induce blood vessel formation is present in fetal cells but is lost or reduced during the course of maturation

Angiogenesis occurs rapidly, assuring survival and growth

Blood vessels entering fetal tissues are influenced to adapt to their new environment

One of the most critical needs in any tissue or organ graft is the ability of the transplanted tissue or origin to become established in the new environment and to receive the nutrients it needs for survival and growth.

The ability to induce blood vessel formation and penetration, once thought to be primarily restricted to tumors, has now been shown to be present in all or virtually all fetal tissues. When a chick embryonic heart, for example, is grafted into a different site it becomes established within 2 days, vessels from the host fusing with those of the graft to yield patent vessels filled with circulating red blood cells. Similarly, embryonic mouse heart fragments when implanted into the ear of an adult mouse will rapidly become vascularized and start rhythmic contractions within a few days.

IV. Immunological Compatibility

Many antigens are not present until late in development or arise postnatally

Those antigens that do exist are frequently shared by the host, and therefore do not elicit an immune reaction

Leukocytes that trigger host immune reactions also develop late during fetal life

Lymphocytes that can cause immune reactions develop late during fetal life

Antigens, those chemical moieties such as proteins that can elicit an immune reaction, are in large part produced only after a tissue or organ has reached maturity. There is always some degree of "foreignness", but the extent of it and the degree to which it leads to immune rejection is much lower early in development and only gradually increases during fetal life. Thus embryonic and fetal tissues are less likely to evoke an immune reaction leading to rejection than are adult tissues.

Those antigens that are present early in development are frequently shared by adult cells and tissues. When this is the case, the immune response is either very weak or absent.

One cause of immune reactivity by the host is the presence within the grafted tissue of certain types of white blood cells (passenger leukocytes). These cells are absent from embryonic and early fetal organs or tissues.

Graft-versus-host reactions occur when the transplanted tissue contains lymphocytes that are capable of carrying out immune reactions. These cells recognize the recipient as "foreign" and thus mount an immunological attack that is frequently lethal. Lymphocytes competent to carry out immune reactions arise relatively late during fetal development, and thus pose no problem when young embryonic or fetal tissues are transplanted.

V. Other Properties

Fetuses develop in a protective environment

There is little likelihood of undiagnosed pathology

Storage and recovery of viable fetal tissues is readily achieved

One of the unique features of mammals is that embryonic and fetal development take place in a protective environment. Protection is afforded both because development takes place within the uterus and because the placenta provides for selective transfer not only of nutrients but of protective substances such as antibodies and antiviral substances.

Because of this generally healthy and uniform environment, tissues and organs obtained before parturition are almost universally devoid of pathology.

Because of their propensity for growth and adaptation, embryonic and fetal cells and tissues are amenable to storage conditions. In many instances cells and small tissue fragments can be maintained almost indefinitely in low temperatures (liquid nitrogen storage). One of the best examples of this property is seen by the fact that the Jackson Laboratory, the world's most important repository for inbred and mutant mouse strains, now routinely stores early embryos in this manner, rather than maintaining the large number of animals that would be needed to assure continuation of these animal stocks.

Summary

Embryonic and fetal cells have unique properties that are relevant to their use as a source of material for transplantation. Their plasticity permits them to integrate and be integrated into the physiological environment of the host. Their ability to proliferate and respond to regulatory control lets them grow to the size appropriate to the recipient. Their ability rapidly to evoke blood vessel formation allows them to receive the necessary nutrition for survival. The lack of antigenicity and passenger leukocytes reduces their chance of being rejected as foreign and reduces the risk of death of the recipient from graft-versus-host reactions. And the isolation and protection provided by the intrauterine environment enhances the likelihood that the embryonic and fetal cells and tissues are free of pathology and of contaminating microorganisms.

Foreign Regulations and Guidelines
Summary of presentation by Bernard M. Dickens, Ph.D., LL.D., Faculty of Law and Faculty of Medicine, University of Toronto, Canada

Introduction

This presentation does not aim to offer a comprehensive review of how every country addresses the potential use of tissues taken from the products of induced abortion for purposes of research, particularly into Parkinson's and comparable diseases. The issue is too novel for specific legal provisions to have been enacted; the United States is in the forefront of the movement to apply research or related provisions to this type of procedure.

Legislation, rules of customary legal application (common law) and research guidelines that are applicable to the procedure exist in a number of countries whose experience is particularly relevant to that of the U.S. Before such provisions are reviewed, a number of analytical points have to be made regarding use of tissues derived from induced abortion.

Analysis

The colonizing effect of controversies about induced abortion in several countries is such that it often imposes itself on adjacent activities to which induced abortion is secondary. Protagonists of different views about the propriety of induced abortion employ instrumental arguments for and against related practices in order to advance their preferences, and counter those they oppose. Accordingly, legal provisions and ethical guidelines become scrutinized to serve purposes for which they were not designed.

Fetal tissue transplantation presupposes that the fetus is determined to be dead by appropriate medical criteria, and raises legal questions primarily concerning the acquisition of such tissues rather than concerning the uses to which they are put. Whether sufferers from Parkinson's disease, diabetes, sickle-cell anemia and other conditions that fetal-cell transplantation is proposed to relieve are receiving innovative therapy or primarily a research procedure is subordinate to the question of the legality of fetal tissue acquisition. The same legal issues of acquisition would arise were such tissues to be used for an established therapeutic procedure. Even if such uses are classified as research uses, this does not involve the fetus itself in research; that is, the sometimes complex provisions of legislation and/or guidelines that several countries have developed to regulate research on human fetuses or embryos are applicable only when a fetus *in utero* is placed at risk of damage. The dead fetus that is the source of tissues used in research is not itself the subject of that research, although the woman producing the product of conception may be.

Few legal systems personify ''the fetus'' that is the source of tissues as an entity that has an identity or interests separate from the identity or interests of the mother, although some constitutions claim to recognize individuals ''from conception.'' A fetus, whether viable or not, is recognized to warrant special protection while it is alive *in utero,* but that protective regard ends as a consequence of abortion. That is so even if pregnancy ends by the pregnant woman's request. Accordingly, while several countries have legislation and customary laws that govern medical uses of fetal tissues, their orientation is to protect the wishes and interests of the maternal sources of those tissues regarding their own health and, for instance, confidentiality, rather than to protect the fetuses *per se*. The fate of living fetuses *in utero* is governed by the abortion laws of the country, but following induction of abortion, the fetal tissues have no different legal status from that of the placenta and associated products of conception or other materials recovered from the body of a living human person. If the fetus is at or over a given weight such as 500 grams or over a given gestational age such as 20 weeks, procurement of its miscarriage in some countries will be registered as a stillbirth, and its remains will have to be treated with the dignity appropriate to the remains of a human being, meaning one born alive from its mother's body. As in the case of such newborn human beings, its remains may be used for scientific or therapeutic purposes with parental consent.

There are few instances of legislation that governs acquisition of fetal tissues in particular, and relatively few court decisions in which judges have declared customary laws applicable to fetal tissues. The status as legal property of tissues that have proceeded from the bodies of living persons has been recognized only partially (see B. M. Dickens, ''The Control of Living Body Materials,'' 27 *University of Toronto Law J.*

(1977), 142–198), although the California Court of Appeal decision in *Moore* v. *Regents of the University of California,* 249 Cal. Rptr. 494 (Cal. App. 2 Dist. 1988) may find an echo in a number of other countries, particularly of the Common law tradition. Legal prohibitions of the sale of such materials have been known for about two decades, however, indicating that proprietary interests in them may exist. Tissues from living persons' bodies have not been analogized to dead bodies, in which nothing more than quasi-property rights have generally been recognized. Quasi-property rights are sepulchral rights of burial or cremation.

Human tissue gift laws may be applicable only to *post mortem* donations, and property law is commonly undeveloped on transfer and acquisition of living persons' body products. Accordingly, criminal laws on theft and civil laws on conversion and trespass to property may be difficult to apply. Nevertheless, quite sophisticated codes of conduct that are influenced by ethical perceptions and sensitivities may be given the force of law, by virtue of express or implied terms of contracts.

Researchers are frequently in the salaried employment of institutions such as universities, hospitals and research clinics or laboratories. A term of their contracts of employment, express or implied, will be that they will observe not only applicable laws and regulations, but also ethical codes and guidelines established by the employing institutions, research funding agencies or, for instance, general professional or professional specialty associations. Thus, ethical guidelines that themselves lack enforceability against institutions or individuals except perhaps through financial sanctions may be given the force of law against individuals by virtue of private contractual agreements. Further, when professional licensing authorities have statutory disciplinary powers, for instance when professional misconduct is alleged against licensed physicians, disciplinary tribunals may invoke non-compliance with ethical codes or guidelines as the basis of legally effective sanctions consequent on findings of misconduct.

Ethical codes or guidelines gain legal force when they are incorporated expressly or, as is usual, by reference into contracts of service. Servants are told what to do and the means by which to tackle their tasks. Independent contractors are different in that, while they may be instructed what to do, they make decisions regarding the means to be used. Accordingly, researchers who are independent contractors may deny that they are bound by implied terms of contracts to observe ethical codes or guidelines. If they are health professionals, their licencing or disciplinary authority may nevertheless charge them with professional misconduct if they acquire or use fetal tissues improperly.

Language regarding fetuses is often used imprecisely. As influential a body as the United Kingdom's Peel Committee, for instance, inaccurately wrote in its 1972 Report about, for instance, ''Where a fetus dies after birth'' (Report of the Advisory Group *The Use of Fetuses and Fetal Material for Research,* HMSO 1972, para. 37, p.8). After birth, meaning complete expulsion from a mother's body, no fetus exists in law; a human being has been born (that is, the human entity is ''in being'') with all of the rights of a human being, even if at perhaps premature birth it is not viable or is born dying. A fetus by definition is *in utero* or in the course of delivery, whether spontaneously or by induction. The living product of induced abortion is a human being, no longer a fetus. Accordingly, this text takes fetal remains to mean those of fetuses that never proceeded completely from their mothers' bodies as living entities, even though at delivery certain of their tissues such as cells or organs were live and transplantable.

Legislation

Countries as sophisticated in medical research as the United Kingdom may lack legislation that is applicable to the acquisition of fetal tissues. In England, for instance, the Human Tissue Act 1961 applies to *post mortem* tissue gifts, but not to *inter vivos* gifts, meaning those made by living persons. Since the dead fetus never possessed dispositive autonomy, disposition of its tissues is the responsibility of its mother, since the tissues are determined to be hers, although following stillbirth, meaning in England expulsion of a dead fetus of 28 weeks' gestation, both parents may have powers and responsibilities of disposal. When a non-viable fetus is born alive, however, it becomes a human being, and following its death its remains may be applied according to the Human Tissue Act's provisions regarding a deceased who left no expression of intention regarding bodily disposition. Its parents may make its remains available for therapeutic, scientific research or educational purposes. The tissues may be made available in general by the "person lawfully in possession" of the deceased child's body.

Canadian provinces follow a generally uniform pattern of legislation, modelled on Ontario's Human Tissue Gift Act, which was enacted in 1971. The Act governs "tissue," which is defined to include an organ but not to include any skin, bone, blood, blood constituent or other tissue that is replaceable by natural processes of repair (R.S.O., 1980, c. 210, s. 1(c)). The Act's applicability will accordingly depend on what tissues are proposed to be acquired from a fetus. Different Parts of the Act deal with *inter vivos* and *post mortem* gifts. Part I governs the former, and provides that "A transplant from one living human body to another living human body may be done in accordance with this Act, but not otherwise" (s.2). The following section permits any person aged at least 16 years of age, who is mentally competent to consent and is able to make a free and informed decision, to consent, in writing, to implantation in another of tissue derived from his or her body. A general Part of the Act prohibits commerce in any tissue or any body or part or parts thereof other than blood or a blood constituent, for therapeutic purposes, medical education or scientific research (s. 10), leaving open the question of commerce for other purposes, such as cosmetic treatment.

The lack of specificity in these provisions is representative of the way in which legislation in this area has developed. Historically, human tissue gift legislation was introduced to accommodate the first tissues that became transplantable, namely corneas, but corneal grafting legislation was in time superseded by legislation of far more general scope, although, as remains the case in England, most legislation remains confined to *post mortem* acquisitions. In Australia, early legislation on human tissue transplantation was designed to regulate blood donation for transfusion, leaving the transplantation of other materials from the bodies of live donors to be regulated under the Common law. In New Zealand too, the Human Tissue Act 1964 followed the provisions of the 1961 English Act regarding confinement to *post mortem* donation.

Customary Law (Common Law)

The practice of *inter vivos* tissue donation developed in the context not of specific legislation but of customary (or common) law. English Common law prohibited the cutting of the body under its provisions against wounding, and precluded the infliction of life or health endangering interventions under its law against maim (or mayhem). A maim was not excusable on the ground that the subject consented to it; indeed, the subject then became a participant in the offence. An exception was allowed where the intention was to provide therapeutic treatment or relief, particularly when a physician was involved. This law was inapplicable to donation of materials that left the body naturally, such as stillborn fetuses. When legislation came to permit therapeutic abortion, disposal of the products of conception thereby removed was governed by the prevailing customary or common law.

The ambivalence of such law is expressed in the *Report of the Royal Commission of Inquiry into Contraception, Sterilization and Abortion in New Zealand*, published in 1977. The Report summarized prevailing law in the United Kingdom, to which New Zealand's law was compared. The Report observed that:

> *Where the fetus is born dead there is no statutory requirement to obtain the parent's consent [to research] but equally no power to ignore the parent's wishes. (Report p. 323).*

The Report adds that "The parent should be offered the opportunity to express any special directions about the disposal" but does not give any legal basis for this rule. In default of a woman directing the disposition of the products of conception that result from spontaneous or induced abortion, the legal presumption of abandonment will apply, and the materials will fall under the control of whoever first exercises control over them, which in many cases will be hospital personnel. The Common law is reflected in such U.S. cases as *Hembree* v. *Hospital Board of Morgan County*, 300 So. 2d 823 (Ala. S.C., 1974) which held, where a stillborn child's body was incinerated without consent, that there is no implied contract in the hospital-patient relation preventing disposal without prior permission. See also *Brooks* v. *South Broward Hospital District*, 325 So. 2d 479 (Fla. Dist. C.A., 1975), denying damages when a hospital misplaced the body of a prematurely born baby.

When management of a woman's abortion is proposed to be influenced by the possibility of her fetus being a source of tissues for transplantation, legal doctrines of informed consent and free consent will have to be observed. In 1980 Canada adopted the patient-oriented standard of disclosure (*Reibl* v. *Hughes* (1980), 114 D.L.R. (3d) 1 (S.C.C.)) that originated in such U.S. cases as *Canterbury* v. *Spence*, 464 F. 2d 722 (D.C. Div. 1972), but in England the standard of disclosure remains the so-called "professional standard" (*Sidaway* v. *Bethlem Royal Hospital Governors*, [1985] 1 All E.R. 643 (H.L.)). This requires physicians to give only such information as other physicians in like circumstances would give, which can accommodate a high level of medical paternalism. In contrast, the patient-oriented standard requires disclosure of such information as a prudent person in the patient's circumstances would consider material to know. The latter standard better protects women's interests in knowing whether and how their treatment is intended to maximize the utility of their products of conception for transplantation.

Because patients for abortion often feel vulnerable and dependent on their physicians' good will, the issue of free consent is of particular significance. A physician who will undertake the procedure should either have no interest in availability of resulting tissues for transplantation, or should be able to overcome the legal presumption of exercising undue influence in persuading a patient to endure disadvantage, for instance through delay or use of an inferior method to protect her health, in order to maximize utility of fetal tissues. It is likely that a physician with such a conflicting interest would be in breach of professional ethical guidelines, which may be incorporated by reference into any employment contract with a hospital or clinic.

Guidelines

Particularly in the last few years, many countries have seen the development of ethical guidelines concerning availability of fetal tissues for transplantation. These tend to be more sophisticated than prevailing legislation, and address such issues as limits on management of a patient's abortion, although few if any address such recent scenarios as a woman planning to initiate a pregnancy for the purpose of terminating it and recovering fetal tissues for transplantation in a specific recipient, including arranging the genetic composition of the fetus to minimize risk of rejection in the recipient.

As its 18th sitting in September 1986, the Parliamentary Assembly of the Council of Europe adopted the text of Recommendation 1046 proposed by the Assembly's Legal Affairs Committee, including the recommendation:

> *to limit the use of human embryos and foetuses and materials and tissues therefrom . . . to purposes which are strictly therapeutic and for which no other means exist, according to the principles set out in the appendix, and to bring their legislation into line with these principles or to enact rules in accordance therewith . . . (para 14A ii).*

The appendix to the Recommendation provides in paragraph B vi that:

> *The use of dead embryos or foetuses must be an exceptional measure, justified in the present state of knowledge by the rare nature of the illness treated, the absence of any equally effective therapy and a manifest advantage (such as survival) for the person receiving treatment; it must comply with the following rules:*
>
> a. *the decision to terminate pregnancy and the conditions of termination (date, technique, etc.) must under no circumstances be influenced by the possible or desired subsequent use of the embryo or foetus;*
>
> b. *the use of the embryo or foetus must be undertaken by highly qualified teams in approved hospitals or scientific centres supervised by the public authorities; to the extent that national legislation foresees, these centres must possess multidisciplinary ethical committees;*
>
> c. *total independence between the medical team terminating the pregnancy and the team which might use the embryo or foetus for therapeutic purposes must be guaranteed;*
>
> d. *embryos and foetuses may not be used without the consent of the parents or gamete donors where the latters' identity is known;*
>
> e. *the use of embryos, foetuses or their tissues for profit or remuneration shall not be allowed.*

National practices may conform to this recommendation by, for instance, recognizing that new uses of fetal tissues to treat pathological conditions constitute innovative therapy rather than pure research, and so are "strictly therapeutic." The British Medical Association's Interim Guidelines, going somewhat beyond the Council of Europe recommendation in condemning the generation or termination of pregnancy solely to produce suitable material, is given in the Appendix (see p. 811 below).

In Australia, the National Health and Medical Research Council adopted a report in October 1983 that noted that historically hospital pathologists have frequently supplied fetal tissues to colleagues for research use without parental consent, but that some hospitals have come to insist that requests be considered by an institutional ethics committee. (Medical J. of Australia, May 12, 1984, pp. 612–3). The NHMRC favored the duty to obtain free and informed consent of the woman, and of the father when practicable. The Medical Research Council of Canada's *Guidelines on Research Involving Human Tissues, 1987,* provide that:

> *Separated tissue and placental material may be regarded as routine pathological tissue, and may be used in research, subject to the permission of the mother whenever possible and to provincial human-tissue-gift legislation and hospital regulations. (p. 32).*

This research requirement is applicable by analogy to use of such tissue in therapeutic procedures including therapeutic innovation.

APPENDIX

British Medical Association Interim Guidelines on the Use of Foetal Tissue in Transplantation Therapy

The Association has become aware that a number of research centres are developing therapeutic techniques involving the transplantation of foetal tissue, for treatment of conditions including Parkinson's Disease. Such work has now commenced within the United Kingdom. The Association continues to support the recommendations of the Peel committee on The Use of Fetuses and Fetal Material for Research (1972).

Guidelines

1. Tissue may be obtained only from dead foetuses resulting from therapeutic or spontaneous abortion. Death of the foetus is defined as an irreversible loss of function of the organism as a whole.
2. United Kingdom laws on transplantation must be followed. The woman from whom the foetal material is obtained must consent to the use of the foetal material for research and/or therapeutic purposes.
3. Transplantation activity must not interfere with the method of performing abortions, nor the timing of abortions, or influence the routine abortion procedure of the hospital in any way. Abortions must be performed subject to the Abortion Act, and any subsequent amendments thereof, uninfluenced by the fate of the foetal tissue. The anonymity of the donor should be maintained.
4. The generation or termination of a pregnancy solely to produce suitable material is unethical. There should be no link between the donor and the recipient.
5. There must be no financial reward for the donation of foetal material or a foetus.
6. Nervous tissue may only be used as isolated neurones or tissue fragments for transplantation. Other foetal organs may be used as either complete or partial organs for transplantation.

7. All hospital staff directly involved in the procedures—including the abortion—must be informed about the procedures involved.
8. Every project involving transplantation of foetal tissue must be approved by the local ethical research committee.

Building Ethical Concerns into Protocol Designs
Robert J. Levine, M.D., Professor of Medicine, Yale University School of Medicine, New Haven, Connecticut

I have been asked to show how ethical concerns are reflected and accommodated in the design of protocols that are negotiated between investigators and Institutional Review Boards (IRBs); they are negotiated, not merely reviewed and approved. The ethical concerns I shall deal with are those identified in the March 22, 1988 memo from the Assistant Secretary for Health to the Director, National Institutes of Health. The protocol to which I shall refer is "The Transplantation of Fetal Substantia Nigra into the Caudate Nucleus of Patients with Parkinson's Disease;" this protocol was approved by the IRB at Yale-New Haven Medical Center (YNHMC) on June 30, 1988.

First, a word about the meaning of IRB approval. At Yale, this means simply that the IRB has found the protocol to be in adequate conformity with the ethical and legal standards for research involving human subjects. IRB approval does not constitute authorization to proceed with a project. The power to grant such authorization resides in other individuals and groups within the institution. In this case, the decision as to whether and when this project will begin remains to be made.

I shall first discuss some features of the protocol and then I shall show their relationship to the ethical concerns identified in the Assistant Secretary's memo.

According to the protocol, the population of potential donors is limited to women who present themselves to YNHMC seeking elective abortions. The women must be at least 18 years old and it must be clear that the procedure for termination of pregnancy will be accomplished during the first trimester.

No woman is to be made aware of the possibility that she might be invited to participate in research until all arrangements for the termination procedure—including informed consent—have been accomplished. At this point, a member of the research team, a clinician-investigator, examines her clinic record to determine whether there have yet been detected any exclusion criteria. If not, he or she then initiates contact with the prospective subject to begin a discussion which might lead to her informed consent to become a research subject.

Following are some excerpts from the consent form:

> *Because you have decided to have an abortion, you are invited to donate some tissue from the abortus for use in medical research and to have one additional blood sample drawn to determine the safety of using the tissue in these studies . . .*
>
> *The tissue will be used to study ways to preserve fetal tissues and cells, and to understand fetal development. Some of the tissue may be frozen, thawed, grown in tissue culture, or implanted in animals so that we can learn techniques to use in implanting tissue into humans. Some cells may be implanted . . . in patients with Parkinson's disease. We hope that development of this technology will help us some day to find a*

treatment for Parkinson's disease and possibly other medical disorders. You will not be able to designate the specific use or recipient of the tissue, which might be used for any of the things mentioned. Under no circumstances may you learn the name of the recipient of the tissue, if it is implanted. In the other direction, a possible recipient will not learn your identity . . .

You are free to choose not to donate this tissue and blood sample, and your decision will not adversely affect your relationship with your doctors or this hospital and will have no effect on whether or not you may have an abortion or on how, when, and by whom it will be done. You should know also that even after signing this consent form, you can still change your mind about having the abortion. After the abortion, you can withdraw your permission for the research or transplantation use of the tissue, until such research has actually begun. These decisions would not deprive any recipient of a chance to receive fetal tissue implantation.

Now let us refer to the Assistant Secretary's memo:

7.   What actual steps are involved in procuring the tissue from the source to the researcher? Are there any payments involved? . . .

I have traced the actual steps involved. The financial arrangements are precisely those that prevail at YNHMC for the same patients who are not participating in any research. There is no waiver of fees and no reimbursement for expenses.

6.   In particular, is the optimal or safest way to perform an abortion likely to be in conflict with preservation of the fetal tissue? Is there any way to ensure that induced abortions are not intentionally delayed in order to have a second trimester fetus for research and transplantation?

According to the protocol, there is no necessity to wait for second trimester fetuses. There is to be no change whatever in the procedure or personnel involved in the first trimester abortion procedure. The only difference from the standard procedure is in the disposition of the abortus after the procedure has been completed.

9.   For those diseases for which transplantation using fetal tissue has been proposed, have enough animal studies been performed to justify proceeding to human transplants? Because induced abortions during the first trimester are less risky to the women, have there been enough animal studies for each of those diseases to justify reliance on the equivalent of the second trimester human fetus?

In response to the first question, in the judgment of the YNHMC IRB, the answer is yes. With regard to the second question, our response is incorporated in the response to question 6 *(supra)*.

3.   As a legal matter, does the very process of obtaining informed consent from the pregnant woman constitute a prohibited ''inducement'' to

terminate the pregnancy for the purposes of the research—thus preclud-
ing research of this sort, under HHS regulations?

Under no circumstances is the pregnancy to be terminated for research purposes. No mention of research is made to the woman until she has completed arrangements for an abortion procedure which she has elected to serve her own purposes; whatever these purposes might be, they are not research purposes.

2. Does the use of fetal tissue in research encourage women to have an
abortion they might otherwise not undertake? If so, are there ways to
minimize such encouragement?

The protocol design does not encourage abortions. It is only after the woman has made her choice that she is made aware of the possibility of getting involved in research. Since we are aware of the fact that a small percentage of women may change their minds about abortion, we are careful to reassure them that such a change of mind "would not deprive any recipient of a chance to receive fetal tissue implantation." In this way, we assure the women that they need not feel constrained because they have made what they might consider a commitment.

5. Should there be and could there be a prohibition on donation of fetal
tissue between family members, or friends and acquaintances? Would a
prohibition on donation between family members jeopardize the likeli-
hood of clinical success?

Whether or not there should be a prohibition of such donations, in the Yale protocol there is a *de facto* prohibition. We have taken care to assure anonymity. Women are being invited to donate tissue for a variety of purposes only one of which is implantation in patients with Parkinson's disease. No woman will be able to guess the purposes for which her donated tissues were used.

Moreover there will be substantial delay between the time that the tissue is donated and the time it is implanted in a patient. During this time, various tests are done for (e.g.) infectious diseases. The tissue is to be frozen while awaiting the results of these tests. Thus, because of the delay, even if a woman were to become aware of the fact that some patient had received an implantation of fetal tissue, the delay would be such that she would be unlikely to assume that she was the donor.

Among the exclusion criteria for potential donors are "first degree relatives with Parkinson's disease, or any other neurodegenerative condition . . ." Although this exclusion criterion was established for safety reasons, it has the effect of precluding donations "between family members." We are aware of no evidence that exclusion of family members will jeopardize the likelihood of clinical success.

Time permits only brief responses to the remaining questions.

4. Is maternal consent a sufficient condition for the use of the tissue, or
should additional consent be obtained? . . .

As a general rule, the YNHMC IRB considers maternal consent sufficient authorization for the use for research purposes of the dead fetus, fetal material, or the placenta.

This general rule seems to apply *a fortiori* in instances such as the present case in which there seems to be a greater than usual probability of benefit and this benefit will be realized earlier than in the typical research project for which we find maternal consent sufficient.

> *8.   According to HHS regulations, research on dead fetuses must be conducted in compliance with state and local laws. A few States' enacted version of the Uniform Anatomical Gift Act contain restrictions on the research applications of dead fetal tissue after an induced abortion . . .*

This concern does not arise for research to be done in the State of Connecticut.

> *1.   Is an induced abortion of moral relevance to the decision to use human fetal tissue for research? Would the answer to this question provide any insight on whether and how this research should proceed?*

This is, of course, a very complex question. It is one that was discussed at great length by IRB members as they reviewed this protocol. There were those who suggested that we might consider limiting potential donors to those who had either spontaneous or therapeutic abortions. Parenthetically, I have thus far spoken only of the protocol as it relates to the use of tissues obtained in the course of elective abortions. The protocol also accommodates the possible use of spontaneous or therapeutic abortions.

At the conclusion of our discussion consensus was achieved on the approval of the use—under circumstances I have discussed—of fetal tissues obtained from elective abortions (one member abstained from the final vote). Thus, although many members of the IRB found the nature and the purpose of the abortion relevant morally, none found it decisive in the sense that they wished to prohibit the use of fetal tissues obtained in the course of induced elective abortions.

I want to make one final comment on the point of showing how ethical concerns are reflected and accommodated in the design of protocols. The Yale protocol is designed as a randomized controlled clinical trial. Thus, in contrast to experiences reported earlier, if and when this protocol is completed, it should be possible to make a definitive statement regarding the efficacy of fetal tissue implantation in the treatment of Parkinson's Disease.

Statement on Proposed Uses of Human Fetal Tissue
Stuart A. Newman, Ph.D., Professor of Cell Biology and Anatomy, New York Medical College

In light of the divergence of opinion in U.S. society on the desirability of elective termination of pregnancy, it is not surprising that there is wide disagreement about the appropriateness of putting tissues of deliberately aborted embryos to various uses. In contrast, the medical and scientific use of tissues from spontaneous abortions or miscarriages does not present comparable difficulties, as this is not generally considered to differ in principle from the disposition, subject to the consent of its parents, of the tissues of a deceased child.

I would like to make my own interests in this matter explicit. I am a developmental biologist with a long-term scientific interest in vertebrate embryogenesis. The availability of human embryonic tissue for experimental purposes would greatly benefit my research program by permitting me more directly to explore the basic mechanisms of human skeletal development. I am also a strong supporter of a woman's right to decide for herself whether or not she will become a mother, and consider the option to electively terminate a pregnancy to be inalienable.

Nonetheless, I have a number of reservations about proposed medical and research uses of tissues of electively aborted embyros of fetuses. My misgivings stem from what I see as negative social implications of these activities that are as weighty as their potential benefits. Assigning a utility to the results of an abortion creates contending interests around an otherwise intensely private event. Whether or not women would be encouraged to become pregnant "for medical science," they would certainly experience pressure to undergo abortion procedures that are more invasive and dangerous to them, but more sparing of the fetus. Such pressure might be sweetened by a *quid pro quo* in the form of relief from medical costs.

Moreover, as various interest groups become accustomed to and dependent on supplies of fetal tissue, they will inevitably seek to enforce their rights to this material. Success in the use of embryos of various stages of development would very reasonably cause decisions on the timing of abortions to be influenced by utilitarian concerns beyond those of the woman's well-being. And even if the procurement and distribution of fetal tissues were prevented by law from becoming overtly commercialized, such tissues would come to represent a desirable resource that would inevitably be transformed into a commodity by those vying for it. As long as medical care remains within the market system, no number of middlemen or brokers interposed between the pregnant woman and transplant recipient will negate this commodification [sic] of human embryos.

A related issue concerns the general objectification of the products of human reproduction. A woman's option to terminate a pregnancy is ethically and legally justified by a tradition (held by a majority in the U.S.) that the unwelcome embryo does not represent a socially constituted human individual. But, from a biological viewpoint, neither does it represent the pregnant woman's own tissues. It therefore seems that the concept of "informed consent," and even parental consent, breaks down in these cases. But the elimination of informed consent by the pregnant woman, as has been recommended by some speakers at this forum, threatens to further objectify the embryo. The use of human embryos as sources of biological "spare parts," however laudable the therapeutic goals, is a scenario virtually out of the pages of Aldous Huxley's *Brave New World*. Have we come so far in our collective wisdom that these images are no longer disquieting?

Proposed medical and scientific uses of human embryos and fetuses would necessitate a heightened degree of concern for their safety, intactness, and viability. Given the biological nature of the embryo, these measures would often result in its continued development. Such arrangements philosophically undermine their own necessary condition: the social consensus that permits legal abortion.

Spontaneous abortions represent a legitimate source of fetal tissues for scientific study and potential medical therapy. Although this resource is scarcer than what would be available from elective abortions, its use is consistent with tissue donation programs that have wide social acceptance, and thus avoids most of the ethical problems discussed above. The right to elective abortion is also socially accepted, but not universally so. To burden this essential personal option with extraneous utilitarian aspects only invites further divisiveness.

Public Policy Considerations in the Use of Human Fetal Tissue—
Roundtable Discussion

This summary has been prepared by Kathleen Nolan, M.D., Associate for Medicine at the Hastings Center, Briarcliff Manor, NY. The Hastings Center is a non-profit, non-partison [sic] organization that carries out educational and research programs on ethical issues in medicine, the life sciences, and the professions. The Center does not represent any constituency or advocate positions; moreover, the scholars at the Center rarely attempt to reach consensus judgments and often vigorously disagree. Therefore, the ideas presented here do not represent the Hastings Center's position on this or any of the other questions raised by fetal tissue transplantation. Because of the short time available for preparation, full discussion and review of this paper by the staff at the Center has not been possible. Nonetheless, it is offered to the Human Fetal Tissue Transplantation Research Panel as an example of the type of considerations that are being brought to the Center's on-going dialogue and debate on this issue.

Summary of Presentation

> *ASH Question 1: Is an induced abortion of moral relevance to the decision to use human fetal tissue for research? Would the answer to this question provide any insight on whether and how this research should proceed?*
>
> *Is there any moral distinction between the cadaver of a dead fetus resulting from an induced abortion and any other cadaver?*

There are at least three levels of inquiry suggested by the framing of these two questions. First, what would be necessary for a feature to be *morally* important in this context? Second, what features, in general, distinguish fetal cadavers resulting from elective abortion from other cadavers? And third, are there also important distinctions to be made about the intended *use* of fetal tissue (e.g., research versus transplantation)?

To identify morally important features, let us simplify by requiring only that such features either evoke basic moral principles (e.g., respect for persons) or have potentially morally relevant consequences. That is, let us reason in both deontological and teleological modes, taking into account features that raise claims about inherently right or wrong activities and also those that are considered right or wrong primarily in reference to potential consequences.

Moral distinctions, like others, must be made relative to specific features. That is, to judge that fetal cadavers resulting from elective abortion are either the same or different from other cadavers, we must ask *in what respect* comparisons are to be drawn. For example, fetal cadavers are obviously biologically different from adult cadavers, in ways that many believe can lead to improved outcomes after transplantation. This feature, the properties of fetal tissue, is morally important in that—barring other considerations—the ability to treat and possibly cure serious illness fulfills the moral principle of beneficence and produces good consequences.

Fetal cadavers resemble adult cadavers in their both being dead, and therefore both incapable of being directly harmed by our activities. This relieves us of the burden of respecting their subjective interests, since by definition, they cannot have any. Limiting our attention to cadavers is very helpful in this respect, since the regard due living fetuses as subjects in themselves is highly controverted.

Handling of cadavers is not wholly settled by reference to their status as non-living beings, however. Dead bodies command respect for reasons that are difficult to articulate, yet ancient and powerful.[1] In general, though, autopsy and organ retrieval for research and transplantation are seen as compatible with this principle, presumably for fetuses no less than for adults.

The problematic distinctions, then, are those among different classes of fetal cadavers. The most troubling distinguishing feature looks not to the present state of the cadaver but to its history. The cause of death in a fetal cadaver resulting from an elective abortion may be attributed to a pregnant woman's decision to abort, while the cause of death in a fetal cadaver resulting from a spontaneous abortion is usually attributed to biologic or natural causes. For those who hold that a decision to abort is morally unjustifiable, the moral principle "good ends cannot come from immoral means" precludes use of fetal cadavers resulting from elective abortions.[2]

In addition, opponents of legalized elective abortion worry that allowing tissue from electively aborted fetuses to be used to achieve dramatic benefits may potentially influence individual abortion decisions, or, more likely, cause elective abortion to be viewed more favorably as a means of family planning. An increased number of abortions would be viewed by these individuals (and perhaps by some who favor maintaining a legal option for abortion but have reservations about its morality) as a harmful and distressing consequence.

It may be, however, that different uses for fetal tissue may have quite different implications. Handling of cadavers can be divided into five major categories: 1) disposal (usually cremation); 2) burial; 3) commercial use; 4) research; and 5) therapy. Elective abortion has been claimed to be potentially sensitive to each of these methods of handling the fetal cadaver, as either positive or negative incentives. The most obvious positive incentive would be a financial one, and objections to payment of women for use of fetal tissue have been almost universal. Research on fetal tissues (obtained primarily from fetuses resulting from elective abortion) has been conducted for over a decade without noticeably influencing rates of elective abortion.

Use of fetal tissue for transplantation may be quite different. Although studied and conducted under protocols, transplantation of human fetal tissue has been offered to patients less as a form of research than as a form of innovative therapy.[3] Unlike research, which benefits society in a vague and diffuse way, transplantation as a form of therapy potentially benefits society very concretely. Instead of "saving" statistical lives, transplantation "saves" *individuals,* some of whom have devastating illnesses. The one-to-one quality of some forms of transplantation makes this feature even more graphic.

Suggestions that women be informed about the option of transplantation only *after* an abortion (in order to shield them from its influence on decisionmaking) really miss the point, because the presence of the mass media in our society means that knowledge of this option will be widespread. Even if no single woman would list "the opportunity to save someone's life with a tissue donation" as her reason for deciding to have an abortion, the fear that dramatic transplantation successes with fetal tissue will erode individual and societal inclemency toward abortion seems worth taking quite seriously.

Note.—Footnotes appear at end of summary.

Another difficulty intensified by transplantation efforts as opposed to other forms of research with fetal tissue is that transplantation in the United States has quite consciously been conducted under a framework of "gifts."[4] In fact, use of fetal tissue for transplantation has been explicitly sanctioned under the Uniform Anatomical Gift Act (UAGA) since 1968, although the UAGA was adopted by most states well prior to the Supreme Court's decision in *Roe* v. *Wade*. While placing cadaveric fetal tissue donation squarely within the rubric of other organ and tissue donations has certain attractions, a strange dissonance attends treating as a "gift" tissue considered by the contributor to be worthless.

In relation to the model of gift-giving, consent issues also become particularly thorny. Under the Uniform Anatomical Gift Act, donations from cadavers, including those of stillborn infants and fetuses, may be made by others who would have authority to determine the disposition of the body. Because the Act defines donors as individuals making "a gift" of all or parts of their bodies, the implication is often taken that a caring person speaks as a proxy for the other in authorizing this gift.

With fetal cadavers resulting from elective abortion, the "gift relation" comes into question. If a pregnant woman has opted to end her pregnancy, then ethical objections arise to her claiming the role of mother and serving as a proxy for a fetal donation. A decision to abort almost inevitably requires some degree of objectifying of the fetus, making an offering to "donate" ring somewhat hollow.

Treating offers of such tissue as a type of "contribution," an offering of something not particularly valued to a common fund or store, might make more sense.[5] In fact, some have argued that public policy would be better served if we moved transplantation in general out of the model of altruism and gift-giving and into a model of social utility and appropriation. Substantial resistance to ideas like "presumed consent" for adult organ donation suggest, however, discomfort with the notion that bodies "belong" to society and not to relatives or loved ones.

A compromise solution would be to try to distinguish those uses of fetal tissue that seem to evoke images of transplantation and gift—and concomitantly, those most likely to influence societal attitudes toward abortion—from those that do not. The gift model, with its more stringent requirements for relation of giver to gift, would then be reserved for those cases in which fetal tissue use truly parallels organ transplantation in adults. These cases show themselves through several aspects: a one-to-one relation of source of tissue to recipient, special kinds of tissue (e.g., brain and perhaps heart), and great potential for benefit in members of the recipient pool. One can argue that these are the main features of neural tissue transplantation of Parkinson disease that trigger much of the concern about using tissue from electively aborted fetuses.

A compromise such as this depends on developing another source of tissue to be used when tissue from electively aborted fetuses is restricted under the gift model. Otherwise, ill individuals will be forced to forgo trials of therapy in order to prevent speculative impacts on abortion rates and in order to make a symbolic statement about fetal worth.

Are other sources of tissue potentially available? . . . several other sources of fetal tissue might be considered. Tissue from fetuses that have been spontaneously aborted has been suggested, but the possibility of fetal abnormalities is high, most miscarriages occur prior to a gestational age that would make them useful for transplantation, and much of this tissue is irretrievable. Consent would potentially be complicated by emotional upset, but it is precisely this fact that evidences the woman's standing in a position to offer a "gift" of fetal tissue. (Some women will, of course, be glad to have miscarried; it is worth pondering whether others can ever know when a gift relation truly exists.)

Another potential source that has yet to receive attention is tissue from fetuses obtained at the time of surgery for ectopic pregnancy. Again, fetal abnormalities may be more likely than in the setting of elective abortion, and numbers may be small, but techniques to rule abnormalities must be developed for any source of tissue, and only small amounts of tissue will be needed initially. Obtaining tissue from this source would likely pose hardships for clinician-investigators because surgery is often required on an emergency basis, making it necessary for them to remain ready to come in to the hospital on short notice. The emergency setting would make consent difficult as well. Nonetheless, practical hurdles might be worth addressing, to determine at least whether tissue from electively aborted fetuses is truly the only workable source.

If an alternative source of tissue could be identified and reserved for dramatic, transplantation-like interventions, several benefits would be attained. First, this would make a symbolic statement that fetuses have sufficient value to justify attempts to minimize incentives toward elective abortion. Second, it would indicate to those opposed to abortion that their concerns are taken seriously. Third, it would allow research and forms of transplantation that are unlikely to influence attitudes toward abortion to continue unimpeded. Fourth, procedures that are developed to insure the suitability of less obviously suited tissues can be used to improve safety whatever the source of tissue. Finally, it would insure that patients who might potentially benefit from treatment with fetal tissue have the opportunity to enroll in clinical trials where therapeutic benefit can be fully evaluated.

Since distinguishing "gifts" from "contributions" requires considerable judgment, a national advisory committee, such as the Congressional Biomedical Ethics Board would need to be available for judgments about what source(s) of tissue might be appropriate in given cases. Open, on-going national-level review of possible uses of fetal tissue would offer testimony to wide-spread societal concerns that elective abortion—though legal and available—not be viewed as a morally neutral enterprise.

References

[1] William May, "Attitudes Toward the Newly Dead," *Hastings Center Studies* I (1972) 3–13.

[2] James T. Burtchaell, "Case Study: University Policy on Experimental Use of Aborted Fetal Tissue," *IRB: A Review of Human Subjects Research* 10:4 (July/August, 1988) 7–11.

[3] Robert J. Levine, *Ethics and Regulation of Clinical Research* (Baltimore-Munich: Urban & Schwarzenberg, 1986).

[4] Thomas H. Murray, "Gifts of the Body and Needs of Strangers," *Hastings Center Report* 17 (2) (April, 1987) 30–38.

[5] Kathleen Nolan, "Enough Is Enough: A Fetus Is Not a Kidney," *Hastings Center Report* (in press).

Parkinson's Disease Fetal Tissue Transplant Research, Basic and Clinical Studies

Lars Olson, Department of Histology and Neurobiology, Karolinska Institute, Stockholm, Sweden

Parkinson's disease is a severe progressive neurological disease of unknown cause. Symptoms develop when an area of the brain called the basal ganglia has lost a large part of a specific set of incoming nerve fibers that utilize dopamine as a transmitter and that have their cellular origin in an area called the substantia nigra. The best treatment for Parkinson's disease would obviously be one that detects the disease at an early asymptomatic stage and prevents further degeneration of nerve cells. This, however, is not possible today. A second alternative, which I will describe below, consists of replacing the lost cells by some form of transplantation. A third approach, and the only one that has so far proven effective, is to replace the effects of the lost neurotransmitter pharmacologically. This is the basis of L-dopa therapy and other pharmacological treatments. While effective for some years, current drug therapy has two problems: with time it becomes increasingly difficult and often impossible to maintain normal function and there are also side effects of the treatments such as uncontrolled movements. An estimated 400,000 people suffer from Parkinson's disease in the United States alone, and for many of these patients, who have already lost their dopamine-producing nerve cells, an alternative treatment strategy based on a transplantation procedure would be most valuable.

Parkinson's disease does not exist in animals. However, since it is known precisely which nerve cells that degenerate in this disease in man, it can be replicated with high precision in rodents by injecting the neurotoxin 6-hydroxydopamine stereotaxically into the nigrostriatal dopamine pathway on one side of the brain. Such animals have no overt symptoms of their unilateral deficiency. However, when challenged with drugs that interfere with dopamine neurotransmission, they will show an asymmetrical behavior which can be measured precisely and quantified using so-called rotometers. In 1979 we were able to show that the asymmetrical behavior of such animals could be effectively and permanently counteracted by transplantation of fetal dopamine nerve cells (Perlow et al. 1979). Similar results were reported independently by another group the same year (Björklund and Stenevi 1979) and the techniques for counteracting experimentally induced parkinsonism in rodents by fetal brain tissue grafting has been improved and confirmed in many laboratories over the last 10 years. Soon after the reported success with fetal cells, we developed an alternative approach based on grafting adult chromaffin tissue from the adrenal medulla (Freed et al. 1981; Strömberg et al. 1985). The technique of chromaffin autografting was first applied to patients at the Karolinska Institute in Stockholm in 1982 (Backlund et al. 1985) using implantations into the caudate nucleus and they were continued using implantations into the putamen and caudate nucleus at the Lund University Hospital in Lund (Lindvall et al. 198[7]). Stereotaxic implantation of chromaffin tissue has so far not provided permanent positive effects to patients. The reason may be that the basal ganglia contain too low levels of nerve growth factor to support the chromaffin tissue grafts. Therefore, fetal brain tissue transplants have also been tried. In the following, I shall describe the Swedish experience on use of human fetal tissue transplanted both to rodents and to patients.

Collection of Fetal Material

Tissue for transplantation purposes has been collected after elective early routine vacuum-aspiration abortions. The procedures have been approved by the Swedish Council for Medical Ethics, the Ethical Delegation of the Swedish Association of Physicians, and the ethical committees of involved guidelines hospitals and research centers. The provisional guidelines include informed consent from the woman seeking abortion. She is informed orally and in writing after all decisions regarding her abortion have been made, and is given time before answering yes or no to the collection of material. The provisional guidelines further state that the collection of material must not influence when, how, or why the abortion is being performed. The vacuum-aspiration technique used will cause death and fractionation of the fetus. Material used for research and clinical trials has been collected from the 7th through 10th weeks of gestation. Death of the fetus is caused by the abortion procedure. Strict anonymity is maintained; thus, there is no coupling between the identity of the aborted fetus and the further transplantation experiments.

Almost all women that have been asked have approved of the procedures. They have been informed about the fact that their decision will in no way influence their treatment at the hospital.

The fragmented fetus, together with placental debris, is kept on saline and brought to the laboratory where it is carefully searched for identifiable pieces of brain tissue by an experienced scientist using a stereomicroscope. In approximately 50 percent of the cases it is possible to identify the brainstem area including the mesencephalic flexure and from there dissect small tissue pieces measuring approximately 1 millimeter in diameter, containing the fetal dopamine neuroblasts of the substantia nigra region. In a similar fashion, it is often possible to identify other areas of the central nervous system, including the spinal cord, and prepare small tissue fragments for transplantation purposes.

Grafting Human Fetal Brain Tissue to Rodent Hosts

Extensive studies have been carried out to characterize viability and growth potential of aborted human fetal tissue using rodent hosts. It is then necessary to use immunocompromised hosts. We have tried both athymic, "nude" mice and rats which are unable to reject foreign tissue, and rats whose immune responses have been suppressed by daily injections of the immunosuppressive agent ciclosporin. By grafting minute tissue fragments to the anterior chamber of the eye in such rodents, it becomes possible to follow survival, growth and development by repeated observations and measurements through the cornea of the host animal. These intraocular transplantations do not usually disturb vision of the hosts. Finally, the structural and functional characteristics of such transplants can be evaluated using appropriate techniques. With this approach we have determined optimal stages and dissection techniques for survival of human dopamine neuroblasts and for survival of other cells and tissues from the human fetal central nervous system.

In a second series of experiments, human fetal dopamine neuroblasts were grafted to rats with experimentally induced unilateral parkinsonism. It was shown that the human cells could counteract the symptoms of the disease similarly to what had previously been demonstrated using rat-to-rat allografts. However, the human tissue transplants developed with a human, and thus longer, rather than a rat time course also after grafting to a rat host. Thus in the rat brain, human dopamine neuroblasts develop into mature dopamine nerve cells which extend nerve fibers reinnervating the dopamine-denervated rat striatum. The nerve fibers will form specific synapses as identified by immunohistochemistry at the electron microscopic level. The cells are electrically active, they release dopamine which normalizes firing characteristics and dopamine receptor sensitivity of neurons in rat host striatum. These effects develop within 3 to 5 months in the rat hosts and are paralleled by significantly decreased abnormalities in the rotational behavior of the hosts.

Grafting Human Fetal Tissue to Patients with Parkinson's Disease

In Sweden, two patients with severe, longstanding Parkinson's disease have been given human fetal dopamine neuroblast implantations in 1987. Although information is sparse, we are aware of similar attempts in several countries, including Mexico, China, England, and Cuba. The Swedish patients were two women in their fifties with a disease duration of over 15 years. L-dopa had become less effective and they had severe problems with the so-called "on-off" effects. In November and December 1987, respectively, the two patients were given unilateral injections of substantia nigra cell suspensions prepared from 7- to 10-week-old fetal tissue. For each patient, substantia nigra tissue from four fetuses was made into a cell suspension by gentle trypsination and mechanical dissociation. The cells were used for three deposits, two into putamen and one into the caudate nucleus on one side of the brain. The patients have been kept on immunosuppression since transplantation. The transplantations have been carried out as a joint research project between the Karolinska Institute and the University Hospital of Lund in Lund, Sweden, under the clinical leadership of Dr. Olle Lindvall in Lund. Based on our previous experience with chromaffin autografts, the patients have been and are being followed by a large number of different neurological, neurophysiological and other tests including autoscoring, videotaping, PET-scan evaluations, etc. There have been no adverse side effects to date. It is too early after transplantation to draw any definite conclusions about the outcome. It appears, however, as if the patients are slightly, but significantly improved on several of the tests applied, making these procedures worthy of further clinical trials.

Possible Future Developments

There are several different sources of cells which might be useful for grafting in Parkinson's disease. Here we have described chromaffin tissue grafts and fetal dopamine neuroblasts. In animal experiments, the chromaffin tissue grafts can be made more effective by addition of nerve growth factor (Strömberg et al. 1985). Chromaffin autografts supported by nerve growth factor injections have not been tried in patients. It is also possible to genetically engineer cells and perhaps in the future to generate cell lines useful for grafting which would make it less necessary to obtain fetal tissue. We have recently developed a rat fibroblast cell line which has been transfected with many copies of the gene for nerve growth factor, and which after grafting will secrete nerve growth factor to the surroundings. Such cells might be cografted with nerve growth factor-dependent cells such as chromaffin cells.

It must be pointed out, however, that at present no genetically designed cells are available for grafting to patients. Recombinant human NGF is also not available, and even if it becomes available, grafting chromaffin tissue has several potential drawbacks. Thus, removal of one adrenal gland is a major surgical procedure which might be harmful to an elderly patient. Moreover, chromaffin cells do not produce large amounts of dopamine, something that only dopamine neuroblasts can do. Thirdly, chromaffin cells produce several other substances such as neuropeptides and growth factors with so far not very well characterized effects. Based on the scientific background in animal research, it thus appears that the best chances of obtaining good functional effects in parkinsonian patients are provided by grafting human fetal dopamine neuroblasts. To obtain better functional effects than have so far been noted, it may be necessary to implant a larger number of cells and/or perform such implantations at a larger number of sites in the basal ganglia, perhaps on both sides of the brain.

Comment to Questions Raised by the Assistant Secretary of Health

Question 1: It has been important for the ethical discussion in Sweden to realize that the issue of whether or not to perform induced abortions is a separate issue which should be treated separately from the subject of fetal tissues in research. The activities described above are entirely after the fact, that is, they are an adoption to the fact that induced abortions are being made in Sweden and, as indicated above, collection of tissue does in no way influence the abortion procedures.

Question 2: No. In Sweden approximately every fourth pregnancy is terminated by abortion. The use of cell and tissue grafting from aborted fetuses to certain defined diseases would in no way cause a "demand" for more aborted fetuses. Moreover, it would be of no immunological advantage with fetal tissue from a "related" fetus. Obviously, an aborted fetus can never be the identical twin of a patient. In this context, it might be relevant to emphasize that we still do not know whether or not immuno-suppression is necessary at all. In the first Swedish cases, immunosuppression has been maintained in order to optimize chances of seeing beneficial effects. However, recent grafting of fetal brain tissue in primates suggests that immunosuppression might not be necessary at all.

Question 3: In Sweden, the answer is no.

Question 4: In Sweden, the answer is yes.

Question 5: Prohibition on donation between family members would not jeopardize the likelihood of clinical success. On the other hand, given the number of induced abortions, the issue will probably not arise in Sweden.

Question 6: Since the procedures described above are entirely passive in relation to the abortion, they would have no impact on the activities and procedures employed by abortion clinics. For the purposes of grafting human fetal brain cells, only early fetuses are appropriate; thus, second trimester fetuses would be of no use.

Question 7: In Sweden, no payments are involved. The procedures are still on a research level, procuring the tissue from the source to the laboratory has been the responsibility of the involved scientists.

Question 8: Not applicable to Sweden.

Question 9: For Parkinson's disease, it is our opinion that enough animal studies have indeed been performed to justify proceeding to human transplants. However, continued animal experimentation, both at the rodent and primate level, is also necessary to further improve the techniques.

Question 10: This question cannot be answered precisely. As [alluded] to above, cell cultures might eventually be successful; however, it is also possible that they will never be useful. One severe problem with cell cultures is that cells that can be maintained in culture, i.e. cells that have been "immortalized," are difficult to control also after transplantation and can continue to grow, forming tumors. Thus, probably for many years to come, the only alternative for parkinsonian patients who have already lost their dopamine nerve cells is a grafting procedure involving fresh tissues.

References

Backlund E-O, Granberg P-O, Hamberger B, Knutsson E, Mårtensson A, Sedvall G, Seiger Å, Olson L. Transplantation of adrenal medullary tissue to striatum in parkinsonism. First Clinical trails. *J Neurosurg* 62, 169–173, 1985.

Björklund A, Stenevi U. Reconstruction of the nigrostriatal dopamine pathway by intracerebral nigral transplants. *Brain Res* 177, 555–560, 1979.

Brundin P, Nilsson OG, Strecker RE, Lindvall O, Åstedt B, Björklund A. Behavioural effects of human fetal dopamine neurons grafted in a rat model of Parkinson's disease. *Exp Brain Res* 65:235–240, 1986.

Brundin P, Strecker RD, Widner H, Clarke DJ, Nilsson OG, Åstedt B, Lindvall O, Björklund A. Human fetal dopamine neurons grafted in a rat model of Parkinson's disease: Immunological aspects, spontaneous and drug-induced behaviour, and dopamine release. *Exp Brain Res* 70, 192–208, 1988.

Freed W, Morihisa J, Spoor E, Hoffer B, Olson L, Seiger Å, Wyatt R. Transplanted adrenal chromaffin cells in rat brain reduce lesion-induced rotational behaviour. *Nature* 292, 351–352, 1981.

Lindvall O, Backlund E-O, Farde L, Sedvall G, Freedman R, Hoffer B, Nobin A, Seiger Å, Olson L. Transplantation in Parkinson's disease: Two cases of adrenal medullary grafts to the putamen. *Ann Neurol* 22, 457–468, 1987.

Perlow M, Freed W, Hoffer B, Seiger Å, Olson L, Wyatt R. Brain grafts reduce motor abnormalities produced by destruction of nigrostriatal dopamine system. *Science* 204, 643–647, 1979.

Strömberg I, Herrera-Marschitz M, Ungerstedt U, Ebendal T, Olson L. (1985) Chronic implants of chromaffin tissue into the dopamine-denervated striatum. Effects of NGF on graft survival, fiber growth and rotational behavior. *Exp Brain Res* 60:355–349.

Strömberg I, Bygdeman M, Goldstein M, Seiger Å, Olson L. (1986) Human fetal substantia nigra grafted to the dopamine-denervated striatum of immunosuppressed rats: evidence for functional reinnervation. *Neurosci Lett* 71:271–276.

Strömberg I, Almqvist P, Bygdeman M, Finger T, Gerhardt G, Granholm L, Mahalik T, Seiger Å, Olson L, Hoffer B. (1988) Human fetal mesencephalic tissue grafted to dopamine-denervated striatum of athymic rats: Light- and electron-microscopical histochemistry and in vivo chronoamperometric studies. *J Neurosci* (in press).

State Regulation of Human Fetal Tissue Transplantation

Lori B. Andrews, J.D., American Bar Foundation

A variety of therapeutic innovations may be possible using fetal tissue or organs.[1] Consequently, researchers have sought funding from the National Institutes of Health to pursue research involving fetal tissue and organ transplantation. In carrying out such projects, researchers must adhere to the federal regulations governing fetal research.[2] They must also comply with state regulations governing the acquisition and disposition of fetuses, research on fetuses, and payment for human organs and tissues.

The state laws vary in the type of penalties they impose for violation of the fetal research laws. In some states, violation of the law is considered to be unprofessional conduct,[3] creating the potential for a physician/researcher who violates the law to lose his or her license to practice medicine. In other jurisdictions, the violation of the laws can subject the researcher to a fine and imprisonment.[4]

The first notable feature of the states' regulatory approaches is that they differ dramatically from that of the federal regulations.[5] The federal regulations are fairly precise in their coverage—specifically defining fetus as beginning at implantation and containing a definition of a dead fetus as a "fetus *ex utero* which exhibits neither heartbeat, spontaneous respiratory activity, spontaneous movement of voluntary muscles, nor pulsation of the umbilical cord . . ."[6] The 24 state statutes on fetal research[7] are, for the most part, not as precise. Some contain no definition of fetus, of death, or of research. Others include much broader definitions of the term fetus (or unborn child) so that the laws cover not just post-implantation conceptuses, but (in the words of the Missouri statute) cover "the offspring of human beings from the moment of conception

---

[1] *See, e.g.,* Association of American Medical Colleges, *Fetal Research and Fetal Tissue Research* (June 1988); S.D. Lawler, "Conception and Development of a Fetal Tissue Bank," 34 *J. Clin. Path.* 240–248 (1981); McAuliffe, "A Startling Fount of Healing," 101 *U.S. News & World Report* 68–70 (1986). See also Kay and Constandoulakis, "A Foetal Tissue Bank," 1 *Br. Med. J.* 575 (Supp. 1959).

[2] 45 C.F.R. §§ 46.201–46.211 (1987).

[3] *See e.g.,* Cal. Health and Safety Code § 25956(b) (West 1984).

[4] *See e.g.,* N.M. Stat. Ann. § 24-9A-6 (1981), providing for imprisonment for up to one year or the payment of a fine up to $1,000 or both.

[5] For the background of the development of the federal regulations, *see* National Commission for the Protection of Human Subjects of Biomedical and Behavioral Research, *Report and Recommendations: Research on the Fetus* (1975) (hereinafter Research on the Fetus). This document is reprinted in 40 Fed. Reg. 33,530 (1975). The Commission also published, in a separate volume, *Appendix: Research on the Fetus* (1975), the papers prepared for the Commission during its consideration of the fetal research issue.

[6] 42 C.F.R. § 46.203(f) (1987).

[7] Ariz. Rev. Stat. Ann. § 36-2302 (1986); Ark. Stat. Ann. § 82-436 to -442 (Supp. 1985); Cal. Health & Safety Code § 25956 (West 1984); Fla. Stat. Ann. § 390.001 (6), (7) (West 1986); Ill. Ann. Stat. ch. 38 para. 81-26(7) (Smith-Hurd 1986); Ind. Code § 35-1-58.5-6 (1986); Ky. Rev. Stat. Ann. § 436.026 (Baldwin 1985); Me. Rev. Stat. Ann. tit. 22 § 1593 (1980); Mass. Ann. Laws ch. 112 § 12J (Law. Co-op. 1985); Mich. Comp. Laws Ann. §§ 333.2685–2692 (West 1980); Minn. Stat. Ann. § 145.421 to .422 (West Supp. 1987); Mo. Ann. Stat. § 188.037 (Vernon 1983); Mont. Code Ann. § 50-20-108(3) (1985); Neb. Rev. Stat. § 28-342 to -346 (1985); N.M. Stat. Ann. § 24-9A-1 et seq. (1981); N.D. Cent. Code § 14-02.02-01 to -02 (1981); Ohio Rev. Code Ann. § 2919.14 (Baldwin 1982); Okla. Stat. Ann. tit. 63 § 1-735 (West (1984); Pa. Stat. Ann. tit. 18 § 3216 (Purdon 1983); R.I. Gen. Laws § 11-54-1 (Supp. 1986); S.D. Codified Laws Ann. § 34-23A-17 (1986); Tenn. Code Ann. § 39-4-208 (1982); Utah Code Ann. § 76-7-310 to -311 (1978); and Wyo. Stat. § 35-6-115 (1977).

until birth at every stage of its biological development including the human conceptus, zygote, morula, blastocyst, embryo, and fetus.''[8]

Only one state—New Mexico—has adopted a law patterned on the federal regulations pertaining to fetal research. Other states have enacted a variety of regulatory approaches, with the permissibility of fetal research depending on some or all of the following factors: 1) the purposes of the activities undertaken—for example, whether they are intended to benefit the conceptus on which they are to be performed; 2) the effects of the activities undertaken on the conceptus—whether they impose a risk to the life or health of the conceptus and, if so, the likelihood and seriousness of this risk; 3) the relation of research to an abortion procedure—that is, whether the activity involves a fetus prior to, during, or subsequent to an induced abortion; 4) the location of the research subject—whether it is in the womb or outside of the womb; 5) the stage of development of the conceptus—whether it has reached a point or acquired characteristics which would warrant treating it as a person or has acquired some characteristic such as the capability for experiencing pain, which would give it an important claim to protection (often this factor is put in terms of the fetus's viability or nonviability).

The Significance of Abortion

Under the state laws, the factor which seems most significant for regulating research and for determining the level of restriction imposed is whether or not the research concerns a fetus which is to be or has been aborted. Most of the state fetal research statutes were passed as a part of abortion legislation. Twelve of the twenty-four laws apply to research only where it concerns a fetus prior to or subsequent to a planned abortion.[9] Of the twelve that apply to fetuses more generally, four impose more stringent restrictions on fetal research in conjunction with an abortion.[10] These four statutes allow nontherapeutic research on a fetus *in utero* if it poses no substantial threat to the life and health of the fetus and provided that the fetus is not the subject of a planned abortion (other than one to protect the life of the mother), but forbid research on a fetus prior to or subsequent to an abortion. It is notable that these four statutes explicitly extend to research on embryos and neonates and that the standard of regulation is constant with respect to these different stages of maturity but differs depending upon whether or not the mother is planning an abortion.

Another tactic that has been taken to assure that fetal research does not encourage abortion is to prohibit the performance of an abortion where ''part or all of the consideration for said performance is that fetal remains may be used for experimentation.''[11]

---

[8] Mo. Ann. Stat. § 188.015(5) (Vernon 1983) (defining unborn child). See also the Kentucky law which defines a fetus as a human being from fertilization until birth.

[9] Ariz. Rev. Stat. Ann. § 36-2302(A) (1986) (subsequent); Ark. Stat. Ann. §§ 82-436 to -441 (Supp. 1985) (subsequent); Cal. Health & Safety Code § 25956(a) (West 1984) (subsequent); Fla. Stat. Ann. § 390.001(6) (West 1986) (prior to subsequent); Ind. Code § 35-1-58.5-6 (1986) (subsequent); Ky. Rev. Stat. § 436.026 (Baldwin 1985) (subsequent); Mo. Ann. Stat. § 188.037 (Vernon 1983) (prior or subsequent); Neb. Rev. Stat. § 28-346 (1985) (subsequent); Ohio Rev. Code Ann. § 2919.14(A) (Baldwin 1982) (subsequent); Okla. Stat. Ann. tit. 63 § 1-735(A) (West 1984) (prior or subsequent); Tenn. Code Ann. § 39-4-208 (1982) (subsequent); and Wyo. Stat. Ann. § 35-6-115 (1977) (subsequent).

[10] Mass. Ann. Laws ch. 112 § 12J(a)(I) (Law. Co-op. 1985); Mich. Comp. Laws Ann. § 333.2685(1) (West 1980); N.D. Cent. Code § 14-02.2-01(1) (1981); and R.I. Gen. Laws § 11-54-1(a) (Supp. 1986). The Michigan law extends this standard of regulation to *ex utero* fetuses as well.

[11] Mass. Ann. Laws ch. 112 § 12J(a)(III) (Law. Co-op 1985); Mich. Comp. Laws Ann. § 333.2689 (West 1980); N.D. Cent. Code § 14-02.2-02(2) (1981); R.I. Gen. Laws § 11-54-1(e) (Supp. 1986).

There had been some concern in the deliberations of the National Commission for the Protection of Human Subjects of Biomedical and Behavioral Research that free second trimester abortions were given to poor women in exchange for consent to participate in fetal research.[12]

The question of whether aborted fetuses should be used for transplantation is an important one. In the past, research has been undertaken on fetuses scheduled to be aborted. In particular, the development of prenatal diagnosis techniques has involved pregnant patients about to undergo abortions.[13]

Experimental therapies such as thymus transplantation and other transplant procedures require the removal of fetal tissues and organs as quickly as possible after death.[14] For procedures which rely on obtaining fresh tissue, the use of fetuses from induced abortions will be advantageous.[15] Preparation for the examination or transplantation of fetal tissues can be carried out prior to an abortion in anticipation of a research subject and thereby enhance the possibilities for a successful investigation or therapy.

Some have argued that research involving fetuses resulting from planned abortions, whether the fetus be living or dead, is morally impermissible on the grounds that it constitutes cooperation with an immoral practice. Richard McCormick has made this point in the following way:

> If one objects to most abortions being performed in our society as immoral, is it morally proper to derive experimental profit from the products of such an abortion system? Is the progress achieved through such experimentation not likely to blunt the sensitivities of Americans to the immorality (injustice) of the procedure that made such advance possible, and thereby entrench attitudes injurious and unjust to nascent life? This is, in my judgment, a serious moral objection to experimentation on the products of most induced abortions (whether the fetus be living or dead, prior to abortion or post abortional).[16]

Though McCormick himself acknowledges that this moral evaluation of the use of aborted fetuses for research is not widely shared and is therefore not feasible as a policy position in a morally pluralistic society, a number of the state laws seem to embody just this reasoning in their provisions.[17]

---

[12] Toulmin, "Fetal Experimentation: Moral Issues and Institutional Controls," in *Appendix: Research on the Fetus, supra* n. 5 at 10-14.

[13] The development of chorionic villi sampling, for example, has relied on patients about to undergo first trimester abortions. Jackson "Prenatal Genetic Diagnosis by Chorionic Villus Sampling (CVS)," 9 *Seminars in Perinatology* 209, 214 (April 1985).

[14] Mahoney, "The Nature and Extent of Research Involving Living Human Fetuses," in *Appendix: Research on the Fetus, supra* n. 5 at 1-22, 1-29, 1-35.

[15] Mahoney, *supra* n. 14 at 1-35.

[16] McCormick, "Experimentation on the Fetus: Policy Proposals," in *Appendix: Research on the Fetus, supra* n. 5 at 5-1, 5-5. Similarly, there is concern that allowing research in conjunction with an abortion will lead to science becoming dependent for their research on fetuses who are subjects of abortion, causing science and society not to develop alternatives to abortion. Testimony of Chris Mooney, President, Pregnancy Aid Centers, Inc., in Research on the Fetus, *supra* n. 5 at 46.

[17] Many of the state fetal research laws require research only where it involves a fetus which is the subject of an abortion and some impose a stricter standard on research involving fetuses to be aborted than on research involving fetuses going to term.

Against this view it is possible to argue that even if abortion represents a moral wrong, the use of dead abortuses for certain types of research is not only morally legitimate but obligatory. Marc Lappé has argued that research with fetuses to be aborted is morally justified provided the research is aimed at deriving information potentially beneficial to other fetuses. According to Lappé, by allowing research intended to benefit future fetuses "what we have done is add a moral good to a morally tragic situation."[18]

Research on Dead Fetuses

Of most relevance to the issue of transplantation are the regulations covering research on dead fetuses. Under the federal regulations governing the funding of research, experimental activities involving a dead fetus or fetal material are to be conducted "in accordance with any applicable State or local laws regarding such activities."[19] Under state law, research involving dead fetuses and fetal tissues is regulated under the Uniform Anatomical Gift Act (UAGA) which has been adopted by all fifty states. Research with dead fetuses is also regulated in some states by fetal research statutes. According to the provisions [of] the UAGA, either parent might donate all or any part of a fetus "after or immediately before death," provided that the other parent does not present opposition to the gift.[20]

At least one legal commentator, Alexander Capron, has observed that there may be some question as to whether the requirements for a legally valid consent could be met for donation of fetuses in the context of an abortion procedure.[21] For consent to be valid it must be voluntary. Where consent is sought immediately prior to the abortion, it is unclear whether these requirements could be met.

It might be argued that undergoing an abortion procedure may significantly hinder a pregnant woman's ability to clearly evaluate or freely respond to a request for a donation of her fetus. As Capron points out, this problem need not arise in cases where the research interests do not require prompt examinations of the fetal tissue or the extraction of living tissues and functioning organs, since the woman can be asked for her consent after the abortion. However in research involving the transplantation of viable tissues or organs, there would be an obvious advantage to obtaining consent immediately before or just after fetal death. Capron maintains that consent requirements may still be met if physicians could explain the purposes of their request for a donation at the time they explain the abortion procedure, allowing the woman or couple to reach an informed decision well before the abortion process. The actual request and authorization could then be carried out immediately subsequent to the abortion procedure.[22]

Of the twenty-four state fetal research statutes, thirteen have provisions regulating research with dead fetuses.[23] These laws deviate from the provisions of the UAGA in

---

[18] Lappé, "Balancing Obligations to the Living Human Fetus with the Needs for Experimentation" in *Appendix: Research on the Fetus, supra* n. 5 at 4-6.

[19] 45 C.F.R. § 46.210 (1986).

[20] Under the Uniform Anatomical Gift Act (1968), a 'decedent' is defined to include "a stillborn infant or fetus" (§ 1(b)). The Act covers the donation of all or any portions of the human body (§ 1(e)) for purposes which include both educational and therapeutic benefits (§ 3). Under the consent requirements of the UAGA, either parent might donate all or any part of a fetus "after or immediately before [its] death," provided that the other parent does not present opposition to the gift (§ 2(c)).

[21] Capron, "The Law Relating to Experimentation with the Fetus," in *Appendix: Research on the Fetus, supra* n. 5 at 13-6, 13-16.

[22] *Id.*

[23] Ariz. Rev. Stat. Ann. § 36-2302(A)(C) (1986); Ark. Stat. Ann. §§ 82-438 (Supp. 1985); Ill. Ann. Stat. ch.

one of two ways. Eight of these laws would require the mother's consent for research making no provision for consent or objection by the father.[24] The remaining five states diverge from the UAGA more radically by prohibiting any research with dead fetuses except for pathological examinations or autopsies.[25] The divergences of these laws from the provisions of the UAGA are perhaps attributable to lawmakers' interests in regulating abortion and related practices.

Of the thirteen which regulate research with dead fetuses, seven apply only to research with abortuses.[26] Of the five statutes which prohibit any research except for pathological examinations, four apply exclusively to abortuses,[27] and one puts more restrictions on research with dead fetuses resulting from an induced abortion.[28] In fact, although the Illinois law prohibits the use of a dead aborted fetus for experimental transplantation, it specifically allows the use of a spontaneous aborted fetus for "therapeutic purposes or scientific, research, or laboratory experimentation, provided that the written consent to such use is obtained from one of the parents . . ."[29]

In light of these restrictions, many of the laws which regulate research with dead fetuses seem designed to preclude any medical or social benefits of elective abortion. Because much valuable research would require or benefit from the use of abortuses, the consequences of laws prohibiting research with abortuses are significant.[30]

The attempt to regulate research with dead fetuses raises a fundamental issue concerning the meaning of the terms "living" and "dead" with respect to embryos and fetuses. The definition of fetal death has been a concern primarily in cases where research involves later stage fetuses outside the womb which have no prospects for survival but which possess some signs of life such as a heartbeat or spontaneous respiration. The issue of determining when death has occurred is of particular importance where the fetus might serve as a source of tissue and organs for transplantation.[31] Several commentators have stressed the importance of articulating a definition of death

---

38 para. 81-26(7), 81-32, 81-32.1 (Smith-Hurd Supp. 1986); Ind. Code § 35-1-58.5.5-6 (1986); Mass. Ann. Laws ch. 112 § 12J(a)(II) (Law. Co-op. 1985); Mich. Comp. Laws Ann. § 333.2688(1) (West 1980); N.D. Cent. Code § 14-02.2-02(1) (1981); Ohio Rev. Code Ann. § 2919.14(A) (Baldwin 1982); Okla. Stat. Ann. tit. 63 § 1-735(B) (West 1984); Pa. Stat. Ann. tit. 18 § 3216(b) (Purdon 1983); R.I. Gen. Laws § 11-54-1(d) (Supp. 1986); S.D. Codified Laws Ann. § 34-23A-17 (1986); Tenn. Code Ann. § 39-4-208(a) (1982).

[24] The laws of Arkansas, Massachusetts, Michigan, North Dakota, Pennsylvania, Rhode Island, South Dakota and Tennessee as cited in n. 23.

[25] The laws of Arizona, Illinois, Indiana, Ohio, and Oklahoma as cited in n. 23.

[26] The laws of Arizona, Arkansas, Indiana, Ohio, Oklahoma, Pennsylvania, and Tennessee as cited in n. 23.

[27] Those of Arizona, Indiana, Ohio and Oklahoma as cited in n.23.

[28] In Illinois, research on dead fetuses is prohibited (Ill. Stat. Ann. ch. 38 para. 81-26 (Smith-Hurd Supp. 1986)), but a pathological examination is required (Ill. Ann. Stat. ch. 38 para. 81-32 (Smith-Hurd Supp. 1986)). However, with respect to a fetus whose death did not result from an induced abortion, research can be undertaken on its tissues or cells with the consent of one of the parents (Ill. Ann. Stat. ch. 38 para. 81-32.1 (Smith-Hurd Supp. 1986)).

[29] Ill. Stat. Ann. ch. 30, para 81-32.1 (Smith-Hurd Supp. 1986).

[30] Once the research phase of fetal tissue transplantation is passed and the procedure becomes accepted medical practice, the statutory provisions (for example, of a particular state's Uniform Anatomical Gift Act regarding donation for therapy or transplantation (rather than for research)) would apply. In that context, there may be limitations on some aspects of the donation. For example, under its UAGA, Massachusetts seems to limit donations to situations in which the decedents died in acute care facilities. Mass. Gen. Laws Ann. ch. 113, § 8 (Law Co-op. 1985).

[31] Mahoney, *supra* n. 14 at 1-29, 1-30.

which is independent of or in no way influenced by any proposed future use of the dead subject.[32]

In their concern for distinguishing between live and dead fetuses, the Commission adopted operational criteria for defining death similar to those defining death in adult persons.[33] The subsequent federal regulations followed this course and adopted the following definition:

> *'Dead fetus' means a fetus* ex utero *which exhibits neither heartbeat, spontaneous respiratory activity, spontaneous movement of voluntary muscles, nor pulsation of the umbilical cord (if still attached).*[34]

Such a definition is obviously inadequate for determining the status of early stage embryos and establishes a presumption that embryos and fetuses *in utero* are living. Because the regulations elected not to address research with pre-implantation embryos, defining the fetus as the product of conception from the time of implantation,[35] and explicitly made decisions concerning the funding of IVF research the province of a future national ethics advisory board,[36] the definition of "dead fetus" adopted was perhaps sufficient for their purposes.

In contrast to the federal regulations, most of the state fetal research laws fail to include a definition of the terms "dead" or "living" with reference to the fetus.[37] Those that employ a definition use one similar to that of the federal regulations. By hinging death on the lack of a heartbeat, the laws that would allow experimental procedures on a dead fetus would seem to preclude organ transplants from aborted dying fetuses to premature infants since the transfer could not take place while the donor's organs are still healthy.[38] The provisions regulating research on dead fetuses presumably would not apply to research with living pre-implantation embryos (unless these are considered dead fetuses by virtue of their lack of vital signs).

Research on Living Fetuses

There may be instances in which an experimental protocol as a whole requires that some action be undertaken on a dying or about-to-be-aborted fetus in order to better prepare the fetus for use as a donor of tissue or organs. There are significant ethical questions raised about whether such actions should be permissible. For example, some commentators argue that no research should be permitted on fetuses which are about to be aborted that would not be permissible on fetuses that would go to term.[39]

---

[32] *See e.g.,* Lappé "Balancing Obligations to the Living Human Fetus with the Needs for Experimentation" in Appendix: Research on the Fetus, *supra* n. 5 at 4-7, 4-8.

[33] Research on the Fetus, *supra* n. 5 at 6.

[34] 45 C.F.R. § 46.203(f) (1986).

[35] 45 C.F.R. § 46.203(c) (1986).

[36] 45 C.F.R. § 46.204(d) (1986).

[37] Only nine statutes define "dead" or "living." Ark. Stat. Ann. § 82-501(g), (h); Cal. Health and Safety Code § 25956(a) (West 1984); Me. Rev. Stat. Ann. tit. 22 § 1595 (1980); Mass. Ann. Laws ch. 112 § 12J(a)(I) (Law. Co-op. 1985); Mich. Comp. Laws Ann. § 333.2687 (West 1980); Minn. Stat. Ann. § 145.421(3) (West Supp. 1987); N.M. Stat. Ann. § 24-9A-1(H) (1981); Pa. Stat. Ann. tit. § 3203 (Purdon 1983); R.I. Gen. Laws § 11-54-1(c) (Supp. 1986).

[38] Note, "Fetal Experimentation: Moral, Legal, and Medical Implications," 26 *Stan. L. Rev.* 1191, 1200 (1974).

[39] See *Research on the Fetus,* supra n. 5 at 67.

Additionally, there are state statutory constraints on live fetuses. Even with respect to federally-funded fetal research, the federal regulations provide that these state laws are still applicable.[40]

Of the twenty-four state fetal research laws, twenty-three impose some restriction on experimentation with live fetuses *ex utero*.[41] Fourteen of the laws cover research on the fetus *in utero*.[42]

Of the 23 laws regulating research on *ex utero* live fetuses, 21 would prohibit research involving tissue or organ transplantation (generally because it is not therapeutic to the fetus itself). Two statutes would permit research on a live fetus *ex utero* provided the mother has given her consent.[43]

Of the 14 laws regulating research on *in utero* fetuses, 13 would prohibit research involving tissue or organ transplantation (generally because it is not therapeutic to the fetus itself). One would allow such research if the mother has consented.[44]

Research on Preimplantation Embryos

There may be instances in the future in which researchers may wish to use embryos *in vitro* to serve as sources for the development of cells or tissue for transplantation.[45] In addition to the serious ethical questions such an activity would raise, it would also fall within the reach of the fetal research statutes in some states.[46]

Some statutes specifically mention *in vitro* fertilization (IVF) in their definitions. Minnesota defines a human conceptus as "any human organism, conceived either in the human body or produced in an artificial environment other than the human body, from fertilization through the first 265 days thereafter." [47] The New Mexico "Maternal, Fetal and Infant Experimentation Act" defines "clinical research" to include research involving human *in vitro* fertilization.[48] Despite their inclusion of definitions of *in vitro* fertilization, these laws do not restrict research on the IVF embryo because the laws' sub-

---

[40] 46 C.F.R. § 46.201(b) (1986).

[41] Ariz. Rev. Stat. Ann. § 36-2302(A) (1986); Ark. Stat. Ann. § 82-437, 438 (Supp. 1985); Cal. Health & Safety Code § 25956(a) (West 1984); Fla. Stat. Ann. § 390.001 (6) (West 1986); Ill. Ann. Stat. ch. 38 para. 81-26(7) (Smith-Hurd Supp. 1986); Ind. Code § 35-1-58.5-6 (1986); Ky. Rev. Stat. Ann. § 436.026 (Baldwin 1985); Me. Rev. Stat. Ann. tit. 22 § 1593 (1980); Mass. Ann. Laws ch. 112 § 12J(a) (Law. Co-op. 1985); Mich. Comp. Laws Ann. §§ 333.2685-2692 (West 1980); Minn. Stat. Ann. § 145.421 to .422 (West Supp. 1987); Mo. Ann. Stat. § 188.037 (Vernon 1983); Mont. Code Ann. § 50-20-108(3) (1985); Neb. Rev. Stat. § 28-342, -346 (1985); N.M. Stat. Ann. § 24-9A-3 (1981); N.D. Cent. Code § 14-02.02-01 to -02 (1981); Ohio Rev. Code Ann. § 2919.14(A) (Baldwin 1982); Okla. Stat. Ann. tit. 63 § 1-735 (West 1984); Pa. Stat. Ann. tit. 18 § 3216 (Purdon 1983); R.I. Gen. Laws § 11-54-1(a), (d) (Supp. 1986); S.D. Codified Laws Ann. § 34-23A-17 (1986); Tenn. Code Ann. § 39-4-208 (1982); and Wyo. Stat. § 35-6-115 (1977)).

[42] See the statutes of Florida, Illinois, Maine, Massachusetts, Michigan, Minnesota, Missouri, New Mexico, North Dakota, Oklahoma, Pennsylvania, Rhode Island, and South Dakota, *supra* n. 41 and Utah § 76-7-310 (1978).

[43] S.D. Codified Laws Ann. § 34-23A-17 (1986); Tenn. Code Ann. § 39-4-208(a) (1982). The Tennessee law applies only to research on an aborted fetus.

[44] S.D. Codified Laws Ann. § 34-23A-17 (1986).

[45] There have been instances in which fetal tissue has been used to develop cell lines. Office of Technology Assessment, *New Developments in Biotechnology; Ownership of Human Tissues and Cells* (March 1987).

[46] The types of laws that potentially would cover research involving preimplantation *in vitro* embryos are those that do not limit their coverage to aborted fetuses and that also fail to define "fetus" or that define a fetus to encompass a preimplantation embryo.

[47] Minn. Stat. Ann. § 145.421(2) (West Suppl. 1987).

[48] N.M. Stat. Ann. § 24-9A-1(D), (K) (1981).

stantive provisions specifically apply only to research on fetuses having one or more vital signs.[49] (They were likely adopted to avoid the possibility that researchers would create embryos *in vitro* and allow them to develop to a much later stage and then do research on them.)

Under the Illinois law banning embryo research, a specific exception is made for *in vitro* fertilization.[50] It is unclear how broadly this exception will reach. It is likely that it will be applied only to allow traditional *in vitro* fertilization using a husband's sperm and wife's egg with implantation of the embryo in the wife's uterus, and thus create a barrier to embryo donation to a second woman. It probably will not be interpreted to allow use of *in vitro* embryos for tissue transplantation.

A Louisiana law[51] specifically prohibits the use of human embryos fertilized *in vitro* for research purposes or for any other purpose (including, apparently, transplantation) except for the purpose of human *in utero* implantation. The law also prohibits the farming, culturing or sale of embryos created *in vitro*.

There are six other states' laws that could potentially affect the use of IVP embryos for tissue transplantation.[52] They restrict research with any product of conception and do not limit this restriction to aborted fetuses.

Other Provisions Restricting Fetal Research

In addition to the restrictions on research *per se,* state laws in 15 states prohibit the sales of fetuses, with six of those states additionally prohibiting donations of fetuses.[53] In addition, a law in Nevada prohibits people from making available the remains of an aborted embryo or fetus for any commercial purpose.[54] Another state attempts to protect the sensibilities of the public by providing that experimentation "shall be in a place not open to the public."[55]

---

[49] Another state, Pennsylvania, specifically regulates *in vitro* fertilization (IVF). It does not prohibit the procedure, but rather provides for filing information with the state about attempts at IVF. Pa. Stat. Ann. tit. 18 § 3213(e) (Purdon (1983).

[50] Ill. Stat. Ann. ch. 38 para. 81-26(7) (Smith-Hurd Suppl. 1986). Moreover, it is fairly widely accepted that IVF under these circumstances has evolved from being an experimental procedure to being standard medical practice.

[51] La. Rev. Stat. Ann. § 9:121 (West Suppl. 1987).

[52] Me. Rev. Stat. Ann. tit. § 1593 (1980); Mass. Ann. Laws ch. 112 § 12J (Law. Co-op. 1985); Mich. Comp. Laws Ann. § 333.2685 to .2692 (West 1980); N.D. Cent. Code § 14.02.2-01 to -02 (1981); R.I. Gen. Laws § 11-54-1 (Suppl. 1982); and Utah Code Ann. § 76-7-310 (1978).

[53] Ark. Stat. Ann. §§ 82-439 (Supp. 1985); Fla. Stat. Ann. § 873.05 (West Supp. 1987) (does not apply to donation); Ill. Ann. Stat. ch. 38 para. 81-26(7) (Smith-Hurd Suppl. 1986) (does not apply to donation); Ky. Rev. Stat. § 436.026 (Baldwin 1985) (applies to live or viable fetus); Me. Rev. Stat. Ann. tit. 22 § 1593 (1980) (applies just to selling or donating for experimentation); Mass. Ann. Laws ch. 112 § 12J (a)(IV) (Law. Co-op. 1985) (applies just to selling or donating for experimentation); Mich. Comp. Laws Ann. § 333.2690 (West 1980) (applies just to selling or donating for experimentation); Neb. Rev. Stat. § 28-342 (1985) (applies to live or viable fetus) (applies just to selling or donating for experimentation); N.D. Cent. Code § 14-02.2-02(3) (1981); Ohio Rev. Code Ann. § 2919.14(A) (Baldwin 1982) (does not apply to donation) (applies just to selling or donating for experimentation); Okla. Stat. Ann. tit. 63 § 1-735(A) (West 1984) (does not apply to donation) (applies just to selling or donating for experimentation); R.I. Gen. Laws § 11-54-1(f) (Suppl. 1986) (applies just to selling or donating for experimentation); Tenn. Code Ann. § 39-4-208(b) (1982) (does not apply to donation); Utah Code Ann. § 76-7-311 (1978) (does not apply to donation); Wyo. Stat. Ann. § 35-6-115 (1977) (applies just to selling or donating for experimentation) (applies to live or viable fetus).

[54] Nev. Rev. Stat. Ann. § 451.015 (Michie 1986).

[55] Cal. Health and Safety Code § 25957(a) (West 1984).

Other types of statutes may also influence whether a woman may be paid to transfer her fetus to a researcher for use in tissue transplantation. At least ten states have laws that ban payment in connection with organ transplantation.[56] The California statute prohibits a person from knowingly acquiring, receiving, selling or promoting the transfer or otherwise transferring any organ for transplantation for valuable consideration.[57] The law is directed against the brokering of organs rather than the direct selling from a donor to a recipient. There is an exception allowing purchase by the person who receives a transplant from "the person from whom the organ is removed, . . . or those persons' next-of-kin who assisted in obtaining the organ for purposes of transplantation."[58]

Most of these statutes define organ quite broadly and would cover most types of tissues and organs to be transplanted from fetuses. Other statutes are more limited in the body parts they cover. The Florida statute bans the sale of the kidney, liver, heart, lung, pancreas, bone, and skin or any other organ or tissue specified by rules adopted by the Department of Health and Rehabilitative Services.[59] The New York statute begins with a larger list of items and then provides for regulatory expansion. It defines human organs to mean "the human organ or tissue as may be designated by the commissioner but shall exclude blood."[60] Another Florida statute prohibits the purchase or sale of human embryos.[61] In Louisiana, an additional statute prohibits the buying and selling of corpses and parts of corpses.[62]

Some states also contain restrictions on the transfer of fetal tissues from state to state. An Indiana law, for example, forbids transporting a fetus from an induced abortion to another state "for experimental purposes."[63]

The Significance of the Woman's Consent

One of the most shocking findings of the National Commission was that as a matter of medical practice, women's aborted fetuses were being experimented on without the women's knowledge and consent.[64] Similarly, there is also evidence that embryos removed during the course of medical procedures, such as hysterectomies, have been used without the knowledge or consent of the women undergoing the procedures.[65] This can create psychological harm to women. It can also pose potential physical harm to particular women since, if they do not realize experimentation is intended for the fetus, they may not question potentially risky medical procedures undertaken on them to facilitate the research.[66]

---

[56] CA, DC, FLA, IL, LA, MD, MI, NY, TX, VA. These laws do not limit their application to research activities but rather apply to clinical uses of medically accepted transplant procedures as well.

[57] Cal. Penal Code § 367f (West Suppl. 1987).

[58] Cal. Penal Code § 367f(e) (West Suppl. 1987).

[59] Fla. Stat. Ann. § 873.01(3)(a) (West Suppl. 1987).

[60] N.Y. Pub. Health Law § 4307 (McKinney 1985).

[61] Fla. Stat. Ann. § 873.05(1) (West Supp. 1987).

[62] La. Rev. Stat. Ann. § 17:2280 (West 1982).

[63] Ind. Code Ann. § 35-1-58.5-6 (1986).

[64] Research on the Fetus, *supra* n. 5 at 25.

[65] G. Corea, *The Mother Machine* 102, 135 n. 2 (1984).

[66] It has been charged that some abortionists performed abortion procedures that were more potentially harmful to the pregnant woman in order to obtain a live fetus for research purposes. Schulman, "Editorial: Major Surgery for Abortion and Sterilization," *40 Obstet. Gynecol.* 738, 739 (1972).

A woman should be asked for consent before research is undertaken on her embryo or fetus, even if the conceptus is outside of her body, and should have the right to refuse to permit such experimentation. Stephen Toulmin has argued this point on the grounds that failure to gain a woman's informed consent to experimentation on her conceptus could have emotionally damaging effects. He asserts that "it would be morally wrong to disregard a woman's psychological investment in a pregnancy, and in the issue of that pregnancy. Whatever the circumstances in which a pregnancy is terminated, the mother should have confidence that the issue will be handled and disposed of, both before or after death, in a respectful and humane way; and lack of such an assurance would be a legitimate source of grief and guilt."[67]

Some commentators suggest that the woman who has decided to abort the child is not an appropriate person to give a proxy consent for research on the fetus.[68] However, the Commission pointed out that since women have a constitutional right to abort, "basing maternal disqualification on the exercise of that right may be an unconstitutional penalty."[69]

Constitutionality of Fetal Research Statutes

In considering the potential reach of the state fetal research statutes, their constitutional validity must be assessed. In *Margaret S. v. Edwards,* the U.S. Court of Appeals, Fifth Circuit, declared a Louisiana fetal research law unconstitutional. The court said that the term "experimentation" was impermissibly vague[70] since physicians do not and cannot distinguish clearly between medical experimentation and medical tests.[71] The court noted that "even medical treatment can be reasonably described as both a test and an experiment."[72] This is the case, for example, "whenever the results of the treatment are observed, recorded, and introduced into the data base that one or more physicians use in seeking better therapeutic methods."[73] The case thus raises questions about the continued validity of the laws banning embryo and fetal research.

---

[67] Toulmin, *supra* n. 12 at 10-11.

[68] *See e.g.,* Note, "Fetal Experimentation: Moral, Legal, and Medical Implications," 26 *Stan. L. Rev.* 1191, 1202 (1974); Ramsey, *The Ethics of Fetal Research* 88-99 (1975).

[69] Research on the Fetus, *supra* n. 5 at 26. See also Capron, *supra* n. 21 at 13-1: "Such attempts to take away parental custody and control on the grounds that the mother has abandoned the fetus or is unable to take account of its interests seem unwise (because of the burden placed on state officials which they are ill-equipped to handle), misguided (because it is based on misapprehension of the significance of the decision to abort), unnecessary (because the interests of such fetuses are already protected by the law from parental abuse to the same degree as those of other children), and perhaps unconstitutional (because it chills exercise of the right to have an abortion and operates arbitrarily through presumptions rather than actual facts about parental choices)."

[70] *Margaret S. v. Edwards,* 794 F.2d 994, 999 (5th Cir. 1986).

[71] *Id.* A concurring judge found this analysis to be contrived (id. at 1000) (Williams, J., concurring) and opined that the provision was not unconstitutionally vague. Instead, he suggested that the prohibition was unconstitutional because "under the guise of police regulation the state has actually undertaken to discourage constitutionally privileged induced abortions." *Id.* at 1002 (citing *Thornburgh v. American College of Obstetricians and Gynecologists* 476 U.S. 747, 106 S. Ct. 2169, 2178 (1986)). The concurring judge pointed out that the state had "failed to establish that tissue derived from an induced abortion presents a greater threat to public health or other public concerns than the tissue of human corpses [upon which experimentation is allowed]." *Id.* Moreover, the state had not shown a rational justification for prohibiting experimentation on fetal tissue from an induced abortion, rather than a spontaneous one. *Id.*

[72] *Margaret S. v. Edwards,* 794 F.2d 994, 999 (5th Cir. 1986).

[73] *Id.*

Conclusion

Most of the state laws regulating fetal research are severely inadequate either for dealing with fetal research or for dealing with embryo research.[74] They pay little attention to potentially morally and legally relevant distinctions between different classes of conceptuses and types of research, and frequently lack clarification of important concepts such as fetal life and death. Consequently they fail to provide a set of clear provisions for regulating research. Furthermore, some of these laws may be unconstitutional.

---

[74] The state federal research laws have been criticized as seeming to be "largely the product of haste and emotion." Capron, "The Law Relating to Experimentation with the Fetus," 13-4 in Appendix: Research on the Fetus, *supra* n. 5 at 13-4.

Testimony of Alan Meisel

Alan Meisel, J.D., Professor of Law and Psychiatry, University of Pittsburgh School of Law

Introduction

Although I was asked to address the role of informed consent in fetal research, I want to caution at the outset that the role that informed consent should play in the protection of research subjects should not be overrated. Care must be taken not to place too much weight on informed consent to protect fetal interests. Experience with informed consent in other areas of medical practice and research suggest that it simply does not function well enough to serve as the sole protection of individual rights.[1] In addition, there are some important structural and conceptual reasons why research protections—especially in fetal research—cannot be provided by informed consent. Before turning to these, however, let me discuss informed consent.

What Constitutes Consent?

It is generally acknowledged that three requirements must be met for consent to be valid both morally and legally. First, the party giving consent must have adequate information; second, he or she must be "competent"; and third, consent must be voluntarily given.

INFORMATION   I will not reiterate each of the standard elements of information set forth in the basic federal regulations governing research[2], but emphasize those that I believe to be most important in the area of fetal research, and especially nontherapeutic research.

Most fundamentally, the pregnant woman must be told that the procedures are research. In the case of therapeutic research, the emphasis must be on the fact that the procedures are experimental, and in nontherapeutic research, the emphasis must be on dispelling any possible misconception that the research is for the benefit of either the pregnant woman or the fetus.[3]

Another significant and related feature of discussion must be alternatives. It is essential that the pregnant woman be told that participation is entirely optional and that the alternative to participation is nonparticipation, and that nonparticipation will in no way bring any harm or other disadvantage to her or the fetus. When the research itself will introduce, or has the potential for introducing, added risks or discomforts, it is essential that the pregnant woman be so informed.

The disclosure of information is intended in part to benefit a patient or research subject by assisting him or her in making an informed choice. However, it is essential to keep in mind that patients and research subjects also have a legally protected interest in not being harmed by the disclosure of information. A balance must be struck in obtaining informed consent between providing useful information and harming the pregnant woman by the "gratuitous or inappropriate [disclosure of] information that could be 'cruel, as well as destructive of the physician-patient relationship.' "[4]

The common law protects this interest through two exceptions to ordinary disclosure requirements, the so-called "therapeutic privilege" and "waiver" exceptions. The

---

Note.—Footnotes appear at end of testimony.

former permits the physician to withhold information the disclosure of which would be counterproductive because it would undermine the right of autonomy by so upsetting the patient that she would be unable to make an informed and rational decision.[5] The waiver exception serves the same purpose by permitting the patient or research subject to halt the disclosure of information that he or she does not wish to hear.[6] Another protection is accorded by the recognition in tort law of a cause of action for the infliction of emotional distress caused by the disclosure to a patient of such upsetting information.[7]

The Supreme Court has constitutionalized the common-law exceptions to informed consent by holding that state legislation that specifies in detail the information to be provided to a woman seeking to terminate a pregnancy—information such as the details of fetal development,[8] particular physical and psychological risks associated with abortion,[9] the availability of financial assistance from the father,[10] or the availability of assistance from social service organizations[11]—may not constitute "a 'parade of horribles' " designed "to influence the woman's informed choice between abortion and childbirth."[12] Rather, if patients are to "chart their own course understandably"[13] the idea of informed consent envisions collaborative, mutual, and shared decisionmaking between physician and patient.[14] The core notion of the idea of informed consent is that decisions about the medical care a person will receive, if any, are to be made in a collaborative manner between patient and physician.

COMPETENCY   The existing regulations already require that the mother and father be legally competent to consent.[15] No further protections are required in this regard.

VOLUNTARINESS   Recently, Justice Handler of the New Jersey Supreme Court remarked, in a right-to-die case, that "Voluntariness is . . . a difficult concept. The line between motivations we consider normal and legitimate and those we consider distorting or coercive is not always clear."[16] Nonetheless, for consent to be morally and legally valid, it must be voluntary,[17] freely given,[18] without duress,[19] undue influence,[20] or coercion.[21]

An important consideration has to do with *timing*. Decisions about fetal research need to be separated from decisions about the continuing or terminating [of] a pregnancy. Although the existing regulations recognize this, they may not be adequate in this regard since they merely state that "Individuals engaged in the [research] activity will have no part in . . . [a]ny decisions as to the timing" of pregnancy termination.[22] The regulations should be strengthened by prohibiting a pregnant woman from being asked to participate in fetal research before she has made a decision about pregnancy termination. Only after a decision to terminate a pregnancy has been made should it be legitimate to request participation in fetal research.

Another consideration concerning voluntariness has to do with the *inducements* offered to participate in fetal research. Although improper inducements sought to render consent ineffective, nonetheless this problem does not lend itself to resolution under the aegis of informed consent. The existing regulatory scheme recognizes this in two ways. Existing regulations already prohibit the provision of "inducements, monetary or otherwise," for the termination of a pregnancy.[23] Such a prohibition does not, however, address the problem raised by women who might become pregnant with the sole purpose of aborting the pregnancy in order to serve as a fetal tissue donor, whether for pecuniary gain or not.[24] Existing regulations also impose additional duties on IRBs in the area of fetal research. One of these duties is "[d]etermin[ing] that adequate consideration has been given to the manner in which potential subjects will be selected . . ."[25] Under this heading, IRBs could exercise the authority to prohibit the selection of donees by the donor. If it is felt that this would place too much discretion in the hands of IRBs, an explicit prohibition on this practice should be added to the regulations.

Consent Monitoring

Monitoring of the process of obtaining informed consent is one thing that could be done to enhance the likelihood that no improper influences are exerted on pregnant women. The existing regulations empower IRBs to undertake such monitoring by

> *Overseeing the actual process by which individual consents . . . are secured either by approving induction of each individual into the activity or verifying, perhaps through sampling, that approved procedures for induction of individuals into the activity are being followed . . .*[26]

The National Commission for the Protection of Human Subjects recommended that a "consent auditor" be appointed when research involves subjects who are mentally infirm[27] or children[28] depending on the degree of risk involved in the research. The recommendations concerning the mentally infirm have never been promulgated in regulations. The final rule governing research with children[29] did not adopt this recommendation; however, that is because the regulations concerning basic policy (i.e., subpart A of Part 46) were thought to provide the IRB with authority to adopt such additional protections for children when warranted.[30]

In practice, such monitoring, especially of the actual consent process, is not likely to be simple, but it may not be too high a price to pay to be sure that improper influence is not brought to bear on subjects.

Consent by Whom?

MATERNAL CONSENT   Maternal consent to fetal research is,[31] and should continue to be, required by existing regulations. The pregnant woman may veto the use of the fetus for research just as she might veto the use of a body part for research. The primary purpose of maternal consent is not to protect the fetus per se, but to protect the mother from subjecting herself to an abortion that she may not want. It is the mother's right to decide that is constitutionally protected, and the purpose of that right is so that she can determine what happens to her body. Consent is the mechanism by which society assures that the mother's own interests are protected, that is that she is not pressured to have an abortion or not to have an abortion because of the fact that the fetus might or might not be used in research.

The requirement of maternal consent does provide some protection for the fetus. It interposes a form of "review" between the researchers' need for research subjects and the fetus. It is, however, an incomplete protection.

PATERNAL CONSENT   Paternal consent is also required by existing regulations.[32] However, the protections that it adds to maternal consent are also insufficient to protect societal interests in the fetus.

Furthermore, the requirement of paternal consent may be unconstitutional because such a requirement unduly burdens the woman's right to choose to continue or terminate a pregnancy.[33] First, it is well settled that the father has no right to prohibit the termination of the pregnancy that would precede fetal research. However, what is facially at stake is not the prohibition of an abortion but the disposal of the fetus or fetal remains.

It does not seem to me that the father has any constitutionally protected right to dictate or override the pregnant woman's choice as to disposal of fetal remains. Subject only to societal interests mentioned below, the pregnant woman has the right to dispose of the fetal remains as she sees fit. Thus, for example, a pregnant woman who wished to have the fetal remains buried has the legal right to do so even against paternal opposition. Similarly, a pregnant woman who wishes to have the fetal remains disposed of in the ordinary medical fashion has the right to do so. If a pregnant woman chose the latter course, and a father wanted a funeral, would the father be able so to require?

If the father's wish as to disposal could prevail, and the pregnant woman found that wish offensive, she might decide against an abortion in order to avoid a dispute over the manner of disposal and the possible consequence that disposal would not be in accordance with her wishes. Thus, because a requirement of paternal consent to disposal would unduly burden the woman's right to choose to continue or terminate a pregnancy.[34]

CONSENT BY A THIRD PARTY   Since, in my view, neither maternal nor paternal consent are adequate to protect fetal interests, should consent be required from some other party?

Although it is possible to devise a scheme in which consent (or refusal) would be obtained from a third party to participation of the fetus in research—such as the judicial appointment of a guardian—any such scheme is not only likely to be unwieldy, but most certainly fictional.

The experience over the past ten years or more in right-to-die cases illustrated the futility and vacuity of attempting to use the judicial guardianship process for decision-making for individuals who never have had and never will have the capacity to formulate any sorts of desires. This approach has, therefore, been largely abandoned and should not be resurrected to protect fetal interests. Consequently, protections other than those provided by consent—whether maternal, paternal, or otherwise—need to be more closely examined.

A fetus does not enjoy the full legal protections of personhood. Nonetheless, a fetus does have interests which the law protects. Put another way, society has an interest in according certain protections to the fetus whether or not it is a person, just as certain protections are accorded by law to animals, the environment, and historical and esthetically significant buildings. Sometimes these protections are accorded for *their* sake—such as in the case of protection of animals from cruelty—but often the protection is accorded for *our* sake.

In the case of a fetus, these interests are protected in part by maternal consent, but they cannot be protected fully either by maternal consent or the consent of any other party. Surely, if the pregnant woman, the father, and a court-appointed guardian concurred that the proper means for the disposition of a fetus were "dumping . . . on to garbage piles,"[35] there would still be strong societal reasons for not permitting such a result to occur, such as protection against pain, indignity, and waste.

This is precisely what IRBs are intended to assess. For example, when viewed as a scarce resource, it is socially undesirable for a particular fetal research project to be carried out if it is likely to provide little or no benefit in either an absolute or relative sense (i.e., relative to other potential uses of the resource).

Protections Other than Those Provided by Consent

Although consent is the means by which protection is accorded to a variety of interests, it is not the only means. Consent is not the sole proper or available mechanism for protection of the interests of the fetus. The general scheme of the federal research regulatory process is based on this assumption.

THE GENERAL SCHEME OF FEDERAL RESEARCH REGULATION   The federal regulations governing biomedical and behavioral research are based on a two-tiered scheme. Before research can be undertaken, it must be approved at two different levels: the IRB representing societal interests, and the potential subject representing his or her own interests.

First, the IRB makes a determination whether or not a particular research project ought to be permitted to be undertaken by determining whether the balance of the risks potentially posed by the research and the benefits to be gleaned from it warrants its conduct. If the balance of risks and benefits is unfavorable, further inquiry is ended and the research cannot go forth.

If, however, the balance of risks and benefits is favorable, so that a decision can be made that it is socially desirable to conduct this research, the second tier of the regulatory process is activated in which it is determined who the research subjects are to be. This is where informed consent enters into the regulation of research.

FETAL RESEARCH   The federal regulation of fetal research conforms generally to the two-tier regulatory scheme established in the basic rules governing research. Before a particular research project can be undertaken, it must be approved at two different levels: the IRB representing societal interests, and the potential subject representing his or her own interests, implemented through informed consent.

First, a determination is made by an IRB as to whether or not the balance of risks and benefits is such that the research should be approved. Once approved, a pregnant woman has the right to consent or not, thereby determining whether she and/or the fetus will be a participant.

An important difference between fetal research and most other research is that the party giving consent—the pregnant woman—is not the primary research subject; in ex utero research, she is not a research subject at all. Consequently, in my view, protection of the interests of the fetus must occur predominantly, though not exclusively, at the first tier—at the societal (IRB and or EAB) level.

A fetus does not enjoy the full legal protections of personhood. Nonetheless, a fetus does have interests which the law protects. Put another way, society has an interest in according certain protections to the fetus whether or not it is a person, just as certain protections are accorded by law to animals, the environment, and historical and esthetically significant buildings. Sometimes these protections are accorded for their sake— such as in the case of protection of animals from cruelty—but often the protection is accorded for our sake.

This is precisely what IRBs are intended to assess. For example, when viewed as a scarce resource, it is socially undesirable for a particular fetal research project to be carried out if it is likely to provide little or no benefit in either an absolute or relative sense (i.e., relative to other potential uses of the resource).

References

[1] *See* Meisel & Roth, *Toward an Informed Discussion of Informed Consent: A Review of the Empirical Studies,* 25 Arizona L. Rev. 265 (1983); Meisel & Roth, *What We Do and Do Not Know About Informed Consent,* 246 J.A.M.A. 2473 (1981).

[2] 45 C.F.R. part 46, subpart A, § 46.116.

[3] *See* Appelbaum, Roth, Lidz, Benson, Winslade: *False Hopes and Best Data: Consent to Research and the Therapeutic Misconception,* 17(2) Hastings Center Report 1987.

[4] L. Tribe, American Constitutional Law sec 15-10, at 1343 n.44 (2d ed. 1988).

[5] *See* Meisel, *The "Exceptions" to the Informed Consent Doctrine,* 1979 Wis. L. Rev. 413, 460–70.

[6] *Id.* at 453–60.

[7] *See, e.g., Ferrara v. Galluchio,* 5 N.Y.2d 16, 176 N.Y.S.2d 996, 152 N.E.2d 249 (1958); *see also Molien v. Kaiser Foundation Hospitals,* 167 Cal. Rptr. 831, 27 Cal.3d 916, 616 P.2d 813 (1980).

[8] Akron, 462 U.S. at 444; Thornburgh v. American College of Obstetricians & Gynecologists, 106 S. Ct. 2169, 2178–79 (1986).

[9] Akron, 462 U.S. at 444–45.

[10] Thornburgh, 106 S. Ct. at 2179–80.

[11] *Id.* at 2167–80; Akron at 442.

[12] *Id.* at 443–44.

[13] Canterbury v. Spence, 150 U.S. App. D.C. 263, 464 F.2d 772, 781, *cert. denied,* 409 U.S. 1064 (1972).

[14] *See* Bouvia v. Superior Court (Glenchur), 225 Cal. Rptr. 297, 303 (Ct. App. 1986); *In re* Farrell, 108 N.J. 335, 529 A.2d 404, 418 (1987) (O'Hern, J., concurring) (citing President's Commission for the Study of Ethical Problems in Medicine & Biomedical & Behavioral Research, Deciding to Forego Life-Sustaining Treatment 48 (1983)).

[15] C.F.R. § 46.209(d); *see also* §§ 46.207(b), 46.208(b).

[16] *In re* Jobes, 108 N.J. 394, 529 A.2d 434, 454 (1987) (Handler, J., concurring).

[17] President's Commission for the Study of Ethical Problems in Medicine & Biomedical & Behavioral Research, Making Health Care Decisions 63 *et seq* (1982).

[18] Restatement Torts § 892, at 486 (1939).

[19] Restatement (Second) Torts § 892B(3) (1977).

[20] Jobes, 529 A.2d at 454 (Handler, J., concurring).

[21] Rasmussen v. Fleming, 154 Ariz. 207, 741 P.2d 674, 683 (1987); *In re* Farrell, 108 N.J. 335, 529 A.2d 404, 413 (1987).

[22] 45 C.F.R. § 46.206(a)(3).

[23] *Id.* § 46.206(b).

[24] *See, e.g.,* N.Y. Times, Aug. 16 1987 at 1 (reporting case of a woman who wished to be artificially inseminated with her father's sperm and then to abort the fetus to provide neural tissues to be transplanted to her father who was suffering from Alzheimer's disease).

[25] 45 C.F.R. § 46.205(a)(2).

[26] *Id.*

[27] U.S. Dep't of Health, Education, and Welfare, *Protection of Human Subjects: Research Involving Those Institutionalized as Mentally Infirm,* 43 Fed. Reg. 11,328, 11,357 (1978).

[28] U.S. Dep't of Health, Education, and Welfare, *Protection of Human Subjects: Research Involving Children,* 43 Fed. Reg. 2084, 2087 (1978).

[29] 46 C.F.R. part 46, subpart D.

[30] *See* U.S. Dep't of Health & Human Services, *Additional Protections for Children Involved as Subjects in Research,* 48 Fed. Reg. 9814, 9816 (Mar. 8, 1983) (commentary).

[31] *See* 45 C.F.R. § 46.209(d); *see also* 45 C.F.R. §§ 46.207(b), 46.208(b).

[32] *See id.* § 46.209(d); *see also* §§ 46.207(b), 46.208(b).

[33] Planned Parenthood Ass'n v. Fitzpatrick, 401 F. Supp. 554, 573 (E.D.Pa. 1975), *aff'd sub nom.* Franklin v. Fitzpatrick, 428 U.S. 901 (1976).

[34] *Id.*

[35] Akron v. Akron Center for Reproductive Health, Inc., 452 U.S. 416, 451 (1983) (quoting Planned Parenthood Ass'n v. Fitzpatrick, 401 F. Supp. 554, 573 (E.D. Pa. 1975), *aff'd mem. sub. nom.* Franklin v. Fitzpatrick, 428 U.S. 901 (1976)).

Statement of the American College of Obstetricians and Gynecologists on Human Fetal Tissue Transplantation

Presented by Robert C. Park, Col., M.C. USA

I am Robert C. Park, MD, an obstetrician-gynecologist and President of the American College of Obstetricians and Gynecologists (ACOG), I am pleased to be here on behalf of ACOG to discuss ethical issues in human fetal tissue transplantation research.

In my statement I will address a number of questions first raised by the Assistant Secretary of Health in his memorandum withholding approval of an experiment in which human fetal neural tissue would have been implanted in an adult patient suffering from Parkinson's disease. This panel has since been charged with responding to these questions. Among them is the question of whether or not the use of fetal tissue in research encourages a woman to have an abortion she might not otherwise undertake. Also, whether maternal consent is sufficient to permit the use of the tissue or if consent should be obtained from additional persons, whether the optimal or safest way to perform an abortion may conflict with preservation of the fetal tissue, and, finally, whether existing research procedures and regulations are adequate to deal with issues raised by research involving tissue obtained via induced abortion, as well as spontaneous abortions and stillbirths.

My testimony will provide a framework for responding to these questions from the perspective of clinicians whose central concern is the welfare of the pregnant woman and the fetus. I will also describe the rationale for our conclusion that existing laws on the donation of human fetal tissue and regulations on the protection of pregnant women and fetuses in biomedical research are both applicable to and appropriate for handling the complex questions raised by fetal tissue transplantation. In an appendix to my statement I am providing the committee with information on the overall incidence of abortion in the U.S., the incidence of abortion by gestational age, and the most common methods by which abortion is induced.

My statement today draws heavily from principles set forth in the ACOG statement of policy "Ethical Considerations in Perinatal Research," which was initially presented to the National Commission for the Protection of Human Subjects of Biomedical and Behavioral Research in February, 1975, and the 1977 ACOG Statement of Policy "Further Ethical Considerations in Induced Abortion."

Although the statement on "Ethical Considerations in Perinatal Research" was developed for situations in which the fetus itself is the subject of research, it sets forth two important principles to which we subscribe that are relevant to this discussion. First, it is important to distinguish between ethical issues involved in patient care and those involved in research. In the current context, the ethical issues involved in abortion should be viewed separately from those involved in research related to the transplantation of fetal tissue, whether obtained through induced abortion, spontaneous abortion, or stillbirth. Second, the welfare of the patient (woman, fetus or infant) is always the primary concern. This means that the most appropriate clinical management of the patient (the decision to have an abortion, its timing or the method employed) should not be affected by research goals.

Ethical Issues in Abortion

All medical and surgical procedures, abortion included, share certain common ethical issues. These include concerns such as whether a particular treatment is best for the welfare of the patient, whether the physician is fully qualified to perform the treatment and whether the patient is fully aware of its advantages and disadvantages. Because of the unique nature of the fetus, abortion also raises ethical issues that differ from those of other medical and surgical procedures. Even though our society has not reached a consensus on the status of the fetus, we believe there is broad consensus that the fetus has a different nature and value from that of other human tissue or organs. This qualitative difference derives at least in part from the potential of the fetus to develop into a member of the human family.

The central issue in abortion is reconciling conflicts between the welfare of the pregnant woman and that of the fetus. Pregnancy often involves medical, social, and economic factors which impact adversely on the welfare of the woman. Given the widely divergent theological and philosophical views on the value of the fetus, we believe it is best to allow the pregnant woman to exercise her beliefs in resolving these conflicts. Induced abortion is a legal option and one that can be ethically justified.

In responding to a patient who has an unwanted pregnancy, a physician has an ethical responsibility to assure that the patient receives quality counseling presenting the practical alternatives for managing her pregnancy. Counseling directed solely toward either promoting or preventing abortion does not sufficiently reflect the full nature of the problem or the range of options to which the patient is entitled, nor does it afford her the opportunity to make a truly informed choice. As part of this counseling a woman choosing to terminate her pregnancy should be provided with an explanation of the procedure, and its risks and benefits.

Ethical Issues in Fetal Tissue Research

Our statement on "Ethical Considerations in Perinatal Research" addresses the issue of balancing the goals of patient care and those of research and firmly concludes that the welfare of the patient is always the primary concern. The desirable goals of research should not affect advice about the decision to have an abortion, its timing, or the method employed to induce the abortion. Rather, these decisions should be made with the primary concern directed toward the welfare of the patient. Involvement in a research protocol in no way modifies the physician's responsibility for the most appropriate clinical management of the patient.

Early induced abortion, performed during the first trimester of pregnancy, involves the least risk. Major complications occur in fewer than one in 100 women after suction curettage, the most common method of first trimester abortion. Abortion later in pregnancy is linked with a higher rate of serious complications, occurring in about 2 women in 100. By comparison, the risk of a woman dying from full-term pregnancy and childbirth is at least 10 times greater than that from early abortion.

Aside from the ethical issues common to all biomedical research, research involving human fetal tissue obtained from the dead fetus or infant, whether from induced or spontaneous abortion or stillbirth, is of ethical concern only if it fails to preserve respect for human remains or tissue. Local laws on autopsy, health statistics reporting and disposal of human remains or tissue should be followed. The donation of all or part of a dead fetus or infant is specifically authorized by the Uniform Anatomical Gift Act (UAGA) under which each of the 50 states and the District of Columbia regulate the gift of all or part of a human body. Such research required informed consent. The ACOG believes that consent of the woman is sufficient.

Adequacy of Existing Research Procedures and Regulations

The principle enunciated in the ACOG statement on Ethical Considerations in Perinatal Research that the desirable goals of research should not affect the clinical management of patients who choose to have an induced termination of pregnancy is embodied in existing federal regulations for the Protection of Human Subjects. Specifically, the regulations state at Sec. 42.206(a) that:

(3)   Individuals engaged in the [research] activity will have no part in: (I) any decisions as to the timing, method, and procedures used to terminate the pregnancy, and (II) determining the validity of the fetus at the termination of the pregnancy; and

(4)   No procedural changes which may cause greater than minimal risk to the fetus or the pregnant woman will be introduced into the procedure for terminating the pregnancy solely in the interest of the [research] activity.

(b)   No inducements, monetary or otherwise, may be offered to terminate pregnancy for the purposes of the activity.

Although these regulations, like the ACOG policy statement on "Ethical Considerations in Perinatal Research", were developed for situations in which pregnant women or fetuses are themselves research subjects, the principles remain sound in these new situations in which tissue or organs from fetal remains are employed in research on a wide range of subjects. If the foregoing regulations are adhered to, the ACOG sees no likelihood that the potential use of fetal tissue obtained from induced terminations of pregnancy will encourage women to have abortions that they would not have sought otherwise. Moreover, adherence to these regulations would preclude physicians from recommending that pregnancy termination be delayed for the purposes of obtaining fetal tissue of increased gestational age for use in research.

ACOG reaffirms its support for these regulations and concludes that research carried out in accordance with these regulations involving organs or tissue obtained from fetal remains does not present new ethical problems. This concludes my statement. I would be happy to respond to any questions from the panel.

Appendix

It has been estimated recently that as many as one in three pregnancies miscarries (aborts spontaneously) sometimes even prior to the woman's knowledge that she is pregnant. A more conservative estimate is that 15 percent of all confirmed pregnancies result in spontaneous abortion. Most of these fetal deaths occur in the first trimester, and as gestational age increases, spontaneous abortion is less likely to occur.

Approximately 1.5 million induced abortions occur in the U.S. annually, or approximately 30 percent of all pregnancies (excluding those ending in fetal death). The National Center for Health Statistics reports that 90 percent of induced abortions are performed during the first 12 weeks of gestation. The median duration of gestation was 9.2 weeks for women having induced abortions in 1984. Almost half (47 percent) of induced abortions were for pregnancies of 8 weeks duration or less, and 43 percent were for pregnancies of 9–12 weeks duration. Only 11 percent of induced abortions involved pregnancies of more than 12 weeks.

The most commonly performed abortion procedures are suction curettage, a method employed until 12 weeks of pregnancy, dilation and evacuation (D&E), a method employed after 12 weeks of pregnancy, and medication-induced abortions, performed after 16 weeks of pregnancy. More than 9 out of 10 abortions are performed by suction curettage.

For all methods of induced pregnancy termination, the risk of maternal death increases with advancing gestational age. Early abortions by suction curettage are the safest and least expensive. Delays for any reason, administrative, social or medical, increase the risk and cost. Regardless of advances in abortion technology, mid-trimester terminations are likely to remain more hazardous, expensive, and more emotionally disturbing for women than early abortions.

Appendix III _____
Excerpts from the Supreme Court Decision in *Webster v. Reproductive Health Services*

Rehnquist for the Majority

This appeal concerns the constitutionality of a Missouri statute regulating the performance of abortions. The United States Court of Appeals for the 8th Circuit struck down several provisions of the statute on the ground that they violated this court's decision in *Roe* v. *Wade* and cases following it. We noted probable jurisdiction and now reverse . . .

Section 188.210 provides that "[i]t shall be unlawful for any public employee within the scope of his employment to perform or assist an abortion not necessary to save the life of the mother," while § 188.215 makes it "unlawful for any public facility to be used for the purpose of performing or assisting an abortion not necessary to save the life of the mother." The court of appeals held that these provisions contravened this court's abortion decisions. (851 F. 2d, at 1082–1083.) We take the contrary view . . .

In *Maher* v. *Roe, supra,* the court upheld a Connecticut welfare regulation under which Medicaid recipients received payments for medical services related to childbirth but not for nontherapeutic abortions. The court rejected the claim that this unequal subsidization of childbirth and abortion was impermissible under *Roe v. Wade* . . .

We think that this analysis is much like that which we rejected in *Maher, Poelker* and *McRae.* As in those cases, the state's decision here to use public facilities and staff to encourage childbirth over abortion "places no governmental obstacle in the path of a woman who chooses to terminate her pregnancy." (*McRae,* 448 U.S. at 315.) Just as Congress' refusal to fund abortions in *McRae* left "an indigent woman with at least the same range of choice in deciding whether to obtain a medically necessary abortion as she would have had if Congress had chosen to subsidize no health-care costs at all," (*id.*, at 317) Missouri's refusal to allow public employees to perform abortions in public hospitals leaves a pregnant woman with the same choices as if the state had chosen not to operate any public hospitals at all.

The challenged provisions only restrict a woman's ability to obtain an abortion to the extent that she chooses to use a physician affiliated with a public hospital. This circumstance is more easily remedied, and thus considerably less burdensome, than indigency, which "may make it difficult—and in some cases, perhaps, impossible—for some women to have abortions" without public finding. (*Maher*, 432 U.S. at 474.) Having held that the state's refusal to fund abortions does not violate *Roe v. Wade*, it strains logic to reach a contrary result for the use of public facilities and employees. If the state may "make a value judgment favoring childbirth over abortion and . . . implement that judgment by the allocation of public funds" (*Maher, supra,* at 474), surely it may do so through the allocation of other public resources, such as hospitals and medical staff . . .

"Constitutional concerns are greatest," we said in *Maher, supra,* at 476, "when the state attempts to impose its will by the force of law; the state's power to encourage actions deemed to be in the public interest is necessarily far broader." Nothing in the Constitution requires states to enter or remain in the business of performing abortions. Nor, as appellees suggest, do private physicians and their patients have some kind of constitutional right of access to public facilities for the performance of abortions. (Brief for appellees 46–47.) Indeed, if the state does recoup all of its costs in performing abortions and no state subsidy, direct or indirect, is available, it is difficult to see how any procreational choice is burdened by the state's ban on the use of its facilities or employees for performing abortions . . .

Thus, we uphold the act's restrictions on the use of public employees and facilities for the performance or assistance of nontherapeutic abortions . . .

Section 188.029 of the Missouri Act provides:

"Before a physician performs an abortion on a woman he has reason to believe is carrying an unborn child of 20 or more weeks gestational age, the physician shall first determine if the unborn child is viable by using and exercising that degree of care, skill and proficiency commonly exercised by the ordinarily skillful, careful and prudent physician engaged in similar practice under the same or similar conditions. In making this determination of viability, the physician shall perform or cause to be performed such medical examinations and tests as are necessary to make a finding of the gestational age, weight and lung maturity of the unborn child and shall enter such findings and determination of viability in the medical records of the mother" . . .

We think the viability-testing provision makes sense only if the second sentence is read to require only those tests that are useful to making subsidiary findings as to viability. If we construe this provision to require a physician to perform those tests needed to make the three specified findings *in all circumstances,* including when the physician's reasonable professional judgment indicates that the tests would be irrelevant to determining viability or even dangerous to the mother and the fetus, the second sentence of § 188.029 would conflict with the first sentence's *requirement* that a physician apply his reasonable professional skill and judgment. It would also be incongrous to read this provision, especially the word "necessary," to require the performance of tests irrelevant to the expressed statutory purpose of determining viability . . .

The viability-testing provision of the Missouri Act is concerned with promoting the state's interest in potential human life rather than in maternal health. Section 188.029

creates what is essentially a presumption of viability at 20 weeks, which the physician must rebut with tests indicating that the fetus is not viable prior to performing an abortion. It also directs the physician's determination as to viability by specifying consideration, if feasible, of gestational age, fetal weight and lung capacity. The District Court found that "the medical evidence is uncontradicted that a 20-week fetus is *not* viable" and that "23½ to 24 weeks gestation is the earliest point in pregnancy where a reasonable possibility of viability exists." (662 Supp., at 420.) But it also found that there may be a four-week error in estimating gestational age, (*id.,* at 421), which supports testing at 20 weeks.

In *Roe* v. *Wade,* the court recognized that the state has "important and legitimate" interests in protecting maternal health and in the potentiality of human life. (410 U.S., at 162.) During the second trimester, the state "may, if it chooses, regulate the abortion procedure in ways that are reasonably related to maternal health." (*Id.* at 164.) After viability, when the state's interest in potential human life was held to become compelling, the state "may, if it chooses, regulate and even proscribe abortion except where it is necessary, in appropriate medical judgment, for the preservation of the life or health of the mother." (*Id,* at 165.)

In *Colautti* v. *Franklin, supra,* upon which appellees rely, the court held that a Pennsylvania statute regulating the standard of care to be used by a physician performing an abortion of a possibly viable fetus was void for vagueness. (439 U.S., at 390–401). But in the course of reaching that conclusion, the court reaffirmed its earlier statement in *Planned Parenthood of Central Missouri* v. *Danforth,* [428 U.S. 52, 64 (1976)], that " 'the determination of whether a particular fetus is viable is, and must be, a matter for the judgment of the responsible attending physician.' " (439 U.S., at 396.)

The dissent, *post,* at 9, n. 6, ignores the statement in *Colautti* that "neither the legislature nor the courts may proclaim one of the elements entering into the ascertainment of viability—be it weeks of gestation or fetal weight or any other single factor—as the determinant of when the state has a compelling interest in the life or health of the fetus." (439 U.S., at 388–389.) To the extent that § 188.029 regulates the method for determining viability, it undoubtedly does superimpose state regulation on the medical determination of whether a particular fetus is viable. The Court of Appeals and the District Court thought it unconstitutional for this reason. (851 F. 2d, at 1074–1075; 662 F. Supp., at 423.) To the extent that the viability tests increase the cost of what are in fact second-trimester abortions, their validity may also be questioned under *Akron,* 462 U.S., at 434–435, where the court held that a requirement that second-trimester abortions must be performed in hospitals was invalid because it substantially increased the expense of those procedures.

We think that the doubt cast upon the Missouri statute by these cases is not so much a flaw in the statute as it is a reflection of the fact that the rigid trimester analysis of the course of a pregnancy enunciated in *Roe* has resulted in subsequent cases like *Colautti* and *Akron* making constitutional law in this area a virtual Procrustean bed. Statutes specifying elements of informed consent to be provided abortion patients, for example, were invalidated if they were thought to "structur[e] . . . the dialogue between the woman and her physician." *Thornburgh* v. *American College of Obstetricians and Gynecologists,* [476 U.S. 747, 763 (1986)]. As the dissenters in *Thornburgh* pointed out, such a statute would have been sustained under any rational standard of judicial review, *id*, at 802 (WHITE, J., dissenting), or in any other surgical procedure except abortion, *id.*, at 783 (Burger, C. J., dissenting).

Stare decisis is a cornerstone of our legal system, but it has less power in constitutional cases where, save for constitutional amendments, this court is the only body able to make needed changes. See *United States v. Scott* [437 U.S. 2, 101 (1978)]. We have not refrained from reconsideration of a prior construction of the Constitution that has proved "unsound in principle and unworkable in practice." *Garcia v. San Antonio Metropoliton Transit Authority*, [469 U.S. 528, 546 (1985)]; see *Solorio v. United States*, [483 U.S. 435, 448–450 (1987)]; *Erie R. Co. v. Tompkins*, [304 U.S. 64, 74–78 (1938)]. We think the *Roe* trimester framework falls into that category.

﹒In the first place, the rigid *Roe* framework is hardly consistent with the notion of a Constitution cast in general terms, as ours is, and usually speaking in general principles, as ours does. The key elements of the *Roe* framework—trimesters and viability—are not found in the text of the Constitution or in any place else one would expect to find a constitutional principle. Since the bounds of the inquiry are essentially indeterminate, the result has been a web of legal rules that have become increasingly intricate, resembling a code of regulations rather than a body of constitutional doctrine. As Justice [Byron R.] White has put it, the trimester framework has left this court to serve as the country's "*ex officio* medical board with powers to approve or disapprove medical and operative practices and standards throughout the United States." *Planned Parenthood of Central Missouri v. Danforth* [428 U.S., at 99], opinion concurring in part and dissenting in part. Cf. *Garcia, supra*, at 547.

In the second place, we do not see why the state's interest in protecting human life should come into existence only at the point of viability and that there should therefore be a rigid line allowing state regulation after viability but prohibiting it before viability. The dissenters in *Thornburgh*, writing in the context of the *Roe* trimester analysis, would have recognized this fact by positing against the "fundamental right" recognized in *Roe* the state's "compelling interest" in protecting potential human life throughout pregnancy. "[T]he State's interest, if compelling after viability, is equally compelling before viability." [*Thornburgh*, 476 U.S., at 795 (White, J., dissenting); see *id.*, at 828 (O'Connor, J., dissenting)]. ("State has compelling interests in ensuring maternal health and in protecting potential human life, and these interests exist 'throughout pregnancy' "). [citation omitted].

The tests that § 188.029 requires the physician to perform are designed to determine viability. The state here has chosen viability as the point at which its interest in potential human life must be safeguarded. See Mo. Rev. Stat. § 188.030 (1986). ("No abortion of a viable unborn child shall be performed unless necessary to preserve the life or health of a woman.") It is true that the tests in question increase the expense of abortion and regulate the discretion of the physician in determining the viability of the fetus. Since the tests will undoubtedly show in many cases that the fetus is not viable, the tests will have been performed for what were in fact second-trimester abortions. But we are satisfied that the requirements of these tests permissibly furthers the state's interest in protecting potential human life, and we therefore believe § 188.029 to be constitutional.

The dissent takes us to task for our failure to join in a "great issues" debate as to whether the Constitution includes an "unenumerated" general right to privacy as recognized in such cases as *Griswold v. Connecticut*, 381 U.S. 479 (1965), and *Roe*. But

Griswold v. Connecticut, unlike *Roe,* did not purport to adopt a whole framework, complete with detailed rules and distinctions, to govern the cases in which the asserted liberty interest would apply. As such, it was far different from the opinion, if not the holding, of *Roe v. Wade,* which sought to establish a constitutional framework for judging state regulation of abortion during the entire term of pregnancy. That framework sought to deal with areas of medical practice traditionally subject to state regulation, and it sought to balance once and for all by reference only to the calendar the claims of the state to protect the fetus as a form of human life against the claims of a woman to decide for herself whether or not to abort a fetus she was carrying.

The experience of the court in applying *Roe v. Wade* in later cases, see *supra,* at 20, n. 15, suggests to us that there is wisdom in not necessarily attempting to elaborate the abstract differences between a "fundamental right" to abortion, as the court described in *Akron,* 462 U.S. at 420, n. 1, a "limited fundamental constitutional right," which Justice Blackmun's dissent today treats *Roe* as having established, *post,* at 18, or a liberty interest protect by the due-process clause, which we believe it to be. The Missouri testing requirement here is reasonably designed to ensure that abortions are not performed where the fetus is viable—an end which all concede to be legitimate—and that is sufficient to sustain its constitutionality.

The dissent also accuses us, *inter alia,* of cowardice and illegitimacy in dealing with "the most politically divisive domestic legal issue of our time." [*Post,* at 23.] There is no doubt that our holding today will allow some governmental regulation of abortion that would have been prohibited under the language of cases such as *Colautti v. Franklin,* 439 U.S. 379 (1979), and *Akron v. Akron Center for Reproductive Health, Inc., supra.* But the goal of constitutional adjudication is surely not to remove inexorably "politically divisive" issues from the ambit of the legislative process, whereby the people through their elected representatives deal with matters of concern to them. The goal of constitutional adjudication is to hold true the balance between that which the Constitution puts beyond the reach of the democratic process and that which it does not. We think we have done that today. The dissent's suggestion, *post,* at 1–2, 21–22, that legislative bodies, in a nation where more than half of our population is women, will treat our decision today as an invitation to enact abortion regulation reminiscent of the dark ages not only misreads our views but does scant justice to those who serve in such bodies and the people who elect them.

Both appellants and the United States as *Amicus Curiae* have urged that we overrule our decision in *Roe v. Wade.* [Brief for Appellants 12–18; Brief for the United States as *Amicus Curiae* 8–24.] The facts of the present case, however, differ from those at issue in *Roe.* Here, Missouri has determined that viability is the point at which its interest in potential human life must be safeguarded. In *Roe,* on the other hand, the Texas statute criminalized the performance of *all* abortions, except when the mother's life was at stake. [410 U.S., at 117–118.] This case therefore affords us no occasion to revisit the holding in *Roe,* which was that the Texas statute unconstitutionally infringed the right to an abortion derived from the due-process clause, *id.,* at 164, and we leave it undisturbed. To the extent indicated in our opinion, we would modify and narrow *Roe* and succeeding cases.

Because none of the challenged provisions of the Missouri Act properly before us conflict with the Constitution, the judgment of the Court of Appeals is *Reversed.*

O'Connor, Concurring in Part

. . . In its interpretation of Missouri's "determination of viability" provision, Mo. Rev. Stat. § 188.029 (1986), see *ante,* at 15–23, the plurality has proceeded in a manner unnecessary to deciding the question at hand . . .

Unlike the plurality, I do not understand these viability-testing requirements to conflict with any of the court's past decision concerning state regulation of abortion. Therefore, there is no necessity to accept the state's invitation to reexamine the constitutional validity of *Roe v. Wade* [410 U.S. 113 (1973)]. Where there is no need to decide a constitutional question, it is a venerable principle of this court's adjudicatory processes not to do so for "[t]he Court will not 'anticipate a question of constitutional law in advance of the necessity of deciding it.' ". [*Ashwander v. TVA,* 297 U.S. 288, 346 (1936) (Brandeis, J., concurring), quoting *Liverpool, New York and Philadelphia S.S. Co. v. Commissioners of Emigration,* 113 U.S. 33, 39 (1885)]. Neither will it generally "formulate a rule of constitutional law broader than is required by the precise facts to which it is to be applied." [297 U.S., at 347.]

Quite simply, "[i]t is not the habit of the court to decide questions of a constitutional nature unless absolutely necessary to a decision of the case." [*Burton v. United States,* 196 U.S. 283, 295 (1905)]. The court today has accepted the state's every interpretation of its abortion statute and has upheld, under our existing precedents, every provision of that statute which is properly before us. Precisely for this reason, reconsideration of *Roe* falls not into any "good-cause exception" to this "fundamental rule of judicial restraint . . ." [*Three Affiliated Tribes of Fort Berthold Reservation v. Wold Engineering, P.C.,* 467 U.S. 138, 157.] See *post,* at 4 (Scalia, J., concurring in part and concurring in judgment). When the constitutional invalidity of a state's abortion statute actually turns on the constitutional validity of *Roe v. Wade,* there will be time enough to reexamine *Roe.* And to do so carefully . . .

I do not think the second sentence of § 188.029, as interpreted by the court, imposes a degree of state regulation on the medical determination of viability that in any way conflicts with prior decisions of this court. As the plurality recognizes, the requirement that, where not imprudent, physicians perform examinations and tests useful to making subsidiary findings to determine viability "promote(es) the State's interest in potential human life rather than in maternal health." *Ante,* at 17. No decision of this court has held that the state may not directly promote its interest in potential life when viability is possible. Quite the contrary.

In *Thornburgh v. American College of Obstetricians and Gynecologists,* 476 U.S. 747 (1986), the court considered a constitutional challenge to a Pennsylvania statute requiring that a second physician be present during an abortion performed "when viability is possible." [*Id.,* at 769–770.] For guidance, the court looked to the earlier decision in *Planned Parenthood Assn. of Kansas City, Missouri, Inc. v. Ashcroft,* 462 U.S. 476 (1983), upholding a Missouri statute requiring the presence of a second physician during an abortion performed after viability. [*Id.,* at 482–486 (opinion of Powell, J.); *id.,* at 505 (opinion concurring in judgment in part and dissenting in part)]. The *Thornburgh* majority struck down the Pennsylvania statute merely because the statute had no exception for emergency situations and not because it found a constitutional difference between the state's promotion of its interest in potential life when viability is possible and when viability is certain. [476 U.S., at 770–771.]

Despite the clear recognition by the *Thornburgh* majority that the Pennsylvania and

Missouri statutes differed in this respect, there is no hint in the opinion of the *Thornburgh* court that the state's interest in potential life differs depending whether it seeks to further that interest postviability or when viability is possible. Thus, all nine members of the *Thornburgh* court appear to have agreed that it is not constitutionally impermissible for the state to enact regulations designed to protect the state's interest in potential life when viability is possible. [See *id.*, at 811 (White, J., dissenting); *id*, at 832 (dissenting opinion)]. That is exactly what Missouri has done in § 188.029.

Similarly, the basis for reliance by the District Court and the Court of Appeals below on *Colautti v. Franklin*, 439 U.S. 379 (1979), disappears when § 188.029 is properly interpreted. In *Colautti*, the court observed:

"Because this point [of viability] may differ with each pregnancy, neither the legislature nor the courts may proclaim one of the elements entering into the ascertainment of viability—be it weeks of gestation or fetal weight or any other single factor—as the determinant of when the state has a compelling interest in the life or health of the fetus. Viability is the critical point." [*Id.*, at 388-389.]

The courts below, on the interpretation of § 188.029 rejected here, found the second sentence of that provision at odds with this passage from *Colautti*. [See 851 F. 2d, at 1074; 662 F. supp., at 423.] On this court's interpretation of § 188.029, it is clear that Missouri has not substituted any of the "elements entering into the ascertainment of viability" as "the determinant of when the state has a compelling interest in the life or health of the fetus." All the second sentence of § 188.029 does is to require, when not imprudent, the performance of "those tests that are useful to making *subsidiary* findings as to viability." [*Ante*, at 16 (emphasis added)]. Thus, consistent with *Colautti*, viability remains the "critical point" under § 188.029.

Finally, and rather halfheartedly, the plurality suggests that the marginal increase in the cost of an abortion created by Missouri's viability testing provision may make § 188.029, even as interpreted, suspect under this court's decision in *Akron*, 462 U.S., at 434–439, striking down a second-trimester hospitalization requirement. [See *ante*, at 19.] I dissented from the court's opinion in *Akron* because it was my view that, even apart from *Roe's* trimester framework which I continue to consider problematic, see *Thornburgh, supra*, at 828 (dissenting opinion), the *Akron* majority had distorted and misapplied its own standard for evaluating state regulation of abortion which the court had applied with fair consistency in the past: that, previability, "a regulation imposed on a lawful abortion is not unconstitutional unless it unduly burdens the right to seek an abortion." [*Akron, supra*, at 453 (dissenting opinion). (internal quotations omitted)].

It is clear to me that requiring the performance of examinations and tests useful to determining whether a fetus is viable, when viability is possible, and when it would not be medically imprudent to do so, does not impose an undue burden on a woman's abortion decision. On this ground alone, I would reject the suggestion that § 188.029 as interpreted is unconstitutional. More to the point, however, just as I see no conflict between § 188.029 and *Colautti* or any decision of this court concerning a state's ability to give effect to its interest in potential life, I see no conflict between § 188.029 and the court's opinion in *Akron*.

The second-trimester hospitalization requirement struck down in *Akron* imposed, in the majority's view, "a heavy, and unnecessary, burden," 462 U.S., at 438, more than doubling the cost of "women's access to a relatively inexpensive, otherwise accessible and safe abortion procedure." [*Ibid.;* see also *id.*, at 434.] By contrast, the cost of examinations and tests that could usefully and prudently be performed when a woman is 20–24 weeks pregnant to determine whether the fetus is viable would only marginally, if at all, increase the cost of an abortion. [See Brief for American Association of Prolife Obstetricians and Gynecologists et al. as *Amici Curiae* 3 ("At 20 weeks gestation, an ultrasound examination to determine gestational age is standard medical practice. It is routinely provided by the plaintiff clinics. An ultrasound examination can effectively provide all three designated findings of sec. 188.029"); *id.,* at 22 ("A finding of fetal weight can be obtained from the same ultrasound test used to determine gestational age"); *id.,* at 25 ("There are a number of different methods in standard medical practice to determine fetal lung maturity at 20 or more weeks gestation. The most simple and most obvious is by inference. It is well known that fetal lungs do not mature until 33–34 weeks gestation . . . If an assessment of the gestational age indicates that the child is less than 33 weeks, a general finding can be made that the fetal lungs are not mature. This finding can then be used by the physician in making his determination of viability under section 188.029"); cf. Brief for American Medical Association et al. as *Amici Curiae* 42 (no suggestion that the fetal weight and gestational age cannot be determined from the same sonogram); *id.,* at 43 (another clinical test for gestational age and, by inference, fetal weight and lung maturity, is an accurate report of the last menstrual period), citing Smith, Frey, & Johnson, Assessing Gestational Age, 33 Am. Fam. Physician 215, 219–220 (1986).

Moreover, the examinations and tests required by § 188.029 are to be performed when viability is possible. This feature of § 188.029 distinguishes it from the second-trimester hospitalization requirement struck down by the *Akron* majority. As the court recognized in *Thornburgh,* the state's compelling interest in potential life postviability renders its interest in determining the critical point of viability equally compelling. [See *supra,* at 7–8.] Under the court's precedents, the same cannot be said for the *Akron* second-trimester hospitalization requirement. As I understand the court's opinion in *Akron,* therefore, the plurality's suggestion today that *Akron* casts doubt on the validity of § 188.029, even as the court has interpreted it, is without foundation and cannot provide a basis for reevaluating *Roe.* Accordingly, because the Court of Appeals misinterpreted Mo. Rev. Stat. § 188.029, and because, properly interpreted, § 188.029 is not inconsistent with any of this court's prior precedents, I would reverse the decision of the Court of Appeals.

Scalia, Concurring in Part

. . . I share Justice Blackmun's view, *post,* at 20, that it effectively would overrule *Roe v. Wade,* 410 U.S. 113 (1973). I think that should be done but would do it more explicitly. Since today we contrive to avoid doing it, and indeed to avoid almost any decision of national import, I need not set forth my reasons, some of which have been well recited in dissents of my colleagues in other cases . . .

The outcome of today's cases will doubtless be heralded as a triumph of judicial statesmanship. It is not that, unless it is statesmanlike needlessly to prolong this court's self-awarded sovereignty over a field where it has little proper business since the answers to most of the cruel questions posed are political and juridical—a sovereignty which therefore quite properly, but to the great damage of the court, makes it the object of the sort of organized public pressure that political institutions in a democracy ought to receive.

Justice O'Connor's assertion, *ante,* at 5, that a "fundamental rule of judicial restraint" requires us to avoid reconsidering *Roe,* cannot be taken seriously. By finessing *Roe,* we do not, she suggests, *ante,* at 5, adhere to the strict and venerable rule that we should avoid " 'decid[ing] questions of a constitutional nature.' " We have not disposed of this case on some statutory or procedural ground but have decided, and could not avoid deciding, whether the Missouri statute meets the requirements of the United States Constitution. The only choice available is whether, in deciding that constitutional question, we should use *Roe v. Wade* as the benchmark or something else . . .

The real question, then, is whether there are valid reasons to go beyond the most stingy possible holding today. It seems to me there are not only valid but compelling ones. Ordinarily, speaking no more broadly than is absolutely required avoids throwing settled law into confusion; doing so today preserves a chaos that is evident to anyone who can read and count. Alone sufficient to justify a broad holding is the fact that our retaining control, through *Roe,* of what I believe to be, and many of our citizens recognize to be, a political issue, continuously distorts the public perception of the role of this court.

We can now look forward to at least another term with carts full of mail from the public, and streets full of demonstrators, urging us—their unelected and life-tenured judges who have been awarded those extraordinary, undemocratic characteristics precisely in order that we might follow the law despite the popular will—to follow the popular will. Indeed, I expect we can look forward to even more of that than before, given our indecisive decision today. And if these reasons for taking the unexceptional course of reaching a broader holding are not enough, then consider the nature of the constitutional question we avoid: In most cases, we do no harm by not speaking more broadly than the decision requires. Anyone affected by the conduct that the avoided holding would have prohibited will be able to challenge it himself and have his day in court to make the argument.

Not so with respect to the harm that many states believed, pre-*Roe,* and many may continue to believe, is caused by largely unrestricted abortion. That will continue to occur if the states have the constitutional power to prohibit it and would do so, but we skillfully avoid telling them so. Perhaps those abortions cannot constitutionally be proscribed. That is surely an arguable question, the question that reconsideration of *Roe v. Wade* entails. But what is not at all arguable, it seems to me, is that we should decide now and not insist that we be run into a corner before we grudgingly yield up our judgment. The only sound reason for the latter course is to prevent a change in the law—but to think that desirable begs the question to be decided.

It was an arguable question today whether § 188.029 of the Missouri law contravened this court's understanding of *Roe v. Wade,* and I would have examined *Roe* rather than examining the contravention. Given the court's newly contracted abstemiousness, what will it take, one must wonder, to permit us to reach that fundamental question? The result of our vote today is that we will not reconsider that prior opinion, even if most of the justices think it is wrong, unless we have before us a statute that in fact contradicts it—and even then (under our newly discovered "no broader than necessary" requirement), only minor problematical aspects of *Roe* will be reconsidered, unless one expects state legislatures to adopt provisions whose compliance with *Roe* cannot even be argued with a straight face. It thus appears that the mansion of constitutionalized abortion-law, constructed overnight in *Roe v. Wade,* must be disassembled door-jamb by door-jamb and never entirely brought down, no matter how wrong it may be.

Of the four courses we might have chosen today—to reaffirm *Roe,* to overrule it explicitly, to overrule it *sub silentio* or to avoid the question—the last is the least responsible. On the question of the constitutionality of § 188.029, I concur in the judgment of the court and strongly dissent from the manner in which it has been reached.

Blackmun, Concurring and Dissenting

Today, *Roe v. Wade* . . . and the fundamental constitutional right of women to decide whether to terminate a pregnancy, survive but are not secure. Although the court extricates itself from this case without making a single, even incremental, change in the law of abortion, the plurality and Justice Scalia would overrule *Roe* (the first silently, the other explicitly) and would return to the states virtually unfettered authority to control the quintessentially intimate, personal and life-directing decision whether to carry a fetus to term. Although today, no less than yesterday, the Constitution and the decisions of this court prohibit a state from enacting laws that inhibit women from the meaningful exercise of that right, a plurality of this court implicitly invites every state legislature to enact more and more restrictive abortions regulations in order to provoke more and more test cases, in the hope that, sometime down the line, the court will return the law of procreative freedom to the severe limitations that generally prevailed in this country before Jan. 22, 1973. Never in my memory has a plurality announced a judgment of this court that so foments disregard for the law and for our standing decisions.

Nor in my memory has a plurality gone about its business in such a deceptive fashion. At every level of its review, from its effort to read the real meaning out of the Missouri statute, to its intended evisceration of precedents and its deafening silence about the constitutional protections that it would jettison, the plurality obscures the portent of its analysis. With feigned restraint, the plurality announces that its analysis leaves *Roe* "undisturbed," albeit "modif[ied] and narrow[ed]." *Ante,* at 23. But this disclaimer is totally meaningless. The plurality opinion is filled with winks and nods and knowing glances to those who would do away with *Roe* explicitly but turns a stone face to anyone in search of what the plurality conceives as the scope of a woman's right under the due-process clause to terminate a pregnancy free from the coercive and brooding influence of the state. The simple truth is that *Roe* would not survive the plurality's analysis and that the plurality provides no substitute for *Roe's* protective umbrella.

I fear for the future. I fear for the liberty and equality of the millions of women who have lived and come of age in the 16 years since *Roe* was decided. I fear for the integrity of, and public esteem for, this court.

I dissent.

The plurality parades through the four challenged sections of the Missouri statute *seriatim.* I shall not do this but shall relegate most of my comments as to those sections to the margin. Although I disagree with the plurality's consideration of §§ 1.205, § 188.210 and § 188.215 and am especially disturbed by its misapplication of our past decisions in upholding Missouri's ban on the performance of abortions at "public facilities," the plurality's discussion of these provisions is merely prologue to its consideration of the statute's viability-testing requirement, § 188.029—the only section of the Missouri statute that the plurality construes as implicating *Roe* itself. There, tucked away at the end of its opinion, the plurality suggests a radical reversal of the law of abortion, and there, primarily, I direct my attention.

In the plurality's view, the viability-testing provision imposes a burden on second-trimester abortions as a way of furthering the state's interest in protecting the potential life of the fetus. Since under the *Roe* framework, the state may not fully regulate abortion in the interest of potential life (as opposed to maternal health) until the third trimester, the plurality finds it necessary, in order to save the Missouri testing provision, to throw out *Roe's* trimester framework. [*Ante,* at 19–22.] In flat contradiction to *Roe,* 410 U.S., at 163, the plurality concludes that the state's interest in potential life is compelling before viability and upholds the testing provision because it "permissibly furthers" that state interest. [*Ante,* at 21.]

At the outset, note that in its haste to limit abortion rights, the plurality compounds the errors of its analysis by needlessly reaching out to address constitutional questions that are not actually presented. The conflict between § 188.029 and *Roe's* trimester framework, which purportedly drives the plurality to reconsider our past decisions, is a contrived conflict: the product of an aggressive misreading of the viability-testing requirement and a needlessly wooden application of the *Roe* framework . . .

The plurality's reading of the provision, according to which the statute requires the physician to perform tests only in order to determine *viability,* ignores the statutory language explicitly directing that "the physician *shall* perform or cause to be performed such medical examinations and tests as are *necessary to make a finding of the gestational age, weight and lung maturity* of the unborn child and shall enter such findings" in the mother's medical record. [§ 188.029 (emphasis added)]. The statute's plain language requires the physician to undertake whatever tests are necessary to determine gestational age, weight and lung maturity, regardless of whether these tests are necessary to a finding of viability and regardless of whether the tests subject the pregnant woman or the fetus to additional health risks or add substantially to the cost of an abortion.

Had the plurality read the statute as written, it would have had no cause to reconsider the *Roe* framework. As properly construed, the viability-testing provision does not pass constitutional muster under even a rational-basis standard, the least restrictive level of review applied by this court. [See *Williamson v. Lee Optical Co.,* 348 U.S. 483 (1955)]. By mandating tests to determine fetal weight and lung maturity for every fetus thought to be more than 20 weeks gestational age, the statute requires physicians to undertake procedures, such as amniocentesis, that, in the situation presented, have no medical justification, impose significant additional health risks on both the pregnant woman and the fetus and bear no rational relation to the state's interest in protecting fetal life. As written, § 188.029 is an arbitrary imposition of discomfort, risk and expense, furthering no discernible interest except to make the procurement of an abortion as arduous and difficult as possible. Thus, were it not for the plurality's tortured effort to avoid the plain import of § 188.029, it could have struck down the testing provision as patently irrational irrespective of the *Roe* framework.

The plurality eschews this straightforward resolution, in the hope of precipitating a constitutional crisis. Far from avoiding constitutional difficulty, the plurality attempts to engineer a dramatic retrenchment in our jurisprudence by exaggerating the conflict between its untenable construction of § 188.029 and the *Roe* trimester framework.

No one contests that, under the *Roe* framework, the state, in order to promote its interest in potential human life, may regulate and even proscribe nontherapeutic abortions once the fetus becomes viable. [Roe, 410 U.S., at 164–165.] If, as the plurality appears to hold, the testing provision simply requires a physician to use appropriate and

medically sound tests to determine whether the fetus is actually viable when the estimated gestational age is greater than 20 weeks (and therefore within what the District
Court found to be the margin of error for viability, *ante,* at 19), then I see little or no
conflict with *Roe.* Nothing in *Roe* or any of its progeny holds that a state may not
effectuate its compelling interest in the potential life of a viable fetus by seeking to
ensure that no viable fetus is mistakenly aborted because of the inherent lack of precision in estimates of gestational age.

A requirement that a physician make a finding of viability, one way or the other,
for every fetus that falls within the range of possible viability does no more than preserve the state's recognized authority. Although, as the plurality correctly points out,
such a testing requirement would have the effect of imposing additional costs on second-
trimester abortions where the tests indicated that the fetus was not viable, these costs
would be merely incidental to, and a necessary accommodation of, the state's unquestioned right to prohibit nontherapeutic abortions after the point of viability. In short, the
testing provision, as construed by the plurality is consistent with the *Roe* framework
and could be upheld effortlessly under current doctrine.

How ironic it is, then, and disingenuous, that the plurality scolds the Court of
Appeals for adopting a construction of the statute that fails to avoid constitutional difficulties. [*Ante,* at 16.] By distorting the statute, the plurality manages to avoid invalidating the testing provision on what should have been noncontroversial constitutional
grounds; having done so, however, the plurality rushes headlong into a much deeper
constitutional thicket, brushing past an obvious basis for upholding § 188.029 in search
of a pretext for scuttling the trimester framework. Evidently, from the plurality's perspective, the real problem with the Court of Appeals' construction of § 188.029 is not
that it raised a constitutional difficulty but that it raised the wrong constitutional difficulty, one not implicating *Roe.* The plurality has remedied that, traditional canons of
construction and judicial forbearance notwithstanding.

Having set up the conflict between § 188.029 and the *Roe* trimester framework,
the plurality summarily discards *Roe's* analytic core as " 'unsound in principle and
unworkable in practice.' " [*Ante,* at 20, quoting *Garcia v. San Antonio Metropolitan
Transit Authority,* 469 U.S. 528, 546 (1985)]. This is so, the plurality claims, because
the key elements of the framework do not appear in the text of the Constitution, because
the framework more closely resembles a regulatory code than a body of constitutional
doctrine and because under the framework the state's interest in potential human life is
considered compelling only after viability, when, in fact, that interest is equally compelling throughout pregnancy. [*Ante,* at 21–22.] The plurality does not bother to explain
these alleged flaws in *Roe.* Bald assertion masquerades as reasoning. The object, quite
clearly is not to persuade, but to prevail.

The plurality opinion is far more remarkable for the arguments that it does not
advance than for those that it does. The plurality does not even mention, much less
join, the true jurisprudential debate underlying this case: whether the Constitution includes an "unenumerated" general right to privacy as recognized in many of our decisions, most notably *Griswold v. Connecticut* and *Roe,* and more specifically, whether
and to what extent such a right to privacy extends to matters of childbearing and family
life, including abortion . . . These are questions of unsurpassed significance in this
court's interpretation of the Constitution, and mark the battleground upon which this
case was fought, by the parties, by the solicitor general as *amicus* on behalf of petition-

ers and by an unprecedented number of *amici*. On these grounds, abandoned by the plurality, the court should decide this case.

But rather than arguing that the text of the Constitution makes no mention of the right to privacy, the plurality complains that the critical elements of the *Roe* framework—trimesters and viability—do not appear in the Constitution and are, therefore, somehow inconsistent with a Constitution case in general terms. [*Ante,* at 20.] Were this a true concern, we would have to abandon most of our constitutional jurisprudence. As the plurality well knows, or should know, the "critical elements" of countless constitutional doctrines nowhere appear in the Constitution's text. The Constitution makes no mention, for example, of the First Amendment's "actual malice" standard for proving certain libels . . . or of the standard for determining when speech is obscene . . . Similarly, the Constitution makes no mention of the rational-basis test or the specific verbal formulations of intermediate and strict scrutiny by which this court evaluates claims under the equal-protection clause. The reason is simple. Like the *Roe* framework, these tests or standards are not, and do not purport to be, rights protected by the Constitution. Rather, they are judge-made methods for evaluating and measuring the strength and scope of constitutional rights or for balancing the constitutional rights of individuals against the competing interests of government.

With respect to the *Roe* framework, the general constitutional principle, indeed the fundamental constitutional right, for which it was developed is the right to privacy, see, *e.g., Griswold v. Connecticut,* 381 U.S. 479 (1965), a species of "liberty" protected by the due-process clause, which under our past decisions safeguards the right of women to exercise some control over their own role in procreation. As we recently reaffirmed in *Thornburgh v. American College of Obstetricians and Gynecologists,* 476 U.S. 747 (1986), few decisions are "more basic to individual dignity and autonomy" or more appropriate to that "certain private sphere of individual liberty" that the Constitution reserves from the intrusive reach of government than the right to make the uniquely personal, intimate and self-defining decision whether to end a pregnancy. [*Id.,*. at 772.]

It is this general principle, the " 'moral fact that a person belongs to himself and not others nor to society as a whole,' " *id.,* at 777 n. 5 (Stevens, J., concurring), quoting Fried, Correspondence, 6 Phil. & Pub. Aff. 288–289 (1977), that is found in the Constitution. [See *Roe,* 410 U.S., at 152–153.] The trimester framework simply defines and limits that right to privacy in the abortion context to accommodate, not destroy, a state's legitimate interest in protecting the health of pregnant women and in preserving potential human life. [*Id.,* at 154–162.] Fashioning such accommodations between individual rights and the legitimate interests of government, establishing benchmarks and standards with which to evaluate the competing claims of individuals and government, lies at the very heart of constitutional adjudication. To the extent that the trimester framework is useful in this enterprise, it is not only consistent with constitutional interpretation, but necessary to the wise and just exercise of this court's paramount authority to define the scope of constitutional rights.

The plurality next alleges that the result of the trimester framework has "been a web of legal rules that have become increasingly intricate, resembling a code of regulations rather than a body of constitutional doctrine." [*Ante, at* 20.] Again, if this were a true and genuine concern, we would have to abandon vast areas of our constitutional jurisprudence. The plurality complains that, under the trimester framework, the court has distinguished between a city ordinance requiring that second-trimester abortions be performed in clinics and a state law requiring that these abortions be performed in hospitals, or between laws requiring that certain information be furnished to a woman by a physician or his assistant and those requiring that such information be furnished by the physician exclusively. [*Ibid.*, at n. 15, citing *Simopoulos v. Virginia*, 462 U.S. 506 (1983), and *Akron, supra*].

Are these distinctions any finer, or more "regulatory," than the distinctions we have often drawn in our First Amendment jurisprudence where, for example, we have held that a "release time" program permitting public school students to leave school grounds during school hours to receive religious instruction does not violate the Establishment clause, even though a release-time program permitting religious instruction on school grounds does violate the Clause? . . . Our Fourth Amendment jurisprudence recognizes factual distinctions no less intricate . . . . That numerous constitutional doctrines result in narrow differentiations between similar circumstances does not mean that this court has abandoned adjudication in favor of regulation. Rather, these careful distinctions reflect the process of constitutional adjudication itself, which is often highly fact-specific, requiring such determinations as whether state laws are "unduly burdensome" or "reasonable" or bear a "rational" or "necessary" relation to asserted state interests.

In a recent due-process case, the chief justice wrote for the court: "[M]any branches of the law abound in nice distinctions that may be troublesome but have been though nonetheless necessary: 'I do not think we need trouble ourselves with the thought that my view depends upon differences of degree. The whole law does so as soon as it is civilized.' "

These "differences of degree" fully account for our holdings in *Simopoulos, supra*, and *Akron, supra*. Those decisions rest on this court's reasoned and accurate judgment that hospitalization and doctor-counseling requirements unduly burdened the right of women to terminate a pregnancy and were not rationally related to the state's asserted interest in the health of pregnant women, while Virginia's *substantially less restrictive* regulations were not unduly burdensome and did rationally serve the state's interest. That the court exercised its best judgment in evaluating these markedly different statutory schemes no more established the court as an " '*ex officio* medical board' " . . . than our decisions involving religion in the public schools established the court as a national school board or our decisions concerning prison regulations establish the court as a bureau of prisons . . . If, in delicate and complicated areas of constitutional law, our legal judgments "have become increasingly intricate" . . . it is not, as the plurality contends, because we have overstepped our judicial role. Quite the opposite: The rules are intricate because we have remained conscientious in our duty to do justice carefully, especially when fundamental rights rise or fall with our decisions.

Appendix IV
Freedom of Choice Bill

This bill was originally presented to Congress November 6, 1989. It was recently re-submitted and is presently before Congress.

    101st Congress, 1st Session

S. 1912

To protect the reproductive rights of women, and for other purposes.

In the Senate of the United States: November 17 (legislative day, November 6), 1989—Mr. Cranston (for himself, Mr. Packwood, Mr. Metzenbaum, Mr. Adams, Mr. Simon, Mr. Pell, Ms. Mikulski, Ms. Kassebaum, Mr. Matsunaga, Mr. Wilson, Mr. Inouye, Mr. Chafee, Mr. Glenn, Mr. Cohen, Mr. Kerry, Mr. Stevens, Mr. Wirth, Mr. Burdick, Mr. Robb, Mr. Bingaman, Mr. Lautenberg and Mr. Kennedy) introduced the following bill; which was read twice and referred to the Committee on Labor and Human Resources.

A Bill to Protect the Reproductive Rights of Women, and for Other Purposes.
    Be it enacted by the Senate and House of Representatives of the United States of America in Congress assembled.

Section 1. Short Title
    This Act may be cited as the ''Freedom of Choice Act of 1989''.

Section 2. Right to Choose

IN GENERAL.—Except as provided in subsection (b), a State may not restrict the right of a woman to choose to terminate a pregnancy—

(1)   before fetal viability; or
(2)   at any time, if such termination is necessary to protect the life or health of the woman.
(3)   MEDICALLY NECESSARY REQUIREMENTS.—A State may impose requirements medically necessary to protect the life or health of women referred to in subsection (a).

Section 3. Definition of State.

As used in this Act, the term "State" includes the District of Columbia, the Commonwealth of Puerto Rico, and each other territory or possession of the United States.

Appendix V ───────────────
Excerpts from the Supreme Court Decision in *Planned Parenthood of Southeastern Pennsylvania v. Casey*

Justices O'Connor, Kennedy and Souter for the Majority

Liberty finds no refuge in a jurisprudence of doubt. Yet 19 years after our holding that the Constitution protects a woman's right to terminate her pregnancy in its early stages, Roe v. Wade, 410 U. S. 113 (1973), that definition of liberty is still questioned. Joining the respondents as amicus curiae, the United States, as it has done in five other cases in the last decade, again asks us to overrule Roe.

At issue in these cases are five provisions of the Pennsylvania Abortion Control Act of 1982 as amended in 1988 and 1989. The Act requires that a woman seeking an abortion give her informed consent prior to the abortion procedure, and specifies that she be provided with certain information at least 24 hours before the abortion is performed. For a minor to obtain an abortion, the Act requires the informed consent of one of her parents, but provides for a judicial bypass option if the minor does not wish to or cannot obtain a parent's consent. Another provision of the Act requires that, unless certain exceptions apply, a married woman seeking an abortion must sign a statement indicating that she has notified her husband of her intended abortion. The Act exempts compliance with these three requirements in the event of a "medical emergency," which is defined in Sections 3203 of the Act. In addition to the above provisions regulating the performance of abortions, the Act imposes certain reporting requirements on facilities that provide abortion services.

Before any of these provisions took effect, the petitioners, who are five abortion clinics and one physician representing himself as well as a class of physicians who provide abortion services, brought this suit seeking declaratory and injunctive relief. Each provision was challenged as unconstitutional on its face. The District Court entered a preliminary injunction against the enforcement of the regulations, and, after a 3-day bench trial, held all the provisions at issue here unconstitutional, entering a permanent injunction against Pennsylvania's enforcement of them. The Court of Appeals for the Third Circuit affirmed in part and reversed in part, upholding all of the regulations except for the husband notification requirement. . . .

And at oral argument in this Court, the attorney for the parties challenging the statute took the position that none of the enactments can be upheld without overruling Roe v. Wade. We disagree with that analysis; but we acknowledge that our decisions after Roe cast doubt upon the meaning and reach of its holding. Further, the Chief Justice admits that he would overrule the central holding of Roe and adopt the rational relationship test as the sole criterion of constitutionality. State and Federal courts as well as legislatures throughout the union must have guidance as they seek to address this subject in conformance with the Constitution. Given these premises, we find it imperative to review once more the principles that define the rights of the woman and the legitimate authority of the state respecting the termination of pregnancies by abortion procedures.

After considering the fundamental constitutional questions resolved by Roe, principles of institutional integrity, and the rule of stare decisis, we are led to conclude this: the essential holding of Roe v. Wade should be retained and once again reaffirmed.

It must be stated at the outset and with clarity that Roe's essential holding, the holding we reaffirm, has three parts. First is a recognition of the right of the woman to choose to have an abortion before viability and to obtain it without undue interference from the State. Before viability, the state's interests are not strong enough to support a prohibition of abortion or the imposition of a substantial obstacle to the woman's effective right to elect the procedure. Second is a confirmation of the state's power to restrict abortions after fetal viability, if the law contains exceptions for pregnancies which endanger a woman's life or health. And third is the principle that the state has legitimate interests from the outset of the pregnancy in protecting the health of the woman and the life of the fetus that may become a child. These principles do not contradict one another; and we adhere to each.

Men and women of good conscience can disagree, and we suppose some always shall disagree, about the profound moral and spiritual implications of terminating a pregnancy, even in its earliest stage. Some of us as individuals find abortion offensive to our most basic principles of morality, but that cannot control our decision. Our obligation is to define the liberty of all, not to mandate our own moral code. The underlying constitutional issue is whether the state can resolve these philosophic questions in such a definitive way that a woman lacks all choice in the matter, except perhaps in those rare circumstances in which the pregnancy is itself a danger to her own life or health, or is the result of rape or incest.

It is conventional constitutional doctrine that where reasonable people disagree the Government can adopt one position or the other. That theorem, however, assumes a state of affairs in which the choice does not intrude upon a protected liberty. Thus, while some people might disagree about whether or not the flag should be saluted, or disagree about the proposition that it may not be defiled, we have ruled that a state may not compel or enforce one view or the other.

Our cases recognize "the right of the individual, married or single, to be free from unwarranted governmental intrusion into matters so fundamentally affecting a person as the decision whether to bear or beget a child." Eisenstadt v. Baird. Our precedents "have respected the private realm of family life which the state cannot enter." Prince

v. Massachusetts. These matters, involving the most intimate and personal choices a person may make in a lifetime, choices central to personal dignity and autonomy, are central to the liberty protected by the Fourteenth Amendment. At the heart of liberty is the right to define one's own concept of existence, of meaning, of the universe, and of the mystery of human life. Beliefs about these matters could not define the attributes of personhood were they formed under compulsion of the State.

These considerations begin our analysis of the woman's interest in terminating her pregnancy but cannot end it, for this reason: though the abortion decision may originate within the zone of conscience and belief, it is more than a philosophic exercise. Abortion is a unique act. It is an act fraught with consequences for others: for the woman who must live with the implications of her decision; for the persons who perform and assist in the procedure; for the spouse, family, and society which must confront the knowledge that these procedures exist, procedures some deem nothing short of an act of violence against innocent human life; and, depending on one's beliefs, for the life or potential life that is aborted. Though abortion is conduct, it does not follow that the State is entitled to proscribe it in all instances. That is because the liberty of the woman is at stake in a sense unique to the human condition and so unique to the law. The mother who carries a child to full term is subject to anxieties, to physical constraints, to pain that only she must bear.

·   ·   ·

Although Roe has engendered opposition, it has in no sense proven "unworkable," representing as it does a simple limitation beyond which a state law is unenforceable.

·   ·   ·

But to do this would be simply to refuse to face the fact that for two decades of economic and social developments, people have organized intimate relationships and made choices that define their views of themselves and their places in society, in reliance on the availability of abortion in the event that contraception should fail. The ability of women to participate equally in the economic and social life of the nation has been facilitated by their ability to control their reproductive lives. The Constitution serves human values, and while the effect of reliance on Roe cannot be exactly measured, neither can the certain cost of overruling Roe for people who have ordered their thinking and living around that case be dismissed.

No evolution of legal principle has left Roe's doctrinal footings weaker than they were in 1973. No development of constitutional law since the case was decided has implicitly or explicitly left Roe behind as a mere survivor of obsolete constitutional thinking.

·   ·   ·

We have seen how time has overtaken some of Roe's factual assumptions: advances in maternal health care allow for abortions safe to the mother later in pregnancy than was true in 1973, and advances in neonatal care have advanced viability to a point somewhat earlier. But these facts go only to the scheme of time limits on the realization of competing interests, and the divergences from the factual premises of 1973 have no bearing on the validity of Roe's central holding, that viability marks the earliest point at which the state's interest in fetal life is constitutionally adequate to justify a legislative ban on nontherapeutic abortions.

The soundness or unsoundness of that constitutional judgment in no sense turns on whether viability occurs at approximately 28 weeks, as was usual at the time of Roe, at 23 to 24 weeks, as it sometimes does today, or at some moment even slightly earlier in pregnancy, as it may if fetal respiratory capacity can somehow be enhanced in the future. Whenever it may occur, the attainment of viability may continue to serve as the critical fact, just as it has done since Roe was decided; which is to say that no change in Roe's factual underpinning has left its central holding obsolete, and none supports an argument for overruling it.

The sum of the precedential inquiry to this point shows Roe's underpinnings un-weakened in any way affecting its central holding. While it has engendered disapproval, it has not been unworkable. An entire generation has come of age free to assume Roe's concept of liberty in defining the capacity of women to act in society, and to make reproductive decisions; no erosion of principle going to liberty or personal autonomy has left Roe's central holding a doctrinal remanant; Roe portends no developments at odds with other precedent for the analysis of personal liberty; and no changes of fact have rendered viability more or less appropriate as the point at which the balance of interests tips. . . .

Our analysis would not be complete, however, without explaining why overruling Roe's central holding would not only reach an unjustifiable result under principles of stare decisis, but would seriously weaken the Court's capacity to exercise the judicial power and to function as the Supreme Court of a nation dedicated to the rule of law. . . .

The root of American Governmental power is revealed most clearly in the instance of the power conferred by the Constitution upon the Judiciary of the United States and specifically upon this Court. As Americans of each succeeding generation are rightly told, the Court cannot buy support for its decisions by spending money and, except to a minor degree, it cannot independently coerce obedience to its decrees. The Court's power lies, rather, in its legitimacy, a product of substance and perception that shows itself in the people's acceptance of the judiciary as fit to determine what the nation's law means and to declare what it demands.

The underlying substance of this legitimacy is of course the warrant for the Court's decisions in the Constitution and the lesser sources of legal principle on which the Court draws. That substance is expressed in the Court's opinions, and our contemporary understanding is such that a decision without principled justification would be no judicial act at all. But even when justification is furnished by apposite legal principle, something more is required. Because not every conscientious claim of principled justification will be accepted as such, the justification claimed must be beyond dispute.

The Court must take care to speak and act in ways that allow people to accept its decisions on the terms the Court claims for them, as grounded truly in principle, not as compromises with social and political pressures having, as such, no bearing on the principled choices that the Court is obliged to make. Thus, the Court's legitimacy depends on making legally principled decisions under circumstances in which their principled character is sufficiently plausible to be accepted by the nation.

The need for principled action to be perceived as such is implicated to some degree whenever this, or any other appellate court, overrules a prior case. This is not to say, of course, that this Court cannot give a perfectly satisfactory explanation in most cases. People understand that some of the Constitution's language is hard to fathom and that the Court's Justices are sometimes able to perceive significant facts or to understand principles of law that eluded their predecessors and that justify departures from existing decisions. However upsetting it may be to those most directly affected when one judicially derived rule replaces another, the country can accept some correction of error without necessarily questioning the legitimacy of the Court.

In two circumstances, however, the Court would almost certainly fail to receive the benefit of the doubt in overruling prior cases. There is, first, a point beyond which frequent overruling would overtax the country's belief in the Court's good faith. Despite the variety of reasons that may inform and justify a decision to overrule, we cannot forget that such a decision is usually perceived (and perceived correctly) as, at the least, a statement that a prior decision was wrong. There is a limit to the amount of error that can plausibly be imputed to prior courts. If that limit should be exceeded, disturbance of prior rulings would be taken as evidence that justifiable re-examination of principle had given way to drives for particular results in the short term. The legitimacy of the Court would fade with the frequency of its vacillation.

That first circumstance can be described as hypothetical; the second is to the point here and now. Where, in the performance of its judicial duties, the Court decides a case in such a way as to resolve the sort of intensely divisive controversy reflected in Roe and those rare, comparable cases, its decision has a dimension that the resolution of the normal case does not carry. It is the dimension present whenever the Court's interpretation of the Constitution calls the contending sides of a national controversy to end their national division by accepting a common mandate rooted in the Constitution.

The Court is not asked to do this very often, having thus addressed the nation only twice in our lifetime, in the deicions of Brown and Roe. But when the Court does act in this way, its decision requires an equally rare precedential force to counter the inevitable efforts to overturn it and to thwart its implementation. Some of those efforts may be mere unprincipled emotional reactions; others may proceed from principles worthy of profound respect.

But whatever the premises of opposition may be, only the most convincing justification under accepted standards of precedent could suffice to demonstrate that a later decision overruling the first was anything but a surrender to political pressure, and an unjustified repudiation of the principle on which the Court staked its authority in the first instance. So to overrule under fire in the absence of the most compelling reason to re-examine a watershed decision would subvert the Court's legitimacy beyond any serious question.

•   •   •

The Court's duty in the present case is clear. In 1973, it confronted the already-divisive issue of governmental power to limit personal choice to undergo abortion, for which it provided a new resolution based on the due process guaranteed by the Fourteenth Amendment. Whether or not a new social consensus is developing on that issue, its divisiveness is no less today than in 1973, and pressure to overrule the decision, like pressure to retain it, has grown only more intense. A decision to overrule Roe's essential holding under the existing circumstances would address error, if error there was, at the cost of both profound and unnecessary damage to the Court's legitimacy, and to the nation's commitment to the rule of law. It is therefore imperative to adhere to the essence of Roe's original decision, and we do so today.

From what we have said so far it follows that it is a constitutional liberty of the woman to have some freedom to terminate her pregnancy. We conclude that the basic decision in Roe was based on a constitutional analysis which we cannot now repudiate. The woman's liberty is not so unlimited, however, that from the outset the State cannot show its concern for the life of the unborn, and at a later point in fetal development the state's interest in life has sufficient force so that the right of the woman to terminate the pregnancy can be restricted.

• • •

Yet it must be remembered that Roe v. Wade speaks with clarity in establishing not only the woman's liberty but also the state's "important and legitimate interest in potential life." That portion of the decision in Roe has been given too little acknowledgement and implementation by the Court in its subsequent cases.

Those cases decided that any regulation touching upon the abortion decision must survive strict scrutiny, to be sustained only if drawn in narrow terms to further a compelling state interest. Not all of the cases decided under that formulation can be reconciled with the holding in Roe itself that the state has legitimate interests in the health of the woman and in protecting the potential life within her.

In resolving this tension, we choose to rely upon Roe, as against the later cases.

• • •

Some guiding principles should emerge. What is at stake is the woman's right to make the ultimate decision, not a right to be insulated from all others in doing so.

Regulations which do no more than create a structural mechanism by which the state, or the parent or guardian of a minor, may express profound respect for the life of the unborn are permitted, if they are not a substantial obstacle to the woman's exercise of the right to choose. Unless it has that effect on her right of choice, a state measure designed to persuade her to choose childbirth over abortion will be upheld if reasonably related to that goal.

Regulations designed to foster the health of a woman seeking an abortion are valid if they do not constitute an undue burden. That is to be expected in the application of any legal standard which must accommodate life's complexity. We do not expect it to be otherwise with respect to the undue burden standard. We give this summary:

(a) To protect the central right recognized by Roe v. Wade while at the same time accommodating the state's profound interest in potential life, we will employ the undue burden analysis as explained in this opinion. An undue burden exists, and therefore a provision of law is invalid, if its purpose or effect is to place a substantial obstacle in the path of a woman seeking an abortion before the fetus attains viability.

(b) We reject the rigid trimester framework of Roe v. Wade. To promote the state's profound interest in potential life, throughout pregnancy the state may take measures to ensure that the woman's choice is informed, and measures designed to advance this interest will not be invalidated as long as their purpose is to persuade the woman to choose childbirth over abortion. These measures must not be an undue burden on the right.

(c) As with any medical procedure, the state may enact regulations to further the health or safety of a woman seeking an abortion. Unnecessary health regulations that have the purpose or effect of presenting a substantial obstacle to a woman seeking an abortion impose an undue burden on the right.

(d) Our adoption of the undue burden analysis does not disturb the central holding of Roe v. Wade, and we reaffirm that holding. Regardless of whether exceptions are made for particular circumstances, a State may not prohibit any woman from making the ultimate decision to terminate her pregnancy before viability.

(e) We also reaffirm Roe's holding that "subsequent to viability, the State in promoting its interest in the potentiality of human life may, if it chooses, regulate, and even proscribe, abortion except where it is necessary, in appropriate medical judgment, for the preservation of the life or health of the mother." Roe v. Wade, 410 U. S., at 164 165.

Justice Stevens Concurring in Part and Dissenting in Part

The portions of the Court's opinion that I have joined are more important than those with which I disagree. I shall therefore first comment on significant areas of agreement, and then explain the limited character of my disagreement.

The Court is unquestionably correct in concluding that the doctrine of stare decisis has controlling significance in a case of this kind, notwithstanding an individual justice's concerns about the merits. The central holding of Roe v. Wade, has been a "part of our law" for almost two decades. It was a natural sequel to the protection of individual liberty established in Griswold v. Connecticut. The societal costs of overruling Roe at this late date would be enormous. Roe is an integral part of a correct understanding of both the concept of liberty and the basic equality of men and women.

* * *

I also accept what is implicit in the Court's analysis, namely, a reaffirmation of Roe's explanation of why the state's obligation to protect the life or health of the mother must take precedence over any duty to the unborn. The Court in Roe carefully considered, and rejected, the state's argument "that the fetus is a 'person' within the language and meaning of the Fourteenth Amendment."

After analyzing the usage of "person" in the Constitution, the Court concluded that that word "has application only postnatally." Commenting on the contingent property interests of the unborn that are generally represented by guardians ad litem, the Court noted: "Perfection of the interests involved, again, has generally been contingent upon live birth. In short, the unborn have never been recognized in the law as persons in the whole sense." Accordingly, an abortion is not "the termination of life entitled to Fourteenth Amendment protection."

From this holding, there was no dissent, indeed, no member of the Court has ever questioned this fundamental proposition. Thus, as a matter of Federal constitutional law, a developing organism that is not yet a "person" does not have what is sometimes described as a "right to life." This has been and, by the Court's holding today, remains a fundamental premise of our constitutional law governing reproductive autonomy.

Justice Blackmun Concurring in Part and Dissenting in Part

Three years ago, in Webster v. Reproductive Health Serv., four members of this Court appeared poised to "cas(t) into darkness the hopes and visions of every woman in this country" who had come to believe that the Constitution guaranteed her the right to reproductive choice. All that remained between the promise of Roe and the darkness of the plurality was a single, flickering flame. Decisions since Webster gave little reason to hope that this flame would cast much light. But now, just when so many expected the darkness to fall, the flame has grown bright.

I do not underestimate the significance of today's joint opinion. Yet I remain steadfast in my belief that the right to reproductive choice is entitled to the full protection afforded by this Court before Webster. And I fear for the darkness as four Justices anxiously await the single vote necessary to extinguish the light.

Make no mistake, the joint opinion of Justices O'Connor, Kennedy, and Souter is an act of personal courage and constitutional principle. In contrast to previous decisions in which Justices O'Connor and Kennedy postponed reconsideration of Roe v. Wade, the authors of the joint opinion today join Justice Stevens and me in concluding that "the essential holding of Roe should be retained and once again reaffirmed."

In brief, five members of this Court today recognize that "the Constitution protects a woman's right to terminate her pregnancy in its early stages." A fervent view of individual liberty and the force of stare decisis have led the Court to this conclusion.

. . .

At long last, the Chief Justice admits it. Gone are the contentions that the issue need not be (or has not been) considered. There, on the first page, for all to see, is what was expected: "We believe that Roe was wrongly decided, and that it can and should be overruled consistently with our traditional approach to stare decisis in constitutional cases." If there is much reason to applaud the advances made by the joint opinion today, there is far more to fear from the Chief Justice's opinion.

The Chief Justice's criticism of Roe follows from his stunted conception of individual liberty. While recognizing that the Due Process Clause protects more than simple physical liberty, he then goes on to construe this Court's personal-liberty cases as establishing only a laundry list of particular rights, rather than a principled acount of how these particular rights are grounded in a more general right of privacy.

. . .

Under the Chief Justice's standard, states can ban abortion if that ban is rationally related to a legitimate state interest, a standard which the United States calls "deferential, but not toothless." Yet when pressed at oral argument to describe the teeth, the best protection that the Solicitor General could offer to women was that a prohibition, enforced by criminal penalties, with no exception for the life of the mother, "could raise very serious questions." Perhaps, the Solicitor General offered, the failure to include an exemption for the life of the mother would be "arbitrary and capricious."

If, as the Chief Justice contends, the undue burden test is made out of whole cloth, the so called "arbitrary and capricious" limit is the Solicitor General's "new clothes."

Even if it is somehow "irrational" for a state to require a woman to risk her life for her child, what protection is offered for women who become pregnant through rape or incest? Is there anything arbitrary or capricious about a state's prohibiting the sins of the father from being visited upon his offspring?

But, we are reassured, there is always the protection of the democratic process. While there is much to be praised about our democracy, our country since its founding has recognized that there are certain fundamental liberties that are not to be left to the whims of an election. A woman's right to reproductive choice is one of those fundamental liberties. Accordingly, that liberty need not seek refuge at the ballot box.

In one sense, the Court's approach is worlds apart from that of the Chief Justice and Justice Scalia. And yet, in another sense, the distance between the two approaches is short—the distance is but a single vote. I am 83 years old. I cannot remain on this Court forever, and when I do step down, the confirmation process for my successor well may focus on the issue before us today. That, I regret, may be exactly where the choice between the two worlds will be made.

Chief Justice Rehnquist Dissenting in Part and Concurring in Part

The joint opinion, following its newly minted variation on stare decisis, retains the outer shell of Roe v. Wade, but beats a wholesale retreat from the substance of that case. We believe that Roe was wrongly decided, and that it can and should be overruled consistently with our traditional approach to stare decisis in constitutional cases. We would adopt the approach of the plurality in Webster v. Reproductive Health Services, and uphold the challenged provisions of the Pennsylvania statute in their entirety.

• • •

The joint opinion of Justices O'Connor, Kennedy, and Souter cannot bring itself to say that Roe was correct as an original matter, but the authors are of the view that "the immediate question is not the soundness of Roe's resolution of the issue, but the precedential force that must be accorded to its holding."

Instead of claiming that Roe was correct as a matter of original constitutional interpretation, the opinion therefore contains an elaborate discussion of stare decisis.

• • •

In our view, authentic principles of stare decisis do not require that any portion of the reasoning in Roe be kept intact. "Stare decisis is not . . . a universal, inexorable command," especially in cases involving the interpretation of the Federal Constitution. . . . Erroneous decisions in such constitutional cases are uniquely durable, because correction through legislative action, save for constitutional amendment, is impossible. It is therefore our duty to reconsider constitutional interpretations that "depar(t) from a proper understanding" of the Constitution.

• • •

Our constitutional watch does not cease merely because we have spoken before on an issue; when it becomes clear that a prior constitutional interpretation is unsound we are obliged to re-examine the question.

•   •   •

In the end, having failed to put forth any evidence to prove any true reliance, the joint opinion's argument is based solely on generalized assertions about the national psyche, on a belief that the people of this country have grown accustomed to the Roe decision over the last 19 years and have ''ordered their thinking and living around'' it. As an initial matter, one might inquire how the joint opinion can view the ''central holding'' of Roe as so deeply rooted in our constitutional culture, when it so casually uproots and disposes of that same decision's trimester framework.

•   •   •

There is also a suggestion in the joint opinion that the propriety of overruling a ''divisive'' decision depends in part on whether ''most people'' would now agree that it should be overruled. Either the demise of opposition or its progression to substantial popular agreement apparently is required to allow the Court to reconsider a divisive decision. How such agreement would be ascertained, short of a public opinion poll, the joint opinion does not say. But surely even the suggestion is totally at war with the idea of ''legitimacy'' in whose name it is invoked.

The Judicial Branch derives its legitimacy, not from following public opinion, but from deciding by its best lights whether legislative enactments of the popular branches of Government comport with the Constitution. The doctrine of stare decisis is an adjunct of this duty, and should be no more subject to the vagaries of public opinion than is the basic judicial task.

There are other reasons why the joint opinion's discussion of legitimacy is unconvincing as well. In assuming that the Court is perceived as ''surrender(ing) to political pressure'' when it overrules a controversial decision, the joint opinion forgets that there are two sides to any controversy. The joint opinion asserts that, in order to protect its legitimacy, the Court must refrain from overruling a controversial decision lest it be viewed as favoring those who oppose the decision. But a decision to adhere to prior precedent is subject to the same criticism, for in such a case one can easily argue that the Court is responding to those who have demonstrated in favor of the original decision.

Justice Scalia Dissenting in Part and Concurring in Part

My views on this matter are unchanged from those I set forth in my separate opinions in Webster v. Reproductive Health Services and Ohio v. Akron Center for Reproductive Health. The states may, if they wish, permit abortion-on-demand, but the Constitution does not *require* them to do so.

The permissibility of abortion, and the limitations upon it, are to be resolved like most important questions in our democracy: by citizens trying to persuade one another and then voting. As the Court acknowledges, ''where reasonable people disagree the Government can adopt one position or the other.''

The Court is correct in adding the qualification that this "assumes a state of affairs in which the choice does not intrude upon a protected liberty," but the crucial part of that qualification is the penultimate word. A state's choice between two positions on which reasonable people can disagree is constitutional even when (as is often the case) it intrudes upon a "liberty" in the absolute sense.

Laws against bigamy, for example—which entire societies of reasonable people disagree with—intrude upon men and women's liberty to marry and live with one another. But bigamy happens not to be a liberty specially "protected" by the Constitution.

That is, quite simply, the issue in this case: not whether the power of a woman to abort her unborn child is a "liberty" in the absolute sense; or even whether it is a liberty of great importance to many women. Of course it is both. The issue is whether it is a liberty protected by the Constitution of the United States. I am sure it is not.

I reach that conclusion not because of anything so exalted as my views concerning the "concept of existence, of meaning, of the universe, and of the mystery of life." Rather, I reach it for the same reason I reach the conclusion that bigamy is not constitutionally protected—because of two simple facts: (1) the Constitution says absolutely nothing about it, and (2) the longstanding traditions of American society have permitted it to be legally proscribed.

●   ●   ●

The Court's description of the place of Roe in the social history of the United States is unrecognizable. Not only did Roe not, as the Court suggests, *resolve* the deeply divisive issue of abortion; it did more than anything else to nourish it, but elevating it to the national level where it is infinitely more difficult to resolve.

Subject Index

Case Name Index

Case names are filed letter-by-letter. Locators followed by the letter "*n*" and an *italic* number indicate footnotes.

LINCOLN CHRISTIAN COLLEGE AND SEMINARY